June 25–29, 2012
San Servolo Island, Venice, Italy

**Association for
Computing Machinery**

Advancing Computing as a Science & Profession

ICS '12

Proceedings of the 2012 ACM

International Conference on Supercomputing

Sponsored by:
ACM SIGARCH

Supported by:
**Intel, Cineca, Università degli Studi di Padova,
IBM Research, IBM Italia, Eurotech,
& Bertinoro International Center for Informatics**

**Association for
Computing Machinery**

Advancing Computing as a Science & Profession

ISBN: 978-1-4503-1316-2

Additional copies may be ordered prepaid from:

ACM Order Department
PO Box 30777
New York, NY 10087-0777, USA

Phone: 1-800-342-6626 (USA and Canada)
+1-212-626-0500 (Global)
Fax: +1-212-944-1318
E-mail: acmhelp@acm.org
Hours of Operation: 8:30 am – 4:30 pm ET

ACM Order Number: 415121

Printed in the USA

Cover photo by: Didier Descouens as posted on Wikipedia

Message from the General Co-chairs

Welcome to the 26th ACM International Conference on Supercomputing on the beautiful island of San Servolo near the heart of Venice, Italy. The first edition of this conference was held in Athens, Greece, in 1987. Over the years it has grown to be the premier international forum for the presentation of research results in high-performance computing systems. Some of us have been involved with ICS since the very beginning, and we take great pride and joy in its longevity and success. We are happy to report that, with its program of high quality original research papers and two days of tutorials and workshops, this year's conference continues the rich tradition and promises to be another effective and enriching event for the supercomputing community.

No conference of this size and magnitude can come into being without the concerted teamwork of a large number of dedicated individuals. We offer our sincere gratitude and appreciation to the Program Co-chairs Gianfranco Bilardi and Manolis Katevenis, for their tireless work in creating a truly outstanding technical program, and to Workshops and Tutorials Co-chairs Claudia Di Napoli and David Sehr, for assembling a collection of state-of-the-art workshops and illuminating tutorials.

Sincere thanks are also due to Finance Chair Carlo Fantozzi and Local Arrangements Co-chairs Marco Bressan and Luca Pretto for their skill and determination in dealing with the innumerable contractual and logistical tasks required to make the conference an enjoyable and memorable experience. We thank Publications Chair Enoch Peserico for his tactful persistence in ensuring the timely contributions of all concerned and his work in support of producing these Proceedings. Submissions Co-chairs Francesco Silvestri and Francesco Versaci, Web Chair Marc Gonzalez Tallada and Publicity Co-chairs Kazuki Joe, Ben Juurlink, and Arun Kejariwal efficiently and effectively collected and disseminated conference submissions and information and we thank them for their efforts.

It is almost impossible to base the budget of a large international conference on registration fees alone. We deeply appreciate receiving financial support from the Intel Corporation, CINECA, IBM Research, the Department of Information Engineering at the University of Padova, Eurotech, IBM Italia, and the Bertinoro international Center for informatics (BiCi). We thank ACM for its continuing support and sponsorship of the conference. Finally, ICS Steering Committee Chair, Alex Veidenbaum, has provided constant guidance and assistance throughout the planning of the conference for which we are very grateful.

Utpal Banerjee
University of California, Irvine, USA
ICS'12 General Co-Chair

Kyle A. Gallivan
Florida State University, USA
ICS'12 General Co-Chair

Message from the Program Chairs

On behalf of the Program Committee, we are pleased to introduce the technical program of the *2012 ACM International Conference on Supercomputing (ICS)*, the 26th in the series. The conference is by now a well established forum to present and discuss explorations that aim at pushing the limits of performance and capacity in large-scale computing systems, while preserving power efficiency, reliability, and programmability. In this context, papers have been solicited and submitted on parallel applications, architecture, hardware, accelerators, systems software, large scale installations, data center, grid and cloud computing, reliability, power efficiency, models of computation and of programming, and theoretical foundations of performance, for terascale to exascale systems.

This year's program includes 36 technical papers selected out of 161 submissions (a 22.3% acceptance rate). There were more submissions of high quality and relevance than could be accommodated in a three-day technical program. Under these constraints, a Program Committee of 70 world experts on the variety of topics of interest to the conference has worked very hard to select a high quality program, assisted by 134 external reviewers and by the Submission Chairs, Francesco Silvestri and Francesco Versaci. The task was carried over a period of two months, with two rounds of reviews–the second deepening the results of the first one–and one week of email discussion among PC members to further refine the evaluation and prepare a preliminary synthesis on each submission. A total of 641 reviews were provided in the process, with each paper receiving at least 3 reviews, and half the papers receiving 5 reviews. Final deliberations were made during the Program Committee meeting, held at the University of Padova, Italy, on March 9, 2012. The meeting was attended by nearly two-thirds of the PC members; most of the other members participated via conference call.

The technical program is further enriched by the two keynote addresses. Yale Patt will reflect on avenues to improve the performance of the individual core that will benefit even exascale class systems. Michael Gschwind will present the Blue Gene/Q supercomputer design, and how it addresses the memory, power, scalability, communication, and reliability "walls".

The Best Paper Award will be given according to the selection made by the audience among all papers. Thus, we invite you to carefully attend all talks, and to vote according to each paper's content, relevance, and presentation quality.

A scientific event can only be as good as its scientific content. Thus, for the excellent technical program of the Conference, we want to express our appreciation to the large number of authors who submitted their work to ICS 2012, to the program committee members and to the external reviewers, as well as to the speakers who have accepted to deliver keynote addresses. We welcome all of you to this year's ICS technical program, and hope you will enjoy it and learn from it as much as we did in the process of assembling it.

Gianfranco Bilardi
Università di Padova, Italy
ICS'12 Program Co-Chair

Manolis Katevenis
FORTH and Univ. of Crete, Greece
ICS'12 Program Co-Chair

Table of Contents

Keynote Address 1

Session 1: Micro-Architecture 1

Session 2: GPUs, Compilers

Session 3: Fault Tolerance

Session 4: Micro-architecture 2, Interconnection Networks

Session 5: Runtime, Dependences, Load Balancing

Session 6: Communication, HPC Applications

Keynote Address 2

Session 7: Workloads

Session 8: Memory Hierarchies & Interconnects

Session 9: GPUs & Parallel Programming

Session 10: GPUs, CPUs, & Linear Algebra

ICS 2012 Organization

General Chairs:	Utpal Banerjee *(University of California at Irvine, USA)*
	Kyle A. Gallivan *(Florida State University, USA)*
Program Chairs:	Gianfranco Bilardi *(Università degli Studi di Padova, Italy)*
	Manolis G. H. Katevenis *(FORTH and University of Crete, Greece)*
Workshops and Tutorials Chairs:	Claudia Di Napoli *(IC-CNR, Italy)*
	David Sehr *(Google, USA)*
Finance Chair:	Carlo Fantozzi *(Università degli Studi di Padova, Italy)*
Registration and Local Arrangements Chairs:	Marco Bressan *(Università degli Studi di Padova, Italy)*
	Luca Pretto *(Università degli Studi di Padova, Italy)*
Publication Chair:	Enoch Peserico *(Università degli Studi di Padova, Italy)*
Submission Chairs:	Francesco Silvestri *(Università degli Studi di Padova, Italy)*
	Francesco Versaci *(Università degli Studi di Padova, Italy)*
Web Chair:	Marc Gonzalez Tallada *(Universitat Politecnica de Catalunya, Spain)*
Publicity Chairs:	Kazuki Joe *(Nara Women's University, Japan)*
	Ben Juurlink *(TU Berlin, Germany)*
	Arun Kejariwal *(Netflix, USA)*
Steering Committee Chair:	Alex Veidenbaum *(University of California at Irvine, USA)*
Steering Committee:	Eduard Ayguade *(Universitat Politecnica de Catalunya, Spain)*
	Utpal Banerjee *(University of California at Irvine, USA)*
	Bronis R. De Supinski *(Lawrence Livermore National Lab., USA)*
	Kyle Gallivan *(Florida State University, USA)*
	Jim Goodman *(University of Auckland, New Zealand)*
	Mike Gschwind *(IBM Research, USA)*
	David K. Lowenthal *(University of Arizona, USA)*
	Sally A. McKee *(Chalmers University of Technology, Sweden)*
	Avi Mendelson *(Microsoft, Israel)*
	Jose Moreira *(IBM Research, USA)*
	Alex Nicolau *(UC Irvine, USA)*
	Constantine Polychronopoulos *(UIUC, USA)*
	Valentina Salapura *(IBM Research, USA)*
	John Sopka *(EMC, USA)*
	Mateo Valero *(Universitat Politecnica de Catalunya, Spain)*
	Alex Veidenbaum *(University of California at Irvine)*
	Harry Wijshoff *(Leiden University, The Netherlands)*

Program Committee (continued): David Padua *(University of Illinois at Urbana-Champaign, USA)*
Keshav Pingali *(University of Texas at Austin, USA)*
Dionisios Pnevmatikatos *(Technical University of Crete, Greece)*
Viktor Prasanna *(University of Southern California, USA)*
Markus Pueschel *(ETH Zurich, Switzerland)*
Abhiram Ranade *(Indian Institute of Technology Bombay, India)*
Larry Rudolph *(ReDigi Inc. & CSAIL/MIT, USA)*
Daniele Scarpazza *(D.E. Shaw Research, USA)*
Fabio Schifano *(University of Ferrara, Italy)*
Yanos Sazeides *(University of Cyprus, Cyprus)*
Michael C. Shebanow *(NVIDIA, USA)*
Henk Sips *(Delft University of Technology, The Netherlands)*
Ioannis Sourdis *(Chalmers University of Technology, Sweden)*
Y.C. Tay *(National University of Singapore, Singapore)*
Raffaele Tripiccione *(University of Ferrara, Italy)*
Dan Tsafrir *(Technion, Israel)*
Henry M. Tufo III *(Univ. Colorado & NCAR, USA)*
Eli Upfal *(Brown University, USA)*
Jeffrey S. Vetter *(Oak Ridge National Laboratory & Georgia Tech, USA)*
Weng Fai Wong *(National University of Singapore, Singapore)*
Qing Yi *(University of Texas San Antonio, USA)*
Xiaodong Zhang *(Ohio State University, USA)*
Huiyang Zhou *(North Caroline State University, USA)*

Additional reviewers:

Mark Adams	James Elliott
Mauricio Alvarez	Toshio Endo
Nadav Amit	Nina Engelhardt
Angelos Arelakis	Montse Farreras
Matthew Badin	Kurt Ferreira
Jayaram Bobba	David Fiala
Ali Bakhoda	Adam Fidel
Leonardo Bautista Gomez	Bjoern Franke
Muli Ben-Yehuda	Vincent Freeh
Andrew Boktor	Wilson Fung
Aydin Buluc	Vladimir Gajinov
Antal Buss	Thilan Ganegedara
Harold Cain	Hongliang Gao
Rosario Cammarota	Miles Gould
Feng Chen	Saurabh Gupta
Chi Ching Chi	Sean Halle
Jeffrey Cook	Nadav Har'El
Tamer Dallou	Damien Hardy Harshvardhan
Xiaoning Ding	Stefan Hauser
Christophe Dubach	Tayler Hetherington
Ahmed El-Shafiey	Mohammad Hossain

Additional reviewers (continued):

Victoria Howle
Jen-Cheng Huang
Joe Hummel
Nikolas Ioannou
Yasuo Ishii
Hideyuki Jitsumoto
Gangwon Jo
Troy Johnson
Mohammad Hadi Jooybar
Gokul Kandiraju
Kise Kenji
Hongjune Kim
Jungwon Kim
Ilia Kravets
Rakesh Krishnaiyer
Arvind Krishnaswamy
Jun Lee
Myungho Lee
Tian Luo
Spyros Lyberis
Nam Ma
Kamesh Madduri
Alberto Magni
Alirad Malek
Manmohan Manoharan
Hiroki Matsutani
Fei Meng
Jamin Nagmouchi
Priya Nagpurkar
Lifeng Nai
Eyee Hyun Nam
Bogdan Nicolae
Chrysostomos Nicopoulos
David Oehmke
Zhong Liang Ong
Andreas Panteli
Ioannis Papadopoulos
Jungho Park
Giorgos Passas
Arash Rezaei
German Rodriguez
Pooja Roy
Silvius Rus
Jose Carlos Sancho

Abhik Sarkar
Hitoshi Sato
Kento Sato
Toshinori Sato
Nicolas Schier
Sangmin Seo
Nak Hee Seong
Shishir Sharma
Mark Silberstein
Inderpreet Singh
Artyom Skrobov
Timmie Smith
Suriya Subramanian
Lucia Sun
Zhenyu Sun
Mitsugu Suzuki
Shinichoro Takizawa
Nathan Tallent
Kiyofumi Tanaka
Ilie Tanase
Gervin Thomas
Xinmin Tian
Ruben Titos-Gil
Daniel Tomkins
Stavros Tzilis
Ana Lucia Varbanescu
Ugo Varetto
Frédéric Vivien
Tobias von Koch
Steven Vormwald
Chundong Wang
Kaibo Wang
Zheng Wang
Xing Wu
Gala Yadgar
Shinichi Yamagiwa
Yi Yang
Sungkap Yeo
Jin Hyuk Yoon
Yuan Yuan
Yonghao Yue
Mani Zandifar
Zhao Zhang
Aviad Zuck

ICS 2012 Sponsor & Supporters

Sponsor:

Supporters:

High Performance Supercomputers: Should the Individual Processor be More than a Brick?

Yale N. Patt
The University of Texas at Austin, USA
patt@ece.utexas.edu

KEYNOTE ADDRESS SUMMARY

The world of supercomputing is rightfully caught up in the notion of exascale computing, and the number of cores being touted keeps growing. As a result, there there is less and less attention being paid to what the individual core can or can not provide. The argument goes: The core is but a brick; we are constructing buildings. I submit that the two vectors are orthogonal, and we throw away a lot of potential if we don't also address what the individual core can provide. I do not argue for one ox to pull the plow rather than a thousand chickens. I ask for yokes of oxen.

To address the inherent capabilities of the individual core, I find the transformation hierarchy enlightening. I identified the concept 30 years ago, reflecting that although (a) problems are described in natural language, it is really (b) the electrons that solve these problems as they move from one voltage potential to another. To get from (a) to (b) requires working through several layers, requiring several transformations. That was 1981, long before the era of multi-core. In those days, the layers provided safe abstractions – people worked within their own layer, not paying much attention to the other layers. In my view, part of the solution to the exascale computing requirement requires expanding the awareness at each layer to what goes on beneath that layer.

In this talk, I hope to suggest several steps for improving performance if every layer of the transformation hierarchy is allowed to help. They include: multiple interfaces to the "bare metal", the importance of ILP (which is not dead, incidentally), directives from the compiler, and run-time systems that are intrinsically coupled to the microarchitecture. Although I address these issues from the standpoint of the single core, there is nothing to preclude them from being considered at a higher level of abstraction where they can be applied with thousands of cores at our disposal. If time permits, I may have a few words to add about that.

ABOUT THE SPEAKER

Yale Patt is Professor of Electrical and Computer Engineering and the Ernest Cockrell, Jr. Centennial Chair in Engineering at UT Austin. He enjoys thoroughly teaching both the 400+ freshmen in the required intro to computing course and the 25 graduate students in his advanced microarchitecture course. He has also taught intensive courses to graduate students at many campuses in the US and Europe. He has been teaching for 45 years, and as he now approaches mid-career, he is looking forward to another 45 years as a professor and teacher. He has earned appropriate degrees from reputable universities and has received more than enough awards for his research and teaching. More detail is available on his website: www.ece.utexas.edu/~patt.

Categories and Subject Descriptors

C.5.1 [**Computer System Implementation**]: Large and Medium ("Mainframe") Computers—*Super (very large) computers*

General Terms

Design, Performance

Keywords

exascale, transformation hierarchy, abstraction layers, microarchitecture, compiler, run-time, instruction level parallelism

ICS'12, June 25–29, 2012, San Servolo Island, Venice, Italy.
ACM 978-1-4503-1316-2/12/06.

Distributed Replay Protocol for Distributed Uniprocessors

Mengjie Mao, Hong An, Bobin Deng, Tao Sun, Xuechao Wei, Wei Zhou, Wenting Han
School of Computer Science and Technology
University of Science and Technology of China
mjmao@mail.ustc.edu.cn, han@ustc.edu.cn,
{bbdeng, suntaos, xcwei, greatzv}@mail.ustc.edu.cn

ABSTRACT

Data speculation technique has been heavily exploited in various scenarios of architecture design. It bridges the time or space gap between data producer and data consumer, which gives opportunities to processors to gain significant speedups. However, large instruction windows, deep pipeline and increasing latency of on-chip communication make data misspeculation very expensive in modern processors.

This paper proposes a Distributed Replay Protocol(DRP) that addresses data misspeculation in a distributed uniprocessor, named TFlex. The partition feature of distributed uniprocessors aggravates the penalty of data misspeculation. After detecting misspeculation, DRP avoids squashing pipeline; on the contrary, it retains all instructions in the window and selectively replays the instructions that depend on the misspeculative data. As one possible use of DRP, We apply it to recovery from data dependence speculation. We also summarize the challenges of implementing selective replay mechanism on distributed uniprocessors, and then come up with two variations of DRP to effectively solve these challenges. The evaluation results show that without data speculation, DRP achieves 99% of the performance of perfect memory disambiguation. It speeds up diverse applications over baseline TFlex(with a state-of-art data dependence predictor) by a geometric mean of 24%.

Categories and Subject Descriptors

C.1.3 [**Processor Architectures**]: Other Architecture Styles

Keywords

Selective replay, selective recovery, selective re-execution, data misspeculation, distributed uniprocessors

1. INTRODUCTION

Data speculation plays a critical role in architecture design. It bridges the time or space gap between data producer and data consumer. Once the consumer receives a speculative data, it can drive a speculative execution, which would lead to considerable performance improvements.

Many types of data speculation have been proposed for alleviating the latency penalty caused by on-chip communication or sequential execution. Data dependence prediction[6][18][32]is considered a major technique for tolerating the latency incurred by maintaining sequential memory semantics within a thread. Continual Flow Pipeline (CFP)[11][28] is a means of exposing Memory-Level Parallelism (MLP) that speculates the consecutive independent instructions after cache miss. Data speculation is also employed by Thread-Level Speculation (TLS)[29] and Transactional Memory (TM)[19][20] for relieving from frequent aborts or data conflicts.

Data speculation gives an opportunity to system to gain significant speedup if speculations are correct. However, large instruction windows, deep pipeline and long-latency of on-chip communication make data misspeculation much expensive in modern processors. Large instruction windows allow hundreds or thousands of instructions to issue after the speculative point that may be declared a misspeculation in future. Moreover, the growing latency of on-chip communication enlarges the time gap between misspeculation detection and report[9], which enables more "dirty" instructions to go into pipeline. As instruction windows increase, data predictor bears more burdens and then results in descendant accuracy. Once a misspeculation is asserted, tremendous computations after the misspeculation point will be discarded. Therefore, data misspeculation becomes a prominent obstacle that prevents systems from getting higher performance scalability.

Figure 1 shows the downgrade of performance along with the increase of data dependence misprediction across various window sizes on TFlex, a distributed tiled architecture[14]. As the window size scales, the load dependence misprediction rate climbs up slightly, but the performance downgrades drastically. With an one core configuration(up to 128 instructions, up to 32 of which can be memory instructions), TFlex achieves about 99% of ideal performance of oracular memory disambiguation with less than 1% load dependence misprediction. When the window size increases to 2046, of which 512 instructions can be loads or stores, the performance of TFlex drop to 82% of ideal performance but the misprediction rate only increases about 1%, which indicates that the entire system performance is very sensitive with data dependence prediction.

In this paper, we propose a selective replay protocol, called Distributed Replay Protocol(DRP), for a novel distributed microarchitecture-TFlex-to efficiently recover from data dependence misprediction. DRP enables TFlex to aggressively issue all the load instructions and provides a lightweight recovery mechanism for load violations. DRP makes TFlex ap-

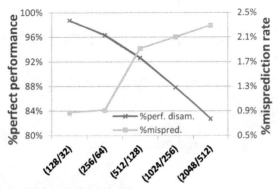

Figure 1: Performance scalability and predictor accuracy with increasing window sizes of TFlex

proximate the performance of perfect memory disambiguation without any data speculation.

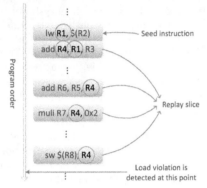

Figure 2: An example of replay slice which derives from a load violation

As Figure 1 shown, TFlex is vulnerable to data dependence misprediction, which lends DRP a great potential to exploit the hiding performance improvements. Recent study[21] points out that distributed architectures confront a major bottleneck of fetch stalls. Squashing the pipeline due to data misprediction contributes a large part of fetch stalls. Figure 2 shows a section of a program code, in which the shaded instructions are data dependent on the speculative load instruction through register or memory locations. After detecting load violation, DRP avoids squashing the pipeline and also obviates the necessity of redoing all the works after the load instruction. The correctness of execution is promised by selectively replaying the instructions depended on the mispredicted load value. DRP speeds up the original TFlex, which deploys state-of-the-art data dependence predictor, with affordable hardware cost. It achieves about 99% of the performance of perfect memory disambiguation with thousands of window size, and outperforms the performances gained by various idealize predictors listed in [22].

The replay protocol we propose for TFlex is not limited to data dependence misprediction recovery; it can apply to all data speculations including value prediction[16], predicate prediction[10] etc. It can also be a part of implementation of control independence[23] or system reliability. This paper systematically details the challenges of implementing selective replay on dataflow machines and demonstrates that DRP is able to tackle these challenges thoroughly, which implies that it is a competitive candidate of selective replay protocol for distributed dataflow-driven architectures[30][31].

The rest of this paper is organized as follows. Section 2 lists the related works; section 3 provides a simple background of TFlex architecture; we describe DRP in section 4; section 5 and 6 then present the evaluation; section 6 concludes the paper.

2. RELATED WORK

Selective replay has been widely investigated for tolerating the cost of data misspeculation. Early study[4] showed that selective replay with data prediction can approach the performance of perfect disambiguation in processors that have small window size. Several commercial processors had introduced limited selective replay mechanisms for recovery from load scheduling misspeculation[13][17]. Zhou et al. [33] summarized the challenges about selective recovery from value misspeculation in superscalar processors, which include the identification and reservation of dependent instructions, and the replay mechanism itself. Kim et al.[15] pointed out that aggressive selective replay was not feasible for large instruction windows based on current designs. TFlex, on which we implement a universal distributed replay scheme, is free from above constrains by its architecture characteristics, which we will extend on section 3.

CFP-set architectures[11][28] employ limited replay. Generally, this set of architectures buffer the forward slice driven by cache miss and continue executing following independent instructions. The forward slice will not be executed until its seed instruction (often is load) retrieves the value from cache. Sun's ROCK Processor[5] has introduced CFP to exploit thread-level parallelism. CFP has to speculate which instructions belong to a specific forward slice. If misspeculation is detected, it squashes the pipeline and rolls back to former checkpoint(if it is a checkpoint-based system) without selective replay.

ReSlice[24] enables CFP to support thorough replay-it replays the forward slice after misspeculation. Reslice can also be applied to other checkpoint systems. However, ReSlice imposes rigorous conditions only under which replay will be correct and successful. Additionally, it has to dynamically collect forward slice. In TFlex, neither buffering nor rebuilding replay slice is necessary, since instructions in TFlex do not retire until they are committed. The replay slice in TFlex is exposed automatically by the dataflow execution model adopted by TFlex.

DRP is inspired by Distributed Selective Re-Execution (DSRE)[7]. DSRE is the first replay protocol proposed for TRIPS processor[3], which also implements the ISA of T-Flex. We will detail DSRE and compare it with DRP in section 4.3.3. We transplant DSRE into TFlex and compare the performance of it with that of DRP in section 6.

RETCON[2] exploits replay in the context of TM. Unlike above instruction-based replay mechanisms, it uses symbolic tracking to repair transaction. Selective replay is additionally used for control independence architectures[1][12]. In this paper we only evaluate DRP for memory dependence prediction, but it is easily adopted for supporting other misspeculation recovery mechanisms.

3. BACKGROUND

TFlex is a Composable Lightweight Processor(CLP)[14] that has up to 32 distributed simple cores. It implements EDGE ISA[3] that defines block-atomic execution and direct instruction communication. Block-atomic execution allows TFlex to manipulate instruction block(we refer block in the rest of this paper) as the basic operative element, so the fetch and commit protocols in TFlex operate on block rather than single instruction. TFlex uses tournament-extended branch predictor to predict the next block, several blocks can be executed simultaneously. Direct instruction communication means that all instructions within a block communicate with each other directly without accessing register file; inter-block communications are via register file and memory. Within a block, each instruction encodes its consumers' identifiers in its bits. EDGE ISA restricts a block to possess no more than 32 register reads, 32 register writes and 128 normal instructions, up to 32 of which can be loads/stores. In the rest of this paper, we refer input instruction (register read & load) as seed instruction which can drive or propagate speculative execution slices; we refer branch, register write and store as output instruction, which can alter the program state; and we refer all the other instructions as intermediate instruction.

TFlex combines inter-block control flow and intra-block data-flow, which make itself easily capture replay slices. Intra block, replay slice is exposed by direct instruction communication; inter block, TFlex uses register forward units and partitioned LSQs[25] to trace the replay slice that stretches several blocks. Each TFlex core contains a register forwarding unit and a piece of LSQs, as shown in figure 3.

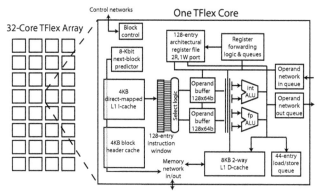

Figure 3: Microarchitectural components of single core of a 32-core TFlex[14]

TFlex is able to fuse several cores to a logical big core to run an application. When running in the merged mode, all on-chip resources of participated cores are shared by each other and are addressed interleavely. The instructions of a block are mapped to participated cores interleavely, thus, all instructions within that block execute and communicate across cores. For example, a memory instruction computes address in one core, and then routes to the appropriate core containing the cache associated with its memory address. In order to charge the fetch and commit stage of blocks, each block is designated a Coordinator Core (CC) indexed by that block's sub-PC bits when it is fetched.

4. DISTRIBUTED REPLAY PROTOCOL (DRP)

In this section, we first introduce how selective replay works on TFlex. We then analyze why correct replay is challenging and review former proposed DSRE. We details DRP and show how it addresses these challenges at the end of this section.

4.1 Overview of selective replay

Dataflow execution is born with suitability for selective replay. If an instruction inside a Data Flow Graph (DFG) computes a new result, its children, which belong to the sub-tree of that instruction, will all be re-driven and then finally generate new output(s) at the bottom of the DFG. If the instructions are not expelled from window until committing, the replay mechanism will be unnecessarily to dynamically collect the replay slices derived from any seed instructions. TFlex embraces above two assumptions, which enable it to easily implement distributed replay protocol.

As mentioned in section 3, TFlex instantiates EDGE ISA that defines dataflow execution within blocks. Instructions, as well as their operands, are buffered in window. When an instruction receives an operand, it tags the corresponding bit as valid. An instruction issues only all bits for operands are valid. When detecting a seed instruction computed with a wrong speculative operand, TFlex reissues this instruction that then re-sends the correct result to its children and triggers their reissues, in which they execute just like the first time they executed. So the replay has been easily implemented intra blocks.

Replay slice derives from seed instruction inside a block, and always stretches out following blocks through register file or memory (except for the situation that that slice eventually generate only one output-branch-in a block). Thus, the replay slice is a collection of small, statical DFGs from each related block[7], and the flow arcs connecting these small DFGs are virtualized by inter-block communication via resgister file and memory. TFlex does not include register renaming, EDGE ISA defines 128 architecture registers. Moreover, each TFlex core possesses a register forwarding unit that accelerates register forwarding. Memory dependences are forced by partitioned LSQs. All of these promise efficient selective replay on inter-block level.

Figure 4 is an example of selective replay. The left part of this figure is a source code of a loop with the corresponding EDGE assembly code[1]. This loop is packed into a block. Multiple blocks can be executed simultaneously on TFlex, of which one is non-speculative and the rest are speculative, as shown in the right part of figure 4 (for space limitation, we cut off the sub-tree of N[12] in each DFG). Three inter-block dependences are carried by the loop, one for register (variable i) and the other two are for memory (a[i] and b[i]). Speculatively loading b[n-1] in block n (N[4]) would result in violation if b[n-1] had not been written in block n-1 (N[10]). If violation occurs, TFlex without DRP will squash block n and its followers, and then re-fetches, re-dispatches, re-issues and re-executes all instructions of these blocks. On the contrary, with DRP, TFlex needlessly squash any blocks, it re-executes N[4] in block n, which then evokes a execution flow that will submerge all old computations (shaded nodes in block n) depending on the former incorrect result produced by N[4]. Once this flow reaches N[10], LSQ forwards new value to N[4] in block n+1. Eventually, all blocks following block n-1 will repair their states.

---

[1]The assembly presented here is modified to meet the space limitation

```
for (i = 1; i < 100; i++)
{
    a[i] += a[i - 1];
    b[i] += b[i - 1];
    if (a[i] > 0) b[i] = a[i] + i;
    else b[i] *= 2;
}
```

EDGE Assembly:

```
R0   G[20]  N[0], N[1], N[2], N[8], N[12]  ; read i
N[0]  lw     $(a[i])  N[5]   ; load a[i]
N[1]  lw     $(b[i])  N[6]   ; load b[i]
N[2]  subi   1  N[3]  N[4]   ; i-1
N[3]  lw     $(a[i-1]) N[5]  ; load a[i-1]
N[4]  lw     $(b[i-1]) N[6]  ; load b[i-1]
N[5]  add    N[7]  N[8]  N[9]  N[11]  ;a[i] + a[i-1]
N[6]  add    N[9]           ; b[i] + b[i-1]
N[7]  tgz    N[8]  N[9]     ; if( a[i] > 0 )
N[8]  add_t  N[10]          ; a[i] + i
N[9]  muli_f N[10]          ; b[i] * 2
N[10] sw     &(b[i])        ; store b[i]
N[11] sw     &(a[i])        ; store a[i]
N[12] addi   1  N[13]  W[0]  ; i + 1
N[13] teqi   100  N[14]  N[15]  ; if( i ==100 )
N[14] bro_f  loop
N[15] bro_t  exit
W[0]  wr     G[20]
```

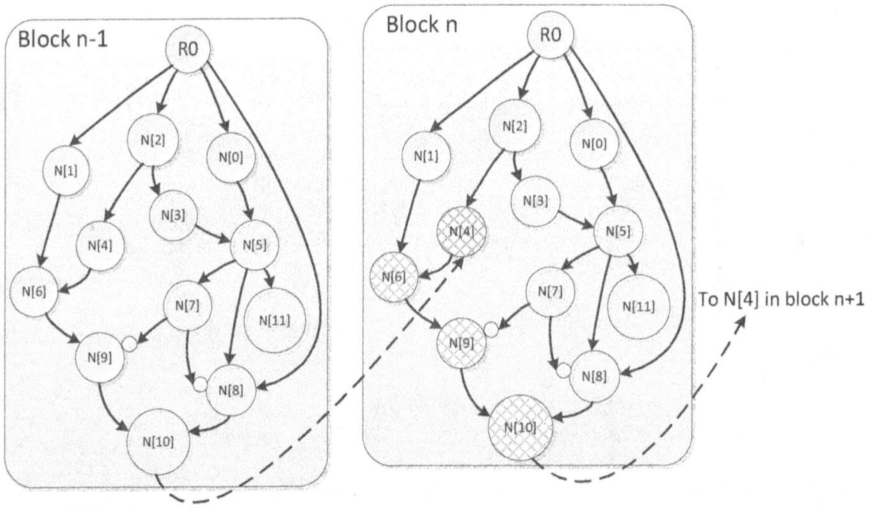

Figure 4: An example of selective replay on EDGE Architecture

4.2 The challenges of correct replay

4.2.1 The first challenge : detecting block completion

TFlex determines whether a block completes or not by counting the outputs of that block has been produced. When a block is dispatched, CC records the number of its outputs. Each time an output instruction issues, it sends an output report to CC. Once CC receives the expected number of output reports of a block, it labels that block as completion. If a block is the oldest one among inflight blocks, which indicates that it is non-control-speculative, and it is labeled as completion, CC then will broadcast a signal to all participated cores for committing the output results(register writes or stores) of that block, after which all participated cores will release the resources occupied by that block.

Selective replay breaks up this commit protocol, because an output instruction is allowed to issue more than once, which makes CC disable to figure out which report it receives from that output instruction is correct. For example, in figure 4, N[4] in block n may reissue several times and then N[10] will report corresponding times to block n's CC.

4.2.2 The second challenge: out-of-order messaging

In an in-order messaging network, CC can treat the last report of an output instruction as the correct one, since the seed instruction which evokes multiple replay slices will definitely generate a correct, non-speculative value in the last time of issue. TFlex promises operand messages are routed in-order and never drops any messages.

However, predication[27] makes in-order messaging turn to be out-of-order, so the last output report may be incorrect. For example, in block n of figure 4, N[3] issues without waiting for N[11] in block n-1. N[7], a predication-generated instruction, then predicates N[8] can issue. N[3] then reissues as misprediction, this time N[7] receives another operand derived from N[3] and predicates N[8] should not issue but N[9]. Let's assume in last execution flow, N[8] computed a result with an incorrect value and had sent it to N[10], but N[10] has not received N[8]'s message. In cur-

rent execution flow, N[9] also sends a operand to N[10], this operand has reached N[10] before that sent by N[8]. After a while N[8]'s message eventually arrives at N[10] and immerses the one sent by N[9] (it can happen if the location of N[8] is far away from that of N[10] or the path between N[8] and N[10] is in traffic jam). In this case, N[10] computes with an old false operand even the operand is received lately.

4.3 Correct selective replay

4.3.1 Sufficient information for correct replay

If CC knows the output report is the exact one computed with non-speculative operands, the first challenge mentioned above will be perfectly solved. Only receiving the exact report does CC increase the output counter for the corresponding block, otherwise, it discards that report. If CC can pick up the only appropriate report, then the order among messages turns to be meaningless-only output instructions can modify program states, CC promises to commit the correct results of output instructions. Thus, the second challenge is also unraveled.

In order to determine whether a report sent by output instruction is the exact one, CC must hold three pieces of information about this report: 1) the set of seed instructions that can reach the output instruction; 2) whether the report is computed with the most-updated operands derived from that set of seed instructions; 3) whether all instructions within that set are non-speculative.

Combing information 1) and 2), CC can determine whether a report is most-updated or not. We revisit the example from section 4.2.2, CC first receives a report from N[10], which is computed with a operand sent by N[9]. According information 1), CC knows this report is derived from R0, N[0], N[1], N[3] and N[4](they are the sources of N[10]); according information 2), CC notes this report is most-updated. When another report from N[8] arrives, whose corresponding set of seed instructions is R0, N[0] and N[3], CC discovers it use old version of operand provided by N[3], thus it is thrown by CC. However, at this moment, CC is still unable to know whether new report will come from N[10]

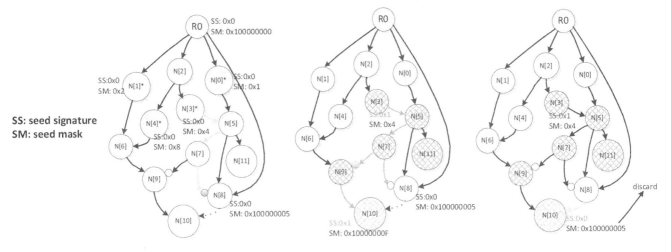

SS: seed signature
SM: seed mask

*load is an intermediate but also an input instruction, so it possesses two pairs of SM&SS for both status,
we only present one pair SM&SS of load for its input instruction status here due to space limitation.

(a)   (b)   (c)

Figure 5: Using seed mask and seed signature to filter outdated message: (a) N[3] speculatively issues first, execution flow reach N[8]; (b) N[3] violates and drives a replay slice; (c) outdated message from N[8] is discarded by CC.

since N[3] or N[4] may reissue later. The presenting of information 3) enables CC to figure out which report is the final, exact one sent by N[10], since the set of seed instructions(N[0], N[1], N[3], N[4] and R0) for N[10] have been non-speculative, which means these seed instructions will never reissue.

4.3.2 Seed mask and seed signature

To satisfy information 1), we designate each seed instruction a mask that is exclusive intra-block, namely seed mask, and let CC holds all seed masks of its slave blocks. Each operand message sent by seed instruction is attached with that instruction's seed mask, which indicates where this operand comes from. Intermediate instruction ORs the seed masks of the operands it receives, and attaches the accumulative mask to its result that will be sent to consumer instructions. Eventually, output instruction sends a final mask along with original report to CC. Since CC holds all seed masks of seed instructions of that block, it can use the received mask to extract a set of seed instructions that are responsible for that output report.

We use the raw ID of seed instruction, which is statically allocated by compiler, to assign seed mask exclusively in block-scope. Inside a block, the IDs of register reads/writes vary from 0 to 31, so as that of loads/stores, so we define 64-bit for a seed mask to allow it embraces all seed instructions of a block. For load, its mask is computed as follow:

$$load.mask = 1 \ll load.ID$$

As the ID range of register read overlays with that of load, register read should shift left by 32-bit from the original mask. The mask computing formula for read is:

$$read.mask = 1 \ll (read.ID + 32)$$

When fetching a block, CC calculates and stores the block's seed masks before it is dispatched.

Again, to satisfy information 2), each time a seed instruction (re)issues, it attaches a signature to its result, which exactly distinguishes this result among all results, including past and future ones computed by all seed instructions of

that block. To guarantee every signature is unique intra-block, CC is responsible for dispatching signature for its slave blocks. Therefore, each operand message sent by seed instruction should first route to CC to register a signature, then route to its consumer. CC pluses a 64-bit signature register for a block, each time a signature is dispatched, the register shifts left by 1. Intermediate instruction ORs the signatures of operands it receives. Output instruction, finally, gains a comprehensive signature. Output instruction also sends signature to CC along with seed mask and report mentioned above.

Assuming R0 has reissued several times in figure 4(for example, R0 was forwarded by register write in previous block, in which the write depended on a frequent-reissue load), which drives N[0], N[1], N[3] and N[4] to reissue corresponding times. More seriously, if the sub-tree of R0 contains much more amount of loads(it often appears in real applications), the signature register of that block will overflow at high rates. So we restrict that only can 1)reissue reads and 2)violated loads change their signatures. This restriction implies that normal execution of loads and the first issue of register reads are both unnecessarily to route to CC, they keep their former signature(for read, its first signature is 0) and send it to consumer directly.

Once CC receives a pair of seed mask and signature from an output report, it uses the seed mask to extract a set of seed instructions, and then calculates the expected aggregate signature by ORing the individual signatures of that set of instructions. If the expected signature is the same with the received one, that report must be most-updated; otherwise, it would be discarded by CC as outdated.

Figure 5 revisits the case in 4.2.2 and illustrates how seed mask and seed signature address the problem raised in that case. In figure 5(a), R0 first issues with a signature 0x0, N[0], N[1], N[3] and N[4] receive corresponding operands and issue aggressively without waiting the completions of stores in previous block n-1. At this slice, N[7] allows N[8] to issue. In figure 5(b), N[3] reissues due to violation, it obtains a new signature 0x1 from CC. The replay slice reaches N[7] and then re-selects N[9] to issue. The operand message sent by N[9] transmits much faster than that sent by N[8] in former slice, so N[10] receives the operand sent by N[9] first. In figure 5(c), N[8]'s message arrives at N[10] and N[10] then also sends a report to CC, but CC forsakes this report, because the expected signature for that report is 0x1 but not 0x0.

To satisfy information 3), CC should know the speculative statuses of all seed instructions of its slave blocks. The output instruction that sends out a most-updated report can be committed if the corresponding set of seed instructions of this report are all non-speculative. For example, in figure 5(b), if R0, N[0], N[1], N[3] and N[4] become non-speculative, which means none of them will reissue, then N[10] is safe to commit and the counter of that block will increase one.

A load is non-speculative only all its logical-pervious stores are non-speculative; a register read is non-speculative only the register write that forwards value to it is non-speculative or, it directly reads a value from register file. We adopt the distributed protocol described in [22] to propagate the commit statuses of inflight stores among merged cores. If a register write instruction is notified to commit(non-speculative) by CC, the write then will mark following reads which read its target as non-speculative through register forwarding unit. Once a read is labeled as non-speculative, it sends a message to inform CC. The latency induced by these communications will be evaluated in section 6.3.

4.3.3 Former work of selective replay for EDGE architecture

Distributed Selective Re-Execution[7] introduces commit wave to detect block completion. Commit wave is generated by seed instruction once it becomes non-speculative; this wave traverses the whole DFG. When it passes an output instruction, that instruction can be committed. To handle out-of-order messaging, DSRE let each instruction maintain an incremental version number, which increases one each time the instruction (re)issues. An operand message attached with a bigger version number is newer, so operand messages is re-ordered by their version numbers, older messages are automatically discarded by executing cores.

DSRE provides a preliminary solution for the two major challenges listed in section 4.2. However, the latency incurred by transmission of commit wave limits its potential of performance outburst, and forces it to return speculation for accelerating commit wave; numerical version number of individual instruction only takes effect if communications are strict one-to-one[8]. Predication enables an instruction to receive the same operand from different producers, which makes version number meaningless. DSRE requires each instruction backup its result for predication-caused disorder messaging, since commit wave should refresh the operands of instructions locating on its trace, which may cause additional computations and open another window for downgrading the whole system performance.

4.4 Masks overlapping

In order to reduce the overflow of signature register, we have imposed two restrictions for signature dispatching. Unfortunately, these restrictions induce a side effect. We excerpt a snip of figure 5(b) and show it in figure 6. In figure 5(b), we assume N[8] receives a new predication from N[7] first, which prevents it from reissuing. However, if N[8] receives new operand from N[5] first, a ambiguity will happen, because the computed result will falsely become the most-

updated one that should be throttled by new predication value, which has not reach N[8] yet, as shown in figure 6(a). This ambiguity propagates to N[10] and eventually reach C-C, then makes CC disable to discriminate outdated reports.

The seed masks of operands overlapping inside an instruction is the factor causing above ambiguity. To throttle ambiguity produced by overlapping masks, each participated core should buffer the most-updated signatures of all seed instructions of all inflight blocks. If an instruction has overlap seed masks, as well as at least one of whose signatures is outdated, that instruction will be postponed by its executed core. After assigning a signature to a seed instruction, CC broadcasts the signature to all participated cores. The latency of waiting the newest signatures is ignorable, for example, in figure 6(a), the newest signature of corresponding seed instruction is always sent along with the operand message(the message from N[5]) that first arrives at instruction. Otherwise, if an instruction possesses non-overlap seed masks, it will be allowed to issue even though it computes with outdated operands, since its outdated result will be eventually discriminated and discarded by CC. With the 2-D mesh operand networking, the instructions which need the newest signatures most urgently are always satisfied in time.

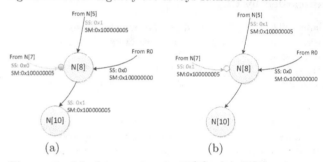

(a)   (b)

Figure 6: Masks overlap in N[8]: (a) N[8] reissues due to receiving a new operand from N[5]; (b) N[8] receives a new predication from N[7] that throttles its issue

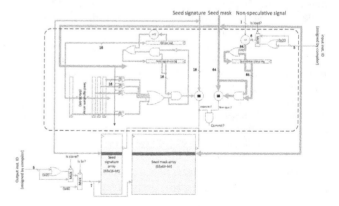

Figure 7: Added logic diagram of CC used for determining output instruction committing

Aggregating all above descriptions, the implementation of CC tackling arrival report of output instruction is shown in figure 7. The incoming seed mask filters out a set of seed signatures from buffer array, and then the expected signature of that report is ORed by the set of signatures. The speculative statuses of seed instructions are stored in a 64-bit register(one bit for one instruction, if this instruction is speculative then its bit will be set to 0, otherwise it will be set to 1). If the incoming seed signature is 1)the same with the expected one, and 2)the selective set of seed instructions is non-speculative, the output instruction, which sends out this report, can commit its results to corresponding register file bank or cache bank. Otherwise, the report will be buffered for further review if it satisfies 1), or, it will be discarded if not. We limit one CC can master no more than 2 blocks, so a CC has two replications of the logic presented in figure 7.

4.5 Avoid signature broadcasting: coupling seed mask and seed signature

Signature broadcasting effectively addresses the problems of signature overflow and mask overlapping, but it requires additional broadcasting network and more register resources to buffer signatures in each participated core. There is a tradeoff between signature overflow and hardware cost: if we slacken the restriction on signature dispatching, the buffers of signatures for tackling mask overlapping will be no longer necessary.

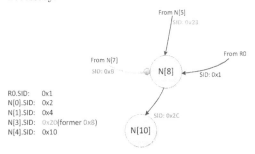

Figure 8: Using SID to address mask overlapping, the SID of each seed instruction is presented in the left

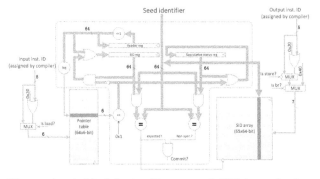

Figure 9: Added logic diagram of CC introducing SID to determine output instruction committing

We extend the conditions under which a seed instruction can accept a new signature: 1)reissued read, 2)violated load and 3)seed instruction that never issues before. With the slack restrictions, we can combine seed mask and seed signature into one 64-bit word, called Seed IDentifier(SID), to ensure correct selective replay. Qualified seed instruction routes to CC to acquire a SID, which not only distinguishes itself from multiple instantiations but also distinguishes its result among those of other seed instructions. Figure 8 shows how SID addresses signature overlapping. Even though N[8] still sends out a outdated value that should be inhibited by the coming predication, but CC will be able to identifies the outdated report derived from N[8], since the SID of that report should be 0x23(R0.SID *OR* N[0].SID *OR*

N[3].SID) but not 0x2C. The implementation of CC deploying SID to check arrival reports is shown in figure 9.

If incoming SID is a non-empty subset of the word ORed by all SID of seed instructions that belong to a block, the report accompanied with that SID is most-updated. In order to extract the set of responsible seed instructions for determining if the report is safe to commit, the speculative bit of each seed instruction, which is stored in a specific spot of the speculative status register, should locate at the same spot with that it occupies in SID, which means that we should provide a pointer table to index a specific spot in speculative register associated with that seed instruction, as shown in figure 9. For space efficiency, one CC master no more than 2 blocks so that two replications of the logic presented in figure 9 are required.

5. EVALUATION METHODOLOGY

We implement DRP-SB, which employs Signature Broadcasting, and DRP-SID, which employs Seed IDentifier, on a cycle accurate TFlex microarchitecture simulator. Table 1 expresses the parameters of one TFlex core[14]. Avoid favoring the performance advantage of DRP, we deploy the most optimistic dependence predictor[22] into baseline TFlex configuration, called Counting Dependence Predictor(CDP). We also transplant the DSRE protocol[7] into TFlex, along with a modified predictor derived from[22] to speculate commit bit, to compare with our protocol.

The hardware costs of three replay schemes are shown in table 2. Without pointed, the length of seed signature in DRP-SB is 16 bits. DRP-SB inflates hardware about 3.7 times over DSRE, and 2.2 times over DRP-SID. DRP-SID is hardware-efficient than DRP-SB, because DRP-SID has no necessary to buffer all seed signatures in each merged core, and it requires less resources to buffer operand-relevant bits(64-bit identifier versus 80-bit mask&signature) in each instruction slot. The hardware cost of DSRE is underestimated, we rule out the extra cost added to LSQs when introducing CDP in DSRE. The original DSER relies on central LSQ to force memory disambiguation, it requires more ancillary resources when running with partitioned LSQs on TFlex, which we also exclude in the table.

For DSRE, we exclude all latencies incurred by differences between TRIPS and TFlex, which implies that DSRE runs in a near oracular manner. We do not simulate the contentions of assigning signature or identifiers at CCs, these contentions have been reflected by on-chip network latency. And we do not simulate the contentions of checking output reports at CCs, since the arrival frequencies of reports are relatively low and we can increase the read ports of the implementations in figure 7 and 9, or even replicate the dash areas of both figures to enlarge the number of reports that a CC can process in one time.

We select a subset of SPEC 2000(with the Ref input data set) and EEMBC codes for evaluation. All SPEC benchmarks are simulated with single SimPoints[26]; the iteration of each EEMBC benchmark is carefully tailored for proper instruction count.

6. RESULTS
6.1 Performance evaluation

Figure 10 shows the performances obtained by CDP, DSRE, DRP-SB and DRP-SID, normalized to the performance of perfect disambiguation. All applications run on 16-core

Table 1: Single core TFlex microarchitecture parameter

Parameter	Configuration
Instruction Supply	Partitioned 8KB I-cache (2-cycle hit); Local/Gshare Tournament predictor(8K+256 bits, 3 cycle latency) with speculative updates; Num.entries: Local: 64(L1)+128(L2), Global: 512, RAS: 16, CTB:16, BTB: 128, Btype:256.
Execution	Out-of-order execution, RAM structured 128-entry issue window, dual-issue (up to 1 INT and 1 FP).
Data Supply	Partitioned 8KB D-cache(2-cycle hit, 2-way set-associ-1-read port and 1-write port); 64-entry LSQ bank; 4MB ative,decoupled S-NUCA L2 cache (8-way set-associative, LRU-replacement);L2-hit latency varies from 5 cycles to 27 cycles depending on memory address; average (unloaded) main memory latency is 150 cycles.

Table 2: Hardware consumption/core

item	DSRE	DRP-SB	DRP-SID
inst. slot	19b/ver.buf*3 64b/res.buf*1	64b/sm.buf*3 16b/ss.buf*3	64b/sid.buf*3
total	1.89kB	3.75kB	3kB
cc	-	16b/ss.buf*64 80b/o.buf*65	6b/pt*64 64b/o.buf*65
total	-	0.76*2kB	0.55*2kB
seed sig.	-	16b*64/blk 30blk/core	-
total	-	3.75KB	-
DP	0.55kB	-	-
overall	2.44kB	9.02kB	4.1kB

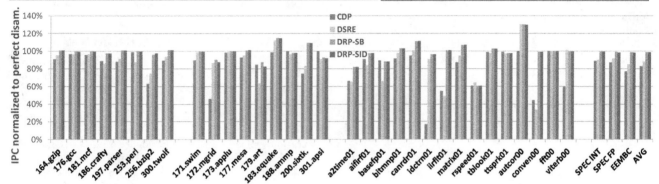

Figure 10: Performances of different applications running on 16-core TFlex with different configurations

TFlex, in which there are up to 2048 instruction windows, up to 512 of which can be loads/stores. CDP achieves 88%, 87%, 77% of the perfect performance in SPEC INT, SPEC FP and EEMBC respectively, and average 82% for all applications; DSRE moderately scale the performance in these three categories; it achieves 90%, 92% and 85% of perfect performances respectively, 88% for overall average. DRP-series extremely approximate the perfect disambiguation performance: DRP-SB achieves 99% of perfect performance in SPEC INT and SPEC FP, and 98% in EEMBC, 99% for average; DRP-SID achieves 99% in SPEC INT, and 98% in SPEC FP and EEMBC, 98% for overall average.

The accuracy of CDP is very high, indeed, figure 1 shows that it accurately predicts 97.7% of the dynamic load issues. We define misprediction as a load 1)violates or 2)should be issued aggressively but conservatively. We find that the portion of 1) contributing to misprediction is trivially small, only less than 0.5%. However, the system is significantly sensitive to misprediction when it adopts large instruction window, which makes CDP only achieve 82% of perfect performance even with a high accuracy. On the other hand, these data implies that it is worth digging performance from those 2.3% misprediction.

DSRE employs CDP for commit wave prediction and s-elective replays after misprediction, both of which lend it achieve 88% of perfect performance. In this case, we do not simulate the flow control that is indispensable because commit wave may surpass execution wave, which will eventually destroy the completion detection mechanism of block. Moreover, we do not consider the situations under which instruction should re-computes its result due to predication-incurred out-of-order messaging. Combing above factors and those described in section 5, we can see that DSRE only gains extra 6% performance with an ideal setting, which

indicates that, with a thorough distributed substrate, the latency of commit wave propagation heavily limits the performance scalability of DSRE. Additionally, we note that the CDP loses a little accuracy when it is applied to DSRE, which counteracts the performance improvement it obtains.

Both of the DRP configurations outperform CDP and D-SRE. The reasons why DRPs achieve high performance are 1)issuing all loads aggressively that covers the loads that falsely wait for prior independent stores in CDP, and applying selective replay, instead of pipeline squashing, to recover from load violation; 2)unlike DSRE, no speculation is required to assist detecting block completion, efficient block completion detection in DRPs ensures output instructions are always committed in time without non-trivial latency. Theoretically, DRP-SB could achieve 100% of the perfect performance, or even exceed perfect performance due to some positive side effects. We will analyze this topic in section 6.3.2.

DRP-SB outperforms DRP-SID a little even the former includes broadcasting, which attests our supposition that broadcasting doesn't introduce any latency. On the other hand, broadcasting seed signature to participated cores allows DRP-SB to throttle some outdated replay slices that are allowed under DRP-SID(the execution in figure 8 is always ceased by DRP-SB), so the operand network of DRP-SID suffers from more traffic jams, which slightly downgrades its performance.

Table 3 presents the statistics well profiling the performance improvements of each replay scheme. Column 2 of table 3 presents the total amount of instructions fetched by DSRE and DRPs, normalized to the amount of those fetched by CDP. Commonly, selective replay techniques fetch less instructions than CDP, because they retain instructions in window that would be re-fetched regardless after data de-

Table 3: Characterizing the execution of applications running on 16-core TFlex with different replay schemes

bench.	%saved fetch			%saved commit			%reissue			squash/k inst.			speedup		
	DSRE	SB	SID	DSRE	SB	SID	DSRE	SB	SID	DSRE	SB	SID	DSRE	SB	SID
gzip	95.06	88.99	89.04	12.90	21.12	21.11	32.72	41.87	41.94	1.27	0.00	0.01	1.048	1.106	1.106
gcc	97.71	145.31	145.56	7.47	9.08	8.95	15.77	17.96	18.11	0.75	0.12	0.00	0.998	1.028	1.027
mcf	104.76	98.28	98.32	3.58	4.24	4.23	6.89	7.97	7.99	0.60	0.00	0.00	1.011	1.041	1.041
crafty	102.56	83.76	83.89	23.13	33.20	33.24	20.00	17.68	17.70	1.25	0.12	0.01	0.968	1.101	1.097
parser	105.53	84.44	84.55	13.42	17.33	16.60	9.44	10.14	10.14	2.41	0.04	0.00	1.035	1.143	1.142
perl	109.78	99.92	100.72	5.91	11.80	11.69	54.44	42.67	44.68	2.46	0.00	0.00	0.885	1.010	1.008
bzip2	89.88	52.52	52.63	16.57	47.77	47.40	23.06	13.46	14.50	2.90	1.48	0.04	1.185	1.520	1.548
twolf	97.61	88.73	88.74	26.49	31.75	31.70	25.34	23.48	23.52	0.56	0.00	0.00	1.049	1.130	1.129
SPEC INT	100.36	92.74	92.93	13.68	22.04	21.87	23.46	21.90	22.32	1.53	0.22	0.01	1.019	1.126	1.127
swim	98.06	98.97	98.97	0.00	0.00	0.00	0.00	0.00	0.00	0.00	0.00	0.00	1.101	1.109	1.109
mgrid	99.82	84.84	84.50	67.69	82.36	82.75	37.55	33.30	27.86	0.36	0.03	1.12	1.883	1.955	1.897
applu	99.47	100.07	100.02	0.00	0.00	0.00	0.00	0.00	0.00	0.00	0.00	0.00	1.012	1.016	1.016
mesa	96.58	91.40	91.27	16.31	21.42	21.49	17.34	17.23	17.27	0.51	0.00	0.00	1.027	1.086	1.087
art	222.95	99.86	99.92	0.73	10.19	10.20	46.88	21.14	21.19	2.65	3.64	0.00	0.752	1.033	0.973
equake	94.95	91.65	91.66	65.54	59.20	59.41	8.49	7.87	7.85	0.07	0.00	0.00	1.139	1.167	1.165
ammp	105.03	100.04	100.05	7.41	7.88	7.88	26.99	25.76	25.76	0.35	0.00	0.00	0.966	0.977	0.977
sixtk.	95.81	61.91	62.19	10.54	24.71	24.57	28.68	19.25	19.25	1.59	0.11	0.00	1.117	1.468	1.463
apsi	156.78	140.39	140.83	8.91	10.06	10.03	277.16	249.62	253.31	0.85	3.00	1.16	0.909	0.926	0.918
SPEC FP	118.83	96.57	96.60	19.68	23.98	24.04	49.23	41.57	41.39	0.71	0.75	0.25	1.068	1.161	1.148
a2time	193.66	91.46	91.38	39.11	93.93	94.02	31.47	21.33	21.30	2.68	0.00	0.00	0.984	1.236	1.236
aifirf	111.38	94.22	93.85	8.11	9.88	10.02	4.40	4.99	4.87	0.17	0.00	0.00	0.927	1.074	1.074
basefp	133.98	96.38	96.33	25.10	36.61	36.65	157.20	109.04	108.90	1.17	0.00	0.00	0.738	0.987	0.986
bitmnp	95.03	90.50	90.50	6.00	6.88	6.88	51.99	47.82	47.82	0.18	0.00	0.00	1.068	1.124	1.124
canrdr	88.11	78.44	78.41	47.24	58.32	58.39	15.21	14.65	14.54	1.59	0.00	0.00	1.065	1.176	1.177
idctrn	109.57	67.74	67.80	13.37	71.27	70.85	54.83	25.36	25.32	1.64	0.02	0.00	5.397	5.717	5.718
iirflt	165.59	66.16	66.16	29.71	91.11	90.98	12.36	7.22	7.22	3.15	0.25	0.00	0.896	1.835	1.834
matrix	86.55	71.76	71.70	9.48	21.07	21.14	27.72	16.53	16.56	0.54	0.06	0.00	1.086	1.224	1.226
rspeed	132.79	70.23	70.25	37.62	84.35	84.34	43.53	24.68	24.77	4.11	6.70	0.00	1.057	0.994	0.994
tblook	99.01	91.47	91.48	18.87	21.15	21.23	12.80	12.33	12.29	0.32	0.00	0.00	0.992	1.039	1.039
ttsprk	100.82	99.99	100.17	8.88	9.11	9.18	36.36	35.93	35.59	0.14	0.00	0.00	0.982	0.986	0.985
autcor	66.22	66.22	66.22	0.02	0.03	0.03	24.69	26.46	26.42	0.00	0.00	0.00	1.307	1.309	1.300
conven	144.48	47.77	47.77	29.75	91.54	91.54	18.35	7.20	7.22	5.41	0.00	0.00	0.759	2.229	2.233
fft	97.35	97.34	97.34	0.12	0.12	0.12	56.64	56.45	56.44	0.00	0.00	0.00	1.000	0.999	0.999
viterb	69.01	68.10	68.27	6.69	8.65	8.69	129.69	120.46	123.11	0.40	0.01	0.00	1.703	1.679	1.673
EEMBC	112.90	79.85	79.84	18.67	40.27	40.27	45.15	35.36	35.49	1.43	0.47	0.00	1.138	1.369	1.368
overall	111.43	87.78	87.83	17.71	31.13	31.10	40.87	33.75	33.86	1.25	0.49	0.07	1.088	1.245	1.241

pendence misprediction. Column 3 presents the percentage of committed instructions covered by selective replay. Note that the values in column 2 are different from those in column 3, for example, although an instruction is not squashed by data misprediction, perhaps it would be squashed by other events, for example, branch misprediction, which is not covered by our replay mechanisms. Column 4 indicates the portion of saved instructions(column 3) that should be reissued, since they belong to replay slices driven by reissued seed instructions. Column 5 shows Overflow Per Kilo Instructions(OPKI) of seed signature register in DRP-SB, OPKI of SID register in DRP-SID, and Commit wave misprediction Per Kilo Instructions(CPKI) in DSRE. Note that overflow of corresponding registers in DRPs doesn't result in pipeline flush; we simply reset all states of the blocks after the overflow block, and then completely re-execute them again. On the contrary, when DSRE mispredicts commit wave, it should recover in traditional way that CDP performs. The last column indicates speedup over CDP.

We observe that, low amount of instructions fetched into windows, or high amount accompanied with low reissued percentage of saved committed instructions often lead to dramatic performance improvements. Fetching fewer instructions means less cycles, and even less power are wasted on re-fetching the instructions that should not be squashed after data misprediction. Lower reissued percentage of saved instructions implies more saved instructions do not need to

re-executing, which also indicates more cycles and power are saved. *bzip2, mgrid, equake, sixtrack, a2time01, canrdr01, idctrn01, iirflt01, conven00* and *viterb00* can be clustered into this category. Note that *viterb00* has high branch misprediction rate(nearly 17%) that counteracts the amount of committed instructions covered by selective replay.

On contrast, applications, which 1)fetch more instructions, 2) reissue enormous instructions, or 3) overflow frequently, usually result in few improvement or even downgrade performance. For example, *apsi* possesses above three characteristics, which makes it result in obvious performance downgrade. Some applications that enjoy positive side effects generated by selective replay, can surpass their perfect performances. For example, when running with replay configurations, *equake* and *sixtrack* both increase 2% branch prediction accuracy that lets them outperform the performances of perfect memory disambiguation. In some case replay slices alter the original control flows, which change the local or global history of branch predictor and eventually improve branch prediction accuracy.

We note that 2 applications display interesting characteristics. There is no data misprediction when running *autcor00* and *swim* on 16-core TFlex, however, with selective replay, *autcor00* improves its branch predication accuracy from 95% to 100%, swim enjoys much lower L1 and L2 Dcache miss rates. We suggest that different NoC traffics and different

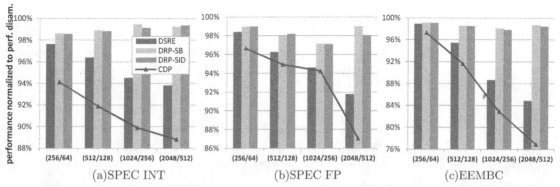

(a)SPEC INT   (b)SPEC FP   (c)EEMBC

Figure 11: The performances of selective replay schemes with increasing window size

commit detection technique exert some invisible impacts on system performance.

Across all applications, DRP-SB obtains a 24.5% of geometric mean speedup over the most aggressive CDP; DRP-SID uses about a half resources of DRP-SB to achieve a 24.1% speedup; with an ideal configuration, DSRE achieves an 8.8% of geometric mean improvement over CDP.

6.2 Performance scalability

Figure 11 shows the average performances of different replay schemes as the window size increases from two-core TFlex configuration(256 instruction windows, up to 64 of which can be loads/stores) to 16-core configuration(2048/512). The figure also shows the CDP performance to compare it with the performances of the other three replay schemes. As instruction window scales, the performances of DRPs consistently maintain at high level, for three types of applications(SPEC INT/FP, EEMBC) running across all configurations, DRPs always achieve more than 96% of the performance of perfect disambiguation. The rest replay scheme-DSRE, and CDP increase their vulnerabilities as the instruction window scales.

CDP performs poorly when running EEMBC with large instruction window, since the memory footprints of these applications are too various to trace. DSRE relies on CDP to speculate the commit waves, so it manifests the same trend with that of CDP.

6.3 Architectural parameter effects

6.3.1 Length limitation of seed signature

For DRP-SB, the length of seed signature register determines how many times a block can generate or propagate replay slices. Once a block's seed signature register overflows, all states of following blocks, including current overflow block, should be cleaned. These blocks then are re-executed with individual reset seed signature register. The intuition is that longer signature is better, however, refer to figure 12, we find that there is an optimal point of signature length.

Figure 12 shows the best average performance of SPEC FP can be obtained with a 32-bit seed signature; the performance decreases when the length of signature climbs up to 64-bit. The performance of EEMBC becomes stable when the length of signature reaches 16-bit; the performance then scales a little as the length of signature continues to grow, and the best average performance is given at the point of 32-bit. The performance doesn't permanently increase with the increasing length of seed signature because longer signature allows more seed instructions to reissue, which pluses

more burdens onto operand network and results in network contention. For hardware consideration, we choose 16-bit signature for the baseline configuration of DPR-SB.

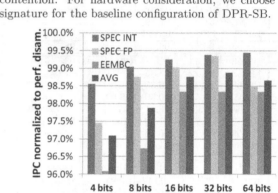

Figure 12: Performance scaling with increasing signature length

6.3.2 Perfect architectural settings

DRPs require the operand messages sent by seed instructions must route to CC under some conditions, as mentioned in section 4.3, 4.4 and 4.5. Additionally, we introduce a distributed protocol for notifying the speculative statues of stores and writes between participated cores. We examine the performance impacts the above techniques introduce into DRPs.

Figure 13 shows the speedups DRPs achieve across different window sizes over realistic DRPs configurations, discounting the extra route cost and latency of speculative status notifying. From figure 13(a) we can see that DRP-SB benefits little from these perfect settings, its performance even slightly slows down in some cases. Compared with DRP-SB, DRP-SID is more sensitive with perfect settings, but is also trivial. So we conclude that the reason why DRPs can't achieve the performance of perfect memory disambiguation is the traffic jams of operand transmission induced by replay slices.

7. CONCLUSION

Distributed uniprocessors are vulnerable to data mispredictions that squashes hundreds or thousands inflight instructions following mispredicted seed instructions. However, only a few instructions depend on the values produced by seed instructions(column 4 in table 3), simple squashing all instructions is a great waste. Selective replay technique is a promising approach to reduce this waste. In this paper, we first characterize the challenges of implementing selective replay on a dataflow-like distributed architecture-TFlex; we

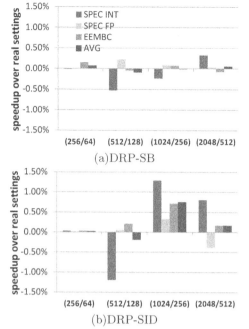

(a)DRP-SB

(b)DRP-SID

Figure 13: The impact of perfect environment for DRPs' performance

then propose a set of distributed replay protocols-DRP-SB and DRP-SID-to reduce the penalty of data dependence misprediction in TFlex.

Compared with former replay protocol, DRPs completely solve the challenges that hinder efficient replay. The evaluation results show that DRP-SB(DRP-SID) achieve about 99%(98%) of the performance of perfect memory disambiguation across various applications running on 16-core T-Flex. DRPs outperform former replay protocol-DSRE, and the state-of-art data dependence predictor. Moreover, DRP-SID reduces the hardware cost by 54% with an ignorable performance downgrade, when compared with DRP-SB.

The DRPs we propose are suitable for all types of data misspeculation recovery. And this protocol is a competitive candidate of selective replay for other dataflow-like distributed uniprocessors.

8. ACKNOWLEDGMENT

We highly appreciate Dr. Doug Burger, Prof. Stephen W. Keckler and the members of TRIPS team, for their generosities sharing the EDGE simulators and their helps consummating this article. This work is supported financially by the National Basic Research Program of China under contract 2011CB302501, the National Natural Science Foundation of China grants 60970023, the National Hi-tech Research and Development Program of China under contracts 2012AA010902 and 2012AA010303, the National Science & Technology Major Projects 2009ZX01036-001-002 and 2011ZX01028-001-002-3.

9. REFERENCES

[1] A. S. Al-Zawawi, V. K. Reddy, and E. Rotenberg et al. Transparent control independence (tci). In *ISCA-34*, 2007.

[2] C. Blundell, A. Raghavan, and M. M. K. Martin. Retcon: Transactional repair without replay. In *ISCA-37*, 2010.

[3] D. Burger, S. W. Keckler, and K. S. McKinley et al. Scaling to the end of silicon with edge architecture. *IEEE Computer*, 37(7):44–55, July 2004.

[4] B. Calder and G. Reinman. A comparative survey of load speculation architectures. *JILP*, 2, 2000.

[5] S. Chaudhry, R. Cypher, and M. Ekman et al. Simultaneous speculative threading: A novel pipeline architecture implemented in sun's rock processor. In *ISCA-36*, 2009.

[6] G. Z. Chrysos and J. S. Emer. Memory dependence prediction using store sets. In *ISCA-25*, 1998.

[7] R. Desikan, S. Sethumadhavan, and D. Burger et al. Scalable selective re-execution for edge architectures. In *ASPLOS-11*, 2004.

[8] Rajagopalan Desikan. *Distributed Selective Re-Execution for EDGE Architecture*. Doctoral dissertation, UT-Austin, 2005.

[9] D. Ernst and T. Austin. Practical selective replay for reduced-tag schedulers. In *Proceedings of the 2nd Annual Workshop on Duplicating, Deconstructing, and Debunking*, 2003.

[10] H. Esmaeilzadeh and Doug Burger. Hierarchical control flow speculation: Support for aggressive predication. In *Proceedings of the 2009 Workshop on Parallel Execution of Sequential Programs on Multi-core Architectures*, 2009.

[11] A. D. Hilton, S. Nagarakatte, and A. Roth. icfp: Tolerating all-level cache misses in in-order processors. In *HPCA-14*, 2008.

[12] A. D. Hilton and A. Roth. Ginger: Control independence using tag rewriting. In *ISCA-34*, 2007.

[13] J. B. Keller and R. W. Haddad et al. Scheduler which discovers non-speculative nature of an instruction after issuing and reissues the instruction. United States Patent 6,564,315, May 2003.

[14] C. Kim, S. Sethumadhavan, and M.S. Govindan et al. Composable lightweight processors. In *MICRO-40*, 2007.

[15] I. Kim and M. Lipasti. Understanding scheduling replay schemes. In *HPCA-10*, 2004.

[16] M. Lipasti, C. B. Wilkerson, and J.P. Shen. Value locality and load value prediction. In *ASPLOS*, 1996.

[17] A. A. Merchant, D. J. Sager, and D. D. Boggs. Computer processor with a replay system. United States Patent 6,163,838, December 2000.

[18] A. Moshovos and G. S. Sohi. Dynamic speculation and synchronization of data dependences. In *ISCA-24*, 1997.

[19] S. M. Pant and G. T. Byrd. Extending concurrency of transactional memory programs by using value prediction. In *CF-6*, 2009.

[20] S. M. Pant and G. T. Byrd. Limited early value communication to improve performance of transactional memory. In *ICS-23*, 2009.

[21] B. Robatmili, S. Govindan, and D. Burger et al. Exploiting criticality to reduce bottlenecks in distributed uniprocessors. In *HPCA-17*, 2011.

[22] F. Roesner, D. Burger, and S. W. Keckler. Counting dependence predictors. In *ISCA-35*, 2008.

[23] E. Rotenberg, Q. Jacobson, and J. Smith. A study of control independence in superscalar processors. In *HPCA-5*, 1999.

[24] S. R. Sarangi, W. Liu, and J. Torrellas et al. Rslice: Seletive re-execution of long-retired misspeculated instructions using forward slicing. In *MICRO-38*, 2005.

[25] S. Sethumadhavan, F. Roesner, and J. S. Emer et al. Late-binding: Enabling unordered load-store queues. In *ISCA-34*, 2007.

[26] T. Sherwood, E. Perelman, and B. Calder. Basic block distribution analysis to find periodic behavior and simulation points in applications. In *PACT*, 2001.

[27] A. Smith, R. Nagarajan, and K. Sankaralingam et al. Dataflow predication. In *MICRO-39*, 2006.

[28] S. T. Srinivasan, R. Rajwar, and H. Akkary et al. Continual flow pipelines. In *ASPLOS-11*, 2004.

[29] J. G. Steffan, C. B. Colohan, and A. Zhai et al. Improving value communication for thread-level speculation. In *HPCA-8*, 2002.

[30] S. Swanson, K. Michelson, and A. Schwerin et al. Wavescalar. In *MICRO-36*, 2003.

[31] Y. Watanabe, J. D. Davis, and D. A. Wood. Widget: Wisconsin decoupled grid execution tiles. In *ISAC-37*, 2010.

[32] A. Yoaz, M. Erez, and R. Ronen et al. Speculation techniques for improving load related instruction scheduling. In *ISCA-26*, 1999.

[33] H. Zhou, C. Fu, and E. Rotenberg et al. A study of value speculative execution and misspeculation recovery in superscalar microprocessors. Technical report, ECE Department, N. C. State University, January 2001.

Characterizing and Improving the Use of Demand-Fetched Caches in GPUs

Wenhao Jia
Princeton University
wjia@princeton.edu

Kelly A. Shaw
University of Richmond
kshaw@richmond.edu

Margaret Martonosi
Princeton University
mrm@princeton.edu

ABSTRACT

Initially introduced as special-purpose accelerators for games and graphics code, graphics processing units (GPUs) have emerged as widely-used high-performance parallel computing platforms. GPUs traditionally provided only software-managed local memories (or scratchpads) instead of demand-fetched caches. Increasingly, however, GPUs are being used in broader application domains where memory access patterns are both harder to analyze and harder to manage in software-controlled caches. In response, GPU vendors have included sizable demand-fetched caches in recent chip designs. Nonetheless, several problems remain. First, since these hardware caches are quite new and highly-configurable, it can be difficult to know when and how to use them; they sometimes degrade performance instead of improving it. Second, since GPU programming is quite distinct from general-purpose programming, application programmers do not yet have solid intuition about which memory reference patterns are amenable to demand-fetched caches.

In response, this paper characterizes application performance on GPUs with caches and provides a taxonomy for reasoning about different types of access patterns and locality. Based on this taxonomy, we present an algorithm which can be automated and applied at compile-time to identify an application's memory access patterns and to use that information to intelligently configure cache usage to improve application performance. Experiments on real GPU systems show that our algorithm reliably predicts when GPU caches will help or hurt performance. Compared to always passively turning caches on, our method can increase the average benefit of caches from 5.8% to 18.0% for applications that have significant performance sensitivity to caching.

Categories and Subject Descriptors

C.1.2 [**Processor Architectures**]: Multiple Data Stream Architectures

General Terms

Performance, Measurement, Algorithms

Keywords

GPU cache, CUDA, GPGPU, compiler optimization

1. INTRODUCTION

Graphics processing units (GPUs) were introduced to efficiently handle computer graphics workloads in specialized applications such as image rendering and games. In most early GPUs, software-managed local memories (or scratchpads) instead of traditional demand-fetched caches were provided for two reasons. First, traditional GPU workloads involved large amounts of streaming and were deemed difficult to cache [7]. Second, graphics/game programmers were willing to meticulously orchestrate memory access behavior and hand-tune use of software-managed caches [6].

More recently, GPU software has broadened and often includes memory access patterns that are both hard to analyze and hard to manage in software-controlled caches. In response, GPU vendors have included demand-fetched caches in their recent chip designs. For instance, the NVIDIA Fermi models introduced a relatively large (up to 48 KB per core) and configurable L1 cache not previously seen on GPUs [12]. Likewise, AMD's Fusion GPUs also offer a 16 KB L1 cache per core [5]. Both vendors' recent GPUs have sizable, globally coherent L2 caches.

Although the introduction of these seemingly intuitive demand-fetched caches is appealing, several problems remain. First, since these hardware caches are quite new and highly configurable, reasoning about when they will improve or harm application performance is still difficult. Second, since GPU programming is quite distinct from general-purpose programming, application programmers do not yet have widespread intuition about which memory reference patterns in their code are most amenable to demand-fetched caches and which should be optimized in other ways.

Defying conventional wisdom about caches built up over years of their use on general-purpose CPUs, our experiments show that caches are not always helpful to GPU applications, and in many cases they may even hurt performance. For a suite of 12 general-purpose GPU (GPGPU) programs on an NVIDIA Tesla C2070 GPU with L1 caches turned on and off, we find that only 3 of them see substantial performance improvements from caching. Meanwhile, another 3 of them actually see non-trivial performance degradations. This lack of performance predictability is so well-known that it is reflected in GPU vendor directions to application programmers—NVIDIA's programming manual specifically suggests that software developers experiment with cached and uncached versions of their code to see which one works better [14]. Such ad hoc approaches are clearly unappealing because they are time-consuming and error-prone, and they do not work well for software that must run well across many data set sizes and GPUs.

This paper provides methods for efficiently utilizing the newly provided demand-fetched GPU caches despite their seemingly difficult-to-predict payoff. In particular, we start by characterizing GPU application performance on a real GPU system with L1 caches turned on and off. Our results show the degree to which L1 caches may either improve or hurt program performance. Then, based on observations about GPU program access patterns, we provide a taxonomy of GPU memory access locality that can help programmers reason about when caches are likely to be helpful. We also note that since GPUs typically have extensive latency-tolerance mechanisms using multi-threading, it is memory bandwidth rather than latency that often determines cache utility. From our measurements and taxonomy, we develop methods that enable automated compile-time optimizations to determine when to use (or *not* to use) L1 caches in GPUs. Overall, this paper makes the following contributions.

First, we present a systematic taxonomy of GPU memory access patterns. Inspired by the "three C's" of general-purpose CPU caches, the taxonomy helps GPU compiler writers and application developers build intuition about the best ways to improve their application's memory access performance on cache-enabled GPUs.

Noting that memory bandwidth, more so than latency, is an important determinant of cache utility, our work demonstrates compile-time methods to analyze GPU programs and calculate "estimated memory traffic". Our estimates serve as indicators of when caches are likely to be beneficial.

Third, we propose a compile-time algorithm which automatically uses the traffic estimates to predict how caches will affect applications' performance and controls caching accordingly. Our method increases the benefit of using L1 caches from 5.8% to 18.0% for applications that experience significant changes in performance when caches are used.

The remainder of the paper is structured as follows. Section 2 gives background information on GPU hardware and software. Section 3 details our measurement methodology. In Section 4, we present real-system GPU cache characterizations and use those results to develop a GPU memory access locality taxonomy. Based on this taxonomy, Section 5 develops an automatable compile-time algorithm for determining whether/when to employ L1 caching on each global memory load of a GPU program. Section 6 gives experimental results of applying this algorithm. Section 7 discusses related work, and Section 8 concludes the paper.

2. BACKGROUND

This section gives background details on GPU architectures. For consistency, we primarily use NVIDIA and CUDA terminology in this paper. Our techniques are, however, applicable to a broader range of GPUs from different vendors.

2.1 GPU Hardware Characteristics

A modern GPU is a many-core processor optimized for throughput computing. Each core, or Streaming Multipro-

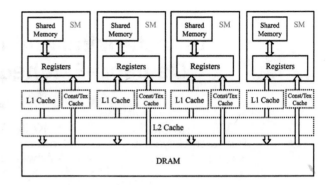

Figure 1: A typical GPU memory hierarchy. Arrows indicate data-flow paths.

cessor (SM) in NVIDIA terminology, is capable of executing a large number of threads in parallel. SMs have internal memory units, including registers private to each thread and software-managed local memories (shared memory) accessed by all threads running on the same SM. Figure 1 shows a typical GPU memory hierarchy as well as possible data flow paths among these components. A GPU program consists of many thread blocks. A thread block is always scheduled to run on a single SM so that threads in that block can cooperate through the use of shared memory in that SM. When threads access data in the large off-chip DRAM called global memory, their accesses go through a two-level cache hierarchy. Each L1 cache is private to its SM. L1 caches in different SMs are *not coherent* with each other. The L2 cache is shared by and coherent across all SMs on the chip.

Current NVIDIA GPUs have configurable L1 caches whose size can be either 16 KB or 48 KB. The L1 cache in each SM shares the same total 64 KB of memory cells with shared memory, giving users dynamically configurable choices regarding how much storage to devote to the cache versus the shared memory. AMD GPU L1 caches have a fixed size of 16 KB. The NVIDIA Tesla GPU we use has a non-configurable 768 KB L2 cache, while L2 caches on AMD GPUs have a size of 64 KB per core. Finally, a GPU has constant and texture caches; these are separate from the two-level demand-fetched caches and are only accessed through special constant and texture instructions.

Because L1 caches are not coherent across SMs, current NVIDIA GPUs treat every global memory store as a write-through transaction (write through L1 caches to the L2 cache) followed by an invalidate transaction (invalidate the copy in the L1 cache). In other words, global memory stores ignore L1 caches and this behavior is not configurable at the hardware level. For that reason, in this paper we only study global memory loads—not stores—in GPU programs.

2.2 GPU Software Characteristics

Each GPU program has one or more kernel functions that are launched and executed on the GPU. Each kernel divides its work into identically sized thread blocks. The size of a thread block is the number of software threads in that block. From a programmer's perspective, each instruction in the kernel is executed by all threads in the same thread block concurrently. However, on the real hardware, because of the limited number of SIMD units, software threads are actually executed in groups of threads called warps. A warp has 32 threads on current NVIDIA GPUs, and the SIMD units execute one warp at a time, switching to other warps when long-latency instructions are encountered. Because threads within the same warp execute instructions concurrently on the hardware, their global memory accesses are "coalesced" into the smallest number of unique memory requests. Memory accesses from different warps do not get coalesced, so they may result in redundant memory traffic if the memory fetches are not cached. Finally, each thread executes exactly the same binary instructions as other threads in the program, so it has to use thread ID and thread block ID variables to find out its own identity and operate on its individual data accordingly. Thread ID and block ID variables can be one- or multi-dimensional, but they must take consecutive values in their respective ranges.

GPU programmers are usually encouraged to declare and use shared memory variables as much as possible, because the on-chip shared memories have much shorter latency and much higher bandwidth than the off-chip global memory. Small, repeatedly-used data are good candidates to be declared as shared memory objects. However, because shared memories have limited capacity and an SM cannot access another SM's shared memory, many programs cannot use shared memories due to the algorithmic characteristics of these programs. In these situations, the global memory is always a bigger, slower fallback choice.

2.3 An Example GPU Program: BFS

As an example, Figure 2 shows the CUDA version of the breadth-first search (BFS) application taken from the Rodinia benchmark suite [3]. We revisit BFS later in the paper to explain our work. This program does breadth-first graph traversal to search for a specified item. More details about this program can be found in [9], but here we give a brief summary of its execution flow.

When the program runs, two kernels are called repeatedly in a cyclic fashion. Both kernels have a thread block size of 512 threads. The first kernel expands the search frontier to the next node level of the graph, and the second kernel does the actual visit (`visit()`) and then sets up conditions for the next run of the first kernel. The program terminates when a certain number of calls are performed, corresponding to the total number of node levels in the graph. The arrays `now[]`, `visited[]`, and `next[]` are used for tracking node visit status, and they are stored in global memory. The other global memory array `children[]` stores the child node IDs of each node consecutively. In this example, each node of the graph has a fixed number of 8 children.

2.4 Why Study GPU Caches?

Since GPU caches have considerable configurability, multiple decisions must be made to determine how to use them. For example, NVIDIA programmers can select whether or not to turn on caching depending on overall data access patterns. Additionally, they can select the size of the L1 cache when it is used. This configurability gives programmers flexibility but also introduces performance uncertainties.

GPU programs usually have hundreds of threads running concurrently on the same processor core. The cache capacity per thread is very small, despite the relatively large overall cache size. This makes it difficult to fit the entire working set into caches. Such capacity constraints challenge the conventional wisdom gained from CPU caches. To get the most benefit from limited per-thread cache capacity, programmers

```
#define TRUE 1
#define FALSE 0
kernel( int now[], int visited[], int next[],
        int children[] ) {
  int nodeID = blockIdx.x * 512 + threadIdx.x;
  if ( now[nodeID] == TRUE ) {
    now[nodeID] = FALSE;
    for ( int i = 0; i < 8; i++ ) {
      int childID = children[nodeID * 8 + i];
      if ( visited[childID] == FALSE )
        next[childID] = TRUE;
    }
  }
}
kernel2( int next[], int now[] ) {
  int nodeID = blockIdx.x * 512 + threadIdx.x;
  if ( next[nodeID] == TRUE ) {
    next[nodeID] = FALSE;
    now[nodeID] = TRUE;
    visit(nodeID);
    visited[nodeID] = TRUE;
  }
}
```

Figure 2: An example breadth-first search GPU program. The global load instructions are underlined.

Parameters	Values
CPU model	Intel Core 2 Duo E8500
System DRAM capacity	4 GB
GPU model	NVIDIA Tesla C2070
SM count	14
SM SIMD width	32
SM clock rate	1.15 GHz
L1 cache size	16 KB or 48 KB
Shared memory size	48 KB or 16 KB
L2 cache size	768 KB
GPU DRAM capacity	6 GB
GPU DRAM clock rate	1.5 GHz
GPU DRAM bandwidth	144 GB/sec
Single-/Double-precision floating point performance	1030/515 GFLOPS
CUDA version	4.0

Table 1: Our CPU/GPU measurement platform.

must determine which portions of the working set will benefit from caching and only cache these portions (Section 3.1).

Because experimentally choosing the desired cache configuration and deciding which instructions should load data into the cache has many drawbacks, our work seeks to build better programmer intuition as well as to help automate cache configuration and data caching decisions.

3. METHODOLOGY

3.1 Real-System Measurement Infrastructure

All of our experiments are performed using a real running system, with an NVIDIA Tesla C2070 GPU and an Intel Core 2 Duo E8500 CPU. Table 1 lists the details.

The L1 cache in this GPU is controllable in several ways. First, it shares storage cells with shared memory, and we can configure the partitioning to select the size of each unit. Specifically, one can have a 16 KB L1 cache with a 48 KB shared memory, or one can have a 48 KB shared memory with a 16 KB L1 cache. The second way to control the L1 cache is to turn it on or off for an entire program. We refer to this as "cache all" or "cache none" respectively. This is done

Kernels	Thread block sizes	Shared memory use per block
backprop-1	16 × 16	0
backprop-2	16 × 16	1088 B
bfs-1	512	0
bfs-2	512	0
cfd-1	192	0
cfd-2	192	0
cfd-3	192	0
cfd-4	192	0
heartwall	512	11872 B
hotspot	16 × 16	3072 B
kmeans-1	256	0
kmeans-2	256	0
leukocyte-1	320	14568 B
leukocyte-2	175	0
leukocyte-3	176	0
lud-1	32	3072 B
lud-2	16	1024 B
lud-3	16 × 16	2048 B
nw-1	16	2180 B
nw-2	16	2180 B
particlefilter	128	0
srad-1	512	4096 B
srad-2	512	0
srad-3	512	0
srad-4	512	0
srad-5	16 × 16	6144 B
srad-6	16 × 16	6144 B
streamcluster	512	1024 B

Table 2: Rodinia programs and kernel attributes.

by passing the compiler flags -dlcm=ca or -dlcm=cg to the Parallel Thread Execution (PTX) assembler. (PTX is the CUDA ISA [13].) Finally, one can also select whether each individual global load instruction's memory access should go through the L1 cache or not, by using the global memory access modifiers available in PTX 2.x.

3.2 Applications

Our experiments use the CUDA version of the applications in the Rodinia 1.0 benchmark suite [3]. Rodinia contains a diverse set of real-world GPU programs. Each program in the suite has one or more GPU kernels, and our methods analyze each kernel independently. (Cross-kernel optimizations are rare in GPUs and could be a topic for future work.) Table 2 lists the programs and some per-kernel characteristics; different kernels in an application are distinguished by numbering. All measured numbers are hardware performance counter values collected with NVIDIA Visual Profiler. All reported kernel runtimes are the time between kernel launch and finish, excluding CPU work and CPU-GPU communication time, which are not the focus of this study. Because programs have nearly identical execution times from one run to another (less than 1% variance), we present results from a single program run. Within a single run, a particular kernel may be invoked several times; when this occurs, we present the runtime as total time accumulated over all launches of this kernel in the entire run.

4. CHARACTERIZING GPU CACHE USE

This section experimentally characterizes when L1 caches help and hurt performance of a suite of GPGPU kernels. From this, we determine cache prediction metrics, and we construct a model that helps programmers understand how different types of memory accesses interact with GPU caches.

4.1 L1 Cache Performance Impact

To measure the impact of L1 caches on GPU application performance, we run the entire Rodinia benchmark suite on our platform with the L1 caches turned on and off. The suite's applications use the GPU memory system in widely varying ways. Some of the kernels load data only into the texture and constant caches; on the NVIDIA hardware, these data never enter the L1 demand-fetched cache. Other kernels use explicit software management to pull data from global memory into the software-managed shared memory. While such data pass through the L1 cache en route to shared memory, they are only accessed from shared memory from that point on. For a third group of kernels, accesses are made directly to global memory without making use of shared memory. In such cases, data are implicitly demand-fetched into the L1 cache through the global memory accesses; caching of these data is similar to how data are managed by CPU caches. It is the L1 hits to these data that offer the largest potential payoff in performance.

Figure 3 presents the speedup obtained when 16KB L1 caches are used relative to when they are not used. The bars in the graph are grouped to indicate how each kernel uses the memory system based on the three usage categories from the preceding paragraph. Values smaller than 1 indicate that an L1 cache offers speedup over the no-cache case.

Among the three groups of kernels, the performance of the first group of kernels is expected to be unaffected by whether L1 caches are present or not, because their memory accesses do not go through L1 caches. This expectation is confirmed by our results: almost no performance variation is seen.

The second group of kernels shows very small responses to the use of L1 caches. This is because the initialization phases of these kernels, during which accesses go through L1 caches, are usually much shorter than the computation phases of these kernels, during which accesses focus on the shared-memory and no longer go through L1 caches. Notably, the srad kernels show up to 10% performance variations caused by the use of L1 caches. This is because these kernels have fairly short computation phases, and even the initialization phases affect the total runtime.

The third group of kernels (solid bars in Figure 3) are of the most interest to us, because they should have the greatest potential benefit from caching—they all use global memory (rather than shared memory) to hold their working sets, and so they continue to have global memory accesses even during the main computation phases. Because these global memory accesses can use the L1 cache, these are the cases where a demand-fetched L1 cache can be most helpful. However, instead of seeing uniform benefits from caching, we see much more variable performance. In particular, when the cache is turned on, backprop-1 and particlefilter show significant speedup while bfs-1, cfd-1, and kmeans show noticeable slowdown.

To investigate such varying cache effects, Figure 4 plots the L1 cache hit rates of these kernels. There is no clear relationship between performance changes and L1 hit rates. Two kernels with large performance variations (kmeans-2 at 0.59× and particlefilter at 1.9×) do show the smallest (0.2%) and the largest (99%) L1 hit rates respectively. For the other programs, however, the hit rate cannot be directly related to performance. For example, backprop-1 and bfs-1 show opposing performance trends, though they have similar cache hit rates. In fact, while it might be appealing to

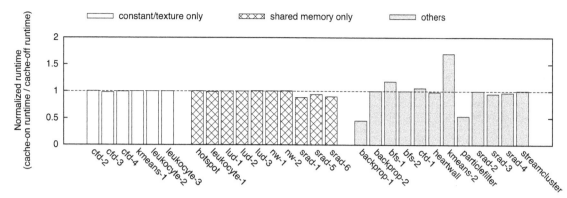

Figure 3: 16 KB L1 caches have little or unpredictable performance impact on the Rodinia benchmark suite. Lower bars indicate better performance (i.e. shorter runtime) when the L1 caches are turned on.

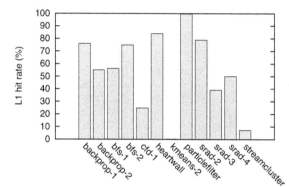

Figure 4: The L1 hit rate is not a good predictor of program performance variations.

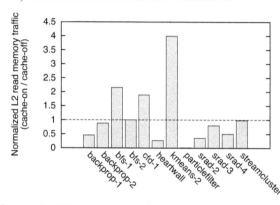

Figure 5: The amount of L2 read memory traffic better indicates cache impact on program runtime.

devise a caching policy based on a hit rate threshold—turn on caching if profiling shows a hit rate above the threshold and turn off caching otherwise—there is no reasonable threshold to choose for these results.

To find a better indicator of caching's performance influence, we look more closely at bfs-1. In fact, the performance slowdown stems from the 128 B L1 cache line size, which is quite long relative to the amount of spatial access locality in the kernel. The default input graph supplied with the benchmark causes threads in bfs-1 to issue random, scattered 4 B accesses to main memory. When the L1 cache is off, each 4 B access is turned into a 32 B memory request and sent to the L2 cache and DRAM. However, when the L1 cache is on, each thread has to fetch an entire 128 B cache line for the same 4 B access. This quadruples the required L2-to-L1 traffic, and results in much higher DRAM-to-L2 traffic as well. However, much of this increased memory traffic goes unused because the graph's access locality is low. Since bfs-1 is a memory bandwidth bound application, extra wasted memory traffic leads to a 18% performance slowdown in Figure 3. The observation made using bfs-1 inspires the use of memory traffic as an estimator of caching's benefit.

Figure 5 shows the relative reduction in memory traffic from L2 to L1 when the L1 cache is turned on, compared to when the L1 cache is off, for the third group of kernels. This is obtained by multiplying the observed number of L2 read requests and the request size (32 B or 128 B). The graph shows that the amount of L2 read memory traffic is better correlated (than hit rate) with the L1 cache's performance impact. In kernels where L1 caches harm performance (bfs-

1, cfd-1, and kmeans-2), the amount of memory traffic increases. The opposite is true for kernels that benefit from L1 caches (backprop-1 and particlefilter). The rest of the programs are not memory bandwidth bound, and so their memory traffic changes are inconsequential.

Across the test suite, it is generally true that increased L2-to-L1 memory traffic results in equal or worse performance and reduced traffic results in equal or better performance. Using memory traffic as a metric for driving our caching policy algorithm is intuitive in several ways. First, if computation is identical whether caching is turned on or off, the difference in memory traffic can be expected to determine runtime changes. Second, at compile-time, aggregate traffic estimates for GPU programming models are easier to collect than cache hit rate estimates. Finally, while we are the first to apply traffic estimation to caching decisions, they have seen prior use for other GPU optimizations [1].

4.2 A Taxonomy of Memory Access Locality

CPU programmers have long used the three C's (compulsory, conflict, and capacity) taxonomy for cache misses to help them understand and reduce the cache miss rates of their programs [10]. Since L1 cache hit rates are not particularly predictive of a GPU cache's potential benefit, a new model is needed to help GPU programmers understand how global memory accesses interact with the cache and how they can modify their program to improve performance.

Our characterization experiments show that memory traffic can be indicative of how the L1 cache impacts performance. The new model therefore needs to translate how different memory access patterns result in different amounts of memory traffic and how those levels of traffic change with the use of caches. Because of the complex execution model used to program and execute work on GPUs (e.g. threads, warps, and blocks), this model must also relate memory traffic to how computation is scheduled.

Instead of using different types of cache misses, our taxonomy for GPUs introduces three types of locality.

- *Within-warp data locality* applies to a single load instruction being executed by threads within the same warp. If these threads access data mapped to the same cache line, they are said to have within-warp locality.

- *Within-block (cross-warp) data locality* applies to a single load instruction being executed by threads within the same thread block but in *different* warps. If these threads access data mapped to the same cache line, they are said to have within-block locality.

- *Cross-instruction data reuse* applies to more than one instruction (including the same instruction being executed more than once) being executed by the same or different threads within the same thread block. If these threads access data mapped to the same cache line, they are said to have cross-instruction data reuse.

To understand each type of locality, recall how threads are organized into warps. Threads in the same block have consecutive IDs. Warps are formed as groups of 32 threads with consecutive IDs. For example, if `tid` is the thread ID variable, the threads in the first warp of a block will have `tid` from 0 to 31, the second warp will be 32 to 63, etc. *Within-warp locality* is frequently due to threads in a warp (32 threads per warp) sharing contiguous elements of an array (e.g. `array[tid]`), resulting in coalesced accesses to the same cache line. *Within-block locality* results from threads having IDs with a distance greater than 32 accessing the same cache line (e.g. `array[tid % 32 * 32]`. The critical difference between within-warp locality and within-block locality is that, without an L1 cache, two identical requests from the same warp (bearing within-warp locality) generate only one L2 request while two identical requests from the same block but different warps (bearing within-block locality) generate two L2 requests. Turning caches on may exploit within-block locality by reducing the number of L2 requests from two to one, but it cannot exploit within-warp locality because the number of L2 requests is already at its minimum due to coalescing. Hence within-warp locality does not benefit from caches while within-block locality does.

Cross-instruction reuse always exists between multiple instructions executing at different moments in time, similar to temporal locality in CPUs. However, due to the small per-thread cache capacity, instructions with cross-instruction reuse have a much smaller chance of retaining their data in the cache. Consequently, it is difficult to exploit cross-instruction reuse through caching on GPUs.

Finally, if an instruction executed by a whole thread block exhibits none of the locality above, it is said to have *non-locality*. Instructions with non-locality should not use the cache, because turning off the cache for them results in smaller (32 B) request sizes than turning on the cache would (128 B). The random accesses in BFS are examples of such non-locality; this program benefits from the lower overall bandwidth of non-cached operation.

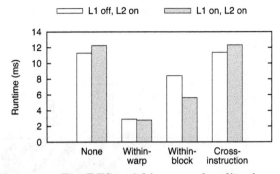

Figure 6: For BFS, within-warp locality improves program performance regardless of whether the L1 cache is turned on. Caches are helpful to within-block locality. The L1 cache is too small for cross-instruction reuse.

4.3 Taxonomy Example: BFS

Below we use the BFS example (Section 2.3) to quantitatively demonstrate the caching benefits for each type of locality. Experimental results confirm our analysis of locality and motivate our caching strategy in Section 5.4.

We use different data layouts in a special BFS input set to vary the types of memory access locality and test their amenability to caching. The special input graph is a carefully designed directed octree. Its graph structure is manipulated to contain *one and only one* type of locality at a time. For example, to produce cross-instruction reuse, a thread is directed by `children[]` to access 8 adjacent elements in `visited[]` over 8 iterations of a loop. However, different threads in the same thread block (including those in the same warp) access random 8-element groups to make sure no within-warp or within-block locality is present. Likewise, graphs with *only* within-warp or *only* within-block locality can be constructed, while the degree of locality is kept at 8 to ensure *fair* comparisons across different types of locality. For within-warp locality, this means every 8 threads in the same warp access adjacent elements in `visited[]`; for within-block locality, this means 8 threads from 8 distinct blocks access adjacent elements in `visited[]`. Finally, a randomly structured tree is used as the non-locality input.

As shown in Figure 6, when BFS runs on an input with no locality, the use of an L1 cache slightly hurts its performance (8.5% slowdown) due to the long cache line size resulting in an almost 2× increase in L2 traffic. The same program running on an input having within-warp locality sees greatly improved performance—3.9× in the cache-off case caused by a 3.6× traffic reduction, compared to the non-locality input. Turning the L1 cache on, however, has a negligible effect on performance, since within-warp locality uses coalescing instead of caching to reduce memory traffic. For the third input (within-block locality), the L1 cache successfully exploits the locality (2.2× runtime reduction due to 3.1× traffic reduction, relative to non-locality case). Even when the L1 cache is off, the always-on L2 cache can still exploit the locality to a lesser degree (1.3× runtime reduction). Lastly, caches cannot exploit the cross-instruction reuse even if it exists in the input—a thread's cache lines are evicted from the cache before they get reused. These experiments reinforce our analysis of locality and show, in a real application, the relative performance benefits of caching for each type of locality.

5. A COMPILE-TIME ALGORITHM FOR IMPROVING GPU CACHE USE

This section presents an algorithm that performs compile-time analysis of GPU memory access patterns and accurately predicts whether caching would be useful to each load instruction in a program. Even though here we apply our algorithm to the kernels manually, it can be easily carried out automatically by a compiler. The algorithm is designed using the following abstract GPU execution model.

First, we assume all threads in a thread block execute an instruction simultaneously, before they move on to the next instruction together. Even though in real hardware, threads execute instructions in units of warps instead of blocks, and a warp may execute a few instructions consecutively before it stalls and gets swapped out by another warp, the simpler model without warps is intuitive and accurate enough for our cache analysis and optimization.

Second, our model considers each SIMD load instruction in isolation from other instructions, as if the cache is flushed before and after each instruction is executed by all threads in a block. (This assumption has no effect on analyzing within-warp locality, within-block locality, and scattered accesses, because they all exist within the scope of a single instruction.) Thus, our algorithm does not directly aim to exploit cross-instruction data reuse, but the final step may optionally use some heuristics to try to cache for it (Section 5.4).

Finally, minor effects such as cache line mapping conflicts are ignored; our results show this is generally acceptable.

5.1 Algorithm Overview

For a given GPU program kernel, our algorithm first discovers the memory access patterns of each individual SIMD load instruction. It achieves this by representing the data address of each load instruction as a function of the thread ID variables. Based on that information, the algorithm then estimates how much memory content will be transferred when the instruction is executed by an entire thread block, with the cache on and off. Based on these traffic estimates, the algorithm decides whether the data of each load instruction should be cached or not.

The algorithm has 3 steps: analyze access patterns, estimate memory traffic, and determine which instructions should use the cache. They can be applied to both high-level (such as the pseudocode below) and low-level (such as PTX code in our experiments) GPU program representations.

5.2 Step 1: Analyze Access Patterns

Our access pattern analysis takes advantage of the fact that GPU threads rely on their thread IDs and block IDs to identify and load their own data. Consequently, when a thread executes a load instruction, the data address that instruction loads is usually a function of its thread ID, its block ID, and some other values that are the same for all threads in the entire thread block (such as kernel input arguments). Thus, one can analyze a particular single thread's behavior and extrapolate the overall kernel behavior.

Values passed by heap (e.g. input data stored in global memory) may cause uncertainties. However, these values have to be explicitly loaded, and hence they are identifiable and can be marked as unanalyzable. We find that these values often lead to either scattered accesses (such as looking up children nodes in `bfs`) or instances of cross-instruction

reuse (such as iterating over elements of multi-dimensional input points in `k-means`), and our algorithm does not cache them (Section 5.4). `cfd-1` is the only exception in which unanalyzable accesses have caused problems (Section 6).

To simplify the analysis, we assume the block ID variable is 0, meaning we use the first thread block's access patterns to estimate access patterns of all other thread blocks. Future work can look into using statistical sampling to estimate the average thread block behavior.

The analysis step is shown in Algorithm 1. For brevity, it uses a one-dimensional thread block to explain the execution flow. Multi-dimensional thread blocks can easily be handled by using multiple thread ID variables. In the pseudocode, there are three special notations. τ is the thread ID variable itself, and $f(\tau)$ is a computable function of τ which may be a combination of τ, constants and basic arithmetic operations ($+$, $-$, $\times$, $/$, $\%$ and their combinations in our experiments). The symbol ϕ represents any unprocessed variable. The symbol ∞ represents an unknown value. Similar to the "Not a Number (NaN)" data value, an instruction with at least one ∞ as its input operand produces a result of ∞. In this algorithm, an ∞ is an unanalyzable variable which blocks the compiler from analyzing values produced from that ∞. These unknown values are usually caused by loading content from the heap.

Algorithm 1 Analyze the memory access patterns of global load instructions in a kernel

---

initialize all variables in the kernel to ϕ
delete all loop back edges and set loop induction variables to 0
set kernel input arguments to user-supplied sample values
set results of all memory load instructions to ∞
set thread ID variables to τ
repeat
  for all instructions in the program **do**
    if all source operands of an instruction have known values: constant, $f(\tau)$, or ∞ **then**
      define the result of this instruction by executing the arithmetic operation represented by this instruction
      propagate this definition to all of its uses in instructions dominated by this instruction
    end if
  end for
until no new propagation or definition happens
mark all ϕ variable as ∞
output the data addresses of all load instructions

This algorithm is iterative like common constant folding and propagation compiler optimizations. It sets "seeds" (loop induction variables, kernel input arguments, thread ID variables and memory load results) to known values in the initialization phase and then uses data-flow analysis to fold and propagate these known values. The deletion of loop back edges in Algorithm 1 lets us analyze inside loops at the cost of using the first iteration to estimate the overall loop behavior. This is generally not a problem because loops usually correspond to cross-instruction reuse which we do not aim to analyze. When the algorithm has converged and terminated, it outputs data addresses of computable load instructions and marks the rest as unknown (∞).

5.3 Step 2: Estimate Memory Traffic

Based on Step 1's analysis output, Step 2 estimates the amount of memory traffic resulting from these memory access patterns for both cache-on and cache-off cases.

21

Algorithm 2 shows the process of estimating the cache-on memory traffic. It makes use of the fact that when a sufficiently large cache is on, no content would be loaded repeatedly. So the memory traffic is equal to the number of unique bytes the instruction needs.

Algorithm 2 Estimate the amount of memory traffic generated by threads in one block when cache is on

---

set M to 128, the memory request size when cache is on
for all global load instructions in the kernel **do**
  let N = the number of threads in each block
  declare tags[N] which stores the upper bits of the memory
  addresses threads load when they execute this load
  for i = 0; i < N; i++ **do**
    use the data address expression to compute which memory
    address thread i is loading and assign that address to addr
    tags[i] = addr / M
  end for
  count the total number of unique values in tags[] and store
  it in U, counting each ∞ as one unique value
  U is the total number of unique memory requests of this load
  output U × M, the total amount of memory traffic generated
  by all threads executing this load instruction when the cache
  is turned on for it
end for

Algorithm 3 estimates the cache-off memory traffic. It first calculates the amount of traffic generated by each warp, and then it simply adds these amounts together because there is no caching to prevent loading redundant data.

Algorithm 3 Estimate the amount of memory traffic generated by threads in one block when cache is off

---

set M to 32, the memory request size when cache is off
set B to the thread block size
for all global load instructions in the kernel **do**
  set W to B / 32, the number of warps in the block
  set nreqs, the total number of memory requests sent by all
  warps in the block, to 0
  for all W warps in this thread block **do**
    declare tags[32] which is used to store the upper bits of
    the memory addresses threads of this warp load when they
    execute this load instruction
    for i = 0; i < 32; i++ **do**
      use the data address expression to compute which mem-
      ory address thread i is loading and assign it to addr
      tags[i] = addr / M
    end for
    count the total number of unique values in tags[] and
    store it in n, counting each ∞ as one unique value
    nreqs = nreqs + n
  end for
  output nreqs × M, the total amount of memory traffic generated by all threads executing this load instruction when
  the cache is turned off for it
end for

As an example, Table 3 lists the access patterns, locality types, and estimated cache-on and cache-off traffic for a few typical instructions found in the Rodinia benchmarks.

5.4 Step 3: Determine Cache Use

The final step of the algorithm uses the following strategy to decide whether each instruction should use the cache or not, depending on the estimated memory traffic and access patterns of this instruction.

1. *If the cache-on memory traffic is equal to the cache-off memory traffic of this instruction:* This occurs because this instruction only has within-warp locality and has no within-block locality. If the cache-on memory traffic is larger than cache capacity, we do not let this instruction use caches. If the cache-on memory traffic is smaller than cache capacity, we have two choices. The conservative strategy does not turn on caches, reasoning that within-warp locality does not need caching and caching may accidentally evict useful cross-instruction reuse of other instructions. The aggressive strategy turns on caches, hoping to exploit cross-instruction reuse which may exist between this and some other instructions. Section 6 evaluates both strategies.

2. *If the cache-on memory traffic is smaller than the cache-off memory traffic:* This occurs because this instruction has some amount of within-block locality. Note that it may have an arbitrary amount of within-warp locality at the same time. If the cache-on traffic is smaller than cache capacity, we turn on caching for this instruction; otherwise we turn off caching to prevent cache thrashing.

3. *If the cache-on memory traffic is larger than the cache-off memory traffic:* We have successfully identified a scattered access. We turn caching off for this instruction.

4. *If an instruction has unknown (∞) memory access data addresses:* We assume that it is likely to issue scattered or cross-instruction reuse accesses (Section 5.2) and we do not use caching for this instruction.

Our algorithm does not try to identify cross-instruction data reuse, though it does have an optional heuristic which aggressively tries to cache for cross-instruction reuse existing across instructions having within-warp locality. A complete analysis of cross-instruction reuse must account for how each instruction affects other instructions in relation to their relative positions in the program's control flow graph and their respective required cache sizes. This is beyond the scope of this paper but is certainly of value for future work.

Table 3 lists the cache-on and cache-off traffic for each instruction. Their caching decisions can be easily computed based on the rules above.

6. EXPERIMENTAL RESULTS

In Figure 3, 5 kernels show unpredictable performance influence from caches and need an intelligent cache management algorithm. We apply our analysis algorithms to these kernels and the results are shown in Figure 7. Both 16 KB and 48 KB L1 cache sizes are tested. Results *less than 1* indicate performance improvements from caching.

Compared to not having caches (white bars in Figure 7), simply keeping caches on for all kernels (cross-hatched bars) results in only 5.8% performance improvement on average, due to the harmful effects caches have on some kernels. Our conservative strategy (gray bars), which keeps within-block locality cached and scattered accesses uncached, is able to identify and modify these harmed kernels. Consequently, the average benefit of caching increases to 16.9%—a 2.9× boost. Further caching within-warp locality with the aggressive approach (black bars) offers an 18.0% speedup. This is consistent with our analysis that within-warp locality does not benefit much from caching, even though backprop-1 and bfs-1 still show clear improvements (5.5% on average).

As a matter of fact, for most kernels, our method can reliably achieve performance close to the better result of the two fixed choices—cache-all and cache-none—without the need for pre-run profiling. In addition, our method actually outperforms both choices on bfs-1, because bfs-1 has a mix

Kernels	Instructions	Access patterns	Types of locality	Warp count	Cache-on traffic	Cache-off traffic
bfs-1	`now[nodeID]`	τ	within-warp	16	2 KB	2 KB
	`children[nodeID * 4]`	4τ	within-warp	16	8 KB	8 KB
	`visited[childID]`	∞	none	16	64 KB	16 KB
backprop-1	`delta[index_x]`	$\tau \% 16$	within-warp, within-block	8	128 B	512 B
	`ly[index_y]`	$\tau/16$	within-warp, within-block	8	128 B	256 B
kmeans-2	`input[point_id * nfeatures]`	34τ	none	8	32 KB	8 KB

Table 3: Example instructions and their locality. τ is the thread ID variable. ∞ is an unknown access. The warp count is the number of warps in a thread block. All array elements are 4-byte types (int or float).

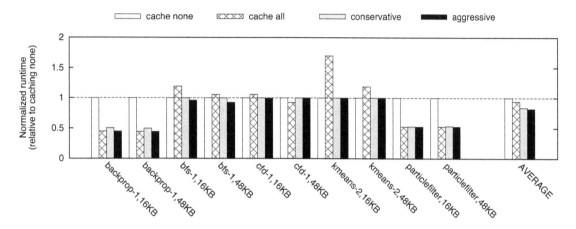

Figure 7: Normalized runtime of different caching approaches. Results less than 1 indicate caching is helpful. Caching all data improves performance by 5.8%. Our analysis algorithms improve performance much more: 16.9% or 18.0%. Both 16 KB and 48 KB L1 caches are tested.

of load instructions that need caching and load instructions that do not need caching. A kernel-wide decision for caching or not always helps one type of instruction but hurts the other, losing to the instruction-level decisions we use here.

Finally, `cfd-1` with a 48 KB L1 cache is the only case in which our method performs worse than the better result of the two fixed choices. This is because this kernel has some scattered accesses, along with some other cross-instruction reuse which can only be cached by a sufficiently large cache. With the 16 KB cache, the cache-all choice has worse performance caused by the scattered accesses, while the cross-instruction reuse cannot be cached by this smaller cache. With the 48 KB cache, the cache-all choice caches enough cross-instruction reuse that it actually overcomes the harm from scattered accesses and the overall performance comes out ahead. Our method is unable to analyze both access types and chooses not to use caches for unknown loads, and so its performance is the same as the cache-none choice with both cache sizes. Overall, we conclude these results by noting the degree to which our method can offer significant performance improvements without the need for profiling.

7. RELATED WORK

As GPUs have gained wider use, there has been research aiming to characterize and improve their memory hierarchies. Brook [2] and Merrimac [4] represent two early efforts at utilizing GPUs for general purpose computing. They both derive their methods based on GPUs which rely exclusively on software-managed on-chip storage. Hong and Kim build an analytical GPU architecture model with memory-level

parallelism awareness, but their model does not consider demand-fetched caches [11]. Wong et al. use microbenchmarking techniques to discover and describe many undocumented features of NVIDIA GPUs, including memory structures and cache parameters [19].

A large body of work studies how to transform data layout to improve GPU memory system efficiency. Various compile-time and runtime algorithms are proposed to improve GPU program memory access patterns, aiming at different parts of the memory system including reducing irregular memory accesses [21], coalescing loop nest accesses [1], improving coalescing [20], and increasing memory controller parallelism [16]. However, none of this work targets caches. In addition, these studies usually change the programs themselves, while our work attempts to analyze memory behaviors of given programs. One study [17] provides a limited observation of GPU cache impact on a handful of simple kernels. In contrast, our work provides a more systematic characterization of GPU cache effectiveness and uses that to develop an algorithm for automating the choice of how and when to use demand-fetched caches.

Software-managed on-chip storage such as shared memory on NVIDIA GPUs has been present on a number of modern parallel processors [15]. In embedded systems, where it is called scratchpad memory, this type of storage is even more commonplace than on GPUs and has been carefully studied [18]. On GPUs, some work studies high-level programming models which partially automate the use of shared memory [8]. However, none of this work includes caches in their systems. A systematic study of comparisons and tradeoffs between GPU shared memory and caches can guide future GPU designs. Our work on characterizing the use of GPU caches provides groundwork for achieving this goal.

8. CONCLUSIONS

Though L1 caches are being included in current GPUs, little work has been done to study their effectiveness. In this paper, we evaluate the performance impact of using L1 caches on the Rodinia benchmark programs, and we provide an automatable algorithm for exploiting caches to reliably improve performance. L1 caches improve the performance of some programs while hurting or not affecting others. Our analysis shows that instead of cache hit rate, the metric commonly used in CPUs to describe cache effectiveness, memory traffic is a more indicative predictor of GPU cache benefits.

To help GPU programmers understand cache impacts, we develop a GPU-oriented locality taxonomy reminiscent of the three C's model for CPU caches. The taxonomy's three types of memory access locality (within-warp, within-block, and cross-instruction reuse) help programmers reason about memory accesses in GPU execution models. Within-block locality has the greatest potential for benefiting from caching based on memory traffic reduction. Cross-instruction reuse has the possibility of benefiting from caching depending on the working set size relative to cache capacity. Within-warp locality does not benefit from caching.

We present a compile-time algorithm which analyzes load instructions in a GPU kernel and determines whether each load should use the cache. For kernels that previously experienced unpredictable performance variations from using L1 caches in an all-or-nothing fashion, our algorithm offers significant performance improvements. Compared to a 5.8% caching benefit gained by turning caches on all the time, our algorithm improves performance by 16.8% (conservative) or 18% (aggressive) by more carefully analyzing data transfers and using the per-load caching control provided in real GPUs. Furthermore, our approach can be implemented at compile-time and requires no dynamic execution profiling.

9. ACKNOWLEDGMENTS

We thank Carole-Jean Wu and the anonymous reviewers for their comments on this work. This work was supported in part by the National Science Foundation under Grant No. CCF-0916971. The authors also acknowledge the support of the Gigascale Systems Research Center, one of six centers funded under the Focus Center Research Program (FCRP), a Semiconductor Research Corporation entity. Finally, we acknowledge equipment donations from NVIDIA.

10. REFERENCES

[1] M. M. Baskaran et al. A compiler framework for optimization of affine loop nests for GPGPUs. In *Proc. 22nd ACM Intl. Conf. on Supercomputing*, 2008.

[2] I. Buck et al. Brook for GPUs: Stream computing on graphics hardware. In *31st Intl. Conf. on Computer Graphics and Interactive Techniques*, 2004.

[3] S. Che et al. Rodinia: A benchmark suite for heterogeneous computing. In *Proc. IEEE Int. Symp. Workload Characterization*, 2009.

[4] W. J. Dally et al. Merrimac: Supercomputing with streams. In *Proc. 2003 ACM/IEEE Conf. Supercomputing*, 2003.

[5] E. Demers. Evolution of AMD graphics, 2011. Presented at AMD Fusion Developer Summit.

[6] K. Fatahalian and M. Houston. A closer look at GPUs. *Communications of the ACM*, 51(10):50–57, October 2008.

[7] M. Gebhart et al. Energy-efficient mechanisms for managing thread context in throughput processors. In *Proc. 38th Ann. Int. Symp. Computer Architecture*, 2011.

[8] T. D. Han and T. S. Abdelrahman. hiCUDA: High-level GPGPU programming. *IEEE Trans. on Parallel and Distributed Systems*, 2011.

[9] P. Harish and P. J. Narayanan. Accelerating large graph algorithms on the GPU using CUDA. In *Proc. 14th Intl. Conf. High Performance Computing*, 2007.

[10] M. D. Hill and A. J. Smith. Evaluating associativity in CPU caches. *IEEE Transactions on Computers*, 38(12):1612–1630, December 1989.

[11] S. Hong and H. Kim. An analytical model for a GPU architecture with memory-level and thread-level parallelism awareness. In *Proc. 36th Ann. Int. Symp. Computer Architecture*, 2009.

[12] NVIDIA Corp. *NVIDIA's Next Generation CUDA Compute Architecture: Fermi*, 2009.

[13] NVIDIA Corp. *PTX: Parallel Thread Execution ISA Version 2.3*, March 2011.

[14] NVIDIA Corp. *Tuning CUDA Applications for Fermi*, May 2011. Page 3.

[15] S. Seo et al. Design and implementation of software-managed caches for multicores with local memory. In *IEEE 15th Intl. Symp. on High Performance Computer Architecture*, 2009.

[16] I.-J. Sung, J. A. Stratton, and W.-M. W. Hwu. Data layout transformation exploiting memory-level parallelism in structured grid many-core applications. In *Proc. 19th Int. Conf. on Parallel Architectural and Compilation Techniques*, 2010.

[17] Y. Torres and A. Gonzales-Escribano. Understanding the impact of CUDA tuning techniques for Fermi. In *2011 Intl. Conf. on High Performance Computing and Simulation*, 2011.

[18] S. Udayakumaran, A. Dominguez, and R. Barua. Dynamic allocation for scratch-pad memory using compile-time decisions. *ACM Trans. on Embedded Computing Systems*, 2006.

[19] H. Wong et al. Demystifying GPU microarchitecture through microbenchmarking. In *IEEE Intl. Symp. on Performance Analysis of Systems Software*, 2010.

[20] Y. Yang et al. A GPGPU compiler for memory optimization and parallelism management. In *Proc. 2010 ACM SIGPLAN Conf. on Programming Language Design and Implementation*, 2010.

[21] E. Z. Zhang et al. Streamlining GPU applications on the fly—thread divergence elimination through runtime thread-data remapping. In *Proc. 24th ACM Intl. Conf. on Supercomputing*, 2010.

One Stone Two Birds: Synchronization Relaxation and Redundancy Removal in GPU-CPU Translation

Ziyu Guo[*]
Qualcomm CDMA
Technologies, San Diego, CA,
USA
guoziyu@qualcomm.com

Bo Wu
Computer Science
Department
College of William and Mary,
VA, USA
bwu@cs.wm.edu

Xipeng Shen
Computer Science
Department
College of William and Mary,
VA, USA
xshen@cs.wm.edu

ABSTRACT

As an approach to promoting whole-system synergy on a heterogeneous computing system, compilation of fine-grained SPMD-threaded code (e.g., GPU CUDA code) for multicore CPU has drawn some recent attentions. This paper concentrates on two important sources of inefficiency that limit existing translators. The first is overly strong synchronizations; the second is thread-level partially redundant computations. In this paper, we point out that both kinds of inefficiency essentially come from a single reason: the non-uniformity among threads. Based on that observation, we present a thread-level dependence analysis, which leads to a code generator with three novel features: an instance-level instruction scheduler for synchronization relaxation, a graph pattern recognition scheme for code shape optimization, and a fine-grained analysis for thread-level partial redundancy removal. Experiments show that the unified solution is effective in resolving both inefficiencies, yielding speedup as much as a factor of 14.

Categories and Subject Descriptors

D.3.4 [**Programming Languages**]: Processors—*optimization, compilers*

General Terms

Performance,Experimentation

Keywords

GPU-CPU translation, heterogeneous computing, redundancy removal, synchronization, optimization

---

*This work was done when Ziyu Guo was in The College of William and Mary.

1. INTRODUCTION

The quick rise of heterogeneous computing systems creates urgent demands for support of code portability between CPU and accelerators, for for avoiding device-specific code rewriting and promoting across-device cooperations.

Among many efforts along this line [2, 8, 11, 13, 19, 20], SPMD-translation has drawn some recent attentions. An SPMD-translation takes a program written in a fine-grained SPMD-threaded programming model—such as CUDA [1]—as the base code, and generates programs suitable for multicore CPUs or other types of devices. In a fine-grained SPMD-threaded program, it is typical that a large number of threads execute the same kernel function but on different data sets. Because the task per thread is usually small, parallelism among tasks are often exposed to an extreme extent. From such a form, it is relatively simple to produce code for platforms that require larger task granularities by task aggregation. SPMD-translation simplifies coding for heterogeneous devices, and meanwhile, enables seamless collaboration of different devices (e.g., CPU and GPU) as tasks can be smoothly partitioned or migrated across devices. Recent efforts in this direction have yielded translators at both the source code level (e.g., MCUDA [20,21]) and below (e.g., Ocelot [8].) A main type of target architecture of the translation is multicore CPU, in which case, the translators are also called GPU-CPU translators.

Due to the architectural differences among different types of devices, some coding tradeoff suitable for exploiting one type of processors may not fit another well. An SPMD-translation that is oblivious to such differences may end up producing code of inferior efficiency. In this work, we concentrate on two main sources of inefficiency that limits existing GPU-CPU translators.

The first source of inefficiency is in the redundant computations in GPU programs (Section 3.2.) In GPU programs, there are typically more redundant computations than in CPU programs: As GPU is strong in supporting massive parallelism but weak in handling conditional branches, it is common for a GPU program to allow some threads to carry some useless computations because otherwise, some conditional branches would have to be introduced—and these statements often hurt GPU performance substantially due to the weakness of GPU in handling conditional branches. In the parallel reduction code in CUDA SDK [1], for instance, more than half of all threads conduct some useless computations (elaborated in Section 3.2.) Such redundancies are often acceptable on GPU as they overlap with useful calculations for the massive parallelism of GPU. But when getting into the translated CPU code, they may cause serious inefficiency. In the case of parallel reduction, the useless computations in the execution of the translated CPU code weights more than half of the entire execution time. Such a redundancy differs from the traditional concept of redundancy in that they are thread-dependent. We call it *thread partial redundancy*.

The second relates with synchronizations in GPU programs (Section 3.3.) A GPU kernel is usually executed simultaneously by thousands of threads. Fine-grained synchronizations (e.g., locks) are rarely used—they are especially error-prone for large scale parallelisms. And furthermore, they often require the insertion of some thread-ID-based conditional statements for distinguishing threads with different synchronization needs. As a result, many GPU programs employ barriers, causing *overly strong synchronizations* whose constraints are stronger than necessary. In this paper, we sometimes call these synchronizations *relaxable synchronizations*.

In this paper, we propose a unified solution to both issues (Section 4.) The key insight is that the two kinds of inefficiency essentially come from a single reason: the non-uniformity among GPU threads. At a relaxable synchronization point, some but not all threads really need to synchronize; at a thread partially redundant instruction, some but not all threads really need to execute that instruction. Examining the behaviors of each individual thread is hence necessary for a GPU-CPU translation to avoid both sources of inefficiency.

Based on the insight, we develop a thread-level fine-grained analysis framework to address both types of inefficiency. Unlike existing GPU-CPU translations, the analysis target of our framework is not the static instructions but their instances executed by each thread. The framework uses *thread-level dependence graphs (TLDG)* (Section 4.1) to model the relations among the dynamic instances of GPU instructions in the executions of different threads. TLDG has a bounded size, with edges capturing critical dependences.

Based on the TLDG, we develop a CPU code generator with three novel features. The first feature is an instance-level instruction scheduler (Section 4.2), which produces a schedule for the instances of all instructions in a TLDG. The schedule is free of barriers but obeys all critical dependences. In another word, it automatically reduces the strength of overly strong synchronizations but without compromising correctness. As usually more than one legitimate schedules exist, we develop three scheduling algorithms and present a systematic comparison of their influence on the locality and performance of the generated code.

The second feature is the use of graph pattern matching and instance-level conditional branch elimination for the optimization of the generated code. The graph pattern matching works on TLDG. It automatically recognize regular patterns in the TLDG and reduces them to loops to control the size of the generated CPU code (Section 4.3). The conditional branch elimination works on instruction instances exposed by the TLDG. It precomputes some conditional statement results to reduce runtime overhead.

The third feature is a scheme for identifying thread partial redundancy from the TLDG and preventing them from getting into the generated CPU program through an integration with the code generator (Section 4.4.)

We evaluate the instance-level analysis framework on a set of GPU programs. By comparing with the codes produced by prior techniques [11, 20], we demonstrate that the techniques are able to address both types of inefficiency effectively, improving the performance of the produced CPU program by as much as a factor of 14 (Section 5.)

To the best of our knowledge, this TLDG-based framework provides the first comprehensive solution to relaxable synchronizations and thread partial redundancy problems in GPU-CPU translations. This study demonstrates the large potential of instance-level analysis, which may open many other opportunities for program optimizations in heterogeneous computing systems.

2. BACKGROUND ON GPU AND SYNCHRONIZATIONS

In this work, we concentrate on GPU programs written in CUDA due to its broad usage. This section provides some basic background on CUDA and GPU that is closely relevent to the following discussions.

Overview of CUDA. CUDA is a typical example of fine-grained SPMD-threaded programming models. It is designed for GPU, a type of massively parallel device containing hundreds of cores. CUDA is mainly based on the C and C++ languages, with several minor grammar extensions. A CUDA program is composed of two parts: the host code to run on CPU, and some kernels to run on GPU. A GPU kernel is a C function. When it is invoked, the runtime system creates thousands of GPU threads, with each executing the same kernel function. Each thread has a unique ID. The use of thread IDs in the kernel differentiates the data that different threads access and the control flow paths that they follow. The amount of work for one thread is usually small; GPU rely on massive parallelism and zero-overhead context switch to achieve its tremendous throughput.

GPU Threads and Synchronizations. When a GPU kernel is launched, the runtime usually creates thousands of GPU threads. These threads are organized hierarchically. A number of threads (32 in NVIDIA GPU) with consecutive IDs compose *a warp*, a number of warps compose *a thread block*, and all thread blocks compose *a grid*.

There are two main types of synchronizations on GPU. Threads in a warp run in the single instruction multiple data (SIMD) mode: No threads can proceed to the next instruction before all threads in the warp have finished the current instruction. Such a kind of synchronization is called **implicit synchronization**: No statements are needed to trigger them; they are enabled by hardware implicitly. There is another type of synchronization. By default, different warps run independently. CUDA provides a function "__syncthreads()" for cross-warp synchronizations. That function works like a barrier, but only at the level of a thread block. In another word, no thread in a block can pass the barrier unless all threads in that block has reached that barrier. Such synchronizations are called **explicit synchronizations**.

3. SOURCES OF INEFFICIENCY

Due to architectural differences between GPU and CPU, some coding tradeoff suitable for exploiting GPU features

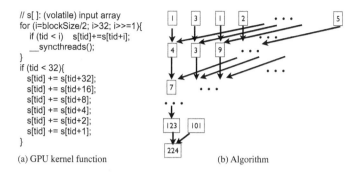

```
// s[ ]: (volatile) input array
for (i=blockSize/2; i>32; i>>=1){
    if (tid < i)    s[tid]+=s[tid+i];
    __syncthreads();
}
if (tid < 32){
    s[tid] += s[tid+32];
    s[tid] += s[tid+16];
    s[tid] += s[tid+8];
    s[tid] += s[tid+4];
    s[tid] += s[tid+2];
    s[tid] += s[tid+1];
}
```

(a) GPU kernel function   (b) Algorithm

Figure 1: Parallel reduction with explicit and implicit synchronizations. (warp size=32.)

may not fit CPU well. Without careful treatments, such tradeoffs, after being translated into CPU code, may cause substantial inefficiency on CPU. In this section, we examine two main sources of the inefficiency.

3.1 An Example: Parallel Reduction

To make explanation concrete, we will use the parallel reduction in the CUDA SDK [1] as an example throughout the following discussions. Parallel reduction represents a class of important operations that reduce many numbers into one or a few.

The example code from the CUDA SDK computes the sum of an input array. The execution of a thread block computes the sum of a chunk of data in the input array. The algorithm is the classic tree-shaped algorithm, as shown in Figure 1 (b). Every level of the tree computes a part of the sum.

Figure 1 (a) contains a piece of code from the GPU kernel of the reduction program in the CUDA SDK [1]. Each iteration of the "for" loop corresponds to the reduction at one level of the tree. Due to the dependences between levels, an explicit synchronization is invoked at the end of each iteration (the "_syncthreads()" call at the bottom of the loop body.)

The six lines of code at the bottom of Figure 1 (a) are for the bottom six levels of reduction. Note that there are no explicit synchronizations among the six lines, even though the same types of dependences exist among those levels as among the upper levels. This missing of synchronizations is not a coding error: Only the first warp executes these instructions and there are already implicit warp-level barriers between every two instructions. Inserting explicit synchronizations would only introduce unnecessary overhead.

This example illustrates two typical features that may cause existing GPU-CPU translators to produce inefficient code. We explain them as follows.

3.2 Thread Partial Redundancy

Thread partial redundancy refers to the case where the instances of an instruction executed by some but not all threads are useful. For instance, even though all threads in the first warp executes the bottom line of code in Figure 1 (a), only the result of the first thread's execution is useful. The redundancy is even more prominent in the reduction loop in Figure 1 (a): In all iterations except the first one, no more than half of all the threads conduct useful calculations. These redundancies are tolerable on GPU given its massive

parallelism. In fact, to remove them, some thread-ID–based conditional statements have to be inserted, lengthening the critical path. However, if these useless calculations get into the generated CPU code, they may consume significant portion of CPU time, hurting the overall computing efficiency.

Thread partial redundancy differs from the concept of redundancy in the traditional compiler terminology: The instruction itself is not redundant as some threads need it to conduct some useful work. It resembles the partial redundancy in traditional compiler terms, but the distinction between being redundant or useful is not due to variances in execution paths, but due to the identity of GPU threads. As traditional partial redundant removal techniques (e.g., Lazy Code Motion [7]) are all designed to exploit execution path variations, they are not directly applicable to solve this problem.

Most existing SPMD-translations are oblivious to thread partial redundancies. Such redundancies simply become part of the generated CPU code. It is important to notice that because the instructions are not redundant (just some of their instances are), current CPU compilers do not consider them redundancy, as confirmed by our experiments in Section 5. As a consequence, these thread partial redundancies slow down the CPU executions by as much as a factor of 14 as Section 5 will show.

3.3 Relaxable Synchronizations

The second source of inefficiency, *relaxable synchronizations*, refers to the use of overly strong synchronizations in GPU programs. The two types of main synchronization schemes described in Section 2 are both barriers: one at the thread block level (explicit synchronizations), the other at the warp level (implicit synchronizations.) But in many cases, synchronizations are only needed between some rather than all threads in a block or warp. At the third level (i.e., the second iteration of the reduction loop) of the reduction tree in Figure 1 (b), for instance, the first thread only needs two numbers on the second level of the tree, $s[0]$ and $s[blockSize/2 - 1]$, which are computed by the first thread and the thread whose ID equals $blockSize/2 - 1$ in the previous iteration of the reduction loop. In the same vein, it is easy to see that every thread in every iteration of the parallel reduction loop may start its calculation as soon as two (or fewer) corresponding threads have finished their calculations in the previous iteration. The explicit synchronizations in the loop, as well as the implicit synchronizations between every two instructions in the bottom six lines of the code, cause unnecessarily strong constraints by requiring all threads in a thread block or warp to synchronize at those points.

The overly strong synchronizations can be relaxed with fine-grained locks. However, such locks are extremely difficult to use and error-prone at such a large scale of parallelism. Meanwhile, they would require the insertion of some conditional statements so that threads requiring different synchronizations can be distinguished from one another. These statements often hurt performance substantially due to the weakness of GPU in handling conditional branches. As a result, it is a common practice to use explicit and implicit barriers in place of fine-grained synchronizations on GPU.

3.4 Existing Treatments

Even though the thread partial redundancy and overly

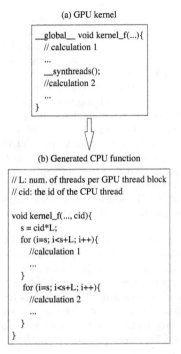

(a) GPU kernel

```
__global__ void kernel_f(...){
   // calculation 1
   ...
   __synthreads();
   //calculation 2
   ...
}
```

(b) Generated CPU function

```
// L: num. of threads per GPU thread block
// cid: the id of the CPU thread

void kernel_f(..., cid){
   s = cid*L;
   for (i=s; i<s+L; i++){
      //calculation 1
      ...
   }
   for (i=s; i<s+L; i++){
      //calculation 2
      ...
   }
}
```

Figure 2: Treatment to synchronizations in existing SPMD-translations.

strong synchronizations are reasonable to occur on GPU programs and are often unavoidable, they may jeopardize the efficiency of the translated CPU code when not handled carefully. In Section 5, we will see that a careful treatment to them may yield performance improvement as much as a factor of 14.

Existing SPMD-translators, however, have not given appropriate treatments to either of the two issues. They handle an explicit synchronization in a way that preserves its original semantics. For instance, MCUDA [20,21] is a translator from CUDA kernels to C code for multicore CPU. After its translation, each code segment between two adjacent explicit synchronization points (including the start and end of a kernel) in the GPU kernel becomes a serial loop in the generated CPU code. Each of such loops has L iterations (L is the number of threads per GPU thread block), which correspond to the tasks of a thread block during the GPU kernel execution. Figure 2 illustrates this loop fission-based translation scheme. By putting the two sections of work into two loops, the translation maintains the semantics of the "__synchthreads()"—that is, no task below the synchronization point is executed before all tasks above the point have finished. Such a treatment is adopted by all other existing SPMD-translators [8,11].

The preservation of the overly strong synchronizations in the generated CPU code has three-fold shortcomings. *First*, the loop fission limits the scope and flexibility of instruction scheduling. Merging the two loops is beyond the capability of typical compilers due to the existence of data dependences across the loops. Even though compilers and hardware may be able to schedule instructions across loop boundaries, the cross-loop instruction reordering is usually limited to the end of the earlier loop and the beginning of the later loop. *Second*, the loop fission may impair data locality. The existence of data dependences across the two loops implies data reuses between the two loops. The loop fission lengthens reuse distances and hence hurts the data temporal locality. *Finally*, the fission creates more loops and hence more loop overhead.

Implicit synchronizations in GPU code makes the efficiency problem even worse. Most prior SPMD-translations [8, 20] simply ignore implicit synchronizations. As a recent work [11] points out, such a treatment may cause violations of data dependences and hence errors in the generated CPU code. The authors propose a data dependence theorem to identify those implicit synchronizations that cannot be ignored and uses the same loop fission approach as described in the previous paragraph to tackle them. Although the approach fixes the correctness issue, it is subject to the same three efficiency issues of loop fission.

None of previous SPMD-translators has considered the thread-level partial redundancy problem. Their generated CPU code inherits these redundancy completely. As mentioned earlier, these redundancies differ from the partial redundancies current compilers handle. They may end up causing a substantial amount of useless computation on CPU.

4. A UNIFIED SOLUTION

One option to tackle the problems is to work on the generated CPU program by extending the current CPU C compilers so that it can recognize and remove the thread partial redundancy and overly strong synchronizations. Although this option may be feasible to a certain degree, it needs changes to the third-party CPU C compilers, and it has to deal with the extra complexities the code generation introduces, including the fissioned loops with partial data dependences and the interplays between the produced loop iteration space and the partial redundancy of instructions it contains.

We choose to work on the original GPU code. Besides the solution will be independent to third-party CPU compilers, there are two more reasons. First, GPU code clearly reveals the computation assignment among threads and relations among the threads, making analysis simpler. Second, the two kinds of inefficiency are essentially two forms of the non-uniformity among GPU threads: At a relaxable synchronization point, some but not all threads really need to synchronize with one another; at a thread partially redundant instruction, some but not all threads really need to execute that instruction. This key insight leads to a unified framework for solving both problems.

In the framework, we use a dependence graph at the GPU thread level (rather than statement level) to enable the examination of the behaviors of every thread and the data dependences among all dynamic instances of each GPU instruction. Such a fine-grained analysis is resilient to the non-uniformity among GPU threads, making it possible for code generator to produce CPU programs with both types of inefficiency resolved.

In the rest of this section, we will first present the thread-level dependence graph since it is the underlying vehicle for all analyses. We will then describe a set of instruction scheduling algorithms and some code shape optimization techniques for generating efficient code in the presence of synchronizations. Finally, we will discuss how thread partial redundancy can be removed easily on the TLDG framework.

4.1 Thread-Level Dependence Graphs (TLDG)

TLDG is a concept similar to traditional program dependence graphs (PDG) but with some important differences. A TLDG for a GPU kernel consists of a number of nodes and directed edges between nodes. Unlike nodes in a PDG which correspond to static statements, each node in a TLDG corresponds to a dynamic instance of an instruction in the GPU kernel. Roughly speaking, the number of TLDG nodes an instruction equals the number of threads in the scope of the TLDG. For example, for a block-level TLDG, that number is the size of a thread block. Explicit synchronization instructions have no node in a TLDG; they are treated separately. Let $node_1$ and $node_2$ represent two nodes in a TLDG, corresponding to two instructions I_1 and I_2 respectively. There is an edge from $node_1$ to $node_2$ if (1) the two nodes belong to the same thread (i.e., the same thread conducts both I_1 and I_2) and there is a control dependence from I_1 to I_2, or (2) there is a data dependence between I_1 and I_2, and I_1 may occur earlier than I_2 in an execution. Figure 3 shows an example TLDG. (For illustration purpose, the example uses source code statements rather than actual low-level instructions.)

Constructing a TLDG from a GPU kernel is straightforward. We just mention two complexities. *First*, a GPU kernel sometimes contain data races that do not hurt the correctness of executions. Upon a data race, I_1 and I_2 may happen in any order in an execution, but the edge between the two nodes can still have only one direction. The direction is arbitrarily determined by the TLDG constructor, which causes no correctness issues to the generated code because either order is allowed in the case of data races. *Second*, if there is a loop inside the kernel, it is fully unrolled before the construction of the TLDG. For a loop with large or unknown trip-counts so that it is hard to unroll, the whole loop is taken as a single node in the TLDG. Because of the regularity of data-level parallel computations on GPU, such hard-to-unroll loops are uncommon. With these operations, the resulting TLDG is directed and acyclic.

A TLDG has several properties. *First*, it exposes much more detailed dependences than traditional PDG does. In PDG, each node is a statement and there is an edge between two statements as long as some instances of the two statements have dependences. With dependences exposed for every instance and every thread, TLDG lays the foundation for tackling thread-level dependences and redundancies. *Second*, a TLDG may consist of multiple separate graphs when some threads are independent with some others. At an extreme case, when there are no cross-thread data dependences, a TLDG consists of L graphs (L equals the number of threads it models.) *Finally*, TLDG, although modeling dynamic instances, has a bounded and usually small size. Apparently, it is enough for a TLDG to contain just the nodes for a single thread block (e.g., for handling explicit synchronizations) if the dependence patterns of all blocks are identical. When some thread blocks (or warps) show different dependence patterns, a TLDG needs to be created for each class of blocks. Fortunately, thanks to the regular data-parallelism of typical GPU programs, the thread blocks of a GPU program usually follow a single pattern. The size of the TLDG of a GPU kernel is bounded by the product of the size of a thread block and the number of kinds of thread blocks in terms of dependence patterns. Due to hardware constraints, a thread block on modern GPUs contains no more than one thousand threads. A TLDG hence contains nodes and edges at the order of thousand, easy to construct and manage. When used for handling implicit synchronizations, TLDG should be created at the level of a warp. The size of such a TLDG is usually even smaller than that at the level of thread blocks.

4.2 Relaxing Synchronizations through Instance-Level Instruction Scheduling

A typical SPMD-translation result exploits parallelisms among the tasks executed by different GPU thread blocks. The computations conducted by one thread block are usually sequentially executed by a CPU thread when the translated code runs on a CPU.

The goal of instance-level instruction scheduling is to produce an order of the nodes in a TLDG so that their sequential executions produce the same results as what the executions of the corresponding GPU thread block produces. With all dependences captured by the TLDG, the code generator just needs to produce an order of the nodes such that those dependences are obeyed. *Such an order automatically relaxes the overly strong synchronizations*: No loop fission is needed any more because the successful preservation of instance-level dependences by the node order effectively eliminates the need for a whole block synchronization.

Many orders of the nodes may be legitimate. At a first glance, the scheduling problem may seem identical to traditional instruction scheduling problem except that the dependence graphs encode dependences among dynamic instances of instructions rather than static statements. Traditional list-based scheduling algorithms [7] seem to be directly applicable.

However, a careful examination shows that some unique features of our problem add some special complexities. In traditional list-based scheduling, each node in the dependence graph is labeled with some weight typically equaling the length (in terms of cycles) of the shortest path from the node to a root (i.e., a node with no outgoing edges) of the dependence graph. These weights are used as guidance for scheduling. On a TLDG of a GPU kernel, however, often hundreds of nodes have the same weights. The reason is that many threads in a block have the same dependence patterns and instructions due to the regular data-level parallel computations in most GPU kernels. The implication is that if list-based scheduling is used, the mechanism for tie-breaking will play an especially important role in the scheduling. Another important feature of TLDG is that a TLDG often consists of many separate graphs. As a consequence, some practices natural to traditional list-based scheduling will show some new effects on TLDG. For instance, if we apply the basic list-based scheduling to TLDG so that every time the node with the largest weight is taken, then the largest-weight nodes from different graphs (corresponding to different threads) will tend to be scheduled close in time, even though they may have no dependences (hence data reuses) among one another.

We design three scheduling algorithms to meet the special complexities of the TLDG scheduling problem. These algorithms are based on different heuristics, but with the same goal as to enhance data locality in the generated code.

Breadth-First Scheduling.
The first algorithm is a breadth-first scheduling algorithm.

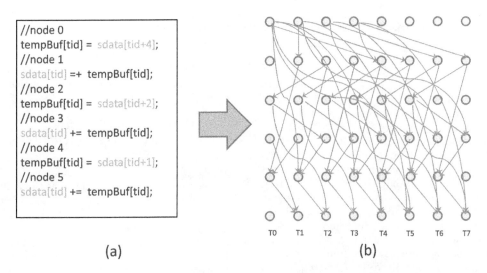

```
//node 0
tempBuf[tid] = sdata[tid+4];
//node 1
sdata[tid] =+ tempBuf[tid];
//node 2
tempBuf[tid] = sdata[tid+2];
//node 3
sdata[tid] += tempBuf[tid];
//node 4
tempBuf[tid] = sdata[tid+1];
//node 5
sdata[tid] += tempBuf[tid];
```

(a)

(b)

Figure 3: (a) The bottom three statements of Figure 1 with shared memory references broken into pieces; (b) the corresponding TLDG with only eight threads shown.

It partitions the TLDG nodes into a number of groups and imposes strict order among groups. In each round, the algorithm finds all nodes that have no incoming edges and put them into a group. It schedules the nodes in the group based on an ascending order of their GPU thread IDs. It then removes all the nodes in the group along with their outgoing edges from the TLDG and proceeds to the next round. The process continues until the TLDG becomes empty. It is easy to see that the produced code maintains the source-sink relationships of all the dependences in the original TLDG. This algorithm is called *breadth-first* because during its scheduling, nodes of different threads but at a level similar to the level of the current node are often preferred over the successors of the current node.

The breadth-first scheduling can be viewed as a variation of the basic list-based scheduling. When all threads have the same instruction sets and dependence patterns, the basic list-based scheduling algorithm, coupled with the use of thread ID as the tie-breaker, will produce the same results as the breadth-first algorithm does.

The intuition of the breadth-first algorithm is that even though the nodes in a group tend to come from different threads, they often reside at the same level in the TLDG, hence likely corresponding to the instances of the same memory access instruction in a GPU kernel. Because many GPU programs conduct coalesced memory references (i.e., adjacent threads access memory locations close to one another), a memory reference instruction in a GPU kernel often produces relatively regular memory accesses: Locations accessed by threads with adjacent IDs tend to be close in memory. Therefore, the breadth-first scheduling algorithm, by ordering nodes based on their thread IDs in each round, is likely to yield good spatial locality.

Depth-First Scheduling.

While the breadth-first algorithm may offer good spatial locality, it considers no temporal data reuses. Furthermore, it requires many temporal variables to store the intermediate computing results, and the consumption of the results is likely in another round and many instructions later.

The depth-first scheduling algorithm emphasizes intra-

thread data reuses. It starts by taking a node that has the largest weight but has no incoming edges. It then removes that node and its outgoing edges from the TLDG. In each of the following steps, it tries to find a node of the same thread that the last-taken node belongs to. (The tie-breaking is thread ID.) If none of such nodes is free (i.e., having no incoming edges), the scheduler will switch to the nodes of a different thread and continue this process.

The selection of which thread to switch to is important for the performance of the produced schedule. The criterion used in the depth-first algorithm is based on the number of useful nodes in a thread. A useful node is a node containing non-redundant instructions. (The recognition of useful nodes will be described in the next section.) Because the goal of this scheduler is to divide the nodes of a thread into as few partitions as possible, the scheduler selects the thread with the fewest useful nodes left. The rationale is that by choosing such a thread, we have a better chance of removing all the nodes of that thread from the TLDG early so that the nodes in that thread will not affect the scheduling of the nodes of other threads any further.

Length-First Scheduling.

The length-first algorithm is a variation of the depth-first algorithm. Instead of limiting the selection of nodes within one thread, this algorithm prefers the selection of nodes on the longest uninterrupted path. A path is uninterrupted if all the nodes in the path have one incoming edge and that edge comes from a node in this path. The nodes in a path may belong to different threads.

Both the depth-first and length-first algorithms follow the dependence edges in the graph. The difference is that the former emphasizes intra-thread dependences, while the latter does not. As dependences means data reuses, both algorithms tend to produce code with temporal data locality highlighted.

4.3 Code Shape Optimization

With the support of the TLDG, two optimizations can be easily materialized to enhance the code shape of the generated program.

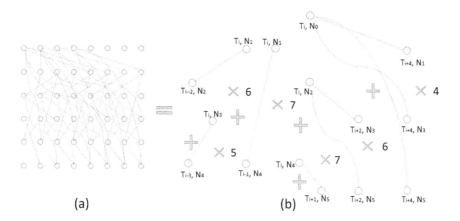

Figure 4: The original TLDG (a) broken down into six basic patterns (b), each of which retains its shape and orientation in the whole graph, only repeated in the horizontal direction.

The first optimization is enabled by the instance-level code generation. With each instance of an instruction explicitly expressed, it becomes possible to compute the results of some thread-ID–dependent conditional statements (e.g., "if (tid<32)"), and hard-code the results into the generated code. This optimization help reduce the number of instructions and branches in the generated CPU code.

The second optimization is based on the observation that a TLDG typically consists of some identical subgraphs. For example, the TLDG in Figure 4 (a) is essentially composed of the many copies of the several subgraphs in Figure 4 (b). Each of the subgraphs repeats multiple times horizontally. Such repetitions stem from the similarity of the control flows taken by the GPU threads. Such a similarity is common due to the data-level parallel computations in the kernel. The patterns can be discovered through heuristic graph pattern matching algorithms [23]. This optimization can help reduce the size of the CPU code: n copies of a subgraph can be implemented with a loop of n iterations. The application of this optimization is optional. It can be used to help strike a good tradeoff between code size and loop unrolling benefits.

4.4 Thread Partial Redundancy Removal

The TLDG provides a convenient representation for detecting thread partial redundant calculations. Because every instance of an instruction becomes a node in the TLDG, thread partial redundancy becomes complete redundancy at some nodes. The redundancy removal problem turns into the detection of useless nodes and the prevention of them from getting into the generated code.

With the support of TLDG, the detection of the redundant nodes is similar to traditional redundancy removal. The process starts with marking the initial set of useful nodes, which consists of three classes of nodes: the nodes containing returning instructions, the nodes modifying the kernel function arguments, and the nodes storing data into pinned memory (i.e., a segment of host memory directly accessible by GPU kernels.) All these nodes are very likely to contain operations useful for the program final output. The compiler then starts from these "useful" nodes and traces upwards to the top of the TLDG, marking all the nodes encountered as useful. All the unmarked nodes are then removed

from the TLDG. Figure 5 illustrates this process. This optimization should happen before the instruction scheduling.

It is easy to see that both the thread partial redundancy removal and the scheduling-based relaxation of synchronizations are applicable at the levels of both thread blocks and warps. The only difference is at which level the TLDG is created.

5. EVALUATION

We evaluate the TLDG-based optimizations on five CUDA programs. Three of them come from NVIDIA CUDA SDK [1]: *Reduction* is the fifth version of parallel reduction in the SDK, *Transpose* implements parallel matrix transposing, *SortingNetworks* is an implementation of the standard sorting network model which uses a network of wires and comparator modules to sort a sequence of numbers in parallel. The program *CG* is the conjugate gradient program from NPB benchmark suite, recently ported to CUDA under the HPCGPU project. The program *Nw* implements a widely used sequencing algorithm in bioinformatics. It is part of the Rodinia benchmark suite [6]. We select these programs mainly because they form a set containing the typical GPU program features that are relevant to this work: non-trivial explicit and implicit synchronizations, and thread partial redundancy.

We compare the performance of four versions of the SPMD-translated code. Three of them are the versions from the TLDG-based methods described in this paper. They are named *breadth-first*, *depth-first*, and *length-first*, corresponding to the three scheduling algorithms presented in Section 4.2 respectively. By default, thread partial redundancy removal has been applied to all these TLDG-based methods. The baseline for our comparison is the state of the art—that is, to use the MCUDA approach [20] to do normal translation, and use statement-level dependence analysis [11] to identify potentially critical implicit dependences and treats them with loop fission. The generated version is named *splitting-oriented*. Recent explorations [11] have shown that among all existing GPU-CPU translation methods, this approach generates the most efficient code that runs correctly.

All our experiments are carried out on a quad-core Intel Xeon E5460 machine, with Linux 2.6.33 and GCC 4.1.2

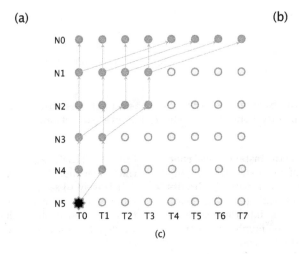

```
1 {
2 T*data,
3 hash<int, T> tempBuf)
4 if(tid[128]<256) tempBuf.insert(<0>, data[128]);
5 if(tid[129]<256) tempBuf.insert(<1>, data[129]);
......
3458 if(tid[239]<32) data[239] += tempBuf.pop(239);
3459 if(tid[255]<32) data[255] += tempBuf.pop(255);
3460}
```

(a)

```
1 {
2 T*data,
3 hash<int, T> tempBuf)
4 tempBuf.insert(<0>, data[128]);
5 tempBuf.insert(<1>, data[129]);
......
511 data[1]+=tempBuf.pop(1);
512 tempBuf.insert(<0>, data[1]);
513 data[0]+=tempBuf.pop(0);
514 }
```

(b)

(c)

Figure 5: (a). The original generated code before redundancy removal. (b). Pruned code where all useless computations are removed. (c). Bottom-up redundancy removal, starting with the initial useful nodes, marked black.

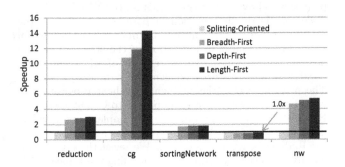

Figure 6: Performance of the benchmarks normalized by the *splitting-oriented* performance. The thread partial redundancy removal is applied.

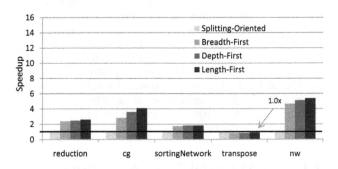

Figure 7: Performance of the benchmarks normalized by the *splitting-oriented* performance. The thread partial redundancy removal is not applied.

installed. The compilations always use the highest level of optimization.

5.1 Overall Speedup

Figure 6 reports the overall performance of the benchmarks. By breaking the thread tasks into many nodes, the TLDG-based methods do introduce additional overhead, especially in loading and storing intermediate results when two adjacent nodes from the same GPU thread are separated apart by some other nodes scheduled by the TLDG-based methods. In the case of *transpose*, with only four memory references per GPU thread and no redundant calculations, the benefits by the TLDG methods turn out to be not enough to outweigh the overhead, resulting in slightly lower

performance than the code produced by the statement-level method.

However, on all the other four benchmarks, the TLDG-based methods consistently outperform the statement-level, splitting-oriented method. Since the TLDG method converts all operations in a GPU block to a piece of linear CPU code, the scope for compiler optimizations on such CPU code is much larger than in the thread loop structure generated by MCUDA-like methods. Instruction re-scheduling and merging on both compiler and processor pipeline level will have sufficient space to operate. It further reduces loop overhead. The instance-level redundancy removal proves to be a powerful tool in reducing unnecessary operations in the translated CPU code. Its effectiveness shows up in the results of *Reduc-*

tion and *CG*, both of which contains a non-trivial amount of thread partial redundant computations. For comparison, Figure 7 reports the speedups of the benchmarks without thread partial redundancy removal applied.

The breadth-first scheduler delivers the lowest performance among all TLDG-based methods. It is mainly because the scheduling algorithm is more oriented at processing the TLDG itself rather than the GPU program the TLDG stands for. Although it tries to take advantage of the largely well-arranged access patterns of the GPU kernels by sorting within each round, the benefit of that sorting turns out to be not as significant as temporal locality in the CPU code it generates. The depth-first scheduler generally performs better than the breadth-first scheduler. It is better at handling intra-thread control dependences by trying to put adjacent nodes of the same thread together in the CPU code, which eliminates the need for many temporary buffer accesses. However, it still ignores the inter-thread data dependence edges, which constitute a majority of the edges in a typical TLDG. By taking advantage of such dependence edges, the length-first scheduler achieves the highest speedup overall. The length-first scheduling generally adapts better to dependence patterns, and is therefore exposed to more temporal-reuse opportunities than other scheduling algorithms. Recall that both depth-first and length-first schedulers use GPU thread ID as the tie breaker. Because there are a large number of ties in a typical TLDG, these two methods turn out to achieve most of the spatial locality benefits that the breadth-first method obtains, even though neither of them does intra-round sorting explicitly.

From the benchmark aspect, the tested kernels of *CG* and *Reduction* are both implementation of the classic parallel reduction algorithms, but CG has more complicated computation in each iteration, and a larger block size, which translates into more data dependence edges and partial redundancy. Both factors contribute to the more prominent gains of the TLDG-based methods on *CG* than on *Reduction*. *SortingNetworks* and *Transpose* have no instance-level redundant computation, but *SortingNetworks* has a much denser graph than *Transpose*, leading to considerable benefits of the TLDG-based methods. *Nw* has few threads in a block but a large number of nodes in a thread. More than half of the dependence edges in its TLDG connect two nodes of the same thread. All three TLDG-based methods perform well on this program.

Overall, the length-first scheduling algorithm performs the best. Paired with the thread partial redundancy removal and other optimizations, it produces performance improvements from a factor of 1.9 to 14.2 on four of the five benchmarks. Although it results in a slight slowdown on one benchmark, that negative effect can be mostly avoided by simply not applying TLDG-based optimizations to small kernels—such as those with fewer than six memory operations.

5.2 Code Shape Optimization

The capability of the code shape optimization is demonstrated by applying this optimization on *SortingNetworks*, a benchmark with the densest TLDG among all the five benchmarks. As stated in earlier sections, this optimization seeks to reduce the size of the generated code by extracting those vertically non-overlapping, horizontally repetitive

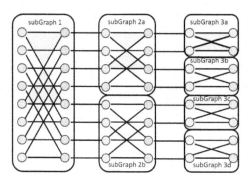

Figure 8: The repetitive subgraphs in the TLDG for *SortingNetworks*.

sub-graphs in the TLDG, and use a loop in the generated code to represent their repetitive occurrences.

The optimization is applied to *SortingNetworks* TLDG, then a modified breadth-first instruction scheduler is used to generate the CPU code. The experimental result shows a two-fold reduction in the size of the code. The reason for such a substantial reduction is attributed partly to the dependence patterns in the benchmark. *SortingNetworks* employs a butterfly network approach to parallelize the comparison and swapping. In this iterative process, every entry is compared to another entry that is s entries away from itself. The variable s is reduced by half in each iteration, which essentially divides the operations in each iteration into several independent and homomorphous partitions, as shown in Figure 8 (the yellow in the figure highlights the butterfly-shape patterns.)

The reduced code shows no measurable performance difference compared to the version without code size reduction. This is due to the large instruction cache on the host machine. The benefits of code reduction are expected to be more prominent on mobile CPUs.

6. RELATED WORK

SPDM-translation has received a number of recent explorations. MCUDA [21] is one of the first studies trying to translate GPU CUDA code into C code for multicore CPU. The authors later developed a set of optimizations to enhance the code quality [20]. Ocelot [8] tries to do the translation at the CUDA PTX level. Neither of the two explorations has considered relaxable synchronizations or thread partial redundancies—the main focus of this current work.

Neither MCUDA nor Ocelot has provided appropriate treatments to implicit synchronizations in a GPU kernels. They are subject to translation errors on a program with critical implicit synchronizations.

A recent study [11] points out the correctness pitfall and proposes a dependence theorem to help identify critical implicit synchronizations—that is, those synchronizations that cannot be ignored during the translation. The authors further compare the efficiency of two code generation methods that handle critical synchronizations correctly. There are several significant differences between that study and our current work. First, all the methods proposed in the previous study are based on static statements in a GPU kernel. This current work focuses on dynamic instances of instructions. Second, this work tackles both explicit and implicit synchronizations, while the previous study has only implicit synchronizations as its target. Third, the previous study does not deal with thread partial redundancy. Finally, none of the techniques proposed in this work—including the use of TLDG, instance-level instruction scheduling, code shape optimizations, thread partial redundancy removal—is proposed in the previous study. As Section 5 has shown, these new techniques help produce code significantly more efficient than what the previous approach generates.

There is a body of work trying to simplify GPU programming. Some [3, 13] try to develop automatic compilers to translate CPU code into GPU code. They usually use pragmas to incorporate programmers knowledge. Some other work add extensions to CUDA or OpenCL (e.g. [19].) Some work exploits cooperation of CPU and GPU for whole system synergy [15, 17, 24]. Most of them assume the code for both devices are given or consider only CPU-to-GPU code translation.

There have been many studies in optimizing GPU programs for high efficiency. Some propose hardware extensions (e.g. [9, 16, 22]), but more rely on software analysis, transformations, and tuning (e.g. [4, 5, 12, 14, 18, 25–27].)

None of these studies have concentrated on the two issues this work addresses: thread partial redundancy and relaxable synchronizations. Our recent workshop paper [10] raises the two issues for the first time, but in a preliminary manner. Mainly to express our position on the issues, the workshop paper briefly discusses the properties of the two issues and the basic concept of TLDG. This current paper provides a much more comprehensive explorations to the problems in almost every aspect. (1) In the TLDG concept and construction, this paper describes how to handle hard-to-unroll loops, data races, and reveals several important properties of TLDG by comparing with traditional PDG. (2) In instruction scheduling, this paper presents three scheduling algorithms and a set of empirical comparisons among the algorithms, while only the breadth-first algorithm is mentioned in the previous workshop paper. Furthermore, this current paper systematically analyzes the difficulties for traditional list-based scheduling algorithms to apply to the instruction scheduling problem. (3) In code optimizations, the previous workshop paper contains no code shape optimizations at all. (4) Finally, this paper gives a more comprehensive evaluation of the techniques.

7. CONCLUSION

This paper has presented an exploration for enhancing the treatment of two important features of GPU kernels during SPMD-translations, namely overly strong synchronizations and thread partial redundancy. It first explains the concepts of the two features and their influence on the quality of SPMD-translation results. It then points out that the two features essentially come from a single reason: the non-uniformity among threads. It introduces the use of TLDG as a convenient representation for analyzing both issues, and proposes a set of techniques on TLDG for addressing the inefficiency caused by those features. These techniques include three instance-level instruction scheduling algorithms, some code shape optimizations, and the detection of thread partial redundancies. Together, these techniques lead to

an approach which systematically relaxes overly strong synchronizations (both explicit and implicit ones) and removes thread partial redundancies for SPMD-translations. In an experiment on five programs, these techniques enhance the efficiency of the SPMD-translation results by up to a factor of 14, demonstrating the promise for improving the quality of existing SPMD-translators. The instance-level analysis proposed in this work may open many other opportunities for promoting the whole-system synergy in modern heterogeneous computing systems.

Acknowledgment

We owe the anonymous reviewers our gratitude for their helpful suggestions on the paper. This material is based upon work supported by the National Science Foundation Grant (0811791), NSF CAREER (0954015), DOE Early Career Award, and IBM CAS Fellowship. Any opinions, findings, and conclusions or recommendations expressed in this material are those of the authors and do not necessarily reflect the views of NSF, DOE, or IBM.

8. REFERENCES

[1] NVIDIA CUDA. http://www.nvidia.com/cuda.

[2] OpenCL. http://www.khronos.org/opencl/.

[3] E. Ayguade, R. M. Badia, D. Cabrera, A. Duran, M. Gonzalez, F. Igual, J. Jimenez, Daniel andLabarta, X. Martorell, R. Mayo, J. M. Perez, and E. S. Quintana-Ortí. A proposal to extend the openmp tasking model for heterogeneous architectures. In *Proceedings of the 5th International Workshop on OpenMP: Evolving OpenMP in an Age of Extreme Parallelism*, IWOMP '09, pages 154–167, 2009.

[4] M. M. Baskaran, U. Bondhugula, S. Krishnamoorthy, J. Ramanujam, A. Rountev, and P. Sadayappan. A compiler framework for optimization of affine loop nests for GPGPUs. In *ICS'08: Proceedings of the 22nd Annual International Conference on Supercomputing*, pages 225–234, 2008.

[5] S. Carrillo, J. Siegel, and X. Li. A control-structure splitting optimization for gpgpu. In *Proceedings of ACM Computing Frontiers*, 2009.

[6] S. Che, M. Boyer, J. Meng, D. Tarjan, J. W. Sheaffer, S.-H. Lee, and K. Skadron. Rodinia: A benchmark suite for heterogeneous computing. In *IISWC*, 2009.

[7] K. Cooper and L. Torczon. *Engineering a Compiler*. Morgan Kaufmann, 2003.

[8] G. Diamos, A. Kerr, and M. Kesavan. Translating gpu binaries to tiered simd architectures with ocelot. 2009.

[9] W. Fung, I. Sham, G. Yuan, and T. Aamodt. Dynamic warp formation and scheduling for efficient gpu control flow. In *MICRO '07: Proceedings of the 40th Annual IEEE/ACM International Symposium on Microarchitecture*, pages 407–420, Washington, DC, USA, 2007. IEEE Computer Society.

[10] Z. Guo and X. Shen. Fine-grained treatment to synchronizations in gpu-to-cpu translation. In *Proceedings of the International Workshop on Languages and Compilers for Parallel Computing*, 2011.

[11] Z. Guo, E. Zhang, and X. Shen. Correctly treating synchronizations in compiling fine-grained

spmd-threaded programs for cpu. In *Proceedings of International Conference on Parallel Architectures and Compilation Techniques*, 2011.

[12] A. Hormati, M. Samadi, M. Woh, T. Mudge, and S. Mahlke. Sponge: portable stream programming on graphics engines. In *Proceedings of the International Conference on Architectural Support for Programming Languages and Operating Systems*, 2011.

[13] S. Lee, S. Min, and R. Eigenmann. Openmp to gpgpu: A compiler framework for automatic translation and optimization. In *Proceedings of ACM SIGPLAN Symposium on Principles and Practice of Parallel Programming*, 2009.

[14] Y. Liu, E. Z. Zhang, and X. Shen. A cross-input adaptive framework for gpu programs optimization. In *Proceedings of International Parallel and Distribute Processing Symposium (IPDPS)*, pages 1–10, 2009.

[15] C. Luk, S. Hong, and H. Kim. Qilin: Exploiting parallelism on heterogeneous multiprocessors with adaptive mapping. In *Proceedings of the International Symposium on Microarchitecture*, 2009.

[16] J. Meng, D. Tarjan, and K. Skadron. Dynamic warp subdivision for integrated branch and memory divergence tolerance. In *ISCA*, 2010.

[17] V. Ravi, W. Ma, D. Chiu, and G. Agrawal. compiler and runtime support for enabling generalized reduction computations on heterogeneous parallel configurations. In *Proceedings of the ACM International Conference on Supercomputing (ICS)*, 2010.

[18] S. Ryoo, C. I. Rodrigues, S. S. Baghsorkhi, S. S. Stone, D. B. Kirk, and W. W. Hwu. Optimization principles and application performance evaluation of a multithreaded GPU using CUDA. In *PPoPP '08: Proceedings of the 13th ACM SIGPLAN Symposium on Principles and Practice of Parallel Programming*, pages 73–82, 2008.

[19] M. Steuwer, P. Kegel, and S. Gorlatch. Skelcl âĂŞ a library for portable high-level programming on multi-gpu systems. In *Proceedings of International Parallel and Distribute Processing Symposium (IPDPS)*, 2011.

[20] J. Stratton, V. Grover, J. Marathe, B. Aarts, M. Murphy, Z. Hu, and W. Hwu. Efficient compilation of fine-grained spmd-threaded programs for multicore cpus. In *CGO '10: Proceedings of the International Symposium on Code Generation and Optimization*, 2010.

[21] J. Stratton, S. Stone, and W. Hwu. Mcuda: An efficient implementation of cuda kernels for multi-core cpus. 2008.

[22] D. Tarjan, J. Meng, and K. Skadron. Increasing memory miss tolerance for simd cores. In *SC*, 2009.

[23] G. Valiente. *Combinatorial Pattern Matching Algorithms in Computational Biology Using Perl and R.* CRC Press, 2009.

[24] B. Wu, E. Zhang, and X. Shen. Enhancing data locality for dynamic simulations through asynchronous data transformations and adaptive control. In *Proceedings of the International Conference on Parallel Architecture and Compilation Techniques (PACT)*, 2011.

[25] Y. Yang, P. Xiang, J. Kong, and H. Zhou. A gpgpu compiler for memory optimization and parallelism management. In *PLDI*, 2010.

[26] E. Zhang, Y. Jiang, Z. Guo, K. Tian, and X. Shen. On-the-fly elimination of dynamic irregularities for gpu computing. In *Proceedings of the International Conference on Architectural Support for Programming Languages and Operating Systems*, 2011.

[27] E. Z. Zhang, Y. Jiang, Z. Guo, and X. Shen. Streamlining gpu applications on the fly. In *Proceedings of the ACM International Conference on Supercomputing (ICS)*, pages 115–125, 2010.

Fast Loop-level Data Dependence Profiling

Hongtao Yu
Department of Computer Science
Purdue University
West Lafayette, IN 47907
htyu@purdue.edu

Zhiyuan Li
Department of Computer Science
Purdue University
West Lafayette, IN 47907
zhiyuanli@purdue.edu

ABSTRACT

Execution-driven data dependence profiling has gained significant interest as a tool to compensate the weakness of static data dependence analysis. Although such dependence profiling is valid for specific inputs only, its result can be used in many ways for program parallelization. Unfortunately, traditional hash-based dependence profiling can take tremendous memory and machine time, which severely limits its practical use. In this paper, we propose new compiler-based techniques to perform fast loop-level data dependence profiling. Firstly, using type consistency and alias information, our compiler embeds memory tags into the data structures in the original program such that memory addresses can be efficiently compared for dependence testing. This approach avoids the bytewise hashing overhead in conventional profiling methods. Secondly, we prove that a partial dependence graph obtained from profiling is sufficient for loop-level reordering transformations and parallelization. Such partial dependence graph can be obtained very fast, without having to exhaustively enumerate all dependence edges. Thirdly, our compiler partitions the profiling task into independent slices. Such slices can be profiled in parallel, producing subgraphs which are eventually combined automatically into the complete data dependence graph by the compiler. Experiments show that these techniques significantly reduce the memory use and shorten the profiling time (by an order of magnitude for several SPEC2006 benchmarks). Benchmarks too big to profile at all loop levels by previous methods can now be profiled fully within several hours.

Categories and Subject Descriptors

D.3.4 [**Programming Languages**]: Processors—*Compilers, run-time environments*; F.3.2 [**Logics And Meanings Of Programs**]: Semantics of Programming Languages—*Program Analysis*

General Terms

Algorithms, Languages, Performance

Keywords

Software parallelization, profiling, data dependence, instrumentation

1. INTRODUCTION

One of the key steps in parallelization of existing software is to gain a thorough understanding of the data dependences which constrain the potential parallelism in a program. Unfortunately, the ability of existing compilers to analyze data dependence is quite limited, due to difficulties such as complicated aliasing patterns and unknown symbolic relationships that govern data references. Execution-driven data dependence profiling, on the other hand, has gained significant interest in recent years [2,6,7,8,13,16,18,23,27,28,29,31,34] because memory access ambiguity can be resolved exactly during program execution, which allows data dependence to be analyzed exactly. Although such dependence profiling is valid for specific inputs only, programmers can use the profiling result to identify the most promising loops for hand parallelization. Profiling is especially important to speculative parallelization techniques, due to the heavy penalty in case the speculation is wrong. If dependence profiling shows a loop to be parallelizable for representative inputs, then we have high confidence that speculative parallelization will likely succeed at run time. Lastly, by comparing the profiling result with the compiler analysis result, compiler developers can identify the weaknesses in their static dependence analyzers. Improvements can then be made.

To date, the most common approach to data dependence profiling is based on pairwise checking. Given a loop, a pairwise profiler records all the memory addresses visited within the loop. For memory accesses with regular strides, stride information may also be recorded to speed up profiling, as explained below. Since regular strides often happen only in the innermost loops, a hash table is used for checking memory addresses in more common cases. With the hash table, each memory address that stores the original program's data is associated with an *access record* which keeps track of the program statements reading/writing at that address. The loop iteration in which each access takes place is also indexed and recorded. Every time a new statement accesses the same memory address, the profiler searches the access record in order to find data dependences on previous accesses. With such conventional approach, the profiling cost, in terms of memory requirement and execution time, can be prohibitive even for programs with modest-sized inputs.

Conventional profiling suffers from two major sources of inefficiency. Firstly, it does not utilize any type information in a program. As a result, an access record must be allocated for each byte in a data item in the original program. An 8-byte double word data item, therefore, will need eight access records. As mentioned above, such an access record must be large enough to store all the statements (and the associated iteration indices) that have ever visited that byte. Although there exist various ways to compress the records, their sizes remain significant. Furthermore, during data dependence profiling, a single load or store instruction in the original program must be accompanied by at least one hash operation and a series of comparisons with previously-executed instructions accessing the same address. This usually results in hundreds or thousands of extra instructions and potentially excessive cache misses. Therefore, hash-based pairwise dependence profiling is often slower than the original program execution by a factor of hundreds or thousands. The memory required to run the profiler is also greater than the original run by the factor of hundreds. These memory and time costs are especially pronounced when profiling is applied to loops at outer levels which are often exactly those needing parallelization. The second source of inefficiency is exhaustive enumeration of all dependence instances while, as we will prove, a subset of information is sufficient for correct loop-level reordering transformations and parallelization.

In this paper, we propose three new complementary methods to significantly enhance both the memory use and the speed for data dependence profiling. Firstly, using type consistency and alias information, our compiler embeds memory tags into the data structures in the original program such that memory addresses can be efficiently compared for dependence testing. Secondly, we prove that a partial dependence graph obtained from profiling is sufficient for loop-level reordering transformations and parallelization. Such partial dependence graph can be obtained very fast. Thirdly, our compiler partitions the profiling task into independent slices. Such slices can be profiled in parallel, producing sub-graphs which are eventually combined automatically into the complete data dependence graph by the compiler. Experiments show that these techniques significantly reduce the memory use and shorten the profiling time (by an order of magnitude for several SPEC2006 benchmarks). Several benchmarks are too big to be profiled at all loop levels by previous methods even with several days of running, but they can now be profiled fully within a few hours.

The rest of this paper is organized as follows. Section 2 gives an overview of concepts and issues in dependence profiling. We then present our new techniques, i.e. type-based memory tagging (in Section 3), partial dependence graphs (in Section 4), and parallel multi-slicing (in Section 5). Experimental results are given in Section 6. We discuss related work in Section 7 and conclude in Section 8.

2. BACKGROUD

For the purpose of program parallelization, we are interested in three kinds of data dependences, namely flow(i.e. read-after-write, or RAW), anti- (i.e. write-after-read, or WAR), and output(i.e. write-after-write, or WAW) dependences. If a dependence happens between two statements (or two memory operations) denoted by $S1$ and $S2$, respectively, which are executed in the same loop iteration, it is said to be *loop-independent*. If they happen in different iterations, the dependence is said to be *loop-carried*. In particular, if a load from an address is covered by a previous store to the

same address in the same loop iteration, the load is said to be covered by the store and thus is prevented from being involved in any loop-carried RAW dependence. If none of the dependences due to loads and stores for a memory location are loop-carried RAW, then such dependences do not fundamentally impede loop parallelization, because even if the same memory location is overwritten in different loop iterations, memory duplication (also called variable privatization) can be performed to remove the dependences without changing the program correctness. Certain loop transformations that enhance parallelization opportunities and execution efficiency need to know the shortest distances of dependences. We record such information in our profiler.

2.1 Pairwise Dependence Profiling

Figure 1 gives an example to illustrate how pairwise dependence profiling works. Immediately before each memory operation, a call to the function *check_address* is inserted to record the accessed memory address and to check the operation's dependence on previously recorded accesses at the same address. In this example, for brevity, such calls are inserted for array accesses only. Note that the basic profiling does not benefit from any alias analysis and hence must conservatively profile all memory accesses except those to temporary registers introduced by the compiler. At each loop entry or exit, a call to the function *update_loop* is inserted in order to count the number of iterations of each loop. If more than one loop are profiled at the same time, a loop stack is maintained to record the current loop nest during profiling in order to check dependences that occur within the loop nest.

```
main()
{
    L1:    int a[100];
    L2:    a[0] = 0;
    L3:    for (int i=1;  i < 100; i++)
    L4:        a[i] = a[i-1] + 1;
}
```

(a) A sample program

```
main()
{
    L1:    int a[100];
    L5:    check_address (&a[0], 1,"write");
    L2:    a[0] = 0;
    L3:    for (int i=1;  i < 100; i++) {
    L6:        update_loop("enter");
    L7:        check_address(&a[i-1],2,"read");
    L8:        check_address(&a[i],3,"write");
    L4:        a[i] = a[i-1] + 1;
           }
    L9:    update_loop("exit");
}
```

(b) The sample program after instrumentation

Figure 1: Basic instrumentation.

As mentioned in the introduction, hash-based pairwise profilers use hash tables to allow fast search for memory accesses that are indexed using memory addresses as the keys. Whenever a load/store occurs, it is checked against each statement recorded in the hash table entry for the accessed memory address. The checking determines whether a RAW, WAW or WAR dependence is found and whether the dependence is loop-independent or loop-carried. The checking also determines whether the dependence distance is constant. If not, the shortest distance found so far between the specific pair of statements is determined. After the checking, the new iteration number replaces the old one for the specific load or store recorded in the hash table. It is important to note that, as soon as a loop-independent RAW dependence is found at a specific memory address, the subsequent loads at the same memory address in the same iteration will no longer have any loop-carried RAW dependences. The profiler does not need to search further for such RAW dependences at this address, because a store in the same iteration has *covered* all the subsequent loads at the same address. Whenever a dependence is found, the current global dependence graph is checked to see whether it is already represented. If not, the new dependence edge is added. If the edge exists, we update its distance if the new distance is shorter.

Suppose M memory locations are accessed during the execution of a loop. M hash entries are needed in the local hash table for the loop. Suppose on average there are N memory accesses to each memory location. Assuming that a hash operation takes constant time, checking dependences on memory operations registered at each hash entry takes $O(N^2)$ time on average, giving an $O(M \times N^2)$ time complexity and an $O(M \times N)$ storage overhead to profile that loop.

2.2 Stride-based Dependence Profiling

It has been recently shown [13] that, when iteratively executed load/store instructions access memory addresses in regular strides, data dependences between such instructions can be checked by comparing the strides. Such checking method, used in the SD^3 profiler [13], consumes much less memory and execution time than checking on memory address hash tables. When applied to the 20 hottest loops in each SPEC2006 program, the stride checking approach is reported to keep the profiling overhead at about 100 times the original program execution time.

During profiling, SD^3 tries to compute a stride expression for each load/store instruction such that all the memory addresses visited by the instruction can be inferred without recording each address in a hash table. For irregular accesses, i.e., accesses which do not show a regular stride, SD^3 stores each memory address into a hash table because a stride expression cannot be obtained. If all the accesses to a memory block (e.g. an array) are regularly strided, then SD^3 is able to summarize memory accesses to the memory block in a highly-compact way and therefore can significantly reduce the memory usage for profiling that memory block. However, if some of the accesses have irregular strides, SD^3 may fail to compress. Worse yet, without knowing which variables may be aliased, potential data dependences between different memory blocks must be checked. Even if accesses to one of the blocks are regularly strided, others may not. The dependence checking will have to compare entries in the hash table against those with regular strides, which is as time consuming as pairwise checking. For this reason, SD^3 is much more effective for profiling inner loops than outer loops. As data dependence profiling proceeds to outer loops, irregular strides become more frequent, again making a thorough data dependence profiling extremely expensive.

3. OBJECT-BASED PROFILING

Instead of allocating an access record for every byte, we perform compiler analysis to obtain type and alias information such that an access record can be allocated for a *fixed object* (defined below) but not for each of its bytes. This is obviously more efficient in both memory use and processing time.

DEFINITION 1. *In a program written in a typed language, we call a data item a **fix-sized data object**, or simply a **fixed object**, if it is always accessed in its entirety by every load/store instruction.*

According to Definition 1, a scalar variable a with integral or floating-point type in the C language is a fixed object if the memory unit storing a is of a fixed size. (If it is ever cast to a type of a different size or it is *unioned* with another variable of a different size, then it is not considered a fixed object.) Similarly, the following data items can be fixed objects if their sizes are fixed and are always accessed in their entirety: (i) a scalar array element $arr[i]$; (ii) a scalar structure field $s.a$; and (iii) a scalar member of an allocated memory chunk, such as $*p$, $p \to arr[i]$ and $p \to a$. For dependence profiling, we do not need to keep the access record of a fixed object in a hash table. Instead, we can use a *memory tag* (or a *tag* in short) whose access is much faster than hashing. Such a memory tag is co-allocated with the fixed object with a predetermined offset. We say the tag is embedded in the fixed object. Every time a fixed object is constructed, its tag is created at the same time; when the fixed object is freed, its tag is also discarded. Therefore no tags are reused when the same memory address is reused for a new data object, and therefore no spurious dependence between logically-independent dynamic data structures will be reported. This is an improvement over several previous methods which do not differentiate logically-independent objects which happen to be assigned the same memory address. We promote a fixed scalar data object to a structure object whose first field is the original data object while the second field being the tag. For the example in Figure 1(a), the promoted version is shown in Figure 2. Other than the profiling operations, the transformed program has the same semantics as the original program. The *TAG_SIZE* is determined according to the desired dependence profiling details.

```
#define TAG_SIZE 8
struct INT {
  int data;
  char tag[TAG_SIZE];
};
main()
{
    struct INT a[100], i;
    a[0].data = 0;
    for (i.data=1;  i.data < 100; i.data++)
      a[i].data = a[i-1].data + 1;
}
```

Figure 2: The transformed program with memory tags embedded.

Next, we discuss the issues of identifying fixed objects and promoting such objects.

3.1 Object Identification

Object identification aims to find fix-sized data objects, either constructed statically or allocated on the heap. We perform alias classification [24] to divide program statements into *alias classes*. If two references in the same alias class access data units of different sizes, then it is possible that at run time the two statements access the same physical memory block, with their values simultaneously live but with two different data widths. In such a case we conservatively regard the alias class as containing varied objects instead of fixed objects. In contrast, if references in an alias class always access data units of the same size, we recognize them as accessing fixed objects. We perform object promotion for alias classes containing references to fixed objects. For references to varied objects, we fall back to bytewise hash-based profiling. For C programs we employ an inexpensive flow- and context-insensitive pointer analysis [1] for alias classification. Clearly, object-based profiling can potentially benefit from using a more precise pointer analysis [11, 32] and a more precise liveness analysis.

3.1.1 Declaration Collection

For a heap-allocated object we must identify its type in order to correctly promote it. Take the following C program as an example.

```
int N=2;
struct S {
        int a;
        int b;
} *p;
p = malloc(N*sizeof(struct S));
p[0].a=1;
((short*)&p[1].b)[0]=0;
((short*)&p[1].b)[1]=1;
```

For this example, field-sensitive alias classification can only tell us that memory operations p[0].a and p[1].b are not aliased and that the type of p[0].a is int. In order to correctly promote the field, we need to further recognize that the int type comes from the first field a of struct S. The second field b can not be promoted because of the conflicting type sizes. We perform a simple data flow analysis on the actual parameter of the malloc call. If such identification fails, then the corresponding alias class is not promoted. If identification succeeds, we mark the malloc call as a heap variable declaration with type struct S[N] and collect it for promotion. Note that we do not need to know the concrete value of N.

3.2 Object Promotion

Object promotion aims to adjust the type of a fixed object so that the corresponding tag can be inserted in a memory location adjacent to the original object. After collecting all variable declarations, we proceed to promote their types. If the original type of a declaration is a scalar type, e.g., *char*, *short*, *int*, *float* in C, we promote it to a structure type as shown in Figure 2. If the original type is an array type, we promote the element type correspondingly. Similarly if the original type is a structure type we promote its field types. If the original type is a pointer type, we first check to see whether all the objects which the pointer points to are fixed objects. If so, we must promote the pointee type before promoting the pointer type. Otherwise, we promote the pointer type only. The whole promotion process proceeds recursively because there may exist various combinations of aggregate types and pointer types.

Figure 3 lists the promotion rules. Figure 4 lists the auxiliary functions used in Figure 3. We apply promotion to all variable declarations in a program, including global variable declarations, local variable declarations, formal parameter declarations and heap variable allocations. The *Decl Scalar* rule is for all scalar variables of built-in types, such as *char*, *short*, *int*, *float* and so on. We list only the rules for the *int* type. Generalization to the other built-in types is straightforward. After promoting all declarations, we adjust each reference site to make sure that the statements of the program after promotion make reference to the same data as in the original program. As shown in those *Ref* and *Deref* rules, this is done by replacing each original reference by a reference to the *data* field if its type is promoted. We do not list rules for all kinds of references here. Instead we use *store* assignments to illustrate the idea. *Load* sites and call-site argument passing are processed similarly. Structure assignments are expanded to assignments for corresponding fields since they can be viewed as a series of scalar assignments.

---

is_promotable(e):
  let $T=$**type**(e) **in**
  let $n=$pointer_level(T) **in**
    $\forall i \in [0..n] : p[i] =$ alias_class_compatible$(\textbf{deref}_i(e))$
  return $p[1..n]$

promote$(t, p[0..n])$:
  case t **of**
    $[int]$:
      if $p[0]=$**true**
        return struct(int *data*, char *tag*$[N]$)
      else return t
    $[T*]$:
      if $p[0]=$**true**
        return struct(promote$(T, p[1..n])*$ *data*,
                         char *tag*$[N]$)
      else return promote$(T, p[1..n])*$

type(e) :
    return the type of expression e
deref$_i(e)$:
    return the dereference of e with level i
alias_class_compatible(e) :
    report, based on alias analysis, whether there exist
    conflicting data types that access what e refers to
pointer_level(T) :
    return the pointer level of a type T.

Figure 4: Auxiliary functions in promotion rules.

The *tag* field of a promoted fixed object keeps the memory tag and it must be initialized. The initialization is done in several stages, along with the initialization of the original fixed objects. A global *tag* field can be initialized when the global data section is initialized. In programming languages such as C/C++, local variables are never initialized automatically. Therefore our compiler inserts explicit initialization instructions in a function body for local *tag* fields. Heap *tag* fields are either initialized in the promoted object constructor or, if no constructors are invoked, by our compiler generated initializer.

40

$$\frac{\begin{array}{c}\textbf{[Decl Scalar]}\\ \Gamma \vdash v : \textbf{int}\\ p[0] = \text{is\_promotable}(v)\end{array}}{\Gamma' \vdash v : \text{promote}(\textbf{int}, p[0])} \qquad \frac{\begin{array}{c}\textbf{[Decl Pointer]}\\ \Gamma \vdash v : T*\\ p[0:n] = \text{is\_promotable}(v)\end{array}}{\Gamma' \vdash v : \text{promote}(T*, p[0:n])} \qquad \frac{\begin{array}{c}\textbf{[Decl Array]}\\ \Gamma \vdash v : T[N]\\ p[0:n] = \text{is\_promotable}(v)\end{array}}{\Gamma' \vdash v : \text{promote}(T, p[0:n])[N]}$$

$$\frac{\begin{array}{c}\textbf{[Decl Struct]}\\ \Gamma \vdash v : \textbf{struct}(f_1 : T_1, ..., f_m : T_m)\\ \forall i \in [1..m] : p[i][0:n_i] = \text{is\_promotable}(v.f_i)\end{array}}{\Gamma' \vdash v : \textbf{struct}(f_1 : \text{promote}(T_1, p[1][0:n_1]), ..., f_m : \text{promote}(T_m, p[m][0:n_m]))} \qquad \frac{\begin{array}{c}\textbf{[Decl Heap]}\\ \Gamma \vdash v = \textbf{new } T\\ p[0:n] = \text{is\_promotable}(*v)\end{array}}{\Gamma' \vdash v = \textbf{new } \text{promote}(T, p[0:n])}$$

$$\frac{\begin{array}{c}\textbf{[Decl Function]}\\ \Gamma \vdash f_m : T_m\ func(f_1 : T_1, ..., f_{m-1} : T_{m-1})\\ \forall i \in [1..m] : p[i][0:n_i] = \text{is\_promotable}(func.f_i)\end{array}}{\Gamma' \vdash f_m : \text{promote}(T_m, p[m][0:n_m])\ func(f_1 : \text{promote}(T_1, p[1][0:n_1]), ..., f_{m-1} : \text{promote}(T_{m-1}, p[m-1][0:n_{m-1}]))}$$

$$\frac{\begin{array}{c}\textbf{[Ref Scalar]}\\ \Gamma \vdash v : \textbf{int}\\ \Gamma \vdash v = val\\ \text{is\_promotable}(v)\end{array}}{\Gamma' \vdash v.data = val} \quad \frac{\begin{array}{c}\textbf{[Ref Pointer]}\\ \Gamma \vdash v : T*\\ \Gamma \vdash v = val\\ \text{is\_promotable}(v)\end{array}}{\Gamma' \vdash v.data = val} \quad \frac{\begin{array}{c}\textbf{[Ref Array]}\\ \Gamma \vdash v : T[N]\\ \Gamma \vdash v[i] = val\\ \text{is\_promotable}(v)\end{array}}{\Gamma' \vdash v[i].data = val} \quad \frac{\begin{array}{c}\textbf{[Ref Field]}\\ \Gamma \vdash v : \textbf{struct}(f_1 : T_1, ..., f_m : T_m)\\ \Gamma \vdash v.f_i = val\\ \text{is\_promotable}(v.f_i)\end{array}}{\Gamma' \vdash v.f_i.data = val} \quad \frac{\begin{array}{c}\textbf{[Deref Pointer]}\\ \Gamma \vdash v : T*\\ \Gamma \vdash *v = val\\ \text{is\_promotable}(*v)\end{array}}{\Gamma' \vdash v \rightarrow data = val}$$

Figure 3: Object promotion rules.

4. PARTIAL DEPENDENCE PROFILING

Profiling for a complete dependence graph incurs significant cost because of the intrinsics invoked for capturing dependence relationship between every possible pair.

We observe that a partial dependence graph which contains only the latest data dependence concerned with each statement is sufficient for loop parallelization. The access record for each monitored memory address can be simplified to keep only the most recent load and store. Under such simplification we are able to capture the most recent instance of loop-independent or loop-carried dependence. Algorithm 1 gives the detail of such partial profiling.

Algorithm 1 Partially Check Address.

1: **procedure** check_address($addr$, $opid$, $kind$)
2: **begin**
3: **if** $iterno > 0$ **then**
4:   $< id_1, iterno_1, kind_1 > = hash[addr].last\_load$
5:   $< id_2, iterno_2, kind_2 > = hash[addr].last\_store$
6:   check whether $< addr, opid, kind >$ depends on either/both of the above triplets
7:   **if** $kind == $"read" **then**
8:     $hash[addr].last\_load = < opid, iterno, kind >$
9:   **else**
10:     $hash[addr].last\_store = < opid, iterno, kind >$
11:   **end if**
12: **end if**
13: **end**

Partial dependence profiling works because of the following theorem [12]:

THEOREM 1. *(Fundamental Theorem of Dependence) Any reordering transformation that preserves every dependence in a program preserves the meaning of that program.*

Based on Theorem 1, we prove the following theorem which states that loop transformations and loop execution schedules based on our partial dependence graph are also correct.

THEOREM 2. *A reordering transformation or a loop execution schedule violates a dependence in the partial dependence graph if and only if it violates a dependence in the complete dependence graph.*

PROOF. The "only if" part is obvious because any dependence edge in the partial dependence graph is also a dependence edge in the complete dependence graph.

To prove the "if" part, suppose A and B are the source and sink statements, respectively, of a dependence edge in the complete dependence graph that is violated by a certain loop transformation or loop execution schedule. Such an invalid transformation or schedule will result in the execution of a B instance preceding the execution of an A instance. We prove that there must exist a sequence of dependence edges $C_0 = A, C_1, C_2 .. C_{n-1}, C_n = B$ in the partial graph such that $\forall i.0 < i \leq n$, C_i depends on C_{i-1} and at least one of them is violated by the said transformation or execution schedule.

The existence of the sequence is due to the way our partial dependence graph is constructed: we capture only the closest dependence edge reaching a statement in the partial graph and we always record the shortest distance for each data dependence. The existence of a dependence edge (A, B) in the complete dependence graph means that a pair of instances of A and B access the same memory address. If (A, B) is absent from the partial dependence graph, then it means that the A instance is not the most recent access to that address prior to the B instance and there must exist another statement C whose instance happens between A and B which accesses the same address. Inductively, we will find a dependence sequence $A, ... C, B$ in the partial dependence graph. By transitivity, unless one of these dependences is violated, the B instance must execute after the A instance. □

5. PARALLELIZATION

Object-based profiling and partial dependence graphs are combined into our new profiling tool. We now further improve the profiling efficiency by a novel parallel scheme which partitions the job of runtime profiling on a single program into multiple profiling tasks. These tasks execute simultaneously on parallel processors. The idea of parallelizing dynamic profiling through partition was explored previously by SuperPin [30]. However, the partitioning strategy proposed here is based on alias equivalence classes and is different from that of SuperPin.

As menthioned in Section 3.1, with an alias analysis, a program's memory space is divided into *alias classes* which are disjoint sets of locations. Two memory operations performed on different alias classes never visit the same data object and therefore can never have a data dependence. Hence, we are allowed to profile different alias classes independently. The immediate benefit of such an approach is the reduced memory requirement for running a single profiling task. An accompanying benefit is the reduced complexity in the profiling operations. For example, when used in conjunction with the pairwise profiling method, the size of the runtime hash table is reduced after partitioning, which decreases the overhead of a hash operation and the penalty of hash failure.

Furthermore, utilizing a cluster of computers or a multicore machine, we can profile different alias classes simultaneously to shorten the profiling time. We use a benchmark program, CPU2000/256.bzip2, as an example to illustrate such alias partitioning method. This benchmark program performs computation on three big arrays, `block`, `quadrant`, and `zptr` (Figure 5). Using alias analysis, we determine that these different arrays have no overlap in the memory. Hence, we can decompose profiling into at least three sub tasks, which saves memory by a factor of three when running on three different computers. When profiling them simultaneously on three processors, we expect to speed up by a factor of three as well.

```
void allocateCompressStructures ( void )
{
    Int32 n   = 100000 * blockSize100k;
    block     = malloc ( (n + 1 + 20) * 8 );
    quadrant  = malloc ( (n     + 20) * 16 );
    zptr      = malloc ( n            * 32 );
    ftab      = malloc ( 65537        * 32 );
    ...
}
```

Figure 5: Non-aliased Arrays in 256.bzip2.

5.1 Task Scheduling

After partitioning memory operations into different alias classes, we perform instrumentation on each class and generate a binary code for each instrumentation. Note that the binary code for each instrumentation includes both the original operations in the program and those responsible for profiling a specific alias class. Both the instrumentation and the profiling can be performed on different processors for dif-

ferent alias classes. After profiling, we collect results from each processor and combine them to produce the dependence graph for the entire program. To avoid unnecessary repetition of the re-execution of the original program operations, we fix the number of "native runs", i.e., the execution of the original program to drive the profiling, and make it equal to the number of available processors. A single native run is used to drive the profiling of multiple alias classes if the number of processors is less than that of alias classes. After binding alias classes to native runs, the instrumented codes are sent to the corresponding processors and run concurrently. At the compile time, it is difficult to predict the "weight" of an alias class which refers to the profiling time of the alias class, because the dynamic instruction count is unknown. Instead, we take a pre-profiling step, using the same program input for the dependence profiling, to obtain the weight. This step collects native instruction count, loop trip-count, branch misses and so on to compute the weight information. The technique in this step is quite mature and it increases the program execution time by less than 10% [19].

5.1.1 Dispatching

After getting the weight of an alias class through pre-profiling, we assign alias classes to native runs such that weights are evenly distributed among different participating processors. The optimal assignment problem is equivalent to the *Min Number Partition* problem [9] in computer science.

The Min Number Partitioning problem can be defined as the following: Given a set of n positive integer numbers $\{a_1, ..., a_n\}$, find a partition of A, i.e. a subset $A \subset \{1, ..., n\}$ such that discrepancy

$$E(A) = |\sum_{i \in A} a_i - \sum_{i \notin A} a_i| \qquad (1)$$

is minimized. Finding an optimal solution for the problem is known as NP-complete [9].

In our problem, the integer numbers $\{a_1, ..., a_n\}$ are the weights of the alias classes. Equation 1 represents the case of two processors. A *K-Way Partitioning* [14] is to partition a set of numbers into K mutually exclusive and collectively exhaustive subsets, such that the difference between the largest subset sum and the smallest subset sum is minimized. We have adopted a greedy heuristic similar to the one proposed in [14] in order to quickly find an approximate solution. The greedy heuristic first sorts the numbers in decreasing order and then places the largest number in one of the K subsets chosen arbitrarily. Each remaining number is then placed in the subset with the smallest total sum thus far, until all numbers are assigned. While placing numbers, if the sum of numbers in a subset exceeds a threshold value $\lceil \frac{\sum_{1 \le i \le n} a_i}{n} \rceil$, the subset will no longer accept new members. The greedy algorithm runs in $O(n \log n)$ time.

6. EXPERIMENT

We have implemented the techniques presented above in the GCC compiler, version 4.6. In order to assess how these techniques speed up data dependence profiling, we have performed experiments on all twelve C benchmark programs in the SPEC CPU2006 suite. The benchmark characteristics are listed in Table 1. Columns 2 and 3 show the total number of lines, counted by thousands, and the number of files of

Benchmark	#KLOC	#File	#Loop	Loop profiled	#Run	#Iter	%Time
400.perlbench	170	126	1361	perl.c, 4751:4833	279	1.96	1%
401.bzip2	8	12	234	spec.c, 329:377	1	3	99.71%
403.gcc	521	278	4621	c-parse.c, 1874:4510	1	609709	99.80%
429.mcf	3	25	53	mcf.c, 48:104	1	6	99.33%
433.milc	15	89	445	update.c, 40:94	2	2	90.82%
445.gobmk	197	96	1359	interface/gtp.c, 82:135	1	484	99.98%
456.hmmer	36	72	897	hmmcalibrate.c, 499:518	1	500000	99.99%
458.sjeng	14	23	306	epd.c, 313:334	1	9	99.99%
462.libquantum	4	31	102	expn.c, 45:54	1	21	97.81%
464.h264ref	51	81	1963	lencod.c, 305:424	1	62	99.95%
470.lbm	1.3	6	23	main.c, 39:51	1	300	99.16%
482.sphinx3	25	94	599	spec_main_live_pretend.c:167,189	1	24	99.81%

Table 1: Benchmark characteristics.

a benchmark, respectively. Column 4 gives the total number of loops. Column 5 shows the location of the profiled loops, including the source file name, and the starting/ending line number. Most of these loops are the heaviest outermost loops according to a lightweight preprofiling which provides the trip count and the percentage of running time for each loop under the reference input set. Column 6 lists how many times a loop is executed and Column 7 lists the average iteration counts per execution. The last column gives the percentage of running time for the loop with respect to the whole program. Note that all individual loops in 400.perlbench constitute little execution time, with the heaviest one taking less than 1% of the execution time of the whole benchmark. This is because almost all the execution time is spent on deep recursive calls.

Our experiment is conducted on a multi-core machine with two 2.00GHz Quad-Core AMD Opteron 8350 processors and 32GB RAM. All benchmarks are executed under the reference input. Table 2 compares the elapsed time and memory consumption among different profiling techniques. All the timing results include both the compilation time and the execution time. The column marked by "Native" refers to the original program execution without any profiling work. The column marked by "SD^3" refers to profiling runs by directly implementing the sequential SD^3 technique [13]. For the majority of the benchmark programs, it turns out to be prohibitively expensive to directly use SD^3. None of the benchmarks except 400.perlbench finishes profiling within 15,000 minutes. We emphasize that this result does not contradict with previously published results [13], because in our new experiments we profile data dependences for the heaviest outermost loop which takes almost all the computations of an entire benchmark.

The column marked by "Hash" in Table 2 refers to a hash-based bytewise partial dependence profiler. Previous result [13] indicate that hash-based pairwise profiling is extremely expensive in comparison to the SD^3 profiler. Therefore we do not replicate the comparison in this paper. Instead we implement a hash-based bytewise partial dependence profiler, without benefiting from type information and alias analysis. We see from Table 2 that even hash-based implementation of partial profiling is much more efficient than SD^3. Still, the hash-based partial profiling method fails to complete the profiling of 403.gcc, 429.mcf, 433.milc and 470.lbm because

the memory requirement has reached 28GB (which is near the 32GB quota of the whole system memory). The method also fails to complete the profiling of 462.libquantum within 15,000 minutes.

The column marked by "Tag" in Table 2 refers to the profiler that integrates both object-based profiling and partial dependence profiling, but without partitioning the profiling tasks for parallel execution. This profiler is much more efficient, in both time and memory, than using partial profiling alone. It takes just about 10 times more time than the original program (i.e., the native run) for most of the benchmarks. However, for some benchmarks, e.g, 401.bzip2 and 403.gcc, even this integrated profiler is still too slow. The tool fails to profile 403.gcc because the excessive memory consumption. This is due to the weakness in the alias analysis in our implementation which does not recognize the main data structure as fixed objects. In 403.gcc, a GNU compiler, most computation is performed on two main data structures, namely $tree\_node$ and rtx_def. The structure $tree\_node$ is used as a high-level intermediate program representation, which is implemented as a union. Our alias analyzer was unable to decide whether two fields of a union variable may be live at the same time. Therefore it is unable to recognize a $tree\_node$ variable as a fixed object. The structure rtx_def is used as a register-level intermediate representation. Most of its fields are bit fields, which cannot be separated by bytewise profiling. As for 401.bzip2, a popular compression tool, the key data structures are two large buffers, namely $Estate.arr1$ and $Estate.arr2$. Although both are declared as integer type, there are various type castings to the two buffers. For example, $Estate.mtfv$ is a short integer pointer which is also used for accessing $Estate.arr1$. $Estate.block$ and $Estate.zbits$ are character pointers. Both of them are used for visiting $Estate.arr2$. As a result we have to perform hash-based bytewise profiling to all statements accessing $Estate.arr1$ and $Estate.arr2$.

Table 3 shows the execution time when running the "Tag" profiler in parallel on two cores, four cores and eight cores, respectively. The "Serial" time is copied directly from Table 2. Based on Table 3, Figure 6 shows the slowdowns against the execution time of native programs. For most benchmarks, running on two cores achieves good speedup. For some, e.g. 456.hmmer and 464.h264ref, the parallel speedup is almost linear. As the number of cores increases over eight

Benchmark	Time(Minutes)				Memory(MB)			
	Native	SD³	Hash	Tag	Native	SD³	Hash	Tag
400.perlbench	13.26	34.15	16.26	15.48	227	234	275	249
401.bzip2	9.16	>15000	364.46	319.65	849	×	1536	1487
403.gcc	4.97	>15000	×	×	846	×	>28G	>28G
429.mcf	18.31	>15000	×	203.43	1600	×	>28G	4812
433.milc	48.22	>15000	×	331.72	679	×	>28G	2048
445.gobmk	4.46	>15000	306.06	33.49	31	×	5222	99
456.hmmer	43.83	>15000	7858.14	829.61	3.8	×	1536	18
458.sjeng	39.72	>15000	2025.18	337.64	175	×	1945	629
462.libquantum	45.71	>15000	>15000	804.93	64	×	×	241
464.h264ref	7.84	>15000	634.07	88.54	18	×	730	63
470.lbm	2.88	>15000	×	43.38	409	×	>28G	1200
482.sphinx3	86.72	>15000	4687.52	564.38	41	×	18432	119

Table 2: Timing and memory usage result of different profiling techniques.

cores, however, the speedup increases little for most benchmarks. The main reason seems to be the number of alias classes not being very large, due in part to imprecise alias analysis and to the relatively few data structures declared in those benchmarks.

Benchmark	Serial	2-core	4-core	8-core
400.perlbench	15.48	15.38	15.22	15.26
401.bzip2	319.65	231.6	221.07	210.22
429.mcf	203.43	133.40	108.26	89.9
433.milc	331.72	191.31	163.61	151.68
445.gobmk	33.49	21.55	15.64	14.46
456.hmmer	829.61	424.67	264.88	175.41
458.sjeng	337.64	260.18	240.89	233.61
462.libquantum	804.93	612.90	576.39	550.26
464.h264ref	88.54	45.07	24.08	18.64
470.lbm	43.38	26.41	17.99	16.91
482.sphinx3	564.38	368.87	231.89	212.40

Table 3: Time of profiling with memory tags, counted by minutes.

7. RELATED WORK

To date, data dependence profiling techniques are based on either compiler instrumentation or binary instrumentation. Software tools such as Pin [17], Valgrind [22] and DynamoRIO [3] can be used to perform customized instrumentation on binary codes. To keep and update the profiling information pertaining to memory locations and registers of interest, most profilers store *shadow values* in the *shadow address space* which is logically separated from the application address space. With hash-based methods, the hash table can be viewed as the shadow address space with the hashing operation being the mapping mechanism. For data dependence profiling, the shadow approach has two main shortcomings. Firstly, without type and alias information, bytewise association must be kept between the application address space and the shadow address space. As Table 2 in our previous section shows, the bytewise association can be extremely costly in both time and memory, and the mapping

between the two address spaces is quite complicated. The experimental results in [35] show that even the relatively efficient mapping mechanisms in Umbra [35] and Valgrind [21] incur three and nine times slowdown, respectively, to the program execution. In contrast, with our object-based technique, the mapping has almost no time overhead.

Chen *et al* [5] perform compiler-based instrumentation. They use dependence profiling to guide optimizations such as code scheduling and partial redundancy elimination. Their method is hash-based but not pairwise. They show that, for code scheduling and partial redundancy elimination, a partial dependence graph like ours is sufficient. Their work also evaluates various sampling techniques as means to improve the efficiency of profiling. However the sampling may cause dependences to be missed. Shadow Profiling [20] is another sampling technique. It takes advantage of multi-cores to perform sampling on long traces of instrumented code in parallel with normal execution. Each instrumented sample can be many millions of instructions in length. They report an average profiling accuracy between 83% to 93% for path-profiling and 94% for value profiling. They have not applied the technique to data dependence profiling.

SuperPin [30] also employs parallelization techniques to reduce the time overhead of instrumentation-based dynamic analyses. In SuperPin, several non-overlapping program slices of an application are launched as separate instrumentation threads and are executed in parallel. The publication [30] refers to a generalized framework without technical details on how to divide a whole program into program slices. PiPA [36] parallelizes profiling in a pipelined style. It first divides the whole profiling task into several stages, similar to out-of-order instruction processing pipelines on superscalar processors. It then uses multiple threads to run different stages in that pipeline in order to construct the full profile. Unlike Shadow Profiling, PiPA does not rely on sampling for achieving efficiency and, thus, provides 100 % accurate analysis results. However they have not addressed the memory issue.

SD³ [13] is the most efficient dependence profiler prior to our work. It takes advantage of regular memory access strides to reduce both runtime and memory overhead. In addition to the use of stride expressions when possible, to speed up profiling, they employ multiple threads to exploit both

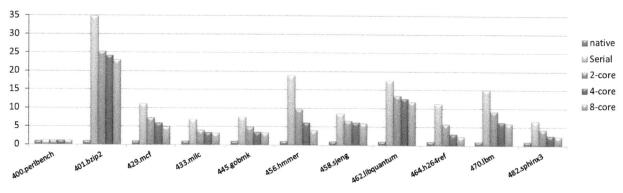

Figure 6: Slowdowns of profiling with memory tags.

pipeline parallelism and data parallelism. Their pipelining method divides the profiling work into several pipelined stages, and their data-parallel execution divides the entire address space into blocks of a certain size, e.g. 2^k bytes, allowing a separate thread to analyze the memory references to each block. Applied to 20 hottest loops in each SPEC2006 program, they report a speedup of 4.1 on eight cores and 9.7 on 32 cores respectively. Although with this level of parallelism SD^3 seems still below the speed of our technique, it may prove beneficial to combine their pipelined and data-parallel methods with ours, because these methods are essentially orthogonal. We do not have evidence to support this hypothesis, however, since we have yet to implement the pipelined and data-parallel methods to verify the combined effect.

A number of techniques have been proposed to reduce the time for collecting program traces and compression of the collected traces for off-line analysis [4, 15, 33]. Such trace-based profiling can potentially be used for data dependence checking. However, their algorithms are specifically for compressing memory streams. Tallam *et al.* [25, 26] extended the program traces to support data dependence profiling. However, their concept of data dependence refers to def-use chains, not a general loop-level dependence. They have not provided performance results in comparison with hash-based method. Unlike these methods, the current trend in loop-level data dependence profiling seems to favor the use of execution-driven memory address checking without having to produce the traces first.

There exist prior efforts making use of dependence profiling to guide optimizations and parallelization. Peng *et al.* [31] employ profile-based analysis of data dependences to aid compiler-driven task selection for thread-level speculation. They propose a cost model for estimating the probability of successful speculation. Zhang *et al.* [34] propose a data dependence distance profiler called Alchemist and use it to automatically detect available concurrency in C programs. Alchemist operates in a way that is completely transparent to applications, and it identifies program constructs at various levels of granularity as candidates for asynchronous execution. Tournavitis *et al.* [28] propose a dependence profiling mechanism to understand the limitations of automatic parallelization. They show that data dependence profiling exposes significantly more parallel loops than state-of-the-art parallelizing compilers can and that parallelism exposed by dependence profiling is close to that is embedded in manually-parallelized counterparts. Embla [7]

and Embla 2 [18] take advantage of dependence profiling to assist the programmer in parallelization by identifying appropriate source-level synchronization points. By mapping dynamic dependencies back to the program source, they estimate the potential speedup for parallelization using frameworks such as Cilk and OpenMP. Thies *et al.* [27] and Rul *et al.* [23] use dependence profiling to find coarse-grained pipeline parallelism in C programs. Kremlin [8, 10] is a dependence profiling tool to assist the parallelization of serial programs. Given a serial version of a program, Kremlin makes recommendations to the user as to what regions of the program to be parallelized first.

8. CONCLUSION

We have proposed a fast scheme for profiling loop-level data dependence. The speedup is achieved from (1) safely embedding memory tags into the data structures (based on type and alias information) in order to rapidly test dependence; (2) tracing a subset of data dependence which we prove to be sufficient for loop-level reordering transformations and loop parallelization; and (3) parallelizing the profiling tasks based on static alias classification. Experiments with SPEC CPU 2006 benchmarks show that these techniques not only significantly shorten the profiling time but also reduce the memory use considerably. Except for the benchmark 403.gcc, our profiling runs all finish within a few hours on a desktop machine, which is faster than the fastest previous profiler by an order of magnitude or more. With the parallelization technique, the profiling runs just about five times slower than the original program for most of the benchmarks. We believe that our work has made dependence profiling much more useful in practice for guiding program parallelization. For future work, we plan to design more aggressive static and symbolic analysis to further improve the efficiency such that even the most difficult benchmarks can be profiled within practical time constraints. Furthermore, profiling dependences to expose parallelism between recursive calls may worth investigation, because at least one of the SPEC CPU benchmarks spend most of time on recursive calls.

9. ACKNOWLEDGMENTS

We thank Chunlei Sang for implementing part of the SD^3 profiler. We also thank Xinmin Tian and Bob Kuhn for offering insights from the perspective of industry. Our work is sponsored in part by the National Science Foundation through grants CNS-0915414, CCF-0811587, and CCF-0702245, and by an Intel research grant and an Intel gift.

10. REFERENCES

[1] ANDERSEN, L. Program analysis and specialization for the c programming language. *PhD Thesis, DIKU, University of Copenhagen* (1994).

[2] BRIDGES, M., VACHHARAJANI, N., ZHANG, Y., JABLIN, T., AND AUGUST, D. Revisiting the sequential programming model for multi-core. In *MICRO* (2007).

[3] BRUENING, D., GARNETT, T., AND AMARASINGHE, S. An infrastructure for adaptive dynamic optimization. In *CGO* (2003).

[4] BURTSCHER, M. Vpc3: a fast and effective trace-compression algorithm. In *SIGMETRICS* (2004).

[5] CHEN, T., LIN, J., DAI, X., HSU, W., AND YEW, P. Data dependence profiling for speculative optimizations. In *CC* (2004), Springer.

[6] CROSTHWAITE, P., WILLIAMS, J., AND SUTTON, P. Profile driven data-dependency analysis for improved high level language hardware synthesis. In *International Conference on Field-Programmable Technology* (2009).

[7] FAXÉN, K.-F., POPOV, K., JANSSON, S., AND ALBERTSSON, L. Embla - data dependence profiling for parallel programming. In *CISIS* (2008).

[8] GARCIA, S., JEON, D., LOUIE, C. M., AND TAYLOR, M. B. Kremlin: rethinking and rebooting gprof for the multicore age. In *PLDI* (2011).

[9] GAREY, M. R., AND JOHNSON, D. S. *Computers and Intractability: A Guide to the Theory of NP-Completeness.* W. H. Freeman & Co., New York, NY, USA, 1979.

[10] JEON, D., GARCIA, S., LOUIE, C., KOTA VENKATA, S., AND TAYLOR, M. B. Kremlin: like gprof, but for parallelization. In *PPoPP* (2011).

[11] KAHLON, V. Bootstrapping: a technique for scalable flow and context-sensitive pointer alias analysis. In *PLDI* (2008).

[12] KENNEDY, K., AND ALLEN, J. R. *Optimizing compilers for modern architectures: a dependence-based approach.* Morgan Kaufmann Publishers Inc., 2002.

[13] KIM, M., KIM, H., AND LUK, C.-K. Sd3: A scalable approach to dynamic data-dependence profiling. In *MICRO* (2010).

[14] KORF, R. E. From approximate to optimal solutions: a case study of number partitioning. In *Proceedings of the 14th international joint conference on Artificial intelligence - Volume 1* (1995).

[15] LARUS, J. R. Whole program paths. In *PLDI* (1999).

[16] LIU, W., TUCK, J., CEZE, L., AHN, W., STRAUSS, K., RENAU, J., AND TORRELLAS, J. Posh: a TLS compiler that exploits program structure. In *PPoPP* (2006).

[17] LUK, C.-K., COHN, R., MUTH, R., PATIL, H., KLAUSER, A., LOWNEY, G., WALLACE, S., REDDI, V. J., AND HAZELWOOD, K. Pin: building customized program analysis tools with dynamic instrumentation. In *PLDI* (2005).

[18] MAK, J., FAXÉN, K.-F., JANSON, S., AND MYCROFT, A. Estimating and exploiting potential parallelism by source-level dependence profiling. In *EuroPar* (2010).

[19] MELLOR-CRUMMEY, J. M., AND LEBLANC, T. J. A software instruction counter. In *ASPLOS* (1989).

[20] MOSELEY, T., SHYE, A., REDDI, V. J., GRUNWALD, D., AND PERI, R. Shadow profiling: Hiding instrumentation costs with parallelism. In *CGO* (2007).

[21] NETHERCOTE, N., AND SEWARD, J. How to shadow every byte of memory used by a program. In *Proceedings of the 3rd international conference on Virtual execution environments* (2007), VEE.

[22] NETHERCOTE, N., AND SEWARD, J. Valgrind: a framework for heavyweight dynamic binary instrumentation. In *PLDI* (2007).

[23] RUL, S., VANDIERENDONCK, H., AND DE BOSSCHERE, K. A profile-based tool for finding pipeline parallelism in sequential programs. *Parallel Comput. 36* (September 2010).

[24] STEENSGAARD, B. Points-to analysis in almost linear time. In *POPL* (1996).

[25] TALLAM, S., AND GUPTA, R. Unified control flow and data dependence traces. *ACM Trans. Archit. Code Optim. 4* (September 2007).

[26] TALLAM, S., GUPTA, R., AND ZHANG, X. Extended whole program paths. In *PACT* (2005).

[27] THIES, W., CHANDRASEKHAR, V., AND AMARASINGHE, S. A practical approach to exploiting coarse-grained pipeline parallelism in C programs. In *MICRO* (2007).

[28] TOURNAVITIS, G., WANG, Z., FRANKE, B., AND O'BOYLE, M. F. Towards a holistic approach to auto-parallelization: integrating profile-driven parallelism detection and machine-learning based mapping. In *PLDI* (2009).

[29] VANDIERENDONCK, H., RUL, S., AND DE BOSSCHERE, K. The Paralax infrastructure: automatic parallelization with a helping hand. In *PACT* (2010).

[30] WALLACE, S., AND HAZELWOOD, K. Superpin: Parallelizing dynamic instrumentation for real-time performance. In *CGO* (2007).

[31] WU, P., KEJARIWAL, A., AND CAŞCAVAL, C. Compiler-Driven Dependence Profiling to Guide Program Parallelization. In *LCPC* (2008).

[32] YU, H., XUE, J., HUO, W., FENG, X., AND ZHANG, Z. Level by level: making flow- and context-sensitive pointer analysis scalable for millions of lines of code. In *CGO* (2010).

[33] ZHANG, X., AND GUPTA, R. Whole execution traces and their applications. *ACM Trans. Archit. Code Optim. 2* (September 2005).

[34] ZHANG, X., NAVABI, A., AND JAGANNATHAN, S. Alchemist: A transparent dependence distance profiling infrastructure. In *CGO* (2009).

[35] ZHAO, Q., BRUENING, D., AND AMARASINGHE, S. Umbra: efficient and scalable memory shadowing. In *CGO* (2010).

[36] ZHAO, Q., CUTCUTACHE, I., AND WONG, W.-F. Pipa: pipelined profiling and analysis on multi-core systems. In *CGO* (2008).

Apricot: An Optimizing Compiler and Productivity Tool for x86-compatible Many-core Coprocessors

Nishkam Ravi
NEC Laboratories
America
Princeton, NJ, USA
nravi@nec-labs.com

Yi Yang
Dept. of ECE
North Carolina State
University
yyang14@ncsu.edu

Tao Bao
Dept. of Computer
Science
Purdue University
tbao@cs.purdue.edu

Srimat
Chakradhar
NEC Laboratories
Princeton, NJ, USA
chak@nec-labs.com

ABSTRACT

Intel MIC (Many Integrated Core) is the first x86-based co-processor architecture aimed at accelerating multi-core HPC applications. In the most common usage model, parallel code sections are offloaded to the MIC coprocessor using LEO (Language Extensions for Offload). The developer is responsible for identifying and specifying offloadable code regions, managing data transfers between the CPU and MIC and optimizing the application for performance, which requires some amount of effort and experimentation. In this paper, we present *Apricot*, an optimizing compiler and productivity tool for x86-compatible many-core coprocessors (such as Intel MIC) that minimizes developer effort by (i) automatically inserting LEO clauses for parallelizable code regions, (ii) selectively offloading some of the code regions to the coprocessor at runtime based on a cost model that we have developed, (iii) applying a set of optimizations for minimizing the data communication overhead and improving overall performance. Apricot is intended to assist programmers in porting existing multi-core applications and writing new ones to take advantage of the many-core coprocessor, while maximizing overall performance. Experiments with SpecOMP and NAS Parallel benchmarks show that Apricot can successfully transform OpenMP applications to run on the MIC coprocessor with good performance gains.

Categories and Subject Descriptors

D.3.4 [**Programming Languages**]: Processors—*Compilers, Optimization*

Keywords

Intel MIC, Compiler, Offload, Many-core, Optimizations

1. INTRODUCTION

Intel Many Integrated Core Architecture (MIC) has been inspired by the Intel Larrabee GPGPU processor [28] that is widely considered a hybrid between a GPU and a multi-core CPU. It can be summarized as an x86-based many-core architecture that is intended for use as a coprocessor in much the same way as GPUs are used for general purpose computing in conjunction with CPUs. Unlike GPUs, which require significant programming effort, MIC is designed to leverage the x86 experience and benefit from existing parallelization tools and programming models (e.g., OpenMP [9], OpenCL [8], Intel Cilk Plus [14]), with the help of a few additional keywords that constitute the MIC programming model, henceforth LEO (Language Extensions for Offload).

Intel MIC and the LEO programming model represent the next step in the evolution of high performance computing using heterogeneous processors. The programming model (described in Section 2) is simple and general enough to be used with any x86-based coprocessor architecture with a suitable runtime implementation. In the most common usage model, highly parallel code regions in an application are offloaded to the Intel MIC coprocessor over PCIe. The developer identifies and marks such code regions using `#pragma offload` and specifies data transfers between the host and coprocessor using `in/out/inout` clauses (as shown in Fig. 2). The goal is to improve overall application performance by taking advantage of the large number of cores on Intel MIC (for multi-threading) and the wide SIMD units (for vectorization). Intel offload compiler and runtime manage the actual code and data transfer.

Although Intel MIC is a big step forward in terms of programmability as compared to GPUs, some amount of developer effort is required in order to get performance gains with MIC. First, due to the communication overheads between the host and the coprocessor, it is important to ensure that the code regions for offload are carefully selected, so that the speedup obtained by running them on Intel MIC is not offset by offload overheads. Not only does this require extra effort on the part of the developer at compile time, it also poses a performance risk due to the unavailability of runtime information (such as input data sizes) crucial to assessing communication overheads at compile time. Second, specifying the data transfers between the host and coprocessor requires effort; moreso when minimizing data communication overhead is important. Finally, once the code and data transfers have been specified, it is necessary to optimize the application in order to obtain good performance on MIC.

The solution proposed in this paper aims to maximize programmer productivity and application performance by partially automating the three steps. We present *Apricot*, an optimizing compiler for x86-based many-core coprocessors (such as Intel MIC) that minimizes developer effort by (i) automatically inserting conditional `#pragma offload` to mark code regions for offload, (ii) automatically inserting the corresponding `in/out/inout` clauses for data transfer for the marked code regions, (iii) selectively offloading some of the code regions to the coprocessor at runtime based on a cost-benefit analysis model that we have developed, (iv) applying a set of optimizations for minimizing the data communication overhead and improving overall performance. Apricot takes a best-effort approach for populating `in/out/inout` clauses. When the analysis fails to determine if a certain variable should to be transferred to the coprocessor, it prints out a comment next to the `pragma offload` asking the developer to handle it themselves.

Unlike multi-core, where identifying a parallelizable loop with sufficient amount of work is generally enough to guarantee performance, a lot more effort is needed to guarantee performance for many-core coprocessors. Apricot is intended to assist programmers in porting existing multi-core applications and writing new ones to take advantage of many-core coprocessors, while maximizing overall performance. Experiments with SpecOMP and NAS Parallel benchmarks show that Apricot can successfully transform OpenMP applications to run on the MIC coprocessor with performance gains.

2. BACKGROUND

The first Intel MIC prototype, codenamed Knights Ferry, is built at 45 nm and consists of 32 in-order x86 cores running at 1.2GHz with four threads per core, thus allowing 128 threads to run in parallel. Each core has a 32KB L1 instruction cache, 32KB L1 data cache and 256KB L2 cache. The L2 caches are kept coherent by a bi-directional ring network, effectively creating a shared 8MB L2 cache. The ring network also connects to the four on-die memory controllers. Knights Ferry is implemented on a PCIe card. A total of 2GB on-chip memory is present on the Knights Ferry board. There is no shared memory in hardware between Knights Ferry and the host processor. Each core has a newly designed SIMD vector unit consisting of 32 512-bit wide vector registers. The first MIC-based product, codenamed Knights Corner, would be built at 22nm and consist of more than 60 cores. It would have more memory, faster data transfer rates over PCIe, larger L2 cache per core and better single-thread performance as compared to Knights Ferry.

Intel MIC coprocessor runs its own Linux-based Operating System that manages MIC-side resources. A device driver is installed on the host processor that is responsible for managing device initialization and communication over PCIe. A set of runtime libraries provide buffer management and communication capabilities between the CPU and MIC. The library invocations are auto-generated by the Intel Compiler for an application, thereby hiding the architectural complexity from the developer. Fig. 1 shows the overview of the MIC software stack.

2.1 Programming Model

In order to take advantage of the Intel MIC coprocessor, the developer must identify regions of code in the application that can benefit from executing on MIC. A straightforward example would be a highly parallel hot loop. The developer can *mark* such regions using `#pragma offload` (as shown in Fig. 2). The corresponding data/variables to be copied and direction of copy can be specified using `in/out/inout` clauses. The size of the data/variable to be copied can be specified using the `length` clause. Execution on the host

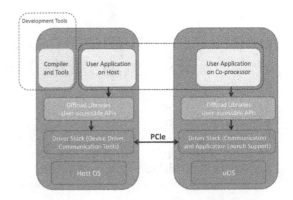

Figure 1: MIC Software Stack and Execution Model

```
#pragma offload target(mic) in(B,C:length(n))
   out(A:length(n))
{
  #pragma omp parallel for shared(A,B,C) private(i)
  for (i=0; i<n; i++){
      A[i] = B[i] * C[i];
  }
}
```

Figure 2: Pragma Offload Example

processor is suspended when such a marked code region is encountered, continued on the Intel MIC coprocessor and then resumed on the host processor after the code region on MIC has executed to completion. The actual transfer of code and data over PCIe is managed by the runtime libraries supplied with the MIC software stack, as noted earlier. The Intel Compiler auto-generates invocations to the libraries for code and data transfer for marked regions. All the marked code regions are transferred to Intel MIC over PCIe in one shot at runtime when the first `pragma offload` is encountered. However, data transfers for every marked code region, as specified through the `in/out/inout` clauses, are managed individually as and when they are encountered, thus creating significant communication overhead.

As noted above, the programming model for Intel MIC (i.e., LEO) includes a small number of programming language extensions/keywords to enable code and data transfer between CPU and MIC. The main LEO keywords are shown in Table 1. The Fortran equivalent of `#pragma offload` is `!dir$ omp offload`. In addition to explicit data/memory transfer using `in/out/inout` clauses, implicit memory transfers can be specified using the `_Shared` construct. A variable marked as `_Shared` can be used by both the host and coprocessor code. This is accomplished by reserving a section of memory at the same virtual address on both the host and coprocessor, which is automatically synchronized by the runtime on entry to or exit from an offload call. All variables marked as `_Shared` are allocated to this memory section. The implicit copy model simplifies programming, but has a number of limitations. First, it only works with the `_Offload` construct that is used for marking an entire function for offloading, which severely limits applicability. Second, the argument evaluation is consistent with Cilk [14], in that the arguments are always evaluated on the host-side even if marked `_Shared`. Third, it has poor performance as compared to the explicit copy model, due to the overheads of redundant synchronization. Fourth, in practice it would only be helpful when there is ample memory on

Table 1: Main LEO keywords– Programming Language Extensions for MIC

Keyword	Description
#pragma offload <clauses>	Execute next code block on coprocessor
target(mic)	Specify MIC coprocessor as the target for offload
in (<var-list>:<length(size)>	Copy from host to coprocessor
out (<var-list>:<length(size)>	Copy from coprocessor to host
inout (<var-list>:<length(size)>	Copy from host to coprocessor and back
nocopy (<var-list>:<length(size)>	Prohibit copying from host to coprocessor
length (<size>)	Specify the size of the pointer data to be copied
alloc_if (<condition>)	Allocate memory on coprocessor for the given pointer only if condition is true
free_if (<condition>)	Free memory on coprocessor for the given pointer only if condition is true
__attribute__((target(mic)))	Allocate variable or function on both host and coprocessor
!dir$ offload <clauses>	Fortran equivalent of offload pragma
_Shared <variable/function>	Variable/function is visible on both host and coprocessor
_Offload <function>	Execute function on coprocessor

the coprocessor side to accommodate the longer lifetime of _Shared variables. In this paper, we focus on the mainstream programming model that uses pragma offload and in/out/inout clauses.

OpenACC [7] is an emerging standard for accelerometers and coprocessors. It bears strong resemblance to the LEO programming model. Apricot, with some front-end modifications, can potentially be used to port and optimize OpenACC applications as well.

3. APRICOT OVERVIEW

The primary input to Apricot is a C/C++/Fortran application, where the parallelizable loops have been annotated with OpenMP [9] or CilkPlus [14] constructs. The output is an optimized application that runs on the (multi-core processor + MIC coprocessor) and yields better performance. The modifications needed for porting the application to MIC and the performance optimizations are applied by Apricot, as described below.

For each parallelizable code section (marked with OpenMP or CilkPlus), Apricot performs liveness analysis to determine the variables that need to be copied in to MIC (live-in variables) and copied out of MIC (live-out variables), if the code section were to to be offloaded. This would be needed for populating the in/out/inout clauses used for specifying data transfers (described in Section 4). It then performs *array bound analysis* to determine the start and end location of each array/pointer used in the code section. This is done for the purpose of populating the length clause that specifies the number of bytes to be copied starting from a particular memory location (described in Section 4.1).

In the second phase, Apricot inserts #pragma offload right before the offloadable code section, along with the in/out/inout and length clauses. The code section is guarded by an if condition that invokes our *cost-benefit analysis* function (at runtime) to determine if offloading this particular code section to the coprocessor would be beneficial. The original unmodified code section is placed in the else branch and gets executed on the host processor if the if condition returns false. Figure 6 shows the transformed code. We call this transformation *conditional offload insertion* (described in Section 4.2). The code in the then branch is further optimized for performance. Conditional offload insertion is carried out for every parallelizable code section, and obviates the developer effort required for (i) experimentally identifying the code sections that would benefit from Intel MIC, (ii) inserting pragma offload and determining the parameters of the in/out/inout and length clauses.

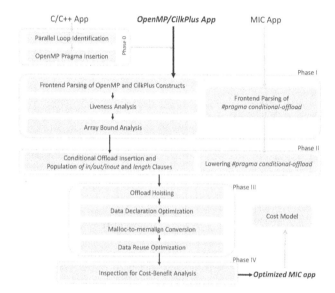

Figure 3: Apricot Design Overview

In the third phase, Apricot applies a number of performance optimizations to the code in the then branch, namely: (i) Offload Hoisting– pragma offload is hoisted out of the parent loop when legal and profitable, (ii) Data Declaration Optimization– certain data declarations are moved inside the offload code section to reduce data transfer overhead, (iii) Data Reuse Optimization– if two successive offload code sections share data, the data transfers are combined, and (iv) Malloc-to-memalign Conversion– DMA transfers are triggered whenever possible. These optimizations are crucial to performance; we describe them in Section 4.3. Please note that the traditional compiler optimizations (including vectorization) are performed by the Intel Compiler independent of our optimizations.

In order to decide if a code section should be offloaded at runtime, the cost-model function would need information about the amount of work being done in the code section and the amount of data being transferred in to and out of it. Apricot has a fourth phase that inspects every offload code section after all the transformations have been applied, determines the amount of computation being performed, the amount of data transfer needed and populates the parameter list for the cost-benefit analysis function (as described in Section 4.4). The cost-benefit analysis function invokes a set of heuristics to determine if it would be profitable to offload the code section to MIC, as described in Section 4.4.2.

In addition to taking OpenMP applications as input, Apricot also accepts applications that have already been modified for MIC, and optimizes them for performance. We introduce a construct called #pragma conditional-offload that extends the semantics of #pragma offload (Section 4.2.2). The semantics of #pragma conditional-offload state that a code block will be offloaded only if the cost-model finds it profitable to do so at runtime. This allows the developer to freely put a pragma conditional-offload before any parallelizable section without worrying about performance consequences and let the compiler and runtime decide which of them should be offloaded. The code is optimized for performance by applying the optimizations mentioned above.

Finally, if the input application is a C/C++ application with no OpenMP/CilkPlus constructs, Apricot invokes a module for identifying parallelizable code sections. In the current design, this translates to invoking the Intel Compiler's auto-parallelizer [1], which identifies *some* of the parallelizable code sections. Once the parallelizable code sections are identified, Apricot inserts #pragma omp parallel for every such code section and then goes on to apply conditional offload insertion and performance optimizations in the same way as for an OpenMP application. This approach broadens the scope of Apricot. The component for identifying parallelizable code sections can be developed over time.

Fig. 3 shows the overall design. The primary input to Apricot is (i) OpenMP/CilkPlus applications written for multi-core that get transformed and optimized to take advantage of MIC, and (ii) unoptimized MIC applications that get enhanced with our cost-model and optimized for performance. Apricot has limited handling for vanilla C/C++ applications, which are first annotated with OpenMP pragmas and then treated the same way as OpenMP applications.

4. APRICOT DESIGN

Apricot is implemented on top of gcc [3] as a source-to-source compiler, and intended for use as a pre-processing tool by developers. In this section, we present the design of the different phases and components of Apricot.

4.1 Phase I

We add support for parsing pragma offload, cilk_for, !omp parallel do and pragma conditional-offload to gcc fronted. In order to simplify analysis, we ignore compiler generated variables that are introduced in the process of lowering OpenMP pragmas. For every offloadable code section marked with OpenMP/CilkPlus, liveness analysis is carried out followed by array bound analysis. The results are stored in a data structure called offload_regions created during parsing. In order to trigger phase I, the developer has to specify -gencodeMIC flag during compilation, which tells Apricot that the input is an OpenMP/CilkPlus application that needs to be transformed and optimized for Intel MIC.

4.1.1 Liveness Analysis

Liveness analysis [23] is performed before creation of SSA, and handles simple arrays and pointers in addition to scalars. We leverage the existing gcc modules for live-in/live-out analysis for scalars, tailor them for our purpose and extend them to handle pointers and arrays. This is done with the help of the *memory tag* infrastructure in gcc, which can be used for tracking reads and writes to pointers. There is no special representation for arrays in the gcc IR, so for the pur-

```
void f(){
    ...
    // candidate code section
    #pragma omp parallel for ..
    for(i=0; i < 100; i++){
        int x = a;
        A[i] = B[i];
        C[i] = D[i];
        D[i] = x*i;
    }

    ...
    E[k] = A[k]*x;
    F[k] = D[k]*k;
    ...
}

LIVE_IN = {a, B, D}, LIVE_OUT = {x, A, D}
IN = {a, B}, OUT = {x, A}, INOUT = {D}

State of pragma offload after liveness analysis (length
clauses are populated afterwards); note that array A is
added to the inout clause:

#pragma offload target(MIC) in(a) in(B:length(..))
        out(x) inout(A:length(..),D:length(..))
```

Figure 4: Example of Liveness Analysis

pose of liveness analysis, they are handled the same way as pointers: a *write* to a memory location serves as a *def* for the pointer/array that points to that memory location. Indirect memory references, nested arrays and structs are not handled in the current implementation, due to the limitations of the array bound analysis pass (described next).

Bitmaps are used to record LIVE_IN and LIVE_OUT sets for each basic block. At the end of the analysis, the LIVE_IN set for the first basic block of the offload code section is stored as the IN set for the code section. The LIVE_OUT set of global variables is computed a little differently. Since our inter-procedural analysis is limited in its capability, we cannot guarantee the absence of the *use* of a global variable in the rest of the application. To err on the conservative side, the LIVE_OUT set includes all global variables that are defined/re-defined inside the code section. The LIVE_OUT set of the last basic block of the offload code section is stored as the OUT set for the code section.

The variables that are common to both the IN and OUT sets are used for populating the inout clause, which signifies the set of variables that should be copied into Intel MIC prior to the execution of the code section and copied out of MIC after completion. The variables that are present only in the IN set are used for populating the in clause, which signifies the set of variables that should be copied into MIC. The scalars present only in the OUT set populate the out clause, which signifies the set of variables that should be copied out of MIC after the code section executes to completion. Note that all the pointers/arrays that are only present in the OUT set are added to the inout clause (instead of the out clause as expected). The reason for this is as follows: when an array is copied back to host memory, any unassigned memory locations (on the MIC side) will cause null/garbage to be written onto corresponding memory locations on the host side. To prevent this from happening, it is important to copy the contents of the array into MIC memory, even if there are no reads to it. Fig 4 shows a simple example of liveness analysis in Apricot.

```
for(i=30; i < 100; i++){
    x = A[i];
}

Simplified IR:

a = 30;
loop_1
  b = phi(a,c)
  x = A[b];
  c = b + 1;
  if(c > 100) exit_loop
endloop

Scalar Evolution Rep. for b: {30,+,1}
⟹  initial value=30, increment=+1
Upper Bound of loop: 100
Bounds of array A: {30,100}
```

Figure 5: Simple Example of Array Bound Analysis

4.1.2 Array Bound Analysis

For any non-scalar variable, i.e. arrays and pointers, the size of the memory to be copied is specified using the `length` clause, as shown in Fig. 6. Estimating the section of memory that would be used inside a code section, for a given pointer, is non-trivial. A simple approach is to trace the declaration of the array/pointer and pass the entire size of the array/pointer (when available) to the `length` clause. This, however, would result in redundant data transfers. We attempt to solve this problem by estimating the section of memory being accessed inside the offload code section for a given pointer. We leverage existing gcc modules for this purpose. The basic idea is to identify the memory access pattern of a pointer by parsing it as a function of the loop indices using scalar evolution representation [26] (which bears resemblance to the polyhedral model [15]). For each loop index, the corresponding stride, lower bound and upper bound are extracted. This allows us to estimate the bounds of the pointer/array. As mentioned before, arrays and pointers are handled in the same way. Fig. 5 shows a simple example. This approach is similar to array section analysis [20, 27, 16], commonly used for array privatization.

Discussion: Indirect memory references, structs and nested arrays are not handled in the current implementation. This would be gradually improved over time as we beef up liveness and array bound analyses. In order to keep the coverage high, we conform to a best effort semi-automatic approach for populating `in/out/inout` clauses. Since Apricot outputs transformed source code, the developer can make further changes as needed. If Apricot is unable to estimate the liveness or size of a given pointer for an offload code section, it prints out a comment next to the `pragma offload` clause asking the developer to handle it themselves.

4.2 Phase II

The first round of code transformations are applied in phase II. As mentioned earlier, when -gencodeMIC flag is used, the input is assumed to be an OpenMP/CilkPlus application. Apricot carries out conditional offload insertion for every offload code region parsed in phase I. If -optimizeMIC flag is used, the input is assumed to be a MIC application. In this case, Apricot lowers all `#pragma conditional-offload` statements in the application, which is similar to conditional offload insertion with a few minor differences.

```
#pragma omp parallel for shared(A,B,C) private(i)
  for (i=0; i<n; i++){
    A[i] = B[i] * C[i];
  }
```

(a) Original Code

```
if(cbf()){
  #pragma offload target(mic) in(B,C:length(n))
      out(A:length(n))
  {
    #pragma omp parallel for shared(A,B,C) private(i)
    for (i=0; i<n; i++){
      A[i] = B[i] * C[i];
    }
  }
}else{
  #pragma omp parallel for shared(A,B,C) private(i)
  for (i=0; i<n; i++){
    A[i] = B[i] * C[i];
  }
}
```

(b) Transformed Code

Figure 6: Conditional Offload Insertion

```
#pragma conditional-offload target(mic) in(B,C:length(n))
      out(A:length(n))
{
  #pragma omp parallel for shared(A,B,C) private(i)
  for (i=0; i<n; i++){
    A[i] = B[i] * C[i];
  }
}
```

(a) Original Code

```
if(cbf()){
  #pragma offload target(mic) in(B,C:length(n))
      out(A:length(n))
  {
    #pragma omp parallel for shared(A,B,C) private(i)
    for (i=0; i<n; i++){
      A[i] = B[i] * C[i];
    }
  }
}else{
  #pragma omp parallel for shared(A,B,C) private(i)
  for (i=0; i<n; i++){
    A[i] = B[i] * C[i];
  }
}
```

(b) Transformed Code

Figure 7: Lowering #pragma conditional-offload

4.2.1 Conditional Offload Insertion

Conditional offload insertion consists of three steps. In the first step, an `if-then-else` block is created, the original code section is placed in the `else` branch and a copy of the code section is placed in the `then` branch. An invocation to the cost-benefit analysis function (`cbf()`) is introduced as the predicate. The parameter list for `cbf()` is empty at this point. In the second step, `#pragma offload` is inserted at the beginning of the `then` branch along with empty `in/out/inout` and `length` clauses. In the third step, the information stored in `offload_regions` created during phase I is used to populate `in/out/inout` and `length` clauses. Fig 6 shows the transformation for a simple code snippet.

```
for(j=0; j<100; j++){
  #pragma offload target(mic) in(B,C:length(n))
      out(A:length(n))
  {
    #pragma omp parallel for shared(A,B,C) private(i)
    for (i=0; i<n; i++){
        A[i] = B[i] * C[i];
    }
  }
  ...
  #pragma offload target(mic) in(A,B:length(n))
      out(D:length(n))
  {
    #pragma omp parallel for shared(A,B,D) private(i)
    for (i=0; i<n; i++){
        D[i] = A[i] + B[i];
    }
  }
  ...
}
```

(a) Original Code

```
#pragma offload target(mic) in(A,B,C:length(n))
      out(A,D:length(n))
{
  for(j=0; j<100; j++){
    #pragma omp parallel for shared(A,B,C) private(i)
    for (i=0; i<n; i++){
      A[i] = B[i] * C[i];
    }
    ...
    #pragma omp parallel for shared(A,B,D) private(i)
    for (i=0; i<n; i++){
      D[i] = A[i] + B[i];
    }
  }
}
```

(b) Transformed Code

Figure 8: Offload Hoisting

4.2.2 Lowering #pragma conditional-offload

This is very similar to conditional offload insertion. An `if-then-else` block is created, the original code section is placed in the `else` branch and a copy of the code section is placed in the `then` branch. An invocation to the cost-benefit analysis function (`cbf()`) is introduced as the predicate. The `#pragma conditional-offload` is replaced by `#pragma offload` in the `then` branch, and deleted from the `else` branch. An entry is made into `offload_regions` for this code section. The transformation is shown in Fig. 7.

4.3 Phase III

The code generated from phase II is optimized for performance in this phase. We outline a few prominent optimizations that have been experimented with so far. These optimizations are targeted towards minimizing the communication overheads between the host processor and MIC. Traditional compiler optimizations (e.g, vectorization) are performed by the Intel Compiler independently.

4.3.1 Offload Hoisting

Optimal placement of `pragma offload` is essential for performance. Consider the code snippet in Fig. 8(a). The offload overhead for the `pragma offload` as shown in Fig. 8(a) is $100*(t_1+t_2)$, where t_1 and t_2 represent the time it takes to complete offload/data transfer for the two code sections respectively. Hoisting `pragma offload` out of the parent loop

```
double C[1000];
...
#pragma offload target(mic) in(B,C:length(1000))
{
    #pragma omp parallel for shared(B,C) private(i)
    for (i=0; i<1000; i++){
        C[i] = f(B[i]);  //initialization of array C
    }
    ...
}
... /* no reads/writes to C  */
```

(a) Original Code

```
...
#pragma offload target(mic) in(B:length(1000))
{
    double C[1000];
    #pragma omp parallel for shared(B,C) private(i)
    for (i=0; i<1000; i++){
        C[i] = f(B[i]);
    }
    ...
}
...
```

(b) Transformed Code

Figure 9: Data Declaration Optimization

(as shown in Fig. 8(b)), would reduce the data transfer time to $t_1 + t_2$, significantly improving performance.

In general, this optimization aims to exploit opportunities for work consolidation by constructing one large code section for offload from several small ones, in order to minimize the communication overheads between the host processor and MIC. In the current design, this is implemented as iterative hoisting of `pragma offload`'s. If a code region marked by `pragma offload` is found to have a parent loop, analysis is carried out to determine if it would be profitable to hoist the `pragma offload` outside the parent loop. If so, the `pragma offload` is hoisted out and all the `pragma offload`'s inside the parent loop are deleted. Liveness and array bound analyses are invoked on-demand for the outer loop in order to populate the `in/out/inout` clauses.

For offload hoisting to be profitable, it is important to make sure that all the hot inner loops are parallelizable and that the serial code between them is minimal. We have interfaced the *GNU gprof* [4] profiler with Apricot in order to determine profitability of this optimization. Gprof is invoked from within Apricot before Phase III. The generated profile information is processed and stored on a per-loop basis for use by later optimizations. Currently, offload hoisting is the only optimization that makes use of profile information. If t_1 is the time spent in the outer loop, and t_2 is the total time spent in the inner parallelizable loops (marked by OpenMP pragma's), offload hoisting is performed only when $t_1/t_2 > c$. The value of c is currently set to 0.8.

4.3.2 Data Declaration Optimization

Data declaration optimization is a very simple but effective transformation for reducing communication overheads. For all the variables in the `LIVE_IN` set of an offload code section that are declared outside, we try to ascertain if the variable is used *only* inside the code section. This is done by looking at the *use-def* chain and making sure that the declaration is local to the function and that there are no

```
double *data = (double*) malloc(dsize*sizeof(double))
...
#pragma offload target(mic) inout(data: length(dsize))
{
  ...
}
```

(a) Original Code

```
int mult64(int n){
  int k = n/64;
  if(k*64 == n){
    return n;
  }
  return (k+1)*64;
}

posix_memalign((void **)&data, 4096, mult64(size)
                                      *sizeof(double))
...
#pragma offload target(mic) inout(data:length(mult64(size)))
{
  ...
}
```

(b) Transformed Code

Figure 10: Malloc-to-memalign Conversion

uses/definitions of the variable outside the code section, except for the declaration itself. We move the declaration of such variables inside the offload code block to avoid the redundant copy-in. Fig. 9 shows the transformation. In C/C++, it is common practice to declare a data variable at the top of a function, which creates opportunities for applying this optimization.

4.3.3 Malloc-to-memalign Conversion

The use of DMA can significantly improve performance. In order for the Intel Compiler to generate DMA transfers, the pointer address must be 64-byte aligned and the data size must be a multiple of 64, which can be done using posix_memalign. Malloc-to-memalign optimization traces the malloc for a given data pointer in the in/inout clause, and replaces it by a suitable posix_memalign when possible. Function mult64 is defined to round off the size of the allocated pointer to the next multiple of 64. Fig. 10 shows the transformation.

4.3.4 Data Reuse Optimization

When a data variable is copied into MIC, memory is allocated for it by default unless otherwise specified using the alloc_if clause; alloc_if allows memory to be conditionally allocated based on the truth value of the predicate. Similarly, after an offload section finishes to completion, the memory is deallocated by default, unless otherwise specified using the free_if clause, which allows memory to be conditionally deallocated.

If a data variable is shared between multiple offload code sections or between successive executions of a code section, such that there are no writes to it on the host side (in between those executions), it is generally beneficial to retain the data in MIC memory and consequently delete all redundant data transfers associated with it. This can be done with the help of alloc_if, free_if and nocopy clauses. A nocopy clause indicates that a variable's value already exists in MIC memory and prohibits copy-in.

In order to apply the Data Reuse optimization for a given data variable, we need to ensure that there are no definitions of the variable on the host side in between two occurrences

```
#pragma offload target(mic) in(m:length(1000))
        out(a:length(1000))
{
  #pragma omp parallel for shared(a,m) private(i)
  for(i=0; i < 1000; i++){
    a[i] = m[i];
  }
}

... /* no writes to m */

#pragma offload target(mic) in(m:length(1000))
        out(b:length(1000))
{
  #pragma omp parallel for shared(b,m) private(i)
  for(i=0; i < 1000; i++){
    b[i] = m[i]*m[i];
  }
}
```

(a) Original Code

```
#pragma offload target(mic) in(m:length(1000) free_if(0))
        out(a:length(1000))
{
  #pragma omp parallel for shared(a,m) private(i)
  for(i=0; i < 1000; i++){
    a[i] = m[i];
  }
}

... /* no writes to m */

#pragma offload target(mic) nocopy(m:length(1000) alloc_if(0))
        out(b:length(1000))
{
  #pragma omp parallel for shared(b,m) private(i)
  for(i=0; i < 1000; i++){
    b[i] = m[i]*m[i];
  }
}
```

(b) Transformed Code

Figure 11: Data Reuse: Transformation 1

(i.e., uses or definitions) on MIC side. This can be done by inspecting the *use-def* chain for the variable. The analysis needed for data reuse across two successive executions of an offload code section (e.g, in a loop) is simpler than the analysis for data reuse across two difference code sections. The complexity arises due to the conditional nature of offload as introduced by our compiler– whether a code section will execute on the host processor or be offloaded to MIC is not known at compile time. The data reuse optimization creates a dependence between two code sections. If only one of them gets offloaded to MIC, incorrect results may be generated. It is important to ensure that both the code sections, for which data reuse optimization is being applied, get offloaded to MIC or neither does.

For applying data reuse optimization across two different code sections, *if-fusion* is performed. Since cbf() is part of Apricot, if-fusion can be applied without danger of side-effects. Data reuse analysis is then applied to the two code sections in the **then** branch by inspecting the *use-def* chains for all variables in the in/out/inout clauses. The variables that get defined on the host side in between the two code sections are not considered as candidates for reuse.

If a data variable m occurs in the in/inout clause of the first pragma and the in clause of the second pragma, a free_if(0) is inserted in the first pragma and a nocopy along with alloc_if(0) is inserted in the second pragma. This informs the compiler that m is not to be deallocated after the completion of first code section and that it is not to be copied in or allocated for the second code section. The

```
#pragma offload target(mic) in(k) inout(m:length(1000))
        out(a:length(1000))
{
  #pragma omp parallel for shared(a,m) private(i)
  for(i=0; i < 1000; i++){
    m[i%100] = k*i;
    a[i] = m[i];
  }
}

... /* no reads or writes to m */

#pragma offload target(mic) inout(m:length(1000))
        out(b:length(1000))
{
  #pragma omp parallel for shared(b,m) private(i)
  for(i=0; i < 1000; i++){
    b[i] = m[i]*m[i];
  }
}
```

(a) Original Code

```
#pragma offload target(mic) in(k) in(m:length(1000) free_if(0))
        out(a:length(1000))
{
  #pragma omp parallel for shared(a,m) private(i)
  for(i=0; i < 1000; i++){
    m[i%100] = k*i;
    a[i] = m[i];
  }
}

... /* no reads or writes to m */

#pragma offload target(mic) nocopy(m:length(1000) alloc_if(0))
        out(b,m:length(1000))
{
  #pragma omp parallel for shared(b,m) private(i)
  for(i=0; i < 1000; i++){
    b[i] = m[i]*m[i];
  }
}
```

(b) Transformed Code

Figure 12: Data Reuse: Transformation 2

```
for(i=0; i < N; i++){
  ...
  #pragma offload target(mic) inout(m:length(1000))
  {
    #pragma omp parallel for ..
    for(i=0; i < 1000; i++){
      a[i] = m[i];
      ...
      m[i] = a[i] * m[i];
      ...
    }
  }
  ...
}
```

(a) Original Code

```
int first_p = 1;
for(i=0; i < N; i++){
  ...

  if(first_p){
    #pragma offload target(mic) inout(first_p) in(m:length(1000)
                                                  free_if(0))
    {
      first_p = 0;
    }
  }

  #pragma offload target(mic) nocopy(m:length(1000) alloc_if(0)
                                                  free_if(0))
  {
    #pragma omp parallel for ..
    for(i=0; i < 1000; i++){
      a[i] = m[i];
      ...
      m[i] = a[i] * m[i];
      ...
    }
  }

  ...
}

#pragma offload target(mic) out(m:length(1000)) alloc_if(0)
{
}
```

(b) Transformed Code

Figure 13: Data Reuse: Transformation 3

transformation is shown in Fig. 11. If a data variable m occurs in the inout clause of both the pragmas, such that there are no uses of it in between on the host side, then m is moved from the inout to the in clause of the first pragma and from the inout to the out clause of the second pragma. A free_if(0) is inserted for it in the first pragma and a nocopy along with alloc_if(0) is inserted in the second pragma. This tells the compiler that m is to be reused between the first and second code section and that it should be copied out only after the completion of the second code section. Fig. 12 shows the transformation.

In order to apply data reuse analysis across successive executions of an offload code section inside a loop, the *use-def* chains for all variables in the in/out/inout clause are inspected. If a data variable in the in/inout clause does not get defined outside the code section within the surrounding loop, data reuse optimization is applied to the code section. An empty code section (surrounded by pragma offload) is created and placed right before the original code section. The empty code section only gets executed for the first iteration of the loop. All data variables in the in clause that do not get defined outside the code section in the surrounding loop are moved to the in clause of the empty code section. Corresponding nocopy, free_if(0) and alloc_if(0) clauses are inserted as shown in Fig. 13. All data variables in the inout clause that do not get defined outside the code sec-

tion in the surrounding loop (but *may* get used) are moved to the in clause of the empty code section and the out clause of the original code section. If any of those data variables get neither defined nor used outside the code section in the surrounding loop, another empty code section is created and placed right after the loop, and all such variables are moved from the out clause of the original code section to the out clause of this empty code section. Since the two empty code sections are only executed once, the copy-in/copy-out and memory allocation of the data variables is done once per loop as opposed to once per iteration.

4.4 Phase IV

In the final phase of compilation with Apricot, all the optimized offload code sections are inspected and the parameter list for the cost-benefit analysis function (cbf()) is populated for each code section.

4.4.1 Inspection for Cost-benefit Analysis

The idea behind this analysis is to come up with estimates for the amount of work done and data communicated per code section and pass them as parameters to the cost model.

```
Input:   For all loops in code section:  number of loop iterations
{num_iter_1,..,num_iter_n}, number of cpu operations {cpu_ops_1...,cpu_ops_n},
number of memory operations {mem_ops_1,..,mem_ops_n}; data transfer size
dsize; thresholds: k_1, k_2, k_3, k_4
Output: TRUE or FALSE
Procedure cbf()
    for i = 1 → n do
        if (num_iter_i ≤ k_1) then
            return FALSE;
        end if
    end for
    total_work ← ∑_i((cpu_ops_i + mem_ops_i) * num_iter_i)
    if (total_work ≤ k_2) then
        return FALSE;
    end if
    total_cpuops ← ∑_i(cpu_ops_i * num_iter_i)
    if ((total_cpuops/dsize) ≤ k_3) then
        return FALSE;
    end if
    total_memops ← ∑_i(mem_ops_i * num_iter_i)
    if ((total_cpuops/total_memops) ≤ k_4) then
        return FALSE;
    end if
    return TRUE;
```

Figure 14: Cost Model

A code section is typically a parallelizable loop or a set of parallelizable loops with limited serial code in between.

In order to get an estimate for the amount of work done in the code section, Apricot identifies (i) the set of cpu operations (i.e., addition, subtraction, multiplication, exponentiation, etc) in the code section and condenses them into a single number (cpu_ops) per loop based on relative weights (that are experimentally obtained) for the different operations, (ii) the set of memory operations (i.e., loads/stores) condensed into a single number (mem_ops) per loop, and (iii) the number of loop iterations (num_iter) for each loop. The estimate for data transfer size (dsize) is obtained by adding up the data sizes of all the scalars, arrays and pointers specified the in/out/inout clauses. This information is passed as a set of parameters to cbf() for each code section.

4.4.2 Cost Model

In order to ascertain if a code section should be offloaded to MIC, a simple cost model is invoked by cbf() at runtime. The cost model consists of a set of heuristics to determine profitability, as shown in Fig. 14. Four conditions should be satisfied for a code section to be profitably offloaded to MIC: (i) the number of iterations of every loop in the code section should be greater than a certain threshold k_1, (ii) the total amount of work done in the code section over all loops, i.e. $\sum_i((cpu\_ops_i + mem\_ops_i) * num\_iter_i)$ should be greater than a threshold k_2, (iii) the ratio of total cpu operations to total data transfer size, i.e. $\sum_i(cpu\_ops_i * num\_iter_i)/dsize$ should be greater than a threshold k_3, and (iv) the ratio of total cpu operations to memory operations, i.e. $\sum_i(cpu\_ops_i * num\_iter_i)/\sum_i(mem\_ops_i * num\_iter_i)$ should be greater than a threshold k_4. The fourth check has been added because our experiments suggest that memory intensive code regions do not perform very well on the current MIC hardware. Values of k_1 through k_4 are experimentally obtained. In the current cost model, the values of k_1, k_2, k_3 and k_4 are set to 100, 10^{10}, 1000, and 2 respectively. The cost model would evolve over time as more data is obtained. Also, since Intel MIC has 512-bit wide vector registers, modeling the difference in vectorization capabilities should improve the accuracy of the cost-model.

5. EVALUATION

Apricot has been implemented on top of the gcc infrastructure. The analyses are performed with gcc IR, but the actual transformations are applied to the source code. We take advantage of the IR-to-source mapping capabilities in gcc. Output from the different analyses are stored and maintained in the offload_regions data structure and used during transformation. This approach allows the user to make further modifications to the optimized source code and have a final say in what gets executed, thereby allowing Apricot to function as a pre-processor/best-effort compiler and be used as a productivity tool as much as a performance tool. Moreover, generating optimized source code provides additional flexibility as to how, where and when the optimized source code is eventually compiled. All the different phases and optimizations presented in the paper have been implemented and tested.

We carry out the experiments with a Quadcore Xeon E5620 server equipped with a Knights Ferry Card. Knights Ferry has been made available to a few groups for the purpose of debugging and optimizing the runtime, compiler and other libraries for Intel MIC in order to pave the way for Knights Corner. Due to confidentiality reasons, we can only report the relative gains obtained with our optimizations.

We use the Knights Ferry card to (i) test out correctness of conditional offload insertion, and (ii) evaluate the four optimizations presented in the paper. We have experimented with SpecOMP [11] benchmarks and NAS Parallel benchmarks [6], in addition to a number of micro-benchmarks. Our experiments show that Apricot can successfully transform OpenMP applications to run on Intel MIC by applying conditional offload insertion. In the rest of the section, we present our experimental results for two SpecOMP benchmarks: 321.equake_l and 313.swim_l and two NAS parallel benchmarks: FT and MG. For all the benchmarks, code modifications are made to convert multi-dimensional arrays to one-dimensional arrays (since Apricot currently handles only one-dimensional arrays during array-bound analysis). The benchmarks were all compiled at -O3. A number of loops were auto-vectorized by icc in each of the four benchmarks. No MIC-specific vector intrinsics were used.

321.equake_l: Finite element simulation of elastic wave propagation in large valleys due to seismic events. There is a total of 12 loops marked with #pragma omp for. The compiler auto-generates conditional #pragma offload and corresponding in/out/inout/length clauses for these loops and the benchmark executes successfully on MIC. The cost model finds that only 2 of the 12 loops would benefit from offloading to MIC. This version serves as the baseline for evaluating the four optimizations.

Figure 15(a) shows the results with the four optimizations applied individually and together. The Y-axis represents the time of execution of the benchmark (in timeunits) such that it is proportional to the actual time of execution (omitted for confidentiality). The numbers are averaged over multiple runs and reported with num_threads set to 64. The baseline (offload version without any optimizations applied) takes 234 timeunits to execute. A speedup of 2.4X, 5.2X, 11.7X and 17.3X is obtained with malloc-to-memalign conversion, data declaration optimization, offload hoisting and data reuse optimization respectively. When all the optimizations are applied together, a speedup of 24.5X is achieved.

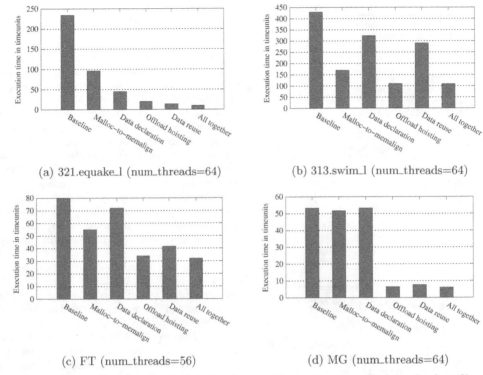

(a) 321.equake_l (num_threads=64)

(b) 313.swim_l (num_threads=64)

(c) FT (num_threads=56)

(d) MG (num_threads=64)

Figure 15: Performance gains obtained with the four optimizations applied to the baseline offload version

The reason why performance gains from the different optimizations are not additive is because application of one optimization affects the applicability as well as performance headroom of other optimizations. For example, when offload hoisting is applied, the gains obtained by data reuse optimization diminish because less data is transferred.

313.swim_l: Weather prediction program, used for comparing performance of supercomputers. There is a total of 11 loops marked with `!omp parallel do`. iThe cost model finds that only 2 of the 11 loops would benefit from offloading to MIC. This version serves as the baseline for evaluating the four optimizations. Figure 15(b) shows the results with the four optimizations applied individually and together. The baseline (offload version) takes 429 timeunits to execute. A speedup of 2.5X, 1.33X, 3.89X and 1.45X is obtained with malloc-to-memalign conversion, data declaration optimization, offload hoisting and data reuse optimization respectively. When all the optimizations are applied together, a total speedup of 3.91X is obtained.

FT: Time integration of a three-dimensional partial differential equation using FFT. There is a total of 6 loops marked with `#pragma omp for`, of which 3 are found to benefit from offloading to MIC by our cost-model. Figure 15(c) shows the results with the four optimizations applied. The baseline version takes 80 timeunits to execute. A speedup of 1.45X, 1.1X, 2.3X and 1.9X is obtained with malloc-to-memalign conversion, data declaration optimization, offload hoisting and data reuse respectively. When all the optimizations are applied together, a total speedup of 2.47X is obtained.

MG: Multigrid solver for a 3-dimensional potential field. There is a total of 12 loops marked with `#pragma omp for`, of which 5 are found to benefit from offloading. Figure 15(d) shows the results with the four optimizations applied. The baseline (offload version) takes 53 timeunits to execute. A speedup of 8.2X and 7X is obtained with offload hoisting and data reuse optimization respectively. A 3% gain is obtained with malloc-to-memalign conversion, while data declaration optimization does not yield any performance gains for this benchmark. A total speedup of 8.75X is obtained with all the optimizations applied together.

These experimental results indicate the significant potential of the optimizations proposed in the paper. The results are reported for 56-64 threads which yield best performance for these benchmarks (for certain benchmarks 88-96 threads yield slightly better performance). The gains may vary as the hardware evolves but communication overheads would continue to be a performance bottleneck.

6. RELATED WORK

Donaldson et al [18] illustrate the use of *Offload C++* extensions for offloading C++ code to Cell BE. This work is nearly identical (as well as contemporary) to Intel's LEO programming model and the corresponding compiler and runtime. Apricot is complementary to both and can be used alongside Offload C++, in the same way as it is used alongside LEO. Apricot focuses on the automatic insertion of the offload constructs, optimization of the generated code and selective offloading at runtime.

General purpose programming for GPUs (GPGPU) has received a lot of attention lately. Consequently, a number of GPGPU compilers have been developed [25, 12, 21, 17, 10]. The idea behind these compilers is to reduce the programming effort and maximize performance for GPUs. LEO and the Intel Offload Compiler are in their infancy and have significant room for improvement. Apricot shares the goal of improving programmer productivity and application performance for this new generation of many-core coprocessors, as well as the design rationale, with GPGPU compilers. However, the manner in which the ideas are formulated and applied is very different due to the difference in the programming models as well as target architectures.

Apricot builds on top of prior work in the area of static analysis [23, 20], multi-core programming [9, 14] and heterogeneous computing [17, 13]. The idea of conditional offload is inspired by the problem of automatic partitioning of applications for CPU/coprocessor model [22]. Minimizing communication overhead [19, 21] between host processor and MIC coprocessor is the main goal of the optimizations introduced in the paper. The inspection phase for cost-benefit analysis is inspired by auto-parallelization [5, 1]. The liveness analysis phase bears resemblance with the approach used for automatic generation of MPI messages from OpenMP [24].

The idea of conditional offload, the cost model as well as the compiler optimizations introduced in this paper are novel. To the best of our knowledge, this is the first attempt at investigating LEO and suggesting extensions and optimizations. These optimizations can potentially also be applied to C++ Amp [2], which is a set of programming language extensions (similar to LEO) being proposed by Microsoft for GPGPU.

7. CONCLUSION AND FUTURE WORK

In this paper, we give an overview of the new Intel MIC architecture and the associated programming model for offload. We present the design of Apricot, an optimizing compiler and productivity tool for many-core coprocessors such as Intel MIC. The key features of Apricot are: (i) automatic insertion of offload constructs to take advantage of MIC coprocessor (ii) cost model and analysis for selective offload of code regions to the coprocessor at runtime (iii) optimization of code regions for minimizing data communication overheads. We evaluate the optimizations with respect to Knights Ferry, a MIC prototype developed by Intel as a precursor to Knights Corner and observe upto 24X speedup. Apricot can be extended to other offload models, such as OpenACC [7], Offload C++ [18] and C++ Amp [2].

The current implementation of liveness and array bound analysis only handles simple pointers and arrays; nested arrays and structures of pointers are not handled. We plan to extend the implementation to handle more complex cases to further improve coverage. The cost model is currently tuned with respect to Knights Ferry. We need to refine and reevaluate the cost model (as well as the optimizations) with respect to Knights Corner. We also plan to design and evaluate an auto-parallelizer for many-core.

8. ACKNOWLEDGEMENTS

We thank Intel for providing us with the MIC KNF boards and for an early review of the paper. We thank Ozcan Ozturk for some of the early discussions. We thank our shepherd Albert Cohen and the anonymous reviewers for their valuable feedback.

9. REFERENCES

[1] Automatic parallelization with intel compilers. http://software.intel.com/file/39655.
[2] C++ accelerated massive parallelism. http://msdn.microsoft.com/en-us/library/hh265137
[3] Gnu compiler collection. http://gcc.gnu.org.
[4] Gnu gprof. http://sourceware.org/binutils/docs/gprof.
[5] Intel c++ compiler. http://www.intel.com/Compilers.
[6] Nas parallel benchmarks. http://nas.nasa.gov/Software/NPB.
[7] Openacc: Directives for accelerators. http://www.openacc-standard.org/.
[8] Opencl. http://www.khronos.org/opencl.
[9] The openmp api. http://www.openmp.org.
[10] R-stream compiler. https://www.reservoir.com/rstream.
[11] Spec openmp benchmark suite. http://www.spec.org/omp2001.
[12] M. M. Baskaran, J. Ramanujam, and P. Sadayappan. Automatic c-to-cuda code generation for affine programs. In *Compiler Construction (CC)*, pages 244–263, 2010.
[13] M. Becchi, S. Byna, S. Cadambi, and S. Chakradhar. Data-aware scheduling of legacy kernels on heterogeneous platforms with distributed memory. In *Proceedings of the 22nd ACM Symposium on Parallelism in Algorithms and Architectures (SPAA)*, pages 82–91, 2010.
[14] R. D. Blumofe, C. F. Joerg, B. C. Kuszmaul, C. E. Leiserson, K. H. Randall, and Y. Zhou. Cilk: An efficient multithreaded runtime system. In *Proceedings of the Fifth ACM SIGPLAN Symposium on Principles and Practice of Parallel Programming (PPoPP)*, pages 207–216, 1995.
[15] U. Bondhugula, A. Hartono, J. Ramanujam, and P. Sadayappan. A practical automatic polyhedral parallelizer and locality optimizer. In *Proceedings of the 2008 ACM SIGPLAN conference on Programming Language Design and Implementation (PLDI)*, pages 101–113, 2008.
[16] B. Creusillet and F. Irigoin. Interprocedural array region analyses. *International Journal of Parallel Programming*, 24(6):513–546, 1996.
[17] G. Diamos, A. Kerr, S. Yalamanchili, and N. Clark. Ocelot: A dynamic compiler for bulk-synchronous applications in heterogeneous systems. In *Proceedings of The Nineteenth International Conference on Parallel Architectures and Compilation Techniques (PACT)*, 2010.
[18] A. F. Donaldson, U. Dolinsky, A. Richards, and G. Russell. Automatic offloading of c++ for the cell be processor: A case study using offload. In *Proceedings of the 2010 International Conference on Complex, Intelligent and Software Intensive Systems*, pages 901–906, 2010.
[19] I. Gelado, J. H. Kelm, S. Ryoo, S. S. Lumetta, N. Navarro, and W.-m. W. Hwu. Cuba: an architecture for efficient cpu/co-processor data communication. In *Proceedings of the 22nd Annual International Conference on Supercomputing (ICS)*, pages 299–308, 2008.
[20] W. H. Harrison. Compiler analysis of the value ranges for variables. *IEEE Trans. Softw. Eng.*, 3:243–250, May 1977.
[21] T. B. Jablin, P. Prabhu, J. A. Jablin, N. P. Johnson, S. R. Beard, and D. I. August. Automatic cpu-gpu communication management and optimization. In *Proceedings of the 32nd ACM SIGPLAN conference on Programming Language Design and Implementation (PLDI)*, pages 142–151, 2011.
[22] J. H. Kelm and I. Gelado et al. Cigar: Application partitioning for a cpu/coprocessor architecture. In *Proceedings of the 16th International Conference on Parallel Architecture and Compilation Techniques (PACT)*, pages 317–326, 2007.
[23] G. A. Kildall. A unified approach to global program optimization. In *Proceedings of the 1st annual ACM SIGACT-SIGPLAN symposium on Principles of Programming languages (POPL)*, pages 194–206, 1973.
[24] O. Kwon, F. Jubair, R. Eigenmann, and S. Midkiff. A hybrid approach of openmp for clusters. In *Proceedings of the 17th Symposium on Principles and Practice of Parallel Programming (PPoPP)*, pages 75–84, 2012.
[25] S. Lee, S.-J. Min, and R. Eigenmann. Openmp to gpgpu: a compiler framework for automatic translation and optimization. In *Proceedings of the 14th Symposium on Principles and Practice of Parallel programming (PPoPP)*, 2009.
[26] S. Pop, A. Cohen, and G.-A. Silber. Induction variable analysis with delayed abstractions. In *In 2005 International Conference on High Performance Embedded Architectures and Compilers (HiPEAC)*, pages 218–232, 2005.
[27] R. Rugina and M. Rinard. Symbolic bounds analysis of pointers, array indices, and accessed memory regions. In *Proceedings of the ACM SIGPLAN 2000 conference on Programming Language Design and Implementation (PLDI)*, pages 182–195, 2000.
[28] L. Seiler and D. Carmean et al. Larrabee: a many-core x86 architecture for visual computing. In *ACM SIGGRAPH*, pages 18:1–18:15, 2008.

UniFI: Leveraging Non-Volatile Memories for a Unified Fault Tolerance and Idle Power Management Technique

Somayeh Sardashti
Department of Computer Sciences
University of Wisconsin-Madison
somayeh@cs.wisc.edu

David A. Wood
Department of Computer Sciences
University of Wisconsin-Madison
david@cs.wisc.edu

ABSTRACT

Continued technology scaling presents new challenges for system-level fault tolerance and power management. Decreasing device sizes increases the likelihood of both transient and permanent faults. Increasing device count, together with the end of Dennard scaling, makes power a critical design constraint. Techniques that seek to improve system reliability frequently use more power. Similarly, many techniques that reduce power hurt system reliability. Ideally system designers should seek out techniques that mutually benefit both fault tolerance and power management.

In this paper, we develop a unified technique, called UniFI, for fault tolerance and idle power management in shared memory multi-core systems. UniFI leverages emerging non-volatile memory technologies to provide an energy-efficient lightweight checkpointing technique. In addition to tolerating a large class of faults, UniFI's frequent checkpoints permit near-instant transition to a deep sleep mode to reduce idle power. UniFI incurs very low performance and energy overheads during fault-free execution—less than 2%—while taking checkpoints every 0.1ms. For typical server workloads (such as DNS), UniFI reduces average power by 82% by shutting off during idle periods.

Categories and Subject Descriptors

C.1 [**Processor Architectures**]: General

Keywords

Energy, Reliability, Checkpointing, Idle power management.

1. INTRODUCTION

Continuing advances in technology scaling promise significantly higher levels of system integration, but to effectively exploit this potential requires concomitant advances in fault tolerance and power management. Decreasing feature sizes pose new challenges to system reliability, due to increased rates of transient and permanent faults [4]. Future multicore systems must also treat power as a first-class design constraint, and should seek not only to limit the maximum power dissipation but also to make power - proportional to performance by managing idle power. The twin challenges of fault tolerance and power management motivate our work towards a unified technique that addresses both.

Power has become a primary design constraint for multicore processors and systems, and is projected to become ever more important as technology continues to scale [10]. Shrinking transistor dimensions results in the exponential growth of leakage power, while dynamic power no longer follows Dennard's classical scaling trend [36]. In addition, due to scaling conventional memory technologies encounter scaling difficulties and power issues. To answer these issues, emerging resistive memory technologies — such as Phase-Change Memory (PCM) and Spin-Torque Transfer Magneto-resistive RAM (STT-MRAM) – have been proposed [11-23]. They promise to not only eliminate the major sources of leakage power, but to also make main memory and caches non-volatile [14,20].

Server power is also a critical factor at data centers, where power consumption is growing rapidly [35]. In most data centers, servers have relatively low utilization, but exhibit bursty behavior and are rarely idle for long. Conventional idle power management techniques, such as OS-directed ACPI power modes, are insufficient due to high transition overheads. What is needed are low-overhead idle power management techniques, which rapidly transition between idle and active power modes [34]. On the other hand, power management techniques may degrade reliability if applied aggressively due to decreased noise margins and thermal cycling [42].

Technology scaling and power management both impact system reliability. Shrinking semiconductor feature sizes results in a higher possibility of process and operating condition variations, and increases the susceptibility of system components to both transient and permanent faults. In a data center, power management may also interrupt server power due to power outages, power over-subscription (e.g., power capping), or thermal emergencies [11]. To recover from a wide range of failures, various checkpointing techniques have been proposed operating at different software or hardware layers [7,24,25,26,27]. However, conventional checkpointing techniques incur high performance and power overheads or require high disk bandwidth and capacity [27].

This paper proposes UniFI, a Unified Fault tolerance and Idle power management technique for shared-memory multicore systems. UniFI helps both system reliability and power by exploiting the synergy between backward error recovery and idle power management. It leverages resistive memory and provides a lightweight energy-efficient checkpointing mechanism to recover from a wide range of transient and permanent faults. Relying on its light-weight global checkpoint mechanism, UniFI allows almost instant transition of the system to a deep sleep mode during idle periods and at power emergencies. Unlike other power management mechanisms, UniFI's checkpoint mechanism also helps tolerate any fault due to increased thermal cycling.

Table 1. Taxonomy of fault tolerance and power management techniques.

		System Reliability		
		Tends to hurt	Neutral	Tends to help
System Power	Tends to hurt	N/A	N/A	High-overhead global checkpointing [7],[24],[25], and redundancy [40] mechanisms
	Neutral	N/A	N/A	Power-aware reliability techniques [41], Rebound [45]
	Tends to help	Aggressive power management techniques [38][42]	Razor [39], MS-ECC [47], Word-disable and Bit-fix schemes [48], heterogeneous LLC [46]	UniFI [New]

We evaluate UniFI's performance and energy overheads using full-system simulation with SPEComp [3], PARSEC and commercial workloads [2] running on an 8-processor multicore system. For continuous fault-free execution, UniFI incurs very low performance and energy overheads, less than 1% on average and less than 2% for the worst performing workloads. For low-utilization server workloads, we use Meisner, et al.'s power model [34] to show that UniFI significantly eliminates idle power.

The main contributions of this paper are as follows:

• To the best of our knowledge, UniFI is the first unified technique that addresses the synergies between fault-tolerance and idle power management.

• UniFI proposes an efficient checkpointing technique—using a novel combination of lazy flushing, in-cache logging, and safe replacement—that incurs low performance and energy overheads in the common case of fault-free execution, allowing frequent checkpointing.

• UniFI exploits the unique characteristics of resistive memories to efficiently recover from a wide range of permanent and transient faults and to provide efficient idle power management.

In the rest of the paper, we study the synergies between fault tolerance and power management techniques in Section 2, describe the background in non-volatile memories in section 3, present UniFI and its mechanisms in Section 4, give evaluation methods in Section 5, provide experimental results in Section 6, discuss related work in Section 7, and conclude the paper in Section 8.

2. SYNERGY BETWEEN FAULT TOLERANCE AND POWER MANAGEMENT

With continued transistor scaling, designers face new challenges in both system reliability and system power. Despite decades of fault-tolerance research, most studies on reliability have paid little attention to power overheads [27]. Similarly, recent power management techniques, which reduce average power and temperature, may degrade reliability due to decreased noise margins and thermal cycling [42]. System designers should seek solutions that synergistically improve both system reliability and power.

The taxonomy in Table 1 categorizes various fault tolerance and power management techniques based on their impacts on reliability and power. Different fault tolerance techniques can be categorized into Forward Error Recovery (FER), which uses redundant computation, and Backward Error Recovery (BER), which maintains checkpoints or logs. FER (e.g., ECC and triple-modular redundancy) tends to consume additional power [40]; however some recent work uses dynamic adaptation to provide a target reliability level with minimum resources and power [41]. Traditional BER techniques such as SafetyNet [25] and ReVive [24] incur significant power overhead for large on-chip log buffers [25], flushing caches and writing logs to main memory [24]. In a recent work, although Dong et al. use PCM for checkpointing [7], their proposed technique has also high power and performance overheads, and so low checkpoint frequency. More recently, Rebound reduces both performance and power overhead by using coordinated local, rather than global, checkpoints [45].

Aggressive power management techniques can hurt system reliability by increasing both transient and hard faults. For instance, aggressive idle power management techniques, such as PowerNap, can increase hard error rates due to thermal cycling [42]. Active power management techniques, such as DVFS and drowsy cache [49], can also hurt transient fault rates if being used aggressively[38]. Recent work has proposed using additional redundancy and/or selective reconfiguration to improve the reliability of caches in low-power operating modes [39,46,47,48].

UniFI seeks to help both system reliability and power by exploiting the synergy between backward error recovery and idle power management. It provides a light-weight global checkpoint mechanism, and unlike other aggressive idle power management techniques, it leverages its checkpoint mechanism to tolerate possible faults due to increased thermal cycling.

3. BACKGROUND IN NON-VOLATILE MEMORY TECHNOLOGIES

Since conventional memory technologies encounter scaling difficulties and power issues as semiconductor feature sizes shrink, the research community has proposed using resistive memory technologies, such as PCM, STT-MRAM, Resistive RAM (RRAM), and memristors, at different levels of the memory hierarchy [11-23]. While still relatively early in the technology development cycle, these technologies all promise scalability, non-volatility, high density, and energy-efficiency.

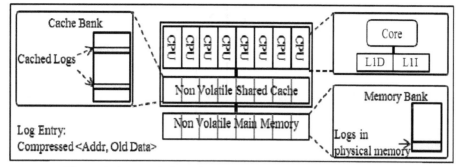

Figure 1. A general view of a multicore system with UniFI's support.

While UniFI is largely independent of which technologies ultimately dominate the market, it does assume that both main memory and the last level cache are non-volatile. To make our work concrete, we focus on PCM and STT-MRAM, which are two promising alternatives.

As DRAM technology faces scalability and power issues, PCM has gained attention in the research community as a DRAM replacement for main memory [11-19]. In comparison with DRAM, PCM is scalable, denser, non-volatile, and has near zero leakage power. On the other hand, it has lower write endurance, higher latency and higher writing power. Different techniques have been proposed to make PCM competitive with DRAM [12,13,15,16,17,19].

As vendors increase the number of cores per die, there is a commensurate demand for larger and low power on-chip caches. Conventional SRAM-based caches cannot meet both objectives due to their low density and high leakage power. Recent studies show that STT-MRAM is a good candidate for the next generation of large on-chip caches [20-22]. STT-MRAM is scalable, fast (similar to SRAM) and dense (similar to DRAM), and has near zero leakage power and very high write endurance. On the other hand, it takes longer than SRAM to write, which can be addressed by different techniques [20,21].

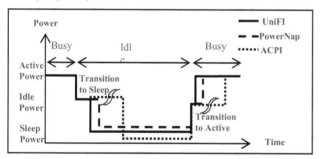

Figure 2. Different idle power management techniques.

4. UNIFI: A UNIFIED TECHNIQUE FOR FAULT TOLERANCE AND IDLE POWER MANAGEMENT

In this section, we first describe a general overview of UniFI. We then provide a detailed explanation of all UniFI mechanisms.

4.1 UniFI Overview

We propose UniFI, a unified mechanism that helps provide high availability and power proportionality. UniFI's main goals are providing low-overhead checkpointing and recovery, rapid transition to/from low-power mode, and recovery from a wide range of faults. To achieve these goals, UniFI proposes different

mechanisms, all described below. UniFI leverages emerging non-volatile memory technologies to make both the last-level cache and main memory persistent across power outages. It provides a low-overhead global checkpointing mechanism, and creates safe checkpoints (i.e., stored in non-volatile storage) periodically without ever quiescing the system. Using its checkpointing mechanism, it recovers from a wide range of faults, described in Section 4.5, including power outages.

Figure 2 shows how different idle power management techniques eliminate idle power. To provide an efficient idle power management mechanism for server workloads with short idle periods, deep sleep mode and rapid transition between sleep and active modes are required. To eliminate idle power efficiently, UniFI provides very rapid transition (almost instant) of the system to/from a very deep sleep mode. UniFi's system-level idle power management mechanism, described in Section 4.4, treats transitions to deep low-power states much like unintentional power outages. When an idle period is detected, it rapidly transitions the system to a very deep sleep mode with powered-off cores, caches, and main memory. In response to instantaneous load, it quickly transitions the system to the high-performance active state by recovering the system to the last safe checkpoint. Unlike other power management techniques (such as PowerNap), UniFI compensates for the possible higher error rates caused by its aggressive power management with its efficient checkpoint recovery mechanism.

UniFI is largely independent of any specific fault detection mechanism [43]. It keeps multiple checkpoints, so it can support relatively long-latency, signature-based fault detection mechanisms. In addition, to keep I/O consistent, UniFI leverages existing techniques, e.g., ReViveIO [44], that buffer input and output in non-volatile buffers until they are known to be safe. As UniFI's checkpointing interval is short (e.g., 0.1ms), buffering outputs has little impact on most application's performance.

4.2 UniFI System Model

Figure 1 shows a general view of a shared-memory multi-core system with UniFI's support. Cores have one or more levels of private, volatile caches, and share a non-volatile last-level cache and non-volatile main memory.

Each core has volatile, private L1 instruction and (write-back) data caches implemented using conventional SRAM. They share non-volatile STT-MRAM L2 cache and PCM main memory. To hide STT-MRAM high write latency, we use multiple banks and sub-bank buffers in the L2 cache [21].

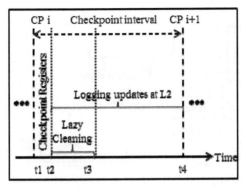 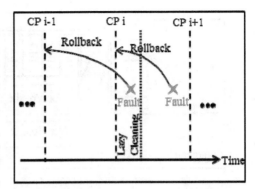

Figure 3. different phases of creating a checkpoint (a) and rollback recovery from different faults.

In addition, to make PCM main memory competitive with DRAM, we apply different techniques including: multiple narrow buffer rows in memory banks and word-level dirty bits in the caches, to mitigate PCM's high write latencies and to improve its energy and endurance [13].

4.3 UniFI Checkpointing Mechanisms

Figure 3 (a) illustrates different phases of creating a checkpoint with UniFI. Checkpoints occur at a logical time (e.g., time t1 in Figure 3) defined as the edge of a checkpointing clock, which is a loosely synchronized clock received at different modules (e.g., caches and cores). A checkpoint can be used as a recovery point when it is safe in non-volatile memory, which is any time after all checkpoint state resides in stable storage (e.g., at time t3 in Figure 3 (a)). UniFI ensures that there is always a safe checkpoint by keeping at least two checkpoints at a time.

4.3.1 Checkpointing at Processors

To establish a new persistent checkpoint, UniFI checkpoints processor registers first. As there are a limited number of registers, performance overhead of register checkpointing is negligible. Therefore, processors checkpoint their registers explicitly, storing them into their private caches via their load/store units. Register checkpoints will be safe in stable storage (i.e., non-volatile L2 and main memory) once the L1 caches are cleaned (described next).

4.3.2 Lazy Cleaning of Volatile Private Cache

To create a safe checkpoint, UniFI makes all updates preceding that checkpoint persistent before they are modified or lost. Figure 4 illustrates UniFI's checkpointing mechanism at caches. To keep checkpointing overhead low, UniFI handles it entirely within the hardware. It augments the L1 cache tags with a flash clear bit column (CP bit in Figure 4) [31] indicating if the line has been cleaned in the current checkpointing interval.

UniFI uses a lazy checkpointing mechanism at caches, and cleans L1 caches without stopping the running applications. It uses a simple state machine in the L1 cache controller to walk through the L1 cache and clean a cache line (i.e., copy it to the non-volatile L2 cache) if it is dirty and not cleaned yet (e.g., Cache Line A in Figure 4). If there is an update request to such a line UniFI first makes it safe by copying it back to the non-volatile L2 before processing the new request. Since update requests are not on the critical path, as shown in Section 6, its overhead is negligible.

4.3.3 Logging Updates at the Shared Cache.

Between two successive checkpoints, UniFI logs data updates to the L2 cache by storing their physical addresses and old data as log entries. UniFI keeps logs as part of the physical address space (e.g., in an address assigned at boot time). To provide low-overhead checkpointing and fast recovery, UniFI caches logs in the L2 cache, in the same bank as the original cache line resides. By caching the logs, UniFI avoids extra costs of special log buffers [7][25] and high energy and performance overheads of storing logs in the main memory [24]. Also, since most of the logs reside in the cache, as shown in Section 6, recovery is fast and energy efficient.

To reduce the possible overheads of caching logs (e.g., cache pollution), UniFI employs two techniques: logging only first updates in a checkpointing interval and compressing logs. During a checkpointing interval, UniFI only logs on the first update to a cache line using the CP bit added to the L2 cache (Figure 4). UniFI also compresses logs using Frequent Pattern Compression (FPC) [1], which is a hardware-based low overhead compression technique. FPC achieves high compression ratio for most applications by compressing frequent patterns (e.g., consecutive 0s and 1s) of data [1]. By applying these techniques, and due to the fact that UniFI creates checkpoints frequently and keeps a limited number of them (e.g., two), its overhead due to polluting the cache is low. As shown in Section 6, each UniFI's checkpoint is about 23 KB or 1.14% of the L2 cache on average.

Since UniFI cleans L1 caches lazily, it keeps two active checkpoints (the previous and the current checkpoints). It logs updates generated by cleaning the L1 caches as part of the previous checkpoint, while logging others in the current checkpoint.

4.3.4 Safe Data Replacements

Although UniFI assumes non-volatile shared cache and main memory, there are usually volatile buffers in between, such as write-back buffers and buffers in the memory controller. To achieve recovery from instant power-off, UniFI ensures that data in these buffers are not lost using a safe replacement policy. In a directory-based coherence protocol with 1-phase write-back technique, which the cache controller sends the replaced address and data to the memory controller at the same time, or 3-phase write-back technique, which the cache controller waits for an acknowledgement from the memory controller before sending the data and unblocking the cache line, UniFI adds one more phase to ensure data is safe. It basically blocks the cache line until it

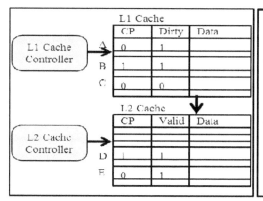

L1 Cache		
CP	Dirty	Data

	CP	Dirty	Data
A	0	1	
B	1	1	
C	0	0	

L2 Cache		

	CP	Valid	Data
D	1	1	
E	0	1	

1. When establishing a new checkpoint, all CP bits in the L1 and L2 caches are cleared.
2. L1 cache controller lazily makes updates to the cache safe by copying them back to L2.
3. Line A (not B neither C) will be copied back to the L2 cache before processing any request on this line.
4. When copying back Line A, L2 cache controller logs its old value.
5. L2 cache controller logs on the first update to Line E.

Figure 4. UniFI checkpointing mechanism.

receives an unblock acknowledgment message from the memory controller indicating that it has issued the request to the persistent main memory (i.e., 2-phase or 4-phase write-back). In this way, even in the case of power-off, data can be found in the cache.

4.3.5 Synchronization

Since UniFI logs all updates at the L2 cache, unlike global checkpointing techniques such as SafetyNet [25], it needs a simple synchronization technique. To create globally synchronized checkpoints, UniFI needs processors and cache controllers to receive a checkpointing clock at which they start creating a new checkpoint. Since the L2 cache controller handles all logs, a loosely synchronized clock (i.e., it could have skew) can be used at different modules. In addition, as UniFI lazily cleans the L1 caches, when L1 cache controllers complete cleaning the caches, they need to notify the L2 cache controller (e.g., by sending an ack) of the new safe checkpointing.

4.3.6 Rollback Recovery

When a fault is detected, UniFI recovers the system to a safe checkpoint preceding the fault. The system first diagnoses the error (e.g., using a service processor), reconfigures it in case of permanent failure, and reinitializes the hardware. These steps are beyond this paper's scope. UniFI handles recovery entirely within the hardware. To recover a checkpoint, as shown in Figure 3 (b), processors first restore their register checkpoints in parallel, reading and unrolling them via their load/store units. The L2 cache controller then reads and undoes the checkpoint logs in reverse order from the most recent checkpoint to the recovery point.

UniFI provides rapid recovery using different techniques including: caching logs, parallel undo, and pipelined recovery. Since UniFI caches logs, it finds most of the logs in the L2 cache at the time of recovery. UniFI also keeps logs in the same bank as the original cache line resides, so it can unroll them in parallel. In addition, it pipelines reading logs, decompressing them, and restoring their data to the cache or processors in order to reduce recovery overhead.

4.4 UniFI Idle Power Management Mechanisms

UniFI leverages non-volatile memory technologies and its efficient checkpointing mechanism to provide both fast transitioning and very low power system-level sleep mode. Figure 5 illustrates two mechanisms to eliminate idle power with UniFI.

In the first mechanism, shown in Figure 5 (a), UniFI instantly transitions the system to the deep sleep mode in case of a power emergency or a detected idle period. Later, when there is a new job to process or the power failure is fixed, UniFI rapidly transitions the system to the active mode by recovering the system to the most recent safe checkpoint before the transition (CPi in Figure 5 (a)). It then finishes the previous job (i.e., redo the lost work), and starts the new job. This mechanism is mostly useful for emergencies, such as thermal emergencies and power outage, since it does not let the previous job commit (i.e., buffer its I/O outputs) until the system transitions back to the active mode and it creates another safe checkpoint.

On the other hand, when there is no emergency (e.g., to eliminate a detected idle period), UniFI can let the previous job commit before transitioning to the sleep mode. In this mechanism, shown in Figure 5 (b), UniFI makes a new safe checkpoint just before switching to the sleep mode by checkpointing processors' registers, flushing their L1 caches, and committing buffered I/O outputs. On a new job arrival, it activates the system by recovering to this safe point, which only includes restoring registers. In addition to system level power management, UniFI can provide fine-grained power management at core level by checkpointing registers of a core and flushing its L1 caches. That core or even another core (e.g., using server consolidation) can later continue running by reloading its register.

4.5 UniFI Fault model

UniFI is designed to recover from a wide class of faults. It recovers from multiple simultaneous transient or permanent faults at any part of the system as long as it can access a safe checkpoint. As UniFI keeps checkpoints in the non-volatile shared cache and main memory, it must assume they are error free. Fortunately, UniFI can leverage well-known techniques, ranging from conventional ECC to RAID-like memories [24], to protect memory.

UniFI tolerates various transient or permanent faults including those result in loss of all data in volatile caches (e.g., due to a glitch on reset signal), permanent failure of a core and its private cache. In addition to transient and permanent faults, one of our goals is recovering from instant power-off. Instant power-off may happen unintentionally due to power failures (e.g., power outage or thermal emergencies), or intentionally for idle power management. In all of these cases, UniFI recovers the system state to a consistent fault-free state preceding the fault or the sleep mode.

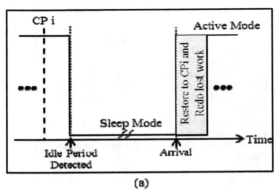 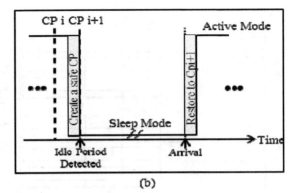

(a)   (b)

Figure 5. Two different mechanisms to eliminate idle power with UniFI.

5. EVALUATION SETUP

In order to evaluate UniFI, we use two mechanisms: full system simulation and analytical modeling. To evaluate UniFI's fault tolerance mechanism, we have implemented UniFI in a full-system simulator based on GEMS [28]. We use CACTI [30] and McPAT [50] to model power at 32nm. We model a multi-core system with 8 cores, shared STT-MRAM L2 cache, and PCM main memory (Figure 1) modeled after the parameters in Table 2. We also consider overheads of FPC compression, which take 0.41ns and consumes 0.112nJ for compressing/decompressing 64-byte data [6]. We use a similar system with same configurations but without UniFI's support as our baseline. We have also enhanced our simulator to model the energy and delay of STT-MRAM and PCM with the parameters in Table 3. In this Table, the STT-MRAM cache cells are optimized for density and access energy, while its corresponding SRAM-based cache is designed for low leakage and high speed access [21].

Table 2. Simulation Parameters

Cores	8 OOO cores, 4GHz frequency, 4-wide issue, 192 physical registers
L1 Caches	Private, 32-KB iL1/dL1, 4-way associative, 3-cycle access latency
L2 Caches	Shared, 4-MB, 8-way associative, 8 banks, 8-cycle Read latency, 24-cycle Write latency, MESI Coherency
Main Memory	4GB, 16 banks, 400MHz bus frequency
Checkpointing Parameters	2 checkpoints, 400K cycles (0.1ms) checkpointing interval

We evaluate UniFI's checkpointing mechanism with a large variety of applications from PARSEC with simlarge input sets (Blackscholes, Bodytrack, Canneal, Fluidanimate, Freqmine, Streamcluster, and Swaptions), SPEComp (Ammp, Applu, Equake, Fma3d, Gafort, Mgrid, Swim, and Wupwise), and commercial workloads (Apache, Oltp, Jbb, and Zeus). Since these benchmarks are multi-threaded, we use a work-related metric, run each workload for a fixed number of transactions/iterations (for approximately 100M instructions), and report the average of 15-20 runs using randomized memory delays to address workload variability [37]. We evaluate UniFI's overheads with a very frequent checkpointing, creating a checkpointing every 0.1 ms (i.e. checkpoint frequency of 10KHz or 400K core cycles). We keep two checkpoints (one active, one safe). In this way UniFI can support long fault detection techniques with latency of up to 800,000 cycles.

To evaluate power savings of UniFI's power management, we extend the power model presented in Meisner et al. [34], which model power saving in a server using an M/G/1 queuing model. Their model calculate power savings of an idle power management technique based on workload parameters (e.g., the work-load's average busy time), and the power management mechanism's parameters (e.g., transition latency between active and sleep modes, and sleep power). We use this model, which we skip its details here, and augment it with UniFI's checkpointing power and performance overheads to find UniFI's power savings in a typical blade. We also find UniFI's impact on response time using the model presented in their paper [34].

Table 3. STT-MRAM cache and PCM memory parameters

L2 Cache Parameters	4MB SRAM	4MB STT-MRAM
Rd/Wrt Latency (core cycle)	10/10	8/24
Energy per Rd/Wrt (pJ/64B)	1268/1268	798/952
Leakage Power (mW)	6578	3343
Memory Parameters	**DRAM**	**PCM**
tCL/tRCD/tWTR/tWR/tRTP/ tRP/tCCD/tWL (mem cycle)	5/5/3/6/3/5/ 4/4	5/22/3/6/3/60/4 /4
Energy per Rd/Wrt (pJ/bit)	1.17/0.39	2.47/16.82

Table 4 shows the power consumption of a typical blade [34], which has two cores operating at 2.4 GHz and eight DRAM DIMMS. We use the RAILS power supply units (PSU) [34], which significantly reduces energy costs of PSU when idle power management techniques are being used. We evaluate UniFI and compare it with PowerNap using different server workloads [34].

6. EVALUATION

In this section, we first evaluate our baseline system and study impacts of using non-volatile memories. We then evaluate UniFI's checkpointing mechanism and idle power management.

6.1 Evaluation: Baseline

To study impacts of using non-volatile memories in the system, we evaluate four baseline configuration listed in Table 5 with the parameters in Table 2. The last two configurations employ sub-bank buffers at the STT-MRAM L2 cache [21], buffer reorganization and partial writes at PCM main memory [13].

Table 4. Component power consumption of a typical blade with/without power management techniques

Blade Components	Active Power	Idle Power	Sleep Power with PowerNap	Sleep Power with UniFI
CPU Chip	80-150W	12-20W	6.8W	0W
DRAM DIMMs	3.5-5W	1.8-2.5W	1.6W	0W
Other modules (PSU, SSD, etc.)	110-262W	210-230W	2W	2W
Total	**450W**	**270W**	**10.4W**	**2W**

Figure 6 and Figure 7 illustrate performance and energy of baseline configurations normalized to SRAM-DRAM baseline system. A baseline of STT-MRAM and PCM system without any extra technique (the second configuration) is on average 1.5x slower and requires 1.2x more energy than a SRAM-DRAM system. Applying different techniques in non-volatile memories reduce this delay and energy gap to 1.08x and 0.92x, and makes the baseline competitive with SRAM-DRAM system. To evaluate UniFI, we use this configuration as our baseline system.

Table 5. Baseline Configurations

SRAM-DRAM	4-MB SRAM L2$, DRAM memory
STT-PCM w/o techs	4-MB STT-MRAM L2$, PCM memory
STT-PCM w techs (our baseline)	4-MB SRAM L2$, PCM memory, extra techniques applied
STT-PCM w large cache	8-MB SRAM L2$, PCM memory, extra techniques applied

In addition to these techniques, a large DRAM buffer can be used before PCM main memory to hide its high latencies and energy overheads [16]. In the last configuration, we study using a larger STT-MRAM on-chip cache instead since STT-MRAM is scalable, energy efficient and non-volatile with similar density

comparing to DRAM. This configuration further reduces the energy and delay gap to 0.95x and 0.88x.

6.2 Evaluation: UniFI

Figure 8 and Figure 9 show the breakdown of UniFI's performance and energy overheads over the baseline system during fault-free execution. UniFI incurs less than 2% (0.5% on average) performance and energy overheads for all the workloads (0.08% for PARSEC, 0.45% for SPEComp, and 1.46% for commercial workloads) while it creates checkpoints frequently (every 400K cycles or 0.1ms). UniFI also increases Energy-Delay product (ExD) up to 3.7% for OLTP, and 1.02% on average. The main sources of UniFI's overheads are caching logs in the L2 cache and cleaning L1 caches. Compressing logs and lazy cleaning significantly reduce these overheads. Compressing logs reduces performance overhead of caching logs by up to 4.1% (for OLTP) and 0.64% on average for all the workloads. In addition, lazy cleaning improves performance by up to 2.1% and 0.3% on average. Similarly, these techniques reduce energy overhead by up to 4.5% and on average 1%.

For workloads with large footprints in the L2 cache, such as commercial workloads and some of SPEComp (e.g., Swim) and PARSEC workloads (e.g., Canneal), UniFI's overhead is mainly due to caching logs in the L2 cache, and so increasing cache miss ratio. For instance, UniFI increases miss ratio by 1.41% to 80

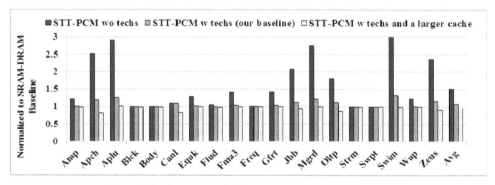

Figure 6. Performance of different baseline configurations.

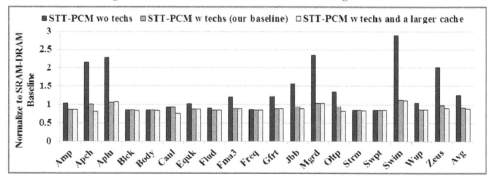

Figure 7. Energy of different baseline configurations.

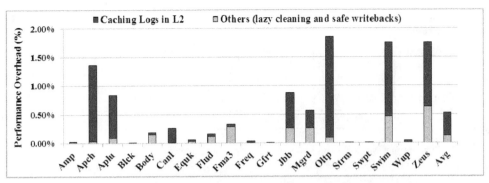

Figure 8. Breakdown of UniFI's performance overhead over the baseline.

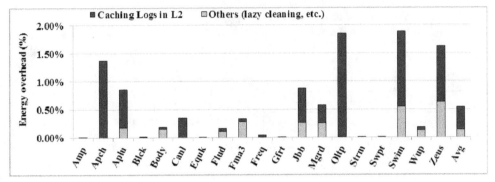

Figure 9. Breakdown of UniFI's energy overhead over the baseline.

MPKI (misses per kilo instructions) for Swim. This overhead is also a function of checkpoint size, which is fairly small for most of the workloads (23 KB or 1.14% of the L2 cache on average). For OLTP, UniFI creates checkpoints with average size of 117KB (5.7% of the L2 cache), which explains its high performance and energy overheads in comparison with other workloads.

As UniFI lazily cleans the L1 caches in the background, its overhead due to cleaning caches is low (on average 0.1%). This overhead is related to the number of dirty lines copied back when establishing a checkpoint, and so is higher for those with more dirty lines (such as Zeus, Swim, and Fma3d). Since access to the main memory is not on the critical path, safe data replacements at the L2 cache has negligible effects.

To estimate the overhead of recovery and unavailability of the system due to an error, we consider the worst case recovery scenario. For example, when an error occurs after establishing the first checkpoint and is detected at the end the second checkpoint interval (i.e., detection latency of about 800K cycles), UniFI unrolls both checkpoints. Since most the logs reside in the L2 cache (on average 99.5% of logs stay in the cache), the overhead of unrolling a checkpoint is low. It takes less than 40K cycles (10us) to unroll one checkpoint on average. Considering approximately 0.2ms for lost work (2 checkpointing intervals), UniFI provides about 99.999999% availability if one of these faults occurs per day.

In addition to evaluating UniFI's checkpointing mechanism, we study how it saves power by eliminating idle power. Figure 10 illustrates power saving (part (a)) and relative response time (part (b)) with UniFI and PowerNap in a typical blade with parameters in Table 4 for different server applications. UniFI's transition time between sleep and active states, and checkpointing overhead are very low, however we conservatively assume 0.1ms transition time and 2% performance/energy overheads. As shown in Figure

10, UniFI provides better power saving and response time than PowerNap for most applications because of its rapid transition to the deep sleep mode and leveraging non-volatile memories. Due to UniFI's rapid transitions, its checkpointing overhead is mostly amortized for most of the workload except Cluster as it has longer service time and higher utilization.

7. RELATED WORK

UniFI improves the standard global checkpointing technique proposed in SafetyNet and ReVive [24][25] to provide low-power checkpointing. UniFI provides frequent checkpointing with much less energy, performance and area overheads. In addition to leveraging non-volatile memory technologies, UniFI differs from ReVive by caching compressed logs in LLC (similar to regular data), and so significantly reducing power and memory bandwidth overheads of writing and recovering logs into/from the main memory. UniFI also eliminates the high overhead of flushing caches in ReVive by lazily cleaning dirty cache lines only in the private caches. In comparison with SafetyNet, UniFI eliminates the extra power and area costs of separate log buffers. Regarding to leveraging non-volatile memories, the technique proposed in [7] also leverages PCM, however unlike UniFI, they use special 3D stacked PCM storage as checkpoint buffers. They also have a costly mechanism to create a checkpoint, which stalls the system periodically and copies DRAM content to the PCM buffers.

UniFI also leverages its checkpointing mechanism to save power for server workloads comparably to PowerNap idle power management. Unlike PowerNap and other aggressive power management techniques, UniFI compensates the possible higher error rates due to aggressive power management with its low overhead checkpoint recovery mechanism.

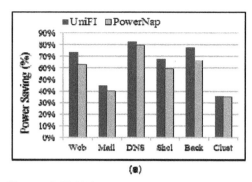 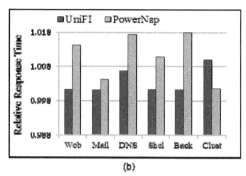

(a)   (b)

Figure 10. UniFI's power savings and relative response time for server workloads Breakdown of UniFI's

8. CONCLUSIONS

We propose UniFI, a unified technique that addresses two critical challenges of reliability and power management together. UniFI exploits resistive memory technologies, and proposes a light-weight energy-efficient checkpointing to recover from transient and permanent faults, and power failures. Exploiting UniFI's ability to recover from instant power-off, we use UniFI to eliminate idle power of servers with short idle periods. We demonstrate that it incurs less than 2% performance and energy overheads for a wide range of applications. We also show that for typical server workloads with short idle periods, UniFI can reduce average power by up to 82% by leveraging its low overhead checkpointing mechanism and non-volatile memories.

9. REFERENCES

[1] Alameldeen, A., and Wood, D. 2004. Adaptive Cache Compression for High-Performance Processors. In *Proc. of the 31st Annual Intnl. Symp. on Computer Architecture* (June 2004).

[2] Alameldeen, A., Mauer, C., Xu, M., Harper, P., Martin, M., Sorin, D., Hill, M., and Wood, D. 2002. Evaluating Non-deterministic Multi-threaded Commercial Workloads. In *Proc. of the 5th Workshop on Computer Architecture Evaluation Using Commercial Workloads* (Feb. 2002).

[3] Aslot, V., Domeika, M., Eigenmann, R., Gaertner, G., Jones, W., and Parady, B. 2001. SPEComp: A New Benchmark Suite for Measuring Parallel Computer Performance. *In Workshop on OpenMP Applications and Tools* (July 2001).

[4] Borkar, S. 2005. Designing Reliable Systems from Unreliable Components: the Challenges of Transistor Variability and Degradation. *IEEE Micro* (November 2005).

[5] Borkar, S., Jouppi, N., and Stenstrom, P. 2007. Microprocessors in the era of terascale integration. In *Proc. of the conference on Design, automation and test in Europe*.

[6] Das, R., Mishra, A., Nicopoulos, C., Park, D., Narayanan, V., Iyer, R., Yousif, M., and Das, C. 2008. Performance and power optimization through data compression in Network-on-Chip architectures. In *Proc. of the 14th IEEE Symp. on High-Performance Computer Architectur*.

[7] Dong, X., Muralimanohar, N., Jouppi, N., Kaufmann, R., and Xie, Y. 2009. Leveraging 3D PCRAM technologies to reduce checkpoint overhead for future exascale systems. In *Proc. of the Conference on High Performance Computing Networking, Storage and Analysis*.

[8] Fernandez-Pascual, R., Garcia, J., Acacio, M., and Duato, J. 2007. A Low Overhead Fault Tolerant Coherence Protocol for CMP Architectures. In *Proc. of the 13th IEEE Symp. on High-Performance Computer Architecture* (February 2007).

[9] Hagersten, E., and Koster, M. 1999. WildFire: A Scalable Path for SMPs. In *Proc. of the 5th IEEE Symp. on High-Performance Computer Architecture* (January 1999).

[10] International technology roadmap for semiconductors. Process integration, devices, and structures, 2009.

[11] Condit, J., Nightingale, E., Frost, C., Ipek, E., Lee, B., Burger, D., and Coetzee, D. 2009. Better I/O through byte-addressable, persistent memory. In *Proc. of the ACM SIGOPS 22nd symposium on Operating systems principles*.

[12] Ipek, E., Condit, J., Nightingale, E., Burger, D., and Moscibroda, T. 2010. Dynamically replicated memory: building reliable systems from nanoscale resistive memories. In *Proc. of the fifteenth edition of ASPLOS on Architectural support for programming languages and operating systems*.

[13] Lee, B., Ipek, E., Mutlu, O., and Burger, D. 2009. Architecting phase change memory as a scalable dram alternative. In *Proc. of the 36th Annual Intnl. Symp. on Computer Architecture*.

[14] Lee, B., Zhou, P., Yang, J., Zhang, Y., Zhao, B., Ipek, E., Mutlu, O., and Burger, D. 2010. Phase-Change Technology and the Future of Main Memory. *IEEE Micro*.

[15] Qureshi, M., Karidis, J., Franceschini, M., Srinivasan, V., Lastras, L., and Abali, B. 2009. Enhancing lifetime and security of PCM-based main memory with start-gap wear leveling. In *Proc. of Micro*.

[16] Qureshi, M., Srinivasan, V., and Rivers, J. 2009. Scalable high performance main memory system using phase-change memory technology. In *Proc. of the 36th Annual Intnl. Symp. on Computer Architecture*.

[17] Schechter, S., Loh, G., Straus, K., and Burger, D. 2010. Use ECP, not ECC, for hard failures in resistive memories. In *Proc. of the 37th Annual Intnl. Symp. on Computer Architecture*.

[18] Zhang, W., and Li, T. 2009. Characterizing and mitigating the impact of process variations on phase change based memory systems. In *Proc. of Micro*.

[19] Zhou, P., Zhao, B., Yang, J., and Zhang, Y. 2009. A durable and energy efficient main memory using phase change memory technology. In *Proc. of the 36th Annual Intnl. Symp. on Computer Architecture*.

[20] Zhou, P., Zhao, B., Yang, J., and Zhang, Y. 2009. Energy reduction for STT-RAM using early write termination. In

Proc. of the 2009 International Conference on Computer-Aided Design.

[21] Guo, X., Ipek, E., and Soyata, T. 2010. Resistive computation: avoiding the power wall with low-leakage, STT-MRAM based computing. In *Proc. of the 37th Annual Intnl. Symp. on Computer Architecture.*

[22] Zhu, J. 2008. Magnetoresistive Random AccessMemory: The Path to Competitiveness and Scalability. In *Proc. of the IEEE.*

[23] Mohan, C., and Bhattacharya, S. 2010. Implications of Storage Class Memories (SCM) on Software Architectures. In *HPCA 2010 Workshop on the use of Emerging Storage and memory Technologies (WEST).*

[24] Prvulovic, M., Zhang, Z., and Torrellas. J. 2002. ReVive: Cost-Effective Architectural Support for Rollback Recovery in Shared-Memory Multiprocessors. *In Proc. of the 29th Annual Intnl. Symp. on Computer Architecture.*

[25] Sorin, D., Martin, M., Hill, M., and Wood, D. 2002. SafetyNet: Improving the Availability of Shared Memory Multiprocessors with Global Checkpoint/Recovery. In *Proc. of the 29th Annual Intnl. Symp. on Computer Architecture* (May 2002).

[26] Teodorescu, R., Nakano, J., and Torrellas, J. 2006. SWICH: A Prototype for Efficient Cache-Level Checkpointing and Rollback. *IEEE Micro.*

[27] Torrellas, J. 2009. Architectures for Extreme-Scale Computing. *Computer.*

[28] Martin, M., Sorin, D., Beckmann, B., Marty, M., Xu, M., Alameldeen, A., Moore, K., Hill, M., and Wood, D. 2005. Multifacet's General Execution-driven Multiprocessor Simulator (GEMS) Toolset. *Computer Architecture News.*

[29] Brooks, D., Tiwari, V., and Martonosi, M. 2000. Wattch: A Framework for Architectural-Level Power Analysis and Optimizations. In *Proc. of the 27th Annual Intnl. Symp. on Computer Architecture* (June 2000).

[30] Shyamkumar, T., Muralimanohar, N., Ahn, J., and Jouppi, N. 2008. *CACTI 5.1.* Technical Report HPL-2008-20, Hewlett Packard Labs.

[31] Lee, D., and Katz, R. 1991. Using Cache Mechanisms to Exploit Nonrefreshing DRAM's for On-Chip Memories. *IEEE Journal of Solid-State Circuits* (April 1991).

[32] Xie, Y., Loh, G., Black, B., Bernstein, K. 2006. Design space exploration for 3D architectures. *ACM Journal on Emerging Technologies in Computing Systems (JETC).*

[33] Meixner, A., Bauer, M., and Sorin, D. 2007. Argus: Low-Cost, Comprehensive Detection of Errors in Simple Cores. In *Proc. of Micro.*

[34] Meisner, D., Gold, B., and Wenisch, T. 2009. PowerNap: Eliminating Server Idle Power. In *Proc. of the 14th International Conference on Architectural Support for Programming Languages and Operating Systems (ASPLOS)* (Mar. 2009).

[35] Barroso, L., and Holzle, U. 2007. The case for energy-proportional computing. *IEEE Computer* (Jan 2007).

[36] Dennard, R., Gaensslen, F., Rideout, V., Bassous, E., and LeBlanc, A. 1974. Design of Ion-Implanted MOSFET's with Very Small Physical Dimensions. *IEEE Journal of Solid-State Circuits* (Oct. 1974).

[37] Alameldeenand A., Wood, D. 2003. Variability in architectural simulations of multi-threaded workloads. In *HPCA.*

[38] Degalahal, V., Lin, L., Narayanan, V., Kandemir, M., and Irwin, M. 2005. Soft errors issues in low-power caches. *IEEE Transactions on Very Large Scale Integration (VLSI) Systems.*

[39] Das, S., Pant, S., Rao, R., Pham, T., Ziesler, C., Blaauw, D., Austin, T., Flautner, K., and Mudge, T. 2004. Razor: A Low-Power Pipeline Based on Circuit-Level Timing Speculation, *IEEE MICRO* (Dec. 2004).

[40] Gomaa, M., Scarbrough, C., and Vijaykumar, T. 2003. Transient-Fault Recovery for Chip Multiprocessors. In *Proceedings of ISCA-30* (June 2003).

[41] Miller, T., Surapaneni, N., Teodorescu, R., and Degroat, J. 2009. Flexible Redundancy in Robust Processor Architecture, *Workshop on Energy-Efficient Design (WEED), in conjunction with ISCA* (June 2009).

[42] Srinivasan, J., Adve, S., Pradip, B., Rivers, J. 2005. Lifetime reliability: toward an architectural solution. *IEEE Micro.*

[43] Mukherjee, S. 2008. Architecture Design for Soft Errors. *Elsevier Inc.*

[44] Nakano, J., Montesinos, P., Gharachorloo, K., and Torrellas, J. 2006. ReViveI/O: Efficient handling of I/O in highly-available rollback-recovery servers. *Intl. Symp. on High-Perf. Com, Arch.*

[45] Agarwal, R., Garg, P., and Torrellas, J. 2011. Rebound: Scalable Checkpointing for Coherent Shared Memory, *ISCA* (June 2011).

[46] Ghasemi, H., Draper, S., and Kim, N. 2011. Low-Voltage On-Chip Cache Architecture using Heterogeneous Cell Sizes for Multi-Core Processors. In *HPCA.*

[47] Chishti, Z., Alameldeen, A., Wilkerson, C., Wu, W., and Lu, S. 2009. Improving Cache Lifetime Reliability at Ultra-Low Voltages, In *Proc. of Micro* (December 2009).

[48] Wilkerson, C., Gao, H., Alameldeen, A., Chishti, Z., Khellah, M., and Lu, S. 2008. Trading Off Cache Capacity for Reliability to Enable Low Voltage Operation, *35th Annual International Symposium on Computer Architecture* (June 2008).

[49] Flautner, K., Kim, N., Martin, S., Blaauw, D., and Mudge, T. 2002. Drowsy Caches: Simple Techniques for Reducing Leakage Power. *Proc. IEEE/ACM 29th Intl. Symposium on Computer Architecture* (May 2002).

[50] Li, S., Ahn, J., Strong, R., Brockman, J., Tullsen, D., Joupp, N. 2009. McPAT: An Integrated Power, Area, and Timing Modeling Framework for Multicore and Manycore Architectures. In *Proc. of Micro.*

Fault Tolerant Preconditioned Conjugate Gradient for Sparse Linear System Solution *

Manu Shantharam
The Pennsylvania State
University
(shanthar@cse.psu.edu)

Sowmyalatha
Srinivasmurthy
The Pennsylvania State
University
(sowmya@cse.psu.edu)

Padma Raghavan
The Pennsylvania State
University
(raghavan@cse.psu.edu)

ABSTRACT

In scientific applications that involve dense matrices, checksum encodings have yielded "algorithm-based fault tolerance" (ABFT) in the event of data corruption from either hard or transient (soft) errors in the hardware. However, such checksum-based ABFT techniques have not been developed when sparse matrices are involved, for example, in sparse linear system solution through a method such as preconditioned conjugate gradients (PCG). In this paper, we develop a new sparse checksum encoded algorithm-based fault tolerant PCG, S-ABFT-PCG. Our checksum based approach can be applied to all the key operations in PCG, including sparse matrix-vector multiplication (SpMV), vector operations and the application of a preconditioner through sparse triangular solution. We prove that our approach detects a single error in the matrix and vector elements and in the metadata representing the sparse matrix row or column indices, when the linear system has a coefficient matrix that is symmetric positive definite and strictly diagonally dominant. The overhead of S-ABFT-PCG is proportional to the cost of a few $O(n)$ vector operations, a value that is relatively low compared to the total cost of a PCG iteration with an SpMV and two triangular solutions. However, if an error is detected, then the underlying PCG iteration must be recomputed because our approach does not enable checksum encoded recovery from the error. We compare our S-ABFT-PCG with a classical ABFT-PCG (C-ABFT-PCG) that detects and recovers from a single error in the SpMV kernel, but does not provide fault tolerance for the sparse triangular solution kernel. Our experimental results indicate that in the event of no errors, compared to a PCG with no ABFT, the overheads of S-ABFT-PCG are 11.3% and lower than the 23.1% overheads of C-ABFT-PCG. Furthermore, in the event of a single error in the application of the preconditioner through triangular solution, C-ABFT-PCG

*This research is supported in part by grants MRI 0821527, SHF 0963839 and CCF 0830679 from the National Science Foundation.

suffers from significant increases in iteration counts, leading to performance degradations of 63.2% on average compared to 3.2% on average for S-ABFT-PCG.

Categories and Subject Descriptors

G.4 [**Mathematical Software**]: Algorithm design and analysis, Efficiency, Reliability and robustness; G.1.3 [**Numerical Linear Algebra**]: Sparse, structured, and very large systems (direct and iterative methods)

General Terms

Theoretical underpinning, Algorithms, Reliability

Keywords

Algorithm based fault tolerance, Iterative methods, Soft errors

1. INTRODUCTION

Current large-scale high performance computing (HPC) installations have over 100,000 processor cores [1] and some may soon have over a million cores [2]. Increasing transistor densities per unit area and smaller feature sizes have resulted in increased core performance, and thus overall improved performance of the HPC installations. However, the performance benefit comes at the expense of higher susceptibility to hardware errors including, especially, transient or soft errors. For example, the BlueGene/L experiences one transient error in its L1 cache every 4-6 hours [3]. Consequently, long running scientific applications on large-scale HPC installations are more susceptible to transient errors.

Several algorithm-based fault tolerance (ABFT) techniques have been proposed for scientific applications with numeric computing involving dense matrix operations [4–7]. Typically, these techniques are based on checksum encoding to detect and recover from data errors for various dense matrix operations, such as, matrix-matrix multiplication and matrix factorization. However, such checksum encoding based ABFT techniques have not been developed when sparse matrices are involved, for example, in sparse linear system solution through methods such as preconditioned conjugate gradients (PCG). These are often used to solve PDE models in a variety of application such as those found in structural mechanics and computational fluid dynamics [8].

Recent work [3, 9, 10] show the differential impact of transient errors on sparse linear system solution. Bronevetsky et al. [3] show that a sparse linear solver affected by a transient error can have a wide range of behavior, from having no effect to application crash. More specially for PCG, Shantharam et al. [9] show that performance degradation can be as high as a factor of 250 relative to the case with no error, for a single transient error, i.e., there is a very large increase in the number of iterations to convergence. Thus, there is a strong need for protection mechanisms against such errors.

In this paper, we develop a new checksum encoded sparse ABFT PCG, S-ABFT-PCG, with checksum encodings for all its key operations, including, sparse matrix-vector multiplication (SpMV), vector operations and in particular, sparse triangular solution. Our formulation differs from the traditional encodings for dense matrices in the following ways. First, our method allows only for the detection and not the correction of a single error; however, such detection extends to a single error in metadata specific to sparse systems, including row and column subscript information. Second, we construct a formulation that enables single error detection in sparse triangular solution. Third, we seek to manage the tradeoffs between fault tolerance and the overheads of ABFT in a way that benefits PCG instances that may be more susceptible to soft errors, i.e., on systems of large dimension with hundreds to thousands of iterations to convergence. We have made the overhead of our scheme per iteration of PCG lower at the expense of having to recompute a single iteration if an error is detected.

The remainder of this paper is organized as follows. In Section 2, we first provide classification of faults. Next, we present recent work related to the ABFT techniques and discuss the relevance of our work. Section 3 contains our main contributions, namely, the development of our sparse checksum encoded algorithm-based fault tolerant PCG, S-ABFT-PCG, and analytic proofs indicating that the underlying checksum properties will enable the detection of a single error in each key operation within PCG. In Section 4, we provide empirical evaluation to illustrate the tradeoffs between the overheads of ABFT versus the benefits of fault tolerance, including comparisons with the traditional ABFT technique. In Section 5, we conclude this paper with a brief summary of our findings and directions for future work.

2. RELATED WORK AND BACKGROUND

Faults or errors can be broadly classified as permanent and transient. Henceforth, we use faults and errors interchangeably. The permanent faults that are often caused by aging hardware, such as, non functional memory cells, can only be overcome by avoiding the use of faulty hardware. In contrast, a transient fault is a temporary error that can occur due to several reasons such as cosmic radiation and voltage fluctuation. Both types of faults can leave the computing system state corrupt by either causing a fail-stop failure [11] or a silent error [3, 9]. In a fail-stop failure, the process that encounters a fault stops working. However, silent errors do not interrupt the process, but can eventually lead to incorrect computation. It is very difficult to find the actual faulty elements (permanent or transient) within a HPC system with billions of hardware components. Thus, it is important to develop fault tolerance techniques [4–7, 12–19] to improve the resilience of HPC systems.

Many ABFT techniques have been used for application specific fault tolerance [4,6,7,15]. Although, developing such techniques require a thorough understanding of the application, the low overhead costs and scalability of ABFT techniques make them an attractive alternative to the fault toler-

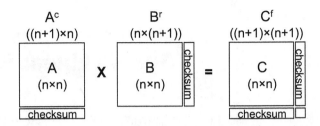

Figure 1: The C-ABFT technique.

ance techniques based on checkpoint/restart [12,13]. One of the common ABFT methods is to encode the input data such as matrices using checksums and verify that the output has a valid encoding. Huang et al. [4] propose an ABFT technique to handle errors in numerical computation, in particular, to detect and correct errors in dense matrix computations using checksum-encoded matrices. These methods use the linear transformation property of matrix computations to detect and correct a single error. Subsequently, a number of ABFT schemes have been proposed for error detection in different computations such as Fourier transforms [17] and dense matrix factorizations solvers [5]. Many build upon the ABFT proposed by Huang et al [4]. Chen et al. [6] show that the ScaLAPACK matrix-matrix multiplication kernel can tolerate fail-stop process failures without checkpointing or message logging. Yeh et al. [7] propose the use of ABFT techniques within matrix inversion with maximum pivoting.

Most of the prior work on ABFT has concerned dense linear algebra as indicated above. However, many scientific applications typically involve sparse linear algebra operations such as a sparse linear system solution. Hence, it is very important to develop and analyze the efficacy of ABFT techniques on such sparse computations. To the best of our knowledge, there has been very little development of such sparse ABFT techniques. The earliest work that we know of is that of Roy-Chowdhury et al. [15] that proposes an ABFT successive over relaxation (SOR) scheme for solving the Laplace equation on a model 5-point finite difference grid. More recently, Bronevetsky et al. [3] consider checksum-based ABFT in the context of sparse solvers as a relatively minor component of a complex set of fault tolerant approaches, including checkpointing and prediction of errors. In their work, they primarily apply the traditional checksum encoding of Huang et al. ([4]) to the SpMV kernel and vector operations. ABFT of sparse triangular solution, an operation that is required to apply popular incomplete factorization preconditioners is not considered. In contrast to their work, the focus of our paper is primarily on developing a sparse checksum encoding for all the key operations of PCG, including triangular solves. Additionally, unlike the checksum encoding of Huang et al. [4] that is also used in [3], we propose a lower overhead encoding tailored to PCG instances where convergence often depends on many hundreds of iterations, as explained later in Section 3.

Background: Classical ABFT. We now provide a brief overview of the algorithm-based fault tolerance technique of Huang et al. [4], as it forms the building block of many ABFT techniques. We call this technique *classical* ABFT or C-ABFT in this paper. Figure 1 illustrates C-ABFT for a dense matrix-matrix multiplication operation. In this technique, the input matrices are augmented with row or column checksums. In Figure 1, Matrix **A** is augmented with a row vector whose elements are the checksum of the corresponding columns (called $\mathbf{A}^c$), whereas, Matrix $\mathbf{B}$ is augmented with a column vector whose elements are the checksum of the corresponding rows (called $\mathbf{B}^r$), i.e.,

$$\mathbf{A}^c_{n+1,j} = \sum_{i=1}^{n} \mathbf{A}_{ij} \text{ and } \mathbf{B}^r_{i,n+1} = \sum_{j=1}^{n} \mathbf{B}_{ij}$$

Given $\mathbf{C} = \mathbf{A} * \mathbf{B}$ and $\mathbf{C}^f = \mathbf{A}^c * \mathbf{B}^r$, the output matrix, $\mathbf{C}^f$, has the following properties:

$$\text{i) } \mathbf{C}^f_{n+1,j} = \sum_{i=1}^{n} \mathbf{C}^f_{ij}, \quad \text{ii) } \mathbf{C}^f_{i,n+1} = \sum_{j=1}^{n} \mathbf{C}^f_{ij}.$$

These properties ensure that a single erroneous element in any of the matrices will be detected and corrected. Huang et al. [4] give a formal proof that indicates the ability of the checksum encoded dense matrix-matrix multiplication operation to detect and recover from a single error in one of the matrix elements.

3. A SPARSE CHECKSUM ENCODING FOR ABFT-PCG

We present the main contributions of our work in this section and it is organized as follows. In Section 3.1, we provide an overview of a PCG algorithm and explain key kernel operations. In Section 3.2, we discuss the issues with the C-ABFT technique with respect to sparse operations. In Section 3.3, we describe in detail our sparse checksum encoded ABFT technique with respect to the sparse matrix vector multiplication (SpMV) and triangular solve operations and prove the correctness of our technique. Theorem 1 proves that our technique detects a single error in an SpMV operation. Theorems 3-5 prove the error detection property of our technique for a sparse triangular solution. As the vector operations: addition and dot product are performed on dense vectors, we do not consider these operations when analyzing our technique. Note that we do not explicitly provide the pseudocode for our sparse checksum encoded ABFT-PCG (S-ABFT-PCG) as it can be obtained by combining our fault tolerance technique and the PCG algorithm presented in Section 3.1.

3.1 Overview of PCG and its primary operations

In this section, first, we give a brief overview of a PCG algorithm. Next, we explain the basic matrix and vector operations that comprise the PCG algorithm.

Algorithm 1 illustrates the pseudocode of a typical PCG algorithm used to solve a large sparse linear system. The algorithm takes several input parameters; a coefficient matrix $\mathbf{A}$ (which is sparse and symmetric positive definite), a known vector $\mathbf{b}$, the solution vector $\mathbf{x}$ initialized to random values, a preconditioner matrix $\mathbf{M}$, the maximum number of iterations allowed $maxit$ and a tolerance TOL, to detect the convergence of the algorithm. The primary operations in Algorithm 1 are: SpMV (line 9), triangular solve (line 15, note that computing matrix inverse is expensive, hence a triangular solve is use in practice) and vector operations like vector additions and dot products (lines 10, 11, ...).

Sparse matrix-vector multiplication (SpMV). SpMV is the most compute intensive operation in the PCG algorithm. It multiplies a sparse matrix ($\mathbf{A}$) in a compressed

---

Algorithm 1 Preconditioned Conjugate Gradient

procedure PCG(A,b,x,M,maxit,TOL)
1: $r = b - A * x$
2: $z = M^{-1} * r$ {solve using a triangular solve}
3: $iters = 0$
4: $nb = norm(b)$
5: $rsq = r' * r$
6: $p = z$
7: **while** iters < maxit && sqrt(rsq)/nb > TOL **do**
8: $\quad iters = iters + 1$
9: $\quad t = SpMV(A, p)$
10: $\quad v = r' * z$
11: $\quad alpha = v/(p' * t)$
12: $\quad x = x + alpha * p$
13: $\quad r = r - alpha * t$
14: $\quad rsq = r' * r$
15: $\quad z = M^{-1} * r$
16: $\quad beta = (r' * z)/v$
17: $\quad p = z + beta * p$
18: **end while**

storage format (CSR) [20] with a dense vector ($\mathbf{p}$). It is important to note here that, unlike the dense matrix-vector multiplication, SpMV loads the matrix indices to access corresponding data. The computational complexity of an SpMV operation is $O(nnz)$, where, nnz represents the number of nonzero elements in $\mathbf{A}$.

Preconditioning. Preconditioning is an essential part of PCG as it ensures fast convergence of the conjugate gradient method. In Algorithm 1, line 15 represents the preconditioning operation. This operation could be an SpMV operation or a triangular solve depending on the preconditioner matrix. For a diagonal preconditioner, it is an SpMV operation as computing $\mathbf{M}^{-1}$ is simple, however, for a more complex preconditioner, computing $\mathbf{M}^{-1}$ is expensive. Typically, $\mathbf{z}$ is obtained as follows

$$z = M^{-1} * r \implies M * z = r$$
$$L * L^T * z = r \quad (1)$$
$$L * y = r \quad (2)$$
$$L^T * z = y \quad (3)$$

Equation 1 represents the incomplete Cholesky factorization [21] of $\mathbf{M}$ into $\mathbf{L}$ and $\mathbf{L}^T$. Note that this incomplete factorization is performed only once per linear system following which sparse triangular solves are performed in Equations 2 and 3 to obtain $\mathbf{z}$. The complexity of a sparse triangular solution (Equations 2, 3) is proportional to the number of non-zeroes in $\mathbf{L}$.

Vector operations. There are two types of vector operations within an iterative linear solver. First, an inner product which involves multiplying the corresponding elements of two vector to yield a scalar. For example, if $\mathbf{a}$ and $\mathbf{b}$ are n×1 vectors, then the inner product $\mathbf{a}^T * \mathbf{b} = \sum_{i=1}^{n} \mathbf{a}_i * \mathbf{b}_i$.

Second, a vector addition which involves adding the corresponding elements of two or more vectors to yield a vector. Note that these operations take $O(n)$ operations.

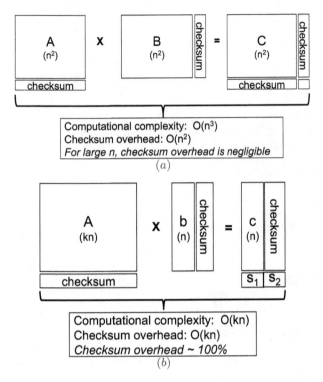

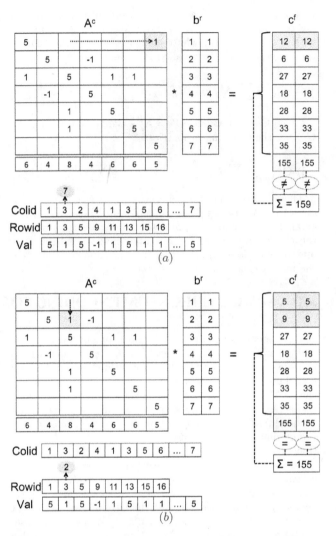

Figure 2: C-ABFT technique and its overheads for (a) dense matrix-matrix multiplication, (b) sparse matrix-vector multiplication.

3.2 Issues with application of C-ABFT to PCG

Recall that most earlier related work on ABFT have used C-ABFT or its variants to protect dense matrix-matrix operations. However, there are several issues related to the applicability of such techniques in the context of a sparse PCG. First, overheads of C-ABFT for the SpMV kernel are relatively high. Second, C-ABFT does not consider fault tolerance of the metadata that is a part of the sparse matrix representation. Third, C-ABFT does not include the sparse triangular solution kernel. In the remainder of this section, we explain the first two issues. We address the last issue is Section 3.3.2.

The dense matrix-matrix operations like matrix multiplication have computational complexity of $O(n^3)$ for an $n \times n$ matrix. The overhead of C-ABFT on such operations is $O(n^2)$ due to an additional matrix-vector multiplication. In Figure 2(a), this additional multiplication corresponds to $\mathbf{A}*$(checksum of $\mathbf{B}$). Therefore, asymptotically, the overhead of C-ABFT on dense matrix-matrix operations is relatively small. In contrast, the overhead of C-ABFT on an SpMV operation is directly proportional to the number of non-zero elements in the sparse matrix (kn), i.e., $O(n)$. However, an SpMV operation takes $O(n)$ time, making the C-ABFT overhead significantly high[1]. This is illustrated in Figure 2(b). Consequently, especially for long running PCG instances on large sparse systems with hundreds to thousands of iterations to convergence, we focus on developing a new sparse ABFT that has lower overheads. Our scheme

---

[1] Although analytically this overhead is at 100% the computational cost of a single SpMV, in practice, an efficient implementation with locality of data accesses can reduce this to a small fraction.

Figure 3: An illustration of the ABFT technique when there is an error in the metadata (a) column index, (b) row index.

(developed in Section 3.3.1) trades off a lower overhead per SpMV operation and PCG iteration to provide detection of a single error in all PCG operations, at the expense of having to recompute the PCG iteration in the event an error does occur.

The sparse matrices used within an iterative solver are stored in a compressed representation and requires the use of metadata to access the actual matrix elements. For example, an $n \times n$ sparse matrix with nnz non-zeroes requires two arrays of sizes nnz and n representing column and row pointers respectively, in addition to the nnz data elements. As the size of the metadata is almost half the size of the actual data, there is need to detect an error in the metadata. C-ABFT is vulnerable to an error in the metadata during an operation such as SpMV. For example, consider Figures 3(a) and 3(b). Figure 3(a) shows an instance of an error in the column index. Observe that such an error is equivalent to changing the non-zero structure of the matrix. As we can see from the figure, C-ABFT detects this error; however, it may not detect an error in the row index (see Figure 3(b)). Note that a single error in the row index could manifest as multiple errors in the output, hence C-ABFT may not be able to detect it.

In the following section, we address these issues in C-ABFT by developing sparse checksum encoding schemes proven to detect a single error in PCG operations and the sparse matrix metadata.

3.3 Sparse-ABFT for PCG operations

In this section, we describe our ABFT technique for the SpMV and sparse triangular solve operations. We provide theoretical analysis and prove that S-ABFT works for SpMV and sparse triangular solve.

3.3.1 SpMV Operation

Typically, an SpMV operation is of the form, $\mathbf{t} \leftarrow \mathbf{A} \cdot \mathbf{p}$, where, $\mathbf{t}$ and $\mathbf{p}$ are output and input vectors, respectively, and $\mathbf{A}$ is a sparse matrix. Thus, a fault tolerance technique should take in account an error in any of these three data structures. Additionally, as the elements in $\mathbf{A}$ (data) are accessed through metadata (column and row indices), it is important to protect the metadata. First, we discuss fault tolerance considerations for the metadata during an SpMV operation. Next, we present our ABFT technique for the SpMV operation that focuses on the actual matrix data.

Fault tolerance for the metadata. As illustrated earlier in Figure 3(a), an error in an element of *Colid* results in exactly one error in the output vector, hence it is detected by C-ABFT. Later in this section, we prove that our technique will also detect such an error. Now, let us consider an error in *Rowid* that may not be detected by C-ABFT. To protect against this case, our technique does the following: (i) computes and stores the checksum of *Rowid* before an SpMV operation in a variable (say Row_{cksm}) and (ii) during the SpMV operation, whenever an element of *Rowid* is accessed, subtracts the value of the accessed element from Row_{cksm}. After the SpMV operation, a non-zero value of Row_{cksm} indicates an error. It is important to note here that an error in either vector (*Rowid* or *Colid*) can change the value of the affected element to an arbitrary value. However, we consider only the cases wherein the changed value is in the range $[1, n]$. On the other hand, an out-of-range value can potentially cause fail-stop failures such as segmentation faults. As the focus of this paper is on silent errors, we ignore the cases that could lead to fail-stop failures.

Low overhead fault tolerance for SpMV. Figure 4 shows the S-ABFT technique for an SpMV operation. Unlike C-ABFT that has two SpMV operations, S-ABFT has one SpMV operation and a vector dot product. This reduces the fault tolerance overhead significantly. The following theorems show that our technique detects a single error (in the matrix elements or the vectors) during an SpMV operation when the matrix is symmetric positive definite [2] (SPD) and strictly diagonally dominant.

THEOREM 1. *Consider an encoded SpMV operation, $\mathbf{t}^c = \mathbf{A}^c * \mathbf{p}$, where $\mathbf{A}^c$ is the $(n+1) \times n$ checksum encoded matrix of a sparse SPD and diagonally dominant matrix $\mathbf{A}$, $\mathbf{p}$ and $\mathbf{t}^c$ are input and output vectors, respectively. By definition of a checksum matrix, $\mathbf{A}^c_{(n+1)j} = \sum_{i=1, A_{ij} \neq 0}^{n} \mathbf{A}_{ij}$ for $1 \leq j \leq n$.*

---

[2] A symmetric matrix $\mathbf{A}$ is positive definite if $\mathbf{x}^T \mathbf{A} \mathbf{x} > 0$ for all non-zero vectors $\mathbf{x}$, where $\mathbf{x}^T$ denotes the transpose of $\mathbf{x}$.

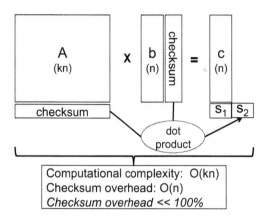

Figure 4: S-ABFT technique and its corresponding overhead for an SpMV operation.

Let $\mathbf{p}^r = \mathbf{p}$ and $dotp = \sum_{i=1}^{n} \mathbf{A}^c_{(n+1)i} * \mathbf{p}^r_i$. *A single error in the encoded SpMV operation causes one of the following conditions to fail:*

$$(i) \ \mathbf{t}^c_{n+1} = \sum_{i=1}^{n} \mathbf{t}^c_i, \qquad (ii) \ dotp = \sum_{i=1}^{n} \mathbf{t}^c_i$$

PROOF. We consider the following three error scenarios that can affect an SpMV operation, a single error in (a) $\mathbf{t}^c$, (b) $\mathbf{A}^c$, and (c) $\mathbf{p}$.

Case (a): Without loss of generality, let us assume an error in the jth element of $\mathbf{t}^c$ and denote it by $\hat{\mathbf{t}}^c_j$. Let the error prone output vector be $\hat{\mathbf{t}}^c$. Therefore, $\hat{\mathbf{t}}^c_i = \mathbf{t}^c_i$ for $1 \leq i \leq n+1$ and $i \neq j$. $\hat{\mathbf{t}}^c_j = \mathbf{t}^c_j + \delta$, where, δ is change in the value of $\mathbf{t}^c_j$ due to an error. Now, adding the elements of $\hat{\mathbf{t}}^c$, we have,

$$\sum_{i=1}^{n} \hat{\mathbf{t}}^c_i = \sum_{i=1, i \neq j}^{n} \mathbf{t}^c_i + \hat{\mathbf{t}}^c_j = \sum_{i=1}^{n} \mathbf{t}^c_i + \delta = \mathbf{t}^c_{n+1} + \delta$$

As, $\hat{\mathbf{t}}^c_{n+1} = \mathbf{t}^c_{n+1}$, $\sum_{i=1}^{n} \hat{\mathbf{t}}^c_i \neq \hat{\mathbf{t}}^c_{n+1}$. Hence condition (i) fails and the error is detected.

Case (b): Without loss of generality, let us assume an error in the element $\mathbf{A}^c_{jk}$. By definition of the SpMV operation, this translates to an error in the jth element of output vector. Hence, the proof follows from **Case (a)**.

Case (c): Without loss of generality, let us assume an error in the jth element of $\mathbf{p}$ and denote it by $\hat{\mathbf{p}}_j$. Let the error prone input vector be $\hat{\mathbf{p}}$. Therefore, $\mathbf{p}^r_i = \hat{\mathbf{p}}_i$ for $1 \leq i \leq n$ and $i \neq j$. $\hat{\mathbf{p}}_j = \mathbf{p}_j + \delta = \mathbf{p}^r_j + \delta$, where, δ is change in the value of $\mathbf{p}_j$ due to an error. Given the encoded SpMV operation, $\mathbf{t}^c = \mathbf{A}^c * \hat{\mathbf{p}}$, consider $\sum_{i=1}^{n} \mathbf{t}^c_i$.

$$\sum_{i=1}^{n} \mathbf{t}^c_i = \sum_{i=1}^{n} \sum_{k=1, A_{ik} \neq 0}^{n} \mathbf{A}^c_{ik} \hat{\mathbf{p}}_k$$

$$= (\sum_{i=1}^{n} \sum_{k=1, k \neq j, A^c_{ik} \neq 0}^{n} \mathbf{A}^c_{ik} \hat{\mathbf{p}}_k) + \sum_{i=1, A^c_{ij} \neq 0}^{n} \mathbf{A}^c_{ij} \hat{\mathbf{p}}_j$$

$$= (\sum_{i=1}^{n} \sum_{k=1, k \neq j, A^c_{ik} \neq 0}^{n} \mathbf{A}^c_{ik} \mathbf{p}^r_k) + \sum_{i=1, A^c_{ij} \neq 0}^{n} \mathbf{A}^c_{ij} (\mathbf{p}^r_j + \delta)$$

$$= (\sum_{i=1}^{n} \sum_{k=1, A^c_{ik} \neq 0}^{n} \mathbf{A}^c_{ik} \mathbf{p}^r_k) + \sum_{i=1, A^c_{ij} \neq 0}^{n} \mathbf{A}^c_{ij} \delta$$

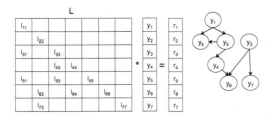

Figure 5: An example triangular solve system. The graph on the right represents the dependence among the solution elements.

$$= (\sum_{k=1}^{n} \sum_{i=1, A_{ik}^c \neq 0}^{n} \mathbf{A}_{ik}^c \mathbf{p}_k^r) + \delta \sum_{i=1, A_{ij}^c \neq 0}^{n} \mathbf{A}_{ij}^c$$

$$= (\sum_{k=1}^{n} (\mathbf{p}_k^r \sum_{i=1, A_{ik}^c \neq 0}^{n} \mathbf{A}_{ik}^c)) + \delta \sum_{i=1, A_{ij}^c \neq 0}^{n} \mathbf{A}_{ij}^c$$

$$= (\sum_{k=1}^{n} \mathbf{p}_k^r \mathbf{A}_{(n+1)k}^c) + \delta \sum_{i=1, A_{ij}^c \neq 0}^{n} \mathbf{A}_{ij}^c$$

$$= dotp + \delta \sum_{i=1, A_{ij}^c \neq 0}^{n} \mathbf{A}_{ij}^c$$

Therefore,

$$\sum_{i=1}^{n} \mathbf{t}_i^c = dotp + \delta \sum_{i=1, A_{ij} \neq 0}^{n} \mathbf{A}_{ij}^c$$

Condition (ii) fails if, $\delta \sum_{i=1, A_{ij}^c \neq 0}^{n} \mathbf{A}_{ij}^c \neq 0$. As $\mathbf{A}$ is strictly diagonally dominant, we have,

$$|\mathbf{A}_{jj}^c| > \sum_{i=1, A_{ij}^c \neq 0, i \neq j}^{n} |\mathbf{A}_{ij}^c|.$$

From this inequality, it follows that $\sum_{i=1, A_{ij}^c \neq 0}^{n} \mathbf{A}_{ij}^c \neq 0$, thus condition (ii) fails and the error is detected. $\square$

3.3.2 Sparse triangular solution

The sparse triangular solve operation involves solving a linear system of the form $\mathbf{L} * \mathbf{y} = \mathbf{r}$, where $\mathbf{L}$ is an $n \times n$ lower triangular matrix, $\mathbf{y}$ is an unknown vector $n \times 1$ and $\mathbf{r}$ is an $n \times 1$ known vector. Figure 5 gives an example of a lower triangular solve system. The graph on the right represents the dependence among the solution elements during the triangular solve process using forward substitution. For example, the solution element $\mathbf{y}_5$ depends on the already solved values $\mathbf{y}_1$ and $\mathbf{y}_3$. We present a graph-based formulation of a sparse lower triangular solve process, the impact of an error on the solution vector, and theoretical analysis of our ABFT technique for triangular solve, in the following subsections.

Graph Representation. Consider a linear system $\mathbf{L} * \mathbf{y} = \mathbf{r}$. Define a graph representation of $\mathbf{L}$, $\mathbf{G}(\mathbf{L}) = (V, E)$, where, $V = \{v_1..v_n\}$ is the vertex set; $E = \{(v_i v_j) : i > j, 1 \leq i, j \leq n, \mathbf{L}_{ij} \neq 0\}$ is the edge set. Note that $\mathbf{G}$ is a directed graph. Let $reach[S]$ represent the set of all the immediate neighbors of a set of vertices S, i.e., $reach[S] = \{v_j | v_j \in V, (v_i v_j) \in E, v_i \in S\}$.

Algorithm 2 illustrates the partitioning the elements in $\hat{\mathbf{y}}$ into *fault* (FS) and *correct* (CS) sets due a fault in $\mathbf{L}$. The input to the algorithm are: $\mathbf{G}(V, E)$ - directed graph

---

Algorithm 2 Fault set construction
function BuildFaultSet $(G(V,E),k,\hat{\mathbf{y}})$
1: **if** $k > |V|$ **then**
2:    $CS = V$
3:    **return**
4: **end if**
5: $CS = \phi$ {set of correctly solved elements in $\hat{\mathbf{y}}$}
6: $VS = V$
7: $i = 1$
8: **while** $i < k$ **do**
9:    $CS = CS \bigcup \{\hat{\mathbf{y}}_i\}$
10:   $VS = VS \backslash \{v_i\}$
11: **end while**
12: $FS = \{\hat{\mathbf{y}}_i\}$ {set of corrupted elements in $\hat{\mathbf{y}}$}
13: $VS = VS \backslash \{v_i\}$
14: $RS = reach(\{v_i\})$
15: **while** $RS \neq \phi$ **do**
16:   $FS = FS \bigcup \{\hat{\mathbf{y}}_j : v_j \in RS\}$
17:   $VS = VS \backslash RS$
18:   $RS = reach(RS)$
19: **end while**
20: $CS = CS \bigcup \{\hat{\mathbf{y}}_j : v_j \in VS\}$
21: **return**

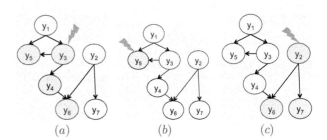

Figure 6: The effect of the error occurrence position on the solution vector. The grey elements are corrupt. (a) FS = $\{\mathbf{y}_3, \mathbf{y}_4, \mathbf{y}_5, \mathbf{y}_6\}$, (b) FS = $\{\mathbf{y}_5\}$, (c) FS = $\{\mathbf{y}_2, \mathbf{y}_6, \mathbf{y}_7\}$.

representing $\mathbf{L}$, k - implying $\hat{\mathbf{y}}_k$ is corrupt due a fault in one of elements in $\mathbf{L}_{k*}$, and $\hat{\mathbf{y}}$ - the corrupt vector. Figures 6(a), 6(b), 6(c) illustrate the differential impact of an error on the solution vector based on the error occurrence position. Note that the number of corrupt elements vary based on the error position as indicated by the size of FS. The following theorems use the sets FS and CS to illustrate the protection mechanism that can detect a single transient error in any of the data structures.

Fault tolerance for sparse triangular solve. Figure 7 shows the S-ABFT technique for a sparse triangular solve operation. In this technique, we first encode the triangular matrix, $\mathbf{L}$ by augmented it with a row representing the column checksum of $\mathbf{L}$. Next, we compute the solution, $\mathbf{y}$ and perform a dot product operation between the augmented row (checksum) and $\mathbf{y}$. We compare the value of this dot product with S ($S = \sum_{i=1}^{n} \mathbf{r}_i$). In the case of a single error, this value will not match and we detect an error. We prove the correctness of this fault tolerance technique in the following theorems.

In an attempt to improve the readability of the following theorems, we use a vector, $\mathbf{p}$, to represent the checksum

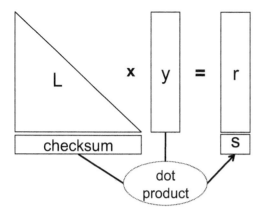

Figure 7: S-ABFT technique for a sparse triangular solve.

augmented row in $\mathbf{L}$, i.e., $\mathbf{p}_j = \sum_{i=1, \mathbf{L}_{ij} \neq 0}^{n} \mathbf{L}_{ij}$. Although we prove our scheme for a lower triangular solution ($\mathbf{L} * \mathbf{y} = \mathbf{r}$), similar results hold for solving an upper triangular system ($\mathbf{L}^T * \mathbf{z} = \mathbf{y}$).

THEOREM 2. *Consider a linear system* $\mathbf{L} * \mathbf{y} = \mathbf{r}$, *where,* $\mathbf{L}$ *is an* $n \times n$ *sparse lower triangular matrix and* $\mathbf{r}$ *is an* $n \times 1$ *known vector. Assume that* $\mathbf{y}$ *is solved correctly without any errors. Then, the value of the inner product of* $\mathbf{p}$ *and* $\mathbf{y}$ *is equal to the sum of the elements of* $\mathbf{r}$, *i.e.,* $\mathbf{p}^T \mathbf{y} = \sum_{i=1}^{n} \mathbf{r}_i$.

PROOF. Let us expand the linear system $\mathbf{L} \mathbf{y} = \mathbf{r}$ into a set of n linear equations:
$$\sum_{\forall j : \mathbf{L}_{1j} \neq 0} \mathbf{L}_{1j} \mathbf{y}_j = \mathbf{r}_1 \ ,$$
$$\sum_{\forall j : \mathbf{L}_{2j} \neq 0} \mathbf{L}_{2j} \mathbf{y}_j = \mathbf{r}_2$$
$$\vdots$$
$$\sum_{\forall j : \mathbf{L}_{nj} \neq 0} \mathbf{L}_{nj} \mathbf{y}_j = \mathbf{r}_n.$$
Adding the equations, we get,
$$\sum_{i=1}^{n} \sum_{\forall j : \mathbf{L}_{ij} \neq 0} \mathbf{L}_{ij} \mathbf{y}_j = \sum_{i=1}^{n} \mathbf{r}_i.$$
Consider LHS,
$$\sum_{i=1}^{n} \sum_{\forall j : \mathbf{L}_{ij} \neq 0} \mathbf{L}_{ij} \mathbf{y}_j = \sum_{j=1}^{n} \sum_{\forall i : \mathbf{L}_{ij} \neq 0} \mathbf{L}_{ij} \mathbf{y}_j \text{ (row summation is}$$
same as the column summation)
$$= \sum_{j=1}^{n} \{ \mathbf{y}_j \sum_{\forall i : \mathbf{L}_{ij} \neq 0} \mathbf{L}_{ij} \}$$
$$= \sum_{j=1}^{n} \mathbf{y}_j \mathbf{p}_j = \mathbf{p}' \mathbf{y}$$
Therefore, $\mathbf{p}^T \mathbf{y} = \sum_{i=1}^{n} \mathbf{r}_i$ (theorem proved). $\square$

THEOREM 3. *Consider a linear system* $\hat{\mathbf{L}} * \hat{\mathbf{y}} = \mathbf{r}$, *where,* $\hat{\mathbf{L}}$ *is an error prone* $n \times n$ *sparse lower triangular matrix, i.e.,* $\mathbf{L}$ *affected by exactly one error, and* $\mathbf{r}$ *is an* $n \times 1$ *known*

vector. Let $\hat{\mathbf{y}}$ be the incorrect solution to the linear system. Then, $\mathbf{p}' \hat{\mathbf{y}} \neq \sum_{i=1}^{n} \mathbf{r}_i$.

PROOF. Consider a single error in $\mathbf{L}$ during the triangular solve. Let us assume without loss of generality that the error occurs in $\mathbf{L}_{ij}$ and $\mathbf{L}_{ij} \neq 0$. Essentially, we are solving a modified system $\hat{\mathbf{L}} \mathbf{y} = \mathbf{r}$. Let the error prone solution be $\hat{\mathbf{y}}$. We know that some of the elements in $\hat{\mathbf{y}}$ will be error prone. Let FS and CS represent sets of elements of $\hat{\mathbf{y}}$ that are affected and unaffected by the error, respectively (as in Algorithm 2). From Theorem 2 we have,

$$\mathbf{p}^T \hat{\mathbf{y}} = \sum_{i=1}^{n} \mathbf{r}_i.$$
$$\implies \sum_{\forall k : \hat{\mathbf{y}}_k \in CS} \mathbf{p}_k \hat{\mathbf{y}}_k + \sum_{\forall k : \hat{\mathbf{y}}_k \in FS} \mathbf{p}_k \hat{\mathbf{y}}_k = \sum_{i=1}^{n} \mathbf{r}_i.$$
This is equivalent to,
$$\sum_{\substack{\forall k : \hat{\mathbf{y}}_k \in CS \\ k \neq j}} \mathbf{p}_k \hat{\mathbf{y}}_k + \sum_{\substack{\forall k : \hat{\mathbf{y}}_k \in FS \\ k \neq j}} \mathbf{p}_k \hat{\mathbf{y}}_k + \mathbf{p}_j \hat{\mathbf{y}}_j = \sum_{i=1}^{n} \mathbf{r}_i. \quad (4)$$

As $\hat{\mathbf{y}}$ is the solution for $\hat{\mathbf{L}} \hat{\mathbf{y}} = \mathbf{r}$, we have $\hat{\mathbf{L}} \hat{\mathbf{y}} = \mathbf{r}$. Expanding this similar to Theorem 2, we have:
$$\sum_{j=1}^{n} \{ \hat{\mathbf{y}}_j \sum_{\forall i : \mathbf{L}_{ij} \neq 0} \hat{\mathbf{L}}_{ij} \} = \sum_{i=1}^{n} \mathbf{r}_i.$$
Hence,
$$\sum_{\substack{\forall k : \hat{\mathbf{y}}_k \in CS \\ k \neq j}} \mathbf{p}_k \hat{\mathbf{y}}_k + \sum_{\substack{\forall k : \hat{\mathbf{y}}_k \in FS \\ k \neq j}} \mathbf{p}_k \hat{\mathbf{y}}_k + \hat{\mathbf{p}}_j \hat{\mathbf{y}}_j = \sum_{i=1}^{n} \mathbf{r}_i. \quad (5)$$

Note that $\hat{\mathbf{p}}_j$ in the above equation is due an error in $\mathbf{L}_{ij}$. Equations 4 and 5 are not equal unless $\mathbf{p}_j = \hat{\mathbf{p}}_j$, hence, an error is detected as Equation 4 does not hold. This test can be used to detect an error in matrix $\mathbf{L}$. $\square$

THEOREM 4. *Consider a linear system* $\mathbf{L} * \hat{\mathbf{y}} = \mathbf{r}$, *where,* $\mathbf{L}$ *is an* $n \times n$ *sparse lower triangular matrix,* $\mathbf{r}$ *is an* $n \times 1$ *known vector and* $\hat{\mathbf{y}}$ *is the error prone solution. Then,* $\mathbf{p}^T \hat{\mathbf{y}} \neq \sum_{i=1}^{n} \mathbf{r}_i$.

PROOF. Consider a single error in $\mathbf{y}$, say, in $\mathbf{y}_j$. Let the solution be $\hat{\mathbf{y}} = [\hat{\mathbf{y}}_1, \hat{\mathbf{y}}_2, ..., \hat{\mathbf{y}}_j, ..., \hat{\mathbf{y}}_n]$. Let FS and CS represent sets of elements of $\hat{\mathbf{y}}$ that are affected and unaffected by the error, respectively. From Theorem 2 we have,

$$\mathbf{p}^T \hat{\mathbf{y}} = \sum_{i=1}^{n} \mathbf{r}_i. \quad (6)$$

Expanding the LHS of Equation 6, we have,
$$\mathbf{p}^T \hat{\mathbf{y}} = \sum_{\forall i : \hat{\mathbf{y}}_i \in CS} \mathbf{p}_i \hat{\mathbf{y}}_i + \sum_{\forall i : \hat{\mathbf{y}}_i \in FS} \mathbf{p}_i \hat{\mathbf{y}}_i.$$
$$= \sum_{\substack{\forall i : \\ \hat{\mathbf{y}}_i \in CS}} \sum_{\substack{\forall k : \\ \mathbf{L}_{ki} \neq 0}} \mathbf{L}_{ki} * \hat{\mathbf{y}}_i + \sum_{\substack{\forall i : \\ \hat{\mathbf{y}}_i \in FS}} \sum_{\substack{\forall k : \\ \mathbf{L}_{ki} \neq 0}} \mathbf{L}_{ki} * \hat{\mathbf{y}}_i$$

Since the first $j - 1$ elements of $\hat{\mathbf{y}}$ are not affected by the error, we have

$$= \sum_{k=1}^{j-1} \mathbf{r}_k + \sum_{\substack{\forall i: \\ \hat{\mathbf{y}}_i \in CS}} \sum_{\substack{\forall k: \\ k \geq j \\ \mathbf{L}_{ki} \neq 0}} \mathbf{L}_{ki} * \hat{\mathbf{y}}_i + \sum_{\substack{\forall i: \\ \hat{\mathbf{y}}_i \in FS}} \sum_{\substack{\forall k: \\ \mathbf{L}_{ki} \neq 0}} \mathbf{L}_{ki} * \hat{\mathbf{y}}_i$$

Although, we know that some elements $\hat{\mathbf{y}}_i$ for $i > j$ could be corrupt due an error in $\mathbf{y}_j$, the equations represented by $\mathbf{r}_i$ for $i > j$, still hold, i.e., $\sum_{\forall l: \mathbf{L}_{il} \neq 0} \mathbf{L}_{il} \hat{\mathbf{y}}_l = \mathbf{r}_i$ for $i > j$, hence

$$= \sum_{k=1, k \neq j}^{n} \mathbf{r}_k + \sum_{\substack{\forall i: \hat{\mathbf{y}}_i \in CS \\ \mathbf{L}_{ji} \neq 0}} \mathbf{L}_{ji} * \hat{\mathbf{y}}_i + \sum_{\substack{\forall i: \hat{\mathbf{y}}_i \in FS \\ \mathbf{L}_{ji} \neq 0}} \mathbf{L}_{ji} * \hat{\mathbf{y}}_i$$

$$= \sum_{k=1, k \neq j}^{n} \mathbf{r}_k + \sum_{\substack{\forall i: \hat{\mathbf{y}}_i \in CS \\ \mathbf{L}_{ji} \neq 0}} \mathbf{L}_{ji} * \hat{\mathbf{y}}_i + \mathbf{L}_{jj} \hat{\mathbf{y}}_j$$

$$\mathbf{p}^T \hat{\mathbf{y}} = \sum_{k=1, k \neq j}^{n} \mathbf{r}_k + \sum_{\substack{\forall i: \hat{\mathbf{y}}_i \in CS \\ \mathbf{L}_{ji} \neq 0}} \mathbf{L}_{ji} * \hat{\mathbf{y}}_i + \mathbf{L}_{jj} \hat{\mathbf{y}}_j \qquad (7)$$

Equations 6 and 7 are equivalent if

$$\mathbf{r}_j = \sum_{\substack{\forall i: \hat{\mathbf{y}}_i \in CS \\ \mathbf{L}_{ji} \neq 0}} \mathbf{L}_{ji} * \hat{\mathbf{y}}_i + \mathbf{L}_{jj} \hat{\mathbf{y}}_j.$$

However,

$$\mathbf{r}_j = \sum_{\substack{\forall i: \hat{\mathbf{y}}_i \in CS \\ \mathbf{L}_{ji} \neq 0}} \mathbf{L}_{ji} * \hat{\mathbf{y}}_i + \mathbf{L}_{jj} \mathbf{y}_j.$$

Hence, if $\hat{\mathbf{y}}_i \neq \mathbf{y}_i$, $\mathbf{p}^T \hat{\mathbf{y}} \neq \sum_{k=1}^{n} \mathbf{r}_k$. Consequently, the error will be detected. This test can be used to detect an error in the vector $\mathbf{y}$. $\square$

THEOREM 5. *Consider a linear system* $\mathbf{L} * \hat{\mathbf{y}} = \hat{\mathbf{r}}$, *where,* $\mathbf{L}$ *is an* $n \times n$ *lower triangular matrix,* $\hat{\mathbf{r}}$ *is an error prone* $n \times 1$ *known vector. Let* $\hat{\mathbf{y}}$ *be the incorrect solution to the linear system. Define an* $n \times 1$ *vector* $\mathbf{p}$, *such that,* $\mathbf{p}_j = \sum_{k=1}^{n} \mathbf{L}_{kj}$. *Then,* $\mathbf{p}^T \hat{\mathbf{y}} \neq \sum_{k=1}^{n} \mathbf{r}_k$.

PROOF. Consider a single error in $\mathbf{r}_j$ leading to an error in $\mathbf{y}_j$. The proof follows from Theorem 4. $\square$

3.4 Overheads: C-ABFT-PCG vs S-ABFT-PCG

We analyze the fault tolerance overheads of C-ABFT-PCG and S-ABFT-PCG and develop analytical models that capture these overheads. First, we define the following notation and terms that are used in our models. Subscripts b, s and c are used to denote *base*, S-ABFT-PCG, and C-ABFT-PCG methods respectively. For example, T_b represents the time to convergence of the base method. Similarly, superscripts *spmv*, *vec* and *trisol* are used to denote the SpMV, vector operations and sparse triangular solution kernels. For example, t_b^{vec}, represents the time spent in the vector operations for the base method. Let T_x^o represent the absolute overhead of method 'x' compared to the base method.

Consider the total time per iteration of PCG for each method: $T_b = t_b^{spmv} + t_b^{vec} + t_b^{trisol}$, $T_c = t_c^{spmv} + t_c^{vec} + t_c^{vec} + t_c^{trisol}$ and $T_s = t_s^{spmv} + t_s^{vec} + t_s^{vec} + t_s^{trisol}$. Note that the execution time of each kernel could vary based on

the fault tolerance method. We know that, $t_x^{spmv} = \alpha_x nnz$, $t_x^{vec} = \beta_x n$ and $t_x^{trisol} = \gamma_x nnz$, for a method 'x' and α_x, β_x and γ_x are method specific constants. Thus, we have, $T_b = \alpha_b nnz + \beta_b n + \gamma_b nnz$, $T_c = \alpha_c nnz + \beta_c n + \gamma_c nnz$ and $T_b = \alpha_s nnz + \beta_s n + \gamma_s nnz$. Now, we compute the overheads of C-ABFT-PCG as, $T_c^o = T_c - T_b = (\alpha_c - \alpha_b)nnz + (\beta_c - \beta_b)n + (\gamma_c - \gamma_b)nnz$. As C-ABFT-PCG does not protect the triangular solve operation, $\gamma_c = \gamma_b$. Thus,

$$T_c^o = (\alpha_c - \alpha_b)nnz + (\beta_c - \beta_b)n. \qquad (8)$$

For S-ABFT-PCG, $T_s^o = T_s - T_b = (\alpha_s - \alpha_b)nnz + (\beta_s - \beta_b)n + (\gamma_s - \gamma_b)nnz$. From the previous sections, we know that the encoded SpMV and sparse triangular solution operations in S-ABFT-PCG can be considered equivalent to the SpMV and sparse triangular solution operations of the base method plus some extra vector operations. Using this information, we have, $T_s^o = (\beta_s - \beta_b)n + \zeta n$, where, ζ denotes the extra vector operations. Thus,

$$T_s^o = (\zeta + \beta_s - \beta_b)n. \qquad (9)$$

Comparing Equations 8 and 9, for a large average non-zero density per row of a matrix, i.e., for large $\frac{nnz}{n}$, we expect that C-ABFT-PCG will have higher overheads than S-ABFT-PCG. This analysis considers the overheads in the event of no error. In the event of an error, C-ABFT-PCG can detect or correct a single error in SpMV without additional overheads; however, it cannot detect and correct a single error in the application of the preconditioner through sparse triangular solution. In contrast, S-ABFT-PCG will require an additional PCG iteration to correct an error that it detects, but, it guarantees detection and correction of an error in all kernels of PCG including triangular solution.

4. EXPERIMENTAL EVALUATION

We present our experimental setup in Section 4.1. In Sections 4.2 and 4.3, we present the experimental results on overheads for error-free and a single error prone instances of PCG. We compare overheads for S-ABFT-PCG relative to PCG implementation with no ABFT and C-ABFT-PCG.

4.1 Experimental Setup

We use PCG with incomplete Cholesky preconditioner with thresholding [21] as a representative iterative linear solver. We evaluate the runtime of PCG using C-ABFT-PCG and S-ABFT-PCG techniques. We use 20 SPD matrices from The University of Florida Sparse Matrix Collection [22]. Table 1 lists the properties of the these matrices. The first column represents matrix ids and the second column gives matrix names. The third and fourth columns represent, respectively, the matrix dimension and number of non-zero elements in the matrix.

4.2 Overheads for Error-Free PCG instances

We present experimental results comparing C-ABFT-PCG and S-ABFT-PCG to traditional PCG without fault tolerance. We refer to the PCG implementation without fault tolerance as our *base scheme*. Figure 8 shows the relative performance degradation of three different fault tolerant techniques with respect to the base scheme. The technique, S-ABFT-SpMV-PCG, refers to our S-ABFT-PCG with no

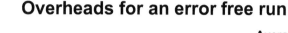

Overheads for an error free run

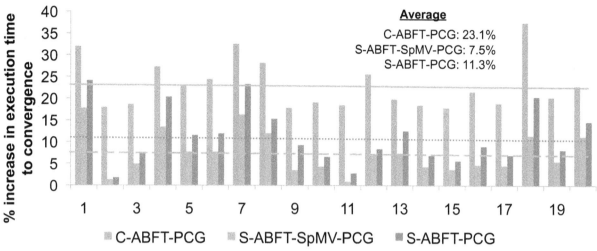

Average
C-ABFT-PCG: 23.1%
S-ABFT-SpMV-PCG: 7.5%
S-ABFT-PCG: 11.3%

■ C-ABFT-PCG　■ S-ABFT-SpMV-PCG　■ S-ABFT-PCG

Figure 8: Performance degradation due to overheads of ABFT, in terms of the percentage increase in execution time to convergence.

Matrix ID	Matrix	N	NNZ
1	cvxbqp1	50,000	349,968
2	crankseg_1	52,804	10,614,210
3	nasasrb	54,870	2,677,324
4	Andrews	60,000	760,154
5	qa8fm	66,127	1,660,579
6	cfd1	70,656	1,828,364
7	finan512	74,752	596,992
8	thermal1	82,654	574,458
9	consph	83,334	6,010,480
10	s3dkq4m2	90,449	4,820,891
11	shipsec8	114,919	6,653,399
12	ship_003	121,728	8,086,034
13	cfd2	123,440	3,087,898
14	boneS01	127,224	6,715,152
15	shipsec1	140,874	7,813,404
16	Dubcova3	146,689	3,636,649
17	shipsec5	179,860	10,113,096
18	thermomech_dM	204,316	1,423,116
19	hood	220,542	10,768,436
20	offshore	259,789	4,242,673

Table 1: The UFL benchmark matrices with their dimension (N) and number of non-zeroes (NNZ).

fault tolerance for the sparse triangular solution operation. This technique gives a fair comparison between S-ABFT and C-ABFT as both protect the same kernels (SpMV and vector operations) within PCG, whereas, S-ABFT-PCG protects all kernels within PCG, including sparse triangular solution. Observe that fault tolerance overheads for an error free run can be as high as 37.4%, 17.8% and 24.1% for C-ABFT-PCG, S-ABFT-SpMV-PCG and S-ABFT-PCG techniques, respectively. The average fault tolerance overheads are 23.1%, 7.5% and 11.3%, for C-ABFT-PCG, S-ABFT-

SpMV-PCG and S-ABFT-PCG techniques, respectively, as indicated by the horizontal lines.

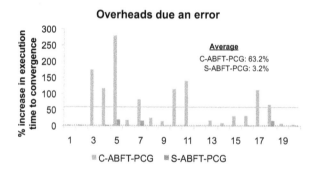

Average
C-ABFT-PCG: 63.2%
S-ABFT-PCG: 3.2%

■ C-ABFT-PCG　■ S-ABFT-PCG

Figure 9: Percentage increase in execution times of PCG due to a single error in sparse triangular solution. The increase in execution time is from a corresponding increase in the number of iterations to convergence.

4.3 Overheads for Single Error PCG instances

We now evaluate the benefits to the performance of PCG in the event of a single error. Recall that differential impacts are expected only for errors in the triangular solve kernel because both C-ABFT-PCG and S-ABFT-PCG can detect and recover from an error in SpMV. Results in [9] indicate that the component in which error occur impacts convergence, with greatest degradations corresponding to rows with high norm values. In Figure 9, we report the maximum observed performance degradation of C-ABFT-PCG and S-ABFT-PCG with an error in the component corresponding to a median value of the row norm during sparse triangular solution. Observe that C-ABFT-PCG can have significantly high performance degradation of over 250% increase in iteration counts in the worst case and 63.2% on average. Overheads of S-ABFT-PCG are 3.2% on average for recovering from the error by recomputing one iteration of PCG.

5. CONCLUSION AND FUTURE WORK

Resiliency is a key issue as we move toward peta-to-exascale HPC systems that are expected to encounter multiple faults within a day [23], with faults ranging from fail-stop failures to silent errors. A natural concern is the vulnerability of long running scientific applications on such HPC systems, often involving computations with very large sparse matrices [8]. Such applications can benefit from algorithm-based fault tolerance (ABFT) techniques that offer detection and recovery from errors at the expense of low overheads. Although ABFT techniques have been developed for dense matrix operations, they have been largely ignored for sparse matrix operations.

We consider sparse linear system solution using preconditioned conjugate gradients, a popular choice when the coefficient matrix is sparse and symmetric positive definite. We develop a new sparse checksum encoded algorithm-based fault tolerant PCG, S-ABFT-PCG, that can provably detect a single error in the data for PCG when the matrix is strictly diagonally dominant. Our approach trades-off the ability to correct a single error in the data in favor of lower overheads per PCG iteration at the expense of recomputing a single PCG iteration when an error occurs. Our experimental evaluations indicate that in the event of no errors, compared to a PCG with no ABFT, the overheads of S-ABFT-PCG are 11.3% on average. For comparison, the overheads of applying the classical ABFT to the SpMV kernel of PCG, C-ABFT-PCG, are on average higher at 23.1%. Furthermore, in the event of a single error in the application of the preconditioner through triangular solution, C-ABFT-PCG suffers from significant increases in iteration counts to convergence, with overheads of 63.2% on average compared to 3.2% on average for S-ABFT-PCG. Our evaluations motivate the need for further study of algorithm-based fault tolerance approaches for widely used sparse computations in large-scale computational modeling and simulation software.

6. REFERENCES

[1] "http://www.nccs.gov/jaguar/."
[2] "http://en.wikipedia.org/wiki/ibm_sequoia."
[3] G. Bronevetsky and B. de Supinski, "Soft error vulnerability of iterative linear algebra methods," in *ICS*, 2008, pp. 155–164.
[4] K.-H. Huang and J. Abraham, "Algorithm-based fault tolerance for matrix operations," *IEEE Trans. on Computers*, vol. C-33, no. 6, pp. 518 –528, June 1984.
[5] F. T. Luk and H. Park, "An analysis of algorithm-based fault tolerance techniques," *J. Parallel Distrib. Comput.*, vol. 5, pp. 172–184, April 1988.
[6] Z. Chen and J. Dongarra, "Algorithm-based fault tolerance for fail-stop failures," *IEEE Trans. Parallel Distrib. Syst.*, vol. 19, pp. 1628–1641, December 2008.
[7] Y.-M. Yeh and T. yun Feng, "Algorithm-based fault tolerance for matrix inversion with maximum pivoting," *Journal of Parallel and Distributed Computing*, vol. 14, no. 4, pp. 373 – 389, 1992.
[8] M. A. Heroux, P. Raghavan, and H. D. Simon, *Parallel Processing for Scientific Computing (Software, Environments and Tools)*. Philadelphia, PA, USA: Society for Industrial and Applied Mathematics, 2006.
[9] M. Shantharam, S. Srinivasmurthy, and P. Raghavan, "Characterizing the impact of soft errors on iterative methods in scientific computing," in *ICS*, 2011, pp. 152–161.
[10] K. Malkowski, P. Raghavan, and M. T. Kandemir, "Analyzing the soft error resilience of linear solvers on multicore multiprocessors," in *IPDPS*, 2010, pp. 1–12.
[11] R. D. Schlichting and F. B. Schneider, "Fail-stop processors: an approach to designing fault-tolerant computing systems," *ACM Trans. Comput. Syst.*, vol. 1, pp. 222–238, August 1983.
[12] Z. Chen and J. Dongarra, "Highly scalable self-healing algorithms for high performance scientific computing," *IEEE Trans. Comput.*, vol. 58, pp. 1512–1524, November 2009.
[13] G. Bronevetsky, K. Pingali, and P. Stodghill, "Experimental evaluation of application-level checkpointing for openmp programs," in *ICS*, 2006, pp. 2–13.
[14] J. Anfinson and F. T. Luk, "A linear algebraic model of algorithm-based fault tolerance," *IEEE Trans. Comput.*, vol. 37, pp. 1599–1604, December 1988.
[15] A. Roy-Chowdhury and P. Banerjee, "A fault-tolerant parallel algorithm for iterative solution of the laplace equation," *Parallel Processing, International Conference on*, vol. 3, pp. 133–140, 1993.
[16] P. Banerjee, J. Rahmeh, C. Stunkel, V. Nair, K. Roy, V. Balasubramanian, and J. Abraham, "Algorithm-based fault tolerance on a hypercube multiprocessor," *Computers, IEEE Transactions on*, vol. 39, no. 9, pp. 1132 –1145, Sep 1990.
[17] Y.-H. Choi and M. Malek, "A fault-tolerant fft processor," *IEEE Trans. Comput.*, vol. 37, pp. 617–621, May 1988.
[18] J.-L. Sung and G. R. Redinbo, "Algorithm-based fault tolerant synthesis for linear operations," *IEEE Trans. Comput.*, vol. 45, pp. 425–438, April 1996.
[19] J. N. Glosli, D. F. Richards, K. J. Caspersen, R. E. Rudd, J. A. Gunnels, and F. H. Streitz, "Extending stability beyond cpu millennium: a micron-scale atomistic simulation of kelvin-helmholtz instability," in *SC*, 2007, pp. 58:1–58:11.
[20] A. George and J. Liu, *Computer Solution of Large Sparse Positive Definite Systems*. Prentice Hall, 1981.
[21] I. Lee, P. Raghavan, and E. G. Ng, "Effective preconditioning through ordering interleaved with incomplete factorization," *SIAM J. Matrix Anal. Appl.*, vol. 27, pp. 1069–1088, December 2005.
[22] T. Davis, "The University of Florida Sparse Matrix Collection," *NA Digest*, vol. 97, 1997.
[23] F. Cappello, A. Geist, B. Gropp, L. Kale, B. Kramer, and M. Snir, "Toward exascale resilience," *Int. J. High Perform. Comput. Appl.*, vol. 23, pp. 374–388, November 2009.

Data-driven Fault Tolerance for Work Stealing Computations

Wenjing Ma
Comp. Sci. and Math. Div.
Pacific Northwest National Lab
wenjing.ma@pnnl.gov

Sriram Krishnamoorthy
Comp. Sci. and Math. Div.
Pacific Northwest National Lab
sriram@pnnl.gov

ABSTRACT

Work stealing is a promising technique to dynamically tolerate variations in the execution environment, including faults, system noise, and energy constraints. In this paper, we present fault tolerance mechanisms for task parallel computations, a popular computation idiom, employing work stealing. The computation is organized as a collection of tasks with data in a global address space. The completion of data operations, rather than the actual messages, is tracked to derive an idempotent data store. This information is also used to accurately identify the tasks to be re-executed in the presence of random work stealing. We consider three recovery schemes that present distinct trade-offs — lazy recovery with potentially increased re-execution cost, immediate collective recovery with associated synchronization overheads, and noncollective recovery enabled by additional communication. We employ distributed-memory work stealing to dynamically rebalance the tasks onto the live processes and evaluate the three schemes using candidate application benchmarks. We demonstrate that the overheads (space and time) of the fault tolerance mechanism are low, the costs incurred due to failures are small, and the overheads decrease with per-process work at scale.

Categories and Subject Descriptors

C.4.2 [**Computer Systems Organization**]: Performance of Systems—*Fault tolerance*; C.4.6 [**Computer Systems Organization**]: Performance of Systems—*Reliability, availability, and serviceability*

Keywords

fault tolerance, load balancing, work stealing

1. INTRODUCTION

As the component count of large-scale systems increases, the mean time between failures (MTBF) plummets, and will soon result in MTBFs becoming less than the typical application execution time. This has necessitated application design principles that consider faults as common occur-

rences rather than rare events that can be ignored or handled through expensive mechanisms.

The traditional approach to fault tolerance employs coordinate checkpoint coupled with collective restart. Uncoordinated techniques employ message logging to avoid the need for collective synchronization to derive a consistent checkpoint. These approaches introduce synchronization costs or message logging overheads. More importantly, collective restart approaches typically roll back all processes to the previous consistent checkpoint in the event of a failure. These overheads increase with process count, making them prohibitively expensive on large systems [11].

Dynamic load balancing through work stealing involves an idle process randomly stealing work from another active process. Work stealing offers a natural approach to even out variations in the parallel execution environment introduced by effects such as system noise, energy or temperature constraints, or faults. It has been well researched in terms of space and time overheads, synchronization costs, and parallelizability in shared memory and distributed memory contexts [15, 27].

In this paper, we present data driven approaches to tolerate faults in task parallel computations employing work stealing. Task parallelism — computation organized as a collection of parallel tasks — is a popular idiom commonly found in applications and supported in parallel languages and runtime libraries.

In this paper, we describe an approach to fault tolerance for task parallel computations in the presence of work stealing that does not require frequent synchronizations, message logging, or rolling back all processes to a prior consistent state. Using an active message implementation, we track ongoing and completed communication operations. In addition to creating an *idempotent data store*, which enables re-execution of tasks without affecting correctness, the mechanisms support accurate and efficient determination of tasks to be re-executed in the event of a failure. We identify the causes for re-execution and present techniques to efficiently determine the groups of tasks associated with each such cause.

We present alternative recovery mechanisms that expose the trade-offs in the costs incurred. The three algorithms presented employ lazy recovery that minimizes execution time overhead while potentially resulting in increased re-execution, collective immediate recovery which incurs the cost to synchronize all live processes, and noncollective recovery that requires additional communication operations throughout the execution.

Our algorithms exhibit good performance on two candidate application benchmarks. In the absence of faults, the proposed algorithms incur an overhead up to 4% as compared to a non-fault-tolerant implementation. Failure of one node introduces an additional overhead of 4% on average, which varies depending on the point of failure and the algorithm employed.

2. COMPUTATION MODEL

Work stealing involves processes, equivalently threads in a multi-threaded environment, switching between worker and thief roles. A worker actively executes tasks from a local efficiently accessible collection of tasks. When a worker runs out of local tasks, it becomes a thief trying to steal tasks from other workers. Random work stealing has been actively studied in both shared memory and distributed memory systems to minimize task creation costs, synchronization overheads, and space bounds [10, 16, 27].

Collections of parallel tasks constitutes common computation idiom widely observed in scientific applications. While not sufficient to express dependences, the idiom's importance is illustrated by the support for parallel loops, iterators, slices, and task parallel regions in parallel programming models such as TBB [25], OpenMP [1], X10 [7], and Chapel [6]. In this paper, we present mechanisms to tolerate faults for work stealing computations on parallel task collections.

The algorithms presented are designed and evaluated in a distributed memory work stealing framework. A function pointer and task-specific information, encapsulated in a task descriptor uniquely describe a task. A collection of such tasks, coupled with global information shared amongst all tasks in the collection, constitutes the computation of interest. Rather than assuming a functional task execution model, in which the tasks execute without side-effects, we tackle the scenario typical in scientific applications — tasks operating on parallel data structures. To enable task migration in a distributed memory setting, these data structures are constructed in a globally accessible address space. Any worker can obtain the inputs and communicate the outputs in global data structures as part of a task's execution. The task collection is executed using a distributed memory work stealing model until termination is detected. Barring the output to the global address space, the tasks are side-effect free. While seemingly severe, note that local data can often be placed in global address space but directly accessed locally.

All communication and work stealing operations in the computation are performed using active messages [28], with callback functions executed on the remote node. This simplifies the data structures employed and allows coalescing of multiple messages and lock operations, as compared to an algorithm restricted to remote memory operations [10]. While flexible, the active message model also supports efficient zero-copy data transfer.

In addition to *putting* data, which involves copying local data to global memory, tasks are allowed to contribute their outputs through these active messages. This functionality, equivalent to inlets in Cilk [16], greatly increases the flexibility provided and the challenge faced in ensuring fault tolerance.

We do not require the tasks to be explicitly enumerated — they could be arbitrary random-access iterators [25], that en-able a task descriptor to be recreated from an index. This is required only when recovering from a fault, allowing the use of an efficient sequential iterator in the place of a random-access iterator.

We assume a fail-stop failure model in which a worker stops execution once it fails, never to rejoin the computation. Several techniques exist to recover the data in the global address space, including checkpointing (possibly in-memory) or checksumming of individual data structures. These can be employed to recover the loss of any state available prior to execution of the tasks, including global data and the collection of tasks. We focus on the complementary problem of fault tolerance within a task parallel phase.

When simulating failures, a process marked as failed notifies one arbitrary other process before turning *mute*. Once mute, the process waits for termination detection and does not participate in the computation. The data and the task queue on the failed process are assumed to be unavailable subsequent to the failure.

This work complements efforts on fault detection. In particular, we assume a mechanism to notify different layers of the software stack of a failure and enable continued execution in a well-defined state. The fault tolerance support proposed in the MPI-3 standard should provide us with one such substrate.

3. PROBLEM STATEMENT

Given such a computation model, the objective is to ensure continued execution to successful completion of tasks in the presence of failures. In this paper, we focus on tolerating the loss of state with respect to the control system responsible for the task queues and their execution state, including any updates to global data performed as part of the execution of tasks. We would like to achieve fault tolerance with minimal overheads including communication (such as duplicating data communication and tracking task completion) and memory consumption (such as duplicating modified data structures and operations on them). Several questions need to be answered in tolerating faults in such a computation:

1. How to identify the tasks to re-execute to recover the lost data?
2. How to find and recover partial data updates due to a failure during the execution of a task?
3. How to correctly identify tasks enqueued on the failed process in the presence of work stealing?
4. How to efficiently recover from faults with minimal performance degradation?
5. How to minimize overheads in the normal non-fault execution path?

4. IDEMPOTENT DATA STRUCTURES

When a process fails, it could be running a task that has already updated some of the outputs. Re-execution of these tasks will result in such data regions being updated with the output from the task multiple times. Operations such as *put*, possibly using network-supported RDMA mechanisms, are idempotent with multiple updates producing the same result. However, duplicated non-idempotent operations can lead to incorrect results. Examples of such operations include operations that add to the result or invoke an arbitrary function, such as a Cilk inlet.

We overcome this challenge by tracking updates using non-idempotent operations, i.e., anything beyond gets or puts, to global data structures. Duplicated updates from the same task to the same data regions are identified and ignored.

A *marker* identifies update operations from a task's execution. The marker protocol guarantees that an update operation is reflected as a marker before the update begins. This ensures correct identification of data corrupted as a result of ongoing update operations from a failed process.

Intuitively, the markers can be organized as a matrix of size $N \times M$, where N is the number of tasks, and M is the total number of data regions in global space. On a failure, the markers help deduce which tasks modified what data regions, and the status of each such data region. If a data region is to be updated by a task, but its status shows that it is not updated, or the task has not finished updating that region, the data need to be restored to the initial state, and the task re-executed.

However, there are several issues with a direct implementation of such an approach that hinder scalability. First, if a data region has partial updates, all the tasks that have updated that region need to be re-executed, even though the data region is on a live process. Second, the marker needs to be updated before the communication operation, so that all data updates are accurately reflected in the event of a failure. This requires an expensive fence operation before each data communication. Third, the marker matrix is space inefficient, quickly becoming large with increase in the number of data regions. Fourth, determining the set of processes the tasks communicate with would require re-executing every task.

We address these challenges through several improvements. First, we colocate the markers with their associated data regions. This precludes any "dirty" data, data whose state is not known, since any data alive after a fault will have its corresponding markers, eliminating the need to roll back all updates on such data.

Second, the data, together with the markers, are updated using active messages. The sequential execution of the active message elides the fence operation, while the colocation ensures that any live data also has its markers. More importantly, it coalesces the marker operation with the data update operation, eliminating the need for additional communication operations.

Third, rather than associate markers with data regions, we track the update operations initiated during each task's execution. A sequence number is associated with each update operation for a task. These sequence numbers are stored in a collection at the target process, which significantly reduces the space overhead, proportional to the number of update operations rather than the number of data regions.

Fourth, in addition to individual sequence numbers employed as update markers, we store the total number of update operations. On a failure, whether a task's execution updated data on one of the failed processes can be computed by comparing this total count with the number of update markers recorded for this task on all the live processes. When not all markers are found, one or more updates from the task were lost. This scheme avoids the need to re-execute tasks to determine whether a given task performed an update to any lost data.

Combining these improvements, each process maintains

```
int nUpdates; //#updates in ongoing task execution
map<int,int> MarkerTotal; //map task id to #updates
map<int,set<int>> UpdateSet; //incoming updates

on start of task execution ():
   nUpdates=0

on each task update(proc,updateOp,taskId) :
   piggyBackAm(proc,updateOp,taskId,nUpdates)
   nUpdates+=1

on task completion (taskId) :
   MarkerTotal[taskId] = nUpdates

piggyBackAm(proc,updateOp,taskId,seqNumber):
   @proc :
      /*executed on remote process proc*/
      updateOp()
      UpdateSet[taskId].insert(seqNumber)
```

Figure 1: Marker management protocol through piggybacking on user-initiated active message

two data structures associated with the marker information. Every process stores the total number of update operations it initiated, for each task it executed. For each incoming update operation, the process also stores the operation's sequence number in a map with the corresponding task identifier.

A user-level operation on the data structure can translate into multiple update operations. For example, an update to a portion of an array distributed on multiple processes could result in several communication operations. Constraints on the communication libraries in terms of size and count of buffers they employ could further split a communication operation. In order to handle these constraints, the sequence numbers are managed at the lowest level of the communication substrate — a single active message.

Figure 1 shows the various operations involved in the management of the markers. The number of update operations initiated by each task is maintained locally by the executing process. This count is used as the sequence number for the update operation. The sequence number for incoming active messages is updated by piggybacking the marker operation on the active message initiated by application action. Thus the additional communication cost is minimized. On completion of the task's execution, the total number of updates is stored locally.

5. RESILIENT TASK COLLECTIONS

In the event of a failure, the tasks in the task collection can be classified into the following categories.

XS: Tasks executed by live processes, successfully finished without data/meta-data loss

XD: Tasks executed by live processes, but with data/meta-data loss

XF: Tasks executed by failed processes

NL: Tasks enqueued on live processes

NF: Tasks enqueued on failed processes

Tasks in these categories are illustrated in Figure 2, on three processes (process k failed, while processes i and j are live), each with its own task queue. The head pointer iden-

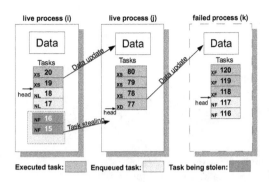

Figure 2: Classification of tasks when one of three processes fail, together with locally stored portion of global data and tasks. The classification for each task is shown next to the task identifier. Dashed boxes indicate tasks "in-flight" due to a steal operation

tifies the position in the queue that splits the executed and enqueued tasks, which are numbered using their identifiers. Tasks 15 and 16 are being migrated between processes as part of an ongoing steal operation. Tasks executed by live processes that did not perform any updates on the failed process (category XS, eg., task 19) and tasks enqueued on live processes (category NL, eg., task 17) do not require re-execution or any restoration of the book-keeping. Upon restoration of the data on the failed nodes, tasks executed by live processes that contributed to data on the failed ones (category XD, eg., task 77) need to be re-executed to update their contributions to the data structures on the failed nodes. The idempotent global data structures enable selective updates to the restored data, so that duplicated updates are avoided. Tasks enqueued on the failed processes at the time of the failure (category NF, eg., task 117) need to be identified and populated on the queues of the live processes. Tasks executed by the failed processes (category XF, eg., task 120) also need to be identified and re-executed by a live process. Task stolen by failed processes can be considered as being enqueued on the failed processes (category NF) and recovered accordingly. Any tasks successfully stolen from a failed node are classified into categories XS, XD, or NL, depending on their execution status. Therefore the categories presented above include tasks participating in ongoing steal operations (eg., tasks 15 and 16).

Successful recovery of the task collection state involves accurate identification of tasks in these categories. The idempotent data stores make the mis-identification of executed tasks as enqueued tasks a performance and not a correctness criterion. Partially executed tasks on the failed node will need to be correctly identified as tasks enqueued on or executed by the failed node rather than as completed tasks. Enqueued tasks need to be correctly identified so they are executed at least once.

We consider two points of recovery — lazy and immediate. Lazy recovery ignores failures until all available tasks are executed, at which point recovery is attempted if failures were detected during the task parallel execution. In the immedi-

ate recovery model, the live processes recover immediately upon notification of failure, identifying and redistributing the tasks, before continuing execution.

5.1 Collective Recovery — Lazy vs Immediate

The markers corresponding to each task are reduced using the following expression:

$$\text{sum}_t = \text{MarkerTotal}_t + \text{queue}_t - |\text{UpdateSet}_t|$$

where MarkerTotal_t is one more than the number of update operations performed during task t's execution. queue_t is max if task t is in the current task queue of this process, zero otherwise. max is a value larger than the largest possible value take by MarkerTotal. The checks for the tasks are partitioned amongst the processes with each process computing the sum for a disjoint subset of the tasks. Note that valid values for MarkerTotal_t are constrained to be either 0 (the task has not been executed and no entry exists in the set) or positive (number of updates plus one), and it is set exactly once per task.

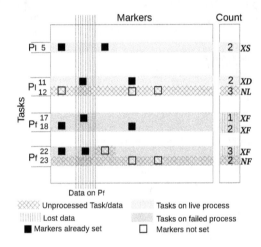

Figure 3: Status of data and meta-data after failure

We now associate the anticipated values of the sum_t to the various categories of tasks presented earlier. The categories are illustrated using the tasks shown in Figure 3. The filled squares denote data and corresponding markers that are already set, while hollow squares indicate incomplete or anticipated update operations. Note that the anticipated update operations are only shown for illustration and are not known at runtime until the tasks initiate the operations. A column corresponds to data and markers on each process. Pf is a failed process, all of whose data and markers are lost. The tasks executed by Pf, together with the data contained in Pf are shown in the figure. Similar information is depicted for a live process Pl. The figure also shows each tasks' classification into the categories, as explained below.

1. sum_t=max: When the task is in some live process' queue, it contributes max to the reduction. Without such a contribution, by construction, sum_t will be less than max. Therefore, tasks satisfying this condition are classified into category NL (in some live process' queue) and are not considered for re-execution. Task 12 in Figure 3 is an example of such a task.

2. $\text{sum}_t \in [2, \text{max}-1]$: This condition is valid for a task when it is not in any live process' queue ($\text{queue}_t=0$), has been executed by a live process providing the positive contribution to the reduction, but not all updates are available. Such tasks are classified into category XD, with some lost data and are enqueued for re-execution. Task 11 in the figure falls into this category.

3. $\text{sum}_t=1$: This condition implies that the task is not in any live process' queue, some of the markers exist, and the process that executed the task is alive. As mentioned above, MarkerTotal_t is one plus the total number of data updates. If all updates were not to live processes, MarkerTotal_t will exceed 1. Thus tasks satisfying this condition are those executed by live processes with updates to only live processes (category XS). No further action is required for these tasks. Task 5 in the figure is an example of this case.

4. $\text{sum}_t=0$: Given that an executed task registers a positive count, this equality identifies tasks that have no markers, no count, and are not in any live process' queue. This implies either a task that is enqueued on a failed process (category NF), illustrated by task 23 in the figure, or a task executed by a failed process with all its update contained in failed processes, illustrated by task 17 in the figure. Since an executed task all of whose updates and meta-data are lost cannot be distinguished from a non-executed task, tasks satisfying this equality are classified to be category NF and are enqueued for re-execution.

5. $\text{sum}_t<0$: This condition is true when the task is not in any live process' task queue and the count is lost. Such a scenario, illustrated by tasks 18 and 22 in the figure, occurs for tasks executed by a failed process. Note that while task 18 has completed its execution, task 22 crashed without completing its updates. The idempotent data stores ensure that such tasks are also identified as failed tasks. This condition identifies all such tasks in category XF, which are then enqueued for re-execution by live processes.

Thus tasks in all categories are correctly identified by the observed values in the reduction. Most importantly, these conditions provide an assertional mechanism to verify the state of the computation and do not depend on the order of operations. In particular, evaluating the reductions does not require ongoing data transfer and steal operations to be stalled, canceled, or completed. Any markers not included in the reduction, possibly due to them being in flight, only result in the relevant task being marked as incompletely executed, requiring re-execution. Any stolen tasks in flight will not appear in any live process' task queue and will be classified into category NF. This will lead to redundant execution of these tasks, but will not result in incorrect execution. Flushing of ongoing communication can alleviate these challenges, but is a performance rather than a correctness constraint.

Failures encountered during the recovery are handled by initiating another round of recovery involving the processes that are still alive. The procedure does not suffer from any single point of failure and can tolerate arbitrary number of failures, assuming at least one process remains alive to continue the execution.

Lazy Recovery: Under lazy recovery, failures are ignored while in the task parallel phase. On termination detection, recovery is initiated using the reduction describe above, if any failures were observed during the execution of the phase just terminated. The tasks to re-execute are distributed amongst the live processes, which re-enter the task parallel phase. This continues until a phase is terminated without any failures. Note that no tasks remain in the queue of any live processes when lazy recovery is undertaken. Failures require recovery of lost global data from stable storage (in-memory copy, checkpoint, checksum) before the tasks can continue execution.

Immediate recovery: Lazy recovery enables collective recovery of data when no tasks are being executed, potentially simplifying the recovery. However, after a failure, the live processes continue executing tasks, even those that contribute to data on the failed process. These tasks will need to be re-executed after the lost data is restored. Thus lazy recovery potentially incurs increased re-execution costs. The immediate recovery algorithm notifies all processes of a failure immediately upon detection. The notification is broadcast using active messages. All processes, when notified of a failure, enter the recovery phase, perform the reduction and classify the tasks as described above. Unlike lazy recovery, tasks in the live process' queue are encountered and classified into category NL, as described above.

5.2 Noncollective Recovery

In both algorithms above, a reduction operation among all live processes is required. In this section, we present a noncollective recovery algorithm in which global recovery is achieved by each process independently acting on a fault notification.

In addition to the markers associated with update operations, we employ two data structures. First, we replace the total number of update operations per task (MarkerTotal in the discussion above) by the set of processes containing the update operations. Second, we define a home for each task. The completion of a task's execution, by any process, is reported to the task's home.

The modifications to the task execution procedure shown in Figure 1 for the noncollective recovery mechanism are presented in Figure 4. piggyBackAm is the mechanism to manage markers together with the update operation in the same active message. home() is a method to determine the home process for each task. It could be the result of pre-computed task distribution, or a function that evenly divides the total number of tasks amongst the processes. On each process, HomedTasks maintains the status of processes that executed the tasks homed on that process.

Compared to the collective recovery model, this approach incurs higher space overheads due to storage of the set of processes communicated to for each task and the home information. An additional communication call is introduced to maintain the status of task completion on the home node. We choose the home of each task to be the process on which it is enqueued at the start of the task parallel phase. This minimizes the number of communications to only the stolen tasks, potentially reducing the communication overhead introduced.

On notification of failure, each process looks up its local records to evaluate the following conditions:

1. $\text{TaskRecord}[t] \cap \text{FailedSet} = \emptyset$: These are tasks that have not incurred any failures and belong to category XS.

2. $\text{TaskRecord}[t] \cap \text{FailedSet} \neq \emptyset$: If a task t executed by a process contributed an update to one of the failed processes, it is classified into category XD and populated into the local task queue for re-execution.

```
int nUpdates; //#updates in ongoing task execution
map<int, set<int>> TaskRecord; //set of processes
    communicated to for each task
map<int,int> HomedTasks; //map of homed task ids to
    their executors

on start of task execution ():
  nUpdates=0

on each task update(proc,updateOp,taskId) :
  piggyBackAm(proc,updateOp,taskId,nUpdates)
  TaskRecord[taskId].insert(proc)
  nUpdates+=1

on task completion (taskId) :
  @home(taskId): /*executed as an active message*/
    HomedTasks[taskId] = me //initiator of the active
        msg

piggyBackAm(proc,updateOp,taskId,seqNumber):
  @proc: /*executed on remote process proc*/
    updateOp()
    UpdateSet[taskId].insert(seqNumber)
```

Figure 4: Marker management with noncollective recovery

3. HomeTasks[t] ∈ FailedSet: These tasks were executed by a failed process, precluding verification of their TaskRecord. They are classified into category NF and are marked for re-execution.

4. home(t) ∈ FailedSet: All processes are assumed to know the initial distribution of tasks. On a failure, all tasks homed on a failed process are entered into the task queue on its mirror, which now becomes the home for all such tasks. The mirrors can be specified by a simple function, such as shift by a constant that is co-prime to the number of processes. This ensures successful execution even if only one process is alive.

5. Enqueued on this process: These tasks, classified into category NL, are executed as without failures.

6. Termination and HomeTasks[t]=null: These are tasks that were not executed by any process when termination was detected. Such tasks are classified to be enqueued on the failed processes (category NF). These tasks are reseeded into the queue for another round of execution to complete the task parallel phase.

We now discuss the key properties of the algorithm. Formal proofs are not presented due to space limitations. A task could satisfy many of these conditions. If a task satisfies any of the above conditions that require re-execution, it is enqueued for re-execution. Unlike in the collective algorithms, the markers only contribute to the idempotence of the data structure and not to the task collection's recovery. In addition, an additional round of execution is required to complete execution if any tasks satisfy condition 6.

We observe that all failed tasks are recovered as long as all processes are eventually notified of all faults. Since fail-stop failures are stable duplicated notifications of the same fault can be ignored. Conditions 2, 3, 4, and 6 ensure re-execution of all tasks with any failures. These correspond to cases with lost data, lost executor, lost home, or lost owner

(process on whose tasks queue it belonged) for a given task, respectively. These can be independently verified by the processes involved (executor, home, and mirror), possibly at different points in time. The actions for the different failure scenarios for a given executed task are shown below:

Process state			Action
Executor	Home	DataOwner	
live	live	live	Ignore (category XS)
live	live	failed	Enqueued by executor
*	failed	*	Enqueued by mirror
failed	live	*	Enqueued by home

We observe that need for re-execution of an executed task is identified by at least one process, which adds the identified task to its own queue. A task homed on a failed node could have been stolen and reside in a live process' queue. Such tasks could be redundantly executed by multiple live processes. This is a potentially significant additional overhead as compared to the collective recovery schemes. This is also the only case of duplicated re-execution.

Any meta-data operations in flight will be considered as being lost and the corresponding tasks enqueued for re-execution. Similar treatment is rendered to stolen tasks in flight. Pending communication operations during recovery are therefore a performance and not a correctness issue.

Note that local addition of tasks by a process performing noncollective recovery appear unforeseen and complicate termination detection. For example, a process could detect a failure after termination has been detected by some other processes and the notification is being broadcast. Some of the processes might leave such a computation while a process is still recovering from the observed failure. Such left-over tasks are parceled into the additional round required by this algorithm, necessitated by condition 6.

6. EXPERIMENTAL EVALUATION

We evaluated the proposed schemes using two benchmarks. Self Consistent Field (SCF) is a widely used kernel that forms the initial stage of many *ab initio* quantum chemistry simulations. Tensor Contraction Expressions (TCE) constitute the Coupled Cluster methods, employed in accurate descriptions of many-body systems in electronic structure calculations. Both benchmarks involve parallel task collections with tasks of widely varying computation requirements. The data is obtained from and results updated in global address space, through active messages over MPI.

Unlike SCF, whose execution times showed little variation, TCE showed nontrivial variance. We therefore report the average over five runs, together with minimum and maximum times as error bars, for the execution times for the TCE benchmark.

The tests are conducted on NERSC Hopper, a Cray XE6 system. Each compute node consists of two 12-core AMD "MagnyCours" 2.1-GHz CPUs, connected with "Gemini" interconnect.

All results presented in this paper rely on an active message implementation on MPI. In particular, we employ a multi-threaded configuration with one process per SMP node and one thread per core. Each thread maintains its local queue of tasks and participates in random work stealing. We evaluated several configurations and report results for the configuration that produced the best performance for the non-fault-tolerant version of both benchmarks — one process per node with 23 worker threads, each pinned to a core, performing application work and one helper thread serving incoming active message requests. For SCF, we used between 200 and 1600 nodes for the tests. For TCE, we used 100 and 800 nodes. In the figures and tables, we denote the number of cores, as the number of nodes multiplied by 24.

A node is considered as the unit of failure with all threads in the node failing simultaneously. Failures are simulated with the "failed" processes notifying process 0 at the point of failure. Subsequently, the failed processes wait for termination of the task parallel phase, without executing incoming active messages except to vote for termination detection. The global data, matrices in SCF and tensors in TCE, were backed up in memory to enable continued execution after failure.

We consider three different failure points: (a) beginning — the chosen processes fail after executing one task; (b) middle — the chosen processes fail at roughly the mid-point in their execution; (c) end — where the failure is simulated upon termination detection. Failure at the "middle" is simulated by estimating the total execution time with a prior run, followed by failure notification at roughly the midpoint of execution. Note that the actual midpoint could be altered by stealing or long running tasks, which are not interrupted.

In the figures and tables, *Lazy*, *Imm*, and *Noncoll* denote lazy, immediate, and noncollective recovery, respectively. *beg*, *mid*, and *end* denote failures at the beginning, middle, and end of execution.

6.1 Single-node Failure

Figures 5 and 6 show the execution times for the various schemes and failure points on different numbers of cores for SCF and TCE, respectively. The figures include execution times for the benchmark with no additions to support fault tolerance. Since the non-fault execution of the two collective schemes is identical, they are depicted once.

For SCF, the fault tolerance mechanism introduces less than 5% overhead for all cases with the non-collective recovery and for tests on less than 38,400 cores with the collective recovery. The three failure points result in similar performance due to the trade-off between increased re-execution cost caused by late failures as compared to longer execution with fewer processes due to early failures. The noncollective version performs slightly better than the other schemes due to the absence of the collective reduction involving all the tasks. The lazy and immediate recovery mechanisms show similar performance at smaller scales with the difference increasing gradually with scale. At 38,400 cores, lazy recovery is up to 18% slower than immediate.

For the TCE benchmark, the additional overheads in the absence of faults are often within the variation observed in the baseline implementation without fault tolerance support. Comparing the average times, immediate recovery imposed less than 6% overhead in all cases of failure except when failure happens at the end on 19,200 cores (15% overhead in this case). Noncollective recovery incurred less than 8% overhead in all cases. Failures at the end of execution caused more overhead, mainly because every task has a significant amount of computation, making the time for re-execution longer. Lazy recovery is generally worse than the other schemes when failure happens at the beginning, due to relatively larger number of re-executed tasks.

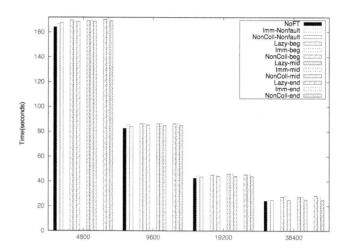

Figure 5: Performance of fault tolerance algorithms for SCF

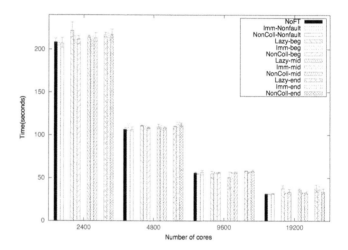

Figure 6: Performance of fault tolerance algorithms for TCE

To better understand the overheads involved, Tables 1 and 2 show the total number of tasks, across all processes, executed at each failure point, and total number of re-executed tasks. We measure the total number of tasks executed at a failure point by synchronizing all processes. This would also be the cost incurred due to collective rollback when a conventional checkpoint-restart approach is employed. This anticipated cost of collective rollback is shown in the second and fourth columns. The actual number of re-executed tasks with our algorithm are listed in the third and fifth columns. We do not include the tasks processed at the failure point for lazy recovery, because the recovery always happens after termination.

Work stealing causes the execution profile to vary across runs due to differences in the tasks executed by a given process across runs. This, together with the approximation involved in simulating failure in the middle, with failure at half the anticipated execution time, is observed as the different number of tasks executed at the failure point, which, in principle, should stay the same across process counts.

We can see that the actual number of re-executed tasks by using our algorithm is much less than the expected number of re-executed tasks with checkpointing. When failure happens at the beginning, the number of processed tasks (the expected re-executed tasks by checkpointing) grows with number of cores, because if every thread exits after executing 1 task, the total number of tasks processed at that time is proportional to the number of cores.

On the other hand, our algorithm only re-executes the tasks with corrupted data, so the re-executed tasks are very few. When failure happens in the middle or end, the total number of tasks processed does not change much according to the number of cores, because the total amount of finished work is the same. In these situations, we can also see that all our algorithms execute less tasks with the increase in core counts, due to the decrease in the data stored and tasks executed per core. Lazy recovery re-executes more tasks, especially when failure happens earlier. This is because the recovery does not happen until the end of execution, and the processes keep updating data on the failed node after its failure. In some cases, noncollective recovery has more re-executed tasks, potentially due to duplicated re-execution.

No. cores	Imm processed	Imm re-exe	Lazy re-exe	NonColl processed	NonColl re-exe
Failure at beginning					
4800	6844	23	3358	6828	23
9600	14.7K	23	2806	13.9K	23
19200	35.9K	25	720	30.6K	22
38400	58.9K	39	1581	56.6K	25
Failure in the middle					
4800	32.3M	165K	168K	31.6M	163K
9600	32.0M	82.4K	85.0K	31.9M	81.5K
19200	31.8M	40.8K	41.4K	31.5M	40.2K
38400	29.7M	18.9K	20.1K	29.1M	18.7K
Failure at the end					
4800	84.9M	436K	450K	84.9M	429K
9600	84.9M	223K	219K	84.9M	215K
19200	84.9M	109K	107K	84.9M	107K
38400	84.9M	56.0K	55.6K	84.9M	54.7K

Table 1: Number of tasks processed at failure time and tasks re-executed for SCF (84.9M tasks in total)

The memory required by meta-data for immediate/lazy recovery includes marker sets (1 byte for sequence number per update, 4 bytes for task identifier per executed task) and update counts (4 bytes for task identifier per executed task, 1 byte for number of updates per executed task). For noncollective recovery, it includes the marker set as above, task record (4 bytes for process rank per update, 4 bytes for task identifier per executed task) and HomedTasks array (4 bytes for task identifier per executed task). Thus, for SCF, the total memory required for the meta-data on all the nodes is 427MB for immediate recovery, and 1.02GB for noncollective recovery. For TCE, the entire memory requirement on all processes for keeping the meta-data is 21.3MB for immediate recovery, and 26.5MB for noncollective recovery. The space overhead per node goes down with the increase in the number of cores, becoming manageable even at 1,000 cores.

6.2 Multi-node Failure

We also evaluated the schemes when 5% of all the comput-

No. cores	Imm processed	Imm re-exe	Lazy re-exe	NonColl processed	NonColl re-exe
Failure at beginning					
2400	2717	42	13.2K	2909	43
4800	4709	53	8840	4734	53
9600	9897	54	6634	10.2K	54
19200	18.7K	53	1677	18.7K	52
Failure in the middle					
2400	360K	6756	16.6K	378K	7039
4800	224K	2268	7839	223K	2366
9600	429K	2030	4229	448K	2102
19200	426K	1031	2164	400K	968
Failure at the end					
2400	1.33M	26.2K	25.2K	1.33M	28.3K
4800	1.33M	13.2K	13.3K	1.33M	14.6K
9600	1.33M	6404	6306	1.33M	7109
19200	1.33M	3190	3239	1.33M	3533

Table 2: Number of tasks processed at failure time and tasks re-executed for TCE (1.33M tasks in total)

ing nodes failed, representing a large failure scenario. For example, when running on 4,800 cores (200 nodes), we bring 240 cores (10 nodes) out of execution. The tests on SCF and TCE are shown in Figure 7 and 8. It can be seen that even with such large number of failed processors, the overhead is tolerable. For SCF, when failure happens at the beginning and in the middle, in most cases the immediate recovery and noncollective recovery imposes less than 10% overhead, except when immediate recovery is used for 38,400 cores. Since the number of failed processes is proportional to the total number of nodes, it is understandable that the runs on larger processes have more data/tasks to recover. Lazy recovery generally takes longer time, due to more re-executed tasks. For the same reason, failure happens at the end leads to more re-executed tasks, so the overhead is mostly between 20% and 25% on 38,400 cores, though less than 15% on smaller number of cores. With TCE, we have similar observations. In most cases, the overhead is less than 10%. When executing on 19,200 cores, where we kick out 960 cores, the overhead is a little higher, mostly between 15% and 20%. Some exceptions exist, which are within the noise range according to the nature of this application.

Table 3 and Table 4 list the number of re-executed tasks and processed tasks at failure time. Similar to the single failure cases, we can see that the re-executed tasks are much less than the processed tasks at failure time, which is the anticipated re-execution of check-pointing. When failure happens in the beginning, very few tasks are re-executed. Though failure after termination brings more re-executed tasks, it is only 5% for SCF, and about 10% for TCE. The reason that we have a higher percentage of re-execution for TCE is that the intensive data update caused more tasks to be re-executed.

7. RELATED WORK

Coordinated and non-coordinated checkpointing approaches have been widely studied [12]. These include system-level [17, 20], user-directed [18] and compiler-oriented [4] approaches. The primary benefit of these approaches is their generality and the simplicity with which they can be integrated into existing applications. The primary limitations are the cost of synchronizing processes, or logging messages, and storing checkpoints, and the work lost due to collective rollback.

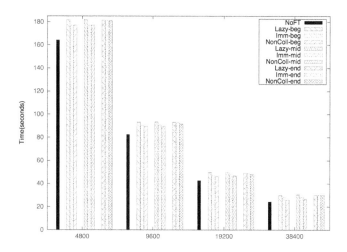

Figure 7: Performance of fault tolerance algorithms with multiple failures for SCF

	Imm processed	Imm re-exe	Lazy re-exe	NonColl processed	NonColl re-exe
Failure at beginning					
4800	6.29K	227	20.6K	6314	215
9600	13.2K	442	20.9K	16.1K	446
19200	79.3K	915	20.1K	33.5K	923
38400	92.3K	1825	26.8K	78.1K	1810
Failure in the middle					
4800	32.1M	1.59M	1.16M	32.0M	1.59M
9600	32.4M	1.60M	1.62M	32.1M	1.59M
19200	32.2M	1.58M	1.60M	31.9M	1.57M
38400	31.5M	1.46M	1.48M	30.6M	1.44M
Failure in the end					
4800	84.9M	4.24M	4.24M	84.93M	4.27M
9600	84.9M	4.25M	4.28M	84.93M	4.27M
19200	84.9M	4.26M	4.28M	84.93M	4.27M
38400	84.9M	4.26M	4.26M	84.93M	4.28M

Table 3: Number of tasks processed at failure time and tasks re-executed with multiple failed nodes for SCF

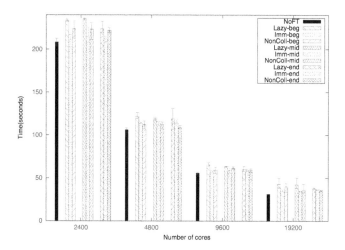

Figure 8: Performance of fault tolerance algorithms with multiple failures for TCE

	Imm processed	Imm re-exe	Lazy re-exe	NonColl processed	NonColl re-exe
Failure at beginning					
2400	2737	181	63.3K	2665	180
4800	5596	509	63.4K	5404	358
9600	12.3K	1071	63.6K	11.7K	736
19200	27.8K	2280	64.0K	34.0K	15.9K
Failure in the middle					
2400	354K	22.7K	76.7K	347K	22.7K
4800	449K	40.0K	81.5K	462K	29.0K
9600	485K	42.0K	82.0K	528K	44.6K
19200	538K	45.4K	81.5K	598K	48.4K
Failure in the end					
2400	1.33M	132K	128K	1.33M	139K
4800	1.33M	130K	129K	1.33M	138K
9600	1.33M	130K	129K	1.33M	137K
19200	1.33M	129K	129K	1.33M	138K

Table 4: Average number of tasks processed at failure time and tasks re-executed with multiple failed nodes for TCE

People also made efforts to address these limitations, such as through cooperative checkpointing [23] or avoiding job relaunching [29].

Proactive fault tolerance approaches attempt to preclude the penalties incurred by fault tolerance through monitoring and migration away from nodes susceptible to faults [5, 22].

Recent results on the prohibitive cost of checkpoint-restart under high failure-rate conditions [12] have motivated alternative system-level solutions. One such approach is the use of shadow processes [14], together with redundant communication. While tolerating much lower mean time between failure, this approach also eliminates the need for frequent checkpoints and collective rollback. The primary disadvantage of this application-independent approach is the significant redundancy cost incurred through duplicated execution.

An alternative approach is the design of a fault tolerant application architecture, with multiple layers of the software stack cooperating to tolerate faults. While inherently more expensive to design, this approach could potentially manage faults at a lower cost. Efforts towards the design of fault tolerant MPI [3, 13] target such implementations. Algorithm-based fault tolerance (eg., [19, 30]) is a kernel-dependent approach that exploits the algorithmic properties of individual kernels to selectively incorporate redundancies and tolerate faults. The approach presented in this paper is similar in spirit to algorithmic techniques, although focusing on a computation idiom rather than a specific algorithm.

RAID [24] ensures fault tolerance for data on disks, which could be applied in memory. The fundamental challenges are the space overhead and the redundancy requirement in each communication operation that modifies data. For non-memory bound applications that can overlap communication, duplicated storage in memory, in the spirit of RAID 1, might be a suitable approach.

A fundamental alternative to the proposed approach to overcoming data corruption is the use of write-once data structures. Log-structured file systems [26] avoid contamination of data and ensure data consistency by appending writes, rather than modifying old versions. In addition to increasing the space overhead, application of this technique in memory could potentially increase cache pressure. Key-value stores employed in several programming models [8, 9, 21] can discard subsequent writes to a key already in the key-value store. Our approach to marker-based idempotent data is similar in spirit to key-value stores, but focused on distributed data structures encountered in scientific applications.

Cilk-NOW [2] is a scheduler for Cilk programs on networks of workstations. It supports fault tolerance for recursive applications organized as *return transactions*, with results passed up the call tree. Sub-trees of a recursive computation are checkpointed (without coordination) into stable storage. Faults result in identification of checkpoints and re-execution of sub-trees to recover and continue execution. Our approach assumes data in an orthogonal data space and recovers individual tasks rather than sub-trees.

8. CONCLUSIONS AND FUTURE WORK

We presented an approach to data-driven fault tolerance for work stealing computations on parallel task collections. Recovery from failure employed an idempotent data store coupled with an inversion of the task-to-data mapping, to identify the tasks that contributed to data on the failed processes. We presented and evaluated algorithms with distinct recovery points and associated trade-offs were shown to be small and scalable at large core counts. We believe the overheads incurred are low enough to treat a detected transient error as a simulated fail-stop failure within the current task parallel phase. As future work, we intend to optimize the algorithms to reduce the space overhead and adapt them to more efficiently handle transient errors.

ACKNOWLEDGEMENTS

This work was supported in part by the DOE Office of Science, Advanced Scientific Computing Research, under award number 59193. This research used resources of the National Energy Research Scientific Computing Center, which is supported by the Office of Science of the U.S. Department of Energy under Contract No. DE-AC02-05CH11231.

9. REFERENCES

[1] E. Ayguade, N. Copty, A. Duran, J. Hoeflinger, Y. Lin, F. Massaioli, X. Teruel, P. Unnikrishnan, and G. Zhang. The design of OpenMP tasks. *Parallel and Distributed Systems, IEEE Transactions on*, 20(3):404 –418, march 2009.

[2] R. D. Blumofe and P. A. Lisiecki. *Adaptive and Reliable Parallel Computing on Networks of Workstations*, page 10. USENIX Association, 1997.

[3] G. Bosilca, A. Bouteiller, F. Cappello, S. Djilali, G. Fedak, C. Germain, T. Herault, P. Lemarinier, O. Lodygensky, F. Magniette, V. Neri, and A. Selikhov. MPICH-V: Toward a Scalable Fault Tolerant MPI for Volatile Nodes. In *Proceedings of the 2002 ACM/IEEE conference on Supercomputing*, Supercomputing '02, pages 1–18, Los Alamitos, CA, USA, 2002. IEEE Computer Society Press.

[4] G. Bronevetsky, D. Marques, K. Pingali, and P. Stodghill. Automated application-level checkpointing of MPI programs. In *Proceedings of the ninth ACM SIGPLAN symposium on Principles and practice of parallel programming*, PPoPP '03, pages 84–94, New York, NY, USA, 2003. ACM.

[5] S. Chakravorty, C. Mendes, and L. Kalé. Proactive Fault Tolerance in MPI Applications via Task Migration. In *High Performance Computing - HiPC 2006*, volume 4297, pages 485–496. 2006.

[6] B. Chamberlain, D. Callahan, and H. Zima. Parallel programmability and the Chapel language. *International Journal of High Performance Computing Applications*, 21(3):291–312, 2007.

[7] P. Charles, C. Grothoff, V. Saraswat, C. Donawa, A. Kielstra, K. Ebcioglu, C. Von Praun, and V. Sarkar. X10: An object-oriented approach to non-uniform cluster computing. In *ACM SIGPLAN Notices*, volume 40, pages 519–538. ACM, 2005.

[8] J. Dean and S. Ghemawat. Mapreduce: simplified data processing on large clusters. *Commun. ACM*, 51(1):107–113, Jan. 2008.

[9] G. DeCandia, D. Hastorun, M. Jampani, G. Kakulapati, A. Lakshman, A. Pilchin, S. Sivasubramanian, P. Vosshall, and W. Vogels. Dynamo: Amazon's highly available key-value store. In *Proceedings of twenty-first ACM SIGOPS symposium on Operating systems principles*, SOSP '07, pages 205–220, New York, NY, USA, 2007. ACM.

[10] J. Dinan, D. B. Larkins, P. Sadayappan, S. Krishnamoorthy, and J. Nieplocha. Scalable work stealing. In *Proceedings of the Conference on High Performance Computing Networking, Storage and Analysis*, SC '09, pages 53:1–53:11, New York, NY, USA, 2009. ACM.

[11] E. Elnozahy and J. Plank. Checkpointing for peta-scale systems: a look into the future of practical rollback-recovery. *Dependable and Secure Computing, IEEE Transactions on*, 1(2):97 – 108, April-June 2004.

[12] E. N. Elnozahy, L. Alvisi, Y.-M. Wang, and D. B. Johnson. A survey of rollback-recovery protocols in message-passing systems. *ACM Comput. Surv.*, 34(3):375–408, 2002.

[13] G. Fagg and J. Dongarra. FT-MPI: Fault Tolerant MPI, Supporting Dynamic Applications in a Dynamic World. In *Recent Advances in Parallel Virtual Machine and Message Passing Interface*, volume 1908. 2000.

[14] K. Ferreira, J. Stearley, J. H. Laros, III, R. Oldfield, K. Pedretti, R. Brightwell, R. Riesen, P. G. Bridges, and D. Arnold. Evaluating the viability of process replication reliability for exascale systems. In *Proceedings of 2011 International Conference for High Performance Computing, Networking, Storage and Analysis*, SC '11, pages 44:1–44:12, New York, NY, USA, 2011. ACM.

[15] M. Frigo. *Portable High-Performance Programs*. PhD thesis, MIT, Cambridge, MA, USA, 1999.

[16] M. Frigo, C. E. Leiserson, and K. H. Randall. The implementation of the Cilk-5 multithreaded language. *SIGPLAN Not.*, 33:212–223, May 1998.

[17] R. Gioiosa, J. C. Sancho, S. Jiang, F. Petrini, and K. Davis. Transparent, incremental checkpointing at kernel level: a foundation for fault tolerance for parallel computers. In *Proceedings of the 2005 ACM/IEEE conference on Supercomputing*, SC '05, pages 9–, Washington, DC, USA, 2005. IEEE Computer Society.

[18] P. H. Hargrove and J. C. Duell. Berkeley Lab Checkpoint/Restart (BLCR) for Linux clusters. In *Journal of Physics: Conf. Series (SciDAC)*, volume 46, pages 494–499, June 2006.

[19] K.-H. Huang and J. Abraham. Algorithm-based fault tolerance for matrix operations. *Computers, IEEE Transactions on*, C-33(6):518 –528, June 1984.

[20] O. Laadan and J. Nieh. Transparent checkpoint-restart of multiple processes on commodity operating systems. In *USENIX Annual Technical Conference*, 2007.

[21] A. Lakshman and P. Malik. Cassandra: a decentralized structured storage system. *SIGOPS Oper. Syst. Rev.*, 44:35–40, April 2010.

[22] A. B. Nagarajan, F. Mueller, C. Engelmann, and S. L. Scott. Proactive fault tolerance for hpc with xen

virtualization. In *Proceedings of the 21st annual international conference on Supercomputing*, ICS '07, pages 23–32, New York, NY, USA, 2007. ACM.

[23] A. J. Oliner, L. Rudolph, and R. K. Sahoo. Cooperative checkpointing: a robust approach to large-scale systems reliability. In *Proceedings of the 20th annual international conference on Supercomputing*, ICS '06, pages 14–23, New York, NY, USA, 2006. ACM.

[24] D. Patterson, G. Gibson, and R. Katz. *A case for redundant arrays of inexpensive disks (RAID)*, volume 17. ACM, 1988.

[25] J. Reinders. *Intel Threading Building Blocks: outfitting C++ for multi-core processor parallelism*. O'Reilly Media, Inc., 2007.

[26] M. Rosenblum and J. Ousterhout. The design and implementation of a log-structured file system. *ACM Transactions on Computer Systems (TOCS)*, 10(1):26–52, 1992.

[27] V. A. Saraswat, P. Kambadur, S. Kodali, D. Grove, and S. Krishnamoorthy. Lifeline-based global load balancing. In *Proceedings of the 16th ACM symposium on Principles and practice of parallel programming*, PPoPP '11, pages 201–212, New York, NY, USA, 2011. ACM.

[28] T. von Eicken, D. E. Culler, S. C. Goldstein, and K. E. Schauser. Active messages: a mechanism for integrated communication and computation. In *Proceedings of the 19th annual international symposium on Computer architecture*, ISCA '92, pages 256–266, New York, NY, USA, 1992. ACM.

[29] C. Wang, F. Mueller, C. Engelmann, and S. L. Scott. A Job Pause Service under LAM/MPI+BLCR for Transparent Fault Tolerance. In *IPDPS*, pages 1–10, 2007.

[30] S.-J. Wang and N. Jha. Algorithm-based fault tolerance for FFT networks. *Computers, IEEE Transactions on*, 43(7):849 –854, Jul 1994.

Fault Resilience of the Algebraic Multi-Grid Solver

Marc Casas, Bronis R. de Supinski, Greg Bronevetsky and Martin Schulz

Lawrence Livermore National Laboratory
7000 East Avenue
Livermore, CA, 94550

ABSTRACT

As HPC system sizes grow to millions of cores and chip feature sizes continue to decrease, HPC applications become increasingly exposed to transient hardware faults. These faults can cause aborts and performance degradation. Most importantly, they can corrupt results. Thus, we must evaluate the fault vulnerability of key HPC algorithms to develop cost-effective techniques to improve application resilience.

We present an approach that analyzes the vulnerability of applications to faults, systematically reduces it by protecting the most vulnerable components and predicts application vulnerability at large scales. We initially focus on sparse scientific applications and apply our approach in this paper to the Algebraic Multi Grid (AMG) algorithm. We empirically analyze AMG's vulnerability to hardware faults in both sequential and parallel (hybrid MPI/OpenMP) executions on up to 1,600 cores and propose and evaluate the use of targeted pointer replication to reduce it. Our techniques increase AMG's resilience to transient hardware faults by 50-80% and improve its scalability on faulty computational environments by 35%. Further, we show how to model AMG's scalability in fault-prone environments to predict execution times of large-scale runs accurately.

Categories and Subject Descriptors

B.8 [**Performance and Reliability**]: Reliability, Testing, and Fault-Tolerance; G.1.3 [**Numerical Linear Algebra**]: Sparse, Structured, and Very Large Systems

Keywords

Algebraic Multi-Grid Solver, Resilience, Transient Faults.

1. INTRODUCTION

Exascale systems are expected to have hundreds of millions of cores with feature sizes as low as 12nm [1, 14]. These feature sizes and growing total feature count will significantly increase variability in circuit behavior and, thus, the probability that some circuit produces an incorrect result. Today's systems are already vulnerable to *soft faults* [4, 5].

A large BlueGene/L system experienced an L1-cache bit flip every five hours [10] and the ASCI Q machine experienced 26.1 cache errors per week [18]. Industry cannot justify the cost to harden circuitry to the levels that exascale systems would require since commodity systems will have many fewer components. Thus, we must develop software techniques to allow applications to tolerate soft faults.

Soft faults can reduce performance, which increases energy consumption. They can also cause aborts, which require re-executions that waste more time and energy, and can cost significant debugging efforts that seek phantom coding errors. Most importantly, they can corrupt results. Thus, we must study the soft fault vulnerability of scientific applications to identify their most vulnerable components and to design techniques that reduce the vulnerabilities.

We present a general approach that evaluates an application's vulnerability to soft faults, hardens it against the most critical errors and models its effective scalability. We focus on an important numerical method, specifically Algebraic Multi-Grid (AMG) [6]. AMG iteratively solves linear systems by applying a linear solver, such as conjugate gradient or Jacobi, to finer and coarser variants of the same linear system to compute increasingly more accurate solutions.

We evaluate the resilience of AMG's implementation in the Hypre [9] library by observing the effect of random injected faults. These faults can cause a segmentation fault or increase the time to converge. Our evaluation shows that AMG is naturally resilient to soft faults: 50% of runs converge without significant performance loss even when subjected to hundreds of faults per second. However, since AMG is typically used with sparse matrices, it is vulnerable to pointer corruptions. We thus evaluate a resilience algorithm that selectively triplicates the most critical pointers and the operations that access them. We show that triplication of a few pointers significantly reduces the probability of segmentation faults in AMG to improve its resilience at little cost. Overall, we make the following contributions:

- A methodology to explore fault vulnerability.
- A detailed vulnerability study of AMG's solver phase.
- The design and implementation of resilience techniques for AMG's most vulnerable components.
- An evaluation of AMG's scalability in a faulty environment, with and without our resilience techniques.
- A Markov model that predicts the impact of faults on application scalability, which we apply to AMG.

We show that simple techniques reduce AMG's fault vulnerability by 50-80% and only increase execution time 23%

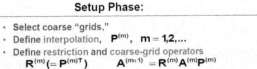

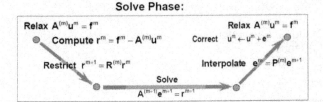

Figure 1: V-cycle of the AMG Solver

when no faults occur. For parallel executions, we improve AMG's scalability in faulty environments by 35% when AMG is scaled to 100 nodes (1,600 cores). Finally, we show that our model accurately predicts large-scale execution time based on small-scale fault injection experiments.

This paper is structured as follows. Section 2 explains the characteristics of the AMG solver. Section 3 presents our fault injection methodology. Section 4 evaluate the vulnerability of AMG's phases and Section 5 shows that a simple algorithm-based fault tolerance technique increases AMG's resilience. Section 6 evaluates the impact of soft faults and our fault tolerant techniques on AMG's scalability.

2. ALGEBRAIC MULTI-GRID

Iterative linear solvers compute the solution, x, of a linear system, $Ax = b$, by iteratively refining an initial guess for x until the residual, $Ax - b$, is below some bound. In contrast, direct solvers solve the system in a fixed, large number of steps. Thus, iterative solvers are in general much faster for large sparse systems. Algebraic Multi-Grid (AMG) quickly refines the guess based on coarse versions of the system to improve traditional techniques such as conjugate gradient [11] or the generalized minimal residual (GMRES) [24] method.

Although each step of a traditional iterative solver reduces the residual, the reductions are typically local. Some regions of x can have much more error than others. Thus, many small-scale corrections must smooth out large-scale differences. AMG overcomes this problem by applying traditional solvers such as CG to coarser versions of the linear system and interpolating to the finer ones. This approach reduces error and significantly improves the speed of convergence.

AMG consists of two phases: a *setup* and a *solve* phase, as Figure 1 illustrates. The setup phase computes matrices that the solve phase uses. Often, several solve phases use those matrices. Thus, we focus on the AMG solve phase; evaluation of setup phase vulnerability is future work.

The solve phase is divided into three phases, as Figure 1 shows. First, the *relaxation phase* applies a few steps of a traditional iterative solver at one coarseness level. The *restriction phase* (operations Compute and Restrict in the figure) then moves the algorithmic state to a coarser grid by multiplying the error of the previous phase by a coarsening matrix (computed in the setup phase). Another *relaxation phase* (denoted Solve in the figure) estimates the error

with larger-scale information incorporated. The *interpolation phase* (operations Interpolate and Correct in the figure) then maps this coarser estimate to the finer version and adjusts the current solution x with the new error information.

This algorithm repeats until the error is below a threshold. It is directly extended to use multiple coarseness levels, ranging from the original problem to one with few entries in the matrix and vectors. A single AMG V-cycle starts with the original problem and repeats the relaxation and restriction steps $m - 1$ times through m coarsening levels. After a solve step, the reverse order of these steps estimates x for the original problem. AMG repeats this V cycle until the estimate's residual error $Ax - b$ is sufficiently small.

AMG can use a variety of other algorithms. For example, the solver at each level can depend on the linear system's properties. Further, the restriction and interpolation techniques that move the algorithm between coarseness levels can use simple averaging or complex graph algorithms [26].

3. FAULT INJECTION

We evaluate the resilience of AMG routines by injecting errors into their execution. Soft faults can manifest themselves as corruptions in system memory or as errors in instruction results. Since error correcting codes can efficiently detect and correct the former, we focus on errors in computations, for which no general, efficient checks exist.

We use a fault injection infrastructure [8] that simulates soft faults by compiling application into the Low Level Virtual Machine (LLVM) typed bytecode [15]. This bytecode is transformed to allow a bit flip in each instruction's output with some probability P. The time between injections is thus exponentially distributed with period $\frac{1}{P}$.

While the basic fault injector can corrupt any instruction with equal probability, this choice is unrealistic since the clock cycles per instruction vary. A more accurate model adjusts the probability of injecting an error into each instruction to be proportional to the time that the instruction takes to execute. Our novel algorithm, presented in Section 3.1, computes the average number of cycles for each LLVM instruction type. Section 3.2 compares the results of injecting errors using constant probability distribution and the more accurate cycle-weighted distribution.

3.1 Generation of Instruction Weights

The total cycles spent during a given application code region is the sum of the total cycles spent in each instruction type. Thus, if I_i is the number of executions of a particular instruction type i and α_i is the average number of cycles to execute i, the total number of cycles in a given time period C is their linear combination:

$$I_1\alpha_1 + I_2\alpha_2 + ... + I_n\alpha_n = C$$

We measure I_i and C with performance counters and solve for each α_i. Since this system is underdetermined (one equation and n unknowns), we must measure at least $m \geq n$ regions of the application or $m \geq n$ application runs to produce the full linear system:

$$I_{11}\alpha_1 + I_{21}\alpha_2 + ... + I_{n1}\alpha_n = C_1$$
$$I_{12}\alpha_1 + I_{22}\alpha_2 + ... + I_{n2}\alpha_n = C_2$$
$$...$$
$$I_{nm}\alpha_1 + I_{2m}\alpha_2 + ... + I_{nm}\alpha_n = C_n$$

where I_{ij} is the number of times that instruction type i

executed during the jth measurement and C_j is the number of cycles in the jth measurement. The solution of this system estimates the expected value of each α across all observations [20]. We can only solve this system if it is fully-determined, which is equivalent to requiring that each measurement has a different instruction mix. We can ensure this property by running the application on multiple inputs or scheduling measurements so that no two capture exactly the same code region, which is the approach that we use. Since the estimate's accuracy improves as the number of observations increases, m should be much larger than n. We compute the solution using a least squares approximation.

Our initial experiments use the AMG implementation in the Hypre [9] library, executed on a linear problem that corresponds to solving the Laplace equation [21] in a cube using a 7 point stencil and a regular discretization in which all elements are the same size. The problem size of the finest level is 15,625, which corresponds to solving for 15,625 variables. The number of non-zero coefficients of the matrix is less than the 0.1% of its entries. We used a V-cycle of depth 6, which means that AMG performs 5 restrictions and 5 interpolations and 6 relaxation phases for each V-cycle. We used conjugate gradient for 5 iterations during each relaxation phase. The coarsest version is a 4x4 matrix with all non-zero coefficients. AMG converges on this system in 3 V-cycles when no faults are injected.

We choose the problem and the structure of the V-cycle to represent a typical small-scale AMG use case. The problem is structured and is representative of a partial differential equation. Since the execution only takes a few minutes, we can conduct fault injection campaigns that include thousands of application runs. Unless otherwise noted, all experiments that we present focus on this system.

3.2 Comparison of Fault Injection Scenarios

We evaluate the difference between cycle-weighted and constant-probability fault injection for AMG's restriction phase. Constant-probability injection selects each instruction with equal probability. Cycle-weighted injection ensures each cycle has an equal fault probability as determined through the method described in Section 3.1.

We execute AMG 10,000 times, injecting faults into randomly chosen instructions and output locations with probability 5.4×10^{-8}, which corresponds to an injection rate of 300 errors/sec. We change the initial seed to obtain different randomly chosen fault injections for each execution. Both schemes inject 15 faults on average into each execution.

Errors in AMG lead to three possible outcomes. First, the algorithm can converge to an approximate solution in the same number of V-cycles and, thus, the execution time is equal to a non-faulty execution. AMG takes 3 V-cycles on our target problem, so we categorize executions that converge in 3 V-cycles as *normal*. Second, the algorithm can take longer to converge than normal, which means AMG must perform additional work to find an approximate solution. Most such cases require 4 V-cycles so we categorize executions that take more than 4 V-cycles separately. Finally, the error can lead to a segmentation fault that aborts AMG, typically because a pointer was corrupted, leading to access of an invalid memory address.

The constant probability approach leads to segmentation faults in 30% of the executions. The AMG solver required 4 V-cycles in 4% of the executions and only 3 V-cycles in

	Restriction	Interpolation	Relaxation
Rate 1	200 f, 4273 e/s	100 f, 5128 e/s	200 f, 1666 e/s
Rate 2	100 f, 2136 e/s	50 f, 2564 e/s	100 f, 833 e/s
Rate 3	20 f, 427 e/s	10 f, 513 e/s	20 f, 167 e/s
Rate 4	10 f, 214 e/s	5 f, 256 e/s	10 f, 83 e/s
Rate 5	2 f, 43 e/s	1 f, 51 e/s	2 f, 17 e/s
Rate 6	1 f, 21 e/s	0.5 f, 25 e/s	1 f, 9 e/s
Rate 7	0.2 f, 4 e/s	0.1 f, 5 e/s	0.2 f, 2 e/s

Table 1: Error Rates and Injected Faults Counts

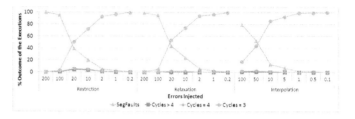

Figure 2: Vulnerability of the AMG Phases

66% of the executions. Using the cycle-weighted approach reduced the occurrence of segmentation faults to 28% of the executions while 4% still required 4 V-cycles and 68% needed 3. Although the exact numbers vary, the qualitative behavior of both injection scenarios is similar. However, this result depends on the instruction mix and we anticipate the difference would be more significant for applications with a lower percentage of load/store operations.

4. VULNERABILITY OF AMG ROUTINES

We evaluate the resilience of the *restriction*, *relaxation* and *interpolation* phases of the AMG solver phase individually. We use the fault injection methodology described in Section 3 to inject errors in that phase and study how these errors propagate through the entire execution. Each experiment involves 10,000 AMG runs. We use seven error rates so the evaluation of three phases requires 210,000 total runs.

4.1 Evaluation

Our error injection rates range from a few errors per run (0.1 errors expected in the target phase during a 3 V-cycle AMG run on the Laplace 7 point stencil) to many errors (200 errors expected per run). Table 1 presents the error rates and the total number of errors injected in each phase, which ranges from 2 errors/sec to 5,128 errors/sec.

We use these error rates for three reasons. First, the large number of injection events simplifies observation of error effects, similarly to a particle accelerator performing many collisions to improve its observational power. Second, although no individual computing device suffers from such high error rates, supercomputing systems that utilize millions of such chips could approximate these error rates. For example, in the context of long-running computations, each month-long run on an exascale system will be exposed to tens or hundreds of such errors. Finally, studying extremely high error rates informs hardware designers about the flexibility of applications with respect to soft faults and enables consideration of a wider range of design-space tradeoffs.

Figure 2 presents the result of injecting errors into each

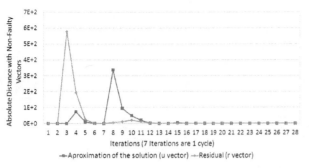

Figure 3: Propagation of Error (Linear)

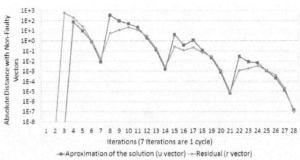

Figure 4: Propagation of Error (Logarithmic)

of the three phases. When the *restriction* phase experiences 200 errors, all runs terminate due to a segmentation fault. If we inject 100 errors, 3% of executions converge normally (3 V-cycles), and 2% take longer than normal to converge. As the number of injected errors drops to 20, 10 and finally 2 errors per run we see that AMG runs much more productively. It converges normally in 51% of the runs at 20 errors, and 93% for 2 errors. It aborts due to segmentation faults in 40% of the runs with 20 errors, 20% with 10 errors and only 5% with 2 errors and most runs converge in 3 V-cycles.

The *relaxation* and *interpolation* phases have similar behavior to the *restriction* phase. In both experiments, the percentage of executions that converge normally within 3 V-cycles is more than 90% when we inject 1 or 3 faults.

We derive three lessons from these experiments. First, AMG is naturally resilient to errors: if a segmentation fault does not occur, it always finds a correct solution. Even high error rates do not impact convergence, with few non-aborted runs taking more than 3 V-cycles. Thus, AMG does not require relatively expensive algorithm-based fault tolerance (ABFT) checksum error detection and correction [12, 13, 23]. AMG's resilience arises from its multilevel structure: errors increase the impact of high-frequency components of the residual (errors that vary on a small scale), but relaxation corrects these component on each grid. Relaxation on coarser grids more effectively corrects these high-frequency errors than relaxation over finer grids. Thus, our results complement related work on ERSA [16], application robustification [25] and code perforation [22], which also show that some applications are naturally resilient.

Second, since AMG correctly converges despite numerical errors, we can most improve its resilience by reducing its rate of segmentation faults. Section 5 presents and evaluates our solution for protecting AMG memory accesses.

Finally, our experiments show that the *restriction* phase is the least resilient. More of its executions take abnormally long to converge, relative to the other phases. Thus, the errors that are injected into this phase are more easily propagated. Section 4.2 analyzes this behavior in more detail.

4.2 Error Propagation

Error propagation is an important aspect of an algorithm's resilience since the corruption of a single data value can spread throughout the algorithm's state. Depending on the application's numerical stability, a corruption's effects may amplify to corrupt the entire state severely or may be dampened out and vanish as the execution advances. Our experiments show that AMG is resilient to errors; we now in-

vestigate this effect more precisely by looking at how the magnitude of the errors propagates through AMG's state.

We evaluate error propagation through AMG by examining the difference between its key data structures during normal execution and when we inject an error. We focus on vectors u^m and r^m that appear in Figure 1. Vector u^m is the intermediate solution of the iterative method at level m and r^m is the residual of this intermediate solution. As discussed in Section 2, the *restriction phase* computes the residual r^m and its restriction to a coarser grid. In this experiment, we inject a fault into each execution of the restriction phase and observe how the values of u^m and r^m change. In order to observe fault propagation through many algorithmic steps, we choose a larger variant of the problem than we used in earlier experiments. It corresponds to a system with 421,875 unknowns and we use 4 V-cycles of depth 7.

Figures 3 presents the absolute difference between the vectors u^m and r^m during normal execution and their values during a single representative run of AMG with injected faults. The x-axis corresponds to instances of the restriction phase in iterations at different depths, with 7 such iterations per V-cycle. We do not inject an error during the first two iterations in which AMG computes on the finest and the second finest grids. Thus, vectors u and r equal their counterparts in the non-faulty execution. In iteration 3, while vector u equals its non-faulty counterpart, r is significantly different, meaning that a fault was injected during the residual computation. In the next iteration, once the algorithm has already performed 5 steps of the CG solver in the 4th level grid, the vectors u and r are both different from their counterparts in the non-faulty execution. However, the difference in the r vector is significantly smaller. This trend continues in subsequent iterations until the difference almost disappears. In iteration 8, the first restriction of the second V-cycle, the difference in vector u increases significantly, which has little effect on the residual. However, these differences vanish as the execution progresses. At the end, both vectors are near their counterparts and the algorithm converges in 4 V-cycles in both executions.

The logarithmic chart on the right of Figure 4 clearly shows the dynamics of error propagation. We can see the effect of each V-cycle, with error magnitude dropping as AMG iterates over the coarsest grids. Although the error spreads among the variables when AMG's execution returns to the finest levels, the correction on the coarsest grids is more significant than this subsequent contamination, which illustrates the reasons that AMG is naturally resilient. Traditional iterative methods effectively reduce the highest fre-

Variable	# of corruptions
y_data	18
A_data	53
x_data	118
A_j	227
jj	0
other	0
Total	395

Table 2: Corruptions

Original Code of Matrix-Vector Multiplication
```
for(jj = A_i[i]; jj < A_i[i+1]; jj++) {
    y_data[i] += A_data[jj] * x_data[A_j[jj]];
}
```

Transformed Code With Pointer Triplication
```
for(jj = A_i[i]; jj < A_i[i+1]; jj++) {
    y_data[i] += A_data[jj] * x_data[triplication(A_j, A_j_p1, A_j_p2)[jj]];
}
```

Table 3: Source Code Before and After Triplication

quency (most localized) errors, but may have trouble overcoming the large high-frequency error that a soft fault may introduce. AMG's coarsening smooths out the effects of these large local errors at the coarser levels of the problem and allows the traditional methods to use global information to dampen the local error. Thus, coarse-level computations, which represent a small portion of the algorithm's execution and thus have low fault vulnerability, are the most instrumental to protecting finer-level computations from errors.

5. POINTER REPLICATION

Our experiments show that we should protect AMG from segmentation faults. Thus, we implement a simple algorithm that protects key pointers through replication. We maintain multiple copies of a protected pointer and compare them before every memory access. This general technique is easy to implement and has low overhead, as we show in Section 5.3.

In this study we specifically evaluate pointer triplication, in which we maintain three copies of each key pointer. On each memory access that uses a pointer, we read all three copies. We then perform the memory access on the majority value among the copies. This algorithm, which we can extend to any number of copies, can detect errors if they only affect a minority of the copies (one copy for triplication). The number of copies used must balance their effectiveness at reducing the rate of segmentation faults against their cost in storage and performance as well as increased application vulnerability due to longer execution times. In the next section, we explore a detailed example that shows how pointer replication can protect the AMG solver.

5.1 Protection of the Restriction Phase

To protect a code region, we must identify its most vulnerable variables. We inject faults to determine the variables that are corrupted when a segmentation fault occurs. Consider the effect of faults on AMG's restriction phase. We run AMG 10,000 times, injecting 20 errors into this phase in each execution (427 errors/sec). 395 executions abort due to a segmentation fault. Table 2 shows several variables that the phase uses and the number of runs in which the the variable is corrupted when the run aborts. Variable A_j, the most vulnerable, is corrupted in 227 of the 395 aborted runs, followed by x_data, A_data and y_data.

These variables belong to the most internal loop of the matrix-vector multiplication routine $y = Ax$ in the Hypre library [9]. The top of Table 3 shows the pseudocode of this loop. This non-trivial implementation of this operation exploits the sparsity of the A matrix by putting its non-zero entries in the dense vector A_data and indexing them with the vectors A_i and A_j. The bottom of Table 3 shows the

System	Domain	Stencil	Discretization
Rotate1	2D	7-points	Regular
Rotate2	2D	7-points	Irregular
Laplace1	3D	7-points	Regular
Laplace2	3D	7-points	Irregular
9pt1	2D	9-points	Regular
9pt2	2D	9-points	Irregular
27pt1	3D	27-points	Regular
27pt2	3D	27-points	Irregular

Table 4: Description of the Linear Systems

modified source code in which we protect the A_j pointer through triplication. Two extra copies of the pointer A_j, A_j_p1 and A_j_p2, appear in the source code and the *triplication* function performs the comparisons and voting.

5.2 General Protection Method

We use these ideas to create a general methodology to identify and to protect the most critical application variables. Similarly to how we protect the most critical variable in Table 2, we can protect the second most critical variable and so on, until we reach the required resiliency. However, the protection of one variable affects the criticality of other variables since protecting the first still leaves the application vulnerable to corruptions in others. Thus we must repeat the fault injection experiment after we protect each variable to ensure that we protect the next most critical variable. Our general procedure for protecting applications from errors consists of these steps:

1. Perform a fault injection campaign on the code region;

2. Identify the most vulnerable pointers by checking whether their values are correct in runs that abort;

3. If the code region is insufficiently resilient, protect the most vulnerable pointer and return to Step 1, else stop.

While we could protect all pointers from corruption, full protection is often undesirable since the replica checking code is also vulnerable to errors. As we replicate more pointers, the fraction of execution time spent in the checks increases, making it likely that many errors will occur during them rather than in the original code. Thus, we miss errors or more segmentation faults occur. However, since most errors occur in a few pointers, as Table 2 shows, we can choose a replication level that balances the cost and effectiveness of protection to make faults irrelevant to developers.

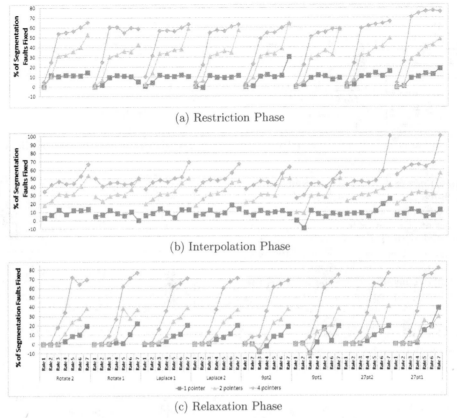

(a) Restriction Phase

(b) Interpolation Phase

(c) Relaxation Phase

Figure 5: Evaluation of Pointer Replication

5.3 Evaluation

This section evaluates our pointer replication and critical variable selection algorithms for each of the phases of the AMG solver: *restriction, relaxation* and *interpolation*. In each experiment we inject one phase with errors at the frequencies that Table 1 shows. We use these error rates rather than the absolute number of errors to reflect how pointer replication increases AMG's runtime, making it vulnerable to more errors. It also enables direct comparison of the utility of replicating different numbers of critical pointers.

We evaluate the algorithms for 8 linear systems that represent different problems. Table 4 lists, for each linear system, the dimensions of their problem domain, the chosen stencil and the kind of discretization performed. In general, stencils with more points correspond to denser linear systems because each discretized element must exchange information with the same number of elements as points in the stencil. Regular discretization leads to structured matrices and irregular to unstructured matrices. Finally, domains with bigger dimensions allow more flexibility in choosing the stencil or the discretization. This set of 8 linear systems is representative for workloads typically executed by the AMG solver, since it covers a range of problem sparsities as well as both structured and unstructured matrices. Our previously described experiments use the `Laplace1` problem of this set.

Figure 5 presents the effect of the replication algorithm in these contexts, showing the relative reduction in the number of application runs that aborted with a segmentation fault: $\frac{\text{\# unprotected runs that aborted} - \text{\# protected runs that aborted}}{\text{\# unprotected runs that aborted}}$. Each data point is computed from 10,000 AMG runs. The graphs

cover 8 linear systems, 7 error rates, AMG's 3 main phases and 5 replication schemes (from no replication to the replication of 4 pointers) for a total of 8,400,000 AMG executions.

Figure 5(a) shows results for the *restriction* phase. Protecting the 4 most critical pointers reduces segmentation faults between 59% and 78%, depending on the matrix, when we inject errors at the lowest rate (4 errors/sec). As the error rate rises by a factor of 5, replication of the top 4 pointers still reduces segmentation faults by 59-83%. However, for the highest error rates (2,136 and 4,273 errors/sec), the improvement drops to just 23%-32% and 3%-10% because errors are likely to occur during pointer checks at such high rates. Our technique is thus most effective at intermediate and lower error rates, which most closely model exascale systems and are still significantly higher than what is experienced on commodity hardware.

Figure 5(b) shows the improvement in segmentation fault rates during the *interpolation* phase. Pointer replication also improves these rates by more than 50% when faced with low error rates and between roughly 30%-50% for higher rates. The four-pointers protection scheme fixes most segmentation faults against rates of several errors per second with problems `27pt1` and `27pt2`. Although we use similar error rates as with the *restriction* phase, the *interpolation* phase is generally more reliable since it performs fewer computations. Thus, the same error rate results in a fewer total error injections. The total number of errors rather than the physical error rate is a better predictor of the algorithm's vulnerability. Replicating only one pointer can actually degrade the resilience of the interpolation phase under high error rates, as we see with the `9pt1` input matrix. This ef-

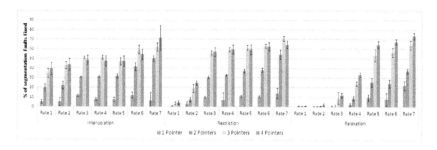

Figure 6: Pointer Replication Evaluation Summary

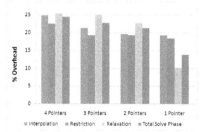

Figure 7: Protection Overheads

fect occurs because replication of only one pointer does not tolerate errors sufficiently to compensate for the increased vulnerability of AMG due to reduced performance.

Figure 5(c) shows the effect of pointer replication on the *relaxation* phase. Our techniques improve the phase's resilience to segmentation faults by over 60% for error rates of equal or lesser than 17 errors/sec, dropping to 30% improvement for 83 errors/sec. Against several thousands or hundreds of errors per second, our techniques do not improve the phase's resilience significantly.

Finally, Figure 6 summarizes the above data, plotting the average reduction in segmentation fault rate and confidence interval bars that show the range taken up by 95% of the reduction values for each phase and fault rate. These intervals are generally small, showing that our technique is consistently effective. The only exception is 4 pointer replication during the *interpolation* phase at the lowest error rate, where our technique is significantly more effective for problems `27pt2` and `27pt1`. Since our experiments cover a heterogeneous set of input problems, the data shows that the effectiveness of pointer replication for AMG is generally independent of the input matrix.

Figure 7 shows the overhead of replicating the top 1 to 4 pointers, focusing on each phase as well as the entire AMG solver. Overhead is closely related to the number of pointers checked. Replicating one increases execution time by 14%, two by 21%, three by 22% and four by 24%.

Overall, our experiments show that pointer replication and critical variable selection improve the resilience of AMG against segmentation faults by 50% to 100% under error rates of a few or tens of errors per second and 30% to 50% under high error rates of hundreds of errors per second. The cost of using these techniques is a 24% reduction in performance, making it a cost-effective choice for use in unreliable computational environments. Our flexible techniques support an easy trade-off between reliability and performance by changing the number of pointers that we replicate and the number of replicas that we maintain for each pointer to target the reliability of specific systems.

6. IMPACT ON PARALLEL EXECUTIONS

In this section we evaluate the impact of faults on parallel AMG executions and the improvement from our pointer triplication technique. We perform several fault injection campaigns in parallel AMG executions and compare the results of runs with the original and the protected routines. To support reasonable scaling on moderate numbers of processors, the experiments in this section use a 100 times extension of the `Laplace1` system used in Sections 4 and 5.

Consistent with our results in Section 5.3, parallel results with other problems are similar.

Since parallel executions require more resources than sequential ones, we perform 100 executions for each configuration instead of 10,000. We replicate the four most critical pointers using the methodology described in Section 5. We use an Infiniband QDR connected Linux cluster that has 800 compute nodes, each with four quad-core 2.3 GHz AMD Opteron processors. AMG is run in a fully-hybrid parallelization mode that uses both OpenMP and MPI. Our experiments cover a range of scales and ratios of MPI processes to OpenMP threads, ranging from fully sequential (1 process x 1 thread), single-node (1 process x 16 threads) and hybrid runs at 2x16, 4x16 and 100 MPI tasks x 16 OpenMP threads each. We inject faults in each thread of the parallel run at the same rate of 1 error/sec. Figures 8, 9 and 10 show the results for the *restriction* phase; results for the *interpolation* and *relaxation* phases are similar.

Figures 8 presents the percentage of runs that result in segmentation faults. As the level of parallelism increases, the fraction of runs with segmentation faults decreases even for unprotected routines. Further, although run times decrease when running on more processors, the total number of injected faults increases since the application does not exhibit perfect speedup. Thus, the decrease in segmentation faults does not arise from a decrease in the number of faults. Instead, this decrease arises from communication between processes, which increases as we increase the degree of parallelism. Each process receives data from other processes that can replace corrupted data. Although the new data may also be corrupted, the probability is low.

Importantly, pointer replication still increases the routine's resilience. The improvement increases with the parallel scale. In particular, the improvement is close to 80% in the executions with 40 MPI tasks and 16 OpenMP threads per task and with 100 MPI tasks and 16 OpenMP threads per task. Figure 8 also shows bars that represent the 95% confidence interval (Gaussian distribution assumed). Since each experiment consists of only 100 executions, the intervals are larger than in Section 5. However, we still have statistical confidence that our pointer replication technique significantly improves resilience of our parallel executions.

6.1 Impact on Scalability

Soft errors impact the scalability of AMG. The ultimate speedup of the solver is impacted by both segmentation faults and the extra V-cycles that may be required to correct data corruptions. In this section, we evaluate these effects and the speedup of the solver in the face of faults with unprotected and protected routines.

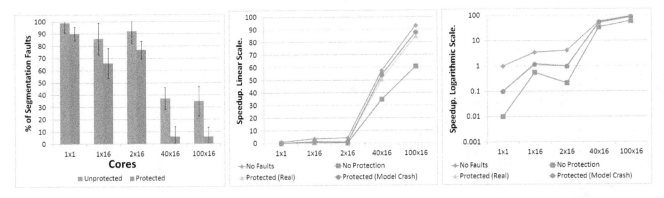

Figure 8: Vulnerability of AMG at Different Scales

Figure 9: Application Speedup at Different Scales (linear)

Figure 10: Application Speedup at Different Scales (logarithmic)

The following scenario illustrates how we compute the slowdown due to soft errors. Imagine that a particular execution crashes when it has completed 30% of the required work (for example 3 out of 10 V-cycles) so that AMG must be completely re-executed. Assume that in this second execution the algorithm determines the solution with the same number of cycles as the non-faulty execution. The slowdown would be 1.3 and the final speedup would be $\frac{S}{1.3}$ where S is AMG's speedup when no faults are injected. We run this kind of experiment 100 times for each degree of parallelism to make sure that we capture AMG's behavior.

Figures 9 and 10 compare the speedup when no faults are injected ("No Faults" bar), when we inject faults in the *restriction* phase with a fault injection rate of 1 error/sec without pointer replication ("No Protection" bar) and with triplication of the 4 most critical pointers ("Protected Real" bar). Figure 9 shows the speedups on a linear scale and Figure 10 shows the same data using a logarithmic scale. We achieve a significant improvement of the speedup in all parallel environments. The results using 40 and 100 MPI tasks (640 and 1,600 total cores, respectively) are especially remarkable because the pointer replication technique accounts for 35% of the speedup. While the protected routines achieve a lower speedup than the non-faulty executions, the difference is generally small and is significantly better than in faulty executions with no protection.

While the above experiments are illuminating, they are far too expensive to be used at large scales. Measuring the application's rate of segmentation faults and convergence slowdowns requires many executions (100 to 10,000 in our experiments) at the desired scale, each of which may be slowed down by the injected faults. For example, in the experiments that use 2 MPI tasks and 16 OpenMP threads, 4.07 executions were required on average across the 100 experiments to complete an AMG run successfully, totaling in 407 AMG executions. Overall, the required computational resources make such studies prohibitively expensive at the scales of interest for typical HPC applications. However, as Figure 8 shows, AMG's vulnerability to faults converges to a constant for scales above 40 MPI tasks (640 cores). Thus, we can model the application's vulnerability at any scale analytically based on its vulnerability at smaller scales. Section 6.2 shows how we use stochastical models based on Markov Chains [17] to model the application's vulnerability behavior and to predict faults' impact on its scalability.

6.2 Using Markov Chains to Model Slowdown

We derive a model that estimates the impact on the speedup of a parallel application given some probability that a crash occurs (e.g., due to a segmentation fault). We assume that for a given fault injection rate r the probability that the application crashes is p_r. We can obtain p_r by performing a fault injection campaign with the application at a representative scale, such as the data presented in Figure 8.

We model the application's behavior by a Markov Chain that has 3 possible states: *Begin, End, Fault*. The AMG solver is initially in the *Begin* state, which means it will be executed. It exits this execution by either completing with a valid solution (probability $1 - p_r$) or crashing (probability p_r). If it completes successfully, it transitions to state *End*. If the application crashes it transitions to state *Fault*, in which case the application must be re-executed. This repeated execution may fail with probability p_r and may need to be re-executed an arbitrary number of times before it transitions successfully to state *End* with probability $1 - p_r$.

We can solve this Markov Chain to compute the expected number of AMG executions required to produce valid output, given a crash probability of p_r. Let X be a random variable that represents the number of AMG executions required to compute valid output. $E(X)$ is its expected value, the average of all possible values of X, weighted by their probabilities. The probability of obtaining a valid solution after the first execution is $1 - p_r$, which is the probability of no crash. The probability of success after two executions is $p_r(1 - p_r)$ since it involves recovering from one crash, followed by a fully successful run. Finally, the probability of success after exactly n executions is $p_r^{n-1}(1 - p_r)$. Thus, the expected number of executions before a valid output is

$$E(X) = \sum_{n=1}^{\infty} nP(X = n) = \sum_{n=1}^{\infty} n(1 - p_r)p_r^{n-1} =$$

$$= (1 - p_r)\sum_{n=1}^{\infty} np_r^{n-1} = (1 - p_r)\frac{1}{(1 - p_r)^2} = \frac{1}{1 - p_r}$$

Note that $\sum_{n=1}^{\infty} np_r^{n-1} = \frac{1}{(1-p_r)^2}$ when $0 < p_r < 1$.

If AMG achieves speedup S in fault-free execution in a particular parallel environment then the slowdown due to faults equals $\frac{1}{E(X)}$. That is, the final speedup in a faulty environment is $\frac{S}{E(X)} = S(1 - p_r)$.

We use probabilities derived from the results in Figure 8

to parameterize the model. Figures 9 and 10 (bar "Protected - Model Crash") show its predictions. The data shows that the model is highly accurate in predicting the real speedups obtained in Section 6.1. These predictions are significantly less expensive than full fault injection studies since they only require one run of the application at the desired scale plus fault injection experiments at a much smaller scale to measure fault probabilities, as opposed to the many full-scale runs required via traditional fault injection.

7. RELATED WORK

The research community has explored many algorithm-based solutions for fault tolerant computing. One of the simplest approaches is the checksum procedure by Huang and Abraham [12]. It can detect single transient errors in linear algebra operations. This approach adds an extra row and an extra column to a matrix A. Each cell of the extra row contains a checksum of the cell's column and each cell of the extra column contains a checksums of the cell's row. This scheme can detect a single error in a particular matrix cell a_{ij} by comparing the sum of the ith row and the jth column to the values in the extra column and row. This checksum approach has been extended to use more sophisticated encodings [13]. The weighted checksum approach, which adds d extra weighted checksum rows or columns, can detect at most d transient data corruptions and correct at most $\lfloor \frac{d}{2} \rfloor$. Subsequent work adds more rigor to these contributions [3] by showing that any linear error correcting code can be used. However, these approaches are difficult to apply efficiently to sparse methods, such as AMG, for which the O(n) overhead of error detection and correction is significant.

Al-Yamani et al [2] compare the performance of several ABFT schemes as well as recomputation for many error rates. They present, implement and evaluate early detection ABFT schemes. Their results show that such techniques improve the performance of the algorithm for intensive computations and high error rates.

Roy-Chowdhury et al [23] developed an ABFT technique for the Gauss-Jacobi iterative solver for linear systems obtained from the discretization of the Poison differential equation on a rectangular grid. Exploiting some of the problem's symmetries, they derive an invariant expression that they use to detect data corruptions or other causes leading to invalid temporal solutions.

This work has been extended by Mishra and P. Banerjee [19] to the general Multi-Grid (MG) method. They derive an invariant to detect data corruptions that is applied during the relaxation phase of the MG algorithm. This invariant only works in regular grids. They also obtain checks for the restriction and the interpolation phases. They report that the overhead of these checks is negligible since it grows linearly with the size of the problem while the multigrid algorithm needs $O(n^2)$ operations to solve a nxn linear system. However, the checks developed in this contribution only protect MG algorithms against data corruptions, not against corrupted pointers. Even more, we have seen in Section 4.1 that AMG is resilient against data corruptions, which means that the invariant approach does not increase AMG's resilience and only adds overhead.

Turmon and Granat explored analytical models of error propagation for linear algebra operations [27]. These models are a basis for using checksum methods to validate the output of some routines. Interestingly, this work supports

methods to separate errors caused by a soft error from those caused by finite-precision numerical calculations.

Other approaches analyzed the vulnerability of sparse iterative methods to soft errors [7] and considered a variety of soft error detection and tolerance techniques, including checkpointing, linear matrix encodings, and residual tracking techniques. This work showed that the evaluated algorithms converged to an incorrect result approximately in 10% of the experimental runs and diverged in another 10% when injected with a single bit error in application memory. This result is superficially different from our conclusions that AMG is naturally resilient. The difference arises from two reasons. First, that study injected errors into application memory rather than computations. Such errors are persistent: once injected they continually corrupt the application's execution until the algorithm terminates. If such an error corrupts the inputs then the iterative solver will converge to the solution of a different problem. Further, that study looked at traditional linear solvers that work only at the problem's finest level. As we show in this work, the key to AMG's resilience to errors is in its coarse-grain relaxation steps. One way in which the studies validate each other is that both observe that segmentation faults are common in sparse linear algebra algorithms, further motivating our work on pointer replication.

8. CONCLUSION

We presented a methodology to evaluate the vulnerability of scientific applications to soft faults, efficiently improving their resilience and modeling their resulting scalability in faulty environments. We applied our approach to the Algebraic Multi-Grid algorithm, a powerful tool for solving large linear systems. To evaluate AMG's vulnerability we injected faults into its execution and demonstrated that AMG is naturally resilient to numerical errors. In particular, in most cases in which AMG converged correctly, it did so in the same number of V-cycles as during non-faulty runs. By visualizing the difference between the values of key variables in normal and corrupted runs we demonstrated that the reason for AMG's high resilience is that it performs relaxation over coarse grids. This approach dampens the large local errors introduced by error injection. In contrast, traditional iterative solvers only relax on the fine grid, which is much less effective at overcoming such errors.

Since AMG is primarily vulnerable to segmentation faults, we developed a novel targeted methodology to improve the resilience of its data structures. We used fault injection studies to identify the pointers that are most critical to the application's reliability and triplication to verify their correctness every time they were read. Our experiments show that this technique reduces the fraction of AMG runs affected by segmentation faults by 50% to 80% when AMG is exposed to hundreds of errors per second. Further, we applied this methodology to parallel runs of AMG on up to 1,600 cores using both OpenMP and MPI parallelization, showing it improves AMG's scalability by 35% and enabling it to scale almost as well as it does in the absence of faults. Finally, we presented a modeling methodology that uses fault injection experiments conducted at smaller scales to predict the application's scalability at large scales accurately. Our models further showed that segmentation faults explain most of the effect of soft faults on application scalability, while slowdowns due to extra V-cycles have a much smaller influence.

9. ACKNOWLEDGEMENTS

This article (LLNL-CONF-546331) has been authored in part by Lawrence Livermore National Security, LLC under Contract DE-AC52-07NA27344 with the U.S. Department of Energy and partially supported by the Department of Energy Office of Science (Advanced Scientific Computing Research) Early Career Grant, award number NA27344. Accordingly, the United States Government retains and the publisher, by accepting the article for publication, acknowledges that the United States Government retains a non-exclusive, paid-up, irrevocable, world-wide license to publish or reproduce the published form of this article or allow others to do so, for United States Government purposes.

10. REFERENCES

[1] International Technology Roadmap for Semiconductors. White Paper, ITRS, 2010.

[2] A. A. Al-Yamani, N. Oh, and E. J. McCluskey. Performance Evaluation of Checksum-Based ABFT. In *16th IEEE International Symposium on Defect and Fault-Tolerance in VLSI Systems*, 2001.

[3] C. J. Anfinson and F. T. Luk. A Linear Algebraic Model of Algorithm-Based Fault Tolerance. *IEEE Transactions on Computers*, 37(12):1599–1604, 1988.

[4] A. Avritzer, F. P. Duarte, R. M. M. Leao, E. de Souza e Silva, M. Cohen, and D. Costello. Reliability Estimation for Large Distributed Software Systems. In *Conference of the Center for Advanced Studies on Collaborative Research*, 2008.

[5] L. N. Bairavasundaram, R. G. Goodson, B. Schroeder, A. C. Arpaci-Dusseau, and R. H. Arpaci-Dusseau. An Analysis of Data Corruptions in the Storage Stack. In *USENIX Conference on File and Storage Technologies, (FAST)*, 2008.

[6] W. L. Briggs, V. E. Henson, and S. F. McCormick. *A Multigrid Tutorial*. 2000.

[7] G. Bronevetsky and B. R. de Supinski. Soft Error Vulnerability of Iterative Linear Algebra Methods. In *International Conference on Supercomputing (ICS)*, pages 155–164, 2008.

[8] M. de Kruijf, S. Nomura, and K. Sankaralingam. Relax: An Architectural Framework for Software Recovery of Hardware Faults. In *International Symposium on Computer Architecture (ISCA)*, 2010.

[9] R. Falgout, J. E. Jones, and U. M. Yang. The design and implementation of hypre, a library of parallel high performance preconditioners. *Numerical Solution of Partial Differential Equations on Parallel Computers*, (51), 2006.

[10] J. N. Glosli, K. J. Caspersen, J. A. Gunnels, D. F. Richards, R. E. Rudd, and F. H. Streitz. Extending Stability Beyond CPU Millennium: A Micron-Scale Atomistic Simulation of Kelvin-Helmholtz Instability. In *Proceedings of the 2007 ACM/IEEE conference on Supercomputing*, SC '07, pages 58:1–58:11, New York, NY, USA, 2007. ACM.

[11] G. H. Golub and Q. Ye. Inexact Preconditioned Conjugate Gradient Method with Inner-Outer Iteration. *SIAM Journal of Scientific Computing*, pages 1305–1320, 1999.

[12] K. H. Huang and A. J. Abraham. Algorithm Based Fault Tolerant for Matrix Operations. *IEEE Transactions on Computers*, C33:518–528, 1984.

[13] J. Y. Jou and A. J. Abraham. Fault-Tolerant Matrix Arithmetic and Signal Processing on Highly Concurrent Computing Structures. *Proc IEEE*, 74:732–741, 1986.

[14] P. Kogge. ExaScale Computing Study: Technology Challenges in Achieving Exascale Systems. Technical report, DARPA IPTO, September 2008.

[15] C. Lattner and V. Adve. LLVM: A Compilation Framework for Lifelong Program Analysis and Transformation. In *International Symposium on Code Generation and Optimization (CGO)*, 2004.

[16] L. Leem, H. Cho, J. Bau, Q. A. Jacobson, and S. Mitra. ERSA: Error Resilient System Architecture for Probabilistic Applications. In *Conference on Design, Automation and Test in Europe (DATE)*, pages 1560–1565, 2010.

[17] S. P. Meyn and R. L. Tweendie. *Markov Chains and Stochastic Stability*. 2008.

[18] S. Michalak, K. W. Harris, N. W. Hengartner, B. E. Takala, and S. A. Wender. Predicting the Number of Fatal Soft Errors in Los Alamos National Laboratory's ASC Q Supercomputer. *IEEE Transactions on Device and Materials Reliability*, 5(3), September 2005.

[19] A. Mishra and P. Banerjee. An Algorithm-Based Error Detection Scheme for the Multigrid Method. *IEEE Transactions on Computers*, 52(9):1089–1099, 2003.

[20] D. C. Montgomery, E. A. Peck, and G. G. Vining. *Introduction to Linear Regression Analysis*. Wiley, 2006.

[21] A. D. Polyanin. *Handbook of Linear Partial Differential Equations for Engineers and Scientists*. 2002.

[22] M. Rinard, H. Hoffmann, S. Misailovic, and S. Sidiroglou. Patterns and Statistical Analysis for Understanding Reduced Resource Computing. In *Conference on Object-Oriented Programming, Systems, Languages, and Applications (OOPSLA)*, 2010.

[23] A. Roy-Chowdhury, N. Bellas, and P. Banerjee. Algorithm-Based Error-Detection Schemes for Iterative Solution of Partial Differential Equations. *IEEE Transactions on Computers*, 45(4), 1996.

[24] Y. Saad and M. Schultz. GMRES: A Generalized Minimal Residual Algorithm for Solving Nonsymmetric Linear Systems. *SIAM Journal of Scientific Computing*, 7, 1986.

[25] J. Sloan, D. Kesler, R. Kumar, and A. Rahimi. A Numerical Optimization-Based Methodology for Application Robustification: Transforming Applications for Error Tolerance. In *IEEE/IFIP International Conference on Dependable Systems and Networks (DSN)*, pages 161–170, 2010.

[26] H. D. Sterck, R. Falgout, J. W. Nolting, and U. M. Yang. Distance-Two Interpolation for Parallel Algebraic Multigrid. *Numerical Linear Algebra with Applications*, 15:115–139, 2008.

[27] M. Turmon, R. Granat, D. S. Katz, and J. Z. Lou. Tests and Tolerances for High-Performance Software-Implemented Fault Detection. *IEEE Transactions on Computers*, 52(5):579–591, 2003.

Overcoming Single-Thread Performance Hurdles in the Core Fusion Reconfigurable Multicore Architecture

Janani Mukundan[†]
mukundan@csl.cornell.edu

Saugata Ghose[†]
ghose@csl.cornell.edu

Robert Karmazin[†]
rob@csl.cornell.edu

Engin İpek[*]
ipek@cs.rochester.edu

José F. Martínez[†]
martinez@cornell.edu

[†]Computer Systems Laboratory
Cornell University
Ithaca, NY 14853 USA
http://m3.csl.cornell.edu/

[*]University of Rochester
Rochester, NY 14627 USA
http://cs.rochester.edu/~ipek/

ABSTRACT

Though the prime target of multicore architectures is parallel and multithreaded workloads (which favors maximum core *count*), executing sequential code fast continues to remain critical (which benefits from maximum core *size*). This poses a difficult design trade-off. *Core Fusion* is a recently-proposed reconfigurable multicore architecture that attempts to circumvent this compromise by "fusing" groups of fundamentally independent cores into larger, more aggressive processors dynamically as needed. In this way, it accommodates highly parallel, partially parallel, multiprogrammed, and sequential codes with ease. However, the sequential performance of the original fused configuration falls quite short of an area-equivalent, monolithic, out-of-order processor.

This paper effectively eliminates the fusion deficit for sequential codes by attacking two major sources of inefficiency: collective commit and instruction steering. We demonstrate in detail that these modifications allow Core Fusion to essentially match the performance of an area-equivalent monolithic out-of-order processor. The implication is that the inclusion of wide-issue cores in future multicore designs may be unnecessary.

Categories and Subject Descriptors

C.1.3 [**Processor Architectures**]: Other Architectural Styles—*adaptable architectures*; B.7.1 [**Integrated Circuits**]: Types and Design Styles—*microprocessors and microcomputers*

Keywords

microarchitecture, multicore, software diversity, Core Fusion, collective commit, instruction steering, genetic programming

1. INTRODUCTION

Core Fusion [16] is a recently-proposed reconfigurable multicore architecture where four fundamentally independent two-issue out-of-order cores can fuse on demand into larger "supercores." Core Fusion supports software diversity because it may be configured for fine-grain parallelism (by providing more lean cores), coarse-grain parallelism and multiprogramming (by providing fewer, but more powerful 4-issue supercores, up to capacity), and sequential execution (by executing on one 8-issue supercore). Core Fusion scales with the number of cores on chip not by providing ever-wider-issue supercores, but by providing the ability to instantiate more supercores simultaneously.

The original paper compares Core Fusion against a multitude of competing symmetric and asymmetric multicore configurations of different granularities for sequential, multiprogrammed, and parallel codes. In all cases, Core Fusion is either the fastest or second fastest configuration; and all other configurations trail significantly from Core Fusion in performance for at least one type of workload. Moreover, for codes with significant parallel and serial sections, Core Fusion's dynamic reconfiguration capability compares favorably against any other static design.

However, the original paper also shows that, when executing sequential code, Core Fusion's performance is still noticeably lower than that of an area-equivalent monolithic out-of-order processor. This paper effectively eliminates Core Fusion's sequential performance deficit by attacking two major sources of its inefficiency—distributed commit (through efficient ROB storage) and remote operand communication (through improved instruction steering). We generate transistor-level netlists and simulate the circuit using HSPICE, verifying that our proposed steering mechanism operates within a single cycle with margins in a 4 GHz implementation at 22 nm.

We show that the performance of our improved Core Fusion architecture is within 98% of that of an area-equivalent monolithic out-of-order processor for both SPEC2000 Int and FP applications (vs. 88% and 82%, respectively, for the original Core Fusion proposal). The implication of this result is that the inclusion of wide-issue cores in future multicore designs may effectively be unnecessary, since a Core Fusion organization can now match their sequential performance when needed while retaining the ability to offer fine-grain parallelism on demand.

2. BACKGROUND: CORE FUSION

Core Fusion [16] provides the capability to dynamically fuse four two-issue out-of-order cores to form a large "supercore" with up to four times the fetch, execute, and commit width, as well as four times the aggregate cache and branch prediction capacity (Figure 1). In this section, we provide an abridged, non-comprehensive

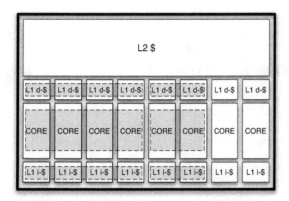

Figure 1: Conceptual depiction of an eight-core Core Fusion chip (not an actual floorplan). At left, four independent cores are fused to form a larger "supercore." To the right of them, two independent cores are fused into a smaller "supercore." The two rightmost cores are shown operating independently as distinct processing elements.

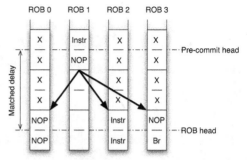

Figure 2: In this distributed ROB, a fetch group with four inserted NOPs is preparing to commit. The pair in ROB 1 is not ready to commit, so it broadcasts a a *Stall* signal to the other ROBs. Pre-commit and ROB heads are spaced to match the communication delay; the signal arrives just in time to prevent the other cores' pairs from committing. When the pair in ROB 1 becomes ready, a *Resume* signal is broadcast as the pair advances to the ROB head. The delay matching allows all of the ROBs to retire the entire fetch group in sync.

summary of the behavior of Core Fusion in fused mode as proposed originally; more details can be found in that paper.

Collective Fetch — When a four-core group transitions into fused mode, their instruction caches are flushed and they begin fetching code in a distributed fashion: On an instruction cache miss, a cache block of eight words is distributed across the four cores (a two-word sub-block for each core), and the tag for the cache block is replicated across cores. A centralized *fetch management unit* (FMU) coordinates collective fetch by receiving and communicating fetch information across cores. The collective fetch mechanism allows each core to fetch two instructions every cycle. Instruction fetch is aligned: Core 0 is responsible for the oldest two instructions, Core 1 for the next two, and so on. On a branch or jump, the oldest instruction in the fetch group might not be mapped to Core 0. In such cases, to preserve fetch alignment, the appropriate lower order cores skip fetch for that cycle. On a branch, the appropriate core accesses its own branch predictor, and BTB prediction table events are communicated to all other cores along with the target program counter. When events occur that stall the front end or require a pipeline flush (e.g. branch mispredictions, replay traps, fetch stalls), the cores send the program counter of the instruction causing the event to the FMU, which coordinates either the flush or stall by sending appropriate messages to each core.

Steer & Rename — After fetch, each core pre-decodes two instructions and sends the source and destination register specifiers to a common *steering management unit* (SMU). The SMU stage in the pipeline is similar to the rename stage of an out-of-order superscalar processor. It includes the rename map table and free lists for register allocation. Additionally, the SMU is also responsible for distributing instructions across cores. For this, the SMU uses a *global steering table*, which keeps track of the mapping between architectural registers and cores. The steering logic responsible for assigning instructions to cores also resides with the SMU. No more than two instructions are dispatched to each core every cycle. The SMU is also responsible for generating copy instructions to transfer operands to consumers that are not co-located with their producers. The copy instruction injection bandwidth is restricted to two per core, per cycle. The original paper identifies the overhead associated with remote operand communication between producer-consumer pairs steered to different cores as one important source of performance degradation (which we improve in this paper).

Collective Execution — Once the instructions have been steered and renamed, they are sent to their respective back ends based on the steering decisions. The cores make use of an operand crossbar to support remote operand communication using the SMU-

generated copy instructions. Additionally, the back end also includes copy-in and copy-out queues for incoming and outgoing copy instructions, respectively.

Collective Memory Access — Memory accesses are handled by the cores' data caches and load-store queues in a distributed fashion, using a bank-by-address approach. This allows the architecture to keep data coherent without requiring data cache flushes after dynamic reconfiguration, and to elegantly support store forwarding and speculative loads. The core issuing each load/store is determined using the effective address, and memory disambiguation is handled mostly locally at that core. Because effective addresses are generally not known when instructions are steered, a bank prediction mechanism is employed.

Collective Commit — The four cores can synchronously commit a fetch group of eight instructions (two per core) in one cycle. When instruction commit is blocked in one of the cores, commit of the fetch group in all cores must be stalled to guarantee (later) synchronous commit. This is done via *Stall/Resume* signals. Each ROB is equipped with a *pre-commit head pointer* placed ahead of the actual ROB head. Instruction pairs that are not ready to commit at the time they reach the pre-commit head will stall in place and send *Stall* signals to the other cores. Once they are ready, they send *Resume* signals to the other cores and continue moving toward the ROB head. The number of ROB entries between the pre-commit head and the actual ROB head is enough to cover the number of cycles it takes for the *Stall/Resume* signal to reach the other cores (2 cycles, requiring 4 entries).

In the next few sections we discuss two sources of inefficiencies in the Core Fusion pipeline and provide solutions to overcome them.

3. DISTRIBUTED COMMIT

Recall that, to simplify collective commit, Core Fusion commits one fetch group at a time (eight instructions, two per core). However, fetch groups are often not filled up to capacity, due to branch mispredictions and PC redirections after predict-taken branches. When this happens, Core Fusion inserts NOPs into the ROBs at the end of the fetch stage, so that each fetch group still occupies exactly two slots in each core's ROB.

Figure 2 shows an example of a fetch group padded with NOPs. The second instruction in ROB 1's pair is the target of a branch (not shown); thus, the ROB slots that precede this instruction are filled with NOPs to preserve alignment. Also, the first instruction in ROB 3's pair is a taken branch, and thus the subsequent instructions in the fetch group (only one in this case) have been nullified.

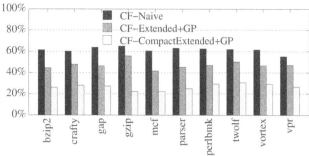

Figure 3: **Percentage of ROB entries occupied by NOPs when instruction fetch stalls due to a full ROB while running SPEC-Int applications. GP stands for the steering algorithm derived from genetic programming (see Section 4).**

The main downside of this approach is that the effective size of a core's ROB may be significantly reduced because of NOP insertions. Figure 3 shows that during fetch stalls caused by a full ROB, on average, 60% of the ROB entries are taken up by NOPs for SPEC-Int applications (CF-Naive shows the original Core Fusion mechanism). The original Core Fusion proposal already identifies NOP insertions as one important source of performance degradation [16]. In this section, we propose three new mechanisms to achieve synchronous commit of fetch groups while reducing the storage overhead of fetch group alignment in the ROBs. We do this by compacting the representation of such NOPs in the ROBs.

CF-Naive — This is the mechanism in the original Core Fusion proposal. NOPs inserted at the end of fetch for fetch group alignment occupy one ROB entry each, taking up to two ROB slots per core per fetch group. The top row of Figure 4 shows possible ways in which an instruction pair can be represented in a core's ROB according to this scheme.

CF-Compact — In this organization, an attempt is made to lessen storage overhead for the NOP+NOP pair case as follows: (i) Legitimate instruction pairs in each core take up two ROB slots as usual. (ii) A NOP+instruction pair is encoded by systematically storing the instruction in the first ROB slot, followed by the NOP. This is true even for a misaligned fetch where, strictly speaking, the inserted NOP should precede the instruction; notice that such reordering does not change the program semantics in any case. (iii) A NOP+NOP pair is encoded by a single NOP in the first ROB slot, in which case the second ROB slot becomes the first ROB slot for the next pair. When pre-commit and ROB heads encounter a pair for which the first ROB slot contains a NOP, they can easily recognize that the NOP encodes a NOP+NOP pair (case iii), and when appropriate they move one slot forward (instead of the usual two) in order to process the next pair. Thus, the Compact configuration halves the ROB storage requirement for the NOP+NOP pair case. The second row of Figure 4 shows possible ways in which an instruction pair can be represented in a core's ROB according to CF-Compact.

CF-Extended — In this organization, each ROB slot is extended with one NOP bit. (i) Legitimate instruction pairs in each core still take up two ROB slots as always; their NOP bits are set to zero. (ii) A NOP+instruction pair is encoded in a single ROB slot, by having the instruction take up the ROB slot and setting the NOP bit. (iii) The NOP+NOP pair is also encoded in a single ROB slot, by storing a NOP in the ROB slot proper and setting the NOP bit as well. Thus, in the Extended configuration, pairs with one or two NOPs (cases ii and iii) can be represented with a single ROB slot. The third row of Figure 4 shows possible ways in which an instruction pair can be represented in a core's ROB using this scheme.

CF-CompactExtended — In this configuration, we attempt to reduce the storage overhead even further for the NOP+NOP case. Each ROB slot is again extended with one NOP bit as follows:

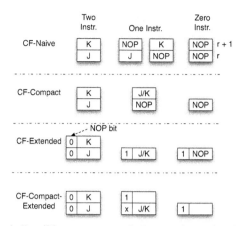

Figure 4: **Possible ways to encode instruction pairs, including any inserted NOPs at the end of the collective fetch phase, in the original (CF-Naive) and proposed ROB management schemes.**

(i) As before, legitimate instruction pairs in each core take up two ROB slots; their NOP bits are set to zero. (ii) A NOP+instruction pair is encoded by having the instruction take up the first ROB slot and setting the NOP bit for the *next* ROB slot, which becomes the new tail of the ROB. (iii) The NOP+NOP pair is encoded, by setting the NOP bit for the *current* ROB slot, without advancing the ROB tail. Thus, a NOP+NOP pair does not really occupy an ROB slot. (In situations where there are back-to-back NOP pairs, the first NOP pair is represented by setting the NOP bit of the ROB entry, and the second NOP pair is represented by inserting an actual NOP instruction in the ROB entry.) The bottom row of Figure 4 shows possible ways in which an instruction pair can be represented in a core's ROB according to this scheme.

At retirement, we must distinguish between the NOP+instruction and the NOP+NOP scenarios. While retiring instructions, the head slot of the ROB is first checked. If it contains an instruction, and the NOP bit is not set, we retire the instruction, move the head pointer, and check the next slot. If the second slot also contains an instruction and the NOP bit is not set (in the case of a legitimate instruction pair), we retire the instruction and advance the head pointer by one. If, however, the NOP bit is set for the second slot, this means that the bit was set as a result of a NOP+instruction pair, so we simply clear the NOP bit, but do not advance the ROB head pointer. On the other hand, while checking the first slot, if we find the NOP bit to be set, this means that the bit was set because of a NOP+NOP pair. In such a case, we clear the NOP bit and do not move the head pointer to the next subsequent ROB entry. Finally, recall that a ROB slot containing a proper NOP instruction also encodes a NOP+NOP case. In that case, assuming that the NOP bit was already reset during the last cycle (corresponding to the earlier NOP+NOP pair), the head slot is retired as a second NOP+NOP pair.

3.1 Branch Handling

Two details need to be addressed for the space-saving configurations to handle branches correctly. Notice that the number of ROB entries across cores is no longer in sync, because cores with NOPs will now try to encode them more efficiently. This presents a problem upon branch misprediction handling, for those cores which do not hold the offending branch: Where is the ROB slot beyond which everything must be squashed? Fortunately, the original Core Fusion proposal can readily accommodate this. Recall that, to keep the Global History Register consistent across cores, Core Fusion already uses a mechanism very similar to Alpha 21264's Outstanding Branch Queue (OBQ) [16, 19]. In our space-saving configurations, we can easily extend each OBQ entry with a pointer to the appropriate ROB entry in each core. That way, upon notification by the FMU of a misprediction, each core can, through the OBQ, easily identify the location beyond which everything must be squashed.

Second, for CF-CompactExtended, in the same ROB slot, we must be careful not to mix a pre-branch NOP bit with a post-branch instruction in those cores which do not directly store the branch instruction. Should we allow that, on a branch misprediction, we would be unable to figure out whether that NOP bit pertains to code before or after the branch. To resolve this, at the time the FMU notifies each core of a branch, if the ROB tail points to an entry with its NOP bit set, the core resets the NOP bit and explicitly stores a NOP in it, unequivocally making it part of the code preceding the branch. (Later at retirement, this special case of a NOP instruction with NOP bit = 0 can be easily recognized and processed.)

3.2 Area Analysis

The CF-Compact organization requires minimal hardware additions over CF-Naive—mainly a means for the pre-commit and ROB heads to recognize the NOP+NOP case. There is no additional raw storage overhead. In the CF-Extended organization, we do increase raw storage in each core's ROB by one bit per ROB slot. Assuming that each ROB entry takes on the order of 50 bits (32-bit PC, 6-bit destination register, 6-bit recycle register, 1-bit valid field, 1-bit exception field, 4-bit interrupt field), the ROB storage overhead of CF-Extended is 2%. (Later, in Section 6, we compensate for this overhead by providing CF-Naive and CF-Compact with extra ROB slots.) We also add six bits to each OBQ entry, for a total of 72 bits per core. The CF-CompactExtended has the same additional overhead as the CF-Extended setup.

4. INSTRUCTION STEERING

Instruction steering must strike a delicate balance between minimizing remote operand communication and making effective use of all cores. Excessive operand co-location in any one core reduces remote operand communications at the expense of load balancing. Conversely, excessive load balancing may result in high communication overheads. Optimal instruction steering is provably NP-complete [37]. Although several heuristics have been proposed and compared against each other, there is no known way to establish a tight upper bound to instruction steering performance. Moreover, Core Fusion's architecture differs in important aspects from the clustered architectures that served as context to most of these proposals.

Rather than engaging in (yet another) "expert" analysis of a problem of such complexity using strictly human intuition, we propose to take an automated approach. We use genetic programs (GP) [22, 23] to search for a static, high-performance steering policy that suits our context and whose hardware implementation is simple enough to execute within a single processor cycle. To our knowledge, this is the first paper to address instruction steering systematically in this way.

4.1 Original Steering Algorithm

The original Core Fusion steering algorithm is a modified version of the dependence-based algorithm [27]. Each steering link has an instruction queue, drained at a rate of two instructions per cycle (matching the destination core's issue width). If the instruction has one operand, it is sent to the least-loaded of the queues whose core has a *copy* of the source operand or producer instruction. If the instruction has two operands, it is sent to the least-loaded queue whose core has both; if no such core exists, it is sent to the least-loaded queue whose core contains a copy of either $source_1$ or $source_2$. This algorithm considers dependencies, copies, and load balancing, with several levels of decisions.

Algorithm 1 Improved instruction steering policy for CF-CompactExtended, derived via genetic programming.

```
 1: for all instructions in the fetch group
 2:     if instruction contains both source₁ and source₂ operands then
 3:         steeredCluster ← core where source₁ operand produced
 4:     else
 5:         if instruction contains a source₁ operand only then
 6:             steeredCluster ← core where source₁ operand produced
 7:         else
 8:             steeredCluster ← least-loaded core (at beginning of cycle)
 9:         end if
10:     end if
11: end for
```

4.2 Steering Policy Derivation

4.2.1 Genetic Programming Setup

For the GP mechanism to explore the design space of tree-based steering policies, we first codify a set of 28 functions (which make decisions) and 18 terminals (which assign a particular value for the destination core). These functions and terminals are derived from previously-proposed steering policies. Example functions include checking the type of an instruction (e.g., if it is a branch), determining the number of valid source operands the instruction has (0, 1, or 2), checking to see if each source operand value is ready, or evaluating if the instruction is dependent on a load. Examples of terminals include the least-loaded core (i.e., the core with the least number of instructions in flight), the core that produced either the first source operand or the second one, a random core, the core with the least copy bandwidth filled, or the least-loaded core that contains a copy of both source operands.

We use these states and terminals to come up with an initial random population of 100 steering policies. These are then evaluated on a training set of three integer and three floating-point applications from the MinneSPEC suite [21],[1] using IPC as a fitness function, as measured in detailed simulation models (see Section 5). We select parent policies for the next generation using a fitness-proportional selection methodology called tournament selection, coupled with elitist selection [23]. The parent policies are then evolved using crossover and mutation to get the next generation [22, 23, 24]. The new generation of steering policies is again evaluated on our training set, and so forth.

We stop the training phase after evolving 200 generations, at which point, convergence is observed. Among the policies that perform within 2% of the best-performing policy, we manually select one whose hardware implementation is simple enough that its latency is less than one clock period. This then becomes our policy of choice for our final evaluation (see Section 6). We apply this process separately for the CF-Naive, CF-Compact, CF-Extended and CF-CompactExtended configurations (see Section 5), yielding four steering policies that are best optimized for each case. The rest of this section discusses the policy for CF-CompactExtended.

In order to consider the feasibility of the hardware implementation, we correlate the tree structure to the expected hardware design as a rough approximation—a larger number of terminal nodes will require a larger hardware area, whereas a larger tree depth requires not only greater area, but greater latency as well. Figure 5 shows a scatter plot of the top ten policies, plotting their tree depth versus IPC. Of these, we select the policy in the upper left corner, mini-

---

[1]The MinneSPEC suite features reduced versions of the full SPEC CPU 2000 [10] applications, which we use in our final evaluation (see Section 5.2). To avoid overfitting, we ensure that (a) the number of applications used in our final evaluation is significantly larger; (b) the applications used for training are simulated for different regions of code than in our final evaluation; and (c) we use reduced input sets for training.

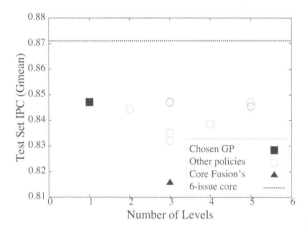

Figure 5: Scatter plot of the top 10 GP-derived steering policies for CF-CompactExtended. The number of levels acts as a corollary to the expected latency of the policy.

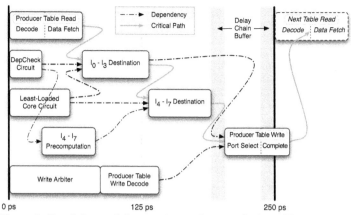

Figure 6: Breakdown of the steering cycle, to scale for a 22 nm process (Borkar scaling). Arrows indicate data dependencies. The gray bars illustrate the buffer used to tolerate the susceptibility of delay chains to process variation. (A delay chain is used to trigger the write port select.)

mizing complexity with near-peak performance. As we will see in Section 4.3, simplicity will be important to make steering implementable in an aggressive 4 GHz, 22 nm pipeline design.

4.2.2 Selected Algorithm

Algorithm 1 lists the procedure for our selected policy. For every instruction that needs to be steered, the algorithm determines the core where its source operands are produced. If they happen to be produced in the same core, we steer the instruction to this common producer core. If not, we pick the core where the first operand is produced, and steer the instruction there. If the instruction does not have source operands, we steer it to the least-loaded core.

The resulting algorithm has a number of interesting features:

- Consumers always follow the producer instruction, even if an operand replica may be available elsewhere. This contradicts earlier proposals for instruction steering in the context of clustered processors [1, 8, 30]. While following replicas may improve load balancing, we identified situations where this practice is counter-productive. Consider, for example, an instruction I_1 that produces a value consumed by otherwise independent instructions I_{2a} and I_{2b}. Instruction I_3 uses the values produced by both I_{2a} and I_{2b}. If I_{2a} and I_{2b} are steered to different cores, I_3 will be forced to receive at least one of its operands from a remote core. If, however, both I_{2a} and I_{2b} are steered to I_1's core, steering I_3 to that same core easily avoids the costly remote operand communication.

- The cores' load is not taken into account, except when there are no operands to follow. This also contradicts some of the earlier proposals of instruction steering [1, 3, 8]. Notice that the way Core Fusion does instruction steering already provides a form of load balancing, by assigning a maximum of two instructions per core, per cycle.[2] In this context, the GP procedure did not find that monitoring a core's load was productive in the general case.

- Algorithm 1, as depicted, favors $source_1$ over $source_2$ for two-source-operand instructions (Step 3). Experiments show that picking either operand yields the same performance. The GP did not generate any superior algorithms that checked both source operands (e.g., algorithms that check the load of each operand's core [1]), or even algorithms that picked a source operand randomly. Thus, we favor systematically

picking the same operand because it simplifies hardware (see Section 4.3).

- The algorithm is simple, which leads to a hardware implementation that can meet high-speed timing constraints.

4.3 Hardware Implementation

Instruction steering is a critical mechanism that cannot be easily pipelined, as steering decisions typically must know the decisions for immediately-preceding instructions. As a result, it is important to demonstrate that all instructions within a fetch group can be processed within a single cycle. Even with as few decision tree levels as our chosen policy (see Figure 5), we find that steering fits into a single cycle with little slack. Therefore, simplicity is of the essence.

Steering eight instructions using Algorithm 1 requires two operations: (a) determining which cores contain the registers that $source_1$ of each instruction references, and (b) finding the core with the least number of instructions pending for issue. To complete successfully within the given clock period, part (a) is split into two steps—determining the cores containing the desired registers at the beginning of the cycle (before any of the current instructions are steered), and then modifying these destinations based on read-after-write dependencies within the fetch group.

Our implementation requires four major components:

- a **producer table**, mapping architectural registers to cores,

- a **least-loaded core circuit**, which compares issue queue occupancies amongst the four cores,

- a **dependency-checking circuit** that tracks read-after-write dependencies within the fetch group, and

- a **destination core circuit**, for aggregating the information from the first three components and determining which core to send the instructions to.

All combinational logic in the steering mechanism was designed using static CMOS logic, optimized to reduce logic depth. We implemented this logic using a NAND-NAND topology. We parallelize many of the basic building blocks within the steering stage; Figure 6 shows our sequence of operations. We elaborate on the producer table and the destination core circuit in the following sections, as they fall on the critical path of the steering circuit. An area and delay analysis is presented in Section 4.4.

4.3.1 Producer Table

The producer table is a 32x2b SRAM structure with eight read and eight write ports. Each entry holds the ID of the core that produces the corresponding architectural register. Within a single

---

[2] If the steering algorithm assigns more than two instructions from the same fetch group to any one core, steering for subsequent fetch groups stalls until all instructions from the current fetch group are injected. This was introduced in the original Core Fusion proposal as a means to achieve a simpler and more feasible hardware implementation.

clock cycle, the steering management unit (SMU) must read from the table and write back new values before the next read occurs.

The large number of read and write ports required for this design would create an unreasonably large capacitance on the data-storing nodes of a traditional SRAM cell, affecting access times as well as write stability. The need for fast read and write latencies forces us to abandon the 6T SRAM cell and use a modified version. An inverter is added to each bitcell to buffer the output, isolating all of the read ports from the data-storing nodes. Dedicated *set* and *reset* transistors are also added to every cell to enable fast writes. In all, these changes allow us to remove the bitlines and wordlines found in typical SRAM structures, thus removing the latency of charging and discharging highly-capacitive wires. Though this design is less dense than a traditional SRAM structure, given the criticality of latency minimization for this application and the relatively small storage requirements (only 64 bits), this is a worthwhile trade-off.

The producer table read begins at the start of the SMU cycle. From the pre-decode pipeline stage, each core front-end will provide two *source$_1$* register specifiers to the SMU (one for each instruction), which will be used to index the table. Once the address is decoded, the core ID is fetched. To ensure that setup and hold times are met for the registers at the end of the SMU steering stage, transparent Earle latches (which are off the critical path) are used, allowing the table to be re-used while the clock is low.

Data write-back technically starts with the write arbiter, which resolves write-after-write register dependencies within the same fetch group. The arbiter grant signals are then processed by the write decoders, to determine which data value to send to the *set/reset* transistors for the modified rows. All this can be completed in parallel with the critical path, as the destination register for each instruction is known at the start of each cycle. Once the destination core calculation has completed, a delay chain triggers the write enable pulse, asserting the appropriate *set/reset* signals on the bitcells themselves. After a certain pulse width, the bitcell will have passed its switching threshold, and will settle to its intended value even if the enable signal is de-asserted before the bitcell completes its transition. We exploit this completion stage for improved latency, as discussed in Section 4.4.2.

4.3.2 Least-Loaded Core & Dependency-Checking Circuits

The least-loaded core is calculated using the issue queue occupancy values at the beginning of the cycle. In case of a tie, the core with the lower ID is statically chosen (using less-than-or-equal-to comparators). The dependency-checking circuit identifies read-after-write dependencies within the current fetch group, comparing *source$_1$* registers with the destination registers. This circuit consists of 28 5-bit comparators. Neither circuit falls on the critical path (see Figure 6).

4.3.3 Destination Core Circuit

For our steering algorithm, an instruction can be sent to one of two places: (a) if the first source operand exists, to the core that produced that value; otherwise (b) to the least-loaded core. The producer table provides a stale value for the core containing the first source operand of each instruction, which we will refer to as S_n, where I_n is the nth instruction being steered in the current cycle. We also know whether the instruction has a valid *source$_1$* operand (from the pre-decode stage), which we will refer to as V_n.

For instruction I_0, computing the destination core C_0 simply involves choosing either the least-loaded core (LLC) or S_0:

$$C_0 = (LLC \wedge \neg V_0) \vee (S_0 \wedge V_0) \qquad (1)$$

Subsequent instructions involve more complex logic, as they may also have read-after-write dependencies on instructions steered in the same fetch group—remember that the value of S_n is not up-

dated after each steering decision. To fit within a cycle, we choose to "unroll" the destination core equations and use deeper Boolean logic gates—while this does replicate some calculations, we reduce the total number of logic levels (and thus, signal transitions) needed to compute each core. This is conceptually similar to how outputs are constructed in a carry-lookahead circuit. For example, the logic to steer I_1 is:

$$C_1 = (LLC \wedge \neg V_1) \vee (S_1 \wedge V_0 \wedge \neg I_1 DI_0) \vee (C_0 \wedge I_1 DI_0) \quad (2)$$

where $I_1 DI_0$ is whether the *source$_1$* operand of I_1 is produced by I_0. If we substitute Equation 1 in for C_0, we can flatten the gates for C_1, removing the need for serialization:

$$\begin{aligned} C_1 =&(LLC \wedge \neg V_1) \vee (S_1 \wedge V_0 \wedge \neg I_1 DI_0) \\ &\vee (LLC \wedge \neg V_0 \wedge I_1 DI_0) \vee (S_0 \wedge V_0 \wedge I_1 DI_0) \end{aligned} \qquad (3)$$

Likewise, this technique can be applied up to instruction I_3.

While instructions I_4 through I_7 could also be calculated in this flattened manner, the corresponding circuits would become relatively large (for example, I_7 would involve the sum of 256 logic products, some of which include 9 logic terms, themselves requiring four gates to compute). Instead, we compute the destination cores for these instructions once the destination cores C_0 through C_3 are computed. While this does perform a serialization step, we find that we can significantly reduce the area while still meeting timing constraints (I_7 now contains 48 logic products). Furthermore, many of the control signals in these products can be partially pre-computed off of the critical path.

4.4 Circuit Analysis

The entire steering mechanism has been implemented at the transistor level, and its functionality and performance have been verified using HSPICE simulations [34]. Given the tight timing constraints, low-V_t transistors are used for every circuit except for the SRAM cells in the producer table and keepers on dynamic gates, in order to minimize the latency of all the components. All simulations were run using custom transistor-level netlists, with transistor models provided by IBM for their 45 nm 12SOI process [36].

Every transistor was carefully sized in order to balance drive strength with parasitics. Gate capacitances and diffusion capacitances are accounted for in the transistor models themselves, and accurately scale with transistor size, gate topology, and fanout. An additional 4 fF of load capacitance is added to every gate to model wiring parasitics. This value has been extracted from previously-fabricated designs in this process technology.

We assume a 22 nm process technology for all of our steering circuitry. ITRS forecasts are used to used to scale delays from 45 nm to 22 nm technology (conservatively using planar bulk transistor models as opposed to multi-gate transistors, and using 2014 forecasts for 24 nm) [17]. We also use a conservative 22 nm scaling factor from Borkar [2].

4.4.1 Area

In total, the steering mechanism uses 21,340 MOSFET transistors. This represents a very tiny area overhead within a processor. Table 1 breaks down the transistor count by each component. Many of the larger units (e.g., dependency-checking circuit, write arbiter) are the result of logical unrolling, where common sub-circuits have been repeated to improve performance.

4.4.2 Delay

Figure 6 not only shows the timings of each component to scale, but it also illustrates the data dependencies between these blocks. The critical path travels through the producer table read, destination core computation, and producer table write. Unless otherwise noted, all latencies in this section use the more conservative scaling

Table 1: Transistor counts for the steering circuit components.

Circuit	Transistor Count
Producer Table	11872
Least-Loaded Core	914
Dependency Check	2520
Write Arbiter	2706
$I_0 - I_3$ Dest. Core	776
$I_4 - I_7$ Dest. Core	1564
$I_4 - I_7$ Precompute	412
Earle Latches	576
TOTAL	21340

Table 2: Steering circuit latencies (ps). 45 nm values are only provided for circuits simulated using the IBM 12SOI model in HSPICE. Critical path circuits italicized.

Circuit		45 nm	32 nm		22 nm	
			Conservative	Traditional	Borkar	ITRS
Producer Table Read	*Decode*	40.50	36.99	34.90	34.09	30.08
	Data Fetch	41.45	37.86	35.72	34.89	30.78
Producer Table Write	*Decode*	65.65	59.96	56.58	55.26	48.75
	Port Select	40.00	36.53	34.47	33.67	29.70
	Completion	32.07	29.29	27.64	26.99	23.82
Least-Loaded Core		67.72	61.85	58.36	57.00	50.29
Dependency Check		36.83	33.64	31.74	31.00	27.35
Write Arbiter		101.79	92.96	87.72	85.68	75.59
$I_0 - I_3$ Destination Core		74.39	67.94	64.11	62.62	55.24
$I_4 - I_7$ Destination Core		69.89	63.83	60.23	58.83	51.90
CRITICAL PATH		266.23	243.15	229.44	224.10	197.70

proposed by Borkar [2], and target a 22 nm technology. A conservative FO4 ring oscillator scaling and the traditional NMOSFET scaling, both from ITRS, are used to provide 32 nm latencies as a reference. Table 2 summarizes these numbers, and includes latencies for scaling methods in both 32 nm and 22 nm technology.

Along the critical path, a total of 224.10 ps is required for the circuit to execute. Since the critical path includes the use of a delay chain to trigger the producer table write (see Section 4.3.1), extra timing margins must be left in place. Increased process variations at smaller technologies may shift the trigger time in either direction. To account for this, the extra time left over in the cycle (currently 25.90 ps) is partitioned equally on both sides of the table write. Setup times for the end-of-stage registers are masked by the write, as they only require the output of the destination core circuits.

An important aspect of our circuit timing is the overlap between the producer table write completion and the read decode for the next cycle, as seen in Figure 6. We note that the data inside the table must be stable for reading only after the read ports have finished decoding, as the bitcells are not accessed up to that point. We can take advantage of our observation in Section 4.3.1 by asserting write enable just long enough to cross the switching threshold of the bitcell. Write completion can therefore overlap with the read decode of the next cycle without introducing any data hazards, since the decode latency is longer than the completion time.

5. EXPERIMENTAL METHODOLOGY

5.1 Architectural Setup

We design our experiments assuming a 22 nm process technology. We increase the L2 cache size from 4 MB to 8 MB, and increase associativity from 8 ways to 16. However, we do not change the pipeline structure of the cores from the ones described in İpek et al. [16] for 65 nm. This is in line with recent trends observed in industry [13, 15, 18]: As process technology scales, frequency has stopped scaling beyond the 4 GHz range, and the additional slack achieved in the clock period is typically put to use not by redesigning the pipelines, but by lowering the chip supply voltage, thereby consuming less power per core and enabling more cores to be simultaneously active on the chip with the smaller feature size.

All our experiments have been carried out using a highly-detailed and heavily-customized version of the SESC simulator [29]. We evaluate the performance of the *CF-Naive*, *CF-Compact*, *CF-Extended*, and *CF-CompactExtended* configurations, with both GP-generated steering (*+GP*) and the original Core Fusion steering solution (see Section 4.1). To compensate for extending each ROB entry by one NOP bit, we allocate two additional ROB entries to CF-Naive and CF-Compact. Table 5 shows the various configurations evaluated, and Table 3 describes the microarchitecture of the two-issue base core used in Core Fusion.

We use the performance of an area-equivalent monolithic processor (*Monolithic*) as reference. It is a six-issue out-of-order processor with three times the amount of core resources as the two-issue base core, but four times the size of the base core's L1 cache, branch predictor, and BTB. We model wake-up and selection delays in the base core to be one cycle each, and extrapolate such delays for the six-issue core to 3 and 2 cycles, respectively, using trends presented in the literature [11, 12, 26]. We assume that wake-up and select are fully pipelined for the six-issue core [33].

Across different configurations, we always maintain the same parameters for the shared portion of the memory subsystem (system bus and lower levels of the memory hierarchy; see Table 4). All configurations are clocked at the same speed.

5.2 Applications

Since we focus on improving the performance of sequential applications, we evaluate our proposal using the SPEC CPU 2000 application suite for the MIPS ISA [10]. We use the *ref* input sets, and simulate one billion instructions for each workload, skipping the initialization phase. The SimPoint toolset [32] was used to ensure that the simulated instructions were a representative sample of the entire application.

5.3 Core Fusion Overheads

Area — We estimate the area overhead of all original Core Fusion additions pessimistically. To calculate the area overheads from wiring, we use the wiring area estimation methodology described by Kumar et al. [25], assuming a 22 nm technology and global wires with a 81 nm wire pitch, as projected by ITRS [17]. The delay of global wires with repeater links is obtained from Chen et al. [5]. Accordingly, we calculate the area of fetch wiring (92 bits/link) to be 0.21 mm^2, the area of rename wiring (250 bits/link) to be 0.60 mm^2, the area of the operand crossbar (80 bits/link) to be 1.09 mm^2, and the commit wiring overhead (20 bits/link) to be 0.02 mm^2. The wiring area overhead amounts to 1.92 mm^2 for a single fusion group of four cores. Scaling from the original paper, the extra cache tags, copy-in/copy-out queues and the bank predictors to be 0.24 mm^2, 0.13 mm^2, 0.08 mm^2 and 0.12 mm^2, respectively, for a fusion group of four cores. This amounts to a total of 0.57 mm^2 for the group. Adding these to the wiring overheads, we estimate an overall area overhead to be 2.49 mm^2 per fusion group for the Core Fusion architecture, including our proposed extensions.

Assuming a reticle-limited 400 mm^2 die size,[3] one fusion group takes up an area of 49 mm^2. For the original Core Fusion architecture, with two fusion groups, the area overhead (4.98 mm^2) is less than half that of a two-issue core (12.25 mm^2)—smaller than the overhead reported in İpek et al. [16], which targeted a (now obsolete) 65 nm technology node. The result is reassuring that the overhead of our enhanced Core Fusion solution remains manageable.

---

[3] Some server multicore chips today, such as Intel's Xeon or IBM's Power7, have a die area in excess of 500 mm^2 [6, 14].

Table 3: Parameters of the base two-issue core.

Frequency	4 GHz
Fetch/issue/commit width	2/2/2
Int/FP/AGU/Br Units	1/1/1/1
Int/FP Multipliers	1/1
Int/FP issue queue size	16/16 entries
ROB (reorder buffer) entries	48
Int/FP registers	32 + 40 / 32 + 40 (Arch. + Phys.)
Ld/St queue entries	12/12
Bank predictor	2,048 entries
Max. br. pred. rate	1 taken/cycle
Max. unresolved br.	12
Br. mispred. penalty	7 cycles min., 14 cycles when fused
Br. predictor	Alpha 21264 (tournament)
RAS entries	32
BTB size	512 entries, 8-way
iL1/dL1 size	16 kB
iL1/dL1 block size	32 B/32 B
iL1/dL1 round-trip latency	2/3 cycles (uncontended)
iL1/dL1 ports	1 / 2
iL1/dL1 MSHR entries	8
iL1/dL1 associativity	direct-mapped/4-way
Memory Disambiguation	Perfect
Coherence protocol	MESI
Consistency model	Release consistency

Table 4: Parameters of the shared L2 and DRAM subsystem.

System bus transfer rate	32 GB/s
Shared L2	8 MB, 64 B block size
Shared L2 Associativity	16-way
Shared L2 banks	16
L2 MSHR entries	16/bank
L2 round-trip	32 cycles (uncontended)
Memory access latency	328 cycles (uncontended)

Table 5: Configurations evaluated.

CF-Naive	4×2-issue with (48+2)-entry ROB / core
CF-Naive+GP	— + custom GP steering
CF-Compact	4×2-issue with (48+2)-entry ROB / core
CF-Compact+GP	— + custom GP steering
CF-Extended	4×2-issue + 48-entry Extended ROB / core
CF-Extended+GP	— + custom GP steering
CF-CompactExtended	4×2-issue + 48-entry Extended ROB / core
CF-CompactExtended+GP	— + custom GP steering
Monolithic	Area-equivalent monolithic core (Section 5.1)

Delay — To calculate the wire delays we assume the worst-case cross-core communication distance. From Friedman [9], we find the delay of global wires with repeater links to be 31.8 ps/mm in 22 nm technology. As aforementioned, one fusion group of four cores takes up an area of 49 mm^2. We expect to floorplan the processor such that all cross-core communicating logic will sit in the quadrant of the core—1.75 mm on each side—closest to the center of the chip. Therefore, the worst-case cross-core communication distance will be 7 mm. Assuming the widest possible link, the worst-case communication distance can be traversed in one cycle. However, we conservatively set the communication latencies for fetch, rename, operand transfer, and commit to be two cycles each.

6. EVALUATION

Figures 7 and 8 show the performance obtained by the various CF configurations considered in this study, relative to Monolithic on SPEC CPU 2000 applications. From Figure 8, we see that CF-CompactExtended+GP is the CF configuration that performs best: it improves performance over CF-Naive by 11.5%, and it is within 98% of Monolithic for the SPEC-Int applications. For SPEC-FP, we improve performance over CF-Naive by 19%, and we are again within 98% of Monolithic. In contrast, the performance of CF-Naive is only within 88% and 82% of Monolithic for SPEC-Int and SPEC-FP, respectively. Note that we see some speedups over the 6-issue baseline as in fused mode, Core Fusion can provide 8-wide issue.

As Figure 8 shows, the results for SPEC-Int applications suggest a somewhat synergistic effect between the proposed mechanisms for distributed commit and instruction steering. (SPEC-FP applications, which typically respond very well to mechanisms that exploit instruction-level parallelism, benefit primarily from the ability of the extended ROB to support more in-flight instructions.) These two mechanisms attack different stages of the pipeline: The retirement scheme was added to improve throughput in the fetch stage of the pipeline, by reducing NOP insertions and thereby increasing useful instructions being fed into the subsequent pipeline stages. The improved instruction steering algorithm focuses on improving throughput in the execution stage, by increasing the probability of producers and consumers being co-located in a core. Naturally, only freeing a bottleneck in one stage while allowing the other to persist will not improve performance as effectively. When the two techniques are coupled together, the opportunity to co-locate dependent instructions increases, as does the number of useful instructions in the pipeline. By co-locating more dependent instruc-

tions, we reduce the wait time involved for consumers to issue after their producers complete, thereby improving issue rate, and hence commit rate. An increase in commit rate frees up ROB entries faster, which in turn helps prevent fetch stalls, which increases the ROB occupancy. This positive feedback leads to a more free-flowing pipeline, due to a decrease in pipeline stalls in both stages, resulting in better overall performance for CF-CompactExtended+GP than the sum of the two effects separately (CF-CompactExtended and CF-Naive+GP).

Next, we analyze CF-CompactExtended+GP in more detail. For brevity, we provide analysis for SPEC-Int applications only—the findings are consistent with the results for SPEC-FP as well.

6.1 Inside Distributed Commit

Recall that the new retirement scheme was added to the baseline architecture (CF-Naive) to reduce unnecessary NOP insertions in the ROB. If the number of NOPs inserted is reduced, the ROB can be filled with more useful instructions, which may result in more in-flight instructions (and hence higher potential for exploiting instruction-level parallelism). This is particularly important for handling long-latency load operations: With more NOPs filling up the ROB, there are fewer in-flight loads in the pipeline, and thus the possibility of exploiting memory-level parallelism (MLP) by overlapping long-latency loads is smaller. Higher MLP often results in better overall performance [28]. Figures 3 and 9 show that the new retirement scheme indeed increases the effective use of the ROB with respect to CF-Naive, and in particular it improves memory-level parallelism.

6.2 Inside Instruction Steering

In order to understand the effect of the GP-generated steering algorithm, we introduce a metric called *communication penalty*. Every cycle, for each core, we count the number of instructions that are issued. For every free issue slot that is not filled, we check to see if an instruction is not issued due to a source operand not being available. For such instructions, we check if the producer has already completed execution in another remote core. This means that, if the producer and consumer were co-located, the consumer could have issued immediately after the producer; but now it has to wait for the copy instruction to arrive at the consumer core. If an issue slot is not filled for such a scenario, we assign a communication penalty of one. Thus, the maximum penalty a core can be assigned each cycle is two, as each core has two issue slots it can fill every cycle.

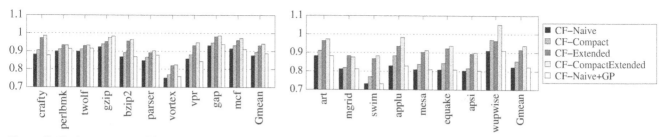

Figure 7: Performance resulting from applying our proposed configurations in isolation, normalized to that of an area-equivalent monolithic core configuration (Section 5.1), for SPEC-Int (left) and SPEC-FP (right) applications.

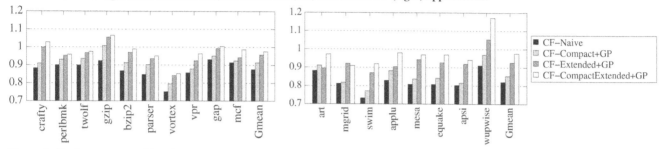

Figure 8: Performance resulting from the synergy between improved commit and improved steering, normalized to that of an area-equivalent monolithic core configuration (Section 5.1), for SPEC-Int (left) and SPEC-FP (right) applications.

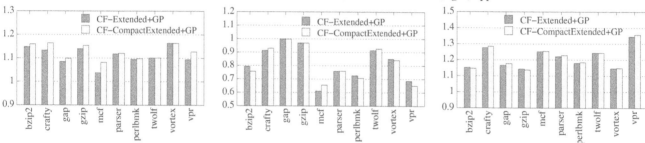

Figure 9: Increase in memory-level parallelism (MLP) when running SPEC-Int applications, relative to CF-Naive.

Figure 10: Stall time due to remote operand communication for SPEC-Int applications, relative to CF-Naive.

Figure 11: Increase in locally co-located producer-consumer pairs for SPEC-Int applications, relative to CF-Naive.

Figure 10 gives us the communication penalty observed relative to CF-Naive. The results show that CF-CompactExtended+GP incurs a lesser penalty than CF-Naive for all applications; the improvement is rather significant in some of them. This is because the steering algorithm in CF-CompactExtended+GP improves the probability of co-locating producers and consumers (Figure 11). By reducing communication delays among producers and consumers in this way, we issue instructions at a faster rate, which leads to improved performance.

7. RELATED WORK

Reconfigurable multicore architectures — TFlex [20] is a novel reconfigurable architecture comprised of distributed composable tiles that communicate with each other via control and operand networks. While TFlex can use its dataflow-based ISA to track dependent instructions, this custom ISA requires extensive binary modifications and additional compiler support.

Federation [35] is another reconfigurable architecture along the lines of Core Fusion that proposes fusing a pair of scalar cores into a two-way out-of-order processor. Salverda and Zilles demonstrate the fundamental challenges in reconfiguring in-order cores into larger cores, on demand, even under ideal conditions, as it necessitates very complex instruction steering hardware [31].

Clustered architectures — One of the very first approaches to clustering involved designing a microarchitecture that would simplify the wakeup and selection logic by introducing multiple in-order issue queues, and placing chains of dependent instructions in them [27].

Another early approach extended the floating-point cluster to execute simple integer instructions, resulting in a clustered architecture [3]. The steering schemes used are a combination of reducing workload imbalance and inter-cluster communications.

The Multicluster architecture introduced a dynamically-scheduled partitioned architecture which allowed the register file of one cluster to be accessed by instructions being executed on another cluster, by distributing an instruction to multiple clusters [7].

Canal et al. [4] have proposed various dynamic code partitioning mechanisms for clustered microarchitectures. The basic idea of dynamic code partitioning is to steer instructions present in either a *LdSt slice* or a *Br slice* within a register dependence graph to the same cluster. They also experimented with static steering algorithms, and their results indicate that dynamic steering algorithms outperform static cluster assignments in general. Moreover, static cluster assignment tends to be less flexible and needs compiler support as well as extensions to the ISA.

Baniasadi and Moshovos investigated various non-adaptive and adaptive instruction steering techniques for quad-cluster dynamically-scheduled superscalar processors [1]. They studied the sensitivity of steering heuristics to relevant architectural parameters, such as inter-cluster communication latency and pipeline depth, and found that performance is much more sensitive to inter-cluster communication.

8. CONCLUSION

In this paper, we attack two important inefficiencies of Core Fusion—collective commit storage and cross-core operand communication overheads. We introduce a new commit scheme that reduces the storage requirement associated with NOP insertions, thereby increasing the number of ROB entries available to useful instructions. This in turn increases the number of in-flight load instructions, allowing a greater possibility of overlapping long-latency loads, and improving memory level parallelism in the system. The improved performance is achieved with virtually negligible area and delay overheads. We also introduce an improved instruction steering algorithm, which reduces the communication penalty by increasing the probability of co-locating producers and consumer instructions. We derive this algorithm systematically using genetic programming, verify the steering circuit implementation using HSPICE, and provide a detailed area and delay analysis. By combining these two techniques, the performance of our improved Core Fusion architecture comes within 98% of that of an area-equivalent monolithic machine for both SPEC-Int and SPEC-FP. The implication is that Core Fusion may effectively render the inclusion of wide-issue cores in future multicore designs unnecessary, since it can match their sequential performance when needed while retaining the ability to offer fine-grain parallelism on demand through its narrow-width base cores.

9. ACKNOWLEDGEMENTS

This research was supported in part by NSF CAREER Award CCF-0545995, NSF Award CNS-0720773, and gifts from IBM, Intel, and Microsoft. Saugata Ghose was supported in part by DoD, Air Force Office of Scientific Research, National Defense Science and Engineering Graduate (NDSEG) Fellowship, 32 CFR 168a.

10. REFERENCES

[1] A. Baniasadi and A. Moshovos. Instruction distribution heuristics for quad-cluster, dynamically-scheduled, superscalar processors. In *MICRO*, 2000.

[2] S. Borkar. Major challenges to achieve exascale performance. In *Salishan Conf.*, 2009. Presentation.

[3] R. Canal, J.-M. Parcerisa, and A. González. A cost-effective clustered architecture. In *PACT*, 1999.

[4] R. Canal, J.-M. Parcerisa, and A. Gonzalez. Dynamic cluster assignment mechanisms. In *HPCA*, 2000.

[5] G. Chen, H. Chen, M. Haurylau, N. Nelson, P. M. Fauchet, E. G. Friedman, and D. Albonesi. Predictions of CMOS compatible on-chip optical interconnect. In *SLIP*, 2005.

[6] EUROSOI Newsletter. IBM's Power7 heats up server competition at Hot Chips. http://www.eurosoi.org/public/Newsletter_AugSept2009.pdf.

[7] K. I. Farkas, P. Chow, N. P. Jouppi, and Z. G. Vranesic. The Multicluster architecture: Reducing processor cycle time through partitioning. *International Journal of Parallel Programming*, 27(5):327–356, 1999.

[8] B. Fields, S. Rubin, and R. Bodik. Focusing processor policies via critical-path prediction. In *ISCA*, 2001.

[9] E. G. Friedman. Predictions, challenges, and opportunities in CMOS compatible on-chip optical interconnect. In *STEP Conf. on Optical Computer Developments*, 2008.

[10] J. L. Henning. SPEC CPU2000: Measuring CPU performance in the new millennium. *IEEE Computer*, 33(7):28–35, July 2000.

[11] G. Hinton, D. Sager, M. Upton, D. Boggs, D. Carmean, A. Kyker, and P. Roussel. The microarchitecture of the Pentium 4 processor. *Intel Technology Journal*, Q1 2001.

[12] M. S. Hrishikesh, N. P. Jouppi, K. I. Farkas, D. Burger, S. W. Keckler, and P. Shivakumar. The optimal logic depth per pipeline stage is 6 to 8 FO4 inverter delays. In *ISCA*, 2002.

[13] Intel Corporation. First the tick, now the tock: Next-generation Intel microarchitecture (Nehalem). http://www.intel.com/technology/architecture-silicon/next-gen/whitepaper.pdf.

[14] Intel Corporation. Intel Xeon 7400 Processor series. http://www.intel.com/p/en_US/products/server/processor/xeon7000.

[15] Intel Corporation. Introducing the 45nm Next-Generation Intel Core Microarchitecture. http://www.citrix.com/site/resources/dynamic/partnerDocs/Intel_45nm-core2_whitepaper.pdf.

[16] E. İpek, M. Kırman, N. Kırman, and J. F. Martínez. Core Fusion: Accomadating software diversity in chip multiprocessors. In *ISCA*, 2007.

[17] ITRS. International Technology Roadmap for Semiconductors: 2010 update. http://www.itrs.net/reports.html.

[18] H. Iwai. Roadmap for 22nm and beyond (invited paper). *Microelectron. Eng*, 86:1520–1528, Nov. 2009.

[19] R. E. Kessler, E. J. McLellan, and D. A. Webb. The Alpha 21264 microprocessor architecture. In *International Conference on Computer Design*, pages 90–95, Austin, Texas, Oct. 1998.

[20] C. Kim, S. Sethumadhavan, M. S. Govindan, N. Ranganathan, D. Gulati, D. Burger, and S. W. Keckler. Composable lightweight processors. In *MICRO*, 2007.

[21] A. KleinOsowski, J. Flynn, N. Meares, and D. Lilja. Adapting the SPEC 2000 benchmark suite for simulation-based computer architecture research. In *Workshop on Workload Characterization*, Austin, TX, Sept. 2000.

[22] J. R. Koza. *Genetic Programming: A Paradigm for Genetically Breeding Populations Of Computer Programs to Solve Problems - Technical Report*. Stanford University, Computer Science Department, 1990.

[23] J. R. Koza. *Genetic Programming: On the Programming of Computers by Means of Natural Selection*. MIT Press, Cambridge, MA, 1992.

[24] J. R. Koza, M. A. Keane, M. J. Streeter, W. Mydlowec, J. Yu, and G. Lanza. *Genetic Programming IV: Routine Human-Competitive Machine Intelligence*. Kluwer Academic Publishers, 2003.

[25] R. Kumar, V. Zyuban, and D. M. Tullsen. Interconnections in multi-core architectures: Understanding the mechanisms, overheads and scaling. In *ISCA*, 2005.

[26] S. Palacharla, N. Jouppi, and J. E. Smith. *Technical Report: Quantifying the Complexity of Superscalar Processors*. University of Wisconsin - Madison, 1996.

[27] S. Palacharla, N. P. Jouppi, and J. E. Smith. Complexity-effective superscalar processors. In *ISCA*, 1997.

[28] M. K. Qureshi, D. N. Lynch, O. Mutlu, and Y. N. Patt. A case for MLP-aware cache. In *ISCA*, 2006.

[29] J. Renau, B. Fraguela, J. Tuck, W. Liu, M. Prvulovic, L. Ceze, S. Sarangi, P. Sack, K. Strauss, and P. Montesinos. SESC simulator, January 2005. http://sesc.sourceforge.net.

[30] P. Salverda and C. Zilles. A criticality analysis of clustering in superscalar processors. In *MICRO*, 2005.

[31] P. Salverda and C. Zilles. Fundamental performance constraints in horizontal fusion of in-order cores. In *HPCA*, 2007.

[32] T. Sherwood, E. Perelman, G. Hamerly, and B. Calder. Automatically characterizing large scale program behavior. In *ASPLOS*, 2002.

[33] J. Stark, M. D. Brown, and Y. N. Patt. On pipelining dynamic instruction scheduling logic. In *MICRO*, 2000.

[34] Synopsys. HSPICE: Circuit simulation. http://www.synopsys.com/Tools/Verification/AMSVerification/CircuitSimulation/HSPICE/.

[35] D. Tarjan, M. Boyer, and K. Skadron. Federation: Repurposing scalar cores for out-of-order instruction issue. In *DAC*, 2008.

[36] The MOSIS Service. IBM 45 nanometer 12SOI CMOS process. http://www.mosis.com/ibm/12soi/.

[37] V. V. Zyuban and P. M. Kogge. Inherently lower-power high-performance superscalar architectures. *IEEE Trans. Computers*, 50(3):268–285, 2001.

CVP: An Energy-Efficient Indirect Branch Prediction with Compiler-Guided Value Pattern

Mingxing Tan, Xianhua Liu, Dong Tong, Xu Cheng
Microprocessor Research and Development Center, Peking University, Beijing, China
{tanmingxing, liuxianhua, tongdong, chengxu}@mprc.pku.edu.cn

ABSTRACT

Indirect branch prediction is becoming increasingly important in modern high-performance processors. However, previous indirect branch predictors either require a significant amount of hardware storage and complexity, or heavily rely on the expensive manual profiling.

In this paper, we propose the *Compiler-Guided Value Pattern (CVP)* prediction, an energy-efficient and accurate indirect branch prediction via compiler-microarchitecture cooperation. The key of CVP prediction is to use the compiler-guided value pattern as the correlated information to hint the dynamic predictor. The value pattern reflects the *pattern regularity* of the value correlation, and thus significantly improves the prediction accuracy even in the case of deep pipeline stage or long memory latency. CVP prediction relies on the compiler to automatically identify the primary value correlation based on three high-level program substructures: *virtual function calls, switch-case statements* and *function pointer calls*. The compiler-identified information is then fed back to the dynamic predictor and is further used to hint the indirect branch prediction at runtime. We show that CVP prediction can be implemented in modern processors with little extra hardware support.

Evaluations show that CVP prediction can significantly improve the prediction accuracy by 46% over the traditional BTB-based prediction, leading to the performance improvement of 20%. Compared with the state-of-the-art aggressive ITTAGE and VBBI predictors, CVP prediction can improve the performance by 5.5% and 4.2% respectively.

Categories and Subject Descriptors

C.1.0 [**Processor Architectures**]: General;
C.5.3 [**Computer System Implementation**]: Microcomputers—*Microprocessors*

Keywords

Indirect branch prediction, compiler-guided value pattern.

1. INTRODUCTION

In modern high-performance processors, accurate branch prediction can improve both the performance and energy efficiency. As indirect branches are widely used in modern applications [10, 21], an accurate indirect branch predictor is becoming an important component of modern processors [14]. Unfortunately, indirect branches are hard to predict because each indirect branch may correspond to multiple targets [18, 21]. As a special kind of indirect branches, function return instructions can be predicted using return-address-stack [19], but other indirect branches used for virtual function calls, switch-case statements, and function pointer calls are hard to predict. As a result, indirect branch mispredictions usually make up a sizable fraction of overall branch mispredictions [18, 21]. We evaluate the Mispredictions Per Kilo Instructions (MPKI) for conditional branches, function returns and indirect branches[1] in a 4-issue, 16-stage processor with a 4-way, 4K-entry Branch Target Buffer (BTB). Figure 1 shows the results. On average, the indirect branch MPKI accounts for 42% of total mispredictions.

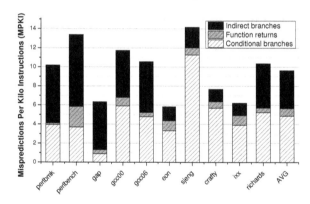

Figure 1: MPKI for different kinds of branches.

Previous indirect branch predictors mainly require a significant amount of extra hardware storage and complexity. History-based predictors such as TTC predictor [5], Cascade predictor [7] and ITTAGE predictor [28] generally require large extra storage; while value-based ARVI predictor [6] and VBBI predictor [11] heavily rely on the complex control logics or manual profiling. These predictors mainly focus on hardware-only approach, because they hope to be readily deployed into existing architectures and maintain bina-

---

[1]In the rest of this paper, an "indirect branch" refers to a non-return unconditional indirect branch instruction.

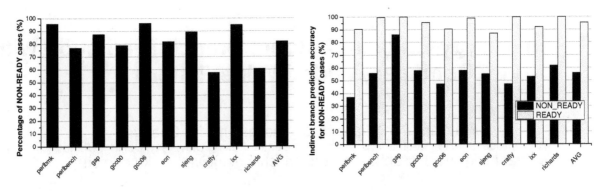

Figure 2: Percentage (left) and prediction accuracy (right) for NON-READY cases.

ry compatibility. However, as energy efficiency is becoming the fundamental performance limit of modern processors [4], their significant hardware complexity actually deters their adoption in modern processors [25].

We observe that the inefficiency of previous hardware-only predictors mainly comes from the lack of high-level control-flow and dataflow information. For example, the state-of-the-art ITTAGE predictor [28] uses thousands bits of global history to track distant branch correlation, but few branches actually make effective use of that very long history information [25]. Especially, previous value-based predictors rely on complex hardware to track data dependence, but such dependence can be easily and effectively identified by the compiler based on high-level dataflow information. Based on this observation, we argue that a compiler-microarchitecture cooperative approach can be more accurate and more efficient than previous hardware-only branch predictors.

In this paper, we propose a compiler-microarchitecture cooperative indirect branch prediction, called Compiler-Guided Value Pattern (CVP) prediction. It relies on the cooperation between the compiler and the dynamic predictor to utilize the effective value pattern information. The compiler automatically identifies primary value correlation based on high-level program substructure and explicitly inserts guiding instructions to indicate the primary value correlation. At runtime, the predictor uses a low-cost filter table and a simple global register to maintain the value pattern according to the compiler-guided information. Unlike previous value-based predictors, CVP prediction combines multiple data values to form a value pattern and then uses the value pattern rather than a single value to hint the dynamic predictor. The value pattern reflects the pattern regularity of the value correlation, which significantly improves the prediction accuracy even in the case of long pipeline or memory latency. We show that CVP prediction is energy-efficient, requiring only little extra hardware support. Evaluations show that CVP prediction can significantly improve the prediction accuracy and performance over the traditional BTB-based predictor. Compared with those aggressive ITTAGE [28] and VBBI [11] predictors, it still performs better with much lower hardware complexity.

The remainder of this paper is organized as follows: Section 2 explains the motivation. Section 3 discusses the details of our approach, including both the compiler support and predictor hardware. Section 4 provides experimental methodology and Section 5 shows results. Section 6 discusses related work and section 7 concludes.

2. MOTIVATION

2.1 Looking At the Value Correlation

Correlation-based predictors are the most widely used branch predictors [5, 6, 7, 11, 21]. Recent research [11] has shown value correlation is more effective than traditional history correlation for indirect branch prediction. However, there are two limitations for the value correlation. The first limitation is that it is very difficult to find proper data values that have strong correlation with branch targets. Previous predictors generally rely on large storage buffer [34], complex control logics [6] or expensive manual profiling [11] to identify proper value correlation, and they are usually ineffective even with aggressive hardware support. In this paper, we propose to identify effective value correlation based on high-level dataflow information at compile time.

Another important limitation is that the latest data values are usually unavailable at the prediction time because of the long pipeline and memory latency in modern high-performance processors. We call it NON-READY problem. The NON-READY problem is inherent for value-base predictors and it is especially significant in large issue width and deep pipeline superscalar processors. We evaluate the NON-READY cases (the latest data values are not available) and READY cases (the latest data values are available) on a 4-issue, 16-stage pipeline superscalar processor. Figure 2 shows the percentage and prediction accuracy. On average, NON-READY cases account for 78% of all cases, but their prediction accuracy is almost 40% lower than READY cases.

2.2 Our Cooperative Approach

In this paper, we propose the *compiler-guided value pattern*, a novel value correlation for indirect branch prediction. The idea of value pattern is derived from the central concept of history-based predictors, in which multiple resolved branch outputs are combined to distinguish dynamic occurrences of each branch [5]. Our approach combines multiple correlated data values to form a *value pattern* and then uses the value pattern to distinguish dynamic occurrences of each indirect branch. To our knowledge, it is the first time to utilize the *value pattern* in indirect branch prediction, even though the context based value prediction technique [27] has adopted similar policy. Our approach explores the correlation between indirect branch targets and the *pattern regularity* of the value correlation rather than a single data value, so even if the latest single data value is unavailable at the prediction time, it still achieves high prediction accuracy.

The compiler-guided value pattern relies on the cooperation between the compiler and the microarchitecture. First, it relies on the compiler to automatically identify effective primary value correlation based on high-level dataflow information. Through analyzing the three widely used program substructures: *virtual function calls, switch-case statements* and *function pointer calls*, we show that indirect branches in different program substructures are usually correlated to different data values . Second, the value pattern also relies on a low-complexity filter table and a global value pattern register to maintain the value pattern. We show that the extra hardware storage is small and the control logic is simple.

2.3 Source Code Example

Figure 3 shows an example taken from 458.sjeng benchmark in SPEC CPU 2006 suite [32]. The indirect branch (*jmp*) has strong correlation with the variable t. However, the value of t is generally unavailable at the time of indirect branch prediction, especially when the condition of the *if-statement* is false. As a result, traditional value-based predictors [6, 11, 34] perform low accuracy ($\leq 54\%$) for those NON-READY cases. In contrast, our CVP prediction can achieve the prediction accuracy of 93% by correlating the predicted target addresses to the value pattern.

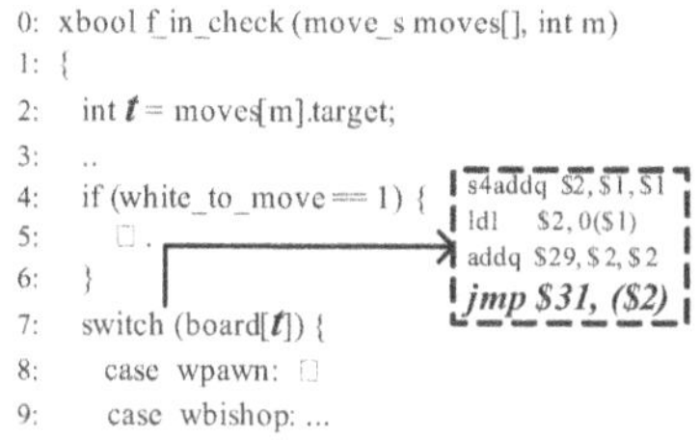

```
0:  xbool f_in_check (move_s moves[], int m)
1:  {
2:      int t = moves[m].target;
3:      ..
4:      if (white_to_move == 1) {           s4addq $2, $1, $1
5:          □                                ldl    $2, 0($1)
6:      }                                    addq $29, $2, $2
7:      switch (board[t]) {                  jmp $31, ($2)
8:          case wpawn: □
9:          case wbishop: ...
```

Figure 3: A source code snippet from 458.sjeng.

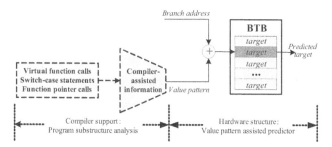

Figure 4: A scene of the branch target prediction.

Figure 4 shows a scene for the NON-READY branch listed in Figure 3. There are two dynamic targets $T1$ and $T2$, which correspond to two date values: $\{a \rightarrow T1, b \rightarrow T2\}$. However, the latest values are always unavailable at the prediction time. In this example, both the traditional BTB predictor and the traditional value-based predictor will perform low prediction accuracy. In contrast, our CVP prediction combines multiple data values (e.g. two values) to form the value pattern: $\{aa, ab, bb, ba\}$. Results show that such a simple value pattern can well reflect the pattern regularity and this value pattern has strong correlation with the predicted targets: $\{aa \rightarrow T2, ab \rightarrow T2, bb \rightarrow T1, ba \rightarrow T1\}$. After the warm-up time t_6, CVP prediction can always predict the correct target if data values keep this pattern regularity.

3. CVP PREDICTION

3.1 Overview

CVP prediction relies on the cooperation between the hardware and the compiler to utilize the value pattern. Figure 5 shows the overview of CVP prediction. At compile time, the compiler identifies the correlated data values based on three program substructures: *virtual function calls, switch-case statements* and *function pointer calls*. The compiler-assisted information is passed to the dynamic predictor using a special *nop* instruction, called *guiding instruction*. At runtime, the processor combines those data values to form the value pattern according to the compiler-assisted information. When an indirect branch instruction is fetched, the predictor uses the hash value of the branch address and the value pattern to get the final predicted target address from the Branch Target Buffer (BTB).

Figure 5: Overview of CVP prediction.

3.2 Compiler Support for CVP Prediction

3.2.1 Program Substructure Analysis

Program substructures illustrate the high-level control-flow and dataflow features for a local code region. In this paper, we mainly study three widely used program substructures: *virtual function calls, switch-case statements* and *function pointer calls*. These three program substructures cover most of indirect branches in modern applications [8]. The compiler identifies the effective value correlation based on two principles: first, the identified data value should better have one-to-one correspondence to the branch target address; second, the data value should be produced as early as possible. Specifically, the compiler identifies the primary value correlation as follows:

Virtual function calls: The compiler usually implements a virtual function call as a serial of load operations followed by an indirect branch. Figure 6 shows the execution of a virtual function, which contains four steps [26]: O(Object), V(Vtable), F(Function) and C(Call). Given a virtual object, it first loads the start address of the vtable from a fixed offset of the virtual object, then it loads the function address from the vtable and jumps to the target function by an indirect call. The object address is not strongly correlated to the target address because many objects can branch to the same target address. The offset to the vtable is constant for each virtual call, so the start address of the vtable has one-to-one correspondence to the final branch target address. As a result, the compiler treats the start address of the vtable as the final correlated data value.

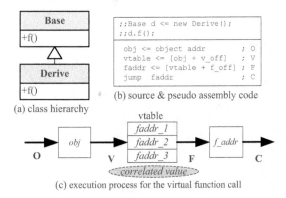

(a) class hierarchy

```
;;Base d <= new Derive();
;;d.f();

obj   <= object addr        ; O
vtable <= [obj + v_off]     ; V
faddr <= [vtable + f_off]   ; F
jump   faddr                ; C
```

(b) source & pseudo assembly code

(c) execution process for the virtual function call

Figure 6: The process of virtual function call.

```
switch(k)
{
  case 0...3:
    ...//action 1
  case 4...7:
    ...//action 2
  case 8...11:
}
```

(a) source code

```
bv <= k                   ; C
nv <= bv/4                ; N
caddr <= [ctable+nv]      ; G
jump  caddr               ; J

L1:···  ;;action 1
L2:···  ;;action 2
```

(b) pseudo assembly code

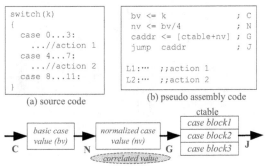

(c) Execution process for the switch-case statement

Figure 7: The process of switch-case statement.

Switch-case statements: Figure 7 shows the process of a switch-case statement, which contains four steps: C (Case value), N (Normalized value), G (Global case table) and J (Jump). The basic case value is firstly normalized to a serial of enumerable values such as 0, 1, 2, 3 ... The normalized value is used as index to get the case block address from the global case table. At last, an indirect branch is executed to transfer the control flow to the corresponding case block. Multiple original case values can be mapped into one case block, but each one case block corresponds to exactly one normalized case value. In other words, the normalized value has strongly correlation with branch target, so the compiler takes the normalized case value as the value correlation.

Function pointer calls: The process of a function pointer call usually contains a load operation followed by an indirect branch. The target of a pointer call is decided by the pointer value, so the compiler usually identifies the pointer value as the correlated value. However, when a serial of function pointer calls are organized as a constant pointer array, the compiler will treat the array index as the value correlation.

3.2.2 Guiding Instruction Encoding

After the program substructure analysis, the compiler should pass the value correlation to the dynamic predictor. Modifying existing instructions [33] and adding new instructions are two common approaches to pass the compiler-assisted information in previous compiler-microarchitecture cooperative

techniques. In our simulation, the compiler-assisted information is passed by a special *nop* instruction, called *guiding instruction*. The special *nop* instruction consists of an opcode and some unused bits, in which the compiler-assisted value correlation information is encoded. We mainly investigate those correlated data values that reside in the register file, so the register number (rn) is the only extra information encoded in the special *nop* instruction. These special *nop* instructions do nothing to the semantics of the program and they are simply stripped out of the instruction stream after their execution, so their negative impact on the overall performance is limited.

Similar to other cooperative techniques, our approaches may raise the compatibility problem. Previous research [17] has shown such problem can be addressed through decoupling the architected and physical instruction set architecture with binary translation system. In-depth study is beyond the scope of this paper, so we assume such problem has been addressed and the extra overhead is acceptable.

3.2.3 Guiding Instruction Inserting and Scheduling

The compiler explicitly inserts guiding instructions to transfer the compiler-assisted information. For each indirect branch instruction, the compiler computes the Definition-Use chain for its corresponding correlated variables, which can be the start address of vtable, the normalized case value or the function pointer value. Then, the compiler inserts a guiding instruction immediately after the definition instruction. For those inter-procedure variable definitions, the compiler simply inserts a guiding instruction into function prologue to avoid the inter-procedure analysis. At last, the compiler schedules the guiding instruction using the global instruction scheduling technique [3]. If the guiding instruction is a precedent node of the indirect branch, then the guiding instruction is scheduled as far as possible to the branch; otherwise, it is scheduled as near as possible to the branch. In other words, it targets to increase the dynamic distance between the guiding instruction and its corresponding indirect branch instruction.

3.3 Hardware Design

3.3.1 Basic Hardware Structure

Figure 8 shows the hardware structure of CVP prediction. It mainly consists of four components: the Register file (Regfile), the Global Value Pattern Register (GVPR), the Filter Table (FT) and the Branch Target Buffer (BTB). Both the Regfile and the BTB are existing components in modern superscalar processors, so only the GVPR and the FT are two extra components for the CVP prediction.

The GVPR is a global register which is used to maintain the value pattern information. It is updated when guiding instructions are executed and then accessed in the fetch stage. When a guiding instruction is executed, the GVPR is updated by concatenating a part of the original GVPR bits and a part of data value bits indicated by the guiding instruction. When an indirect branch instruction is fetched, the processor uses the value pattern in the GVPR to guide the target address prediction. Since the value pattern has strong correlation with indirect branch target addresses, the GVPR always provides effective correlated information no matter whether it has been updated by the single latest data value at the prediction time.

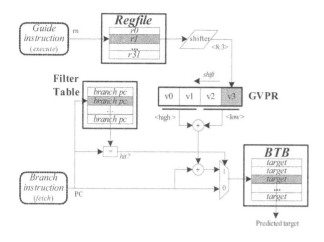

Figure 8: Hardware structure for CVP prediction.

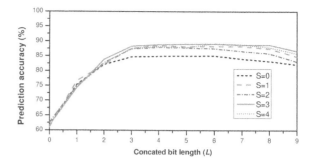

Figure 9: Prediction accuracy on different concatenating policy.

The FT is used to pick out indirect branches that are hard-to-predict using traditional BTB predictor. Hard-to-predict indirect branches correspond to multiple dynamic targets and these targets change frequently, so they usually behave low prediction accuracy in traditional BTB predictor. In our CVP prediction, only hard-to-predict indirect branches are predicted using value pattern, while other regular branches are predicted in the same way as traditional BTB predictor. The FT contains a serial of *branch_pc*, i.e., the address of hard-to-predict branches. Only those indirect branches whose corresponding Program Counter (PC) exist in the FT are considered as hard-to-predict indirect branches, while the others are considered as regular branches. The FT can be implemented as direct-map or way-associate. In our simulation, we implement the FT as 2-way set associative; each entry only contains the pc tag and its output is a simple 'hit-or-miss'. The FT is read in the fetch stage and updated in the retire stage. When an indirect branch is fetched, the processor looks up the FT to decide whether it is a hard-to-predict branch. Subsequently, when the indirect branch is retired, the processor updates the FT using the branch address if it is a hard-to-predict indirect branch.

As shown in Figure 8, CVP prediction also requires a simple control logic, which mainly consists of the following components: (i) a comparator for the Filter Table lookup; (ii) two XOR gates and a MUX for the target address prediction; (iii) a shifter and an OR gate for the GVPR update. In addition, CVP prediction reuses the existing BTB to store predicted target addresses (similar to [11, 21]), so no extra large target cache storage is required.

3.3.2 Value Pattern Update

Value pattern is updated by guiding instructions. When a guiding instruction is executed, the processor immediately reads out the primary data value from the Regfile. The primary data value is preprocessed by right shifting some bits. Then, the processor concatenates the original GVPR with the primary data value by left shifting the GVPR and OR-ing the low bits of the primary data value. After that, the guiding instruction is stripped out of the instruction stream. Note that to update the value pattern as earlier as possible, the processor may actually execute guiding instructions in the issue stage, which is the earliest time that its dependent register is ready.

The GVPR update process is affected by the concatenating policy. Assuming L is the length of bits shifted into the GVPR and S is the starting bit position from where L bits are taken from the primary data value. Figure 9 shows the prediction accuracy on different L and S. Results show that the prediction accuracy is stable when $4 \leqslant L \leqslant 7$ and $2 \leqslant S \leqslant 4$, meaning that these concatenating policies can reflect the pattern regularity very well. In our simulation, we set $L = 6$ and $S = 3$, so the part of $<8:3>$ bits are extracted from the primary data value for GVPR updating. However, both P and L can be implemented as configurable to adapt to various applications.

Since the GVPR register is updated before retirement, it may potentially get polluted by incorrectly fetched guiding instructions from the wrong path of execution. Generally, such issue can be addressed using the repair mechanism by referring to the return-address-stack repair mechanism [31]. However, our evaluations show that such cases are rare (less than 2%) and the negative impact is negligible, so we don't repair the GVPR for the sake of hardware complexity in our simulation.

3.3.3 Target Address Prediction and Update

The indirect branch target address is predicted in the fetch stage and updated in the retire stage. When an indirect branch instruction is fetched, the processor generates the predicted target address from the BTB at the index of hashing result of the value pattern and the branch address. The filter table is used to distinguish hard-to-predict indirect branches and other regular branches. The prediction flow is completed within two cycles. In the first cycle, the processor looks up the FT and the BTB in parallel at the index specified by the indirect branch instruction's PC. If the FT lookup result is a miss, which means the instruction is a regular branch, then the prediction is finished in one cycle and the processor continues to fetch the next instruction using the predicted target address produced in the first cycle. If the FT lookup result is a hit, then the processor cancels the BTB lookup result in the first cycle, and restarts a new BTB lookup process in the second cycle at the index computed by hashing the instruction's PC with the folded value pattern resided in the GVPR register. The second BTB lookup is needed only for hard-to-predict indirect branches, so it does not affect the regular conditional or indirect branch prediction.

When the indirect branch instruction is retired, the corresponding BTB entry is updated with the actual target (if

Table 1: Characteristics of evaluated benchmarks

	perlbmk	perlbench	gap	gcc00	gcc06	eon	sjeng	crafty	ixx	richards	AVG
Language type	C	C	C	C	C	C++	C	C	C++	C++	-
Static indirect jumps	343	11	57	460	65	129	96	9	232	11	125
Dynamic indirect jumps (K)	1790	2000	1333	1216	1029	1462	689	221	290	912	1012
Baseline IPC	1.00	1.16	1.68	1.48	1.79	1.60	1.35	1.42	1.73	1.51	1.47

different from the predicted target) using the same BTB index computed in the fetch stage.

3.3.4 Filter Table Update

CVP prediction relies on the Filter Table (FT) to distinguish between regular branches and hard-to-predict indirect branches. The FT is updated in the retire stage. When an indirect branch instruction is retired, the processor compares the predicted target address with the actual target address. If the predicted target address is different from the actual target address, and the corresponding BTB lookup is 'hit', then the indirect branch must have corresponded to multiple different target addresses. In such a case, the current indirect branch instruction is identified as an hard-to-predict indirect branch, and the corresponding branch instruction PC is written into the FT. If the filter table is full, then an existing entry is evicted out according to the First-in-First-Out (FIFO) replacement policy.

3.3.5 Implementation Cost

The extra overhead includes the compilation cost and the hardware cost. The compilation complexity is low, requiring only intra-function level dataflow analysis and instruction scheduling. In our simulation, the additional compile time overhead is less than 1% of overall compile time with -O2 optimization level. Note our approach does not require profiling, so it is applicable to modern processors.

The hardware cost of CVP prediction mainly comes from the Global Value Pattern Register (GVPR) and the Filter Table (FT). In our simulation, the GVPR is a 32-bit register with some shifting components. The FT is implemented as a 32-entry, 2-way associative and tagged hardware structure. Each entry contains 32-bit *branch_pc*, so the total size of the FT structure is 1024 bits. Besides the GVPR and the FT, CVP prediction also requires a simple control logic consisting of a comparator, a shifter, a mux and two XOR gates. The full control logic is shown in Figure 8. Furthermore, CVP prediction only adds minor modification to the BTB index component. Compared with previous BTB-reused predictors [21] that add significant link structure modification to the exiting BTB, CVP prediction is much low-complexity.

In conclusion, we show that the CVP prediction requires only 1024 bits extra storage, a global register and a simple control logic consisting of a few muxes, comparators and shifters, so it is low-complexity and applicable to modern energy-efficient processors.

4. EXPERIMENTS METHODOLOGY

We extend the SimpleScalar/Alpha [2] to evaluate CVP prediction. Table 2 shows the parameters of the baseline processor. The baseline processor uses a 4K-entry, 4-way BTB to predict conditional and indirect branch targets. Function return instructions are predicted using a 32-entry return-address-stack [19], while other indirect branches are predict-

Table 2: Baseline processor configuration

Front End	4 instructions per cycle; fetch ends at the first predicted taken branch or indirect jump
Execution Core	4-wide decode/issue/execute/commit; 512-entry ROB; 128-entry LSQ
Branch Predictor	12KB hybrid pred. (8K-entry bimodal and selector, 32K-entry gshare); 4K-entry, 4-way BTB with LRU; 32-entry return address stack; 15 cycle min. branch misprediction penalty
On-chip Caches	16KB, 4-way, 1-cycle L1 D-cache and L1 I-cache; 1MB, 8-way, 10-cycle unified L2 cache; All caches have 64B block size with LRU replacement
Memory	150-cycle latency (first chunk), 15-cycle (rest)

ed using the traditional BTB predictor [22]. We also compare our technique with those state-of-the-art aggressive indirect branch predictors including VBBI predictor [11], and ITTAGE predictor [30, 28].

CVP prediction is evaluated using 5 SPEC CPU 2000 INT benchmarks, 3 SPEC CPU 2006 INT benchmarks [32] and 2 other C++ programs. We choose those benchmarks in SPEC INT2000 and SPEC INT2006 suites that gain at least 5% performance with a perfect indirect branch predictor. The other two selected C++ benchmarks, *richards* and *ixx*, are widely used for indirect branch prediction evaluation [11, 21]. *Richards* simulates the task dispatcher in the kernel of an operation system and *ixx* is a translator from IDL to C++. We use the SimPoint [9] to select a representative simulation region for each benchmark using the reference input set. Each benchmark is run for 100M instructions. Table 1 shows the characteristics of the evaluated benchmarks on the baseline processor.

We extend GCC-4.2 [13] compiler toolchain to provide the compiler support including program substructure analysis, guiding instruction inserting and scheduling. The final binaries are compiled with the -O2 optimization level.

5. RESULTS

5.1 Timing

We evaluate the timing impact of CVP prediction based on the CACTI-6.5 tool [24] using the 32 nm technology. Results show that the access latency for the extra Filter Table is about $0.144ns$, which is much smaller than the original 4K-entry BTB latency ($0.438ns$).

We also evaluate the timing impact of CVP prediction in a commercial 4-issue, 8-stages 64-bit superscalar processor, which runs about 1GHz under TSMC 65nm technology. It employs a 512-entry, 4-way BTB structure with 1-cycle access latency. We extend the existing components in the processor front-end to implement our CVP prediction. All components of the branch predictor are fully synthesizable rather than customized, so the estimated timing would be a little longer than real chips. Results show that the FT access latency is $0.520ns$, which is much smaller than the original BTB latency ($1.112ns$).

Table 3: MPKI: baseline vs. CVP prediction

	perlbmk	perlbench	gap	gcc00	gcc06	eon	sjeng	crafty	ixx	richards	AVG
Conditional branch MPKI (baseline)	3.9	3.7	0.9	5.9	4.8	3.3	11.3	5.7	3.9	5.2	4.87
Indirect jump MPKI (baseline)	6.1	7.5	5.0	4.9	5.3	1.5	2.2	1.3	1.3	4.7	3.98
Conditional branch MPKI (CVP)	4.1	3.9	1.2	6.1	4.9	3.4	11.3	5.8	3.9	5.3	4.99
Indirect jump MPKI (CVP)	2.9	1.7	0.7	2.0	1.4	0.3	0.6	0.4	0.5	0.6	1.05

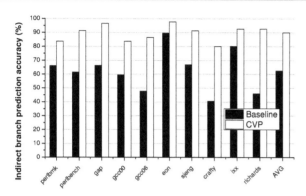 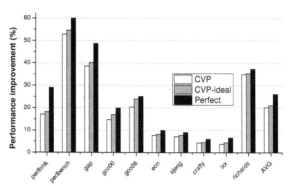

Figure 10: Performance of CVP prediction: prediction accuracy (left) and performance improvements (right).

Evaluation results in both the commercial processor and the CACTI tool show that our CVP prediction only slightly increase the prediction latency. However, to maximize the extra latency impact, we assume 2-cycle prediction latency for CVP prediction in our following simulation: one cycle for the FT lookup and one cycle for BTB lookup.

5.2 Performance

Figure 10 shows the indirect branch prediction accuracy and the performance of CVP prediction. On average, CVP prediction significantly increases the indirect branch prediction accuracy by 46% and improves the performance by 20% over the baseline-BTB prediction. The outstanding performance shows that our compiler-guided value pattern information has strong correlation with target addresses.

To investigate the impact of the 2-cycle prediction latency, we evaluate the CVP-ideal prediction, which assumes 1-cycle prediction latency rather than 2-cycle latency. The comparison between CVP and CVP-ideal prediction shows that the extra one cycle prediction latency leads to about 0.8% performance penalty. Such negligible performance penalty can be ignored compared with the great overall performance improvements. Furthermore, we also evaluate the perfect predictor, which perfectly predicts the correct target address for all indirect branches. Results show that our CVP prediction can significantly reduce the performance gap between the actual predictor and the perfect predictor by adding little extra hardware support.

Table 3 shows the Misprediction Per Kilo Instruction (MPKI) for conditional and indirect branches in the baseline BTB prediction and CVP prediction. CVP prediction reuses the existing BTB structure to store multiple target addresses for each indirect branch instruction, so it will interfere with the original conditional branch prediction. On average, the conditional branch MPKI of CVP prediction is slightly increased by 2.5% (from 4.87 to 4.99). However, CVP prediction can significantly reduce the indirect branch MPKI by 74% (from 3.98 to 1.05). As a result, CVP prediction still significantly reduces the total branch mispredictions.

5.3 Impact of Guiding Instructions

Table 4 shows the percentage of guiding instructions in the simulated region. On average, dynamic guiding instructions make up about 1.73% of all executed instructions. Since the percentage of guiding instructions is small, its negligible performance overhead can be ignored. Note that results in Figure 10 have counted the extra overhead caused by guiding instructions. The outstanding overall performance has shown guiding instructions are effective.

In processors that do not support CVP prediction, guiding instructions will be treated as *nop* instructions and it will be stripped out in the decode stage. Our evaluations show that these *nops* will cause about 0.92% performance penalty. We argue that such performance penalty is acceptable.

5.4 NON-READY problem study

Figure 11 shows the percentage of NON-READY cases on different pipeline depths, issue widths and memory latencies. Results show that the NON-READY problem is especially significant in aggressive high-performance processors with deep pipeline, wide issue and long memory latency. Pipeline depth has strong impact on the NON-READY problem because a deep pipeline will greatly increase the pipeline latency from processor front-end stages to back-end stages. Since data values are usually produced in processor back-end stages (e.g. the write-back stage), while branches are usually predicted in front-end stages (e.g. the fetch stage), a long pipeline latency makes a large number of data values unavailable at the prediction time. As pipeline stages increase from 8-stage to 64-stage, the percentage of NON-READY cases also increases from 65% to 94%. Similarly, a large issue width will also increase the pipeline latency, so the percentage of NON-READY cases increases from 70% to 88% when the issue width increases from 2-issue to 8-issue. Memory latency mainly affects those indirect branches that depend on some cache-miss load/store instructions. On average, as the memory latency increases from 100-cycle to 800-cycle, the percentage of NON-READY cases also increases from 78% to 85%.

Table 4: Statistics of Guiding Instructions (g_inst)

	perlbmk	perlbench	gap	gcc00	gcc06	eon	sjeng	crafty	ixx	richards	AVG
Percentage of dynamic g_inst (%)	1.7	2.7	1.5	2.2	2.4	1.3	1.5	1.6	1.5	0.9	1.73
Performance penalty of g_inst (%)	1.3	1.7	0.7	1.1	1.0	0.6	0.9	0.9	0.6	0.4	0.92

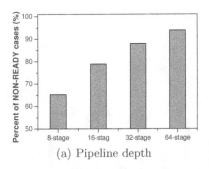

(a) Pipeline depth

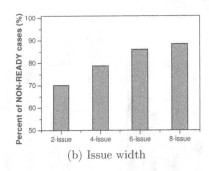

(b) Issue width

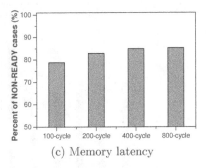

(c) Memory latency

Figure 11: Percent of NON-READY cases on different pipeline depths, issue widths and memory latencies.

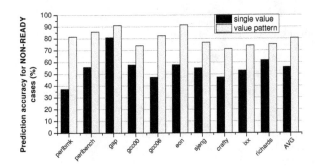

Figure 12: Prediction accuracy for NON-READY cases.

To deal with the NON-READY problem, our CVP prediction makes use of the value pattern rather than the single value to hint indirect branch prediction. Figure 12 shows the prediction accuracy for NON-READY cases. Compared with traditional single value correlation, our value pattern can improve the prediction accuracy by 41% for NON-READY cases. This is because our value pattern reflects the pattern regularity of the value correlation, so it always has strong correlation with indirect branch targets even if the latest single value is not available at the prediction time.

5.5 CVP with Different Filter Table Sizes

Table 5 shows the performance of CVP prediction with different Filter Table (FT) sizes. Generally, CVP prediction can achieve better performance with large filter table sizes, because a large filter table can buffer more hard-to-predict indirect branches. As the number of filter table entries increases from 16 to 128, the indirect branch MPKI reduction increases from 68.5% to 76.2%, which leads to the performance improvement from 17.9% to 21.5%. Recent research [11, 21] show that most of mispredictions are caused by only a few static indirect branches, so even a small filter table can still achieve considerable performance improvement.

Table 5: Performance of CVP on different FT sizes

Number of FT entries	16	32	64	128
MPKI reduction (%)	68.5	73.2	75.1	76.2
Performance improvement (%)	17.9	20.3	21.3	21.5

5.6 CVP with Different BTB Sizes

CVP prediction is sensitive to BTB size because it reuses the BTB structure to store all indirect branch target addresses. Table 6 shows the performance of CVP prediction with different BTB sizes. The BTB structure is always configured as 4-way associative and tagged. As the BTB size increases from 1K to 8K entries, both the indirect branch MPKI and performance are improved more substantially. However, even with a small size BTB (1K entries), it can still reduce the MPKI by 69.4% and improve the performance by 18.3%.

Table 6: Performance of CVP with different BTB sizes

Number of BTB entries	1K	2K	4K	8K
MPKI reduction (%)	69.4	71.4	73.2	74.5
Performance improvement (%)	18.3	19.5	20.3	20.9

5.7 Comparison with Aggressive Predictors

We compare our CVP prediction with two state-of-the-art indirect branch predictors: ITTAGE [30, 28] and VBBI [11]. Table 7 shows their configuration and Figure 13 shows their MPKI and performance. On average, CVP prediction reduces the indirect branch MPKI by 49% over ITTAGE predictor and 45% over VBBI predictor, which leads to performance improvements of 5.5% and 4.2% respectively.

ITTAGE predictor [30, 28] is the state-of-the-art history based indirect branch predictor. It stores indirect branch targets into several tagged tables and produces target address using the aggressive Prediction by Partial Matching (PPM) algorithm. ITTAGE predictor can achieve very high prediction accuracy in some benchmarks, such as perlbmk, sjeng and richards. However, it also performs poor in some benchmarks because its history-based correlation may be not strongly correlated with indirect branches. For example, the gap benchmark contains 7 hard-to-predict indirect branches, which cause most of indirect branch mispredictions. These indirect branches are surrounded by some unrelated loops and procedure calls, so it is difficult to catch the effective branch history for ITTAGE predictor. On the contrary, CVP prediction can accurately predict these indirect branches, because it is easy to identify effective value correlation based on high-level program substructures. On average,

Table 7: Configuration of ITTAGE and VBBI predictors

ITTAGE	256 Kbits, including 15 tagged tables and 1 tagless table. Tables are indexed with hashing of the global branch history, path history and branch address. No compiler support or profiling is required.
VBBI	1040 bits storage with target overriding support. Benchmarks are profiled using the same reference input data set.

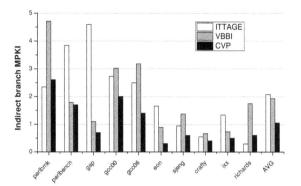 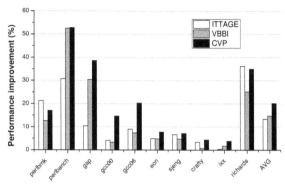

Figure 13: Comparison for different predictors: indirect branch MPKI (left) and performance improvement (right).

CVP prediction reduces the indirect branch MPKI by 49% and improves the performance by 5.5% over ITTAGE predictor. Furthermore, CVP prediction is much low-complexity compared with the aggressive 256 Kbits ITTAGE predictor.

VBBI predictor [11] is a recently proposed value-based indirect branch predictor. It heavily depends on the manual profiling to mark the value correlation. To maximum the performance of VBBI predictor, we profile benchmarks using the same reference input data set, so the VBBI performance shown in Figure 13 is a little better than expected. On average, CVP prediction reduces the indirect branch MPKI by 45% and improves the performance by 4.2% over VBBI predictor. CVP prediction can perform better because it makes use of compiler-guided value pattern information to hint indirect branch prediction, while VBBI predictor utilizes single data value. When the latest single data value is unavailable at the prediction time, VBBI predictor has to use the previously buffer single value as the correlated information, which significantly reduces the prediction accuracy and performance. Although its target overriding mechanism can slightly reduce the misprediction penalty, the performance overhead caused by misprediction is still significant. On the contrary, CVP prediction makes use of the value pattern to deal with such problem and it can achieve high prediction accuracy even if the latest single data value is unavailable at the prediction time. Furthermore, our CVP prediction does not require any profiling, so it is much more applicable than VBBI predictor.

6. RELATED WORK

Since the seminal work explored by Lee and Smith [22], a great number of indirect branch predictors are proposed. Chang et al. [5] firstly propose the history-based TTC predictor, which stores multiple targets in a special target cache and then uses branch history to index the target cache. Subsequently, many history-based indirect branch predictors such as Cascade predictor [7], Rehashable predictor [23] and PPM predictor [20] are proposed to improve the effectiveness of the history-based correlation by adding large storage

or complex algorithm. VPC prediction [21] tries to reduce the indirect branch predictor complexity by reusing existing processor components, but it requires significant modification to the conditional branch predictor and the BTB structure. Furthermore, its additional long prediction latency significantly reduces the overall performance [35]. Recently, Seznec [30, 28] proposes the ITTAGE predictor by extending their aggressive TAGE predictor [30, 29]. ITTAGE predictor can achieve high prediction accuracy and it is well studied in the 3rd Championship Branch Prediction [28]. However, it also requires large storage and complex logics to implement the Prediction by Partial Match (PPM) algorithm. These aggressive predictors are usually inefficient because of their large storage and complexity [25].

Value-based branch predictors are firstly studied in [15] and [16]. Gonzalez et al. [15] investigate the potential performance benefits of value correlation, and suggest some branches should be predicted using the data value correlation. Heil et al. [16] propose a hybrid predictor, which uses the data value history to complement the global branch history. Subsequently, a number of aggressive value-based predictors are proposed, such as BPVR+BPRU predictor [34], ARVI predictor [6], EXACT predictor [1]. These predictors are mainly used to complement conditional branch prediction. Recently, Farooq et al. [11] propose the value-based VBBI predictor. It points out that the value correlation is more effective for indirect branches and such value correlation can be identified by profiling. Unfortunately, the correlated data values may be unavailable at the prediction time because of the pipeline and memory latency. Although recently proposed address-branch correlation [12] and active update [1] can slightly reduce the impact of those long-latency branches, they usually rely on large storage or complex logics. Recently, Joao et al. [18] propose the Dynamic Indirect branch Predication (DIP), which predicates multiple targets rather than predicts a single target. It can eliminate the pipeline flush if the branch would actually have been mispredicted, but it requires complex hardware support for dynamic predication.

7. CONCLUSION

This paper proposed and evaluated the CVP prediction, an energy-efficient and accurate indirect branch prediction via compiler-microarchitecture cooperation. The key idea of CVP prediction is to use the compiler-guided value pattern as the correlated information to guide indirect branch prediction. As such, it can make use of the strong correlation between indirect branch targets and the pattern regularity of value correlation. CVP prediction relies on the cooperation between the compiler and the microarchitecture. The compiler identifies effect value correlation based on high-level program substructures. At runtime, the processor dynamically maintains the value pattern using a low-complexity filter table and a global register. We show that CVP prediction can be implemented in modern processors with little extra hardware support.

Evaluations show that CVP prediction significantly improves the indirect branch prediction accuracy and the performance with little extra hardware support. Compared with the state-of-the-art ITTAGE and VBBI predictors, CVP prediction can improve the performance by 5.5% and 4.2% respectively with less hardware storage and complexity.

8. ACKNOWLEDGMENTS

We would like to thank the anonymous reviewers for their constructive feedback. This work was partially supported by the National Science and Technology Major Project of the Ministry of Science and Technology of China under grant 2009ZX01029-001-002 and Beijing Natural Science Fund under grant 4123098.

9. REFERENCES

[1] M. Al-Otoom, E. Forbes, and E. Rotenberg. EXACT: Explicit dynamic-branch prediction with active updates. In *CF'10*, pages 165–176, 2010.

[2] T. Austin, E. Larson, and D. Ernst. SimpleScalar: an infrastructure for computer system modeling. *IEEE Computer*, 35(2):59–67, 2002.

[3] D. Bernslein and M. Rodeh. Global instruction scheduling for superscalar machines. In *PLDI'91*, pages 241–255, 1991.

[4] S. Borkar and A. A. Chien. The future of microprocessors. *Communications of the ACM*, 54(5):67–77, 2011.

[5] P.-Y. Chang, E. Hao, and Y. N. Patt. Target prediction for indirect jumps. In *ISCA-24*, pages 274–283, 1997.

[6] L. Chen, S. Dropsho, and D. H. Albonesi. Dynamic data dependence tracking and its application to branch prediction. In *HPCA-9*, pages 65–76, 2003.

[7] K. Driesen and U. Holzle. The cascaded predictor: Economical and adaptive branch target prediction. In *MICRO-31*, pages 249 – 258, 1998.

[8] K. Driesen and U. Holzle. Improving indirect branch prediction with source- and arity-based classification and cascaded prediction. *Technical Report in University of California at Santa Barbara*, 1998.

[9] E.Perelman, G.Hamerly, M. Biesbbrouck, T.Sherwood, and B.Calder. Using SimPoint for accurate and efficient simulation. In *SIGMETRICS'03*, pages 318–319, 2003.

[10] M. A. Ertl and G. David. Optimizing indirect branch prediction accuracy in virtual machine interpreters. In *PLDI'03*, pages 278–288, 2003.

[11] M. U. Farooq, L. Chen, and L. K. John. Value Based BTB Indexing for indirect jump prediction. In *HPCA-16*, pages 1–11, 2010.

[12] H. Gao, Y. Ma, M. Dimitrov, and H. Zhou. Address-Branch Correlation: A novel locality for long-latency hard-to-predict branches. In *HPCA-14*, pages 74 – 85, 2008.

[13] GCC. The GNU Compiler Collection. http://gcc.gnu.org/.

[14] S. Gochman, R. Ronen, I. Anati, A. Berkovits, T. Kurts, A. Naveh, A. Saeed, Z. Sperber, and R. C. Valentine. The Intel Pentium M processor: Microarchitecture and performance. *Intel Technology Journal*, 7(2), 2003.

[15] J. Gonzalez and A. Gonzalez. Control-flow speculation through value prediction for superscalar processors. In *PACT'99*, pages 2–10, 1999.

[16] T. H. Heil, Z. Smith, and J. E. Smith. Improving branch predictors by correlating on data values. In *MICRO-32*, pages 28–37, 1999.

[17] R. Huang, A. Garg, and M. Huang. Software-hardware cooperative memory disambiguation. In *HPCA-12*, pages 244–253, 2006.

[18] J. A. Joao, O. Mutlu, H. Kim, R. Agarwal, and Y. N. Patt. Improving the performance of object-oriented languages with dynamic predication of indirect jumps. In *ASPLOS-XIII*, pages 80–90, 2008.

[19] D. R. Kaeli and P. G. Emma. Branch history table prediction of moving target branches due to subroutine returns. In *ISCA-18*, pages 34–42, 1991.

[20] J. Kalamatianos and D. R. Kaeli. Predicting indirect branches via data compression. In *MICRO-31*, pages 272–281, 1998.

[21] H. Kim, J. A. Joao, O. Mutlu, C. J. Lee, Y. N. Patt, and R. Cohn. VPC prediction: reducing the cost of indirect branches via hardware-based dynamic devirtualization. In *ISCA-34*, pages 424–435, 2007.

[22] J. K. F. Lee and A. J. Smith. Branch prediction strategies and branch target buffer design. *IEEE Computer*, 17(1):6–22, 1984.

[23] T. Li, R. Bhargava, and L. K. John. Adapting branch-target buffer to improve the target predictability of java code. *ACM Transactions on Architecture and Code Optimization*, pages 109–130, 2002.

[24] N. Muralimanohar, R. Balasubramonian, and N. P. Jouppi. CACTI 6.0: A tool to model large caches. *HP Tech Report HPL-2009-85.*, 2009.

[25] L. Porter and D. M. Tullsen. Creating artificial global history to improve branch prediction accuracy. In *ICS-23*, pages 266–275, 2009.

[26] A. Roth, A. Moshovos, and G. S. Sohi. Improving virtual function call target prediction via dependence-based pre-computation. In *ICS-13*, pages 356–364, 1999.

[27] Y. Sazeides and J. E. Smith. The predictability of data values. In *MICRO-30*, pages 248 – 258, 1997.

[28] A. Seznec. A 64-kbytes ITTAGE indirect branch predictor. In *the 3rd Championship Branch Prediction*. http://www.jilp.org/jwac-2/.

[29] A. Seznec. A new case for the TAGE branch predictor. In *MICRO-44*, 2011.

[30] A. Seznec and P. Michaud. A case for (partially) TAgged GEometric history length predictors. *Journal of Instruction-Level Parallelism (JILP)*, 2006.

[31] K. Skadron, P. S. Ahuja, M. Martonosi, and D. W. Clark. Improving prediction for procedure returns with return-address-stack repair mechanisms. In *MICRO-31*, pages 259–271, 1998.

[32] SPEC. Standard Performance Evaluation Corporation. http://www.spec.org.

[33] M. Tan, X. Liu, Z. Xie, D. Tong, and X. Cheng. Energy-efficient branch prediction with compiler-guided history stack. In *DATE'12*, pages 449–454, 2012.

[34] R. Thomas, M. Franklin, C. Wilkerson, and J. Stark. Improving branch prediction by dynamic dataflow-based identification of correlated branches from a large global history. In *ISCA-30*, pages 314–323, 2003.

[35] Z. Xie, D. Tong, M. Huang, X. Wang, Q. Shi, and X. Cheng. TAP prediction: Reusing conditional branch predictor for indirect branches with target address pointers. In *ICCD-29*, pages 119–126, 2011.

Congestion Avoidance on Manycore High Performance Computing Systems

Miao Luo   Dhabaleswar K. Panda
Ohio State University
{luom, panda}@cse.ohio-state.edu

Khaled Z. Ibrahim   Costin Iancu
Lawrence Berkeley National Laboratory
{kzibrahim,cciancu}@lbl.gov

ABSTRACT

Efficient communication is a requirement for application scalability on High Performance Computing systems. In this paper we argue for incorporating proactive congestion avoidance mechanisms into the design of communication layers on manycore systems. This is in contrast with the status quo which employs a reactive approach, e.g. congestion control mechanisms are activated only when resources have been exhausted. We present a core stateless optimization approach based on open loop end-point throttling, implemented for two UPC runtimes (Cray and Berkeley UPC) and validated on InfiniBand and the Cray Gemini networks. Microbenchmark results indicate that throttling the number of messages in flight per core can provide up to 4X performance improvements, while throttling the number of active cores per node can provide additional 40% and 6X performance improvement for UPC and MPI respectively. We evaluate inline (each task makes independent decisions) and proxy (server) congestion avoidance designs. Our runtime provides both performance and performance portability. We improve all-to-all collective performance by up to 4X and provide better performance than vendor provided MPI and UPC implementations. We also demonstrate performance improvements of up to 60% in application settings. Overall, our results indicate that modern systems accommodate only a surprisingly small number of messages in flight per node. As Exascale projections indicate that future systems are likely to contain hundreds to thousands of cores per node, we believe that their networks will be underprovisioned. In this situation, proactive congestion avoidance might become mandatory for performance improvement and portability.

Categories and Subject Descriptors

C.2.0 [**Computer Systems Organization**]: Computer-Communication Networks—*General*; D.4.4 [**Software**]: Operating SystemsCommunications Management[Network Communication]

Keywords

Congestion, Avoidance, Management, High Performance Computing, Manycore, Multicore, InfiniBand, Cray

1. INTRODUCTION

The fundamental premise of this research is that contemporary or future networks for large scale High Performance Computing systems are likely to be underprovisioned with respect to the number of cores or concurrent communication requests per node. In an underprovisioned system, when multiple tasks per node communicate concurrently, it is likely that software or hardware networking resources are exhausted and congestion control mechanisms are activated: the performance of a congested system is usually lower than the performance of a fully utilized yet uncongested system.

In this paper we argue that, to improve performance and portability, HPC runtime implementations need to employ novel node level congestion avoidance mechanisms. We present the design of a proactive congestion avoidance mechanism using a network stateless approach: end-points limit the number of messages in flight using only local knowledge, without global information about the state of the interconnect. The communication load is allowed to reach close to the threshold where congestion might occur, after which it is throttled. Our node level mechanism is orthogonal to the traditional congestion control mechanisms [12, 2] deployed for HPC, which reason in terms of the overall network (switch) load rather than the Network Interface Card load. Our work makes the following contributions:

- We are the first to present evidence that on existing multicore systems maximal network throughput cannot be achieved when all cores are active.

- We propose, implement and evaluate mechanisms to handle node level congestion, ranging from completely distributed control to coordinated control.

- We describe the end-to-end experimental methodology to empirically derive the control algorithms for node level congestion control.

The rest of this paper is organized as follows. In Section 2 we discuss related work and in Section 3 we present our experimental setup. In Section 4 we describe microbenchmarks to understand the variation of network performance with the number of messages in flight, to recognize congestion and to derive heuristics used for message throttling. As shown, techniques to limit the number of in-flight messages per core can improve performance up to 4X. In addition, restricting the number of cores concurrently active per node from 32 to 16 provides additional performance improvements of up to 40% on our InfiniBand testbed. For MPI on Cray Gemini, restricting the number of active cores per "node" from 48 to 12 provides as much as 6X performance improvement.

We then present several designs for congestion avoidance mechanisms implemented in two Unified Parallel C [23] runtimes on different networks: the Berkeley UPC [9] implementation on InfiniBand and the Cray UPC implementation on Cray XE6 systems with the Gemini interconnect. In Section 5.1 we discuss the design of a message admission control policy using rate or count based metrics. In Section 5.2 we present *inline* and *proxy* based implementations of the admission control policy. With *inline* mechanisms, each task is responsible for managing its own communication requests using either task or node level information. With *proxy* based mechanisms, any communication request can be initiated and managed by any task: intuitively this scheme provides communication servers that perform node-wide communication management on behalf of client pools.

In Sections 6 and 7 we discuss the performance implications of the multiple runtime designs considered. In Sections 8 and 9 we demonstrate how our congestion avoiding runtime is able to provide both performance and performance portability for applications. We transparently improve all-to-all collective performance by 1.7X on InfiniBand system and 4X on Cray Gemini systems, using a single implementation. In contrast, obtaining best performance on each system requires completely different hand tuned implementations. Furthermore, our automatically optimized implementation performs better than highly optimized third party MPI and UPC all-to-all implementations. For example, using 1,024 cores on the InfiniBand testbed, our implementation provides more than twice the bandwidth of the best available library all-to-all implementation for 1,024 byte messages. We also demonstrate 60% performance improvements for the HPCC RandomAccess [3] benchmark. When running the NAS Parallel Benchmarks [15, 4], our runtime improves performance by up to 17%.

As Exascale projections indicate that future systems are likely to contain hundreds to thousands of cores per node, we believe that their networks are likely to be underprovisioned. In this situation, proactive congestion avoidance might become mandatory for performance and performance portability.

2. RELATED WORK

"but I always say one's company, two's a crowd..."

Congestion control in HPC systems has received a fair share of attention and networking, transport or runtime layer techniques to deal with congestion inside high speed networks have been thoroughly explored. Congestion control mechanisms are universally provided at the networking layer. For example, the IB Congestion Control mechanism [2] specified in the InfiniBand Architecture Specification 1.2.1 uses a closed loop reactive system. A switch detecting congestion sets a *Forward Explicit Congestion Notification* (FECN) bit that is preserved until message destination. The destination sends a backward ECN bit to the message source, which will temporarily reduce the injection rate. Dally [12] pioneered the concept of wormhole routing and his work has been since extended with congestion free routing alternatives on a very large variety of network topologies. For example, Zahavi et al [27] recently proposed a fat-tree routing algorithm that provides a congestion-free all-to-all shift pattern for the InfiniBand static routing.

A large body of research proposes algorithmic solutions, rather than runtime approaches. Yang and Wang [25, 26] discussed algorithms for near optimal all-to-all broadcast on meshes and tori. Kumar and Kale [18] discussed algorithms to optimize all-to-all multicast on fat-tree networks. Dvorak et al [13] described techniques for topology aware scheduling of many-to-many collective operations. Kandalla et al [16] discussed topology aware scatter and gather for large scale InfiniBand clusters. Thakur et al [22] discussed the scalability of MPI collectives and described implementations that use multiple algorithms in order to alleviate congestion in data intensive operations such as all-to-all.

A common characteristic of all these approaches is that they target congestion in the network core (or switches): the low level mechanisms use reactive flow control while the "algorithmic" approaches use static communication schedules that avoid route collision. Systems with enough cores per node to cause NIC congestion have been deployed only very recently and we believe that our study is the first to propose solutions to this problem.

The work closest related to ours in the HPC realm has been performed for MPI implementations and mostly on single core, single threaded systems. In 1994 Brewer and Kuszmaul [7] discuss how to improve performance on the CM-5 data network by delaying MPI message sends based on the number of receives posted by other ranks. Chetlur et al [10] propose an active layer extension to MPI to perform dynamic message aggregation on unicores. Pham [20] also discusses MPI message aggregation heuristics on unicore clusters and compares sender and receiver initiated schemes. These techniques use a message aggregation threshold and timeouts with a result equivalent to message rate limitation within a single thread of control. In this paper we advocate for node wide count based message limitation and empirically compare it with rate limitation extended to multi-threaded applications. Furthermore, in MPI information about the system wide state is available to feedback loops (closed control) mechanisms by matching Send and Receive operations. Since in one-sided communication paradigms this type of flow control is not readily available, our techniques use open loop control with heuristics based only on node local knowledge.

2.1 Node Level Proactive Congestion Avoidance

The basic premise of our work is that manycore parallelism breeds congestion and additional techniques for congestion management are required in such clusters. First, the Network Interface Card is likely to be underprovisioned with respect to the number of cores per node and techniques to avoid NIC congestion are required. Second, congestion inside the network proper is likely to become the norm, rather than the exception and congestion control mechanisms are likely to become even harder to implement.

While the former reason is validated throughout this paper, the latter is more subtle. With more cores per node, the likelihood of any node sending messages to multiple nodes at any time is higher, thus making "all-to-all" patterns the norm. These patterns are dynamic, while the whole body of work in algorithmic scheduling [25, 26, 18, 13, 16, 22] addresses only static patterns. Second, the low level congestion control mechanisms [2] already require non-trivial extensions to handle multiple concurrent flows and to deal with runtime software artifacts such as multiplexing processes, pthreads on multiple endpoints or "interfaces".

In this paper we argue that proactive congestion avoidance mechanisms are required in conjunction with reactive congestion control mechanisms. In a reactive approach, congestion control is activated when resources are exhausted or performance degrades below an acceptable threshold. In a proactive approach, traffic is policed such that, ideally, congestion never occurs. We propose several designs incorporated into a software layer interposed between applications and their runtime. In order to provide scalability, we explore only designs where congestion is managed at endpoints (nodes in the systems), using open loop control without any knowledge of the state of the network core or the system load. All of our implementations are designed to avoid first and foremost congestion at the Network Interface Card, rather than network core congestion. By throttling traffic at endpoints, we also alleviate congestion in the core.

3. EXPERIMENTAL SETUP

We use two large scale HPC systems for our evaluation. Trestles is a 324 compute nodes cluster at the San Diego Supercomputing Center. Each compute node is quad-socket, each with a 8-core 2.4 GHz AMD Magny-Cours processor, for a total of 32 cores per node and 10,368 total cores for the system. The compute nodes are connected via QDR InfiniBand interconnect, fat tree topology, with each link capable of 8 GB/s (bidirectional). Trestles has a theoretical peak performance of 100 TFlop/s.

NERSC's Cray XE6 system, Hopper, has a peak performance of 1.28 Petaflops/sec and 153,216 cores organized into 6,384 compute nodes made up of two twelve-core AMD 'MagnyCours'. Hopper uses the Cray 'Gemini' interconnect for inter-node communication. The network is connected in a mesh topology with adaptive routing. Each network interface handles data for the attached node and relays data for other nodes. The "edges" of the mesh network are connected to each other to form a "3D torus." The Gemini message latency is $\approx 1\mu s$ and two 24 core compute nodes are attached to the same NIC, thus 48 cores share one Gemini card.

All the software described in this paper is implemented as a thin layer interposed between applications and runtimes for the Unified Parallel C (UPC) language. On the InfiniBand network we use the Berkeley UPC runtime [ ], version 2.12.2. BUPC is free software and it uses for communication the GASNet [ ] layer which provides highly optimized one-sided communication primitives. In particular, on InfiniBand GASNet uses the OpenIB Verbs API. On the Cray system, we use the Cray UPC compiler, version 5.01 within Cray Compiling Environment (CCE) 7.4.2. The Cray UPC runtime is built using the DMAPP[1] layer. We also experiment with MPICH, Cray MPI and OpenMPI.

4. NETWORK PERFORMANCE CHARACTERIZATION

We explore the variation of network performance using a suite of UPC microbenchmarks that vary: i) the number of active cores per node; ii) the number of messages per core; iii) the number of outstanding messages per core; and iv) the message destination. We consider bi-directional traffic,

i.e. all cores in all nodes perform communication operations and we report the aggregate bandwidth. We have performed experiments where each core randomly chooses a destination for each message, as well as experiments where each core has only one communication partner. Both settings provide similar performance trends and in the rest of this paper we present results only for the latter.

Figure 1(a) shows the aggregate node bandwidth on InfiniBand when increasing the number of cores. Each core uses blocking communication and we present three runtime configurations ('Proc', 'Hyb' and 'Pth') that are characterized by increasing message injection overheads as first indicated by Blagojevic et al [ ]. The series labeled 'Proc' shows results when running one process per core, the series labeled 'Hyb' shows one process per socket with pthreads within the socket and the series 'Pth' shows one process per node. In general, best communication performance [ ] is obtained when threads within a process are mapped on the same socket, rather than spread across multiple sockets. For lack of space, we only summarize the performance trends without detailed explanations.

For all message sizes, the throughput with 'Pth' keeps degrading when adding more sockets. With 'Hyb', the throughput slightly increases up to two sockets active, after which it reaches a steady state. With 'Proc', which has the fastest injection rate, the throughput increases up to two sockets, after which it drops dramatically. In the best configuration, 'Proc' has 3X better throughput than 'Hyb' and 15X better throughput than 'Pth'. The performance difference between best and steady state 'Proc' throughput is roughly 2X. Similar behavior is observed across all message sizes.

These trends are a direct result of congestion in the networking layers. When running pthreads, runtimes such as BUPC or MPI use locks to serialize access to the networking hardware: the larger the number of threads, the higher the contention and the higher the message injection overhead. The UPC 'Proc' configuration running with one process per core[2] on InfiniBand, does not use any locks to mitigate the network accesses and the drop in throughput is caused by either low level software (NIC driver) or hardware. Since one process per core provides the best default performance for UPC and it is the default for MPI, the results presented in the rest of this paper are for this particular configuration.

Figure 1(a) indicates that there is a temporal aspect to congestion and throughput drops when too many endpoints inject traffic concurrently. We refer to this as *Concurrency Congestion* (CC) and informally define its threshold measure as the number of concurrent transfers from distinct endpoints (with only one transfer per endpoint) that maximize node bandwidth. For example, any 'Proc' or 'Pth' run with more than 20, respectively four, cores active at the same time is said to exhibit *Concurrency Congestion*. On Cray Gemini, congestion is less pronounced and it occurs when more than 40 of the 48 cores per NIC are active. We believe that ours is the first study to report this phenomenon.

Avoiding CC requires throttling the number of active endpoints and Figure 1(b) shows the performance expectations of a simple optimization approach. Assuming N cores per node, there are N messages to be sent and we plot the speed-up when using only subsets of C cores to perform the communication. There are $\frac{N}{C}$ rounds of communication and we

---

[1]Distributed Memory Application API for Gemini

[2]One thread per process, rather.

plot $\frac{T(N)-T(C)*\frac{N}{C}}{T(N)}$. Positive values on the z axis indicate performance improvements. For example, on InfiniBand using 16 cores to send two stages of 16 messages each is up to 37% faster than allowing each core to send its own message.

Optimized applications use non-blocking communication primitives to hide latency with communication-communication and communication-computation overlap. Figure 2 shows results for a two node experiment where we assume each core has to send a large number of messages. The figure plots the relative differences between communication strategies: N outstanding messages compared with $\frac{N}{D}$ rounds of communication, each with D outstanding messages: $\frac{T(D)*\frac{N}{D}-T(N)}{T(N)}$. In the first setting each core initiates N non-blocking communication requests then waits for completion, while in the second it waits after initiating only D requests.

Intuitively, congestion occurs whenever performing multiple rounds of communication is faster than a schedule that initiates all the messages at the same time. On the Infini-Band system this occurs whenever there is more than one message outstanding per core and best throughput is obtained using blocking communication. Increasing the number of outstanding messages per core decreases throughput, e.g. two outstanding messages per core deliver half the throughput of blocking communication. Asymptotically, the throughput difference is as high as 4X. The Cray Gemini network can accommodate a larger number of messages in flight and there is little difference between one and two outstanding messages per core; with more than two messages per core throughput decreases by as much as 2X. These results indicate that when all cores within the node are active, best throughput is obtained when using blocking communication.

On both systems, reducing the number of active cores determines an increase in the number of outstanding messages per core that provides best throughput, e.g. on InfiniBand with *one* core active, best throughput is observed with 40 outstanding messages.

Intuitively, the behavior with non-blocking communication illustrates the spatial component of congestion, i.e. there are limited resources in the system and throughput drops when space is exhausted in these resources. For the purposes of this study, we refer to this *Rate Congestion*. As with CC, we define the threshold for *Rate Congestion* as the number of outstanding messages per node that maximize throughput. Note than while CC distinguishes between the traffic participants, RC does not impose any restrictions.

The behavior reported for the UPC microbenchmarks is not particular to one-sided communication or caused solely by implementation artifacts of GASNet or DMAPP. Similar behavior is shown in Figure 3 for MPI on both systems. Note the very high speedup (250% on InfiniBand and 700% on Gemini) of MPI throughput when restricting the number of cores: Overall, it appears that MPI implementations exhibit worse congestion than the UPC implementations.

Increasing the number of nodes participating in traffic and varying the message destinations does not change the trends observed using a two node experiment. For lack of space we do not include detailed experimental results but note that on both systems, best throughput when using a large number of nodes is obtained for workloads that have a similar or lower number of outstanding messages per node than the best number required for two nodes. Workloads with small messages tend to be impacted less at scale than workloads containing large messages. In summary, congestion happens first in the Network Interface Card, with secondary effects inside the network when using large messages.

5. CORE STATELESS CONGESTION AVOIDANCE

As illustrated by our empirical evaluation, network throughput drops when tasks initiate too many communication operations. We interpose a proactive congestion avoidance layer between applications and the networking layer that allows traffic to be injected into the network only up to the threshold of congestion.

Our implementation redefines the UPC level communication calls and it is transparently deployed for the BUPC and the Cray runtimes. While the UPC language specification allows only for blocking communication, e.g. `upc_memget()`, all existing implementations provide non-blocking communication extensions. Avoiding *Concurrency Congestion* requires instrumenting the blocking calls, while avoiding *Rate Congestion* requires instrumenting the non-blocking calls.

The first component is an admission control policy that determines whether a communication request can be injected into the network. In order to provide scalability, we explore core stateless policies: communication throttling decisions are made using open-loop control[3] with only task or node knowledge and without any information about the state of the outside network. In contrast, previous work [7, 10, 20] tries to correlate MPI Send and Receive events. We derive the congestion thresholds and heuristics to drive the admission control policy from the results reported by the microbenchmark described in Section 4.

For each communication call, e.g. `upc_memget`, our implementation consults the admission control policy. To address both *Rate* and *Concurrency Congestion* we present a count based policy that uses node level information for message access. Mostly for comparison with delay based techniques (and for the few scenarios where node level network state information is not available to endpoints), we design a rate based policy that allows each endpoint to inject traffic based only on knowledge about its own history. While providing the most scalable runtime design, rate based admission is expected to be able to avoid only *Rate Congestion*.

We have implemented the admission control policy using multiple designs. In the inline design, each task is directly responsible for managing its own communication operations, e.g. the task that initiates a `upc_memget` is also the only one capable of deciding it has completed. Note that this is the functionality implicitly assumed and supported by virtually all contemporary communication layers and runtimes. In the proxy based design, a set of communication "servers" manage client requests. We provide a highly optimized implementation that uses shared memory between tasks (even processes) and allows any task to initiate and retire any communication operation on behalf of any other task. To our knowledge, we are the first to present results using this software architecture within a HPC runtime. The approach is facilitated by GASNet, which provides a communication library for Partitioned Global Address Space Languages. We wish to thank the GASNet developers for providing the modifications required to enable any task to control any communication request.

---

[3]No monitoring or feedback loop.

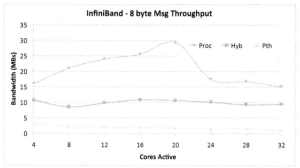

(a) Variation of node throughput with the number of active cores

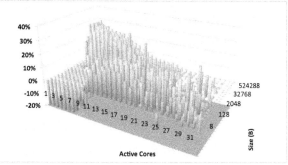

(b) Throughput Improvement when Restricting Active Cores: InfiniBand

Figure 1: *Concurrency Congestion: node throughput drops when multiple cores are active at the same time. We assume each core has one message to send and we plot the speedup of using cores/x rounds of communication over all cores active.*

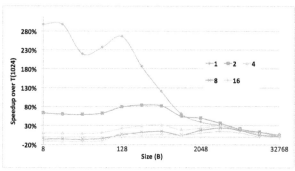

(a) Throughput Variation with Msg/Core - InfiniBand

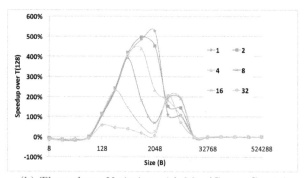

(b) Throughput Variation with Msg/Core - Gemini

Figure 2: *Rate Congestion: node throughput drops when cores have multiple outstanding messages. We assume each core has to send 1,024 messages and we plot the speedup of using 1,024/x rounds of communication with x = (1,2,4..) messages over sending 1,024 messages at the same time.*

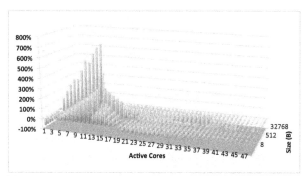

(a) Throughput Improvement when Restricting Active Cores: MPI on Gemini

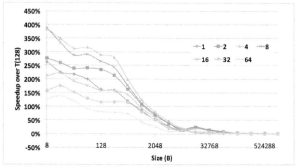

(b) Throughput Variation with Msg/Core - InfiniBand MPI Isend/Irecv with 1,2, 4 ... outstanding messages at a time compared with 128 outstanding messages

Figure 3: *Concurrency and Rate Congestion in MPI. Note that MPI (two-sided) exhibits even larger performance degradation, up to 600%, than UPC (one-sided).*

5.1 Admission Control Policies

Count Limiting: In the count based approach, each node has a predetermined set of tokens. Any task has to acquire enough tokens before being allowed to call into the low level communication API. The number of tokens can either be fixed, *i.e.* one token per request, or can be dynamically specified based on the message size; larger messages are associated with more tokens. Completion of a request involves relinquishing the tokens consumed at posting. Given that we provide a single token pool per node, unfairness is certainly a concern as it reduces the performance of SPMD programs by increasing the synchronization time. To reduce the likelihood of such behavior, we use a ticket-based token allocation that guarantees a first-come first-serve policy. Specifically, threads that are denied network access are given a numbered ticket with the tokens requested. Completion of requests is associated with activation of the next ticket in-line.

We have explored both one token per message and "size proportional" allocations. Achieving optimal performance requires to use for each message a number of tokens proportional to its size. We have implemented a benchmark that performs a guided sweep of different token allocation strategies and synthesizes a total number of tokens per node as well as the number of tokens required by any size. As we explore a multidimensional space [$nodes$, $cores\_per\_node$, $msgs\_per\_core$, msg_size], this is a very labor intensive process which we plan to automate in future work. The parameters determined by the offline search are then used to specialize the control avoidance code.

Rate Limiting: In the rate limiting approach, tasks are not allowed to call into the low level API for certain periods of time in an attempt to throttle the message injection rate. If the time difference between the last injection time-stamp and the current time is less than a specified threshold, the thread waits spending its time trying to retire previously initiated messages. To determine the best self-throttling injection rates we implemented a benchmark that for each message size sweeps over different values of injection delay using a fine-grained step of 0.5 μs. For each message size we select the delay that maximizes node throughput.

5.2 Admission Control Implementations

Inline Admission Control: We implement two variants of inline enforcement of the admission control policy. The first variant, which is referred to in the rest of this paper as *inline rate throttling* (IRT) uses rate control heuristics based on task local knowledge with synchronous behavior with respect to message injection. IRT is provided mostly for comparison with the related optimization [7, 10, 20] approaches. The second variant, referred to as *inline token throttling* (ITT) uses count limiting heuristics based on node-wide information and it has synchronous behavior with respect to message injection. We did not implement IRT with node knowledge due to the lack of synchronized node clocks.

Proxy Based Admission Control: We implement a proxy based admission control that provides non-synchronous behavior with respect to message injection at the application level. The design is presented in Figure 4. We group tasks in pools and associate a communication server with each task pool. Besides being a client, each application level task can act as a server. Each task has an associated request

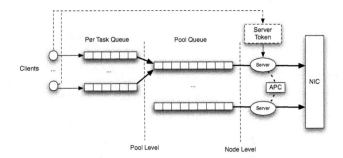

Figure 4: *Software architecture of the Proxy implementation. An admission control policy layer can be easily added behind the servers.*

queue and whenever it wants to perform a communication operation, it will place a descriptor in its "Per Task Queue". Afterwards, the task tries to grab the "Server Token" associated with its pool. If the token is granted, the task starts acting as a server, polls all the queues in the pool and initiates and retires communication operations. When a task masquerades as a server, it serve queues in a round-robin manner, starting with its own. This approximates the default best-effort access to the NIC provided by the underlying software layers. If a token is denied, control is returned to the application and the request is postponed.

Another possibility we have still to experiment with is to have a server issue all the messages within a queue before proceeding to the next queue. This strategy has the effect of minimizing the number of active routes when a task has only one communication partner within a "scheduling" window,

Such a software architecture is able to avoid both types of congestion. In addition, having the requests from multiple tasks aggregated into a single pool increases the opportunity of more aggressive communication optimizations such as message coalescing or reordering. *Concurrency Congestion* is clearly avoided by controlling the number of communication servers. The question remains whether the overhead and throttling introduced by the proxy indirection layer is able to prevent *Rate Congestion* by itself or supplementary avoidance mechanisms are required behind the server layer. *Rate Congestion* avoidance might require controlling the number of requests in flight per server.

In the experimental evaluation section, this implementation is referred to as *Proxy*.

6. MICROBENCHMARK EVALUATION

Figure 5 shows the performance when running the microbenchmark described in Section 4 on top of our congestion avoiding runtime on InfiniBand. We plot the speedup of congestion avoidance over the default runtime behavior. The parameters controlling the behavior of congestion avoidance are obtained using sweeps as described in Sections 5.1 and 5.2.

Figure 5(a) shows the impact of IRT for microbenchmark settings with an increasing number of operations per task, i.e. for the series "2" each task issues two non-blocking operations at a time. As expected, IRT it is not able to avoid *Concurrency Congestion* (series "1"). When tasks issue a larger number of transfers IRT provides a maximum of 2X performance improvements. The largest improvements are observed for messages shorter than 2KB.

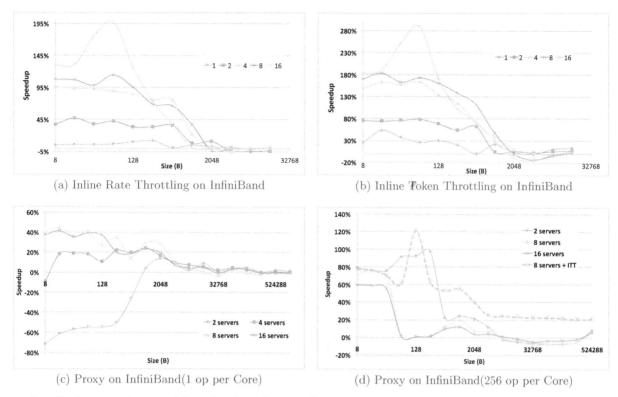

(a) Inline Rate Throttling on InfiniBand

(b) Inline Token Throttling on InfiniBand

(c) Proxy on InfiniBand(1 op per Core)

(d) Proxy on InfiniBand(256 op per Core)

Figure 5: *Performance impact of Rate (IRT), Token (ITT) and Proxy congestion avoidance on InfiniBand. We plot the speedup of applying our congestion avoidance while increasing the number of outstanding messages per core (1, 2, 4, 8, 16).*

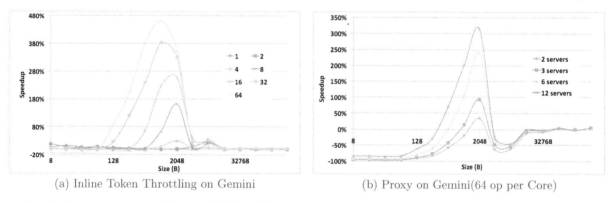

(a) Inline Token Throttling on Gemini

(b) Proxy on Gemini(64 op per Core)

Figure 6: *Performance impact of Token (ITT) and Proxy congestion avoidance on Gemini. We allow an increasing number of outstanding messages per core and plot the speedup of applying our congestion avoidance mechanisms.*

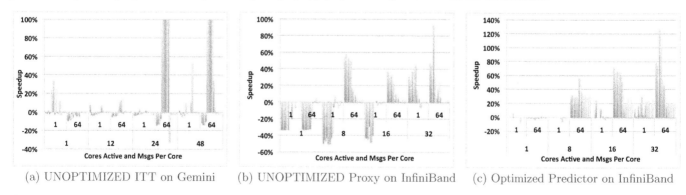

(a) UNOPTIMIZED ITT on Gemini   (b) UNOPTIMIZED Proxy on InfiniBand   (c) Optimized Predictor on InfiniBand

Figure 7: *Overhead of Congestion Avoidance with Active Cores. We plot the speedup for an increasing number of active cores, number of messages per core and message sizes. We vary the message size from 8B to 512KB in increasing powers of 2 and there is one data point per 8, 16, ..., 512KB.*

Figure 5(b) shows that ITT avoids both types of congestion and we observe as much as 3X speedups. Note the 50% speedup obtained when throttling blocking communication.

Figures 5(c) and (d) show the impact of the Proxy implementation for settings where we allow one and 256 outstanding operations per core. We plot the speedup obtained when using two, four, eight and 16 servers per node and observe speedups as high as 1.6X. When the degree of communication concurrency per core is low, e.g. blocking communication, Proxy performs best when the number of active servers (16) is close to the concurrency congestion threshold. When the communication concurrency per core is high (256 outstanding messages), Proxy by itself cannot prevent *Rate Congestion* and best performance is obtained with two servers. The series "8 serves + ITT" shows that implementing an additional admission control layer behind the servers enables the Proxy design to handle both Rate and Concurrency Congestion.

Figure 6 shows the performance on Gemini. ITT is able to improve performance whenever tasks issue more than two outstanding messages and by as much as 5X when issuing 64 outstanding messages. The Proxy implementation improves performance for workloads with at least four outstanding messages per core.

Our approach delays message injection and it might decrease throughput when the communication load is below the congestion thresholds. Figure 7(a) and Figure 7(b) show the impact of **unoptimized ITT** on Gemini and **unoptimized Proxy** on InfiniBand throughput when increasing the number of active sockets per node and the number of messages per core. In this case we are using a predictor independent of the message size, i.e. one token per message. For short messages, ITT on Gemini decreases throughput by at most 10% independent of core concurrency. The data indicates that, although it introduces only a low overhead, it is be beneficial to disable our congestion avoidance mechanism for certain message sizes when only a subset of cores is active.

7. BUILDING A CONGESTION AVOIDANCE POLICER

The microbenchmarks presented throughout the paper indicate that congestion avoidance should be driven by the following control parameters: i) concurrency congestion threshold ($CCT[size]$) measured as the number of cores that when active decrease throughput of blocking communication; ii) node congestion threshold ($NRCT[size]$) measured as the total number of outstanding messages per node that "maximizes" throughput; iii) core congestion threshold ($CRCT[active\_cores][size]$) measured as the number of non-blocking operations per core that "maximize" throughput at a given core concurrency. Intuitively, these parameters capture the minimal amount of communication parallelism required to saturate the network interface card.

Algorithm 1 shows the pseudo code for the control decisions in our mechanism. We give priority to dealing with *Concurrency Congestion* and then we try to avoid *Rate Congestion*. The "procedures" avoid_* use internally a count based predictor for both ITT and the Proxy implementation. For Proxy we add an admission control layer behind the servers. All parameters, including the tokens per node, are determined by iteratively executing the microbenchmarks

---

Algorithm 1 Pseudo code for congestion avoidance.

```
1:  procedure MSG_INIT( size : In,  dest : In)
2:      if active_cores < CCT[size] then
3:                              ▷ no concurrency congestion
4:          if   active_node_msgs   <   NRCT[size]   AND
        active_msg < CRCT[active_cores][size] then
5:              inject(size, dest)            ▷ no congestion
6:          else
7:              avoid_RC(size,dest)
8:                              ▷ rate congestion detected
9:          end if
10:     else
11:         avoid_CC_RC(size,dest)
12:                   ▷ concurrency and rate congestion detected
13:     end if
14:
15: end procedure
```

---

using manual guidance. At this point, the predictor we synthesize in practice contains thresholds that are independent of the message size, i.e. one token per message. For Proxy, we also search for the best server configuration. Our results on the InfiniBand cluster indicate that eight servers per node produce good results in practice, while on Gemini, 24 servers per node are required. This amounts to a ratio of four, respectively two tasks per server.

The behavior on InfiniBand using the tuned predictors is shown in Figures 7(c). When varying the number of active cores, messages per core and size of the message, our implementation improves performance in most of the cases. In very few cases it introduces a small overhead, at most 4%. We are still investigating the behavior of ITT when using eight cores with blocking communication. Similar trends are observed on Gemini. When comparing with Figure 7(a) and 7(b) which show unoptimized ITT and Proxy performance, tuning reduces drastically the number of configurations where performance is lost. For the configurations where our implementation actually slows down the microbenchmark execution, the predictor causes an average slowdown of 2% across varying core concurrencies, message sizes and messages per core.

As we have only partially processed a large volume of experimental data, we believe that we can further tune the predictors and improve the performance of our mechanisms.

8. ALL-TO-ALL PERFORMANCE

All-to-all communication is widely used in applications such as CPMD [11], NAMD [21], LU factorization and FFT. MPI [22, 17] and parallel programming languages such as UPC [19] provide optimized implementations of all-to-all collective operations. Most if not all of the existing implementations use multiple algorithms selected by message size. Bruck's algorithm [8] is used for latency hiding for small messages and it completes in $log(P)$ steps, where P is the number of participating tasks. For medium message sizes an implementation overlapping [22] all the communication operations is used. In this implementation, tasks use non-blocking communication and initiate $P - 1$ messages. For large message sizes, a pairwise exchange [22] algorithm is used where pairs of processors "exchange" data using blocking communication.

To demonstrate the benefits of our congestion avoidance runtime, we compare the performance of a single algorithm all-to-all against the performance of library implementations.

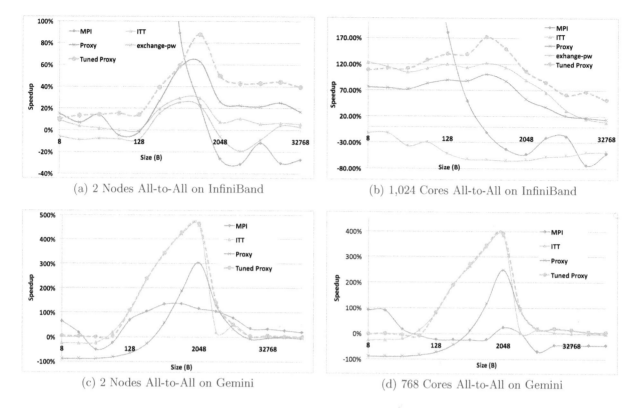

(a) 2 Nodes All-to-All on InfiniBand (b) 1,024 Cores All-to-All on InfiniBand

(c) 2 Nodes All-to-All on Gemini (d) 768 Cores All-to-All on Gemini

Figure 8: *Impact of IRT, ITT and Proxy congestion avoidance on all-to-all performance. We plot the speedup of MPI and that of single implementation running on top of congestion avoidance (IRT, ITT, Proxy). The performance baseline is a overlapped implementation in UPC.*

Our baseline implementation is the overlapping "algorithm" with each processor starting to communicate with $MYTHREAD + 1$. In Figure 8 we plot the speedup of multiple implementations over the baseline implementation running on the native UPC runtime layers. For reference, the series labeled MPI presents the performance of the MPI_Alltoall on the respective system. The performance of the UPC library all-to-all is similar to MPI and not shown. On both systems the library calls implement Bruck's algorithm for small messages. The series labeled "exchange-pw" presents the performance of a handwritten pairwise exchange implementation in UPC. We have also implemented pairwise exchanges in MPI, the results are similar to exchange-pw and omitted for brevity. The series labeled "ITT" and "Proxy" show the performance of the overlapping algorithm with a runtime that implements ITT and Proxy congestion avoidance respectively. These implementations are not tuned and use a simple count based predictor enabled for all core concurrencies and message sizes. The series labeled "Tuned Proxy" shows the behavior of a tuned implementation of Proxy and it illustrates the additional benefits after a significant effort to mine the experimental data.

On the InfiniBand network, "Tuned Proxy" provides best performance and we observe speedups as high as 90% and 170% for 512 byte messages on two nodes and 1024 cores respectively. Furthermore, our implementation is faster than any all-to-all deployed on the system for medium to large messages. For example, "Tuned Proxy" is roughly 5X faster than the MPI library at 1KB messages. We omit any rate throttling results (IRT) since IRT provides only modest performance improvements.

On Gemini, our congestion avoiding runtime provides again the best performance. The MPI library is not as well tuned on Gemini and our implementation is as much as 6X faster than MPI for medium sized messages. ITT provides better performance than Proxy and IRT provides the least improvements. Except for small messages where MPI uses Bruck's algorithm, ITT is faster than any communication library deployed on the Cray, by as much as 25% for 2KB messages when using 768 cores.

These results indicate that our congestion avoiding runtime is able to improve performance and provide performance portability. We have obtained best performance on two systems using one implementation when compared against multi-algorithm library implementations.

9. APPLICATION BENCHMARKS

We evaluate the impact of our congestion avoiding runtime on several application benchmarks written by outside researchers. The HPCC RandomAccess benchmark [ ] uses fine grained communication, while the NAS Parallel Benchmarks [ ] are optimized to use large messages. Fine-grained communication is usually present in larger applications during data structure initializations, dynamic load balancing, or remote event signaling.

The current UPC language specification does not provide non-blocking communication primitives and all publicly available benchmarks use blocking communication. On the other hand, both BUPC and Cray provide nonblocking extensions. We have modified each benchmark implementation to exploit as much communication overlap as possible. All the performance models and heuristics described in this

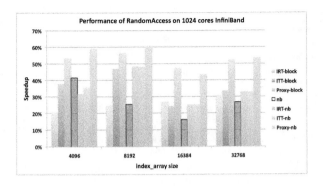

Figure 9: *RandomAccess on 1,024 cores InfiniBand. We plot the speedup relative to a baseline implementation using blocking communication.*

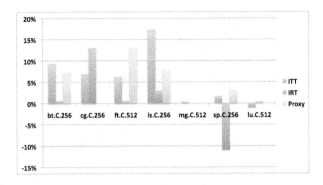

Figure 10: *The NAS Parallel Benchmarks on Infini-Band. We plot the speedup relative to a baseline implementation using blocking communication.*

paper have been implemented in a thin layer between the application and the runtimes for Berkeley UPC and Cray UPC, which is transparent to the application developer.

RandomAccess: The RandomAccess benchmark is motivated by a growing gap in performance between processor operations and random memory accesses. This benchmark intends to measure the peak capacity of the memory subsystem while performing random updates to the system memory. The benchmark performs random read/modify/write accesses to a large distributed array, a common operation in parallel hash table construction or distributed in-memory databases. The amount of work is static and evenly distributed among threads at execution time. Figure 9 presents the results on InfiniBand when using 1,024 cores. We plot the speedup relative to a baseline implementation that uses only blocking communication primitives. The x-axis plots the number of indirect references per thread. The message size for every single operation is 16 byte. The first three bars (IRT-block, ITT-block, Proxy-block) plot the speedup observed when running the baseline implementation with congestion avoidance and illustrate the capability of our runtime to avoid *Concurrency Congestion*. Proxy is able to provide speedup as high as 57%. The series labeled "nb" plots the performance of a hand optimized implementation in which the inner loops are unrolled and communication is pipelined and overlapped with computation and other communication. This is the de facto communication optimization strategy that is able to improve performance by as much as 40%. The series IRT-nb, ITT-nb and Proxy-nb show the additional performance improvements of congestion avoidance for *Rate Congestion* and Proxy-nb is able to provide as much as 60% speedup. As indicated by Figure 2, the small messages in RandomAccess do not generate congestion on Gemini and our runtime does not affect its performance.

The behavior of RandomAccess illustrates an interesting performance inversion phenomenon: an implementation with blocking communication and congestion avoidance is able to attain better performance than an implementation hand optimized for communication overlap. Best performance is obtained by the implementation optimized for overlap and using congestion avoidance.

NAS Benchmarks: All implementations are based on the official UPC [1, 15] releases of the NAS benchmarks, which we use as a performance baseline. For brevity we do not provide more details about the NAS Parallel Benchmarks, for a detailed description please see [1, 14]. The

benchmarks exhibit different characteristics. FT and IS perform all-to-all communication. SP and BT use scatter-gather communication patterns. SP issues requests (Put) to transfer a variable number of mid-size contiguous regions. The requests in BT (Put and Get) vary from small to medium sizes. In MG, the communication granularity varies dynamically at each call site. CG uses point to point communication with constant message sizes. For all benchmarks, the count and granularity of messages varies with problem class and system size. Vetter and Mueller [24] indicate that large scientific applications show a significant amount of small to mid-size transfers and all the benchmark instances considered in this paper exhibit this characteristic.

Figure 10 presents the results on InfiniBand. As discussed, the implementations that use `upc_memput` show no performance improvement. Best performance improvements are observed for the communication intensive benchmarks (CG, FT, IS) and we observe as much as 17% speedup for IS.

10. DISCUSSION

Most of the previous work [2, 12, 27, 25, 26, 18, 13, 10] addresses congestion in the core (switches) of HPC networks. As our experimental evaluation shows, the advent of multicore processors introduces congestion at the edge of these networks and mechanisms to handle *Concurrency Congestion* are required for best performance on contemporary hardware. Our count based heuristic can handle both *Rate* and *Concurrency Congestion* and it has been easily incorporated into software architectures using either task level (ITT) or node level (Proxy) mechanisms. While ITT is simple to implement and provides good performance, we favor in the long run the Proxy with ITT design which allows for further optimizations such as coalescing and reordering of communication operations. We also believe that the admission control policy heuristics can be further improved.

All the experimental results illustrate the challenges of writing performance portable code in a multi-system, hybrid-programming model environment and we have shown that our congestion avoiding runtime provides both performance and performance portability. The current optimization dogma advocates for exposing a large concurrency and hiding latency (with multi-threading or other optimizations) by overlapping communication with other work. Our experiments indicate that each system supports only a very limited amount of communication concurrency without significant performance degradation. Our techniques allow developers to expose the maximum "logical" concurrency at the application level and throttle it at runtime for optimal performance. Also, note that without congestion avoidance, our evaluation indicates that overlap is becoming harder to achieve with portability on manycore systems.

Examining the design tradeoffs of congestion avoidance mechanisms, and in general application optimization tradeoffs, we see two main design criteria: 1) optimizing for overlap; and 2) optimizing for throughput. As overlap requires fast message injection and throughput requires throttling and delays, these two have contradictory requirements. The status-quo in runtime and optimizations design favors overlap and fast injection. For the systems examined in this paper we observe a performance inversion between injection speed and throughput: the networking layers allowing the fastest injection rate observe the highest throughput degradation. We have re-implemented all of our microbenchmarks using the vendor APIs OpenIB Verbs and DMAPP. While calling the native API provides the fastest injection rate, those benchmarks achieve lower throughput than either GASNet, UPC or MPI. The detailed results are omitted for brevity. We believe that increasing the number of cores per node will require a shift towards optimizations for throughput using new approaches and performance metrics. Our congestion avoiding runtime samples points in the space of throughput oriented designs and we believe the Proxy design can provide both fast injection/overlap and throughput.

The microbenchmark results in Section 4 indicate that congestion is observable independently of the implementation, i.e. GASNet, MPI or native APIs, or the communication paradigm, i.e. one-sided in GASNet and two-sided in MPI. On the InfiniBand system we have experimented with multiple NIC resource knobs controlled by software: the settings used in this study provide the best default performance. The MPI implementations (Cray MPI, MPICH, OpenMPI) seem to be affected even more than the one-sided runtimes (GASNet and Cray UPC). Thus, deploying similar mechanisms into MPI implementations is certainly worth pursuing. The implicit flow control provided by MPI Send and Receive operations allows for extensions using closed loop control techniques.

Our congestion avoidance mechanisms implement a core stateless approach where decisions are made at the edge of the network (nodes), without global state information about actual congestion in the network core (switches). The results indicate that we can provide good performance at scale, but the question remains how close to optimal we can get and whether mechanisms using global state can do better. While we do not have conclusive evidence, our conjecture is that addressing congestion at the edge of the network is likely to provide similar or better performance than global state mechanisms at scale. Another question is that of fairness when not all the nodes in the system use congestion avoiding runtimes. Our experiments were run on capacity systems and the benchmarks were competing directly against applications using unmodified runtimes. This indicates that a congestion avoiding runtime competes well with greedy traffic participants.

This work also raises the question whether the runtime can displace the algorithm. Previous work proposes application algorithmic changes that affect the communication schedule to reduce the chance of route collision. Our implementation throttles communication operations and implicitly re-

duces the chance of collisions. Furthermore, Proxy can be extended with node-wide message reordering and coalescing optimizations and mechanisms to avoid route collision can be provided at that level. Understanding the tradeoffs between these alternatives is certainly important and is the subject of future work.

Finally, we believe that our open loop runtime congestion avoidance mechanisms are orthogonal to the vendor provided closed loop congestion control mechanisms. In all of our experiments the vendor congestion control mechanisms (e.g. IB CCA) were enabled. However, the question remains if there are any undesired interactions between the two mechanisms.

11. CONCLUSION

Efficient communication is required for application scalability on contemporary High Performance Computing systems. One of the most commonly employed and advocated optimization techniques is to hide latency by overlapping communication with computation or other communication operations. This requires exposing a large degree of communication concurrency within applications.

In this paper, we show that contemporary networks or runtime layers are not very well equipped to deal with a large number of operations in flight and suffer from congestion. We distinguish two types of congestion: *Rate Congestion* happens when tasks inject too many concurrent messages, while *Concurrency Congestion* happens when too many cores are active at the same time. We propose a runtime design using proactive congestion avoidance techniques: a thin software layer is interposed between the application and the runtime to limit the number of concurrent operations. This approach allows the communication load to increase to the point where native congestion control mechanisms might have been triggered, without actually triggering them.

We implement a congestion avoiding runtime for one-sided communication on top of two UPC runtimes for two networks: InfiniBand and Cray Gemini. We discuss heuristics to limit the number of messages in flight and present implementations using either task inline or server based mechanisms. Our runtime is able to provide performance and performance portability for all-to-all collectives (2x improvements), fine grained application benchmarks (60% improvements), as well as implementations of the NAS Parallel Benchmarks (up to 17% improvements).

As Exascale projections indicate that future systems are likely to contain hundreds to thousands of cores per node, we believe that their networks are likely to be underprovisioned and applications are likely to suffer from both *Rate Congestion* and *Concurrency Congestion*. In this situation, proactive congestion avoidance might become mandatory for performance and performance portability.

12. REFERENCES

[1] The GWU NAS Benchmarks.
http://threads.hpcl.gwu.edu/sites/npb-upc.

[2] The InfiniBand Specification. Available at
http://www.infinibandta.org.

[3] V. Aggarwal, Y. Sabharwal, R. Garg, and
P. Heidelberger. HPCC Randomaccess Benchmark For
Next Generation Supercomputers. In *Proceedings of
the 2009 IEEE International Symposium on
Parallel&Distributed Processing*, pages 1–11,
Washington, DC, USA, 2009. IEEE Computer Society.

[4] D. H. Bailey, E. Barszcz, J. T. Barton, D. S.
Browning, R. L. Carter, D. Dagum, R. A. Fatoohi,
P. O. Frederickson, T. A. Lasinski, R. S. Schreiber,
H. D. Simon, V. Venkatakrishnan, and S. K.
Weeratunga. The NAS Parallel Benchmarks. *The
International Journal of Supercomputer Applications*,
5(3):63–73, Fall 1991.

[5] F. Blagojević, P. Hargrove, C. Iancu, and K. Yelick.
Hybrid PGAS Runtime Support for Multicore Nodes.
In *Proceedings of the Fourth Conference on
Partitioned Global Address Space Programming Model*,
PGAS '10, 2010.

[6] D. Bonachea. GASNet Specification, v1.1. Technical
Report CSD-02-1207, University of California at
Berkeley, October 2002.

[7] E. A. Brewer and B. C. Kuszmaul. How to Get Good
Performance from the CM-5 Data Network. In
IPPS'94, pages 858–867, 1994.

[8] J. Bruck, S. Member, C. tien Ho, S. Kipnis, E. Upfal,
S. Member, and D. Weathersby. Efficient algorithms
for all-to-all communications in multi-port
message-passing systems. In *IEEE Transactions on
Parallel and Distributed Systems*, pages 298–309, 1997.

[9] Berkeley UPC. Available at http://upc.lbl.gov/.

[10] M. Chetlur, G. D. Sharma, N. B. Abu-Ghazaleh,
U. K. V. Rajasekaran, and P. A. Wilsey. An Active
Layer Extension to MPI. In *PVM/MPI*, 1998.

[11] Available at http://www.cpmd.org/.

[12] W. J. Dally and C. L. Seitz. The Torus Routing Chip.
Distributed Computing, pages 187–196, 1986.

[13] V. Dvorak, J. Jaros, and M. Ohlidal. Optimum
Topology-Aware Scheduling of Many-to-Many
Collective Communications. *International Conference
on Networking*, 0:61, 2007.

[14] A. Faraj and X. Yuan. Communication Characteristics
in the NAS Parallel Benchmarks. In *14th IASTED
International Conference on Parallel and Distributed
Computing and Systems (PDCS 2002)*, November
2002.

[15] H. Jin, R. Hood, and P. Mehrotra. A Practical Study
of UPC with the NAS Parallel Benchmarks. *The 3rd
Conference on Partitioned Global Address Space
(PGAS) Programming Models*, 2009.

[16] K. C. Kandalla, H. Subramoni, A. Vishnu, and D. K.
Panda. Designing Topology-Aware Collective
Communication Algorithms for Large Scale InfiniBand
Clusters: Case studies with Scatter and Gather. In
IPDPS Workshops'10, pages 1–8, 2010.

[17] R. Kumar, A. Mamidala, and D. K. Panda. Scaling
alltoall Collective on Multi-Core Systems. *2008 IEEE
International Symposium on Parallel and Distributed
Processing*, pages 1–8, 2008.

[18] S. Kumar and L. V. KalÃľ. Scaling All-to-All
Multicast on Fat-tree Networks. In *ICPADS'04*, pages
205–214, 2004.

[19] R. Nishtala, Y. Zheng, P. Hargrove, and K. A. Yelick.
Tuning Collective Communication for Partitioned
Global Address Space Programming Models. *Parallel
Computing*, 37(9):576–591, 2011.

[20] C. D. Pham. Comparison of Message Aggregation
Strategies for Parallel Simulations on a High
Performance Cluster. In *In Proceedings Of The 8th
International Symposium On Modeling, Analysis And
Simulation Of Computer And Telecommunication
Systems, August-September*, 2000.

[21] J. C. Phillips, G. Zheng, S. Kumar, and L. V. Kalé.
NAMD: Biomolecular Simulation on Thousands of
Processors. In *Proceedings of SC 2002*, Baltimore,
MD, September 2002.

[22] R. Thakur, R. Rabenseifner, and W. Gropp.
Optimization of Collective Communication Operations
in MPICH. *IJHPCA*, pages 49–66, 2005.

[23] UPC Language Specification, Version 1.0. Available at
http://upc.gwu.edu.

[24] J. Vetter and F. Mueller. Communication
Characteristics of Large-Scale Scientific Applications
for Contemporary Cluster Architectures. *Proceedings
of the 2002 International Parallel and Distributed
Processing Symposium (IPDPS)*, 2002.

[25] Y. Yang and J. Wang. Efficient All-to-All Broadcast in
All-Port Mesh and Torus Networks. In *Proceedings of
the 5th International Symposium on High Performance
Computer Architecture*, HPCA '99, pages 290–,
Washington, DC, USA, 1999. IEEE Computer Society.

[26] Y. Yang and J. Wang. Near-Optimal All-to-All
Broadcast in Multidimensional All-Port Meshes and
Tori. *IEEE Trans. Parallel Distrib. Syst.*, 13:128–141,
February 2002.

[27] E. Zahavi, G. Johnson, D. J. Kerbyson, and M. L.
0003. Optimized InfiniBand^{TM} Fat-Tree Routing For
Shift All-To-All Communication Patterns.
*Concurrency and Computation: Practice and
Experience*, 22(2):217–231, 2010.

Channel Borrowing: An Energy-Efficient Nanophotonic Crossbar Architecture with Light-Weight Arbitration *

Yi Xu   Jun Yang
Department of Electrical and Computer Engineering
University of Pittsburgh
{yix13, juy9}@pitt.edu

Rami G Melhem
Department of Computer Science
University of Pittsburgh
melhem@cs.pitt.edu

ABSTRACT

The emerging on-chip optical interconnection has become a promising candidate for future network design because of its advantages in high bandwidth density, low propagation delay and dynamic power consumption. However, a key challenge of on-chip optics is the high static power consumption which dominates the total network power. Hence, it is imperative to design an energy-efficient optical network architecture with high throughput while consuming low static power. In conventional optical crossbars, static channel allocation results in low channel utilization and network throughput, while full channel sharing requires a significant number of microrings, which incurs high static power.

To obtain high network throughput with low power consumption, this paper proposes a nanophotonic crossbar architecture with light-weight distributed arbitration. Network channels are allocated to an owner node, but can also be used by a few other nodes during idle time. The number of microring resonators is greatly reduced compared to the full channel sharing architecture. The arbitration is also simplified due to the small number of nodes sharing a channel. Every node can use the statically assigned channel to avoid starvation and borrow an additional idle channel to improve the utilization of the network. We intelligently select the network nodes that should share a channel to increase the chance of successful borrowing with low probability of conflict. The energy efficiency of the proposed network architecture is evaluated in terms of energy efficiency (throughput/watt) and Energy-delay^2(ED^2) using synthetic traces and traffic traces from PARSEC benchmarks. The simulation results show that our design can improve energy efficiency by 34% and 26% and improve ED^2 by 73% and 45% compared to Single-write-multi-read (SWMR) crossbars and Multi-write-multi-read (MWMR) crossbars respectively.

*This work is supported in part by NSF 0747242 and 1012070.

Categories and Subject Descriptors

C.1.2 [**Computer Systems Organization**]: Multiprocessors, Interconnection architectures; B.4.3 [**Hardware**]: Input/Output and Data Communications—*Interconnections (subsystems)*

Keywords

Network-on-Chip, Nanophotonics, Crossbar

1. INTRODUCTION

As technology scales into deep submicron domain, electrical wires start to face critical challenges in latency and power since they do not scale well compared to transistors [9]. Much recent research has shifted focus to optical on-chip interconnection, for its promises regarding high bandwidth density, low propagation delay, distance-independent power consumption, and natural support for multicast and broadcast. Compared to traditional electrical networks, photonic networks can achieve two to six times more performance and reduce the power significantly in many-core chips [22]. In addition, large scale systems require high memory bandwidth, which is limited by the number of electrical I/O pins and their high power consumption. Photonic connections could alleviate this problem as they can support high data rate and Dense Wavelength Division Multiplexing (DWDM) to provide enormous bandwidth and improved energy efficiency [4, 5]. There have also been studies exploiting the nanophotonic network topologies [8, 10, 12, 19, 20, 23] as well as nanophotonics interconnection for chip-to-chip communication [14]. In many cases, an optical crossbar is favored as the network backbone for cache coherence management [15, 24, 25] and data transmission as it provides natural support for broadcast, as well as short and uniform latency that simplifies protocol design.

However, while optical interconnects provide many attractive and promising features, they also face several key challenges. Thermal sensitivity and process variation of silicon photonic devices are two difficult hurdles for robust and reliable on-chip communication [16, 17, 26]. Another major challenge is the high static power consumption which dominates the total on-chip network power. The static power is mainly attributed to the off-chip laser source and on-chip microring resonators. A laser source supplies light of multiple wavelengths that traverse the waveguides. Laser power needs to compensate for a variety of light losses along its path. Microring resonators, the basic components in optical networks, are very sensitive to temperature variations. They require additional trimming power to maintain their resonant wavelength [16]. The laser power and trimming power, contributing 74% of network power [20], are determined by the network bandwidth, the number of microrings and temperature variation etc. On the other hand, future large-scale CMPs (Chip Multiprocessor) require the optical network to provide high network bandwidth to handle increasing on-chip communications. Hence, it is imperative to design energy-efficient network architectures to achieve high throughput with low static power.

Conventional crossbar designs such as Single-Write-Multi-Read (SWMR) and Multi-Write-Single-Read (MWSR) [12, 22, 19] statically allocate a channel to a particular node. Those designs fail to deliver high network throughput due to poor channel utilization. Increasing throughput would require overprovisioning of channels, waveguides, laser powers, and microrings. Multi-Write-Multi-Read (MWMR) crossbars can improve the channel utilization by sharing all channels among all network nodes. However, this design results in an excessive number of microrings because every node should be able to modulate light in all channels. Though most of the microrings are idle, they still consume significant trimming power, which is proportional to the number of nodes and channels. Furthermore, MWMR requires arbitration and existing token-based arbitration schemes present a significant unfairness due to the fixed priorities of tokens, as discussed later in section 4.

This paper proposes an energy-efficient optical crossbar design that aims to achieve high network throughput with low static power consumption. The design approaches the network throughput of a MWMR crossbar while using only slightly more microrings than a SWMR or MWSR crossbar. To achieve high throughput, we propose a *channel borrowing* scheme that, instead of having full sharing of channels among all network nodes, allows only a few nodes to share a channel. A channel is allocated to an owner node and can be borrowed by sharers when the channel is idle. The owner always has the highest priority over the channel to avoid starvation. We intelligently select the network nodes that can share a channel, with low probability of contention among the nodes. Arbitration is still necessary. However, the complexity and latency are much lower than in MWMR due to the greatly reduced sharing degree. This scheme achieves high channel utilization, and hence high network throughput, while removing the dependency between the number of microrings per sender and the network node count. The result is a significant reduction in both laser power and trimming power for microrings. In summary, the major contributions of this paper are:

- The design of an energy-efficient optical crossbar architecture that improves network throughput by increasing the channel utilization with low static power.

- The introduction of a simple arbitration scheme to resolve the conflicts among the nodes that share the channel fairly and efficiently.

- The evaluation of the energy efficiency of the proposed channel borrowing design relative to other alternative crossbar architectures using synthetic traffic patterns and traces from PARSEC benchmarks.

Using synthetic traces, our experimental results show that, compared with SWMR and MWMR crossbars, the proposed network design can improve energy efficiency by 34% and

Crossbar Designs	Laser Power	Trimming Power
Radix-32 SWMR	35% [20]	38% [20]
Radix-64 MWSR (Corona)	5.4% [1]	54% [1]
Radix-16 MWMR (FlexiShare)	23% [20]	42% [20]

Table 1: Power breakdowns of laser source and microring trimming.

26%. Under real traffic traces extracted from PARSEC benchmarks [6], the average network latency is reduced by 51%, when compared with SWMR. Our channel borrowing scheme also achieves comparable or even better performance than a MWMR crossbar with only 44% of its microrings because of light-weight and fair arbitration. Finally, energy-delay^2 (ED^2) is reduced by 73% and 45% compared to SWMR and MWMR respectively.

The remainder of this paper is organized as follows. Section 2 presents the background of nanophotonics. Section 3 discusses the designs, implementation details of network architecture, arbitration as well as the router micro-architecture. The experimental results are analyzed in Section 4. Section 5 summarizes the related work. Finally, Section 6 concludes this paper.

2. BACKGROUND

Recent advances in photonic devices and integration technology have made optical links a feasible solution for future global interconnects. A basic optical network includes an off-chip laser source that provides on-chip light, waveguides that route and guide optical signal, microring modulators that convert electrical signals to optical ones, and microring filters to detect light and translate it to electrical signals. Though on-chip light sources exist [27], we select off-chip laser as it reduces on-chip power and area [15]. Light of different wavelengths can be transmitted and modulated in a single waveguide, so dense wavelength division multiplexing (DWDM) technology is employed to enable multiple data channels per waveguide, thus providing high network bandwidth density. Wavelength-selective silicon modulators convert the digital signals to the laser light by varying the absorption of corresponding wavelength, which is determined by the size of the microring, temperature and injection charge density. At the receiving end, an optical filter extracts the light of a specific wavelength from the waveguide and transfers it to the photo detector to convert optical signal to electrical one.

Power Consumption

For conventional electrical networks, dynamic power, which depends on the activities of routers and channels, typically dominates the total network power, whereas for optical networks, static power surpasses dynamic power and becomes dominant in the total network power. The static power of an optical network is mainly comprised of laser source power and microring trimming power. The laser power is determined by the total number of wavelengths, the conversion efficiency from electrons to photons of the laser, and all types of transmission losses including both on-resonance microrings and scattered losses from off-resonance microrings [1]. Hence, laser power increases with the total number of microrings. The resonance wavelength of a microring drifts with temperature variation. Such drift can be corrected, or *trimmed*, via either heating or carrier injection. Both methods consume power. Hence, the total power spent in trimming all microrings also increases with the total number of microrings. Recent studies have shown that laser and trimming power together contribute over 60% of the total on-chip network power, as shown in Table 1, which summarizes the percentages of power spent in laser source and trimming for different crossbar designs. For example, the Corona network in 17-nm technology from HP [1, 22] is estimated to consume ~26W in trimming microrings, out of ~48W of the total network power. Even with optimistic microring heating efficiency, e.g. using in-plane heaters and air-undercut [4, 10], it is estimated that microring heating still consumes 38% of the total network power [20]. Hence, it is unwise to increase the throughput of an optical network through increasing the number of channels (and microrings) since the idle channels still consume significant static power. Instead, an *energy-efficient* optical network that achieves high throughput via improved *channel utilization*, which does not increase static power, is preferred and is what we develop in this paper.

3. CHANNEL BORROWING

In this section, we will present the proposed channel borrowing architecture with the distributed arbitration and implementation details of routers. We first discuss the conventional crossbars and their physical layout used in this paper.

3.1 Overview of Optical Crossbars

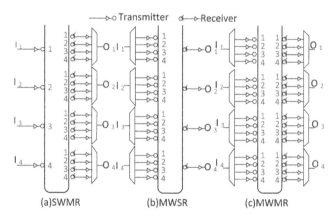

Figure 1: Crossbar microarchitectural design [3].

We classify previous crossbar designs into two main categories: static and dynamical channel allocation. The channel defined here is a set of wavelengths used to transfer one flit (flit is the smallest unit of the transmission). The number of wavelengths per channel depends on the flit size and modulation speed of microrings. Crossbars using static channel allocation include SWMR and MWSR. The microarchitectural designs of the crossbars are shown in Fig. 1(a) and (b), using a radix-4 crossbar as a simple example. I_n and O_n represent the sending and receiving interface of the optical router at node n. The different indices of rings in Fig. 1 indicate different optical channels. There are a total of 4 channels for the 4 network nodes in this example. Each node in SWMR has one dedicated channel to send data and can receive data from all channels. On the contrary, MWSR provides each node with a dedicated channel to read data and allows any node to write to the given channel. With exclusive sending channels, SWMR avoids starvation and does

not need global arbitration to handle contention, which reduces design complexity and network latency. When traffic loads on the channels are evenly distributed, SWMR and MWSR can perform well and provide high channel utilization. However, because SWMR/MWSR assigns dedicated channels to every sender/receiver, those channels are idle if the sender/receiver does not have data to send/receive, thus reducing the utilization of the channel and the total network throughput. Increasing throughput would require over provisioning of channels and causes proportional static power increase. Therefore the low channel utilization of SWMR and MWSR results in low energy efficiency.

Dynamic channel allocation design, e.g. MWMR shown in Fig. 1(c), can improve channel utilization and network throughput with channel sharing. In the figure, we can see that each network node can write to or read from any channel via more transmitters/receivers and MUXes than in SWMR and MWSR. Thus, under uneven traffic distribution, the nodes with high injection rate can utilize multiple channels to improve channel usage. However, as we can observe in Fig. 1(c), full channel sharing also requires more microring resonators than SWMR or MWSR as in SWMR because every node can modulate light on all channels. Most of the time, the majority of microring modulators are idle as only M out of NM (N is the crossbar radix, M is the number of channels) transmitters are used simultaneously. But idle microrings still consume significant trimming power which is proportional to NM and cause more light losses in the waveguide. Hence, full sharing architectures also have low energy efficiency because of a large number of microrings.

To achieve high energy efficiency, we still employ dynamic channel allocation to improve channel utilization. However, instead of having full sharing of channels among all network nodes, we allow only a few nodes to share a channel so that there are much fewer microrings than in MWMR and the dependency between the number of transmitters per channel and the number of network nodes is removed. The next question is how to select the nodes to share the channels in order to achieve high network throughput. The cumulative traffic on the shared channel should be high enough to obtain high channel utilization. On the other hand, the possibility of contention among the nodes to compete for the same channel should be low to avoid throughput loss. Before we analyze the traffic distribution on the channels and introduce the selection policy of sharing nodes, we briefly describe the physical channel design of nanophotonic crossbars.

Waveguide Layout

Since optics are more cost-effective for many-core CMPs, we choose to model in this paper a 64-core chip with die size of $400mm^2$ [12, 22]. Concentration [2, 11] is employed to let 4 cores share one optical router so that network size is reduced from 64 to 16. Downsizing the network reduces the number of microrings and static power cost. SWMR, MWMR and the proposed channel borrowing network use the same ring-shaped waveguide layout to connect all 16 routers across the chip, as shown in Fig. 2(a).

There are two ways to implement a data channel, namely single-serpentine and double-serpentine layouts [3]. They are illustrated in Fig. 2(b) and (c). The single-serpentine layout has two separate channels for upstream and downstream transmission. The direction of increasing router index is defined as downstream, otherwise the direction is

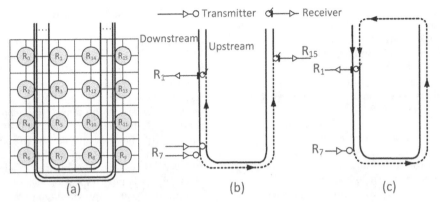

Figure 2: (a)Waveguide layout for a 16-node crossbar. (b) Single-Serpentine layout.(Data transmission: $R_7 \to R_1$ and $R_7 \to R_{15}$ via upstream and downstream channels)(c) Double-Serpentine layout.

defined as upstream. For example, in Fig. 2(b), R_7 sends message to R_1 through upstream channel and to R_{15} via downstream channel. The message path is illustrated by the dotted line. The alternative layout is double-serpentine that doubles the length of optical paths and lets the light traverse each node twice. During the first pass, the transmitter modulates the light to send a message. Then the receiver detects the light and converts it to digital signal in the second pass. The first option is usually adopted as it reduces the length of waveguide, the light loss and transmission latency. Hence, each channel actually is composed of two subchannels for upstream and downstream directions. Next, we will analyze the traffic distribution on each subchannel and introduce selection policy of nodes that share a given channel.

3.2   Selection Policy of Sharing Nodes

Fig. 3(a) shows the channel utilization on upstream (Up_1)/ downstream ($Down_1$) subchannel assigned to node 1 in a SWMR crossbar. R_1 is the owner node of the two channels. Static channel allocation does not allow any other node to write to the two channels. The physical location of R_1 relative to the waveguide determines that the upstream channel is only used for communication with R_0 and the downstream channel is used for $R_2 \sim R_{15}$. So there is a great chance that the traffic load on $Down_1$ is much higher than the traffic on Up_1. Under uniform random traffic, the traffic loads on Up_1 and $Down_1$ are $\frac{1}{15}$ and $\frac{14}{15}$, respectively. Thus, one of the subchannels is more utilized than the other. That is why the network throughput of SWMR is only 60% of MWMR (measured from Fig. 7). MWMR achieves better channel utilization through dynamically allocating the under-utilized Up_1 to other nodes.

In our design, we allow a small-degree of sharing. R_1 is still the owner of $Down_1$ and Up_1, but other sharers can borrow the channels during their idle time. The channel utilization can benefit from high borrowing opportunities. As mentioned in the previous section, our aim is to intelligently pick the network nodes with low probability of contention among the sharing nodes. In this case, we want to pick the node generating high traffic volume on the upstream channel to improve the usage of Up_1 but low traffic on the downstream channel to avoid competing with R_1 for $Down_1$. In other words, a node that produces the complementary traffic load of R_1 on two directions is a perfect candidate to share channel resources. Thus we pick R_{14}, which has the required traffic distribution.

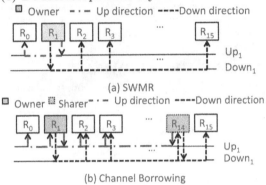

Figure 3: Channel utilization for (a) SWMR (b) channel borrowing crossbar.

Fig. 3(b) shows that with R_{14} sharing the two subchannels with R_1, the amount of traffic flows traveling through Up_1, i.e. $R_1 \to R_0$, $R_{14} \to R_0 \sim R_{13}$ is the same as the amount of the traffic flows traversing along $Down_1$, i.e. $R_1 \to R_2 \sim R_{15}$ and $R_{14} \to R_{15}$. Then, under uniform random traffic, where the traffic load of each traffic flow— source and destination pair is the same, the average traffic loads of the two channels are exactly the same, which leads to a much better channel utilization. We pair the remaining network nodes based on the same policy, letting R_i and R_{N-1-i} (N is the radix of optical crossbar) share their dedicated channel resources. By allowing one more node to share the channels, our design can achieve network throughput comparable with MWMR due to balanced traffic as shown later in section 4.

Increasing the sharing degree requires more microrings and higher power but it also provides more opportunity to improve the channel utilization, especially under unbalanced traffic loads. We will study the energy and performance tradeoff by varying the sharing degree in the evaluation section. How should we select nodes to form a small group and share channels, when the number of nodes sharing one channel increases? We will add one more pair of nodes into each existing group. For example, if 4 nodes can share one channel, then we combine the original pair of R_0 and R_{15} together with their neighboring node pair: R_1 and R_{14} to form a new group. The reason of such combination is that it is more convenient for two adjacent nodes to exchange information such as the channel idleness. Arbitration can benefit from quick notification. Eventually, we partition the network nodes into small groups. The size of the group is the sharing degree of the channel. Each group is assigned a set of sending channels that can only be written by nodes in the same group. With better selection of sharing nodes, small-sized group still can approach channel utilization of the fully-shared design with much fewer microrings. The dependency between the number of nodes and channels can be removed by allowing fewer channels in each group. For example, to implement a radix-16 crossbar with 8 channels, the number of channels dedicated for each pair of nodes is reduced from two to one. The priority used in the arbitration is also modified accordingly.

Arbitration is necessary since small-degree sharing still results in contention in the optical channels among the sharing nodes. Next we will discuss the proposed arbitration to resolve the conflict efficiently and fairly.

3.3 Arbitration

As a channel is shared by multiple nodes, arbitration is necessary to make sure that only one of the nodes can send data on the channel. Efficient arbitration should allocate the channel to the nodes fairly and provide high channel utilization with low latency, power and control overhead. Previous MWSR and MWMR crossbars [20, 22, 23] leverage token-based arbitration that uses a photonic token to represent the right of exclusive access to the channel during a data slot. Each node that wants to transmit data has to grab the token by removing light from the token channel. A token is injected every cycle to form a continuous token stream so that the network throughput is not limited by round-trip delay of token traversal. The main drawback of the arbitration is that routers closer to the injection point of tokens always have higher priority than the remote ones, which could lead to starvation and unfairness.

FlexiShare [20] proposed two-pass token arbitration for MWMR crossbars. It eliminates starvation with dedicated tokens owned by each network node. A token passes all network nodes twice. During the first pass, a token can only be removed by its owner node. For example, in the 1st pass, T0,T1 ...Tn are assigned to R_0, R_1...R_n respectively. In the case that the owner node does not require the channel, the reserved token is recycled in the second pass as a free one. So if T0 is still available in the 2nd round, it can be used by any node that does not have a dedicated token in the current cycle. However two-pass arbitration is still unfair because of the fixed priority in the second pass of token traveling. Besides, the arbitration latency varies depending on the pass in which the token is obtained. Specifically, if the node gets the reserved token in the 1st round, it has to wait one more cycle during which the token completes the second pass, before it actually writes to the data channel, assuming 1 cycle latency for token to travel across the chip. While if the node grabs the free token during the 2nd pass, it can use the channel in the next cycle.

In our proposed network architecture, control and latency overhead of arbitration are much lower than in MWMR due to the greatly reduced sharing degree. Each network node is assigned a dedicated channel consisting of two unidirection subchannels to avoid starvation. In the network with sharing degree of two, the arbiter resolves the contention between two nodes locally. If the channel is idle, the arbiter grants the request. Otherwise, it rejects the node that wants to borrow the channel. The information is sent via a separate channel, which is implemented as continuous tokens. Note

Channel	0	1	2	3	Sum of Priority
R0	1	0	–	–	1
R1	0	1	–	–	1
R2	–	–	1	0	1
R3	–	–	0	1	1

Table 2: Priority vector of routers in a radix-4 crossbar with sharing degree of 2.

that the token in our arbitration represents the availability of the corresponding channel. The decision of channel allocation is still made by the proposed arbitration. For each channel, each node has different arbitration priority with the owners' being the highest. For each node, its priority over each network channel is also different. For instance, in a network with 4-way sharing, R_2, R_3, R_{12} and R_{13} are partitioned as a group to share their assigned channels. R_2 and R_3 are the owners of $Down_2$ and $Down_3$, respectively. The priorities of R_2, R_3, R_{12} and R_{13} are 3, 0, 1, 2 for $Down_2$ and 0, 3, 2, 1 for $Down_3$. The average priority value of each node is the same to ensure all network nodes have equal right to access channel resources. Table 2 shows the priority vector of routers in a radix-4 crossbar with sharing degree of two. The "1" and "0" represents the highest and lowest priority of a particular channel. Since only two routers are sharing the same channel, "–" indicates that the channel is not available. In the table, the cumulative priority values of each of the 4 nodes are the same, which proves that the arbitration is fair.

In summary, channel borrowing network architecture improves the energy efficiency of optical crossbar by allowing channel sharing by a few nodes. Each channel is allocated to an owner node and can be borrowed by other nodes. To improve the channel utilization, we intelligently select R_i and R_{N-1-i} (N is the radix of the crossbar) as a pair to share channels. The pairing policy reduces the probability of contention among the nodes and balances the traffic loads on each subchannel. When the sharing degree increases, neighboring node pairs are selected to share channels. In the following parts of the paper, we will only focus on the network architectures with the sharing degree of two, unless we explicitly state other types of network setting. With a small degree of sharing, arbitration is much simpler than MWMR. The contention among shared nodes can be solved locally with the fixed priority and idleness information of the channels. The priorities of network nodes are set to ensure overall fairness of arbitration. Through this scheme, we are able to achieve high channel utilization, and high network throughput, while removing the dependency between the number of transmitting microrings per channel and the number of network nodes. This results in significant reduction in both laser power and trimming power for microrings.

Optical crossbars in general do not scale well since the number of microrings grows quadratically with the crossbar radix. However, they are still promising designs for small to medium size networks because of their high throughput and low network latency. Channel borrowing is more scalable than SWMR/MWSR/MWMR crossbars due to better energy-efficiency, as will be shown later. When the number of network nodes increases, the throughput of SWMR/MWSR tends to degrade as the traffic on different channels becomes less even, causing lower channel utilization. Also,the chance for each node to use all channels is small, which makes full sharing schemes such as MWMR less beneficial. However, the small sharing degree in channel borrowing could still balance the traffic loads toward two directions effectively without having to use a large number of microrings.

In the next section, we will describe implementation details of channel borrowing and its light-weight arbitration.

3.4 Implementation

Router Microarchitecture

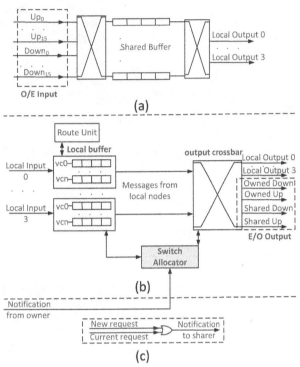

Figure 4: Electrical router microarchitecture. (a) Receiving module, (b) transmitting module, (c) notification generation unit.

Figure 4 shows the microarchitecture of the electrical router, which connects to four local cores and the global optical network. In SWMR, the router consists of two main modules: one for receiving the messages from the optical network and forwarding them to the local cores, as shown in Fig. 4(a); the other for transmitting the local messages to the optical network, illustrated in Fig. 4(b). The transmitting unit also requires a notification signal that indicates whether the node will use the optical network. This signal is sent to the sharer and also to the switch allocator to guide switch allocation, as shown in Fig. 4(c).

In Fig. 4(a), the messages collected from all optical channels are first converted to electrical ones. Then, packets are stored into a shared buffer [20] before being transferred through the second stage of the switch to the input ports of local cores. Compared to SWMR, the overhead of the switch comes from the increased number of input ports, which results in higher radix of the first crossbar. MWMR requires more ports than the channel borrowing topology since full channel sharing allows each node to receive messages from any of the subchannels. The power overhead of the crossbar is evaluated in Section 4.2.

For the transmitting process, messages generated by local cores are initially stored in the router buffers. Next, the switch allocation (SA) unit arbitrates the flits head-

	Optical channel (λ)	Microrings
SWMR	9376	156K
MWMR	9392	553K
Channel borrowing	9408	246K

Table 3: Component count in SWMR, MWMR and channel borrowing

ing to the same output port. The winner is transmitted through the output crossbar to either local cores or optical network. SWMR, MWMR and channel borrowing topologies require different number of output ports for E/O conversion. SWMR only needs to access two unidirectional subchannels. The sharing degree of the channel borrowing network is two, so it requires one more set of output ports per router, which increases the radix of output crossbar by two, as shown in Fig. 4(b). MWMR, allowing full sharing, has the largest crossbar size among the three network designs. The SA unit is also designed differently for the three types of crossbars. SWMR only requires local arbitration because there is no conflict on optical channels. Our arbitration adds a fixed priority arbitration unit—a 2:1 MUX with 1-bit notification from the owner node as the control signal for each direction. The notification signal, indicating if the shared channel is idle, is generated as shown in Fig. 4(c). The inputs of the notification unit include the remaining requests in the buffer which can be determined one cycle in advance and the new incoming requests. The extra control logic for SA in channel borrowing does not introduce huge overhead, because (1) simple circuits are sufficient; (2) crossbar and buffers dominate the area and power cost of the router. MWMR employs a state machine for its token-based arbitration, which is more complicated than our SA design.

SWMR and channel borrowing design require 4 pipeline stages: (1) buffering/routing/notification, (2) reservation, (3) crossbar traversal and (4) transferring to remote router/local node. In MWMR, the additional token arbitration stage may take one or two cycles as explained in section 3.3. To complete the transmission in a single cycle, the cycle time should accommodate the transmission delay in the worst case plus the small control delay. Considering a 400 mm^2 die size, the speed of light is 10.45ps/mm and the latency of O/E/O is 75ps [12]. Therefore the transmission can complete at 1GHz network frequency.

Optical Resource Costs

In addition to the costs of electrical routers, we also analyzed the overheads of optical components. Table 3 lists the network bandwidth in terms of the number of wavelengths and the number of microrings of the three evaluated crossbars. Given a radix-N network with M W-bit channels, the channel width for sending data, reservation and buffer credit information in SWMR crossbars are $2NMW$, $2N\log N$ and $2N$, respectively [20] (M=N in this paper). MWMR requires additional token channels, which needs M bits. The proposed channel borrowing network uses a total of $2N$ bits to send notifications of channel status. The bandwidth overhead of the token channel is small, but the token channels in MWMR employ two round waveguides which require higher laser power than one round waveguides. MWMR allows global channel sharing, so the number of transmitters is $16\times$ of SWMR and $8\times$ of channel borrowing in a radix-16 crossbar. The number of receivers is also increased, compared to SWMR. For example, for upstream channel assigned to R_7

(Up_7), only $R_0 \sim R_6$ needs to read from Up_7 in SWMR. But Up_7 is not allocated to any node in MWMR, so every router has receivers to access Up_7. Therefore, MWMR uses more than twice the number of microring resonators used in the two alternative designs.

4. EVALUATION

In this section, we evaluate the energy-efficiency, channel utilization, performance and fairness of SWMR, MWMR and the proposed channel borrowing crossbar, BORROW, using both synthetic traffic and real traffic traces from PARSEC [6] benchmarks.

4.1 Simulation Methodology

We extend a cycle-accurate NoC simulator Noxim [18] into a 64-tile network with parameterized radix-16 optical crossbar similar to the one shown in Fig. 2(a). We assume separated control and data networks with flit sizes being 8B and 64B, respectively. The number of optical channels M in our experiment is the same as the crossbar radix, following the settings in SWMR and MWSR. The shared buffer shown in Fig. 4(a) holds 4 flits per receiving channel. Credit-based flow control is employed to avoid flit loss upon fully occupied buffer. The round trip delay including request and reply is collected as network latency. The network frequency is 1GHz to accommodate 1-cycle propagation delay. We experiment with uniform random traffic where each node uniformly injects packets into the network with random destinations. We also experiment with several permutation traffic types, where each node has specific destination nodes. We evaluate bit-complement, transpose, bit-reversal, shuffle and two types of hotspot traffic. The first type of hotspot traffic lets all nodes send requests only to the four nodes at the left corner in the network. For the other type, each tile sends messages to one node with higher probability than others. The network throughput is measured as the average receiving rate at each core. Thus, an optical channel consisting of two subchannels can send at most two requests per cycle, even though the four cores can generate up to 4 messages per cycle.

To evaluate BORROW under various traffic conditions including uneven traffic load distribution, we also use PARSEC [6] benchmarks to generate traffic traces. We extend PTLsim [28], a user level simulator to support many-core simulation. For each PARSEC workload, we use *sim-large* input set and collected all L2 cache transactions into trace files. A 1024-thread simulation environment is setup to test the performance and energy efficiency of SWMR, MWMR and BORROW. Each tile in the network contains one shared L2 cache which is shared by four multithreaded cores with private L1 caches. With a concentration degree of 4, 64 tiles are connected with a radix-16 optical crossbar. The simulation configuration is listed in Table 4.

4.2 Power Model

We estimate the power consumption of laser, microrings, electrical router and links to evaluate the energy efficiency of different crossbar designs. We adopt the nanophotonics power model from [4]. The dynamic energy cost of optical transmission is 158 fJ/bit including modulation, detection and amplification. The static power of the optical network consists of trimming power to maintain corresponding wavelength, which introduces 16∼32fJ/bit/heater [10]

Number of threads	1024
Network organization	64 tiles, 4 cores per tile
Cores	4-thread, 1 GHz
Crossbar Radix	16
Private L1I/D	32KB per core, 2-cycle hit time, write-through
Shared L2	2MB per tile, 16-way, 64B line, 10-cycle hit time, write-back
Memory Controller	Four, located in the edges of the chip
Router	1GHz frequency, 4-stage pipeline.
Packet size	1 flit
Buffer space	4 flits/VC, 2VCs/input

Table 4: System configuration.

thermal tuning energy cost and laser power. Based on the data of microring count in Table 3, we obtain the trimming power of SWMR, MWMR and BORROW to be 3.12W, 11.06W, 4.92W, respectively. The power of the off-chip laser should be large enough to overcome all types of light losses before the detector can receive sufficient optical power. In Table 5, we list the loss values for the optical components, following the work in [10, 13]. Since off-tune microrings lead to non-negligible insertion and scattering losses, MWMR requires higher laser power due to the large number of idle microrings. Besides, the waveguide length of token and credit channel is longer than data channel, which results in higher light losses. We perform detailed laser power calculation for the optical networks that we consider. The estimated laser power for SWMR, MWMR and BORROW to be 5.76W, 8.01W and 5.82W respectively. The power estimations of buffers, crossbars and electrical links are from the model implemented in HSPICE with 45nm PTM (www.eas.asu.edu/~ptm/interconnect.html) device models at 1.1V and a temperature of 90°C. Due to the large number of receivers and transmitters per router, the buffer and crossbar size in MWMR is also larger than in SWMR and BORROW. Thus the static power of electrical routers is also higher than other compared crossbar designs.

Photonic device	Loss (dB)	Photonic device	Loss (dB)
Waveguide loss	1.0/cm	Waveguide bend	0.005
Splitter	0.2	Coupler	1
Insertion	0.017	Scattering	0.001
Filter drop	1.5	Ring through	0.01
Laser efficiency	30%	detector sensitivity	$10\mu w$

Table 5: Optical loss of optical components [4, 13, 23].

4.3 Channel Utilization

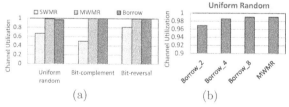

(a)　　　　　　　　(b)

Figure 5: Channel utilization of (a) SWMR, MWMR and BORROW (b) BORROW with varying sharing degree.

Our design aims to achieve high network throughput with high channel utilization, so we measure the channel utilization of SWMR, MWMR and BORROW under uniform random, bit-complement traffic and bit-reversal traffic. As shown in Fig. 5(a), BORROW can achieve channel utilization comparable to MWMR that allows full channel sharing. For uniform random traffic, the injection rate of each tile is the same, but the number of downstream and upstream messages may be different at each router. Especially in SWMR, the traffic loads on two dedicated subchannels are quite different. Thus one of the channels is underutilized, which results in the lowest utilization among the three designs. BORROW allows two routers with complementary traffic load to borrow channels from each other. Hence, the aggregate traffic on each subchannel is the same. However, traffic loads may be uneven during a short period of time. For example, the sharer may not need to borrow the idle channel from the owner. That is the reason that BORROW does not achieve the utilization of MWMR. MWMR provides the highest channel utilization among the three designs as it has the highest sharing degree and flexibility. Even during intermittent uneven traffic, other nodes can still use the idle channels. For permutation traffic such as bit-complement, each core sends requests to a fixed destination. The two nodes in the same pair may send requests toward opposite direction. Then they have 100% chance to borrow channels from each other and improve channel utilization. SWMR only achieves 50% channel usage as it sends requests only through one of the two dedicated subchannels.

To approach the high channel utilization of MWMR, we can increase the sharing degree of each channel, as shown in Fig. 5 (b). BORROW_n indicates n nodes sharing their assigned channels. We observe from the figure that channel utilization improves when sharing increases. However, to achieve a 2% higher utilization, transmitters and trimming power are increased by a factor of 4. Therefore, we will use BORROW_2 in the remaining evaluations.

4.4 Network Latency and Throughput

Network Latency

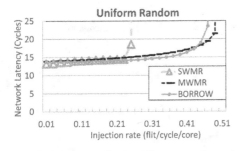

Figure 6: Latency under uniform random traffic.

Fig. 6 shows the network latencies under uniform random traffic. Although MWMR achieves the highest throughput, it incurs higher network latency than SWMR and BORROW before the saturation point due to the propagation latency of tokens in the two-pass token arbitration. If a router grabs a dedicated token during the first pass, it still has to wait for the second pass to start data transmission. As the injection rate increases, the network nodes require more bandwidth and use the dedicated tokens more frequently. Hence, the arbitration often requires an extra cycle, which causes larger latency difference between MWMR and BORROW.

Network Throughput

Fig. 7 compares the throughput of SWMR, MWMR and

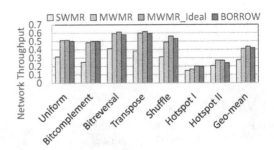

Figure 7: Throughput under synthetic traffic.

BORROW under various traffic traces. Note that the extra arbitration delay in MWMR has an impact on network throughput for the following reasons. The delay of the credit loop increases upon the extra arbitration cycle. The latency of the backward credit path impairs buffer utilization because it increases buffer idle time between uses, which leads to throughput loss. In addition, the head flit of the buffer blocks the following flit from entering the arbitration stage due to the extra arbitration cycle. In order to show the achievable network throughput with full channel sharing, we added to Fig. 7 a comparison with MWMR_Ideal, which is a mutation of MWMR that removes throughput loss due to additional delay of token arbitration. On average, BORROW can achieve 96% network throughput of MWMR_Ideal with 1/8 the number of transmitters.

Energy Efficiency

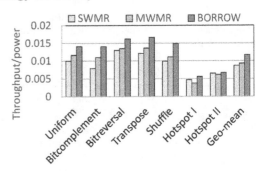

Figure 8: Energy efficiency in throughput/power under synthetic traffic.

We compare the energy efficiency with the metric "throughput/power" in Fig. 8. The power value including dynamic and static power of both optical and electrical components is measured when the network is fully activated. On average, BORROW outperforms SWMR and MWMR by 34% and 26%, respectively. This is because it achieves high channel utilization, and hence high throughput with small-degree of sharing using fewer microrings and incuring less trimming and laser power than in MWMR.

4.5 Evaluations with Real Workloads

Network Latency

Under synthetic traces, each node injects a similar number of messages into the network. So the dedicated channels have equal opportunities to be utilized by their owners. However, real benchmark traffic may show uneven injection rates among network nodes, which hurts channel utilization in the designs with static channel allocation. We examine our crossbar design with PARSEC benchmarks to see if network performance degrades significantly under unbalanced traffic. Fig. 9 shows the normalized network latency of the

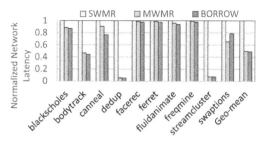

Figure 9: Latency normalized to SWMR for PARSEC benchmarks.

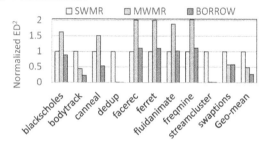

Figure 10: ED^2 normalized to SWMR for PARSEC benchmarks.

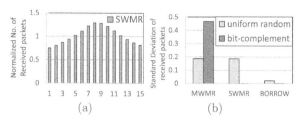

Figure 11: (a) Number of and (b) standard deviation of received packets of each network node under uniform random traffic.

three crossbars. Through all tested benchmarks, MWMR and BORROW show better performance than SWMR due to high channel utilization. Especially, when traffic injection is beyond the network throughput of SWMR, the network latency increases exponentially, because of contention delay. The improvement of BORROW over SWMR can reach up to 94%. For benchmark Swaptions, MWMR outperforms BORROW mainly because of its higher channel utilization with global channel sharing. Occasionally, both paired nodes in BORROW generate heavy traffic toward the same direction, causing arbitration contention. Overall, BORROW achieves similar or even better performance due to its low-overhead arbitration.

Energy Delay Product

We evaluate energy efficiency of the 3 crossbar designs using the ED^2 metric as shown in Fig. 10. High ED^2 indicates low energy efficiency. The energy consumed by the off-chip laser and heaters to trim resonance wavelengths of microrings dominates the total energy costs. SWMR requires the least microrings and incurs the lowest static power among the three designs. For some benchmarks such as facerec, the small delay improvement cannot overcome the high energy cost. Therefore, SWMR shows the highest energy efficiency, while for other applications such as dedup, the network latency of SWMR is increased significantly when traffic load is above the network throughput. In addition, the energy cost drops with shorter execution time. Thus BORROW improves the energy efficiency of SWMR by up to 99.6%. Overall, the geometric mean value of ED^2 in BORROW is improved by 73% and 45% compared to SWMR and MWMR, respectively.

4.6 Fairness

SWMR does not require arbitration, so the uneven traffic distribution on two subchannels causes the uneven throughput of each node, which is indicated by different numbers of received packets per node, as shown in Fig. 11(a). The nodes attached to the middle part of the waveguide generate more balanced traffic loads on two subchannels than the

nodes at the two ends of the waveguide, since the middle nodes have similar number of destination nodes toward two opposite directions. Fig. 11(b) shows the comparisons of the standard deviation of network throughput per node in the 3 crossbar designs under uniform random and bit-complement traffic. The uneven throughput of MWMR comes from the unfairness of token arbitration. The routers closer to the injection point of tokens always have advantage to grab tokens over other routers. For bit-complement traffic, MWMR shows a larger throughput difference because of uneven distribution of free tokens. Free tokens contributed by half of the network nodes are always obtained by the routers with higher priority. Hence these router have higher chances to use the optical channels and receive more packets. BORROW shows the least throughput variation among the three designs, which indicates the fairness of the proposed arbitration. SWMR also has similar throughput among network nodes under bit-complement traffic, but the throughput is only half that of BORROW.

5. RELATED WORK

Global crossbar topology provides fast all-to-all connection [12, 22] but the overhead of microrings becomes a serious issue for high node count, requiring high laser and thermal tuning power. Many works build different topologies such as Clos [10], mesh [8] or stars [7] to reduce the number of optical devices but incurs higher dynamic energy cost due to intermediate routers. A 2D torus topology was proposed using wavelength-based routing with passive wavelength-routers [13]. Retransmission is applied when multiple senders communicate with the same receiver at the same time, which brings long contention delay. The circuit-switch based photonic network [21] presented a hybrid topology that arranges large messages transmitted through optical network and small messages are delivered by electrical wires to improve overall energy efficiency. However, the setup time overcomes the benefit of optical transmission and makes it suitable for off-chip communications. The hybrid networks [19, 15] that leverage both metal and OP-I connections, and utilize OP-I in global communication where long-range metal wires or multi-hop metal network are originally adopted and clustering [12] are proposed to shrink the crossbar size. A reservation mechanism [19] that can tune off the idle receivers was introduced to avoid optical energy loss of broadcast on the data channels. In this paper we adopt reservation and clustering techniques to improve the utilization of network channels, but we focus on optical crossbar designs for global communications because even with the reduced radix, the static power cost still contributes a significant portion of the power consumption of the entire network.

The MWSR crossbar architecture [22, 23] allocates a dedicated receiving channel to each network node and leverages the fair token slot arbitration to solve channel contention fairly. The SWMR [12, 19] crossbar architecture provides each network router with a dedicated sending channel to obtain contention-free communications. However, both designs limit the channel utilization under unbalanced traffic distribution due to the static channel allocation. Increasing throughput would require overprovisioning of channels, which is less energy-efficient because of the dominant static power cost. FlexiShare (MWMR) topologies [20] allow global channel sharing among the network nodes to improve channel utilization. In addition, they remove the dependency between the number of channels and network node count present in SWMR and MWSR. Thus, they can achieve high energy efficiency when a small number of channels are enough for a large network. However, if that is the case, we can also reduce the number of channels by applying concentration and clustering techniques to downsize the network. Moreover, the static power cost is further reduced because smaller network size results in fewer microrings. The major drawback of MWMR is the large number of microrings that degrades the energy efficiency of the network.

6. CONCLUSIONS

The proposed "channel borrowing" optical crossbar architecture and its light-weight distributed arbitration can approach the throughput of MWMR under most of the tested traffic types with much fewer transmitters. It removes the dependency between the number of microring modulators and the radix of crossbar by employing a small-degree of channel sharing. Network channels are allocated to an owner node, but can also be used by a few other nodes during idle time. The network nodes that share a channel are selected based on low probability of conflict. Our simulation results show that compared with SWMR and MWMR crossbars, the proposed network design can improve energy efficiency by 34% and 26% using synthetic traces. Under real traffic traces extracted from PARSEC benchmarks, ED^2 is reduced by 73% and 45% compared to the two alternative architectures. This demonstrates that channel borrowing is an energy-efficient optical crossbar design that can achieve high throughput with low static power consumption.

7. REFERENCES

[1] J. Ahn et al. Devices and architectures for photonic chip-scale integration. *Appl. Phy. A*, pages 989–997, 2009.

[2] J. Balfour and W. J. Dally. Design tradeoffs for tiled cmp onchip networks. In *ICS*, 2006.

[3] C. Batten. Designing nanophotonic interconnection networks. In *Workshop on the Interaction between Nanophotonic Devices and Systems*, 2010.

[4] C. Batten et al. Building manycore processor-to-dram networks with monolithic silicon photonics. In *Hot Interconnects*, pages 21–30, 2008.

[5] S. Beamer et al. Re-architecting dram memory systems with monolithically integrated silicon photonics. In *ISCA*, pages 129–140, 2010.

[6] C. Bienia et al. The parsec benchmark suite: Characterization and architectural implications. In *PACT*, pages 72–81, 2008.

[7] D. Chiarulli et al. Multiprocessor interconnection networks using partitioned passive star topologies and distributed control. In *Int'l Workshop on MPPOI*, 1994.

[8] Cianchetti et al. Phastlane: a rapid transit optical routing network. In *ISCA*, pages 441–450, 2009.

[9] ITRS. International technology roadmap for semiconductors. Technical report, 2010.

[10] A. Joshi et al. Silicon-photonic clos networks for global on-chip communication. In *3rd NOCS*, pages 124–133, 2009.

[11] J. Kim et al. Flattened butterfly topology for on-chip networks. In *MICRO*, 2007.

[12] N. Kirman et al. Leveraging optical technology in future bus-based chip multiprocessors. In *MICRO*, pages 492–503, 2006.

[13] N. Kirman and J. F. Martínez. A power-efficient all-optical on-chip interconnect using wavelength-based oblivious routing. In *ASPLOS*, pages 15–28, 2010.

[14] P. Koka et al. Silicon-photonic network architectures for scalable, power-efficient multi-chip systems. *SIGARCH Comput. Archit. News*, 38, 2010.

[15] G. Kurian et al. Atac: a 1000-core cache-coherent processor with on-chip optical network. In *PACT*, pages 477–488, 2010.

[16] C. Nitta et al. Addressing system-level trimming issues in on-chip nanophotonic networks. In *HPCA*, pages 122–131, 2011.

[17] C. Nitta et al. Resilient microring resonator based photonic networks. In *MICRO*, 2011.

[18] M. Palesi et al. Noxim, an open network-on-chip simulator. http://noxim.sourceforge.net.

[19] Y. Pan et al. Firefly: Illuminating future network-on-chip with nanophotonics. In *ISCA*, pages 429–440, 2009.

[20] Y. Pan et al. Flexishare: Channel sharing for an energy-efficient nanophotonic crossbar. In *HPCA*, pages 1–12, 2010.

[21] A. Shacham et al. Photonic networks-on-chip for future generations of chip multiprocessors. *IEEE Trans. Comput.*, 57:1246–1260, September 2008.

[22] D. Vantrease et al. Corona: System implications of emerging nanophotonic technology. In *ISCA*, pages 153–164, 2008.

[23] D. Vantrease et al. Light speed arbitration and flow control for nanophotonic interconnects. In *MICRO*, pages 304–315, 2009.

[24] D. Vantrease et al. Atomic coherence: Leveraging nanophotonics to build race-free cache coherence protocols. In *HPCA*, pages 132–143, 2011.

[25] Y. Xu et al. A composite and scalable cache coherence protocol for large scale cmps. In *ICS*, pages 285–294, 2011.

[26] Y. Xu et al. Tolerating process variations in nanophotonic on-chip networks. In *ISCA*, 2012.

[27] J. Xue et al. An intra-chip free-space optical interconnect. In *ISCA*, pages 94–105, 2010.

[28] M. T. Yourst. Ptlsim: A cycle accurate full system x86-64 microarchitectural simulator. In *ISPASS*, pages 23–24, 2007.

HiRe: Using Hint & Release
to Improve Synchronization of Speculative Threads

Liang Han[*]
Qualcomm
San Diego, California
liangh@qualcomm.com

Xiaowei Jiang[†]
Intel
Hillsboro, Oregon
xiaowei.jiang@intel.com

Wei Liu
Intel
Santa Clara, California
wei.w.liu@intel.com

Youfeng Wu
Intel
Santa Clara, California
youfeng.wu@intel.com

James Tuck
North Carolina State Univ.
Raleigh, North Carolina
jtuck@ncsu.edu

ABSTRACT

Thread-Level Speculation (TLS) is a promising technique for improving performance of serial codes on multi-cores by automatically extracting threads and running them in parallel. However, the speculation efficiency as well as the performance gain of TLS systems are reduced by cross-thread data dependence violations. Reducing the cost and frequency of violations are key to improving the efficiency of TLS. One method to keep a dependence from violating is to predict it and communicate the value via synchronization. However, prior work in this field still cannot handle enough violating dependences, especially hard-to-predict ones and those in non-loop TLS tasks. Also, they suffer from over-synchronization and/or introduce complicated hardware. The major reason is that these techniques are highly sensitive to the accuracy of the dependence prediction, which is hard to improve in the face of irregular dependence and task patterns.

In this paper, we propose a novel synchronization technique that avoids over synchronization and works for irregularly occurring dependences. We use a profiler to find and mark store-load pairs that generate data dependences. Then, the compiler schedules a *hint* instruction in advance of the store to inform successor threads of a possible pending write to a specific address; in this way, later loads only wait for a store if the loading location has been hinted. The compiler also schedules a *release* instruction that notifies the load when it should proceed. It places the *release* both after the store and on every path leading away from the *hint* that does not pass through the store. By placing it on all such paths, we limit the cost due to over synchronization. To-

gether, the *hint* and *release* form our proposal, called *HiRe*. We implemented the *HiRe* scheme on a well-tuned TLS system and evaluated it on a set of SPEC CPU 2000 applications; we find that *HiRe* suffers only 22% of the violations that occur in our base TLS system, and it cuts the instruction waste rate of TLS in half. Furthermore, it outperforms prior approaches we studied by 3%.

Categories and Subject Descriptors

C.1.4 [**Processor Architectures**]: Parallel Architectures; D.1.3 [**Programming Techniques**]: Concurrent Programming; D.3.4 [**Processors**]: Compilers

General Terms

Algorithms, Design, Measurement, Performance

Keywords

Synchronization, Dependence Prediction, Thread-Level Speculation, multi-core architecture

1. INTRODUCTION

Given the abundance of multi-core architectures and the relatively large number of programs that are not capable of exploiting them effectively, techniques for automatic and semi-automatic parallelization are increasingly important. Parallelizing compilers attempt to decompose a program into threads (or tasks) that can execute in parallel when there are no cross-thread control or data dependences. Despite their advances, such compilers still fail to parallelize many codes. Examples of such codes are accesses through pointers, inter-procedural dependences or input-dependent access patterns. Parallelizing compilers [7, 11, 16, 20] that target architectures with support for dynamic speculation of data dependences [3, 4, 8, 11, 14, 15, 17, 18, 21] have shown promise for coping with these kinds of programs.

However, even if the compiler and hardware are capable of speculating on unknown data dependences, blind speculation is not a good idea. A variety of techniques for data dependence prediction and synchronization have identified common patterns and how to detect them on the fly. For example, some memory locations are updated repeatedly, and by detecting an access to such a location, threads can stall

---

[*]This work was done while he was a student at NCSU.
[†]This work was done while he was a student at NCSU.

and handle the pending write [1] to prevent violations. Another behavior is that of store-load pairs (SLPs). SLPs can be identified and synchronized when they occur again [9]. Other proposals ([19, 20]) have exploited SLPs by using the compiler to insert signal&wait that force the load and store to synchronize and communicate their values.

However, these prior works have two major shortcomings. The first shortcoming is that they rely on data dependences to occur relatively frequently and in a simple pattern. Dependences that occur infrequently or occur in complicated patterns are hard to handle either because they introduce too much synchronization overhead or they cannot be detected by hardware as relevant. Ignoring these dependences is detrimental because *good compilers for speculative parallelism are likely to produce code with relatively more infrequent dependences and fewer frequent ones*. Second, prior techniques imagined fairly regular tasking behavior, like loops. However, irregular codes (that you would want to parallelize using TLS or similar techniques) tend to need highly dynamic and irregular tasking patterns [10, 13] made up of loops, function calls, and continuations of loops and function calls. Therefore, simple dependence prediction techniques that rely on frequent and easy to anticipate patterns are insufficient in such a system.

In this paper, we propose a novel synchronization technique that doesn't highly depend on dependence prediction. Compared to prior work, it can handle most hard-to-predict dependences and is good for irregular TLS tasking patterns.

This work makes the following contributions. (i) We propose a new data dependence synchronization technique called *HiRe*, that provides novel synchronization properties in the context of speculative parallelization. (ii) We describe the architectural and compiler designs needed to support *HiRe*. (iii) We evaluate *HiRe* with a subset of the SPEC 2000 benchmark suite on a cycle-accurate execution-driven simulator.

The rest of the article is organized as follows. Section 2 provides background on TLS and previous dependence prediction and synchronization techniques; Section 3 provides a high level description of our proposal. Section 4 describes the compiler algorithms, and Section 5 describes the new architectural support. Section 6 introduces our methodology, Section 7 presents our evaluation results, and Section 8 concludes the paper.

2. BACKGROUND

2.1 Data Dependences in TLS

Loads and stores in a TLS program must read and write memory in the same order they would in a serial execution of the program. If a load executes for a memory location before the preceding write to that location, then the load's task must rollback and re-execute in the correct order. In addition, if successor tasks had already consumed data created by the load's task, then they would have to re-execute on a mis-speculation as well. Avoiding such a rollback is desirable since it would prevent wasted work in the load's own task and possibly in successor tasks as well.

This creates a dilemma when executing a load: has the last write to the load's effective address already occurred or has it not? If it has not yet occurred, will it occur in the near future? Is it better to synchronize the load or let it speculate? In general, such a decision is non-trivial. Overall, there are a few possible behaviors. (1) The last write has occurred, so the load may proceed. This case occurs much of the time. (2) The last write will occur after the load, so

the load should wait. Or, (3) the last write will occur after the load, but the load goes ahead using a predicted value [5, 6, 8, 11] for either prefetching benefit or parallelism in the event the prediction is correct. This last case is problematic because it demonstrates that some benefit can be extracted from speculating even when a dependence is violated. However, case (3) tends to be the exception and not the rule [7]. In this paper, we are mostly considered with distinguishing case (1) and case (2).

2.2 Dependence Prediction and Synchronization

There are two overall strategies that have been proposed for predicting/synchronizing dependences: store-load-pair (SLP) centric [9, 19] and address centric synchronization [1]. SLP-centric techniques are based on the observation that data dependences usually occur between a small set of loads and stores in a program, and that often a specific store communicates to a specific load. Hence, if these SLPs are identified, then only loads that participate in an SLP need to be synchronized. Furthermore, if their associated store has already occurred, then it likely falls into case (1), otherwise it likely falls into class (2). Address-centric predictors first determine which memory locations tend to suffer from violations. Then, any load to such a location is forced to synchronize.

Moshovos *et al.*'s hardware predictor [9] adopts an SLP-centric approach. When a squash occurs, an SLP is stored in a centralized table in the processor, called the Memory Dependence Predictor Table (MDPT), and trained. If a load instruction's PC is found in the MDPT as part of an SLP, then it checks the Memory Dependence Synchronization Table (MDST) to see if its matching store has already occurred. If it has, the load accesses memory and continues executing. If the store has not occurred yet, then the load stalls to wait for it. If the SLP synchronizes properly, the entry for the SLP in the MDPT is re-enforced by incrementing a saturating counter. If the SLP fails to synchronize because the store is on the un-taken path, then the counter in the MDPT for the SLP is decremented. Over time, this mechanism learns which SLPs are common and synchronizes them. For example, Figure 1(a) is a case detected and handled by this predictor, assuming it occurs frequently. However, it may over-synchronize loads when their store never occurs or when the load and store occur to different memory locations (Fig. 1(b)). To mitigate the case in which the store does not occur, they propose using a timeout and tracking the dependence distance. However, this predictor will still not work well in Figure 1(c) since the store may not occur frequently enough to train the MDPT.

Zhai *et al.* provide a compiler based approach that schedules signal&wait instructions at SLPs to force synchronization between tasks. Using high-speed core-to-core communication queues, they send the address of the store and its value to the synchronizing load. If the load's address matches the store address, the sent value is used. Otherwise, the load proceeds by accessing memory. This scheme forces the load to wait until the store executes. If the store and load are accessing different addresses, then the load stalled for nothing, as is the case in Fig. 1(b). Furthermore, it is necessary that communication is guaranteed between the store and the load. For example, in Fig. 1(c), the signal must be placed before the if condition. However, in general, such placement is not always possible with irregular task patterns (e.g. if the store is located in a subroutine).

Finally, Cintra and Torrellas [1] propose an address-centric scheme called Stall&Release and Stall&Wait. If a memory

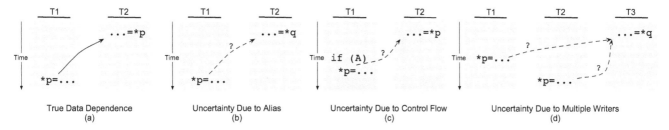

Figure 1: Data Dependence Patterns in TLS Programs.

location is frequently involved in a dependence violation, then Stall&Release forces a load to wait until a write occurs to an address, and Stall&Wait forces a load to wait until its task becomes safe (is the oldest one in the system). Stall&Release would work in Figures 1(a)-(c) if p usually has the same address (or one of a few addresses). Stall&Wait will work in Fig. 1(d) where there are multiple writers. However, if the locations involved in the dependence change frequently, then this approach will not catch many dependences.

3. MAIN IDEA: HINT & RELEASE

We propose a flexible synchronization scheme that is able to relieve the over-synchronization problem in the prior work and robustly cover a larger set of dependence patterns.

Our idea is inspired by the strengths of both SLP-centric and Address-centric synchronization schemes. SLP-centric techniques are powerful because they identify specific locations in the code that may trigger a dependence violation. In particular, knowing which store is likely to produce the value needed by a load enables timely and efficient synchronization when the store actually executes. This is a feature worth preserving. Address-centric strategies are powerful in their ability to only stall loads that are accessing a location likely to be involved in a dependence. Stalling only those loads that are accessing a location likely to be written is also a feature worth preserving.

Figure 2 shows the basic idea of our scheme. Rather than trying to synchronize a SLP, it identifies a window of execution that contains a store with the potential to trigger a misspeculation. This window (a.k.a. the sync window) begins at a point in execution when a store is *anticipated* to occur and will be marked with a *hint*. The window extends until a point after the store occurs, called the *release*. The placement of *hint* and *release* is SLP-centric in the sense that it is placed around a store for a specific SLP.

Because *hint* and *release* both specify a specific address for synchronization, any load that tries to access the *hinted* address will be forced to stall. Hence, loads are synchronized in an address-centric manner. Once the address is *released*, loads are allowed to proceed with execution again.

The *hint* and *release* instructions delineate the execution of a load into 3 regions, as Figure 2 shows. The load will act differently at run time in different regions. In **Region A**, the hint has not been observed and the load will blindly speculate. This region occurs on any non-synchronized load or when a *hint* is not observed in a timely way. In **Region B**, the load will wait to be released, providing synchronization for the load. We hope most loads that have a late arriving dependence execute in this region. Finally, in **Region C**, the load will proceed with execution confidently since the dependence has been satisfied.

Our scheme achieves the ability to handle infrequent and

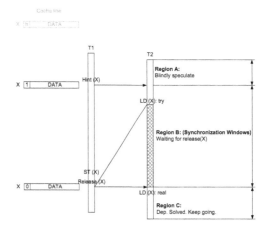

Figure 2: Basic Idea of *HiRe*

complicated-patterned dependences without causing over-synchronization from three aspects. First, we enlist the help of the compiler to find and mark stores that generate data dependence violations. In this way, no run-time training is needed to identify the SLPs, and irregular patterns are handled. Although, we do need a profiler to help identify important SLPs. Second, rather than synchronize every time the load in a SLP executes, our mechanism only synchronizes a load when it detects that a likely store to the same address may occur in the future. We achieve this by using a *hint* instruction that informs hardware of a possible pending write. The compiler inserts a *hint* before the store and hoists it as early as possible to warn successor threads in advance. With this flexible way of synchronization, infrequent dependences are identified and handled very cheaply – with less likelihood of over-synchronization. Third, our mechanism also provides a way to wake-up the waiting load and let it resume execution as soon as the store executes or is known not to occur. We achieve this via the *release* instruction. The *release* is scheduled just after a store and on every path leading away from a hint in which the store does not occur. In this way, the over synchronization issue is resolved. Together, *hint & release* form the *HiRe* synchronization mechanism. This strategy is very tolerant of arbitrary tasking patterns since it makes no assumption on the relative ordering or location of stores and loads in the code.

3.1 Design Overview

To work effectively, *HiRe* must accomplish tasks which rely on a mix of compiler and hardware support. A compiler coordinates insertion and scheduling of the *hint* and *release* to create the desired synchronization window, and the hardware must track the *hint* and *release* information and stall dependent loads if they are located within the sync window. We briefly consider these goals but leave detailed discussions for the next section.

A compiler will carry out several tasks in order to insert *hint* and *release* pairs. First, it will identify loads and stores that are likely to participate in a data dependence using program profiling. Given that few loads and stores (from 10s to 100s) actually cause violations, this is a relatively simple task through program profiling [9, 19]. For each store, the *hint* must be hoisted early enough in execution that it occurs before a dependent load in a successor. To do this, a backward slice for the store address can be hoisted to an earlier program point along with the *hint* instruction. Finally, the *release* follows the execution of *hint*. Ideally, it will occur just after the store itself or on a side-exit that guarantees the store will not occur.

The hardware is responsible for tracking the *hint* and *release* on any given address and synchronizing dependent loads. Ideally, such support should be cost effective for a large number of addresses and for many concurrent synchronizations. In addition, the *hint* and *release* should not add much overhead. To accomplish these goals, *HiRe* adds one bit to the cache state to track *hint* and *release* operations per address, as is shown Figure 2. Because the information is tracked with cache line state, the TLS coherence protocol can be leveraged to synchronize remote loads. Furthermore, since coherence operations are highly distributed, it can support many concurrent synchronizations. The following section describes these mechanisms in detail.

4.   *HIRE* COMPILER

HiRe's compiler support consists of a set of passes in GCC that perform TLS task selection, SLP selection and scheduling of the hint and release in the code. It includes a profiler which collects information about TLS tasks and data dependences for selection of tasks and SLPs.

4.1   Task Selection and SLP Selection

During compilation, two kinds of tasks are extracted from the program: loops and subroutine continuations. For loop selection, the compiler selects either outer or inner loops, depending on task characteristics. Subroutine-continuations with easy-to-speculate return values are also selected. Next, during task pruning, some tasks which are expected to offer little parallelism are eliminated. To do this, we adopted a profiling strategy very similar to [7]. The profiler executes the TLS binary sequentially and analyzes tasks according to several key properties: (1) the size of the task (t_{size}), (2) the overlap (parallelism) achieved with its predecessors ($t_{overlap}$), (3) the likelihood of mis-speculation (p_{sq}), and the time saved due to prefetching from a squashed execution ($t_{prefetch}$). Overall, we keep a task if $t_{size} > t_{szMin}$, $p_{sq} < p_{sqMax}$, and Benefit $= t_{overlap} + t_{prefetch} > 0$.

To identify SLPs that need synchronization, all loads and stores are monitored during profiling. For each dependence violation that occurs, the profiler creates a record for the SLP and counts the number of occurrences. The record includes the store PC, the load PC, and the source and destination task IDs. Even if a load or store occurs in multiple pairs, the information for each pair is tracked separately. All stores detected that ever occur in an SLP are candidates for *HiRe*. Then, a pair of *hint* and *release* are inserted around each of such stores. However, the compiler may choose to discard some pairs for cost reasons (see Section 7.4).

4.2   Hint Scheduling

The Hint hoisting algorithm tries to schedule the Hint instruction as early as possible. The algorithm must overcome the difficulty of precomputing the store's address, and it must choose a location for the hint that increases the chances it will execute before the dependent load.

One problem is that the store's address calculation places a limit on the Hint's placement; therefore, we construct a backward slice for the store's address calculation to enable a greater motion. Figure 3(a) shows a store and its nearby address calculation. Using a precomputation slice, we can move the Hint a bit earlier (Fig. 3(b)). The slice computation algorithm, compute_slice, in shown in Figure 3(e). It takes as input a stmt, an existing slice, and a location, earliest, above which we cannot hoist the hint. Starting from stmt, it traverses backward in the Program Dependence Graph (PDG) [2], recursively, gathering nodes to add into the slice. During the traversal, it will visit an ancestor at most once and decide how to process it. If the ancestor node is before earliest, a phi node, or a node that could cause an exception (i.e. memory load), it can move no further back and it determines the new earliest location which it cannot move beyond. Otherwise the node is added to the slice subject to data dependence constraints. When compute_slice finishes its PDG traversal, we can place the slice at earliest.

However, the earliest possible location in the serial program is not always the best choice when considering its parallel execution. The dynamic task structure must be considered to ensure that *hint* actually executes before the load. In Figure 3(c), the *hint* is properly placed to execute before the load. However, Figure 3(d) shows what happens if we hoist the hint before the beginning of Task B. Now, it is actually located at the end of Task A and will occur *after* both the dependent load and the store! Hence, task boundaries must be considered as a limiting factor in *hint* placement. The get_earliest_loc_for_hint function determines the nearest task boundary which cannot be crossed. For a loop task, the boundary is placed at the beginning of the loop header. For other tasks, starting from the store, we traverse the dominator tree looking for a parent task and stop when the boundary basic block is found. If one is found, the beginning of the task-starting basic block is set as the hoist limit; otherwise, the first block in the function (found at the root of the dominator tree) is chosen.

The hoist_hint function pulls all this functionality together. First, it determines the earliest possible location for the hint subject to task boundary constraints. Next, it computes the slice for the store address. Finally, the full slice, including the *hint* instruction, is scheduled just after the earliest location.

4.3   Release Scheduling

The purpose of *release* is to notify any stalled load that it may proceed. It is scheduled immediately following the store and on every side-exit between *hint* and store.

The *release* after the store may appear redundant since the store could be modified to toggle the hint bit. However, in some cases, it is needed because the *hint* may calculate an address other than what is updated by the store. (For example, a function call in between the hint(&X) and the store(X) may update a global variable which is a part of the calculation of &X.) It is important to release the same address that was hinted so that stalled loads on the incorrectly hinted address are released. For simplicity, we always place a *release* after the store to catch this case even when the hinted and stored address can be proven to match.

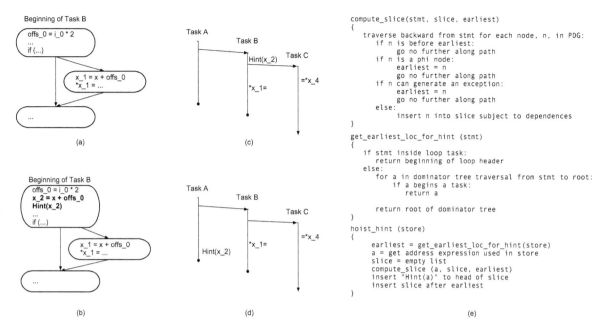

```
compute_slice(stmt, slice, earliest)
{
    traverse backward from stmt for each node, n, in PDG:
        if n is before earliest:
            go no further along path
        if n is a phi node:
            earliest = n
            go no further along path
        if n can generate an exception:
            earliest = n
            go no further along path
        else:
            insert n into slice subject to dependences
}
get_earliest_loc_for_hint (stmt)
{
    if stmt inside loop task:
        return beginning of loop header
    else:
        for a in dominator tree traversal from stmt to root:
            if a begins a task:
                return a

        return root of dominator tree
}
hoist_hint (store)
{
    earliest = get_earliest_loc_for_hint(store)
    a = get address expression used in store
    slice = empty list
    compute_slice (a, slice, earliest)
    insert "Hint(a)" to head of slice
    insert slice after earliest
}
```

Figure 3: *hint* hoisting examples and pseudo code.

We would like to release the load as soon as possible. So, we devised an algorithm that places *release* immediately following the store and at the earliest point on every path that will not pass through the store. This is easily implemented using depth-first traversal of the CFG starting from the *hint* and enumerating all side-exits on the path to the store.

5. *HIRE* ARCHITECTURE

We extend a CMP with a TLS coherence protocol and versioned L1 data caches, much like [13]. The overall system is shown in Figure 4(a). We extend this system to support *HiRe* by adding three new instructions, extending the cache state to support a H bit, and modifying the TLS coherence protocol to stall a load when it encounters a set H bit. The following sections describe the architecture for these extensions in detail.

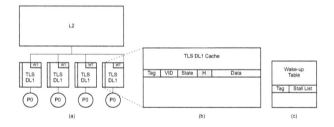

Figure 4: *HiRe* architectural support.

5.1 Hint and Release

We add an H-bit to each cache line to record the presence of a *hint*; and the H-bit is reset to indicate that *hint* has been released. Figure 4(b) shows the resulting organization for one cache line. It includes a tag, a speculative version identifier (VID) that determines the task, the speculative state for each byte in the line, support for *HiRe*, and the data.

The *hint* instruction executes as soon as its address is resolved in order to update the cache line status as early as possible. However, the *release* instruction waits until all prior store addresses are resolved and only executes after any preceding store. Once there are no preceding stores with the same address, it can execute. This policy ensures that it will follow a prior store to the same line, but, otherwise, will execute early and allow stalled loads to resume. Both the *hint* and *release* instructions work like a non-faulting prefetch and will not generate an exception if the input address is invalid. Due to aggressive slice construction, such an invalid address is possible.

Most interactions at the task level are kept as simple as possible. When a task completes and commits its data or when a task is squashed, all H bits are reset. They are not passed from one task to another, and they are not preserved across task boundaries. They are associated with the VID in the cache line they are written into. However, some additional interaction is needed to support stalling a load.

5.2 Stalled Load Support

In the TLS coherence protocol, when a thread reads an address for the first time, it must identify the most recent writer (in program order) and obtain a copy of the data from that task. We extend this mechanism with an additional rule — if an *executing* predecessor thread has set the H bit for the line, the request to read the line is nacked rather than returning stale data. When the requesting thread receives the nack, it knows to wait. Because such a mechanism is already provided in coherence protocols, adding this support is trivial.

Without any additional changes, we get the following behaviors. After waiting for a pre-determined timeout period after a nack, the load is retried. If the same predecessor is found with its H bit cleared or if the same predecessor finished executing without clearing its H bit, the load will check if the dirty bit is set; if so, the load will now succeed since it has found the latest version. Otherwise, it will keep searching in older predecessors. It is possible that a more recent predecessor has set its H bit during the previous load stall. On detection of such a case, the load will stall for that task's write (this is the multiple writer support). The load will continue to stall and retry as long it finds an H bit set for a running task. If the search reaches the oldest predecessor and still doesn't find any Hint, the load proceeds speculatively. Also, if the stalled task becomes safe, it must proceed since no violation is possible.

5.3 Wake-up Table: Load Behavior Optimization

Requiring the load to busy wait is undesirable and inefficient. If we make it retry frequently, we waste power and energy; if it is infrequent, we sacrifice performance by unnecessarily delaying the load. The data in Section 7.3 shows that the average synchronization time fluctuates greatly from load to load. It is hard to set a unified time-out duration even for different loads in the same application. In order to reduce the wait time for the load, we add a small table near each DL1 cache that detects requests to cache lines with the H bit set. The Wake-up Table is shown in Figure 4(c). When such a load request occurs, the requesting task's id number is added to the table in an entry tagged with the requested line. When the H bit is cleared for that line or when the task finishes execution, the stalled task is sent a message to proceed. When the stalled task receives this message, it tries to load again in the method described in the previous section.

It would be nice to avoid re-executing the stalled load yet again by forwarding the entire cache state immediately. However, such an approach would bypass the TLS coherence mechanism and could lead to an incorrect execution if another task, later in program order, wrote the data in the time since the load's first request. Therefore, it is necessary to check again for the nearest writer rather than forwarding the line.

Since the table will be small, it may not be able to hold all pending hints at all times during execution. Therefore, we support a timeout mechanism. We adopt a naive timeout in which a load waits at most for a fixed period of time before it tries again. We set the interval high enough that it will not retry many times while waiting for the wake-up signal.

In an empirical study, we found that 4-entries is nearly identical to an unlimited-sized wake-up table. Therefore, we do not evaluate this part of the architecture in order to save space.

5.4 A Runtime Example

Figure 5 shows how the *HiRe* scheme works at run-time. When a load instruction executes in thread C, it checks for any local write first (0). If it is an exposed read, it checks its predecessor's versioned cache in reversed speculative order (1). When the request reaches core 2, synchronization logic there checks the cache and finds that the H bit of location X is set (2). Entry "&X: thread C" is thus added into the wakeup table on core 2 (3). On being notified of this (3), core 3 suspends thread C (4).

When the *release*(&X) instruction (without updating X) executes later on core 2 (5), it updates the cache line by clearing the H-bit (6). When a hinted location is released, the wakeup table on core 2 is checked and thread C is found suspended on this location (7). At that moment, a release message is sent to core 3 to wake up thread C (8). Once resumed, the load instruction re-executes and checks the previous versions again (9). This time, it will not stop on core 2 since neither Hint bit nor Dirty bit is set, which means that no write to location X happened although thread B

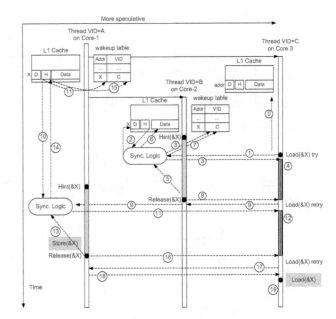

Figure 5: *HiRe* Run-Time Actions

suspected there would be one. (Otherwise, if the dirty bit is set, the read request would consume this value and stop searching further backwards since the latest store has been located.) The request continues to check for an older version, say thread A running on core 1 (9). Similar to what happened on core 2 by the synchronization logic (10,11), thread C is suspended again (12).

When a *release*(&X) instruction executes in thread A later (13), it clears H-bit, and wakes up thread C (14,15,16). Once C resumes execution, it re-executes the load(&X) instruction and checks again. Since this time only the D-bit is set on core 1, it means core 1 has the latest update to location X in the system at this moment, the search is stopped, and the value on cache 1 is consumed by the load (18). Now, thread C can move forward (19).

6. METHODOLOGY

6.1 Compiler Infrastructure

We implement our compiler in a copy of the POSH [7] compiler we obtained from the original authors, and we have ported it to GCC 4.3. We use the compiler to generate 4 different binaries for each application evaluated, shown in Table 1. The *Base* case is a sequential binary that we normalize all of our plots against. *TLS* shows the result of the POSH compiler with all of its optimizations enabled. During profiling, we use a $p_{sq} = 0.55$ and a $t_{szMin} = 30$.

HiRe adds Hint-Release synchronization support to the POSH on the SLPs selected by the profiler and compiler. *SWsync* adds Signal&Wait synchronization to SLPs with occurring frequency greater than 50% in the profiling.

Table 1: Compile Settings.

Name	Description
Base	-O2
TLS	Base + POSH optimizations
SWsync	TLS + Signal&Wait Sync
HiRe	TLS + *HiRe* support

6.2 Simulated Architecture

We target our compiler to the SESC simulator [12], a cycle accurate execution driven simulator. The simulator models out-of-order superscalar processors and memory systems with cycle-accurate precision. It also contains a TLS architecture model as shown in Table 2. Each processor is a 3-issue core and has a private L1 cache that buffers the speculative data. The L1 caches are connected through a crossbar to an on-chip shared L2 cache. All communication between cores occurs through the TLS coherence protocol which implements lazy task commit similar to [13]. Our baseline TLS architecture supports silent stores [5].

Table 2: Architectural Details. (Cycle counts are in processor cycles.)

Frequency	4 GHz	ROB	132
Fetch width	8	I-window	68
Issue width	3	LD/ST queue	48/42
Retire width	3	Mem/Int/Fp unit	1/2/1
Branch predictor:		Spawn Overhead	12 cycles
Mispred. Penalty	14 cycles	Squash Overhead	20 cycles
BTB	2K, 2-way		
Private L1 Cache:		Shared L2 Cache:	
Size, assoc, line	32KB, 4, 64B	Size, assoc, line	2MB, 8, 64B
Latency	3 cycles	Latency	10 cycles
		Memory:	
Lat. to remote L1	at least 8 cycles	Latency	500 cycles
		Bandwidth	10GB/s
HiRe parameters:		*HiRe* parameters:	
Wakeup Table (per core)	4 entries	Stalled load timeout	1600 cycles
Hardware Dependence Predictors:			
MBVS: Moshovos *et al.* style predictor with unlimited size MDPT. [9](twolf,vpr)			
HybridMBVS: MBVS predictor that only synchronizes on memory locations likely to			
have a violation.(bzip2,gap,equake)			
Stall&Release: Cintra&Torrellas style predictor, with dynamically tuned			
release delay.(gzip,mcf,mesa)			

6.3 Benchmark

We evaluate our proposal on a set of SPEC CPU 2000 applications that work in the POSH compiler and the SESC simulator as provided by their original implementers. To accurately compare the performance of the different binaries, simply timing a fixed number of instructions is incorrect. Instead, simulation markers are inserted in the code of each binary, and simulations are run for a given number of markers. After skipping the initialization (typically 1-6 billion instructions), a certain number of markers are executed, so that the baseline binary graduates from 500 million to 1 billion instructions. We use *train-* input set for the profiling, and *ref-* input set for the simulation.

6.4 Implementation of Prior Work

To compare HiRe with Zhai *et al*'s proposal[19], we implement an approximation of their scheme in our framework. *SWsync* binary in Table 1 is generated by adding Signal&Wait synchronization to SLPs that occur with a frequency greater than 50% during the profiling. Although they find 25% or 5% is the best threshold, our compiler selects both subroutine continuations and loops for TLS tasks. We explored the design space for *SWsync* with thresholds of 5%, 25%, 50%, 75%, and 90%, and found it gets the best performance on a threshold of 50%. Also, we assume special high speed signal&wait hardware to give it an additional advantage.

To compare HiRe to hardware predictors, we implement three hardware dependence predictors, shown at the bottom of Table 2. We do not have space to fully evaluate and characterize these designs. Therefore, when we compare against the hardware based predictors (labeled *HWpred*), we give each application the predictor that works the best for it. While this is unfair to us, we believe it may represent a

highly tuned hybrid predictor that a clever chip designer may be able to develop. The applications that use a predictor are shown in parentheses above.

7. EVALUATION

We compare four sync schemes. The *SWsync* and *HWpred* bars are the sync schemes we compare against, as described in the previous section. The *HiRe* bar shows our *HiRe* scheme. The *HiRe+HWpred* bar shows a combination result of *HiRe* scheme and hardware dependence predictor. The *TLS* bar, if we don't normalize sync schemes to it, shows the basic *TLS* scheme without any synchronization support.

7.1 Speculation Efficiency and Performance

The most direct impact of *HiRe* is the reduction of dependence violations. We counted the number of violations for each application and normalized it to that of basic *TLS* scheme. Figure 6 shows the normalized violation rate and compares 4 sync schemes.

We find that every technique decreased the violation rates from *TLS*, and *HiRe* beats *HWpred* and *SWsync* by a considerable margin. *mcf* and *vpr* drop dramatically under *HiRe* scheme; and *twolf* also has an outstanding decrease. Overall, *HiRe* has, by geometric mean, only 23% of the violations that TLS does. Whereas, *HWpred* has a rate of 53% and *SWsync* has a rate of 93%. Interestingly, Figure 6 shows that we can get the best violation rate if *HiRe* is combined with *HWpred* scheme, bringing it down to only 15%. This suggests that the two schemes handle some complementary dependence patterns, as expected.

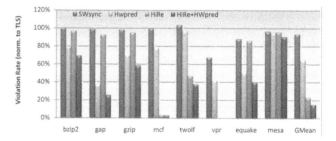

Figure 6: Violation Rate Comparison.

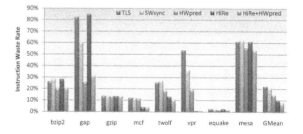

Figure 7: Wasted Instruction Rate

To further understand the importance of reducing violation rate, we measured the Instruction Waste Rate. It is defined as the number of squashed instructions divided by the number of useful instructions. This is an indicator of the efficiency of speculation. Figure 7 compares the waste rate across the same experiments. Overall, *HiRe* has an average waste rate of only 10%, while *TLS* has a waste rate of 22%,

SWsync has a waste rate of 21%, and *HWpred* has a waste rate of 14%. Again, we can get the lowest waste rate under the combined scheme of *HiRe* and *HWpred*.

We also measured the overall performance of these systems. Since the task selection policy is tuned for a TLS system without support for dependence prediction, we do not expect large speedups. Rather, we expect only modest speedups. *HiRe* is the best performing synchronization technique overall. Figure 8 shows the percentage of performance improvement for each system normalized to that of basic TLS. Note, bars above the line mean speedup and bars below mean slowdown from *TLS*. Table 3 gives speedup of base TLS from serial execution. Overall, *HiRe* achieves an average performance improvement of 3.2% over *TLS*. The largest single gains are in *vpr*, *mcf*, *equake*, and *twolf*. Also, the best gain of *HiRe* is on par with the best gains of *HWpred*. Interestingly, *HiRe* does not have the negative effects the other schemes have on application performance. This is important because a good dependence predictor should avoid slowdowns if it does not provide speedup. The worst degradation for an application on *HiRe* is -4.4% on *gap*.

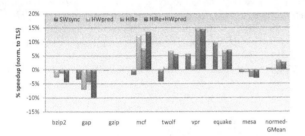

Figure 8: Performance Comparison.

Table 3: *TLS* Speedup over Serial Execution.

Benchmarks	bzip2	gap	gzip	mcf	twolf	vpr	equake	mesa	G-mean
TLS speedup	1.1187	1.181	1.0296	1.3225	1.5567	0.994	3.3677	1.333	1.3712

Table 4: *Release* Efficiency

Benchmarks	addedRelease	addedWakeup	RelWakeup
bzip2	23.89%	2.36%	64.49%
gap	0.00%	0.00%	0.00%
gzip	0.00%	0.00%	0.00%
mcf	87.30%	1.54%	37.94%
twolf	0.07%	2.36%	0.02%
vpr	47.27%	43.38%	53.83%
equake	0.00%	0.00%	0.00%
mesa	0.00%	0.00%	0.00%

Table 5: # of Tasks.

Benchmarks	nAllTask	nSelTask	nPrefTask
bzip2	35	12	0
gap	24	13	3
gzip	37	17	0
mcf	6	5	3
twolf	44	22	0
vpr	14	5	0
equake	8	7	4
mesa	23	19	1

To explain how our scheme decreases violations without having performance suffer much, we collected statistics for release operations, shown in Table 4. The second column shows, for each application, how frequent a *Hint* is released from a side-exit *release* operation rather than the one following the store instruction. Since some of these releases could happen before the load occurs and thus the load need not stall at all, we show, in the third column, what percentage of such releases are going to really wake up a stalled load. And the last column shows the percentage of all the stalled loads that are released in this way. Because *HiRe* selects infrequent SLPs too, it is very important to provide a release on side-exits so that the load can proceed when

Table 6: Dependence Statistics

APP	nAllDep	nSW	nHIRE	nStatHints	nDyncHints
bzip2	85	2	12	6	1641167
gap	236	6	134	8	2497839
gzip	102	4	12	0	0
mcf	27	3	5	4	16444042
twolf	124	6	56	6	4493541
vprman	43	2	24	8	11080543
equake	30	2	6	6	6616380
mesa	85	25	33	2	1530322

the store doesn't happen. We will come back to these data along with the discussion in later sections.

7.2 *HiRe* Characterizations

In this section, we will characterize several aspects of the *HiRe* system. Table 5 shows the breakdown of selected TLS tasks. For each application, the second column shows the number of tasks chosen by the first phase of profiling; the third column is the number of tasks remaining after the second phase; the fourth column shows the number of tasks selected for prefetching. When these prefetching tasks execute, any synchronization in them is ignored so that the benefit of data prefetching can be explored.

Table 6 characterizes the dependences selected for *HiRe* and *SWsync*. For each application the second column *nAllDep* shows the total number of dependences detected by the profiler. *nSW* is the number of dependences selected and handled by *SWsync* scheme occurring at the frequency threshold of 50%. *nHIRE* is the number of dependencies pre-selected by *HiRe* scheme. Even though many dependences are pre-selected, we only handle a few of them in the end to control the cost (see Section 7.4 for details). *nStatHints* is the number of *Hint* instructions that are finally placed in the code – generally they had a sufficient hoist distance. *nDyncHints* is the dynamic number of *Hint* instructions executed and successfully committed at run time.

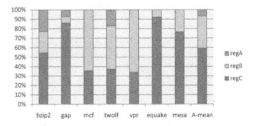

Figure 9: *HiRe* Regions Breakdown

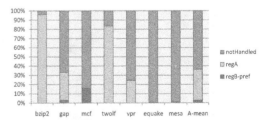

Figure 10: Violations Breakdown

To evaluate the efficiency of *HiRe* scheduling algorithm, for the dependences synchronized using *HiRe*, we classify how often each dependence occurs in Region A, B, or C (defined in Section 3). Figure 9 shows the fraction in each region summed up over all dependences finally selected for *HiRe*. We removed *gzip* since there is no SLP selected for it. A large majority are captured in Region B and Region C. This means that most stores we marked using *HiRe* are successfully synchronized with their loads. Only *bzip2*, *gap*, and *twolf* had an appreciable fraction of dependences that occurred in Region A. For these applications, our compiler failed to take away some SLPs that cannot be handled well in the system because the compiler is using unified thresholds for all applications. Dynamically deciding the thresholds individually for these applications remains as the future work.

We also characterized the dependences that did violate into three categories, as shown in Figure 10. *NotHandled* are dependences for which we made no attempt; *regA* are dependences that occurred in region A and cannot be handled by *HiRe*; *regB-pref* are dependences that occurred in Region B and thus could be handled by *HiRe* but we chose not to synchronize them for their prefetching benefits. *bzip2*, *gap*, *twolf*, and *vpr* have a significant fraction of dependences in Region A. Their hints are not hoisted far enough for these cases. *gap*, *mcf*, and *mesa* all have a significant number of prefetching based violations; this is expected since they all had prefetching tasks. *gap*, *gzip*, *mcf*, *twolf*, *vpr*, *equake*, and *mesa* had the majority of their dependence violations fall into the *NotHandled* category. Even so, the violation rate for *HiRe* is only 23% of that for *TLS*. Some of these remaining may need to be handled using a dynamic technique, or improvements are needed in the overall process of selecting SLPs and hoisting hints.

7.3 *HiRe* Window Size and Sync. Time

We show detailed timing statistics for SLPs in this section. Before looking at the figures, we need to define a few terms.

A HiRe window (*HireWin*) is defined as the code region between a hint instruction and its corresponding release instruction. We measure the execution time of a *HireWin* to characterize its behavior(s). A *HireWin* can be further classified into 2 types: A Store-Released HiRe Window (*St-Win*) is a *HireWin* that really contains an update of the hinted memory location; a Release-Released HiRe Window (*Rel-Win*) is the case that the hinted location is not updated by any store instruction. We call the time, in number of cycles, from a hint instruction to its release instruction the HiRe window size. We measure the HiRe window size with 3 average parameters as defined in line 1-3 in Figure 11(a). *avgHireWin* is the overall average window size of *Rel-Win* and *St-Win*.

We also characterize the time it takes to synchronize a load with a store. At the load side, we measure the average waiting time for each synchronized load if it falls into region B (the same region as the HiRe window). We define Sync Time as the period that starts with a load finding a hint and ends when it is resumed by a release instruction. Sync Time is similarly classified depending on the source of the *release*. If the hinted location is actually updated it is classified as Store-Released Sync Time (*StSyn*). Otherwise, if no update occurs, it is Release-Released Sync Time (*RelSyn*). *avgHireSyn* is the overall average Sync Time for both cases. Line 4-6 in Figure 11(a) shows their formulas.

Other subfigures in Figure 11 show these 6 parameters for each application. For each HiRe window identified by an ID

number on the X-axis, the Y-axis shows its 6 parameters in simulated cycles.

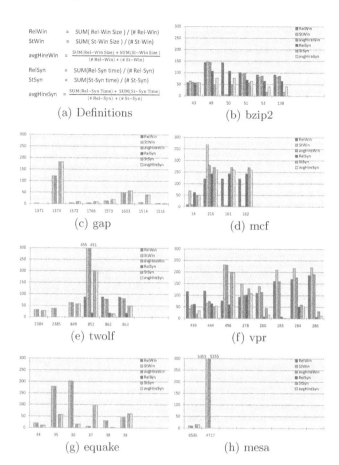

(a) Definitions   (b) bzip2

(c) gap   (d) mcf

(e) twolf   (f) vpr

(g) equake   (h) mesa

Figure 11: Sync. Time of *HiRe* Windows.

The first thing we learn from Figure 11 is that the Sync Time varies greatly from window to window even in the same application. This shows how hard it will be to use a naive time-out mechanism to resume suspended loads – it is impossible to find a single, fixed unified time-out time. And it is also hard to find an easy rule or a common pattern for this variation so as to train hardware to adjust the time-out time effectively. However, *HiRe* solves the over-sync problem easily by introducing the *release* instruction. This is the key reason why it doesn't hurt the performance while reducing the violations greatly via synchronization.

In *bzip2*, *mcf*, *vpr*, and *twolf*, release instructions play important roles. For some HiRe windows in these applications, for example *HireWin* 278 of *vpr* in Figure 11(f), the average values of window size (*avgHireWin*) and Sync Time (*avghireSyn*) are mostly dominated by the release bars (*Rel-Win* and *RelSyn*), but not by the store bars. In *HireWin-278* of *vpr*, the release instructions release the synchronized loads after 102 cycles of them being suspended since there is no corresponding store instruction that will be executed. Without such releases, the majority of the suspended loads would have to either wait for a time-out (1600 cycles in our experiments) or until the loading thread becomes a safe thread, which could be hundred of cycles. In these windows, release instructions are the key to avoid over synchronization. This result is consistent with Table 4, where we see the percentage of active release instructions is large.

On the other hand, however, some applications, such as *equake*, *mesa*, and *gap*, have almost no synchronization occurring via a release instruction because they do not suffer from the over synchronization problem. That also explains why *SWsync* outperforms *HiRe* in these cases.

There are also some windows, in which the *release* plays a small role. For example, in *HireWin* 456 of *vpr* in Figure 11(f), the store-based release is the dominating behavior.

Note that for some windows, the Sync Time is even greater than the window size. For example, *HireWin* 162 of *mcf* in Figure 11(d). This is because for some windows the hint and release instructions can execute much more frequently than the load. Although the window size is always greater than the Sync Time when synchronization actually occurs, for most cases, when there is no sync, the window sizes are small. Thus, on average, we see a smaller window size and a larger Sync Time.

Also, for some windows, such as *HireWin* 50 of *bzip2* in Figure 11(b), the *release* takes much longer to release the *hint* than the *store* does. This is because the *hint* and *store* are located in a loop task, and a *release* for a side-exit is scheduled on the loop exit-edge; also, the *store* is not always updating the hinted location. Mostly the *store* keeps updating the location that is hinted and releases the *load* in a short time (thus a small StWin size). But, occasionally, if the *store* is not updating that location, the *load* will have to wait until the loop exits and the *release* is reached. In that case, we see a big RelWin size. This also explains why the StWin dominates the average window size in this case.

7.4 Overhead of HiRe

We calculated the overhead added to the *TLS*, *SWsync*, and *HiRe* binaries respectively. This is calculated using f_{bloat} as defined in [13]. The G-mean of f_{bloat} for *TLS* in our experiments is 1.25, on average. This means that *TLS* dynamically executes 25% more instructions to complete the same amount of work. For *HiRe*, the bloat factor increases to 1.35, on average. This increase in bloat is enough to reduce the performance gains of *HiRe* in our experiments. To keep the cost this low, we removed less useful *HiRe* code. Table 6 gives statistics for SLPs removed to keep costs low.

8. CONCLUSION

If data dependence prediction can achieve the same or better accuracies as branch prediction, automatic parallelization techniques like TLS may become ever more attractive. However, this is not easy because there are always many infrequent and complicated patterned dependences, especially in TLS systems supporting irregular task patterns. Existing synchronization techniques cannot achieve high speculation efficiency in such TLS systems either because they rely on highly-predictable dependence patterns or/and because they suffer from over-synchronization.

In this paper, we propose a novel synchronization technique which does not rely on the accuracy of dependence prediction. This is achieved by inserting and hoisting a *hint* on a *store* which is likely to trigger a dependence violation. The *hint* enables a *load* to the same address to wait for the *store* or speculate with a high confidence, according to the run-time situation. Also, we resolve the over synchronization problem by scheduling a *release* for a each hint. The *HiRe* mechanism provides a way to wake up a waiting *load* and let it resume execution as soon as the *store* executes or

is known to never occur. We evaluated the *HiRe* scheme on a set of SPEC 2000 applications and find that a TLS system supporting *HiRe* suffers from only 22% of the violations that occur in our base TLS system, and it cuts the waste rate of TLS in half. Furthermore, it outperforms the prior approaches by 3%, on average.

9. REFERENCES

[1] M. Cintra and J. Torrellas. Eliminating squashes through learning cross-thread violations in speculative parallelization for multiprocessors. In *HPCA*, 2002.

[2] J. Ferrante, K. J. Ottenstein, and J. D. Warren. The program dependence graph and its use in optimization. *ACM Transactions on Programming Languages and Systems*, 1987.

[3] L. Hammond, M. Willey, and K. Olukotun. Data Speculation Support for a Chip Multiprocessor. In *ASPLOS*, 1998.

[4] V. Krishnan and J. Torrellas. A Chip-Multiprocessor Architecture with Speculative Multithreading. *IEEE Trans. on Computers*, pages 866–880, September 1999.

[5] K. M. Lepak and M. H. Lipasti. On the value locality of store instructions. In *ISCA*, 2000.

[6] K. M. Lepak and M. H. Lipasti. Temporally silent stores. In *ASPLOS*, 2002.

[7] W. Liu, J. Tuck, L. Ceze, W. Ahn, K. Strauss, J. Renau, and J. Torrellas. POSH: a TLS Compiler that Exploits Program Structure. In *PPoPP'06*.

[8] P. Marcuello, J. Tubella, and A. GonzÃ¡lez. Value prediction for speculative multithreaded architectures. In *MICRO*, 1999.

[9] A. Moshovos, S. E. Breach, T. N. Vijaykumar, and G. S. Sohi. Dynamic speculation and synchronization of data dependences. In *ISCA*, 1997.

[10] J. T. Oplinger, D. L. Heine, and M. S. Lam. In search of speculative Thread-Level parallelism. In *PACT*, 1999.

[11] C. G. QuiÃ±ones, C. Madriles, J. SÃ¡nchez, P. Marcuello, A. GonzÃ¡lez, and D. M. Tullsen. Mitosis Compiler: an Infrastructure for Speculative Threading Based on Pre-Computation Slices. In *PLDI*, 2005.

[12] J. Renau, B. Fraguela, J. Tuck, W. Liu, M. Prvulovic, L. Ceze, S. Sarangi, P. Sack, K. Strauss, and P. Montesinos. SESC Simulator, January 2005. http://sesc.sourceforge.net.

[13] J. Renau, J. Tuck, W. Liu, L. Ceze, K. Strauss, and J. Torrellas. Tasking with out-of-order spawn in TLS chip multiprocessors: microarchitecture and compilation. In *ICS*, 2005.

[14] G. Sohi, S. Breach, and T. Vijayakumar. Multiscalar Processors. In *ISCA*, 1995.

[15] J. Steffan, C. Colohan, A. Zhai, and T. Mowry. A Scalable Approach to Thread-Level Speculation. In *ISCA*, 2000.

[16] J. G. Steffan, C. Colohan, A. Zhai, and T. C. Mowry. The STAMPede Approach to Thread-Level Speculation. *ACM Trans. Comput. Syst.*, 2005.

[17] M. Tremblay. MAJC: Microprocessor Architecture for Java Computing. Hot Chips, August 1999.

[18] J. Tsai, J. Huang, C. Amlo, D. Lilja, and P. Yew. The Superthreaded Processor Architecture. *IEEE Trans. on Computers*, 1999.

[19] A. Zhai, C. B. Colohan, J. G. Steffan, and T. C. Mowry. Compiler optimization of Memory-Resident value communication between speculative threads. In *CGO*, 2004.

[20] A. Zhai, S. Wang, P. Yew, and G. He. Compiler Optimizations for Parallelizing General-Purpose Applications under Thread-Level Speculation. In *PPoPP*, 2008.

[21] Y. Zhang, L. Rauchwerger, and J. Torrellas. A Unified Approach to Speculative Parallelization of Loops in DSM Multiprocessors. Technical report, 1998.

Enhancing the Performance of Assisted Execution Runtime Systems through Hardware/Software Techniques

Gokcen Kestor
Barcelona Supercomputing
Center
C/ Jordi Girona 34
08034 Barcelona, Spain
gokcen.kestor@bsc.es

Roberto Gioiosa[*]
Pacific Northwest National
Laboratory
902 Battelle Boulevard
Richland, WA 99352
roberto.gioiosa@pnnl.gov

Osman Unsal
Barcelona Supercomputing
Center
C/ Jordi Girona 34
08034 Barcelona, Spain
osman.unsal@bsc.es

Adrian Cristal
IIIA - CSIC - Spanish National
Research Council
C/ Jordi Girona 34
08034 Barcelona, Spain
adrian.cristal@bsc.es

Mateo Valero
Universitat Politecnica de
Catalunya
C/ Jordi Girona 34
08034 Barcelona, Spain
mateo@ac.upc.edu

ABSTRACT

To meet the expected performance, future exascale systems will require programmers to increase the level of parallelism of their applications. Novel programming models simplify parallel programming at the cost of increasing runtime overheard. Assisted execution models have the potential of reducing this overhead but they generally also reduce processor utilization.

We propose an integrated hardware/software solution that automatically partition hardware resources between application and auxiliary threads. Each system level performs well-defined tasks efficiently: 1) the runtime system is enriched with a mechanism that automatically detects computing power requirements of running threads and drives the hardware actuators; 2) the hardware enforces dynamic resource partitioning; 3) the operating system provides an efficient interface between the runtime system and the hardware resource allocation mechanism. As a test case, we apply this adaptive approach to STM^2, an software transactional memory system that implements the assisted execution model.

We evaluate the proposed adaptive solution on an IBM POWER7 system using Eigenbench and STAMP benchmark suite. Results show that our approach performs equal or better than the original STM^2 and achieves up to 65% and 86% performance improvement for Eigenbench and STAMP applications, respectively.

Categories and Subject Descriptors

D.1.3 [**Software**]: Programming Techniques—*Concurrent Programming*

Keywords

Exascale, Assisted execution, Transactional Memory, Performance

---

[*]Dr. Gioiosa was at BSC during this work.

1. INTRODUCTION

In order to achieve 10^{18} FLOPS with a limited power budget (25MW) [18], exascale systems will push thread level parallelism (TLP) to the extreme. Exascale systems are expected to feature a total of 10^8 - 10^9 high-efficient, high-density, low-power cores per systems, with 1-10 thousands cores just within a single node. The complexity of such high level of concurrency poses considerable challenges to programmers: classical message-passing or lock-based programming models, such as MPI or Pthreads, do not seem to have the capability of expressing the desired TLP. In particular, at least within a single node, it seems reasonable to leverage the use of shared memory to reduce synchronization overhead. Shared memory programming models, such as OpenMP, PGAS [25] (e.g., UPC and GA), and Transactional Memory [14], that have the potentiality to simplify parallel programming and to enable users to extract higher level of parallelism are seeing wider use in HPC. While simplifying parallel programming, however, these richer runtime systems introduce runtime overhead that may reduce applications speedups. Moreover, even for systems with limited runtime overhead, the theoretical speedup computed with the Amdahl's Law may not justify the use of all available cores/hardware threads. Both programming model runtime overhead and the Amdahl's Law limit on the theoretical speedup suggest the use of assisted execution models [11], in which some of the computing elements (cores or hardware threads) are used to support computation rather than being devoted to running additional application threads [22, 31]. The intuition behind assisted execution models is that some of the computing elements can accelerate sequential part of the application and/or relieve application threads from handling runtime functionalities, therefore pushing further the theoretical Amdahl's Law's speedup. The main drawback of assisted execution models is the generally low processor utilization and the waste of resources, especially in phases when applications could use all available hardware threads. Waste of hardware resources cannot be tolerated for exascale systems that need to achieve an efficiency of 40 GFLOPS/Watt. A tighter interaction between hardware and software is essential to reach this level of system efficiency.

This paper explores the use of fine-grained hardware resource allocation to increase overall processor utilization and application's performance for assisted execution runtime systems. As opposed to coarse-grained resource allocation (adding or removing cores/hardware threads to a particular task) that can be implemented at software level, fine-grained resource allocation (partitioning renaming registers, load/store queue entries, ROB slots, etc.) requires a collaboration between the software and the underlying hardware. Although this fine-grained resource allocation requires a deep understanding of all the layers involved, from the hardware to the applications, it has the potential to provide higher performance and better adapt to frequent changes in the application's behavior.

Transactional memory (TM) has recently received considerable interest, which eventually motivated the development of processors with hardware support for TM, such as IBM BG/Q [13]. Software-only solutions (STMs) are especially compelling because they remove some of the hardware transactional memory limitations [7, 9] and provide high portability. STM systems, however, usually suffer from high overhead, which makes them good candidates for assisted execution models. As a test case, we apply fine-grained hardware resource partitioning to STM^2 (*Software Transactional Memory for Simultaneous Multithreading* processors), an assisted execution STM system [17]. With STM^2, transactional operations are divided between *application* and *auxiliary* threads: application threads optimistically perform computation, while time-consuming TM management operations, such as read-set validation, are handled by auxiliary threads. Application and auxiliary threads run on separate but paired hardware threads, thus computation and TM management operations are effectively performed in parallel.

In this work, we propose an integrated hardware/software approach where system functionalities are divided among three different components: 1) STM^2 is enriched with a mechanism that automatically detects computing demand of application and auxiliary threads and drives the underlying hardware actuators; 2) the hardware enforces resource partitioning among the running threads; 3) the OS provides an interface between STM^2 and the hardware. We leverage the IBM POWER7 *hardware thread prioritization* [2, 5, 28] to dynamically partition hardware resource (e.g., renaming registers or load/store queue entries) between the running threads.

We begin by proposing a set of static techniques that can be applied when configuring STM^2 to partition hardware resources between application/auxiliary thread pairs. We show that static techniques work for simple applications but might not work for applications with irregular transaction structures. Hence, we propose an adaptive solution that automatically partitions hardware resources between application and auxiliary threads at run time, transparently to the programmer and with no need of manual reconfiguration. Our adaptive solution monitors the computing power demand of application and auxiliary threads and adapts to 1) phases within an application, 2) different behaviors of each application/auxiliary threads pair within the same application, and 3) the structure of the particular transaction executed by a thread at a given moment.

We test our proposals on a IBM POWER7 system using two sets of benchmarks: first, we explain the potentialities of fine-grained resource allocation using Eigenbench [15] and then we apply our solutions to STAMP applications [24]. Experimental results show that static approaches are only effective for simple scenarios while more realistic and complex applications require the use of adaptive solutions. The adaptive solution matches static approaches for simple cases, and outperforms the original STM^2 for complex scenarios, up to 65% and 85% for Eigenbench and STAMP applications.

This work is organized as follows: Section 2 describes IBM POWER7 hardware thread priority mechanism. Section 3 and Section 4 introduce static and adaptive solutions for assisted execution systems, respectively. Section 5 provides experimental results. Section 6 details the related work and Section 7 concludes.

Table 1: Hardware thread priority levels for IBM POWER7.

Priority	Priority level	Privilege level	or-nop inst.
0	Thread shut off	Hypervisor	-
1	Very low	Supervisor	or 31,31,31
2	Low	User	or 1,1,1
3	Medium-Low	User	or 6,6,6
4	Medium	User	or 2,2,2
5	Medium-high	Supervisor	or 5,5,5
6	High	Supervisor	or 3,3,3
7	Very high	Hypervisor	or 7,7,7

2. HARDWARE RESOURCE PARTITIONING

Fine-grained hardware resource allocation generally requires hardware support to dynamically partition resources at run time with acceptable latency. A wide range of mechanisms to control hardware resources allocated to a particular core or hardware thread have been proposed in the literature [6, 19, 20]. Some of these proposals have been implemented in real IBM [12, 28, 29] or Intel [16] processors, which allows system developers to implement fine-grained resource allocation solutions on real systems. In this work fine-grained hardware resource allocation for STM^2 is implemented upon IBM POWER7 processors, using the hardware thread prioritization mechanism to dynamically assign processor resources to the running threads at run time.

IBM POWER7 [1] processors are out-of-order, 8-core design with each core having up to 4 SMT threads. IBM POWER7 provides a mechanism to partition hardware resource within a core by fetching and decoding more instructions from one hardware thread than from the others [28]. Each hardware thread in a core has a *hardware thread priority*, an integer value in the range of 0 to 7, as illustrated in Table 1. The amount of hardware resources assigned to a hardware thread is proportional to the difference between the thread's priority and the priorities of the other hardware threads in the same core. The higher the priority of a hardware thread, the higher the amount of hardware resources assigned to that thread.

The priority value of a hardware thread in IBM POWER7 can be controlled by software and dynamically modified during the execution of an application. IBM POWER7 processors provide two different interfaces to change the priority of a thread: or-nop instructions or *Thread Status Register* (TSR). As Table 1 shows, not all hardware thread priority values can be set by applications: user software can only set priority levels 2, 3, 4; the operating system (OS) can set 6 out of 8 levels, from 1 to 6; the Hypervisor can span the whole range of priorities. In order to use all possible levels of priorities, a special Linux 2.6.33 kernel patched with the Hardware Managed Threads priority (HMT) patch [2, 3, 4] is required. This custom kernel provides two interfaces (a `sysfs` and a system call) through which the users can set the current hardware thread priority, including the ones that require OS or Hypervisor privilege (the OS issues a special Hypervisor call to set priority 0 and 7). The system call interface (`hmt_set()`) is more suitable for the purpose of this work because it introduces lower overhead.

3. STATIC FINE-GRAINED RESOURCE PARTITIONING

Runtime systems benefit from the assisted execution model if application threads often require support to perform time-consuming operations [22, 31]. Under these hypothesis, devoting hardware threads to perform runtime operations rather than main computation may provide higher performance than using all available hardware resources to run application threads. STM^2, in particular, provides significant speedups over canonical STM systems (between

1.8x and 5.2x on average) [17] for applications that spend a considerable amount of time performing transactions. However, similarly to other assisted execution systems, STM^2 may not fully utilize the processor's resources for some cases.

This section describes fine-grained resource allocation techniques that can be applied to STM^2 at configuration time to improve processor utilization and efficiency when auxiliary threads are mostly idle or overloaded.[1] Applying these techniques requires an comprehensive understanding of the IBM POWER7 hardware thread priority mechanism. In order to better explain the effects of fine-grained resource partitioning, this section follows a step-by-step approach. Experiments are performed using Eigenbench [15], a simple TM micro-benchmark that allows programmers to tune orthogonal TM characteristics, such as the number of local accesses outside or inside transactions, the conflict level, or the number of transactional operations per transaction. Eigenbench performs N consecutive iterations of a computation block, where each block consists of an embarrassingly parallel computation part and a transaction. We properly tune Eigenbench to create challenging scenarios for STM^2. We then leverage the IBM POWER7 hardware thread priority mechanism to improve STM^2's performance in these challenging scenarios. In the following sections, AT_p denotes the priority of an application thread, AxT_p the priority of an auxiliary thread, and $\Delta_p = AT_p - AxT_p$ the difference between the priority of an application thread and its corresponding auxiliary thread.

3.1 Embarrassingly parallel phases

During embarrassingly parallel phases, threads perform computation on private data and do not need to protect accesses to memory locations. In STM^2, auxiliary threads paired with application threads not performing transactions at a given time sit idle, waiting for a new transaction to start. Since each thread runs on a dedicated hardware thread and the system is not over-provisioned, this design may lead to overall processor under-utilization. In fact, waiting auxiliary threads do not perform any useful work but consume hardware resources. A naïve solution to this problem consists of suspending waiting auxiliary threads and resuming their execution as soon as their paired application threads enter a transaction. This approach usually reduces responsiveness, which may limit overall performance, especially if the application frequently alternates short transactions and embarrassingly parallel phases. Moreover, suspending idle auxiliary threads, in general, does not increase processor utilization: the hardware thread that was running the auxiliary thread is released back to the operating system (OS) which may decide to either run another task or leave it idle. If there is no other runnable task available to the idle hardware thread, the OS may reduce the priority of the idle hardware thread, implicitly increasing the performance of the other hardware thread. This decision is not under the control of STM^2 and depends on the system status at the time of suspending an auxiliary thread. On the other hand, spinning usually guarantees higher responsiveness at the cost of unnecessarily consuming hardware resources without making any progress. To increase processor utilization while maintaining high responsiveness, we reduce the hardware priority of spinning auxiliary threads (AxT_p) and restore it to its initial value as soon as the corresponding application threads start a new transaction.

The impact of reducing AxT_p during embarrassingly parallel phases on the performance of the whole application depends on the percentage of time the application spends performing embarrassingly parallel computation and the amount of extra hardware resources assigned to application threads (Δ_p). Figure 1 shows the perfor-

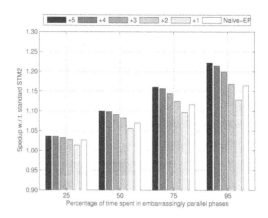

Figure 1: Performance impact of reducing AxT_p when varying the percentage of time spent performing embarrassingly parallel computation and the value of Δ_p.

mance improvement of Eigenbench over STM^2 when running 1000 iterations per thread, with one transaction per iteration. In this experiment, the number of transactional operations per iteration is fixed to 20.[2] We then vary the percentage of time spent by Eigenbench in embarrassingly parallel phases from 25% to 95% and the value of the AxT_p while keeping $AT_p = 6$. This experiment only focuses on the performance improvement obtained from reducing the AxT_p during embarrassing parallel phases, hence $AT_p = AxT_p = 6$ inside transactions. As expected, reducing AxT_p during embarrassingly parallel computation phases provides performance improvements proportional to the percentage of time the application spends in embarrassingly parallel computation. Figure 1 also shows that the best performance values are obtained with $\Delta_p = 5$ (i.e., $AT_p = 6$ and $AxT_p = 1$). This is an important design point because this value of Δ_p can only be achieved through the HMT Linux patch. Had we limited the use of priority to the user-available levels, the maximum Δ_p would have been 2 ($AT_p = 4$ and $AxT_p = 2$), meaning that the performance improvement would have been 16.8% instead of 22.3%. This performance improvement comes essentially free of any drawbacks, as reducing hardware resources does not have any impact on the performance of waiting auxiliary threads.

The graph also reports the performance improvement obtained suspending idle auxiliary threads (*naïve-EP*) and resuming them as new transactions begin. Suspending waiting auxiliary threads provides some performance improvement, mainly because the system only runs one application and, thus, there is a high probability that the OS will reduce the hardware thread priority of the hardware thread previously running the waiting auxiliary thread. However, the performance improvement achieved with this approach does not match the one obtained with $\Delta_p = 5$. This is due to two main reasons: first, the OS is free to schedule any other process or kernel daemon on idle hardware threads previously occupied by the waiting auxiliary threads. This external process may introduce even larger slowdown on the applications threads (data cache lines eviction, TLB entries eviction, resource contention). Second, the overhead of resuming auxiliary threads may reduce the overall benefit.

3.2 Load imbalance inside transactions

In STM^2, each application/auxiliary thread pair needs to synchronize at the end of each transaction (`commit()`) before moving to the next phase. For each application/auxiliary thread pair, load imbalance may occur because: 1) the application thread issues TM

---

[1] No application's source modification is required in order to apply these techniques.

[2] Here, and in the rest of the paper, Eigenbench is configured to perform 10% of transactional writes.

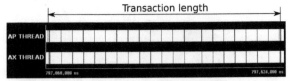

(a) Standard Case: Application threads issue TM operations at a low rate.

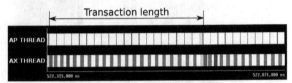

(b) Static allocation of extra hardware resources to application threads.

Figure 2: Frequently idle auxiliary threads within a transaction. In this trace white denotes local computation while gray bars denote transactional reads or writes. The elapsed time in both traces is the same.

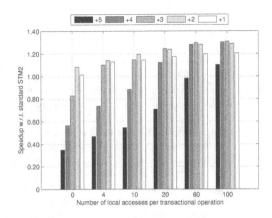

Figure 3: Performance impact of reducing AxT_p in presence of load imbalance (overloaded application threads) when varying the number of local accesses per transactional operation and Δ_p.

operations at a low rate, thus its corresponding auxiliary thread is frequently idle (Section 3.2.1), and 2) the auxiliary thread has not completed all TM management operations when the corresponding application thread reaches the commit phase (Section 3.2.2). The next sub-sections explain these scenarios with details.

3.2.1 Overloaded application threads

Figure 2 shows a partial execution trace (one transaction) of a scenario in which application threads perform TM operations at a low rate. In this figure, local computation (operations on private variables) is depicted in white and TM operations are drawn as gray bars. To obtain these execution traces, we instrumented STM^2 and produced traces that can be visualized with Paraver [26], a performance analysis tool used to study parallel applications. In this experiment Eigenbench is configured in such a way that application threads perform N_{local} local operations for every shared access (N_{shared}). In the example shown in Figure 2, $N_{local} = 300$ and $N_{shared} = 20$ (the total number of operations is $N_{local} \times N_{shared} + N_{shared} = 6,020$), which results in the auxiliary thread being idle for 95% of the time during the execution of a transaction.

Figure 2a shows the standard STM^2 case: the auxiliary thread is frequently idle but consumes hardware resources by spinning on the communication channel for incoming read/write messages. The application thread, on the other hand, can only use a partial amount of the shared hardware resources, with the results that its speed is limited. In this simple scenario the programmer could configure STM^2 to reduce the AxT_p, therefore assigning more hardware resources to the application thread. Figure 2b shows the effect of setting $AT_p = 6$ and $AxT_p = 1$ ($\Delta_p = 5$): Although the auxiliary thread proceeds at slower speed than the one in Figure 2a (the trace shows that each TM operation now takes longer), the application thread does not have to wait and can proceed with its computation. This happens because the auxiliary thread has still enough time to complete all TM operations before its corresponding application thread reaches the commit phase, thus the application thread does not wait to complete the transaction.

Unfortunately, setting the correct values of AT_p and AxT_p is not always straightforward: since the internal design of the IBM POWER7 hardware thread priority mechanism is not symmetric [2], the performance degradation of the lower priority thread is usually higher than the performance improvement of the higher priority thread. This design does not lead to performance degradation when reducing the priority of auxiliary threads that are actually not doing any progress, like in embarrassingly parallel computation phases. How-

ever, applying the wrong set of priorities when both threads are performing useful work may reverse the imbalance, with the final effect of worsening the overall performance.

In order to quantify the effect of fine-grained resource allocation on applications with imbalanced transactions, we performed a complete design space exploration, varying the number of accesses to local variables (N_{local}) per TM operation (N_{shared}) within a transaction and the priority values of the auxiliary threads (AxT_p); $AT_p = 6$ in all cases. The result of this design space exploration is reported in Figure 3. When the number of local accesses is limited or null, excessively reducing AxT_p reverses the imbalance: auxiliary threads become the bottleneck and application threads have to wait at commit phase for their auxiliary threads to complete their work. This often leads to performance degradation, especially when the priority difference is large (e.g., $\Delta_p \geq 4$). For $N_{local} = 0$, reducing the hardware thread priority of auxiliary threads degrades performance up to 63% ($AT_p = 6$ and $AxT_p = 1$, $\Delta_p = 5$). As the number of local accesses per TM operation increases, auxiliary threads are able to complete their work even with fewer hardware resources: for $N_{local} = 100$, aggressive settings achieve overall performance improvement of 30%.

3.2.2 Overloaded auxiliary threads

Some TM management operations, such as read-set validation or conflict detection, require a variable amount of time to be completed. For example, the read-set validation overhead depends on the number of individual shared memory locations read during a transaction and the number of concurrent writers. The former determines the size of the read-set while the latter determines the frequency with which read-set validation is performed.

STM^2 is an eager-conflict detection STM, thus read-set validation is performed when a potential conflict arises. Note that, although required, not all read-set validations result in aborting the transaction. If an application triggers several read-set validations, auxiliary threads may not be able to complete all their TM operations before the corresponding application threads reach the commit phase. If such a situation arises, application threads are forced to wait at commit phase. Figure 4a illustrates this case: the auxiliary thread is not able to complete all TM management operations before its corresponding application thread reaches the commit phase, thus the application thread is forced to wait, effectively serializing part of computation and TM management operations. In

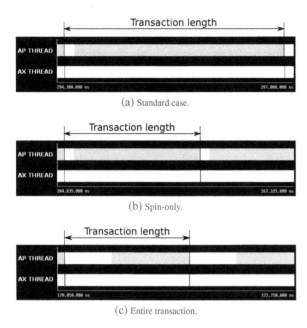

(a) Standard case.

(b) Spin-only.

(c) Entire transaction.

Figure 4: Overloaded auxiliary threads. In the traces, white denotes transaction computation (both local and shared accesses) while light gray denotes application threads' waiting time at commit phase. The elapsed time is the same for all the traces.

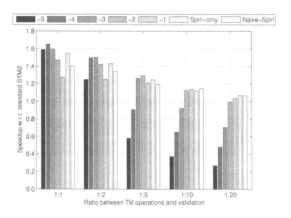

Figure 5: Performance impact of increasing the AxT_p when varying the number of read-set validations per transactional operation and Δ_p.

the trace, application thread's waiting time at commit phase is denoted with light gray while white depicts the execution of a transaction (both local computation and transactional operations). As shown in Figure 4a, prioritizing auxiliary threads ($\Delta_p < 0$) may provide performance benefits. This technique can be applied just at commit phase (Spin-only) or throughout the whole transaction (Entire Transaction).

Spin-only: Figures 4b shows how reducing AT_p while an application thread is waiting at commit phase speeds up the execution of TM management operations and improve overall performance. This solution, similarly to the case described in Section 3.1, is straightforward and does not introduce any performance degradation because application threads do not perform useful work while waiting at commit phase. In particular, the figure shows the case in which $AT_p = 1$ and $AxT_p = 6$ ($\Delta_p = -5$). Comparing Figures 4a and 4b, there is no performance degradation for the application thread computing phase (white in the traces), while the spinning time (light gray) is considerably reduced. Performance improvement, in this case, is proportional to the spinning time reduction.

Entire transaction: Figure 4c shows a solution that decreases AT_P at the beginning of the transaction and maintains $\Delta_p < 0$ for the entire transaction execution. This approach is more aggressive than the previous spin-only solution: the performance of application threads considerably reduces by prioritizing auxiliary threads during the transaction computation phase. This can be observed by comparing Figures 4a and 4c: the application thread computing phase (white) takes considerably longer than in the standard case. On the other hand, the auxiliary thread does not accumulate too many pending TM operations, hence its corresponding application thread has to spin for less time at commit phase. The net result is that performance improves with respect to both the baseline (65%) and the safe, spin-only approach (7%).

Figure 5 shows the impact of statically increasing AxT_p ($\Delta_p < 0$) at the beginning of the transaction when the number of read-set validations per TM operation decreases. The graph also shows the performance of reducing AT_p to one ($\Delta_p = -5$) when application

threads wait at commit phase (i.e., the case depicted in Figure 4b). Finally, the graph reports the effect of suspending waiting applications threads and resuming them once the transaction is ready to commit (*naïve-spin*). The figure reports the performance improvement over the standard STM^2 when performing one read-set validation every N transactional operations (1:N) and varying the value of Δ_p. These experiments show that increasing AxT_p for transactions that require a high number of validations generally provides higher performance improvements than just reducing AT_p at commit phase or suspending/resuming waiting applications. For example, when performing one validation for every transactional operation (1:1), increasing AxT_p from the beginning of the transaction provides performance improvement of 65% over the standard STM^2 while reducing AT_p to one at commit phase provides 55% performance improvement and suspending/resuming waiting application threads provides 40% performance improvement. On the other hand, reducing AT_p when an application thread is spinning at commit phase is a safe operation that does not introduce any measurable performance degradation. This technique can, therefore, be applied as fall-back mechanism in case a perfect balance between application and auxiliary threads cannot be achieved by increasing AxT_p at the beginning of a transaction.

Finally, the best value of Δ_p is not always the same for all ratios and aggressive settings are only possible when the number of read-set validations per transactional operations is high. Figure 5 shows, in fact, that incorrect settings of AT_p and AxT_p when prioritizing auxiliary threads may lead to considerable performance degradation (up to 70%), especially if the number of read-set validations per transaction is low. As for the case of reducing AxT_p for frequently idle auxiliary threads (Section 3.2.1), manually setting AT_p and AxT_p is a complicated task, even for simple micro-benchmarks.

4. ADAPTIVE FINE-GRAINED RESOURCE PARTITIONING

Section 3 shows that, for simple scenarios, setting the best values of AT_p and AxT_p can be set at configuration time by an expert programmer. For complex scenarios, instead, setting the right value of Δ_p is not trivial and depends on the actual work performed by application and auxiliary threads.

Figure 6a shows an execution trace of a Eigenbench transaction with a burst of accesses to shared memory locations roughly starting in the middle of the transaction: the application thread performs

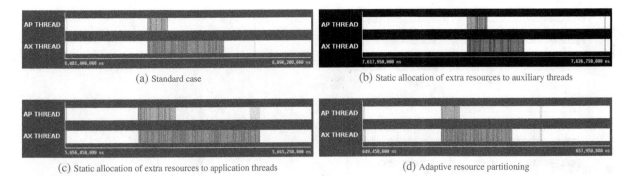

(a) Standard case

(b) Static allocation of extra resources to auxiliary threads

(c) Static allocation of extra resources to application threads

(d) Adaptive resource partitioning

Figure 6: Irregular transactions with bursts of transactional operations in the middle. White denotes local computation within transaction, gray bars denote transactional reads and writes, the light gray at the end of the transaction denotes application threads waiting at commit phase.

some local computation (white in the trace) followed by a burst of shared memory accesses (the gray bars in the trace denote transactional read and write operations), and then performs computation on local data. This simple example shows that a large part of the execution of TM operations overlaps with the application computation. However, the same trace shows that the auxiliary thread is mainly idle during the local computation phases and considerably overloaded when the sudden burst of shared memory accesses starts. As with many static approaches, the main problem in this example is that it is not trivial to configure, at compile time, the values of AT_p and AxT_p that provide the best performance for both local computation and bursts of shared memory accesses.

Noticing that the burst of shared accesses results in a considerable amount of work for the auxiliary thread, one possible approach is to increase AxT_p ($\Delta_p < 0$). Figure 6b shows the effect of setting $AT_p = 5$ and $AxT_p = 6$ ($\Delta_p = -1$): although the performance of the auxiliary thread improves considerably during the execution of the TM operations, the performance degradation suffered in the local computation phases outweighs the improvement, which results in an overall 27% slowdown with respect to the standard STM^2 design. The opposite approach consists of reducing the priority of the auxiliary thread to benefit the application thread. Figure 6c shows that the performance of the application thread during the local computation phase improves by 12%, while, obviously, the performance of the auxiliary thread when performing TM operations decreases. In fact, the trace shows that the auxiliary thread is still performing TM operations when the application thread reaches the end of the transaction, thus, the application thread has to wait at commit phase. Although local computation phases are predominant in this transaction structure and part of the TM operations overlaps with the second local computation phase, there is still a slight performance degradation. Neither solution is optimal, as both of them gain and suffer in opposite phases during the execution of the transaction. The common problem to both solutions is that static approaches seldom adapt to non-uniform structures, such as the one presented in Figure 6a.

This section introduces an automatic solution that adapts, at run time, to the transaction's structure and automatically sets the best values of AT_p and AxT_p. This adaptive solution is based on heuristics and on the lessons learned when applying the static solutions described in Section 3. The proposed heuristics are designed according to the following key principles:

P1 Reducing the hardware thread priority of either application or auxiliary threads introduces an asymmetric performance degradation [2]. Thus, we need to be careful when decreasing the priority of a thread, especially for large values of $|\Delta_p|$.

P2 Reducing the priority of a waiting auxiliary thread considerably improves performance (up to 30%) without any performance degradation. The heuristics should decrease AxT_p whenever the application enters a (large) embarrassingly parallel section.

P3 If application threads issue bursts of TM operations, their corresponding auxiliary threads may not be able to complete all TM operations before the application threads reach commit phase. The heuristics should consider prioritizing auxiliary threads ($\Delta_p < 0$) in such scenarios. However, auxiliary thread prioritization reduces application threads performance and must be done judiciously.

P4 Large values of Δ_p provide higher performance improvements. However, this required the use of the system call `hmt_set()`, which introduces some overhead. We tend to modify the priority of waiting threads (mainly the auxiliary threads), as this directly affects the value of $\Delta_p = AT_p - AxT_p$.

Besides these basic key principles, the adaptive solution employs the static mechanisms that do not depend on the actual application and auxiliary thread structure, such as reducing AxT_p during embarrassingly parallel phases or reducing AT_p when spinning at commit phase. For short embarrassingly parallel sections or for cases in which all TM operations are completed when an application thread reaches the commit phase, the overhead of invoking a system call may outweigh the performance improvement. To avoid such situations, the adaptive solution snoozes for a short time before actually issuing the system call. At the beginning of a transaction the initial values are $AT_p = AT_p(0) = 5$ and $AxT_p = AxT_p(0) = 5$. Since AT_p remains constant during the execution of a transaction ($P4$), these settings allow the enriched STM^2 to reach large positive values of Δ_p ($P2$) but also to be able to prioritize auxiliary threads ($P3$), depending on the structure of the transaction.

Detecting load imbalance: The first problem towards the development of an adaptive solution is how to determine if there is load imbalance and which thread is the bottleneck. To this extent, we monitor the number of messages queued in the communication channel between application and auxiliary threads, which introduces negligible overhead. In fact, if the application thread issues transactional operations at a low rate, the queue would be frequently empty. Conversely, if the application thread issues TM operations at a rate higher than the rate at which the auxiliary thread completes its work, the queue would gradually fill up.

Reducing the priority of auxiliary threads: In case it is determined that an auxiliary thread is often idle (i.e., the queue is empty most of the time), the heuristic aims at reducing AxT_p so that the paired application thread receives more hardware resources. In order not to reverse the load imbalance, the heuristic decreases AxT_p only after a certain amount of consecutive attempts to dequeue a message that reveal that the queue is empty. This quantity is denoted as *snooze_time*. A constant *snooze_time* would decrease the priority regardless of the current value of AxT_p, however, according to principle $P1$, the priority of a thread should be decreased judiciously, especially if the priority difference Δ_p is already large. On the other hand, Figure 3 shows that, even for small values of N_{local}, decreasing AxT_p provides benefits. The solution adopted here is to make *snooze_time* variable: every time the auxiliary thread decreases its priority, the heuristic computes a new *snooze_time* value as a function of Δ_p. The general idea is that the larger the value of Δ_p, the larger the value of *snooze_time*, i.e., the value of AxT_p is reduced less often if the Δ_p is large. The heuristics used in this work to compute *snooze_time* is the following:

$$snooze\_time = a + b * (\Delta_p + 1)^c$$

where $a = 40$, $b = 10$ and $c = 3$ have been computed empirically.

Increasing the priority of auxiliary threads: In this adaptive system, the value of AxT_p at time t may be lower than its initial value $AxT_p(0)$. This may happen because the auxiliary thread was frequently idle before t and the heuristic decreased its hardware thread priority. If a burst of TM operations such as the one depicted in Figure 6a arises, the heuristic should increase the value of AxT_p or else the auxiliary thread will not be able to complete its work before its corresponding application thread reaches the commit phase (see Figure 6c). Raising the value of AxT_p should not be too impulsive as, if the burst is particularly short, it might be worth keeping $AxT_p < AxT_p(0)$ (Figure 3). The heuristic increases the value of AxT_p until it reaches $AxT_p(0)$ if there are more than `QS_THRESHOLD` elements in the queue (in the current implementation this value is 20), which denotes that the auxiliary thread is potentially accumulating work. Additionally, auxiliary threads are allowed to increase their priority up to $AxT_p = 6$ (i.e., $\Delta_p = -1$) if the number of pending messages in the queue is larger than `QS_THRESHOLD_CRITICAL` (128 in our implementation). Notice that higher values of $|\Delta_p|$ (i.e., $\Delta_p = -2, -3, ..$) are also possible but cumbersome. Instead, in case the load cannot be balanced with $\Delta_p = -1$, the heuristic reduces the priority of the application thread while spinning at commit phase (see Figure 4b).

Figure 6d shows that the dynamic solution is able to adapt to the irregular structure of the transaction and provides higher performance than both static approaches. First, the adaptive solution reduces the priority of the auxiliary thread during the initial local computation phase, therefore improving the performance of the application thread. Next, when the sudden burst of accesses to shared memory locations starts, the adaptive solution gradually increases AxT_p and, if necessary, reaches values higher than AT_p ($\Delta_p < 0$). Finally, once the auxiliary thread has completed all its TM operations, the adaptive mechanism reduces AxT_p again, improving the performance of the application thread in the last part of the transaction. The overall result is performance improvement of 15%, where static approaches result in performance degradation when decreasing or increasing AxT_p, respectively (based on the best values among all possible settings of AT_p and AxT_p).

The adaptive solution's heuristics can be evaluated with two different metrics: 1) the convergence to the best value of Δ_p, and 2) the speed at which the heuristics reach that value. Figure 7 shows the value of AxT_p ($AT_p = AT_p(0)$ throughout the execution) as function of the elapsed time since the beginning of the transaction, for

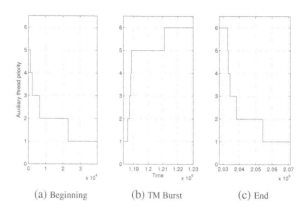

(a) Beginning	(b) TM Burst	(c) End

Figure 7: The adaptive solution automatically changes the value of AxT_p according to the structure of the transaction and the computing demand of application and auxiliary threads. These graphs show the values of AxT_p during one transaction for the case discussed in Figure 6d. The x-axis reports time since the beginning of the transaction.

a transaction with a burst of TM operations in the middle (the same case reported in Figure 6d). As Figure 7a shows, the adaptive solution successfully converges to $AxT_p = 1$ (stable state), first quickly and then, as Δ_p increases, more slowly (the steps get larger as Δ_p increases). When the sudden burst of TM operations starts (Figure 7b), the heuristic quickly adapts to the new scenario and converges to $AxT_p = 5$. Since increasing AxT_p does not depend on Δ_p, the steps are much smaller than in Figure 7a. In the meanwhile, the auxiliary thread has accumulated a considerable amount of work, thus, the heuristic further increases $AxT_p = 6$ ($\Delta_p = -1$), giving more hardware resources to the auxiliary thread. Finally, once all the accumulated work has been processed, the heuristic automatically reduces the auxiliary thread priority until it reaches the value $AxT_p = 1$ (Figure 7c), similarly to what happens in the first part.

5. EXPERIMENTAL RESULTS

This section presents the evaluation of the static and adaptive solutions on an IBM POWER7 system (8 cores, 4 hardware threads/core) equipped with 64 GB of RAM. STM^2 and all the applications are compiled with GCC 4.3.4 with optimization level O3; the results reported for each application are the average of 25 runs. In order to use all hardware priority levels, all tests are performed on a custom version of the Linux 2.6.33 kernel patched with the HMT patch [3]. In all the experiments, Eigenbench and STAMP applications use all the 32 available hardware threads: 16 application threads and 16 auxiliary threads.

5.1 Eigenbench

Figure 6 shows the effect of statically increasing (Figure 6b) and decreasing (Figure 6c) AxT_p for transactions with irregular structures. For this particular example, neither statically decreasing nor increasing AxT_p provides performance improvement over the standard STM^2, while the adaptive solution effectively allocates hardware resources on demand and improves performance by 15%.

For transactions with burst of TM operations, the performance improvement depends on both the size and the position of the burst. The size of the burst clearly affects whether prioritizing application/auxiliary threads provides higher performance. In the extreme cases (bursts of 0% or 100%), the examples degenerate to the cases presented in Section 3. If a short burst of TM operations occurs at the beginning of a transaction, the auxiliary thread has enough time to complete all TM management operations before the ap-

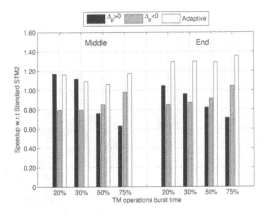

Figure 8: Performance of static (best values among all combinations) and adaptive solutions for application with irregular transaction structures and varying size/position of burst of shared accesses.

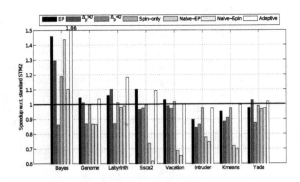

Figure 9: Performance impact of static (best values among all combinations) and adaptive solutions for STAMP applications.

plication thread reaches the commit phase, even without applying fine-grained resource allocation. As the burst of TM operations moves towards the end of the transaction, the auxiliary thread may not be able to complete all the TM operations before its corresponding application thread reaches the commit phase. If that happens, the application thread will spin at commit phase, which leads to sub-optimal performance. Obviously, the worst case occurs when the burst of TM operations appears at the end of the transaction: in this case application and auxiliary threads essentially run sequentially, invalidating most of the advantages of assisted execution.

Figure 8 shows the performance of the best combination for the proposed static approaches and the adaptive solution over the standard STM^2 design, when varying the size of the burst (from 20% to 75% of the transaction execution time) and the position of the burst (middle and end of the transaction). The experiments in the graph show that statically partitioning hardware resources provides performance improvement only for extreme cases (20% and 75%), either because there is a large part of the transaction in which the auxiliary thread is mainly idle, or because the burst is large enough to cause the application thread to spin at commit phase for a considerable amount of time. In the other scenarios (30% and 50%), STM^2 effectively runs TM operations and computation in parallel. The dynamic approach, on the other hand, 1) provides performance improvement over both static approaches and 2) more importantly, always outperforms the standard STM^2 for both the "Middle" and the "End" cases. This experiment shows that the automatic solution is able to adapt to the structure of the transaction, properly increasing or decreasing the value of AxT_p on demand. In a nutshell, the adaptive solution provides performance improvements between 6% and 38% over the standard STM^2 and outperforms the best performance provided by both static techniques.

5.2 STAMP applications

In this section we apply static and adaptive fine-grained resource allocation to STAMP applications [24]. Figure 9 reports the performance impact of (separately) applying the static approaches and the adaptive solution. The graph reports, for each static technique, the best values of the pair (AT_p, AxT_p) among all possible configurations. For several applications, applying fine-grained resource allocation results in performance improvement (*Bayes*, *Genome*, *Yada*, *Labyrinth*, and *SSCA2*). Others applications (*Vacation*, *Intruder*, and *Kmeans*), instead, show limited or no performance improvement. These applications are well balanced and the original STM^2

design already provides optimal performance. In these cases, the adaptive solution aims at not worsening performance.

Statically decreasing AxT_p during embarrassingly parallel phases generally improves performance, up to 46% for *Bayes*. Even in this simple case, however, static solutions may suffer from the overhead of unnecessary changing the values of AT_p, e.g., if the application present back-to-back transactions with a short interval time between transactions, which may lead to performance degradation up to 10% (*Intruder*). The same scenario arises when application threads are waiting at commit phase: if the auxiliary thread has already performed all the TM operations when the application thread reaches the commit phase, the system call overhead may induce performance degradation. Suspending idle auxiliary threads (*naïve-EP*) or spinning application threads (*naïve-Spin*) introduces an even larger overhead: in the worst cases (large number of small transactions) the performance slowdown can be up to 38% (*SSCA2*). In general, *naïve-EP* and *naïve-Spin* perform worst or equal than their hardware thread priority counterparts (*EP* and *Spin-only*, respectively). In order to avoid these situations, the adaptive solution snoozes for a short time before reducing the priority of waiting application/auxiliary threads. In particular, the adaptive solution reduces AT_p only if there are at least SPIN_THRESHOLD messages (20 in the current implementation) in the communication channel when an application thread reaches the commit phase. Similarly, the adaptive solution reduces AxT_p in embarrassingly parallel phases only after EP_THRESHOLD cycles.

Within transactions, static techniques do not usually provide performance improvement: Prioritizing auxiliary threads ($\Delta_p < 0$) always reduces application's performance while prioritizing application threads ($\Delta_p > 0$) provides speedups for *Bayes*, *Labyrinth* and *Yada*. Spinning at commit phase provides measurable performance improvement only for *Bayes*, which suggests that auxiliary threads are not usually overloaded and AxT_p should not generally be greater than AT_p. For well-balanced applications, such as *Vacation*, static approaches provide performance degradation or have almost no effect. In these cases, the adaptive solution does not detect load imbalance and, therefore, does not priority change.

Among the STAMP applications, *Labyrinth*, *SSCA2* and *Bayes* are the most interesting cases for this study. *Labyrinth* presents very large, back-to-back transactions with a large number of local accesses followed by a burst of transactional accesses. Figure 10a depicts the execution trace of one of *Labyrinth*'s transaction: the picture clearly shows that the local computation phase (white in the trace) is predominant, which explains why statically reducing AxT_p provides some performance improvements (Figure 9). Figure 10b shows a close-up of the final part of the transaction, the burst of

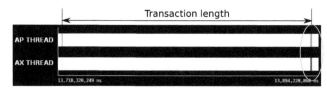

(a) Labyrinth's transaction execution trace   (b) Labyrinth's execution trace: close-up of the final part of a transaction

Figure 10: Labyrinth's transactions alternate a large local computation phase (white in the figure) with a burst of transactional operations (gray bars) at the end.

TM operations. Since the burst is at the end of the transaction, the application thread has to wait at commit phase for the auxiliary thread to complete all TM management operations, though the auxiliary thread is mainly idle during the transaction (which explains the small performance improvement for the spin-only case in Figure 9). While static solutions fail to capture the application's characteristics due to the irregular structure of the transaction, the adaptive solution is able to lower AxT_p in the first part of the transaction, reaching $AxT_p = 1$, and increase AxT_p when the application thread issues the burst of TM operations. Overall the adaptive solution outperforms the standard STM^2 by 19%.

SSCA2 presents two separate execution phases: in the first phase, the application generates the graph that will be solved in the second phase. Both phases are parallel but, while the second phase uses transactions to protect shared memory locations, the first phase is embarrassingly parallel, as each thread works on its local portion of the graph. The original STM^2 assigns half the available hardware threads to run auxiliary threads even in the embarrassingly parallel phase: by statically reducing the priority of the auxiliary threads in the first phase, static solutions achieve 10.3% of performance improvement over the standard STM^2 design. In the second part of the application, *SSCA2* performs very short and balanced transactions with a low conflict rate and several concurrent writers. In this phase, the application is well balanced and applying static solutions decreases performance. The adaptive solution also lower AxT_p in the first phase but does not detect load imbalance in the second phase, hence it does not react. The net result is a performance improvement of 9.8% over STM^2. For this application, suspending waiting application or auxiliary threads has a dramatic impact on performance caused by the large number of short transactions.

Bayes is the application that shows the largest performance improvement: Even static approaches achieve improvement in the order of 30-45%. *Bayes* implements an algorithm for learning the structure of Bayesian networks from observed data through a hill-climbing strategy. Similarly to *SSCA2*, the applications performs two parallel parts: the first is mainly embarrassingly parallel and devoting more hardware resources to application threads considerably increases performance (up to 45%). In the second part, instead, the applications uses a few large transactions. However, similarly to *Labyrinth*, auxiliary threads are frequently idle, thus decreasing AxT_p provides benefits. For *Bayes* the adaptive solution precisely captures the application's structure and combine the positive effects observed for *Labyrinth* and *SSCA2*, providing a final performance improvement of 85% over the standard STM^2.

The examples shown in this section demonstrate that there are cases in which fine-grained hardware resource partitioning can be used to improve the performance of assisted execution systems, such as STM^2. For not well-balanced applications, like *Labyrinth* and *Bayes*, and for applications with large (sequential or parallel) independent computing phases, like *SSCA2* and *Bayes*, the adaptive solution successfully employs dynamic fine-grained hardware

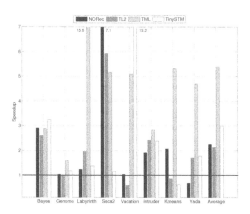

Figure 11: Speedup of adaptive fine-grained hardware resource allocation with respect to other state-of-the-art STMs.

resource partitioning and provides considerable performance improvements without any effort from the programmer, modification of the applications or library re-linking. Only *Intruder* among all the STAMP applications shows minimal performance degradation. Finally, Figure 11 shows the speedup of adaptive hardware resource allocation with respect to other state-of-the-art STMs. The adaptive solution outperforms, on average, TinySTM [27], NORec [8], TL2 [10], and TML [30], by 3x, 2.3x, 2.1x, and 5.4x, respectively.

6. RELATED WORK

Hardware thread prioritization [2, 29] has been introduced by IBM in the POWER5 processor family. AIX provides the users with an interface to modify hardware thread priorities. Linux kernels use hardware prioritization when 1) a thread is spinning on a lock, 2) a thread is waiting for another thread to complete a required operation (`smp_call_function()`), or 3) a thread is idle. Linux resets the priority of a thread after receiving an interrupt or an exception and does not keep a per-process priority status. Moreover, Linux does not consider the priority of the paired thread and, since the prioritization mechanism works with the priority difference, arbitrarily modifying the priority of one hardware thread may invalidate the decision taken on the other. Boneti et al. [2] characterized the use of hardware thread prioritization for POWER5 processors running micro-benchmarks and SPEC benchmarks. Other researchers [23] have also investigated the effect of hardware thread priorities on the execution time of co-scheduled application pairs on a trace-driven simulator of the POWER5 processor. Moreover, in a follow-up work, Boneti et al. used hardware prioritization to transparently balance high performance computing applications [3, 4], achieving up to 18% performance improvement.

Mann et al. [21] proposed a holistic approach that aims at reducing OS jitter by utilizing the additional threads or cores in a system. The authors reduce jitter through different approaches, one of which sets the hardware priorities of the primary and secondary hardware thread to 6 and 1, respectively, in order to reduce jitter caused by SMT interference.

7. CONCLUSIONS

Assisted execution systems aim at improving overall performance by relieving application threads from the overhead of performing system functionalities. These approaches are promising especially for runtime systems of novel programming models that help programmers expose a higher level of parallelism but whose runtime systems may introduce considerable overhead.

In this paper we examine the use adaptive fine-grained resource allocation to improve the efficiency and the performance of assisted execution systems. In particular, we propose an integrated hardware/software approach to dynamically partition hardware resources at run time among the running threads. We implement static and adaptive solutions for STM^2, a parallel STM system that offloads time-consuming TM operations to auxiliary threads.

While static solutions provide performance improvements only for simple cases, the proposed adaptive solution improves performance and resource utilization for applications that prove to be challenging for the original STM^2. Results obtained on a state-of-the-art IBM POWER7 system with 32 hardware threads show that adaptive fine-grained resource allocation provides performance improvement up to 65% and 86% over the standard STM^2 design for Eigenbench and STAMP applications, respectively.

Finally, we remark that, although we applied fine-grained hardware resource allocation to STM^2, this approach can be used for other assisted execution systems, such as OS exception handlers [31] or dynamic check in Java Script [22].

Acknowledgment

We would like to thank Dr. Robert W. Wisniewski from IBM, Nehir Sonmez and Vasileios Karakostas from BSC for their helpful comments. This work is supported by the cooperation agreement between the BSC and Microsoft Research, by the Ministry of Science and Technology of Spain and the European Union (FEDER funds) under contracts TIN2007-60625, JCI-2008-3688, 2009501052, and TIN2008-02055-E, by the HiPEAC European Network of Excellence (IST-004408) and by the European Commission FP7 project VELOX (216852). Gokcen Kestor is also supported by a scholarship from the Government of Catalonia.

8. REFERENCES

[1] J. Abeles, L. Brochard, L. Capps, D. DeSota, J. Edwards, B. Elkin, J. Lewars, E. Michel, R. Panda, R. Ravindran, J. Robichaux, S. Kandadai, and S. Vemuganti. Performance guide for HPC applications on IBM power 755 system, 2010.

[2] C. Boneti, F. Cazorla, R. Gioiosa, C.-Y. Cher, A. Buyuktosunoglu, and M. Valero. Software-Controlled Priority Characterization of POWER5 Processor. In *Proc. of the 35th IEEE Intl. Symp. on Computer Architecture*, pages 415–426, Beijing, China, June 2008.

[3] C. Boneti, R. Gioiosa, F. Cazorla, J. Corbalan, J. Labarta, and M. Valero. Balancing HPC applications through smart allocation of resources in MT processors. In *Proc. of the 22nd IEEE Intl. Parallel and Distributed Processing Symp.*, Miami, FL, 2008.

[4] C. Boneti, R. Gioiosa, F. Cazorla, and M. Valero. A dynamic scheduler for balancing HPC applications. In *Proc. of the 2008 ACM/IEEE Conf. on Supercomputing*, 2008.

[5] J. M. Borkenhagen, R. J. Eickemeyer, R. N. Kalla, and S. R. Kunkel. A multithreaded PowerPC processor for commercial servers. *IBM Journal of Research and Development*, (6):885–898, 2000.

[6] F. J. Cazorla, P. M. W. Knijnenburg, R. Sakellariou, E. Fernandez, A. Ramirez, and M. Valero. QoS for high-performance SMT processors in embedded systems. *IEEE Micro*, (4), 2004.

[7] L. Dalessandro, F. Carouge, S. White, Y. Lev, M. Moir, M. L. Scott, and M. F. Spear. Hybrid NOrec: A case study in the effectiveness of best effort hardware transactional memory. In *Proc. of the 16th Intl. Conf. on Architectural Support for Programming Languages and Operating Systems*, Newport Beach, CA, USA, Mar. 2011.

[8] L. Dalessandro, M. F. Spear, and M. L. Scott. NOrec: Streamlining STM by abolishing ownership records. In *Proc. of the 15th ACM SIGPLAN Symp. on Principles and Practice of Parallel Programming*, Jan. 2010.

[9] P. Damron, A. Fedorova, Y. Lev, V. Luchangco, M. Moir, and D. Nussbaum. Hybrid transactional memory. In *Proc. of the 12th Intl. Conf. on Architectural Support for Programming Languages and Operating Systems*, 2006.

[10] D. Dice, O. Shalev, and N. Shavit. Transactional locking II. In *Proc. of the 20th Intl. Symp. on Distributed Computing*, Stockholm, Sweden, Sept. 2006.

[11] M. Dubois and H. Song. Assisted execution. Technical Report GENG-98-25, University of Southern California, Los Angeles, 1998.

[12] H. Q. Le, W. J Starke, J. S. Fields, F. P. O'Connell, D. Q. Nguyen, B. J. Ronchetti, W. M. Sauer, E. M. Schwarz, and M. T. Vaden. IBM POWER6 microarchitecture. *IBM Journal of Research and Development*, (6), 2007.

[13] R. Haring. The Blue Gene/Q compute chip. In *The 23rd Symposium on High Performance Chips (Hot Chips)*, 2011.

[14] M. Herlihy and J. E. B. Moss. Transactional memory: Architectural support for lock-free data structures. In *Proc. of the 20th IEEE Annual Intl. Symp. on Computer Architecture*, 1993.

[15] S. Hong, T. Oguntebi, J. Casper, N. Bronson, C. Kozyrakis, and K. Olukotun. Eigenbench: A simple exploration tool for orthogonal TM characteristics. In *Proc. of the IEEE Int. Symp. on Workload Characterization*, 2010.

[16] Intel Corporation. Intel AtomTM processor n450, d410 and d510 for embedded applications, 2010. Document Number: 323439-001 EN, revision 1.0.

[17] G. Kestor, R. Gioiosa, T. Harris, A. Crystal, O. Unsal, I. Hur, and M. Valero. STM2: A parallel STM for high performance simultaneous multithreading systems. In *Proc. of the 20th IEEE Int. Conference on Parallel Architectures and Compilation Techniques*, 2011.

[18] P. Kogge, K. Bergman, S. Borkar, D. Campbell, W. Carlson, W. Dally, M. Denneau, P. Franzon, W. Harrod, K. Hill, J. Hiller, S. Karp, S. Keckler, D. Klein, R. Lucas, M. Richards, A. Scarpelli, S. Scott, A. Snavely, T. Sterling, R. S. Williams, and K. A. Yelick. Exascale computing study: Technology challenges in achieving exascale systems. Technical Report DARPA-2008-13, DARPA IPTO, September 2008.

[19] K. Luo, M. Franklin, S. S. Mukherjee, and A. Seznec. Boosting SMT performance by speculation control. In *Proc. of the 15th IEEE Int. Parallel & Distributed Processing Symposium*, pages 2–, 2001.

[20] M. Moreto, F. J. Cazorla, A. Ramirez, and M. Valero. MLP-Aware Dynamic Cache Partitioning. *Int. Conference on High Performance Embedded Architectures and Compilers*, 2008.

[21] P. D. V. Mann and U. Mittaly. Handling OS jitter on multicore multithreaded systems. In *Proc. of the 2009 IEEE Inter. Symp. on Parallel and Distributed Processing*, pages 1–12, 2009.

[22] M. Mehrara and S. A. Mahlke. Dynamically accelerating client-side web applications through decoupled execution. In *Proc. of the 9th IEEE Int. Symp. on Code Generation and Optimization*, pages 74–84, 2011.

[23] M. R. Meswani and P. J. Teller. Evaluating the performance impact of hardware thread priorities in simultaneous multithreaded processors using SPEC CPU2000. In *Workshop on Operating System Interference in High Performance Applications*, 2006.

[24] C. C. Minh, J. Chung, C. Kozyrakis, and K. Olukotun. STAMP: Stanford transactional applications for multi-processing. In *Proc. of the IEEE Intl. Symp. on Workload Characterization*, 2008.

[25] J. Nieplocha, B. Palmer, V. Tipparaju, M. Krishnan, H. Trease, and E. Aprà. Advances, applications and performance of the global arrays shared memory programming toolkit. *Int. J. High Perform. Comput. Appl.*, 20:203–231, 2006.

[26] V. Pillet, J. Labarta, T. Cortes, and S. Girona. PARAVER: A tool to visualize and analyze parallel code. Technical report, In WoTUG-18, 1995.

[27] T. Riegel, C. Fetzer, and P. Felber. Time-based Transactional Memory with scalable time bases. In *19th ACM Symp. on Parallelism in Algorithms and Architectures*, 2007.

[28] B. Sinharoy, R. Kalla, W. J. Starke, H. Q. Le, R. Cargnoni, J. A. Van Norstrand, B. J. Ronchetti, J. Stuecheli, J. Leenstra, G. L. Guthrie, D. Q. Nguyen, B. Blaner, C. F. Marino, E. Retter, and P. Williams. IBM POWER7 multicore server processor. *IBM J. Res. Dev.*, pages 191–219, May 2011.

[29] B. Sinharoy, R. N. Kalla, J. M. Tendler, R. J. Eickemeyer, and J. B. Joyner. POWER5 system microarchitecture. *IBM Journal of Research and Development*, (4/5):505–521, 2005.

[30] M. F. Spear, A. Shriraman, L. Dalessandro, and M. L. Scott. Transactional mutex locks. In *Proc. of the 4th ACM SIGPLAN Workshop on Transactional Computing*, Raleigh, NC, USA, Feb. 2009.

[31] C. B. Zilles, J. S. Emer, and G. S. Sohi. The use of multithreading for exception handling. In *Proc. of the 32nd annual ACM/IEEE Intl. Symp. on Microarchitecture*, 1999.

CATS: Cache Aware Task-Stealing based on Online Profiling in Multi-socket Multi-core Architectures

Quan Chen
Shanghai Key Laboratory of
Scalable Computing and
Systems,
Department of Computer
Science, Shanghai Jiao Tong
University, China
chen-quan@sjtu.edu.cn

Minyi Guo[*]
Shanghai Key Laboratory of
Scalable Computing and
Systems,
Department of Computer
Science, Shanghai Jiao Tong
University, China
guo-my@cs.sjtu.edu.cn

Zhiyi Huang
Department of Computer
Science,
University of Otago,
New Zealand
hzy@cs.otago.ac.nz

ABSTRACT

Multi-socket Multi-core architectures with shared caches in each socket have become mainstream when a single multi-core chip cannot provide enough computing capacity for high performance computing. However, traditional task-stealing schedulers tend to pollute the shared cache and incur severe cache misses due to their randomness in stealing. To address the problem, this paper proposes a Cache Aware Task-Stealing (CATS) scheduler, which uses the shared cache efficiently with an online profiling method and schedules tasks with shared data to the same socket. CATS adopts an online DAG partitioner based on the profiling information to ensure tasks with shared data can efficiently utilize the shared cache. One outstanding novelty of CATS is that it does not require any extra user-provided information. Experimental results show that CATS can improve the performance of memory-bound programs up to 74.4% compared with the traditional task-stealing scheduler.

Categories and Subject Descriptors

C.4 [**Performance of Systems**]: Measurement Techniques

Keywords

Cache Aware, Task-stealing, Online Profiling, Multi-socket Multi-core, Cache misses

1. INTRODUCTION

Multi-core processors have become mainstream since they have better performance per watt and larger computational capacity than complex single-core processors. However, a single CPU die can hardly contain too many cores (e.g., more than 128 cores) due to the physical limitations in industrial manufacture. To fulfill the urgent desire on powerful computers, many multi-core CPUs are integrated together into a Multi-socket Multi-core (MSMC) architecture. In an MSMC architecture, each CPU die is plugged into a socket and the cores in the same socket have a shared cache; however, the cores from different sockets can only share the main memory.

To fully utilize the MSMC architectures, many parallel programming environments have been proposed. In some of them, such as Pthread [8], MPI [16] and Maotai [29], parallelism is expressed through multithreading. Programmers need to launch threads and assign tasks to these threads manually in multithreading. However, the manual assignment of tasks is often burdensome for developing applications. To relieve the burden of parallelization and task assignment, parallel programming environments, such as Cilk [7], Cilk++ [20], TBB [25], X10 [19], and OpenMP [2], assign and schedule tasks automatically. *Task-sharing* [2] and *task-stealing* (also known as work-stealing[1]) [14] are the two most famous task scheduling strategies.

In task-sharing, workers (i.e. threads) push new tasks into a central task pool when they are generated. Tasks are popped out from the task pool when workers are free to execute them. The push and pop operations need to lock the central task pool, which often causes serious lock contention.

Task-stealing, on the other hand, provides an individual task pool for each worker. Most often each worker pushes tasks to and pops tasks from its own task pool without locking. Only when a worker's task pool is empty, it tries to steal tasks from other workers with locking. Since there are multiple task pools for stealing, the lock contention is much lower than task-sharing even at task steals. Therefore, task-stealing performs better than task-sharing as the number of workers increases.

However, both task-sharing and task-stealing strategies schedule tasks randomly to different cores. This randomness can cause shared cache misses and degrade the performance of memory-bound applications on MSMC architectures (to be discussed in detail in Section 2). For example, two tasks with shared data may be allocated to different sockets due to the randomness in these strategies. In this case, both tasks

---

*Minyi Guo is the correspondence author of this paper.

---

[1]We use "task-stealing" in this paper for the consistency of terms.

cannot share the data loaded to the shared cache but have to read the shared data from the main memory which could be hundreds times slower than the shared cache. If the two tasks are scheduled to cores in the same socket, only one of them needs to read the shared data from the main memory while the other task can access the shared data from the shared cache directly.

Based on this observation, this paper proposes a Cache Aware Task-Stealing (CATS) scheduler that automatically schedules tasks with shared data into the same socket for memory-bound applications based on Jacobi method. CATS is proposed for systems like MIT Cilk and targets applications with tree-shaped execution DAG (Directed Acyclic Graph). CATS consists of two parts: an *online DAG partitioner* and a *bi-tier task-stealing scheduler*. The online DAG partitioner automatically divides the execution DAG of a parallel program into the inter-socket tier and the intra-socket tier based on the profiling information collected during execution. The bi-tier task-stealing scheduler allows tasks in the inter-socket tier to be stolen across sockets, while tasks in the intra-socket tier are scheduled within the same socket. Since tasks from the intra-socket tier often share data, CATS uses the shared cache efficiently.

The contributions of this paper are as follows.

- We propose an online profiling method that automatically collects run-time profiling information for cache aware task scheduling. It enables the task scheduler to optimally utilize the shared cache without extra user-provided information.

- We propose an online DAG partitioner that optimally divides tasks into the inter-socket tier and the intra-socket tier based on the profiling information, and a bi-tier task-stealing algorithm that schedules tasks with shared data to the same socket.

- We demonstrate that CATS significantly reduces the shared cache misses and thus improves the performance of memory-bound applications. The experiment shows that CATS can achieve a performance gain of up to 74.4% for memory-bound applications.

The rest of this paper is organized as follows. Section 2 describes the problem and explains the motivation of CATS. Section 3 presents CATS, including the online DAG partitioner and the bi-tier task-stealing scheduler. Section 4 shows the experimental results and the limitations of CATS. Section 5 discusses the related work. Section 6 draws conclusions and sheds light on future work.

2. PROBLEM AND MOTIVATION

For many parallel programming environments such as Cilk, the execution of a parallel program can often be expressed by a Directed Acyclic Graph (DAG) $G = (V, E)$, where V is a set of nodes, and E is a set of directed edges [15]. Each node in a DAG represents a task (i.e., a set of instructions) that must be executed sequentially without preemption, and the edges in a DAG correspond to the dependence relationship among the nodes. Fig. 1 shows execution DAG of a general parallel program. In the figure, the solid lines represent the task generating relationship and the strings by the side of nodes are the identifiers of the corresponding tasks.

2.1 The problem

We use Fig. 1 as an example to explain the problem of shared cache pollution in an MSMC architecture. In many parallel programs based on the *Jacobi iteration algorithm*, neighbor tasks need to access some shared data. For example, *Five-point heat distribution* and *Successive Over-Relaxation* are examples of such parallel programs. Therefore, γ_1 and γ_2, γ_3 and γ_4 in Fig. 1 have shared data respectively.

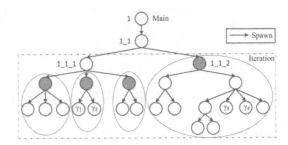

Figure 1: A general execution DAG for iteration-based parallel programs.

We assume the parallel program in Fig. 1 runs on a dual-socket dual-core architecture. If γ_1, γ_2, γ_3 and γ_4 are scheduled as shown in Fig. 2(a), the shared data between γ_1 and γ_2 and the shared data between γ_3 and γ_4 is only read into the shared cache once from the main memory. Since most tasks can access the shared data in the shared cache of the socket, cache misses are reduced.

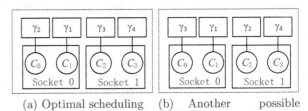

(a) Optimal scheduling   (b) Another possible scheduling

Figure 2: Two possible scheduling of γ_1, γ_2, γ_3 and γ_4 on a dual-socket dual-core architecture. The first scheduling can gain performance improvement due to cache sharing and reduction of memory footprint.

However, for random task-stealing, since it randomly chooses a victim to steal tasks, γ_1, γ_2, γ_3 and γ_4 are likely to be scheduled to the cores as shown in Fig. 2(b). In this case, each task needs to read all its data from the main memory. This larger memory footprint leads to more compulsory cache misses. Even worse, if the memory footprint exceeds the capacity of the shared cache, the situation leads to more capacity cache misses and increases the chances of conflict cache misses. The resulted larger number of cache misses leads to worse performance of memory-bound applications.

Though there were some task schedulers proposed [5, 6, 10] to reduce cache misses, they either need extra user-provided information [10], or are not general enough for MSMC architectures [5, 6].

2.2 Proposed solution

If a task-stealing scheduler can ensure tasks with shared data are scheduled to the same socket as shown in Fig. 2(a), the shared cache misses will be minimized and the performance of memory-bound applications can be improved. To achieve the purpose, we propose the *Cache Aware Task-Stealing* (CATS) scheduler in this paper.

CATS is proposed based on the following three observations of the execution of parallel programs as shown in Fig. 1. First, parallel tasks create child tasks recursively until the data set for each leaf task is small enough. During the procedure, only the leaf tasks physically touch the data. Second, a parallel program often works on the same data set for a large number of iterations. Finally, neighbor tasks usually share some data.

Based on the runtime profiling information, CATS can divide an execution DAG into the inter-socket tier and the intra-socket tier. For example, CATS may divide the execution DAG in Fig. 1 into two tiers separated by the shaded tasks. The shaded tasks are called *leaf inter-socket tasks*. Tasks above the leaf inter-socket tasks, including the leaf inter-socket tasks, are called *inter-socket tasks*, which belong to the inter-socket tier. Tasks in a subtree rooted with a leaf inter-socket task are called *intra-socket tasks*, which belong to the intra-socket tier. A subtree rooted with a leaf inter-socket task is called an *intra-socket subtree*. For example, in Fig. 1, tasks in an ellipse consist in an intra-socket subtree. The goal of CATS is to schedule tasks in the same intra-socket subtree within the same socket. In this way, CATS can ensure γ_1 and γ_2 (or γ_3 and γ_4) to be executed in the same socket.

However, to achieve the optimal scheduling, it is very challenging to find the proper leaf inter-socket tasks so that tasks in the same intra-socket subtree will be able to utilize the shared cache efficiently. If an intra-socket subtree is too large, the involved data can be too large to fit into the shared cache of the socket. On the other hand, if an intra-socket subtree is too small, the workload of the subtree can be too small to get better balanced among the cores of the same socket.

CATS uses an online DAG partitioner to find leaf inter-socket tasks and partition an execution DAG into two tiers. When CATS starts to execute a parallel program, the partitioner first profiles the program in the first iteration. Based on the profiling information, the online DAG partitioner adaptively divides the execution DAG into two tiers (to be discussed in Section 3.2). According to our first observation of parallel programs, the collected profiling information in the first iteration can be used to predict the execution behavior of the following iterations. Therefore, an optimal partitioning of DAG based on the profiling information of the first iteration will also be optimal for the following iterations.

After the runtime partitioning of the DAG, a bi-tier task-stealing algorithm is adopted in CATS to schedule tasks in the two tiers differently. The inter-socket tasks are scheduled across sockets, while the tasks in the same intra-socket subtree are scheduled within the same socket. CATS ensures that each socket can only execute one intra-socket subtree at the same time to avoid cache pollution. In this way, the shared data can be reused without reloading among tasks within an intra-socket subtree. That is, the scheduling in Fig. 2(a) can be enforced to reduce cache misses. Fig. 3 illustrates the detailed processing flow of a parallel program in CATS.

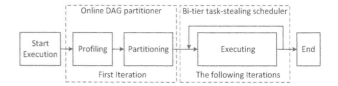

Figure 3: The processing flow of a parallel program in CATS.

3. CACHE AWARE TASK-STEALING

This section presents CATS, a Cache Aware Task-Stealing scheduler. First, we give the CATS runtime environment. Then we describe an online DAG partitioner for dividing the execution DAG into two tiers. Lastly, we present the bi-tier task-stealing algorithm, the task-generating policy and the implementation details in CATS.

3.1 CATS runtime environment

To support the processing flow in Fig. 3, we have built a runtime environment for CATS as follows. For an M-socket N-core architecture, CATS launches $M \times N$ workers (i.e., threads) at runtime and affiliates each worker with one individual hardware core as shown in Fig. 4. For convenience of presentation, we use the term *core* to mean a worker in the rest of the paper.

In each socket, only one core is selected as the head core of the socket to look after the inter-socket task scheduling. In CATS, we choose "core 0" in each socket as the socket's header core.

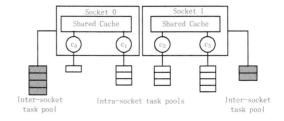

Figure 4: CATS runtime environment in a dual-socket dual-core architecture. Each socket has an inter-socket task pool and each core has an intra-socket task pool.

In order to schedule inter-socket tasks and intra-socket tasks in different ways in bi-tier task-stealing, CATS creates an *inter-socket task pool* for each socket to store inter-socket tasks, and an *intra-socket task pool* for each core to store intra-socket tasks, as shown in Fig. 4. A task pool is a double-ended queue for storing tasks.

During the first iteration of a parallel program, all the tasks are generated and pushed into intra-socket task pools when they are generated. In this case, tasks are scheduled adopting traditional task-stealing policy. That is, in the first iteration, tasks in intra-socket task pools can be scheduled across sockets since the profiling information has not been collected and thus the execution DAG has not been partitioned. In the following iterations, tasks are generated and pushed into different pools accordingly. If core c in socket ρ generates a task γ that is an inter-socket task, γ is pushed into ρ's inter-task pool. Otherwise, if γ is an intra-socket task, it is pushed into c's intra-socket task pool.

We present the online DAG partitioner and the bi-tier task-stealing scheduler in detail in the following sections.

3.2 Online DAG partitioner

As explained in Section 2, to partition an execution DAG into the inter-socket tier and the intra-socket tier optimally, the most challenging problem is to find the proper leaf inter-socket tasks. Once the proper leaf inter-socket tasks are identified, the DAG can be easily divided into two tiers: all the tasks above the leaf inter-socket tasks (including the leaf inter-socket tasks) belong to the inter-socket tier, and those tasks in the subtrees rooted with leaf inter-socket tasks belong to the intra-socket tier.

An optimal partitioning of an execution DAG should satisfy two constraints. The first constraint is that, for any intra-socket subtree ST, the involved data of all the tasks in ST is small enough to fit into the shared cache of a socket. The second constraint is that an intra-socket subtree ST should be large enough to allow a socket to have sufficient intra-socket tasks.

To fulfill the two constraints when dividing an execution DAG, for any task γ in the execution DAG, CATS should collects its involved data size. For convenience of description, we use *Size Of Involved Data* (SOID) to represent the involved data size of a task γ. That is, SOID includes the data accessed by all tasks in the subtree rooted with γ. Once the SOIDs for all tasks in the execution DAG are known, the online DAG partitioner can divide the execution DAG into two tiers optimally.

3.2.1 Online Profiling

In order to collect SOIDs of all the tasks, CATS profiles the program during the first iteration of the execution. During the online profiling, we use the hardware Performance Monitoring Counters (PMC) [3] to collect cache misses, based on which the SOIDs for all tasks are calculated. The performance counter event we have used is the last level private data cache (e.g. L2 in AMD Quad-core Opteron 8380) misses. That is, we have used the performance counter event "07Eh" with mask of "02h" to collect the last level private data cache misses in AMD Quad-core Opteron 8380. For detailed information of the performance counter events, refer to *BIOS and Kernel Developer's Guide* of the corresponding processor. Though it is straightforward to collect the event statistics of the last level private data cache misses in modern multi-core machines like X86_64, it is very tricky to calculate the SOIDs of the tasks based on the last level private data cache misses.

First, limited by the hardware PMCs, a core can only collect the cache misses of its own, but a task may have multiple child tasks executing on different cores. Therefore, it is impossible to collect the overall cache misses for a task directly.

Second, it is nontrivial to relate the private cache misses to the SOID of a task. For a task γ that runs on a core c in socket ρ, if γ fails to get its data from the last level private cache of c, it requests the data from the shared cache of ρ. Since c does not execute other tasks when it is executing γ, the last level private cache misses of c are totally caused by γ. The last level private cache misses of c can be used to approximate to the size of data accessed by γ for the following reasons. Many memory-bound applications adopt data parallelism. As mentioned in our second observation in

Section 2.2, only the leaf tasks physically access data. The data of leaf tasks do not have much overlapping with each other. Even when two neighbor leaf tasks have a small portion of shared data, the chances for them to be executed in the same core are small in a random task-stealing scheduler, which is adopted during the profiling stage. Therefore, the above approximation is accurate enough for us to calculate the SOIDs of all tasks.

Based on the collected last level private cache misses of γ, its SOID is calculated as follows. If γ is a leaf task, the number of cache misses of γ times the cache line size (e.g., 64 bytes in AMD Quad-core Opteron 8380) is γ's SOID. Otherwise, if γ is not a leaf task, its SOID is the sum of its cache misses times the cache line size plus the SOIDs of all its child tasks. Given a task β with n sub-tasks β_1, β_2, ..., β_n. Suppose M is β's number of cache misses times the size of cache line, and the SOIDs of its child tasks are S_1, S_2, ..., S_n respectively, then β's SOID, denoted by S_β, is calculated as in Eq. (1).

$$S_\beta = M + \sum_{i=1}^{n} S_i \qquad (1)$$

Based on Eq. (1), Fig. 5 presents an example of calculating SOIDs for all the tasks. In the figure, S_i is the SOID for leaf task γ_i, but represents the size of data physically accessed by the task itself for non-leaf tasks. In fact, for many memory-bound applications, S_i for non-leaf tasks is very small, if it is not zero, since non-leaf tasks do not physically access data.

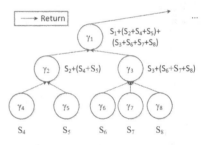

Figure 5: Collect Size Of Involved Data (SOID) for tasks.

As shown in Fig. 5, the SOID of a task is returned to its parent task when it is completed. For example, in Fig. 5, γ_2's SOID is added to γ_1's SOID when γ_1 is completed. Therefore, when all the tasks in the first iteration are completed, the SOIDs of all the tasks can be calculated.

3.2.2 DAG Partitioning

Based on the SOIDs of tasks that are collected in the first iteration, the online DAG partitioner divides the execution DAG into inter-socket tier and intra-socket tier automatically.

To satisfy the aforementioned constraints, the online DAG partitioner identifies leaf inter-socket tasks as follows. For a task α and its parent task α_p, let D_α and D_{α_p} represent SOIDs of α and α_p respectively. α is a leaf inter-socket task if and only if D_α is smaller than the size of the shared cache and D_{α_p} is larger than the size of the shared cache.

More precisely, given a task α and its parent task α_p, our DAG partitioning method determines α's tier as follows.

- If both D_{α_p} and D_α are larger than the shared cache of a socket, α is an inter-socket task, as shown in Fig. 6(a).

- If D_{α_p} is larger than the shared cache and D_α is smaller than the shared cache of a socket, α is a leaf inter-socket task, as shown in Fig. 6(b).

- If both D_{α_p} and D_α are smaller than the shared cache, α is an intra-socket task, as shown in Fig. 6(c).

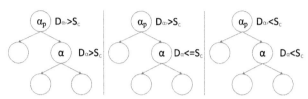

(a) α is an inter-socket task   (b) α is a leaf inter-socket task   (c) α is an intra-socket task

Figure 6: Conditions that α is an inter-socket task, leaf inter-socket task or intra-socket task.

After the profiling and the partitioning, the online DAG partitioner has already divided the execution DAG into two tiers optimally. Then, based on the partitioning, bi-tier task-stealing can be adopted to schedule tasks for optimizing shared cache in the following iterations.

In order to identify the same task in the following iterations, during the execution of a parallel program, each task is given an identifier (a string) according to the spawning relationship between tasks. If a task γ's identifier is S, then its ith sub-task's identifier is S_i. For example, Fig. 1 shows the way of constructing identifiers for tasks. The strings beside the tasks are the identifiers in Fig. 1. The identifiers of all the completed tasks are saved in a hash table with their SOIDs. When a new task is spawned, CATS tries to find its identifier in the hash table. If the identifier is found, it means the first iteration has completed since a new task in the same location of the execution DAG has been spawned. In this case, CATS uses the bi-tier task-stealing scheduler to schedule tasks based on their tiers which are decided according to their SOIDs as shown above.

It is worth noting that, in our implementation, we obtain the size of the shared cache from */proc/cpuinfo* by the CATS runtime system. To this end, all the needed information for optimal bi-tier task-stealing is obtained automatically by the runtime system of CATS. In this way, CATS can automatically improve the performance of parallel application without human intervention.

3.3 Bi-tier task-stealing scheduler

Task-stealing algorithm is used by a free core to obtain or steal a new task. When CATS starts to execute a parallel program, during the first iteration, CATS has not partitioned its execution DAG into two tiers. Therefore, the cores adopt the traditional task-stealing algorithm to obtain or steal a new task in the first iteration. In the following iterations, CATS adopts a bi-tier task-stealing algorithm to schedule tasks so that tasks in a subtree rooted with a leaf inter-socket task are scheduled to the same socket. Since traditional task-stealing has been discussed in detail in [14], this section only presents the bi-tier task-stealing in CATS.

When a core c in socket ρ is free, it first tries to obtain a task from its own intra-socket task pool. If its own task pool is empty, c tries to steal a task from the intra-socket task pools of other cores in ρ. If the task pools of all the cores in ρ are empty, the head core of ρ tries to obtain a task from its own inter-socket task pool. If its inter-socket task pool is empty, the head core tries to steal an inter-socket task from other sockets.

In CATS, only the head core of each socket can steal inter-socket tasks so that the lock contention of the inter-socket task pools is reduced. In addition, cores in the same socket are not allowed to execute tasks in different intra-socket subtrees at the same time. This policy can avoid the situation where different intra-socket subtrees pollute the shared caches with different data sets. The downside of the policy is that some cores in a socket may be idle waiting for other cores to finish their tasks. An alternative policy is to allow a socket to execute tasks from more than one intra-socket subtrees at the same time. This alternative policy can ensure most cores are busy, but different intra-socket subtrees may pollute the shared caches, which leads to more cache misses. For the memory-bound applications that CATS is targeting, the cache misses are more critical to the performance according to our experimental results. Therefore, we have adopted the first policy in CATS.

3.4 Task generating Policy

Two types of task-generating policies, parent-first and child-first, can be adopted for task stealing. In the parent-first policy, a core continually executes the parent task after spawning a child task, leaving the child task for later execution or for stealing by other cores. One such example is the help-first policy in [17, 18]. Parent-first policy works better when the steals are frequent and the execution DAG is shallow [17]. In the child-first policy, a core executes the child task immediately after the child is spawned, leaving the parent task for later execution or for stealing by other cores. For example, MIT Cilk uses the child-first policy, a.k.a. work-first in [7]. Child-first policy works better when the steals are infrequent [17].

During the first iteration of a parallel program, tasks have not been divided into inter-socket tasks and intra-socket tasks. For the convenience of collecting SOID, we choose to adopt the parent-first policy in the first iteration.

After the execution DAG has been divided into two tiers, CATS generates inter-socket tasks with the parent-first policy and generates intra-socket tasks with the child-first policy. CATS adopts the parent-first policy for generating inter-socket tasks so that leaf inter-socket tasks can be generated as soon as possible. The parent-first policy is more efficient in this case because inter-socket tasks take short time and thus are frequently stolen. On the other hand, CATS adopts the child-first policy to generate intra-socket tasks. The child-first policy works better in this case because the leaf tasks take longer time and thus the steals are infrequent. Also the child-first policy is more space efficient.

3.5 Implementation

We implement CATS in MIT Cilk that is one of the earliest task-stealing programming environments [14]. MIT Cilk consists of a compiler and a scheduler. Cilk compiler, named as *cilk2c*, is a source-to-source translator that transforms a

Cilk source into a C program. Cilk programs can run with CATS without any modifications.

The compiler is modified to support both the parent-first and the child-first task-generating policy. At each spawn, CATS finds out whether the spawn happens in the first iteration of the program. If it is in the first iteration, the to-be-spawned task is spawned with the parent-first policy. If it is not in the first iteration and the to-be-spawned task's SOID is smaller than the size of the shared cache, CATS spawns the task with the child-first policy and pushes the task into the intra-socket task pool of the current core. Otherwise, CATS spawns the task with the parent-first policy and pushes the task into the inter-socket task pool of the current socket.

Since CATS aims to reduce shared cache misses, CATS may not work very well for CPU-bound applications since the cache misses have neutral effect on their performance. On the contrary, CATS may adversely affect the performance of the CPU-bound applications. To avoid the problem, an interface could be provided for users so that they can tell CATS that whether the to-be-executed program is CPU-bound or not through command line. However, even if the users could not figure out if the program is memory-bound or CPU-bound, CATS has provided the following mechanism to identify whether it is CPU-bound based on the profiling information collected in the first iteration. Given an MSMC architecture with k levels of caches and the cache miss penalty (i.e. the delay) of the ith level cache is p_i. Let n_i represent the ith level cache misses of γ. The normalized cache misses of γ is $M = \sum_{i=1}^{k} (n_i \times \frac{p_i}{p_1})$. Suppose the number of instructions in γ is N, we can use CMPI (*Cache Misses Per Instruction*), $CMPI_\gamma = \frac{M}{N}$, to decide γ is CPU-bound or memory-bound. If $CMPI_\gamma$ is smaller than a predefined threshold, γ is CPU-bound. If most tasks are CPU-bound, CATS treats the program as a CPU-bound program. In this case, CATS simply generates and schedules tasks of CPU-bound programs in traditional task-stealing. We have also discussed ways to optimize the performance of CPU-bound programs in [9] by balancing workloads among cores. Experiment results in Section 4.3 show that the extra overhead in CATS for CPU-bound programs is negligible.

4. EVALUATION

We use Otago's Dell 16-core computer that has four AMD Quad-core Opteron 8380 processors (codenamed "Shanghai") running at 2.5 GHz to evaluate the performance of CATS. Each Quad-core socket has a 512K private L2 cache for each core and a 6M L3 cache shared by all four cores. The computer has 16GB RAM and runs Linux 2.6.29.

Since CATS is proposed to reduce cache misses, we use memory-bound benchmarks to evaluate the performance of CATS. However, CPU-bound benchmarks are also used to measure the extra overhead of CATS compared with random task-stealing.

To evaluate the performance of CATS in different scenarios, we use only benchmarks that have both balanced and unbalanced execution DAGs in the experiments, although CATS can improve the performance of many similar programs (e.g., almost all the stencil-based programs [4]). Table 1 lists the used CPU-bound and memory-bound benchmarks. *Heat-ub*, *GE-ub* and *SOR-ub* implement the same algorithm as *Heat*, *GE* and *SOR* respectively, except their execution DAGs are unbalanced trees. For example, we im-

Table 1: Benchmarks used in the experiments

Name	Bound	Description
Mandelbrot	CPU	Calculate Mandelbrot Set
Queens(15)	CPU	N-queens problem
FFT	CPU	Fast Fourier Transform
GA	CPU	Island Model of Genetic Algorithm
Knapsack	CPU	0-1 knapsack problem
Heat	Memory	Five-point heat
Heat-ub	Memory	Five-point heat (unbalance)
SOR	Memory	Successive Over-Relaxation
SOR-ub	Memory	Successive Over-Relaxation (ub)
GE	Memory	Gaussian elimination
GE-ub	Memory	Gaussian elimination (unbalance)

plement *Heat-ub* in Algorithm 1. According to the algorithm, the branching degree of tasks created from cilk procedure *heat* is 2 while the branching degree of tasks created from cilk procedure *heat2* is 4. Obviously, *Heat-ub*'s DAG is an unbalanced tree. *GE-ub* and *SOR-ub* are implemented in the similar way.

Algorithm 1 The source code skeleton of *Heat-ub*

```
cilk void heat (int start, int end) {
    int mid = (start + end) / 2;
    spawn heat2 (start, mid);
    spawn heat (mid, end);
    sync; return;
}
cilk void heat2 (int start, int end) {
    int quad = (end - start) / 4;
    spawn heat (start, start + quad);
    spawn heat (start + quad, start + 2 * quad);
    spawn heat2 (start + 2 * quad, start + 3 * quad);
    spawn heat (start + 3 * quad, end);
    sync; return;
}
```

As mentioned before, CATS affiliates each worker with a hardware core. However, MIT Cilk does not affiliate workers with the cores. Therefore, we have modified the MIT Cilk (denoted as *Cilk* for short) to affiliate each worker with a hardware core (denoted as *Cilk-a* for short) in order to ensure fair comparison, since the affiliation of workers with cores can improve the performance of memory-bound applications (to be shown in Fig. 7).

Cilk-a uses the pure child-first policy to schedule tasks, while CATS flexibly uses both the child-first and parent-first policies to achieve the best performance. We implement Cilk-a and CATS based on MIT Cilk. The MIT Cilk programs run with Cilk-a and CATS without any modification.

All benchmarks are compiled with "cilk2c -O2" based on gcc 4.4.3. Furthermore, for each test, every benchmark is run ten times. Since the execution time is very stable, the average execution time is used in the final results.

4.1 Performance of memory-bound programs

Fig. 7 shows the performance of memory-bound benchmarks in Cilk, Cilk-a and CATS with a 1024×512 matrix as the input data. For *GE* and *GE-ub*, the used input data is a 1024×1024 matrix.

From the figure we can find that Cilk-a provides much better performance compared with Cilk for all the benchmarks. For memory-bound applications, the better performance in Cilk-a results from the affiliation of the workers with the cores. In the rest of our experiments, we only compare the performance of CATS with Cilk-a.

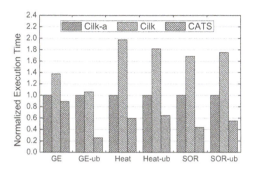

Figure 7: The performance of memory-bound benchmarks in Cilk-a, Cilk and CATS.

As we can see from Fig. 7, CATS can significantly improve the performance of memory-bound applications compared to Cilk-a while the performance improvement ranges from 35.3% to 74.4%.

To explain why CATS can improve the performance of memory-bound applications compared with Cilk-a, we collect the cache misses of all the benchmarks and list them in Table 2. Observed from the table, we can find that the shared cache (L3) misses are prominently reduced while the private cache (L1 and L2) misses are also slightly reduced in CATS compared with Cilk-a. Since CATS schedules tasks with shared data into the same socket, the shared cache misses have been significantly reduced.

Table 2: Cache misses in Cilk-a and CATS (*1E6)

Application	Scheduler	L1	L2	L3
GE	Cilk-a	60.8	58.8	14.5
	CATS	53.9	50.3	2.94
GE-ub	Cilk-a	37.2	37.1	10.7
	CATS	23.9	20	2.15
Heat	Cilk-a	82.7	79.6	24.8
	CATS	71.1	67.5	5.9
Heat-ub	Cilk-a	82.2	78.7	29.7
	CATS	71.3	67.6	3.72
SOR	Cilk-a	88.5	85	29.6
	CATS	70.7	66.2	4.75
SOR-ub	Cilk-a	89.8	85.5	30.7
	CATS	73.6	67.4	8.27

Although scheduling tasks with shared data to the same socket only reduces the shared L3 cache misses, the affiliation of an intra-socket subtree with a socket in CATS can help reduce the L2 cache misses slightly. In CATS, for a task γ_i in an intra-socket subtree, if it is executed by core c in socket ρ, its neighbor tasks (i.e., γ_{i-1} and γ_{i+1}) are also executed by c as well unless they are stolen by other cores in ρ. Compared with random task-stealing where any free cores can steal γ_i's neighbor tasks, there are fewer cores that can steal γ_i's neighbor tasks in CATS. Therefore, the probability that neighbor tasks are executed by the same core is

larger in CATS. For this reason, the private cache (e.g., L2) misses have also been slightly reduced in CATS.

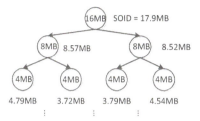

Figure 8: Calculated SOIDs of tasks in *Heat* with a 1024×512 matrix as input data.

Fig. 8 shows the SOIDs of *Heat* with a 1024×512 matrix as input data that are calculated with Eq. (1). The real involved data size of tasks in Fig. 8 are shown in the circles. Since *Heat* uses two matrices of "double" during the execution, the overall input data size is $1024 \times 512 \times 16 \times 2 = 16$MB. Then the real data set is evenly divided every time when the tasks are spawned. From the figure, we can find that the calculated SOIDs are close to the real involved data sizes, which shows our online DAG partitioner is reasonably accurate. In future, to calculate SOIDs more accurately, we will explore more hardware performance counters. Another possible way to improvement is to adopt the technique in [26] in our online DAG partitioner.

4.2 Scalability of CATS

To evaluate scalability of CATS in different scenarios, we use benchmarks that have both balanced and unbalanced execution DAGs. In this experiment, we execute benchmarks with different input data sizes in CATS and Cilk-a to compare their scalability.

During the execution of all the benchmarks, every task divides its data set into several parts by rows to generate child tasks unless the task meets the cutoff point (i.e., the data set size of a leaf task). Since the data set size of the leaf tasks affects the measurement of scalability, we should ensure that the data set size of the leaf tasks is constant in our experiment. To satisfy this requirement, we use a constant cutoff point, 8 rows, for the leaf tasks, and a constant number of columns, 512, for the input data. We only adjust the number of rows of the input matrix in the experiment. In this way, we can measure the scalability of CATS without the impact of the granularity of the leaf tasks. In all the following figures, the x-axis represents the number of rows of the input matrix.

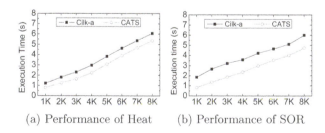

(a) Performance of Heat   (b) Performance of SOR

Figure 9: Performance of Heat and SOR with different input data sizes.

4.2.1 Balanced execution DAGs

We use *Heat* and *SOR* as benchmarks to evaluate the s-calability of CATS for applications with balanced execution DAGs. Other benchmarks, such as *GE*, have similar results.

Fig. 9 shows the performance of *Heat* and *SOR* with different input data sizes in Cilk-a and CATS. From Fig. 9, we can see that *Heat* and *SOR* achieve better performance in CATS for all sizes of the input data up to 8192 rows compared with Cilk-a. When the input data size is small (i.e., 1024 × 512), CATS reduces 40.4% execution time of *Heat* and reduces 56.1% execution time of *SOR*. When the input data size is large (i.e., 8192 × 512), CATS reduces 12.3% execution time of *Heat* and reduces 21.1% execution time of *SOR*.

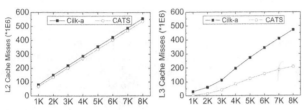

(a) L2 cache misses of Heat (b) L3 cache misses of Heat

Figure 10: L2 and L3 cache misses of Heat with different input data sizes.

Fig. 10 shows the L2 and L3 cache misses of *Heat* with different input data sizes in Cilk-a and CATS. Observed from the figure, we can find that both the shared cache misses and the private cache misses are reduced in CATS compared with Cilk-a. The better performance of *Heat* in CATS results from the less cache misses in CATS compared with Cilk-a. When the input data size is small (1024 × 512), CATS can reduce 76.1% L3 cache misses and 15.2% L2 cache misses compared with Cilk-a. When the input data size is large (8192 × 512), CATS can reduce 55.9% L3 cache misses and 3.6% L2 cache misses compared with Cilk-a. Therefore, when CATS schedules regular applications with balanced execution DAGS, it is scalable. Other benchmarks show similar results of cache misses. We omit them here due to limited space.

4.2.2 Unbalanced execution DAGs

We use *Heat-ub* and *SOR-ub* as benchmarks to evaluate the scalability of CATS for applications with unbalanced execution DAGs. Other benchmarks, such as *GE-ub*, have similar results.

Fig. 11 shows the performance of *Heat-ub* and *SOR-ub* with different input data sizes in Cilk-a and CATS. From Fig. 11 we can find that *Heat-ub* and *SOR-ub* also achieve better performance in CATS for all input data sizes compared with Cilk-a. When the input data size is small (i.e., 1024 × 512), CATS reduces 35.3% execution time of *Heat-ub* and reduces 44.9% execution time of *SOR-ub*. When the input data size is large (i.e., 8192 × 512), CATS reduces 11.4% execution time of *Heat-ub* and reduces 18% execution time of *SOR-ub*.

Fig. 12 shows the L2 and L3 cache misses of *SOR-ub* with different input data sizes. Observed from the figure, we can find that both the shared cache misses and the private cache misses of *SOR-ub* are reduced in CATS compared with Cilk-

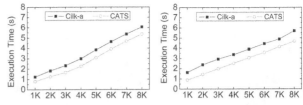

(a) Performance of Heat-ub (b) Performance of SOR-ub

Figure 11: Performance of Heat-ub and SOR-ub with different input data sizes.

a. The better performance of *SOR-ub* in CATS results from the less cache misses in CATS compared with Cilk-a. When the input data size is small, CATS can reduce 73.1% L3 cache misses and 21.2% L2 cache misses compared with Cilk-a. When the input data size is large, CATS can reduce 38.2% L3 cache misses and 5.2% L2 cache misses compared with Cilk-a. Other benchmarks show similar results of cache misses. We omit them here due to limited space.

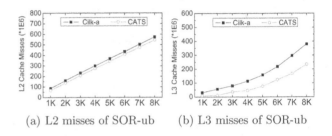

(a) L2 misses of SOR-ub (b) L3 misses of SOR-ub

Figure 12: L2 and L3 cache misses of SOR-ub with different input data sizes.

As illustrated in Fig. 9 and Fig. 11, the execution times of the benchmarks in both Cilk-a and CATS increase linearly to the input data size, because the execution times of the memory-bound benchmarks in both Cilk-a and CATS are determined by the input data size. However, for all the input data sizes, CATS can reduce the execution times of the memory-bound applications accordingly. Therefore, CATS is scalable in scheduling both balanced execution DAGs and unbalanced execution DAGs.

In addition, Fig. 10 and Fig. 12 further verify that CATS can also slightly reduce private cache misses by scheduling tasks with shared data into the same socket, which is due to the same reason explained previously.

4.3 Performance of CPU-bound programs

Since CATS is proposed to reduce shared cache misses of memory-bound applications, it is neutral to CPU-bound applications. Therefore, for CPU-bound applications, CATS uses child-first policy to schedule the tasks as Cilk-a.

Fig. 13 shows the performance of CPU-bound benchmarks listed in Table 1 in Cilk-a and CATS. By comparing the performance of CATS with Cilk-a, we can find the extra overhead of CATS. Observed from Fig. 13, we see the extra overhead of CATS is negligible compared with Cilk-a. The extra overhead of CATS mainly comes from the profiling overhead in the first iteration of a parallel program, when CATS can determine if the program is CPU-bound or memory-bound based on the profiling information.

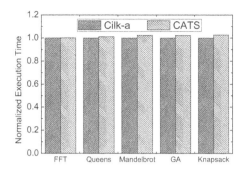

Figure 13: Performance of CPU-bound benchmarks in Cilk-a and CATS.

4.4 Discussion

As mentioned before, CATS targets memory-bound programs whose execution DAGs are tree-shaped. Therefore the most important limitation of CATS is that CATS is not suitable for programs whose DAGs are not tree-shaped since the DAG partitioner is not applicable to non-tree DAGs. CATS is applicable to divide-and-conquer programs because they have tree DAGs. We have modified *cilk2c* to check for the divide-and-conquer programs at compile time by analyzing the task generating pattern in the source code. If any function in the source code generates new tasks that run the same function as itself, the program is assumed to be a divide-and-conquer program. For programs that do not follow the divide-and-conquer pattern, CATS can simply adopt the traditional task-stealing in the execution. Therefore, the above limitation does not affect the applicability of CATS with the compiler identifying the class of programs that are suitable for CATS.

5. RELATED WORK

Reducing cache misses of parallel programs in parallel architectures is a popular research issue. However, many of the existing works either need extra user-provided information or are not general enough for MSMC architectures.

In [22], MTS (Multi-Threaded Shepherds) was proposed to reduce cache misses in MSMC architecture. In MTS, when all the cores in a socket are free, the head core of the socket steals a batch of tasks from other sockets. However, MTS cannot ensure tasks executed by cores in the same socket have shared data, and thus cannot reduce shared cache misses in MSMC. In [5], CONTROLLED-PDF was proposed to reduce cache misses in single-socket multi-core architecture. The scheduler divided nodes of a DAG into *L2-supernodes* that contain data fit for the shared L2 cache. By executing L2-supernodes sequentially, the cache misses can be reduced. The scheduler needed users to provide space complexity function of the executed program and was only applicable to single-socket multi-core architecture. Also the paper did not evaluate the proposed scheduler through experiments. In [28], another task scheduler is proposed to improve the cache performance for single-socket multi-core architectures. The scheduler needs users to provide working set size of tasks. However, CATS obtains the required information automatically. In [27], a less reused cache filter was proposed to filter out the less reused data so that the frequently reused data can stay in the cache.

Based on page-coloring, many works enable programmers

to manage shared cache explicitly. In [23], a cache partitioning method was proposed. Based on the method, a cache control tool is implemented so that users can control the partitioning of cache. In [13], ULCC was proposed to explicitly manage and optimize last level cache usage by allocating proper cache space for different data sets of different threads. Although programmers may improve their programs by managing last level cache , the management is burdensome for programmers. In contrast, CATS can improve the last level cache (L3) performance of memory-bound applications automatically without extra user-provided information.

Task-stealing is popular for automatic load balancing inside parallel applications due to its high performance. Many works have been done on its improvement [21, 18].

There are also some works aiming to reduce cache misses in task-stealing on parallel architectures. In [1], a theoretical bound on the number of cache misses for random task-stealing was presented and a locality-guided task-stealing algorithm was implemented on a single-socket SMP. In [12], the authors analyzed the cache misses of algorithms using random task-stealing, focusing on the effects of false sharing. In [11], cache behaviors of task-stealing and a parallel depth-first scheduler were compared and analyzed. It was proposed to promote constructive cache sharing through controlling task granularity. However, the above studies did not take the MSMC architecture into consideration, and thus did not target the reduction of shared cache misses as CATS does.

In [24], PWS (Probability Work-Stealing) and HWS (Hierarchical Work-Stealing) were proposed to reduce communications among different computers for hierarchical distributed platform. In PWS, processors had higher probability to steal tasks from processors in the same computer. HWS used a rigid boundary level to divide tasks into global tasks and local tasks which are similar to inter-socket tasks and intra-socket tasks in CATS. However, the boundary level in HWS must be given by users manually. It is also worth noting that PWS and HWS were proposed for reduction of communications in distributed environments.

In [10], a task-stealing scheduler, called CAB, is proposed to reduce shared cache misses in MSMC. Similar to HWS, CAB used a rigid boundary level to divide tasks into global tasks and local tasks. Though the boundary level is calculated at run-time, users have to provide a number of command line arguments for the scheduler to calculate the boundary level. If the arguments are not correct, the performance of applications may degrade seriously. In addition, CAB is not as adaptive as CATS since it cannot work with irregular and unbalanced execution DAGs that CATS works with.

6. CONCLUSIONS

The traditional task-stealing algorithm steals tasks randomly from other cores. Although the random stealing works efficiently in a multi-core processor, it tends to pollute the shared caches in MSMC architectures. To solve the problem, we have designed and implemented the CATS scheduler that reduces cache misses but requires no extra user-provided information. By profiling a parallel program at its first iteration, CATS uses an online DAG partitioner to automatically divide the execution DAG into inter-socket tier and intra-socket tier. Scheduling tasks of an intra-socket subtree within the same socket, CATS can reduce the shared cache misses significantly. Experimental results show that CATS can achieve up to 74.4% performance gain for memory-bound applications compared with random task-stealing. The extra overhead of CATS for CPU-bound applications is negligible.

One future research direction is to improve CATS for more complex architectures such as NUMA and cc-NUMA architectures. Another interesting future work is to explore task-stealing in asymmetric architectures and to design a task-stealing scheduler to allocate tasks with different features onto different asymmetric cores optimally in order to better utilize the system resources.

Acknowledgment

This work was partially supported by Shanghai Excellent Academic Leaders Plan(No. 11XD1402900), 863 program 2011AA01A202, NSFC (Grant No. 60725208, 61003012) and National Science Fund for Distinguished Young Scholars with Grant Nos. 61028005.

7. REFERENCES

[1] U. Acar, G. Blelloch, and R. Blumofe. The data locality of work stealing. *Theory of Computing Systems*, 35(3):321–347, 2002.

[2] E. Ayguadé, N. Copty, A. Duran, J. Hoeflinger, Y. Lin, F. Massaioli, X. Teruel, P. Unnikrishnan, and G. Zhang. The design of openmp tasks. *IEEE Transactions on Parallel and Distributed Systems*, 20(3):404–418, 2009.

[3] R. Azimi, M. Stumm, and R. Wisniewski. Online performance analysis by statistical sampling of microprocessor performance counters. In *ICS'05*, pages 101–110. ACM, 2005.

[4] M. Berger and J. Oliger. Adaptive mesh refinement for hyperbolic partial differential equations. *Journal of computational Physics*, 53(3):484–512, 1984.

[5] G. Blelloch, R. Chowdhury, P. Gibbons, V. Ramachandran, S. Chen, and M. Kozuch. Provably good multicore cache performance for divide-and-conquer algorithms. In *SODA'08*, pages 501–510. Society for Industrial and Applied Mathematics, 2008.

[6] G. Blelloch, J. Fineman, P. Gibbons, and H. V. Simhadri. Scheduling irregular parallel computations on hierarchical caches. In *SPAA'11*, San Jose, California, June 2011.

[7] R. D. Blumofe, C. F. Joerg, B. C. Kuszmaul, C. E. Leiserson, K. H. Randall, and Y. Zhou. Cilk: An efficient multithreaded runtime system. *Journal of Parallel and Distributed computing*, 37(1):55–69, Aug. 1996.

[8] D. Butenhof. *Programming with POSIX threads*. Addison-Wesley Longman Publishing Co., Inc. Boston, MA, USA, 1997.

[9] Q. Chen, Y. Chen, Z. Huang, and M. Guo. WATS: Workload-Aware Task Scheduling in Asymmetric Multi-core Architectures. In *IPDPS'12*. IEEE, 2012.

[10] Q. Chen, Z. Huang, M. Guo, and J. Zhou. CAB: Cache-aware Bi-tier task-stealing in Multi-socket Multi-core architecture. In *ICPP'11*, Taipei, Taiwan, 2011. IEEE.

[11] S. Chen, P. Gibbons, M. Kozuch, V. Liaskovitis, A. Ailamaki, G. Blelloch, B. Falsafi, L. Fix, N. Hardavellas, T. Mowry, et al. Scheduling threads for constructive cache sharing on CMPs. In *SPAA'07*, page 115. ACM, 2007.

[12] R. Cole and V. Ramachandran. Analysis of Randomized Work Stealing with False Sharing. *ArXiv e-prints*, Mar. 2011.

[13] X. Ding, K. Wang, and X. Zhang. ULCC: a user-level facility for optimizing shared cache performance on multicores. In *PPoPP'11*, pages 103–112, 2011.

[14] M. Frigo, C. E. Leiserson, and K. H. Randall. The implementation of the Cilk-5 multithreaded language. In *PLDI'98*, pages 212–223, Montreal, Canada, June 1998. ACM.

[15] A. Gerasoulis and T. Yang. A comparison of clustering heuristics for scheduling directed acyclic graphs on multiprocessors. *Journal of Parallel and Distributed Computing*, 16(4):276–291, 1992.

[16] W. Gropp, E. Lusk, and A. Skjellum. *Using MPI: portable parallel programming with the message passing interface*. MIT Press, 1999.

[17] Y. Guo, R. Barik, R. Raman, and V. Sarkar. Work-first and help-first scheduling policies for async-finish task parallelism. In *IPDPS'09*, pages 1–12. IEEE, 2009.

[18] Y. Guo, J. Zhao, V. Cave, and V. Sarkar. Slaw: a scalable locality-aware adaptive work–stealing scheduler. In *IPDPS'10*, 2010.

[19] J. Lee and J. Palsberg. Featherweight X10: a core calculus for async-finish parallelism. In *PPoPP'10*, pages 25–36. ACM, 2010.

[20] C. Leiserson. The Cilk++ concurrency platform. In *DAC'09*, pages 522–527. ACM, 2009.

[21] M. M. Michael, M. T. Vechev, and V. A. Saraswat. Idempotent work stealing. In *PPoPP'09*, pages 45–54. ACM, 2009.

[22] S. L. Olivier, A. K. Porterfield, K. B. Wheeler, and J. F. Prins. Scheduling task parallelism on multi-socket multicore systems. In *ROSS'11*, pages 49–56. ACM, 2011.

[23] S. Perarnau, M. Tchiboukdjian, and G. Huard. Controlling cache utilization of hpc applications. In *ICS'11*, pages 295–304. ACM, 2011.

[24] J.-N. Quintin and F. Wagner. Hierarchical work-stealing. In *EuroPar'10*, pages 217–229. Springer-Verlag, 2010.

[25] J. Reinders. *Intel threading building blocks*. O'Reilly, 2007.

[26] D. Tam, R. Azimi, L. Soares, and M. Stumm. Rapidmrc: Approximating l2 miss rate curves on commodity systems for online optimizations. *ACM Sigplan Notices*, 44(3):121–132, 2009.

[27] L. Xiang, T. Chen, Q. Shi, and W. Hu. Less reused filter: improving l2 cache performance via filtering less reused lines. In *ICS'09*, pages 68–79. ACM, 2009.

[28] T. Yang, C. Lin, and C. Yang. Cache-aware task scheduling on multi-core architecture. In *VLSI-DAT'10*, pages 139–142. IEEE, 2010.

[29] J. Zhang, Z. Huang, W. Chen, Q. Huang, and W. Zheng. Maotai: View-Oriented Parallel Programming on CMT processors. In *ICPP'08*, pages 636–643. IEEE, 2008.

CRQ-based Fair Scheduling on Composable Multicore Architectures

Tao Sun, Hong An, Tao Wang, Haibo Zhang
School of Computer Science and Technology
University of Science and Technology of China
Hefei, 230027, China
suntaos@mail.ustc.edu.cn, han@ustc.edu.cn,
{tao36, kopcarl}@ mail.ustc.edu.cn

Xiufeng Sui
Advanced Computer Systems Laboratory
Institute of Computing Technology
Chinese Academy of Sciences
Beijing, 100190, China
suixiufeng@ncic.ac.cn

ABSTRACT

As different workloads require different processor resources for better execution efficiency, recent work has proposed composable chip multiprocessors (CCMPs), which provide the capability to configure different number and types of processing cores at system runtime. However, such composable architecture poses a new significant challenge to system scheduler, that is, how to ensure priority-based performance for each task (i.e. fairness), while exploiting the benefits of composability by dynamically changing the hardware configurations to match the parallelism requirements in running tasks (i.e. resource allocation). Current multicore schedulers fail to address this problem, as they traditionally assume fixed number and types of cores.

In this work, we introduce centralized run queue (CRQ) and propose an efficiency-based algorithm to address the fair scheduling problem on CCMP. Firstly, instead of using distributed per-core run queues, this paper employs CRQ to simplify the scheduling and resource allocation decisions on CCMP, and proposes a pipeline-like scheduling mechanism to hide the large scheduling decision overhead on the centralized queue. Secondly, an efficiency-based dynamic priority (EDP) algorithm is proposed to keep fair scheduling on CCMP, which can not only provide homogenous tasks with performance proportional to their priorities, but also ensure equal-priority heterogeneous tasks to get equivalent performance slowdowns when running simultaneously. To evaluate our design, experimental studies are carried out to compare EDP on CCMP with several state-of-art fair schedulers on symmetric and asymmetric CMPs. Our simulation results demonstrate that, while providing good fairness, EDP on CCMP outperforms the best performing fair scheduler on fixed symmetric and asymmetric CMPs by as much as 11.8% in user-oriented performance, and by 12.5% in system throughput.

Categories and Subject Descriptors

C.1.3 [*Other Architecture Styles*] Adaptable Architectures;
D.4.1 [*Operating Systems*]: Process Management – Scheduling

General Terms

Design, Performance, Algorithms

Keywords

Composable Multicore, Fair Scheduling, Resource Allocation, Centralized Run Queue

1. INTRODUCTION

As a chip multiprocessor (CMP) will be at its most efficient when the types of processing cores match the granularities of parallelism in the tasks, recent research has proposed composable chip multiprocessors (CCMPs) [6, 8, 9, 12]. Instead of placing fixed heterogeneous cores at chip design time, CCMP consists of small homogenous *physical cores*, but provides *dynamic heterogeneity* [4,5] at runtime by aggregating different number of physical cores into different sized *logical cores*. This enables CCMP to adapt the processing resources as the workload mix or application parallelism requirements changed. Figure 1 shows a 16-physical core CCMP and its two possible dynamic configurations. For ease of description, we use the terminology *P-N* to refer to a logical core which is composed of N physical cores, and we say P-x and P-y at different *type* when x≠y. Typically, a logical core P-N will have N-times issue width, instruction window, and level-1 I/D cache capacity than P-1. The system software can dynamically configure different number and types of logical cores at runtime by calling the hardware primitives *create/free logical core*.

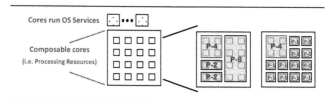

Figure 1. Example 16-physical core CCMP and its two dynamic configurations.

However, such composability poses a new challenge to system scheduling on CCMP. First, to gain the benefits of dynamic heterogeneity, the scheduler must decide logical core allocations, including (1) how many logical cores to be configured, (2) what type of each logical core should be, (3) when to create a new logical core or free an allocated logical core, and (4) when to resize logical core. Furthermore, in order to make the allocations more fitted to the characteristics of running workloads, the core-type requirements of *all* tasks should be known by the scheduler. But such global information is expensive to be collected upon distributed per-core run queues (DRQs), which are widely adopted by the schedulers on symmetric CMPs (SCMPs) and fixed asymmetric CMPs (ACMPs).

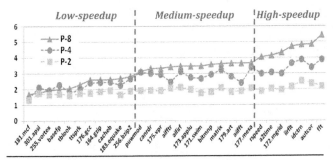

Figure 2. Speedups of different types of cores (P2/ P4/ P8) over P-1 running a subset of SPEC 2K and EEMBC applications. Some applications present super-linear speedup on P-2 mainly due to the larger L1 I/D cache.

Second, as Figure 2 shows, since different applications (or different phases in an application) probably run on different types of logical cores, and the speedup-gains also vary widely across different applications even on same core type, ensuring priority-based performance for each task (i.e. fairness) on CCMP becomes more challenging.

In this paper, we introduce centralized run queue (CRQ) and propose an efficiency-based algorithm to address these two problems. Firstly, instead of using DRQs, CRQ is employed to help the scheduler exploit the benefits of dynamic heterogeneity in a simple but effective way. Furthermore, this paper also proposes a pipeline-like scheduling mechanism to hide the large scheduling decision overhead on the centralized queue.

Secondly, since fairness is important in multiprogram system to avoid starvation and provide predictable per-task performance, an efficiency-based dynamic priority (EDP) algorithm is proposed to provide priority-based fair scheduling on CCMP. Here we define fairness in two features: it provides homogeneous tasks with performance proportional to their priorities; while it ensures equal-priority heterogeneous tasks to get equivalent performance slowdowns when running simultaneously, i.e. multi-program affects per-task performance equally if they have equal priorities. The basic idea of EDP fair scheduling is to keep each application running at similar execution efficiencies, and consume applications' time slices in different speeds depending on their core types.

Finally, to evaluate our design, a 32-physical core CCMP, a $8\times$(P-4) SCMP, and a $4\times$(P-4)$+8\times$(P-2) ACMP are modeled by a cycle-accurate composable multicore simulator (TFlex [6]) in the experiments. Besides EDP on CCMP, several state-of-art fair schedulers, CFS, O(1) sched., DWRR, are implemented on SCMP, while ADWRR is implemented on ACMP and CFS on CCMP. These schedulers are compared in scheduling fairness, user-oriented performance (metric *ANTT*) and system throughput (metric *WSU*) under several homogenous and heterogeneous workloads. Our evaluation results present that, while providing good priority-based fairness, EDP also gives the best performance among all the evaluated schedulers.

The contribution of this work is threefold:

1. This paper introduces CRQ to make the scheduling on CCMP simple but effective. Furthermore, a pipeline-like scheduling mechanism is proposed to hide the large scheduling decision overhead on CRQ. Most of existing scheduling algorithms (e.g. CFS) can be rebuilt on such scheduling mechanism with moderate modifications.

2. This paper proposes an EDP algorithm to provide fair scheduling on CCMP, and demonstrates that the disregarding of per-application's execution efficiency will cause unfair scheduling on

performance-asymmetric multicores, no matter if the heterogeneity is fixed or dynamic (shown by ADWRR results in Section 6.1).

3. This paper provides a comprehensive comparison across different multicore architectures (SCMP, ACMP and CCMP) under several state-of-art fair schedulers and EDP.

The rest of paper is organized as follows. Section 2 discusses the background and related work. Section 3 describes the CRQ-based scheduling and the pipeline-like scheduling mechanism on CCMP. Section 4 firstly describes an adapted algorithm to allocate *suitable core-type* for each task, then discusses how EDP scheduler can provide system-wide fairness. Section 5 discusses our experimental methodology, and Section 6 presents the evaluation results. Section 7 concludes and makes more discussions.

2. BACKGROUND AND RELATED WORK
2.1 Composable Multicore Architectures

Several composable CMPs (CCMPs) have been proposed recently, including Core Fusion [8], TFlex [6], Voltron [9], and WiDGET [12]. These CCMPs allow system software to dynamically form different number and types of (performance asymmetric) logical cores to gain better performance/power trade-off. Current CCMPs allow only single thread to run on each logical core each time (i.e. logical core does not support SMT), while multiple threads can run simultaneously on different logical cores.

The system software (e.g. scheduler) can reconfigure (i.e. create/free/resize) logical cores by using hardware primitives (*create/ free logical core*). Typically, different composable architectures have different implementations to support these primitives. Since this paper takes TFlex as our experimental platform, we make a short introduction on how the TFlex architecture supporting composability. More details of TFlex can be found in [6, 7].

ISA support. TFlex uses Explicit Data Graph Execution (EDGE) ISA, which employs block-atomic execution: the blocks execute and commit in control-flow, while the instructions within each block explicitly encode their consumers and execute in explicitly data-flow. The instructions in each block are interleaved across all participating physical cores of a logical core.

Microarchitectural support. To provide composability, TFlex shares no structures across cores. Each logical core's instruction window, register file, L1 I/D cache and branch predictor are all interleaved (addressed partitioned) over the participating physical cores. It relies on distributed microarchitectural protocols to provide the necessary instruction fetch, execution, memory access/ disambiguation, and commit capabilities. The hardware also implements a virtualization layer that keeps the distributed execution upon physical cores transparent to the thread on logical core.

As the states in register files, L1 caches, etc., are distributed (interleaved) over participating physical cores, these states must be flushed when reconfiguring (create/free/resize) logical core. The reconfiguration overhead is discussed in Section 3.4 in detail.

2.2 Scheduling on SCMP, ACMP and CCMP

On symmetric CMP (SCMP), the fair scheduling has been widely studied. O(1) scheduler [17] is adopted by Linux before 2.6.23, and completely fair scheduler (CFS) [14] is adopted by the latest Linux distributions. DWRR [15] is also proposed to provide proportional fairness on SCMP. These three algorithms are implemented in our experiments to give the reference of state-of-art fair schedulers on SCMP.

On fixed asymmetric CMP (ACMP), several works [2, 18, 19, 23] have proposed to consider applications' execution efficiencies (or speedup) in scheduling decision. This paper differs from these

Table 1. Comparison of several fair schedulers.

Architectures	SCMP			ACMP	CCMP
Fair Schd Alg.s	O(1)	CFS	DWRR	ADWRR	EDP
Task_Prio Aware?	Y	Y	Y	Y	Y
Processor Asymmetry?	N	N	N	Y	Y
Execution Efficiency?	N	N	N	N	Y online

works in two aspects. First, the method evaluating efficiency differs. HASS [18] obtains application's efficiency on different types of cores by using off-line architectural signatures, while CAMP [23] uses on-line last-level cache miss rates and Bias [2] employs CPI stack [21]. Our method is a little similar to the sampling-based way in [19], but the application does not need to run on all types of cores to find the *suitable core-type* (Section 4.1). Second, the works in [2, 18, 19, 23] aim to maximize the system throughput, the scheduling fairness is less concerned. But our scheduling algorithm, EDP, considers fairness in the first place.

ADWRR [1] is proposed to make fair scheduling on ACMP and it has shown good fairness on DVFS-modeled ACMP. In this paper, we model ACMP with microarchitectural heterogeneous cores, and implement ADWRR to give the reference of state-of-art fair scheduler on ACMP.

On composable CMP (CCMP), there are few works studying scheduling problem yet. Gulati et al. [7] extend EQUI and PDPA algorithm from [20] to assign core-types to applications on CCMP. But system-level scheduling is not supported in their work [7]. This paper further adapts the PDPA (performance driven procesor allocation) algorithm to find a *suitable core-type* for each application in each phase, and mainly study OS scheduling on CCMP.

Table 1 shows a comparison of the discussed fair schedulers by listing whether the scheduler considers the priorities of tasks, the performance-asymmetry of processors, and the execution efficiency of each application.

2.3 Many-core Operating System

As the many-core chip will contain 100s~1000s cores in near future, the design trend of operating system is replacing time-sharing with space-sharing for scalability. FOS [11] proposes to implement each system service (e.g. page allocator, process management, file system) in a parallel set of message passing *servers*, and bind each *server* to a distinct core. In this paper, we study the CCMP scheduling under the assumption of such an OS design framework and run OS scheduler on dedicated core.

3. CRQ-BASED SCHEDULING MECHANISM ON CCMP

3.1 Overview

Distributed per-core run queues (DRQs) are widely adopted by the schedulers on SCMP and ACMP, including the state-of-art fair schedulers, CFS [14], DWRR [15], and ADWRR[1]. However, as the scheduler on CCMP is demanded not only to make task scheduling, but also to manage the logical core allocations (listed in first column of Table 2), the information of the resource (i.e. core-type) requirements of *all* tasks is needed by the scheduler to make the allocations more fitted to the characteristics of running workloads. But such system-wide global information is expensive to be collected upon DRQs.

Instead, such information can be easily got if a centralized run queue (CRQ) is used. As illustrated in Figure 3, the scheduler can

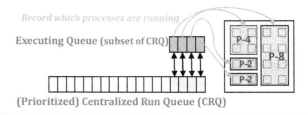

Record which processes are running

Executing Queue (subset of CRQ)

(Prioritized) Centralized Run Queue (CRQ)

Figure 3. Example prioritized CRQ, which can also be maintained as R-B tree in CFS.

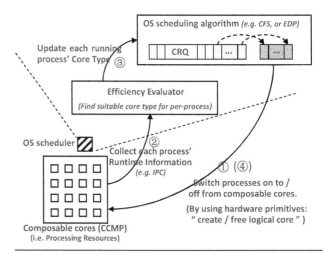

Figure 4. Overview of the scheduling procedure on CCMP.

also easily capture the changing number and types of logical cores by maintaining an additional executing queue, which is simply a subset of the CRQ but records the current running processes. Furthermore, the CRQ can also be implemented as the prioritized queue for fair scheduling.

Figure 4 presents an overview of the scheduling procedure on CCMP with CRQ. Each new process will be assigned the smallest core type (i.e. P-1) when created. At the beginning of every schedule-tick (e.g. 1ms), the OS scheduler collects the runtime information of each running process (shown by ②), evaluates the execution efficiencies (defined in Eq.2) and updates the core-types (shown by ③); then, the scheduler switches processes based on scheduling decision and puts the selected ones to run on composable cores by calling the hard-ware primitives "*create/free logical core*" (shown by ①&④). It is worth mentioning that in this procedure, only the OS scheduler can access the CRQ. A task's *execution efficiency* is calculated as:

$$Speedup_{P-N} = \frac{IPC_{P-N}}{IPC_{P-1}} \qquad \text{(Eq. 1)}$$

$$ExecutionEfficiency_{P-N} = \frac{Speedup_{P-N}}{N} \qquad \text{(Eq. 2)}$$

In this paper, we adapted a processor allocation algorithm [20] to find *suitable core-type* for each application in each phase. Here *suitable* means a good trade-off between task performance (e.g. IPC) and execution efficiency (details in Section 4.1). The scheduler takes these core-types as the resource requirements (i.e. core-type demands) of tasks. For example, if a process has core-type demand of P-2, this means the scheduler should allocate a P-2 core to run this process.

To show how CRQ can simplify the resource allocation decisions on CCMP, let's assume all processes in CRQ are tracked by two arrays, an *active* and an *expired* array. Only the processes in

Table 2. Logical core allocation decisions with CRQ.

Allocation Issues	Logical core allocation decisions with CRQ
What type of logical core to be configured?	The type equals to the *core-type demand* of the process to be running on it.
The *core-type demand* of each process?	Determined by evaluating application's execution efficiency. (This paper uses adapted PDPA algorithm to make such evaluation.)
How many logical cores to be configured?	Greedily assigning logical cores if there are runnable processes left in active array and enough idle physical cores to satisfy the core-type demands of the processes.
When to create a new logical core?	A process is selected to switch in. (A new logical cores is created to run it.)
When to free an allocated logical core?	The process which ran on it is selected to switch out.
When to resize a logical core?	The *core-type demand* of the process running on it changes.

active array can be selected to run, and the process will be moved to expired array once it uses up its time slice. When active array becomes empty, the pointers of active and expired array switch. Then, the scheduler can decide logical core allocation as Table 2 shows. A detail example of resource allocation and task scheduling on CCMP is shown in Figure 10 in Section 4.2.

Besides the above benefits, CRQ also brings larger scheduling decision overhead and the scalability issue [25]. Furthermore, as using the capability of reconfiguring logical core, a natural question is, whether (or how much) the performance will be lost due to logical core reconfigurations. In following subsections, we discuss and address these three issues, respectively.

3.2 Pipeline-like Scheduling Mechanism

Shown in previous Figure 4, OS services run on separate cores. This provides an opportunity to "pipeline" the OS scheduling decision with the processes running on composable cores. Such pipeline-like mechanism is based on two facts. First, since the processes' core types are unchanged between two adjacent OS schedule-ticks, once the scheduler finishes process-switching, it in fact accurately knows the core type of each running process in this schedule period and the remaining time slice after this period. Second, once scheduler finishes process-switching, the core running scheduler becomes idle.

Thus, as shown in Figure 5, while processes running on composable cores, the scheduler can correctly pre-calculate the dynamic priority (or key in CFS [14]) of each process, and pre-maintain the CRQ to be prioritized as the new-calculated priorities. When next schedule-tick arrives, since the CRQ has been properly pre-sorted, the scheduler only needs to update the core-types of processes that ran in last period, and then simply put processes one by one to composable cores from the head of CRQ (if process-switching happens), until there is no enough resources to form the demanded core-type. Therefore, the large scheduling decision overhead caused by the CRQ can be well hidden by such pipeline-like scheduling mechanism.

It is worth mentioning that most of existing scheduling algorithms, e.g. CFS [14], can be rebuilt on top of the pipeline-like scheduling mechanism with moderate modifications.

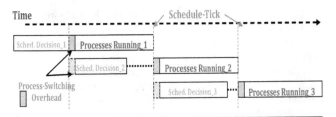

Figure 5. Pipeline-like scheduling mechanism. The scheduling decision overhead may vary but typically shorter than the period between two OS schedule-ticks.

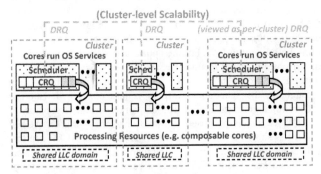

Figure 6. CRQ in each cluster and cluster-level scalability.

3.3 Scalability of using CRQ

This paper assumes that the future many-core OS will divide the cores into clusters and provide a set of OS services for each individual cluster in parallel [11]. Thus, the OS scheduling can be done at two levels: intra- and inter- clusters. In each cluster, the CRQ-based pipeline-like mechanism can be well used because of the limited number of cores (due to dividing). Between clusters, the CRQ in each cluster can be used as the per-cluster DRQ at cluster-level to support load balancing and cluster-level scalability. This idea is illustrated in Figure 6.

This paper focuses on the fair scheduling problem within one cluster under multiprogram environment. We leave the study of the scalability of CRQ-based scheduling under parallel workloads and between clusters for future work.

3.4 Performance Affected by Reconfiguration

The logical core reconfiguration happens in two situations: process-switching happens (*create/free* logical core), or the core-type demands of running processes change (*resize* logical core). The costs incurred in reconfiguration include two components: (1) **hard-costs** of saving register/TLB states to memory, configuring a new-sized logical core, and restoring register/TLB states from memory; (2) **soft-costs** of recreating branch predictor (BP) and L1 cache states on the new logical core.

Because the *soft-costs* not only occur in reconfiguration, but also occur in process-switching (no matter CMP is composable or not), we can show a worst case of losing performance due to logical core reconfiguration, by setting:

   • only one task runs in system, no process switching,

while • forcing to configure a new P-4 core every schedule-tick. For comparison, we also show the ideal performance, by setting:

   • the task runs on a static P-4 core, no process switching, and no reconfiguration.

Figure 7 shows the completion time of three applications under different system schedule-ticks. (Other applications appeared in Figure 2 share the similar results). The reconfiguration-caused

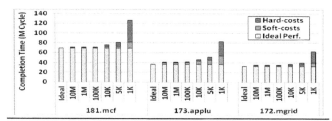

Figure 7. Performance loss caused by logical core reconfiguration. The reconfiguration costs is break down into *hard-* and *soft-* costs. *hard-costs* is roughly 550 cycles when reconfiguring one logical core.

performance loss is also broken down into *hard-* and *soft-* costs. We can see that, when schedule-tick is 1K cycles (i.e. reconfiguration happens every 1000 cycles), logical core reconfiguration causes large performance loss. However, when schedule-tick is longer than 1M cycles (i.e. 1ms when CMP runs at 1GHz), almost **no** performance loss is caused by the reconfiguration. The reason is that, the longer the schedule-tick is, the smaller number of reconfigurations happens (reducing *hard-costs*), and the *soft-costs* (of recreating BP/ L1 cache states) is more likely to be amortized. The work in [26] gives the similar concludes.

As the schedule-tick in a multi-program system is typically at milliseconds, this evaluation shows that the logical core reconfiguration actually affects overall performance slightly under common multi-program environments.

4. EDP FAIR SCHEDULING ON CCMP

This paper proposes an efficiency-based dynamic priority (EDP) algorithm to make fair scheduling on CCMP, which aims to provide homogeneous tasks with performance proportional to their priorities, as well as ensure equal-priority heterogeneous tasks to get equivalent performance slowdowns when running together.

EDP fair scheduling has two basic ideas: first, it keeps all tasks running at efficiencies around a given threshold (typically given by OS scheduler); second, it consumes tasks' time slices in different speeds depending on their core types, in order to ensure the tasks to get proportional amounts of processing resources to their priorities. Following two sections discuss the two ideas in detail.

4.1 Keep Tasks Running at Similar Efficiencies

The composability of CCMP allows system software to dynamically configure processing resources (i.e. physical cores) into different number and types of logical cores. This provides an opportunity to keep different applications running at similar efficiencies by assigning them different types of logical cores.

Figure 8 presents the speedups and efficiencies of three typically different applications running on different types of cores. We can see that, although each application commonly gets higher speedup at bigger core type, its execution efficiency continuously decreases. This suggests that if a system-wide efficiency threshold is given, different applications are able to achieve the threshold by running on different types of cores. E.g., *mcf* can reach the efficiency shown by the red line in Figure 8 when running on P-2, while *applu* on P-4 and *fft* on P-8.

As execution efficiency decreases when core type increases, in this paper we adapts a PDPA algorithm [20] to find the biggest core-type for each application (in each phase) when a system efficiency threshold is given. The basic idea of the adapted PDPA algorithm is "try". Every task begins at running on P-1, but it will try to run on bigger type of core next time as long as its efficiency on current core type is higher than the efficiency threshold.

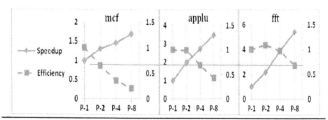

Figure 8. Speedup (left Y-axis) and execution **Efficiency (right Y-axis)** of different types of cores (P-1/P-2/P-4/P-8) running three applications. Figures are aligned in right Y-axis. The *fft* presents super-linear speedup on P-2 mainly due to the larger L1 I/D cache.

The adapted algorithm implements a state machine shown in Figure 9, which aims to find a STABLE state for each application in each phase. Then the *suitable core-type* is set to the core-type when application in STABLE state. If a phase-change is detected, the state will transfer from STABLE to JITTER and re-look for STABLE state in the new phase. Since program exhibits unstable and unique behavior during phase-change [27], the JITTER state is used to avoid sampling task's efficiency in these intervals.

In the algorithm, the given system efficiency threshold is taken as *target_eff*, while a *high_eff* is also introduced to avoid over-aggressive trying of bigger core-type, i.e. the task is prevented from trying bigger core-type if its efficiency below the *high_eff*.

The efficiency thresholds used in this paper are empirically determined by considering both the offline collected characteristics of workloads (i.e. speedups in Figure 2) and the system load status (i.e. number of runnable processes). The selection of the system efficiency threshold (i.e. *target_eff*) strikes a balance between giving each task higher performance by assigning core-type bigger (with lower *target_eff*), and letting more tasks run simultaneously by assigning core-type smaller (with higher *target_eff*). If the system load is

<=4,	*target_eff*=0.3 ,	*high_eff*=0.53
>4,<=8,	*target_eff*=0.53,	*high_eff*=0.8
>8,	*target_eff*=0.8,	*high_eff*=0.95

Although the efficiency thresholds are determined by the offline profiled data, the execution efficiency of each task is evaluated on-line. The evaluation state and other evaluation-assisted information (e.g. *last_speedup* shown in figure) are saved to process control blocks (PCBs) when switching processes. The state evaluations are only done for the processes that have run in last period. Further details of the original PDPA algorithm can be found in [20, 7].

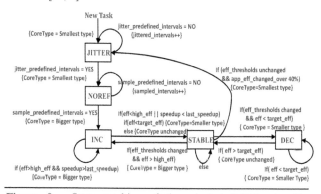

Figure 9. State machine of the adapted PDPA algorithm. The *jitter_predefined_intervals* / *sample_predefined_intervals* will be set to *True* if the evaluated task has stayed in JITTER / NOREF state for pre-defined (1 in this paper) intervals.

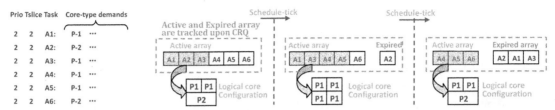

(a) All processes (A1~A6) have same priority and unchanged core-type demands. The running processes are shown in green.

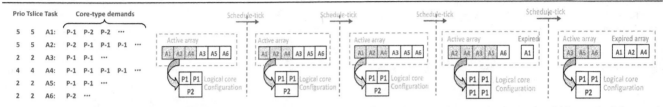

(b) Processes have different priorities and core-type demands. Leftmost table list each process' core-type demands within a *schedule round*.

Figure 10. Example the EDP scheduling on six processes (A1~A6). In both examples, we show every interval within a *schedule round*. For simplicity, time slice (Tslice) is equal to priority value (Prio), and the bigger Prio means higher priority in examples.

4.2 EDP Algorithm

As shown in Figure 8, the speedup-gains vary widely across different applications. Thus, we argue that the fair scheduling on CCMP must consider per-task's execution efficiency (recall Eq.2). Based on this idea, the EDP algorithm takes the cores' heterogeneity (i.e. core types), the tasks' priorities and the tasks' execution efficiencies all into scheduling decision.

EDP keeps track of all runnable processes in CRQ by two arrays, an active array and an expired array, like O(1) scheduler [17] does. Let's say a new *schedule round* begins when the pointers of expired and active array switched, i.e. the active array in last round becomes the expired array in current round and vice versa.

```
FUNCTION EDP_scheduling
1. halt_all_logical_cores( );
//update and save all processes ran in last interval
2. for each p_switch_out in executing_queue do
      2.1 type = evaluate_core_type_demand(p_switch_out);
      2.2 update_core_type_demand(p_switch_out, type);
      2.3 save_context(p_switch_out);
      2.4 free_logical_core(p_switch_out);
3. executing_queue.Clear( );
4. remain_resources = TOTAL_RESOURCES;
5. p_switch_in = active_array.Head( );
6. core_type_demand = p_switch_in.core_type_demand;
//select process from the head of active array to run
7. while ( p_switch_in != NULL
            and remain_resources >= core_type_demand) do
      7.1 lcid = create_logical_core(core_type_demand);
      7.2 load_context(p_switch_in, lcid);
      7.3 remain_resources -= core_type_demand;
      7.4 executing_queue.Enqueue(p_switch_in);
      7.5 p_switch_in = active_array.Next( );
      7.6 core_type_demand = p_switch_in.core_type_demand;
//process-switching and logical core reconfiguring done
8. continue_all_logical_cores( );
//utilize the pipeline_like scheduling mechanism in Sec 3.2
9. pre_maintain_active_and_expired_array_for_next_sched(CRQ);   // O(n)

FUNCTION pre_maintain_active_and_expired_array_for_next_sched(CRQ)
1. for each task in executing_queue do
      1.1 pre_calculate_dynamic_priority(task);
      1.2 re_sort_task_in_active_array(task);
      1.3 task.time_slice -= task.core_type_demand;
      1.4 if (task.time_slice <= 0) do
            1.4.1 task.time_slice += initial_time_slice(task.static_prio);
            1.4.2 move_from_active_and_insert_to_expired_array(task);
2. if(active_array.Size()<PRE_DEFINE_NUMBER and expired_array.Nonempty())do
      2.1 for each actask in active_array do
            2.1.1 actask.time_slice += initial_time_slice(task.static_prio);
            2.1.2 promote_dynamic_priority(actask);
            2.1.3 move_from_active_and_insert_to_expired_array(actask);
      2.2 switch_active_and_expired_array(&active_array, &expired_array);
```

Steps 1~8 are marked O(1); step 9 is marked // O(n).

Figure 11. Pseudo-code of EDP scheduling algorithm (upon CRQ).

Figure 11 presents the pseudo-code of EDP scheduling algorithm upon CRQ. Since the maximum number of logical cores is always less than the number of physical cores on chip (which is a constant), the *step 1~8* in algorithm have *O(1)* time-complexity. As maintaining CRQ to be prioritized may cause the traversal on whole queue in worst case, *step 9* takes *O(n)* time-complexity (*n* is the number of all runnable tasks). However, the overhead of *step 9* can actually be moved from system critical path by using the pipeline-like scheduling mechanism proposed in Section 3.2.

More detail, EDP schedules processes with following features:

① It uses the same algorithm as O(1) scheduler [17] to give each process a dynamic priority to avoid starvation. But it does not give any additional time slice when promoting the dynamic priority of one waiting process.

② It always selects to execute the processes in active array with higher dynamic priorities, and schedules the equal dynamic priority processes as first-in-first-out order in each round.

③ It assigns each process proportional amount of time slice according to its static priority (100~139).

④ It assigns each process different speed to consume its time slice, depending on its core type. For example, when a process runs on P-4, its time slice is reduced by 4 after one schedule-tick. Such a scheduling decision ensures equal-priority tasks to get equivalent amounts of processing resources. This idea is similar to scaled-CPU-time in ADWRR [1].

⑤ When a process uses up its time slice in this round, EDP will reset its time slice and move it from active array to expired array.

⑥ To avoid wasting of processing resources, when there are less than a pre-defined number (4 in this work) of processes in active array but the expired array is nonempty, EDP will add each remaining process in active array with its time slice in new round, promote its dynamic priority (10 in this work), and move it to expired array. Then the active and expired array are switched and new schedule round begins. This method may cause unfairness in each round, but fairness can be maintained among several rounds.

Figure 10 shows two examples of EDP scheduling six processes (A1-A6) on a 4-physical core CCMP. For simplicity, in examples we assume the time slice assigned to process equal to its priority value, and assume the bigger value means higher priority. In Figure 10 (a), all the six processes have the same priority, and their core-type demands are never changed during execution.

Table 3. The parameters of TFlex single physical core and shared L2 cache

Single Physical-Core parameters	
Instruction Supply	L1 I-cache (8KB, 1-cycle hit); Local/Gshare Tournament predictor (8K+256 bits, 3 cycle), Local: 64(L1) + 128(L2), Global: 512, Choice: 512, RAS: 16, CTB: 16, BTB:128, Btype: 256.
Execution	Out-of-order execution; RAM structured 128-entry issue window; dual-issue; INT-ALU: 2. FP-ALU: 1.
Data Supply	L1 D-cache (8KB, 2-cycle hit, 2-way set-associative, 1-read port and 1-write port); 44-entry LSQ bank.
Shared L2-Cache parameters Decoupled Static-NUCA; 4MB capacity, 8-way set-associative, 64B cache line, LRU-replacement; Hit latency varies 5 ~ 27 cycles depending on memory address; average main memory latency is 150 cycles.	

Table 4. Platforms and scheduling algorithms

Platforms	SCMP	ACMP	CCMP
Platform Configuration	8×(P-4)	4×(P-4) +8×(P-2)	32 physical core
Scheduling Algorithms	CFS O(1) schd DWRR	ADWRR	CFS EDP

Table 5. Workload Construction. Each line presents a workload and its components, and the second column gives it an ID.

Fairness Evaluation	wkld ID	Workload Construction	Low speedup (L)			Medium speedup (M)			High speedup (H)		
			mcf	tblook	cacheb	canrdr	applu	matrix	rspeed	mgrid	fft
Homo. Tasks (same prio)	w1	30L	-	30	-	-	-	-	-	-	-
	w2	30M	-	-	-	30	-	-	-	-	-
	w3	30H	-	-	-	-	-	-	-	-	30
Homo. Tasks (diff. prio)	w4	30L (15+15)	-	30	-	-	-	-	-	-	-
	w5	30M (15+15)	-	-	-	30	-	-	-	-	-
	w6	30H (15+15)	-	-	-	-	-	-	-	-	30
Heter. Tasks (same prio)	w7	15L+15M	3	6	6	6	3	6	-	-	-
	w8	15L+15H	3	6	6	-	-	-	6	3	6
	w9	15M+15H	-	-	-	6	3	6	6	3	6
	w10	10L+10M+10H	2	4	4	4	2	4	4	2	4

In Figure 10 (b), processes have different priorities while their core-type demands are also changing. We can see that, EDP is able to schedule each process running at its demanded core-type, while ensure the processes receiving proportional amounts of physical cores to their priorities.

5. EXPERIMENTAL METHODOLOGY

5.1 Modeling SCMP, ACMP and CCMP

In experiments, we use an execution-driven, cycle-accurate composable multicore simulator, TFlex [6], to model SCMP, ACMP and CCMP with equal amounts of processing resources (i.e. total 32 physical cores). Table 3 lists the microarchitectural parameters of a single physical core and the shared L2 cache. The parameters are kept same as in [6].

Table 4 lists the modeled CMPs: SCMP is modeled as 8 symmetric P-4 cores; ACMP is modeled as 4 big cores (P-4) plus 8 small cores (P-2); and CCMP is modeled as 32 physical cores. It is worth mentioning that the P-4 logical core has the similar performance as Power4 processor core [10].

Four types (P-1/P-2/P-4/P-8) of logical cores can be formed dynamically. Since we believe the number of cores on future ACMP will be comparable to (less than but not much less than) CCMP if they have equal amounts of processing resources, the maximum number of logical cores in CCMP is also limited to 16, which is matchable to the number of cores in ACMP (12).

5.2 Reconfiguring and Scheduling Overheads

The overheads of logical core reconfiguration and process-switching are all counted in final results. An analysis on reconfiguration overhead can be found in Section 3.4. Since the pipeline-like scheduling mechanism is able to hide the scheduling decision overhead in CCMP system, to further analyze the benefits of EDP fair scheduling, our experiments also do not count the decision overheads of schedulers on SCMP and ACMP.

To faithfully keep TFlex architecture designs unchanged, this work takes a conservative assumption on reconfiguring logical cores: when any logical core needed to be created, freed, or resized, all logical cores are halted. Then the necessary logical core reconfigurations are done serially. The processes can continue to execute until all logical cores finish reconfiguring.

Table 4 presents the scheduling algorithms implemented in the experiments. To study the importance of efficiency awareness for fair scheduling on composable multicore, CFS algorithm is also implemented on CCMP. The interval of time slice in O(1) scheduler and EDP is remapped ranging from 4 to 16, while DWRR and ADWRR keep the 4-level weights. All schedulers are triggered by the cycle interruption at period of 0.5M cycles (i.e. schedule-tick is 0.5M cycles). The sensitivity of schedulers to tick lengths is studied in work [16].

5.3 Workload Construction

We classified the applications from a subset of SPEC 2K and EEMBC (shown in previous Figure 2) into three classes, low (L), medium (M) and high (H) speedup applications. Three typical applications are then selected from each class to construct workloads. Some applications like *mcf* and *applu* are memory-bounded [18, 19], while some applications like *rspeed* and *fft* are CPU-intensive [7]. The *simpoint* tool [22] is used for SEPC applications, and each task is chosen to be the length of 100M cycles of an application running on P-1.

Table 5 presents the ten workloads used in our experiments. Each line presents the components of each workload, and the workload ID is shown in second column. (There are less SPEC tasks in W7~W10 because our simulator uses checkpoint to load machine states at each *simpoint* [22], but this will cause simulator memory overflow when more than ten SPEC applications being loaded simultaneously).

Workloads 1~3 are homogenous and each consists of 30 copies of a task with same priority (120). Each of workloads 4~6 also consists of 30 homogeneous task but half of them have high priority (100) while the other have low priority (120). These six workloads are used to evaluate proportional fairness. Workloads 7~10

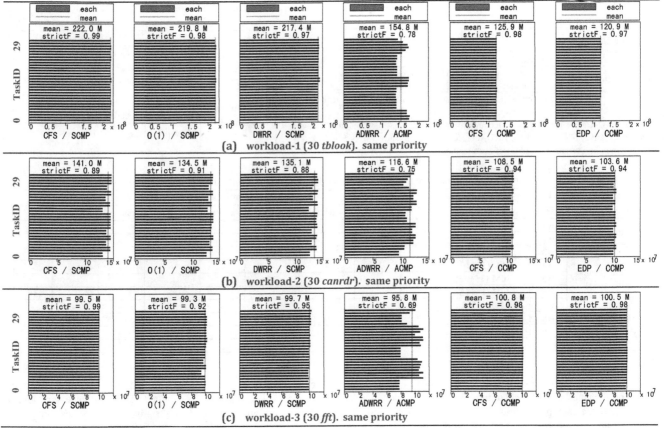

Figure 12. Fairness evaluation under homogenous workloads (1~3). All tasks have same priority (120).

are heterogeneous but with equal priority (120), which are used to evaluate if the schedulers can ensure equivalent performance slowdowns for equal-priority tasks.

5.4 Evaluation Methodology and Metrics

In experiments, all the 30 tasks in each workload become runnable at the same time. Whenever a process exits, a new one is started to keep the co-execution environment unchanged.

Fairness evaluation. Besides showing the completion time of each of 30 evaluated tasks, *StrictFairness* [24] is also used in this work to quantify the scheduling fairness, which defined as:

$$StrictF = \frac{\min_i RelativePerf_i}{\max_i RelativePerf_i} \overset{\text{(this paper)}}{=\joinrel=} \frac{CompletionTime_{best}}{CompletionTime_{worst}} \quad (\text{Eq. 3})$$

The $RelativePerf_i$ is the ratio of task's completion time when running under multiprogram mode and running alone.

StrictF measures the maximum deviation between the best and worst task performance under multiprogram mode. It is a value between 0 (completely unfair) and 1 (completely fair).

For evaluating user-oriented performance, we use the metric *average normalized turnaround time (ANTT)* proposed in [3]. Typically, a multiprogram system with *ANTT* of X means the application runs X-times slower than it running alone on average. Thus, *ANTT* is a lower-is-better metric.

For evaluating system-oriented performance, we use *weighted speedup (WSU)* [3, 24] as the metric. *WSU* is a higher-is-better metric.

ANTT and *WSU* are calculated as in Eq. 4, where C_i^{SP} and C_i^{MP} denote the cycles to execute program *i* alone on P-4 and under multiprogram mode, respectively.

$$ANTT = \frac{1}{n}\sum_{i=1}^{n}\frac{C_i^{MP}}{C_i^{SP}}, \quad WSU = \sum_{i=1}^{n}\frac{C_i^{SP}}{C_i^{MP}} \quad (\text{Eq. 4})$$

6. EXPERIMETAL RESULTS
6.1 Fairness Evaluation under Homo. Wklds

In this section, we evaluate if the schedulers can ensure priority-based fairness for homogenous tasks. Figure 12 shows the completion time of each task in workloads 1 ~ 3 under different schedulers. The 30 evaluated tasks in each workload will get the same completion time if an ideal fair scheduler is used. The red lines in figures give the average completion time (i.e. *mean*).

We can see that CFS, O(1), DWRR on SCMP, and CFS, EDP on CCMP are all able to provide good fairness under homogenous workloads (i.e. all tasks completed at almost same time). Furthermore, EDP gives the best (min) average completion time.

In Figure 12 (b), we can also find that the completion time of tasks (*canrdr*) are relatively instable under CFS etc. schedulers on SCMP. In fact, CFS did give the equal chance for each task to execute, but we found that some of tasks (e.g. task# 0) experienced unequal execution progress by occupying relatively more shared L2 cache resource (shown by less L2 miss rates, not list here). Such effect is weakened under EDP (on CCMP) because the *canrdr* finds its *suitable core-type* as P-2 and then more tasks are able to run simultaneously.

Table 6 shows the average completion time of tasks in homogenous workloads (4~6) in different priorities. The high-priority is set to 100 while low-priority is 120. This means the performance of high-priority task will be twice as low-priority task if an ideal fair scheduler is used. We can see that EDP is able to keep almost precise 2:1 performance depending on tasks' priorities.

Table 6. Fairness evaluation under homogenous workloads (4~6). Half of tasks have *low_prio* (120), the other have *high_prio* (100). For each workload, *Mean* completion time of *low/ high_prio* tasks are listed.

Metric	*Low_prio* **Mean** (million cycles)						*High_prio* **Mean** (million cycles)					
Scheduler \ Platform	SCMP			ACMP	CCMP		SCMP			ACMP	CCMP	
	CFS	O(1)	DWRR	ADWRR	CFS	EDP	CFS	O(1)	DWRR	ADWRR	CFS	EDP
workload-4 (*tblook, L/H_prio*)	330.8	323.7	334.2	220.0	186.8	180.1	164.4	161.1	163.5	121.0	91.6	90.0
workload-5 (*canrdr, L/H_prio*)	210.2	198.7	212.1	168.8	161.3	153.7	102.5	97.3	102.0	91.2	78.4	77.7
workload-6 (*fft, L/H_prio*)	148.8	145.7	149.2	145.9	150.0	150.0	74.6	71.0	75.4	71.7	74.6	74.0

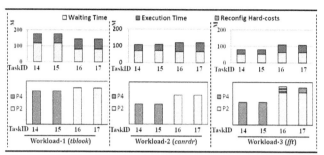

Figure 13. Runtime breakdown (shown in first row) of task#14~task#17 in workloads 1~3 under ADWRR scheduling. The second row shows the types of cores occupied by each task when executing. ("*Reconfig Hard-costs*" is too small to see).

Figure 12 also shows that ADWRR fails in keeping fairness on the microarchitectural heterogeneous ACMP modeled in this work, where different applications typically have different speedups (efficiencies) on same bigger core. ADWRR assumes uniform speedup for different applications, which is approximately true on DVFS-modeled ACMP, but causes unfairness when cores have different microarchitectures.

We show this in detail by breaking down the run-time of task#14 ~ task#17 in each workload 1~3. Figure 13 shows the breakdown and the core types occupied by each task when executing. ADWRR uniformly reduces the time slices by 3 when tasks running on P-4 and by 2 on P-2. So under workload-1 (*tblook*), tasks 14~15 (running on P-4) complete later than tasks 16~17 (on P-2) because of their low-speedup character, where tasks on P-4 get only 1.9x speedup by consuming 3 units in their time slices, while tasks on P-2 can get 1.6x speedup by consuming just 2 units. In contrary, tasks 14~15 (on P-4) in workload-3 (*fft*) complete earlier because of their high-speedup character, where they can get 3.73x speedup on P-4 by consuming just 3 units in time slices. These experimental results demonstrate that the execution efficiency (speedup) of each task must be considered by a fair scheduler on generous ACMP.

It is a little surprising that CFS on CCMP also keeps good fairness under workloads 1~6, although it does not consider per-task's efficiency. The reason is that the tasks in each workload (1~6) are homogeneous and will find the same *suitable core-type*, thus they in fact share the same efficiency. However, in next section we can see that disregarding of per-task's efficiency will result in great unfairness when tasks are heterogeneous.

6.2 Fairness Evaluation under Heter. Wklds

In this section, heterogeneous workloads 7~10 are used to evaluate if the schedulers can ensure equal-priority tasks to be affected equally under multi-programming. As discussed in Section 5.3, each task has the same execution time on P-1 (100M cycles), so they should also have similar completion time when running together if the scheduler provides the fairness described above.

Figure 14 presents the completion time of each task on CCMP under EDP and CFS schedulers, while run-time breakdowns are also shown in each bar. We can see that EDP is able to provide the demanded fairness to keep different tasks having similar completion time. Since EDP provides equal-priority tasks with equal amounts of processing resources, it can balance a task's execution time and waiting time by assigning it different type of logical core. As time-breakdown shows, EDP gives low-speedup tasks (e.g. *mcf*) more chance to execute (shown by less waiting time), while scheduling the higher-speedup tasks (e.g. *fft*) to wait longer.

Figure 14 also presents that CFS on CCMP fails to provide fairness under heterogeneous workloads because of the lack of per-task execution efficiency. CFS gives higher-speedup tasks (e.g. *fft*) the same executing chances as low-speedup ones, which leads to unfairness because the higher-speedup tasks actually occupy more processing resources (higher-speedup task gets bigger *suitable core-type*). This results in higher-speedup tasks having both shorter execution time and waiting time.

The average completion time (i.e. *mean*) and *StrictF* of other schedulers are briefly listed in Figure 14. Sharing the same reason as CFS on CCMP, lack of considering per-task's efficiency leads to unfair scheduling under heterogeneous workloads.

In Figure 14, the EDP results also show that the homogenous tasks of some medium-speedup applications, e.g. *canrdr*, *matrix*, even *cacheb*, may have different execution time. This shares the same reason discussed in Section 6.1, as these applications are more sensitive in sharing L2 cache. This can lead the logical core allocation algorithm (in Section 4.1) selecting different *suitable core-types* for even homogeneous tasks, if the co-running environments are different when these evaluated tasks are in their evaluation states (e.g. NOREF state). Then the execution time of tasks varies as their *suitable core-type*s vary. We will further study this problem in future work.

6.3 Performance Evaluation

In this section, we evaluate both the user-oriented performance by metric *ANTT* and system-oriented performance by metric *WSU* across different schedulers. The metrics are discussed in Sec 5.4.

Workloads 4~6 are not used in performance evaluation, since it has no clear meaning to compare the performance under the workload mixed of high- and low- priority tasks with another workload which consists of only same-priority tasks.

Figure 15(a) shows the user-oriented performance results under different workloads (1~3 and 7~10). Y-axis shows the *ANTT* (lower-is-better). Because of the capability of maintaining good fairness, EDP gets the best performance in 6 of all seven cases. The only exception lies in workload-3 (*fft*), since *fft* selects P-4 as its *suitable core-type*, which provides higher speedup (3.73x) but lower efficiency (0.93) than P-2 (1.09). Then ADWRR on ACMP slightly wins although it is unfair. On average in *ANTT* evaluation, EDP on CCMP outperforms the best performing scheduler on SCMP by 26.2%, outperforms ADWRR on ACMP by 11.8%, and outperforms CFS on CCMP by 6.3%.

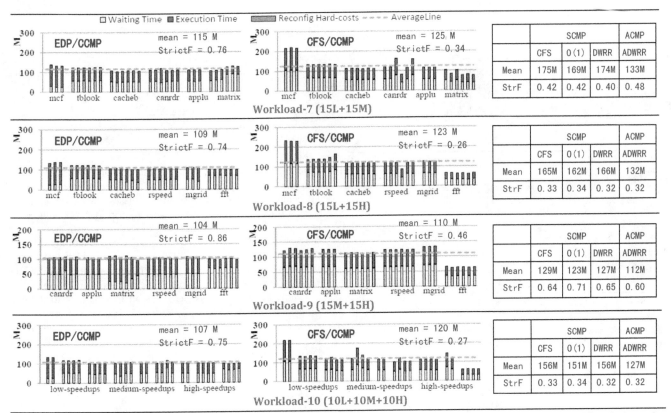

Figure 14. Fairness evaluation under heterogeneous workloads (7~10), comparing between EDP and CFS on CCMP. All tasks have the equal completion time on P-1. ("*Reconfig Hard-costs*" is too small to see in figure).

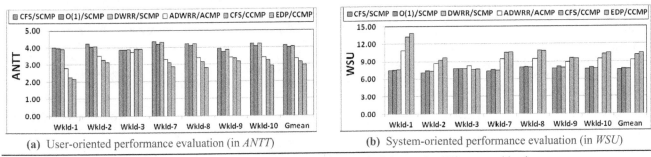

(a) User-oriented performance evaluation (in *ANTT*)　　　　**(b)** System-oriented performance evaluation (in *WSU*)

Figure 15. Performance evaluation across different schedulers under different workloads.

Figure 15(b) shows the system-oriented performance results, where Y-axis shows the *WSU* (higher-is-better). ADWRR wins in workload-3 with the same reason discussed previously, while EDP and CFS on CCMP wins in other 6 of seven cases due to the capability of keeping tasks running at higher execution efficiency (by reconfiguring logical cores). On average in *WSU* evaluation, EDP on CCMP outperforms the best performing scheduler on SCMP by 33.6%, outperforms ADWRR on ACMP by 12.5%, and outperforms CFS on CCMP by 3.4%.

6.4 Summarize Evaluation

Figure 16 summarizes the fairness and performance evaluation in this paper. To show the results more clearly, we show 1/*ANTT* instead of *ANTT* in the figure, as 1/*ANTT* becomes a higher-is-better metric as *WSU* and *StrictF*. Sharing the same reason discussed in Section 6.3, the *Gmean*s shown in figure are calculated using the results under workloads (1~3 and 7~10).

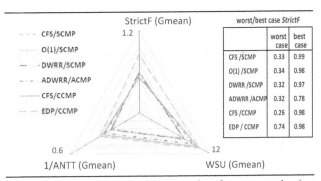

Figure 16. Summarizes the fairness and performance evaluation. we show 1/*ANTT* to keep all three axes are bigger-is-better.

Figure 16 also lists the worst-case and best-case *StrictF* of each scheduler under different workloads. We can see that EDP on CCMP provides much better worst-case *StrictF* than other evaluated schedulers. As shown by *Gmean*s, we can find that EDP on CCMP gives the best tradeoff in scheduling fairness, user-oriented performance and system-oriented performance among all the evaluated schedulers.

7. CONCLUSIONS AND FUTURE WORK

Emerging composable multicore architecture poses new scheduling challenge to operating system due to its capability of dynamic heterogeneity. To address the fair scheduling problem on CCMP, firstly, this paper introduced CRQ to simplify the scheduling and resource allocation decisions on CCMP, and proposed a pipeline-like scheduling mechanism to hide the large scheduling decision overhead on CRQ. Secondly, this paper proposed an efficiency-based dynamic priority (EDP) algorithm, which employs *suitable core-type* to provide priority-based fairness under homogeneous and heterogeneous workloads. In our experiments, several state-of-art fair schedulers were implemented on SCMP and ACMP to make a comprehensive comparison with EDP on CCMP. Our experimental results present that, while ensuring good priority-based fairness, EDP on CCMP outperforms the best performing fair scheduler on SCMP and ACMP by 11.8% in user-oriented performance (*ANTT*), and by 12.5% in system throughput (*WSU*).

We see two main areas of focus in future work. First, as discussed in Section 3.3, we assume that the future operating system will divide the CCMP physical cores into clusters and provide a set of OS services for each cluster in parallel. This paper focuses on the fair scheduling problem within one cluster under multi-program environment; we will study the scalability of the CRQ-based scheduling under parallel workloads and across clusters in future work.

Second, EDP scheduler in this paper does not consider the interaction between multiple programs on shared last level cache (LLC), but our experiments show that some medium-speedup applications (e.g. *canrdr*, *matrix*) are sensitive to cache sharing. In the future work, we will further study the online methods to detect program behavior more accurately under multi-program environment, by co-considering the programs' abnormal behaviors (if happened) in shared LLC.

8. ACKNOWLEDGMENTS

We thank Doug Burger, Aaron Smith and Yongqing Ren for their valuable suggestions and the help in experiments. We are also grateful to anonymous reviewers for their constructive comments. This work is financially supported by the NBR Program of China under contract 2011CB302501, the NNSF of China under grant 60970023, the NHRD Program of China under 2012AA010902 and 2012AA010901, and the NSTM Projects of China under contact 2009ZX01036-001-002 and 2011ZX01028-001-002-3.

9. REFERENCES

[1] T. Li, P. Brett, R. Knauerhase, D. Koufaty, D. Reddy, and S. Hahn. Operating system support for overlapping-ISA heterogeneous multi-core architectures. In *proc. of HPCA'10*, pages 1-12, Jan 2010.

[?] D. Koufaty, D. Reddy, S. Hahn. Bias scheduling in heterogenous multi-core architectures. *In EuroSys'10*, pages 125-138, 2010.

[3] S. Eyerman and L. Eeckhout. System-level performance metirc for multiprogram workloads. *IEEE Micro*, 28(3): 42-53, 2008.

[4] F. A. Bower, D. J. Sorin, and L. P. Cox. The impact of dynamically heterogeneous multicore processors on thread scheduling. *IEEE Micro*, 28(3):17–25, 2008.

[5] P. Wells, K. Chakraborty, G. S. Sohi. Dynamic heterogeneity and the need for multicore virtualization. *ACM OS Rev.* 43(2):5-14, 2009.

[6] C. Kim, S. Sethumadhavan, M. Govindan, N. Ranganathan, D. Gulati, S. W. Keckler, and D. Burger. Composable lightweight processors. In *proc. of MICRO'07*, pages 281-294, Dec. 2007.

[7] D. Gulati, C. Kim, S. Sethumadhavan, S. W. Keckler, D. Burger. Multitasking workload scheduling on flexible-core chip multiprocessors. In *proc. of PACT'08*, pages 187-196, Oct. 2008.

[8] E. Ipek, M. Kirman, N. Kirman, and J. F. Martínez. Core fusion: accommodating software diversity in chip multiprocessors. In *proc. of ISCA'07*, pages 186–197, June 2007.

[9] H. Zhong, S. A. Lieberman, and S. A. Mahlke. Extending multicore architectures to exploit hybrid parallelism in single-thread applications. In *proc. of HPCA'07*, pages 25–36, Feb. 2007.

[10] M. S. Sibi, B. Robatmili, H. Esmaeilzadeh, B. Maher, D. Li, A. Smith, S. W. Keckler, and D. Burger. Scaling power and performance via processor composability. *Department of Computer Sciences TR-10-14, UT Austin*, 2010.

[11] D. Wentzlaff and A. Agarwal. Factored operating systems (fos): the case for a scalable operating system for multicores. *ACM SIGOPS OS Rev.* 43(2):76-85, 2009.

[12] Y. Watanabe, J. D. Davis, and D. A. Wood. WiDGET: Wisconsin Decoupled Grid Execution Tiles. In *proc. of ISCA'10*. June 2010.

[13] Y. Kwon, C. Kim, S. Maeng, J. Huh. Virtualizing performance asymmetric multi-core systems. In *proc. of ISCA*, p 45-56, June 2011.

[14] I. Molnar, "Modular Scheduler Core and Completely Fair Scheduler [CFS]," http://lwn.net/Articles/230501, 2008.

[15] T. Li, D. Baumberger, S. Hahn. Efficient and scalable multiprocessor fair scheduling using distributed weighted round-robin. In *proc. of PPoPP'09*, pages 65-74, Feb. 2009.

[16] T. Sun, H. An, Y. Ren, M. Mao, Y. Liu, M. Xu, and Q. Li. FACRA: Flexible-core Architecture Chip Resource Abstractor. In *Workshop on Prog. Models and App. for Multicores and Manycores*, Dec 2010.

[17] IBM Developer Works, Inside the linux scheduler, http://www.ibm.com/developerworks/linux/library/l-scheduler, 2006.

[18] D. Shelepov, J. C. Saez Alcaide, S. Jeffery, A. Fedorova, N. Perez, Z. F. Huang, S. Blagodurov, and V. Kumar. HASS: a scheduler for heterogeneous multicore systems. *ACM OS Rev. 43(2):66–75*, 2009.

[19] R. Kumar, D. M. Tullsen, P. Ranganathan, N. P. Jouppi, and K. Farkas. Single-ISA heterogeneous multicore architectures for multithreaded workload performance. In *proc. of ISCA*, June 2004.

[20] J. Corbalan, X. Martorell, and J. Labarta. Performance-driven processor allocation. *IEEE Transactions on Parallel and Distributed Systems*, 16(7):599–611, 2005.

[21] S. Eyerman, L. Eeckhout, T. Karkhanis, and J. E. Smith. A top-down approach to architecting CPI component performance counters. *IEEE Micro*, 27(1):84–93, 2007.

[22] T. Sherwood, E. Perelman, and B. Calder. Basic Block Distribution Analysis to Find Periodic Behavior and Simulation Points in Applications. In *proc. of PACT'01*, pages 3–14, 2001.

[23] J. C. Saez, M. Prieto, A. Fedorova, and S. Blagodurov. A comprehensive scheduler for asymmetric multicore systems. In *proc. of EuroSys'10*, pages 139–152, April 2010.

[24] H. Vandierendonck, and A. Seznec. Fairness metrics for multi-threaded processors. *IEEE Comp. Arch. Letter, issue 1.* 2011.

[25] S. P. Dandamudi. Reducing Run Queue Contention in Shared Memory Multiprocessors. *IEEE Computer, (30)3: 82-89*, 1997.

[26] J.A. Brown, L. Porter, and D.M. Tullsen. Fast thread migration via cache working set prediction. In *proc. of HPCA'11*, Feb 2011.

[27] J. Lau, S. Schoenmackers, and B. Calder. Transition Phase Classification and Prediction. In *proc. of HPCA'05*, pages 278-289, Feb 2005.

Quantifying the Effectiveness of Load Balance Algorithms *

Olga Pearce*†, Todd Gamblin†, Bronis R. de Supinski†,
Martin Schulz†, Nancy M. Amato*

*Department of Computer Science and Engineering, Texas A&M University, College Station, TX, USA
{olga,amato}@cse.tamu.edu
†Center for Applied Scientific Computing, Lawrence Livermore National Laboratory, Livermore, CA, USA
{olga,tgamblin,bronis,schulzm}@llnl.gov

ABSTRACT

Load balance is critical for performance in large parallel applications. An imbalance on today's fastest supercomputers can force hundreds of thousands of cores to idle, and on future exascale machines this cost will increase by over a factor of a thousand. Improving load balance requires a detailed understanding of the amount of computational load per process *and* an application's simulated domain, but no existing metrics sufficiently account for both factors. Current load balance mechanisms are often integrated into applications and make implicit assumptions about the load. Some strategies place the burden of providing accurate load information, including the decision on when to balance, on the application. Existing application-independent mechanisms simply measure the application load without any knowledge of application elements, which limits them to identifying imbalance without correcting it.

Our novel load model couples abstract application information with scalable measurements to derive accurate and actionable load metrics. Using these metrics, we develop a cost model for correcting load imbalance. Our model enables comparisons of the effectiveness of load balancing algorithms in any specific imbalance scenario. Our model correctly selects the algorithm that achieves the lowest runtime in up to 96% of the cases, and can achieve a 19% gain over selecting a single balancing algorithm for all cases.

Categories and Subject Descriptors

C.4 [**Performance of Systems**]: Performance attributes, Modeling techniques; I.6.8 [**Simulation and Modeling**]: Types of Simulation—*Parallel*; D.1.3 [**Programming Techniques**]: Concurrent Programming—*Parallel programming*

Keywords

load balance, performance, modeling, simulation, framework

*The research of Amato and Pearce supported in part by NSF awards CRI-0551685, CCF-0833199, CCF-0830753, IIS-096053, IIS-0917266, NSF/DNDO award 2008-DN-077-ARI018-02, by the DOE NNSA under the Predictive Science Academic Alliances Program, by grant DE-FC52-08NA28616, by THECB NHARP award 000512-0097-2009, and by Chevron, IBM, Intel, Oracle/Sun. Pearce supported in part by an NSF Graduate Research Fellowship and the Lawrence Scholar Program Fellowship.

1. INTRODUCTION

Optimizing high-performance physical simulations to run on ever-growing supercomputing hardware is challenging. Large modern parallel simulation codes use message passing frameworks such as MPI, and dynamic behavior can lead to imbalances in computational load among processors. On current machines with hundreds of thousands of processors, this cost can be enormous. Future machines will support even more parallelism and efficiently redistributing and balancing load will be critical for good performance.

Prior work has explored tools to measure large-scale computational load [12, 24] efficiently. These tools can provide insight into the source location that caused an imbalance [23] and into the distribution of the load, but this knowledge alone is insufficient to correct the load. Existing load metrics do not account for constraints on rebalancing imposed by application elements and their interaction. Applications may only be able to rebalance load by moving simulated entities between nearby processors. Because this requires knowledge of application elements, statistical metrics or ones based solely on MPI ranks cannot guide correction of the imbalance. Thus, many applications resort to custom load balancing schemes and build their own workload model to guide the assignment of work to processes. In these custom schemes, application developers estimate the costs of the computation, but their estimates typically only capture the developer's best guess and often do not correspond to the actual costs. As an alternative, applications can supply their workload model to partitioners [9, 19, 25], which leaves the burden of providing accurate load information, including the decision on when to balance, on the application.

Applications need information on both *when* and *how* to rebalance; the three load balancing steps are:

1. Evaluate the imbalance;
2. Decide how to balance if needed;
3. Redistribute work to correct the imbalance.

We address the first two requirements and derive complete information on how to perform the third; the application must be able to redistribute its work units as instructed by our framework (a requirement also imposed by partitioners [9, 19]). Our load model couples abstract application information with scalable load measurements. We derive actionable load metrics to evaluate the accuracy of the information. Our load model evaluates the cost of correcting load imbalance with specific load balancing algorithms. We use it to select the method that most efficiently balances a particular scenario. We demonstrate this methodology on two large-scale production applications that simulate molecular dynamics and dislocation dynamics. Overall, we make the following contributions:

- An application-independent load model that captures application load in terms of the application elements;

Algorithm 1 Using the Load Model *(Application code in Italics)*

Input. $G \leftarrow$ graph of work units and interactions
1: **for** timesteps **do**
2:    *execute application iteration*
3:    *send G to LB Framework*
4:    update Load Model based on iteration measurements and G
5:    use Cost Model for cost-benefit analysis of available LB algorithms
6:    **if** benefit of rebalancing > cost of rebalancing **then**
7:       provide selected LB algorithm with accurate input
8:       send instructions on how to rebalance to application
9:    **end if**
10:   **if** *instructed to rebalance* **then**
11:      *rebalance as directed by LB Framework*
12:   **end if**
13: **end for**

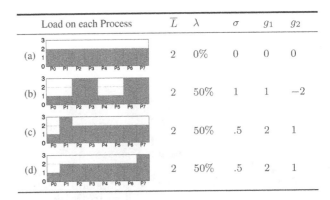

Table 1: Example Load Distributions and Their Moments

- Metrics to evaluate application-provided load models and to compare candidate application models;
- A methodology to evaluate load imbalance scenarios, and how efficiently particular load balance schemes correct it;
- A cost model to evaluate balancing mechanisms and to select the one most efficient for a particular imbalance scenario;
- An evaluation of load balance characteristics in the context of two large-scale production simulations.

We show that *ad hoc* application models can mispredict imbalance by up to 70% and the widely used ratio of maximum load to average load incompletely represents imbalance. Our models provide insight into the cost of algorithms such as diffusion [7] and partitioning [19]. Our model correctly selects the algorithm that achieves the lowest runtime in up to 96% of the cases, and can achieve a 19% gain over selecting a single balancing algorithm.

The remainder of this paper is organized as follows. We give an overview of our method in Section 2 and demonstrate the shortfalls of current load metrics in Section 3. We define our application-independent load model in Section 4 and our cost model for load balancing algorithms in Section 5. We describe our target applications and their balancing algorithms in Section 6. We evaluate application models and demonstrate how to use our load model to select the appropriate load balancing algorithm in Section 7.

2. OVERVIEW OF APPROACH

The computational load in high-performance physical simulations can evolve over time. Our novel model, which represents load in terms of application elements, provides a cost-benefit analysis of imbalance correction mechanisms. Thus, it can guide the application developer on *when* and *how* to correct the imbalance.

Algorithm 1 summarizes the steps of our method. The core of our load model is a graph that abstractly represents application elements (vertices) and dependencies or communication between them (edges). The application elements are the entities that can be migrated to correct imbalance. A developer only needs to provide the work units and their interactions (the same input that they would provide to a partitioner) (Alg. 1, line 3). Our framework then builds a graph to represent this abstract information.

Our load model combines the abstract application representation with existing tools' measurements of the *degree* of imbalance to evaluate the load accurately in terms of the application elements (Alg. 1, line 4). We perform a cost-benefit analysis of available load balancing algorithms to determine if rebalancing the application would be beneficial at a given time, and, if so, which load balancing algorithm to use (Alg. 1, line 5). We give accurate load information to the load balancing algorithm to determine how the application should be rebalanced (Alg. 1, line 7). We instruct the application to

rebalance (answering the *when* question) with that load balancing algorithm (answering the *how* question) (Alg. 1, line 8).

We show that evaluation of the imbalance and correction mechanisms requires awareness of application information. Our general framework characterizes load imbalance and augments existing load metrics by facilitating the evaluation of developer-provided load estimation schemes. Thus, a developer can use it to refine *ad hoc* load models and to understand their limitations. We demonstrate this process for two large-scale applications in Section 7.1. The developer can then use our cost model to select from available load balancing algorithms, as we show in Section 7.2.

3. DEFICIENCIES OF LOAD METRICS

Formally, load imbalance is an uneven distribution of computational *load* among tasks in a parallel system. In large-scale SPMD applications with synchronous time steps, imbalance can force all processes to wait for the most overloaded process. The performance penalty grows linearly as the number of processors increases, so regularly balancing large-scale synchronous simulations is particularly important as their load distribution evolves over time.

Load balance metrics characterize how unevenly work is distributed. The *percent imbalance* metric, λ, is most commonly used:

$$\lambda = \left(\frac{L_{max}}{\overline{L}} - 1 \right) \times 100\% \qquad (1)$$

where L_{max} is the maximum load on any process and $\overline{L}$ is the mean load over all processes. This metric measures the performance lost to imbalanced load or, conversely, the performance that could be reclaimed by balancing the load. Percent imbalance measures the *severity* of load imbalance. However, it ignores statistical properties of the load distribution that can provide insight into how quickly a particular algorithm can correct an imbalance.

Statistical moments provide a detailed picture of load distribution that can indicate whether a distribution has a few highly loaded outliers or many slightly imbalanced processes. These properties impact which balancing algorithm will most efficiently correct the imbalance. Diffusive algorithms [7] can quickly correct small imbalances while the presence of an outlier in the load distribution may require more drastic, global corrections. Figure 1 shows the three most common statistical moments, standard deviation σ, skewness g_1 and kurtosis g_2, where n is the number of processes and L_i is the load on the ith process. Positive skewness means that relatively few processes have higher than average load, while negative skewness means that relatively few processes have lower than average load. A normal distribution of load implies skewness of 0. Higher kurtosis means that more of the variance arises from infrequent extreme deviations, while lower kurtosis corresponds to fre-

$$\sigma = \sqrt{\frac{1}{n}\sum_{i=0}^{n}(L_i - \overline{L})^2} \qquad (2)$$

$$g_1 = \frac{\frac{1}{n}\sum_{i=0}^{n}(L_i - \overline{L})^3}{\left(\frac{1}{n}\sum_{i=0}^{n}(L_i - \overline{L})^2\right)^{3/2}} \qquad (3)$$

$$g_2 = \frac{\frac{1}{n}\sum_{i=0}^{n}(L_i - \overline{L})^4}{\left(\frac{1}{n}\sum_{i=0}^{n}(L_i - \overline{L})^2\right)^2} - 3 \qquad (4)$$

Figure 1: Statistical Moments

quent modestly sized deviations. A normal distribution has kurtosis of 0. Statistical moments capture key information about load distribution but are insufficient to evaluate the speed with which we can correct imbalance because they do not include information about the proximity of application elements in the simulation space.

Table 1 uses several load distributions to show how the statistical moments fail to distinguish key properties. For simplicity, we show a one-dimensional interaction pattern of processes $P_0 \ldots P_7$ in which P_i and P_{i+1} perform computation on neighboring domains. The figure shows that load metrics cannot distinguish cases (c) and (d) while the difficulty of correcting these load scenarios varies greatly if the computation is optimal when neighboring portions of the simulated space are assigned to the neighboring processes. In case (c), we could simply move the extra load on P_1 to P_0, while in (d) the extra load from P_7 must first displace work to P_6, P_5, and so on through P_1 until the under-loaded P_0 receives enough work.

4. ELEMENT-AWARE LOAD MODEL

Parallel scientific applications decompose their physical domain into work units, which, in different applications, can be elements representing units of the simulated physical space, particles modeled, or random samples performed on the domain. Some application elements may involve more or less computation than others due to their physical properties or spatial proximity. Section 3 shows that a load model must be aware of the application elements and their interactions and placement in order to understand load imbalance and, more importantly, how to correct it. A model that does not include this information will fail to capture the effects of the proximity of elements in the simulation space and the mapping of the simulation space onto the process space.

Our investigation of large-scale scientific applications has shaped our novel application-element-aware, application-independent load model that represents application elements and interactions between them. Our API enables the application to provide our framework with abstract application information at the granularity of application domain decomposition. This granularity allows our model to reflect application elements, their communication and dependencies, and their mapping to processes. Most load balancing algorithms analyze and redistribute work with the same granularity, which enables our framework to guide them. We provide a general methodology to map observed application performance accurately to the application elements at the appropriate granularity level.

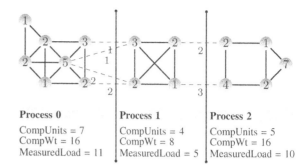

Figure 2: Application Element-Aware Load Model

Figure 2 illustrates our load model: the edges represent bidirectional interactions between application elements. Solid edges represent interactions within a process, while dashed edges represent interprocess communication. The relationships between application elements within the domain decomposition provide the communication structure and the relative weights of computation in the model. Node weights indicate the computation required for each element as anticipated by the application (i.e., the application load model). Importantly, we can correlate this information to wall-clock measurements of the load on each process. The example in Figure 2 shows that Process 0 has 7 work units with an application anticipated load or relative computation weight of 16, and its work units have 4 channels of communication with elements on Process 1 with a total relative communication cost of 6. For example, we measure the load on Process 0 to be 11.

We must carefully consider the difference in modeled and measured load. If the model is accurate, the two are linearly related. If they are not directly proportional, the application model is incomplete and could be improved. We discuss our methodology to evaluate abstract application information in Section 7.1. When we are satisfied with the model accuracy, we can use it to compute the load distribution metrics and to observe how the load is distributed throughout the process space in terms of application elements.

Table 2 illustrates the versatility of our model by showing work unit mappings for three major types of scientific applications.

Unstructured Mesh. In unstructured mesh applications, each cell in the mesh is an element. We represent the mesh connectivity with edges. In some unstructured mesh applications, the cells may require similar computation and we would anticipate unit computation per mesh cell. In others, the computation per cell may be proportional to the cell's volume, and we reflect this in the weight of each node in our model. Table 2(a) shows an unstructured mesh application that performs a Monte Carlo algorithm on its mesh. In this case, the work is proportional to the number of samples in each mesh cell, so we use the sample count as the node weight. We show communication between neighboring grid cells as edges.

Molecular Dynamics. In classical molecular dynamics applications and other N-body simulations, each individual body is an element. Edges reflect the simulated neighborhood of the bodies: each body is connected to others within a cutoff radius (i.e., those with which it interacts), as Table 2(b) shows. As we discuss in Section 7.1, we can select from several models for computation per element. Simple models assume that the work per body is constant, while others reflect the density of the body's neighborhood.

Empirical Model. Some applications, such as ParaDiS [6], use empirical models to anticipate computation per element. An application developer can construct this type of model by placing timers around important computation regions. Table 2(c) shows how *ad hoc* placement of timers may omit important load constituents.

Type of Application, elements and interactions	Sample Application Image	Representation in App.	Our Representation
(a) Unstructured Mesh • e.g., particle transport or finite element applications • elements: cell volume or number of samples in each cell (Monte Carlo algorithms) • interactions: mesh connectivity			
(b) N-body • e.g., Molecular Dynamics Applications • elements: (sampled) molecules • interactions: molecules within range of interaction r (as defined by the application)			
(c) Other - Empirical Model • e.g., ParaDiS (Section 6.3) • interactions: graph of process communication • elements: time in developer-defined 'key' routines (green); incomplete coverage of application behavior (red)			

Table 2: Applications and Their Representation in Our Load Model

5. LOAD BALANCE COST MODEL

In this section, we use our load model to evaluate the cost of two types of load balancing algorithm. Our cost model can guide selection of the best algorithm for specific imbalance scenarios.

5.1 Types of Load Balancing Algorithms

Global Algorithms. A global balancing algorithm [9, 19, 25] takes information about the load on all tasks and decides how to redistribute load evenly in a single step. Global decisions can be costly. Sequential implementations must process data for an entire parallel system. Parallel implementations can communicate excessively. Global algorithms also can require substantial element movement. However, if the cost of balancing is low, global algorithms balance load in a single step and correctly handle local minima and maxima.

Diffusive Algorithms. A diffusive balancing algorithm [7] performs local corrections at each step and only moves elements within a local neighborhood in the logical simulation domain. Diffusive algorithms can take many steps to rectify a large imbalance because load can only move a limited distance. However, diffusive algorithms are scalable because they only require local information, and element movements can be mapped to perform well on high diameter mesh and torus networks used in the largest machines.

5.2 Cost Model for Balancing Algorithms

Our cost model captures the rebalancing characteristics of diffusive and global algorithms. Developers typically choose balancers based on their intuition about the scalability of particular algorithms. For example, one might expect the cost of a global balanc-

ing scheme to be higher than that of a diffusive algorithm at scale because the time required for an immediate rebalance outweighs the amortized cost of local diffusive balancing. The intuition is approximate and sometimes inaccurate. Our cost model provides a quantitative basis for selecting among algorithms. Table 3 summarizes the variables that we use to define this cost model.

Our cost model only considers the current imbalance. Future imbalances are highly dependent on how the simulation evolves. Predicting them is generally infeasible (otherwise we could predict the result of the simulation). We assume a continuous evaluation of the imbalance in an application's load leading to new balancing decisions when necessary. These decisions can consider the (observed) rate at which the application becomes imbalanced, and apply a global balancer when drastic changes are necessary or a diffusion scheme to handle more modest imbalances.

A load balancing algorithm's cost is the time to decide which elements to move plus the time required to move the elements:

$$C_{BalAlg} = C_{LbDecision} + C_{DataMvmt} \qquad (5)$$

where *BalAlg* can be *global* or *diffusion* (i.e., C_{global} or $C_{diffusion}$).

$C_{LbDecision}$, the time to run the balancing algorithm, can be known *a priori* or derived using a performance model, such as a regression model over timings that vary the algorithm's input parameters [15]. Typical parameters for the modeling approach include the input size (e.g., the number of vertices in the load model graph and the average number of edges per vertex) and the number of processes that a parallel balancing algorithm uses.

Variable	Definition	How Determined
L_{ave}	Average process load	$\frac{1}{procs} \sum_{i=0}^{procs} L_i$
L_i	Load of process i	Measured or estimated by Algorithm 2
D_i	Set of processes with elements that can be moved to process i	Derived from edges in load model
L_{ij}	Load of process $j \in D_i$	Measured or estimated by Algorithm 2
γ	Load shifting coefficient in Algorithm 2	Provided by application, $\gamma \leq 1$
convergence_steps	Number of steps for diffusive algorithm to converge	Derived by simulating diffusion, Algorithm 2
L_{max_i}	Maximum process load at step i	Simulated (diffusion); $\approx L_{ave}$ (global)
$ElementsMoved_i$	Largest number of elements moved to a process at step i	Simulated (diffusion); $\approx Elements_{max} \frac{L_{ave}}{L_{max} - L_{ave}}$ (global)
$C_{DataMvmt}$	Time required to send $ElementsMoved_i$	Modeled empirically, $\alpha + \beta ElementsMoved$
$C_{LbDecision}$	Runtime of load balancing algorithm, e.g., C_{global} and C_{diff}	Measured or modeled empirically
$C_{BalAlgo}$	Balancing algorithm cost: algorithm time plus redistribution time	$C_{LbDecision} + C_{DataMvmt}$
$AppTime_{BalAlg}$	Total application runtime under $BalAlg$, e.g., $AppTime_{diff}$	Modeled by cost model
steps	Number of time steps that the application takes	Arbitrary, same for global and diffusion algorithms

Table 3: Cost Model Variables

We define $C_{DataMvmt}$ as:

$$C_{DataMvmt} = \alpha + \beta ElementsMoved_{max} \times elementsize \quad (6)$$

where the application provides $elementsize$, α is the start-up cost of communication (latency), and β is the per-element send time (bandwidth), determined empirically per platform. A more detailed model could capture network contention. For global balancing algorithms, we approximate the number of elements moved as:

$$ElementsMoved_{global} \approx Elements_{max} \frac{L_{ave}}{L_{max} - L_{ave}} \quad (7)$$

where $Elements_{max}$ is the number of elements on the process with L_{max}. We approximate the portion of the elements that we must move from the most loaded process as proportional to the load imbalance, which assumes that the load per element is approximately constant. Although this assumption is coarse (load balance would be trivial), we find this simplification works well in practice.

The total cost of a load balancing algorithm is the application runtime when using the algorithm, which is the time to perform each computation step plus the cost of the algorithm at each step:

$$AppTime_{BalAlg} = \sum_{i=0}^{steps} \left(C_{BalAlg_i} + L_{max_i} \right) \quad (8)$$

where $steps$ is the number of timesteps that the application takes, C_{BalAlg_i} is load balancing algorithm's cost at step i, which is zero for a global algorithm in all steps other than the one in which load balancing is performed. The time for each step of the computation is the time taken by the most heavily loaded process, L_{max}.

For a global scheme, the total cost reduces to:

$$AppTime_{global} = C_{global_1} + steps \times L_{ave} \quad (9)$$

since we assume that the global load balancing algorithm is only invoked in the first step. We estimate the time per computation step as L_{ave} under the assumption that imbalance is corrected.

For diffusion, we compute the total application time as:

$$AppTime_{diff} = \sum_{i=0}^{steps} \left(C_{diff_i} + L_{max_i} \right) \quad (10)$$

To compute the total application time for diffusion, we have developed a diffusion simulator that mimics the behavior of diffusive load balancing algorithms. Algorithm 2 gives a high level overview of our diffusion simulator. We apply Algorithm 2 to our load model

---

Algorithm 2 Diffusion Simulation [7]

Input. $L_i \leftarrow$ load of process i
$D_i \leftarrow$ neighborhood of process i, defined in Load Model graph
$L_{ij} \leftarrow$ load of process $j \in D_i$
$\gamma \leftarrow$ coefficient for how much load can be moved in one timestep
$threshold \leftarrow$ lowest attainable level of imbalance for the application
$convergence\_steps \leftarrow 0$

1: All processes in **parallel do**
2: **for** timesteps **do**
3:    **if** imbalance > threshold **then**
4:      $convergence\_steps$++
5:    **end if**
6:    $L_i = L_i + \sum_{j \in D_i} \gamma(L_i - L_{ij})$
7:    $ElementsMoved_i = NumElements_i \sum_{j \in D_i} \gamma(L_i - L_{ij})$
8:    $NumElements_i = NumElements_i + ElementsMoved_i$
9:    $L_{max_i} = max(L_i) \,\forall$ processes at timestep i
10:    $ElementsMoved_{max_i} = max(ElsMoved_i) \forall$ procs at step i
11: **end for**

---

to simulate the movement of load at each iteration. At each step, process i moves a portion of its load to its neighboring processes. We define a coefficient, γ, to model the amount of load that can be moved in one time step to reflect any application limitations (e.g., the maximum amount that domain boundaries can move in one time step). If the application does not limit element movement, $\gamma = 1$. Our algorithm accounts for local minima and maxima because it moves the simulated load through our graph based model similarly to data motion under an actual diffusive algorithm.

Algorithm 2 records L_{max_i} and $ElementsMoved_{max_i}$ at each simulated step. We use those values in Equation 10. Additionally, Algorithm 2 defines an important metric, *convergence steps*, or the number of steps a diffusion algorithm takes to balance the load. This metric differentiates scenarios that a diffusion algorithm can correct quickly from those for which diffusion performs poorly.

Algorithm 2 determines the costs required for Equation 10 much faster than the actual diffusion can be performed. We can evaluate its cost without perturbing the application. If the simulation predicts that diffusion will take too long, we can use a different load balancing algorithm such as a global load balancing scheme.

We compare $AppTime_{diff}$, $AppTime_{global}$, and $AppTime_{none}$ to determine which load balance algorithm to use, where:

$$AppTime_{none} = steps \times L_{max_1} \quad (11)$$

We report the effectiveness of this decision in Section 7.2.

Algorithm 3 Benchmark

Input. $G \leftarrow$ graph of elements, where each process P is assigned a sub-graph G_P and remote edges represent interprocess communication

```
1:  for P ∈ processes in parallel do
2:      for timesteps do
3:          for remote edges of G_P do
4:              Irecv/Isend messages
5:          end for
6:          for v ∈ G assigned to process P do
7:              do_work(weight_v)
8:          end for
9:          MPI_Wait(all messages)
10:         if directive to rebalance then
11:             rebalance
12:         end if
13:         update info for load balancing framework
14:      end for
15: end for
```

---

6. BENCHMARKS AND APPLICATIONS

To evaluate our load and cost models, we conduct experiments with two large-scale scientific applications, ddcMD and ParaDiS, as well as a synthetic load balance benchmark that allows us to evaluate a larger variety of load scenarios and the performance of various load balancing algorithms for those scenarios.

6.1 Load Balance Benchmark

We use a benchmark to represent classes of load imbalance scenarios that occur in parallel scientific applications. Scientific applications can encounter varying initial load configurations, different patterns of element interactions, and different scenarios of how the imbalance evolves throughout the program. Our benchmark controls these variations to ensure a wide range of experiments.

The main input to our benchmark is a directed graph with vertices that represent application elements and edges the communication/dependencies between them. We derive input graphs from a variety of meshes from actual simulations. We use a simple *do_work(time)* function that accesses an array in a random order. We tune this function for each architecture such that *do_work(1)* executes for one second. Algorithm 3 outlines our benchmark, which calls *do_work* for each graph vertex with the appropriate weights to represent the load scenario. We send an MPI message for each edge that connects vertices on different processes.

Our experiments vary the size of the graph, vertex and edge weights, and the initial distribution. We can reassign each vertex to any process, as determined by the load balance framework.

6.2 ddcMD

ddcMD [8, 11] is a highly optimized molecular dynamics application that has twice won the Gordon Bell prize for high performance computing [11, 22]. It is written in C and uses the MPI library for interprocess communication. In the ddcMD model, each process owns a subset of the simulated particles and maintains lists of other particles with which its particles interact.

To allocate particles to processes, ddcMD uses a *Voronoi* domain decomposition. Each process is assigned a point as its center; it "owns" the particles that are nearer to its center than any other. A *Voronoi cell* is the set of *all* points nearest to a particular center. Figure 3(a) shows a sample decomposition, with cells outlined in black and particles shown in red. Around each cell, ddcMD also maintains a *bounding sphere* that has a radius of the maximum distance of any atom in the domain to its center.

During execution, atoms that a process owns can move outside of their cell. When this happens, ddcMD uses a built-in diffusion

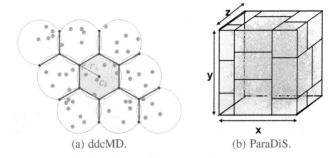

(a) ddcMD. (b) ParaDiS.

Figure 3: Domain Decomposition in ddcMD and ParaDiS

load balancer that uses a load particle density gradient calculation to reassign load. The balancer moves the Voronoi centers so that the walls of the Voronoi cells shift towards regions of greater density. Voronoi centers can only move a limited amount closer to neighboring cells. Voronoi constraints on the shape of cells also limit the possible distributions. To represent elements and the associated load, ddcMD uses three application-specific models:

1. *Molecules*: number of particles (molecules) per process;
2. *Barriers*: time each process spends outside of barriers;
3. *Forces*: time spent calculating interactions on each process.

For our global load balancing algorithm, we use a point-centered domain decomposition method developed by Koradi [14]. Each step, we calculate a bias b_i for each domain i. When the bias increases (decreases), the domain radius and volume increase (decrease). We assign each atom (with position vector x) to the domain that satisfies:

$$|x - c_i|^2 - b_i = minimal, \qquad (12)$$

where c_i is the center of domain i, and we calculate the new centers as the center of gravity for the atoms in each cell.

Although the Koradi algorithm is diffusive, we can run its steps independently of the application execution until it converges. Thus, our implementation is a global method since it only applies the final center positions in the application. We further optimize the algorithm by parallelizing it and executing it on a sample of the atoms rather than the complete set.

Our experiments use a range of decompositions that exhibit different load balance properties by varying the placement of Voronoi cell centers. We evaluate all three models in Section 7.1, and vary load distributions in Section 7.2. We used two problem sets for ddcMD, a nanowire simulation and a condensation simulation. The *nanowire* simulation is a finite system of 133,280 iron (Fe) atoms that incurs imbalance due to uneven partitioning of the densely populated cylindrical body surrounded by vacuum. Atom interaction is modeled with EAM potentials. We ran the nanowire problem on 64 processes. The *condensation* simulation is a Lennard-Jones condensation problem with 2.5e+6 particles and the interactions modeled with Lennard-Jones potentials [13]. It incurs imbalance due to condensation droplets forming in some of the simulated domains. We ran the condensation simulation on 512 processes.

6.3 ParaDiS

ParaDiS [6] is a large-scale dislocation dynamics simulation used to study the fundamental mechanisms of plasticity. It is written primarily in C and uses MPI for interprocess communication. ParaDiS simulations grow in size as more time steps are executed. Thus, the application domain is spatially heterogeneous and the distribution is recalculated periodically to rebalance the workload. ParaDiS uses a 3-dimensional recursive sectioning decomposition that first segments the domain in the X direction, then in the Y direction within X slabs, and finally in the Z direction within XY slabs. Figure 3(b) illustrates this decomposition method.

ParaDiS uses an *empirical model* as an input to its load balancing algorithm. It estimates load using timing calipers around the computation that the developers consider most important for load balance. The load balancing algorithm adjusts work per process by shifting the boundaries of the sections. The size of neighboring domains constrains the magnitude of a shift and the algorithm does not move a boundary past the end of a neighboring section. This constraint makes the ParaDiS balancer a diffusion algorithm. For our experiments, we vary the distributions of the domain by varying the *xyz decomposition* of the domain such that $x * y * z = nProcs$.

We use a highly dynamic crystal simulation input set for ParaDiS, with 1M degrees of freedom at the beginning of the simulation growing to 1.1M degrees of freedom by the end of the run. We ran this simulation on 128 processes.

7. EVALUATION

For all ParaDiS experiments, we use a Linux cluster that has 800 compute nodes, each with four quad-core 2.3 GHz AMD Opteron processors, connected by Infiniband. We use a similar cluster that has 1,072 compute nodes, each with four dual-core 2.4 GHz AMD Opteron processors connected by Infiniband for all ddcMD runs in Section 7.1. On both Linux systems, we use gcc 4.1.2 and MVAPICH v0.99 for the MPI implementation. We use a Blue Gene/P system with 1,024 compute nodes with 4 32-bit PPC450d (850MHz) cores each and 64 32-bit PPC450d I/O nodes for all ddcMD experiments in Section 7.2. On this system, we use gcc 4.1.2 for our measurement framework and compile ddcMD with xlC 9.

To validate application models, we measure the work per process using Libra [10], a scalable load balance measurement framework for SPMD codes. Libra measures the time spent in specific regions of an application per time step using the *effort model*. In this model, time steps, or *progress steps*, model each step of the synchronous parallel computation, and fine-grained *effort regions* within these steps model different phases of computation.

We extend Libra's effort model to serve as input to our load model and add an interface to query load information during execution. We measure the computational load on each process by summing the time spent in all effort regions. Our load model couples these measurements with the application abstractions, allowing us to validate the abstractions against empirical measurements.

We use P^NMPI [20] to integrate Libra with our load model infrastructure. P^NMPI stacks independent tools that use the MPI profiling interface [4], which we apply to combine Libra with our new load model component. P^NMPI also supports direct communication among tools, which we use to exchange element interaction and performance information. Our tool stack imposes 3% overhead on average, an insignificant perturbation of application behavior.

7.1 Evaluating Application Abstractions

In this section, we evaluate the quality of *ad hoc*, developer-provided application load abstractions by comparing them with empirical measurements obtained from Libra. To quantify the quality of the abstractions, we report the accuracy with which they capture the measured load imbalance and the statistical moments of the measured load distribution, as defined in Section 3.

For additional analysis, we validate application abstractions with a *rank correlation* metric. Rank correlation measures how accurately the abstraction ranks each process's load relative to that of

Table 4: RMSE for Plots in Figure 4

	Molecules	Barriers	Forces
imbalance	15.917	25.769	16.095
kurtosis	0.444	0.079	0.057
rank corr.	0.138	0.008	0.007

other processes. To calculate the rank correlation r of process loads between the application abstraction M and measured load L as, we first order all ranks based on the values of the developer-provided load abstraction and the measured load data. The resulting rank number for process i is stored in l_i and m_i respectively, as is the mean rank in $\bar{l}$ and $\bar{m}$. We then calculate the correlation with:

$$r = \frac{\sum_{i=0}^{n}(m_i - \bar{m})(l_i - \bar{l})}{\sqrt{\sum_{i=0}^{n}(m_i - \bar{m})^2 \sum_{i=0}^{n}(l_i - \bar{l})^2}} \tag{13}$$

To accommodate tied ranks correctly, we use Pearson's correlation coefficient [17]. We now apply our abstraction evaluation methodology to ddcMD and ParaDiS.

Figure 4(a) demonstrates how well the ddcMD abstractions capture the imbalance in the problem. Table 4 shows root mean squared error (RMSE) of load imbalance and the statistical moments calculated over our experiments. Abstractions based on the number of molecules and force computation overestimate the imbalance in the system, while the abstraction based on execution time excluding time spent at barriers underestimates the imbalance. Underestimating the imbalance leads to slower imbalance correction with a diffusion scheme because it is less aggressive than necessary. Alternately, overestimation pushes the limits of how much the load can be redistributed at each time step, and thus converges faster, as long as the overestimation correctly captures the *relative* loads.

Figure 4(b) shows how the three ddcMD abstractions capture the kurtosis of the load distributions for each run; Table 4 shows the RMSE. The abstraction based on the number of molecules does most poorly, because much of the imbalance arise from imbalanced neighbor communication, which that abstraction omits.

Figure 4(c) shows the rank correlation between the modeled and measured distributions for each of our test cases; Table 4 shows the corresponding RMSE. Again, abstractions based on time and force computation detect any outliers fairly well, while the abstraction based solely on the number of particles does worse.

Overall, our analysis indicates that the force computation abstraction is the most accurate and, thus, the most suitable for use as input to the diffusion mechanism. To validate our conclusions, Figure 4(d) shows the number of *steps to converge* when the diffusion algorithm uses the three abstractions as input. We use a threshold of 12% imbalance because, as mentioned, ddcMD's best achievable balance is limited by constraints on the shape of Voronoi cells in its domain decomposition. As predicted, the abstraction based on the force calculation is the most accurate and thus corrects the load most quickly. The abstraction based on the number of molecules outperforms the Barrier abstraction, partly because the former overestimates the imbalance making the diffusion scheme take more drastic measures and arrive at a balanced state sooner.

Figure 5(a) shows the accuracy with which the ParaDiS application abstraction represents its load imbalance. Figure 5(b) shows the rank correlation of actual and modeled load distributions. The figures show that the abstraction is somewhat inaccurate, which we suspected because it does not include certain major phases of the computation that are captured by the measurements; the develop-

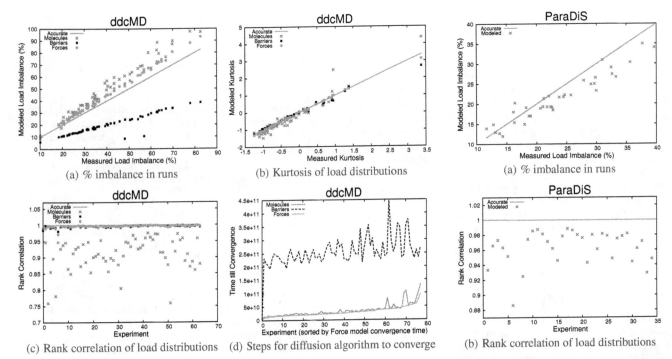

(a) % imbalance in runs (b) Kurtosis of load distributions (a) % imbalance in runs

(c) Rank correlation of load distributions (d) Steps for diffusion algorithm to converge (b) Rank correlation of load distributions

Figure 4: Evaluation of Three ddcMD Models   **Figure 5: ParaDiS Model Evaluation**

ers only measure the main force computation. Our load model in conjunction with Libra's data shows that this fails to capture the behavior of communication, collision detection, and remesh phases. When we compare ParaDiS's calipers to Libra's measurements of only the force computation, the model is quite accurate. Depending on the problem, these omitted regions comprise up to 15% of the execution time. We have communicated our findings to the application developers, and are working with them to optimize how the application reports load to the load balancer.

7.2 Cost Model Case Study

In this section, we evaluate how well our model selects the most effective load balancer for particular imbalance scenarios, and we further evaluate the net performance improvement achieved using our model. We use the cost model defined in Section 5 to select the load balancing algorithm that would lead to the shortest runtime of our benchmark. We then apply our cost model to the global and diffusive load balancing schemes in ddcMD.

For our benchmark, we compare total application runtime when using the following load balancing algorithms:

1. **Global:** Correcting imbalance during the first time step using Zoltan's graph partitioner [9]; modeled by Equation 9;

2. **Diffusive:** Correcting imbalance at every time step using the Koradi method [14]; modeled by Equation 10;

3. **None:** No correction; modeled by Equation 11.

We conduct runs spanning 2 to 64 processes with graphs with between 8,000 and 512,000 vertices and varying weights and initial decompositions. Figure 6(a) shows initial imbalance in the benchmark runs; we chose these initial imbalance scenarios because they are representative of some of the application runs we observed.

Figure 6(b) shows that our load model correctly selects the algorithm that achieves the lowest runtime in 87% of the cases, tracing the curve with highest performance improvement for most of the

experiments. In most cases, our model chooses the global algorithm. This algorithm performs very well in 96% of the cases, but 4% of the time, its high algorithmic and redistribution cost (as modeled by Equation 5) outweighs the performance benefit so it incurs a 35% performance penalty. In these cases, the diffusive algorithm outperforms the global algorithm, and our model correctly chooses it instead. In the only cases where our model does not choose the correct algorithm, it only suffers a penalty of 5.43% because these were scenarios where the global and diffusive algorithm performed within 6% of each other.

On average, using our model can achieve a 49% performance gain while the next best alternative, the global algorithm, achieves 48% overall improvement in runtime. While the diffusive algorithm performed much worse than either of these overall (averaging net gains of only 3% over doing nothing), our model is still able to exploit it in the rare cases where it *did* outperform the global algorithm, leading to significant gains in these scenarios and more reliable performance across the board. For these cases, the diffusive algorithm performs significantly better than Zoltan, and using our model can prevent performance loss for workloads that contain many such pathological runs.

For evaluating the performance of our model for ddcMD, we applied it to the input sets also used in Section 7.1; their initial load properties are demonstrated in Figures 4 (a-c). Our model selected among the following load balancing algorithms:

1. **Global:** Correcting imbalance during the first time step using the Koradi method [14] several times to mimic a method that corrects the imbalance in one step; modeled by Equation 9;

2. **Diffusive:** Correcting imbalance at every time step using the *ad hoc* Voronoi decomposition method with the *Forces* abstraction evaluated in Sec. 7.1 as input; modeled by Eqn. 10;

3. **None:** no correction; modeled by Equation 11.

Table 5 shows runtimes of the load balancing algorithms for several imbalance scenarios in the nanowire simulation. These

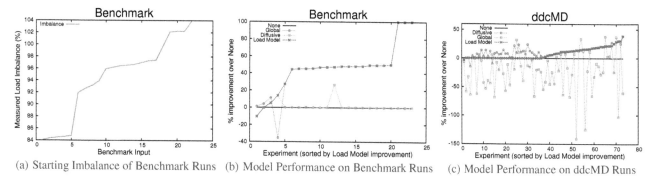

(a) Starting Imbalance of Benchmark Runs   (b) Model Performance on Benchmark Runs   (c) Model Performance on ddcMD Runs

Figure 6: Evaluation of our Load Model on Benchmark and ddcMD

	Load on each Process	Orig.	Diffus.	Global	Model
(a)		226	212	248	diff.
(b)		344	459	269	global
(c)		286	355	239	global
(d)		270	267	235	global

Table 5: Sample ddcMD Imbalance Scenarios (seconds)

cases ran on 64 processors organized as a 4x16 process grid. Table 5 shows the relative load in the beginning of the simulation, with darker sections representing higher load and lighter blue representing lower load for the particular process. For each of these, we show the execution time without load balancing, the execution time with the diffusion algorithm, and the execution time using the global algorithm. We run the nanowire simulation for 200 time steps. The diffusion algorithm has a cost (as defined in Equation 5) of 0.01 seconds per simulation step. The global load balancing method incurs a one-time cost of 9 seconds. In all cases, our cost model guides the selection of the appropriate balancing algorithm.

Figure 6(c) shows that our load model correctly selects the best algorithm in 96% of the cases, tracing the curve of the best performing algorithm. Because the *ad hoc* Voronoi algorithm improves the performance in 82% of the cases with an average performance gain of 14%, our model correctly selects it in most cases. The Koradi algorithm consistently performs worse and is only selected by the model in a few cases where its performance improvement outweighs the high cost of Koradi; overall, the model achieves a 19% gain over the Koradi algorithm.

While our experiments are designed to explore a range of values, a suite of production runs might contain a variety of pathological cases, and our model will allow for a code to perform well even in the cases where the otherwise preferred balancing algorithm will perform poorly. Our model provides a means to select the appropriate load balancing algorithm at runtime without developer intervention, correctly selecting the algorithm that achieves the lowest runtime in up to 96% of the cases, achieving a 19% gain over selecting a single balancing algorithm for all cases.

8. RELATED WORK

Previous work has focused on load measurement and finding sources of imbalance. Efficient, scalable measurement of load [12, 24] identifies whether load imbalance is a problem for a particular application. Imbalance attribution [23] provides insight into the source code locations that cause imbalance. Our load model takes advantage of existing tools [10] and their measurements, and combines them with knowledge of the application elements and their interactions. This combination improves understanding of computational load in terms of application elements.

Many applications that suffer from load imbalance implement their own load balancing algorithms that are usually tightly coupled with application data structures and cannot be used outside of the application. Some rely heavily on geometric decomposition of the domain (i.e., hierarchical recursive bisection [6]). AMR applications can order boxes according to their spatial location by placing a Morton space filling curve [16] through the box centroids to increase the likelihood that neighboring patches reside on the same process after load balancing [27]. N-body simulations either explicitly assign bodies to processes or indirectly assign bodies by assigning subspaces to processes using orthogonal recursive bisection [2], oct-trees [21, 26], and fractiling [1]. These examples require application developers to construct an *ad hoc* model of per-task load. These abstractions are frequently inaccurate because they omit a significant subset of computational costs, or they fail to consider the platform. Our load model enables evaluation of the application abstractions, thus ensuring that the computation costs are correctly assigned prior to being used to correct the imbalance.

Another common approach to load balancing uses suites of partitioners that work with mesh or graph representations of computation in the applications (e.g., ParMetis [19], Jostle [25], Zoltan [9]). Users of these partitioners must supply information about the current state of the application and the system, which again must be application specific. Thus, they may provide inaccurate or incomplete information. Further, partitioners do not have sufficient information to decide when to load balance, placing a further burden on the application developer. Our load model enables actionable evaluation of load imbalance, and can help a developer decide when to rebalance and whether the repartitioner is a good balancing algorithm for a particular type of imbalance.

Charm++ [3, 5] provides a measurement-based load balancing framework that records the work represented by objects and object-to-object communication patterns. The load balancer can migrate the objects between process queues. While this approach may work well when the application developers can decompose their computation into independent objects, many applications cannot. In other cases, Charm++ can over-decompose the domain [18] and then balance load by moving virtual processors from overloaded physical processors to the underloaded ones. This approach can impose extra communication overhead for tightly coupled applications. In more recent work, Charm++ explores hierarchical approaches to load balancing [28]. Our model's ability to evaluate the load in an actionable manner could thus provide a sound basis to choose the best level at which to balance the load.

9. CONCLUSIONS

We have presented a novel load model based on application elements and their interactions. Our load model establishes a mapping between application elements and computation costs while maintaining information on dependencies between application elements. Our load model enables an application-independent representation of load distribution and can form the basis for a new generation of generic, yet element-aware load balance tools. We have shown that our element-aware approach overcomes deficiencies of conventional statistical load metrics, which fail to represent the element interaction information. Using our element-aware load model, we developed a new set of actionable metrics that accurately characterize load distribution.

We have demonstrated the effectiveness and versatility of our load model on several case studies. We have provided a mechanism to evaluate and to contrast several application-provided abstractions. We have used our load model to analyze the load imbalance in two production applications. Finally, we evaluated the ability of available load balance schemes to correct imbalance. In all experiments, adding the application element interaction information to the load data was critical to understanding and analyzing the application's load behavior.

10. REFERENCES

[1] I. Banicescu and S. Flynn Hummel. Balancing processor loads and exploiting data locality in N-body simulations. In *ACM/IEEE Conf. on Supercomputing*, 1995.

[2] M. J. Berger and S. H. Bokhari. A partitioning strategy for nonuniform problems on multiprocessors. *IEEE Transactions on Computers*, 1987.

[3] A. Bhatelé, L. V. Kalé, and S. Kumar. Dynamic topology aware load balancing algorithms for MD applications. In *ACM SIGARCH Intl. Conf. on Supercomputing*, 2009.

[4] S. Browne, J. Dongarra, N. Garner, G. Ho, and P. Mucci. A portable programming interface for performance evaluation on modern processors. *Intl. Journal of High Performance Computing Applications*, 14(3), 2000.

[5] R. K. Brunner and L. V. Kalé. Handling application-induced load imbalance using parallel objects. *Par. and Distr. Comp. for Symbolic and Irregular Applications*, 2000.

[6] V. Bulatov, W. Cai, J. Fier, M. Hiratani, G. Hommes, T. Pierce, M. Tang, M. Rhee, K. Yates, and T. Arsenlis. Scalable line dynamics in ParaDiS. In *Supercomp.*, 2004.

[7] G. Cybenko. Dynamic load balancing for distributed memory multiprocessors. *Journal of Par. and Distr. Comp.*, 1989.

[8] B. R. de Supinski, M. Schulz, V. V. Bulatov, W. Cabot, B. Chan, A. W. Cook, E. W. Draeger, J. N. Glosli, J. A. Greenough, K. Henderson, A. Kubota, S. Louis, B. J. Miller, M. V. Patel, T. E. Spelce, F. H. Streitz, P. L. Williams, R. K. Yates, A. Yoo, G. Almasi, G. Bhanot, A. Gara, J. A. Gunnels, M. Gupta, J. Moreira, J. Sexton, B. Walkup, C. Archer, F. Gygi, T. C. Germann, K. Kadau, P. S. Lomdahl, C. Rendleman, M. L. Welcome, W. McLendon, B. Hendrickson, F. Franchetti, S. Kral, J. Lorenz, C. W. Uberhuber, E. Chow, and U. Catalyurek. BlueGene/L applications: Parallelism on a massive scale. *Intl. Journal of High Performance Computing Applications*, 22(1), 2008.

[9] K. Devine, E. Boman, R. Heaphy, B. Hendrickson, J. Teresco, J. Faik, J. Flaherty, and L. Gervasio. New challanges in dynamic load balancing. *Applied Numerical Mathematics*, 52(2-3), 2005.

[10] T. Gamblin, B. R. de Supinski, M. Schulz, R. Fowler, and D. A. Reed. Scalable load-balance measurement for SPMD codes. In *ACM/IEEE Conf. on Supercomputing*, 2008.

[11] J. N. Glosli, K. J. Caspersen, J. A. Gunnels, D. F. Richards, R. E. Rudd, and F. H. Streitz. Extending stability beyond CPU millennium: A micro-scale atomistic simulation of Kelvin-Helmholtz instability. In *Supercomputing*, Nov. 2007.

[12] K. A. Huck and J. Labarta. Detailed load balance analysis of large scale parallel applications. In *Par. Processing*, 2010.

[13] J. E. Jones. On the determination of molecular fields. II. From the equation of state of a gas. *Royal Society of London Proceedings Series A*, 106:463–477, Oct. 1924.

[14] R. Koradi, M. Billeter, and P. GÃijntert. Point-centered domain decomposition for parallel molecular dynamics simulation. *Computer Physics Communications*, 2000.

[15] B. C. Lee, D. M. Brooks, B. R. de Supinski, M. Schulz, K. Singh, and S. A. McKee. Methods of inference and learning for performance modeling of parallel applications. In *Principles and Practices of Parallel Programming*, 2007.

[16] G. Morton. A computer oriented geodetic data base and a new technique in file sequencing. *IBM tech report*, 1966.

[17] J. L. Myers and A. D. Well. Research design and statistical analysis. *Lawrence Erlbaum Associates Publishers*, 2003.

[18] E. R. Rodrigues, P. O. A. Navaux, J. Panetta, A. Fazenda, C. L. Mendes, and L. V. Kale. A comparative analysis of load balancing algorithms applied to a weather forecast model. In *Comp. Architecture and High Perf. Comp.*, 2010.

[19] K. Schloegel, G. Karypis, and V. Kumar. A unified algorithm for load-balancing adaptive scientific simulations. In *ACM/IEEE Conf. on Supercomputing*, 2000.

[20] M. Schulz and B. R. de Supinski. P^NMPI tools: A whole lot greater than the sum of their parts. In *Supercomputing*, 2007.

[21] J. P. Singh, C. Holt, J. L. Hennessy, and A. Gupta. A parallel adaptive fast multipole method. In *Supercomputing*, 1993.

[22] F. Streitz, J. Glosli, M. Patel, B. Chan, R. Yates, B. de Supinski, J. Sexton, and J. Gunnels. 100+ TFlop solidification simulations on BlueGene/L. In *Supercomputing*, 2005.

[23] N. R. Tallent, L. Adhianto, and J. M. Mellor-Crummey. Scalable identification of load imbalance in parallel executions using call path profiles. In *Supercomputing*, 2010.

[24] N. R. Tallent, J. M. Mellor-Crummey, M. Franco, R. Landrum, and L. Adhianto. Scalable fine-grained call path tracing. In *Intl. Conf. on Supercomputing*, 2011.

[25] C. Walshaw and M. Cross. Parallel optimisation algorxithms for multilevel mesh partitioning. *Parallel Computing*, 2000.

[26] M. S. Warren and J. K. Salmon. A parallel hashed oct-tree N-body algorithm. In *Conf. on Supercomputing*, 1993.

[27] A. M. Wissink, D. Hysom, and R. D. Hornung. Enhancing scalability of parallel structured AMR calculations. In *ACM SIGARCH Intl. Conf. on Supercomputing*, 2003.

[28] G. Zheng, A. Bhatele, E. Meneses, and L. V. Kale. Periodic hierarchical load balancing for large supercomputers. *Journal of High Perf. Comp. App.*, 2010.

Sparse Matrix-Vector Multiply on the HICAMP Architecture

John P. Stevenson
Stanford University
jpeter@stanford.edu

Amin Firoozshahian
HICAMP Systems
aminf13@hicampsystems.com

Alex Solomatnikov
HICAMP Systems
sols@hicampsystems.com

Mark Horowitz
Stanford University
horowitz@stanford.edu

David Cheriton
Stanford University
cheriton@stanford.edu

ABSTRACT

Sparse matrix-vector multiply (SpMV) is a critical task in the inner loop of modern iterative linear system solvers and exhibits very little data reuse. This low reuse means that its performance is bounded by main-memory bandwidth. Moreover, the random patterns of indirection make it difficult to achieve this bound. We present sparse matrix storage formats based on deduplicated memory. These formats reduce memory traffic during SpMV and thus show significantly improved performance bounds: 90x better in the best case. Additionally, we introduce a matrix format that inherently exploits any amount of matrix symmetry and is at the same time fully compatible with non-symmetric matrix code. Because of this, our method can concurrently operate on a symmetric matrix without complicated work partitioning schemes and without any thread synchronization or locking. This approach takes advantage of growing processor caches, but incurs an instruction count overhead. It is feasible to overcome this issue by using specialized hardware as shown by the recently proposed Hierarchical Immutable Content-Addressable Memory Processor, or HICAMP architecture.

Categories and Subject Descriptors

G.1.3 [**Numerical Linear Algebra**]: Sparse, structured, and very large systems—*direct and iterative methods*

Keywords

SpMV, Deduplication, HICAMP

1. INTRODUCTION

The ability to quickly invert a large sparse matrix is strongly desired by many computing applications. In practice, this reduces to finding the vector x which satisfies $y = Ax$, i.e., an explicit inverse is not computed. Direct approaches factor the matrix into upper and lower triangular components and then do forward and back-substitution. The cost of the direct approach can be amortized by solving several vectors

against the same matrix. Unfortunately, finding the matrix factors can be quite costly, which motivates the use of iterative approaches. Iterative approaches propose a trial solution x_0, calculate the residual $r = y - Ax_0$, and update the trial solution based on the residual. The process repeats until the norm of the residual is brought to a satisfactorily low value. Computing the matrix-vector product on each pass comprises the bulk of the work in such a method. This fact has motivated much research into optimizing the performance of sparse matrix-vector multiply, or SpMV.

SpMV is typically limited by memory bandwidth because there is very little data reuse. If the total size of the working set exceeds the capacity of the last-level cache, the cache is effectively rendered useless: each matrix value must be brought in from DRAM, to be used exactly once, on each pass through the SpMV kernel. Much effort has focused on maximizing the attained bandwidth when using a matrix representation such as compressed sparse row (CSR) [3, 12, 19, 20, 22, 25], while relatively little work has focused on reducing memory traffic [2,13–15,24]. Using current techniques, SpMV execution time is set by the ratio of the working set size to the maximum sustainable memory bandwidth of a given system [23]. This motivates research into new methods that work around the bandwidth limitation.

This paper investigates one such method using matrix formats based on fine-grained memory deduplication. Our work is informed by the recently proposed Hierarchical Immutable Content-Addressable Memory Processor, or the HICAMP architecture [9]. The HICAMP architecture provides improved concurrent programming semantics and reduces the cost of inter-process communication by providing an interface to a main memory that is *snapshotted* or *versioned* on every update. To achieve this, without requiring an exorbitant amount of DRAM, HICAMP implements fine-grained in-memory deduplication. Such a deduplicated memory is useful in other domains as well: by introducing another level of indirection, it enables large pages *and* fine-grained sharing of page content in a virtualized server environment.

Such a memory suppresses duplicate zero values and thus inherently provides *sparsity oblivious* hardware support for compact representation of sparse matrices. Because some aspects of the HICAMP architecture may prove useful in fully realizing the potential of our method, we start by describing deduplicated memory and then briefly describe key hardware components used by HICAMP. We then describe several new matrix formats that rely on a deduplicated backing store and investigate their storage efficiency. One such format leverages the deduplicated memory to automatically

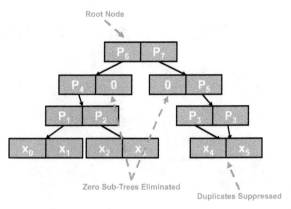

$$v = \begin{bmatrix} x_0 & x_1 & x_2 & x_3 & 0 & 0 & 0 & 0 & 0 & 0 & 0 & 0 & x_4 & x_5 & x_4 & x_5 \end{bmatrix}$$

Figure 1: HICAMP DAG Storage: vector v is stored in the leaf nodes of the DAG

detect symmetric matrix components and recursive patterns of content. Our best compaction result is an improvement of 5700x. These results encouraged us to implement a custom SpMV kernel that emulates the HICAMP data access pattern while running on a standard x86/Linux server. Using this kernel, we achieve an average speedup of 1.5x and a best-case speedup of 3.7x. We investigate the speedup and our performance limits using profiling techniques. Through this paper, we hope to provide insight to how a deduplicated memory could be used in conjunction with certain hardware components to further accelerate SpMV.

2. DEDUPLICATED MEMORY

The HICAMP architecture [8, 9] provides the abstraction of a linear memory, but deduplicates memory content at a fixed granularity that we refer to as a *memory line*. To do this, a level of indirection is introduced. In particular, a given linear array is stored in the leaf nodes of a directed acyclic graph (DAG). The DAG itself is comprised of unique and immutable memory lines. To provide efficient addressing of the fixed granularity memory lines, we use line addresses that we individually refer to as a *physical line id* or PLID. To provide efficient reclamation, each PLID has an affiliated reference count. Figure 1 shows an example of some content (a sparse vector) mapped to a HICAMP DAG.

In Figure 1, the root node contains PLIDs 6 and 7. The memory line containing content (values) x_4 and x_5 is referred to by PLID 3 and has a reference count of two. The zero-valued PLIDs imply zero-valued subtrees. Although we illustrate here using an internal node fanout of two, this conceptual view of memory can use any branching factor. If all leaf nodes were unique and non-zero, the DAG shown in Figure 1 would be a fully balanced binary-tree. Using this observation, we adopt the following convenient (if informal) terminology for use in this paper: when necessary to specify the branching factor, we describe a DAG such as that illustrated in Figure 1 as a binary-tree (or *b-tree*). We describe a DAG with a branching factor of four as a quad-tree (*q-tree*) and a DAG with a branching factor of eight as an oct-tree (*o-tree*).

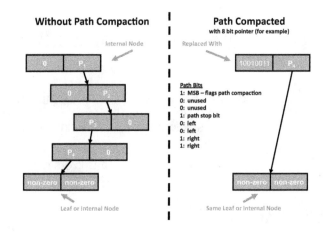

Figure 2: Path Compaction

Because sparse data is common, not just in linear algebra, an optimization is used when internal DAG nodes become underutilized. A path-compacted node replaces a sequence of nodes containing only one PLID each by pointing directly to the PLID at the end and by encoding the path through the DAG. A path compaction is flagged by a single bit sacrificed from the pointer space (example shown in Figure 2).

2.1 HICAMP Architecture

The HICAMP architecture provides hardware support for efficient concurrency-safe access to shared data. Most research has focused on the model of multiple threads accessing data within a single shared address space, but many real applications use multiple separate processes with separate address spaces for fault-isolation and simplified synchronization. HICAMP bridges this discrepancy and provides process-like shared data protection through snapshot isolation and reduces the high cost of inter-process communication by allowing pointer sharing.

HICAMP translates load and store instructions into operations on DAGs of unique and immutable memory lines. The memory lines in the DAG, both internal and leaf, are hardware protected and cannot be modified directly by software. Instead, HICAMP provides a *virtual segment table* that maps from software visible *segment ids* to the DAG root nodes. The segment table provides the interface to software and is somewhat analogous to a TLB.

When a thread begins to access memory referred to by a segment id, it issues a command to hardware that accesses the segment table and issues a reference count increment to the DAG root node. This reference count increment guarantees that the root node, and by extension, any PLID or leaf node referred to by the root node, will not be deallocated or modified. Thus, the thread has a stable and isolated snapshot of the memory content. The thread can modify its view of the DAG, but changes are not globally visible until committed by an update to the virtual segment table. Read-write conflicts are thus eliminated and write-write conflicts can be detected by compare-and-swap (CAS) against the previous root node PLID. This enables snapshot and transactional semantics for arbitrarily large regions of memory, i.e. independent of cache size.

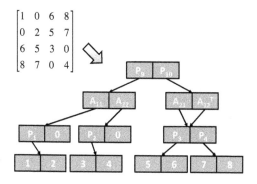

Figure 3: A Sparse Symmetric Matrix Mapped to QTS Format

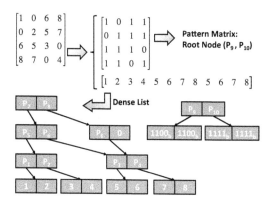

Figure 4: NZD Format using binary-tree and 8 bit nodes

Although we cannot here fully describe all aspects of the architecture, two specific hardware structures are relevant to this paper: the HICAMP memory controller (provides efficient deduplication of content) and the HICAMP iterator register (provides efficient access to DAG leaf nodes).

2.2 HICAMP Memory Controller

The HICAMP memory controller provides an interface to a content addressable memory that is backed by standard DRAM. To implement content lookup, the HICAMP memory controller breaks the address space into hash buckets and performs an efficient hash-based search. The HICAMP memory controller provides two fundamental operations: *lookup by content* (returns a PLID) and *read by PLID* (returns content). The PLID is comprised of the hash bucket index and way number and can be directly converted to a physical address. The HICAMP memory controller also maintains the reference count for each line.

2.3 HICAMP Iterator Register

The HICAMP iterator register accepts load and store instructions from software as operations relative to some *segment id*. A load operation accepts an offset and traverses from the graph root (found in the *virtual segment table*) to the leaf specified by the offset. A store operation implies the insertion (or replacement) of some content as a leaf node. The iterator register issues a lookup to the memory controller and then inserts the returned PLID as an internal node in the DAG. This procedure of lookup-by-content and node insertion continues until the DAG root node is replaced with a new PLID.

As the name implies, the iterator register is meant to provide efficient iteration over leaf elements that are logically contiguous, but actually scattered throughout memory. Besides implementing DAG traversal in hardware, the iterator register maintains a private cache of DAG elements along the path from the root node to the currently referenced leaf node to minimize memory accesses.

3. DEDUPLICATED MATRIX FORMATS

Using the memory structures described in Section 2, a sparse matrix can be efficiently stored with implicit indices (i.e., as if it were dense) because the DAG eliminates zero valued sub-graphs. We call this a logically dense format. A common approach to sparse matrix storage is to store a

list of non-zero values along with arrays that indicate their indices. We call this a compressed format when mapped to a deduplicated memory. A hybrid of these two can be employed – this approach is useful when a large amount of non-zero pattern symmetry exists, but the non-zero values themselves are unique. In this section, we describe the deduplicated matrix formats that we studied. We begin with the logically dense formats (RMA & QTS), then move to hybrid (NZD), and then to compressed (HCSR & HCOO).

3.1 Row Major Array (RMA)

The most basic HICAMP matrix format is row major array. This format logically stores *every* matrix value in row major order; i.e., it is logically dense. Although lacking in sophistication, this method achieves storage efficiency at parity with the canonical CSR format (see Table 2).

3.2 Quad-Tree Symmetric (QTS)

Another logically dense format, quad-tree symmetric, divides the matrix into four quadrants (A_{11}, A_{12}, A_{21}, and A_{22}) and stores each in a separate sub-graph. When the sub-matrix is on diagonal, the storage order is A_{11}, A_{22}, A_{21}, then A_{12}^{T}. In this way, the QTS format automatically exploits the duplicate content found in symmetric matrices. Moreover, because it makes no special provision for explicitly symmetric matrices, it automatically mines out *any amount* of symmetry, i.e., even for non-symmetric matrices. In Figure 3, we show an example mapping a small symmetric matrix to a QTS encoded DAG.

3.3 Non-Zeros Dense (NZD)

The non-zeros dense format is a hybrid format that uses two DAGs: one representing a sparse pattern matrix and the other a dense vector. In NZD, the underlying non-zero pattern is factored out as a pattern matrix in QTS form. Because the pattern matrix leaf elements are logically only one bit in size, 64 leaves can fit in the same space as one double precision floating point value. The non-zero values are then stored in a dense list ordered to correspond to the QTS pattern matrix. In Figure 4, we show the NZD format using the toy matrix from Figure 3.

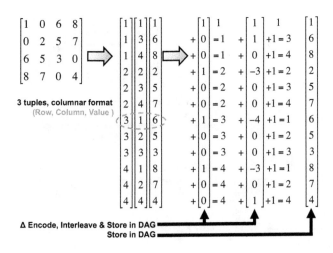

Figure 5: HCOO Format: Delta Encoding and Interleaving Scheme

3.4 HICAMP Compressed Sparse Row (HCSR)

The HICAMP compressed sparse row format maps a list of non-zero values, a corresponding list of column indices, and a shorter list that indicates the positions of row breaks in both of the former lists to the leaf nodes of three separate DAGs. As the name implies, this is a mapping of the canonical compressed sparse row (CSR) format into a deduplicated memory.

To enhance deduplication, the column indices and row breaks are delta encoded. Delta encoding exposes more duplicate values where regular patterns exist. For example, the sequence $1, 2, 3, 4, 10$ becomes $1, 1, 1, 1, 6$ when delta encoded (note that the first value in the list is the seed value). The same sequence can be delta encoded as $1, 0, 0, 0, 5$ with an assumed increment of one. Because the column indices are often clustered in sequential order and because our method favors zero values, we use an assumed increment of one when delta encoding the column indices list.

3.5 HICAMP Coordinate Format (HCOO)

In the traditional coordinate format (COO), each non-zero value is stored along with explicit matrix indices, i.e., as a 3-tuple: (row index, column index, non-zero value). In the HCOO format, we first arrange the tuples in columns so that we have a list of non-zero values, a list of row indices, and a list of column indices. To enhance deduplication, we apply delta encoding to the index lists (with an assumed increment of one for column indices). Although the index lists are logically the same length as the list of non-zero values, the index list data elements are one half the width of the double precision floating point values. Thus, we next interleave the row and column indices so that we have only two lists, each with the same number of bits. We then map these two lists to the leaf nodes of two separate DAGs. We show this delta encoding and interleaving scheme in Figure 5. The two DAGs, thus obtained, are logically the same height – this, by itself, is of no particular importance, but in our software implementation it allows us to track the state of only one DAG and thus reduce our overall instruction count.

3.6 Storage Bounds

Our deduplicated storage formats can achieve a high degree of data compaction, but also provide reasonable bounds in the worst case. Given an m by n matrix A, with nnz random non-zero values, and pessimistically assuming that no deduplication occurs for the row and column indices, we can precisely compute the DAG overhead for the compressed formats HCOO and HCSR using a geometric series:

$$total\_nodes = \begin{cases} 2 & \cdot & num\_leaf\_nodes & b\text{–}tree \\ 4/3 & \cdot & num\_leaf\_nodes & q\text{–}tree \\ 8/7 & \cdot & num\_leaf\_nodes & o\text{–}tree \end{cases} \quad (1)$$

For HCOO and HCSR the number of leaf nodes is $O(nnz)$ and thus the storage is no worse than $O(nnz)$. For logically dense formats, we assume that each non-zero costs one leaf node and that each leaf costs $log(m \cdot n)$ total nodes. With the understanding that n represents the longer dimension of the matrix, the storage cost for a logically dense format is no worse than $O(nnz \cdot log(n))$.

4. CONCURRENT SYMMETRIC SPMV

Using matrix symmetry, traditional matrix storage formats and SpMV kernels can save on storage and bandwidth requirements by storing only the upper (or lower) half of the matrix. The symmetric-CSR format keeps only the upper half and thus achieves an immediate ∼2x storage advantage.

In concurrent SpMV, threads are normally assigned distinct matrix rows. This works well for non-symmetric CSR SpMV because, for each thread, it preserves the property of sequential access along a matrix row. More importantly, this work partition assigns a disjoint write set to each thread, and thus the threads can operate in complete independence with no synchronization.

Unfortunately, this partitioning inhibits performance for concurrent symmetric SpMV: because each thread now owns both one row and one column of the matrix, each thread can write to any value in the output vector. Thus, atomic updates are required for every write operation and synchronization overhead eliminates the benefit of parallelism.

The QTS format described in Section 3.2 neatly avoids these issues. Using QTS, any work partition that is thread-safe for a non-symmetric matrix is inherently thread-safe for a symmetric matrix. To avoid the need for thread synchronization, we partition the QTS matrix by row. In Section 6.9, we demonstrate that our symmetric concurrent SpMV kernel scales with thread-count and exploits the reduction in memory traffic that matrix symmetry enables.

5. SOFTWARE IMPLEMENTATION

5.1 Matrix Encoding

We implemented all of the matrix formats described in Section 3 using software to perform the deduplication. For each format, we implemented binary, quad, and oct-tree variants. For binary internal tree-degree, we used 8-byte memory lines, i.e., wide enough to store one double precision floating point value as a leaf node and enough for two 32-bit pointers in internal nodes. For quad-tree, we used 16-byte memory lines (two doubles per leaf node and four 32-bit pointers per internal node), and for oct-tree, 32-byte memory lines.

```
procedure TraverseDAG( nodes, height ):
  sp = 1                # initialize stack pointer
  ptrStack[0] = 0       # node pointer stack
  offStack[0] = 0       # leaf node offset stack
  lvlStack[0] = height  # DAG level stack
  while( sp ):
    sp -= 1
    level  = lvlStack[ sp ]
    offset = offStack[ sp ]
    ptr    = ptrStack[ sp ]
    node = nodes[ ptr ]
    if level == 0:
      print "offset =", offset, ", leaf =", node
    else:
      if node.left & pathbit:
        # decode path & push new offset, level, & node pointer
      else:
        if node.right:
          ptrStack[ sp ] = node.right
          lvlStack[ sp ] = level
          offStack[ sp ] = offset + 1 << level
          sp += 1
        if node.left:
          ptrStack[ sp ] = node.left
          lvlStack[ sp ] = level
          offStack[ sp ] = offset
          sp += 1
```

Figure 6: DAG Traversal Code

5.2 SpMV Kernel

We implemented an SpMV kernel for each of the HICAMP formats. Due to space limitations, we present results only for HCOO and QTS because they are the most instructive. For SpMV, we used DAGs with internal node fanout of four (quad-tree) because this degree achieves higher data-compaction than oct-tree while exposing more memory parallelism than binary-tree. In Figure 6, we show pseudo-code for traversing a DAG. For simplicity, we show code for binary-tree. This generic code tracks two explicit state variables: the current DAG level (level zero indicates a leaf node) and the offset from the logically leftmost leaf node. In our QTS kernel, we replace the offset state variable with row/column state variables. In the HCOO SpMV kernel, we do not track the offset because the row/column indices are given explicitly in the leaf node data: DAG traversal stops when a zero-valued left subtree is encountered. Further, because the HCOO format stores dense lists, the HCOO kernel does not check for path compactions. Although the HCOO kernel must logically traverse two DAGs, as mentioned in Section 3.5, these DAGs have exactly the same number of leaf nodes and can thus share their state.

6. PERFORMANCE RESULTS

6.1 Methodology

We report performance results for static memory requirements (memory footprint) and for SpMV execution time speedup. In addition to reporting raw performance, we measure memory traffic, instructions executed, and instructions per cycle (IPC). We compare our HCOO SpMV kernel to a multi-threaded CSR SpMV and we compare our QTS SpMV kernel to a symmetry aware CSR SpMV kernel. We measure execution time at nano-second resolution using calls to `clock_gettime()` and average the results over many trials. After the timing run, we measure instruction and cycle count using the Linux `perf` tool and we measure DRAM load and

Sockets	2
Cores	12
Threads	24
LLC	12 MB
f_{clk}	2.93 GHz
Mem Channels	3
f_{mem}	1066 MHZ
Mem BW	25.6 GB/sec

Table 1: Test Platform Specifications

store operations using LIKWID [21] to access uncore performance counters.

6.2 Test Matrices & Performance Metrics

A set of 74 non-symmetric matrices and 12 symmetric matrices were drawn from the UF Sparse Matrix Repository [10]. We ensure that the underlying data span a number of disciplines. For an m by n matrix with nnz non-zero elements, we calculate its non-deduplicated memory footprint as follows:

$$bytes_{csr} = 12 \cdot nnz + 4 \cdot m + 4 \qquad (2)$$

$$working\_set\_size_{csr} = bytes_{csr} + 8 \cdot m + 8 \cdot n \qquad (3)$$

And the deduplicated memory footprint is as follows:

$$bytes_{dag} = bytes\_per\_node \cdot num_{nodes} \qquad (4)$$

$$bytes\_per\_node = \begin{cases} 8 & b-tree \\ 16 & q-tree \\ 32 & o-tree \end{cases} \qquad (5)$$

$$working\_set\_size_{dag} = bytes_{dag} + 8 \cdot m + 8 \cdot n \qquad (6)$$

We compute our key performance metrics as follows:

$$matrix\_compaction = \frac{bytes_{csr}}{bytes_{dag}} \qquad (7)$$

$$working\_set\_compaction = \frac{working\_set\_size_{csr}}{working\_set\_size_{dag}} \qquad (8)$$

$$speedup = \frac{t_{spmv\_csr}}{t_{spmv\_dag}} \qquad (9)$$

$$mem\_traffic = 64 \cdot (num_{dram\_rds} + num_{dram\_wrs}) \qquad (10)$$

$$mem\_traffic\_advantage = \frac{mem\_traffic_{csr}}{mem\_traffic_{dag}} \qquad (11)$$

$$mem_{BW} = \frac{mem\_traffic}{t_{spmv}} \qquad (12)$$

6.3 Compaction Results

Table 2 shows compaction results for non-symmetric matrices for each HICAMP format using binary, quad, and oct-tree. In Figure 7, we plot the best achieved compaction ratio (Equation 7) versus non-deduplicated size (Equation 2). The results in Figure 7 are dominated by the QTS and NZD formats as these two methods simultaneously expose fine and coarse-grained patterns in the underlying matrices and take advantage of what symmetry does exist.

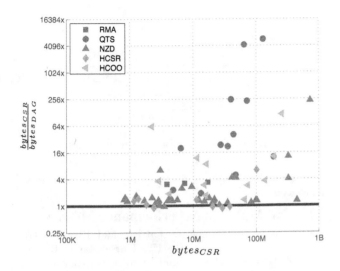

Figure 7: Matrix Data Compaction (Equation 7) vs. Uncompacted Size (Equation 2)

Format	Degree	Geomean	Best	Worst
RMA	b-tree	1.1x	18x	0.45x
	q-tree	0.8x	11x	0.28x
	o-tree	0.6x	8x	0.16x
QTS	b-tree	2.5x	5719x	0.46x
	q-tree	2.3x	5244x	0.29x
	o-tree	1.8x	4028x	0.18x
NZD	b-tree	2.5x	1182x	0.60x
	q-tree	2.8x	1160x	0.79x
	o-tree	2.6x	918x	0.79x
HCSR	b-tree	1.9x	1289x	0.54x
	q-tree	2.2x	1289x	0.76x
	o-tree	2.2x	979x	0.87x
HCOO	b-tree	1.8x	1513x	0.54x
	q-tree	2.2x	3185x	0.65x
	o-tree	2.0x	1141x	0.67x

Table 2: Comparison of HICAMP Matrix Formats

Matrix	Matrix Size	Uncompacted Working Set Size	Matrix Compaction	Working Set Compaction	Speedup
barrier2-1	25 MB	27 MB	0.9x	0.9x	0.9x
poisson3Db	28 MB	29 MB	0.6x	0.7x	0.4x
mc2depi	26 MB	34 MB	1.9x	1.6x	1.6x
TSOPF_RS_b300_c2	34 MB	34 MB	13.4x	11.6x	1.9x
thermomech_dK	33 MB	36 MB	0.9x	0.9x	0.7x
sme3Dc	36 MB	37 MB	0.9x	0.9x	0.7x
stat96v3	38 MB	47 MB	12.5x	4.0x	1.7x
xenon2	45 MB	47 MB	4.4x	3.7x	1.5x
webbase-1M	39 MB	55 MB	1.7x	1.4x	0.9x
rajat29	45 MB	55 MB	1.6x	1.4x	1.1x
stormG2_1000	42 MB	56 MB	6.5x	2.7x	1.6x
Chebyshev4	62 MB	63 MB	1.3x	1.3x	1.1x
largebasis	62 MB	68 MB	3.3x	2.7x	2.3x
pre2	69 MB	79 MB	2.8x	2.3x	1.3x
ohne2	79 MB	82 MB	1.0x	1.0x	0.9x
Hamrle3	69 MB	91 MB	85.9x	4.0x	2.2x
PR02R	94 MB	97 MB	1.1x	1.1x	1.1x
torso1	98 MB	100 MB	1.1x	1.1x	1.2x
Rucci1	97 MB	113 MB	5.7x	3.4x	2.8x
tp-6	133 MB	141 MB	2.3x	2.2x	1.5x
atmosmodl	124 MB	147 MB	3185.0x	6.4x	3.7x
TSOPF_RS_b2383	185 MB	186 MB	12.8x	12.3x	1.8x
circuit5M_dc	184 MB	237 MB	1.7x	1.5x	1.2x
rajat31	250 MB	322 MB	115.1x	4.4x	2.2x
cage14	316 MB	339 MB	2.0x	1.9x	1.0x
FullChip	316 MB	362 MB	1.7x	1.5x	0.9x
RM07R	430 MB	436 MB	1.2x	1.2x	1.1x
circuit5M	702 MB	787 MB	3.0x	2.5x	1.8x
average	n/a	n/a	124.0x	2.5x	1.5x

Table 3: HCOO Compaction and SpMV Speedup

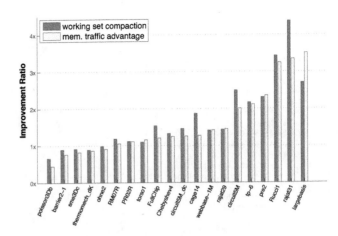

Figure 8: Memory Traffic Advantage and Matrix Compaction for Non-Cacheable Matrices

6.4 SpMV Execution Time

For SpMV performance evaluation, we restrict our attention to the 28 matrices whose working set size exceeds the capacity of the last level cache. Table 3 shows the speedup obtained for these matrices. We achieve an average speedup of 1.5x and a best-case speedup of 3.7x (for matrix *atmosmodl*).

Because our speedup lags the potential improvement indicated by the compaction results, in the remainder of this section, we investigate this discrepancy by analyzing memory traffic, memory bandwidth, instruction count, and IPC.

6.5 Memory Traffic

In Figure 8, we compare memory traffic advantage (Equation 11) to working set compaction (Equation 8). We observe that the reduction in memory traffic is indeed correlated to this compaction metric. As the amount of compaction increases, the probability of evicting a highly deduplicated node from the cache increases. This results in a diminishing return in terms of memory traffic as compared to working set compaction.

In Figure 8, we omit eight matrices whose working sets were compacted to a size smaller than the last level cache capacity. Although we would like to show these on the plot, their memory traffic ratio is heavily skewed in favor of SpMV speedup and the remaining data points are obscured. As a specific example, matrix *stat96v3* had its working set compacted from 47 MB to 12 MB resulting in a memory traffic advantage of 90x. For *stat96v3*, the SpMV execution time speedup was only 1.7x. Obviously, the compaction technique is providing a substantial advantage in terms of memory traffic and one can conclude that DRAM bandwidth is not the performance limiting factor. In the following sections, we investigate performance limits by analyzing sustained bandwidth, instruction count, and IPC.

6.6 Memory Bandwidth

In Figure 9, we plot the sustained memory bandwidth for all matrices in our test set. Additionally, we show the peak theoretical bandwidth of 25.6 GB/sec and the maximum sustainable bandwidth obtained by running the synthetic benchmark *stream* [18]. As expected, the CSR implementa-

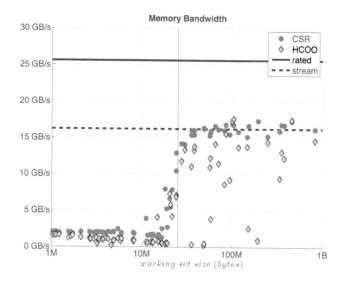

Figure 9: Sustained Bandwidth to DRAM

```
procedure RMA_SpMV( mtxSegID, m, n, y, x ):
  it = IterReg( mtxSegID )
  it.SetSkipZeroValuesOnIncrement()
  while( it.Pos() != it.End() ):
    v = it.Val()
    p = it.Pos()
    r = p / n
    c = p % n
    y[r] += v * x[c]
    it.PosInc()
```

Figure 10: SpMV Using an Iterator Register

tion of SpMV attains the maximum sustainable bandwidth to DRAM (as given by *stream*) when the working set size exceeds twice the capacity of the last level cache (solid vertical line in Figure 9).

6.7 Instruction Count

Although effective at reducing memory traffic, our method imposes the cost of significantly increased instruction count. We find that the CSR implementation executes approximately 9 instructions per non-zero value while our HCOO kernel requires, on average, 26. A significant amount of implementation effort was spent on minimizing the amount of generated code in the performance critical kernel, and despite this, the ratio is still quite unfavorable.

To illustrate that this code overhead would be significantly reduced by implementing hardware such as the HICAMP iterator register, we show pseudo-code for SpMV using the RMA format in Figure 10. Visually comparing to the code in Figure 6, it is clear that there are fewer lines of *source code*. More importantly, because the iterator register implements DAG traversal in hardware, the amount of *generated code* will be far less. In particular, a command such as `it.PosInc()` is reduced to a single hardware instruction. Moreover, the iterator register hardware provisions fast memory for the DAG nodes along the path to the current leaf node and concurrently maintains meta-data such as its offset from the leftmost leaf; the software implementation (Figure 6), is required to maintain a pointer stack, offset stack, and level stack. All of these benefits are retained

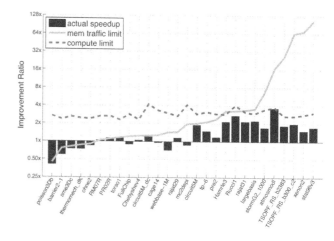

Figure 11: Performance Limits and Speedup

when extending the code shown in Figure 10 to handle other formats such as QTS, NZD, and HCOO.

6.8 Performance Limits

We conclude that the two relevant performance limits are main memory bandwidth and compute:

$$bw\_limit = \frac{mem\_traffic_{csr}}{mem\_traffic_{dag}} \quad (13)$$

$$compute\_limit = \frac{num_{instructions\_csr}/IPC_{csr}}{num_{instructions\_dag}/IPC_{dag}} \quad (14)$$

In Figure 11, we plot the obtained SpMV speedup (Equation 9) and compare it to the memory bandwidth limit (Equation 13) and the compute limit (Equation 14).

The bandwidth limit is plotted under the assumption that our kernel can achieve the maximum sustainable bandwidth as indicated by *stream*. This assumption is justified by the high sustained bandwidth exhibited by the data sets that do not achieve a significant reduction in working set size (see Figure 9). The compute limit is plotted under the assumption that our method can sustain an IPC of 2 (i.e. if not bandwidth limited) and that the CSR method achieves only an IPC of 0.5 (i.e. because it is always bandwidth limited). The average IPC numbers, and other data such as instruction count and DRAM operations, are based on profiling (described in Section 6.1) for the matrices shown in Figure 11.

Prior to the advent of multi-core, SpMV optimization research focused on adding work to the inner loop [22] so that maximum sustainable bandwidth could be attained. Our results shown in Figure 9 indicate that we achieve maximum sustainable bandwidth, but through the use of threads rather than optimizations that generate more memory accesses within a given code block. This is a result of current technology trends: the available memory bandwidth per core is dropping [1]. These technology trends and our results, based on measurements from actual hardware, imply that a HICAMP system provisioned with the same amount of cache as our test platform (Figure 1) could operate at the bandwidth limit and achieve a best-case speedup of 90x. In Figure 12, we simulate further decreases in available bandwidth per core by re-running our experiments using three,

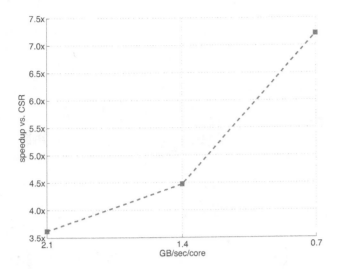

Figure 12: HCOO SpMV speedup vs. multi-threaded CSR as GB/sec/core drops (matrix *atmosmodl*)

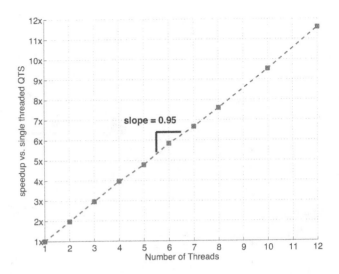

Figure 14: QTS SpMV Scaling With Threads (matrix *nlpkkt120*)

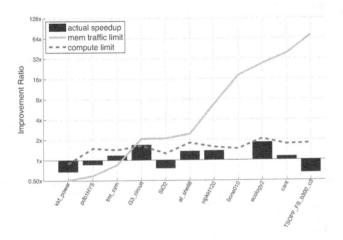

Figure 13: Performance Limits for QTS SpMV on Symmetric Matrices

then two, and then one memory channel: as the cores become more bandwidth starved, our method starts to significantly outperform the traditional CSR method.

6.9 QTS Symmetry Oblivious SpMV

We now assess the performance of our *symmetry oblivious* QTS SpMV kernel. We compare performance to single threaded symmetric CSR SpMV because this kernel achieves the lowest memory traffic. In Figure 13, we show the performance limits versus the speedup achieved. The best-case memory traffic advantage of 71x would be 142x (matrix *TSOPF_FS_b300_c3*) if we compared to a parallelized SpMV kernel without symmetric storage. In some cases, we transfer more data than required by symmetric CSR SpMV due to a combination of cache evictions and less raw compaction.

The QTS SpMV kernel has even more code overhead than our HCOO SpMV kernel with an average of 121 instructions per non-zero matrix element (compared to an average of 26 for HCOO). Because of this, its compute limit is lower and

its raw performance lags. In Figure 14, we show that, when compute limited, our method scales very close to linearly with additional cores (matrix *nlpkkt120*). For many matrices, we have significant headroom to allow this scaling to continue as indicated by Figures 11 and 13.

7. RELATED WORK

The literature on optimizing SpMV is vast: a testament to the difficulty and importance of this task. Historically, it was difficult to achieve peak performance due to the very tight inner loop of SpMV coupled with the indirect and random access pattern into the source vector. This motivated research into methods for adding extra work into the inner loop and regularizing data access patterns. Regularized data access can be achieved by finding dense matrix sub-blocks or through domain specific knowledge that allows a highly customized SpMV kernel to be invoked. Because the bandwidth limitation has long been recognized, research has also focused on methods for reducing memory traffic. Thus, most research into optimizing SpMV can be categorized as either reducing memory traffic, adding work to the inner loop, regularizing data access patterns, or some combination of these.

7.1 Non-Symmetric SpMV

The block compressed sparse row (BCSR) format captures all three of these tactics by using a CSR index structure to point to dense submatrices (or blocks). Because the blocks are fixed size and dense, they exhibit regular data access patterns and allow for optimal loop unrolling. Further, some matrices require less storage because of reduced index data overhead. Vuduc [22] and Williams [25], et al., describe *OSKI*, a framework for autotuning BCSR SpMV kernels.

With the advent of programmable GPUs, researchers have attempted to utilize the high GPU to video-memory bandwidth. Bell and Garland [3] describe methods to approach maximum sustainable bandwidth for SpMV on GPU through several techniques directed at regularizing data access. Because power constraints now force GPUs to include large on-die caches, the regular control flow of our HCOO format makes it an interesting candidate for GPU implementation.

Method	Best Compaction	Best Speedup	Index Compaction	Value Compaction	Data Reuse	Kernel Code
DCSR	1.4x	1.5x	Yes	No	No	Generic
PBR	1.5x	1.5x	Yes	No	Via Code[1]	Per Matrix
RPCSR	1.5x	1.5x	Yes	Yes	Via Code[1]	Per Matrix
CSR-DU	1.3x	1.8x	Yes	No	No	Generic
CSX		1.9x	Yes	No	Via Code[1]	Per Matrix
RSB		2.0x	Yes	No	No	Generic
CSR-VI	2.4x	2.5x	Yes	Yes	Yes	Generic
RBCSR		3.5x	Yes	No	No	Generic
DAG (this work)	5700x	3.7x	Yes	Yes	Yes	Generic
(1) Matrix structure embedded in custom generated code						

Table 4: Comparison of Non-Symmetric SpMV Compaction Techniques

To improve the concurrent scalability of computing $A^T x$, Buluç et al. introduced the new compressed sparse block (CSB) format [6] which has storage and performance similar to CSR. In the reduced bandwidth compressed sparse block (RBCSB) format [7], Buluç et al. use bitmasked register blocks (similar to the NZD pattern matrices in Section 3.3) to reduce the storage requirements of CSB.

Kourtis et al. [13,14], explore the effect of delta-encoding the index values (CSR-DU) and then add value deduplication via an indirection map (CSR-VI). Willcock and Lumsdaine [24] present the delta-coded sparse row (DCSR) method (similar to CSR-DU).

More sophisticated attempts to reduce memory traffic have used offline analysis followed by code generation (resulting in a custom SpMV kernel on a per matrix basis). In the compressed sparse extended (CSX) method [15], Kourtis analyzes each matrix separately to discover the underlying non-zero structure and customizes the delta encoding scheme for the index values. In their row pattern CSR (RPCSR) format [24], Willcock and Lumsdaine exploit macro-scale patterns in each matrix row. Finally, Belgin et al., observe that the underlying physical problem often generates a set of several distinct sub-matrix patterns. They exploit this in their pattern based-representation (PBR) [2].

Recursive matrix layouts, similar to our QTS format, have inspired recent papers [4,17]. In their recursive sparse blocks (RSB) format [17], Martone et al., use a quad-tree with Z-Morton ordering to store pointers to sparse submatrices that are sized to balance the work partitions. Because the quad-tree structure implies an offset (similar to our implicit indices), they use 16 bit index elements in the leaf submatrices.

In Table 4, we compare the techniques using explicit compaction and show the best-case speedup for each method. Data in Table 4 are based on a comparison to multi-threaded CSR when available, otherwise to the best proxy available in the respective paper.

7.2 Concurrent Symmetric SpMV

Several recent papers have also explored techniques for enabling concurrent symmetric SpMV. In addition to improving the CSB format by using register bitmasking, Buluç [7] describes a technique to exploit symmetric storage also using the CSB format. Starting from the observation that a block diagonal symmetric matrix is trivially parallelized, Buluç uses Reverse Cuthill-McKee (RCM) ordering to bring most non-zero elements close to the diagonal. The portions of the matrix, which are in blocks one and two positions off diagonal, are then assigned to separate rounds (coordinated to avoid write-write conflicts) while the elements further off diagonal (few in number) require atomic updates to the destination vector. The cluster scale solution, presented by

Krotkiewski and Dabrowski [16], also starts by using RCM re-ordering and then handles all off-block-diagonal entries with local result buffers and attempts to overlap communication and computation across rounds. Such methods provide the benefit of scaling with threads, up to the memory bandwidth limit, but come at the cost of pre and post-processing steps and still require thread synchronization and either atomic updates or explicit communication.

Tangwongsan et al. [4], introduce a hierarchical storage format that points to the same memory region for off diagonal blocks if the matrix is symmetric (similar to our QTS format). These authors also point out that this kind of matrix storage enables lock and synchronization free concurrent symmetric SpMV. Their method achieves an average of 1.8x less memory traffic when using double precision values. These authors further reduce memory traffic by switching from double to single precision floating point, but do not use any other compaction or deduplication techniques.

8. CONCLUSIONS

In this work, we have shown that fine-grained data deduplication and DAG storage provide efficient representations for sparse matrices and can reduce memory traffic during the bandwidth limited SpMV kernel. Our results indicate that our method improves sparse matrix storage density by a factor of two on average (formats QTS, NZD, HCSR, and HCOO in Table 2). We show that the recursive nature of our data-deduplication technique can provide large advantages in storage density as demonstrated by the 5700x compaction achieved by the QTS format. Our worst-case storage density is $O(nnz)$ for a compressed sparse matrix (HCSR and HCOO) or $O(nnz \cdot log(n))$ for a logically dense or hybrid sparse matrix (RMA, QTS, and NZD).

Using our matrix storage techniques, we demonstrate an average speedup of 1.5x using a custom SpMV kernel running on standard hardware. By measuring DRAM accesses, we show a memory traffic advantage in proportion to the reduction in working set size. The relative benefit of our method depends on the memory traffic required (matrix specific) and the available bandwidth per core (Figure 12). For matrices exceeding LLC capacity (Figure 11), our data indicate an average reduction in memory traffic of 2.8x and best-case reduction of 90x.

For matrices with the highest potential speedup, instruction count overhead prohibits our software kernel from fully exploiting available memory bandwidth. The iterator register, described in the HICAMP architecture [9] (Section 2.3, Figure 10), eliminates this code overhead.

We introduce the novel QTS matrix format that inherently exploits any amount of matrix symmetry. Because the QTS format is *symmetry oblivious*, any thread safe work partitioning for the QTS format is safe for a symmetric matrix. Using this format, we demonstrate symmetric concurrent SpMV without any locks or matrix reordering.

Based on these results, we plan to implement iterator register hardware either as a custom feature in an existing ISA (e.g. using Tensilica TIE instructions [11]) or in an FPGA. For the specific purpose of SpMV, the iterator register functionality can be enhanced by adding a state machine to keep track of implicit matrix indices (for the QTS format) and a separate accumulate and store unit can take the fetch of destination vector elements off of the critical path.

As mentioned, current trends show that processing capability is increasing faster than memory bandwidth [1] and that caches are growing relatively faster than core count [5]. Both larger caches and additional cores benefit the method we have demonstrated. These trends and our data indicate that HICAMP enables otherwise difficult to achieve performance benefits.

9. REFERENCES

[1] A. Bechtolsheim. Technologies for Data-Intensive Computing. In *Proceedings of the 13th International Workshop on High Performance Transaction Systems*. HPTS, October 2009.

[2] M. Belgin, G. Back, and C. J. Ribbens. Pattern-based Sparse Matrix Representation for Memory-Efficient SMVM Kernels. In *Proceedings of the 23rd International Conference on Supercomputing (ICS '09)*, pages 100–109. ACM, June 2009.

[3] N. Bell and M. Garland. Implementing Sparse Matrix-Vector Multiplication on Throughput-Oriented Processors. In *Proceedings of Supercomputing (SC '09)*, pages 18:1–18:11. ACM, November 2009.

[4] G. Blelloch, I. Koutis, G. Miller, and K. Tangwongsan. Hierarchical Diagonal Blocking and Precision Reduction Applied to Combinatorial Multigrid. In *Proceedings of Supercomputing (SC '10)*, pages 1 –12, November 2010.

[5] S. Borkar and A. A. Chien. The Future of Microprocessors. *Communications of the ACM*, 54:67–77, May 2011.

[6] A. Buluç, J. T. Fineman, M. Frigo, J. R. Gilbert, and C. E. Leiserson. Parallel Sparse Matrix-Vector and Matrix-Transpose-Vector Multiplication Using Compressed Sparse Blocks. In *Proceedings of the 21st Annual Symposium on Parallelism in Algorithms and Architectures*, SPAA '09, pages 233–244. ACM, 2009.

[7] A. Buluç, S. Williams, L. Oliker, and J. Demmel. Reduced-Bandwidth Multithreaded Algorithms for Sparse Matrix-Vector Multiplication. In *International Parallel Distributed Processing Symposium (IPDPS), 2011 IEEE International*, pages 721 –733, May 2011.

[8] D. R. Cheriton. Hierarchical Immutable Content-Addressable Memory Processor, January 2010. U.S. Patent 7650460.

[9] D. R. Cheriton, A. Firoozshahian, A. Solomatnikov, J. P. Stevenson, and O. Azizi. HICAMP: Architectural Support for Efficient Concurrency-Safe Shared Structured Data Access. In *Proceedings of the 17th International Conference on Architectural Support for Programming Languages and Operating Systems*, ASPLOS '12, pages 287–300, New York, NY, USA, 2012. ACM.

[10] T. A. Davis and Y. Hu. The University of Florida Sparse Matrix Collection. *ACM Trans. Math. Softw.*, 38:1:1–1:25, November 2011.

[11] R. Gonzalez. Xtensa: A Configurable and Extensible Processor. *Micro, IEEE*, 20(2):60–70, Mar/Apr 2000.

[12] E.-J. Im, K. A. Yelick, and R. Vuduc. SPARSITY: Framework for Optimizing Sparse Matrix-Vector Multiply. *International Journal of High Performance Computing Applications*, 18(1):135–158, February 2004.

[13] K. Kourtis, G. Goumas, and N. Koziris. Improving the Performance of Multithreaded Sparse Matrix-Vector Multiplication Using Index and Value Compression. In *37th International Conference on Parallel Processing (ICPP '08)*, pages 511–519, September 2008.

[14] K. Kourtis, G. Goumas, and N. Koziris. Optimizing Sparse Matrix-Vector Multiplication Using Index and Value Compression. In *Proceedings of the 5th Conference on Computing Frontiers (CF '08)*, pages 87–96. ACM, May 2008.

[15] K. Kourtis, V. Karakasis, G. Goumas, and N. Koziris. CSX: An Extended Compression Format for SpMV on Shared Memory Systems. In *Proceedings of the 16th ACM Symposium on Principles and Practice of Parallel Programming*, pages 247–256, February 2011.

[16] M. Krotkiewski and M. Dabrowski. Parallel Symmetric Sparse Matrix-Vector Product on Scalar Multi-Core CPUs. *Parallel Computing*, 36(4):181 – 198, 2010.

[17] M. Martone, S. Filippone, P. Gepner, M. Paprzycki, and S. Tucci. Use of Hybrid Recursive CSR/COO Data Structures in Sparse Matrix-Vector Multiplication. In *IMCSIT*, pages 327–335, October 2010.

[18] J. D. McCalpin. Memory Bandwidth and Machine Balance in Current High Performance Computers. *IEEE Computer Society Technical Committee on Computer Architecture (TCCA) Newsletter*, pages 19–25, December 1995.

[19] K. K. Nagar and J. D. Bakos. A Sparse Matrix Personality for the Convey HC-1. In *Proceedings of the 19th Annual Symposium on Field-Programmable Custom Computing Machines (FCCM '11)*, pages 1–8. IEEE, May 2011.

[20] S. Toledo. Improving the Memory-System Performance of Sparse-Matrix Vector Multiplication. *IBM Journal of Research and Development*, 41(6):711–725, November 1997.

[21] J. Treibig, G. Hager, and G. Wellein. LIKWID: A Lightweight Performance-Oriented Tool Suite for x86 Multicore Environments. In *Proceedings the International Workshop on Parallel Software Tools and Tool Infrastructures*, 2010.

[22] R. Vuduc, J. W. Demmel, and K. A. Yelick. OSKI: A Library of Automatically Tuned Sparse Matrix Kernels. In *Proceedings of SciDAC 2005*, Journal of Physics: Conference Series, San Francisco, CA, USA, June 2005. Institute of Physics Publishing.

[23] R. Vuduc, J. W. Demmel, K. A. Yelick, S. Kamil, R. Nishtala, and B. Lee. Performance Optimizations and Bounds for Sparse Matrix-Vector Multiply. In *Proceedings of Supercomputing (SC '02)*, Baltimore, MD, USA, November 2002.

[24] J. Willcock and A. Lumsdaine. Accelerating Sparse Matrix Computations via Data Compression. In *Proceedings of the 20th International Conference on Supercomputing (ICS '06)*, pages 307–316. ACM, June 2006.

[25] S. Williams, L. Oliker, R. Vuduc, J. Shalf, K. Yelick, and J. Demmel. Optimization of Sparse Matrix-Vector Multiplication on Emerging Multicore Platforms. In *Proceedings of Supercomputing (SC '07)*, pages 38:1–38:12. ACM, November 2007.

On the Communication Complexity of 3D FFTs and its Implications for Exascale

Kenneth Czechowski[†], Casey Battaglino[†], Chris McClanahan[*],
Kartik Iyer[‡], P.-K. Yeung[†,‡], Richard Vuduc[†]
[*] School of Computer Science
[†] School of Computational Science and Engineering
[‡] School of Aerospace Engineering
Georgia Institute of Technology, Atlanta, GA
{kentcz,cbattaglino3,chris.mcclanahan,kartik.iyer,pk.yeung,richie}@gatech.edu

ABSTRACT

This paper revisits the communication complexity of large-scale 3D fast Fourier transforms (FFTs) and asks what impact trends in current architectures will have on FFT performance at exascale. We analyze both memory hierarchy traffic and network communication to derive suitable analytical models, which we calibrate against current software implementations; we then evaluate models to make predictions about potential scaling outcomes at exascale, based on extrapolating current technology trends. Of particular interest is the performance impact of choosing high-density processors, typified today by graphics co-processors (GPUs), as the base processor for an exascale system. Among various observations, a key prediction is that although inter-node all-to-all communication is expected to be the bottleneck of distributed FFTs, *intra*-node communication—expressed precisely in terms of the relative balance among compute capacity, memory bandwidth, and network bandwidth—will play a critical role.

Categories and Subject Descriptors

D.1 [**Concurrent Programming**]: Distributed programming

General Terms

Algorithms, Performance

Keywords

FFT, Exascale, Performance Model

1. INTRODUCTION

As we progress toward exascale computing, new challenges, such as power and energy constraints, limit the scalability of traditional high performance computing systems. This has spurred the development of various alternative architectures. One noteworthy example is the recent interest in systems comprised of dense, massively parallel processors, such as GPUs. Yet despite the attention surrounding exascale, there is no consensus on which architectural strategies will win out, both on the processor level and on the system-wide level. Furthermore, this uncertainty raises important questions about how these design choices impact algorithms and software implementations.

This paper studies the ways in which the design of future exascale systems will affect applications targeted to run on these machines. To analyze potential architecture and algorithm scenarios, we propose the use of detailed, principled performance models, incorporating both algorithmic and architectural characteristics. This takes a unique approach towards performance modeling by integrating algorithmic communication complexity analysis—including traffic both within the memory hierarchy and across the network—with cost models that are grounded in technology trends. Our overall goal is to use such models to better understand the strengths and weaknesses of a particular algorithmic or architectural approach, and to apply such insights to quantitatively predict performance on future architectures.

To demonstrate this approach, we consider the problem of implementing a large-scale 3-dimensional fast Fourier transform (3D FFT) on a hypothetical future exascale system. We derive and calibrate a suitable analytical performance model, then use it to make predictions about potential scaling outcomes at exascale, based on the extrapolation of current technology trends. Of particular interest is the performance impact of building systems comprised of high-density compute units, as typified today by graphics co-processors (GPUs).

Contributions.

We make what we believe to be two contributions to our current understanding of large-scale FFT computations and the implications for exascale.

1. **Modeling** (§ 3): We derive an analytical performance model of a 3D FFT that includes computation and *both* inter- and intra-node communication costs. The inter-node terms account for topology; the intra-node terms include memory bandwidth, cache, and I/O-bus (PCIe) effects. This gives us a basis for studying how performance changes as machine parameters vary; how alternative 3D FFT algorithms might behave; and

what the future may hold. We instantiate and validate this model experimentally on existing systems. An intuitive interpretation of the model in terms of *processor balance* [6, 8, 11, 33, 35] is given in § 4.

2. **Predictions** (§ 6): Using our model, we consider trends in architecture and FFT performance over the past 30 years and predict what might happen in the year 2020, at exascale. Current debates about exascale architectures suggest two competing designs, or "swim lanes." One design is based on an embedded-CPU-like processor and the other based on a GPU-like design. Barring certain memory technology changes as discussed below, our analysis yields what may be a surprise to some, if not many: the relatively high compute-density of a GPU-like node could cause a global system imbalance. Consequently, a one exaflop/s (EF/s) system based on an extrapolated CPU-like design might actually outperform a one EF/s GPU-like design for 3D FFTs, or any similarly communication bandwidth-bound computation.

Limitations.

Our work has several limitations and qualifications.

First and foremost, we are not oblivious to the notion that, "Prediction is very difficult, especially about the future."[1] Indeed, we rely critically on assumptions that are subject to considerable debate and dramatic shifts. We do discuss some specific threats to validity, including, for instance, viability and impact of stacked memory on intra-node FFT performance. Our real intent in making any predictions at all is to foster discussion and perhaps influence the future, rather than to only obtain the strictly "correct" answer.

Second, our FFT analysis is far from exhaustive. For example, we only consider the pencil decomposition of the transpose method for computing a 3D FFT. Other distributed FFT algorithms exist, but for realistic problem sizes on current and future large-scale systems the pencil decomposition is the best option [17, 22]. We also assume ideal problem sizes: n is a power of two and all dimensions are equally sized. Interested readers are directed elsewhere for examples of how irregular problem sizes can impact performance [9]. Our analysis also omits several factors that could play key roles in future systems. Chief among these are microscopic memory and network contention effects, which we account for implicitly through parameter calibration. These omissions imply that our estimates are optimistic, as we show when we try to validate the model. Nevertheless, our modeling goal is to *bound* performance, in order to understand scalability independent of implementation artifacts that might reasonably disappear by the time we reach exascale. In that sense, the model may still permit interesting conclusions.

Finally, we have framed our Prediction section (§ 6) around "CPUs vs. GPUs," mostly to be topical and provocative. Such comparisons for exascale are in our view a red herring. In fact, our analysis abstracts away the details of CPU and GPU structures and characterizes them simply by balance. The predominant trend in nearly all processor designs is toward greater performance at the cost of increased im-

balance. Our paper serves as a cautionary tale about the consequences of increasing imbalance too aggressively.

2. RELATED WORK

There is a flurry of current research activity in performance analysis and modeling, both for exascale in general and in particular for 3D FFT algorithms and software at all scales of parallelism. Our paper most closely follows three recent studies.

The first study is by Pennycook et al., who also consider inter- vs. intra-node communication for the NAS-LU benchmark (parallel wavefront stencil), leveraging their earlier empirical modeling work [37]. Our model is by contrast more explicit about particular intra-node parameters, such as bandwidth, cache size, and I/O bus factors, and so our model adds improved algorithm-architecture understanding relative to this prior work.

The second study is Gahvari's and Gropp's theoretical analysis of feasible latency and bandwidth regimes at exascale, using LogGP modeling and pencil/transpose-based FFTs as one benchmark [9, 22]. Their model is more general than ours in that it is agnostic about specific architectural forms at exascale; however, ours may be more *prescriptive* about the necessary changes by explicitly modeling particular architectural features.

The third study is Kogge's and Dysart's exascale projection paper [30]. Their paper tracks system characteristics of Top500 supercomputers over the past 18 years to establish technology and architecture trends. Like our analysis, they use historical data to predict exascale technologies, but their paper primarily focuses on classifying supercomputers rather than evaluating the impact of these design choices. We take these projections a step further by combining them with our performance models to make quantitative performance predictions.

Beyond these key studies, there is a vast literature on 3D FFTs [2, 3, 5, 10, 12–15, 19, 20, 24, 25, 27, 32, 39, 40, 43]. We call attention to just a few of these. For large problem sizes, the speed record is 34.7 teraflop/s (TF/s) in 1D set by the 88,126 processor "K computer" manufactured by Fujitsu [1]. For relatively small problem sizes, the most impressive strong scaling demonstration is the 32^3 run on the Anton system, which uses custom ASIC network chips and fixed-point arithmetic, completing a 32^3 3D FFT in 4 μs (614 GF/s) [43], which our codes can only attain for relatively much larger problem sizes (see § 5).

3. 3D FFT PERFORMANCE MODEL

In this section we develop a performance model for a distributed 3D FFT on P nodes and total problem size $N = n^3$. The algorithm is illustrated in Figure 1. It consists of three computation phases which are separated by two communication phases. Each computation phase computes n^2 1D FFTs of size n in parallel. Each communication phase involves $\sqrt{P}$ independent P-node personalized all-to-all exchanges. We describe our model in terms of the time to compute (§ 3.1) and time to communicate (§ 3.2), but focus on dominant terms T_{mem} and T_{net}. In § 5 we identify artifacts of modern architectures, such as the CPU$\leftrightarrows$GPU memory transfer (§ 5.3.1) and local transpose costs (§ 5.2.2), that do not appear in the algorithmic analysis yet can have an impact on performance.

---

[1] Attribution is disputed though often credited to physicist Niels Bohr.

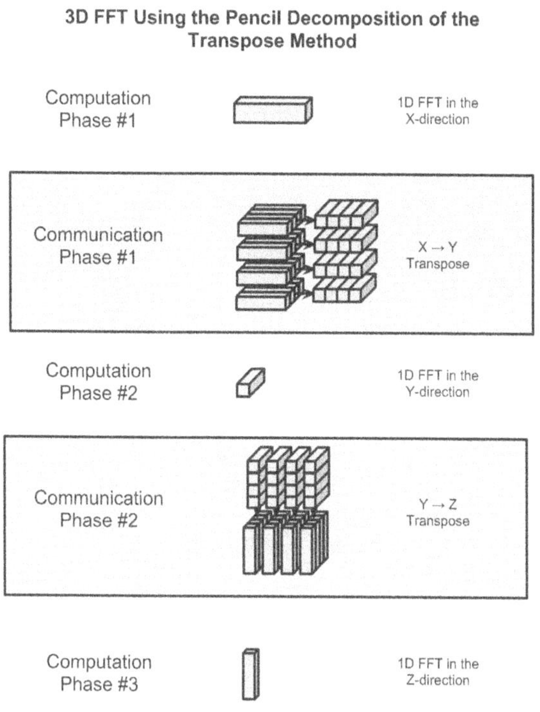

3D FFT Using the Pencil Decomposition of the Transpose Method

Computation Phase #1   1D FFT in the X-direction

Communication Phase #1   X → Y Transpose

Computation Phase #2   1D FFT in the Y-direction

Communication Phase #2   Y → Z Transpose

Computation Phase #3   1D FFT in the Z-direction

Figure 1: An illustration of the Computation and Communication phases in a 3D FFT using a pencil decomposition of the transpose method.

We make an additional simplifying assumption: we assume just one processor per node. The reason is that the cost of communicating between processors within a node versus the cost between nodes may actually be decreasing over time, as suggested in the trend data that appears in § 6.

Note about units of measure.

When counting flops, we assume *scalar flops*. That is, for the multiplication of two complex numbers, we would count 6 flops when using the classical method (4 scalar multiplies and 2 scalar adds). When counting volumes of data, however, we assume each *word* is a *complex* value. We use double-precision flops and double-complex words (16 bytes per word) unless otherwise specified.

3.1 Computation Costs

The 3D FFT is decomposed into $3n^2$ 1D FFTs, each of length n, distributed evenly among the P nodes. To approximate the cost of a local 1D FFT, we must consider both the cost of the floating point operations (T_{flops}) as well as the memory operations (T_{mem}).

3.1.1 Flop Costs

The 1D FFT of size n is computed using $\Theta(n \log n)$ floating point operations. The "radix-2" algorithm, which was originally presented by Cooley and Tukey in 1965, consists of approximately $5n \log_2 n$ flops. Since then numerous FFT algorithms have been presented, most of which reduce the absolute flop count slightly ($\approx 20\%$), but the practical performance benefits come from algorithms that allow the com-

putation to be structured in such a way that fully exploits the caches and SIMD lanes of the processor rather than the improved work load. Therefore, for simplicity we will rely on the conventional constant, which closely matches the observed flop count in § 5.2.1.

Using this approximation of the 1D FFT, we can approximate the total cost of all 1D FFTs during the three computation phases ($3 \times \frac{n^2}{P}$ 1D FFTs per node). If each node can perform C_{node} flops per unit time, then the total time spent on computation is

$$T_{\text{flops}} = 3 \times \frac{n^2}{P} \times \frac{5n \log n}{C_{\text{node}}} \ . \tag{1}$$

3.1.2 Memory Operation Costs

Within each node, we must load and store each data point from memory at least once during a 1D FFT computation. Caches are exploited to prevent an additional DRAM access for each operand of each floating point operation. For a local 1D n-point cache-oblivious FFT in a two-level memory hierarchy, with cache size Z and line size L in words, the number of cache misses grows on the order of $\Theta\left(1 + (n/L)(1 + \log_Z n)\right)$ [21]. This result is I/O-optimal [29], and so represents the best case asymptotic performance for any algorithm and implementation. Note that this bound counts cache misses, each transferring lines of size L, hence the additional factor of L in the equation.

Thus, for some constant A and sufficiently large n, the time spent moving data between main memory and the processor is

$$T_{\text{mem}} \approx 3 \times \frac{n^2}{P} \cdot \frac{A \times n(\max(\log_Z n, 1.0))}{\beta_{\text{mem}}} \ , \tag{2}$$

where β_{mem} is the node's memory bandwidth in words per unit time. The *max* function ensures that the transfers include at least the compulsory misses.

Unfortunately, the relative complexity of the cache hierarchy on modern processors (e.g., multi-levels, replacement policies, address translation, etc.) makes an analytical derivation of the constant prohibitively difficult. Instead, in § 5.2.1 we will approximate the constant $A = 6.3$ by using hardware counters to track the number of DRAM accesses during a 1D FFT computation.

3.1.3 Flops:Byte

Assuming arithmetic and memory operations can be overlapped, $T_{comp} \approx \max(T_{\text{flops}}, T_{\text{mem}})$. However, the computational intensity (flops:byte) of a 1D FFT is generally lower than the machine balance of modern processors, making the computation memory bound. Furthermore, our analysis in § 6 suggests processors will be even more imbalanced in the future. This leads us to focus on T_{mem} instead of T_{flops}.

3.2 Communication Costs

During the communication phase, each node must perform a personalized all-to-all exchange of its data points with $\sqrt{P}$ other nodes on the network. In total, each node sends approximately $\frac{n^3}{P}$ data points.[2]

---

[2]Each node need only send $\frac{(\sqrt{P}-1) \cdot n^3}{P^{\frac{3}{2}}}$ data points, which is approximately $\frac{n^3}{P}$ (all of its data) for the relatively large values of P considered in this paper.

Ideally, on a fully connected network with link bandwidth β_{link}, the time to perform this exchange is

$$T_{\text{net}} \approx 2 \times \frac{n^3}{P \cdot \beta_{\text{link}}} \ , \qquad (3)$$

where the factor of 2 accounts for the two communication phases.

Since a fully connected network is unlikely at exascale, we assume a more realistic 3D torus topology for the analytical sections of this paper. We consider two scenarios. First, a lower-bound on the communication phase on a 3D torus is

$$T_{\text{net}} = \Omega \left(\frac{n^3}{P^{\frac{5}{6}} \cdot \beta_{\text{link}}} \right) \ . \qquad (4)$$

This models the communication phase as simultaneous $\sqrt{P}$-node all-to-all exchanges within $P^{\frac{1}{6}} \times P^{\frac{1}{6}} \times P^{\frac{1}{6}}$ subblocks of the 3D torus (see § 9 for a detailed derivation). For the problem size and machine parameter values we consider in this paper, the latency term will be negligible, and so does not appear in subsequent uses of this formula.

However, the bound of Equation (4) makes strong assumptions about task placement that are not always feasible on shared high-end systems [28]. Thus, we will also consider a second, more realistic approximation by using the cost of a global all-to-all. The communication time is then bound by the bisection bandwidth of a 3D torus, which is $\mathcal{O}\left(P^{\frac{2}{3}} \cdot \beta_{\text{link}}\right)$; thus,

$$T_{\text{net}} \approx 2 \times \frac{n^3}{P^{\frac{2}{3}} \beta_{\text{link}}} \ . \qquad (5)$$

4. INTERPRETING THE MODEL: BALANCED PROCESSORS

This section gives a more intuitive explanation of the high-level features of the model described in § 3.

Suppose we wish to build a machine with a particular peak performance of R_{peak} flops per unit time. Given a node of peak C_{node}, we will choose the number of nodes $P = R_{\text{peak}}/C_{\text{node}}$. Thus, T_{mem} from Equation (2) becomes, in the limit of large n,

$$T_{\text{mem}} \approx \mathcal{O}\left(\frac{1}{R_{\text{peak}}} \cdot \frac{C_{\text{node}}}{\beta_{\text{mem}}} \cdot n^3 \log_Z n \right) \ . \qquad (6)$$

Note the factor $C_{\text{node}}/\beta_{\text{mem}}$. This factor is the classical definition of *balance* [6, 8, 11, 33, 35], which has units of flops / word (or byte), applied here to node performance. When this factor is large (in this case relative to the inherent flop:byte requirements of an FFT), we say the node is *imbalanced*. Thus, the intra-node communication time depends not on the absolute performance of a node but instead on this balance ratio.

A similar argument applies to the inter-node time, T_{net}, yielding from Equation (5),

$$T_{\text{net}} \approx \mathcal{O}\left(\frac{1}{R_{\text{peak}}^{\kappa}} \cdot \frac{C_{\text{node}}^{\kappa}}{\beta_{\text{link}}} \cdot n^3 \right) \ , \qquad (7)$$

where $\kappa = \frac{5}{6}$, using the optimal task-mapping lower-bound of Equation (4), or $\kappa = \frac{2}{3}$, using the bisection bound of Equation (5). Again, a similar kind of balance factor appears, here relative to network bandwidth. Evidently, inter-

node time also depends on balance. However, since $\kappa < 1$, T_{net} is less sensitive to C_{node} than is T_{mem}.

Thus, we may conclude the following: balanced nodes reduce both T_{mem} and T_{net}; and T_{mem} depends more sensitively on C_{node} than T_{net}. Put another way, intra-node design is critical, but in perhaps an unintuitive way: a supercomputer composed of many weak but balanced nodes could perform better than one with the same peak and fewer more powerful but imbalanced nodes.

5. MODEL CALIBRATION

Empirical tests are important for calibrating the analytical model as well as identifying additional hardware and software artifacts that impede performance. In the case of the FFT, we use this opportunity to

- use timing data to estimate effective throughput of both memory bandwidth and network bandwidth;
- use hardware counters to measure the analytical constants in Equation 1 and Equation 2;
- explore hardware and software artifacts that influence performance;
- compare and contrast performance on systems with different underlying architectures —a CPU-based system and a GPU-based system.

5.1 Experiment Setup

The experiments were run on 4,096 nodes (98,304 cores) of "Hopper," a 1.288 PF/s Cray XE6 housed at the the National Energy Research Scientific Computing Center. Each node has two Magny-Cours chips[3] running at 2.1 GHz and 32 GB DDR3 1333-MHz memory. Hopper's 6,392 nodes form a 17×8×24 3D torus with a Gemini interconnect.

In addition to Hopper, the GPU experiments were run on "Keeneland," which consists of HP SL390 servers accelerated with NVIDIA Tesla M2070 GPUs. Keeneland has 120 compute nodes, each with dual-socket, six-core Intel X5660 2.8 GHz Westmere processors and 3 GPUs per node, with 24GB of DDR3 host memory. The interconnect is single rail, QDR Infiniband [41].

We use the P3DFFT (Parallel Three-Dimensional Fast Fourier Transform), an off-the-shelf distributed 3D FFT library, to perform the computations. It implements the distributed memory transpose algorithm using a pencil decomposition [36]. P3DFFT is freely available under a GPL license.[4] A major use of P3DFFT, which could be considered to be our motivating application, is a direct numerical turbulence simulation.

On each node P3DFFT computes local 1D FFTs using third party libraries. We used FFTW 3.2.2, though IBM's ESSL and Intel's MKL libraries can serve as drop-in replacements. For the GPU experiments we developed DiG-PUFFT, [5] a custom wrapper around CUFFT, Nvidia's FFT library for GPUs, making CUFFT an additional option.

5.2 Hopper Performance Results

Here we present our empirical performance results from a large-scale FFT, run on 4096 nodes of Hopper. Figure 2

---

[3]the Magny-Cours chip contains two six-core Istanbul processors on a single die

[4]http://code.google.com/p/p3dfft/

[5]DiGPUFFT is freely available as a set of patches to P3DFFT at http://code.google.com/p/digpufft/

shows the time spent during the Communication and Computation phases over varying problem sizes. To quantify the additional overhead of the 3D FFT, we timed components in an isolated setting. This involved benchmarking the "MPI_AlltoAll()" and FFTW calls individually. The results are shown in Figure 2. Observe that

- network communication time dominates computation time. However, as the problem size increases the computation time grows faster than communication time. This can be explained by the asymptotic complexities of Equation (2) and Equation (5).
- the computation phase incurs a large overhead that is not explained by the analytical model;
- total time is the sum of the computation and communication phases. There is no overlap.

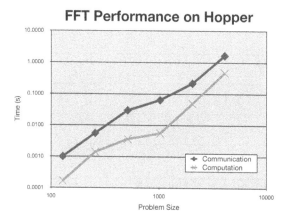

FFT Performance on Hopper

Figure 2: P3DFFT performance on 4096 nodes of Hopper. The plot shows the time spent during the Computation and Communication phases of the 3D FFT.

5.2.1 Measuring Computational Constants

The computational complexity of the FFT and its constant are described in Section 3.1.2. To measure the constant for the FFT's cache complexity (to allow us to model its bandwidth load), we executed FFTW on all arrays of power-of-two size that were too large to fit in L3 cache but small enough to fit in DRAM. We used timing and profiling results and divided by the cache complexity equation to determine the constant A in Equation (2), assuming that the memory bottleneck exists between DRAM and L3 cache.

5.2.2 Local Transpose Artifact

Prior to the personalized all-to-all exchange, each node must compute a *local transpose* to reshuffle the data in addition to performing the local FFT computation. This shuffle can be costly because it involves loading and storing nearly every value in the local data set. For a 3D FFT, where each of the P processors owns $\frac{n^3}{P}$ complex words, the total time spent reshuffling by each processor is

$$T_{\text{shuffle}} \approx 2 \times \frac{2n^3}{P \cdot \beta_{\text{mem}}} , \qquad (8)$$

where β_{mem} is the local main memory bandwidth in words per unit time. There are two factors of 2 here: one accounts

for loads and stores, and the other for the fact that in a 3D FFT there will be two all-to-all exchanges. Figure 4 shows that in DiGPUFFT the local transpose (16%) is nearly as costly as the FFT computation (21%) itself. Other FFT implementations have shown similar relative costs [19, 43].

5.3 Keeneland Performance Results

Here we present our 3D FFT performance results for a GPU cluster. Rather than comparing this data with the results from Hopper, which is much larger and has a more sophisticated interconnect than Keeneland, we also include P3DFFT results from experiments that were run on the CPU processors in Keeneland. The results are shown in Figure 3.

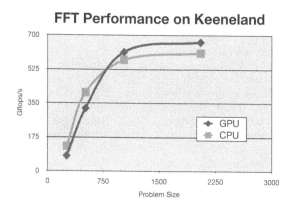

FFT Performance on Keeneland

Figure 3: DiGPUFFT performance on Keeneland.

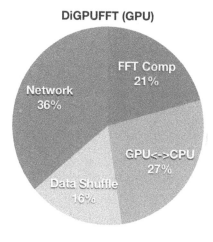

DiGPUFFT (GPU)

Figure 4: Breakdown of execution time in DiG-PUFFT (GPU-based 3D FFT). Results are from a 64 node run on the Keeneland cluster with a problem size of 2048^3, and 3 MPI tasks per node.

5.3.1 The I/O Bus (PCIe) Bottleneck Artifact

An important observation from Figure 3 is that despite the GPU's higher memory bandwidth and floating-point throughput, we observe only a modest overall win from GPU over

CPU, showing just roughly 10% to 20% improvements. Further inspection (see Figure 4) reveals that 27% of the time is spent in CPU⇆GPU communication.

In the case of a 3D FFT of size n^3 evenly distributed across P nodes, this can result in a transfer penalty of

$$T_{\text{PCIe}} \approx \frac{2n^3}{P \cdot \beta_{\text{PCIe}}} \qquad (9)$$

during each computation phase, where β_{PCIe} is the I/O bus bandwidth in words per unit time. The factor of two accounts for both CPU→GPU and CPU←GPU transfers. Since the PCIe bandwidth (β_{PCIe}=8 GB/s) is an order of magnitude slower than the memory bandwidth on the GPU (144 GB/s or more), the PCIe bus can have a significant impact on performance.

Fortunately, the PCIe bottleneck is likely to improve in the near future. The gap in bandwidth between β_{PCIe} and main memory bandwidth is, as it happens, decreasing. Additionally, several approaches are underway to circumvent the CPU⇆GPU memory transfer cost altogether. Early development in MVAPICH-GPU, a MPI implementation that improves the connection between the GPU and network interface, has already shown a 45% performance improvement over the indirect cudaMemcpy() + MPI_Send [42]. Or in a more extreme case, AMD's Fusion architecture discards the notion of a discrete GPU by incorporating CPU and GPU cores on the same processor die. These observations reaffirm generally held views that the effect of PCIe is a short-term artifact, not a long-term barrier to scalability.

6. PROJECTING FORWARD

Recent discussions surrounding the direction of high-end systems has separated into two strategies, sometimes called the exascale processor "swim lanes." Others use the terms *Many-Core* (MC) and *Many-Thread* (MT) designs [16, 23, 26, 30]. MC designs are "CPU-like," in that they replicate embedded CPU-cores, and emphasize latency reduction through traditional memory hierarchy and other techniques that boost instruction-level parallelism. By contrast, MT designs replicate GPU-style processors, with an emphasis on hiding latency via massive multithreading. In this paper, the essential difference is that MC designs have lower absolute performance but may be better balanced than MT designs. Recall that the key design consideration for 3D FFTs, as suggested in § 4, is not absolute per-processor performance, but rather the relative balance among compute capacity per node, intra-node bandwidth, and inter-node bandwidth.

Predictions.

We use our model to see how performance and scaling could change in light of current technology trends. We summarize these trends with respect to various machine parameters in Table 1, which extrapolates from the current configuration of the Keeneland cluster using our own derived trends.[6] We present these extrapolations in terms of the time (in years) for a particular parameter to double and the factor by which current values might increase in ten years. For several parameters, we separate extrapolated CPU-like vs. GPU-like processors. However, since the two are fundamentally based on similar process technologies (e.g., silicon

---

[6] Our precise methodologies for deriving these trends appear in the extended appendix. See § 9.

Table 1: Processor architecture projections, from starting values on the US National Science Foundation's "Keeneland" (GPU-based) and NERSC's Hopper system (CPU-based), both delivered in 2010. Processor/Node counts are scaled to reflect a 4 PF/s machine.

Parameter		2010 values	T_d (years)	10-year increase factor	2020 values
Peak:	C_{CPU}	50.4 GF/s	1.7	59.0×	3.0 TF/s
	C_{GPU}	515 GF/s			30 TF/s
Cores:[a]	ρ_{CPU}	6	1.87	40.7×	134
	ρ_{GPU}	448			18,000
Memory	β_{CPU}	21.3 GB/s	3.0	9.7×	206 GB/s
BW:	β_{GPU}	144 GB/s			1.4 TB/s
Fast	Z_{CPU}	6 MB	2.0	32.0×	192 MB
memory:	Z_{GPU}	2.7 MB[b]			86.4 MB
Line size:	L_{CPU}	64 B	10.2	2.0×	128 B
	L_{GPU}	128 B			256 B
Link BW:	β_{link}	10 GB/s	2.25	21.8×	218 GB/s
Machine peak:	R_{peak}	4 PF/s	1.0	1000×	4 EF/s
System memory:	E	635 TB	1.3	208×	132 PB
Nodes ($\frac{R_{\text{peak}}}{C}$):	P_{CPU}	79,400	2.4	17.4×	1.3M
	P_{GPU}	7,770			135,000

[a] "Cores" refers to the processor manufacturer's own usage rather than, say, floating-point functional units.

[b] Fast Memory refers to the capacity of on-chip cache. In practice, we usually only measure the last-level cache because it dominates the total cache size. However, on the M2070 GPU, the sum of the L1 + registerfiles (2.7 MB) is larger than the L2 (512 KB).

and manufacturing processes), we hypothesize that the *rates* of growth will be identical through 2020 though they start from different values in 2010.

Prediction 1: Under business-as-usual assumptions (Table 1), a 3D FFT will achieve 2.8 petaflop/s (PF/s) on a high-density GPU-like exascale machine in 2020. This value is 0.08% of the 4 EF/s peak, compared to today's best fraction of peak for 3D FFTs, which is about 0.5%.

To obtain this estimate, we extrapolated the various system parameters of Table 1, used them to determine the form (e.g., number of nodes) required to get a system running at 4 EF/s, selected a problem size according to the methodology of Gahvari and Gropp [22], and then evaluated our performance model to estimate execution time. Prediction 2 below further elaborates on this calculation.

Prediction 2: On 4 EF/s systems that are expected in 2020, we predict that the MC or "CPU-like" swim lane will deliver higher performance for a 3D FFT. Our quantitative prediction is that, given MC-style and MT-style systems of 4 EF/s peak each, the MC-style system will deliver about 3.2× better performance.

Figure 5 summarizes our quantitative prediction and shows why we think an MC-style design wins. We consider three scenarios: (i) a GPU-like system vs. a CPU-like system

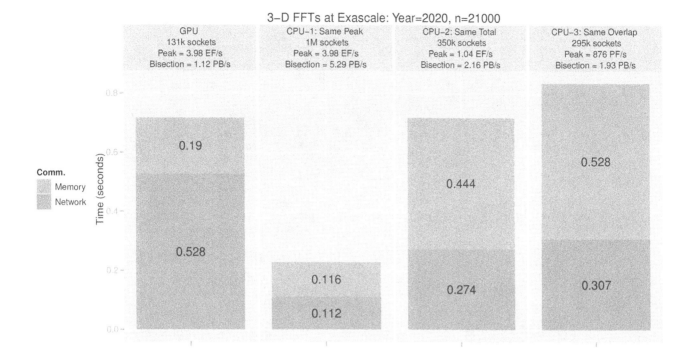

Figure 5: We consider three extrapolated CPU-like systems vs. an extrapolated GPU-like system. CPU-1 has the same peak as GPU; CPU-2 computes the FFT in the same total time as GPU, assuming no overlap of communication; and CPU-3 also yields the same time as GPU, but assuming full overlap. In all cases, the CPU systems actually perform *less* network communication.

matched on peak performance (GPU vs. CPU-1); (ii) a GPU-like system vs. a CPU-like system which both perform the FFT in the same time, assuming inter- and intra-node communication time *cannot* be overlapped (GPU vs. CPU-2); and (iii) a GPU-like system vs. a CPU-like system which both perform the FFT in the same time, assuming inter- and intra-node communication time *can* be overlapped (GPU vs. CPU-3). We fix the problem size to be an n^3 volume with $n = 21,000$. Figure 5 further breaks down the execution time into inter- vs. intra-node time. For the inter-node time, T_{net}, we assume Equation (5) for T_{net}; we revisit this choice in Prediction 3 below. Note that flop-time does not appear; it is practically negligible, as communication time dominates it by roughly three orders of magnitude.

First, consider the case in which the GPU-like and CPU-like systems have the same peak. For the GPU-like design, the values of T_{mem} and T_{net} appear in the leftmost bar of Figure 5. Network time dominates memory time by 2.8×. The CPU-like system, labeled CPU-1, appears as the second bar of Figure 5. This system spends less time than the GPU system in both forms of communication, with its network communication time nearly $\frac{1}{5}$ the time. From the discussion of § 4, the essential reason is better processor balance, which translates into lower memory and network time. However, this advantage is not free: CPU-1 requires over 10× as many processors as the GPU system. The price of such a system could be prohibitive, if dollar cost is proportional to the number of processors.

A more sensible CPU-like configuration might be one in which we match not on *peak* performance but rather on *actual* performance, that is, the actual time to perform the

FFT. In the third bar of Figure 5, we consider a different CPU-based design, CPU-2, in which the total communication time for the FFT, $T_{\text{mem}} + T_{\text{net}}$, exactly matches that of the 4 EF/s GPU system. This change requires fewer processors than CPU-1 (350k vs. 1M) and has a lower overall peak of 1 EF/s, making it perhaps significantly cheaper. More interestingly, observe that relative to the GPU system, CPU-2 trades higher on-chip memory communication time for lower off-chip network communication.

The CPU-2 system may be pessimistic in its execution time, because it assumes that we cannot overlap T_{mem} and T_{net}. The rightmost bar of Figure 5 considers CPU-3, where we assume that the total time to perform the FFT is not the sum, $T_{\text{mem}} + T_{\text{net}}$, but rather $\max\{T_{\text{mem}}, T_{\text{net}}\} = 0.528$ seconds when the two communication phases perfectly overlap. The CPU-3 system loses in total time but reduces off-chip network communication time. This situation can be beneficial if off-chip communication consumes much more energy than on-chip communication [31]. Also, this system uses 295k CPUs, putting it within 2.25× of the total number of processors in the GPU system.

Prediction 3: Time spent moving data within the node could dominate time spent communicating in the network. The implication is that the all-to-all exchange will *not* be the factor that limits FFT scalability; rather, intra-node design will.

To get some intuition for the conditions under which this prediction could come true, consider the ratio $T_{\text{mem}}/T_{\text{net}}$, which is greater than one if main memory communication time dominates network time. Using the simplified analysis

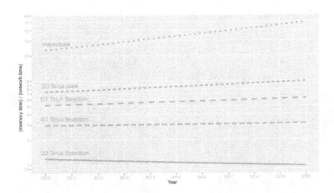

Figure 6: Projected ratio of $T_{\mathrm{mem}}/T_{\mathrm{net}}$ for weakly scaled 3D FFTs. The problem size n^3 starts at 4096^3 and is scaled as the same rate as P.

of § 4, we have

$$\frac{T_{\mathrm{mem}}}{T_{\mathrm{net}}} \propto \left(\frac{C_{\mathrm{node}}}{R_{\mathrm{peak}}}\right)^{1-\kappa} \cdot \frac{\beta_{\mathrm{link}}}{\beta_{\mathrm{mem}}} \cdot \log_Z n \ . \quad (10)$$

The log factor grows slowly, so we can ignore it for the moment. Then, according to Table 1, $C_{\mathrm{node}}/R_{\mathrm{peak}}$ decreases over time, while $\beta_{\mathrm{link}}/\beta_{\mathrm{mem}}$ increases over time.[7] If we wish to control whether the overall product of these two factors increases or decreases, our main "tuning knob" is the network topology, which is captured by κ (recall that $\kappa \leq 1$).

We show how this ratio might grow over time for various topologies in Figure 6, where the base processor is our extrapolated CPU system (as it varies over time). Using the bisection bandwidth estimate given by Equation (5), we see that the overall ratio of $T_{\mathrm{mem}}/T_{\mathrm{net}}$ is less than one for a 3D torus and, furthermore, actually decreases over time, which means the network becomes more and more of a bottleneck. However, under an optimal mapping ("3D Torus Ideal" in Figure 6), a 3D torus could also be as much as $10\times$ faster than suggested by the bisection estimate (compare Equation 4 with Equation 5), and the ratio actually increases over time. Thus, the extent to which the network limits scalability depends on the topology. Figure 6 includes bisection estimates for higher dimensional torii as well, in which cases $T_{\mathrm{mem}}/T_{\mathrm{net}}$ also increase. The slopes of these lines suggest that a 4D torus is well-balanced for an FFT, and that higher-dimensional networks are likely to be over-engineered. However, if there is a severe energy penalty for network communication, then 5D and higher-dimensional FFTs will help provide energy scaling over time, since the $T_{\mathrm{mem}}/T_{\mathrm{net}}$ is tending to increase in those cases.

Note on xPU-memory stacking.

One technology that could disrupt these analyses is xPU-memory die stacking, the leading proposed mechanism for enabling memory bandwidth to scale at the same rate as compute capacity [34]. Applying our model, which is based

---

[7] For us, the fact that β_{link} and β_{mem} are converging is interesting. One explanation for why this happens is that the physical footprint of pins going into a processor or DIMM cannot grow as quickly as the width of, say, wires going into a router or link. This notion is consistent with recent suggestions by interconnect architects, who try to keep the growth in network bandwidth as close to compute capacity increases as costs will permit [7].

on the known I/O complexity estimates for the FFT, we can establish that a node's computation and memory transfers will be balanced when $T_{\mathrm{mem}} \leq T_{\mathrm{flops}}$ [11, 33]. Given a chip with ρ cores, C flop/s per core, β byte/s bandwidth to the chip, and a shared cache of size Z, this balance constraint yields [11]

$$\frac{\rho \cdot C}{\beta} \leq \mathcal{O}\left(\log \frac{Z}{\rho}\right) . \quad (11)$$

In theory, stacked memory makes it possible to keep the left-hand side constant over time. Although ρ grows faster than Z, it enters into this inequality through the log and so will not decrease too quickly. Thus, stacked memory would keep the processing system balanced for FFTs. However, if it is not possible to keep $\rho = \Theta(\beta)$, then stacked memory only delays rather than solves the processor imbalance problem.

7. CONCLUSIONS AND FUTURE WORK

One claim of this paper is that I/O-bus (PCIe) and network bandwidth will not be the true limiters of performance for parallel 3D FFTs. Instead, it is intra-node communication due to main memory bandwidth that will have the biggest impact at exascale. In fact, our key prediction is that if we ignore intra-node balance, as a naïvely extrapolated GPU-style design would do, then we will hurt overall system balance by not taking advantage of the better scaling of network bandwidth relative to memory bandwidth. Thus, more architectural emphasis on intra-node balance will have the biggest pay-off in the long-run for communication bandwidth-bound computations on high-end systems.

In terms of absolute bandwidth values, high-density (GPU-based) compute nodes extend the time until which network bandwidth will outpace main memory bandwidth, but do not fundamentally solve the problem. The most interesting solution for FFT-like computations, which include sorting, is most likely stacked memory if it can indeed deliver proportional scaling of memory bandwidth to core counts.

Interestingly, the most common weak-but-balanced processor designs are those of mobile processors. Our analysis hints strongly that leveraging the volume of production of such processors, combined with high-quality integrated networking, die stacking, and a balanced-throughput design, could be an excellent building block for an exascale system. This notion may, in fact, be part of an emerging view in other large-scale systems, such as data centers [4, 38].

Algorithmically, perhaps the only way forward for FFT type computations is through much more aggressive data or numerical (e.g., low-rank) compression [18].

We believe our basic modeling methodology and its level of detail could provide similar kinds of insights for other computations, particularly if enriched with additional parameters and an explicit accounting of power, energy, and even dollar costs. This style of analysis could be especially useful in the context of algorithm-architecture co-design, a notion that has been outlined for intra-node designs elsewhere [11].

Finally, we would like to emphasize the methodological contribution of this paper over the analytical analysis. While our predictions are provoking and offer a fresh perspective, the results are suggestive rather than conclusive. The intention of this paper is not to fuel the CPU vs GPU debate or dictate microarchitecture design. Instead we are trying to offer a quantitative approach for reasoning about the relationship between hardware and software in future super-computers. In time, as the path toward exascale computing becomes clear, a more rigorous analysis will be possible.

8. ACKNOWLEDGEMENTS

We thank the reviewers for their suggestions. This work was supported in part by the National Science Foundation (NSF) under award number 0833136, NSF CAREER award number 0953100, NSF I/UCRC award number 0934114, NSF TeraGrid allocations CCR-090024 and ASC-100019, joint NSF 0903447 and Semiconductor Research Corporation (SRC) Award 1981, and grants from the U.S. Dept. of Energy (DOE) and the Defense Advanced Research Projects Agency (DARPA). This research also used resources of the Keeneland Computing Facility at the Georgia Institute of Technology, which is supported by the National Science Foundation under Contract OCI-0910735. Any opinions, findings and conclusions or recommendations expressed in this material are those of the authors and do not necessarily reflect those of NSF, SRC, DOE, or DARPA.

9. APPENDIX

We have released a tech report version of this paper which includes an extended appendix with: (1) a more detailed discussion of the the performance model, (2) raw data used to generate the technology tends in Table 1, and (3) code that can be used to reproduce the calculations found in Section 6.

References

[1] The HPC Challenge benchmark. http://icl.cs.utk.edu/hpcc.

[2] R. Agarwal, F. Gustavson, and M. Zubair. An efficient parallel algorithm for the 3-D FFT NAS parallel benchmark. In *Proceedings of IEEE Scalable High Performance Computing Conference*, pages 129–133. IEEE Comput. Soc. Press, 1994.

[3] G. Almasi et al. Cellular supercomputing with system-on-a-chip. In *2002 IEEE International Solid-State Circuits Conference. Digest of Technical Papers (Cat. No.02CH37315)*, pages 196–197. Ieee, 2002.

[4] D. G. Andersen, J. Franklin, M. Kaminsky, A. Phanishayee, L. Tan, and V. Vasudevan. FAWN: A fast array of wimpy nodes. *Communications of the ACM*, 54(7):101–109, July 2011.

[5] C. Bell, D. Bonachea, R. Nishtala, and K. Yelick. Optimizing Bandwidth Limited Problems Using One-Sided Communication and Overlap. In *Proceedings 20th IEEE International Parallel & Distributed Processing Symposium*, pages 1–10. IEEE, 2006.

[6] G. E. Blelloch, B. M. Maggs, and G. L. Miller. The hidden cost of low bandwidth communication. In U. Vishkin, editor, *Developing a Computer Science Agenda for High-Performance Computing*, pages 22–25. ACM, New York, NY, USA, 1994.

[7] R. Brightwell, K. T. Pedretti, K. D. Underwood, and T. Hudson. Seastar interconnect: Balanced bandwidth for scalable performance. *IEEE Micro*, 26:41–57, May 2006.

[8] D. Callahan, J. Cocke, and K. Kennedy. Estimating interlock and improving balance for pipelined architectures. *Journal of Parallel and Distributed Computing*, 5(4):334–358, Aug. 1988.

[9] A. Chan, P. Balaji, W. Gropp, and R. Thakur. Communication analysis of parallel 3d fft for flat cartesian meshes on large blue gene systems. In *Proceedings of the 15th international conference on High performance computing*, pages 350–364. Springer-Verlag, 2008.

[10] C. E. Cramer and J. Board. The development and integration of a distributed 3D FFT for a cluster of workstations. In *Proceedings of the 4th Annual Linux Showcase & Conference*, Atlanta, GA, USA, 2000.

[11] K. Czechowski, C. Battaglino, C. Mcclanahan, A. Chandramowlishwaran, and R. Vuduc. Balance principles for algorithm-architecture co-design. In *USENIX Wkshp. Hot Topics in Parallelism (HotPar)*, pages 1–5, Berkeley, CA, USA, 2011. Usenix Association.

[12] K. Datta, D. Bonachea, and K. Yelick. Titanium Performance and Potential: An NPB Experimental Study. In *Proceedings of the Languages and Compilers for Parallel Computing (LCPC) Workshop*, volume LNCS 4339, pages 200–214, 2006.

[13] H. Q. Ding, R. D. Ferraro, and D. B. Gennery. A Portable 3D FFT Package for Distributed-Memory Parallel Architectures. In *Proceedings of 7th SIAM Conference on Parallel Processing*, pages 70—-71. SIAM Press, 1995.

[14] P. Dmitruk, L.-P. Wang, W. H. Mattaeus, R. Zhang, and D. Seckel. Scalable parallel FFT for spectral simulations on a Beowulf cluster. *Parallel Computing*, 27(14):1921–1936, Dec. 2001.

[15] J. Doi and Y. Negishi. Overlapping Methods of All-to-All Communication and FFT Algorithms for Torus-Connected Massively Parallel Supercomputers. In *2010 ACM/IEEE International Conference for High Performance Computing, Networking, Storage and Analysis*, number November, pages 1–9. IEEE, Nov. 2010.

[16] J. Dongarra et al. The international exascale software project roadmap. *IJHPCA*, 25(1):3–60, 2011.

[17] D. Donzis, P. Yeung, and D. Pekurovsky. Turbulence simulations on $o(10^4)$ processors. 2008.

[18] A. Edelman, P. McCorquodale, and S. Toledo. The Future Fast Fourier Transform? *SIAM Journal on Scientific Computing*, 20(3):1094, 1998.

[19] M. Eleftheriou, B. Fitch, A. Rayshubskiy, T. Ward, and R. Germain. Scalable framework for 3D FFTs on the Blue Gene/L supercomputer: implementation and early performance measurements. *IBM Journal of Research and Development*, 49(2.3):457–464, 2005.

[20] B. FANG, Y. DENG, and G. MARTYNA. Performance of the 3D FFT on the 6D network torus QCDOC parallel supercomputer. *Computer Physics Communications*, 176(8):531–538, Apr. 2007.

[21] M. Frigo, C. E. Leiserson, H. Prokop, and S. Ramachandran. Cache-oblivious algorithms. In *Proceedings of the 40th Annual Symposium on Foundations of Computer Science*, FOCS '99, pages 285–, Washington, DC, USA, 1999. IEEE Computer Society.

[22] H. Gahvari and W. Gropp. An introductory exascale feasibility study for FFTs and multigrid. In *2010 IEEE International Symposium on Parallel & Distributed Processing (IPDPS)*, pages 1–9, Atlanta, GA, USA, Apr. 2010. IEEE.

[23] M. Garland and D. B. Kirk. Understanding throughput-oriented architectures. *Communications of the ACM*, 53(11):58, Nov. 2010.

[24] L. Giraud, R. Guivarch, and J. Stein. Parallel Distributed FFT-Based Solvers for 3-D Poisson Problems in Meso-Scale Atmospheric Simulations. *International Journal of High Performance Computing Applications*, 15(1):36–46, Feb. 2001.

[25] L. Gu, X. Li, and J. Siegel. An empirically tuned 2D and 3D FFT library on CUDA GPU. In *Proceedings of the 24th ACM International Conference on Supercomputing - ICS '10*, page 305, Tsukuba, Japan, 2010. ACM Press.

[26] Z. Guz, E. Bolotin, I. Keidar, A. Kolodny, A. Mendelson, and U. C. Weiser. Many-core vs. many-thread machines: Stay away from the valley. *IEEE Computer Architecture Letters*, 8:25–28, 2009.

[27] J. Hein, H. Jagode, U. Sigrist, A. Simpson, and A. Trew. Parallel 3D-FFTs for multi-core nodes on a mesh communication network. In *Proceedings of the Cray User's Group (CUG) Meeting*, pages 1–15, Helsinki, Finland, 2008.

[28] H. Jagode, J. Hein, and A. Trew. Task placement of parallel multidimensional ffts on a mesh communication network. *University of Tennessee Knoxville, Technical Report No. ut-cs-08-613*, 2008.

[29] H. Jia-Wei and H. T. Kung. I/O complexity: The red-blue pebble game. In *Proceedings of the thirteenth annual ACM symposium on Theory of computing - STOC '81*, pages 326–333, New York, New York, USA, May 1981. ACM Press.

[30] P. Kogge and T. Dysart. Using the top500 to trace and project technology and architecture trends. In *Proceedings of 2011 International Conference for High Performance Computing, Networking, Storage and Analysis*, page 28. ACM, 2011.

[31] P. Kogge et al. Exascale Computing Study: Technology challenges in acheiving exascale systems, Sept. 2008.

[32] S. Kumar, Y. Sabharwal, R. Garg, and P. Heidelberger. Optimization of All-to-All Communication on the Blue Gene/L Supercomputer. In *2008 37th International Conference on Parallel Processing*, pages 320–329. IEEE, Sept. 2008.

[33] H. T. Kung. Memory requirements for balanced computer architectures. In *Proceedings of the ACM Int'l. Symp. Computer Architecture (ISCA)*, Tokyo, Japan, 1986.

[34] G. H. Loh. 3D-Stacked Memory Architectures for Multi-core Processors. In *2008 International Symposium on Computer Architecture*, pages 453–464. IEEE, June 2008.

[35] J. McCalpin. Memory Bandwidth and Machine Balance in High Performance Computers. *IEEE Technical Committee on Computer Architecture (TCCA) Newsletter*, Dec. 1995.

[36] D. Pekurovsky and J. H. Goebbert. P3DFFT – highly scalable parallel 3d fast fourier transforms library. http://www.sdsc.edu/us/resources/p3dfft, November 2010.

[37] S. J. Pennycook, S. D. Hammond, S. A. Jarvis, and G. R. Mudalige. Performance analysis of a hybrid MPI/CUDA implementation of the NAS-LU benchmark. In *Proceedings of the International Workshop on Performance Modeling, Benchmarking and Simulation (PMBS)*, New Orleans, LA, USA, Nov. 2010.

[38] V. J. Reddi, B. C. Lee, T. Chilimbi, and K. Vaid. Web search using mobile cores: Quantifying and mitigating the price of efficiency. *ACM SIGARCH Computer Architecture News*, 38(3):215–314, June 2010.

[39] U. Sigrist. *Optimizing parallel 3D fast Fourier transformations for a cluster of IBM POWER5 SMP nodes*. PhD thesis, The University of Edinburgh, 2007.

[40] D. Takahashi. A Parallel 3-D FFT Algorithm on Clusters of Vector SMPs. In *Proceedings of Applied Parallel Computing: New Paradigms for HPC in Industry and Academia*, volume LNCS 1947, pages 316–323, 2001.

[41] J. Vetter, R. Glassbrook, J. Dongarra, K. Schwan, B. Loftis, S. McNally, J. Meredith, J. Rogers, P. Roth, K. Spafford, et al. Keeneland: Bringing heterogeneous gpu computing to the computational science community. *IEEE Computing in Science and Engineering*, 13(5):90–95, 2011.

[42] H. Wang, S. Potluri, M. Luo, A. Singh, S. Sur, and D. Panda. MVAPICH2-GPU: optimized GPU to GPU communication for InfiniBand clusters. *Computer Science-Research and Development*, pages 1–10.

[43] C. Young, J. Bank, R. Dror, J. Grossman, J. Salmon, and D. Shaw. A 32x32x32, spatially distributed 3D FFT in four microseconds on Anton. In *Proceedings of the Conference on High Performance Computing Networking, Storage and Analysis*, page 23. ACM, 2009.

Composable, non-Blocking Collective Operations on Power7 IH

Gabriel Tanase
IBM TJ Watson Research
Center
Yorktown Heights, NY, US
igtanase@us.ibm.com

Gheorghe Almási
IBM TJ Watson Research
Center
Yorktown Heights, NY, US
gheorghe@us.ibm.com

Hanhong Xue
IBM Systems and Technology
Group
Poughkeepsie, NY, US
hanhong@us.ibm.com

Charles Archer
IBM Systems and Technology
Group
Rochester, MN, US
archerc@us.ibm.com

ABSTRACT

The Power7 IH (P7IH) is one of IBM's latest generation of super-computers. Like most modern parallel machines, it has a hierarchical organization consisting of simultaneous multithreading (SMT) within a core, multiple cores per processor, multiple processors per node (SMP), and multiple SMPs per cluster. A low latency/high bandwidth network with specialized accelerators is used to interconnect the SMP nodes. System software is tuned to exploit the hierarchical organization of the machine.

In this paper we present a novel set of collective operations that take advantage of the P7IH hardware. We discuss non blocking collective operations implemented using point to point messages, shared memory and accelerator hardware. We show how collectives can be composed to exploit the hierarchical organization of the P7IH for providing low latency, high bandwidth operations. We demonstrate the scalability of the collectives we designed by including experimental results on a P7IH system with up to 4096 cores.

Categories and Subject Descriptors

D.1.3 [**Concurrent Programming**]: Parallel Programming

General Terms

Algorithms, Design, Performance

Keywords

Hybrid, Composition, Collectives, Parallel, Libraries, Messaging

This research was supported in part by the Office of Science of the U.S. Department of Energy under contracts DE-FC03-01ER25509 and DE-AC02-05CH11231, and by the DARPA HPCS Contract HR0011-07-9-0002.

1. INTRODUCTION

The need for ever increasing computational power leads major computer vendors, national labs and academia to continuously innovate in the area of high performance computer design and large scale parallel programming. The Productive, Easy-to-use, Reliable Computing System (PERCS) is one of IBM's major high performance computing research programs. Among the notable outcomes of PERCS are the novel Power7-IH supercomputer architecture [6, 18, 19], a powerful programming environment consisting of the X10 language [9] and optimized compilers and runtime systems for existing parallel programming languages like MPI [17] or Unified Parallel C (UPC) [5, 23].

In this paper we describe a design for providing scalable collective communication primitives on the P7IH system. We argue that system software must follow the hierarchical organization of the hardware; efficient parallel algorithms must employ a compositional approach. Thus in our design, algorithms optimized for various levels of the hierarchy are *chained together* to obtain scalable parallel operations.

Another important aspect of a parallel collective operation that we argue for in this paper is the ability to not block threads upon invocation but allow them to further proceed until the result (e.g., reduce, broadcast) or effect (e.g, barrier) of the invocation is required. This has been recognized [5, 13] as an important feature for designing scalable applications on large HPC systems.

We make two different contributions in this paper. First, in Section 3 we describe and analyze three different types of collectives optimized for various components of the P7IH hardware hierarchy: a novel generic design for achieving non blocking collectives using only *point to point* message exchange, *shared memory* non blocking collectives that can achieve very low latency and high bandwidth on the large SMP nodes of the P7IH and collectives that use the novel P7IH *accelerated collective unit* (CAU). We describe for the first time the performance of these collectives on the P7IH architecture.

Our second contribution is in Section 4, where we describe *a novel design for composing existing collectives* to exploit the hierarchical organization of the P7IH. We formalize the process of collective composition and evaluate the performance of a set of hybrid collectives developed in our framework, on a large P7IH system with up to 4096 processor cores.

2. HARDWARE AND SOFTWARE OVERVIEW

P7IH [18] systems employ a hierarchical design allowing highly scalable deployments of up to 512K processor cores. The basic compute node of the P7IH consists of four Power7 (P7) [19] CPUs and a HUB chip, all managed by a single OS instance. The HUB provides the network connectivity between the four P7 Chips participating in the cache coherence protocol. Additionally the HUB acts as a switch supporting communication with other HUBs in the system. There is no additional communication hardware present in the system (no switches). Each P7 CPU has 8 cores and each core can run four hardware threads (SMT) thus leading to a 32 core, 128 threads, and up to 512GB memory compute *nodes*. A large P7IH system is further up organized in *drawers* consisting of 8 compute nodes (256 cores) connected in an all2all fashion, *supernodes* consisting of four drawers (1024 cores) and full system consisting of up to 512 super nodes (524288 cores). Additional hardware description and key parameters are included elsewhere [15, 19, 6, 18].

In this paper we focus on PAMI [2], the IBM parallel messaging library. PAMI is a component of the IBM core system software stack for parallel programming that includes products like PESSL [3], the engineering and scientific subroutine library), GPFS the general parallel file system, the MPI library as well as the UPC [23] and X10 [9] compilers.

The current release of PAMI unifies the functionality of its predecessors, LAPI [1] and DCMF [16] respectively. Thus PAMI provides support for *non blocking* point to point active messages and collectives. The library is not targeted at end users, but is rather intended for system programmers; developers of runtime systems for programing languages and paradigms like MPI, OpenMP, X10, UPC, etc. In terms of collectives the PAMI library supports multiple algorithmic options for a given operation and higher level run time systems are left with the decision of selecting the best choice.

3. COLLECTIVES

Collectives are parallel algorithms performing certain well defined operations like barrier, reduce, broadcast, scatter, gather, prefix sums, all to all exchange, etc., and they are often used as building blocks in users applications. PAMI library provides an extensive collection of such operations tuned for different IBM architectures like BlueGene, Power, x86 clusters. In this section we discuss requirements for the PAMI collectives and the different strategies employed to satisfy these requirements:

Portability: PAMI provides a set of collectives that have minimal assumptions about the underlying architecture, thus ensuring they work on a large spectrum of machines supported by IBM. It is often the case that portability comes at the cost of performance as we will see in this paper.

Efficiency and scalability: collectives have to take advantage of the underlying hardware to provide the best performance for a given architecture. Tuning efforts performed on a given platform cannot always be ported to a different one.

Non blocking: Non blocking collectives have the potential to improve user applications as they allow for better overlap of communication and computation. Supporting this feature has important implications on the collective design as discussed next.

3.1 The PAMI Non Blocking Collectives Interface

In PAMI, both collectives and point to point operations are non blocking. This generally translates into an interface that allows users to start the operation and later on to check for its comple-

tion. Multiple solutions are proposed in the literature to achieve this functionality:

- **handles:** One simple solution starts the operation and returns a handle that the user subsequently checks for completion. Examples of libraries employing this approach are the libNBC [13] discussed more in the related work section, the STAPL library [21] where data structures have non blocking methods and others [5, 13]. The problem with this solution is one of scalability - the number of handles to check grows linearly with the number of simultaneously outstanding operations.

- **counters:** Another solution, employed by LAPI, is to increment designated counters upon completion of non blocking operations. This solution has the problem that counters have to be incremented atomically, causing a very high locking overhead.

- **callbacks:** In this case a callback function is invoked by the library upon completion. This approach is favored by PAMI because of its relative flexibility and scalability. In fact all other solutions can be trivially implemented with appropriately chosen callbacks. Within the callback function, flags can be set to mark the completion of the operation or as we will see later on in Section 4, other non blocking operations can be started to create composed operations.

Figure 1 shows a simple example of a broadcast invocation. We notice the callback (Line 1) as a standalone function where the second argument is the user data that can be modified inside the call. Lines 8-11 prepare the arguments for a broadcast operation, including the callback function, the broadcast buffer, the root, and a particular broadcast algorithm to be used. Line 12 marks a flag variable with zero. The variable subsequently will be assigned a value of one by the callback. Line 13 starts the broadcast and returns immediately. The callback will be invoked when the operation locally finishes. Lines 16, 17 show a possible way to wait for the broadcast's completion. This example is important for understanding hybrid collections described in Section 4.

3.2 PAMI Execution Model

The execution model under which a PAMI program executes is similar to MPI with the following differences. A program consists of a set of *tasks* and not threads or processes. A task can be mapped on a process or a thread and multiple tasks can be advanced by a thread or process. In the example included in Figure 1 the *context* variable is used to distinguish among various tasks of a computation. In this paper a collective operation is invoked from a set of tasks for which the collective is defined. Similar to MPI ranks or thread identifiers a task has an unique identifier and communication or data transfer happens between tasks. Another important aspect about the PAMI library is the progress model. Because collectives are non blocking it is the user responsibility to ensure progress is made by calling PAMI_Context_Advance from all the tasks of a computation [2].

3.3 Generic Non-blocking Collectives

In this section we describe a framework for generic and portable non-blocking collective communication primitives that rely solely on the point-to-point active message primitive [10] provided by PAMI.

One of the key requirements of the collective subsystem is scalability, both in number of participating tasks and in number of si-

```
1  void cb_done (void * ctxt,
2                void * clientdata,
3                pami_result_t err) {
4   int * flag = (int *) clientdata;
5   *flag = 1;
6  }
7  ...
8  broadcast.cb_done = cb_done;
9  broadcast.algorithm = algo_option;
10 broadcast.cmd.xfer_broadcast.buf=buf;
11 broadcast.cmd.xfer_broadcast.root=root_ep;
12 flag = 0;
13 result=PAMI_Collective(context,broadcast);
14 assert(result == PAMI_SUCCESS);
15 ...
16 while (flag)
17   PAMI_Context_advance (context, 1);
```

Figure 1: PAMI non blocking invocation

```
1  struct p2p_state {
2   int    source, dest;
3   void* send_buf;
4   void* recv_buf;
5   ...
6  }
7  class p2p_collective{
8   p2p_state* phases;
9   int phase, num_phases;
10  callback function *cb;
11 public:
12  void reset(data buffers, callback function);
13  void start();
14 };
```

Figure 2: P2P State machine and non blocking interface

multaneously executing collectives. Any single executing collective cannot tie down or block execution threads or processes. This imposes a state machine based implementation. There is a separate state machine for every instance of an executing collective operation on each executing task, and it runs from the starting state to the final state during the execution of the collective. Since the collective state machine cannot block or reserve an execution thread, state changes are always caused by callbacks: completion callbacks from sent messages as well as callbacks for incoming messages. For more details on active message programing models please consult [10, 1, 2].

All our state machines are organized around a number of phases. In each phase the state machine sends and/or receives one active message. When these are complete, the state machine advances to the next phase. The number of required phases for typical algorithms like barriers, reductions, broadcasts, prefix sums is logarithmic in the number of tasks, which ensures that our state machines are scalable with respect to memory use.

Figure 2 shows the main data structure we maintain for each of the phases of a collective for the current implementation. This structure, at minimum, contains the destination where to send the data for a phase, the send data buffer, the source from where it will receive data and the receive buffer.

We implement all collectives as individual classes, each class holding variables describing their internal state. The interface of such a class is shown in Figure 2. It includes two methods: reset() and start(), and a completion callback.

```
1  nphases = ceil(log(T));
2  for (int i=0; i<nphases; i++) {
3    int    dist     = 1<<(nhases-1-i);
4    int    sendmask = (1<<(nphases-i))-1;
5    destrank[i]     = myrank + dist;
6    if ((myrank&sendmask) ||
7        destrank[i]>=nprocs) destrank[i]=NULL;
8  }
```

Figure 3: Initializing state machine for binomial tree broadcast

- The reset() method sets the state machine into the start state and initializes input and output buffers for the collective. This method is completely local (that is, it is not allowed to communicate).

- The state machine starts executing when the start() method is invoked. The start() method is guaranteed by the system to be non blocking: it returns to the user within a finite amount of time, independent of other tasks' progress. The method is allowed to start an arbitrary number of communication operations.

- The completion callback (which is passed in as an argument to the reset() method) is invoked when the state machine reaches the final state (i.e. when the collective is complete). The API contract requires the completion callback to be non blocking as well, but does not prevent it from starting other communication primitives.

Note that completion semantics are *local*, i.e. completion of the state machine on one task does not intrinsically mean that the same instance has completed on any other task. This is completely in line with expected non-blocking collective semantics, e.g. a non-blocking barrier may *complete* on any task as soon as all other tasks have *started* executing it.

Figure 3 illustrates the calculations for building a state machine implementing a binomial tree broadcast from rank 0 to T tasks. In a binomial tree the senders are 0 in the first phase, 0 and T/2 in the second, 0, T/4, T/2 and 3T/4 in the third phase and so on; the destination ranks are T/2 in the first phase, T/4 and 3T/4 in the second phase, and so on. This simple rule is encoded by the dist and sendmask variables, which are calculated with simple shifts and masks. Similar calculations can be made for most well known generic collective algorithms, including butterflies, Bruck's algorithm [8] and others, giving us sufficient coverage for single-ported network algorithms.

3.4 Shared Memory Collectives

For higher level languages and libraries like MPI, UPC, X10, etc., tasks running in a shared memory node may or may not be in the same process. In order to facilitate communication between tasks sharing a node, but not in the same address space, the PAMI library reserves a shared memory region that is accessible from every task on the node. This is done by using standard UNIX primitives such as the shmctl() or mmap() functions. In this section we describe reduction and broadcast algorithms based on the assumption that a pre-allocated shared memory region is shared by all tasks running in an SMP node.

Shared Memory Reduction: We sketch out the code for reduction in Figure 4. Note that the code is incomplete due to space restrictions. The P tasks invoking the collective are logically organized as an n-ary tree, $\{2 \le n < P\}$. Every node in the tree reads and reduces values from its children, and then posts its own

```
1
2  // State machines (one per task)
3  struct {
4    int ctr;
5    TYPE buf;
6  }         * state;      // state machines
7
8  // Static setup (local to task)
9  int       me;           // my index
10 int       nchildren;    // # of my children
11 int       chld[];       // list of my children
12 int       parent;       // idx of my parent
13
14 reduce (me, op) {
15   // 1. wait for children data & reduce
16   val = state[me].buf;
17   for (int c=0; c<nchildren; c++) {
18    WAIT (state[chld[c]].ctr>state[me].ctr);
19    reduce_op(val, state[chld[c]].buf, op);
20   }
21
22   // 2. wait parent to have read prev value
23   WAIT (state[parent].ctr>=state[me].ctr);
24
25   // 3. Post my value
26   state[me].buf= val;
27   __lwsync(); // write barrier
28
29   // 4. update my state counter
30   state[me].ctr++;
31   return val;
32 }
```

Figure 4: Shared memory blocking reduce

```
1  bool reduce_worker (me, op) {
2
3    // 1. test children data readiness.
4    // Bail if not ready.
5    for (int c=0; c<nchildren && finished; c++)
6     if (WAIT_NB(state[chld[c]].ctr <= state[me].ctr))
7      return false;
8
9    // 2. test parent status.
10   // Bail if not ready.
11   if (WAIT_NB(state[parent].ctr < state[me].ctr)))
12    return false;
13
14   // 3. perform reduction
15   val = state[me].buf;
16   for (int c=0; c<nchildren; c++)
17    reduce_op(val, state[chld[c]].buf, op);
18
19   // 4. post result, notify.
20   state[me].buf=val;
21   __lwsync();
22   state[me].ctr++;
23   return true;
24 }
```

Figure 5: Non blocking reduce

value. The data dependency between children and parents requires two synchronization operations: (a) children's contributions should not be read before they are posted and (b) a node's calculated value should not be updated before the parent has read it. The dependency is implemented by monotonically incremented counters, one per task, that are being read by other tasks to assess whether data is available.

Each task busy-waits for data to become available from the children.This is accomplished using the WAIT macro in line 18 which blocks the incoming thread until the associated condition becomes true. Once the data arrives, the children's values are reduced (Line 19). Next, the task waits for the parent to announce having read its *previous* posted value (Line 23). The *new* result can now be posted (Line 26) and announced (Line 30) to parent and children alike. Note the memory sync instruction in line 27. The instruction ensures that data is visible to other tasks before the "data ready" notification.

The algorithm, as depicted here, is blocking. Tasks will not exit the collective until their are done with their contribution. While this in general leads to good performance for the collective considered in isolation, it blocks the task from doing other available work.

We mentioned in Section 3 that all PAMI collectives are non blocking. To transform the algorithm in Figure 4 into a non blocking one we need to replace the busy-waiting-based dependency mechanism. In one potential solution children notify their parents of data readiness by sending an active message. Upon receiving the message the parent increments a (local) counter and when all children are accounted for it performs the reduction and in turn notifies its own parent.

In a second approach, depicted in Figure 5, notification is, as before, by means of incrementing a variable. However, we do not busy-wait indefinitely on these variables. The WAIT_NB macro waits a predefined amount of time for its associated condition to become true. If the condition is still false when the allowed time expires, then WAIT_NB returns false. The reduction operation only takes place if all preconditions are met within a set amount of time. Otherwise the function execution is simply aborted and retried later by the underlying layers of PAMI. In this situation the operation is retried several times until the preconditions are met. This is accomplished by employing the PAMI work queue feature: Arbitrary functions can be queued up here for subsequent execution. A simple mechanism allows us to re-queue the reduction function as long as it keeps returning FALSE [2].

We found the second approach to have *much* higher performance than the first, due to the lower overhead of dependency handling mechanism (e.g, busy-wait). Active messages, even in shared memory, tend to have high overhead, whereas the PAMI task queue is relatively fast. By suitably adjusting the busy-wait time we can ensure that many non-blocking operations can be outstanding at the same time without impacting system performance. For this second approach, individual reduce performance is on par with the blocking version.

Shared Memory Broadcast: Similar with the reduce algorithm presented above we implemented various broadcast algorithms to accommodate both short and large messages. As before, dependencies are handled by monotonically increasing counters. We implemented a binary tree broadcast for small messages and a flat algorithm based on a star topology for large messages. In the flat algorithm the root writes the data and increments a counter while everybody else waits for the counter to be incremented before they start copying data. The advantage of the flat algorithm is that we can accommodate arbitrary large buffers with a minimum number of memory copy operations. A third algorithm we deployed is a variant of the flat broadcast where two buffers are used in an alternated manner. This improves overall performance by a factor of two due to pipelining reads and writes.

Shared Memory Allreduce: A simple allreduce operation can be implemented as a reduction followed by a broadcast. This can be easily achieved using the callback mechanism supported by our

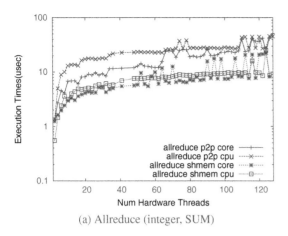

(a) Allreduce (integer, SUM)

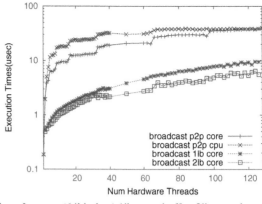

(b) Broadcast Latency (64bit data).1lb - one buffer, 2lb-two alternated buffers

Figure 6: Execution times for shared memory allreduce and broadcast for two different mappings on the machine. Execution time in microseconds for various number of hardware threads

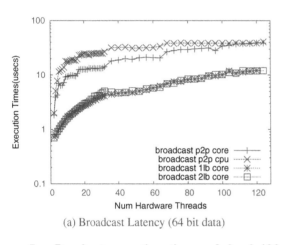

(a) Broadcast Latency (64 bit data)

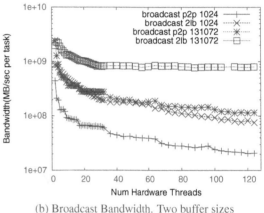

(b) Broadcast Bandwidth. Two buffer sizes

Figure 7: Broadcast execution time and bandwidth when different roots are used. Each iteration uses as root *iteration id%num tasks* **The reported bandwidth is per task.**

collectives. The allreduce will instantiate first a reduce operation whose callback function invokes the broadcast operation. More details on composition are provided in Section 4 as we describe hybrid collectives.

3.5 Evaluation of shared memory algorithms

In this section we analyze the performance of the non blocking shared memory collectives on the P7IH system and compare their performance relative to the generic P2P implementation as described in Section 3.3. We focus the analysis on allreduce and broadcast for which experimental results are included in Figure 6.

To evaluate the performance we employed a simple kernel that repeats the same operation in a loop. A task does not advance to the next iteration until the current one is locally completed. The corresponding code is a while loop around the code included in Figure 1, Lines 12-17. This same kernel has been used for all experiments included in this paper. Individual kernels for performance evaluation were compiled with xlC 11.1 and O3 optimization level.

The performance of shared memory collectives in the context of a multithreaded machine is highly dependent on the mapping between software tasks and hardware threads. On P7IH, for both Linux and AIX, system software provides support to explicitly perform this mapping. In the experiments included in Figures 6, 7, we

consider a P7IH shared memory node with 32 cores configured in a 4-way SMT; thus, 128 hardware threads.

We evaluate two different mappings, called *core* and *CPU* respectively. The *core* mapping allocates first 32 application tasks one per core, on physical thread zero of each of the 32 cores. The next 32 tasks are mapped on physical thread 1 and so on. The *CPU* mapping maps the first four tasks on core zero, the next four tasks on core one and so on.

Figure 6(a) shows the execution time for the shared memory allreduce operation described in the previous section and the corresponding point to point implementation, for two different mappings of the tasks on the machine. The shared memory allreduce is an operation that performs mainly synchronizations with minimal computation. We observe that both collectives scale well across a large number of tasks with the CPU mapping being less susceptible to noise due to cache sharing. For compute intensive application running a task per core may be the preferred way. With 128 tasks the shared memory achieves 9 μs in average while the P2P performance is around 12 μs. As a reference point the POSIX threads barrier is 169 μs on 32 threads.

In Figure 6 (b) and 7 (a) we show the broadcast performance on 8 bytes long messages thus describing the latency characteristics of our algorithm. For P2P we use a binomial tree while for

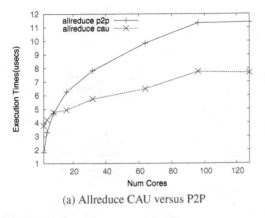

(a) Allreduce CAU versus P2P

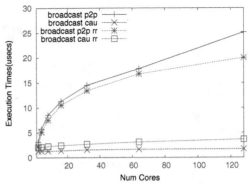

(b) CAU Broadcast 64 bit data (rr - root rotated every iteration)

Figure 8: Execution times for CAU allreduce and broadcast. Execution time in microseconds for various number of nodes; One task per core per node

shared memory we use a flat tree using one (`broadcast_1lb`) or two alternate buffers (`broadcast_2lb`). We also considered two strategies for selecting the root. In Figure 6 (b) we average the execution times for 100000 iterations using the same root zero. The shared memory algorithm with two buffers and core mapping has the lowest latency with 2.23 μs when using 32 tasks. For core mapping the single buffer option achieves 2.65 μs and the P2P is 14 μs, a much higher overhead in this case relative to the allreduce we previously analyzed. We notice the two buffers algorithm benefiting from the pipelining effects that takes place when multiple broadcasts are invoked in succession. In Figure 7 (a), every new iteration uses as root *iteration id%number_of_tasks* to avoid the pipelining effects. In this situation the two buffers version of broadcast doesn't have additional benefits over the single buffer. On 32 cores, using the core mapping the P2P achieves 14.3 μs, the shared memory version using one buffer 4.14 μs and the two buffers version 5.06 μs. The impact of the core mapping versus CPU is included only for the P2P broadcast the other two algorithms considered being less impacted by the mapping. For example on 32 threads the P2P core is 14.3 μs while the cpu is 26.9 μs, for one buffer the core mapping is 4.14 μs and cpu is 3.58 μs, and for two buffers version the core mapping is 5.06 μs while cpu is 3.41 μs. The shared memory version performs better with cpu mapping as the tasks are mapped on fewer cores thus benefiting from the L2 shared caches.

In Figure 7 (b) we look at the bandwidth performance of the broadcast for two buffer sizes in the situation where every iteration uses a different root. The performance of the shared memory version outperforms the P2P in terms of bandwidth for all range of buffer sizes considered. In Figure 7 we exemplify for two buffer sizes but additional results are available in Section 5. The interesting aspect of this experiment is to point out the good scalability of the algorithms on P7IH when scaling across all 128 hardware threads in a node. For a message size of 130K the bandwidth per core with 32 tasks is 1GB/sec and with 128 tasks is 800MB/sec.

3.6 Collective Accelerated Unit (CAU)

The CAU unit integrated in the IBM P7IH HUB provides offload and acceleration for broadcast and reduce up to 64 bytes of data. For reduce, it supports NO-OP, SUM, MIN, MAX, AND, OR and XOR operations with 32-bit/64-bit signed/unsigned fixed-point operands or single/double precision floating-point operands. The CAU device must be correctly initialized before deployment. Once a collective topology (set of nodes) is decided on, PAMI builds a

tree of CAU devices. The maximum fan-out of the tree is 8. CAU hardware provides one unit per SMP node. That is, when multiple tasks on a node are in the topology they need to elect a leader task to operate the CAU. Up to 64 different CAU trees can co-exist in the same device, and they can be used simultaneously. Each CAU packet carries an identifier of the virtual topology it belongs to. Once a CAU tree is established, any of the tasks attached to the tree can issue a broadcast as the root of the operation. Other tasks in the tree will receive the data without any other software involvement. Reductions operate in exactly the opposite manner: all tasks but the root send in data which is combined by the CAU tree and delivered to the root. Obviously, all participants have to agree on the identity of the root.

To implement operations like barriers and all-reduce the CAU tree must be deployed twice in succession, i.e. a reduction followed by a broadcast. This doubles the operation's latency, but as we will see this method still handily outperforms any software-based algorithm we are capable of devising.

In Figure 8 we show the performance for allreduce (a) and broadcast (b) and compare them with P2P implementations. Results are included for up to 128 P7IH nodes, using only one task per node. We observe overall good scalability for both P2P and the CAU collectives, but the CAU outperforms the P2P solution even at this (relatively small) node count. For P2P allreduce the execution time increases from 1.83 μs on two nodes to 11.39 μs on 128, while for CAU allreduce the time increases from 3.78 μs on 2 to 7.66 μs on 128. For all but the smallest number of nodes, the factor of 2 loss in performance of the CAU (reduce followed by broadcast) is more than compensated for by the lower node-to-node latency.

Figure 8 (b) evaluates short broadcast performance for P2P versus CAU. Note that since CAU broadcasts do not require the two deployments of the CAU per operation, results are much better relative to P2P. We evaluate short broadcasts in two situations: using the same root (task=0) in every iteration vs. using rotating roots (a different broadcast root in every iteration). In the case of the CAU algorithm the fixed root test yields better latency than the rotating root test (2.24 vs. 3.6 μs latency on 128 nodes). The reason for this is very simple - in the CAU broadcast packets get pipelined. The P2P algorithm cannot benefit from pipelining because in this case software, not hardware, has to guarantee correct ordering of packets. Thus the P2P algorithm actually includes a set of message exchanges with barrier semantics, preventing any sort of pipelining. The scaling of the P2P algorithm is still logarithmic, but with

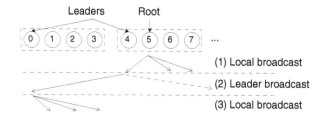

Figure 9: Hybrid broadcast as a three phase composition of local and leader broadcasts

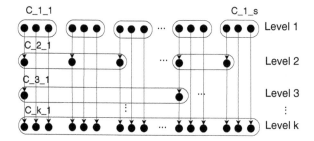

Figure 10: Collective composition

a much higher constant factor, 20 μs to 24 μs per broadcast on 128 nodes.

4. HYBRID COLLECTIVES

In this section we present a *framework* that allows us to compose highly tuned hardware-specific algorithms to obtain proper general purpose collective implementations and yet retain the performance characteristics of their components.

We have so far presented three sets of collective implementations on IBM P7IH: point-to-point messages, shared memory and CAU based. P2P collectives are general and are useful on almost any system. However, they come with built-in efficiency compromises. Shared memory and CAU collectives are designed for proper subsets of the P7IH system hierarchy. In PAMI terminology these are called *local topologies* (for shared memory) and *leader topologies* (one representative task per node), respectively. Topology specific collectives are very efficient, but do not provide a general purpose solution. [1]

To illustrate our approach, consider Figure 9, in which we use a composition of local and leader topologies to execute broadcast across a hybrid system. An initial (shared memory) broadcast within the local topology containing the root is followed by a broadcast across leaders in each node and concluded by a second shared memory broadcast within the nodes whose leaders just received the data.

Our compositional approach rests on the following design features:

Optimized components: Optimized implementations for various subsets of the system hierarchy where high performance can be obtained via hardware support and/or optimized algorithms. In this paper we will consider the shared memory and CAU collectives described in previous sections.

Chaining: The ability to seamlessly connect the completion point of a collective with the start of another without sacrificing performance.

Composition: The ability to decompose a collective to execute on a chained sequence of optimized topologies defined by hardware constraints. This allows us to break down the general problem into pieces that already have optimized solutions.

4.1 Chaining non blocking collectives

The Figure 2 in Section 3.3 shows the proposed application programming interface (API) for non blocking collectives in our framework. The interface includes the `reset` and `start` methods, as well as a callback to be invoked when the collective has terminated.

---

[1] In this paper we restrict ourselves to local and leader topologies. However, PAMI represents many other topologies that carry built-in advantages: for example, on the Blue Gene machines, with its various torus shaped networks, multidimensional rectangular shapes are considered advantageous because of the "broadcast bit" feature of the network [16].

To summarize: `reset()` is guaranteed to be local, `start()` is guaranteed to be non blocking, and the completion callback, provided by the user, is *required* by the API to be non blocking.

The API is carefully crafted to stay invariant under chaining. Our idea of chaining collectives is to use the completion callback of an already executing *primary* collective to start one or more *secondary* collectives. We call such completion callback *continuation functions*, since they don't actually complete the chained collective. Starting a secondary collective involves calls to its `start()` and `reset()` methods. Since these are guaranteed to be non blocking and local respectively, we can satisfy the API contract requirement that our primary completion callback be non-blocking.

4.2 Collective Composition Formalism

In this Section we formalize the compositional process to show its further generality as a methodology for deploying efficient parallel algorithms. As we mentioned already a collective is invoked simultaneously by a set of tasks that we refer in this paper as topology and we use the following notation $T = \{t_1, ..., t_n\}$.

For a given topology T we can compute the local topologies $Local(T) = \{Local_1(T), ..., Local_s(T)\}$ where s is the number of SMP nodes in the system and $Local_j(T) = \{t | t \in T \ and \ t \ mapped \ on \ the \ same \ SMP \ node \ j\}$ (e.g., the subset of tasks mapped on the same SMP node).

The leader topology of a given topology T, $Leader(T)$ is similarly defined as a set of leader tasks from T, one from each SMP node. Yet more topologies can be defined on other architectures. A collective C then will be instantiated with a given topology T and has an associated callback function to be invoked on all members of T when the collective locally completes. We denote this as $C(T, CB)$.

A composed collective then $C_{Composed}(T, CB)$ is defined based on a set of existing collectives and rules on how the collectives are chained together using continuation functions (intermediary callbacks).

Hierarchical chaining: One particularly useful approach to tackle physical hierarchies in the P7IH system is the hierarchical decomposition pattern. In this approach (shown in Figure 10) a composed collective is conceptually organized as a number of levels $\{L_1, L_2, ...L_l\}$. One or more collective instances, executing on different tasks, exist in each level; they are all instances of the same collective, although operating on different topologies and possibly with different callback functions. Thus a level L_k of the composition, $L_k = \{C_{k_1}(T_{k_1}, CB_{k_1}), C_{k_2}(T_{k_2}, CB_{k_2}).. \}$ consists of a set of collectives with their associated topologies and completion callbacks.

Successive levels in the hierarchy are started by continuations of previous levels. In the example included in Figure 10 we have collectives at level 1 employing different continuation functions for different tasks. We see that upon local completion of the collective at level one, certain tasks will start the collectives at level two while other tasks may start collectives at level K. The only requirement is that lower levels can not be re-invoked. The last continuation function invoked by each task invokes the user completion callback.

The performance of such a hierarchically composed collective is ultimately determined by its *critical path*, i.e. the maximum number of distinct levels traversed by any of the tasks involved in the collective.

Pipeline chaining: another useful pattern that emerged during our experiments is pipeline composition. Pipelining allows us to chain together multiple instances of a collective. Specifically, System V shared memory is a precious resource. We cannot internally allocate shared memory chunks to accommodate e.g. arbitrarily large broadcasts. Pipeline chaining allows us to allocate a single instance of a broadcast collective with a limited amount of shared memory, and allow it to restart itself in the continuation function, jumping forward in the user buffer with every new started instance. This can go on until there is no more user buffer to send, in which case the continuation function can revert to calling the next level in the hierarchy.

4.3 Composing hybrid collectives for the P7IH

In this section we present the composition of the P7IH hybrid collectives we actually implemented and tested. We start off with a **low latency allreduce** for short messages on P7IH consisting of four levels: $ShortAllReduce(T, CB) = \{L_1, L_2, L_3, L_4\}$, where:

- **L1 = Initial shared memory reduction**:
  $L_1 = \{SharedMemReduce(LocalTopology_j(T), CF_1\}$,
  where j scans all local topologies (shared memory nodes).

  - CF_1 starts L_2 on all tasks of $LeaderTopology(T)$
  - CF_1 starts L_4 on all tasks of $T \setminus LeaderTopology(T)$,

- **L2 = Leader CAU reduction:**
  $L_2 = \{CAUReduce(LeaderTopology(T), CF_2\}$

  - CF_2 starts L_3 on $LeaderTopology(T)$

- **L3 = Leader result broadcast:**
  $L_3 = \{CAUBroadcast(LeaderTopology(T), CF_3\}$

  - CF_3 starts L_4 on $LeaderTopology(T)$

- **L4 = Final shared memory broadcast:**
  $L_4 = \{SharedMemBroadcast(LocalTopology_j(T), CB\}$

  - CB is the completion callback provided by the user.

In a similar vein, our **low latency broadcast** for P7IH consists of three levels: a shared memory broadcast on the local topology containing the root, followed by a CAU accelerated broadcast across leaders, concluded by shared memory broadcasts on the local topologies not owning the root.

For **high bandwidth hybrid broadcast** optimized for medium to large messages we use the same three phases as for short broadcast, but using a pipelined shared memory broadcast for the first and third phase, and a point to point broadcast across leaders (CAU is primarily useful for short messages).

5. PERFORMANCE EVALUATION

In this section we evaluate the performance of our composed hybrid collectives. We compare the latency and bandwidth of our hybrid allreduce and broadcast against more traditional implementations.

For the experiments in this section we used a different machine than the one introduced in Section 3.5. The P7IH system we employed here has four supernodes, in other words 128 nodes of 32 cores each for a total of $32 \times 128 = 4096$ cores. For the shared memory experiment in Section 3.5 we used a single node machine configured in SMT 4 (each core had all four threads enabled) and using an older network hardware (HFI 2.0). For this section the machine used was configured in SMT 2 (only two hardware threads enabled) and the latest network interconnect (HFI 2.1).

For all experiments on hybrid collective performance we map one application task per process and use the core mapping as described in Section 3.5. All times are averaged over 100000 iterations. For all broadcast experiments included in this section we use as rotating roots (every iteration has a different root) in order to guarantee that latency is measured correctly without pipelining broadcasts.

5.1 Latency study

In Figure 11 we show the performance of the allreduce (a) and short broadcast (b). The short allreduce is of a particular importance to us because it is used by the implementation of the barrier primitive in the UPC language. [2]

Figure 11 (a) shows the scalability of our composed hybrid allreduce. As explained in Section 4.3 the composed allreduce has two shared memory and CAU components each, and we expect to measure the four components' latencies. Thus we expect

$$T \approx T_{CAUreduce} + T_{CAUbcast} + T_{shmreduce} + T_{shmbcast}$$

Drawing on numbers presented earlier in the paper - shared memory reduction on 32 threads is in the 6 μs range; shared memory broadcast in the 2 μs range; and CAU allreduce on 128 nodes is in the 7-8 μs range. Thus we expect 16 μs or so on 4096 tasks. We are actually measuring 18 μs close to the expected value. Thus in our measurements, the overhead of various scaling factors like system noise etc. is 15% or less. The point to point alternative of short allreduce (a non-hybrid, standard butterfly based algorithm) also scales well, but is about 50% behind the optimized algorithm, 24 μs on 4096 cores.

Results for short (8 byte word) broadcast are in Figure 11 (b). Here we compare three versions against each other: a standard binomial algorithm, a composite algorithm with optimized shared memory communication (shmem+P2P) and finally a shmem+CAU algorithm as described in Section 4.3.

All three algorithms show logarithmic scaling behavior. Predictably, the shmem+P2P algorithm has better latency than pure P2P (26 μs vs 40 μs on 4096 cores). Just as unsurprisingly the shmem+CAU combination beats them both (2.8 μs on 4096 cores).

5.2 Bandwidth study

Figure 12 compares the pure P2P binomial tree broadcast with a hybrid shmem+P2P algorithm. We consider both scaling behavior (number of cores from 32 to 4096) and message size (1 KByte to 8 MBytes). We report broadcast bandwidth in MBytes/s/task (not the aggregate number).

We observe that the hybrid algorithm (gray background columns) performs better than its P2P counterpart for all buffer sizes and all number of cores considered. However, the difference varies with scale and message size. With 32 tasks the hybrid algorithm is re-

---

[2] UPC barriers have an optional integer argument. The UPC runtime checks expressions supplied by various UPC participants in the same barrier for equality. This helps UPC programmers to ensure code correctness. A UPC barrier is therefore actually implemented as a PAMI allreduce with a MAX operator rather than an actual barrier.

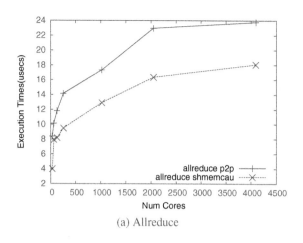

(a) Allreduce

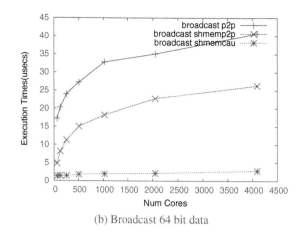

(b) Broadcast 64 bit data

Figure 11: Execution times for hybrid allreduce and broadcast. Execution time in microseconds for various number of cores

Algo	P2P	Hyb	P2P	Hyb	P2P	Hyb	P2P	Hyb	P2P	Hyb	P2P	Hyb	P2P	Hyb	P2P	Hyb
Size/Cores	32	32	64	64	128	128	256	256	512	512	1024	1024	2048	2048	4096	4096
1KB	60	210	47	164	39	97	34	71	25	54	24	43	22	32	19	31
16KB	278	637	158	620	139	486	122	347	112	249	102	208	98	183	80	143
128KB	281	1573	219	1209	191	727	172	575	154	491	140	412	143	359	117	315
1MB	421	1860	400	1146	360	719	329	602	302	520	278	445	208	391	228	344
2MB	490	1756	470	1162	418	726	382	599	348	516	321	450	284	396	260	348
8MB	734	1507	642	1008	564	691	507	574	455	499	418	434	360	382	321	340

Figure 12: Broadcast bandwidth for various buffer sizes and number of cores. The reported bandwidth is in MB/second per task

duced to shared memory only, and hence outperforms the P2P version by a factor between 2 and 5. As the number of nodes increases the relative advantage of the hybrid algorithm diminishes, since the shared memory broadcast contributes a declining proportion of the total execution time as the number of cores is scaled up.

We observe a similar effect for message sizes. Since the chief advantage of the shared memory implementation is lower overhead, larger message sizes tend to wash out the difference between hybrid and P2P only; on 4096 cores with 8MB buffers, the hybrid algorithm only holds a 5% advantage.

5.3 SMT impact on hybrid collectives

Due to lack of space we include only a minimal discussion on the performance of hybrid collectives when using multiple hardware threads per core. For example, when using 4096 cores and 8192 hardware threads the binomial P2P broadcast achieves 68 μs, the hybrid (Shared Memory local and P2P on leaders) is 33 μs and the hybrid version employing CAU is 3.9 μs. Additionally, when using 8192 tasks mapped on as many hardware threads on 4096 cores, the hybrid broadcast algorithm provides 34% more bandwidth relative to P2P for 8MB message size (271MB versus 201MB for P2P). Recall that when not using SMT the hybrid version had only 5% advantage over P2P. Thus when using multiple hardware threads the advantages of shared memory are even bigger.

6. RELATED WORK

Specializing collectives to take advantage of the underlying hardware and specialized networks is a common approach for obtaining the best performance on modern high performance systems [4, 20, 22, 14]. In [4] the authors describe optimization for BlueGene/L. Other major vendors like Cray, Infiniband also provide support for collective acceleration and various academic papers describe opti-

mizations of the MPI library to obtain good performance. For example, in [20, 12] the authors describe a hybrid solution for broadcast using shared memory and Infiniband multicast support.

In [13] the authors present the Non Blocking Collective library (libNBC) as an extension to MPI collectives to provide non blocking functionality. In their model a collective maintains an internal schedule consisting of rounds with operations in a round proceeding only when the previous round completed. Our multi phase mechanism described in Section 3.3 is similar with this approach. The main difference between our approach and this one is the fact that we provide the call back mechanism to signal completion. In libNBC, upon a collective invocation, a handle is initialized and later on the handle can be queried if the collective has finished. We showed in Section 4 that the callback mechanism is essential for us to efficiently compose non blocking collectives to achieve new ones. We can't envision an elegant composition mechanism using the libNBC approach.

Existing parallel programming languages and libraries [11, 7] already exploit shared memory nodes to improve the performance of both point to point and collective operations. In [7] the authors describe performance improvements for point to point operations for the UPC language when optimizing for shared memory intra node communication. However they have only a minimal section on collectives optimizations.

In [15] the authors perform an in depth performance study of the P7IH various intra and inter node communication links describing achievable latencies and bandwidths. They measure the performance using simple point to point kernels and discuss it relative to the maximum specified values. In this paper we discuss for the first time the performance of the collective operations on P7IH, including the novel CAU not presented elsewhere.

In [20], the authors discuss composing collective communication algorithms from primitives. The authors focus there on specific optimization enabled by Infiniband hardware. Our description of collective composition however is more general and establishes the bases under which arbitrary algorithms can be combined to exploit the various levels of a hardware architecture

7. CONCLUSION AND FUTURE WORK

In this paper we have presented an experimental evaluation of collective communication primitives on the IBM P7IH architecture. We presented initial measurements of the collective acceleration unit (CAU) running reduction and broadcast collectives. We also presented collective communication algorithms optimized for the rather large SMP nodes of the P7IH.

Our second contribution in this paper is a novel framework and a formalism that allows us to chain together non blocking collectives optimized for different subsets of the system hierarchy. We demonstrated that the combined hybrid algorithms in our framework offer the best chance to achieve good performance and scalability on the IBM P7IH system.

8. REFERENCES

[1] *Parallel Environment Runtime Edition for AIX, LAPI Programming Guide, Version 1 Release 1.0, IBM.*

[2] *Parallel Environment Runtime Edition for AIX, PAMI Programming Guide, Version 1 Release 1.0, IBM.*

[3] *Parallel ESSL for AIX V4.1 Guide and Reference, IBM.*

[4] G. Almási and all. Optimization of MPI collective communication on BlueGene/L systems. In *Proc. of the 19th International Conference on Supercomputing*, ICS '05, pages 253–262, New York, NY, USA, 2005. ACM.

[5] G. Almasi, P. Hargrove, I. G. Tanase, and Y. Zheng. UPC Collectives Library 2.0. In *Proc. of the Fifth Conference on Partitioned Global Address Space Programming Models*, Oct. 2010.

[6] R. X. Arroyo, R. J. Harrington, S. P. Hartman, and T. Nguyen. IBM Power7 systems. *IBM Journal of Research and Development*, 55(3):2:1 –2:13, may-june 2011.

[7] F. Blagojević, P. Hargrove, C. Iancu, and K. Yelick. Hybrid PGAS runtime support for multicore nodes. In *Proc. of the Fourth Conference on Partitioned Global Address Space Programming Model*, PGAS '10, pages 3:1–3:10, New York, NY, USA, 2010. ACM.

[8] J. Bruck, C.-T. Ho, S. Kipnis, E. Upfal, and D. Weathersby. Efficient algorithms for all-to-all communications in multiport message-passing systems. *IEEE Transactions on Parallel and Distributed Systems*, 8(11):1143 –1156, nov 1997.

[9] P. Charles, C. Grothoff, V. Saraswat, C. Donawa, A. Kielstra, K. Ebcioglu, C. von Praun, and V. Sarkar. X10: An object-oriented approach to non-uniform cluster computing. *SIGPLAN Not.*, 40:519–538, October 2005.

[10] T. Eicken, D. Culler, S. Goldstein, and K. Schauser. Active messages: A mechanism for integrated communication and computation. In *Proc. of the 19th Annual International Symposium on Computer Architecture, 1992*, pages 256 –266, 1992.

[11] E. Gabriel and all. Open MPI: Goals, concept, and design of a next generation MPI implementation. In *Proc. of 11th European PVM/MPI Users' Group Meeting*, pages 97–104, Budapest, Hungary, September 2004.

[12] T. Hoefler and A. Lumsdaine. Optimizing non-blocking Collective Operations for InfiniBand. In *Proc. of the 22nd IEEE International Parallel & Distributed Processing Symposium, CAC'08 Workshop*, Apr. 2008.

[13] T. Hoefler, A. Lumsdaine, and W. Rehm. Implementation and Performance Analysis of Non-Blocking Collective Operations for MPI. In *Proc. of the 2007 International Conference on High Performance Computing, Networking, Storage and Analysis, SC07*. IEEE Computer Society/ACM, Nov. 2007.

[14] N. Karonis, B. de Supinski, I. Foster, W. Gropp, E. Lusk, and J. Bresnahan. Exploiting hierarchy in parallel computer networks to optimize collective operation performance. In *Proc. of the 14th Parallel and Distributed Processing Symposium, 2000. IPDPS 2000.*, pages 377 –384, 2000.

[15] D. Kerbyson and K. Barker. Analyzing the performance bottlenecks of the Power7-IH network. In *Proc. of the IEEE International Conference on Cluster Computing (CLUSTER), 2011*, pages 244 –252, sept. 2011.

[16] S. Kumar and all. The deep computing messaging framework: generalized scalable message passing on the Blue Gene/P supercomputer. In *Proc. of the 22nd International Conference on Supercomputing*, ICS '08, pages 94–103, New York, NY, USA, 2008. ACM.

[17] MPI Forum. MPI:a message-passing interface standard (version 1.1). Technical Report (june 1995). available at: http://www.mpi-forum.org (Jan. 2012).

[18] R. Rajamony, L. B. Arimilli, and K. Gildea. PERCS: The IBM Power7-ih high-performance computing system. *IBM Journal of Research and Development*, 55(3):3:1 –3:12, may-june 2011.

[19] B. Sinharoy, R. Kalla, W. J. Starke, H. Q. Le, R. Cargnoni, J. A. Van Norstrand, B. J. Ronchetti, J. Stuecheli, J. Leenstra, G. L. Guthrie, D. Q. Nguyen, B. Blaner, C. F. Marino, E. Retter, and P. Williams. IBM Power7 multicore server processor. *IBM Journal of Research and Development*, 55(3):1:1 –1:29, may-june 2011.

[20] H. Subramoni, K. Kandalla, S. Sur, and D. Panda. Design and evaluation of generalized collective communication primitives with overlap using connectx-2 offload engine. In *Proc. of the IEEE 18th Annual Symposium on High Performance Interconnects (HOTI), 2010* , pages 40 –49, aug. 2010.

[21] G. Tanase, A. Buss, A. Fidel, Harshvardhan, I. Papadopoulos, O. Pearce, T. Smith, N. Thomas, X. Xu, N. Mourad, J. Vu, M. Bianco, Mauro and N.M. Amato and L. Rauchwerger. The STAPL parallel container framework. In *Proc. of the 16th ACM symposium on Principles and practice of parallel programming*, PPoPP '11, pages 235–246, New York, NY, USA, 2011. ACM.

[22] V. Tipparaju, J. Nieplocha, and D. Panda. Fast collective operations using shared and remote memory access protocols on clusters. In *Proc. of the 17th International Symposium on Parallel and Distributed Processing*, IPDPS '03, pages 84.1–, Washington, DC, USA, 2003. IEEE Computer Society.

[23] UPC language specifications, v1.2. Technical Report LBNL-59208, Lawrence Berkeley National Lab, 2005.

Collective Algorithms for Sub-communicators

Anshul Mittal
Stanford University
Palo Alto, USA.
anmittal@stanford.edu

Nikhil Jain
University of Illinois
Urbana Champaign, USA
nikhil@illinois.edu

Thomas George
IBM Research India
New Delhi, India
thomasgeorge@in.ibm.com

Sameer Kumar
IBM T.J.W. Research Center
Yorktown Heights, USA
sameerk@us.ibm.com

Yogish Sabharwal
IBM Research India
New Delhi, India
ysabharwal@in.ibm.com

ABSTRACT

Collective communication over a group of processors is an integral and time consuming component in many high performance computing applications. Many modern day supercomputers are based on torus interconnects and near optimal algorithms have been developed for collective communication over regular communicators on these systems. However, for an irregular communicator comprising of a subset of processors, the algorithms developed so far are not contention free in general and hence non-optimal.

In this paper, we present a novel contention-free algorithm to perform collective operations over a subset of processors in a torus network. We also extend previous work on regular communicators to handle special cases of irregular communicators that occur frequently in parallel scientific applications. For the generic case where multiple node disjoint sub-communicators communicate simultaneously in a loosely synchronous fashion, we propose a novel cooperative approach to route the data for individual sub-communicators without contention. Empirical results demonstrate that our algorithms outperform the optimized MPI collective implementation on IBM's Blue Gene/P supercomputer for large data sizes and random node distributions.

Categories and Subject Descriptors

D.m [**Software**]: Miscellaneous

Keywords

Collectives, Torus, Sub-communicators

1. INTRODUCTION

Many scientific applications use data movement collectives such as *Broadcast, Scatter, (All)Gather, All-to-all* and computation collectives such as *(All)Reduce, Reduce-scatter* [3]. The performance of these MPI collectives is critical for improved scalability and efficiency of parallel scientific applications. In recent years, there have been an increasing number

of applications such as web analytics, micro-scale weather simulation and computational nanotechnology that involve processing extremely large scale data requiring collective operations with large messages. Performance of such large message collectives is significantly affected by network bandwidth constraints. Our current work is aimed at enabling contention-free communication so as to optimize the performance of such large message collective operations.

Many modern day supercomputers are based on interconnection networks with a k-ary n-cube topology, for example, the Blue Gene/P and Cray XT machines have a 3D torus topology. Applications on such architecture involve collective operations not only on the entire processor partition (MPI_COMM_WORLD or the *full-communicator* in MPI), but also on sub partitions (i.e., sub-communicators in MPI). For example, matrix multiplication and 3D FFT with pencil decomposition are two important applications that have 2D decomposition. Mapping of a 2D decomposition on a 3D torus results in creation of sub-communicators, possibly irregular, for collective operations performed on rows or columns of the 2D decomposition. In the molecular dynamics application NAMD [9], the patch processors broadcast atom coordinates to the compute processors where the interactions are computed and forces are sent back via a reduction to the patch processors. The NAMD load balancer places compute objects on an arbitrary subset of processors to balance load. Even if the load balancer optimizes network hops and places compute objects on neighboring nodes of patch processors, the sub-communicator can still be a random subset.

In the absence of optimized implementations of collective calls for irregular sub-communicators, applications typically use point-to-point messages that also enable applications to overlap computation with communication. As, non blocking collective communication calls are likely to be part of MPI 3.0, more applications will take advantage of such collective calls over sub-communicator if optimized implementations are available.

In this paper, we present a novel technique to build contention free spanning trees on an arbitrary subset of nodes in a torus network. Data can then be pipelined along the spanning tree in order to execute the MPI collectives such as *scatter, broadcast, reduce, gather*. Overlaying spanning tree(s) that are contention free, i.e. no two edges are overlaid on the same link, results in a higher bandwidth utilization. Programming paradigms other than MPI that have sub-communicator collective communication can also take advantage of these techniques.

Our Contributions:

a) We propose an algorithm to construct two edge-disjoint trees in opposite directions that allow contention-free collective operations over a random sub-communicator on a 3D torus network. Our approach guarantees single-link throughput, which we show is the best achievable for "any arbitrary" sub-communicator. To the best of our knowledge, this is the first work to provide theoretical guarantees for such arbitrary sub-communicators. We show a speedup of $2 - 4\times$ for Broadcast and Allreduce operations on Blue Gene/P.

b) We explore a novel co-operative technique that enables sub-communicator collective operations to take advantage of the six spanning trees built on the entire partition. When the root calls broadcast, data is broadcast to all the nodes with full network throughput of the six contention free spanning trees presented in Faraj et.al [4]. Communication threads forward messages on nodes not in the sub-communicator. An empirical evaluation of this approach demonstrates a speedup of $1.7 - 5.8\times$.

c) We explore scenarios with communicators that have random set of nodes, alternate planes and full contiguous rectangles with a node missing. We also explore scenarios where multiple such sub-communicators co-exist and simultaneously participate in collective operations. We demonstrate that good performance is obtained by either: 1) using a novel co-operative scheme over full communicators or 2) independently using our contention-free spanning tree for each irregular sub-communicator.

2. RELATED WORK

Optimizing MPI collectives has been a key topic of interest in high performance computing [10]. Most of the existing algorithms can be grouped into two classes. The first class comprises of generic algorithms such as the binomial algorithm and recursive doubling/halving [13], which work well for most network topologies and a wide range of message sizes. Due to their simplicity and broad applicability, these algorithms are part of many MPI implementations including MPICH [12] and IBM's MPI. The second class of algorithms are specifically tailored for a given network topology. These algorithms outperform the generic algorithms for the specific target topologies and message sizes. For example, Van de Geijn et.al [11] proposed an algorithm for large message broadcast that has been shown to outperform the binomial algorithm [13]. Jain et.al [5] demonstrate that the bucket algorithm [2] can be generalized optimally, both for communication and computation, for an n-dimensional torus.

Optimization schemes for 3D torus networks has been presented in [4] and [5]. Faraj et.al [4] show how to carefully overlay six spanning trees over a 3-dimensional torus without contention. The algorithms in [4] can also be extended to rectangular sub communicators. In general, when multiple spanning trees are directed towards or away from the root, performance improves for *Broadcast, Scatter, Gather and Reduce* because of increased link throughput utilization by multiple trees. Derived collectives, such as *Allreduce* that is performed by pipelining *Reduce* with *Broadcast*, benefit from two edge-disjoint trees, one in each direction towards and away from the root.

3. ALGORITHMS

In this section, we describe two algorithms - the first one is a novel algorithm to construct edge-disjoint spanning trees for arbitrary sub-communicators. The second is an extension of the multi-color algorithm proposed by Faraj et at. [4] to handle special cases of irregular communicators.

We now formally show the construction of the spanning tree for any random sub-communicator. First, we show that it is easy to construct a spanning tree in a mesh instead of a torus, and later highlight the challenges in constructing a spanning tree in a torus. We then present our construction for two dimensions and describe extension for three dimensions.

3.1 Preliminaries

We now introduce some definitions that will be used in this section and also briefly revisit the working of dynamic routing. We consider a 3-dimensional torus of size $d_x \times d_y \times d_z$ and refer to the processing elements in the torus as nodes. The nodes that are part of the communicator under consideration are referred to as *c-nodes*. For a given node u, let $x(u)$, $y(u)$, and $z(u)$, denote the x-coordinate, y-coordinate, and z-coordinate respectively. We say that a node u is to the left of node v in the x dimension if $x(v) - x(u)$ mod $d_x \leq d_x/2$. Similarly node u is to the right of node v in the x dimension if $x(u) - x(v)$ mod $d_x \leq d_x/2$. Similarly, we define the notion of left and right for the y and z dimensions. Let $L_x(u)$ denote the set of all the nodes to the left of u in the x dimension and $R_x(u)$ the set of all the nodes to the right of u in the x dimension. We similarly define the sets $L_y(u)$, $R_y(u)$, $L_z(u)$, and $R_z(u)$.

We define a *line* as the set of points that share the same y and z dimensions. Similarly we define the set of points that share the same z dimension as a *plane*. For a given line ℓ let N_ℓ denote the nodes in line ℓ and C_ℓ, the nodes in line ℓ that are part of the communicator. For a node u in line ℓ, we denote by $r(u)$ the closest c-node to the right of u, i.e., $r(u) = argmin_{v \in C_\ell \cap R_x(u)}\{x(v) - x(u)$ mod $d_x\}$. Similarly, we denote by $l(u)$ the closest c-node to the left of u, i.e., $l(u) = argmin_{v \in C_\ell \cap L_x(u)}\{x(u) - x(v)$ mod $d_x\}$. We say that a line ℓ has a *gap* of $d_x/2+1$ if there exists a node $u \in C_\ell$ such that $R_x(u) \cap C_\ell = \phi$, i.e., there exist two adjacent communicator nodes in the line with a gap of at least $d_x/2 + 1$ between them.

We say that the communicator nodes in a line ℓ form a chain in a tree T if the nodes C_ℓ can be arranged as a sequence $< c_1, c_2, \ldots, c_m >$ where $m = |C_\ell|$ such that $r(c_j) = c_{j+1}$ for all $j = 1, 2, \ldots, m - 1$ and (c_j, c_{j+1}) is an edge in the tree T. Note that the nodes in a line, can always be arranged in such a sequence when the line does not have a gap of $d_x/2+1$. In this case, the sequence could start from any node and go towards right. However, when there is a gap of $d_x/2 + 1$, the chain has to start only from one of the two nodes adjacent to the gap.

Dynamic routing: In dynamic routing, when a node, say a, sends data to another node, say b, each data packet may take any of the shortest paths that connect nodes a and b. The exact path is determined by the congestion in the interconnection network. In general, the set of shortest paths for a 2D-mesh or torus lie in the axis-parallel rectangle with a and b defining the diagonally opposite vertices of this rectangle. For a 3D-mesh or torus, the set of shortest paths define an axis parallel cuboid instead of a rectangle. The necessary and sufficient conditions for a path to be a shortest path are that (i) the number of links it traverses along any dimension is at most half the total length of that dimension; and (ii) it does not traverse any two edges along the same dimension in opposite directions.

In describing a communication pattern, where the underlying routing mechanism is dynamic routing, we say that the communication pattern is contention-free if we can map every pair of processors that exchange data onto the links in such a manner that it constitutes a shortest path between the pair of processors and no link is used more than once. This is one realization of the paths that dynamic routing may take. It is left to the dynamic routing to determine the routes to be taken, but given that there exists such a realization, dynamic routing is expected to do almost as well in the presence of congestion.

3.1.1 Issues with mesh based snake algorithm on torus interconnects

Consider a two dimensional mesh interconnect. It is easy to construct a tree, in fact a chain, with no link contention for a random sub-communicator. A spanning tree with such a *snake like formation* is illustrated in Figure 1. It is straightforward to extend this approach to 3-dimensions. Considering the links to be bi-directional, we can derive two spanning trees, one in each direction as follows. Let r be any one of these nodes. Making r as the root, we obtain one tree by traversing the edges moving away from r. The tree in the opposite direction is obtained by reversing the direction of the edges of this tree. As there is no contention in the undirected tree and every link is used in the opposite direction in the two trees, we obtain two independent trees. As a matter of fact, the degree of any node is at most two in this simple case.

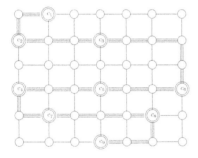

Figure 1: Snake like formation for 2D mesh

We now highlight the challenges in obtaining such a tree when the underlying interconnection is a torus network with wraparound links. Consider the path that connects the c-node c_7 to c_8 in Figure 1. Note that in the case of a torus, there is a wrap-around link so that there is a path of length 3 from c_7 to c_8 by moving left from c_7. However, there is contention between this path and the path connecting c_4 to c_7. Note here that if we only wanted a tree in one direction, then it is fine to have the two paths above as they use the contention links in opposite directions. However, our aim is to build a contention-free undirected spanning tree so that we can extract two directed spanning trees from it – one in each direction. This is considerably more involved than building a single tree and is discussed in detail in the next two sections.

3.1.2 Spanning tree in two dimensions

The algorithm builds a spanning tree over the set of c-nodes by considering them one line at a time. In each iteration it considers one new line; it carefully determines a chain to be formed from these c-nodes and then connects this chain to the previously built spanning tree. There are two crucial decisions that are to be made in each iteration;

the first is to determine which c-nodes will form the *head* and the *tail* of the new chain and the second is to determine the c-node in the previously formed spanning tree to which the head of this chain will be attached as a child; we call this c-node the *connector*. All of this has to be done ensuring that the spanning tree edges can be mapped to torus links constituting shortest paths between the c-nodes connected by the edge and that the set of torus links used by all the edges are disjoint.

The algorithm is presented in Figure 2. The algorithm for building this spanning tree works line by line. In step 1, it first arranges the lines by their y co-ordinates so that the distance between any pair of adjacent lines is no more than $d_y/2$. Let $\ell(i)$ denote the ith line corresponding to y_i for $1 \leq i \leq r$.

In step 2, it builds the chain for the first line. This gives us the first set of edges of the tree.

In step 3, it adds the c-nodes of a new line to the existing tree. Suppose the tree for the first i lines has already been built. This step connects $\ell(i)$ to $\ell(i + 1)$ while continuing to maintain a tree formation. This construction is based on three cases.

In case 1, it checks if there is no gap of $d_x/2+1$ in $\ell(i+1)$. This case is illustrated in Figure 3. In this case, we make any c-node of $\ell(i)$ as a connector. We come down from the connector node and then proceed towards the right in $\ell(i + 1)$. The first c-node encountered in this direction (note that this may be the c-node directly under the connector) is the head c-node and we form a chain proceeding towards the right till we cover all the c-nodes in this new line. More formally, if the connector c-node is selected to be u, then the head c-node is $argmin_{v \in C_{\ell(i+1)} \cap R_x(u)} \{x(v) - x(u) \mod d_x\}$. The tail node happens to be the first c-node of the communicator in the opposite direction from head. In the figure, node c_2 is the connector, node c_1' is the head and node c_3' is the tail.

Case 2 corresponds to the line $\ell(i + 1)$ having a gap of $d_x/2 + 1$. Note that in this case there is only one way to form a chain from the c-nodes in $\ell(i+1)$. Let $< c_1', \ldots, c_{m'}' >$ be the chain of $\ell(i+1)$. This case is handled with 2 subcases.

In case 2(a), the algorithm checks if there is some c-node, u, in $\ell(i)$ such that the node below u is not in the chain of $\ell(i+1)$. More formally if u' be the node below u in $\ell(i+1)$ (having the same x co-ordinate), then $u' \notin R_x(c_1')$. This case is illustrated in Figure 4. In this case, the algorithm makes u the connector node. We come down from the connector node and then proceed in the direction of the closer c-node in $\ell(i + 1)$. The first c-node encountered in this direction is the head c-node and the remaining chain in this new line (obtained by proceeding in the same direction) determines the remaining part of the tree.

Case 2(b) considers the case where the condition of case 2(a) is not satisfied, i.e., every c-node in $\ell(i)$ is directly above the chain of $\ell(i+1)$. Let $< c_1, \ldots, c_m >$ be the chain of $\ell(i)$ and $< c_1', \ldots, c_{m'}' >$ be the chain of $\ell(i+1)$. This scenario is illustrated in Figure 5. Note that it is possible that extra links beyond the chain of $\ell(i)$ are also used in connecting the chain of $\ell(i)$ to the chain of $\ell(i-1)$. Without loss of generality, assume that the rightmost c-node, c_m, is the head of the chain of $\ell(i)$. Therefore, it is possible that the links to the right of c_m are used in connecting c_m to the connector of the chain of $\ell(i-1)$. Let these extra used links be denoted by $\mathcal{E}$. In this case, we consider the other end-point of the chain of $\ell(i)$, i.e., c_1 and make it the connector node. We then proceed left from this node until we are directly above c_1' (it

1. Let $y_1, y_2, \ldots, y_r$ be a sequence of y-coordinates that contain c-nodes such that the y-distance between two consecutive y-coordinates in this sequence $\leq d_y/2$, i.e., $(y_{i+1} - y_i) \bmod d_y \leq d_y/2$ for all $1 \leq i < r$. Let $\ell(i)$ denote the line corresp. to y_i for $1 \leq i \leq r$.

2. Let $< c_1, .., c_m >$ be the chain of c-nodes in line $\ell(1)$. Connect the c-nodes in the chain in a straight line.

3. For $i = 1$ to $r - 1$ do
   Connect $\ell(i)$ to $\ell(i+1)$ based on the following cases:

   Case 1: $\ell(i+1)$ does not have a gap of $d_x/2 + 1$
   a. Select any c-node in $\ell(i)$, say u, as the connector.
   b. Progress down from u to $\ell(i+1)$ and then move towards right in $\ell(i+1)$, say c_1'
   c. Form a chain in $\ell(i+1)$ starting with c_1' and cover all the c-nodes in $\ell(i+1)$ proceeding in the same direction.

   Case 2: $\ell(i+1)$ has a gap of $d_x/2 + 1$
   Let $< c_1, c_2, \ldots, c_m >$ be the chain of $\ell(i)$ where c_1 is the head node and c_m is the tail node

   Case 2(a): there exists a c-node, u, in $\ell(i)$ that is directly above a node not contained in the chain of $\ell(i+1)$
   a. Progress down from u to $\ell(i+1)$ and then move towards the closest node in $\ell(i+1)$.
   c. Form a chain starting with this node and cover all the c-nodes in $\ell(i+1)$ proceeding in the same direction.

   Case 2(b): All c-nodes in $\ell(i)$ are above nodes contained in the chain of $\ell(i+1)$
   Let $u \in \{c_1, c_m\}$ be a node that has an edge adjacent to it in $\ell(i)$ that is not used in the tree
   a. Progress from u in the direction of the unused edge till you reach above the first or last c-node of the chain of $\ell(i+1)$
   b. Progress down to the c-node of $\ell(i+1)$
   c. Form a chain starting with this node and cover all the c-nodes in $\ell(i+1)$

Figure 2: Tree building algorithm in 2 dimensions

is possible that c_1' is directly below c_1) and then move down to connect to c_1'; c_1' is made the head of the new chain. We then proceed right connecting all the c-nodes in the chain, till we reach the last c-node. Let $\mathcal{F}$ denote the set of links to the left of c_1 used in the new chain. The case where the links to the left of c_1 are already used in connecting the chain of $\ell(i)$ to the chain of $\ell(i+1)$ is handled similarly – in this case we make c_m the connector node and proceed right from c_m.

This completes the construction of the spanning tree in two dimensions. In Figure 6, we present an example tree construction using the algorithm described in Figure 2. The rows in the 2-D torus are designated by $l(1), l(2) \cdots l(7)$ as we move from top to bottom. The thick lines represent the links which are used for connecting $l(i)$ to $l(i+1)$ whereas the double stroked lines represent the links used for commu-

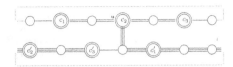

Figure 3: Case 1 - No gap of $d_x/2 + 1$

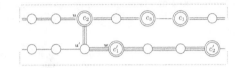

Figure 4: Subcase 2(a) - A c-node in $\ell(i)$ is above gap in $\ell(i+1)$

nication within a row. The algorithm begins with formation of a chain of c-nodes in $l(1)$. The case of connecting $l(1)$ to $l(2)$ falls under case $2(a)$ whereas $l(2)$ is connected to $l(3)$ by steps mentioned for case 1. The usage of case $2(b)$ can be seen in connecting $l(6)$ with $l(7)$.

We now formally show that the tree constructed by the algorithm above is a valid contention free spanning tree.

PROPOSITION 3.1. *Every path connecting adjacent c-nodes in the tree is a candidate shortest path between the c-nodes in the torus and there is no contention along the edges in the torus due to the edges of the tree.*

PROOF. Recall that the necessary and sufficient conditions for a path to be a shortest path are that (i) the number of links it traverses along any dimension is at most half the total length of that dimension; and (ii) it does not traverse any two edges along the same dimension in opposite directions.

The first line is built in step 2 by constructing a chain. Recall that the chain has the property that $c_{j+1} = r(c_j)$ for all $j = 1, \ldots, m-1$. Thus there is no contention amongst the edges of the chain and all the paths between connected pairs of c-nodes are shortest paths (since the distance between connected c-nodes is at most half the total length of the dimension).

We will maintain the invariant that at the end of iteration i (processing of line $\ell(i)$), the x and y edges used so far in the tree all lie between the lines $\ell(1)$ and $\ell(i)$ [both inclusive].

The tree is extended in step 3 to the next line. We consider the correctness for the three cases separately. For case 1, when there is no gap of $d_x/2 + 1$ in $\ell(i+1)$, consider the path from the connector node in $\ell(i)$ to the head of the chain in $\ell(i+1)$ (see Figure 3). As specified by the algorithm the movement along the two dimensions is always along the same direction. The distance covered along the y dimension is no more than $d_y/2$ due to the ordering of the lines in step 1. The distance covered along the x dimension is no more than $d_x/2$ as there is no gap of $d_x/2 + 1$ in $\ell(i+1)$. The only new edges used are below the line $\ell(i)$ and therefore disjoint from all the previously used edges. Also, the x-edges used to connect the connector node of $\ell(i)$ to the head node of $\ell(i+1)$ lie in the gap between the head and tail node of $\ell(i+1)$ and are therefore disjoint from the edges used in the chain of $\ell(i+1)$.

For case 2, the arguments for shortest path and disjoint edges are similar to those of case 1. However, a little more needs to be argued for case $2(b)$ (See Figure 5). In this case, the algorithm uses additional links in $\ell(i)$ while connecting

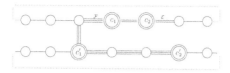

Figure 5: Subcase 2(b) - Every c-node in $\ell(i)$ is directly above the chain of $\ell(i+1)$

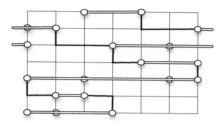

Figure 6: Example tree construction in 2-D torus

$\ell(i)$ to $\ell(i+1)$. Therefore we need to ensure that these links are disjoint from the links used in the tree up to iteration i. Recall that $\mathcal{E}$ denotes the extra links used in $\ell(i)$ outside the chain of $\ell(i)$ in connecting it to $\ell(i-1)$ and $\mathcal{F}$ denotes the extra links used in $\ell(i)$ outside the chain of $\ell(i)$ in connecting it to $\ell(i+1)$. We claim that the set of links in $\mathcal{E}$ and $\mathcal{F}$ are disjoint. This is because $x(c_m) - x(c_1') \mod d_x \leq d_x/2$ as the lower chain is of length at most $d_x/2$; moreover, the links in $\mathcal{E}$ cannot be more than $d_x/2$ as it must be part of a shortest path. This construction ensures that we do not use any link more than once.

This completes the proof of the proposition. $\square$

3.1.3 Spanning tree in three dimensions

We now show how to build the spanning tree in three dimensions. We will reuse the algorithm developed above for two dimensions. For this purpose, consider the 2-dimensional $y - z$ projection, $\mathcal{P}$, of the 3-dimensional torus as shown in Figure 7. This is a 2-D side view of the 3-D torus cuboid; each line along the x dimension is collapsed to a single vertex. Thus a node in $\mathcal{P}$ at location $(\hat{y}, \hat{z})$ will be designated a c-node iff any of the nodes in the corresponding collapsed x-line is a c-node, i.e., if there exists any c-node with y coordinate $\hat{y}$ and z co-ordinate $\hat{z}$. The filled circles in line L of Figure 7 refers to these c-nodes in $\mathcal{P}$. Similarly, notice that an edge in $\mathcal{P}$ is obtained by collapsing a corresponding set of edges that are incident on pairs of nodes with the same y and z co-ordinates, i.e., an edge in $\mathcal{P}$ incident on nodes having co-ordinates $(\hat{y}, \hat{z})$ and $(\hat{y}', \hat{z}')$ is obtained by collapsing all the edges in the 3-D torus incident on nodes having co-ordinates $(\hat{y}, \hat{z})$ and $(\hat{y}', \hat{z}')$. We first apply the 2-d algorithm described in Figure 2 to this projection, $\mathcal{P}$.

Consider a line ℓ in $\mathcal{P}$ that contains some c-nodes. Note that the line ℓ in $\mathcal{P}$ corresponds to a plane in the original 3-D torus as shown by the $x-y$ plane projection in Figure 7. We show how to form the tree in this plane corresponding to ℓ. For this, we shall again use the 2-D algorithm described in Figure 2. Note that each node in ℓ has a unique y coordinate. The horizontal links that form the chain in $\mathcal{P}$ are used to determine the ordering of the y co-ordinates in step 1 of the algorithm. This ensures that when we form the tree for the plane, every y link in the tree will correspond

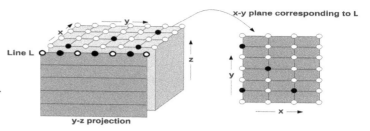

Figure 7: Spanning tree creation in 3-D.

to a unique horizontal link in the projection $\mathcal{P}$. Since the horizontal links used in the projection $\mathcal{P}$ are contention-free, this implies that the y links used in the plane of the 3-D torus are contention free as well. It is easy to see that the x links used in the construction of the individual planes are contention-free as well; this follows from the construction of the tree in the 2-D algorithm of Figure 2.

We now describe how to connect the trees used in different planes together. Consider the connectivity between a pair of c-nodes, a' and b' lying in different lines of the projection $\mathcal{P}$. We pick a pair of c-nodes, a and b, in the original 3-D torus, such that a is collapsed to a' and b is collapsed to b' in $\mathcal{P}$; note that there may be multiple candidates to pick from. For ease of exposition we first handle the simpler case wherein we are able to find c-nodes, a and b have the same x co-ordinate. Thus, we do not need to travel along the x dimension to connect a and b in the 3-D torus. Consider the connectivity between a' and b' in $\mathcal{P}$; this will consist of some vertical edges and horizontal edges. We will map each of these edges to a unique edge in the 3-D torus. This mapping is done as follows. Let e be some horizontal edge in $\mathcal{P}$ along the path from a' to b'; from amongst the set of y-links that collapse to e, we select the link which connects the nodes having the same x co-ordinate as a and b. Similarly, for a vertical edge e in $\mathcal{P}$ along the path; from amongst the set of z-links that collapse to e, we select the link which connects the nodes having the same x co-ordinate as a and b. Essentially, using the path from a' to b' in $\mathcal{P}$, we obtain a path from a to b that traverses nodes in the same x-plane as the co-ordinates as a' and b'. Since the set of edges along the path from a' and b' is contention free in $\mathcal{P}$, the set of edges obtained from a to b is also contention free with respect to all the other links used to construct the trees in the planes so far.

Now let us consider the case where we need to move along the x dimension as well. Again, consider c-nodes a' and b' lying in different lines that are connected in the projection $\mathcal{P}$. We again find nodes a and b as before. Suppose that we cannot find such a pair of nodes having the same x coordinate. As in the previous case, it is easy to show that there is no contention amongst the y links and z links as we can map each of these edges to a unique edge in the 3-D torus, from amongst the edges that collapse to it. The main challenge is to ensure that any x-links that we traverse while connecting a to b do not conflict with any x-links that have been used in the construction of the trees for the individual planes. For this, let us examine the cases used to connect the links a' and b' in the projection $\mathcal{P}$ (refer to the cases in the 2-D algorithm of Figure 2). If a' and b' were connected using case 2(a), then note that the path from a' to b' traverses a node that is not a c-node, i.e., there are no communicator nodes along the line, say ℓ, corresponding to this node in the 3-D torus. Hence all the x-links along ℓ are unused. Therefore, we can use the x-links along this line to perform the x-link traversals, i.e., we move along the derived path from a to the corresponding node on this line while only traversing nodes having the same x co-ordinate as a. Then we move along this line ℓ to the node having the same x co-ordinate as b and finally move along the derived path from this node to the node b while only traversing nodes having the same x co-ordinate as b.

Next, consider case 2(b); refer to Figure 5. Let a' correspond to c_1 and b' to c_1' in the figure. If the path from a' to b' traverses any node that is not a c-node in the projection $\mathcal{P}$, then we can traverse along the x-links along this node as described above. Now suppose that no extra nodes are traversed. This can only happen if a' is directly above b' in projection $\mathcal{P}$ (c_1 is directly above c_1' in Figure 5) and both of them are the end nodes (first or last) of their respective chains. Let ℓ be the line in which a' lies and ℓ' be the line in which b' lies in the projection $\mathcal{P}$. In this case we can view the lines ℓ and ℓ' containing the c-nodes in both these lines as a single line ℓ'' folded at nodes a' and b' using the vertical link between a' and b' in $\mathcal{P}$. Now, we can actually form the spanning tree for the folded plane corresponding to ℓ'' in one go instead of forming them for the two planes corresponding to ℓ and ℓ' separately. Note that the vertical link between a' and b' is selected in forming the tree of projection $\mathcal{P}$. Therefore, the spanning tree for this folded plane in the original 3-D torus will use a z-link that corresponds to one of the edges that was collapsed into the vertical link between a' and b' in $\mathcal{P}$. Clearly this z link will be contention free from other z-links used in case 2(a) as these z-links connect different lines.

Lastly, we consider case 1. This is handled similar to case 2(b). Consider the connectivity between the nodes a' and b' between different lines. As before, if there exists a node that is not a c-node along the path connecting a' to b', we can move along the x-links on the line corresponding to this node. If b' is directly below a', then we can view these adjacent lines in the projection as a single line folded at nodes a' and b' and construct the spanning tree for the corresponding folded plane together. As shown previously, it is not difficult to see that the z-links used in this spanning tree are disjoint from other z-links used in case 1 and 2(b); thus all the links in this spanning tree are contention-free.

Thus, our algorithm for the construction of the spanning tree on a 3-D torus can be summarized as follows. Once we have formed the spanning tree for the projection $\mathcal{P}$, we can partition the lines into bunches of lines which can be folded based on case 1 or case 2(b). We can then construct the spanning trees for the bunches of plane corresponding to these bunches of lines separately considering each bunch to be a single long folded plane using the 2D algorithm. This eliminates the need to handle case 1 and case 2(b) when connecting the trees in different planes together in the original 3-D torus. Case 2(a) is handled as described above.

3.1.4 Number of edge-disjoint trees

We have shown that for any set of communicator nodes, we can construct two edge-disjoint trees; one in each direction with any fixed root. This leads us to ask how many edge disjoint trees can actually be constructed (in one or both directions). Here we show that for a particular choice of communicator nodes, it is not possible to construct two edge-disjoint trees in the same direction (either towards the root or away from the root). The example is very simple; it consists of only two communicator nodes a located at (x_1, y_1, z_1) and b located at $(x_1 + 1, y_1, z_1)$. Note that the shortest path between a and b is a single link that connects them directly. It is straightforward to see that we cannot have two trees in the same direction with either of them as the root. Note that this also rules out having more than one pair of edge-disjoint trees in both directions. Thus, the pair of edge disjoint trees that we construct is the best that can be done for an arbitrary set of communicator nodes.

3.2 Multiple spanning trees for full communicator

Faraj et al. [4] propose multi-color spanning tree algorithms for performing broadcast and reduction operations over full-communicators on a 3D torus interconnect. These algorithms are based on constructing six edge-disjoint spanning trees for any given root. Each of these trees corresponds to an initial traversal along one of the X, Y, and Z dimensions in either direction. Collective operations such as Broadcast, Reduce, and Allreduce involve multiple phases of data transfer along the different dimensions. For example, in an X-color broadcast, the first phase involves data being transferred along the X dimension. In phase 2, the data is transferred along the Y dimension, but not to the Y-neighbors of the root, while in phase 3, the data is transferred along the Z dimension by all the nodes in the 2D plane except the ones along the y-axis containing the root. Finally in phase 4, data is transferred to all the nodes in the YZ plane containing the root from the nearest adjacent YZ plane. Figure 9(b) shows two such trees on a 2D torus. Please refer to [4] for more details. These algorithms have been shown to result in optimal bandwidth utilization.

4. COMMON SUB-COMMUNICATORS

In this section, we demonstrate the use of the algorithms described in Section 3 on a few commonly occurring scenarios. The different scenarios are classified on the basis of the number and kind of simultaneous sub-communicators. We briefly discuss the motivation and use cases for each of the scenarios and describe how to perform collective operations for each of them in detail.

4.1 Single Sub-communicator

Collective operations over a single sub-communicator occur commonly in many parallel applications. We discuss three such scenarios where the algorithms discussed in Section 3 can be used to perform efficient collective operations.
Random communicator: In any dynamic load balancing environment, the placement of processes on the nodes may be arbitrarily changed during the course of the program. This results in situations where a collective may be performed on a sub-communicator which is randomly placed over the network. For example, OpenAtom, which runs on CHARM++ [7], has a phase where only one of the chare arrays is involved in collective communication. This chare array is not large enough to have one chare placed on each processor and owing to load balancing is spread almost randomly in the system. In such cases, the algorithm proposed in Section 3 can be directly used to achieve a single link throughput performance for the collective.
Single communicator with one node missing: The special case of a sub-communicator, where all the nodes except one take part in a collective operation, is frequently encountered in the *master-slave* model of parallelization. Our

solution for this special scenario where master does not take part in collective operations is based on extending the algorithm described in 3.2.

It must be noted that the algorithm cannot be naively used because it is not always possible to obtain six edge-disjoint spanning trees when a node is missing. For example, if the node that is missing in the sub-communicator is used for transmitting the data along any dimension in the original construction, the algorithm breaks down as shown in Figure 8. The missing node is denoted by dashed circle and the root is denoted by the filled circle. The nodes along the Y direction for X-color Broadcast/Reduce (shown in dashed ellipse) will not be able to receive/send the values due to the missing node in the sub-communicator.

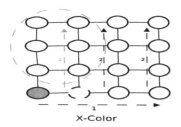

Figure 8: X-Color Broadcast breakdown

However, we can address this problem as we have decoupled the collective operation from the tree creation. In the first step, we follow the same multi-color rectangular approach to create three edge disjoint trees for the collective operation using links only in the X+, Y+ and Z+ direction. However, we start the tree construction using a *pseudo root* that is at least one hop away from the missing node in every dimension. The missing node is hence bypassed during the tree construction. In the second step, the directions of the links is adjusted according to the user specified root. Since the original trees only used the links in the positive direction, reversal of any of the links will not lead to any contention. In this manner, we can guarantee that all the nodes will be present in our tree.

Random subset of parallel planes: This sub-communicator involves a random subset of parallel 2D planes taking part in a collective operation and is encountered in applications such as dense linear solvers and 3D FFT simulations. Most of these applications use parallel planes which are uniformly distributed in the torus. Hence, we deal only with the case where no two planes are separated by a distance of more than $n/2$, where n is the dimension of the axis perpendicular to the planes, so that the complete torus is available for communication.

As before, the approach in Section 3.2 can be extended to handle this special case. Without loss of generality, let us assume that the missing planes are along the Z- axis. Since each of the 2D planes do not have any missing nodes, we first perform phases 1 and 2 of the collective operation where the data is transferred along the X and Y dimensions respectively, as described in [4]. In phase 3, the data is transferred along the Z dimension, with the missing planes in Z dimension being bypassed to transfer the data to the nodes in next 2D plane in the sub-communicator. Phase 4 remains the same as before.

4.2 Multiple Sub-communicators

Many real scientific applications involve more than one sub-communicator performing collective operations simultaneously in a loosely synchronous fashion. Typically, these multiple sub-communicators are disjoint, i.e., no processor is part of two sub-communicators, and exhaustive, i.e., the union of the sub-communicators spans the entire processor group. The performance of collective operations over such multiple sub-communicators critically depends on the composition of the individual sub-communicators.

Contiguous sub-communicator groups: In this case, all the sub-communicators can be readily mapped onto contiguous nodes on the processor space such that there are no overlapping paths. For example, in linear algebra operations a 2D square matrix needs to be mapped onto a 3D torus partition. The row and column sub-communicators in one such mapping can be sets of continuous nodes spanning multiple lines of the torus. For such scenarios, our algorithm 3 for a single random communicator can work independently on the sub-communicators and create multiple edge-disjoint spanning trees. One would expect the performance in this case to be close to that observed in the single random communicator case. However, for certain cases where the contiguous nodes form regular communication patterns on the processor partition, the optimized MPI algorithms will work better than a naive application of our algorithm. For this scenario, suitable modifications of our algorithm, such as the one discussed in Section 4.1, can be adapted to achieve better performance.

Overlapping sub-communicator groups: In certain applications such as molecular dynamics, it is often not possible to have collective operations between sub-communicators that are contiguous, especially if dynamic load balancing schemes are employed. Similarly, a mapping of an $N \times N$ matrix on to a 3D torus partition could result in a scenario where each row of the matrix is mapped onto 2 planes which are not contiguous. Figure 9(a) shows an example where alternate rows of a 2D bidirectional torus belong to different sub-communicators. When collective operations are performed within individual sub-communicators using a simple ring pipelined algorithm, it leads to contention as indicated by the circled area. For such overlapping sub-communicators, we propose a novel approach where multiple sub-communicators co-operate to achieve an optimal performance for the collective operations. Such co-operative schemes can be developed on top of either of the algorithms discussed in Section 3.

One such cooperative schemes that works well for a moderate number of sub-communicators uses the algorithm described in Section 3.2. Specifically, we use up to three edge-disjoint spanning trees and use these trees to pipeline the data for the individual sub-communicators. Figure 9(b) shows the details of our tree construction based approach for performing broadcast operation. Using the multi-color algorithm in [4], we create two trees rooted at R (indicated by the solid and dashed lines) and assign a tree to each of the sub-communicators. Depending on the membership in a sub-communicator, every processor sends, forwards and stores the data along its designated tree. For example, if a processor is part of the communicator containing light circles, then it sends the data along the dashed tree whereas it only forwards data for the solid tree. This approach has been observed to provide good empirical performance for a moderate number of sub-communicators. It is, however, not scalable to a large number of sub-communicators, but the approach outlined for contiguous sub-communicators works well in such cases.

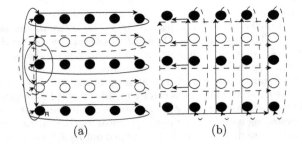

Figure 9: Use of multi-color trees for 2 sub-communicators on a 2D torus.

5. RESULTS

5.1 Empirical Setup

Hardware: All the experiments were performed on IBM's Blue Gene/P [1]. The most important network on BG/P is the torus network, which offers the highest bandwidth in the system. Each node supports 850 MBps bidirectional links (425 MBps in each direction) to each of its nearest neighbors for a total of 5.1 GB/s bidirectional bandwidth per node.

Implementation Specifics: We implemented two versions of our approach; (i) an optimized version which uses a lower level API – SPI and (ii) an MPI version which modifies the MPI stack. SPI is a low level library on BG/P that provides direct access to the DMA and FIFOs [6]. We implemented our algorithms in SPI using DMA direct put and dynamic routing mechanism. For the MPI implementation, we coded our algorithm using a low level messaging interface on BG/P called DCMF [8]. However, the MPI stack uses static routing instead of dynamic routing and does not provide the optimal scenario for the algorithm in Section 3. We refer to our Broadcast implementation using SPI as *BC-SPI* and the MPI stack implementation as *BC-MPI*. Similarly, we refer to our Allreduce implementations as *AR-SPI* and *AR-MPI* respectively.

Evaluation Methodology: We experimented with message sizes from 512 KB to 512 MB and measured the throughput in megabytes/second (MBps) averaged over 10 runs. We use only one core per node to have a fair comparison with the optimized MPI library which uses only a single core. For Broadcast and Allreduce, we experimented with all the options available on BG/P MPI for sub-communicators and picked the best option available among various algorithms (referred as *IBM Product MPI* in our experiments).

5.2 Single Communicator

Random sub-communicator: Figure 10 shows the throughput for various Broadcast algorithms with increasing sub-communicator sizes (up to 1023). The message size for this study was set to 512 MB. The SPI implementation of our algorithms, *BC-SPI*, that exploits dynamic routing, provides a nearly constant throughput value of 350 MBps for Broadcast irrespective of the size of the sub-communicator. The nearly constant throughput is obtained for large messages, since the time taken depends on the available bandwidth and not on the diameter of the tree. The observed value is close to the peak one link throughput of 378 MBps

that can be realized on the Blue Gene/P (only 240 bytes of a 270 byte packet can be user data).

We also observe that the best performance for our MPI implementation, *BC-MPI*, is attained for the cases in which the sub-communicator is either very sparse (< 10 %) or is very dense (> 90%). This performance behavior can be attributed to the fact that our algorithm is more suited for dynamic routing whereas MPI stack uses static routing. Hence, only in the case of extremely sparse or dense sub-communicators, perfect chains can be formed and this leads to better performance in the case of static routing. Note that *BC-MPI* also consistently outperforms *IBM Product MPI* - the best MPI implementation of Broadcast on Blue Gene/P.

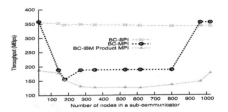

Figure 10: Performance of Broadcast

In Figure 11, we present performance comparison of our Broadcast implementation for increasing message size using a sparse (31/1024 nodes) and a moderately dense (531/1024 nodes) sub-communicator against *IBM Product MPI*. For the sparse sub-communicator, the performance of Broadcast for both *BC-MPI* and *BC-SPI* is close to the peak single link throughput. In comparison to the *IBM Product MPI* implementation, we attain a performance improvement of 2× for large data sizes as shown in Figure 11(a).

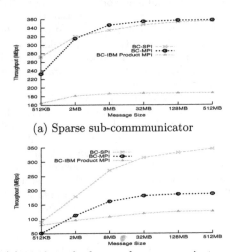

(a) Sparse sub-commmunicator

(b) Moderately dense sub-commmunicator

Figure 11: Performance of Broadcast with variation in message size

For the moderately dense sub-communictor, as presented in Figure 11(b), the drop in throughput is significant for small message sizes. This happens because the constructed spanning tree has a number of branches with not enough data to hide the latency. However, for large message sizes, *BC-SPI* shows close to the peak performance with significantly low performance shown by *BC-MPI* and *IBM Product*

MPI. This can be attributed to the fact that the MPI stack uses static routing whereas SPI implementation utilizes dynamic routing. *BC-MPI* still outperforms *IBM Product MPI* by a factor of 1.5× for large message sizes.

We also performed these experiments for Allreduce and obtained similar results.

Missing Node Communicator: In this section, we present performance results for the special sub-communicator which has a single node missing from the full-communicator. Using the approach outlined in Section 4.1, we used multiple trees for Broadcast and Allreduce algorithms. The observations made in previous section from Figure 10 indicate that for extremely sparse and extremely dense sub-communicators, the performance of our SPI and MPI implementations are fairly close. This is because of the fact that at those density levels, dynamic routing is no longer an advantage for the SPI implementation. Hence, we present results only for SPI implementation in Figure 12(a).

We observe that for the special case with one missing node, the SPI implementation outperforms the optimized MPI routines partly due to the use of multiple spanning trees and partly due to extra overheads associated with the MPI stack. In the case of Broadcast, *BC-SPI* outperforms *IBM Product MPI* by a factor of 5.86× for small messages and by a factor of 4.3× for large messages. For the case of Allreduce, we observe a speedup in the range 2.75×–5.5×. Note that the expected peak performance for Allreduce is two times the expected peak performance for Broadcast.

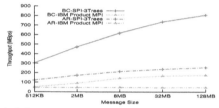

(a) Sub-communicator with one out of 1024 nodes missing

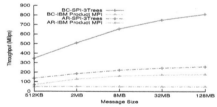

(b) Sub-communicator with 10 out of 16 planes missing

Figure 12: Broadcast and Allreduce for special sub-comms

Missing Planes Communicator: We now present results for another special sub-communicator wherein there are a number of random *2D* parallel planes missing from the full communicator. As shown in Figure 12(b), *BC-SPI* outperforms *IBM Product MPI* for both Broadcast and Allreduce. We observe a factor improvement of 4×–5× for Broadcast and an improvement of 2×–5× for Allreduce. Since we use multiple trees for both Broadcast and Reduce, these results show similar performance trends as in the case of missing node sub-communicator.

5.3 Multiple sub-communicators

As discussed in Section 4.2, several practical scenarios involve the use of multiple sub-communicators operating simultaneously in a loosely synchronous fashion. This section presents results pertaining to a few of those scenarios. We implemented two algorithms for multiple sub-communicators. The first one, with the suffix *SPI-3Trees*, uses multiple trees on the entire partition to route data for individual sub-communicators as discussed in Section 4.2. The second algorithm, with the suffix *SPI*, independently constructs trees for individual sub-communicators using the algorithm detailed in Section 3. The performance of both these algorithms is compared against *IBM Product MPI* for multiple irregular sub-communicators.

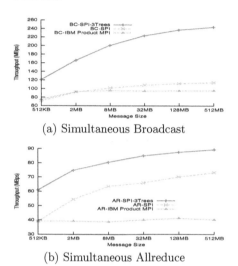

(a) Simultaneous Broadcast

(b) Simultaneous Allreduce

Figure 13: Performance with multiple random sub-communicators

Figure 13 presents the performance of our algorithms for the case when multiple random sub-communicators perform Broadcast and Allreduce simultaneously. We observe that both, *SPI* and *SPI-3Trees*, outperform *IBM Product MPI* since the paths constructed by *IBM Product MPI* causes significant bandwidth contention. The *SPI-3Trees* algorithm routes the data for the sub-communicators along three well defined independent trees and is therefore contention free. The above example clearly shows that while *IBM Product MPI* may perform well for cases with neat patterns in the sets of nodes, it does not fare well when such patterns cannot be extracted.

To further highlight this, we performed an experiment where the number of sub-communicators was increased from 5 to 9 over an 8x8x16 torus partition. The nodes were assigned to sub-communicators in a round robin manner. As shown in Figure 14, *IBM Product MPI* does not perform well in general because of the random placement of nodes belonging to each sub-communicator. However, there is a sudden spike in performance when the number of sub-communicators is 8 (divisor of 16) because the sub-communicators in that case are parallel planes. i

We also performed experiments on some important use cases which occur in real applications such as dense linear solvers. The first such use case that we consider corresponds to a scenario where alternate planes are in the same communicator. As expected for such a scenario, *SPI-3Trees* con-

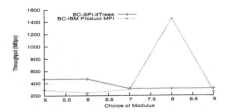

Figure 14: Broadcast performance on dividing nodes in a round robin manner among sub-communicators

sistently outperforms *IBM Product MPI* for both Broadcast and Allreduce as shown in Figure 15.

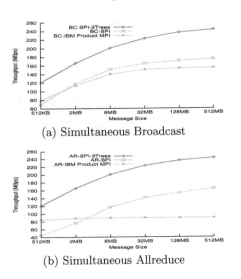

(a) Simultaneous Broadcast

(b) Simultaneous Allreduce

Figure 15: Performance on two simultaneous sub-communicators that have alternate planes

Another example that we consider here maps a 45x45 matrix onto a 8x16x16 torus, and collective operations are performed along the rows of the matrix. The first sub-communicator in this case would map to the first 5 lines and 5 nodes in the *6th* line and so on. This is a special case of non-overlapping sub-communicators because even though the sub-communicators consist of continuous ranks, their physical locations are not neatly aligned so that the optimized MPI algorithms are ineffective. Figure 16 shows the results for this use case. *SPI-3Trees* is not suitable for such cases because the number of sub-communicators is large and is therefore not shown. However, *SPI* performs well for such scenarios in comparison to *IBM Product MPI*.

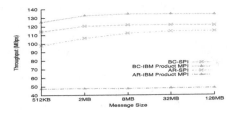

Figure 16: Performance on mapping a square 2D decomposition on a non square 3D torus partition.

6. CONCLUSIONS

We have demonstrated that carefully designed spanning trees can provide significant improvement in the performance of MPI collectives on torus interconnects especially while using adaptive routing. Performance results obtained from an empirical evaluation of our low level API implementation of commonly used collectives such as Broadcast and Allreduce over specialized sub-communicators as well as random sub-communicators of varying sizes show up to factor of 5.8× improvement over the best MPI implementation available on Blue Gene/P. We incorporated our Broadcast and Allreduce algorithms onto the MPI stack and observed a performance boost of up to 3× over the best MPI implementation in some cases. We are exploring further optimizations to the MPI stack to match the SPI performance in all cases.

7. REFERENCES

[1] S. Alam, R. Barrett, M. Bast, M. R. Fahey, J. Kuehn, C. McCurdy, J. Rogers, P. Roth, R. Sankaran, J. S. Vetter, P. Worley, and W. Yu. Early evaluation of IBM BlueGene/P. SC '08, pages 23:1–23:12, 2008.

[2] E. Chan, M. Heimlich, A. Purkayastha, and R. Geijn. Collective Communication: Theory, Practice, and Experience FLAME Working Note #22, 2006.

[3] W. G. et al. MPI2.2. Available online *http://www.mpi-forum.org/docs/docs.html*, Sept 2009.

[4] A. Faraj, S. Kumar, B. E. Smith, A. R. Mamidala, J. A. Gunnels, and P. Heidelberger. MPI collective communications on the Blue Gene/P supercomputer: algorithms and optimizations". In *ICS*, 2009.

[5] N. Jain and Y. Sabharwal. Optimal bucket algorithms for large MPI collectives on torus interconnects. In *ICS*, pages 27–36, 2010.

[6] I. journal of Research and D. staff. Overview of the ibm blue gene/p project. *IBM J. Res. Dev.*, pages 199–220, 2008.

[7] L. Kale and S. Krishnan. Charm++: a portable concurrent object oriented system based on c++. OOPSLA '93, pages 91–108, 1993.

[8] S. Kumar, G. Dozsa, G. Almasi, P. Heidelberger, D. Chen, M. E. Giampapa, M. Blocksome, A. Faraj, J. Parker, J. Ratterman, B. Smith, and C. J. Archer. The deep computing messaging framework: generalized scalable message passing on the blue gene/p supercomputer. ICS '08, pages 94–103, 2008.

[9] S. Kumar, C. Huang, G. Almasi, and L. V. Kalé. Achieving strong scaling with NAMD on Blue Gene/L. In *Proceedings of IEEE International Parallel and Distributed Processing Symposium 2006*, April 2006.

[10] R. Rabenseifner. Automatic Profiling of MPI Applications with Hardware Performance Counters. In *6th European PVM/MPI Users' Group Meeting on Recent Advances in PVM and MPI*, pages 35–42, 1999.

[11] M. Shroff and V. D. Geijn. Collmark: Mpi collective communication benchmark. Technical report, 2000.

[12] R. Thakur and W. Gropp. Improving the performance of collective operations in MPICH. In *Recent Advances in PVM and MPI. 10th European PVM/MPI User's Group Meeting*, pages 257–267, 2003.

[13] R. Thakur, R. Rabenseifner, and W. Gropp. Optimization of collective communication operations in MPICH. *IJHPCA*, 19:49–66, 2005.

Space-Round Tradeoffs for MapReduce Computations

Andrea Pietracaprina
Dip. di Ingegneria
dell'Informazione
Università di Padova
Padova, Italy
capri@dei.unipd.it

Geppino Pucci
Dip. di Ingegneria
dell'Informazione
Università di Padova
Padova, Italy
geppo@dei.unipd.it

Matteo Riondato
Dept. of Computer Science
Brown University
Providence, RI USA
matteo@cs.brown.edu

Francesco Silvestri
Dip. di Ingegneria
dell'Informazione
Università di Padova
Padova, Italy
silvest1@dei.unipd.it

Eli Upfal
Dept. of Computer Science
Brown University
Providence, RI USA
eli@cs.brown.edu

ABSTRACT

This work explores fundamental modeling and algorithmic issues arising in the well-established MapReduce framework. First, we formally specify a computational model for MapReduce which captures the functional flavor of the paradigm by allowing for a flexible use of parallelism. Indeed, the model diverges from a traditional processor-centric view by featuring parameters which embody only global and local memory constraints, thus favoring a more data-centric view. Second, we apply the model to the fundamental computation task of matrix multiplication presenting upper and lower bounds for both dense and sparse matrix multiplication, which highlight interesting tradeoffs between space and round complexity. Finally, building on the matrix multiplication results, we derive further space-round tradeoffs on matrix inversion and matching.

Categories and Subject Descriptors

C.1.4 [**Parallel Architectures**]: Distributed architectures; F.1.2 [**Modes of Computation**]: Parallelism and concurrency; F.1.3 [**Complexity Measures and Classes**]: Relations among complexity measures; F.2.1 [**Numerical Algorithms and Problems**]: Computations on matrices

General Terms

Algorithms, Design, Theory

Keywords

MapReduce, tradeoff, sparse and dense matrix multiplication, matrix inversion, matching

1. INTRODUCTION

In recent years, MapReduce has emerged as a computational paradigm for processing large-scale data sets in a series of rounds executed on conglomerates of commodity servers [6], and has been widely adopted by a number of large Web companies (e.g., Google, Yahoo!, Amazon) and in several other applications (e.g., GPU and multicore processing). (See [20] and references therein.)

Informally, a MapReduce computation transforms an input set of key-value pairs into an output set of key-value pairs in a number of *rounds*, where in each round each pair is first individually transformed into a (possibly empty) set of new pairs (*map step*) and then all values associated with the same key are processed, separately for each key, by an instance of the same reduce function (simply called *reducer* in the rest of the paper) thus producing the next new set of key-value pairs (*reduce step*). In fact, as already noticed in [19], a reduce step can clearly embed the subsequent map step so that a MapReduce computation can be simply seen as a sequence of rounds of (augmented) reduce steps.

The MapReduce paradigm has a functional flavor, in that it merely requires that the algorithm designer decomposes the computation into rounds and, within each round, into independent tasks through the use of keys. This enables parallelism without forcing an algorithm to cater for the explicit allocation of processing resources. Nevertheless, the paradigm implicitly posits the existence of an underlying unstructured and possibly heterogeneous parallel infrastructure, where the computation is eventually run. While mostly ignoring the details of such an underlying infrastructure, existing formalizations of the MapReduce paradigm constrain the computations to abide with some local and aggregate memory limitations.

In this paper, we look at both modeling and algorithmic issues related to the MapReduce paradigm. We first provide a formal specification of the model, aimed at overcoming some limitations of the previous modeling efforts, and then derive interesting tradeoffs between memory constraints and round complexity for the fundamental problem of matrix multiplication and some of its applications.

1.1 Previous work

The MapReduce paradigm has been introduced in [6] without a fully-specified formal computational model for algorithm design and analysis. Triggered by the quickly gained popularity of the paradigm, a number of subsequent works have dealt more rigorously with modeling and algorithmic issues [16, 9, 7].

In [16], a MapReduce algorithm specifies a sequence of rounds as described in the previous section. Somewhat arbitrarily, the authors impose that in each round the memory needed by any reducer to store and transform its input pairs has size $O\left(n^{1-\epsilon}\right)$, and that the aggregate memory used by all reducers has size $O\left(n^{2-2\epsilon}\right)$, where n denotes the input size and ϵ is a fixed constant in $(0,1)$. The cost of local computation, that is, the work performed by the individual reducers, is not explicitly accounted for, but it is required to be polynomial in n. The authors also postulate, again somewhat arbitrarily, that the underlying parallel infrastructure consists of $\Theta\left(n^{1-\epsilon}\right)$ processing elements with $\Theta\left(n^{1-\epsilon}\right)$ local memory each, and hint at a possible way of supporting the computational model on such infrastructure, where the reduce instances are scheduled among the available machines so to distribute the aggregate memory in a balanced fashion. It has to be remarked that such a distribution may hide non negligible costs for very fine-grained computations (due to the need of allocating multiple reducer with different memory requirements to a fixed number of machines) when, in fact, the algorithmic techniques of [16] do not fully explore the larger power of the MapReduce model with respect to a model with fixed parallelism. In [19] the same model of [16] is adopted but when evaluating an algorithm the authors also consider the total work and introduce the notion of work-efficiency typical of the literature on parallel algorithms.

An alternative computational model for MapReduce is proposed in [9], featuring two parameters which describe bandwidth and latency characteristics of the underlying communication infrastructure, and an additional parameter that limits the amount of I/O performed by each reducer. Also, a BSP-like cost function is provided which combines the internal work of the reducers with the communication costs incurred by the shuffling of the data needed at each round. Unlike the model of [16], no limits are posed to the aggregate memory size. This implies that in principle there is no limit to the allowable parallelism while, however, the bandwidth/latency parameters must somewhat reflect the topology and, ultimately, the number of processing elements. Thus, the model mixes the functional flavor of MapReduce with the more descriptive nature of bandwidth-latency models such as BSP [29, 3].

A model which tries to merge the spirit of MapReduce with the features of data-streaming is the MUD model of [7], where the reducers receive their input key-value pairs as a stream to be processed in one pass using small working memory, namely polylogarithmic in the input size. A similar model has been adopted in [5].

MapReduce algorithms for a variety of problems have been developed on the aforementioned MapReduce variants including, among others, primitives such as prefix sums, sorting, random indexing [9], and graph problems such as triangle counting [28] minimum spanning tree, s-t connectivity, [16], maximal and approximate maximum matching, edge cover, minimum cut [19], and max cover [5]. Moreover

simulations of the PRAM and BSP in MapReduce have been presented in [16, 9]. In particular, it is shown that a T-step EREW PRAM algorithm can be simulated by an $O\left(T\right)$-round MapReduce algorithm, where each reducer uses constant-size memory and the aggregate memory is proportional to the amount of shared memory required by the PRAM algorithm [16]. The simulation of CREW or CRCW PRAM algorithms incurs a further $O\left(\log_m(M/m)\right)$ slowdown, where m denotes the local memory size available for each reducer and M the aggregate memory size [9].

All of the aforementioned algorithmic efforts have been aimed at achieving the minimum number of rounds, possibly constant, provided that enough local memory for the reducer (typically sublinear in the input size) and enough aggregate memory is available. However, so far, to the best of our knowledge, there has been no attempt to fully explore the tradeoffs that can be exhibited for specific computational problems between the local and aggregate memory sizes, on one side, and the number of rounds, on the other, under reasonable constraints of the amount of total work performed by the algorithm. Our results contribute to filling this gap.

Matrix multiplication is a building block for many problems, including matching [25], matrix inversion [15], all-pairs shortest path [15], graph contraction [8], cycle detection [30], and parsing context free languages [27]. Parallel algorithms for matrix multiplication of dense matrices have been widely studied: among others, we note [14, 22] which provide upper and lower bounds exposing a tradeoff between communication complexity and processor memory. For sparse matrices, interesting results are given in [23, 21] for some network topologies like hypercubes, in [18] for PRAM, and in [4] for a BSP-like model. In particular, techniques in [22, 18] are used in the following sections for deriving efficient MapReduce algorithms. In the sequential settings, some interesting works providing upper and lower bounds are [13, 17] for dense matrix multiplication, and [12, 31, 11] for sparse matrix multiplication.

1.2 New results

The contribution of this paper is twofold, since it targets both modeling and algorithmic issues.

We first provide a more general and polished version of the MapReduce model of [16]. In particular, we generalize the model by letting the local and aggregate memory sizes be two independent parameters, m and M, respectively. Moreover, we enforce a clear separation between the model and underlying execution infrastructure: for instance, we do not impose a bound on the number of available machines, thus fully decoupling the degree of parallelism exposed by a computation from the one of the machine where the computation will be eventually executed. This decoupling greatly simplifies algorithm design, which has been one of the original objectives of the MapReduce paradigm. (In Section 2, we quantify the cost of implementing a round of our model on a system with fixed parallelism.)

Our algorithmic contributions concern the study of attainable tradeoffs in MapReduce for several variants of the fundamental primitive of matrix multiplication. In particular, we develop deterministic upper and lower bounds for dense-dense, sparse-dense and sparse-sparse matrix multiplication, and a more efficient randomized upper bound for the sparse-sparse case. As a by-product of this latter result, we also obtain a randomized procedure to approximate the number of nonzero entries in the output matrix. Our algorithms are parametric in the m and M, and achieve optimal or quasi-optimal round complexity in the entire range of variability of these parameters. Finally, building on the matrix multiplication results, we derive space-round trade-offs for matrix inversion and matching, which are important by-products of matrix multiplication.

To the best of our knowledge, no previous work in the MapReduce literature has explicitly addressed the above fundamental problems, and the round complexity of our MapReduce algorithms for these problems exhibit a logarithmic improvement upon what could be obtained by simulating the best known PRAM algorithms using the techniques by [16]. Moreover, we show that, for suitable values of the memory parameters, constant number of rounds (the holy grail of algorithmic research in MapReduce) are achievable for both dense and sparse matrix multiplication.

1.3 Organization of the paper

The rest of the paper is structured as follows. In Section 2 we introduce our computational model for MapReduce and describe important algorithmic primitives (sorting and prefix sums) that we use in our algorithms. Section 3 deals with matrix multiplication in our model, presenting theoretical bounds to the complexity of algorithms to solve this problem. We apply these results in Section 4 to derive algorithms for matrix inversion and for matching in graphs.

2. MODEL DEFINITION AND BASIC PRIMITIVES

Our model is defined in terms of two integral parameters m and M, whose meaning will be explained below, and is named $MR(m, M)$. Algorithms specified in this model will be referred to as *MR-algorithms*. An MR-algorithm specifies a sequence of *rounds*: the r-th round, with $r \geq 1$ transforms a multiset W_r of key-value pairs into two multisets W_{r+1} and O_r of key-value pairs, where W_{r+1} is the input of the next round (empty, if r is the last round), and O_r is a (possibly empty) subset of the final output. The input of the algorithm is represented by W_1 while the output is represented by $\cup_{r \geq 1} O_r$, with $\cup$ denoting the union of multisets. The universes of keys and values may vary at each round, and we let U_r denote the universe of keys of W_r. The computation performed by Round r is defined by a *reducer* function ρ_r which is applied independently to each multiset $W_{r,k} \subseteq W_r$ consisting of all entries in W_r with key $k \in U_r$.

Let n be the input size. The two parameters m and M specify the memory requirements that each round of an MR-algorithm must satisfy. In particular, let $m_{r,k}$ denote the space needed to compute $\rho_r(W_{r,k})$ on a RAM, including the space taken by the input (i.e., $m_{r,k} \geq |W_{r,k}|$) and the work space, but excluding the space taken by the output, which contributes either to O_r (i.e., the final output) or to W_{r+1}. The model imposes that $m_{r,k} \in O(m)$, for every $r \geq 1$ and $k \in U_r$, that $\sum_{k \in U_r} m_{r,k} \in O(M)$, for every $r \geq 1$, and that $\sum_{r \geq 1} O_r = O(M)$. Note that the size of the output generated by a reducer is not limited by the local memory m. The complexity of an MR-algorithm is the number of rounds that it executes in the worst case, and it is expressed as a function of the input size n and of parameters m and M. The dependency on the parameters m and M allows for a finer analysis of the cost of an MR-algorithm.

As in [16], we require that each reducer function runs in time polynomial in n. In fact, it can be easily seen that the model defined in [16] is equivalent to the $MR(m, M)$ model with $m \in O(n^{1-\epsilon})$ and $M \in O(n^{2-2\epsilon})$, for some fixed constant $\epsilon \in (0, 1)$, except that we eliminate the additional restrictions that the number of rounds of an algorithm be polylogarithmic in n and that the number of physical machines on which algorithms are executed be $\Theta(n^{1-\epsilon})$, which in our opinion should not be imposed at the model level.

Compared to the model in [9], our $MR(m, M)$ model introduces the parameter M to limit the size of the aggregate memory required at each round, whereas in [9] this size is virtually unbounded, and it imposes a less stringent bound on the output size of each reducer[1]. Moreover, the complexity analysis in $MR(m, M)$ focuses on the tradeoffs between m and M, on one side, and the number of rounds on the other side, while in [9] a more complex cost function is defined which accounts for the overall message complexity of each round, the time complexity of each reducer computation, and the latency and bandwidth characteristics of the executing platform.

2.1 Sorting and prefix sum computations

Sorting and prefix sum primitives are used in the algorithms presented in this paper. The input to both primitives consists of a set of n key-value pairs (i, a_i) with $0 \leq i < n$ and $a_i \in S$, where S denotes a suitable set. For sorting, a total order is defined over S and the output is a set of n key-value pairs (i, b_i), where the b_i's form a permutation of the a_i's and $b_{i-1} \leq b_i$ for each $0 < i < n$. For prefix sums, a binary associative operation $\oplus$ is defined over S and the output consists of a collection of n pairs (i, b_i) where $b_i = a_0 \oplus \ldots \oplus a_i$, for $0 \leq i < n$.

By straightforwardly adapting the results in [9] to our model we have:

THEOREM 1. *The sorting and prefix sum primitives for inputs of size n can be performed in $O(\log_m n)$ rounds in $MR(m, M)$ for any $M = \Omega(n)$.*

We remark that each reducer in the implementation of the sorting and prefix primitives makes use of $\Theta(m)$ memory words. Hence, the same round complexity can be achieved in a more restrictive scenario with fixed parallelism. In fact, our $MR(m, M)$ model can be simulated on a platform with $\Theta(M/m)$ processing elements, each with internal memory of size $\Theta(m)$, at the additional cost of one prefix computation per round. Therefore, $O(\log_m n)$ can be regarded as an upper bound on the relative power of our model with respect to one with fixed parallelism.

In [9], the authors claim that the round complexities stated in Theorem 1 are optimal in their model, as a consequence of the lower bound for computing the OR of n bits on the BSP model [10]. It can be shown that the optimality carries through to our model for any m and any $M = \Omega(n)$.

3. MATRIX MULTIPLICATION

Let A and B be two $\sqrt{n} \times \sqrt{n}$ matrices and let $C = A \cdot B$. We use $a_{i,j}, b_{i,j}$ and $c_{i,j}$, with $0 \leq i, j < \sqrt{n}$, to denote the entries of A, B and C, respectively. In this section we present upper and lower bounds for computing the

---

[1] For clarity, we remark that in [9] M denotes the maximum amount of space used by a reducer, that is, the quantity denoted by m in our model.

product C in $MR(m, M)$. All our algorithms envision the matrices as conceptually divided into submatrices of size $\sqrt{m} \times \sqrt{m}$, and we denote these submatrices with $A_{i,j}$, $B_{i,j}$ and $C_{i,j}$, respectively, for $0 \leq i, j < \sqrt{n/m}$. Clearly, $C_{i,j} = \sum_{h=0}^{\sqrt{n/m}-1} A_{i,h} \cdot B_{h,j}$.

All our algorithms exploit the following partition of the $(n/m)^{3/2}$ products between submatrices (e.g., $A_{i,h} \cdot B_{h,j}$) into $\sqrt{n/m}$ groups: group G_ℓ, with $0 \leq \ell < \sqrt{n/m}$, consists of products $A_{i,h} \cdot B_{h,j}$, for every $0 \leq i, j < \sqrt{n/m}$ and for $h = (i + j + \ell) \mod \sqrt{n/m}$. Observe that each submatrix of A and B occurs exactly once in each group G_ℓ, and that each product in G_ℓ contributes to a distinct submatrix of C.

We focus our attention on matrices whose entries belong to a semiring $(S, \oplus, \odot)$ such that for any $a \in S$ we have $a \odot 0 = 0$, where 0 is the identity for $\oplus$. In this setting, efficient matrix multiplication techniques such as Strassen's cannot be employed. Moreover, for the sake of the analysis, we make the reasonable assumption that the inner products of any row of A and of any column of B with overlapping nonzero entries never cancel to zero.

In our algorithms, any input matrix X ($X = A, B$) is provided as a set of key-value pairs $(k_{i,j}, (i, j, x_{i,j}))$ for all elements $x_{i,j} \neq 0$. Key $k_{i,j}$ represents a progressive index, e.g., the number of nonzero entries preceding $x_{i,j}$ in the row-major scan of X. We call a $\sqrt{n} \times \sqrt{n}$ matrix *dense* if the number of its nonzero entries is $\Theta(n)$, and we call it *sparse* otherwise. In what follows, we present different algorithms tailored for the multiplication of dense-dense (Section 3.1), sparse-sparse (Section 3.2), and sparse-dense matrices (Section 3.3). For suitable values of m and M the algorithms complete in a constant number of rounds. We also derive lower bounds which demonstrate that our deterministic algorithms are either optimal or close to optimal (Section 3.4), and an algorithm for estimating the number of nonzero entries in the product of two sparse matrices (Section 3.2.4).

3.1 Dense-Dense Matrix Multiplication

In this section we provide a simple, deterministic algorithm for multiplying two dense matrices, which will be proved optimal in Subsection 3.4. The algorithm is a straightforward adaptation of the well-established three-dimensional algorithmic strategy for matrix multiplication of [22, 14], however we describe a few details of its implementation in $MR(m, M)$ since the strategy is also at the base of algorithms for sparse matrices. W.l.o.g. we may assume that $m \leq 2n$, since otherwise matrix multiplication can be executed by a trivial sequential algorithm. We consider matrices A and B as decomposed into $\sqrt{m} \times \sqrt{m}$ submatrices and subdivide the products between submatrices into groups as described above.

In each round, the algorithm computes all products within $K = \min\{M/n, \sqrt{n/m}\}$ consecutive groups: namely, at round $r \geq 1$, all multiplications in G_ℓ are computed, with $(r-1)K \leq \ell < rK$. The idea is that in a round all submatrices of A and B can be replicated K times and paired in such a way that each reducer performs a distinct multiplication in $\cup_{(r-1)K \leq \ell < rK} G_\ell$. Then, each reducer sums the newly computed product to a partial sum which accumulates all of the products contributing to the same submatrix of C belonging to groups with the same index modulo K dealt with in previous rounds. At the end of the $\sqrt{n}/(K\sqrt{m})$-th round, all submatrix products have been computed. The

final matrix C is then obtained by adding together the K partial sums contributing to each entry of C through a prefix computation[2]. We have the following result.

THEOREM 2. *The above $MR(m, M)$-algorithm multiplies two $\sqrt{n} \times \sqrt{n}$ dense matrices in*

$$O\left(\frac{n^{3/2}}{M\sqrt{m}} + \log_m n\right)$$

rounds.

PROOF. The algorithm clearly complies with the memory constraints of $MR(m, M)$ since each reducer multiplies two $\sqrt{m} \times \sqrt{m}$ submatrices and the degree of replication is such that the algorithm never exceeds the aggregate memory bound of M. Also, the $(n/m)^{3/2}$ products are computed in $n^{3/2}/(M\sqrt{m})$ rounds, while the final prefix computation requires $O(\log_m K + 1) = O(\log_m n)$ rounds. □

We remark that the multiplication of two $\sqrt{n} \times \sqrt{n}$ dense matrices can be performed in a constant number of rounds whenever $m = \Omega(n^\epsilon)$, for constant $\epsilon > 0$, and $M\sqrt{m} = \Omega(n^{3/2})$.

3.2 Sparse-Sparse Matrix Multiplication

Consider two $\sqrt{n} \times \sqrt{n}$ sparse matrices A and B and denote with $\tilde{n} < n$ the maximum number of nonzero entries in any of the two matrices, and with $\tilde{o}$ the number of nonzero entries in the product $C = A \cdot B$. Below, we present two deterministic MR-algorithms (D1 and D2) and a randomized one (R1), each of which turns out to be more efficient than the others for suitable ranges of parameters. We consider only the case $m < 2\tilde{n}$, since otherwise matrix multiplication can be executed by a trivial one-round MR-algorithm using only one reducer. We also assume that the value $\tilde{n}$ is provided in input. (If this were not the case, such a value could be computed with a simple prefix computation in $O(\log_m n)$ rounds, which does not affect the asymptotic complexity of our algorithms.) However, we do not assume that $\tilde{o}$ is known in advance since, unlike $\tilde{n}$, this value cannot be easily computed. In fact, the only source of randomization in algorithm R1 stems from the need to estimate $\tilde{o}$.

3.2.1 Deterministic algorithm D1

This algorithm is based on the following strategy adapted from [18]. For $0 \leq i < \sqrt{n}$, let a_i (resp., b_i) be the number of nonzero entries in the ith column of A (resp., ith row of B), and let Γ_i be the set containing all nonzero entries in the ith column of A and in the ith row of B. It is easily seen that all of the $a_i b_i$ products between entries in Γ_i (one from A and one from B) must be computed. The algorithm performs a sequence of *phases* as follows. Suppose that at the beginning of Phase t, with $t \geq 0$, all products between entries in Γ_i, for each $i \leq r-1$ and for a suitable value r (initially, $r = 0$), have been computed and added to the appropriate entries of C. Through a prefix computation, Phase t computes the largest K_t such that $\sum_{j=r}^{r+K_t} a_j b_j \leq M$. Then, all products between entries in Γ_j, for every $r \leq j \leq r + K_t$, are computed using one reducer (with constant memory) for each such product.

---

[2]The details of the key assignments needed to perform the necessary data redistributions among reducers are tedious but straightforward, and will be provided in the full version of this abstract.

The products are then added to the appropriate entries of C using again a prefix computation.

THEOREM 3. *Algorithm D1 multiplies two sparse $\sqrt{n} \times \sqrt{n}$ matrices with at most $\tilde{n}$ nonzero entries each in*

$$O\left(\left\lceil \frac{\tilde{n}\min\{\tilde{n},\sqrt{n}\}}{M} \right\rceil \log_m M\right)$$

rounds, on $MR(m,M)$.

PROOF. The correctness is trivial and the memory constraints imposed by the model are satisfied since in each phase at most M elementary products are performed. The theorem follows by observing that the maximum number of elementary products is $\tilde{n}\min\{\tilde{n},\sqrt{n}\}$ and that two consecutive phases compute at least M elementary products in $O(\log_m M)$ rounds. □

3.2.2 Deterministic algorithm D2

The algorithm exploits the same three-dimensional algorithmic strategy used in the dense-dense case and consists of a sequence of phases. In Phase t, $t \geq 0$, all $\sqrt{m} \times \sqrt{m}$-size products within K_t consecutive groups are performed in parallel, where K_t is a phase-specific value. Observe that the computation of all products within a group G_ℓ requires space $M_\ell \in [\tilde{n}, \tilde{n}+\tilde{o}]$, since each submatrix of A and B occurs only once in G_ℓ and each submatrix product contributes to a distinct submatrix of C. However, the value M_ℓ can be determined in $\Theta(\tilde{n})$ space and $O(\log_m n)$ rounds by "simulating" the execution of the products in G_ℓ (without producing the output values) and adding up the numbers of nonzero entries contributed by each product to the output matrix. The value K_t is determined as follows. Suppose that, at the beginning of Phase t, groups G_ℓ have been processed, for each $\ell \leq r-1$ and for a suitable value r (initially, $r = 0$). The algorithm replicates the input matrices $K'_t = \min\{M/\tilde{n}, \sqrt{n/m}\}$ times. Subsequently, through sorting and prefix computations the algorithm computes M_ℓ for each $r \leq \ell < r + K'_t$ and determines the largest $K_t \leq K'_t$ such that $\sum_{\ell=r}^{r+K_t} M_\ell \leq M$. Then, the actual products in G_ℓ, for each $r \leq \ell \leq r + K_t$ are executed and accumulated (again using a prefix computation) in the output matrix C. We have the following theorem.

THEOREM 4. *Algorithm D2 multiplies two sparse $\sqrt{n} \times \sqrt{n}$ matrices with at most $\tilde{n}$ nonzero entries each in*

$$O\left(\left\lceil \frac{(\tilde{n}+\tilde{o})\sqrt{n}}{M\sqrt{m}} \right\rceil \log_m M\right)$$

rounds on $MR(m,M)$, where $\tilde{o}$ denotes the maximum number of nonzero entries in the output matrix.

PROOF. The correctness of the algorithm is trivial. Phase t requires a constant number of sorting and prefix computations to determine K_t and to add the partial contributions to the output matrix C. Each value M_ℓ is $O(\tilde{n}+\tilde{o})$ and the groups are $\sqrt{n/m}$, then $K_t = \Omega\left(\min\{M/(\tilde{n}+\tilde{o}), \sqrt{n/m}\}\right)$ and the theorem follows. □

We remark that the value $\tilde{o}$ appearing in the stated round complexity needs not be explicitly provided in input to the algorithm. We also observe that with respect to Algorithm D1, Algorithm D2 features a better exploitation of the local

memories available to the individual reducers, which compute $\sqrt{m} \times \sqrt{m}$-size products rather than working at the granularity of the single entries.

By suitably combining Algorithms D1 and D2, we can get the following result.

COROLLARY 1. *There is a deterministic algorithm which multiplies two sparse $\sqrt{n} \times \sqrt{n}$ matrices with at most $\tilde{n}$ nonzero entries each in*

$$O\left(\left\lceil \frac{\min\{\tilde{n}^2, \tilde{n}\sqrt{n}, (\tilde{n}+\tilde{o})\sqrt{n/m}\}}{M} \right\rceil \log_m M\right)$$

rounds on $MR(m,M)$, where $\tilde{o}$ denotes the maximum number of nonzero entries in the output matrix.

3.2.3 Randomized algorithm R1

Algorithm D2 requires $O(\log_m M)$ rounds in each Phase t for computing the number K_t of groups to be processed. However, if $\tilde{o}$ were known, we could avoid the computation of K_t and resort to the fixed-K strategy adopted in the dense-dense case, by processing $K = M/(\tilde{n}+\tilde{o})$ consecutive groups per round. This would yield an overall $O((\tilde{n}+\tilde{o})\sqrt{n}/(M\sqrt{m}) + \log_m M)$ round complexity, where the $\log_m M$ additive term accounts for the complexity of summing up, at the end, the K contributions to each entry of C. However, $\tilde{o}$ may not be known a priori. In this case, using the strategy described in Section 3.2.4 we can compute a value $\hat{o}$ which is a $1/2$-approximation to $\tilde{o}$ with probability at least $1 - 1/n$. (We say that $\hat{o}$ ϵ-approximates $\tilde{o}$ if $|\tilde{o} - \hat{o}| < \epsilon\tilde{o}$.) Hence, in the algorithm we can plug in $2\hat{o}$ as an upper bound to $\tilde{o}$. By using the result of Theorem 6 with $\epsilon = 1/2$ and $\delta = 1/(2n)$, we have:

THEOREM 5. *Let $m = \Omega\left(\log^2 n\right)$. Algorithm R1 multiplies two sparse $\sqrt{n} \times \sqrt{n}$ matrices with at most $\tilde{n}$ nonzero entries in*

$$O\left(\frac{(\tilde{n}+\tilde{o})\sqrt{n}}{M\sqrt{m}} + \log_m M\right)$$

rounds on $MR(m,M)$, with probability at least $1 - 1/n$.

By comparing the rounds complexities stated in Corollary 1 and Theorem 5, it is easily seen that the randomized algorithm R1 outperforms the deterministic strategies when $m \in (\Omega(\log^2 n), o(M^\epsilon))$, for any constant ϵ, $\tilde{n} \geq \sqrt{n/m}/\log_m M$, and $\tilde{o} \leq \tilde{n}\min\{\tilde{n}, \sqrt{m}\}\log_m M$. For a concrete example, R1 exhibits better performance when $\tilde{n} > \sqrt{n}$, $\tilde{o} = \Theta(\tilde{n})$, and m is polylogarithmic in M. Moreover, both the deterministic and randomized strategies can achieve a constant round complexity for suitable values of the memory parameters.

3.2.4 Evaluation of the number of nonzero entries

Observe that a $\sqrt{n}$-approximation to $\tilde{o}$ derives from the following simple argument. Let a_i and b_i be the number of nonzero entries in the ith column of A and in the ith row of B respectively, for each $0 \leq i < \sqrt{n}$. Then, $\tilde{o} \leq \sum_{i=0}^{\sqrt{n}-1} a_i b_i \leq \tilde{o}\sqrt{n}$. Evaluating the sum requires $O(1)$ sorting and prefix computations, hence a $\sqrt{n}$-approximation of $\tilde{o}$ can be computed in $O(\log_m \tilde{n})$ rounds. However, such an approximation is too weak for our purposes and we show below how to achieve a tighter approximation by adapting a strategy born in the realm of streaming algorithms.

Let $\epsilon > 0$ and $0 < \delta < 1$ be two arbitrary values. An ϵ-approximation to $\tilde{o}$ can be derived by adapting the algorithm of [2] for counting distinct elements in a stream $x_0 x_1 \ldots$, whose entries are in the domain $[n] = \{0, \ldots, n-1\}$. The algorithm of [2] makes use of a very compact data structure, customarily called *sketch* in the literature, which consists of $\Delta = \Theta(\log(1/\delta))$ lists, $L_1, L_2, \ldots, L_\Delta$. For $0 \le w < \Delta$, L_w contains the $t = \Theta(\lceil 1/\epsilon^2 \rceil)$ distinct smallest values of the set $\{\phi_w(x_i) : i \ge 0\}$, where $\phi_w : [n] \to [n^3]$ is a hash function picked from a pairwise independent family. It is shown in [2] that the median of the values $tn^3/v_0, \ldots tn^3/v_{\Delta-1}$, where v_w denotes the tth smallest value in L_w, is an ϵ-approximation to the number of distinct elements in the stream, with probability at least $1-\delta$. In order to compute an ϵ-approximation of $\tilde{o}$ for a product $C = A \cdot B$ of $\sqrt{n} \times \sqrt{n}$ matrices, we can modify the algorithm as follows. Consider the stream of values in $[n]$ where each element of the stream corresponds to a distinct product $a_{i,h} b_{h,j} \ne 0$ and consists of the value $j + i\sqrt{n}$. Clearly, the number of distinct elements in this stream is exactly $\tilde{o}$. (A similar approach has been used in [1] in the realm of sparse boolean matrix products.) We now show how to implement this idea on $MR(m, M)$.

The MR-algorithm is based on the crucial observation that if the stream of values defined above is partitioned into segments, the sketch for the entire stream can be obtained by combining the sketches computed for the individual segments. Specifically, two sketches are combined by merging each pair of lists with the same index and selecting the t smallest values in the merged list. The $MR(m, M)$-algorithm consists of a number of phases, where each phase, except for the last one, produces set of M/m sketches, while the last phase combines the last batch of M/m sketches into the final sketch, and outputs the approximation to $\tilde{o}$.

We refer to the partition of the matrices into $\sqrt{m} \times \sqrt{m}$ submatrices and group the products of submatrices as done before. In Phase t, with $t \ge 1$, the algorithm processes the products in $K = \min\{M/\tilde{n}, \sqrt{n/m}\}$ consecutive groups, assigning each pair of submatrices in one of the K groups to a distinct reducer. A reducer receiving $A_{i,h}$ and $B_{h,j}$, each with at least a nonzero entry, either computes a sketch for the stream segment of the nonzero products between entries of $A_{i,h}$ and $B_{h,j}$, if the total number of nonzero entries of $A_{i,h}$ and $B_{h,j}$ exceeds the size of the sketch, namely $H = \Theta((1/\epsilon^2)\log(1/\delta))$ words, or otherwise leaves the two submatrices untouched (observe that in neither case the actual product of the two submatrices is computed). In this latter case, we refer to the pair of (very sparse) submatrices as a *pseudosketch*. At this point, the sketches produced by the previous phase (if $t > 1$), together with the sketches and pseudosketches produced in the current phase are randomly assigned to M/m reducers. Each of these reducers can now produce a single sketch from its assigned pseudosketches (if any) and merge it with all other sketches that were assigned to it. In the last phase ($t = \sqrt{n/m}/K$) the M/m sketches are combined into the final one through a prefix computation, and the approximation to $\tilde{o}$ is computed.

THEOREM 6. *Let $m = \Omega((1/\epsilon^2)\log(1/\delta)\log(n/\delta))$ and let $\epsilon > 0$ and $0 < \delta < 1$ be arbitrary values. Then, with probability at least $1 - 2\delta$, the above algorithm computes an ϵ-approximation to $\tilde{o}$ in*

$$O\left(\frac{\tilde{n}\sqrt{n}}{M\sqrt{m}} + \log_m M\right)$$

rounds, on $MR(m, M)$

PROOF. The correctness of the algorithm follows from the results of [2] and the above discussion. Recall that the value computed by the algorithm is an ϵ-approximation to $\tilde{o}$ with probability $1 - \delta$. As for the rounds complexity we observe that each phase, except for the last one, requires a constant number of rounds, while the last one involves a prefix computation thus requiring $O(\log_m M)$ rounds. We only have to make sure that in each phase the memory constraints are satisfied (with high probability). Note also that a sketch of size $H \le m$ is generated either in the presence of a pair of submatrices $A_{i,h}$, $B_{h,j}$ containing at least H entries, or within one of the M/m reducers. By the choice of K, it is easy to see that in any case, the overall memory occupied by the sketches is $O(M)$. As for the constraint on local memories, a simple modification of the standard balls-into-bins argument [24] and the union bound suffices to show that with probability $1 - \delta$, in every phase when sketches and pseudosketches are assigned to M/m reducers, each reducer receives in $O(m + (1/\epsilon^2)\log(1/\delta)\log(n/\delta)) = O(m)$ words. The theorem follows. (More details will be provided in the full version of the paper.) □

3.3 Sparse-Dense matrix multiplication

Let A be a sparse $\sqrt{n} \times \sqrt{n}$ matrix with at most $\bar{n}$ nonzero entries and let B be a dense $\sqrt{n} \times \sqrt{n}$ matrix (the symmetric case, where A is dense and B sparse, is equivalent). The algorithm for dense-dense matrix multiplication does not exploit the sparsity of A and takes $O(n\sqrt{n}/(M\sqrt{m}) + \log_m n)$ rounds. Also, if we simply plug $\tilde{n} = n$ in the complexities of the three algorithms for the sparse-sparse case (where $\tilde{n}$ represented the maximum number of nonzero entries of A or B) we do not achieve a better round complexity. However, a careful analysis of algorithm D1 in the sparse-dense case reveals that its round complexity is $O(\lceil \bar{n}\sqrt{n}/M \rceil \log_m M)$. By using the fastest algorithm, depending on the relative values of the parameters, we obtain:

COROLLARY 2. *The multiplication on $MR(m, M)$ between a sparse $\sqrt{n} \times \sqrt{n}$ matrix with at most $\bar{n}$ nonzero entries and a dense $\sqrt{n} \times \sqrt{n}$ matrix requires a number of rounds which is the minimum between $O(\lceil \bar{n}\sqrt{n}/M \rceil \log_m M)$ and $O(n\sqrt{n}/(M\sqrt{m}) + \log_m n)$.*

The above sparse-dense strategy outperforms all previous algorithms for instance when $\bar{n} = o(n/(\sqrt{m}\log_m M))$.

3.4 Lower bounds

In this section we provide lower bounds for deterministic dense-dense and sparse-sparse matrix multiplication. We restrict our attention to algorithms performing all nonzero *elementary products* $a_{i,k} \cdot b_{k,j}$, which we refer to as *conventional sparse* algorithms, extending a similar terminology introduced in [14] for the dense case. Although this assumption limits the class of algorithms, ruling out Strassen-like techniques, the following lemma generalizes a result in [17] to prove that computing all nonzero elementary products is indeed necessary when entries of the input matrices are from the semiring $(\mathbb{N}, +, \cdot)$. (A similar lemma holds for the semiring $(\mathbb{N} \cup \{\infty\}, \min, +)$, where ∞ is the identity of the min operation, which is usually adopted for shortest path computations.)

LEMMA 1. *Consider an algorithm $\mathcal{A}$ which multiples two $\sqrt{n} \times \sqrt{n}$ matrices A and B with $\tilde{n}_A$ and $\tilde{n}_B$ nonzero entries,* *respectively, from the semiring* $(\mathbb{N}, +, \cdot)$. *Then, for each* $\tilde{n}_A$ *and* $\tilde{n}_B$, *algorithm* $\mathcal{A}$ *must perform all the nonzero elementary products.*

PROOF. The result in [17] focuses on algorithms for multiplying $\sqrt{n} \times \sqrt{n}$ matrices which do not exploit sparsity. The proof in [17] identifies some *specific* pairs of $\sqrt{n} \times \sqrt{n}$ matrices so that any algorithm that does not compute all elementary products is not correct on at least one such pair. Our generalization identifies similar matrix pairs containing $\tilde{n}_A$ and $\tilde{n}_B$ nonzero entries so that any algorithm that does not compute all *nonzero* elementary products is not correct on at least one such pair. More details will be provided in the full version of the paper. $\square$

The following theorem exhibits a tradeoff in the lower bound between the amount of local and aggregate memory and the round complexity of a conventional sparse matrix multiplication algorithm. The proof is similar to the one proposed in [14] for lower bounding the communication complexity of dense-dense matrix multiplication in a BSP-like model: however, differences arise since we focus on round complexity and our model does not assume the outdegree of a reducer to be bounded. In the proof of the theorem we use the following lemma which was proved using the red-blue pebbling game in [13] and then restated in [14] as follows.

LEMMA 2 ([14]). *Consider a parallel algorithm computing the product* $C = A \cdot B$, *where* A *and* B *are two arbitrary matrices. A processor that uses* N_A *entries of* A *and* N_B *entries of* B, *and computes elementary products for* N_C *entries of* C, *can compute at most* $(N_A N_B N_C)^{1/2}$ *elementary products.*

THEOREM 7. *Consider a conventional sparse* $MR(m, M)$-*algorithm* $\mathcal{A}$ *for multiplying two* $\sqrt{n} \times \sqrt{n}$ *matrices. Let* P *and* $\tilde{o}$ *denote the number of nonzero elementary products and the number of nonzero entries in the output matrix, respectively. Then, the round complexity of* $\mathcal{A}$ *is*

$$\Omega\left(\left\lceil \frac{P}{M\sqrt{m}} \right\rceil + \log_m \left(\frac{P}{\tilde{o}}\right)\right).$$

PROOF. Let $\mathcal{A}$ be an R-round $MR(m, M)$-algorithm computing $C = A \cdot B$. We prove that $R = \Omega\left(P/(M\sqrt{m})\right)$. Consider the r-th round, with $1 \leq r \leq R$, and let k be an arbitrary key in U_r and $K_r = |U_r|$. We denote with $o_{r,k}$ the space taken by the output of $\rho_r(W_{r,k})$ which contributes either to O_r or to W_{r+1}, and with $m_{r,k}$ the space needed to compute $\rho_r(W_{r,k})$ including the input and working space but excluding the output. Clearly, $m_{r,k} \leq m$, $\sum_{k \in U_r} m_{r,k} \leq M$, and $\sum_{k \in U_r} o_{r,k} \leq \tilde{o} \leq M$.

Suppose $M/K_r \geq m$. By Lemma 2, the reducer ρ_r with input $W_{r,k}$ can compute at most $m\sqrt{o_{r,k}}$ elementary products, since $N_A, N_B \leq m$ and $N_C \leq o_{r,k}$, where N_A and N_B denote the entries of A and B used in $\rho_r(W_{r,k})$ and N_C the entries of C for which contributions are computed by $\rho_r(W_{r,k})$. Then, the number of terms computed in the r-th round is at most $\sum_{k \in U_r} m\sqrt{o_{r,k}} \leq m\sqrt{MK_r} \leq M\sqrt{m}$, since $K_r \leq M/m$ and the summation is maximized when $o_{r,k} = M/K_r$ for each $k \in U_r$.

Suppose now that $M/K_r < m$. Partition the keys in U_r into K'_r sets $S_0, \ldots S_{K'_r - 1}$ such that $m \leq \sum_{k \in S_j} m_{r,k} \leq 2m$ for each $0 \leq j < K'_r$ (the lower bound may be not satisfied for $j = K'_r - 1$). Clearly, $\lfloor M/2m \rfloor \leq K'_r \leq \lceil M/m \rceil$.

By Lemma 2, the number of elementary products computed by all the reducers $\rho_r(W_{r,k})$ with keys in a set S_j is at most $\sum_{k \in S_j} (m_{r,k} m_{r,k} o_{r,k})^{1/2}$. Since $(xyz)^{1/2} + (x'y'z')^{1/2} \leq ((x + x')(y + y')(z + z'))^{1/2}$ for each non negative assignment of the x, y, z, x', y', z' variables and since $\sum_{k \in S_j} m_{r,k} \leq 2m$, it follows that at most $2m\sqrt{O_{r,j}}$ elementary products can be computed using keys in S_j, where $O_{r,j} = \sum_{k \in S_j} o_{r,k}$. Therefore, the number of elementary products computed in the r-th round is at most $\sum_{j=0}^{K'_r - 1} 2m\sqrt{O_{r,j}} \leq 2m\sqrt{MK'_r} \leq 2M\sqrt{2m}$, since $K'_r \leq \lceil M/m \rceil$ and the sum is maximized when $O_{r,j} = M/K'_r$ for each $0 \leq j < K'_r$.

Therefore, in each round $O(M\sqrt{m})$ nonzero elementary products can be computed, and then $R = \Omega(\lceil P/M\sqrt{m} \rceil)$. The second term of the lower bound follows since there is at least one entry of C given by the sum of $P/\tilde{o}$ nonzero elementary products. $\square$

We now specialize the above lower bound for algorithms for generic dense-dense and sparse-sparse matrix multiplication.

COROLLARY 3. *Consider a conventional sparse* $MR(m, M)$-*algorithm* $\mathcal{A}$ *for multiplying two* $\sqrt{n} \times \sqrt{n}$ *matrices. For input matrices with at most* $\tilde{n}$ *nonzero entries each, the round complexity of* $\mathcal{A}$ *is*

$$\Omega\left(\left\lceil \frac{\tilde{n} \min\{\tilde{n}, \sqrt{n}\}}{M\sqrt{m}} \right\rceil + \log_m \tilde{n}\right).$$

PROOF. Consider two matrices with $\tilde{n}$ nonzero entries each. Depending on which of the two terms in the complexity dominates, we can distribute the nonzero entries in the input matrices so that $P = \tilde{n}\min\{\tilde{n}, \sqrt{n}\}$ or $P/\tilde{o} = \Omega(\tilde{n})$. $\square$

All deterministic algorithms provided in this section comply with the hypotheses of the lower bound, hence the above corollary applies (even in the dense-dense case, by setting $\tilde{n} = n$). Thus, the algorithm for dense-dense matrix multiplication described in Section 3.1 is optimal for any value of the parameters. On the other hand, the deterministic algorithm D2 for sparse-sparse matrix multiplication given in Section 3.2.2 is optimal whenever $\tilde{n} \geq \sqrt{n}$, $\tilde{o} = O(\tilde{n})$ and m is polynomial in M.

4. APPLICATIONS

We now apply the algorithms presented in Section 3 to derive efficient algorithms for inverting a square matrix and for solving several variants of the matching problem in a graph. For specific values of m and M, these MR-algorithms complete in $O(\log n)$ rounds, whereas the corresponding PRAM algorithms [15, 25], simulated using the technique from [16, Theorem 7.1], take $O(\log^2 n)$ rounds.

As done in other parallel models (see e.g. [15]), we assume that each memory word is able to store any value that occurs in the computation. Detailed descriptions of the algorithms and proofs of the theorems will appear in the full version of the paper.

4.1 Inverting a lower triangular matrix

In this section we study the problem of inverting a lower triangular matrix A of size $\sqrt{n} \times \sqrt{n}$. We adapt the simple recursive algorithm which leverages on the easy formula for inverting a 2×2 lower triangular matrix [15, Sect. 8.2]. We have

$$\begin{bmatrix} a & 0 \\ b & c \end{bmatrix}^{-1} = \begin{bmatrix} a^{-1} & 0 \\ -c^{-1}ba^{-1} & c^{-1} \end{bmatrix}. \tag{1}$$

Since Equation (1) holds even when a, b, c are matrices, it is possible to derive a simple recursive algorithm for inverting a lower triangular matrix. Such an algorithm is easily implemented on $\mathrm{MR}(m, M)$ by partitioning A into square matrices of size $\sqrt{m} \times \sqrt{m}$ and proceed from the bottom up. The following theorem formalizes the complexity of such an algorithm.

THEOREM 8. *The above recursive algorithm computes the inverse of a nonsingular lower triangular $\sqrt{n} \times \sqrt{n}$ matrix A in*

$$O\left(\frac{n^{3/2}}{M\sqrt{m}} + \frac{\log^2 n}{\log m}\right)$$

rounds on $\mathrm{MR}(m, M)$.

When $M\sqrt{m}$ is $\Omega\left(n^{3/2}\right)$ and $m = \Omega\left(n^\epsilon\right)$ for some constant ϵ, the complexity reduces to $O(\log n)$ rounds.

It is also possible to compute A^{-1} using the closed formula derived by unrolling a blocked forward substitution. In general, the closed formula contains an exponential number of terms. There are nonetheless special cases of matrices for which a large number of terms in the sum are zero and only a polynomial number of terms is left. This is, for instance, the case for triangular band matrices. A $\sqrt{n} \times \sqrt{n}$ lower triangular band matrix A with bandwidth $b < \sqrt{n}$ is a matrix such that for all entries $a_{i,j}$ with $|i - j| \geq b$ or $i < j$ we have $a_{i,j} = 0$. Note that the inverse of a triangular band matrix is triangular but not necessarily a triangular band matrix. It is possible to compute the inverse of these matrices in a constant number of rounds, as formalized by the following theorem.

THEOREM 9. *Let A be a $\sqrt{n} \times \sqrt{n}$ triangular band matrix with bandwidth $b = n^\epsilon$, for a constant $\epsilon \in (0, 1/2)$. Then, if $m = \Omega\left(n^{2\epsilon+\alpha}\right)$ for any constant $\alpha \in (0, 1 - 2\epsilon)$ and $M = \Omega\left(n^{3/2-\epsilon}\right)$, computing A^{-1} takes $O(1)$ rounds in $\mathrm{MR}(m, M)$.*

4.2 Inverting a general matrix

Building on the inversion algorithm for triangular matrices presented in the previous subsection, and on the dense-dense matrix multiplication algorithm, in this section we develop an $\mathrm{MR}(m, M)$-algorithm to invert a general $\sqrt{n} \times \sqrt{n}$ matrix A. Let the trace $tr(A)$ of A be defined as $\sum_{i=0}^{n-1} a_{i,i}$, where $a_{i,i}$ denotes the entry of A on the i-th row and i-th column. The algorithm is based on the following known strategy (see e.g., [15, Sect. 8.8]).

1. Compute the powers $A^2, \ldots, A^{\sqrt{n}-1}$.
2. Compute $s_k = \sum_{i=1}^{\sqrt{n}} tr(A^k)$, for $1 \leq k \leq \sqrt{n} - 1$.
3. Compute the coefficients c_i of the characteristic polynomial of A by solving a lower triangular system of $\sqrt{n}$ linear equations involving the values s_k (the system is specified below).
4. Compute $A^{-1} = -(1/c_0) \sum_{i=1}^{\sqrt{n}} c_i A^{i-1}$.

We now provide more details on the MR implementation of above strategy. The algorithm requires $M = \Omega\left(n^{3/2}\right)$,

which ensures that enough aggregate memory is available to store all the $\sqrt{n}$ powers of A. In Step 1, the algorithm computes naively the powers in the form A^{2^i}, $1 \leq i \leq \log \sqrt{n}$, by performing a sequence of $\log \sqrt{n}$ matrix multiplications using the algorithm in Section 3.1. Then, each one of the remaining powers is computed using $M/\sqrt{n} \geq n$ aggregate memory and by performing a sequence of at most $\log \sqrt{n}$ multiplications of the matrices A^{2^i} obtained earlier. In Step 2, the $\sqrt{n}$ values s_k are computed in parallel using a prefix-like computation, while the coefficients c_i of the characteristic polynomial are computed in Step 3 by solving the linear system $L \cdot C = -S$ (i.e., computing $C = -L^{-1}S$). L is a lower triangular matrix whose elements are $\ell_{i,j} = s_{i-j}$, for $0 \leq j < i \leq \sqrt{n}$, and $\ell_{i,i} = i + 1$ for $0 \leq i < \sqrt{n}$, C is the vector of the unknown coefficient c_i, and S is the vector of the values s_k. In order to compute the coefficients in C the algorithm inverts the $\sqrt{n} \times \sqrt{n}$ lower triangular matrix L as described in Section 4.1, and computes the product between L^{-1} and S, to obtain C. Finally, Step 4 requires a prefix-like computation. We have the following theorem.

THEOREM 10. *The above algorithm computes the inverse of any nonsingular $\sqrt{n} \times \sqrt{n}$ matrix A in*

$$O\left(\frac{n^2 \log n}{M\sqrt{m}} + \frac{\log^2 n}{\log m}\right)$$

rounds on $\mathrm{MR}(m, M)$, with $M = \Omega\left(n^{3/2}\right)$.

If $M\sqrt{m}$ is $\Omega\left(n^2 \log n\right)$ and $m = \Omega\left(n^\epsilon\right)$ for some constant ϵ, the complexity reduces to $O(\log n)$ rounds.

4.3 Approximating the inverse of a matrix

The above algorithm for computing the inverse of any nonsingular matrix requires $M = \Omega\left(n^{3/2}\right)$. In this section we provide an $\mathrm{MR}(m, M)$-algorithm providing a strong approximation of A^{-1} only assuming the natural constraint $M = \Omega(n)$. A matrix B is a *strong approximation* of the inverse of an $\sqrt{n} \times \sqrt{n}$ matrix A if $\|B - A^{-1}\|/\|A^{-1}\| \leq 2^{-n^c}$, for some constant $c > 0$. The norm $\|A\|$ of a matrix A is defined as

$$\|A\| = \max_{\mathbf{x} \neq 0} \|A\mathbf{x}\|_2/\|\mathbf{x}\|_2$$

where $\| \cdot \|_2$ denotes the Euclidean norm of a vector. The condition number $\kappa(A)$ of a matrix A is defined as $\kappa(A) = \|A\|\|A^{-1}\|$.

An iterative method to compute a strong approximation of the inverse of a $\sqrt{n} \times \sqrt{n}$ matrix A is proposed in [15, Sect. 8.8.2]. The method works as follows. Let B_0 be a $\sqrt{n} \times \sqrt{n}$ matrix satisfying the condition $\|I_{\sqrt{n}} - B_0A\| = q$ for some $0 < q < 1$ and where $I_{\sqrt{n}}$ is the $\sqrt{n} \times \sqrt{n}$ identity matrix. For a $\sqrt{n} \times \sqrt{n}$ matrix C let $r(C) = I_{\sqrt{n}} - CA$. We define $B_k = (I_{\sqrt{n}} + r(B_{k-1}))B_{k-1}$, for $k > 0$. We have

$$\frac{\|B_k - A^{-1}\|}{\|A^{-1}\|} \leq q^{2^k}.$$

By setting $B_0 = \alpha A^T$ where

$$\alpha = \max_i \{ \sum_{j=0}^{\sqrt{n}-1} |a_{i,j}| \} \max_j \{ \sum_{i=0}^{\sqrt{n}-1} |a_{i,j}| \},$$

we have $q = 1 - 1/(\kappa(A)^2 n)$ [26]. Then, if $\kappa(A) = O(n^c)$ for some constant $c \geq 0$, B_k provides a strong approximation when $k = \Theta(\log n)$. From the above discussion, it is easy to derive an efficient MR(m, M)-algorithm to compute a strong approximation of the inverse of a matrix using the algorithm for dense matrix multiplication in Section 3.1.

THEOREM 11. *The above algorithm provides a strong approximation of the inverse of any nonnegative $\sqrt{n} \times \sqrt{n}$ matrix A in*

$$O\left(\frac{n^{3/2} \log n}{M\sqrt{m}} + \frac{\log^2 n}{\log m}\right)$$

rounds on MR(m, M) when $\kappa(A) = O(n^c)$ for some constant $c \geq 0$.

If $M\sqrt{m}$ is $\Omega\left(n^{3/2} \log n\right)$ and $m = \Omega(n^\epsilon)$ for some constant ϵ, the complexity reduces to $O(\log n)$ rounds.

4.4 Matching of general graphs

Given a graph $G = (V, E)$, with $|V| = \sqrt{n}$ and $|E| = k$, a matching is a set of edges without common vertices. Matching problems are natural and ubiquitous in computer science. In this section we present an algorithm to compute, with high probability, a perfect matching of a general graph. A *perfect matching* is defined as a matching containing an edge for each vertex in V. The following strategy to compute a perfect matching with probability at least $1/2$ is presented in [25]:

1. Let the input of the algorithm be the adjacency matrix A of a graph $G = (V, E)$ with $\sqrt{n}$ vertices and k edges.
2. Let B be the matrix obtained from A by substituting the entries $a_{i,j} = a_{j,i} = 1$ corresponding to edges in the graph with the integers $2^{w_{i,j}}$ and $-2^{w_{i,j}}$ respectively, for $0 \leq i < j < \sqrt{n}$, where $w_{i,j}$ is an integer chosen independently and uniformly at random from $[1, 2k]$. We denote the entry on the ith row and jth column of B as $b_{i,j}$.
3. Compute the determinant $det(B)$ of B and the greatest integer w such that 2^w divides $det(B)$.
4. Compute $adj(B)$, the adjugate matrix of B, and denote the entry on the ith row and jth column as $adj(B)_{i,j}$.
5. For each edge $(v_i, v_j) \in E$, compute

$$z_{i,j} = \frac{b_{i,j} \cdot adj(B)_{i,j}}{2^w}.$$

If $z_{i,j}$ is odd, then add the edge (v_i, v_j) to the matching.

An MR(m, M)-algorithm for perfect matching easily follows from the above strategy. To obtain B (Step 2), A is partitioned into square $\sqrt{m} \times \sqrt{m}$ submatrices $A_{\ell,h}$, $0 \leq \ell, h < \sqrt{n/m}$, and then each pair of submatrices $(A_{\ell,h}, A_{h,\ell})$ is assigned to a different reducer. This assignment ensures that each pair of entries $(a_{i,j}, a_{j,i})$ of A is sent to the same reducer. The reducer receiving the pair $(A_{\ell,h}, A_{h,\ell})$ (i.e., receiving the pairs $(a_{i,j}, a_{j,i})$, where $\ell\sqrt{m} \leq i < (\ell+1)\sqrt{m}$, $h\sqrt{m} \leq j < (h+1)\sqrt{m}$), chooses a $w_{i,j}$ independently and uniformly at random from $[1, 2k]$ for each pair $(a_{i,j}, a_{j,i})$ such that $a_{i,j} = a_{j,i} = 1$, and sets $b_{i,j}$ to $2^{w_{i,j}}$ and $b_{j,i}$ to $-2^{w_{i,j}}$. For all the other entries $a_{i,j} = a_{j,i} = 0$, the reducer sets $b_{i,j} = b_{j,i} = 0$. Let c_k, $0 \leq k \leq \sqrt{n}$ be the coefficients of the characteristic polynomial of B, which can be computed

as described in Section 4.2. Using the fact that the determinant of B is c_0 and $adj(B) = -(c_1 I + c_2 B + c_3 B^2 + \cdots + c_{\sqrt{n}} B^{\sqrt{n}-1})$, it is easy to implement Steps 3 and 4. Finally (Step 5), matrices B and $adj(B)$ are partitioned in square submatrices of size $\sqrt{m} \times \sqrt{m}$, and corresponding submatrices assigned to the same reducer, which computes the values $z_{i,j}$ for the entries in its submatrices and outputs the edges belonging to the matching.

Executing this procedure $\Theta(\log n)$ times in parallel allows us to obtain a perfect matching with high probability, as formalized by the following theorem.

THEOREM 12. *The above algorithm computes, with high probability, a perfect matching of the vertices of a graph G, in*

$$O\left(\frac{n^2 \log n}{M\sqrt{m}} + \frac{\log^2 n}{\log m}\right)$$

rounds on MR(m, M), where $M = \Omega\left(n^{3/2} \log n\right)$.

Our algorithm can be extended (as in [25]) to other variants of the matching problem like minimum weight perfect matching and maximum matching. The maximum matching problem in particular was already studied in the MapReduce framework in [19]. The authors of this work present an algorithm to obtain, with high probability, an 8-approximation to the maximum matching in a graph with $k = n^{(1-c)}$ for some constant c. Their algorithm runs in a constant (4) number of rounds if $m = n^{1/2 + 1/(3 - 6c)}$ and $M = k$. In comparison our algorithm runs in $O(\log n)$ rounds if $M\sqrt{m}$ is $\Omega\left(n^2 \log n\right)$ and $m = \Omega(n^\epsilon)$ for some constant ϵ, but computes an exact solution with high probability.

5. CONCLUSIONS

In this paper, we provided a formal specification of a computational model for the MapReduce paradigm which is parametric in the local and aggregate memory sizes and retains the functional flavor originally intended for the paradigm. Performance in the model is represented by the round complexity, which is consistent with the idea that when processing large data sets the dominant cost is the reshuffling of the data. The two memory parameters featured by the model allow the algorithm designer to explore a wide spectrum of tradeoffs between round complexity and memory availability. In the paper, we covered interesting such tradeoffs for the fundamental problem of matrix multiplication and some of its applications. The study of similar tradeoffs for other important applications (e.g., graph problems) constitutes an interesting open problem.

6. ACKNOWLEDGMENTS

The work of Pietracaprina, Pucci and Silvestri was supported, in part, by MIUR of Italy under project AlgoDEEP, by the University of Padova under the Strategic Project STPD08JA32 and Project CPDA099949/09, and by Amazon Web Services in Education grant. The work of Riondato and Upfal was supported, in part, by NSF award IIS-0905553 and by the University of Padova through the Visiting Scientist 2010/2011 grant.

7. REFERENCES

[1] R. Amossen, A. Campagna, and R. Pagh. Better size estimation for sparse matrix products. In *Approximation, Randomization, and Combinatorial Optimization. Algorithms and Techniques*, volume 6302 of *Lecture Notes in Computer Science*, pages 406–419, 2010.

[2] Z. Bar-Yossef, T. S. Jayram, R. Kumar, D. Sivakumar, and L. Trevisan. Counting distinct elements in a data stream. In *Proc. of the 6th Intl. Workshop on Randomization and Approximation Techniques*, pages 1–10, 2002.

[3] G. Bilardi and A. Pietracaprina. Theoretical models of computation. In D. Padua, editor, *Encyclopedia of Parallel Computing*, pages 1150–1158. Springer, 2011.

[4] A. Buluç and J. R. Gilbert. Challenges and advances in parallel sparse matrix-matrix multiplication. In *Proc. of 37th Intl. Conference on Parallel Processing*, pages 503–510, 2008. See also CoRR abs/1006.2183.

[5] F. Chierichetti, R. Kumar, and A. Tomkins. Max-cover in Map-Reduce. In *Proc. of the 19th World Wide Web Conference*, pages 231–240, 2010.

[6] J. Dean and S. Ghemawat. MapReduce: simplified data processing on large clusters. *Communications of the ACM*, 51(1):107–113, 2008.

[7] J. Feldman, S. Muthukrishnan, A. Sidiropoulos, C. Stein, and Z. Svitkina. On distributing symmetric streaming computations. *ACM Transactions on Algorithms*, 6(4), 2010.

[8] J. Gilbert, V. Shah, and S. Reinhardt. A unified framework for numerical and combinatorial computing. *Computing in Science Engineering*, 10(2):20–25, 2008.

[9] M. Goodrich, N. Sitchinava, and Q. Zhang. Sorting, searching, and simulation in the MapReduce framework. In *Proc. of the 22nd International Symp. on Algorithms and Computation*, 2011. See also CoRR abs/1004.470.

[10] M. T. Goodrich. Communication-efficient parallel sorting. *SIAM Journal on Computing*, 29(2):416–432, 1999.

[11] G. Greiner and R. Jacob. The I/O complexity of sparse matrix dense matrix multiplication. In *Proc. of 9th Latin American Theoretical Informatics*, volume 6034, pages 143–156, 2010.

[12] F. G. Gustavson. Two fast algorithms for sparse matrices: Multiplication and permuted transposition. *ACM Transactions on Mathematical Software*, 4(3):250–269, 1978.

[13] J. W. Hong and H. T. Kung. I/O complexity: The red-blue pebble game. In *Proceedings of the 13th ACM Symp. on Theory of Computing*, pages 326–333, 1981.

[14] D. Irony, S. Toledo, and A. Tiskin. Communication lower bounds for distributed-memory matrix multiplication. *Journal of Parallel and Distributed Computing*, 64(9):1017–1026, 2004.

[15] J. JáJá. *An Introduction to Parallel Algorithms*. Addison Wesley Longman Publishing Co., Inc., 1992.

[16] H. Karloff, S. Suri, and S. Vassilvitskii. A model of computation for MapReduce. In *Proc. of the 21st ACM-SIAM Symp. On Discrete Algorithms*, pages 938–948, 2010.

[17] L. R. Kerr. *The Effect of Algebraic Structure on the Computational Complexity of Matrix Multiplication*. PhD thesis, Cornell University, 1970.

[18] C. P. Kruskal, L. Rudolph, and M. Snir. Techniques for parallel manipulation of sparse matrices. *Theoretical Computer Science*, 64(2):135–157, 1989.

[19] S. Lattanzi, B. Moseley, S. Suri, and S. Vassilvitskii. Filtering: a method for solving graph problems in MapReduce. In *Proc. of the 23rd ACM Symp. on Parallel Algorithms and Architectures*, pages 85–94, 2011.

[20] J. Lin and C. Dyer. *Data-Intensive Text Processing with MapReduce*. Morgan & Claypool, 2010.

[21] G. Manzini. Sparse matrix computations on the hypercube and related networks. *Journal of Parallel and Distributed Computing*, 21(2):169–183, 1994.

[22] W. F. McColl and A. Tiskin. Memory-efficient matrix multiplication in the BSP model. *Algorithmica*, 24(3):287–297, 1999.

[23] M. Middendorf, H. Schmeck, H. Schröder, and G. Turner. Multiplication of matrices with different sparseness properties on dynamically reconfigurable meshes. *VLSI Design*, 9(1):69–81, 1999.

[24] M. Mitzenmacher and E. Upfal. *Probability and Computing: Randomized Algorithms and Probabilistic Analysis*. Cambridge University Press, Cambridge MA, 2005.

[25] K. Mulmuley, U. V. Vazirani, and V. V. Vazirani. Matching is as easy as matrix inversion. *Combinatorica*, 7(1):105–113, 1987.

[26] V. Pan and J. Reif. Efficient parallel solution of linear systems. In *Proc. of the 17th ACM Symp. on Theory of Computing*, pages 143–152, 1985.

[27] G. Penn. Efficient transitive closure of sparse matrices over closed semirings. *Theoretical Computer Science*, 354(1):72–81, 2006.

[28] C. Tsourakakis, U. Kang, G. Miller, and C. Faloutsos. DOULION: counting triangles in massive graphs with a coin. In *Proc. of the 15th ACM SIGKDD Intl. Conference on Knowledge Discovery and Data Mining*, pages 837–849, 2009.

[29] L. Valiant. A bridging model for parallel computation. *Communications of the ACM*, 33(8):103–111, Aug. 1990.

[30] R. Yuster and U. Zwick. Detecting short directed cycles using rectangular matrix multiplication and dynamic programming. In *Proc. of 15th ACM-SIAM Symp. On Discrete Algorithms*, pages 254–260, 2004.

[31] R. Yuster and U. Zwick. Fast sparse matrix multiplication. *ACM Transactions on Algorithms*, 1(1):2–13, 2005.

Blue Gene/Q:
Design for Sustained Multi-Petaflop Computing

Michael Gschwind
IBM Corp., Poughkeepsie, NY
mkg@us.ibm.com

Categories and Subject Descriptors
C.5 COMPUTER SYSTEM IMPLEMENTATION

Keywords: Blue Gene, Blue Gene/Q, petascale computing, memory wall, power wall, scalability wall, communication wall, reliability wall, SIMD, quad-vector processing unit (QPU), quad-vector processing extensions (QPX), transactional memory, speculative execution, interconnection networks, design for reliability, supercomputing applications

ABSTRACT
The Blue Gene/Q system represents the third generation of optimized high-performance computing Blue Gene solution servers and provides a platform for continued growth in HPC performance and capability. Blue Gene/Q started with a new design of the hardware platform, while retaining and significantly expanding an established, trusted and successful software environment.

To deliver a system that enables users to fully exploit the promise of high-performance computing for both traditional HPC applications and new commercial application areas, the Blue Gene/Q system architecture combines hardware and software innovations to overcome traditional bottlenecks, most famously the memory and power walls which have become emblematic of modern computing systems. At the same time, to deliver a platform for sustainable petascale computing, and beyond to exascale, we had to address a new set of "walls" with the many innovations described below: a scalability wall, a communication wall, and a reliability wall.

The new Blue Gene/Q system increases overall system performance with a new node architecture: Each node offers more thread-level-parallelism with a coherent SMP node consisting of eighteen 64-bit PowerPC cores with 4-way simultaneous multithreading. Each core provides for better exploitation of data-level parallelism with a new 4-way quad-vector processing unit (QPU). The memory subsystem integrates memory speculation support which can be used to implement both Transactional Memory and Speculative Execution programming models.

The compute nodes are connected in a five dimensional torus configuration using 10 point-to-point links, and a total network bandwidth of 44 GB/s per node. The on-chip messaging unit provides an optimized interface between the network routing logic and the memory subsystem, with enough bandwidth to keep all the links busy. It also offloads communication protocol processing by implementing collective broadcast and reduction operations, including integer and floating point sum, min and max.

Built on the Blue Gene hardware design is an efficient software stack that builds on several generations of Blue Gene software interfaces, while extending these capabilities and adding new functions to support new hardware capabilities. The hardware functions were designed with a focus on providing efficient primitives upon which to build the rich software environment.

To ensure reliable operation of a petascale system, reliability has to be a pervasive design consideration. At the architecture level, new QPX store-and-indicate instructions support the detection of programming errors. To ensure reliable operation in the presence of transient faults, we conducted exhaustive single event upset simulations based on fault injection into the simulated design. The operating system was structured to use firmware in a small on-chip boot eDRAM to avoid silent system hangs.

Together, the hardware and software innovations pioneered in Blue Gene/Q give application developers a platform and framework to develop and deploy sustained petascale computing applications. These petascale applications will allow its users to make new scientific discoveries and gain new business insights, which will be the true measure of the success of the new Blue Gene/Q systems.

ACKNOWLEDGMENTS
The BG/Q project has been supported and partially funded by Argonne National Laboratory and the Lawrence Livermore National Laboratory on behalf of the U.S. Department of Energy, under Lawrence Livermore National Laboratory subcontract no. B554331.

ABOUT THE SPEAKER
Dr. Michael Gschwind is a Senior Technical Staff Member and Senior Manager of System Architecture in the IBM Systems and Technology Group. In his dual role as a technical leader and manager, he is responsible for leading the architecture evolution of IBM's mainframe System z and Power systems and manages the architecture teams for both System z and Power brands. Previously, Dr. Gschwind served as Blue Gene Floating Point Chief Architect and Lead. Dr. Gschwind served as IFU and IDU lead and chief microarchitect for the Komal core which is the foundation for Power7 systems and as architecture lead for Productive, Easy-to-use, Reliable Computing Systems (PERCS) for DARPA's High Productivity Computing Systems (HPCS) initiative where he served as lead architect for IBM's vector/scalar SIMD architecture (VSX). Dr. Gschwind helped initiate the Cell project, served as one of its lead architects for the Cell definition, developed the first Cell compiler and served as technical lead for the software team. He also helped create the Xbox360 chip. Dr. Gschwind received his PhD from Technische Universität Wien. Dr. Gschwind is an IEEE Fellow, an IBM Master Inventor and a member of the IBM Academy of Technology and was named as an industry-leading "IT Innovator and Influencer" by InformationWeek in 2006.

An Analysis of Computational Workloads for the ORNL Jaguar System

Wayne Joubert
Oak Ridge National Laboratory
1 Bethel Valley Road
Oak Ridge, TN 37831
joubert@ornl.gov

Shi-Quan Su
National Institute for Computational Sciences
P.O. Box 2008
Oak Ridge, TN 37831
shiquansu@hotmail.com

ABSTRACT

This study presents an analysis of science application workloads for the Jaguar Cray XT5 system during its tenure as a 2.3 petaflop supercomputer at Oak Ridge National Laboratory. Jaguar was the first petascale system to be deployed for open science and has been one of the world's top three supercomputers for six releases of the TOP500 list. Its workload is investigated here as a representative of the growing worldwide install base of petascale systems and also as a foreshadowing of science workloads to be expected for future systems. The study considers characteristics of the Jaguar workload such as resource utilization, typical job characteristics, most heavily used applications, application scaling and application usage patterns. Implications of these findings are considered for current petascale workflows and for exascale systems to be deployed later this decade.

Categories and Subject Descriptors

K.6.2 [**Management of Computing and Information Systems**]: Installation Management—*performance and usage measurement*; D.2.8 [**Software Engineering**]: Metrics—*complexity measures, performance measures*

General Terms

Measurement; Performance

Keywords

HPC, workload, applications, science, Cray, ORNL, metrics, petascale, exascale, scaling

1. INTRODUCTION

High performance computing (HPC) is now recognized as a third mode of scientific discovery, similar in importance to experiment and theory [1]. Progress in science areas with broad societal impact such as energy, environment, basic science and national security is now seen as intimately connected to the capabilities of the world's most powerful computer systems. Furthermore, many targeted science problems will require exascale-class systems, which are several

orders of magnitude beyond the capabilities of today's top systems [2]. However, building an exascale system within the proposed 2018-2020 timeframe will be extremely challenging and will require hardware innovations on multiple fronts [4], [5].

Anticipated hardware changes on the path to exascale will induce extensive changes to software programming methodologies for building the science applications which serve as the lifeblood of HPC computing. These changes are already being felt through the presence of new programming APIs such as CUDA [6], OpenCL [7] and OpenACC [8] to support emerging heterogeneous compute hardware. Although it is not entirely clear to what extent applications will need to be transformed to reach exascale, it is clear that the starting point of this transition is the reality of how science applications are actually being used currently on petascale systems. Studying petascale application workloads shows not only the requirements these science applications put on exascale hardware but also how the applications will be required to change in order to adapt to the new hardware.

The purpose of this study is to explore these issues through an in-depth report on application workloads for the Oak Ridge Leadership Computing Facility (OLCF) Jaguar system. The Jaguar system was the first petascale HPC platform for open science and has enabled researchers to advance scientific discovery in multiple science areas [22]. Jaguar has repeatedly held the position of one of the world's fastest computers on the TOP500 list [9]. Its primary mission is to provide approximately a billion core-hours annually to the U.S. Department of Energy (DOE) Innovative and Novel Computational Impact on Theory and Experiment (INCITE) Program [10] for scientists and researchers addressing some of the world's most challenging scientific problems. As such, Jaguar provides an ideal opportunity to understand the characteristics of petascale applications solving real science problems.

This study tracks application usage on Jaguar over a period of approximately two years, beginning with Jaguar's upgrade to AMD hex-core Istanbul processors in late 2009 and ending immediately before its upgrade to AMD 16-core Interlagos processors and Gemini interconnect in late 2011. Statistics were gathered using Jaguar's queuing and application launch systems, which record data for every instance of a job launch or application run over this time period. We analyze the data to answer questions such as: What are the most heavily used applications run? How do these applications scale? What are their usage patterns? Answers to these questions will play a role in the broader community dis-

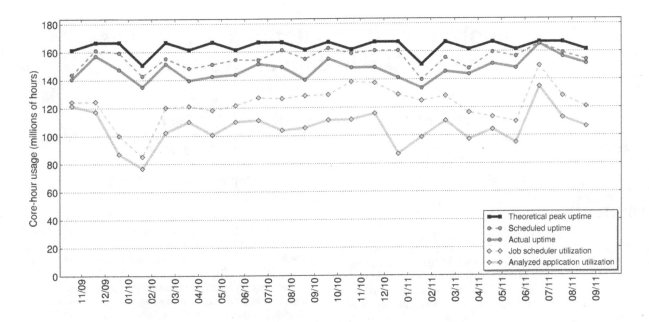

Figure 1: System usage over time.

cussion of application and hardware requirements for solving exascale-class science problems.

The remainder of this paper is organized as follows. After describing the methodology of the study, we begin with a high-level view of Jaguar utilization over time. We then analyze utilization by science area. Following this we investigate usage by science application and then explore in further detail the usage patterns of selected applications. Finally, we discuss the implications of these findings for future petascale and exascale scientific computing.

2. STUDY METHODOLOGY

The ORNL Jaguar Cray XT5 contains 18,688 compute nodes, each containing two hex-core 2.6 GHz AMD Opteron 2345 Istanbul processors and 16 GB of DDR2-800 memory. Each node contains a SeaStar 2+ router with peak bandwidth of 57.6 GB/s. The full system contains 224,256 processing cores, 300 TB of memory, and a peak performance of 2.3 petaflops.

The character of Jaguar's workload is ultimately influenced by usage policies derived from overarching mission goals and implemented through scheduling mechanisms. The Jaguar usage policy emphasizes capability computing, to solve science problems unsolvable on small to midrange HPC systems. Also, the philosophy of the INCITE Program is to support a relatively small number of high-quality projects rather than many small ones. These policies impact system workload, as will be seen below.

The data for this study are taken from a period of nearly two years, from November 2009 through September 2011 inclusive. Two primary sources of data are used. First, the MOAB scheduler [11], which underlies the PBS job queuing system [12] and reserves compute nodes for executing an application, stores entries in a database with information on every PBS job launched on the system. Second, the ALPS scheduler [13] stores entries for every execution of an "aprun"

command which is used to launch an executable code within a PBS job. By matching the entries of these two databases, it is possible to extract data for every execution instance of an application, including job size and duration, user and project name, and filename of the executable code.

Jaguar does not have an automated method for identifying the science application name associated with each executable file that is run. Thus, a manual process was used, merging data from multiple sources, including a secondary database containing the link commands used to build each parallel executable file run on Jaguar, a cross-reference procedure based on the user name and project associated with each job execution, and in some cases interviews with developers and users to clarify the underlying application being used. This process was employed to identify and validate the application names associated with the most heavily run codes on Jaguar.

Although HPC workloads have been studied previously, most studies have been job-centric or user-centric rather than application-centric, have not considered actual in situ workloads, or have been based on secondary evidence rather than hard data. Analysis of application workloads based on system data opens a new door of insight into HPC performance, revealing the connection between workload characteristics and specific science application codes with their distinctive algorithms and science models, thus providing insight into how the computational requirements of each science domain drive the requirements for future hardware.

3. OVERALL SYSTEM UTILIZATION

Jaguar could in theory provide 1.964 billion core-hours per year if the system provided 100% availability and every cycle were used. However, this theoretical peak usage is never attained in practice for working HPC centers for various reasons, such as downtime for system maintenance, unscheduled outages, lack of available jobs of the proper size and duration to fill every "empty hole" of processors and time, and time spent in nonparallel operations in a PBS batch job required to prepare for parallel execution, e.g., reading input files from mass storage.

Figure 1 shows the monthly breakdown of Jaguar usage. The theoretical peak availability is the number of cores multiplied by the number of hours in the month. Scheduled uptime deducts the time spent in scheduled outages, actual uptime deducts the time for all outages, and job scheduler utilization shows the time actually spent running jobs as indicated by the MOAB database. The figure also shows "analyzed application time"—the time spent by applications run using the Cray "aprun" command which is used in this study. For the purposes of this study, incomplete or fragmentary application run data are discarded, such as data that are not fully recorded due to a system failure while the application was running.

Figure 1 shows that Jaguar was very well-utilized over the time period. The system uptime was in excess of 90% of the theoretical maximum, and 83% of the core-hours available during this uptime were consumed executing user jobs. This utilization figure is high compared to typical HPC centers [18] and is especially noteworthy since it is difficult to schedule for high utilization when average job core counts are large relative to system size [16]. Such a high utilization is difficult to improve by scheduler tuning, though an even higher utilization might be obtained from a more variegated job mix supplied by users when possible to fill in the gaps. The high usage is in part fueled by growing demand: in 2011 the number of INCITE core-hours requested by program applicants was over three times the actual number of core-hours granted, and this ratio is increasing every year [17]. This manifestly growing demand as well as the urgency of science need both point to the importance of deploying exascale systems as soon as is practical.

Usage over this period exhibits several specific features. First, usage in the early part of the reporting period was below normal, since new INCITE projects were beginning and users were scaling up their codes to exploit the newly upgraded system for the first time. Second, January 2011 saw a drop in analyzable application time because an uptick in system failures caused loss of system availability as well as loss of job log data. Finally, usage near the end of the reporting period was higher than normal as users intensified efforts to use the system before being taken offline for a processor upgrade.

Over the entire period, the analyzed application utilization total represents a full 86% of the entire MOAB job scheduler utilization. This affirms that the analysis of this study is valid, being based on data that accurately represents nearly the entire core-hour usage of Jaguar over the period studied.

4. USAGE BY SCIENCE DOMAIN

We now consider Jaguar utilization by science domain based on the MOAB job scheduler data. The science domains considered here are based on scientific grand challenges that are a priority for petascale and exascale computing, such as climate, high-energy physics, nuclear physics, fusion energy, materials science, biophysics, national security, and nuclear energy [2]. Each project granted an allocation on Jaguar is categorized by a science domain which is used for the analysis here.

Figure 2 shows Jaguar core-hour usage by science domain. Of the twenty-four categories listed, the top five science domains—chemistry, fusion, computer science, materials and astrophysics—consume over half of Jaguar resources, while the top nine domains consume over three quarters of the total resources. Here the computer science category subsumes a variety of different types of research, such as performance optimization of petascale science applications and the development of next-generation tools. Though some of the science areas show heavy usage due to mandated science priorities, the workload is nonetheless diverse in terms of the types of science being done. Jaguar is similar in this regard to other top systems which must support multiple science domains, such as Tianhe 1A [19] and the Riken K Computer [20], as compared to others which support specialized science domains, e.g., the NOAA Gaea system [21].

Multi-purpose HPC systems like Jaguar necessarily must provide well-balanced hardware capabilities in support of multiple science areas. The OLCF has identified for each science domain and its concomitant models and algorithms a set of specific hardware requirements which must be met in order to run the science applications effectively [22]. Furthermore, some hardware characteristics are growing in importance for multiple science areas as we approach exascale, such as node peak flops, mean time to interrupt, node memory capacity, memory latency, interconnect latency, interconnect bandwidth and memory bandwidth [22]. HPC systems which support general purpose scientific computation across multiple science domains must incorporate well-balanced hardware that necessarily performs well for the differing algorithmic stress points of the diversity of algorithms required by the targeted applications.

5. USAGE BY APPLICATION

In this section we consider Jaguar utilization broken down by individual science applications. We use several measures such as job size (the number of nodes used to execute the application times the number of cores per node), job duration (the number of wallclock time hours used to execute) and job core-hour usage (the product of job size and job duration). Henceforth unless otherwise noted the term "job" is used in an application-centric way to denote the execution of an application using the Cray "aprun" command; note that multiple aprun commands in a single PBS job would be counted here as separate jobs for the purpose of analysis.

A basic workload characteristic is the total number of distinct science applications run on the system. Figure 3 addresses this, showing the cumulative core-hour usage of applications, starting with the most highly used applications on the left side of the graph and accumulating the usage of progressively less used applications toward the right. We omit applications with very low resource usage under 1000 core-hours, which contribute little to Jaguar utilization. The total number of applications measured is less than 700. We also see that core-hour usage per application has a "short tail," with 50% of the core-hours used by a mere 20 science applications, and nearly 80% consumed by the top 50 applications. This concentration of heavily used applications is more pronounced here than at some other centers [23]. This is in line with Jaguar's emphasis on leadership-class applications capable of scaling to a large fraction of the system, for a highly focused set of science problems. In comparison, the number of projects sponsored by INCITE,

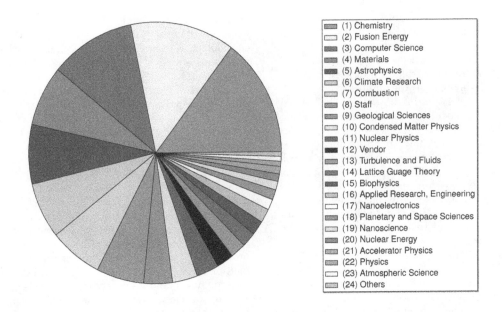

(1) Chemistry
(2) Fusion Energy
(3) Computer Science
(4) Materials
(5) Astrophysics
(6) Climate Research
(7) Combustion
(8) Staff
(9) Geological Sciences
(10) Condensed Matter Physics
(11) Nuclear Physics
(12) Vendor
(13) Turbulence and Fluids
(14) Lattice Guage Theory
(15) Biophysics
(16) Applied Research, Engineering
(17) Nanoelectronics
(18) Planetary and Space Sciences
(19) Nanoscience
(20) Nuclear Energy
(21) Accelerator Physics
(22) Physics
(23) Atmospheric Science
(24) Others

Figure 2: System usage by science domain.

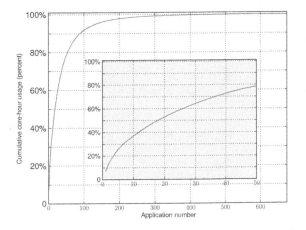

Figure 3: Cumulative core-hour usage by application.

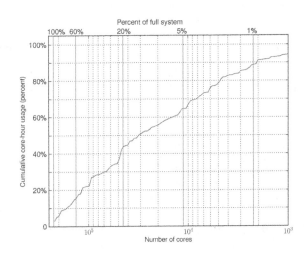

Figure 4: Cumulative core-hour usage by job size.

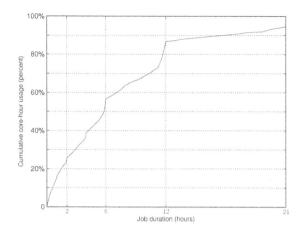

Figure 5: Cumulative core-hour usage as a function of job duration.

the primary vehicle for awarding time on Jaguar, is small in number—for example, 32 projects for Jaguar in 2011 [14]. The picture emerges of science teams each focused on one or a small number of highly scalable codes as the focus of development, tuning and science output. Although the use of multiple codes to provide some level of redundancy for a given science problem is important for validation of science conclusions, it is nonetheless worthwhile to concentrate efforts on a comparatively small set of applications. Since parallel codes can be extremely difficult and time-consuming to scale to the entire system, it is beneficial to concentrate finite developer resources on a comparatively small number of applications. This approach is even more critical for exascale, since hardware, software and science models are becoming increasingly complex, creating more challenges for application development and maintenance. Also, emphasizing a smaller set of applications makes it easier to analyze workload characteristics, to perform meaningful acceptance testing on new systems and to understand requirements for future systems.

A second characteristic of application workload is the profile of job sizes run on the system. The usage policy for Jaguar supports leadership-class jobs, defined to be jobs that run at a large fraction of the entire system.

Figure 4 shows a cumulative graph indicating the job sizes at which core-hours are expended. The lowest core count shown on the graph is 1000 processor cores on the far right, corresponding roughly to sizes of the smallest TOP500 systems in 2011 [9]. Notably, over 90% of core-hours are spent in jobs of at least this size, while over 43% of hours are spent in jobs using at least 20% of the system, i.e., 44,850 cores (this being a specific utilization target), and about 15% of the core-hours are spent on truly large-scale jobs using at least 60% of the system (134,550 cores).

Jaguar is performing leadership-class computing at a very large scale. However, the usage patterns of Jaguar are also evenly balanced across the full spectrum of job sizes shown, as indicated by the relative straightness of the curve in Figure 4. There are several potential reasons for this. Though Jaguar emphasizes leadership-class jobs, some projects may spend significant time at lower core counts performing pre-

liminary runs for leadership job preparation, e.g., software development and testing, code optimization, model validation or parameter studies. Also, some projects may simply generate much of their science at the smaller scale. Additionally, different applications are at different points in their growth curve to higher scalability. As Moore's law and its variants reflect exponential growth of processing power over time, application codes run on these systems are constantly under stress to keep up with this exponential growth curve. Different application codes are at different locations on the growth curve, based on factors such as code size and complexity, code structure and the underlying algorithms. To support this ongoing development process, HPC systems must effectively support the full range of job sizes and application usage patterns. Also, since the graph has no significant bimodal characteristics, there is no clear cutoff which would suggest a smaller system size for servicing a portion of the Jaguar workload.

The duration of jobs is also an important characteristic of application workload. Job duration is relevant to the issue of fault tolerance, which is expected to be a major concern for exascale computing. The sheer number of parts required in an exascale system will tend to drive down the system time between failures. Though it is not entirely clear what will be required of applications in order to adapt to this hardware environment, it will clearly be of value going forward for jobs to be able to execute with short wallclock times, to reduce the risk of encountering hardware failure in a single run.

Figure 5 shows the cumulative number of core-hours spent in jobs of a given duration. This figure shows that about 90% of core-hours are spent in jobs of 12 hours duration or less, and about 50% of Jaguar core-hours are spent in jobs of duration 6 hours or less. Furthermore, comparison of data from Figures 4 and 5 shows that at least 70% of core-hours expended by jobs run on 20% or more of the system are run with duration less than 12 hours, showing that most core-hours spent in large jobs are spent in jobs significantly less than the maximum allowed duration.

During the reporting period, the Jaguar scheduling policy imposed specific duration limits for jobs at 12, 6 or 2 hours depending on job size, with a time limit of 24 hours applied to all jobs. This differs from some other centers which may allow some jobs to run for as long as tens of days uninterrupted [18]. Thus, job durations for the Jaguar workload are in part limited by center queuing policies, though the data indicate that many users are also self-regulating their own job durations to be significantly below these limits.

Jaguar's average mean time to failure (MTTF) over the entire reporting period equals 65 hours, though the value is somewhat higher if unrepresentative time periods with many system failures over a short period of time are excluded. Here, MTTF is a measure of system availability defined as total time in the period minus the duration of unscheduled outages divided by the number of unscheduled outages. Furthermore, the frequency of hardware failures which affect a running application over the reporting period, including both node failures and system-wide failures, is once every 35 hours. These failure rates, currently measured in days, are expected to be pressured downward on the way to exascale as systems are built with increasingly large numbers of parts. Figure 5 shows that users are proactively controlling the duration of their jobs to be far beneath system failure rates, often more aggressively than is required by the

Table 1: Selected Applications

Application	Primary Science Domain	Description
NWCHEM	Chemistry	large scale molecular simulations http://www.nwchem-sw.org
S3D	Combustion	direct numerical simulation of turbulent combustion http://www.nccs.gov/wp-content/training /scaling_workshop_pdfs/ornl_scaling_ws_2007.pdf
XGC	Fusion Energy	particle-in-cell modeling of tokamak fusion plasmas http://w3.physics.lehigh.edu/xgc
CCSM	Climate Research	climate system modeling http://www.cesm.ucar.edu
CASINO	Condensed Matter Physics	quantum Monte Carlo electronic structure calculations http://www.hector.ac.uk/cse/distributedcse/reports/casino
VPIC	Fusion Energy	3-D relativistic, electromagnetic, particle-in-cell simulation http://www.lanl.gov/orgs/hpc/roadrunner/rrinfo/RR%20webPDFs/rr3_bja6.pdf
VASP	Materials	ab-initio quantum mechanical molecular dynamics http://cms.mpi.univie.ac.at/vasp
MFDn	Nuclear Physics	a Many Fermion Dynamics code http://unedf.org/content/PackForest2008_talks/Day1/mfd_unedf.pdf
LSMS	Materials	Wang-Landau electronic structure multiple scattering http://lammps.sandia.gov
GenASiS	Astrophysics	AMR neutrino radiation magneto-hydrodynamics http://iopscience.iop.org/1742-6596/16/1/053/pdf/1742-6596_16_1_053.pdf
MADNESS	Chemistry	adaptive multi-resolution simulation by multi-wavelet bases http://code.google.com/p/m-a-d-n-e-s-s
GTC	Fusion Energy	gyrokinetic toroidal momentum and electron heat transport http://computing.ornl.gov/SC08/documents/pdfs/Klasky_GTC.pdf
OMEN	Nanoelectronics	multi-dimensional quantum transport solver http://docs.lib.purdue.edu/cgi/viewcontent.cgi?article=1513&context=nanopub
Denovo	Nuclear Energy	3-D discrete ordinates radiation transport http://info.ornl.gov/sites/publications/Files/Pub22424.pdf
CP2K	Chemistry	atomistic and molecular simulations http://cp2k.berlios.de
CHIMERA	Astrophysics	modeling the evolution of core collapse supernovae http://astrodev.phys.utk.edu/chimera/doku.php
DCA++	Materials	many-body problem solver with quantum Monte Carlo Carole http://www.nccs.gov/wp-content/training/seminar_series/dcaStory.pdf
LAMMPS	Chemistry	molecular dynamics simulation http://lammps.sandia.gov
DNS	Fluids and Turbulence	direct numerical simulation for fluids and turbulence http://soliton.ae.gatech.edu/people/pyeung
PFLOTRAN	Geological Sciences	multi-phase, multi-component reactive flow and transport http://ees.lanl.gov/pflotran
CAM	Climate Research	global atmosphere models http://www.cesm.ucar.edu/models/cesm1.0/cam
QMCPACK	Materials	diffusive quantum Monte Carlo simulations http://code.google.com/p/qmcpack

scheduler. A common technique used is checkpoint/restart, in which a snapshot of program state data is periodically stored to disk to enable later restart in the event of a system failure. Other reasons for users to run jobs at shorter durations include optimizing throughput of the job scheduler, maximizing code efficiency with respect to the expense of restart dumps or simply responding to the needs of science cases which inherently require short durations. Though it is not clear from these data alone to what degree users are shortening job durations to avoid system or node failures, the fact that users are lowering their job durations is a favorable sign for preparing for a potentially challenging fault tolerance environment on exascale hardware. Furthermore, center policies that restrict the duration for jobs is necessary for petascale systems that unavoidably experiences outages, and these policies also acculturate users for the need to checkpoint/restart their codes on HPC systems going forward.

6. USAGE OF SELECTED APPLICATIONS

Since application usage has a "short tail," the analysis of a handful of heavily used applications is a valid proxy for studying Jaguar application workload as a whole. We thus focus on a set of 22 codes for more in-depth analysis, selected based on two criteria. First, applications are chosen from the largest core-hour consumers on Jaguar. Second, other applications of strategic scientific importance going forward are added. Many of these codes are very well-known in the worldwide HPC community, have a large user base and have been used on multiple HPC systems. Two codes, DCA++ and LSMS, are Gordon Bell prize winners. For details on these applications, including science problems solved, programming models and algorithms, see [22].

These codes are highly relevant to the discussion of exascale computing. Since the INCITE program has a high year-to-year project renewal rate, current applications continue to have impact into the future. Also, many of these codes have already played a key role in planning for the next OLCF system in the 20 petaflop range [15], and it would be natural for them to play a role in planning for 100 petaflop and exaflop systems. Also, some of these codes have development plans out to exascale. These applications are likely to change dramatically through the codesign process on the way to exascale; for some codes, algorithms are already being identified which will need to be replaced. Nonetheless, the current use cases, scaling performance and resource consumption of these applications provides a key starting point for exascale planning.

In total, usage of these applications accounts for approximately 50% of analyzable application core-hours on Jaguar for the reporting period.

The list of applications considered is given in Table 1. This list consists of applications from a very diverse cross-section of science domains, with the 22 applications covering 12 primary science domains. Furthermore, these applications represent a variety of underlying models and algorithms.

Table 2 shows breadth of usage of each application as measured by number of science domains and OLCF projects using the application. Here, the science domains described earlier are used, excluding service categories such as "STAFF" and "VENDOR." On average, the applications are each used by roughly two science domains and four projects. Thus the impact of these applications is broad, involving multiple user

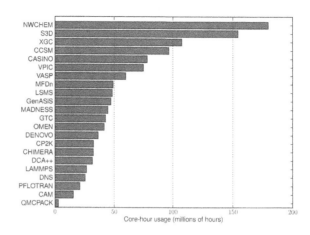

Figure 6: Core-hour utilization for selected applications.

communities. The data show VASP to be most broadly used across science domains and projects. VASP is heavily used to compute material characteristics used in many simulations. Following VASP, the codes LAMMPS and NWCHEM are the most widely-used codes across science domains.

Applications used across multiple science domains and projects are of special significance, as their breadth of use gives them high impact that is not always visible when considering projects individually. They also offer high leverage potential, since improvements to science quality or code performance for these codes have broad cross-cutting impact on many science domains.

Figure 6 shows total core-hour usage of the applications. Of the 2.3 billion core-hours tracked during the 23-month reporting period, NWCHEM is the top user with 197 million core-hours or 7.5% of the total, followed by S3D using 154 million core-hours or 6.3%. By comparison, the average 2011 Jaguar INCITE award was 29 million core-hours, suggesting some codes are heavily used across multiple INCITE projects [17]. The next highest users are XGC, CCSM and CASINO. The data show a mix of heavily used applications across diverse science domains as well as a heavy concentration of usage in a small number of applications. Awareness of the use cases and performance characteristics of top applications is worthwhile for procurement and planning of future systems, since future systems must necessarily perform well for the performance hot spots of these codes.

Scalability characteristics of the applications are shown in Figure 7. For each code, three values are presented. First, the maximum job size ever run is indicated, showing the most ambitious attempt to run the code at a large scale. Second, the job size of the single job consuming the most core-hours is given, which is a better measure of the code's best scalability for a real science job. Finally, the average job size over the reporting period is given. Here and subsequently, averages are weighted by core-hour utilization. This approach differs from other workload studies by reducing the likelihood of skewed data due to many small inconsequential jobs, giving a more realistic measure tied to actual resource utilization of Jaguar.

We can observe the following application scaling charac-

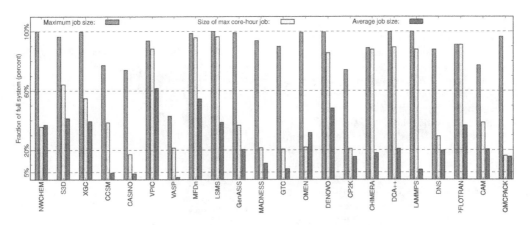

Figure 7: Scalability characteristics of selected applications.

Table 2: Selected Applications Breadth of Usage

Application	Science Domains	Projects
NWCHEM	4	6
S3D	2	3
XGC	1	2
CCSM	2	7
CASINO	2	4
VPIC	3	7
VASP	7	18
MFDn	1	2
LSMS	1	4
GenASiS	1	1
MADNESS	3	5
GTC	1	3
OMEN	1	2
Denovo	1	2
CP2K	3	5
CHIMERA	1	2
DCA++	2	2
LAMMPS	5	9
DNS	1	3
PFLOTRAN	1	2
CAM	2	3
QMCPACK	1	1

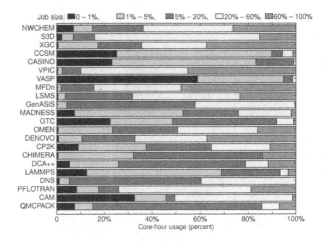

Figure 8: Fraction of time spent at different job sizes for selected applications.

teristics:

1. Every code has been run at 40% or more of the full system. All codes except VASP have been run at 60% of the full system, and over half the codes have been run at 90% of the full system.

2. For every code except CASINO and QMCPACK, the largest core-hour consuming run required at least 20% of the full system. For nearly half the codes, it required 60% of the full system.

3. VPIC, MFDn, Denovo and S3D have average job size in excess of 40% of the full system, thus are typically run at very large scale. Over half the codes have average job size of at least 20% of the full system, thus scaling to leadership size for routine use. Notably, multiple applications already scale successfully to core counts that did not exist on any system a few years ago.

Some codes show a disparity between the best scaling and the average scaling. For some cases, the application scales

well and generates science at the larger scale but also produces much science output at smaller scales. In other cases, the science problems being solved may not provide enough parallelism for the codes to scale well to more cores, for example the case of a strong scaling regime for smaller-sized problems. These codes might benefit from more strenuous code optimization efforts, algorithmic innovations to improve scalability such as latency-hiding techniques, or more powerful compute nodes that might lessen the need for larger factors of inter-node scaling.

Figure 8 gives a more detailed picture of core counts at which the applications are typically run. For each application, the fraction of core-hours consumed for several ranges of job size for that application is shown, for example jobs using 60% or more of Jaguar's cores. About half of the applications spend at least half of their resource usage at 20% or more of the system. The leaders are VPIC, MFDn and S3D. On the other hand, CASINO, VASP, CCSM, and LAMMPS are used most heavily at core counts less than 20% of the full system, though in some cases many small-sized runs may be part of a large ensemble of runs in a single experiment. Some codes use pronounced quantities of resource in specific ranges, for example, S3D and PFLOTRAN in the 20%-60%

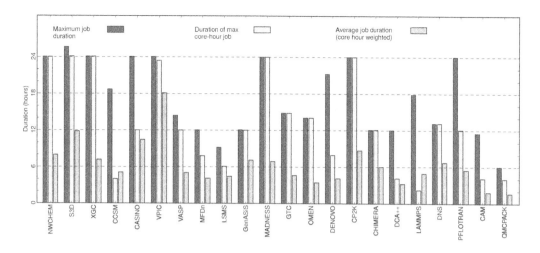

Figure 9: Job duration characteristics of selected applications.

range, or DCA++ and QMCPACK in the 5%-20% range. These latter codes are highly scalable and are used at high core counts but are also heavily used at low core counts. We observe thus a collection of applications with a diverse range of usage patterns, many of which are routinely scaling to large fractions of the full system and thus leading the way to scalability to the exascale regime.

Figure 9 shows the duration at which each of the applications runs. Three statistics for each application are shown: the maximum duration of any job ever run, the duration of the job consuming the maximum number of core-hours, and the average job duration for the given application. About a third of applications have run at least once for 24 hours; however, the typical job duration is much less. The longest running codes on average are VPIC (18 hours) and S3D (12 hours). On the other hand, about half of the codes run on average less than six hours, with the shortest being QMC-PACK and CAM, followed by DCA++ and OMEN. As mentioned earlier, the capability to run applications for shorter time may be strategic for what is expected to be a challenging fault tolerance environment for future exascale systems. However, the actual usage of applications for long job durations does not imply that the long durations are required; for example, VPIC and S3D are run for long durations, though both codes have checkpoint/restart capabilities and can be run effectively for shorter durations.

The codes described here vary in size and complexity, from several thousand to hundreds of thousands of lines of code. Though many are scaling well to Jaguar's 224,256 compute cores, they are likely to require significant restructuring in order to reach exascale. To this end, many of these applications are already being modified for exascale preparedness. In particular, six codes (CAM, DCA++, De-novo, LAMMPS, LSMS and PFLOTRAN) are a spearhead for early readiness for the upcoming 20 petaflop GPU-based ORNL Titan system. [15]. The changes being made to these codes for GPU computing will bring them much closer to readiness for eventual exascale systems, since some of the key exascale issues are being addressed, including exposure of more parallelism and improvement to locality of memory reference.

7. CONCLUSIONS

The following are the major findings of this study:

1. Jaguar has had a productive run as the world's first petascale system for open science, providing high availability and high utilization.

2. The workload of Jaguar has been diverse across science domains, average job sizes, typical job durations and usage patterns.

3. System usage is dominated by a relatively small number of applications.

4. Usage characteristics of applications show promising signs for the transition to exascale. Many applications scale to a large fraction of the system, and workflow patterns show codes are being run effectively within constraints of system uptime characteristics.

We propose the following recommendations:

1. Some applications will require concerted effort to improve scaling behaviors, for current systems and for exascale.

2. Additional log data collected from running applications would be valuable, such as communication and I/O usage and processor counter data. This information can in some cases be collected from science teams but is not always readily available.

3. Rigorous measurement of code efficiency would be very useful. Code teams are naturally incentivized to optimize their codes to make best use of their allocations, and the the OLCF liaison support model [22] assists with this. The DOE Joule Code Project is an effort to improve performance for targeted applications [3]. Code performance improvement is a constant effort driven in part by ongoing algorithmic discovery. Mechanisms for systematically evaluating application efficiency would be useful for maximizing the efficient use of resources.

4. There is room for increasing utilization, whether with more diverse user job mix or possibly scheduler tuning, though utilization is already high.

The road to exascale has multiple challenges, including the power wall, the memory wall, resilience issues and the need for unprecedented levels of parallelism [4]. Developing applications for new hardware paradigms historically has never occurred in a vacuum but has always been based on existing applications. New classes of HPC hardware must provide a migration path for porting existing codes to the new systems. A well-designed science code can embody tens or hundreds of person-years of effort and many years of development time which are not quickly reproduced. Some applications, due to their size, design and modularity, may be moved across the architectural divide with a reasonable amount of refactoring, though codes specifically rewritten for the new hardware are often those that thrive best in the long run. The modifications that are required to port the applications cannot be entirely known in advance and can only be discovered during the process of redesign, rewriting and refactoring. The current study provides one snapshot of application status at the petascale, providing a starting point on the road from petascale to exascale.

8. ACKNOWLEDGEMENTS

The authors thank ORNL staff who provided input to this study, including Buddy Bland, Mark Fahey, Chris Fuson, Al Geist, Mitch Griffith, Rebecca Hartman-Baker, Joshua Hursey, Ricky Kendall, Don Maxwell, Bronson Messer, Maggie Miller, Hai Ah Nam, Jack Wells and Julia White. The authors also thank the reviewers for their helpful comments.

This research used resources of the Oak Ridge Leadership Computing Facility at Oak Ridge National Laboratory, which is supported by the Office of Science of the U.S. Department of Energy under Contract No. DE-AC05-00OR22725. This document describes research performed under contract number DE-AC0500OR22750 between the U.S. Department of Energy and Oak Ridge Associated Universities.

9. REFERENCES

[1] David H. Bailey, "Computing: The Third Mode of Scientific Discovery" presented at University of Newcastle, Australia, August 2009, http://crd.lbl.gov/~dhbailey/dhbtalks/dhb-grinnell.pdf.

[2] —, "The opportunities and Challenges of Exascale Computing: Summary Report of the Advanced Scientific Computing Advisory Committee (ASCAC) Subcommittee," Fall 2010, http://science.energy.gov//media/ascr/-ascac/pdf/reports/Exascale_subcommittee_report.pdf.

[3] —, "US DOE SC ASCR Software Effectiveness," SciDac, San Diego, CA, June 17, 2009, https://hpcrd.lbl.gov/scidac09/talks/joule-scidac09.pdf.

[4] Peter Kogge, ed., *ExaScale Computing Study: Technology Challenges in Achieving Exascale Systems*, DARPA, 2008, http://users.ece.gatech.edu/mrichard/-ExascaleComputingStudyReports/ECS_reports.htm.

[5] Peter Kogge, "Update on Current Trends and Roadblocks," *2011 Workshop on Architectures I: Exascale and Beyond: Gaps in Research, Gaps in our Thinking*, ORAU, 2011, http://www.orau.gov/archI2011/presentations/koggep.pdf.

[6] CUDA, http://www.nvidia.com/object/cuda_home_new.html.

[7] OpenCL, http://www.khronos.org/opencl.

[8] OpenACC, http://www.openacc-standard.org.

[9] TOP500, http://top500.org.

[10] DOE INCITE Program, http://www.doeleadershipcomputing.org/incite-program.

[11] MOAB, http://www.adaptivecomputing.com/products/moab-hpc-suite-basic.php.

[12] Portable Batch System, http://en.wikipedia.org/wiki/Portable_Batch_System.

[13] Michael Karo, "ALPS: Application Level Placement Scheduler," *Cray User Group Meeting*, 2006, http://www.adaptivecomputing.com/products/moab-hpc-suite-basic.php.

[14] 2011 INCITE Awards, http://science.energy.gov/~media/ascr/pdf/incite/docs/2011_incite_factsheets.pdf.

[15] Titan, Oak Ridge Leadership Computing Facility, http://www.olcf.ornl.gov/titan.

[16] James Patton Jones and Bill Nitzberg, "Scheduling for parallel supercomputing: a historical perspective of achievable utilization," in D. Feitelson and L. Rudolph (eds.), *Lecture Notes in Computer Science*, Vol. 1659. Berlin: Springer, 1999, pp. 1–16, http://citeseerx.ist.psu.edu/viewdoc/summary?doi=10.1.1.23.3413.

[17] Julia C. White, "2011 INCITE Process and Awards", ASCAC, March 22, 2011, http://science.energy.gov/~/media/ascr/ascac/pdf/meetings/mar11/White.pdf.

[18] David L Hart, "Measuring TeraGrid: workload characterization for a high-performance computing federation," *International Journal of High Performance Computing Applications*, 25: 451-465, November 2011, http://hpc.sagepub.com/content/25/4/451.

[19] X. J. Yang, X. K. Liao, K. Lu et. al., "The Tianhe-1A supercomputer: Its hardware and software," *Journal of Computer Science and Technology*, 26(3): 344–351, May 2011, http://www.springerlink.com/content/h70244371pr727g0.

[20] K Computer, RIKEN Advanced Institute for Computer Science, http://www.aics.riken.jp/en/kcomputer/what.html.

[21] Gaea, National Climate-Computing Research Center, http://www.ncrc.gov/computing-resources/gaea/.

[22] Wayne Joubert, Douglas Kothe and Hai Ah Nam, *Preparing for Exascale: ORNL Leadership Computing Facility Application Requirements and Strategy*, Oak Ridge National Laboratory ORNL/TM-2009/308, December 2009. http://www.olcf.ornl.gov/wp-content/uploads/2010/03/olcf-requirements.pdf.

[23] Katie Antipas, John Shalf and Harvey Wasserman, "NERSC Workload and Benchmark Selection Process," August 13, 2008, http://escholarship.org/uc/item/7qd192rr.

Multiple Sub-Row Buffers in DRAM: Unlocking Performance and Energy Improvement Opportunities

Nagendra Gulur
Texas Instruments (India)
nagendra@ti.com

Mahesh Mehendale
Texas Instruments (India)
m-mehendale@ti.com

R Manikantan
Indian Institute of Science
rmani@csa.iisc.ernet.in

R Govindarajan
Indian Institute of Science
govind@serc.iisc.ernet.in

ABSTRACT

The twin demands of energy-efficiency and higher performance on DRAM are highly emphasized in multicore architectures. A variety of schemes have been proposed to address either the latency or the energy consumption of DRAMs. These schemes typically require non-trivial hardware changes and end up improving latency at the cost of energy or vice-versa.

One specific DRAM performance problem in multicores is that interleaved accesses from different cores can potentially degrade row-buffer locality. In this paper, based on the temporal and spatial locality characteristics of memory accesses, we propose a reorganization of the existing single large row-buffer in a DRAM bank into multiple sub-row buffers (MSRB). This re-organization not only improves row hit rates, and hence the average memory latency, but also brings down the energy consumed by the DRAM. The first major contribution of this work is proposing such a reorganization without requiring any significant changes to the existing widely accepted DRAM specifications. Our proposed reorganization improves weighted speedup by 35.8%, 14.5% and 21.6% in quad, eight and sixteen core workloads along with a 42%, 28% and 31% reduction in DRAM energy.

The proposed MSRB organization enables opportunities for the management of multiple row-buffers at the memory controller level. As the memory controller is aware of the behaviour of individual cores it allows us to implement coordinated buffer allocation schemes for different cores that take into account program behaviour. We demonstrate two such schemes, namely *Fairness Oriented Allocation* and *Performance Oriented Allocation*, which show the flexibility that memory controllers can now exploit in our MSRB organization to improve overall performance and/or fairness.

Further, the MSRB organization enables additional opportunities for DRAM intra-bank parallelism and selective early precharging of the LRU row-buffer to further improve memory access latencies. These two optimizations together provide an additional 5.9% performance improvement.

Categories and Subject Descriptors

C.1.2 [**PROCESSOR ARCHITECTURES**]: [Multiple Data Stream Architectures (Multiprocessors)]

Keywords

DRAM, Memory Performance, Multi-Core Architecture

1. INTRODUCTION

With the widening gap between processor and memory performance, the memory performance can impact the overall performance of a multicore system in a significant way. Further, the energy consumption of DRAM memory accounts for a non-trivial (greater than 30%) part of the system energy [10], [11]. The importance of energy efficiency and performance of DRAM is emphasized by current trends in high-performance computing which achieve performance scaling via multicores. In both server-class and personal computers, multicore configurations are becoming widespread with several cores sharing DRAM memory that is accessed via one or more memory controllers. Thus a recent research focus has been on improving the performance and energy efficiency of DRAM design which has traditionally been architected to address high density and low cost.

A key component of DRAM that impacts both performance and energy is the row-buffer. When an access request is made to a bank in DRAM, it fetches a large row of data (typically 8KB – 16KB, across all devices accessed in parallel) into the row-buffer. This operation is known as *row-activate*. In the presence of spatial locality, future requests to the same row hit in the row-buffer. In these cases, the row-buffer provides the data, which reduces both access latency and the energy consumed as the row-activate operation is eliminated. A request to a different row in the same bank replaces the row-buffer with the contents of the new row, after the current row-buffer is written back (*precharge*).

The spatial locality exploited in the row-buffer is greatly reduced when accesses from multiple cores get interleaved at the DRAM [13]. A number of memory access re-ordering schemes [1, 2, 3, 25, 4], varying in complexity from the simple FR-FCFS (First Ready-First Come First Served) [5] to the more complex reinforcement learning based approach [25], have been proposed to improve row-buffer hits. Further address re-mapping in hardware or software [8] and memory access re-ordering schemes that are prefetch-aware have also been proposed [9]. While these schemes are effective in improving performance, they do not address the issue of energy reduction directly. Further, they require non-trivial modifications and complex scheduling policies to be implemented at the memory controller.

One significant contributor to the high energy consumption inside DRAMs is the frequent row Activate and Precharge operations to move data back and forth between the row-buffer and the DRAM core. Common methods proposed to reduce DRAM energy include smaller row-buffers [12], storage re-organization [13], and exploiting opportunities for power-down modes of operation [14]. However, these methods generally incur performance degradation and also introduce hardware complexity. For instance, smaller row-buffers reduce the energy consumption at the expense of lower hit rates and a small performance loss.

Though there is a lack of spatial locality, multi-programmed workloads do exhibit considerable temporal locality among memory accesses, at the level of DRAM pages/rows [15]. The observed temporal and spatial locality characteristics make a strong case for having multiple smaller row-buffers per bank instead of a single row-buffer. Such a configuration has been known to provide benefits in the context of Phase Change Memory [15]. However, such a row-buffer reorganization and its impact on performance and energy reduction has not been studied in the context of DRAMs. This is important as the challenge is to accomplish this reorganization under a fairly rigid JEDEC standard [17]. Further, the proposed organization enables a set of optimization opportunities which have not been explored thus far and are relevant specifically for DRAMs.

Our first contribution is to propose a practical design to incorporate multiple sub-row buffers (MSRBs) in DRAMs with minimal changes to the existing DRAM specifications. A study of multiple narrow row-buffers in the context of DRAM shows that it can significantly improve both performance and energy in multi-cores. The performance gains (in terms of weighted speedup) over the baseline are 35.8%, 14.5% and 21% respectively for quad, eight and sixteen cores respectively. This gain in performance is achieved along with an energy reduction of 42%, 28% and 31%. We refer to this organization as MSRB.

The necessary controls for implementing MSRB are incorporated at the memory controller. While this allows the DRAM design changes to be minimal with no changes to the pin interface, it also opens up opportunities for further optimizations to effectively utilize the row-buffers to achieve performance and/or fairness goals. This is because unlike the DRAM, an on-chip memory controller can observe the behavior of various cores and hence can manage the allocation of row buffers to suit the observed beahvior. We demonstrate two such buffer allocation strategies - *Fairness Oriented Allocation* and *Performance Oriented Allocation*. Fairness-oriented Allocation allocates dedicated row-buffers to cores that suffer the most interference thereby improving both performance and fairness. This allocation scheme improves fairness by 43%. Performance-oriented Allocation takes into account the differing memory bandwidth requirements of the various cores and tries to allocate row buffers to cores in line with their demand. Results show that this scheme further improves performance.

Our third contribution is to examine the additional optimizations enabled by our multiple row-buffer design. On a row-buffer miss, it is essential to write back the currently open row, before the newly requested data can be brought into the row-buffer. This precharge latency is typically in the critical path of memory requests. In a multiple row-buffer configuration, it is possible to do an eager precharge of the least recently used row-buffer. This proactive approach, which we refer to as *Early Precharge*, hides the precharge latency that will be experienced by a future request that misses in the row-buffer. This optimization improves performance by an additional 1.8% over MSRB design. A second optimization enabled by the new design is the ability to simultaneously service row-hit requests from one row-buffer while a different row-buffer is being

activated or precharged. This introduces *Intra-Bank Parallelism*, which is in addition to bank-level, rank-level and controller-level parallelism, and improves performance by an additional 4.7% over MSRB. The *Early Precharge* and *Intra-bank Parallelism* optimizations taken together yield an additional performance improvement of 5.9%.

Last, we compare our row-buffer reorganization with two best-in-class memory controller schedulers (Thread Cluster Memory (TCM) scheduling [1] and Parallelism Aware Batch Scheduling (PARBS) [2]) and demonstrate that our design produces far greater system throughput than what is achieved via scheduler optimizations alone. Further, we compare our results against a hypothetical DRAM device which is highly banked (32-banks and 256-columns per bank structure). We observe that our proposed MSRB organization is more effective, in terms of both performance and energy, than a highly banked DRAM with just one small row-buffer per bank.

2. BACKGROUND AND MOTIVATION

In this section, we provide the necessary background and the required motivation for our work.

2.1 Background

We consider the popular JEDEC-style ([17]) DRAM as the baseline architecture throughout the paper. DRAM devices are packaged as Dual In-line Memory Modules (*DIMMs*) which are interfaced typically to an on-chip memory controller. DIMMs contain one or more *ranks*. A rank is a collection of DRAM devices that operate in parallel. Each DRAM device typically serves up a few bits at the specified (row, column) location. Operating together, the devices in a rank match the data bus width. For example, an $x16$ device supplies 16 bits of data and 4 such devices making up a rank can supply data needed to match the 64-bit interface of the memory controller. Each device in a rank is organized into a number (4, 8 or 16) of logically independent banks. Each bank consists of multiple *rows* (also called *pages*) of data. Banks within the same rank can operate in parallel and this provides for some degree of memory level parallelism. Figure 1 shows a diagrammatic description of this organization.

A typical DRAM read request has to first *Activate* the corresponding row by bringing the row data to the row-buffer. This is followed by a column read/write that reads/writes the selected words from/to the row-buffer. Finally *Precharge* writes back the row-buffer to the appropriate row. *Precharge* is needed even on rows that were only read, since row activation depletes the charge in the corresponding row in the DRAM device. Each bank is equipped with its own row buffer and logic to perform row Activate (termed *RAS*), column read/write (termed *CAS*) and Precharge (termed *PRE*) operations. An *open page*[5] policy delays precharging until just before the next row activate has to be performed, while the *closed page* policy eagerly precharges the row soon after the first read-/write operation to this row. The memory controller is responsible for efficient scheduling of requests, as well as for the implementation of the DRAM access protocol. Each cycle, the controller selects a valid command by examining the set of pending requests and issues it to the memory.

2.2 Motivation

A typical DRAM bank is equipped with a large row buffer comprising 1024 to 2048 columns. This large buffer size is an artifact of the original use-model it was intended for, viz., exploiting spatial locality while serving requests from a single core processor. In the multicore scenario wherein requests from multiple workloads are

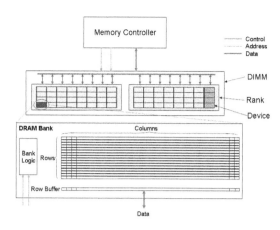

Figure 1: DRAM organization overview

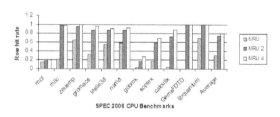

Figure 2: Cumulative stack distance histogram of hits with large (1024 columns) row buffers

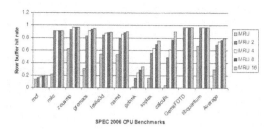

Figure 3: Cumulative stack distance histogram of hits with small (256 columns) row buffers

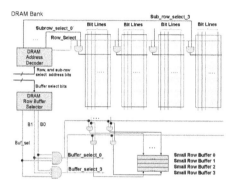

Figure 4: Multipel Sub-Row Buffer Organization

interleaved by the memory controller, there is insufficient reuse of the open row buffer. Further, modern programs have large working sets and even single-core programs could access multiple rows in succession in a bank. These scenarios favor the closed page policy (which precharges and closes the page immediately after the first use) as the de-facto policy, incurring high access time and energy by bringing in a large row for a single word or cacheline. The above observations indicate a potential benefit in using multiple small row-buffers for each bank in the DRAM. Figure 2 shows cumulative stack distance histograms of row hit rates achieved in the top 1, 2, and 4 (Most Recently Used) positions for a representative subset of SPEC 2006 CPU workloads with 1024-columns wide row buffers, while Figure 3 shows the same data for 256-columns wide row buffers. A detailed description of the experimental methodology, simulated configuration, and workloads is included in Section 5.

The graph in Figure 2 shows that, on the average, the hit rate more than doubles as we go from one row-buffer to even just two buffers. This is especially observed in memory intensive programs, e.g. milc, gromacs, soplex, and calculix. Two (or more) row buffers appear to work significantly better at capturing temporal/spatial locality in programs.

The graph in Figure 3 shows the crucial observation for our motivation: *small buffers do nearly as well as their larger counterparts in exploiting spatial locality.* On average, we observed that small buffers captured over 90% of the hits seen with larger ones.

This study reveals that multiple small row-buffers per bank help improve temporal locality without significant loss in spatial locality. Incorporating this into DRAMs within the existing DRAM standards pose certain challenges. At the same time, the MSRB also offers a few additional opportunities such as implementing

different row-buffer management policies for performance and fairness, and optimizations such as Early Precharging and Intra-Bank Parallel accesses. We address these topics in the following sections.

3. MULTIPLE SUB-ROW BUFFER ORGANIZATION

In this section, we describe our MSRB organization for DRAM. Specifically, we replace the one large row-buffer in each bank by four small row-buffers, each one-fourth the size of the original. This organization consists of three components, namely (i) Sub-row activation, (ii) Row-buffer selection, and (iii) Row-Buffer allocation. We describe the first two components in detail below while the row-buffer allocation is deferred to Section 4. Figure 4 provides an overview of a DRAM bank organized to support multiple small row buffers.

3.1 Sub-Row Activation

In order to select the appropriate sub-row, the DRAM needs to have access to both the row address and a part of the column address. Once both are available, the DRAM logic decodes and activates both row_select_i and $sub\_row\_select\_j$ lines and fetches the selected columns to a row buffer. While row_select lines run across the entire length of the row, they need only participate in the sub-row decoding and as such have very little load on them. At the selected sub-row, the traditional wordline is activated to access the entire sub-row. Our implementation of sub-row activation is similar to that described in [12].

To perform sub-row activation, the DRAM needs both the row address (from the RAS command) and a few address bits from the column access command (CAS), since the sub-row selection is dependent on a few column address bits: 2 bits if the size of each sub-row is $\frac{1}{4}$-th the size of the row. In a traditional DRAM interface, the RAS command is issued first and the CAS command follows it a few cycles later. This is done in order to multiplex row and column addresses onto the same set of pins. In the JEDEC standard, a timing parameter termed tRCD specifies the gap between the two commands that has to be met [17], and is typically of the order of 10-15 nano-seconds. With such tRCD delay, a naive scheme which waits for the column address would introduce intolerably high latency to sub-row activation. In order to avoid this, we discuss at least three alternatives that could get the sub-row select address bits to the DRAM without incurring the RAS-to-CAS delay:

- Expanding the address pins by additional sub-row-select pins would address the sub-row selection problem in a straightforward way. Typically, this is an additional 2 to 3 pins depending on the size of the sub-row relative to the full row. Though simple, given the slow growth in pin-count, we do not consider this a feasible option.

- Issue RAS and CAS commands in back to back cycles. The DRAM is expected to latch the addresses issued in these two commands and use them at appropriate times internally. This scheme is termed *Posted-RAS* in [12] and *Posted-CAS* in [24]. There is a 1-cycle delay incurred in this scheme. We chose not to use this scheme due to this 1-cycle latency addition to an already large DRAM access latency.

- Modern DRAMs support double-data-rate transfers on the data pins (hence termed *DDR*). That is, both the DRAM and the memory controller have the capability to transmit/receive data at twice the bus clock. One could extend this capability to address pins as well. A RAS command issued on the rising edge of the bus clock followed by the sub-row-select command issued on the falling of that bus clock serves to transfer all the necessary address bits in one clock cycle and thus incurs no latency in sub-row activation. We term this scheme *Double-Address-Rate*. This is the scheme we assume in our detailed simulations. A similar proposal for fast signalling of address bits appears in [26].

3.2   Row-Buffer Selection

The introduction of multiple row-buffers necessitates a few additional changes in the overall memory organization: i) the memory controller needs to remember the sub-rows in each bank that are currently available in the row-buffers. This is required so that no RAS command is issued for a sub-row that is already available in a row-buffer. ii) when a new sub-row is activated, allocation of a row buffer that will store the newly fetched sub-row data. iii) ensure precharge for the sub-row that is being replaced. Responsibilities (i) and (iii) are necessarily handled by the memory controller even in the case of a single row-buffer. We feel it is natural to let the memory controller handle these responsibilities even for multiple row-buffers. Further, as the controller maintains the book-keeping information regarding open sub-rows, responsibility (ii) can also be handled by the controller. This decision helps in keeping the DRAM logic simple. Essentially, the controller has to maintain cache-like metadata for these buffers: valid bits, row and sub-row tags, and recency bits. We observe that this decision of letting the memory controller manage row-buffer usage not only keeps DRAM logic simple but has several additional benefits, including:

- Enforcement of different row-buffer allocation policies (for instance, the controller could enforce specialized fairness oriented or performance oriented row-buffer allocation policies to suit the memory access characteristics of workloads)

- Holistic management of the pool of row-buffers available across all the DRAM banks in all the DRAM ranks.

In each of the three DRAM access operations (Activate, Precharge, Column Access), a row buffer is accessed. Therefore we look at each operation and discuss signaling and timing issues involved in specifying row-buffer selection information:

- Activate: Row buffer selection is not in the timing critical path for this operation since the DRAM has to first activate the sub-row and start discharging column data onto bit lines. Thus, the row buffer selection should only be ready by the time bit lines have been driven from the storage cells. Thus a simple mechanism such as signaling the row buffer specification bits in the cycle following the RAS command suffices. We call this Posted-Buffer-Selection. This requires no additional pins. Alternatively, the buffer selection bits could be driven along with the sub-row selection bits using the Double-Address-Rate scheme.

- Precharge: In this case, we assume that the row-buffer selection is timing critical. For this operation, the controller needs to specify both the sub-row selection bits as well as the row-buffer selection bits. We propose to use the *double-address-rate* scheme to accomplish this transfer without adding latency.

- Column Access: We assume that row-buffer selection is timing critical to column accesses as well and use the *Double-Address-Rate* mechanism to issue these bits quickly.

The *Double-Address-Rate* scheme thus takes care of signalling both the sub-row selection bits as well as the row-buffer selection bits without incurring additional latency.

3.3   Row-Buffer Allocation

Our MSRB organization requires the memory controller to decide which of the buffers to allocate for a new row activation. For our default configuration, we employ the commonly used *Least Recently Used* (LRU) policy in the memory controller to make this allocation decision. We defer a more detailed discussion of alternative allocation policies to Section 4.

3.4   Sources of Energy Reduction

Energy savings in MSRB are obtained as a combination of:

1. Reduction in the energy consumed by each Activate and Precharge operation due to smaller rows: Since fewer capacitors have to be charged and discharged, and fewer bits have to be latched in the sense amps, the energy consumed reduces.
2. Reduction in the number of Activate and Precharge operations due to fewer row misses: Multiple row-buffers offer higher data retentivity in the buffers thereby reducing the number of times that rows are activated and precharged. Every additional row hit saves the energy that would have been expended in precharging one row and activating another.

Our scheme results in additional energy reduction due to the fact that more row hits lead to fewer total memory cycles, thereby saving additional background power.

3.5   Area Impact

Area overheads comprise the MSRB re-organization overhead in DRAM as well as the book-keeping overhead inside the memory controller, and we discuss each below.

3.5.1 DRAM Area Overhead

In the following discussion, we assume an MSRB organization comprising 4 small row-buffers per bank. Our estimate of the area overhead in MSRB includes: additional decoders for sub-row selection, running additional sub-row selection lines (wires), additional decoders for row-buffer selection, additional multiplexers to control data routing between selected sub-row & selected row-buffer, and additional wiring for data routing.

- *Sub_row_select* lines and AND gates: Since the size of each small row buffer is $\frac{1}{4}$-th the size of the full row buffer, we need to run 4 *sub_row_select* lines and add ($4 \times$ number of rows) AND gates. Each gate adds about 6 additional transistors to the decode logic. As in [12], this was implemented using hierarchical word lines [26] and modeled analytically in CACTI [27]. The CACTI model is set up for exploring the highest density implementation as is the case with commodity DRAMs. With these, we obtain an area overhead of 4.9% to support splitting each row into 4 sub-rows.

- Row-buffer selection demultiplexers, and *buffer_select_n* lines: Since each operation has to access one of the 4 available row-buffers, additional decode circuitry is added to decode two buffer selection bits and drive the appropriate buffer selection lines. While the buffers themselves are sense amps that have a much larger transistor size, the decoder logic transistors are of a smaller transistor size and thus do not significantly increase area. We lay out the 4 small buffers in a 2×2 configuration allowing for efficient wiring of *buffer_select_n* lines. Modeling these overheads in CACTI, we obtain an area overhead of 1.9%.

- Note that in our design, the total storage capacity of the row-buffers (4 buffers of one-fourth the size compared to a single large buffer) does not increase. Thus our design is buffer-capacity-neutral.

Thus the total area overhead of the proposed re-organization is 6.8% per DRAM bank[1].

3.5.2 Area Overhead in the Memory Controller

The memory controller has to maintain certain metadata — tags, valid bits, dirty bits, and recency bits — which constitutes the overhead. This overhead is less than 16 bytes for the 4 row-buffers in a bank. For a 4 GB RAM organized as 4 ranks and 8 banks, this overhead would be $4 \times 8 \times 16 = 512$ bytes. For the baseline with one row buffer per bank, the memory controller still incurs one-fourth of this overhead (128 bytes) since it has to maintain this state information anyway. We consider the additional storage overhead negligible.

4. UNLOCKING PERFORMANCE, ENERGY AND FAIRNESS OPPORTUNITIES

Our MSRB organization opens up the design space for row-buffer *allocation* and *management* — policies for allocation of these resources across the cores for performance and/or fairness benefits. As discussed in Section 3.3, the row-buffer allocation decision is done at the memory controller. While a detailed exploration of allocation policies is outside the scope of this paper, we present two

---

[1]We note here that the commercial DRAM implementations are highly optimized and the area estimates and overheads calculated using tools such as Cactii may differ from these. However, the commercial designs are proprietory and are(almost) never available for research studies (even if they are available such data is seldom published due to business and other reasons).

---

simple schemes below to illustrate the flexibility that row-buffer reorganization facilitates. The first - *Fairness oriented Buffer Allocation* - improves fairness via judicious buffer allocation. The *Performance oriented Buffer Allocation* improves performance of programs with high miss rates. In addition, we discuss a pair of scheduling and hardware optimizations, namely: *Early Precharge* and *Intra Bank Parallelism* that are enabled by MSRB. The net effect of improving performance (via increased row hits) is to also reduce energy consumption. All of these optimizations are implementated at the memory controller [2].

4.1 Fairness-oriented Buffer Allocation

Here, the intuition is that in a typical multicore workload, some cores stand to benefit a lot more from higher row-buffer hit rates than others. Since the interleaving of requests from multiple cores causes cores with lower arrival rates to suffer greater row-buffer misses, this allocation scheme counters the disproportionate increase in miss rate by allocating dedicated buffers for such cores. The scheme works by maintaining on a per-core basis, the actual row-buffer hit rate as well as an estimate of the hit rate had the core been running alone (referred to as *standalone hit rate*). The standalone hit rate is obtained by keeping a shadow row buffer (one per core) in the memory controller which would be updated only with the requests from the given core. The difference between the standalone hit rate and the shared (actual) hit rate provides an estimate of the loss suffered by the core due to interference. If this difference exceeds a threshold (in our case, it is set to 0.5), we classify the core as suffering unfairness. The scheduler then attempts to allocate dedicated buffers to cores suffering unfairness. For instance, if one of 4 cores in a quad-core configuration is unfairly suffering, then the scheduler dedicates one of the 4 row-buffers to this core, while the other 3 row-buffers are made available to all the cores.

For each core c and bank b, the scheme computes the difference $d = $ (standalone hit rate $-$ shared hit rate). Higher values of this measure suggest higher benefits by dedicating buffers to such cores. At each bank, this metric is used to classify the core:

- Type-1: Core with $d \geq threshold$
- Type-2: Core with $d < threshold$

Since the classification is done per-bank, this scheme can inherently self-adjust to variations in bank utilization. The same core could be classified Type-1 in one bank while classified Type-2 in another. This classification is done periodically so as to adapt to program behavior changes. The controller then allocates dedicated row-buffers for Type-1 cores. In our implementation, we chose the below scheme:

- Only 1 Type-1 core in the workload: The Type-1 core gets one dedicated buffer, all cores can access remaining 3 buffers
- Two Type-1 cores in the workload: Each Type-1 core gets one dedicated buffer, all cores can access remaining 2 buffers
- Three or more Type-1 cores in the workload: It defaults to LRU scheme.

Whenever a core needs to activate a new row, the controller looks up the allocated buffers for that core and chooses the LRU buffer from amongst these to bring the new row into.

4.2 Performance-oriented Buffer Allocation

This scheme works by dynamically adapting buffer allocations to the most demanding cores. The scheme estimates the needs of each

---

[2]intraBP requires minor DRAM interfaces changes to permit multiple outstanding accesses to each bank

core periodically on a per-bank basis by taking into account the number of memory requests (i.e., misses from the last-level cache) from each core, and the row-buffer miss rates suffered by each core at each bank. For each core c and bank b, it computes a *rate product* defined as: $rate\_product[c][b] = num\_memory\_requests[c][b] \times row\_miss\_rate[c][b]$. Higher values of this measure suggest higher benefits by improving their hit rates. At each bank, rate products are used to classify cores into one of two types:

- Type-1: Core with $rate\_product \geq threshold$
- Type-2: Core with $rate\_product < threshold$

Several variations of this scheme are possible. We use a simple scheme which defaults to LRU allocation when the number of Type-1 workloads for a bank exceeds half the number of row-buffers per bank (2 in our case). Otherwise, the allocation scheme allows each Type-1 workload to have exclusive use of certain row-buffers (upto 2 in our case) and shared use of the remaining row-buffers by all workloads, similar to the previous scheme.

For both the above schemes, the storage overhead in the memory controller is neglibily small (of the order of $R \times B \times M \times N$ bytes for R ranks, B banks per rank, M buffers per bank, and N cores).

4.3 Early Precharge Scheduling

Traditionally, memory controllers use either an *open page* or *closed page* policy for precharging rows. The policy essentially determines whether to precharge an open page eagerly (closed page) or lazily (open page). Eager policies work better in situations where it is highly likely that the next request would cause a row buffer eviction. Multiple row-buffers open up the possibility to precharge different row-buffers using different policies. We implemented *selective early precharge scheduling* wherein only the LRU row-buffer is precharged early while the rest of the row-buffers follow the open-page policy. The rationale for this is that the LRU row-buffer is most likely to be the candidate for eviction and is better off precharged early while the other row-buffers are more likely to see additional row-hits and therefore are kept open. Eagerly precharging the LRU buffer helps to reduce the latency of a subsequent row-buffer miss. In our implementation, the memory controller looks for idle cycles and inserts precharge operations for the LRU row-buffer in each bank. While this scheduling is orthogonal to the row-buffer allocation schemes described in the earlier section, we only implemented it over the baseline LRU policy for our experiments.

4.4 Intra-Bank Parallelism

Multiple row-buffers permit parallel operations within a bank: column accesses on one row-buffer could occur in parallel with an activate or precharge operation on another. While each individual memory access follows the standard DRAM access protocol, this optimization (abbreviated intraBP) allows pipeling of operations at each bank. It improves the efficiency of data bus utilization by allowing us to issue column accesses faster. Inside each DRAM bank, the necessary circuitry to support this parallelism is already available. The memory scheduler can easily incorporate this enhancement into its scheduling of sub-commands. Figure 5 shows an example timing diagram indicating this parallelism wherein a row activation or a precharge operation occurs concurrently with a column access. This helps to hide some of the activate and precharge latencies via this optimization and it effectively translates to higher bandwidth and lower latency. In particular, programs that have low bank-level parallelism are greatly benefited by this feature since the scheduler is unable to keep multiple banks busy in parallel. Note that exploiting intraBP is not possible without multiple row-buffers.

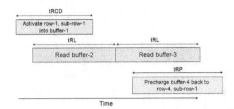

Figure 5: Example of intra-bank parallelism

Processor	3.2 GHz OOO Alpha ISA
L1I Cache	32kB private, 64 byte blocks, Direct-mapped, 3 cycle hit latency
L1D Cache	32kB private, 64 byte blocks, 2-way set-associative, 3 cycle hit latency
L2 Cache	For 1/4/8/16 cores: 1MB/4MB/8MB/16MB 4-way/8-way/16-way/32-way 32/128/256/512 MSHRs 64-byte blocks, 15 cycle hit latency
Controller	On-chip; 64-bit interface to DRAM 256-entry command queue FR_FCFS scheduling [5], open-page policy Address-interleaving: rank-bank-row-column Number of memory controllers for 1/4/8/16 cores: 1/1/2/4
DRAM	DDR3-1600H, BL=8, CL-nRCD-nRP=9-9-9 a rank comprises 4 1GB x16 devices, each device has 8 banks, each bank has 65536 rows, 1024 columns

Table 1: CMP configuration

5. EXPERIMENTAL METHODOLOGY

5.1 Simulation Setup

We evaluate our design using M5 [18] simulator integrated with a detailed in-house DRAM simulator. The DRAM simulator faithfully models both the memory controller as well as the DRAM with accurate timing. Each program in the workload is executed in fast-forward mode for 9 billion instructions, then in warm-up mode for 500 million instructions and finally, in detailed cycle-accurate mode for 250 million instructions. Multi-core simulations are run until all the programs complete 250 million instructions.[3] As is the standard practice, programs that finish early continue to execute but the performance of only the first 250 million instructions is considered for each core.

The baseline machine configuration used in our studies is shown in Table 1. L2 is the last level cache and is shared across all the cores. The baseline configuration (1×1024) has a single large 1024 columns wide row-buffer. Our MSRB configuration (4×256) uses 4 narrow row buffers, each 256 columns wide. MSRB is managed using a LRU buffer allocation policy unless specified otherwise. While the quad-core has one memory controller, the eight and sixteen cores have two and four memory controllers respectively.

5.2 Power Estimation

We estimate the impact of our proposed row-buffer reorganization on DRAM power consumption using Micron's PowerCalculator spreadsheet [19]. The spreadsheet models power consumption of a DRAM configuration by allowing the user to input DRAM

---

[3] Although we run only 250M Instructions per core in cycle-accurate mode, our 4, 8 and 16-core simulations each runs for a total of 1 Billion - 4 Billion instructions in cycle-accurate mode.

Quad-Core Workloads
Q1:(462,459,470,433), Q2:(429,183,462,459), Q3:(181,435,197,473),
Q4:(429,462,471,464), Q5:(470,437,187,300), Q6:(462,470,473,300),
Q7:(459,464,183,433), Q8:(410,464,445,433), Q9:(462,459,445,410),
Q10:(429,456,450,459), Q11:(181,186,300,177), Q12:(168,401,435,464)
Eight Core Workloads
E1:(462,459,433,456,464,473,450,445),
E2:(300,456,470,445,179,464,473,450),
E3:(168,183,437,401,435,445,458),
E4:(187,172,173,410,470,433,444,177),
E5:(434,435,450,453,462,471,164,186),
E6:(181,473,401,172,177,178,179,435),
E7:(437,459,445,454,456,465,171,197),
E8:(429,416,433,454,464,435,444,458)
Sixteen Core Workloads
S1:(462,459,433,179,183,473,450,445,444,470,429,171,168,172,435,458)
S2:(401,433,434,435,444,445,450,300,459,470,471,473,171,181,179,183)
S3:(178,177,168,172,173,187,191,410,429,434,462,473,465,458,464,445)
S4:(186,454,458,482,181,429,255,254,178,197,179,187,173,401,410,437)

Table 2: Workloads

Weighted Speedup (WS) $= \sum_i \frac{IPC_i^{shared}}{IPC_i^{alone}}$

Minimum slowdown $= \min_i \frac{IPC_i^{alone}}{IPC_i^{shared}}$

Harmonic Speedup (HS) $= \frac{N}{\sum_i \frac{IPC_i^{alone}}{IPC_i^{shared}}}$

Maximum slowdown $= \max_i \frac{IPC_i^{alone}}{IPC_i^{shared}}$

Fairness $= \frac{\text{Minimum slowdown}}{\text{Maximum slowdown}}$

Table 3: Performance and Fairness metrics

configuration parameters and system usage values. We obtain the power requirements for both the baseline and the multiple row-buffer organization using this spreadsheet. For the baseline, we use the default settings provided for -125E speed grade. Change to Activate & Precharge power is modeled by adjusting the value of IDD0, the foreground current that drives these operations. Using the equation given in [ ], and conservatively estimating a reduction of IDD0 from 120mA to 95mA, we compute the Activate and Precharge power dissipation for the new organization. We also assume that column access power increases by 5% owing to the addition of row-buffer selection logic. In our studies, we separately estimate the power reductions coming from the two independent factors, namely smaller rows requiring lesser power and fewer Activate/Precharge operations. The power number along with the execution time is used to compute the DRAM energy consumption. We do not model the additional power consumption in the memory controller as the added logic there is marginal and relatively simple.

5.3 Workload and Metrics

We use multi-programmed workloads comprising programs from SPEC [ ] 2000 and SPEC 2006 suites to evaluate our proposal. The workloads are typically a mix of programs with varying levels of memory intensity (based on their L2 MPKI). The workload mix used in our studies is presented in Table 2.

We use weighted speedup [ ] and harmonic speedup [ ] to summarize performance. We report fairness using the ratio of minimum slowdown to maximum slowdown. These terms are defined in Table 3.

6. RESULTS

In this section, we evaluate the impact of MSRB on system performance and the energy benefits[4] provided by it. Further we compare it with state-of-the-art memory access scheduling methods designed to improve row hit rate. A study on the performance improvements due to memory controller side buffer allocation is also presented.

6.1 Performance Benefits of MSRB

The performance of MSRB for the quad-core case is summarized in Figure 6. As can be seen from Figure 6(a), MSRB improves the weighted speedup by 35.8% over 1×1024. The performance gain in terms of harmonic speedup, as shown in Figure 6(b), is 27.5%. All the workloads show improved performance with MSRB. This shows the importance of focusing on the temporal locality (multiple row-buffers) at the cost of spatial locality (narrow row-buffers). MSRB achieves a significantly higher row-buffer hit rate of 0.6 (in Figure 6(c)) as compared to 0.2 observed in the baseline case. The observed gains in performance are typically in line with the improvement in row-buffer hit rate.

Figure 7 shows the performance improvement in terms of weighted speedup for 8 and 16 core workloads. MSRB provides 14.5% and 21.6% improvement in performance for 8 and 16 core workloads respectively over baseline. An interesting case-study is the row-buffer hit rates experienced by the individual programs in the workload E1. Figure 7(b) shows the hit rates experienced by the individual programs for baseline and MSRB. It can be seen that the row-buffer hit rate improves with MSRB for all the individual programs. Last, MSRB improved the performance in terms of IPC of single-core SPEC2000 and SPEC2006 workloads by 7.1% on an average (refer Figure 10 for IPC values obtained for a subset of benchmarks). Observe that programs such as 459.GemsFDTD and 462.libquantum show considerably high gains (148% and 21%).

6.2 Energy Benefits of MSRB

Improved row-hits not only boosts the performance, but also translates into energy savings due to reduced number of activations and precharges. The smaller size of the row-buffers also reduces the energy required for activate and precharge operations. The energy consumption is computed using the methodology described in Section 5.2. Figure 8 shows the DRAM energy gains provided by MSRB for the quad-core workloads. On an average MSRB reduces the energy requirements by 40% compared to the baseline. It is interesting to note that high energy gains are obtained not only for workloads showing high performance gains but also for others due to the narrow row buffers used. Further, as expected improved hit rate not only translates to high performance gains, but also into significant savings in terms of energy consumed. The total activate power reduced on an average from 357mW to 127mW. For 8 core and 16 core workloads, the energy gains are 28% and 31% respectively over the baseline.

6.3 Comparison with Memory-Access Scheduling Schemes

In this section, we compare MSRB with two state-of-the-art memory access scheduling methods, PARallelism aware Batch Scheduling (PARBS) [ ] and Thread Cluster Memory scheduling(TCM) [ ]. We used the same values as in the original paper for the various threshold parameters associated with these schemes. We also compare our scheme to a hypothetical 32 bank DRAM configuration (32-Bank). This is a configuration with a high number of banks,

---

[4]All energy numbers reported in this paper refer to DRAM energy.

263

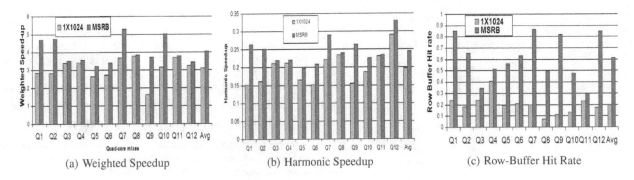

(a) Weighted Speedup   (b) Harmonic Speedup   (c) Row-Buffer Hit Rate

Figure 6: Quad-Core Performance and Row-Buffer Hit Rates

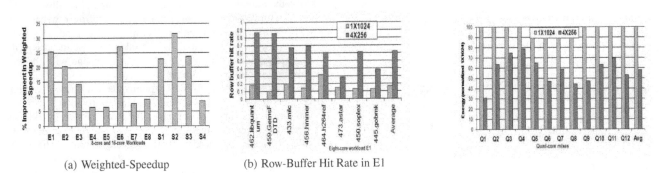

(a) Weighted-Speedup   (b) Row-Buffer Hit Rate in E1

Figure 8: DRAM Energy Consumption.

Figure 7: Eight and Sixteen Core Performance

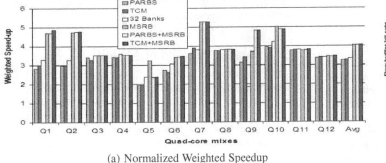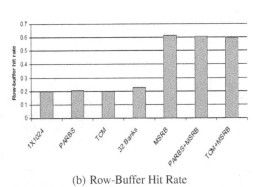

(a) Normalized Weighted Speedup   (b) Row-Buffer Hit Rate

Figure 9: Performance Comparison with Other Scheduling Schemes

with each bank having a 256 column wide row-buffer. 32-Bank has the same number of row-buffers as our 4×256 MSRB configuration which has 8 DRAM banks and 4 row-buffers per bank. In addition, as our scheme is orthogonal to memory-access scheduling schemes to improve row-hit rates, it is possible to have multiple row-buffers in TCM and PARBS. We refer to these configurations of TCM and PARBS enhanced with MSRB (four 256 column wide row-buffers per bank) as TCM+MSRB and PARBS+MSRB respectively.

Figure 9(a) shows the performance in terms of weighted speedup (normalized to the baseline) for PARBS, TCM, 32-Bank, MSRB PARBS+MSRB and TCM+MSRB for quad-core workloads. For all the workloads, it can be seen that MSRB performs better than PARBS and TCM. On an average PARBS and TCM provide gains of only 8.5% and 10.5% over baseline, while MSRB improves the performance by 35.8%. The interesting thing to note is that MSRB can greatly aid the performance of TCM and PARBS, as

can be seen from the significantly better speedups experienced by TCM+MSRB and PARBS+MSRB schemes. The observed trend in performance is also reflected in the row-buffer hit rates exhibited by the various schemes. As can be seen from Figure 9(b), MSRB is more effective in improving row-buffer hit rates compared to PARBS and TCM applied on a top of a single large row-buffer.

It is interesting to note that 32-Bank configuration gives only a 5.9% improvement in performance over baseline (weighted speedup). This is primarily because increasing the number of banks can exploit only a fraction of the temporal locality and the limitations of having only one row-buffer per bank shows up after that.

6.4 Sensitivity Study

Here, we compare the performance of the 4×256 organization with the 2×512 organization. As row-buffer sizes below 256 resulted in noticeable losses even in the case of single-cores, we do

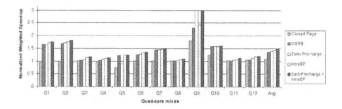

Figure 12: Performance Impact of intraBP and EarlyPrecharge

not evaluate them in detail. Figure 11 shows the row-buffer hit rates experienced by quad-core workloads for MSRB configurations 2×512 and 4×256. 2×512 provides a row hit rate of 0.48 while 4×256 achieves 0.60. In terms of weighted-speedup, 2×512 provided a gain of 34.5% over the baseline configuration of 1×1024.

We also simulated an eight-core system with one memory controller. In the case of a single memory controller, the performance gains provided by MSRB are further enhanced, resulting in an improvement of 16% (weighted-speedup) over the baseline.

6.5 Benefits of Early Precharge and Intra-Bank Parallelism

Figure 12 shows the performance in terms of weighted speedup (normalized to that of 1×1024) for MSRB, EarlyPrecharge, IntraBP and MSRB with both EarlyPrecharge and IntraBP for quad-core workloads. Also included is the performance of the baseline with a closed page policy. This scheme is equivalent to an EarlyPrecharge with a single row-buffer per bank. It can be observed that EarlyPrecharge with MSRB provides a gain of 40% over the baseline on an average. Enabling EarlyPrecharge improves performance by 30% in workload Q9 compared to MSRB. EarlyPrecharge sacrifices some of the row hits to reduce the latency of a future row-buffer miss. In cases where the reduced latency for a row-buffer miss is not sufficient to offset the loss of row-buffer hits, as in Q5, EarlyPrecharge shows a drop in performance compared to MSRB. In summary, EarlyPrecharge yields an additional performance improvement of 1.8% on top of MSRB.

IntraBP has a positive effect on every workload as is to be expected. By utilizing the data bus cycles more efficiently, it achieves an average additional improvement of 4.7% on top of MSRB. While we do not present detailed results here due to lack of space, the average latency for each memory access reduces by 19% due to the increased parallelism. When EarlyPrecharge and IntraBP are both enabled, we observe an average additional improvement of 5.9%. It may also be observed that while EarlyPrecharge faired poorly in workload Q5, the combined optimization restores it to the baseline. Similarly, in workload Q9, EarlyPrecharge gains significantly and that gain is retained in the combined optimization.

6.6 Fairness-oriented and Performance-oriented Allocation Schemes

Figure 13(a) plots fairness of baseline, MSRB , and MSRB with Fairness oriented Allocation (MSRB+Fair) allocation schemes for quad-core workloads. As observed, MSRB improves fairness (over 1×1024 baseline) by 20% while MSRB+Fair improves fairness by an average of 43%. While detailed results are not included here, we observed that in several mixes, latency sensitive cores that suffered significant unfairness got a boost by allocating dedicated buffers to them. Performance oriented Allocation ensures more row-buffers for memory-intensive programs. Figure 13(b) plots

the weighted speedup for the baseline, MSRB , and MSRB with Performance oriented Allocation (MSRB+Perf) allocation schemes for quad-core workloads. MSRB+Perf improves performance by 40.9% over the baseline. This corresponds to an additional improvement of 1.9% over MSRB. In programs with more memory intensive benchmarks, MSRB+Perf can improve performance by as much as 25%. Figure 13(c) shows the IPCs of the individual programs in workload Q9 with MSRB as well as MSRB+Perf. It can be seen that MSRB+Perf improves the performance of memory intensive programs *459.GemsFDTD* and *462.libquantum* without affecting the performance of programs like *445.gobmk* and *410.bwaves* which are relatively less memory intensive.

7. RELATED WORK

There is a large body of work on intelligent memory scheduling to improve row-buffer locality and bank-level parallelism ([ ], [ ], [ ], [ ], [ ]). These methods generally require fairly sophisticated tracking of memory access patterns in the memory controller to drive scheduling decisions. Work on page coloring [ ] and address-mapping techniques ([ ], [ ]) attempt to redistribute pages so as to improve performance ([ ]) or reduce power ([ ], [ ]). Our proposed MSRB organization is orthogonal to all the above schemes and can complement them. Work on phase-change memories in [ ] discusses multiple row buffers as a mechanism to render PCMs as a viable alternative to DRAMs. Though conceptually similar, we propose a practical implementation of this scheme in the context of the widely used DRAM memories without requiring major changes to the rigid JEDEC standard. Further, we illustrate other optimization opportunities enabled by the MSRB organization. The work in [ ] explores the benefit of building a more full fledged SRAM cache in front of the DRAM array to catch more accesses in the cache. However, it necessitates a significant logic addition to the density-optimized DRAM design. Similarly, VCM [ ] memory, introduced briefly in the 90's by NEC, added a set of buffers shared across all the DRAM modules and introduced the notion of foreground and background operations. However it introduced significant changes to the DRAM access standard and the issue of buffer management has not been systematically addressed. Smaller row-buffers for energy-efficiency have received recent attention. Smaller row-buffers result in reduced energy consumption with minimal impact on performance [ ]. Minirank [ ], MC-DIMM [ ] and Adaptive-Granularity [ ] propose alternate data storage to reduce energy consumption while attempting to maintain performance. In contrast, our MSRB organization achieves performance improvement along with energy reduction and fairness improvements.

8. CONCLUSIONS

In this paper we have proposed a row-buffer reorganization for DRAMs which offers significant energy reduction while simultaneously improving performance. These dual benefits make this proposed DRAM architecture an attractive solution for today's DRAM energy and performance issues. We discuss a feasible implementation of this architecture with minimal impact to existing DRAM standards. Our implementation opens up newer optimization opportunities such as Intra-Bank Parallelism and selective Early Precharge. Further, with MSRB different row-buffer allocation schemes can be tried to implement performance and fairness policies. We illustrated this flexibility using a pair of schemes - *Fairness-oriented Allocation* and *Performance-oriented Allocation*.

MSRB showed a performance improvement of 35.8% for quad-core workloads. This improvement was accompanied by an energy

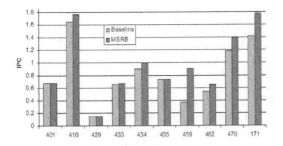

Figure 10: Single-Core IPC

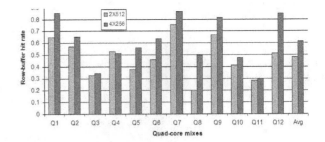

Figure 11: Sensitivity Results for MSRB

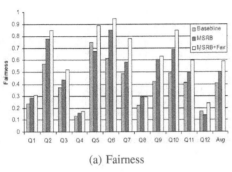

(a) Fairness

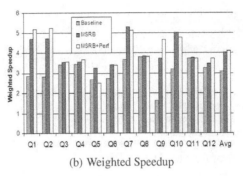

(b) Weighted Speedup

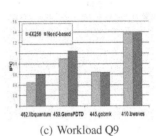

(c) Workload Q9

Figure 13: Fairness and Performance improvements via buffer allocation schemes

reduction of 43% in the DRAM. In comparison, state of the art memory access scheduling schemes TCM [ ] and PARBS [ ] were able to improve the baseline performance by only 10.5% and 8.5%. Further, the additional performance optimizations, namely *Early Precharging* and *Intra-Bank Parallelism* improved the system performance by an additional 5.9%.

9. REFERENCES

[1] Y. Kim, M. Papamichael, O. Mutlu and M. Harchol-Balter. *Thread Cluster Memory Scheduling: Exploiting differences in Memory Access Behavior.* In Micro 2010.

[2] O. Mutlu and T. Moscibroda. *Parallelism-Aware Batch Scheduling: Enhancing both Performance and Fairness of Shared DRAM Systems.* In ISCA 2008.

[3] O. Mutlu and T. Moscibroda. *Stall-Time Fair Memory Access Scheduling for Chip Multiprocessors.* In Micro 2007.

[4] H. Zheng, J. Lin, Z. Zhang, Z. Zhu. *Memory Access Scheduling Schemes for Systems with Multi-Core Processors.* In ICPP 2008.

[5] S. Rixner, W. J. Dally, U. J. Kapasi, P. Mattson, and J. D. Owens. *Memory Access Scheduling.* In ISCA 2000.

[6] K. Sudan, N. Chatterjee, D. Nellans, M. Awasthi, R. Balasubramonian and A. Davis. *Micro-Pages: Increasing DRAM Efficiency with Locality-Aware Data Placement.* In ASPLOS 2010.

[7] M. Awasthi, D. Nellans, K. Sudan, R. Balasubramonian, and A. Davis. *Handling the Problems and Opportunities Posed by Multiple On-Chip Memory Controllers.* In PACT 2010.

[8] Z. Zhang, Z. Zhu and X. Zhang. *A Permutation-based Page Interleaving Scheme to Reduce Row-buffer Conflicts and Exploit Data Locality.* In Micro 2000.

[9] C. J. Lee, O. Mutlu, V. Narasiman and Y. N. Patt *Prefetch-Aware DRAM Controllers.* In Micro 2008.

[10] L. Barroso and U. Holzle. *The Datacenter as a Computer: An Introduction to the Design of Warehouse-Scale Machines.* Morgan & Claypool, 2009.

[11] D. Meisner, B. Gold, and T. Wenisch. *PowerNap: Eliminating Server Idle Power.* In ASPLOS 2009.

[12] A. N. Udipi, N. Muralimanohar, N. Chatterjee, R. Balasubramonian., A. Davis, and N. P. Jouppi. *Rethinking DRAM Design and Organization for Energy-Constrained Multi-Cores.* In ISCA 2010.

[13] H. Zheng, J. Lin, Z. Zhang, E. Gorbatov, H. David, and Z. Zhu. *Mini-Rank: Adaptive DRAM Architecture for Improving Memory Power Efficiency.* In Micro 2008.

[14] H. Huang, K. G. Shin, C. Lefurgy and T. Keller. *Improving Energy Efficiency by Making DRAM Less Randomly Accessed.* In ISLPED 2005.

[15] B. C. Lee, E. Ipek, O. Mutlu and D. Burger. *Architecting Phase Change Memory as a scalable DRAM alternative.* In ISCA 2009.

[16] W. Wong and J-L Baer. *DRAM Caching* Dept of CS and Engg., University of Washington Tech report UW-CSE-97-03-04. 1997.

[17] The JEDEC consortium. *www.jedec.org*

[18] N. L. Binkert, R. G. Dreslinski, L. R. Hsu, K. T. Lim, A. G. Saidi, and S. K. Reinhardt. *The M5 Simulator: Modeling Networked Systems.* In Micro 2006.

[19] Micron. http://download.micron.com/downloads/ misc/ddr3_power_calc.xls

[20] Micron. *Calculating Memory System Power for DDR3* http://download.micron.com/pdf/technotes/ddr3/ TN41_01DDR3%20Power.pdf.

[21] A. Snavely and D. M. Tullsen. *Symbiotic jobscheduling for a simultaneous multithreading processor.* In ASPLOS 2000

[22] K. Luo, J. Gummaraju, and M. Franklin. *Balancing thoughput and fairness in smt processors.* In ISPASS 2001.

[23] The SPEC Consortium. www.spec.org/consortium/

[24] O. La. *SDRAM having posted CAS function of JEDEC standard.* United States Patent, Number 6483769. 2002.

[25] E. Ipek, O. Mutlu, J. F. Martinez, and R. Caruana. *Self-Optimizing Memory Controllers: A Reinforcement Learning Approach.* In ISCA 2008.

[26] D. H. Yoon, M. K. Jeong, and M Erez. *Adaptive Granularity Memory Systems: A Tradeoff between Storage Efficiency and Throughput.* In ISCA 2011.

[27] S. Thoziyoor, N. Muralimanohar, and N. Jouppi. *CACTI 5.0. Technical report.* HP Laboratories 2007.

[28] K. Itoh. *VLSI Memory Chip Design.* Springer 2001.

[29] J. H. Ahn et al. *Multicore DIMM: an Energy Efficient Memory Module with Independently Controlled DRAMs.* In IEEE Computer Architecture Letters 2008.

[30] S. Rixner. *Memory Controller Optimizations for Web Servers.* In IEEE Micro 2004.

Unified Memory Optimizing Architecture:
Memory Subsystem Control with a Unified Predictor

Yasuo Ishii[†‡]   Mary Inaba[†]   Kei Hiraki[†]
The University of Tokyo, 7-3-1 Hongo, Bunkyo-ku, Tokyo, Japan[†]
NEC Corporation, 1-10 Nisshin-cho, Fuchi-shi, Tokyo, Japan[‡]
{yishii, mary, hiraki}@is.s.u-tokyo.ac.jp

ABSTRACT

Data prefetching, advanced cache replacement policy, and memory access scheduling are incorporated in modern processors. Typically, each technique holds recently accessed locations independently and controls the memory subsystem based on the prediction of future memory access. Unfortunately, these specific optimizations often increase the implementation cost, decrease the system performance, and reduce scalability of the processor chip.

In this paper, we propose Unified Memory Optimizing (UMO) architecture to resolve these problems. The UMO architecture is a control architecture for the memory subsystem and takes a unified approach to data prefetching, cache management, and memory access scheduling. On this architecture, we propose a Map-based Unified Memory Subsystem Controller (MUMSC) that is composed of DRAM-Aware prefetching, Prefetch-Aware Cache Line Promotion, and lightweight memory controllers. MUMSC is implemented as the per-core resource to predict future memory access from the per-core memory access history. MUMSC realizes a scalable and high performance memory subsystem with a reasonable hardware cost.

We evaluate MUMSC using a multi-core simulator with multi-programmed workloads of SPEC CPU2006. The results of the simulation show that the system throughput using MUMSC outperforms a combination of state-of-the-art enhancement techniques by 11.5% without increasing the hardware costs and the complexity of the design of the shared resources.

Categories and Subject Descriptors

B.3.2 [**Memory Structures**]: Design Styles—*cache memories*; C.1.0 [**Processor Architectures**]: General

Keywords

multi-core processor, data prefetching, cache management, memory access scheduling

1. INTRODUCTION

With the progress of semiconductor process technology, the performance gap between processor and memory has been increased. To make up for the performance gap, modern processors integrate many techniques to enhance their memory subsystem on a processor chip. Typically, data prefetching, advanced cache replacement policy, and memory access scheduling are incorporated in modern processors.

However, a combination of these three techniques causes the following problems. (1) These three techniques use similar data, such as recently accessed memory locations to predict memory access in the future, and they hold such data independently. Figure 1(A) shows an example of this type of multi-core processor. The processor employs a data prefetcher [6, 22, 10] for each core, shadow tags [25, 32] for last-level cache, and large memory request buffers for memory access scheduling [26, 14, 15, 20]. Each component collects and stores recent memory access independently. Redundant data on each technique increases the total hardware cost. (2) Data prefetching, cache replacement, and memory access scheduling may interfere with each other because all of them control memory access. A combination of these techniques can lead to unexpected situations that do not appear when each technique is used independently, and can decrease the performance of the system significantly [31]. Data prefetching modifies the pattern of memory access, but this modified pattern can confuse modern intelligent cache management systems. However, opportunities to improve performance can also arise. For example, the data prefetching can help the memory access scheduling to improve the available bandwidth [16]. (3) Memory controllers and shared last-level cache memory often take a centralized approach to find the locality of per-core memory access. The history of per-core memory access is useful to exploit memory access locality [15, 11] because memory access from one core has spatial and temporal locality. However, these approaches increase the complexity of the design of the shared resources as the number of cores, the number of cache banks, and the number of memory controllers increase. For example, the Parallelism-Aware Batch Scheduler (PAR-BS) [20] requires communication between different memory controllers. This approach does not scale well when the number of memory controllers increases.

In this paper, we propose Unified Memory Optimizing (UMO) architecture to resolve these problems. The UMO architecture is a memory subsystem control architecture which takes a unified approach to data prefetching, cache replacement policy, and memory access scheduling. Figure

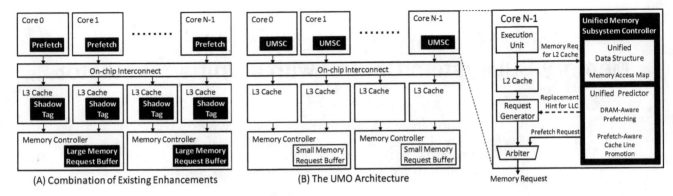

Figure 1: Overview of the UMO Architecture   Figure 2: Core Design

1(B) shows an overview of the UMO architecture. The UMO architecture reduces the functions on the shared resource and unifies these functions into the Unified Memory Subsystem Controller (UMSC) on each core. Figure 2 shows a core design and a block diagram of UMSC. UMSC uses memory access history from the corresponding core and controls the whole memory subsystem via data prefetch and a replacement hint for the last-level cache.

As an implementation of UMSC, we propose a Map-based Unified Memory Subsystem Controller (MUMSC) that is composed of DRAM-Aware prefetching, Prefetch-Aware Cache Line Promotion, and lightweight first-ready first-come-first-serve (FR-FCFS) [26] memory controllers. The DRAM-Aware prefetching reorders the prefetch requests to improve the available memory bandwidth. The Prefetch-Aware Cache Line Promotion gives a replacement hint of usefulness of the cache line based on the previously issued prefetch information.

MUMSC has the following advantages. (1) The unified per-core data structure reduces the redundant run-time information on the chip as shown in Figure 1. This results in a reduction of the total hardware cost of the processor chip. (2) MUMSC improves system performance because both DRAM-Aware prefetching and Prefetch-Aware Cache Line Promotion improve not only their functions (data prefetching or cache management) but also the other system feature such as memory access scheduling. (3) The design complexity of MUMSC is low because MUMSC is implemented as a per-core resource. The UMO architecture is the first unified approach to the integration of data prefetching, cache replacement policy, and the memory access scheduling. The UMO architecture improves system performance without decreasing the scalability of the shared resource and without increasing the total hardware cost.

This paper is organized as follows. In Section 2, our motivation for this study is presented. In Section 3, we propose the concept of the UMO architecture. In Section 4, we propose the design of MUMSC. In Section 5, the evaluation methodology and experimental results are presented. In Section 6, related studies are presented, and finally, we conclude the paper in section 7.

2. BACKGROUND OF THIS WORK

In this section, we explain our motivation for the unified approach. We describe two interactions of modern memory subsystem enhancement techniques. We also describe our previous work that is used in the UMO architecture.

Table 1: Micron MT41J256M8 DDR3 Parameters

	DDR3-800	DDR3-1333	DDR3-1866
tFAW	16 cycle	20 cycle	26 cycle
Available BW	800 MT/s	1066 MT/s	1138 MT/s
Efficiency	100.0%	80.0%	61.5%

2.1 Row Buffer Locality and Data Prefetch

DDR3 devices employ multiple internal banks, which can be accessed independently. Each bank is composed of multiple data blocks called *rows*. When a memory controller reads (or writes) data from a bank, all data in the row is loaded from the DRAM cells into an internal temporal buffer called a *row uffer* in advance of reading (or writing) of the actual data. This operation is called *activation*. Once a corresponding row is activated, the memory controller accesses data stored in the row buffer. Access to a row that is already activated is called *row hit* and its locality is called the *row uffer locality*.

To maximize the available DRAM bandwidth, modern memory controllers have to use row buffer locality due to several timing constraints found in modern DDR3 devices. The most important timing constraint is tF . tF limits the maximum number of activations in a specific timing window. Typically, DDR3 devices allow four activations per an arbitrary 30 ns timing window. In previous DDR3 generations, such as DDR3-800, tF did not limit the available bandwidth because the rate of data transfer is much lower than that of latest DDR3 devices, while the tF delay stays the same. Table 1 shows available bandwidth without row hits for each generation of DDR3 device [18].[1] It shows that the old DDR3 generations, such as DDR3-800, achieve theoretical peak bandwidth without row hits, while DDR3-1866 achieves only 61.5 % of the peak bandwidth. This shows that the modern memory controllers have to exploit row buffer locality to achieve full memory bandwidth in the latest DDR3 generation.[2]

Unfortunately, the row buffer locality tends to decrease as the number of cores increases. This is because a combination of memory access sequences from each core reduces the

---

[1]We suppose burst length (BL) is 8. Without row hits, DDR3 device consumes 4 cycles for each activation and 4 activations consumes 16 cycles (= 4 cycles / activate × 4 activations). The available bandwidth is calculated through the consumed clock cycles (16 clock cycles) per tF .

[2]DDR3-1866 needs 38.5% $(= 1 - 16/tFAW)$ row hit ratio.

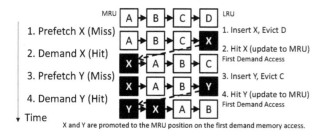

Figure 3: Unexpected Promotion by Prefetch

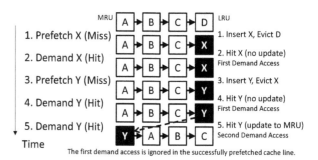

Figure 4: Prefetch-Aware Promotion Strategy

access locality [30]. In order to exploit the row buffer locality from such sequences, memory controllers have to employ large memory request buffers [26, 14, 15, 20]. An alternative approach to increase the row buffer locality is utilization of prefetch requests. The stream prefetcher is used to improve the row buffer locality [13] because it issues consecutive memory addresses as the prefetch requests. However, a simple prefetcher such as a stream prefetch often generates many inaccurate prefetch requests, wasting the memory bandwidth and degrading the overall performance of the system (the accuracy is shown the Section 5.2.4). Other prefetching methods, such as stride prefetching [6], cannot improve the row buffer locality because its prefetch requests are not formed as consecutive address sequences.

2.2 Adaptive Insertion and Prefetched Lines

Generally, a shared last-level cache includes many useless data blocks, which are called dead blocks [17]. Adaptive insertion policy [24] is a cost-effective replacement strategy to eliminate such useless data. In the adaptive insertion policy, most incoming cache lines are inserted into the LRU position when a running workload generates many dead blocks. These cache lines are promoted to the MRU position when the line is accessed repeatedly. Thus, useful cache lines are extracted from all of the inserted cache lines.

However, the adaptive insertion policy creates a new problem when it works with data prefetching. In data prefetching, the prefetched cache lines are expected to be accessed at least once on the cache. The successful prefetched cache lines are always promoted to the MRU position. The advantage of adaptive insertion policy is significantly reduced when most of the cache lines have been prefetched by intelligent prefetchers. In this case, most of the inserted cache lines are promoted to the MRU position, while the adaptive insertion policy is trying to retain most of the inserted cache lines at the LRU position. A simple example is shown in Figure 3. The prefetched lines, X and Y, are promoted to the MRU position by their first demand memory access. This unexpected promotion may generate many dead blocks and degrades the cache efficiency significantly.

To avoid this problem, the cache replacement policy has to be able to identify the prefetched cache lines. A straightforward approach is to attach a flag, which is typically called a prefetch bit, for each cache line. The prefetch bit indicates whether the corresponding cache line has been inserted by a prefetch request. When the prefetched cache line is accessed by a demand memory request, the line should not be moved to the MRU position and the prefetch bit is cleared. Figure 4 shows an example of a desirable promotion strategy. On the first demand access, the prefetched lines, X

and Y, are not promoted to the MRU positions. Therefore, the prefetched lines, X and Y, can be evicted immediately after their demand requests are observed. The prefetched line is promoted to the MRU position at the second demand request. In this replacement strategy, the prefetched data do not undermine the adaptive insertion policy. However, this approach increases the cost of a shared last-level cache because it needs a prefetch bit for each cache line.

The adaptive insertion policy can be also applied for the other replacement policies, such as Dynamic Re-Reference Interval Prediction (DRRIP) [12]. DRRIP represents the LRU-like information of an N-bit counter that is called Re-Reference Prediction Value (RRPV). Large RRPV indicates close to the LRU position and small RRPV indicates close to the MRU position. To apply adaptive insertion policy, DRRIP modifies the initial RRPV of the incoming cache line. Thread-aware adaptive insertion policy [11] is an extension of the adaptive insertion. It takes into account interactions among running threads. These strategies are useful to eliminate dead blocks on the shared last-level cache, but they also suffer from the unexpected cache line promotion. Prefetch-Aware Cache Management (PACMan) [31] coordinates data prefetching and cache replacement. However, it cannot resolve to the problem of the unexpected promotions shown in Figure 3, because it does not identify the prefetched cache lines after the prefetch request has inserted the fetched data into the cache.

2.3 Memory Access Map

A memory access map [7, 8, 9, 10] is a data structure to track memory locations that are accessed in the recent past. Figure 5 shows an overview of the memory access map. On the memory access map, the memory address space is divided into *zones* that are memory regions of fixed size. The memory access map tracks memory access on recently accessed zones, which are called *hot zones*. The history of memory access in the recent past is recorded as a form of 2-bit state. The state diagram of a memory access map is shown in Figure 6(A). The memory access map uses the three states, *Init*, *Prefetch*, and *Access*. Multiple 2-bit states of one hot zone make a state vector. Each state on the vector is attached to all cache lines in the corresponding hot zone. Therefore, one state vector tracks all memory access on the corresponding hot zone. The memory access map is cost-efficient because only 2-bit state is required to track memory access for one cache line. We use 4KB as zone size and 64B for cache line size in this paper. Therefore, each memory access map uses a 64-entry 2-bit state vector to track the 4KB zone.

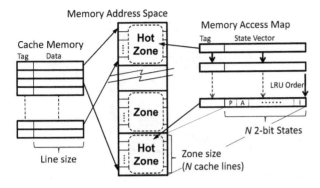

Figure 5: Overview of Memory Access Map

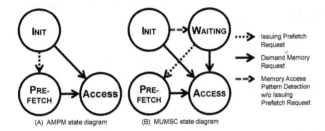

Figure 6: State Diagram of Memory Access Map

Access Map Pattern Matching (AMPM) prefetching is a data prefetching scheme using the memory access map. AMPM uses pattern matching to detect memory access patterns. It works appropriately when the memory access sequence is reordered by microarchitectural techniques such as out-of-order execution. AMPM achieves a higher coverage ratio than the other prefetchers and won the data prefetching championship [1].

Map-based adaptive insertion policy (MAIP) is the enhancement of TADIP [11]. MAIP is also one of the finalists of the previous cache replacement championship [2]. MAIP modifies the insertion position of an incoming cache line based on the recent access history stored in the memory access map. MAIP uses the memory access map as the shadow tags because it holds many previously accessed memory locations. This policy can be applied for other replacement policies such as DRRIP because MAIP modifies only the insertion position of incoming cache lines.

3. THE UMO ARCHITECTURE

3.1 Design Overview

As shown in Figure 1(A), a modern memory subsystem employs multiple functions on the processor chip and interactions among these functions often cause unexpected situations. To optimize the memory subsystem, we propose the Unified Memory Optimizing (UMO) architecture. The UMO architecture unifies data prefetching, cache replacement policy, and memory access scheduling on the Unified Memory Subsystem Controller (UMSC) as shown in Figure 1(B). UMSC realizes two features, which are DRAM-Aware Prefetching and Prefetch-Aware Cache Line Promotion. DRAM-Aware Prefetching reorders prefetch requests to improve row buffer locality of the DRAM devices. Prefetch-Aware Cache Line Promotion eliminates

dead blocks due to the successful prefetch. The UMO architecture also employs first-ready first-come-first-serve (FR-FCFS) memory controllers [26] with small memory request buffers. Figure 2 shows UMSC and the core design of the UMO architecture. UMSC collects all memory requests to the private L2 cache and records the memory access history on the memory access map. On a L2 cache miss, the request generator makes an appropriate demand request for the lower-level cache. Prefetch-Aware Cache Line Promotion attaches a replacement hint to the demand request to improve the cache efficiency. Based on the hint, the shared last-level cache modifies its replacement strategy. UMSC also generates prefetch requests based on the recent memory access sequence. Unlike existing prefetching schemes, DRAM-Aware prefetching reorders prefetch requests to improve row buffer locality.

3.2 DRAM-Aware Prefetching

As described in the previous section, accurate prefetching methods cannot exploit row buffer locality effectively because their prefetch requests are not consecutive. To utilize the row buffer locality with accurate prefetching methods, the memory controller has to reorders these prefetch requests on the large memory request buffers. To optimize these trade-offs, DRAM-Aware prefetching unifies data prefetching and memory access scheduling. DRAM-Aware prefetching reorders issue the timing of prefetch requests to improve the row buffer locality, even if the memory controller employs the small memory request buffer.

The basic concept of DRAM-Aware prefetching is shown in Figure 7. It shows the timing chart of the memory access sequence from two cores. Core 0 and Core 1 generate prefetch requests, a_0, a_1, b_0, and b_1, from their own memory access, A_0, A_1, B_0, and B_1. We assume that prefetch requests a_0 and a_1 access the same row, and prefetch requests b_0 and b_1 access the other row, because memory access from each core has spatial locality [30]. In a normal prefetching scheme, the prefetch request a_0 is immediately issued when Core 0 detects the memory access patterns. In such cases, there is a time-lag between a_0 and a_1. This allows prefetch requests from the other cores to cut in front of the following prefetch request. In Figure 7(A), prefetch request, b_0, cut in front of successive prefetch request, a_1. To reorder a_1 and b_0 in the memory controllers, the memory controllers have to employ large memory request buffers. In DRAM-Aware prefetching, the prefetcher reorders prefetch requests to increase the row hit. Prefetch requests are kept waiting for successive prefetch candidates for the same row. If there are no successive requests, the waiting prefetch request is dropped. In Figure 7(B), prefetch request, a_0, waits for next prefetch request, a_1. After prefetch request, a_1, is detected, the two prefetch requests are issued together. This reduces interruptions by other memory requests and improves row buffer locality. Prefetch request, a_1, results in the row hit in Figure 7(B). This mitigates the necessity of a large memory request buffer in the memory controller.

DRAM-Aware prefetching has the following advantages over existing memory access scheduling methods. (i) The probability of performance-loss is small because it does not postpone the demand requests and it only consumes the timing slack of prefetch requests. As shown in Figure 7(A), prefetch requests often have timing slack between fetch time and use time. DRAM-Aware prefetching reduces only this

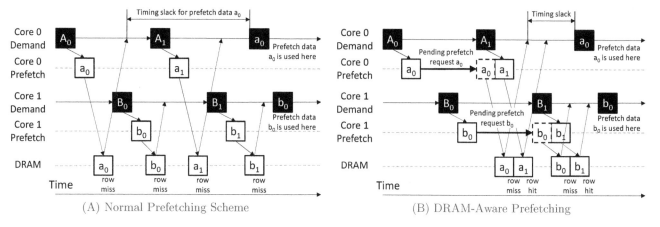

(A) Normal Prefetching Scheme   (B) DRAM-Aware Prefetching

Figure 7: The Concept of DRAM-Aware Prefetching

slack to improve performance. (ii) Pending prefetch requests do not stay in the memory request buffer in the memory controller because the pending prefetch requests wait for appropriate timing in the core resource. This helps to reduce the cost and the design complexity of the memory controllers because the memory controllers can reduce the size of the memory request buffer.

3.3 Prefetch-Aware Cache Line Promotion

Unexpected promotion due to the successful prefetched line can be eliminated by using the prefetch bit. However, this increases the cost of last-level cache. To eliminate the cost of prefetch bit, we propose Prefetch-Aware Cache Line Promotion (PACP). PACP attaches a replacement hint to demand memory requests at request generator on each core (Figure 2), because each core holds the information of recently issued prefetch requests. Based on the attached information, the last-level cache cancels the promotion of accessed cache line, as shown in Figure 4.

Prefetch-Aware Cache Line Promotion has the following advantages over existing cache replacement algorithms. (i) The probability of unexpected promotion is reduced because the information from the prefetch function helps to identify a recently prefetched cache line. (ii) PACP does not require large external costs because it does not add external storage cost to the shared last-level cache, such as prefetch bits.

4. MAP-BASED UNIFIED MEMORY SUB-SYSTEM CONTROLLER

The UMO architecture employs unified functions for the shared resource on UMSC. As an implementation of UMSC, we propose the Map-based Unified Memory Subsystem Controller (MUMSC). As a unified data structure, MUMSC uses a memory access map that is extended to implement the UMO architectures. On the extended memory access map, MUMSC employs a unified predictor that implements a DRAM-Aware Access Map Pattern Matching Prefetching, and Prefetch-Aware Cache Line Promotion with a Map-based Adaptive Insertion Policy.

4.1 Unified Data Structure

To support DRAM-Aware prefetching, we have added a new state to the conventional 2-bit state of the memory access map. The additional state is *Waiting*. The extended

state diagram is shown in Figure 6(B). *Waiting* is used when the prefetch candidates wait for successive prefetch requests, as shown in Figure 7(B). When the data prefetcher detects the prefetch candidates, the corresponding states change to *Waiting* and wait for successive prefetch requests. When the successive requests are detected, the pending prefetch requests are issued and the corresponding state changes to *Prefetch*. The state transitions occur when (1) the actual memory access for the corresponding cache line is observed, (2) the prefetch candidates are detected, and (3) the prefetch request for the corresponding cache line is issued. The memory access map assumes that the state reflects the access history of the corresponding cache line because all recent memory access from the corresponding core is recorded on the state vector. This indicates that the cache line, whose corresponding state is *Access*, is assumed to be stored in the last-level cache because the corresponding location was touched in the recent past. On the *Prefetch*, the corresponding cache line is assumed to be prefetched recently and no demand requests access the prefetched line yet. Therefore, the state transition from *Prefetch* to *Access* indicates the first demand access for the corresponding cache line.

4.2 Unified Predictor

The unified predictor of MUMSC supports DRAM-Aware prefetching and Prefetch-Aware Cache Line Promotion to maximize the performance of the memory subsystem. As the implementation of the unified predictor, we propose DRAM-Aware Access Map Pattern Matching Prefetching and Prefetch-Aware Cache Line Promotion with Map-based Adaptive Insertion.

4.2.1 DRAM-Aware Access Map Pattern Matching Prefetching

MUMSC applies DRAM-Aware prefetching to Access Map Pattern Matching (AMPM) prefetching [10], which is called DRAM-Aware Access Map Pattern Matching (DA-AMPM) prefetching. The DA-AMPM prefetcher moves prefetch candidates to *Waiting* instead of issuing prefetch requests. The corresponding requests wait in *Waiting* until the other prefetch candidates for the same row are detected. When the DA-AMPM detects multiple prefetch requests in the same row, the DA-AMPM issues all prefetch requests for the row and the corresponding state is transit to *Prefetch*. The DA-AMPM modifies the pattern matching logic to support *Waiting*. It detects not only the "stride access pattern" but also *Waiting* as prefetch candidates. The other features are the same as the original AMPM. When the DA-AMPM detects more than two prefetch candidates in the same row, the detected prefetch candidates are issued together.

DA-AMPM has following advantages. (i) The efficiency of memory bandwidth is improved because DA-AMPM improves row buffer locality. Moreover, the DA-AMPM reduces the number of useless prefetch requests from the stream prefetchers because its accuracy is higher than that of the stream prefetchers. (ii) DA-AMPM is low cost and the design of the shared resource remains simple. As described in this section, prefetch requests have to wait for the other prefetch requests. Generally, a buffer for pending requests is required to postpone the issue of prefetch requests. However, DA-AMPM uses *Waiting* to wait for the following prefetch requests. Therefore, DA-AMPM does not employ extra hardware to support DRAM-Aware prefetching.

4.2.2 Prefetch-Aware Cache Line Promotion with Map-based Adaptive Insertion Policy

MUMSC applies Prefetch-Aware Cache Line Promotion to Map-based Adaptive Insertion Policy (MAIP), which is called Prefetch-Aware Cache Line Promotion with Map-based Adaptive Insertion Policy (PA-MAIP). PA-MAIP uses Thread-Aware Dynamic Re-Reference Interval Prediction (TA-DRRIP) [12] as a base replacement policy while the original MAIP uses TADIP because TA-DRRIP has higher performance than TADIP. PA-MAIP strategy can easily be applied for the other adaptive insertion policies such as DIP. However, DRRIP outperforms the other replacement policies and its implementation cost is reasonable. Therefore, we use DRRIP for the baseline algorithm of PA-MAIP in the rest of this paper.

PA-MAIP identifies the location of a prefetched cache line using a corresponding state of the memory access map. PA-MAIP assumes that a cache line, whose state is now *Prefetch*, will have been a recently prefetched line. In the event of cache miss on L2, the core attaches the corresponding 2-bit state recorded on the memory access map to the demand requests. The cache memory uses the attached 2-bit state as a hint to update the Re-Reference Prediction Value (RRPV) of DRRIP. Table 2 shows the insertion and promotion strategy of PA-MAIP for DRRIP. We assume a 3-bit counter for RRPV in the table. Therefore, "7" indicates the 'earliest to evict' position and "0" indicates the 'hardest to evict' position. "Mostly 7" indicates the random insertion policy of DRRIP. When the policy selection counter for set dueling indicates SRRIP, all cache lines are inserted into position 6. When the policy selection counter for set dueling indicates BRRIP, a few randomly selected cache lines are inserted to position 6 and the other cache lines are inserted into 7. "Not Appear" means that the corresponding situation has not appeared because the prefetch requests are issued only for *Init* and *Waiting*.

PA-MAIP has the following advantages over existing cache management strategies. (i) It reduces the unexpected cache promotion of prefetched cache lines because it explicitly uses prefetch information for cache management. PACMan also uses prefetch information for cache management. However, it cannot distinguish the prefetched cache line from all inserted cache lines. Therefore, PACMan cannot resolve the unexpected promotion of the prefetched cache lines. (ii) The

Table 2: Insertion and Promotion (Reuse) Strategy

(a) Demand Request

	State of Memory Access Map		
	Init / Waiting	Prefetch	Access
Insert	Mostly 7	Mostly 7	6
Reuse	0	No Update	0

(b) Prefetch Request

	State of Memory Access Map		
	Init / Waiting	Prefetch	Access
Insert	Mostly 7	Not Appear	Not Appear
Reuse	No Update	Not Appear	Not Appear

implementation cost is reasonable because it shares a data structure with DA-AMPM. Therefore, PA-MAIP does not conflict with the DA-AMPM because it only refers the memory access map. Moreover, PA-MAIP does not increase the complexity of the design of the shared resource because its algorithm is only dependent on the per-core information.

4.3 Implementation Cost and Complexity

An additional hardware cost of MUMSC is the implementation cost of the unified data structure and the unified predictor. The unified data structure is composed of the memory access map that is composed of the storage to hold state vectors and control information. Typically, the memory access map requires several KB to track large memory access history (detailed storage cost is described in the next section). For example, 256-entry 16-way memory access map requires a 5.2 KB storage cost because each memory access map is composed of 64-entry 2-bit state vector, 35-bit tag information, and 4-bit LRU information.

The unified predictor is composed of DA-AMPM and PA-MAIP features. DA-AMPM requires additional pattern matching logic to detect *Waiting*. DA-AMPM also checks whether multiple prefetch requests access the same row. This can be implemented with leading-zero logic that is composed of parallel OR logic to check the attribute of the other prefetch requests. The rest of the pattern matching logic is composed of basic arithmetic components such as shifters and adders. Its implementations cost is in the same range of arithmetic logic units (ALU). PA-MAIP modifies the update logic of the shared last-level cache to support the new update policy shown in Table 2. This logic can be implemented with simple combinational logic and the complexity is in the same range as the other replacement policies such as LRU. Interconnections between the core and the last-level cache are also extended for the 2-bit state of the memory access map. However, this data is much less than the other control information such as the address and the coherence information. Therefore, the additional costs and the design complexities are reasonable for modern processors.

5. EVALUATION

5.1 Methodology

We simulated an 8-core processor using a cycle-accurate processor simulator [23] to evaluate MUMSC. The simulator was extended with a DRAM simulator [27] to simulate detailed DDR3 DRAM behavior. We used MT41J512M8 DDR3-1866 configuration for DRAM system [18]. We used the column centric DRAM address mapping [26]. We also

Table 3: Processor Configuration

Core	x86 out-of-order, 8-core, 4.667 GHz
Pipeline	16 stages, 128 reorder buffers, 64 reservation stations
L1 I-Cache	32 KB, 4-way, 3 cycles, 64B line
L1 D-Cache	32 KB, 4-way, 3 cycles, 64B line
Private L2 Cache	256 KB, 8-way, 8 cycles, 64B line 32 requests per core, inclusive
Shared L3 Cache	8 MB, 16-way, 30 cycles, 4-bank, 64B line 128 requests per bank, non-inclusive
Memory Controller	2 memory controllers per chip DDR3-1866 1 Rank DIMM / controller 8 DDR3-1866 4Gb DRAM chips / DIMM 32 memory request queue, FR-FCFS
DDR3 Device	MT41J512M8, 1866 MT/s, 13-13-13-28 tFAW 26 cycles, tRC 45 cycles

Table 4: 8-core workload mixes

ID	Workload Name
0	milc, grom, calc, sjeng, sjeng, gems, astar, sphin
1	milc, cactus, cactus, sopl, h264, astar, astar, wrf
2	bzip2, bwave, cactus, go, sopl, omnet, omnet, sphin
3	perl, milc, cactus, go, povray, gems, libq, omnet
4	bzip2, milc, cactus, lesl, go, h264, xalan, xalan
5	bzip2, mcf, cactus, namd, go, dealII, sphin, xalan
6	bzip2, gcc, milc, dealII, dealII, hmmer, omnet, wrf
7	perl, games, mcf, lesl, namd, hmmer, gems, omnet
8	games, mcf, go, h264, h264, h264, omnet, sphin
9	bzip2, mcf, grom, cactus, lesl, libq, h264, xalan
10	bzip2, games, mcf, grom, cactus, libq, tonto, sphin
11	gcc, milc, cactus, cactus, cactus, go, sphin, xalan
12	bzip2, lesl, go, povray, sjeng, gems, wrf, sphin
13	bzip2, bwave, milc, lesl, dealII, calc, h264, sphin
14	bwave, lesl, dealII, omnet, astar, wrf, wrf, xalan
15	perl, mcf, grom, grom, go, sopl, h264, sphin

Table 5: Configuration of Memory Subsystem

Baseline	Stream prefetch (distance=64, depth=4) Thread-Aware DRRIP (RRPV 3-bit)
Combi-A	PC/DC (256-entry IT+GHB, depth=2) PACMan with TA-DRRIP (RRPV 3-bit)
Combi-B	AMPM (64-line/map, 256-map, 16-way) MAIP for TA-DRRIP (RRPV 3-bit)
MUMSC	DA-AMPM (64-line/map, 256-map, 16-way) PA-MAIP for TA-DRRIP (RRPV 3-bit)

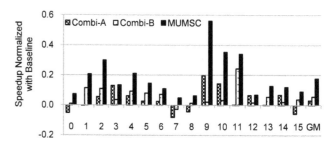

Figure 8: Improvement of Weighted Speedup

implemented MUMSC on the simulator. Table 3 shows the parameter of the simulated processor. We used small memory request buffers like Minimalist [13].

We utilized multi-programmed workload mixes of SPEC CPU2006 suites [3] for our evaluation. We selected 8-core benchmark mixes to saturate the memory bandwidth, which is estimated through single core experiments. Table 4 shows the combination of workloads.

We fast-forwarded all benchmark mixes to the initialization phase. We evaluated the next 100M instructions using the cycle-accurate simulation. The statistics corresponding to the cores are counted in the 100M instructions for each core. We used weighted speedup ($WeightedSpeedup = \sum_i \frac{IPC_i}{IPC_{i,baseline}}$) for the throughput metric. The behavior of shared resources such as DRAM devices is evaluated during the first 1000M instructions after the cycle-accurate simulation is started. DRAM energy consumption is estimated by the power calculating method published by Micron [19].

We compared our scheme with other memory subsystem schemes. The configurations of the evaluated schemes are shown in Table 5. We used the stream prefetcher for the baseline because it requires a small hardware cost and achieves high prefetch coverage. We used PC/DC [22] and AMPM [10] as the more aggressive competitive prefetch-

ers because they can support many memory access patterns. Generally, PC/DC supports higher accuracy than the other existing representative prefetchers. The AMPM supports higher coverage than the other existing representative prefetchers. We aligned the storage budget of the prefetchers, for fairness. The 256-entry GHB requires 5.8 KB and the 256-entry memory access map requires 5.2 KB [10]. As for the cache replacement policy, we used Prefetch-Aware Cache Management (PACMan) for the comparison because it can improve the system performance without increasing the hardware cost, such as prefetch bit. We also used MAIP [9], which is a replacement policy using a memory access map. Both replacement policies use Dynamic Re-reference Interval Prediction as a base replacement policy. Combi-A employs state-of-the-art techniques that do not use a memory access map. Combi-B takes techniques that use memory access map. The difference of Combi-B and MUMSC is whether or not they take unified approach. DA-AMPM and PA-MAIP was implemented as described in the previous section.

5.2 Simulation Result

5.2.1 System Performance

Figure 8 shows the weighted speedups normalized with the baseline performance. MUMSC consistently outperforms the other configurations. MUMSC outperforms the baseline by 17.8%, Combi-A by 14.2%, and Combi-B by 11.5%. In workload 9, MUMSC achieves 56.1% improved performance from the baseline because most memory access is covered by the prefetching and the unexpected eviction is mitigated by the PACP. Mainly, the performance improvement is derived from PA-MAIP, because it reduces useless memory traffic. For further analysis, we analyze the memory traffic in detail in Section 5.2.2.

5.2.2 Traffic Analysis

Figure 9 categorizes the memory traffic on the basis of the prefetch requests. The "cover" refers to the prefetch

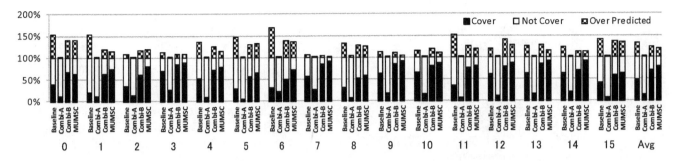

Figure 9: Prefetch Coverage and Prefetch Accuracy for Each Configuration

traffic whose prefetched data are used in the core. The "not cover" refers to the traffic that cannot be covered by the prefetch requests. The "over predicted" refers to the prefetch traffic whose prefetched data are never used before they are evicted. We use "useful" memory traffic as a memory traffic, whose data are actually used in the core. The useful traffic is calculated through the sum of "cover" and "not cover."

In MUMSC, the prefetch requests covers 79.2% of useful memory traffic, but it also increases memory traffic by 20.3% as a result of the over predicted prefetch requests. It outperforms the coverage of AMPM, which achieves 70.8% prefetch coverage with 24.1% of the over predicted prefetch requests. These improvements are not derived from the prefetch algorithm because the prefetch capability of DA-AMPM is in the same range of that of AMPM (detailed analysis is shown in Section 5.2.4). The performance improvements are derived from the difference in the cache replacement policy. PACP unexpectedly reduces evicted cache lines (detailed analysis is shown in Section 5.2.5) and the reduction of unexpected eviction also reduces the opportunities of too early eviction of the prefetched data. This results in an improvement of the prefetch coverage and the prefetch accuracy.

Figure 10 shows the row hit ratio of the DRAM devices. MUMSC achieves a 59.3% row hit ratio and increases the row hit ratio by 1.3% over the baseline, by 34.0% over Combi-A, and by 7.2% over Combi-B. This result confirms that DRAM-Aware prefetching improves row buffer locality with small memory request buffers. The baseline configuration achieves a high row hit ratio that is in the same range of that of MUMSC. However, the baseline uses inaccurate stream prefetching to exploit row buffer locality. The stream prefetcher issues 32.1% more predicted prefetch requests, as shown in Figure 9. Combi-A achieves the most accurate prefetch because it issues only 1.8% more predicted prefetch requests, but its row hit ratio is only 25.3%. When the row hit ratio is small, the energy consumption of activation increases. This limits the available DRAM bandwidth as described in Section 2.1.

5.2.3 DRAM Traffic and Energy Consumption

Figure 11(A) shows a summary of the memory traffic normalized with the baseline. MUMSC reduces the memory traffic by 5.5% over the baseline configuration. MUMSC increases the traffic by 32.5% over Combi-A, but MUMSC reduces the traffic without row hits by 27.9% over Combi-A. Figure 11(B) shows the total energy consumption for the DRAM devices. The energy consumption is classified into three categories. The "background" refers to the energy for the housekeeping such as DRAM refreshing. The "read /

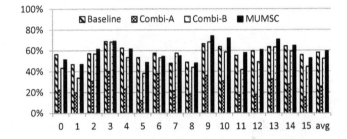

Figure 10: Row Hit Ratio for Each Configuration

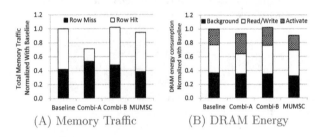

(A) Memory Traffic   (B) DRAM Energy

Figure 11: Memory Traffic and DRAM Energy

write" refers to the energy to transfer reading / writing data between the processor and the memory. The "activate" refers to the energy to activate and precharge the row. MUMSC reduces the energy consumption 6.1% over Combi-A. The reason for this inversion is the number of activations for DRAM access. The activate energy of MUMSC is reduced over Combi-A by 27.8%, because MUMSC increases the row hit with DRAM-Aware prefetching. As well as MUMSC, the baseline also reduces the activate energy over Combi-A by 21.2%. However, the baseline also increases the actual reading / writing energy by 20.8% over Combi-A, because of the inaccurate prefetch requests. These results show that data prefetching should consider both the row buffer locality and the prefetch accuracy to reduce the energy consumption. MUMSC realizes a good balance, resulting in a reduction of total energy consumption over existing memory subsystems.

5.2.4 Performance of DRAM-Aware Prefetching

To discuss the performance of the DA-AMPM prefetching, we compared the performance of existing prefetchers with the same cache replacement policy. We evaluated the stream prefetcher, PC/DC, AMPM, and DA-AMPM with DRRIP replacement policy. The overall speedup from the stream prefetcher is shown in Figure 12. DA-AMPM improves the throughput by 6.6% over the stream prefetcher

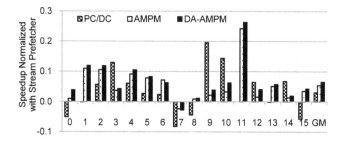

Figure 12: Performance Comparison of Prefetching

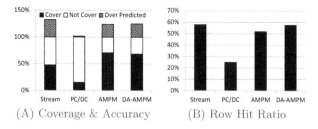

(A) Coverage & Accuracy   (B) Row Hit Ratio

Figure 13: Traffic Analysis for Each Prefetcher

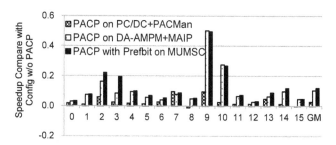

Figure 14: Performance Improvement of PACP

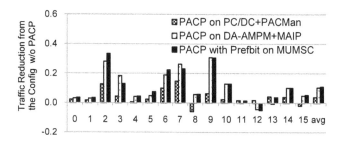

Figure 15: Traffic Reduction of PACP

and outperforms the other existing prefetchers. This performance improvement is much less than in previous work [22, 10] because the narrow memory bandwidth limits the performance improvement in multi-core situations. To analyze the reason for the performance improvements, we evaluated further detailed information.

Figure 13 shows a summary of memory traffic analysis for each prefetcher. Figure 13(A) shows prefetch coverage and prefetch accuracy. The prefetch requests of DA-AMPM cover 68.2% of useful traffic, and the prefetch requests of AMPM cover 70.7% of useful traffic. The difference between DA-AMPM and AMPM is derived from the opportunity loss of the DRAM-Aware prefetching because both methods can detect the same memory access pattern. When DA-AMPM cannot make a group of prefetch requests, as shown in Figure 7(B), the pending prefetch requests are dropped. This decreases the prefetch coverage of DA-AMPM. Figure 13(B) shows the row hit ratio of each prefetcher. DA-AMPM increases row hit memory traffic by 5.6% over AMPM. This results in the increase of the available DRAM bandwidth and an increase in the system throughput. This also contributes to a reduction in the activation power. Compared with the stream prefetcher and PC/DC, DA-AMPM also increases the row hit. DA-AMPM increases row hit by 0.2% over the stream prefetcher and 32.4% over PC/DC. These results are consistent with the result shown in Figure 10. As described in this section, a small row hit ratio results in high DRAM energy consumption and low system performance. DA-AMPM also realizes a good balance between these metrics.

5.2.5 Performance of Prefetch-Aware Cache Line Promotion

We evaluated the performance impact of the Prefetch-Aware Cache Line Promotion (PACP) for the other replacement policies. To emulate PACP for the other replacement policies, we attached a prefetch bit for each cache line. The prefetch requests set the prefetch bit on an insertion, and the demand requests clear the prefetch bit on a cache ac-

cess. The prefetch bit tracks the prefetched cache line completely while the PA-MAIP can drop the prefetch information when the corresponding memory access map is evicted. PACP prevents the cache line from updating RRPV on the first access to the prefetched cache line that is indicated by the prefetch bit. We evaluated PACP on MAIP with DA-AMPM (MUMSC), PACP with a prefetch bit on MAIP with DA-AMPM, and PACP with a prefetch bit on PACMan with PC/DC.

Figure 14 shows the improvement of system throughput with PACP. The result shows that PACP increases the system throughput, except for workload 8 for PACP on PAC-Man. PACP on MAIP increases the throughput by 10.4%, and PACP on PACMan increases system throughput by 2.8%. This result indicates that the performance improvement from Combi-B, compared with MUMSC, is mainly derived from PACP. Figure 15 shows the memory traffic reduction by PACP. PACP on MAIP reduces the memory traffic by 10.4%, and PACP on PACMan reduces the traffic by 3.9%. This result also shows that PACP is consistently useful to improve the cache efficiency for shared last-level cache. These figures also show the effect of the prefetch bit. PACP with the prefetch bit on PA-MAIP increases the system performance by 1.5% over PACP without the prefetch bit, and decreases the memory traffic by 0.8%. However, PACP with the prefetch bit has to pay large external costs for the prefetch bits on the cache. This shows that PACP provides sufficient performance improvement without large additional costs.

5.3 Cost and Scalability Analysis

The additional cost of MUMSC is dominated by the storage cost of a memory access map as described in Section 4.3. This cost is in the same range as other table-based prefetchers, such as stride prefetching [6] and PC/DC (the detailed cost is shown in Table 5.1). The stream prefetcher is a much simpler prefetcher and its implementation cost is lower than MUMSC. However, the stream prefetcher wastes memory bandwidth, as shown in Section 5.2.4. It increases the total operations cost, as shown in Figure 11.

Existing memory controllers tend to employ large scheduling buffers to reorder memory requests and exploit row buffer locality. Such memory request buffers employ more than 100 entries in a multi-core situation [20]. However, MUMSC does not require such aggressive reordering on the memory controller because DA-AMPM reorders memory requests to increase the row hit ratio. As shown in Table 1, DRAM devices can saturate with a few row hits per activation. In DDR3-1866, a 38.5% row hit ratio is enough to saturate the data path. When each core, at least, issues consecutive prefetch requests at the same time, DRAM devices never suffer from the tFAW problem because their row hit ratio becomes larger than 50.0%. Lightweight FR-FCFS memory controllers employ only 32-entry for the memory request buffer, but it achieves a more than 38.5% row hit ratio in Figure 10. Because the requests are already reordered in the memory controller, the memory controller does not need to implement a large memory request buffer in the many-core situation on the UMO architecture.

PA-MAIP also saves hardware resources, compared with existing aggressive replacement techniques such as Burst-Count [17]. BurstCount requires a 3.9 KB dedicated hardware resource to predict dead blocks. PA-MAIP uses similar information to manage a shared last-level cache, but its data is shared with other features such as data prefetching. It saves the total storage cost compared with a replacement policy that requires a dedicated storage cost. Moreover, it simplifies the design of the shared resource. These analyses consistently show that MUMSC reduces the total storage cost and improves the scalability of shared resources.

6. RELATED WORK

6.1 Memory Access Scheduling

First-Ready First-Come-First-Serve (FR-FCFS) [26] exploits row buffer locality to improve the efficiency of DRAM bandwidth. It increases the available memory bandwidth, but it also introduces starvation and unfairness to multi-thread applications. Parallelism-Aware Batch Scheduler (PAR-BS) [20], Thread Cluster Memory Scheduler [15], and Adaptive per-Thread Least-Attained-Service (ATLAS) [14] modify the priority of the memory requests and mitigate the starvation and unfairness. However, these approaches require a large memory request buffer (more than 100 entries are used in their evaluation) in order to exploit row buffer locality. Minimalist [13] limits row buffer locality to improve the throughput of multi-core workloads. It does not require a large memory scheduling buffer and uses prefetch requests to exploits row buffer locality. The Prefetch-Aware DRAM controller [16] also uses the prefetch requests of the stream prefetcher to improve row buffer locality. However, the stream prefetcher often increases useless memory traffic, as shown in Figure 11.

6.2 Cache Replacement Policy

Dynamic Insertion Policy (DIP) [24, 11] is an insertion policy that improves the efficiency of the last-level cache. These techniques insert most incoming cache lines into the LRU position. These techniques improve the system performance significantly, but they conflict with the intelligent prefetchers, as shown in Figure 3. Dead block prediction

(DBP) [12], BurstCount [17], and Less Reused Filter (LRF) [32] are more aggressive approaches. They estimate the usefulness of existing cache lines and evict useless cache lines early. However, these techniques require large hardware costs to predict the usefulness of cache lines. Map-based Adaptive Insertion Policy (MAIP) [9] uses the memory access map to predict the usefulness of incoming cache lines. MAIP uses a memory access map as a shadow tag. MUMSC mitigates the hardware cost for MAIP by sharing the resource with data prefetching. Re-Reference Interval Prediction (RRIP) [12] replaces conventional the LRU stack by a re-reference interval chain. It reduces the cost of a detailed reference order and improves performance. Prefetch-Aware Cache Management (PACMan) [31] is a cache management mechanism that takes prefetch behavior into account. However, it cannot support the unexpected promotions shown in Figure 3, because it cannot distinguish whether the corresponding cache line is inserted by the prefetch requests or not.

6.3 Data Prefetching

Global History Buffer (GHB) [22] is the representative prefetcher because it can support many memory access patterns. GHBs hold all cache miss requests in a circular buffer. When a cache miss occurs, GHB tries to detect the memory access patterns. When the pattern is found, GHB issues prefetch requests to the memory subsystem. C/DC [21] and PC/DC/MG [4] are extensions of GHB. Spatial memory streaming (SMS) has been proposed in [29], and it is extended to a combination of temporal patterns [28]. It holds spatial memory access patterns on the bitmap in order to predict future memory access patterns. This approach is similar to the memory access map, but SMS uses the collected information after the corresponding map is evicted. The evicted map is tagged by the instruction address and stored in the main memory. When the same situation is replicated, the corresponding map is read from the memory and fetches the corresponding data. Spatial memory streaming with rotated patterns [5] tried to reduce the size of the pattern history table, but it did not achieve a higher level of performance in the first data prefetching championship [1].

7. CONCLUSION

In this paper, we have proposed a new architecture for the memory subsystem, called Unified Memory Optimizing (UMO) architecture, which resolves the inefficiency of the current design of the memory subsystem. The UMO architecture integrates data prefetching, cache replacement and memory access scheduling into a per-core Unified Memory Subsystem Controller (UMSC). UMSC controls the whole memory subsystem using a single unified data structure that holds the history of memory access. On the UMO architecture, we have proposed the Map-based Unified Memory Subsystem Controller (MUMSC). MUMSC is composed of DRAM-Aware Access Map Pattern Matching prefetching (DA-AMPM), Prefetch-Aware Cache Line Promotion with Map-base Adaptive Insertion (PA-MAIP), and the lightweight FR-FCFS memory controllers. DA-AMPM reorders prefetch requests in order to exploit row buffer locality. It helps to reduce the size of the memory request buffer on the memory controller. The reordering strategy of memory access is scalable for many-core environments because its algorithm is naturally distributed. PA-MAIP suppresses the update of replacement information on the first demand access at prefetched cache lines. It reduces dead blocks caused by unintended cache promotion and improves the efficiency of the cache. Moreover, the per-core implementation is scalable for many-core environments because its design does not increase the complexity of the design of the shared resources.

Evaluation results of MUMSC show the advantages of the UMO architecture. The unified approach improves system performance, reduces hardware cost, and saves energy consumption for the memory system. The UMO architecture can be applied not only to MUMSC but also to the other data prefetchers, cache replacement policies, and memory access scheduling methods. Moreover, memory subsystem control with a per-core resource is scalable and suitable for many-core processors that employ a multi-banked last-level cache and a multi-channeled memory system. Exploring more efficient unified control strategies for the memory subsystem is a one of the topics of our future work.

8. REFERENCES

[1] The first JILP data prefetching championship (DPC-1). http://www.jilp.org/dpc/.

[2] The first JILP workshop on computer architecture competitions (JWAC-1): http://www.jilp.org/jwac-1/.

[3] SPEC CPU2006. http://www.spec.org/cpu2006/.

[4] P. Diaz and M. Cintra. Stream chaining: exploiting multiple levels of correlation in data prefetching. In C '09, pages 81–92, 2009.

[5] M. Ferdman, S. Somogyi, and B. Falsafi. Spatial memory streaming with rotated patterns. PC-1, 2009.

[6] J. W. C. Fu, J. H. Patel, and B. L. Janssens. Stride directed prefetching in scalar processors. GM CRO ewsl., 23(1-2):102–110, 1992.

[7] Y. Ishii, M. Inaba, and K. Hiraki. Access map pattern matching for data cache prefetch. In C '09, pages 499–500, 2009.

[8] Y. Ishii, M. Inaba, and K. Hiraki. Access map pattern matching prefetch: Optimization friendly method. PC-1, 2009.

[9] Y. Ishii, M. Inaba, and K. Hiraki. Cache replacement policy using map-based adaptive insertion. J C-1, 2010.

[10] Y. Ishii, M. Inaba, and K. Hiraki. Access map pattern matching for high performance data cache prefetch. pecial ssue: he First J P ata Prefetching Championship (PC-1), 2011.

[11] A. Jaleel, W. Hasenplaugh, M. Qureshi, J. Sebot, S. Steely, Jr., and J. Emer. Adaptive insertion policies for managing shared caches. In P C '0 , pages 208–219, 2008.

[12] A. Jaleel, K. B. Theobald, S. C. Steely, Jr., and J. Emer. High performance cache replacement using re-reference interval prediction (RRIP). In C '10, pages 60–71, 2010.

[13] D. Kaseridis, J. Stuecheli, and L. K. John. Minimalist open-page: A dram page-mode scheduling policy for the many-core era. In M CRO 44, pages 24–35, 2011.

[14] Y. Kim, D. Han, O. Mutlu, and M. Harchol-Balter. Atlas: A scalable and high-performance scheduling algorithm for multiple memory controllers. In HPC '10, pages 1–12, 2010.

[15] Y. Kim, M. Papamichael, O. Mutlu, and M. Harchol-Balter. Thread cluster memory scheduling: Exploiting differences in memory access behavior. In M CRO 43, pages 65–76, 2010.

[16] C. J. Lee, O. Mutlu, V. Narasiman, and Y. N. Patt. Prefetch-aware dram controllers. In M CRO 41 pages 200–209, 2008.

[17] H. Liu, M. Ferdman, J. Huh, and D. Burger. Cache bursts: A new approach for eliminating dead blocks and increasing cache efficiency. In M CRO 41, pages 222–233, 2008.

[18] Micron. 4Gb: x4, x8, x16 ddr3 sdram.

[19] Micron. TN-41-01: Calculating Memory System Power for DDR3.

[20] O. Mutlu and T. Moscibroda. Parallelism-aware batch scheduling: Enhancing both performance and fairness of shared dram systems. In C '0 , pages 63–74, 2008.

[21] K. J. Nesbit, A. S. Dhodapkar, and J. E. Smith. AC/DC: An adaptive data cache prefetcher. In P C '04, pages 135–145, 2004.

[22] K. J. Nesbit and J. E. Smith. Data cache prefetching using a global history buffer. In HPC '04, 2004.

[23] A. Patel, F. Afram, S. Chen, and K. Ghose. MARSSx86: A Full System Simulator for x86 CPUs. In C'11, 2011.

[24] M. K. Qureshi, A. Jaleel, Y. N. Patt, S. C. Steely, and J. Emer. Adaptive insertion policies for high performance caching. In C '0 , pages 381–391, 2007.

[25] M. K. Qureshi and Y. N. Patt. Utility-based cache partitioning: A low-overhead, high-performance, runtime mechanism to partition shared caches. In M CRO 39, pages 423–432, 2006.

[26] S. Rixner, W. J. Dally, U. J. Kapasi, P. Mattson, and J. D. Owens. Memory access scheduling. In C '00, pages 128–138, 2000.

[27] P. Rosenfeld, E. Cooper-Balis, and B. Jacob. DRAMsim2: A cycle accurate memory system simulator. Computer rchitecture etters, 10:16–19, 2011.

[28] S. Somogyi, T. F. Wenisch, A. Ailamaki, and B. Falsafi. Spatio-temporal memory streaming. In C '09, pages 69–80, 2009.

[29] S. Somogyi, T. F. Wenisch, A. Ailamaki, B. Falsafi, and A. Moshovos. Spatial memory streaming. In C '06, pages 252–263, 2006.

[30] K. Sudan, N. Chatterjee, D. Nellans, M. Awasthi, R. Balasubramonian, and A. Davis. Micro-pages: increasing dram efficiency with locality-aware data placement. In P O '10, pages 219–230, 2010.

[31] C.-J. Wu, A. Jaleel, M. Martonosi, S. S. Jr, and J. Emer. PACMan: Prefetch-aware cache management for high performance caching. In M CRO 44, pages 442–453, 2011.

[32] L. Xiang, T. Chen, Q. Shi, and W. Hu. Less reused filter: improving l2 cache performance via filtering less reused lines. In C '09, pages 68–79, 2009.

Locality & Utility Co-optimization for Practical Capacity Management of Shared Last Level Caches

Dongyuan Zhan, Hong Jiang, Sharad C. Seth
Department of Computer Science & Engineering
University of Nebraska - Lincoln
Lincoln, NE 68588, USA
{dzhan, jiang, seth}@cse.unl.edu

ABSTRACT

Shared last-level caches (SLLCs) on chip-multiprocessors play an important role in bridging the performance gap between processing cores and main memory. Although there are already many proposals targeted at overcoming the weaknesses of the *least-recently-used* (LRU) replacement policy by optimizing either locality or utility for heterogeneous workloads, very few of them are suitable for practical SLLC designs due to their large overhead of log *associativity* bits per cache line for re-reference interval prediction. The two recently proposed practical replacement policies, TA-DRRIP and SHiP, have significantly reduced the overhead by relying on just 2 bits per line for prediction, but they are oriented towards managing locality only, missing the opportunity provided by utility optimization.

This paper is motivated by our two key experimental observations: (*i*) the *not-recently-used* (NRU) replacement policy that entails only one bit per line for prediction can satisfactorily approximate the LRU performance; (*ii*) since locality and utility optimization opportunities are concurrently present in heterogeneous workloads, the co-optimization of both would be indispensable to higher performance but is missing in existing practical SLLC schemes. Therefore, we propose a novel practical SLLC design, called COOP, which needs just one bit per line for re-reference interval prediction, and leverages lightweight per-core locality & utility monitors that profile sample SLLC sets to guide the co-optimization. COOP offers significant throughput improvement over LRU by 7.67% on a quad-core CMP with a 4MB SLLC for 200 random workloads, outperforming both of the recent practical replacement policies at the in-between cost of 17.74KB storage overhead (TA-DRRIP: 4.53% performance improvement with 16KB storage cost; SHiP: 6.00% performance improvement with 25.75KB storage overhead).

Categories and Subject Descriptors

B.3.2 [**Memory Structures/Design Styles**]: Cache Memories

General Terms

Design, Management, Performance

Keywords

Chip Multiprocessors, Shared Last Level Caches, Practical Capacity Management, Locality & Utility Co-Optimization

1. INTRODUCTION

The shared last level cache (SLLC) organization is commonly adopted in chip multiprocessor (CMP) products, such as AMD's Phenom II X6 and Intel's Core i7, to simplify both cache capacity sharing and coherence support for processing cores. Although the SLLC of a CMP is accessible to all cores, its large aggregate capacity alone cannot guarantee optimal performance without good management strategies. This is especially true when the cores are running a heterogeneous mix of threads that have diverse requirements for SLLC resources, which becomes increasingly common with the widespread deployment of CMPs in complex applications, such as cloud computing [1].

Because of their vital role in minimizing the expensive memory traffic, SLLC capacity management schemes have been extensively studied for a long time by the research community. It has been noticed that the *least-recently-used* (LRU) replacement policy becomes less effective for SLLCs due to the diminished *access locality* [1] at the last cache level [2–5] and the uncoordinationed capacity allocation among heterogeneous threads [6, 7]. In response to LRU's limitations, two approaches have emerged in the literature. First, alternative replacement policies, such as TADIP [2], SDBP [3] and NUcache [5], have been proposed to manage locality by temporally assigning and adjusting lifetime for blocks. Second, working with a different principle, cache partitioning schemes, including UCP [6] and PIPP [7], try to optimize *utility* [2] by spatially partitioning the SLLC capacity among concurrent threads to maximize performance.

Although the aforementioned proposals have demonstrated desirable performance improvement over LRU in simulations, they are not practically useful due to the high storage overhead entailed by them. Specifically, they are all based on the assumption that each cache line has log A bits for its *re-reference interval prediction value* (RRPV) [8] that is used to estimate how soon an accessed block will be reused, where A is the set associativity. But the log A-bit overhead per line is

---

[1] In this paper, locality specifically refers to temporal locality
[2] Utility is defined as a thread's ability to reduce misses with a given amount of allocated cache capacity.

considered prohibitive for SLLCs according to industry standards [4]. As a result, since the uniprocessor era, commodity processors have relied on lightweight LRU approximations for cache management, such as the *not-recently used* (NRU) replacement policy that requires just one-bit overhead in each cache line. It has been experimentally shown that the lightweight NRU is able to perform almost (99.52% [8]) as well as LRU but still cannot provide optimized performance for CMPs either.

Recent efforts have attempted to bridge the gap between the theoretical cache research and practical SLLC designs. Jaleel et al. [8] propose to use 2 bits in each line's RRPV field for a thread-aware dynamic SLLC replacement policy called TA-DRRIP. TA-DRRIP outperforms the baseline LRU and NRU policies by coordinating locality optimization for all of the co-scheduled threads. Rooted in the same two-bit RRPV substrate, the recent work SHiP [9] further improves over TA-DRRIP by accounting for the variations in locality at the finer-grained memory instruction level for re-reference interval prediction, but incurs more overhead than the thread-level TA-DRRIP approach.

Through our analysis of and experimental study on practical SLLC capacity management solutions, we obtain two important insights that counter the previous research: (*i*) since the minimum-overhead NRU achieves almost the same practical performance as LRU but lacks such theoretical traits as the LRU stack property, it is possible to adopt the minimum-overhead 1-bit RRPV substrate in the entire SLLC and utilize monitors with good theoretical properties yet at a slightly more storage cost for just sample sets, so that the goals of overhead reduction and performance improvement can be achieved at the same time; (*ii*) both locality and utility optimization opportunities are present in heterogeneous CMP workloads, but the practical schemes such as TA-DRRIP and SHiP are oriented only towards locality management, missing performance potentials provided by utility optimization.

Hence, we propose a novel practical SLLC management design, called COOP (an acronym for *locality and utility CO-OPtimization*), which achieves higher performance than both TA-DRRIP and SHiP but at comparable or lower overhead. COOP uses a single bit in each line's RRPV field, and employs a classic LRU-stack hit profiler and a novel *logarithmic-distance* BNRU (a.k.a., *bimodal* NRU, for thrashing prevention) hit profiler to monitor the interleaved locality and utility of each thread. Leveraging the information about all co-scheduled threads, COOP spatially allocates SLLC cache ways among the threads and temporally makes the best use of their partitions in an interactive way, so that the highest utility provided by either NRU or BNRU, whichever is better, can be exploited by locality and utility co-optimization for all of the threads. Our evaluation shows that COOP improves the throughput performance for 200 random workloads by 7.67% on a quad-core CMP with a 4MB SLLC, all at the cost of only 17.74KB storage overhead which is comparable to TA-DRRIP (16KB) but lower than SHiP (25.75KB), while outperforming both of them (compared to TA-DRRIP's 4.53% and SHiP's 6.00% throughput improvements).

The rest of the paper is organized as follows. Section 2 elaborates on essential background and research motivations. Section 3 describes the design and implementation of our proposed solution, followed by a thorough performance evaluation in Section 4. Related work is discussed in Section 5 and the paper concludes in Section 6.

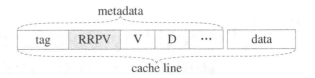

Figure 1: The Structure of a Cache Line

2. BACKGROUND & MOTIVATIONS

Although the entire SLLC capacity can be accessed by all cores, allowing free use, without constraints, does not lead to efficient utilization of SLLC resources. Therefore, various strategies have been proposed to make the best use of the SLLC capacity. We will briefly describe their working principles here but place our research in a broader context of related work in Section 5. Since practical SLLC management is our main focus in the paper, we will analyze the strengths and weaknesses of the state-of-the-art practical schemes and provide quantitative evidence in support of our conclusions.

2.1 Theoretical SLLC Management Proposals

As is illustrated in Figure 1, a cache line typically consists of two parts, *metadata* and a *data block*. The metadata includes such fields as a tag, a *re-reference prediction value* (RRPV), a valid bit, a dirty bit and other information bits (e.g., coherence bits). Given the set associativity A, the LRU replacement policy adopts $\log A$ bits for each line's RRPV field to indicate its current position in the LRU stack. For instance, the RRPVs of the *most-recently-used* and the *least-recently-used* blocks are 0 and $A - 1$ respectively. We note that most previous SLLC management proposals [2, 3, 5–7] are based on the assumption of $\log A$-bit RRPVs. But since this overhead is prohibitive for SLLCs that have large set associativity from the industry's point of view [4], those proposals may arguably only be used for theoretical research. In general, the theoretical proposals can be categorized into either alternative replacement policies for locality management or capacity partitioning schemes for utility optimization, as follows.

Locality-Oriented Alternative Replacement Policies: Because the LRU replacement policy aims to favor cache access recency (or *locality*) only, it can result in thrashing when the working set size of a workload is larger than the cache capacity and the cache access pattern is locality-unfriendly (e.g., a large cyclic working set [10]). Alternative replacement policies, such as TADIP [2], SDBP [3] and NUcache [5], are proposed to optimize locality by temporally assigning and adjusting lifetimes for cached blocks.

Utility-Oriented Capacity Partitioning Schemes: The *utility* of a thread represents its ability to reduce misses with a given amount of allocated SLLC capacity [6]. Although threads may vary greatly in their utility, an LRU-managed SLLC is oblivious of such differences when threads are co-scheduled and their cache accesses are mixed. In response to this shortcoming, several previous studies, such as UCP [6] and PIPP [7], propose to spatially partition the SLLC among competing threads based on the utility information captured by per-thread LRU-stack profilers, notably

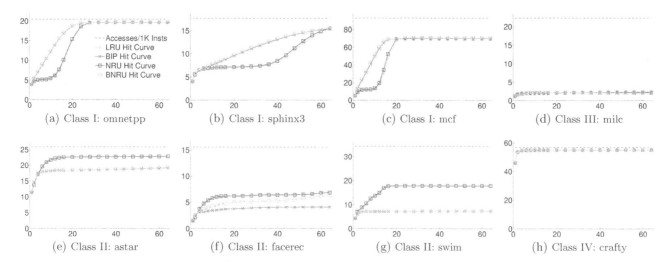

Figure 2: The HPKIs (*hits per thousand instructions*) of LRU, BIP, NRU and BNRU as a function of the SLLC capacity for the SPEC benchmarks. The x-axis shows the SLLC capacity measured in the number of ways (given that the number of sets and line size are fixed), while the y-axis represents *HPKIs*. The dotted roofline in each figure indicates the total number of SLLC accesses per 1k instructions (independent of the SLLC capacity). The 8 benchmarks are divided into four classes according to their locality and utility characteristics.

improving the performance over the baseline LRU replacement policy.

2.2 Practical SLLC Management Schemes

The LRU approximations, such as the *not-recently-used* (NRU) replacement policy, are practically adopted in commodity processors because its RRPV filed requires just a single bit. In NRU, a 0-valued (or 1-valued) RRPV indicates that the block was recently used (or not recently used). Upon a cache hit, NRU updates the block's RRPV bit to 0. In order to select a victim block for eviction followed by a cache miss, there are two possible cases: (*i*) if there are any blocks with 1-valued RRPVs in the target set, the first such block found by scanning the set will be selected as the replacement candidate; (*ii*) otherwise, NRU increments all blocks' RRPVs and then repeats the process (*i*) to find the replacement candidate. Upon a cache fill, the RRPV of the newly-inserted block is set to 0. According to extensive experimental statistics [8], NRU achieves a desirable 99.52% performance approximation to LRU. But since LRU is not performance-effective for CMPs, the NRU replacement policy that closely approximates LRU is not performance-effective for the CMP SLLC management either.

Recently, Jaleel et al. [8] have proposed a high-performance practical replacement policy called RRIP (an acronym for *Re-Reference Interval Prediction*). With 2 bits in the RRPV field, a block can have any of the three different categories of re-reference intervals: *near* (RRPV=0 or 1), *long* (RRPV=2) and *distant* (RRPV=3). RRIP always predicts a long re-reference interval for incoming blocks in an effort to prevent the cache pollution due to a subset of incoming blocks being dead-on-fill. Additionally, the bimodal variant of RRIP (called BRRIP) can prevent thrashing by predicting a distant (or a long) re-reference interval for an incoming block with a high (or a complementarily low) probability. TA-

DRRIP is a thread-aware extension of RRIP to CMPs with SLLCs by coordinating either RRIP or BRRIP for individual threads under set-dueling and feedback control. Rooted in the same 2-bit RRPV substrate, SHiP, proposed in the most recent work [9], assigns either a distant or a long re-reference interval to an incoming block, depending on whether or not it is predicted to be dead-on-fill. Specifically, SHiP leverages a history table and sample sets to dynamically learn which memory instructions (identified by their PC signatures) tend to insert dead-on-fill blocks, and predicts a distant (or a long) re-reference interval for new blocks if they are inserted by those PCs (or otherwise).

2.3 Our New Perspective and Its Supporting Experimental Evidence

If we apply the same categorization in Section 2.1 to TA-DRRIP and SHiP, they are both classified as alternative replacement policies but for practical use in that they aim to optimize locality for SLLCs. While the alternative replacement policies excel in locality management, they are likely unable to coordinate the best capacity provisioning among all co-scheduled threads for utility optimization. This is due to their lack of *utility monitors* [6], a critical component in judicious capacity partitioning, which estimate how many SLLC hits each thread would deliver with various capacity allocated. Therefore, one of our research motivation lies in the question of whether or not locality optimization alone can provide high enough performance for practical SLLC capacity management. The answer to this question, to be shortly backed with workload characterization and performance comparison, is *no*, suggesting that locality and utility co-optimization is indispensable to the best utilization of SLLC resources. Further, if locality and utility co-optimization is out of necessity, another key question is whether or not the minimum-overhead 1-bit RRPV substrate is sufficient for such a purpose. The experiments detailed in the following provide an affirmative answer to this question.

2.3.1 Workload Characterization

Before elaborating on the workload characterization, we supplement a little more background on the *bimodal insertion policy* (BIP) [10] that is a thrashing-prevention replacement alternative to LRU. Based on the log A-bit RRPV substrate, BIP assigns $A - 1$ (or 0) to the RRPV of an incoming block with a high (or complementarily low) probability, in contrast to LRU's constant 0-RRPV assignment for new blocks. LRU and BIP are the two basic optional replacement policies used in *thread-aware dynamic insertion policy* (TADIP) [2] that functions for locality optimization. Given that NRU is shown to closely approximate LRU, we are motivated to propose a new practical replacement policy, called *bimodal NRU* (BNRU), which approximates BIP by filling 1 (or 0) into the RRPV of an incoming block with a high (or complementarily low) probability.

Figure 2 illustrates the SLLC performance in terms of *hits per thousand instructions* (HPKIs), for 8 of the benchmarks in our study, as a function of assigned cache capacity, managed by LRU, BIP, NRU and BNRU respectively (see Section 3 and Section 4 for more details of experimental setups). Here, with fixed 2048 sets and 64B lines assumed, we can measure the capacity in terms of the associativity. Looking at the performance aspects of the 4 policies in Figure 2, we can make the following observations: (1) the NRU and LRU hit curves overlap each other nearly completely for all of the 8 figures, indicating that NRU approximates LRU almost perfectly regardless of the SLLC capacity and associativity configurations; (2) the BNRU and BIP hit curves also match each other very well, except for the benchmark *facerec*, in a variety of SLLC configurations; (3) BNRU is as capable as BIP for thrashing prevention, as evidenced in Figure 2 (a)-(c) where the BNRU and BIP hit curves are higher than the NRU and LRU hit curves for the three benchmarks *omnetpp*, *sphinx3* and *mcf* within certain ranges of SLLC capacity configurations. In addition, *the three observations also hold for other benchmarks in our study* (see Table 2).

From the perspective of benchmark characteristics, the 8 benchmarks can be divided into four classes depending on their locality and utility features. The first two classes represent the cases where the performance can be improved with extra capacity allocated, but they differ in their NRU vs. BNRU utility. The last two classes saturate in performance after a minimal allocation of capacity, but with very different hit rates. In the first class, as indicated in Figure 2 (a)-(c), benchmarks *omnetpp*, *sphinx3* and *mcf* all have inferior locality because their NRU curves are significantly below the BNRU curves within certain capacity ranges (e.g., from associativity 2 to 20 for *mcf*). If any of them runs in a CMP with a mix of co-scheduled threads, an alternative replacement policy such as BNRU can potentially improve the SLLC hit performance over NRU. These are the cases where locality optimization can come into more prominent play for SLLC management. For example, with the replacement policy simply altered from NRU to BNRU for the same allocated capacity of 8 cache ways, the SLLC hit performance of *mcf* can be improved by 2.5x ($\approx \frac{42.4-12.2}{12.2}$).

In contrast, the workloads in the second class, represented by applications *astar*, *facerec* and *swim* (illustrated in Figure 2 (e)-(g)), show good locality since their NRU curves are

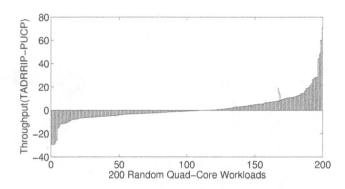

Figure 3: The difference between TA-DRRIP and PUCP in throughput normalized to that of LRU for individual quad-core workloads. Overall, TA-DRRIP and PUCP improve the throughput over LRU by 4.53% and 3.56% respectively. But, TA-DRRIP and PUCP have different performance comfort and discomfort zones due to their fundamentally distinct working principles and optimization objectives of locality vs. utility.

never below the BNRU curves. However, they can still be set apart from each other with respect to their utility. For instance, when assigned 16 ways, *astar* has a higher utility than *facerec* in that *astar* can yield a 22.53 HPKI (corresponding to a hit rate of 87.3%) while *facerec* can deliver only a 6.2 HPKI (with a hit ratio of 40.0%). If a CMP workload consists of applications all from this category, much less room is available for locality improvement that alternative replacement policies are good at, while utility optimization is still likely to make a difference in performance by favoring threads with higher utility in SLLC capacity partitioning (e.g., preferring *astar* to *facerec*).

Figure 2 (d) and (h) illustrate the third and the fourth classes whose applications require very few SLLC resources. In particular, *milc* is a streaming application due to its high miss rate regardless of the amount of allocated SLLC capacity, while *crafty* is CPU-bound and can yield very high hit rates given a small amount of allocated SLLC capacity.

2.3.2 Performance Comparison

The workload characterization experiments above indicate that (i) NRU and its bimodal variant BNRU are competent for favoring good locality and preventing thrashing respectively, and (ii) locality optimization alone cannot work consistently well for heterogeneous CMP workloads consisting of threads with various locality and utility features. To quantitatively demonstrate the limitation of practical alternative replacement policies that are oriented towards locality optimization only, we compose a simple *practical utility-based cache partitioning* (PUCP) scheme and compare it against the locality-oriented TA-DRRIP on 200 random quad-core workloads (see Section 4 for experimental details). In essence, PUCP makes cache-way partitioning decisions for co-scheduled threads by relying on the per-core sampling-based LRU utility monitors (the same as in [6]) and then leverages the NRU replacement policy (instead of LRU in [6]) to manage each thread's allocated ways. More related details will be presented in Section 3. The final performance comparison result is that TA-DRRIP and PUCP improve the throughput performance over LRU by 4.53% and 3.56% on average respectively, which indicates TA-DRRIP is better than PUCP overall. However, if we investigate Figure 3 that illustrates the difference in throughput normalized to that of LRU between TA-DRRIP and PUCP for individual workloads (sorted in ascending order), we can clearly see that there are 112 out of the 200 workloads for which TA-DRRIP underperforms PUCP. Since PUCP does nothing beyond utility optimization with its LRU-based utility monitors and the 1-bit NRU substrate, the detailed view of performance difference in Figure 3 verifies our speculation on the limitation of practical alternative replacement policies with locality management alone. But utility optimization alone as is provided by PUCP is not sufficient either, since TA-DRRIP outperforms PUCP for the remaining 88 workloads, which also contributes to TA-DRRIP's better overall performance in spite of its performance disadvantage for the 112 workloads. In summary, we can infer from this motivational experiment that neither locality nor utility optimizations alone can consistently perform well under a variety of workloads for practical SLLC capacity management due to their different working principles and optimization objectives.

3. DESIGN & IMPLEMENTATION

Our practical scheme, called COOP (an acronym for *locality and utility CO-OPtimization*) is designed to achieve three specific goals: (*i*) to base the SLLC capacity management on the 1-bit RRPV substrate; (*ii*) to be aware of locality and utility features of individual threads by profiling their NRU and BNRU hit curves; and (*iii*) to decide on the SLLC optimal management policy by conducting interactive locality and utility co-optimization for all co-scheduled threads.

3.1 The Overall Architecture

Figure 4 depicts an architectural view of COOP. In the SLLC, every cache line has a single bit in its RRPV field. Associated with each core, there is a *locality & utility monitor* that dynamically profiles both NRU and BNRU hit curves from the core's SLLC reference sequence. In particular, the NRU and the BNRU hit curves are captured by an LRU profiler and a BNRU profiler respectively, both of which are based on *auxiliary tag directories* (ATD) and the *set sampling* technique [10]. On every time interval boundary, the profilers feed the locality and utility information about sampler sets to the *decision unit*. Based on the information, the decision unit makes and enforces the capacity management decisions of cache-way partitions and replacement policies for all co-scheduled threads during the next time period.

3.2 The Locality & Utility Monitor

The *locality & utility monitor* counts the SLLC hits that a thread would contribute if it were running alone, while the amount of space assigned to it and the replacement policy (NRU vs. BNRU) adopted to manage its allocated space are both varied. By doing so, the monitor attempts to capture the runtime interplay between locality and utility optimizations in the SLLC management. Assuming that an SLLC has an associativity of 64, for example, the monitor counts the number of hits a thread would contribute if it were allocated 1-, 2-, ..., or 64-way SLLC space, being managed by NRU and BNRU respectively. Consequently, the monitor is able to deduce both NRU and BNRU hit curves as functions of cache ways, as illustrated in Figure 2 and generalized in

Figure 5. The two curves can jointly convey two critical pieces of information:

- Which replacement policy should be adopted under a given capacity quota for the thread. As depicted in Figure 5, if the thread can get 4 cache ways, then it should apply the NRU replacement policy to manage the given amount of space, since the NRU hit curve (solid) is above the BNRU curve (dotted) when the way count equals 4; but if the assigned way-count is 12, the thread should alter the policy to BRNU that can help it obtain far more hits. Therefore, with the two curves, COOP can implicitly derive a *composite hit curve* (bold) which consists of the higher segments of the NRU or BNRU curves, as illustrated in Figure 5.
- What the preferred utility is under the best replacement policy. For instance, if the hit counts of the derived composite hit curve at the way counts of 10 and 12 are assumed to be 100 and 110 respectively, then we know that the utility of 10 ways is better than that of 12 ways because $\frac{100}{10} > \frac{110}{12}$. In this way, COOP fully exploits the interactions between locality and utility dimensions.

As described below, we apply two different profiling mechanisms to deduce the NRU and the BNRU hit curves of a thread respectively because of their distinct features.

Profiling an NRU Hit Curve: Since NRU and LRU hit curves have been experimentally shown to be almost identical, as exemplified in Figure 2, we approximate an NRU hit curve with its corresponding LRU hit curve, which can be easily obtained by the well-established *LRU utility monitor* (LRU UMON) [6]. In an LRU UMON, an *auxiliary tag directory* (ATD) with an associativity A and a size-A array of *stack-hit counters* are adopted to implement Mattson's *LRU stack algorithm* [11], where A is also the SLLC's set associativity. Here, an ATD structure, with each of its entries containing only a hashed tag, a valid bit and an log A-bit RRPV field mimics the LRU stack of a small group of sampler SLLC sets, as if the monitored thread were exclusively occupying the whole space of these sampler sets. Upon every hit on ATD, it reports the LRU-stack position where the hit takes place so that the corresponding stack-hit counter $h(i)$ can be incremented by one. As a result of the LRU stack property, the values of the NRU and the LRU hit curves at way count i, denoted $NH(i)$ and $LH(i)$ respectively, can be expressed by Equation 1, where $h(k)$ is the hit counter at LRU-stack position k and $1 \leq k \leq i \leq A$.

$$NH(i) \approx LH(i) = \sum_{1 \leq k \leq i} h(k) \quad (1)$$

Profiling a BNRU Hit Curve: The profiling of a BNRU hit curve, on the other hand, is more challenging because BNRU violates the stack property with its nondeterministic 0-valued or 1-valued RRPV assignment for incoming blocks. Thus, the simple stack algorithm cannot be applied to deducing a BNRU hit curve. To resolve this issue, we first propose an exact but complex approach and follow it with an approximate but practical solution.

The *exact approach* is also based on set sampling, and uses a number A of ATD structures representing the A different associativities from 1 to A. Therefore, in the exact approach, we use a group of A ATD structures, {ATD(1), ATD(2),

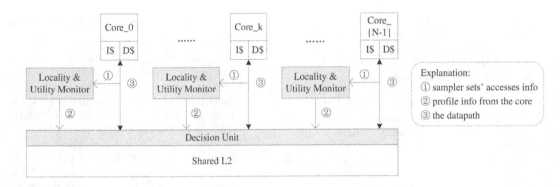

Figure 4: The COOP architecture: the grey boxes are the major extra hardware logic required by COOP on top of the SLLC with 1-bit RRPVs.

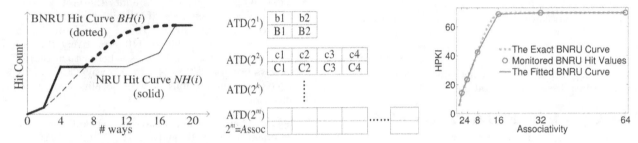

Figure 5: Deriving a *composite hit curve* (bold): the higher segments of either NRU (solid) or BNRU (dotted) hit curves.

Figure 6: Approximately profiling a BNRU hit curve: a 2^k-way ATD structure $\mathrm{ATD}(2^k)$ is used for monitoring at each logarithmic way-count point 2^k, where $1 \leq k \leq \log A$.

Figure 7: Applying the *logarithmic-distance monitoring & curve fitting* approach to profiling the BNRU hit curve for benchmark *mcf* (by approximating the exact curve).

$\mathrm{ATD}(3) \ldots$, $\mathrm{ATD}(A-1)$ and $\mathrm{ATD}(A)\}$, to mimic BNRU's operations on the sampler SLLC sets with an associativity ranging from 1 to A respectively. Although this approach provides an exact measure of the BNRU curve, it requires a significant number A of ATD structures, rendering the implementation prohibitively expensive when A is large.

The *practical solution* is based on four key observations derived from an analysis of the BNRU hit curves for the benchmarks in our study (exemplified in Figure 2): (*i*) the BNRU hit curve is monotonically non-decreasing with respect to the assigned way count; (*ii*) the BNRU hit curve is a concave function, which means that the curve's gradient is always non-increasing as the way count increases. *The intuition behind concave BNRU curves is that, with the high-probability 1-valued RRPV assignment for an incoming block, the block will most likely be victimized due to its 1-valued RRPV upon a subsequent cache miss in the same set, thus preventing other blocks from getting evicted* (namely, *stationary*).; (*iii*) the BNRU hit curve has a long flat tail as the way count approaches a high value; and (iv) it is provable that BNRU and NRU hit curves have the same value at way count 1 ($BH(1) = NH(1)$), since neither of them lets an incoming line bypass the cache. Therefore, it is sufficient to monitor the BNRU hit values at a small number of discrete logarithmic way-count points by using a dedicated ATD for each of these points, and then apply the *curve fitting* technique to deducing the entire BNRU hit curve. Specifically, as illustrated in Figure 6, we employ $m = \log A$ ATD structures $\{\mathrm{ATD}(2^1), \mathrm{ATD}(2^2), \ldots, \mathrm{ATD}(2^m)\}$ to capture the BNRU hit counts $\{BH(2^1), BH(2^2), \ldots, BH(2^m)\}$ in a

small number of way-count cases $\{2^1, 2^2, \ldots, 2^m\}$. We carry out curve fitting based on the m discrete BNRU hit values by linearly interpolating between the two monitored BNRU curve counts $(2^k, BH(2^k))$ and $(2^{k+1}, BH(2^{k+1}))$ for $1 \leq k \leq m-1$. Then, the $BH(i)$ value can be calculated iteratively by Equation 2. Figure 7 shows an example of applying our *logarithmic-distance monitoring & curve fitting* approach with up to 64 ways for benchmark *mcf*.

$$BH(i) = \begin{cases} BH(2^k), \text{ where } i = 2^k \text{ and } BH(2^k) \\ \quad \text{monitored by } \mathrm{ATD}(2^k) \\ \\ BH(i+1) - \Delta, \ \Delta = \frac{BH(2^{k+1}) - BH(2^k)}{2^k} \\ \quad \text{and } 1 \leq 2^k < i < 2^{k+1} \leq 2^m = A \end{cases} \tag{2}$$

The specific design choice of monitoring at logarithmic way-count points stems from our empirical observations mentioned above, suggesting a denser number of monitoring points to more accurately profile the high-gradient portion of the BNRU hit curve when A is small, which is also a property of a logarithmic/geometric series. As a result, the practical solution needs only $m = \log A$, instead of A, BNRU-managed ATD structures at the associativities of 2, 4, ..., $\frac{A}{2}$ and A respectively, as well as m BNRU-hit counters. It is worth remarking that the storage overhead (measured in the total number of ATD ways) required by the practical BNRU profiling is $2 + 4 + 8 + \cdots + \frac{A}{2} + A = \frac{2 \times (A-1)}{2-1} = 2 \times (A - 1) < 2 \times A$, *which is less than twice the storage overhead required by a single A-way ATD structure for the NRU/LRU hit curve profiling and makes our solution very practical in hardware implementation.* It must be noted

Table 2: Selected Benchmarks & Classification

Class	Descriptor	Benchmarks
I	Poor Locality	galgel, libquantum, mcf, omnetpp, sphinx3, xalancbmk
II	Good Utility	astar, ammp, bzip2, calculix, facerec, GemsFDTD, swim, twolf, vpr
III	Streaming	lucas, milc
IV	CPU-Bound	crafty, eon, fma3d

that, (i) the RRPV field of each BNRU-managed ATD entry has only a single bit, and (ii) upon an access to one sampler SLLC set, the LRU-managed ATD and the m BNRU-managed ATDs are operated concurrently to profile both NRU and BNRU hit curves.

3.3 The Decision Unit

With the locality and utility characteristics of co-scheduled threads profiled during each time interval, the decision unit will periodically determine the optimal space partitions and replacement policies for individual threads. Since the space partitioning logic of COOP is also utility-based and targeted at maximizing the overall performance, we adopt but with modification the framework of the *lookahead utility-based cache partitioning algorithm* [6] in the decision unit. The original algorithm evaluates every potential partitioning decision and provisions cache ways to a thread that currently has the highest utility of these ways based on its LRU hit curve. We modify the algorithm to determine the best utility-based partitioning of the cache ways according to the *composite hit curve*, which is composed of the higher segments of the NRU and the BNRU hit curves.

In the decision unit, there is an m-bit *partition quota counter*, an A-bit *global replacement mask* [12] and a single *locality management* bit associated with each core, where $m = \log A$ and A is the associativity. On each time interval boundary, the SLLC's space partitioning result for $Core_i$ is kept in the *partition quota counter*, denoted as Q_i, where $0 \leq i \leq N - 1$. Assuming that A is greater than N, COOP also guarantees that at least one way is provisioned to every core. The *global replacement mask* is used to specify which cache ways are currently allocated to the corresponding core. For example, if a core is allocated with two cache ways, say, Way 0 and Way 1, only the first and the second bits on its *global replacement mask* are set to one. A core can access any lines in an SLLC set but is only allowed to replace a line in its own allocated ways. The *locality management* bit, LM_i, is utilized to indicate whether the NRU (LM_i=0) or BNRU (LM_i=1) policy is adopted for the core to manage its allocated SLLC cache ways. LM_i can be determined by examining the difference between the NRU and BNRU curves at the way count k that is also the value of Q_i: the bit is set 0 if $NH(k) \geq BH(k)$ or 1 otherwise.

4. EVALUATION

In this section, we first briefly describe our simulation-based experimental methodology and then present and analyze the evaluation results.

4.1 Evaluation Methodology

Simulation Setup: We simulate our scheme using the cycle-accurate M5 full system simulator [13] with the key configuration parameters listed in Table 1. We model a quad-core CMP with two levels of on-chip caches. The L1 instruction and data caches adopt a coupled tag & data store organization. For the shared L2 cache, we model decoupled tag and data stores for each L2 slice and also account for the NoC latency when calculating the L2 access time. The SLLC capacity management schemes in comparison include LRU (baseline), NRU, PUCP, TA-DRRIP, SHiP and our proposed COOP scheme. PUCP and COOP make management decisions periodically every 5M cycles [3], and their profiler hit counters are reset upon each periodic decision boundary. We have not found any overflow problems with these 16-bit hit counters in our experiments.

Performance Metrics: We adopt two standard metrics, *throughput* and *fair speedup*, to quantify the CMP performance. Specifically, *throughput* measures the utilization of a system, while *fair speedup* balances both performance and fairness. Let IPC_i be the *instructions per cycle* performance of the ith thread when it is co-scheduled with other threads and $SingleIPC_i$ be the IPC of the same thread when it executes in isolation. Then, for a system where N threads execute concurrently, the formulas for the two metrics are shown in Equation 3 and Equation 4 respectively.

$$\text{throughput} = \sum_{i=1,2,\cdots,N} IPC_i \tag{3}$$

$$\text{fair speedup} = \frac{N}{\sum_{i=1,2,\cdots,N} SingleIPC_i/IPC_i} \tag{4}$$

Workload Construction: As listed in Table 2, we select 20 benchmarks from the SPEC CPU 2000 and 2006 benchmark suites and categorize them into four classes by investigating their locality and utility features via experiments similar to Section 2.3.1. Class I is a collection of benchmarks that exhibit poor locality and can benefit from judicious replacement policies. The benchmarks in Class II have excellent utility and need dedicated SLLC space partitions. Class III is a group of streaming applications that require little SLLC capacity and need to be prevented from polluting the SLLC. Finally, Class IV benchmarks are CPU-bound with small working sets in the SLLC. From the four classes of benchmarks, 200 random quad-core workloads are generated by randomly selecting 200 4-benchmark combinations out of the 20 individual benchmarks.

Simulation Control: In the experiments, all threads under a given workload are executed starting from a checkpoint that has already had the first 10 billion instructions bypassed. They are cache-warmed with 1 billion instructions and then simulated in detail until all threads finish another 1 billion instructions. Performance statistics are reported for a thread when it reaches 1 billion instructions. If one thread completes the 1 billion instructions before others, it continues to run so as to still compete for the SLLC capacity, but its extra instructions are not taken into account in the final performance report. This is in conformation with the standard practice in CMP cache research [2, 3, 5–9].

4.2 Performance Comparison

Figure 8 shows the geometric mean of throughput performance for NRU, PUCP, TA-DRRIP, SHiP and COOP,

---

[3]The period is experimentally tuned.

Table 1: Major Configuration Parameters

Core	four cores, Alpha ISA, in-order, IPC=1 except for memory accesses, 128/128 I/D TLBs, 44-bit physical addresses
L1	2-way, 32KB, 1-cycle delay, 16 MSHRs, write back & 4 write buffer entries for L1D, LRU-managed
L2	16-way, 4MB, 6/8-cycle tag/data store delay, totally 1024 MSHRs, write back & totally 256 write buffer entries
	mesh NoC topology ($1 \times 2, 2 \times 2, 2 \times 4$) with 1 cycle delay per hop; 300-cycle off-chip memory access delay
Schemes	#sample_sets = $\frac{1}{32} \times$ #SLLC_sets for all sampling-based schemes; BNRU's low probability = $\frac{1}{32}$; PUCP/COOP's LRU-managed ATD: 16-bit hit counters, 10-bit hashed tags, 4-bit RRPVs, 1 valid bit; TA-DRRIP: 10-bit saturating counters; SHiP: 16K 3-bit saturating counters in the history table, 14-bit PC signatures + 1 reuse bit in each sampled cache line; COOP's BNRU-managed ATDs: 16-bit hit counters, 10-bit hashed tags, 1-bit RRPVs, 1 valid bit.

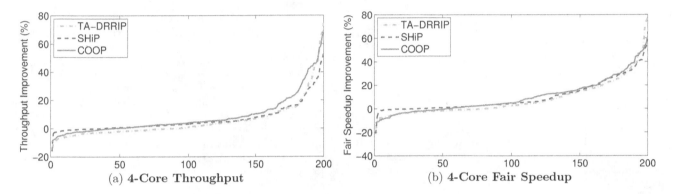

(a) **4-Core Throughput** (b) **4-Core Fair Speedup**

Figure 9: Detailed views of the quad-core throughput and fair speedup improvement for TA-DRRIP, SHiP and COOP. The performance values on each curve are sorted in ascending order.

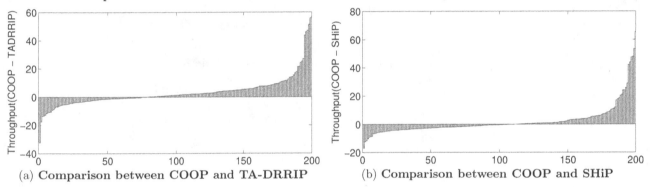

(a) **Comparison between COOP and TA-DRRIP** (b) **Comparison between COOP and SHiP**

Figure 10: The difference between COOP and the two state-of-the-art practical replacement policies in throughput normalized to that of LRU for individual quad-core workloads.

normalized to the baseline (LRU) on the simulated quad-core configuration. Averaged over all of the 200 random workloads, COOP provides a throughput improvement of 7.67%, which is noticeably higher than the improvements achieved by the practical replacement policies (TA-DRRIP: 4.53%, SHiP: 6.00%) and the simple utility-oriented scheme (PUCP: 3.56%). The NRU replacement policy degrades the throughput performance by 0.24%, which indicates that both NRU and LRU are clearly inadequate for CMPs with SLLCs. If we look closer at the details of throughput improvement in Figure 9(a), we can find that the worst case performance of COOP is -9.57% and its best improvement is up to 69.67%, while the (worst, best) performance margins for TA-DRRIP and SHiP are (-15.47%, 74.49%) and (-15.90%, 53.21%) respectively. Figure 9(a) also shows that the throughput performance curve of COOP is almost always above that of TA-DRRIP except for a very small fraction of the 200 workloads (i.e., a very small x-axis range

at the end). COOP's curve is also above that of SHiP except for a small fraction of the 200 workloads (i.e., a small x-axis range at the beginning), which means that COOP offers a consistent and robust throughput performance that is generally better than the two existing practical replacement policies.

Figure 10(a) and Figure 10(b) show the head-to-head comparison between COOP and the two state-of-the-art schemes for individual workloads. COOP outperforms the two practical replacement policies for the majority of the workloads, and in many cases significantly. However, it does not do so in all cases. We speculate that it is because COOP must strike a balance between both locality and utility optimizations. COOP may not optimize locality fully when a workload heavily or exclusively favors locality optimization but does show stronger performance improvement over both of the state-of-the-arts (indicated by the portions of bars above the 0/equal line in Figure 10(a) and Figure 10(b)).

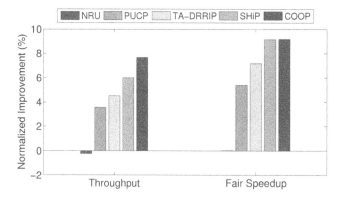

Figure 8: The 4-Core Configuration: the throughput and the fair speedup improvement (over LRU, in geometric mean) averaged over the 200 random quad-core workloads for all of the schemes in comparison.

If we specifically compare Figure 10(a) against Figure 3 in Section 2.3.2, we can make the following two observations: (*i*) COOP significantly boosts the performance beyond capacity partitioning provided by PUCP by additionally adapting to the better replacement policy between NRU and BNRU; (*ii*) it relies on its partitioning module besides the alternative replacement mechanism, which is based on 1-bit RRPVs, to surpass a TA-DRRIP-like replacement policy which only conducts locality optimization even with 2-bit RRPVs. Therefore, COOP is arguably capable of bridging the performance gap between the locality and the utility optimization schemes via its co-optmization strategies.

In terms of the fair speed improvement, COOP improves over LRU by 9.17%, which matches the 9.16% performance improvement of SHiP. Other schemes, NRU, PUCP and TA-DRRIP, improve the fair speedup metric by 0.02%, 5.41%, 7.19% respectively. Figure 9(b) depicts the detailed result of fair speedups for individual workloads. While the curves of COOP and SHiP are both above that of TA-DRRIP in most cases, the difference between the curves of the two bests seems to be minor.

However, we notice in both Figure 9(a) and Figure 9(b) that SHiP's curves are barely below the zero horizontal line, while COOP's curves have a small portion below. This may suggest that SHiP is slightly more robust in the sense that it seldom underperforms LRU. But this robustness may come at the cost of its weakened ability to exploit the highest performance when available, which is evident in Figure 9(a) because the curves of both COOP and TA-DRRIP are above that of SHiP at the end of the *x*-axis range. TA-DRRIP seems to be able to exploit the highest performance, but it underperforms LRU in quite a few cases. In this sense, COOP also shows its ability to strike a reasonable balance between the exploitation of the highest possible performance and keeping performance robust in the worst cases.

4.3 Overhead Analysis

Table 3 gives a detailed comparison of hardware overhead for the various schemes in this paper (see their specific configurations in Table 1). For all of the schemes, the total number of their RRPV bits as well as the extra monitoring logic is counted into their total hardware costs. In partic-

Table 3: Overhead & Throughput

	LRU	NRU	TA-DRRIP	SHiP	COOP
RRPVs	32KB	8KB	16KB	16KB	8KB
Monitors	0	0	5B	9.75KB	9.74KB
Total Overhead	32KB	8KB	16KB	25.75KB	17.74KB
Throughput	1	0.9976	1.0453	1.0600	1.0767

ular, for COOP, since it requires an LRU profiler and an BNRU profiler for per-core locality & utility monitoring, the ATD structures will dominate hardware overhead in its design. But the hashing function that has shown provably low collision rate in [14] and the *logarithmic-distance monitoring* technique in the BNRU profiler contribute to much less cost in the per-core locality & utility monitor. Most importantly, COOP is based on the minimum-overhead 1-bit RRPV substrate, which can greatly help reduce the overhead from the 2-bit RRPV substrate in both TA-DRRIP and SHiP in spite of COOP's extra monitoring logic. As a result, COOP's 3.88KB LRU profiler, 5.86KB BNRU profiler and 8KB RRPVs contribute to its 17.74KB total overhead. In contrast, the recently-proposed practical scheme SHiP, requires more hardware resources due to the large prediction history table (6KB) and also additional PC signature stores (3.75KB), in addition to the 16KB 2-bit RRPVs. Overall, COOP can provide better performance improvement than both TA-DRRIP and SHiP but at a comparable cost of storage overhead to TA-DRRIP and a lower cost than SHiP.

5. RELATED WORK

As our paper focuses on the SLLC capacity management, in what follows, we briefly review the representative work related to the shared LLC organization.

5.1 SLLC Capacity Management

Theoretical Alternative Replacement Policies: As LRU is ineffective in handling workloads with inferior locality, alternative replacement policies have been proposed to adapt management decisions to workloads' specific locality characteristics, by means of sophisticated block insertion, promotion or victimization. The *thread-aware dynamic insertion policy* (TADIP) [2] identifies the locality of individual threads through set-sampling and dueling, and then coordinates locality optimization for all of the co-scheduled threads under feedback control. The *next-use cache* (NUcache) [5] scheme differentiates the locality of individual memory instructions, selects a small group of instructions with superior locality through a cost-benefit analysis and allows their inserted blocks to stay longer in the SLLC by the FIFO replacement policy. Based on LRU-managed set samples and skewed dead-block prediction tables, the *sampling dead block prediction* (SDBP) scheme [3] learns which memory instructions (identified by their PC signatures) tend to access cache blocks that immediately become "dead", victimizes the blocks touched by those PCs prior to default replacement candidates and also bypasses predicted dead-on-fill blocks.

Theoretical Capacity Partitioning Schemes: The commonly used LRU policy implicitly divides the SLLC capacity among competing threads on a miss-driven basis, which is also ineffective in that a thread may occupy much capacity by bringing into the cache a number of missed blocks but without re-referencing them. SLLC capacity partitioning is targeted at allocating LLC resources to threads on a *utility, fairness* or *quality-of-service* (QoS) basis. The *utility-based cache partitioning* (UCP) [6] and the *pseudo insertion/promotion partitioning* (PIPP) schemes are proposed to partition the SLLC space among co-scheduled threads to maximize the throughput performance. With the thread-level utility information profiled by *LRU utility monitors* (LRU UMON) that are based on Mattson's *LRU stack algorithm* [11], UCP partitions SLLC space in the form of assigning cache ways to threads and favors those with higher utility under LRU, while PIPP achieves a similar effect by relying on a combination of insertion and promotion policies. In [15], Kim et al. propose fairness-based cache partitioning so that all threads are slowed down equally from where each thread monopolizes the SLLC. In [16], Nesbits et al. introduce the notion of virtual private caches to facilitate QoS guarantees. Zhou et al. [17] argue that the SLLC miss count, which is a commonly used metric in the literature, is inadequate for QoS considerations. They propose to take into account the measures of both miss count and miss penalty of each thread when performing QoS-oriented SLLC partitioning.

5.2 Hit-Latency Reduction

In the context of *non-uniform cache architecture* (NUCA) [18], the SLLC organization can incur higher hit latencies, because the block being accessed by a core may reside in a non-local SLLC slice. *Victim replication* (VM) [19] reduces SLLC hit latency by retaining/replicating each core's L1 victim blocks in its local SLLC slice if a victim's home slice is non-local. Noticing that blind replication would diminish the effective SLLC capacity and in turn adversely affect performance, the *adaptive selective replication* (ASR) [20] mechanism selectively replicates shared read-only data and adaptively determines the replication level that minimizes hit latency without an obvious increase in cache misses.

5.3 Page-Coloring Management

Page coloring is an OS-based approach to cache management by manipulating an overlapped section (namely the *page color*) between a physical page index and an SLLC set index. First proposed in [21], by using the physical page index rather than the set index in determining a block's home LLC slice, OS-assisted SLLC management is shown to have a direct and flexible impact on CMP's SLLC hit latency and sharing degrees. Lin et al. [22] propose to partition the SLLC capacity to optimize throughput, fairness or QoS for CMPs by allocating page colors to different cores. Awasthi et al. [23] propose to utilize shadow address bits in migrating shared pages to optimal locations. Chaudhuri [24] devises a HW mechanism to support the decision-making on when and where to migrate an entire page so as to amortize the performance overhead. A recent SLLC design called *reactive NUCA* (R-NUCA) [25] classifies SLLC accesses into distinct categories and adapts data placement, replication and migration to individual categories via page coloring.

6. CONCLUSION

The research community has introduced a substantial volume of theoretical proposals to optimize either locality or utility in the SLLC capacity management. But their high storage overhead for re-reference interval prediction discourages the industry from adopting them in practical CMP designs. Although there are already two practical replacement policies TA-DRRIP and SHiP that significantly reduce overhead by relying on a 2-bit RRPV substrate, their performance is suboptimal due to their single-pronged approach of locality optimization. Different from the existing studies, our proposed COOP design (*i*) combines the strengths of both the minimum-overhead 1-bit RRPV substrate and the profilers with good theoretical traits and, importantly, (*ii*) carries out locality and utility co-optimization in capacity management. By employing lightweight monitors that profile both NRU (approximated by LRU) and BNRU hit curves (curve-fitted with *logarithmic-distance monitoring*), our proposed design can exploit the co-optimized locality and utility of concurrent threads and thus effectively manage the SLLC capacity for CMP workloads with heterogeneous resource requirements. Our execution-driven simulation shows that the proposed scheme improves the throughput performance over the baseline LRU for 200 random workloads by 7.67% on a quad-core CMP with a 4MB SLLC, outperforming both TA-DRRIP (4.53%) and SHiP (6.00%), all at the cost of only 17.74KB storage overhead that is slightly higher than TA-DRRIP (16KB) but lower than SHiP (25.75KB).

The present work opens up opportunities for future research. For instance, our current proposed design is evaluated using multiprogrammed workloads for which the heterogeneous capacity requirements of co-scheduled threads are the most important concern. But for multithreaded workloads, the interactions between data sharing and capacity sharing among threads need to be taken into account in the SLLC management [26]. In our future work, the performance impact of COOP on multithreaded workloads will be investigated, for the purpose of devising an amended scheme that incorporates enhancements to promote both data and capacity sharing.

7. ACKNOWLEDGMENTS

We would like to thank the Holland Computing Center of the University of Nebraska - Lincoln for providing the supercomputing facilities. We also greatly appreciate the constructive comments and suggestions from the anonymous reviewers. This work was supported in part by NSF under Grants CCF-0937993, IIS-0916859, CNS-1016609 and CNS-1116606.

References

[1] Iñigo Goiri, Josep Oriol Fitó, Ferran Julià, Ramon Nou, Josep Lluis Berral, Jordi Guitart, and Jordi Torres. Multifaceted Resource Management for Dealing with Heterogeneous Workloads in Virtualized Data Centers. In *Proceedings of the 11th ACM/IEEE International Conference on Grid Computing*, pages 25–32, October 2010.

[2] Aamer Jaleel, William Hasenplaugh, Moinuddin K. Qureshi, Julien Sebot, Simon C. Steely Jr., and Joel S. Emer. Adaptive Insertion Policies for Managing Shared Caches. In *Proceedings of the 17th International Conference on Parallel Architectures and Compilation Techniques*, pages 208–219, October 2008.

[3] Samira M. Khan, Daniel A. Jiménez, Doug Burger, and Babak Falsafi. Using Dead Blocks as a Virtual Victim Cache. In *Proceedings of the 19th International Conference on Parallel Architectures and Compilation Techniques*, pages 489–500, September 2010.

[4] Aamer Jaleel, Eric Borch, Malini Bhandaru, Simon C. Steely Jr., and Joel Emer. Achieving Non-Inclusive Cache Performance with Inclusive Caches: Temporal Locality Aware (TLA) Cache Management Policies. In *Proceedings of the 2010 43rd Annual IEEE/ACM International Symposium on Microarchitecture*, pages 151–162, December 2010.

[5] R. Manikantan, K. Rajan, and R. Govindarajan. NUcache: An Efficient Multicore Cache Organization Besed on Next-Use Distance. In *Proceedings of the 17th International Symposium on High Performance Computer Architecture*, pages 243–254, February 2011.

[6] Moinuddin K. Qureshi and Yale N. Patt. Utility-Based Cache Partitioning: A Low-Overhead, High-Performance, Runtime Mechanism to Partition Shared Caches. In *Proceedings of the 39th IEEE/ACM International Symposium on Microarchitecture*, pages 423–432, December 2006.

[7] Yuejian Xie and Gabriel H. Loh. PIPP: Promotion/Insertion Pseudo-Partitioning of Multi-Core Shared Caches. In *Proceedings of the 36th International Symposium on Computer Architecture*, pages 174–183, June 2009.

[8] Aamer Jaleel, Kevin B. Theobald, Simon C. Steely Jr., and Joel Emer. High Performance Cache Replacement Using Re-Reference Interval Prediction (RRIP). In *Proceedings of the 37th International Symposium on Computer Architecture*, pages 60–71, June 2010.

[9] Carole-Jean Wu, Aamer Jaleel, Will Hasenplaugh, Margaret Martonosi, Simon C. Steely Jr., and Joel Emer. SHiP: Signature-Based Hit Predictor for High Performance Caching. In *Proceedings of the 44th Annual IEEE/ACM International Symposium on Microarchitecture*, pages 430–441, December 2011.

[10] Moinuddin K. Qureshi, Aamer Jaleel, Yale N. Patt, Simon C. Steely Jr., and Joel Emer. Adaptive Insertion Policies for High Performance Caching. In *Proceedings of the 34th International Symposium on Computer Architecture*, pages 381–391, June 2007.

[11] R. L. Mattson, J. Gecsei, D. Slutz, and I. L. Traiger. Evaluation Techniques for Storage Hierarchies. *IBM System Journal*, 9(2):78–117, June 1970.

[12] Derek Chiou, Srinivas Devadas, Larry Rudolph, Boon S. Ang, Derek Chiouy, Derek Chiouy, Larry Rudolphy, Larry Rudolphy, Srinivas Devadasy, Srinivas Devadasy, Boon S. Angz, and Boon S. Angz. Dynamic Cache Partitioning via Columnization. In *MIT CSAIL Computation Structures Group Memo 430*, pages 1–22, November 1999.

[13] Nathan L. Binkert, Ronald G. Dreslinski, Lisa R. Hsu, Kevin T. Lim, Ali G. Saidi, and Steven K. Reinhardt. The M5 Simulator: Modeling Networked Systems. *IEEE Micro*, 26(4):52–60, July 2006.

[14] M. V. Ramakrishna, E. Fu, and E. Bahcekapili. Efficient Hardware Hashing Functions for High Performance Computers. *IEEE Transactions on Computers*, 46:1378–1381, December 1997.

[15] Seongbeom Kim, Dhruba Chandra, and Yan Solihin. Fair Cache Sharing and Partitioning in a Chip Multiprocessor Architecture. In *Proceedings of the 13th International Conference on Parallel Architectures and Compilation Techniques*, pages 111–122, September 2004.

[16] Kyle J. Nesbit, James Laudon, and James E. Smith. Virtual Private Caches. In *Proceedings of the 34th International Symposium on Computer Architecture*, pages 57–68, June 2007.

[17] Xing Zhou, Wenguang Chen, and Weimin Zheng. Cache Sharing Management for Performance Fairness in Chip Multiprocessors. In *Proceedings of the 18th International Conference on Parallel Architectures and Compilation Techniques*, pages 384–393, September 2009.

[18] Changkyu Kim, Doug Burger, and Stephen W. Keckler. An Adaptive, Non-Uniform Cache Structure for Wire-Delay Dominated on-Chip Caches. In *Proceedings of the 10th International Conference on Architectural Support for Programming Languages and Operating Systems*, pages 211–222, March 2002.

[19] Michael Zhang and Krste Asanovic. Victim Replication: Maximizing Capacity while Hiding Wire Delay in Tiled Chip Multiprocessors. In *Proceedings of the 32nd International Symposium on Computer Architecture*, pages 336–345, June 2005.

[20] Bradford M. Beckmann, Michael R. Marty, and David A. Wood. ASR: Adaptive Selective Replication for CMP Caches. In *Proceedings of the 39th IEEE/ACM International Symposium on Microarchitecture*, pages 443–454, Decebmer 2006.

[21] Sangyeun Cho and Lei Jin. Managing Distributed, Shared L2 Caches through OS-Level Page Allocation. In *Proceedings of the 39th IEEE/ACM Internationl Symposium on Microarchitecture*, pages 455–468, December 2006.

[22] Jiang Lin, Qingda Lu, Xiaoning Ding, Zhao Zhang, Xiaodong Zhang, and P. Sadayappan. Gaining Insights into Multicore Cache Partitioning: Bridging the Gap between Simulation and Real Systems. In *Proceedings of the 14th International Symposium on High Performance Computer Architecture*, pages 367–378, Febuary 2008.

[23] Manu Awasthi, Kshitij Sudan, Rajeev Balasubramonian, and John B. Carter. Dynamic Hardware-Assisted Software-Controlled Page Placement to Manage Capacity Allocation and Sharing within Large Caches. In *Proceedings of the 15th International Symposium on High Performance Computer Architecture*, pages 250–261, February 2009.

[24] Mainak Chaudhuri. PageNUCA: Selected Policies for Page-Grain Locality Management in Large Shared Chip-Multiprocessor Caches. In *Proceedings of the 15th International Symposium on High Performance Computer Architecture*, pages 227–238, February 2009.

[25] Nikos Hardavellas, Michael Ferdman, Babak Falsafi, and Anastasia Ailamaki. Reactive NUCA: Near-Optimal Block Placement and Replication in Distributed Caches. In *Proceedings of the 36th International Symposium on Computer Architecture*, pages 184–195, June 2009.

[26] Eddy Z. Zhang, Yunlian Jiang, and Xipeng Shen. Does Cache Sharing on Modern CMP Matter to the Performance of Contemporary Multithreaded Programs? In *Proceedings of the 15th ACM SIGPLAN Symposium on Principles and Practice of Parallel Programming*, pages 203–212, January 2010.

Exploiting Communication and Packaging Locality for Cost-effective Large Scale Networks

Keith D. Underwood
Intel Federal
Knoxville, TN
keith.d.underwood@intel.com

Eric Borch
Intel Federal
Fort Collins, CO
eric.borch@intel.com

ABSTRACT

As processing power increases, maintaining the balance between network and computing is becoming increasingly difficult. The two major contributors to this imbalance are the cost and the power of high bandwidth networks, and both network cost and power are heavily impacted by the type of signaling used. Reducing the length of a network link leads to both lower cost and lower power. Unfortunately, the low dimension mesh and torus topologies that enable the shortest physical links also scale poorly in terms of hop count and global bandwidth. In contrast, topologies with low hop count and high global bandwidth have a large fraction of physical links that are several meters long. We propose the cube collective topology — a hierarchical topology that uses a mesh topology locally to minimize link length and an all-to-all topology globally to minimize global hops. The result is that over 80% of the links can be very short (under 1 meter). This enables significant reductions in both network cost and network power, while still providing a balance of high global and high local bandwidth.

Categories and Subject Descriptors

C.2.1 [**Computer Systems Organization**]: Computer Communications Networks—*Network Architecture and Design*

Keywords

interconnection networks, topology, cube collective

1. INTRODUCTION

The network is a critical ingredient in large scale computer systems. Whether in high performance computing (HPC) or the datacenter, modern systems network together thousands of discrete components to achieve high throughput. Network demands grow at a rate that is comparable to the growth in computing capabilities; however, network performance has not been growing fast enough to meet those demands. More importantly, network cost and power (mW/Gb/s — or energy per bit expressed as pJ/b) have not been decreasing quickly enough to enable high bandwidth systems in a feasible cost or power envelope. Technological solutions are needed for the cost and power problem, while network topology developments will be needed to leverage the new technology.

Top of package connections combined with short flex or microtwinax cables offer a disruptive technology in system level interconnect. The combination of top of package connectivity and short, low loss cables substantially increase signaling density and significantly reduce channel loss. Reduced loss leads directly to improved per-pin bandwidth and reduced power. Today's 10 Gb/s channels require 10 to 15 pJ/b, but research has demonstrated less than 2 pJ/b over 0.5m in 45 nm circuit technology[17]. Similarly, these links are short enough to enable much smaller gauge cables that inherently result in much lower costs.

Leveraging these improvements requires a network topology that can use very short cables. Such network topologies exist: 2D and 3D meshes typically use short connections for the vast majority of their links. Early studies [4] in high performance computing (HPC) indicated that 2D and 3D meshes were the optimal topology; however, many application domains are more sensitive to latency or bisection bandwidth [26]. For bisection bandwidth sensitive applications, 2D and 3D meshes become a major performance bottleneck at even moderate system scales. Furthermore, the growth in per pin bandwidth means that high-radix topologies have drastically lower latency than mesh topologies for small messages [21, 22]. To date, high-radix network topologies have been optimized to maximize the use of cables that are a few meters in length[21, 22].

As technology evolves, it is necessary to evolve network topologies to leverage new capabilities. To leverage sub-one meter links over new materials, we propose to replace the *group* in the dragonfly topology with a local mesh[1] to create the cube collective topology. In our experiments, the mesh is constrained to a 4-ary 3-mesh to ensure sufficient local bandwidth through the mesh. We present how the topology can be scaled to 32K high bandwidth nodes or 256K lower bandwidth nodes using 64 port routers, and we compare the cost and power of the 32K node configuration with the cost and power of a similarly configured dragonfly. Simulations of similarly configured 4K node networks demonstrate that the cube collective outperforms dragonfly on traffic patterns with high locality while underperforming dragonfly on a uniform random traffic pattern. When combined with the superior cost and power profiles, the cube collective topology is shown to have a dramatic advantage in network cost ($/GB/s) and power (W/GB/s) for traffic with locality and a limited downside in these metrics for uniform random traffic. Given the breadth of applications with a larger focus on local bandwidth rather than global bandwidth[31], this is a beneficial trade-off between cost, power, and global bandwidth.

---

[1]Variants using a local torus would also be interesting, because they provide additional local bandwidth; however, variants with a local torus pose more challenging packaging and routing problems.

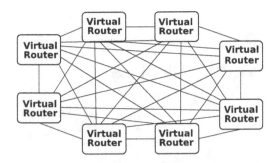

Figure 1: Top level topology for cube collective and dragonfly

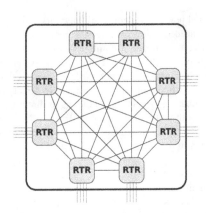

Figure 2: Virtual router topology for dragonfly

2. CUBE COLLECTIVE TOPOLOGY

At a high level, the cube collective topology is similar to a dragonfly topology. Routers are aggregated into groups, and each group acts as a single *virtual router*. Virtual routers are all-to-all connected at the top level, as shown in Figure 1. Inside a group, the dragonfly again leverages an all-to-all connection, as shown in Figure 2, where the size of the group is determined by the radix of the router and the number of links that are dedicated to local links.

In contrast, the cube collective topology optimizes the local topology to exploit very short, very low-power electrical links by using a mesh interconnect within the group. For our simulations and analysis, we chose a 4x4x4 mesh size to maximize performance and minimize cost within reasonable packaging constraints. Since a 4x4x4 mesh is nominally a full bisection topology, it can sustain a relatively high fraction of throughput (larger meshes lose this advantage). Furthermore, the mesh must be symmetric in size, since the bisection bandwidth of misshapen meshes degrades rapidly. As importantly, a 4x4x4 mesh is near the limit of what can be packaged reasonably: it supports 64 nodes that can easily be packaged within one half of a cabinet[21]. Finally, maximizing the size of the local group within the performance and packaging constraints will minimize the number of optical links and, hence, minimize cost. A cube collective using a 4x4x4 local mesh places over 85% of the bandwidth onto short electrical links. Smaller meshes shift a higher fraction of bandwidth to optical links, while larger meshes degrade performance and strain packaging.

Like the dragonfly, the cube collective topology dedicates some links from the local topology (the cube) and connects them as global links. In a full-scale cube collective topology, each global link goes to a different 4x4x4 cube. Due to simulation constraints, the configuration that is modeled uses 8 port routers with the 8th port used

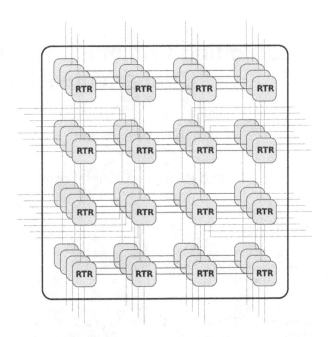

Figure 3: Virtual router topology for cube collective

for global connectivity, as shown in Figure 3. Thus, with a 4x4x4 mesh there are 64 global links (one from each router) to form 65 cubes of 64 nodes each. The local topology is routed as a mesh, and the edge links are unconnected (powered off).

2.1 Routing

For each of the topologies, we evaluated both deterministic and adaptive routing. For deterministic routing on the cube collective topology, messages are routed on the minimal path across the source cube using dimension ordered routing[10] to the router that is connected to the target cube using a global link. In the target cube, the message is once again routed using dimension ordered routing to its final destination.

Adaptive routing is critical for topologies such as the dragonfly and cube collective. The basic adaptive routing concepts from the dragonfly topology[22, 18] apply to the cube collective topology as well. Both use variants of Valiant's[30] algorithm to select an intermediate router and then route the message through that intermediate router to the target node. This use of *indirect* routes balances traffic across the available resources at the expense of using an additional global link.

First, we evaluate an oracle based approach that gives the adaptive routing algorithm full knowledge of the network state. The key component is the ability to see the state of all queues in the network. This allows us to focus on analyzing the topology rather than tuning the adaptive routing algorithm. The oracle adaptive routing algorithm starts by evaluating both local and full-path load on the deterministic path to the destination. If either load exceeds a threshold, then adaptive routes are considered. The use of the threshold is consistent with published algorithms for the dragonfly topology and improves the stability of the adaptive routing algorithm.

When adaptive paths are evaluated, the algorithm randomly selects 4 possible indirect routes. Again, this is consistent with adaptive routing research that suggests only 2 randomly selected routes need to be evaluated to achieve a good result and reduce the computational load (and routing complexity)[20]. The loads of the deterministic path and adaptive paths are compared. If the deterministic path has more "heavily loaded routers" or an equal number of heavily loaded routers and more total network load, then the adaptive path is chosen. Otherwise, the deterministic path is chosen. Load is calculated based on the load of the specific VC a message will pass through at the input port and the full load (across all VCs and all inputs) at each output port. This calculates the load based on all of the traffic that is known to use a resource in this message's path through the network. Like progressive adaptive routing for the dragonfly topology[18], the adaptive routing algorithm can choose an adaptive path at any point along the deterministic path until it leaves the first group (virtual router) in the topology.

We also consider an optimization to the oracle algorithm for the cube collective topology that minimizes the number of hops taken. With the 4x4x4 mesh used for the local connectivity within a group, the number of local hops can be as large as 9. When a message is adaptively routed, it visits 3 different groups (source, intermediate, and destination); thus, the maximum total number of hops is 29 (9*3 local hops + 2 global hops). Rather than randomly selecting 4 indirect routes, the shortest path algorithm selects the 2 shortest indirect routes along with 2 random indirect routes to compare to the deterministic route. This optimization is unnecessary in the dragonfly topology as the all-to-all local connectivity limits the number of hops for any message to a maximum of 5.

While oracle adaptive routing provides an indication of the limit for adaptive routing, it is important to consider a more realistic adaptive routing algorithm. Therefore, we evaluated an adaptation of progressive adaptive routing[18]. Like the dragonfly topology, the message is routed down the deterministic path, and the routing decision is re-evaluated at each router it visits in the source group. Unlike the dragonfly topology, the routing algorithm only considers a router's global link as the sole possible adaptive route. This prevents requiring additional virtual channels for adaptive routing within each cube. If the load on the deterministic path exceeds a threshold, an adaptive route is considered. Load is calculated using the occupancy of the buffers traversed on the next hop. An adaptive route is selected if the adaptive criteria (Deterministic_route_load > 2 * Adaptive_route_load + Threshold) is met[22]. After a message is adaptively routed or crosses a global link, the routing decision can no longer be re-evaluated.

2.2 Building Larger Networks

As simulated, the topology only requires 8 port routers to connect 4,160 nodes. This is a relatively small network by modern high performance computing (HPC) or even datacenter standards. The cost and power models discussed in Sections 5 and 6 assume a higher bandwidth per node and a higher radix router. As noted in [20, 21, 27], higher radix routers are both practical and desirable. Our performance and cost models assume 32K nodes using 64 port routers for the cube collective topology. Eight links are connected to each node and eight links are connected to each neighbor in the local mesh (48 links total). The remaining 8 links on each router are each connected to a unique cube. With 64 routers per cube, this yields 512 global links per cube for a total of 513 cubes. To connect additional nodes, the 8 links to nodes could be connected to 8 unique nodes. This would support up to 256K nodes at lower bandwidth. Bandwidth could then be increased by replicating the network and providing multiple planes to each node, just as would be done for a dragonfly topology[22].

3. METHODOLOGY

We use the ASIM performance simulation infrastructure[12] to simulate the cube collective and dragonfly topologies. ASIM is a generic framework for creating performance models and has been used to model all aspects of system design. It is a cycle based simulation environment where different components can be modeled with different levels of fidelity. This allows the model developer to trade off model accuracy with simulation run time, model development time, or both. The modules themselves model distinct components of the system, and communication between these modules is restricted to ports (analogous to wires in hardware). Because each module is isolated from the other modules, ASIM provides methods to parallelize[8] the performance model itself, which yielded sufficient reductions in run time to enable studies of up to 4K nodes. While many of our network simulations ran for 1 million cycles, we found that runs of 200K cycles were enough to reach a steady state and predict the behavior of the network. To improve our confidence in the results, we ran each simulation for 400,000 cycles.

3.1 Router Model

Each router is modeled as an input and output queued router with independent queue resources at every output for every input. This router model is optimistic, but separates the design of the router itself from its impact on the network topology. The router module is isolated from the topology and routing algorithm module. This enables us to use the same router module for each topology, further removing the router design from the network topology's impact on performance. Queue sizes at the input and output queues are sized to cover the round trip delay across the network link and through the router, respectively. Round-robin arbitration is used at both the input and output queues.

3.2 Networks Modeled

The cube collective network modeled is the same as described in Section 2. Each group, or virtual router, is a 4x4x4 mesh of 8 port routers. 6 ports are local mesh connections (turned off if they are edge connections), 1 port is a global link that connects to a different group, and the remaining port connects to a local node. There are 64 routers in a group, each with 1 global link to a different group. This gives 65 groups of 64 routers for a total of 4,160 routers and with 1 node per router, a similar number of nodes.

The dragonfly we simulated for comparison used the same router model, but was configured so each router had 23 ports. The dragonfly is all-to-all connected within the group, so with 11 ports per router for local connections, there were 12 routers per group. The remaining 12 ports on each router were evenly divided between local nodes and global links. With 6 global links per router and 12 routers per group, each group connects to 72 other groups. This gives a total of 73 groups, 876 routers, and 5256 nodes. The 1:2:1 ratio of local, group, and global connections is consistent with the canonical dragonfly topology.

The number of nodes in our simulated cube collective and dragonfly are noticeably different. Unfortunately, that is a by-product of the inherent topology characteristics. The dragonfly topology typically has twice as many routers in a group as there are global links per router (and nodes per router), while the cube collective topology requires a cube for each group. Following these guidelines only allows a few valid, canonical configurations for each topology. The sizes simulated (4,160 node cube collective and 5,260 node dragonfly) were the most similar that could be simulated and are consistent in size with typical network simulations[21, 22, 5].

3.3 Workloads

A workload module contains network traffic generators to provide stimulus for the topologies. Network traffic is generated across a range of injection rates, which are cumulative over time. Once the network saturates, a flit will be offered every cycle, if the outstanding request limit has not been reached. Outstanding requests are tracked based on responses from the target node. Every request generates a response that retires the request. Each request in the network is modeled as 16 flits and each response is 2 flits.

All networks have pathological traffic patterns, and we model a worst case traffic pattern[18]. The worst case pattern maximizes contention for global links by having all nodes in a given group send messages to nodes on the same target group. It is also critical to determine how the network behaves under workloads that are relevant to the domain. We have chosen three more basic classes of traffic patterns to evaluate: traditional bit permutations, structured patterns with high locality to represent scientific applications[31], and patterns matching HPC benchmarks. These patterns originate in the field of high performance computing (HPC), which is one of the more demanding application domains.

A key metric for networks is how they perform under a variety of permutation patterns. HPC networks have typically been evaluated under permutation patterns that are known to exist in HPC workloads: bit complement, bit reverse, shuffle, and transpose. As a baseline for comparison, we evaluated these "traditional" traffic patterns. Each of these patterns is a static traffic pattern where each node targets one specific other node with a stream of messages.

One type of application communication pattern that is seldom reported in the literature is communications with high locality. However, locality is quite common in many HPC applications[31]. Thus, we chose to model communication patterns where each node communicates with "neighbors" in 2D and 3D. Specifically, we model a 2D pattern with 4 neighbors (north, south, east, west) as well as a 2D pattern that also communicates with the 4 corners (northwest, southwest, southeast, northeast). 2D communication patterns appear in applications such as weather modeling and neutron transport where "pencil" decompositions are common. Two similar types of patterns are also modeled in 3D, which involves communicating with 6 neighbors or with 26 neighbors. Scientific applications ranging from computational fluid dynamics to shock physics[13] use data decompositions that yield 3D traffic patterns. To add a temporal characteristic, which both mimics actual application traffic and stresses adaptive routing, each node sends several flits (512) to each neighbor before moving to the next neighbor.

Finally, we used two scenarios that model stressful benchmark behavior: random access and PTRANS access patterns. In our model of the PTRANS benchmark, we used the communication pattern for a square processor grid (P=Q=64 for a 4096 node network). We modeled a small matrix transpose that was repeated, which models the pipelined communication approach used in the actual PTRANS benchmark.

For any traffic patterns that are sensitive to the network size, the number of injecting nodes is capped to that limit. For example, bit reverse, bit complement, shuffle, and transpose traffic patterns are each dependent on having a power of 2 number of nodes. For topologies larger than 4096 nodes, only the first 4096 nodes participate for these traffic patterns. Similarly, 2D and 3D traffic patterns must have node counts that can be decomposed into 2D and 3D shapes, respectively. The largest 2D or 3D shape that would fit on the modeled network was used. Furthermore, locality in the topology was exploited, with the 2D and 3D layout mapped to the nodes that are local to a router to minimize the communicating surface that leaves the router.

4. PERFORMANCE ANALYSIS

Network performance is one of the key criteria that drives topology selection. However, performance is extremely sensitive to the workload. For each pattern discussed in 3.3, we present simula-

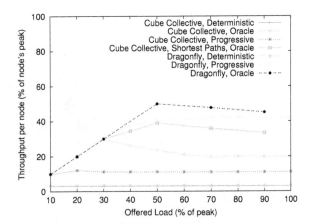

Figure 4: Worst Case Traffic

tion results for both the cube collective topology and the dragonfly topology at various injection rates. Throughput using both deterministic and adaptive routing is presented, since usage models require deterministic routing, but adaptive routing is required to achieve good throughput for many classes of traffic.

4.1 Worst Case Traffic Pattern

When deterministic routing is used with a worst case traffic pattern, the average throughput is limited to one link worth of bandwidth per group — all traffic from a group must go across the one link to the target group. As Figure 4 shows, adaptive routing is able to achieve drastically higher throughput by balancing traffic across all links leaving each group. The dragonfly saturates at 50% throughput — the theoretical maximum when all traffic must take an indirect adaptive route — because all traffic goes through an additional global hop that cuts the theoretical bisection bandwidth in half. In contrast, the cube collective saturates just below 40%. While its global bandwidth (bisection bandwidth) has an identical limit to the dragonfly, the cube collective is further limited by the bandwidth within a cube. Both topologies are further limited when using progressive adaptive routing, but the constraint is much more dramatic in the cube collective topology. Each cube is nominally a "full bisection" cube; however, the theoretical limit for throughput through a mesh is below full bandwidth due to head of line blocking effects. Oracle adaptive routing can compensate for this relatively well, but progressive adaptive routing does not adaptively route through the cube. This bisection limit within each cube will show up in several results.

4.2 Traditional Bit Permutation Patterns

The bit permutation results illustrate a range of interesting phenomena, shown in Figures 5 and 6. In bit reverse, deterministic routing for the cube collective significantly outperforms deterministic routing on the dragonfly — as it does on the transpose pattern. Because the groups for dragonfly and cube collective are of different sizes, the mapping from a bit pattern to groups is different for the two topologies. In stark contrast, bit complement exhibits the opposite characteristics. Adaptive routing algorithms are notoriously difficult to tune to the point that they are uniformly better than deterministic algorithms, and transpose traffic illustrates a case where the general tuning based on prior work[18] is fragile. The shuffle pattern shows a case where deterministic routing on both topologies is poor, and the best adaptive routing algorithms are comparable. In general, progressive adaptive routing works

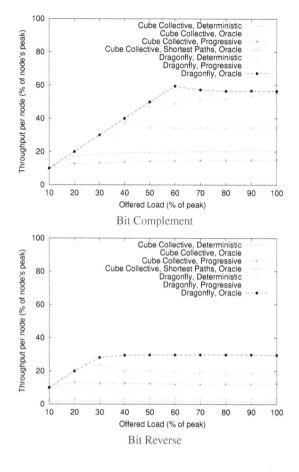

Figure 5: Two standard bit permutations

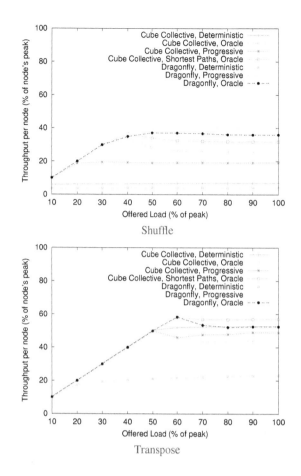

Figure 6: Two standard bit permutations

well for the dragonfly topology, but needs significant additional work for other bit permutations. Clearly, adaptation within the local cube will be needed for these patterns to achieve more of the adaptive routing potential seen with the oracle.

4.3 Structured Communication with Locality

The four communication patterns presented in Figures 7 and 8 represent typical scientific workloads in HPC[31]. As Figure 7 shows, both topologies handle 2D communications patterns comparably well — even when the added contention of communicating with neighbors in the "corners" is added. In contrast, with 3D traffic, the cube collective has a substantial advantage from its natural match to the application's communication pattern. Since the 3D traffic pattern is one of the most important communications patterns in scientific computing, this is an extremely positive result.

For 2D traffic, deterministic routing does relatively well for both the cube collective and dragonfly. There is some benefit from adaptive routing as it is able to route around the congestion on the global links that is induced when a *surface* of the local 2D pattern communicates off node. In the 3D traffic patterns, the natural match between the cube collective and the 3D traffic pattern gives it a substantial advantage in both deterministic and adaptive routing scenarios. Effectively, the symmetric cube at the group level in the cube collective minimizes the surface that must be communicated "off cube". Both the dragonfly and cube collective receive a substantial boost from adaptive routing. Unlike the bit permutation patterns, in all of these cases progressive adaptive routing eas-

ily matches the oracle. Cube collective's improvement is because the *face* of a cube of nodes must communicate with the *face* of a second cube of nodes. Since the two faces are mapped onto two groups, this tends to force all traffic for a face down a single global link between those groups. Adaptive routing is able to avoid this congestion; however, since the cube collective minimizes off-group communication for this pattern, it retains a significant advantage.

4.4 Benchmark Like Traffic Patterns

The random traffic pattern (Figure 9) was modeled on the HPCC RandomAccess benchmark[24, 26, 14] with a random communication pattern of small packets and a limited number of outstanding requests. Similarly, the traffic distribution logic of the HPCC PTRANS benchmark was used for the results in Figure 9. As noted earlier, the limited bandwidth through the 4x4x4 cube in the cube collective topology limits the throughput for bisection limited applications like the random traffic pattern. In contrast, the random traffic pattern is where dragonfly excels. PTRANS, on the other hand, shows a slight advantage for the cube collective topology. While PTRANS performs a matrix transpose operation that may initially seem like the transpose traffic pattern, PTRANS uses a block based decomposition, so its communication pattern uses numerous peers (unlike transpose). Progressive adaptive routing for the cube collective does well on the random traffic, but does not achieve the full potential on PTRANS traffic. This indicates that it has a relatively stiff adaptation criteria[18], which largely comes from the lack of adaptive routing in the cube.

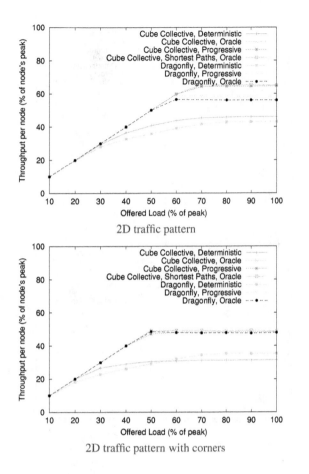

2D traffic pattern

2D traffic pattern with corners

Figure 7: 2D communication patterns

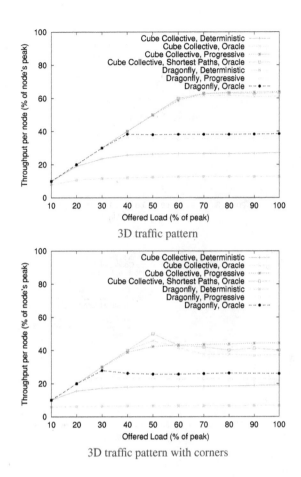

3D traffic pattern

3D traffic pattern with corners

Figure 8: 3D communication patterns

4.5 Performance Summary

The results show several general characteristics. In most of the experiments, the use of some "shortest paths" in the adaptive routing algorithm for the cube collective topology was valuable. Improvements over the base adaptive routing algorithm ranged from a few percent to nearly 50% higher throughput (i.e. 30% when considering 2 short paths and 2 random paths vs. 20% when considering 4 random paths). Comparisons between cube collective and dragonfly were more mixed and are summarized in Table 1, which compares best cases for each. In highly local traffic patterns, the cube collective topology drastically outperformed the dragonfly topology. For some bit permutations and for uniform random traffic, the reverse was true. Notably, however, transpose type traffic patterns performed nominally better on the cube collective than on the dragonfly topology. This is particularly interesting since many scientific applications have a combination of 3D and distributed matrix transpose types of traffic. The use of progressive adaptive routing for the cube collective topology provided similarly mixed results. In many cases, it provides excellent throughput (2D, 3D, HPCC RandomAccess, Transpose); however, some bit permutation patterns did not fare as well. The oracle algorithms clearly indicate more opportunity to create new adaptive routing algorithms to achieve more of the topology's potential.

5. COST ANALYSIS

Network cost is as important as performance. Unfortunately, analyzing cost for rapidly evolving technologies is challenging. There

is almost universal agreement that very short electrical links will continue to be substantially cheaper than optical links; however, the advantages of the cube collective topology depend on relatively new technology (flex or micro-twinax cables with top-of-package connections) reaching the market in a cost effective manner. Similarly, future projections for optical costs vary wildly between sources. Thus, it is necessary to examine the total network cost implications of various potential cost scenarios. Available market data, technology trends, and forecasts by technology companies indicate that optical links will be approximately 8 to 64 times as expensive per unit bandwidth as contemporary, short electrical links. Due to the inherent sensitivity and variability of future cost projections, we present the cost analysis based on ratios between optical and electrical cost. We present a wide range of cost ratios to cover the forecast spectrum.

Table 2 shows the 9 profiles used for comparing the cost of the cube collective topology and the dragonfly topology. Groups of three profiles (1-3, 4-6, 7-9) represent different base costs for short electrical cables (low, medium, and high estimates, respectively) and vary the ratio of optical costs over the expected range. Longer electrical cables (2m) use a fixed ratio of 5x the cost of short electrical cables to account for the substantially larger wire gauge and more complex connector infrastructure required. The ratio of the total cost of signaling/cabling to the total cost of routers for the cube collective point is given for perspective.

In contrast to work that holds bisection bandwidth constant[21, 22], we have chosen to hold node injection bandwidth constant to

	2D	2D w/ corners	3D	3D w/ corners	Bit Comp	Bit Rev	Shuffle	Trans.	Random	PTRANS	WC
Cube Dfly	+16%	+3%	+63%	+61%	+67%	+57%	+14%	+8%	+48%	+7%	+28%

Table 1: Summary of relative performance advantages using adaptive routing

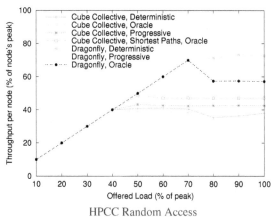

HPCC Random Access

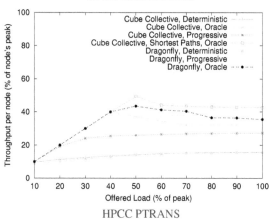

HPCC PTRANS

Figure 9: Benchmark-like traffic patterns

	1	2	3	4	5	6	7	8	9
Opt. to Elect. Ratio	16	32	64	10	20	40	8	16	32
Signaling to Router Ratio	1.2	2	3.6	1.4	2.2	3.8	1.5	2.4	4

Table 2: Cost profile descriptions

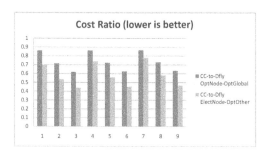

Figure 10: Cost ratio: cube collective to dragonfly

model cost and power. In practice, injection bandwidth is the limiter on traffic patterns with locality, while bisection bandwidth impacts global traffic patterns. Holding injection bandwidth constant results in a dragonfly configuration with bisection bandwidth that matches injection bandwidth, and a cube collective configuration with bisection bandwidth that is 50% of node injection bandwidth. The performance difference is merged with the cost ratio into a single metric to highlight the impact of this choice.

In our cost analysis, we modeled a fixed system size (32K nodes) for both the cube collective and dragonfly topology. The cost of a router was held constant, since both topologies use a 64 port router at this scale. Two physical configurations of the dragonfly topology were considered. In the first, routers in a group were placed close together with a mixture of short electrical connections and longer electrical connections between the routers. In this configuration, all links from routers to nodes and all global links (group to group) use optics. Since a dragonfly topology dedicates 25% of links to nodes, 25% to global links, and 50% to group links, this places 50% of the total network bandwidth on optics, 25% on short electrical links, and 25% on longer electrical links. In the second configuration, connections to the node use short electrical links (25%) and all connections between routers use optical links (75%).

Due to the highly structured nature of the required wiring, the cube collective configuration used short electrical links for all interior links of a cube. The surface links were left unconnected, and the global ports used optics. This makes 86% of the links short electrical links, and 14% optical links.

Despite having over 80% more total link bandwidth in the system, the cube collective topology is lower cost than the dragonfly topology across a wide range of assumptions, as seen in Figure 10. In fact, when optics are relatively more expensive (as they are today), the cube collective topology can be less than half the cost of a dragonfly topology that places the routers near the nodes. Concentrating the routers and reducing the cost of the intra-group links substantially reduces the cost of the dragonfly topology under scenarios where low cost electrical links can be used.

Of course, the cost of a network at fixed injection bandwidth is not the only parameter. If it were, a 3D mesh would be the winner. Instead, it is necessary to evaluate the cost per unit performance under various traffic scenarios. Using the same 9 cost scenarios from Table 2 and the best case performance for each net-

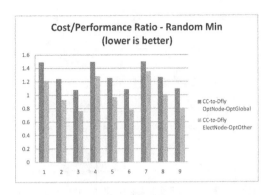

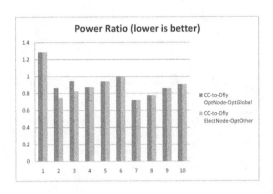

Figure 12: Power ratio: cube collective to dragonfly

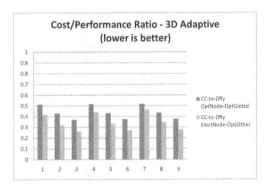

Figure 11: Cost per unit performance analysis expressed as the ratio of cube collective cost to dragonfly cost

work, Figure 11 compares the cost/performance of the cube collective topology to the dragonfly topology. When optics are relatively expensive, the cube collective topology fares well (approaches parity) for even random traffic; however, with lower cost optics, the dragonfly's superior performance on random traffic gives it a stark advantage despite its higher cost. In contrast, the cube collective topology has a 2x to 3x advantage over the dragonfly topology (i.e. is less than 50% of the cost per unit of sustained performance) for 3D traffic.

6. POWER ANALYSIS

Better data is available for power than for cost. Published research has shown 2 pJ/b electrical links over short, low cost interconnects[17] at 10 Gb/s in 45 nm silicon technology. Increases in data rate will increase the power requirement, while improvements in process technology and interconnect technology will decrease it. Thus, for short electrical links, we evaluate profiles of 1, 2, and 3 pJ/b. In practice, longer electrical links using more conventional packaging or advanced board material have taken 10 to 15 pJ/b; however, we always keep long electrical link power at or below optical power, since optics would replace these links if they were lower power. This favors the dragonfly topology slightly in some cases, since the cube collective topology does not use long electrical links. Optical power must include at least the power of one electrical link, and this will require in the range of 10 to 15 pJ/b by

the time the power of the electronics is added to the optics[15]. One profile is used that assumes ring resonators[11] succeed in drastically reducing the power of the optical components, but must add the power of short electrical links to connect to the optics. Finally, router logic will take some power and we consider cases with varying amounts of router logic power from 25W to 45W. The power profiles are summarized in Table 3.

As seen in Figure 12, the power ratio between the cube collective topology and dragonfly topology are much closer to parity. While the cube collective topology has a lower power in all cases except where ring resonators are assumed, the fact that the power ratio between optical links and electrical links is lower than the cost ratio between the two means that the cube collective topology has a smaller advantage in power than it does in cost. This becomes particularly apparent in the power/performance ratios between the cube collective topology and the dragonfly topology that are shown in Figure 13. While the dragonfly topology holds a 25% to 60% lead for the random traffic pattern, the 3D traffic pattern shows substantial improvements across all profiles for the cube collective topology (approximately 2x in many cases).

7. RELATED WORK

Network topologies constantly evolve in response to shifts in technology. At one point, the "correct" answer for topology was to build a mesh or torus[4]. This was driven by the low bandwidth available in a single router package and the fact that many applications had high locality in their communication patterns. Since then, numerous supercomputers have deployed torus technologies, including the recent Cray XT[7, 2] and IBM BlueGene[3] systems. In fact, meshes continue to be used in recent systems due to advantages in packaging and wiring locality; however, higher dimensional 5D[16] and 6D[6] variants are used to improve bisection bandwidth. We build on this tradition of exploiting packaging locality and further improve the bisection bandwidth of the network for large scale systems.

Express cubes[9] extend basic mesh networks by providing links that "skip hops" to improve bisection bandwidth. Unlike express cubes, the cube collective topology does not fully connect a system wide mesh, which eliminates many cables that would cross cabinet boundaries. Whereas express cubes only have links that skip hops within each dimension, the cube collective topology connects every 4x4x4 cube to every other 4x4x4 cube in the system. This significantly improves bisection bandwidth and better leverages optical

	1	2	3	4	5	6	7	8	9	10
Short Electrical (pJ/bit)	1	1	1	2	2	2	2	2	3	3
Long Electrical (pJ/bit)	3	5	5	10	10	10	15	15	15	15
Optical (pJ/bit)	3	10	10	10	10	10	15	15	15	15
Router Logic (W)	25	25	35	25	35	45	25	35	35	45

Table 3: Power profile descriptions

links that are less distance sensitive. Express virtual channels[23] are a logical variant of express cubes in that they attempt to achieve much of the benefit of the express links from express cubes by logically bypassing router logic at intermediate routers rather than using physical bypass. The express virtual channel concept is complementary to the cube collective topology and could be applied to individual cubes.

New topologies have been proposed often; however, the most relevant recent work[1, 21, 22, 5] focuses on both the need for higher radix routers and the advantages that they can provide. The flattened butterfly topology and dragonfly topology both leverage higher line rates and larger router packages to build higher radix routers. Furthermore, these new topologies exploit new technology (cheaper optics) to improve bisection bandwidth. The HyperX makes the assumption that all cables will be optical. We make the same use of optical cables for global links to extend bisection bandwidth, but focus on making the local electrical links short enough to reduce power and cost.

Previous work[25] considered how power may constrain interconnection networks. There have been several prior efforts to reduce power in interconnection networks with a particular focus on reducing power on infrequently used links. Both [19, 29] propose techniques to power down certain links in response to traffic behavior, while [28] investigated using dynamic voltage scaling (DVS) of the links in interconnection networks. We achieve power reductions exclusively through enhancements in topology to enable shorter, more power efficient links. These other efforts are largely orthogonal to a change in topology and could be combined with the topology we propose.

8. CONCLUSIONS

Top-of-package connections and co-designed electrical channels and signaling have the potential to provide disruptive improvements in power, cost, and bandwidth. However, exploiting the technology requires innovations in the basic network topology to take advantage of extremely short (less than 1m) electrical links. We propose the cube collective topology that can use short electrical links for up to 86% of the links in the system. Under several potential cost and technology profiles, the cube collective topology has significantly lower cost and lower power than the dragonfly topology. This is achieved while delivering higher local bandwidth and 50% as much global bandwidth. Combined, this makes the cube collective competitive in terms of cost per unit performance for all traffic patterns and gives it a 2x or more advantage for some traffic patterns. Similarly, it demonstrates up to 2x advantage in power per unit bandwidth for traffic patterns with high locality.

9. REFERENCES

[1] D. Abts, A. Bataineh, S. Scott, G. Faanes, J. Schwarzmeier, E. Lundberg, T. Johnson, M. Bye, and G. Schwoerer. The Cray Black Widow: A highly scalable vector multiprocessor. In *Proceedings of the 2007 Internationa Conference on High-Performance Computing, Networking, Storage and Analysis*, November 2007.

[2] D. Abts, D. Weisser, J. Nowicki, and R. Alverson. Optimized virtual channel assignment in the cray xt. In *Proceedings of the 2007 Cray User Group Annual Technical Conference*, May 2007.

[3] N. Adiga, M. Blumrich, D. Chen, P. Coteus, A. Gara, M. Giampara, P. Heidelberger, S. Singh, B. D. Steinmacher-Burow, T. Takken, M. Tsao, and P. Vranas. Blue gene/l torus interconnection network. *IBM Journal of Research and Development*, 49(2/3):265–276, 2005.

[4] A. Agarwal. Limits on interconnection network performance. *IEEE Trans. Parallel Distrib. Syst.*, 2(4):398–412, 1991.

[5] J. H. Ahn, N. Binkert, A. Davis, M. McLaren, and R. S. Schreiber. Hyperx: Topology, routing, and packaging of efficient large-scale networks. In *SC '09: Proceedings of the 2009 ACM/IEEE conference on Supercomputing*, November 2009.

[6] Y. Ajima, Y. Takagi, T. Inoue, S. Hiramoto, and T. Shimizu. The Tofu interconnect. In *Nineteenth IEEE Symposium on High-Performance Interconnects (HotI'11)*, August 2011.

[7] R. Alverson. Red Storm. In *Invited Talk, Hot Chips 15*, August 2003.

[8] K. C. Barr, R. Matas-Navarro, C. Weaver, T. Juan, and J. Emer. Simulating a chip multiprocessor with a symmetric multiprocessor. In *Boston Area Architecture Workshop (BARC)*, Jan 2005.

[9] W. Dally. Express cubes: improving the performance of k-ary n -cube interconnection networks. *Computers, IEEE Transactions on*, 40(9):1016 –1023, sep 1991.

[10] W. Dally and C. Seitz. Deadlock-free message routing in multiprocessor interconnection networks. *Computers, IEEE Transactions on*, C-36(5):547–553, May 1987.

[11] P. Dong, S. Liao, D. Feng, H. Liang, D. Zheng, R. Shafiiha, X. Zheng, G. Li, K. Raj, A. Krishnamoorthy, and M. Asghari. High speed silicon microring modulator based on carrier depletion. In *Optical Fiber Communication (OFC), collocated National Fiber Optic Engineers Conference, 2010 Conference on (OFC/NFOEC)*, pages 1 –3, march 2010.

[12] J. Emer, P. Ahuja, E. Borch, A. Klauser, C.-K. Luk, S. Manne, S. S. Mukherjee, H. Patil, S. Wallace, N. Binkert, R. Espasa, and T. Juan. Asim: A performance model framework. *Computer*, 35(2):68–76, 2002.

[13] J. E.S. Hertel, R. Bell, M. Elrick, A. Farnsworth, G. Kerley, J. McGlaun, S. Petney, S. Silling, P. Taylor, and L. Yarrington. CTH: A Software Family for Multi-Dimensional Shock Physics Analysis. In *Proceedings*

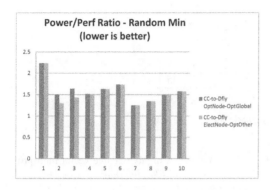

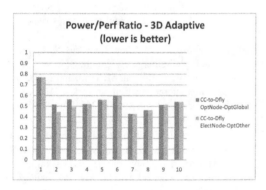

Figure 13: Power per unit performance analysis expressed as ratio cube collective to dragonfly

of the 19th International Symposium on Shock Waves, held at Marseille, France, pages 377–382, July 1993.

[14] R. Garg and Y. Sabharwal. Software routing and aggregation of messages to optimize the performance of the HPCC Randomaccess benchmark. In *2006 ACM/IEEE International Conference for High-Performance Computing, Networking, Storage, and Analysis (SC'06)*, November 2006.

[15] W. M. Green, M. J. Rooks, L. Sekaric, and Y. A. Vlasov. Ultra-compact, low RF power, 10 Gb/s silicon Mach-Zehnder modulator. *Optical Express*, 15:17106–17113, 2007.

[16] P. Heidelberger. The IBM Blue Gene/Q Interconnection Network and Message Unit. In *Invited Talk, Hot Interconnects 19*, August 2011.

[17] J. Jaussi, M. Leddige, B. Horine, F. O'Mahony, and B. Casper. Multi-gbit i/o and interconnect co-design for power efficient links. In *Electrical Performance of Electronic Packaging and Systems (EPEPS), 2010 IEEE 19th Conference on*, pages 1 –4, oct. 2010.

[18] N. Jiang, J. Kim, and W. J. Dally. Indirect adaptive routing on large scale interconnection networks. In *Proceedings of the 36th annual international symposium on Computer architecture*, ISCA '09, pages 220–231, New York, NY, USA, 2009. ACM.

[19] E. Kim, K. Yum, G. Link, N. Vijaykrishnan, M. Kandemir, M. Irwin, M. Yousif, and C. Das. Energy optimization techniques in cluster interconnects. In *Low Power Electronics and Design, 2003. ISLPED '03. Proceedings of the 2003 International Symposium on*, pages 459 – 464, aug. 2003.

[20] J. Kim, W. J. Dally, and D. Abts. Adaptive routing in high-radix Clos network. In *Proceedings of the 2006 ACM/IEEE conference on Supercomputing*, SC '06, New York, NY, USA, 2006. ACM.

[21] J. Kim, W. J. Dally, and D. Abts. Flattened butterfly: a cost-efficient topology for high-radix networks. *SIGARCH Comput. Archit. News*, 35(2):126–137, 2007.

[22] J. Kim, W. J. Dally, S. Scott, and D. Abts. Technology-driven, highly-scalable dragonfly topology. In *ISCA '08: Proceedings of the 35th International Symposium on Computer Architecture*, pages 77–88, Washington, DC, USA, 2008. IEEE Computer Society.

[23] A. Kumar, L.-S. Peh, P. Kundu, and N. K. Jha. Express virtual channels: towards the ideal interconnection fabric. In *Proceedings of the 34th annual international symposium on Computer architecture*, ISCA '07, pages 150–161, New York, NY, USA, 2007. ACM.

[24] P. Luszczek, J. Dongarra, D. Koester, R. Rabenseifner, R. Lucas, J. Kepner, J. McCalpin, D. Bailey, and D. Takahashi. Introduction to the HPC challenge benchmark suite, March 2005.

[25] C. S. Patel, S. M. Chai, S. Yalamanchili, and D. E. Schimmel. Power constrained design of multiprocessor interconnection networks. In *International Conference on Computer Design (ICCD)*, pages 408–416, October 1997.

[26] S. Plimpton, R. Brightwell, C. Vaughan, K. Underwood, and M. Davis. A simple synchronous distributed-memory algorithm for the HPCC RandomAccess benchmark. In *2006 IEEE International Conference on Cluster Computing*, September 2006.

[27] S. Scott, D. Abts, J. Kim, and W. J. Dally. The BlackWidow high-radix Clos network. In *Proceedings of the 33rd Annual International Symposium on Computer Architecture*, ISCA '06, pages 16–28, Washington, DC, USA, 2006. IEEE Computer Society.

[28] L. Shang, L.-S. Peh, and N. Jha. Dynamic voltage scaling with links for power optimization of interconnection networks. In *High-Performance Computer Architecture, 2003. HPCA-9 2003. Proceedings. The Ninth International Symposium on*, pages 91 – 102, feb. 2003.

[29] V. Soteriou and L.-S. Peh. Design-space exploration of power-aware on/off interconnection networks. In *Computer Design: VLSI in Computers and Processors, 2004. ICCD 2004. Proceedings. IEEE International Conference on*, pages 510 – 517, oct. 2004.

[30] L. G. Valiant. A Scheme for Fast Parallel Communication. *SIAM Journal on Computing*, 11(2):350–361, 1982.

[31] J. S. Vetter and F. Mueller. Communication characteristics of large-scale scientific applications for contemporary cluster architectures. In *16th International Parallel and Distributed Processing Symposium (IPDPS'02)*, pages 27–29, April 2002.

Hardware Support for Enforcing Isolation in Lock-Based Parallel Programs

Paruj Ratanaworabhan
Faculty of Engineering
Kasetsart University
paruj.r@ku.ac.th

Martin Burtscher
Texas State University
burtscher@txstate.edu

Darko Kirovski
Microsoft Research
darkok@microsoft.com

Benjamin Zorn
Microsoft Research
zorn@microsoft.com

Abstract

When lock-based parallel programs execute on conventional multicore hardware, faulty software can cause hard-to-debug race conditions in critical sections that violate the contract between locks and their protected shared variables. This paper proposes new hardware support for enforcing isolation of critical section execution. It can detect and tolerate races, allowing programs to execute race-free. Our hardware scheme targets the existing large code base of locked-based parallel programs written in type unsafe languages such as C and C++. Our approach works directly on unmodified executables. An evaluation of 13 programs from the SPLASH2 and PARSEC suites shows that the cost of the additional hardware and the impact on the overall execution time is minimal for these applications. Our mechanism is complementary to hardware transactional memory in that it uses similar structures but focuses on enhancing the reliability of existing lock-based programs.

Categories and Subject Descriptors B.8.1 [Reliability, Testing, and Fault-Tolerance]

General Terms Reliability, performance, experimentation

Keywords Race detection and toleration, hardware support for reliability, transactional memory

1. Introduction

The advent of multicore hardware puts parallel programming in the spotlight. As single-threaded performance has saturated, parallel programs are the new hope for the continued performance improvement in computing and are expected to increasingly become the norm. Traditional lock-based parallel programming, however, is a difficult undertaking. It does not compose well, suffers from all the problems of sequential programming, and introduces additional sources of errors, e.g., deadlock, atomicity violation, and data races. Researchers have therefore proposed a new paradigm called transactional memory (TM) [1] to tame parallel programming. Although it is a promising technology, TM has not yet matured enough to be widely adopted. At present, parallel programmers still use lock-based synchronization, and there exists a large installed code base of lock-based parallel programs, particularly

those written in unsafe languages such as C or C++ with add-on libraries for threading and synchronization. Microsoft is reported to have over 50 million lines of source code in its repository written in this fashion.

This paper focuses on enhancing the reliability of lock-based parallel programs. It proposes a hardware extension to enforce isolation of critical section execution. Normally, when lock-based programs execute, they are vulnerable to race conditions. When a critical section executes, accesses to its protected shared variables may not be mutually exclusive as intended. There may be buggy threads that acquire no locks or the wrong locks, thus concurrently accessing the same "protected" shared variables, which may lead to a race condition. Our proposed scheme, which enforces isolation of critical section execution, can allow a racy program that would otherwise suffer from an isolation violation to execute race-free.

Isolation is a desirable property because it allows programmers to reason about parallel program execution with semantics that match their intuition. With guaranteed isolation, program execution always preserves the data-race-free model (DRF0 to be precise) semantics [2]. This model observes sequentially consistent execution for all synchronization operations while allowing the underlying hardware to be weakly ordered. Violation of isolation can give rise to unexpected behavior. Consider the example in Figure 1. A programmer would expect the value of baseScript to be either default or gScript after the critical section execution. However, Thread 2 can reset gScript to NULL after Thread 1 has evaluated the if condition comparing gScript with NULL but before executing the else body. This unexpected behavior (referred to as Nonrepeatable Read) results from a data race and can crash the program when Thread 1 passes NULL to the compile function. With guaranteed isolation, the system forces the resetting of gScript to NULL to either happen before or after the critical section execution, thus restoring the expected behavior and allowing the execution to proceed correctly. Other unexpected behaviors that could result from isolation violation due to data races in lock-based programs include Intermediate Lost Updates and Intermediate Dirty Reads [3].

```
Thread 1:

CSEnter(mutex_A)

if (gScript == NULL)

  baseScript = default
                                  Thread 2:
else
                           ──────► gScript = NULL
  baseScript = gScript

CSExit(mutex_A)

compile(baseScript)
```

Figure 1: Isolation violation resulting in a nonrepeatable read

This paper makes the following contributions.

1. We propose a hardware extension to enforce isolation of critical section execution. This mechanism builds on top of existing private caches in multicore chips. Preexisting lock-based executables can run on this hardware without modification.

2. We evaluate the proposed hardware on parallel applications taken from the SPLASH2 and PARSEC suites and show that the additional hardware cost is minimal for these programs.

3. We describe how hardware TM can readily be retrofitted to support our mechanism, thus making hardware TM useful not only for new transaction-based code but also for conventional lock-based programs.

2. Theoretical Framework

This section investigates the theoretical framework for handling isolation violations. We first consider harmful interleavings between accesses to shared variables of safe threads and those of non-safe threads. A safe thread only accesses shared variables inside of critical sections that are guarded by the correct locks whereas a non-safe thread might access the same shared variables outside of any critical section or use the wrong lock to guard them. Then, we present a mechanism that enforces isolation by preventing all harmful interleavings. We first consider cases where a single variable is protected and accessed in a non-nested critical section. Then, we extend this theoretical framework to cover cases involving multiple variables and overlapped critical sections. The proposed framework is based on ToleRace [4], a software tool and runtime environment that prevents asymmetric data races.

Let r, w, and x denote read, write, and don't-care operations, respectively, and let lower case letters represent accesses of non-safe threads and upper case letters represent accesses of safe threads. r+ denotes a sequence of at least one read and r* indicates zero or more reads. The operators + and * are equally defined for writes and don't-cares. We note that there are only three ways in which a sequence of operations from a single thread can interact with a single variable: by reading it only (r+), by setting its value regardless of its prior (wx*), and by setting its value based upon its prior (r+wx*). For the r+wx* sequence, we assume that w is dependent upon the value retrieved by r.

Table 1: Data races that result in an isolation violation and the outcome of the resolution function f (see below), attempting to guarantee isolation in the presence of each type of race

	race type	short-hand	serializable	$f(V, V', V'')$	schedule
I	X+ wx* R+X*	XwR	Yes	V	XRw
II	R*WX* r+ R*WX*	WrW	Yes	V'	rWW
III	R+X* wx* WX*	RwW	Yes	V	RWw
IV	R+ r+wx* R+	RrwR	Yes	V	RRrw
V	WX* r+wx* X+	WrwX	Yes	V'	rwWX
VI	X+ r+wx* X+ - {IV + V}	RrwW	No	N.A.	N.A.

Suppose that one of the three possible sequences of operations from a non-safe thread slices the operations of a safe thread into two parts. This results in 27 possible interleavings among the three sequences from both threads, i.e., three possible sequences for the first part of the safe thread, times three sequences for the non-safe thread, times three sequences for the second part of the safe thread. Some of these interleavings are harmful and result in an isolation violation. We classify them in terms of race cases in the first two columns of Table 1. Note that the sequences in capital letters represent the safe thread operations and are combinations of two or more of the three sequences mentioned above. For example, R+X* in race case I corresponds to either an R+ or an R+WX* sequence. The notation used for the sequences in race case VI is slightly overloaded; it denotes the set of interleavings

that can result from an r+wx* intervening sequence from the non-safe thread that does not already belong to cases IV and V.

Column 3 of Table 1 provides a short-hand notation for each race case. It only includes the access operations that matter. For example, in race case II, isolation violation occurs because the read operations from the non-safe thread observe the "dirty" value produced by the first write instead of the second. Operations that are relevant in this case are the read from the non-safe thread and the two writes from the safe thread that sandwich the read (hence the WrW short-hand notation). The motivation for these short-hand notations will become apparent when we explore the mechanism for ensuring isolation next.

Note that our theoretical framework needs to be concerned only with race condition involving 2 threads. Any race condition among K threads where K is greater than 2 can always be reduced to one of the above race cases between two threads shown in Table 1 [4].

2.1 Idealized Mechanism for Ensuring Isolation

The core approach to guaranteeing isolation of critical section execution is to replicate the protected shared state so that the thread that acquires a lock on the shared state has an exclusive copy. This thread continues reading from and writing to this copy until it releases the lock. When the lock is released, the system determines which, if any, isolation violation occurred and decides whether to propagate the value of the local (exclusive) copy or the global copy upon releasing the lock. Isolation can be guaranteed as long as the access operations involved in a race are serializable. If they are not, our system is still able to detect the isolation violation and functions as a race detector in this case. The idealized mechanism for enforcing isolation is described below and shown diagrammatically in Figure 2. Our mechanism is only concerned with enforcing serializable execution and, therefore, cannot fully handle parallel programs that require "stronger" semantics such as linearizability.

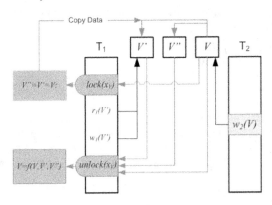

Figure 2: Ensuring isolation by replicating shared state and propagating appropriate copies using the resolution function f

Initialization and Finalization: Assume that the binding of lock x_V to shared variable V is known before the critical section in the safe thread T_1 is entered and that storage for two additional copies (V', V'') of variable V is available. This assumption is only valid with the idealized mechanism. Our implementation relaxes this assumption a great deal.

Lock (Entry): When lock x_V is acquired by T_1, copying V to V' and V'' ($V''=V'=V$) is performed atomically. Note that the copying and the lock acquire may not be performed atomically.

Reads and Writes inside the Critical Section: All instructions in the critical section of T_1 use V' instead of V. V' is the local copy of V for T_1 that cannot be accessed by other threads, not even due to a race. All other threads T_2 are unchanged and continue using V for all accesses. Copy V'' is not accessed by any thread until T_1 exits the critical section.

Unlock (Exit): When T_1 exits the critical section by releasing the acquired lock, the system analyzes the content of V', the original value V'', and the value V that could have been altered by other threads as a consequence of a race. Depending on the relationship of the values in $\{V, V', V''\}$ and knowledge about the specific race case from Table 1 that has occurred, the resolution function $V = f(V, V', V'')$ defines the value of V after T_1 finishes its critical section. The resolution function is executed atomically.

Combining the mechanism outlined above and the knowledge of each race case in Table 1, we can reason about which cases the system can handle and enforce isolation. The last two columns of Table 1 summarize the definition of f and indicate the resulting serializable schedule of operations for cases where isolation can be enforced. We see that a system with this type of resolution function can guarantee isolation in all race cases except the RrwW case. Here, the safe thread and the interleaved part of the non-safe thread both read the value of the shared variable after the safe thread has entered the critical section, and then they execute in parallel. Both threads see the same value returned by the read, which would not be possible if the safe thread had executed its critical section in isolation. This case is, therefore, not serializable under our theoretical framework. (Section 6 discusses the possibility of tolerating this case with re-execution.)

2.2 Multiple Variables and Nested Critical Sections

So far, we have only considered multithreaded, single-variable, non-nested critical section contexts. We now extend our framework to handle all cases, including multiple variables and nested critical sections. Local copies and the resolution function need to be made and executed atomically for multiple variables. Nested critical sections share their local copies with the outermost critical section. However, they have their own resolution function to resolve races for their protected variables.

In general, this mechanism to ensure isolation may lead to inconsistent execution. If it does, the system cannot enforce isolation and reverts to isolation violation detection mode instead. Inconsistent execution arises when the system reorders operations of a non-safe thread such that the operations do not follow their original program order and there are dependencies among the operations that must be observed. This can occur because the proposed mechanism resolves races to each variable independently. Here, dependencies refer to data dependences, i.e., when a write to a given variable depends on a read of another variable.

To understand the general cases involving multiple variables and overlapped critical sections, it suffices to consider a race involving two variables P and Q. Here we provide a summary of the actions involved in each race case. More detailed explanation can be found elsewhere [4].

Let a non-nested critical section protect both variables in a safe thread. In a non-safe thread, let an intervening sequence to P come before an intervening sequence to Q in program order, but the two may overlap each other. Table 2 enumerates all possible P and Q intervening combinations from the non-safe thread. The third column indicates whether the system reorders the intervening operations to P and Q.

Table 2: Enumeration of intervening sequences to P and Q; trailing x* and r+ of P sequence may overlap with Q sequence

P	Q	reorderd by system	dependency from P to Q	enforcing isolation
r+	r+	No	No	Yes
wx*	r+	Yes	No	Yes
r+wx*	r+	If race IV to P	No	Yes
r+	wx*	No	maybe	Yes
wx*	wx*	No	maybe	Yes
r+wx*	wx*	No	maybe	Yes
r+	r+wx*	No	maybe	Yes
wx*	r+wx*	If race V to Q	maybe	No if reordered, Yes otherwise
r+wx*	r+wx*	If race IV to P and V to Q	maybe	No if reordered, Yes otherwise

Note that the presented framework does not disallow orderings that violate sequential memory consistency (SC). If a programmer wants SC to be honored on weakly-ordered hardware, he or she has to use explicit synchronization operations to restrict the ordering of operations.

3. HEI Implementation

Given the ubiquity of multicore chips, it seems expedient to implement our proposed *Hardware for Enforcing Isolation* (HEI) with this microprocessor trend in mind. As we shall see, not much new hardware is needed to realize HEI in a multicore setting. Preexisting multicore components lend themselves well to embrace HEI's functionality. Recall that the mechanism presented in Section 2 involves making thread-local copies of shared variables and operating on those copies. The private data cache in each core naturally serves as thread-local storage. Thus, the central idea behind the design of HEI is to use existing cache components in multicore chips and leverage the already present coherence mechanism that maintains coherency among the private caches of the individual cores. In addition, we want the underlying hardware to be transparent to the running program. The program's executable should be able to run on top of HEI without any modification or user intervention.

The proposed design assumes write-back caches and leverages the MSI snoopy invalidation-based cache coherence protocol. To support the HEI functionality, the cache coherence protocol is augmented with extra states and transitions. We believe that invalidation-based protocols are preferred over update-based protocols and write-back caches are favorable to write-through caches in a multicore environment because both require markedly less inter-core communication bandwidth relative to their counterparts. Hence, we propose the design of HEI per the above assumptions. As the HEI mechanism is tied to bus-based multicore architectures, the scalability of HEI will be limited by it. At present, we target HEI for processors with up to 16 cores.

3.1 Basic Design and Operation

The basic structure of the proposed HEI is shown in Figure 3. The main components represent the safe memory region. This safe memory extends the private cache and is placed at the cache level that handles coherence traffic from other cores. Its structure is similar to that of a victim cache [5]. The design leaves the existing private cache unaltered, but the coherence protocol needs to be augmented.

There are four basic components in the safe memory: the evicted cache block region, the active bit, sets of Access Bit Vectors (ABV), and two status bits.

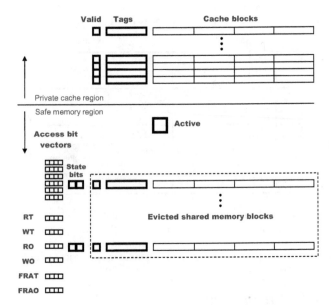

Figure 3: Basic structures of the proposed hardware for enforcing isolation (HEI)

Evicted cache block region: The general structure of this component is the same as the private cache. The key difference is that an entry is searched associatively. Basically, a block is transferred from the private cache to this evicted region in the safe memory whenever the CPU of the core in consideration accesses potentially shared memory locations that reside in this block.

Active Bit: The active bit specifies whether there are valid entries in the safe memory. When this bit is set, HEI signals to the cache controller to also look for cache entries in this region. Whenever the controller receives a request from the CPU or from the bus, it first searches the private cache area. If a miss occurs, it continues the search in the safe memory before proceeding to the lower levels of the memory hierarchy. For performance reasons, searches may be launched simultaneously in multiple levels.

Access Bit Vectors (ABV): There are six cache block bit vectors that serve as bookkeeping mechanism for the types of accesses to each byte in an evicted cache block. They are called: Read This (RT), Write This (WT), Read Others (RO), Write Others (WO), First This Access Read (FTAR), and First Others Access Read (FOAR). The width in bits of each ABV is equal to the size of the cache block in bytes. The purpose of each ABV is explained in Table 3. "This" refers to this core, "Others" to all other cores.

State Bits: The two state bits of each entry reflect the state of the corresponding cache block in the private caches of other cores.

Table 3: Description of each Access Bit Vector

Access Bit Vectors (ABV)	Descriptions
Read This (RT)	Bit i of RT is set when a **read** access from **this** core touches the ith byte
Write This (WT)	Bit i of WT is set when a **write** access from **this** core touches the ith byte
Read Others (RO)	Bit i of RO is set when a **read** access from the **other** cores touches the ith byte
Write Others (WO)	Bit i of WO is set when a **write** access from the **other** cores touches the ith byte
First This Access Read (FTAR)	Bit i of FTAR is set when the **first access** that touches the ith byte from **this** core is a **read**
First Others Access Read (FOAR)	Bit i of FOAR is set when the **first access** that touches the ith byte from the **other** cores is a **read**

3.1.1 Modifications to the Standard MSI Cache Coherence Protocol

The modification depicted in Figure 4 involves (1) adding a new Modified (M) and a new Shared (S) state called Critical Section Modified (CSM) and Critical Section Shared (CSS), which are almost exact replica of the M and S states, (2) modifying some state transition actions between and within the original M and S states, and (3) adding a new set of state transition actions between the CSM and CSS states that are analogous to those of the M and S states. The details pertaining to the standard MSI protocol are omitted for clarity. Interested readers are referred to, e.g., Culler et al. [6]. The underlined actions in Figure 4 relate directly to HEI's functionality. The key points in this augmented protocol are:

1. It adds the two new states CSS and CSM, as mentioned above.
2. It adds transitions from the Invalid (I) state to the two new states, CSS and CSM (transitions 10 and 12 in Figure 4).
3. It dictates that a read hit while in the CSS state needs to propagate a read message on the shared bus (transition 5). In the S state, a read hit does not generate additional bus traffic and is confined to the private cache of the core in consideration.
4. It requires that a read hit and a write hit while in the CSM state place corresponding read and invalidation messages on the bus (transitions 1 and 2). The corresponding transitions in the M state do not propagate such read and invalidation messages.

The changes noted in items 3 and 4 above allow the safe memory in a given cache to snoop for intervening reads or writes that would otherwise be confined to the private caches of the other cores. Note that the cache coherence engine only runs in the private cache region, never in the safe memory region.

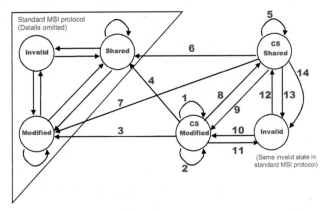

1: CPU read hit; **place read message on bus**
2: CPU write hit; **place invalidation message on bus**
3: CPU write miss; **place write miss on bus and write back**
4: CPU read miss; **place read miss on bus and write back**
5: CPU read hit; **place read message on bus**
6: CPU read miss; **place read message on bus**
7: CPU write miss; **place write miss on bus**
8: **Read miss for block received; write back; place read message on bus**
9: CPU write hit; **place invalidation message on bus**
10: CPU write miss and block found in safe memory; **place write miss on bus**
11: **Write miss for block received; write back**
12: CPU read miss and block found in safe memory; **place read miss on bus**
13: **Write miss for block received**
14: **Invalidation for block received**

Figure 4: Augmenting the MSI protocol to enable HEI; bus requests are in bold; CPU requests in normal font; underlined actions are the key differences from the MSI protocol

3.1.2 Basic Operation

Initially, the safe memory in each core is not active; all the ABVs and the valid bit for each block in the evicted cache region are cleared. When a core detects that:

1. the program starts to execute a critical section, i.e., acquires a lock, and
2. accesses possibly shared memory locations, i.e., non-stack locations,

the hardware evicts the cache block being accessed from the private cache region and sends the block to an entry in the evicted cache region in the safe memory. Detecting the first condition requires hardware that recognizes, for example, the test&test&set lock idiom similar to that used in SLE [7]. Detecting the second condition requires hardware that filters out instructions whose addressing mode is indirect off the stack and frame pointers. We assume that shared variables are accessed via registers other than these two registers.

Once the block is in the safe memory, HEI broadcasts an invalidation message to nullify all other copies of this block in this and all other cores. It also sets the Active Bit in the safe memory.

When the Active Bit is on, there are two cases to consider:

1. subsequent accesses to this block coming from this core, and
2. subsequent accesses to this block coming from another core.

In the first case, the following happens:

1. The accesses never bring the block back into the private cache; they always take a miss in the private cache and use the block in the safe memory. As a consequence, whenever the Active Bit is on, any misses in the private cache need to search the safe memory for a matching entry before going to the next level of the memory hierarchy.
2. The accesses set the appropriate bits in each of the RT, WT, and FTAR bit vectors. Recall that these sets of ABVs are for this core and are updated based on this core's requests.

In the second case, we may potentially have a race. The following happens:

1. The accesses are subject to the augmented cache coherence protocol described above as they are accessing the private cache.
2. The (active) safe memory in each core snoops on the bus for messages that may be relevant and sets the appropriate bits in each of the RO, WO, and FOAR vectors.

Upon exiting from a critical section, HEI resolves races according to the table in Figure 5, which is based on Table 1 in Section 2. Races are resolved at byte granularity using the information from the six Access Bit Vectors. The information from the RT, WT, RO, and WO bit vectors are sufficient to infer some race types. However, for the entries labeled A, B, and C in Figure 5, we need the information stored in the FOAR and FTAR bit vectors to pin down the exact race type. To resolve the race correctly, HEI retrieves the latest block copy that resides outside of the safe memory. This block should be in one of the three states I, CSS, or CSM. To do so, the hardware consults the state bits. If the block is in either the I or CSS state, it obtains the latest copy from the main memory; otherwise, it requests the block from the core that has the block in the CSM state. Upon receiving the latest copy, the hardware inspects the block byte by byte. Based on the race resolution in Figure 5, it determines for each byte whether to pass on the value from the block in the safe memory or from the outside block.

After successfully resolving any possible races for each byte in a block, HEI processes the next valid block in the safe memory until all valid blocks in the evicted cache region have been processed. Then, it resets the valid bits, the ABVs, and the Active Bit. Note

that the hardware needs to ensure that this process happens atomically. A straightforward way of ensuring this is to lock the bus so that only bus transactions from the core that is resolving the race are allowed during this time period. As we will show in the next section, critical section memory accesses constitute only a very small fraction of the total memory accesses, so this simple but seemingly costly way of ensuring atomicity should work well in practice. Furthermore, for most critical sections, the number of entries in the evicted cache region is small.

When encountering the RrwW race case that HEI cannot tolerate, the hardware reverts to detection mode and terminates program execution. The HEI hardware allows logging of quite detailed information including addresses, type, and sequence of accesses involved in the race. Such information can be a helpful debugging aid to identify the cause of the data race offline.

3.1.3 Nested and Overlapped Critical Sections

The HEI mechanism described thus far is designed to handle non-nested non-overlapped critical sections. It may seem like the simplest way to extend the basic hardware to cope with nested critical sections is to flatten them and to add a counter that keeps track of the nesting level. Unfortunately, this simple scheme does not faithfully preserve the original lock-based program semantics (see the example in Section 7) and does not correctly handle overlapped critical sections.

To remedy this situation, we need the ability to perform race resolution at every critical section exit. Thus, we have to associate a lock variable with each access (the term lock variable here refers to the memory location used in the test&test&set operation, which marks the start of a critical section). Since HEI resolves races at byte granularity, having a lock variable associated with each byte in a cache block is potentially costly. If we take a slightly less ambitious approach and decide not to support arbitrary levels of nesting or overlapping, we can scale back the hardware considerably. Based on the benchmark programs we studied, nesting levels greater than two occur rarely. Hence, we believe supporting up to four nesting levels will accommodate the majority of lock-based programs.

WT	RO	WO	Race type (if any)	Serializable execution enforced By HEI	
0	0	0	No race	None	
0	0	1	No race	None	
0	1	0	No race	None	
0	1	1	No race	None	
1	0	0	No race	None	
1	0	1	No race	None	
1	1	0	WrW	rWW	
1	1	1	WrwX, No race	rwWX, None	A
0	0	0	No race	None	
0	0	1	XwR	XRw	
0	1	0	No race	None	
0	1	1	RrwR, XwR	RRrw, XRw	B
1	0	0	No race	None	
1	0	1	XwR	XRw	
1	1	0	WrW	rWW	
1	1	1	WrwX, RrwW, XwR, RwW	rwWX, Not serializable, XRw, RWw	C

Case A:			Case B:			Case C:		
FOAR	Race type		FOAR	Race type		FTAR	FOAR	Race type
0	No race		0	XwR		0	0	XwR
1	WrwX		1	RrwR		0	1	WrwX
						1	0	RwW
						1	1	RrwW

Figure 5: HEI resolution table based on Access Bit Vectors

3.1.4 Fallback Mechanism

If the HEI resources are exhausted while the program is inside of a critical section, there are two possibilities to consider: (1) a race has already been detected, or (2) a race has not yet occurred. In the former case, the fallback is simply to stop program execution and report the race. Resolving the race in the middle of a critical section is not defined in HEI. The focus of the fallback mechanism, therefore, is on the second case where program execution must be allowed to continue. Abruptly stopping the program is not an acceptable solution in this case. After all, the introduction of HEI should not interfere with legitimate race-free runs of programs. The basic idea behind the recovery is to reconcile the copies of each of the active cache blocks in the safe memory region and to update the shared memory before program execution resumes. Consider each cache block residing in the safe memory region. Instances of these cache blocks may exist in (1) one other processor in the CSM state or (2) one or more other processors in the CSS or invalid state. The recovery machinery needs to flush all instances of these cache blocks to memory and make sure that each byte in the blocks holds the latest value from the last write to this byte. To do this correctly, the machinery only needs to consult the two write access bit vectors, WT and WO, associated with each cache block in the safe memory region. To ensure atomicity of the recovery process, the shared bus is locked until the flushing is completed.

4. Discussion

This section compares and contrasts the two other isolation enforcement techniques most closely related to ours, transactional memory (TM) and PACMAN [8]; the former is a well-studied technique whereas the latter is quite new.

General approach: Pacman is a hardware technique that tolerates races by stalling the unsafe threads whose accesses interfere with those in the safe thread that is executing in a critical section. At the heart of Pacman is a centralized piece of hardware (which can be made distributed) called SigTable. An entry in the SigTable stores the signature of the addresses being touched by the safe thread as well as its PID. Pacman monitors accesses from all other threads through coherence transactions to check whether their addresses are in the stored signature. If so, there is a potential race and the access requests from other threads are nacked, thus effectively stalling those threads. Pacman's hardware is placed at the network level so it is unintrusive in the sense that it minimally interferes with the normal processor-cache operations. Pacman could also be used as a race detector, but it is not designed for this purpose as the SigTable holds limited access information and the use of signatures may alias addresses that could result in false positives.

HEI is more intrusive as it is placed directly at the cache level that handles coherence transactions. HEI is distributed among each core's private cache. There is no explicit stalling of threads in HEI; race toleration occurs only at the exit of safe threads' critical sections. HEI readily supports detection and toleration modes as the safe memory contains more access information down to byte granularity and uses full addresses. If it is desirable to have Pacman's style stall-based tolerance, HEI can be modified to emulate it by nacking all external requests that hit in the safe memory.

The HEI mechanism is similar to TM with a lazy versioning policy and lazily detecting conflicts among transactions. However, it is not based on optimistic synchronization as TM is; there is no notion of abort-and-rollback, nor is there a need for contention management. Whereas handling side effect operations and nested transactions are still open issues with TM, HEI handles all I/O operations as well as overlapped critical sections transparently, preserving the semantics of the original lock-based program.

Pacman can also be viewed as pessimistic TM that has no notion of versioning or resolving conflicts (as it prevents them in the first

place). Hence, the TM issues mentioned above become non-issues in Pacman as well.

Isolation enforcement capability: there exist TM mechanisms that guarantee isolation among transactions and between transactions and non-transactions [9]. Pacman, being a pessimistic TM, can also fully enforce isolation in lock-based code. HEI, on the other hand, fails to enforce isolation when it encounters RrwW race cases. In Section 6, we outline a modification to the standard HEI implementation that can tolerate RrwW races.

Speculative execution: TM has this at heart, and, hence, it needs sophisticated techniques to deal with rollback and contention management. In addition, there are open issues with I/O operations. Pacman and HEI never perform speculative execution, so both never have non-undoable actions like I/Os. Encountering of conflicting accesses result in a thread stall in Pacman whereas HEI allows all threads involved in a conflict to progress if it can tolerate the race or terminates the execution and reports the race otherwise.

Starvation and deadlock: this is a major issue in TM that often needs sophisticated contention management to resolve. It is also an issue in Pacman. A simple deadlock case involves two threads using different locks to guard the same protected shared variables, nacking each other while both execute inside of the critical sections. Pacman requires a rather elaborated scheme to deal with this situation. HEI, on the other hand, never encounters such an issue. It always makes forward progress when it can tolerate the race or terminates program execution and reports the race if it cannot. Even when multiple threads exhaust their HEI hardware and need to perform flushing, deadlock cannot occur in HEI as the only resource each thread needs is the bus, which acts as a serialization point that each thread needs to acquire through arbitration before flushing. Once a thread acquires the bus, it does not need to wait for any other resources to perform flushing.

Hardware complexity: it is clear that optimistic concurrency, which needs to satisfy both performance and isolation goals in TM, requires more complex hardware than both Pacman and HEI. The major components in Pacman and HEI, the safe memory and the SigTable, are both regular, table-like structures. The SigTable is a bit more complicated as it works with encoded addresses. However, it is the control logic that makes Pacman more complex than HEI. Pacman's control logic needs to handle deadlock and requires some intrusive hardware addition to be made to the cache hierarchy. In addition, placing the SigTable at the network level makes it tricky to reason about atomicity.

Scalability: HEI has limited scalability as its mechanism is tied to bus-based schemes. Pacman can be made more scalable with a distributed SigTable. Scalable TM has been demonstrated by, for example, Chafi et al. [10].

Executables: Pacman and HEI operate largely on unmodified lock-based executables. They can run code that uses lock-free data structures that contain intentional races and treat them as harmless since these races involve accesses to shared data only outside of lock regions. TM, on the other hand, operates on transactional code. Lock-based code can run on TM hardware, but it first needs to be transactified, i.e., converted from lock-based to transaction-based code. This conversion, however, is not trivial [11].

5. Evaluation
5.1 Benchmarks

We use 13 applications from the SPLASH2 [12] and PARSEC [13] benchmark suites for our evaluation. The eight programs from the SPLASH2 suite were chosen per the minimum set recommended by the suite's guidelines. They are *cholesky*, *fft*, *lu*, *radix*, *barnes*, *ocean*, *radiosity*, and *water*. We replaced the SPLASH2 suite's PARMAC macros with a pthreads library implementation. For each of the eight programs, the default inputs were used. We selected the five programs from the PARSEC suite that use the pthreads library. They are *dedup*, *facesim*, *ferret*, *fluidanimate*, and *x264*. The PARSEC suite aims to provide up-to-date multithreaded programs that focus on workloads in recognition, mining, and synthesis. They are run with the simlarge inputs.

5.2 System and Compiler

All benchmarks are compiled and run on a 32-bit system with a four-core 2.8 GHz Xeon CPU with 16 kB L1 data cache per core, a 2 MB unified L2 cache, and 2 GB of main memory. The operating system is Red Hat Enterprise Linux Release 4 and the compiler is gcc version 3.4.6. We compiled the SPLASH2 and PARSEC programs per each suite's guideline.

5.3 Quantitative Assessment of HEI

This subsection investigates quantitatively the characteristics of the safe memory and the potential overhead when running the benchmark applications under HEI. We first focus on the amount of hardware required to protect the critical sections. Then, we look at the frequency of critical section executions and the effect on the execution time of each application given certain overheads incurred by HEI.

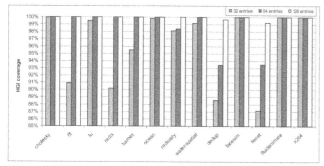

Figure 6: HEI coverage of critical section execution for 64-byte blocks (y-axis not zero based)

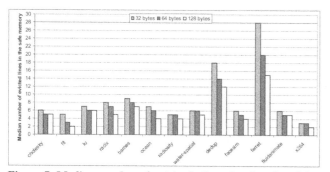

Figure 7: Median number of entries in the evicted cache of the safe memory required by HEI for different block sizes

Figure 6 shows, for each application, the fraction of critical section executions that are fully covered by HEI when the block size is 64 bytes and the number of safe memory entries is 32, 64, or 128. HEI fully covers a critical section execution when, for a given amount of hardware, it does not cause overflow in the safe memory. For 64 entries, over 93% of the critical section executions in each application are covered. When doubling the number of entries to 128, the coverage increases to 99%. Figure 7 shows,

for varying block sizes, the average number of safe memory entries each application operates on. For a 64-byte block, all applications except *dedup* and *ferret* often process less than 8 entries. To obtain the result in Figures 6 and 7, we use our in-house cache simulator that implements the modified MSI protocol as described in the previous section. The simulator is implemented as a Pintool plug-in [14] that runs with the Pin dynamic binary instrumentor.

Table 4: Critical section execution characteristics of each benchmark application

	Avg. Uniq. Mem. Loc. Touched	% Mem. Access	% Time 4-core	% Time 8-core	% Time 16-core
cholesky	14.34	0.06%	0.22%	0.44%	0.88%
fft	6.83	< 0.001%	0.004%	0.007%	0.014%
lu	20.93	< 0.001%	0.02%	0.03%	0.06%
radix	22.57	< 0.001%	0.001%	0.003%	0.006%
barnes	43.05	0.43%	10.94%	19.72%	32.95%
ocean	20.99	< 0.01%	0.03%	0.06%	0.12%
radiosity	4.92	0.49%	23.62%	38.21%	55.30%
water-spatial	15.70	< 0.01%	0.02%	0.03%	0.07%
dedup	121.30	0.73%	4.47%	8.55%	15.76%
facesim	15.40	< 0.01%	0.07%	0.15%	0.29%
ferret	92.76	1.22%	6.93%	12.96%	22.94%
fluidanimate	15.00	1.36%	4.32%	8.29%	15.30%
x264	6.47	< 0.01%	0.01%	0.02%	0.03%

From the simulation result in Figures 6 and 7, we see that covering the majority of critical section execution does not require an excessive amount of hardware. In addition, most critical section executions exercise only a small fraction of the hardware.

Next, we look at the characteristics of critical section executions with a focus on memory accesses. Table 4 summarizes the results. In the first data column, we show the average number of memory locations touched within a critical section. These are the possibly shared locations accessed by each thread. Recall from the previous section that we exclude all stack accesses via frame and stack pointers. Most applications access no more than 20 locations on average. The number for *radix* is slightly above 20 and for *barnes* it is 43. *ferret* and *dedup* perform significantly more accesses than the other applications. These two benchmarks execute loops inside of critical sections whereas all the other programs loop over their critical sections. This access information is in line with the results for the amount of hardware and the coverage shown in Figure 6.

The second column of Table 4 shows the fraction of memory accesses inside critical sections as a percentage of all memory accesses. As we can see, accesses inside of critical sections are relatively infrequent events. The percentage for all the benchmarks except *ferret* and *fluidanimate* is less than 1%. After all, parallel programs try to avoid serial execution, the part where Amdahl's law limits performance. The quantities in the first and second columns are obtained from dynamic program analysis using Pin; we dynamically instrumented all machine instructions – inside and outside of critical sections – that have at least one memory operand not accessed via the stack or frame pointer.

The third, fourth, and fifth columns show the fraction of total execution time spent in critical sections for 4, 8, and 16-core machines. We set the limit at 16 cores as we do not project HEI to be applicable beyond this point. To measure the time, we inserted a call to the clock_gettime() function at each critical section entry and exit point. In case of nested critical sections, we flatten them and measure the time for the outermost critical section. clock_gettime() provides an interface to a high-resolution timer with roughly nanosecond accuracy. To get accurate timing measurement, we configure all the programs to execute with only a single thread. Then, we estimate the time spent outside of the critical sections by assuming that those portions can be fully parallelized. Hence, if each program is to run on an n-core machine, this portion of time is divided by n. The fraction of time spent in the critical sections is calculated as:

$$\frac{(time\ spent\ in\ CS)}{\dfrac{(time\ spent\ outside\ CS)}{n} + (time\ spent\ in\ CS)}$$

We see that only *radiosity*, *barnes*, *dedup*, *ferret*, and *fluidanimate* have a noticeable fraction of time in critical sections, ranging from around 4% to 55%. All the other applications spend less than 1% of their execution time in critical sections. As expected, when the number of cores increases, the fraction of time inside of critical sections becomes more significant, especially when we assume that the code outside of critical sections can be fully parallelized.

The results obtained so far seem to suggest that the HEI overhead should not be significant. The safe memory hardware is small and most of the time only a small fraction of it is exercised. In addition, memory accesses in critical sections are relatively infrequent and most parallel applications spend little time in critical sections.

5.4 Qualitative Argument for HEI Overhead

This subsection offers qualitative arguments as to why the HEI overhead is unlikely to be excessive. We focus on two factors: the HEI memory bandwidth requirement and the HEI overhead when executing inside of critical sections.

To understand the bandwidth requirement, we need to look at the modified MSI protocol in Figure 4. The bottom line is that a system with HEI consumes about as much bandwidth as a system without it. The only time that a system with HEI generates extra coherence messages from cores not executing in critical sections is when the other cores have cache blocks in either CS modified or CS shared states (Figure 4 messages 1, 2, and 5). Since this usually signals a race, it should occur rarely.

Next we look at HEI's critical section execution overhead. The performance penalty of HEI comes primarily from two sources, accessing safe memory and resolving races. As the result in Section 5.3 indicates, the majority of critical section executions exercises fewer than 8 entries in the safe memory. Therefore, the associative search associated with each safe memory access should require only a couple of cycles more than a normal L1 access. This may be a significant overhead for accesses that would have hit in the L1. However, such an access is more likely to first miss in the L1 (after all, it is a shared variable), in which case the overhead becomes insignificant.

The resolution hardware is made of combinational logic that requires only simple AND gates followed by OR gates to process the access bit vector and "filter" bytes in a safe memory entry to pass on. It should take less than one cycle per resolution. If we need faster race resolution, more hardware can be added to resolve races in parallel.

6. Enforcing Isolation for the RrwW Race with Re-execution

As described, HEI is not able to guarantee isolation for the race case RrwW. However, this case can be serialized as rwRW if we have the ability to re-execute the RW operations in the safe thread after having seen the intervening rw operations from the non-safe thread. Assuming we have a mechanism for re-execution, guaranteeing isolation for this race case becomes viable. This section

quantifies the potential to enhance HEI through critical section re-execution on the benchmark programs.

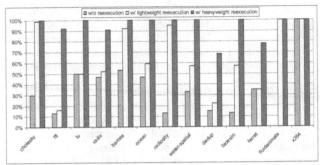

Figure 8: Worst-case measurement for fraction of shared accesses where isolation can be guaranteed

First, consider the re-execution capability of a particular critical section execution. We consider three categories: non-reexecutable, lightweight re-executable, and heavyweight re-executable. A non-re-executable critical section always involves interactive I/O operations that cannot be undone or repeated. A lightweight re-executable critical section does not have calls to library functions that invoke operating system services. Therefore, it can be re-executed by checkpointing the register and memory reads in the critical sections in user code and address space. A heavyweight re-executable critical section contains calls that invoke operating systems services that can potentially be undone by checkpointing the full memory state in both user and OS space, including calls to threading and synchronization operations in the pthread library.

We then measure the fraction of shared accesses where HEI can guarantee isolation in each benchmark application. The results of this experiment for all critical section executions are shown in Figure 8. This is the worst-case measurement, i.e., at least this fraction can be guaranteed. The reading at 50% means that, on average, for a given memory location accessed inside of critical sections, at least half of the accesses can be guaranteed isolation, i.e., they can be serialized with racing accesses.

The first bar in Figure 8 shows, for each application, the measurement without any re-execution. In essence, this bar indicates the fraction of all accesses to a given shared memory location inside of critical sections that do not start with a read that is later followed by a write (which is indicative of RW operations). Recall that when this is the case, it guarantees that race case RrwW cannot happen, and, hence, isolation can always be guaranteed. We find two extreme cases. *fluidanimate* has zero potential whereas *x264* has 100%. *barnes* hovers just above 50% and most of the benchmarks have less than 50% potential. When considering lightweight re-execution, the potential shoots up dramatically in a number of applications, particularly in *fluidanimate* where it jumps from 0% to 100%. Other benchmarks with large improvements are *cholesky*, *barnes*, *radiosity*, and *facesim*. Expectedly, when considering heavyweight re-execution, we see 100% potential in all benchmark applications except those that contain non-reexecutable critical sections, i.e., *fft*, *radix*, *dedup*, and *ferret*.

7. Enabling HEI with Hardware TM

Anticipating the arrival of hardware TM [15], it seems expedient to fit the HEI mechanism into this framework. This section investigates how to accommodate the HEI functionality in this way. A related work albeit with a different focus by Gupta et al. [16] leverages the conflict detection in TM to detect data races.

Because piggybacking on hardware TM requires a minimal increase in hardware budget and complexity, processor manufacturers may be inclined to support both HEI and TM at the same time with the former geared towards enhancing reliability of existing lock-based programs and the latter towards transaction-based parallel applications.

As HEI is designed to work transparently with existing lock-based program binaries, a pre-processing system is needed to "transactify" lock-based programs into transaction-based programs where lock-based critical sections are transformed into atomic blocks marked by transaction constructs recognized by the hardware TM. Note that essentially all this system does is replace lock-based constructs with some constructs recognized by the TM hardware. No knowledge about HEI or TM semantics is incorporated at this point. An example of such a system is HyTM [17]. The following are some necessary conditions for HEI to function on top of hardware TM.

1. Use deferred (a.k.a. lazy) update: To be compatible with HEI, the hardware TM must not modify the shared data directly. Most proposed hardware TMs that buffer updates in private caches satisfy this requirement. However, there exist hardware TM systems such as Wisconsin's LogTM [9] that do not. LogTM uses an eager update protocol that is not compatible with HEI.

2. Support open-nested semantics: To accommodate nested critical sections and follow their lock-based program semantics faithfully, the hardware TM needs to provide support for open nesting. Simple flattening is not sufficient to embrace nested critical sections as it may prevent forward progress in the original lock-based program. To make this more concrete, consider the following (somewhat contrived) example.

```
P = 4;

Lock(mutex_X);

Q++;

Lock(mutex_Y);

P++;

Unlock(mutex_Y);

do {} while (P < 5);

Unlock(mutex_X);
```

In this example, the lock variable mutex_X protects the update to variable Q whereas mutex_Y protects the update to variable P. The mutex_Y critical section is nested in the outer mutex_X critical section and, just before exiting from the outer critical section, there is a do-while loop that spins on the condition (P < 5). If the underlying hardware TM uses a deferred update protocol and flattens nested transactions, when the example code is "transactified", it will keep spinning on the do-while loop after executing the inner critical section as the updated value of the shared variable P will not be made visible until the outer critical section completes.

Unfortunately, recently proposed hardware TM systems handle nested transactions by flattening them. Therefore, for the current generation of TM hardware to accommodate nested critical sections in the way HEI requires, it may need assistance from special hardware as outlined in Section 3.1.3.

3. Disable concurrent transactions: For HEI, there is no notion of concurrent execution of critical sections. To enforce this condition, the hardware TM must disallow concurrent transactions that originate from the same mutex variable. Disabling a given transaction should not be hard to accomplish as the TM hardware already contains structures to track a new transaction that is about to execute in the middle of an outstanding transaction. However, recognizing which transaction to disable requires special treatment. During the "transactification", an atomic block derived from a corresponding critical section needs to be augmented with the mutex variable that is associated with the critical section. When the TM hardware processes a given atomic block, it checks whether the atomic block is generic, i.e., coming from purely transac-

tion-based code, or derived, i.e., coming from lock-based code. It imposes no restriction on the concurrent execution of the former, but prohibits concurrent execution of the latter.

4. Detect conflicts from non-transaction executions: If the hardware TM is only concerned with conflicts among transactions, it needs to be augmented to detect conflicts from non-transaction execution to support HEI. The contention management hardware is not needed when in HEI mode because HEI always guarantees forward progress. However, additional resolution hardware is needed. This is simple hardware whose primary function is to propagate memory writes based on the type of conflict detected.

8. Related Work

8.1 Race Toleration

Krena et al. [18] propose two schemes to dynamically heal data races for Java programs. In one scheme, they reduce the probability of races happening by forcing threads that are about to cause racy accesses to yield. This is done at the byte-code level through yield() calls. In the other scheme, they add extra locks to some common code patterns that are likely to result in races. Rajamani et al. [19] propose a run-time system called Isolator that enforces isolation through page protection. The idea is to protect the pages containing shared variables (that are protected by a lock) so that accesses to them can be intercepted. Then, accesses to those variables that observe the proper locking discipline are redirected to a local copy of the corresponding page. Any improper access will be to the original page and hence raise a page protection fault. Similarly, Abadi et al. [20] use page-level protection to guarantee strong atomicity in software transactional memory. Lucia et al. [21] tolerate some degree of atomicity violation with implicit atomicity by grouping consecutive memory operations into atomic blocks. To avoid concurrency bugs, Yu and Narayanasamy [22] constrain thread interleavings in production runs with Lifeguard Transactions (LifeTx). Legitimate interleavings are determined during the testing phase and LifeTx avoids untested interleavings, which are the sources of concurrency bugs.

8.2 Hardware Transactional Memory

HEI is analogous to hardware TM, which was first proposed by Herlihy and Moss [1]. Their scheme works on a fully associative transaction cache and leverages the cache coherence protocol to detect conflicts. Rajwar and Goodman proposed Speculative Lock Elision (SLE) [7], a form of optimistic synchronization that elides locks in parallel programs and, thus, allows multiple critical sections that were mutually exclusive to execute concurrently. Their follow-up work, Transactional Lock Removal (TLR) [23], extends SLE to address issues with starvation and transactional semantics. The broad introduction of multicore chips around the year 2004 reinvigorated research in hardware transactional memory. Transactional Coherence and Consistency (TCC) [24] is a hardware TM that provides strong isolation and employs deferred policies for both update operations and conflict detections. In contrast to TCC, LogTM [9] uses eager update and eager conflict detection protocols. LogTM's authors argue that commits happen more often than aborts so adopting all eager policies make the common cases fast. Ceze et al. [25] describes a hardware TM that does not rely on cache coherence to track and detect conflicting memory accesses. All the hardware TM schemes described thus far are bounded hardware TM. Cases for unbounded TMs have been described by Ananian et al. [26] and Rajwar et al. [27].

9. Conclusions

This paper presents HEI, a hardware technique for enforcing isolation in lock-based parallel programs that leverages existing multi-core chip components and the cache coherence protocol. We especially target programs written in type unsafe languages, which are prevalent in today's parallel programming world. HEI runs the original, unmodified executables and allows a racy program to execute race-free whenever it can enforce isolation; in the cases where it cannot, it reverts to detecting isolation violations. We evaluate HEI on 13 programs from the SPLASH2 and PARSEC suites and show the additional hardware cost and the overhead to be small. With increasing silicon real estate on a chip, we believe HEI to be a good hardware investment to enhance reliability of lock-based parallel program execution.

10. Acknowledgement

We would like to thank the anonymous reviewers for their insightful comments on this paper. The Computer Systems Laboratory at Cornell University provided some of the computing resources used to obtain the results for this work. Martin Burtscher is supported by grants and gifts from NVIDIA and Intel. Paruj Ratanaworabhan is supported by grants from the Faculty of Engineering, Kasetsart University and a gift from the KSIP laboratory.

11. References

[1] M. Herlihy and J. E. B. Moss, "Transactional Memory: Architectural Support for Lock-Free Data Structures" *International Symposium on Computer Architecture*, 1993.

[2] S. V. Adve and M. D. Hill, "Weak Ordering - A New Definition" *International Symposium on Computer Architecture*, 1990.

[3] T. Shpeisman, V. Menon, A.-R. Adl-Tabatabai, S. Balensiefer, D. Grossman, R. Hudson, K. Moore, and B. Saha, "Enforcing Isolation and Ordering in STM" *ACM SIGPLAN Conference on Programming Language Design and Implementation*, 2007.

[4] P. Ratanaworabhan, M. Burtscher, D. Kirovski, B. Zorn, R. Nagpal, and K. Pattabiraman, "Detecting and Tolerating Asymmetric Races" ACM SIGPLAN Symposium on Principles and Practice of Parallel Programming, 2009.

[5] N. Jouppi, "Improving Direct-Mapped Cache Performance by the Addition of a Small Fully-Associative Cache and Prefetch Buffers" *International Symposium on Computer Architecture*, 1990.

[6] D. Culler, J. P. Singh, and A. Gupta, Eds., *Parallel Computer Architecture: A Hardware/Software Approach*. Morgan Kaufmann, 1998.

[7] R. Rajwar and J. R. Goodman, "Speculative Lock Elision: Enabling Highly Concurrent Multithreaded Execution" *International Symposium on Microarchitecture*, 2001.

[8] S. Qi, N. Otsuki, N. Nogueira, A. Muzahid, and J. Torrellas, "Pacman: Tolerating Asymmetric Data Races with Unintrusive Hardware" *International Symposium on High Performance Computer Architecture*, 2012.

[9] K. E. Moore, J. Bobba, M. J. Moravan, M. D. Hill, and D. A. Wood, "LogTM: Log-Based Transactional Memory" *International Symposium on High-Performance Computer Architecture*, 2006.

[10] H. Chafi, J. Casper, B. Carlstrom, A. McDonald, C. Minh, W. Baek, C. Kozyrakis, and K. Olukotun, "A Scalable, Non-Blocking Approach to Transactional Memory" *International Symposium on High Performance Computer Architecture*, 2007.

[11] C. Blundell, C. Lewis, and M. Martin, "Deconstructing Transactional Semantics: The Subtleties of Atomicity" *Fourth Annual Workshop on Duplicating, Deconstructing, and Debunking*, 2005.

[12] S. Woo, M. Ohara, E. Torrie, J. Singh, and A. Gupta, "The SPLASH-2 Programs: Characterization and Methodological Considerations" *International Symposium on Computer Architecture*, 1995.

[13] C. Bienia, S. Kumar, J. Singh, and K. Li, "The PARSEC Benchmark Suite: Characterization and Architectural Implications" *International Conference on Parallel Architectures and Compilation Techniques*, 2008.

[14] C. Luk, R. Cohn, R. Muth, H. Patil, A. Klauser, G. Lowney, S. Wallace, V. J. Reddi, and K. Hazelwood, "Pin: Building Customized Program Analysis Tools with Dynamic Instrumentation" *ACM SIGPLAN Conference on Programming Language Design and Implementation*, 2005.

[15] D. Dice, Y. Lev, M. Moir, and D. Nussbaum, "Early Experience with a Commercial Hardware Transactional Memory Implementation" *International Conference on Architectural Support for Programming Languages and Operating Systems*, 2009.

[16] S. Gupta, F. Sultan, S. Cadambi, F. Ivancic, and M. Rotteler, "Using Hardware Transactional Memory for Data Race Detection," *International Parallel & Distributed Processing Symposium*, 2009.

[17] P. Damron, A. Fedorova, Y. Lev, V. Luchangco, M. Moir, and D. Nussbaum, "Hybrid Transactional Memory" *International Conference on Architectural Support for Programming Languages and Operating Systems*, 2006.

[18] B. Krena, Z. Letko, R. Tzoref, S. Ur, and T. Vojnar, "Healing Data Races On-The-Fly" *ACM Workshop on Parallel and Distributed Systems: Testing and Debugging*, 2007.

[19] S. Rajamani, G. Ramalingam, V. Ranganath, and K. Vaswani, "ISOLATOR: Dynamically Ensuring Isolation in Concurrent Programs" *International Conference on Architectural Support for Programming Languages and Operating Systems*, 2009.

[20] M. Abadi, T. Harris, and M. Mehrara, "Transactional Memory with Strong Atomicity using Off-the-Shelf Memory Protection Hardware" *ACM SIGPLAN Symposium on Principles and Practice of Parallel Programming*, 2009.

[21] B. Lucia, J. Devietti, K. Strauss, and L. Ceze, "Atom-Aid: Detecting and Surviving Atomicity Violations" *International Symposium on Computer Architecture*, 2008.

[22] J. Yu and N. S., "Tolerating Concurrency Bugs Using Transactions as Lifeguards" *International Symposium on Microarchitecture*, 2010.

[23] R. Rajwar and J. R. R. Goodman, "Transactional Lock-Free Execution of Lock-Based Programs" *International Conference on Architectural Support for Programming Languages and Operating Systems*, 2002.

[24] L. Hammond, V. Wong, M. Chen, B. D. Carlstrom, J. D. Davis, B. Hertzberg, M. K. Prabhu, H. Wijaya, C. Kozyrakis, and K. Olukotun, "Transactional Memory Coherence and Consistency" *International Symposium on Computer Architecture*, 2004.

[25] L. Ceze, J. Tuck, J. Torrellas, and C. Cascaval, "Bulk Disambiguation of Speculative Threads in Multiprocessors" *International Symposium on Computer Architecture*, 2006.

[26] C. S. Ananian, K. Asanovic, B. C. Kuszmaul, C. E. Leiserson, and S. Lie, "Unbounded Transactional Memory" *International Symposium on High Performance Computer Architecture*, 2005.

[27] R. Rajwar, M. Herlihy, and K. Lai, "Virtualizing Transactional Memory" *International Symposium on Computer Architecture*, 2005.

High-Performance Code Generation for Stencil Computations on GPU Architectures

Justin Holewinski   Louis-Noël Pouchet   P. Sadayappan

Department of Computer Science and Engineering
The Ohio State University
Columbus, OH 43210
{holewins, pouchet, saday}@cse.ohio-state.edu

ABSTRACT

Stencil computations arise in many scientific computing domains, and often represent time-critical portions of applications. There is significant interest in offloading these computations to high-performance devices such as GPU accelerators, but these architectures offer challenges for developers and compilers alike. Stencil computations in particular require careful attention to off-chip memory access and the balancing of work among compute units in GPU devices.

In this paper, we present a code generation scheme for stencil computations on GPU accelerators, which optimizes the code by trading an increase in the computational workload for a decrease in the required global memory bandwidth. We develop compiler algorithms for automatic generation of efficient, time-tiled stencil code for GPU accelerators from a high-level description of the stencil operation. We show that the code generation scheme can achieve high performance on a range of GPU architectures, including both nVidia and AMD devices.

Categories and Subject Descriptors

D.1.3 [**Programming techniques**]: Concurrent programming—*Parallel Programming*; D.3.4 [**Programming Languages**]: Processors—*Code Generation, Compilers*

Keywords

GPU, OpenCL, Overlapped Tiling, Stencils, DSL

1. INTRODUCTION

Stencils represent an important computational pattern used in scientific applications in a variety of domains including computational electromagnetics [18], solution of PDEs using finite difference or finite volume discretizations [16], and image processing for CT and MRI imaging [3,4]. A number of recent studies have focused on optimizing stencil computations on multicore CPUs [2,6,8,17,19] as well as GPUs [11–13].

Stencil computations involve the repeated updating of values associated with points on a multi-dimensional grid, using only the values at a set of neighboring points. For multi-core processors, stencil computations are often memory-bandwidth bound when the collective data for all grid points exceeds cache size, since each grid point is accessed at each time step. Time-tiling, i.e., tiling along the time dimension, is useful in enhancing data locality. The standard approach to time-tiling of stencil computations requires loop skewing to make tiling legal and this results in loss of inter-tile concurrency [10], since inter-tile dependences are introduced in the spatial directions due to the skewing. The approach of "overlapped tiling" [10], also called "ghost zone" optimization [3,11], has been used for preserving concurrency in parallel time-tiled execution of stencil computations. However, we are unaware of any fully automated compiler approach for the generation of overlapped-tiling code for execution on GPUs. In this paper, we develop compiler algorithms for automated GPU code generation for stencil computations and demonstrate effectiveness through experimental evaluation using a number of stencils on four GPU platforms.

The paper is organized as follows. In Sec. 2, we provide some background on GPUs and the key issues in achieving high performance with them. In Sec. 3, we formalize the class of stencil computations we consider. The compiler algorithms for generation of overlapped tiled code for GPUs are presented in Sec. 4. Sec. 5 presents experimental results. Related work is covered in Sec. 6, and we conclude in Sec. 7.

2. GRAPHICS PROCESSING UNITS

Graphics Processing Units (GPUs) are massively-threaded, many-core architectures with peak floating-point throughput of over 1 TFLOP/s. NVIDIA GPUs contain hundreds of cores (streaming processors) arranged in tightly coupled groups of 8–32 scalar processors per streaming multi-processor. Threads are grouped into thread blocks that are scheduled on a streaming multi-processor and cannot migrate. A single multi-processor can concurrently handle several blocks of threads using zero-overhead hardware multi-threading to interleave their execution on its cores. Parallelism is exposed both across thread blocks and within thread blocks. Threads within a block are cooperative and can synchronize with each other, but threads in different blocks cannot synchronize, even if they are scheduled on the same streaming multi-processor.

Each thread has access to global, off-chip memory and a shared scratch-pad memory that is shared among all threads within a block. Threads within a block can communicate and exchange data through shared memory. Thread synchronization can be achieved by the use of barrier instructions that cause all threads within a block to stop at the barrier until all threads have reached the barrier. Thread synchronization is, in general, not feasible across thread blocks.

Architectural Model: Low-level programming models are commonly used to write GPU programs. The two most common models are CUDA [14] and OpenCL [9, 15]. In both models, the programmer writes an imperative program (called a *kernel*) that is executed by each thread on the device. Threads are spawned in 1-, 2-, or 3-dimensional rectangular groups of cooperative threads, called blocks (CUDA) or work-groups (OpenCL). A 1- or 2-dimensional grid of blocks is used to schedule the thread blocks. Both the size and number of thread blocks are fixed when launching a GPU kernel and cannot be changed after the threads have launched.

Efficient GPU programs typically involve the scheduling of hundreds of threads per streaming multi-processor to hide memory latency. The streaming multi-processors schedule threads at the granularity of warps, which comprise 32 threads on previous and current generation architectures. The thread scheduler time-shares the streaming multi-processors between all currently active warps, and thread context switches incur no overhead.

Challenges: Several sources of inefficiency can arise when developing GPU applications. GPU devices provide a very high off-chip memory bandwidth (up to 192 GB/sec for the GTX 580), but *this bandwidth is only achievable with coalesced access*. Data from the off-chip memory is transferred to the GPU device in contiguous blocks and therefore high bandwidth can be achieved only when requests by concurrent threads in a warp fall within such contiguous blocks. When non-contiguous memory locations are accessed by threads, the achieved bandwidth can be much lower than the peak, leading to stalling and wasted compute cycles. Branch divergence is another source of inefficiency. Threads within a warp that follow different control paths are serialized, again leading to wasted compute cycles. Traditional approaches to time tiling of stencil computations to enhance data reuse for CPUs do not translate well to GPUs because they lead to uncoalesced memory access and divergent branching of threads.

Another challenge comes from shared scratch-pad memory implemented as a banked memory system. If concurrently executing threads in a block make requests to shared memory locations in the same bank, a bank conflict occurs and the requests are serialized. Therefore, to achieve optimal usage of shared memory, *concurrently executing threads should access data from different banks*. We present in this paper an automated code generation approach to overcome these challenges, for the class of stencil computations as described in Section 3.

3. STENCIL COMPUTATIONS

Recent work has shown promise for high performance by use of overlapped tiling on GPUs [11] for stencil computations. In this paper, we present an automated approach to generate efficient overlapped tiling code for stencil computations on GPUs. We first describe the features of a Domain-Specific Language (DSL) to describe stencil computations, such that any program written in this language can be pro-

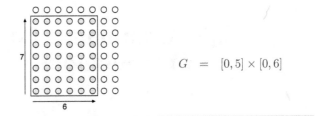

Figure 1: Example of a 2-D grid

cessed automatically by our compiler. The code generation algorithms for overlapped tiling are detailed later in Section 4.

3.1 Stencil DSL

Our stencil DSL models iterative methods operating on (dense) *fields* atop a Cartesian *grid*. In addition to the the data space, we describe the *stencil function* which is applied iteratively on each point of the grid.

We enforce some constraints on the DSL to facilitate transformation to efficient code. First, to enable compile-time generation of overlapped tiled code, we need to model the halo of the stencil, and it needs to be exactly computable at compile time. This implies that the neighboring relationship remains constant during the computation. Second, in order to perform tiling along the time dimension, the computation must iterate a constant number of time steps before any field-spanning operation is performed (e.g., a convergence check). Finally, we remark that to ease code generation, we enforce the use of a second temporary field to store the result of the application of the point function on the input field. Thus in this work, we address Jacobi-like methods, and not Seidel-like methods.

We now define the three key concepts of computation grids, fields, and stencil functions before putting it together to describe a full program using this DSL.

Computation Grid: Every stencil computation that we consider is defined on a *computation grid*, which is a bounded, rectangular region in $\mathbb{Z}^n$. The supporting grid can be seen as a Cartesian coordinate system on a contiguous subset of $\mathbb{Z}^n$. A grid can be defined as a union of "sub-grids". This is particularly relevant to define regions in the space that may have different physical properties, such as boundaries. So we have:

$$G \subset \mathbb{Z}^n$$

Sub-grids G^i of the grid G are non-intersecting subsets of integer points, defining a partition of G.

A sub-grid is defined by an origin point α_i and and end point β_i in each of the n dimensions, with $\alpha_i \leq \beta_i$. That is:

$$G^i = \{[\alpha_1..\beta_1] \times [\alpha_2..\beta_2] \times \ldots \times [\alpha_n..\beta_n], \alpha_i, \beta_i \in \mathbb{Z}, \alpha_i \leq \beta_i\}$$

Fields: Once we have defined our computation grid, we can define the data attached to this grid for a particular computation. This takes the form of a (series of) fields attached to a particular (sub-)grid. Multiple fields are associated with a single grid typically when a stencil uses data from multiple sources during the computation. A field is implemented as a data structure that maps a value to every point in the grid. The type of these values can be simple scalar values or complex recursive types, defined by the following grammar:

$$
\begin{aligned}
ElemType \quad &\longrightarrow \quad \text{real} \mid \text{integer} \mid \text{vector } n \text{ of } ElemType \\
&\qquad\quad \mid StructType \\
StructType \quad &\longrightarrow \quad \{field_1 : ElemType_1, \\
&\qquad\qquad field_2 : ElemType_2, ...\}
\end{aligned}
$$

We denote $\mathcal{F}_G$ a field $\mathcal{F}$ associated to a (sub-)grid G.

Stencil Functions: The last component of a stencil computation is the sequence of *stencil functions* that are applied iteratively to the fields defined on the computation grid. A stencil function defines a computation that is applied to each point of a (sub-)grid. Different functions can be used for different sub-grids, as for instance to handle boundary conditions. The stencil function uses neighboring field points in the same field or other fields in its computation of the new value for the point.

Given a collection of p fields $\mathcal{F}_{G^k}^k$, a stencil function f is a function

$$
f : \mathcal{F}_{G^1}^1 \times \ldots \times \mathcal{F}_{G^p}^p \to T_{\mathcal{F}^p}
$$

where $T_{\mathcal{F}^p}$ is the type of elements in field $\mathcal{F}^p$. The domain of definition G_f of this function is a sub-grid of G^p, and we have $\forall i \in [1..p], G_f \in G^i$. This function is implicitly invoked for each point of G_f.

As an example, consider a simple 2-D stencil function that is defined on the computation grid introduced in Figure 1. We define the stencil as:

$$
\begin{aligned}
f(A_G)[1..N-2, 1..M-2] = &A[-1,0] + A[0,-1] + A[0,0] + \\
&A[+1,0] + A[0,+1]
\end{aligned}
$$

where the notation $A[i,j]$ shows an access to the field A at grid coordinates (i,j) from the current grid point, and $[1..N-2, 1..M-2]$ specifies the range of the grid over which the stencil function should be applied[1]. Since we are using Cartesian grids in $\mathbb{Z}^n$, the grid offsets must be integer values. Furthermore, they must be constant. This notation naturally extends to grids of any dimensionality. This stencil function effectively computes a new value for a grid point based on the immediate neighbors in both the horizontal and vertical directions.

In this example, we assume that the addition operator $(+)$ is well-defined for the value type of elements in the field A. For scalar, vector, and matrix types, the operator is clearly well-defined. However, if our value type is of structure type, the addition operator may not be well-defined in general.

Program Specification: Using the previous definitions of *computation grid, field,* and *stencil function,* we can now define a complete *stencil program*. A stencil program defines the underlying computation grid, a set of one or more fields that are associated to the grid, a sequence of stencil functions that are applied on the (sub-)grids, and the number of steps the iterative process is repeated. For each field, we must define the value type for the points. We must also define the region over which each stencil function operates. Finally, we must define the number of iterations over which the stencil computation will occur, which is attached as an attribute of the grid. In each iteration, every stencil func-

---

[1]Here, it is assumed that N and M are the bounds of the computation grid.

```
1   real A[M];
2   real A_tmp[M];
3
4   copy(A_tmp /* dest */, A /* src */);
5
6   for (n = 0; n < T; ++n) {
7     A[0] = A_tmp[0];
8     for (i = 1; i < M-1; ++i) {
9       A[i] = 0.333 * (A_tmp[i-1] + A_tmp[i] + A_tmp[i+1]);
10    }
11    A[M-1] = A_tmp[M-1];
12    swap(A_tmp, A);
13  }
```

Figure 2: Pseudocode for a simple 3-point stencil.

tion is evaluated in the proper region. Stencil programs in our framework are formally defined as:

$$
\begin{aligned}
Program \quad &\longrightarrow \quad GridDef \; FieldDefs \; Funcs \\
GridDef \quad &\longrightarrow \quad \text{Bounds, TimeSteps} \\
FieldDefs \quad &\longrightarrow \quad \text{Name} : ElemType \; FieldDefs \\
&\qquad\quad \mid \quad \epsilon \\
Funcs \quad &\longrightarrow \quad \text{Name (Arrays) [Bounds]} \\
&\qquad\qquad = Expr \; Funcs \\
&\qquad\quad \mid \quad \epsilon \\
Expr \quad &\longrightarrow \quad \text{FieldAccess} \mid Expr \; \text{Op} \; Expr
\end{aligned}
$$

The bounds assigned to stencil functions define the sub-grids in the computation. A stencil function always operates on a sub-grid of the entire computation grid, and it may span the entire computation grid.

In the presence of multiple stencil functions, the semantics of a stencil program asserts that they are executed in sequential order. That is, the first stencil function is applied to each point in its region and the results are written back to the data grid before any evaluation of the second stencil function occurs. There is no ordering constraint between grid points within a stencil function evaluation. That is, each evaluation of a stencil function within a single outer iteration occurs concurrently.

3.2 Example

As a concrete example, we consider the following stencil program, where M is a parameter:

$$
\begin{aligned}
G \quad &= \quad [0, M-1], 64 \\
A_G \quad &: \quad \text{real} \\
f_1(A_G)[0] \quad &= \quad A[0] \\
f_2(A_G)[1..M-2] \quad &= \quad 0.333 * (A[-1] + A[0] + A[1]) \\
f_3(A_G)[M-1] \quad &= \quad A[0]
\end{aligned}
$$

In this program, we define the computation grid as the region $[0, M-1]$ in $\mathbb{Z}$, where the stencil should be applied iteratively over 64 time steps. We define one field A_G which associates a field of real numbers onto the computation grid. Finally, we define a three stencil functions f_1, f_2 and f_3. f_2 computes an average of grid point values, defined in the range $[1, M-2]$ on the computation grid. The boundary points are updated with specific equations defined by the stencil functions f_1 and f_3.

The semantics of this program is that of the C-like pseudocode as shown in Figure 2. Note the use of the A_tmp array to help implement the semantics of the stencil program. In each iteration (n-loop), the new values for A are computed using the *old* values of A from the previous iteration. Therefore, the `A_tmp` array is used to cache the old values of A. Also, the variable `T` is used as a parameter for the number iterations over which to perform the stencil computation.

4. OVERLAPPED TILING

4.1 Overview

Tiling for stencil computations is complicated by data sharing between neighboring tiles. Cells along the boundary of a tile are often needed by computations in surrounding tiles, requiring communication between tiles when neighboring tiles are computed by different processors. To compute a stencil on a cell of a grid, data from neighboring cells is required. These cells are often referred to as the *halo* region. In general, to compute an $N \times M$ block of cells on a grid, we need an $(N + n) \times (M + m)$ block of data to account for the cells we are computing as well as the surrounding halo region, where n and m are constants derived from the shape of the stencil. For GPU devices, the halo region needs to be re-read from global memory for every time step as surrounding tiles may update the values in these cells. This limits the amount of re-use we can achieve in scratchpad memory before having to go back to global memory for new data. The new cell values produced in each time step must also be re-written to global memory as other tiles may require the data in their halo regions. In addition to the cost of going to global memory for each time step, global synchronization is also required to ensure all surrounding tiles have completed their computation and written their results to global memory before new halo data is read for each tile.

To get around these issues, overlapped tiling has been proposed [10] as a technique to reduce the data sharing requirements for stencil computations by introducing redundant computations. Instead of forcing tile synchronization after each time step to update the halo region for each tile, each tile instead redundantly computes the needed values for the halo region. This allows us to efficiently perform time tiling and achieve high performance on GPU targets.

Consider a simple 2-D Jacobi 9-point stencil like the one shown in Figure 3. In order to compute one time step of an $n \times n$ tile, we need to read $(n + 2) \times (n + 2)$ cells into scratchpad memory, compute the stencil operation on each of the $n \times n$ points, then write back $n \times n$ points to global memory. Now, let us consider the computation of two time steps of the stencils on a single block, without having to go back to global memory between the two time steps. If we read $(n + 4) \times (n + 4)$ cells into memory, we can compute a $(n + 2) \times (n + 2)$ tile of cells in the first time step, which includes the results for our original $n \times n$ tile as well as the halo region needed for the next time step. If we again apply the stencil operation to the $(n+2) \times (n+2)$ tile, we correctly compute the inner $n \times n$ tile for the second time step but the results computed in the halo region for the second time step are not correct. However, this is not a problem since we only care about the inner $n \times n$ region. An illustration of this computation is presented in Figure 4.

4.2 Code Generation

To generate efficient GPU code, we need to tile the data space of the stencil grids into units that can be computed by a single thread block on a GPU device without any needed block synchronization. For each stencil operation, we need

```
1   for(t = 0; t < T; ++t) {
2     for(i = 1; i < N-1; ++i) {
3       for(j = 1; j < N-1; ++j) {
4         A[i][j] = CNST * (B[i ][j ] +
5           B[i ][j-1] + B[i ][j+1] +
6           B[i-1][j ] + B[i-1][j-1] +
7           B[i-1][j+1] + B[i+1][j ] +
8           B[i+1][j-1] + B[i+1][j+1]);
9       }
10    }
11    for(i = 1; i < N-1; ++i) {
12      for(j = 1; j < N-1; ++j) {
13        B[i][j] = A[i][j];
14      }
15    }
16  }
```

(a)   (b)

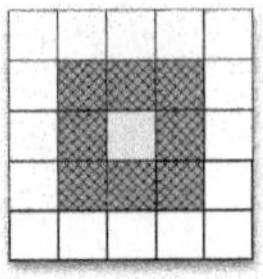

Figure 3: Jacobi 9-Point Stencil. In (a), C code is shown for the stencil, and in (b), the accessed data space is shown for one grid point. The tan cell is the (i, j) point, and each red hashed cell is read during the computation of the (i, j) cell.

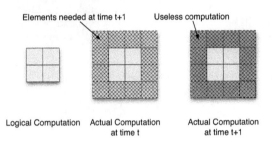

Logical Computation   Actual Computation at time t   Actual Computation at time t+1

Figure 4: Overlapped Jacobi 9-Point Stencil for $T = 2$.

Algorithm 1: Overlapped-tiling code generation algorithm

Input: P : Program, B : Block Size, T : Time Tile Size, E : Elements Per Thread
Output: P_{gpu} : GPU Kernel, P_{host} : CPU function
1 R ← DetermineTileSize(P, B, T)
  //Generate GPU Kernel
2 P_{gpu} ← GenerateGPUKernel (P, B, R, T) (§ 4.3)
  //Generate CPU Function
3 P_{host} ← GenerateHostCode (P, B, R, T) (§ 4.4)

---

to determine the region of grid points that will be computed by each thread block, including any needed redundant computation for intermediate time steps. The input to our code generation algorithm is a sequence of stencil operations and the output is overlapped-tiled GPU code and a host driver function.

Code generation for overlapped tiling on GPU architectures requires us to first identify the footprints of the stencil(s), determine proper block sizes for the target architecture, and then generate the GPU kernel code and host wrapper code. The overall algorithm is presented in Algorithm 1. The following sections describe all of the steps for the code generation algorithm.

Determining Abstract Tiles: To implement overlapped tiling, we need to create tiles such that a single thread block can compute all grid points for all stencil operations for T time steps, where T is the time tile size, without requiring any inter-block synchronization. For single-stencil computations, we only need to worry about the halo regions that are needed in intermediate time steps. However, for multi-stencil computations, we need to account for grid cells that may be needed for later stencil computations.

To determine the required computation for each sub-grid, we work backwards across all stencils and all time steps within our time tile. We start by assuming the last stencil computation in the last time step operates on a rectangular tile that is defined by an origin $\vec{x}_0$ and length $\vec{l}_0$. For each sub-grid used to compute this stencil, we can build a rectangular region that forms a tightest-possible bound on the sub-grid that includes all grid points needed for that stencil computation.

Once rectangular regions have been built for all involved sub-grids, we move onto the previous stencil in execution order and perform the same computation. Once we finish with the first stencil in execution order, we wrap around to the last stencil and continue the process again until we have processed all stencils for all time steps in our time tile. When we generate a new rectangular tile for a sub-grid for which we have already computed a tile, we form the new tile by forming the union of the old and new result and then taking the tightest-possible rectangular bound.

This tile size selection procedure is formalized in Algorithm 2. The `GetUpdatedGrid(s)` function returns the sub-grid that is updated for the given stencil, and the function `GetSourceGrids(s)` returns all sub-grids that are used on the right-hand side of the given stencil. The function `GetRequiredBounds(g, s, \vec{x}, \vec{l})` returns a rectangular region that represents the grid cells that are needed in grid g to compute stencil s in the region defined by $\vec{x}$ and $\vec{l}$. For a given stencil program P, the `ExtractSubGrids(P)` function returns all sub-grids that are touched by any point function. Finally, the `RectangularHull(\cup_i(\vec{x}_i, \vec{l}_i))` function returns the region that forms the tightest-possible rectangular bound on the given (possibly non-rectangular) region.

The results of this algorithm are a set of rectangular regions defined by $\vec{x}_g$ and $\vec{l}_g$, one for each sub-grid g. These regions define the grid cells that must be processed in each time step for each sub-grid in order to properly compute the final stencil in the final time step of the time tile. These regions will later be used to derive the per-block computation code. For the case of multiple grid points processed per thread, the $\vec{l}_g$ quantities are just multiplied by the number of elements per thread, element-wise in each dimension.

Note that to compute the final result for our $(\vec{x}_0, \vec{l}_0)$ region for each sub-grid, we do not need to compute values for the entire $(\vec{x}_g, \vec{l}_g)$ grid in each time step. However, on GPU architectures, it is more efficient to perform this redundant computation and let each thread perform the same amount of work in each time step. Otherwise, threads would contain control-flow instructions that would cause branch divergence and lower overall performance.

1-D Multi-Stencil Example: Let us now consider a multi-stencil computation. In the following example, we use two

---

Algorithm 2: Finding the tile size.

Name: DetermineTileSize
Input: P : Stencil Program, T : Time Tile Size
Output: $(\vec{x}_g, \vec{l}_g) \ \forall$ Sub-Grids

1   S $\leftarrow$ ExtractStencilFunctions (P)
2   DG $\leftarrow$ ExtractSubGrids (P)
3   **foreach** SubGrid $g \in$ DG **do**
4 | $(\vec{x}_g, \vec{l}_g) \leftarrow (\vec{x}_0, \vec{l}_0)$
5   **end**
6   **foreach** TimeStep t in (T, ..., 1) **do**
7 | **foreach** StencilFunction s in Reverse (S) **do**
8 | | $g \leftarrow$ GetUpdatedGrid (s)
9 | | $src \leftarrow$ GetSourceGrids (s)
10 | | **foreach** SubGrid $dg \in src$ **do**
11 | | | $(\vec{x}'_{dg}, \vec{l}'_{dg}) \leftarrow$ GetRequiredBounds $(dg, s, \vec{x}_g, \vec{l}_g)$
12 | | | $(\vec{x}_{dg}, \vec{l}_{dg}) \leftarrow$ RectangularHull $((\vec{x}_{dg}, \vec{l}_{dg}) \cup (\vec{x}'_{dg}, \vec{l}'_{dg}))$
13 | | **end**
14 | **end**
15   **end**

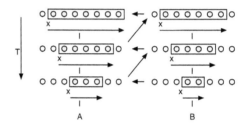

Figure 5: Tile region computation for 1-D multi-stencil.

---

stencil computations operating over two data grids, defined as:

$$f_A(B_G)[1..N-2] \quad = \quad B[-1] + B[0]$$
$$f_B(A_G)[1..N-2] \quad = \quad A[0] + A[1]$$

Again, we use a time tile size of three. We start by assigning an initial tile of $(\vec{x}_B, \vec{l}_B) = (x_0, l_0)$ to grid B. We see that the computation of B only depends on the grid A, so we use the index expressions to compute the needed region of A, which is $(\vec{x}_A, \vec{l}_A) = (x_0, l_0 + 1)$. We then backtrack to the computation for grid A, and determine that the needed region in grid B to compute A is $(\vec{x}_B, \vec{l}_B) = (x_0 - 1, l_0 + 2)$. This completes time step three, so we reverse to time step two and perform the same computation. Backtracking all of the way to the beginning of time step one, we have:

$$(\vec{x}_A, \vec{l}_A) \quad = \quad (x_0 - 2, l_0 + 5)$$
$$(\vec{x}_B, \vec{l}_B) \quad = \quad (x_0 - 2, l_0 + 4)$$

A pictorial representation of this process is shown in Figure 5.

4.3   Generation of GPU Kernel Code

Now that we know the amount of redundant computation that is needed for each sub-grid, we can generate the GPU kernel code for the stencil time tile. For this, we need to

---

Algorithm 3: Generating shared-memory definitions

Name: GenerateSharedMemory
Input: P : GPU Program, $\vec{B}$: Block Size, $\vec{E}$: Elements Per Thread, D : Sub-Grids
Output: P : GPU Program

1 **foreach** SubGrid g *in* D **do**
2   P $\leftarrow$ DeclareSharedRegion (P, NumberOfPoints ($\vec{B}$, $\vec{E}$), g)
3 **end**

---

define a set of parameters that are used as input to the code generation algorithm:

Parameter	Description
E	The number of cells to process per thread
$\vec{B}$	The desired GPU block size (x, y, z)
T	The time tile size

Using the tile regions determined by Algorithm 2, we know that for each sub-grid g, the region of computation for a given thread block is given by $(\vec{x}_g, \vec{l}_g)$. Let us define the region with the maximum size as $(\vec{x}_{max}, \vec{l}_{max})$, where $\vec{x}_{max}$ and $\vec{l}_{max}$ are affine expressions in $\vec{x}_0$ and $\vec{l}_0$, our abstract tile size. Here, our definition of maximum size is the largest number of grid points contained in the region defined by $(\vec{x}_g, \vec{l}_g)$. Then, given that $\vec{B}$ is our desired thread block size, we can solve for $\vec{l}_0$ with:

$$\vec{l}_{max} = \vec{B} \qquad (1)$$

The value $\vec{x}_0$ is still a symbolic entity, but we now have a concrete value for $\vec{l}_0$ which we can use to generate GPU kernel code. An important observation at this point is that the region $(\vec{x}_g, \vec{l}_g)$ defines the region of real computation for the stencil operation writing sub-grid g and the halo region (e.g. the region that is computed redundantly) is defined as:

$$Halo(g) = (\vec{x}_{max}, \vec{l}_{max}) - (\vec{x}_g, \vec{l}_g) \qquad (2)$$

Note that the halo region is, in general, not a rectangular region. It is instead a rectangular bound around the non-halo region.

Shared/Local Memory Size: To take advantage of the GPU memory hierarchy, it is necessary to use shared/local memory to cache results whenever possible. To generate high-performance GPU code using overlapped tiling, we need to determine how much shared memory is needed to cache the redundant computations that are performed. This computation is straight-forward, since we only need to account for the results produced by each thread. Therefore, the amount of shared memory we need for the computation (in number of data elements) is simply:

$$SharedSize = \sum_g (\text{Area}(\vec{B})) \qquad (3)$$

This allows each thread to cache the result it produces for each stencil computation. The Area() function simply returns the number of grid points within the region defined by $(\vec{x}_g, \vec{l}_g)$.

This process is formalized in Algorithm 3. Given a block size and the number of grid points to process per device thread, a shared memory region is declared for each sub-grid. This shared memory region is declared for the GPU

program P. The NumberOfPoints function simply returns the number of integer points contained within the block defined by taking the component-wise multiplication of $\vec{B}$ and $\vec{E}$.

Thread Synchronization: Thread barriers are used between stencil operations to ensure that all threads have finished the computation for a particular stencil operation before any thread starts computing a value for the next stencil operation. The thread blocks compute completely independently, but the threads within a thread block must be synchronized as one thread may produce a result that is needed by another thread in the next stencil operation.

Block Synchronization: Our computation model dictates that for each stencil operation, a snapshot of the data is used as input for every evaluation of every grid point, and writes back to the grid are done after all evaluations have finished. In other words, all reads from global memory must see the same data. Unfortunately, this is hard to guarantee on GPU architectures which lack block synchronization and GPU-wide memory fences. To get around this issue, a buffering approach is used. For each sub-grid used as an output for a stencil computation, two grids are actually maintained in GPU memory. For each time tile, one version is used as input and another is used as output. Between time tiles, the host will swap the buffer pointers before the next kernel invocation. This ensures that all reads within a kernel invocation see the same data and no issues can arise from one thread block completely finishing a computation before another block starts.

Thread Code: We can now generate the per-thread code that will implement the stencil computation. This code implements the computation of all sub-stencils for $\left|\vec{E}\right|$ data elements over T time steps. In the first time step, each thread reads its needed data from global memory, performs the computation of the first stencil operation, and stores the result to shared/local memory. This process is repeated for each stencil operation in the stencil computation. For each subsequent time step, each thread reads its needed data from shared/local memory, performs the computation of each sub-stencil, in order, and stores the result to shared/local memory. In the last time step, *if the thread is not part of the halo*, the final result is written back to global memory.

This process is formalized in Algorithm 4. Here, code is generated for each stencil function evaluation for every time step of our time tile. A new GPU program object is created that represents our generated kernel code, and we generate code to evaluate multiple grid points per thread (if needed), and use shared memory to cache results whenever possible. Different implementations of the generate functions can be used to target different languages, including CUDA, OpenCL, LLVM IR, etc.

Example: As an example, let us consider a Jacobi 5-point stencil over 2 time steps. The stencil function can be defined as:

$$f(A_G)[1..N-1, 1..M-1] = 0.2 * (A[-1,0] + A[0,0] + A[1,0] + A[0,-1] + A[0,1])$$

The generated code for an OpenCL target will apply the stencil function twice, once at time t and again at time $t+1$. Global memory will only be read at the beginning of time

Algorithm 4: Thread code generation

Name: GenerateGPUKernel
Input: P : Stencil Program, $\vec{B}$: Block Size, $\vec{E}$: Elements Per Thread, T : Time Tile Size
Output: P_{gpu} : GPU Program

1   S ← ExtractStencilFunctions (P)
2   D ← ExtractSubGrids (P)
3   P_{gpu} ← NewGPUProgram ()
4   P_{gpu} ← GenerateSharedMemory (P_{gpu}, $\vec{B}$, $\vec{E}$, D) (Algorithm 3)
5   InShared ← ∅
6   **foreach** TimeStep t in T **do**
7 | **foreach** Function f in S **do**
8 | | **foreach** Element e in Iterate $(\vec{E})$ **do**
9 | | | **foreach** SubGrid g in GetSources (f) **do**
10 | | | | **if** $g \in$ InShared **then**
11 | | | | | P_{gpu} ← GenerateSharedMemoryReads (P_{gpu}, g, e, f)
12 | | | | **else**
13 | | | | | P_{gpu} ← GenerateGlobalMemoryReads (P_{gpu}, g, e, f)
14 | | | | **end**
15 | | | **end**
16 | | | P_{gpu} ← GenerateFunctionEvaluation (P_{gpu}, f, e)
17 | | **end**
18 | | P_{gpu} ← GenerateThreadSync (P_{gpu})
19 | | P_{gpu} ← GenerateSharedMemoryWrite (P_{gpu}, g, e)
20 | | InShared ← InShared ∪ GetDestination (f)
21 | | P_{gpu} ← GenerateThreadSync (P_{gpu})
22 | **end**
23   **end**
24   **foreach** SubGrid g in D **do**
25 | **foreach** Element e in Iterate $(\vec{E})$ **do**
26 | | **if** ¬ Halo (g, e) **then**
27 | | | P_{gpu} ← GenerateGlobalMemoryWrite (P_{gpu}, g, e)
28 | | **end**
29 | **end**
30   **end**

Algorithm 5: Host code generation

Name: GenerateHostCode
Input: P : Stencil Program, P_{gpu} : GPU Program, $\vec{B}$: Block Size, $\vec{E}$: Elements Per Thread, T : Time Tile Size, $\vec{N}$: Problem Size, T_{total} : Total Number of Time Steps, $(\vec{x}_0, \vec{l}_0)$
Output: P_{host} : Host Program
Output: P_{host} : Host Program

1   P_{host} ← NewHostProgram ()
2   DG ← ExtractSubGrids (P)
3   NumBlocks ← $(N_x/l_{0,x}, N_y/l_{0,y}, ...)$
4   **foreach** SubGrid g in DG **do**
5 | $g_{gpu,0}$ ← AllocateGPUBuffer (g)
6 | $g_{gpu,1}$ ← AllocateGPUBuffer (g)
7 | P_{host} ← CopyHostToDevice (P_{host}, $g_{gpu,0}$, g)
8 | P_{host} ← CopyHostToDevice (P_{host}, $g_{gpu,1}$, g)
9   **end**
10   Body ← { InvokeKernel (P_{gpu}, NumBlocks); Swap($g_{gpu,0}$, $g_{gpu,1}$) ∀ SubGrid g in DG }
11   P_{host} ← GenerateTimeLoop (P_{host}, T_{total} / T, Body)
12   **foreach** SubGrid g in DG **do**
13 | P_{host} ← CopyDeviceToHost (P_{host}, $g_{gpu,\dagger}$, g)
14   **end**

---

step t, and written at the end of time step $t+1$. The results computed in time step t will be cached in shared memory and read in time step $t+1$. A barrier will be placed between the time steps to ensure all shared memory writes complete before any shared memory reads occur in time step $t+1$.

4.4 Generation of Host Code

To be a complete code generation framework, host code is also needed to properly configure and execute the generated GPU kernels. For our purposes, this involves creating a C/C++ function that is responsible for copying input data to the GPU device before kernel invocation, setting up the proper grid and block sizes, invoking the kernel, and copying output data back to the host after kernel invocation. The general procedure is outlined in Algorithm 5, and details are provided in the following subsections.

Copy In/Out: Copy-in/copy-out code is generated by determining the amount of global halo that is needed, allocating buffers of the appropriate size, and copying data to/from the device at the appropriate time. A global halo is used to eliminate conditional behavior around the boundary in GPU kernel code. When time tiling is used, a thread that would ordinarily access the sub-grid boundary may now read several points beyond the edge of the grid. To make sure these memory accesses stay within bounds and that the intermediate results are correct, the boundary grid cells are replicated into a halo region of width equal to the maximum radius of all stencils that read from the sub-grid.

Thread Blocks: The GPU block size is pre-determined as an input to the code generation algorithm, but we also need to determine the number of thread blocks that will be executed. Remember that each thread block computes a region of $(\vec{x}_{max}, \vec{l}_{max})$ for grid g, where only $(\vec{x}_0, \vec{l}_0)$ is useful work. If $\vec{N}$ is our total problem size, then we need $|\vec{N}/\vec{l}_0|$ total blocks, where the division is performed element-wise and the length is a measure of the total number of blocks in the volume.

Time Loop: The host code is also responsible for implementing the outer time loop. Each invocation of the GPU kernel will compute T time steps of the stencil. If S is the total number of time steps, then the host code will invoke the kernel $\frac{S}{T}$ times. After each time tile, the input and output buffers are swapped to make the output from the previous time tile the input to the next time tile.

5. EVALUATION

In this section, we report on an experimental evaluation of the code generation scheme. using GPU devices from both AMD and nVidia – AMD A8-3850 APU (Radeon HD 6550D GPU), nVidia GTX 280, GTX 580, and Tesla C2050 devices. For the nVidia devices, we used the publicly available CUDA SDK 4.1 RC2 to execute OpenCL programs. For the AMD devices, we used the AMD Accelerated Parallel Processing SDK 2.6. Across all devices, we tested on Red Hat Enterprise Linux 6.2 AMD64 with the kernels and device driver versions recommended by the respective device vendors.

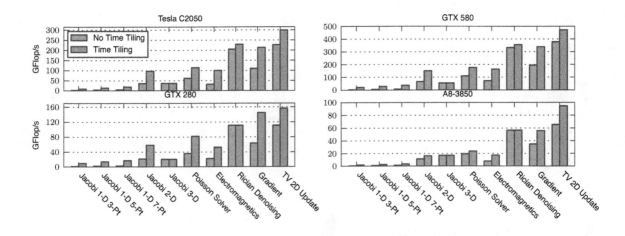

Figure 6: Performance of stencils across architectures

The characteristics of the tested GPU devices are as follows:

	GTX 280	GTX 580	Tesla C2050	AMD A8-3850
Peak SP	933 GF/s	1.58 TF/s	1.03 TF/s	480 GF/s
Peak B/W	141.7 GB/s	192 GB/s	144 GB/s	Variable[2]

The characteristics of the tested stencil programs are as follows:

Program	Elements Per Pt	Number of Arrays	Ops Per Pt	Dim.
Jacobi 1-D 3-Pt	3	1	3	1
Jacobi 1-D 5-Pt	5	1	5	1
Jacobi 1-D 7-Pt	7	1	7	1
Jacobi 2-D	5	1	5	2
Jacobi 3-D	7	1	7	3
Poisson Solver	9	1	9	2
Electromagnetics	2/2/3	3	11	2
Rician Denoising	5	2	44	2
Gradient	5	1	18	2
TV Update 2D	7	1	59	2

The *Jacobi* stencils are synthetic Jacobi-style stencil programs. The *Poisson Solver* stencil is an application of the Poisson PDE in two dimensions. The *Electromagnetics* stencil is an application of the 2-D Finite-Difference Time-Domain method [18]. The *Rician Denoising* and *TV Update 2D* stencils are components of the CDSC CT/MRI imaging pipeline [1]. The *Gradient* stencil is an application of a gradient operator on a two-dimensional grid.

5.1 Performance Analysis

We evaluated the performance improvement of overlapped tiled stencil code as generated by our algorithm by examining the performance over many stencil programs. We performed an exhaustive search of the parameter space (block size, time tile size, and spatial tile sizes) to determine the best performing version. For comparison purposes, we also show the results obtained by only searching in the spatial tile size and not performing time tiling. This allows us to evaluate the effectiveness of time tiling using overlapped tiling for these stencils.

---

[2]The AMD Fusion chips are integrated CPU/GPU devices with the GPU cores using system memory, making the peak bandwidth variable.

Figure 6 shows the results of this experiment. Each graph shows a different GPU devices, and each bar shows performance results for a particular stencil program. Overlapped tiling is particularly effective for 1-D and 2-D stencils, as shown in the Jacobi 1-D, Jacobi 2-D, Poisson, Electromagnetics, TV Update 2D, and Gradient stencils. For 3-D stencils, the computational overhead of overlapped tiling often offsets the savings in global memory access. The same is also true in the 2-D Rician Denoising stencil, where the ratio of computation to memory access is already high.

Peak floating-point performance on a GPU device can only be achieved by issuing a multiply-and-add instruction in each clock cycle. Due to the ratio of floating-point addition to multiplication being quite high in all of the tested stencil programs (often on the order of 5–10), it is expected that the actual performance is significantly lower than device peak. Further, most stencil operations involve multiplying a number by the result of a chain of additions, which does not map well to multiply-and-add instructions (instead, we would need an add-and-multiply instruction). As an example, consider the Gradient stencil program. For each point, there is one reciprocal square-root operation and 17 additions. If we consider only the additions, the achievable peak single-precision floating-point performance of the GTX 580 drops to 790 GFlop/s. Taking this into account, we achieve about 44.3% of the achievable peak on the GTX 580 for the Gradient stencil.

To evaluate our performance results, we compare against the results published in other stencil literature. Datta [5] reports 15.8 GFlop/s and Tang et al. [19] report 19.9 GFlop/s for a 7-point Jacobi 3D stencil on an Intel Nehalem using double-precision. On the GTX 580, we achieve 50 GFlop/s for a 7-point Jacobi 3D stencil in single-precision mode, and 28.7 GFlop/s in double-precision mode. Tang et al. also report a maximum of 5.3 GPoints/s for a 2-D heat equation stencil on an Intel Nehalem, which translates into 31.8 GFlop/s. Our equivalent Jacobi 2-D stencil achieves 49.5 GFlop/s in double-precision mode on the GTX 580. Meng et al. [11] report approximately 2×10^6 cycles per iteration on a GTX 280 for a Poisson stencil that has been manually tiled using overlapped tiling with a time tile size of 3. With a clock speed of 1.3 GHz, this gives approximately 70.2

GFlop/s. In comparison, the Poisson stencil generated by our framework achieves 81.7 GFlop/s on the GTX 280.

In a different work, Datta et al. [6] show 36 double-precision GFlop/s for a 7-point Jacobi 3D stencil on a GTX 280 after aggressive auto- tuning. On the GTX 280, we achieve 20 GFlop/s. We note that the results presented here are shown for automatically generated code that implements overlapped tiling. We do not yet perform some of the manual optimizations performed by Datta et al. in their auto-tuning work. Additionally, 3D stencils are not handled well by overlapped tiling on GPU architectures due to the amount of redundancy computation that is needed for even small time tile sizes. In such cases, the optimizations proposed by Datta el al. are more beneficial than overlapped tiling on GPUs.

5.2 Impact of Tile Size Selection

The proper selection of block size, time tile size, and elements per thread is essential for the performance of the generated code. Figure 7 shows the performance of the Jacobi 2-D stencil for a fixed block size and varying time tile size and elements per thread. The performance on four different architectures is shown: an nVidia GTX 580 (Fermi), Tesla C2050 (Fermi), GTX 280 (GT200), and an AMD A8-3850 APU (Radeon HD 6550D). The block sizes were chosen such that the stencil achieves optimal performance on the architecture for some time tile size and elements per thread.

The trend in each case is that time tiling, through overlapped tiling, improves the performance of the stencil program for increasing time tile sizes up to a point. After this point, the overhead of overlapped tiling offsets the benefits of the time tiling. Therefore, there is an optimal time tile size. The choice for the number of elements per thread to process has an effect on this optimal time tile size, as shown in the graphs. For the GTX 580, this point is at $T = 6$ for 10 and 12 elements per thread, but only $T = 5$ for 6 and 8 elements per thread. For the A8-3850 APU, the optimal time tile size is around 5 for each case.

Insights into this optimal time tile size can be gained by looking at the actual computation being performed on the device for each time tile size. Figure 8 shows normalized GPU performance counter data for a time tile size of 1 to 10 for a fixed elements per thread value of 10 (GTX 280) and 12 (GTX 580). We see that as we increase the time tile size, the total number of global loads generally decreases up to a point and then saturates. For larger time tile sizes, more work is being cached in shared memory resulting in the decrease in global loads. There is a corresponding increase in the number of shared memory loads/stores and total instructions executed as we increase the time tile size. Again, as we increase the time tile size, we are doing more work on data in shared memory, but the percentage of redundant computation also increases, leading to the increase in total instructions executed.

From the GPU time counter, we see that minimum total time spent on the computation is at a time tile size of 6. As we increase this size, we see that the total number of instructions executed continues to increase, but the total number of global loads remains relatively constant. Hence, we begin to increase the overall execution time. It is important to note, however, that the floating-point throughput of the device does continue to increase as we continue to increase the time tile size and hence perform a larger portion of work in shared memory. However, larger time tile sizes also mean that smaller percentages of the total

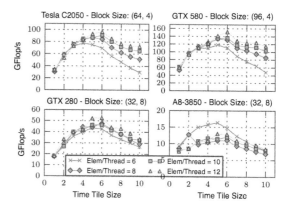

Figure 7: Effects of time tile size selection on performance for the Jacobi 2-D stencil.

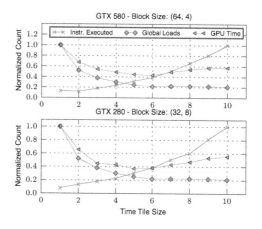

Figure 8: GPU performance counter data for varying time tile sizes

floating-point throughput is actually useful and not just redundant computation. Therefore, after a time tile size of 6, the cost of the redundant computation starts to exceed the savings in global memory transfer. The limiting factor for performance for smaller time tile sizes is thus global memory bandwidth. This changes to floating-point instruction throughput for larger time tile sizes.

Note that even when time tiling through overlapped tiling is not profitable, our code generation algorithm still produces high-performance code. Our framework can still utilize spatial tiling of the stencil computation in order to achieve levels of performance that surpass that of multi-core CPUs.

6. RELATED WORK

A number of recent studies have focused on optimizing stencil computations for multicore CPUs and GPUs [2, 6, 8, 12, 17, 19, 20]. Strzodka et al. [17] use time skewing and cache-size oblivious parallelograms to improve the memory system pressure and parallelism in stencils on CPUs. PA-TUS [2] is a stencil compiler proposed by Christen et al. that uses both a stencil description and a machine mapping description to generate efficient CPU and GPU code for stencil programs. Han et al. [8] propose an extension to OpenMP to allow for pattern-based optimization of stencil programs on CPUs and GPUs. Micikevicius et al. [12] hand-tuned a 3-D finite difference computation stencil and achieved an order of magnitude performance increase over existing CPU implementations on GT200-based Tesla GPUs. Datta et al. [6] developed an optimization and auto-tuning framework for stencil computations, targeting multi-core systems, NVidia GPUs, and Cell SPUs. They proposed autotuning as essential in order to achieve performance levels on GPUs where the benefits outweigh the cost of sending data across the PCIe bus. But neither of these studies considered time-tiled implementations on GPUs.

The work of Tang et al. [19] is perhaps the most closely-related to ours. They propose the Pochoir stencil compiler which uses a DSL embedded in C++ to produce high-performance code for stencil computations using cache-oblivious parallelograms for parallelism. They target x86 using the Intel C++ Compiler and the Intel Cilk Plus library. They show good performance on x86 targets, but do not address issues specific to GPU code generation for stencil computations.

Closely related to our work is that of Meng et al. [11]. They propose a performance model for the evaluation of ghost zones for stencil computations on GPU architectures. They consider the effects of tile size selection on the performance of the final code, and propose an approach based on user provided annotations for GPU code generation, but do not consider fully automated code generation.

Overlapped tiling, the technique used in our automatic code generation framework, was used by Krishnamoorthy et al. [10] for enhancing tile-level concurrency for multicore systems. Nguyen et al. [13] proposed a data blocking scheme that optimizes both the memory bandwidth and computation resources on GPU devices. Peng et al. [7] investigate the selection of tile sizes for GPU kernels, with an emphasis on stencil computations. However, none of these works consider fully automatic, high-performance code generation for stencil computations on GPUs.

7. CONCLUSION

In this paper, we have introduced an automatic code generation scheme for stencil computations on GPU architectures. This scheme uses overlapped tiling to provide efficient time tiling on GPU architectures, which are massively threaded but are susceptible to performance degradation due to branch divergence and a lack of memory coalescing. We have shown that our scheme produces high performance code on a variety of GPU devices for many stencil programs. We further performed an analysis of the resulting code for various time tile sizes to identify the limiting factors, showing that global memory access is the limiting factor for smaller time tile sizes, and computational overhead is the limiting factor for larger time tile sizes.

Acknowledgments

We thank the reviewers for their valuable comments. This work was supported in part by the U.S. National Science Foundation through award 0926688, and by the Center for Domain-Specific Computing (CDSC) funded by NSF "Expeditions in Computing" award 0926127.

8. REFERENCES

[1] CDSC, the Center for Domain-Specific Computing. http://www.cdsc.ucla.edu.

[2] M. Christen, O. Schenk, and H. Burkhart. PATUS: A code generation and autotuning framework for parallel iterative stencil computations on modern microarchitectures. IPDPS '11, pages 676–687, 2011.

[3] J. Cong, M. Huang, and Y. Zou. Accelerating fluid registration algorithm on multi-FPGA platforms. FPL, 2011.

[4] J. Cong and Y. Zou. Lithographic aerial image simulation with FPGA-based hardwareacceleration. FPGA, pages 67–76, 2008.

[5] K. Datta. *Auto-tuning Stencil Codes for Cache-Based Multicore Platforms*. PhD thesis, University of California, Berkeley, 2009.

[6] K. Datta, M. Murphy, V. Volkov, S. Williams, J. Carter, L. Oliker, D. Patterson, J. Shalf, and K. Yelick. Stencil computation optimization and auto-tuning on state-of-the-art multicore architectures. SC '08, pages 4:1–4:12, 2008.

[7] P. Di and J. Xue. Model-driven tile size selection for doacross loops on gpus. In *Euro-Par*, volume 6853, pages 401–412. 2011.

[8] D. Han, S. Xu, L. Chen, and L. Huang. PADS: A pattern-driven stencil compiler-based tool for reuse of optimizations on GPGPUs. In *ICPADS '11*, pages 308–315, dec. 2011.

[9] Khronos OpenCL Working Group. The OpenCL specification - version 1.2. November 2011.

[10] S. Krishnamoorthy, M. Baskaran, U. Bondhugula, J. Ramanujam, A. Rountev, and P. Sadayappan. Effective automatic parallelization of stencil computations. PLDI '07, pages 235–244, 2007.

[11] J. Meng and K. Skadron. A performance study for iterative stencil loops on GPUs with ghost zone optimizations. *IJPP*, 39:115–142, 2011.

[12] P. Micikevicius. 3d finite difference computation on GPUs using CUDA. GPGPU-2, pages 79–84, 2009.

[13] A. Nguyen, N. Satish, J. Chhugani, C. Kim, and P. Dubey. 3.5-d blocking optimization for stencil computations on modern CPUs and GPUs. SC '10, pages 1–13, 2010.

[14] NVIDIA Corporation. CUDA C programming guide - version 4.0. May 2011.

[15] NVIDIA Corporation. OpenCL programming guide for the CUDA architecture. February 2011.

[16] G. Smith. *Numerical Solution of Partial Differential Equations: Finite Difference Methods*. Oxford University Press, 2004.

[17] R. Strzodka, M. Shaheen, D. Pajak, and H.-P. Seidel. Cache oblivious parallelograms in iterative stencil computations. ICS '10, pages 49–59, 2010.

[18] A. Taflove. Computational electrodynamics: The finite-difference time-domain method. 1995.

[19] Y. Tang, R. A. Chowdhury, B. C. Kuszmaul, C.-K. Luk, and C. E. Leiserson. The Pochoir stencil compiler. SPAA '11, pages 117–128, 2011.

[20] J. Treibig, G. Wellein, and G. Hager. Efficient multicore-aware parallelization strategies for iterative stencil computations. *ArXiv e-prints*, Apr. 2010.

An Efficient Work-Distribution Strategy for Gridding Radio-Telescope Data on GPUs

John W. Romein
romein@astron.nl
Netherlands Institute for Radio Astronomy (ASTRON)
Postbus 2, 7990 AA Dwingeloo, The Netherlands

ABSTRACT

This paper presents a novel work-distribution strategy for GPUs, that efficiently convolves radio-telescope data onto a grid, one of the most time-consuming processing steps to create a sky image. Unlike existing work-distribution strategies, this strategy keeps the number of device-memory accesses low, without incurring the overhead from sorting or searching within telescope data. Performance measurements show that the strategy is an order of magnitude faster than existing accelerator-based gridders. We compare CUDA and OpenCL performance for multiple platforms. Also, we report very good multi-GPU scaling properties on a system with eight GPUs, and show that our prototype implementation is highly energy efficient. Finally, we describe how a unique property of GPUs, fast texture interpolation, can be used as a potential way to improve image quality.

Categories and Subject Descriptors

D.1.3 [**Programming Techniques**]: Concurrent Programming; J.2 [**Physical Sciences and Engineering**]: Astronomy

General Terms

Algorithms, Experimentation, Performance

Keywords

Gridding, sky image, convolutions, GPU

1. INTRODUCTION

During the past decades, astronomers, computer scientists, and engineers have been developing new generations of radio telescopes that improve on sensitivity, image resolution, and data quality. The data rates of these telescopes are enormous and increasing with every generation, and so are the processing requirements. New types of radio telescopes like LOFAR [13], that uses tens of thousands of simple receivers rather than some tens of large dishes, even rely more on digital signal-processing techniques than ever before. This trend continues with the development of a telescope more powerful than all other telescopes in the world together — the Square Kilometre Array (SKA) [4].

The imager is a critical component in the data processing pipeline of a telescope. Basically, the sampled data from the telescopes is (after considerable preprocessing) added to a grid, after which the grid is Fourier transformed to create a sky image. It is also one of the most expensive operations, in terms of processing requirements. For LOFAR, roughly half the time of all post-observation processing is spent in creating sky images. For the SKA Phase 1, the required amount of image processing power is estimated to be in the petaflop range [3], and in the exaflop range for the full SKA.

The gridding stage is a good candidate for parallel processing on many-core accelerators like GPUs. However, traditional gridder implementations, designed to run on CPUs, heavily rely on memory caches and high main-memory bandwidth. Accelerators have less bandwidth per FLOP, threatening the efficiency with which this application can be run. Recently, some other work-distribution strategies for accelerators have been published (in this paper, we use the term *algorithm* for sequential algorithm, and the term *work-distribution strategy* or *strategy* for the way in which an algorithm is parallelized). Some of these strategies improve on spatial locality and thus on memory performance, at the cost of additional computations, by sorting and searching data [9, 5, 6, 11]. None of these efforts achieves more than 14% of the peak FPU performance; they are typically closer to 4%. This illustrates that achieving good performance for this algorithm is hard. Moreover, at these efficiencies, one cannot hope to build the SKA.

This paper presents a new, highly efficient work-distribution strategy for GPUs, that grids radio-telescope data typically an order of magnitude faster than other GPU gridders. Our strategy minimizes device-memory accesses, but does not rely on sorting or searching data. We implemented the strategy in CUDA and OpenCL, and compare performance on several high-end platforms. We show that the strategy scales well on an eight-GPU system, and that it is highly energy efficient. We also describe how texture interpolation hardware in GPUs can possibly contribute to a better image quality, and show its effect on performance.

This paper is structured as follows. In Section 2, we explain the basics of imaging radio telescope data. Then, in Section 3, we elaborate on related work. Section 4 explains the new strategy. In Section 5, we briefly discuss our prototype implementation, and in Section 6, we evaluate the per-

Figure 1: Three (out of 36) baselines between nine telescopes.

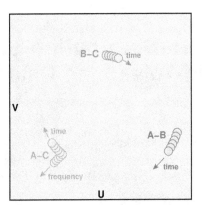

Figure 2: Visibilities from consecutive times and frequencies are placed onto the UV-grid.

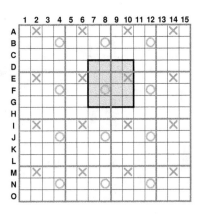

Figure 3: UV-grid divided into subgrids.

formance of the new strategy on multiple platforms, compare with other accelerator-based gridders, show multi-GPU scaling characteristics, and demonstrate that this form of computing is highly "green." Section 7 discusses future work and Section 8 concludes.

2. IMAGING RADIO TELESCOPE DATA

To increase the sensitivity and resolution of images, telescopes often combine data from multiple antennas. Each antenna samples the electromagnetic spectrum at a high rate. The samples are digitized and converted to complex numbers that represent the phase and amplitude of the signal(s) that come from the observed source(s). The data from multiple antennas are correlated by multiplying the samples of each *pair* of antennas. These products are integrated over some time interval, to keep the output data rate manageable. Figure 1 shows a few telescope pairs, which we call *baselines*.

The integrated product of the samples of an antenna pair is called a *visibility*. Each visibility has an associated (u,v,w) coordinate, which depends on the position of the antennas, on the position of the observed source, on the frequency of the observed signal, and on the time. The (u,v,w) coordinates for an antenna pair changes over time due to rotation of the earth, that alters the antenna's positions with respect to the observed source. After correlation, the visibilities undergo some processing (removal of interference, calibration, etc.) to improve data quality.

Since visibilities are sampled in the Fourier domain, they are placed on a *UV*-grid. A final two-dimensional FFT then converts the UV-image to a sky-image. Placement of the visibilities on the UV-grid is the topic of this paper.

A visibility is placed onto the UV-grid using its u and v coordinates. However, the visibility does not contribute to a single grid point, but to neighboring grid points as well. This contribution is computed by *convolving* the visibility with a convolution matrix, i.e., by multiplying the (complex) visibility with each of the (complex) weights in the matrix, and by adding the result to the grid. How the contents of a convolution matrix are obtained, is far beyond the scope of this paper; for interested readers, we refer to [8]. Here, we consider the convolution matrix as a precomputed matrix of complex weights.

Figure 2 shows how visibilities from the three antenna pairs from Figure 1 are placed onto a UV-grid. Consecutive visibilities (in time) from one baseline and one frequency are placed in an elliptic curve over the grid. Visibilities from higher frequencies and larger baselines follow ellipses with larger diameters. Telescope configurations and observation times are typically chosen so that the UV grid is optimally covered with visibility data, to get the best image quality.

For a particular baseline, the convolution matrix slides slowly in time and frequency over the grid. This movement is not too fast, otherwise the visibility would be smeared over a too large area in the UV-grid, reducing image quality. The movement is also not too slow, otherwise the visibilities could have been integrated over a larger time and/or over more frequencies earlier on in the processing pipeline, reducing the data rate and processing time. The speed of the movement depends largely on the baseline length and the grid size, but it generally takes tens of visibilities (in time) to move one grid point away. After (almost) one day of observing, the ellipse is completed, but it is perfectly possible to generate images from shorter observations.

When creating wide-field images, we cannot treat the spheroidal form of the earth and the observed part of the sky as flat planes. In this case, the w coordinate (in the third dimension) is non-zero, and we use a technique called *wide-field imaging*. Using a single convolution matrix is not sufficient then. The *W-projection* algorithm [2] uses different convolution matrices for different values of w. Typically, the W-dimension is partitioned into several tens of W-planes, with different convolution matrices for each W-plane.

Additionally, the W-projection algorithm increases precision in the U and V directions as well. Since the (u,v,w) coordinates of a visibility are floating-point numbers with non-zero fractional parts, the convolved visibility cannot be added exactly at grid points with integer U and V coordinates. To increase accuracy, the W-projection algorithm uses multiple convolution matrices (typically, 8×8 per W-plane) for different fractional parts of u and v. For example, there is a convolution matrix for fractional parts $(.0,.0)$, one for $(.0,.125)$, one for $(.375,.625)$, etc. The convolution matrix that is the closest one to the fractional parts of u and v is then used. The W-projection algorithm increases accuracy by *oversampling* the convolution function when creating the 8×8 convolution matrices. All convolution weights together

```
FOR bl IN baselines DO
  FOR time IN times DO
    FOR chan IN channels DO
      (u,v,w) = getUVWcoordinates(bl, time, chan)
      overSampU = int(8 * frac(u)) // oversampling: use most appropriate convolution matrix
      overSampV = int(8 * frac(v))
      FOR convV IN 0 TO convSize DO
        FOR convU IN 0 TO convSize DO
          weight = convFuncs[int(w)][overSampV][overSampU][convV][convU]
          FOR pol IN {XX,XY,YX,YY} DO
            grid[int(v) + convV][int(u) + convU][pol] += visibilities[time][bl][chan][pol] * weight
```

Algorithm 1: Core of the W-projection algorithm.

form a five-dimensional array, indexed by w, the fractional parts of u and v, and the two coordinates within the convolution matrix.

Typically, telescopes sample the electromagnetic spectrum in two orthogonal polarizations, X and Y. The correlator cross-correlates these polarizations, so that visibilities come in quadruples: XX, XY, YX, and YY. In fact, we create four images from these visibilities, one for each polarization. Each group of four visibilities has the same (u,v,w) coordinates and is convolved using the same convolution matrix, but the results are placed onto different grids.

The W-projection algorithm is summarized in Algorithm 1. It iterates over baselines, times, and frequency channels, looks up the (u,v,w) coordinates of the current four visibilities, determines the most appropriate convolution function, and multiplies the four visibilities with the convolution matrix, and adds the result to the four grids.

3. RELATED WORK

Convolutions are commonly used to implement generic image operations like blurring and edge detection. Here, each pixel of an output image is the sum of weighted neighboring pixels from the input image; the weights are stored in what is called a "mask" or "filter". Generic image-processing convolutions on GPUs (or other many-core hardware) have been studied extensively (for example, [1, 7]), and are commonly used in tutorials on GPU programming (e.g., a sample implementation is distributed in the AMD OpenCL SDK).

However, gridding radio-telescope data is different from generic image convolutions, in the sense that we convolve samples rather than images, that the access patterns are different and less predictable, and that creating a sky image is computationally much more expensive. The output is an image, though (in the Fourier domain). The amount of literature contributions on accelerated radio-telescope convolutions is much smaller. Below, we elaborate on four studies that are related to our work.

The GPU gridder that is being developed for the Murchison Widefield Array (MWA) is one of them. Edgar et. al. [5] describe how visibilities for the MWA are gridded using a gridder written in CUDA. They recognized that actively adding a convolved visibility to a subset of the UV grid is not thread safe on the hardware they use — and if it were, adding convolved visibilities directly to the grid would require a prohibitive amount of (atomic) device-memory accesses. Therefore, their approach is to associate each grid point with a CUDA thread, and search, for all grid points, the visibilities that contribute to a grid point. Since there are, in their case, on average only 60 out of 130,816 visibilities that do contribute something to a grid point, in its basic form, each thread would waste an enormous amount of time

searching for the visibilities of interest. Hence, they sort the visibilities according to their (u,v) coordinates and put them into bins, so that a thread only needs to search nine bins (the "home" bin, plus eight neighboring bins) for the visibilities of interest. However, eight of out of nine searched visibilities will still not contribute to the thread's grid point, but do add to the overhead. The work-distribution strategy presented in this paper, which will be described in the next section, neither needs sorting of visibilities, nor needs searching for visibilities, while keeping the amount of accesses to device memory low.

Varbanescu et. al. [11, 12] implemented the W-projection algorithm on the Cell BE processor. The Cell BE is a many-core processor, but its architecture is rather different from the GPU architectures from AMD and Nvidia. A Cell BE processor essentially consists of a PowerPC CPU, and is assisted by eight vector coprocessors, called SPUs, that run their own code. Asynchronous DMA transfers between CPU and SPU memory are explicitly programmed, and aligned multiples of 128 bytes must be transferred to achieve high bandwidth. Also, the SPUs are (four-word) vector processors that can only load/store efficiently if the words are contiguous and aligned in memory. The nature of Cell BE architecture led to a work-distribution strategy where the parallelism is rather coarse grained: an SPU DMAs a convolution matrix and the relevant part of the grid to its local memory, convolves the visibility and adds it to its partial grid copy, and DMAs the new grid copy back to main memory. They implemented many optimizations: standard optimizations like triple buffering, but also application-dependent optimizations that try to improve locality, so that fewer DMAs between host memory and SPU memory are necessary. Their strategy also (partially) sorts visibilities according to their (u,v,w) coordinates and searches for visibilities that contribute to particular grid points. This is done in a way that the benefits for improved locality outweigh the computational costs for sorting and searching.

The W-projection algorithm was also ported, optimized, and benchmarked on GPUs by van Amesfoort et. al. [9]. Apart from the above-mentioned optimizations to improve locality, they focussed on maximizing the obtained device-memory bandwidth. To avoid race conditions, caused by multiple thread blocks updating device memory concurrently, they gave each thread block a private grid in device memory. Unfortunately, with the memory sizes of present-day GPUs, this implementation limits the grid sizes to very low-resolution images, so this method is not usable for telescopes like LOFAR and the SKA.

Humphreys and Cornwell describe a GPU gridder that is optimized to achieve maximum device memory bandwidth [6]. As with the previously mentioned gridder, this gridder also adds data directly to device memory. Likewise, their gridder is fully memory-bandwidth bound.

4. THE GPU-OPTIMIZED WORK-DISTRIBUTION STRATEGY

We now present a new work-distribution strategy that efficiently convolves and grids the visibility data on the UV-grid, without the necessity to sort or search visibilities, while keeping the number of expensive device-memory accesses very low. The basic idea is to accumulate data in registers rather than in device memory. Unfortunately, this can only be achieved using an unintuitive and complex work-distribution strategy.

The strategy works as follows. We decompose the grid into subgrids that have the same size as the convolution matrix. In the example of Figure 3, we use a 15×15 grid, and a 4×4 convolution matrix; in reality, both are much larger. We also create a number of threads that, for the time being, equals the number of grid points in a subgrid. Conceptually, each thread "monitors" a large number of grid points; one fixed grid point per subgrid. In this example, we create 16 threads, where one of the threads monitors all grid points marked X; another thread monitors all grid points marked O.

The convolution matrix (the gray-shaded area in the figure) slides slowly over the grid. An important insight is that each thread always monitors exactly one grid point covered by the convolution matrix, no more, no less. Consider, for example, the grid point F8, which is monitored by the "O" thread. As the convolution matrix slides, say, to the left, the thread monitors the same grid point until the matrix hits line 4. At this time, the convolution matrix slides off F8, and the O thread switches to grid point F4.

Since the convolution matrix slides slowly, a thread does not often switch to another grid point. An important consequence is that it can accumulate multiple updates (additions) to a grid point locally in registers. Only when the thread switches to another grid point, it (atomically) adds its local sum to the grid point value that resides in device memory. This significantly reduces the number of device memory accesses; a $n \times n$ convolution matrix that slides one grid point away updates only n out of n^2 grid points in device memory.

Algorithm 2 shows simplified pseudo code for the new algorithm. This kernel is invoked for many threads concurrently, where each thread is invoked with different values for $myBL$ (myBaseLine), myU, and myV, the latter two having values between zero and $convSize$ - 1. The kernel initializes four complex accumulators (kept in registers), and iterates over a series of times and frequencies. It computes its convolution function indices and grid coordinates, and checks if the grid coordinates have changed since the previous time. Usually, they are still the same, but sometimes, the thread switches to another grid point an adds its local sums to the grid — atomically, since threads that process different baselines might update the same grid point simultaneously. Then, the thread multiplies the four visibilities with its convolution weight, and adds its them to its local sums. It repeats this, until the visibilities for all times and frequency channels have been processed. Finally, the local sums are once added to the grid.

```
KERNEL convolve(..., myBL, myU, myV) IS
sumXX = sumXY = sumYX = sumYY = (0,0)
prevGridU = prevGridV = 0

FOR time IN times DO
  FOR chan IN channels DO
    (u,v,w) = getUVWcoordinates(myBL, time, chan)
    overSampU = int(8 * frac(u))
    overSampV = int(8 * frac(v))
    myConvU = (int(u) - myU) % convSize // unsigned mod
    myConvV = (int(v) - myV) % convSize
    myGridU = int(u) + myConvU
    myGridV = int(v) + myConvV

    IF prevGridV != myGridV OR prevGridU != myGridV THEN
      atomicAdd(grid[prevGridV][prevGridU][XX], sumXX)
      atomicAdd(grid[prevGridV][prevGridU][XY], sumXY)
      atomicAdd(grid[prevGridV][prevGridU][YX], sumYX)
      atomicAdd(grid[prevGridV][prevGridU][YY], sumYY)
      prevGridU = myGridU, prevGridV = myGridV
      sumXX = sumXY = sumYX = sumYY = (0,0)
    END IF

    weight = convFuncs[int(w)][overSampV][overSampU]...
                              ...[myConvV][myConvU]
    sumXX += visibilities[time][myBL][chan][XX] * weight
    sumXY += visibilities[time][myBL][chan][XY] * weight
    sumYX += visibilities[time][myBL][chan][YX] * weight
    sumYY += visibilities[time][myBL][chan][YY] * weight
  END FOR
END FOR

atomicAdd(grid[prevGridV][prevGridU][XX], sumXX)
atomicAdd(grid[prevGridV][prevGridU][XY], sumXY)
atomicAdd(grid[prevGridV][prevGridU][YX], sumYX)
atomicAdd(grid[prevGridV][prevGridU][YY], sumYY)
```

Algorithm 2: Memory-bandwidth reduced W-projection.

Algorithm 2 illustrates how the amount of memory accesses can be reduced, but it can be improved further. Our GPU implementation prefetches visibilities and UVW coordinates from device memory to fast, shared (local) memory, and precomputes some array indices. Also, we removed the expensive modulo operation from the inner loop, and replaced it by a conditional add.

For small convolution matrices, there is one thread per convolution matrix point. For large convolution functions, we let each thread perform the work for multiple convolution matrix points, because the maximum number of threads per thread block is typically in the 256–1024 range.

The grid is conceptually divided into bins that have the same size as the convolution matrix. The W-projection algorithm allows smaller convolution matrices for short baselines, reducing the amount of computations. Our strategy supports this. The visibilities for different baselines can be gridded independently of each other, and the conceptual division of the grid into subgrids can be different for each baseline.

4.1 Interpolation

Since convolved visibilities must be placed at grid points with integer coordinates, the W-projection algorithm picks the most suitable convolution matrix from a large set, depending on the fractional parts of the u and v coordinates, and on the w coordinate. On GPUs, it seems attractive to take another approach, since the texture units have special-purpose hardware to quickly interpolate values in a one, two, or three-dimensional texture. Instead of using a five-dimensional array to store all convolution weights, we create a three-dimensional texture, organized as a stack of (two-dimensional) convolution functions. Each plane in this stack describes the convolution function for a particular value of w. This way, we create a 3D-texture, that describes the convolution function, for all values of w. By using floating-point indices, the convolution function can be sampled everywhere, using interpolation. This way, we use the fractional parts of the (u,v,w) coordinates to place the convolved visibilities at non-integer grid points. The size of the 3D-texture can be different from the size of the convolved visibility matrix that is added to the grid, since the texture indices can be scaled. A larger texture is more accurate, but causes many misses in the texture cache, especially if the texture is sparsely sampled.

The pseudo codes in Algorithm 1 and Algorithm 2 are slightly modified to allow interpolation. Instead of using *overSampU* and *overSampV* to read *convFuncs*, we call a function *interpolateConvFunc(u,v,w)* that linearly interpolates the eight nearest points in the cube with convolution values, using the floating-point coordinates u, v, and w.

Using a 3D-texture potentially leads to a higher image quality (e.g., with a higher dynamic range), something that we did not yet investigate. Additionally, it is likely that the texture can be significantly smaller than with the classic W-projection algorithm; we think that fewer W-planes are needed, and that the oversampling factors in U and V directions can be much lower than 8×8, because interpolation and oversampling are both techniques that improve accuracy by taking the fractional parts of the (u,v,w) coordinates into account.

5. IMPLEMENTATION DETAILS

We first wrote a reference implementation for the classic W-projection algorithm and the interpolation algorithm in C++. It follows the ideas from a reference implementation by Tim Cornwell, but our implementation is highly optimized: it is multi-threaded and uses AVX vector intrinsics. These eight-word vector instructions are used to efficiently convolve the four complex numbers from the four polarizations in parallel. This way, we compute four complex multiply-adds with four arithmetic AVX instructions. Three additional AVX shuffle instructions are necessary to permute the real and imaginary operands, and one more AVX move instruction stores the result.

The reference implementation still uses the old idea to add the convolved visibility directly to the grid in main memory, and heavily relies on the memory cache to cache the parts of a grid that are actively being added to. To attain high cache-hit ratios, it is of importance to reduce the working set size to something that fits in the L1 cache. This can be achieved by moving the "convV" loop in Algorithm 1 two levels up. Not applying this optimization results in a performance penalty of up to a factor of 18.5. It is important to note that this optimization cannot be applied to GPUs: the large amount of active threads write to many more different locations in main memory than can be cached.

To test our new strategy for the W-projection algorithm on GPUs, we implemented a prototype gridder in both CUDA and OpenCL. The CUDA implementation runs on Nvidia GPUs only. The OpenCL implementation runs on all CPUs and GPUs that support OpenCL. The code that runs on the hosts uses the OpenCL C++ bindings with exception support, which leads to much more concise code than the C bindings.

The convolution matrices are either stored as texture (in OpenCL terminology: image), or a normal array. We only use textures on platforms that support them, and when this actually improves performance. The classic W-projection algorithm does not interpolate the texture.

We distribute the work over the threads (work items) and thread blocks (work groups) as follows. Since the visibilities for different baselines are typically placed on different parts of the grid, we create one thread block per baseline, which are independently processed by the multiprocessors of the GPU. The threads within the thread block then process the visibilities of a number of frequency channels, timesteps, and all polarizations, for a single baseline. This way, we maximize register reuse due to locality on the grid. The kernels transfer visibility and UVW data from mapped host memory through the PCIe bus. Since this data is reused by multiple threads, each kernel first stores the data in shared (local) memory, synchronizes all threads (within the multi-processor), and then performs the convolution computations, This way, the threads have quick access to visibility and UVW data.

6. PERFORMANCE RESULTS

We measured the performance of our new strategy on the following combinations of hardware, programming languages, and platform vendors:

hardware	platform & language	peak GFLOPS	peak GB/s	power Watt
Nvidia GTX 680	Nvidia CUDA	3090	192	195
Nvidia GTX 680	Nvidia OpenCL	3090	192	195
AMD HD 7970	AMD OpenCL	3789	264	230
2× Intel E5-2680	AMD OpenCL	343	102	260
2× Intel E5-2680	Intel OpenCL	343	102	260
2× Intel E5-2680	Intel C++	343	102	260

These are the latest high-end CPUs and GPUs available, manufactured using comparable technologies (28–32 nm).

We used real (u,v,w) coordinates from a six-hour LOFAR observation with 44 antennas (946 baselines; 10 s. integration time, and one subband of 16 frequency channels). A full observation consists of hundreds of subbands, thus the amount of time to grid an entire observation would be several hundreds of times higher than the execution times mentioned below.

6.1 Performance measurements of the W-projection algorithm

We first measured the performance of our strategy for the W-projection algorithm. On the X-axes of Figures 4, 5, and 7, we vary the convolution matrix size. Although the implementation supports baseline-dependent convolution matrix sizes, we use fixed sizes for all performance measurements, to better understand the performance results. All performance measurements were done using a quad polarized, 2048×2048 grid. We use a fixed 8×8 oversampling rate and 32 W-planes, because the execution times hardly depend on these parameters, while these parameters are supported by all platforms.

Figure 4 shows the performance of our prototype implementations. The left graph shows the gridding execution times for one subband of the six-hour observation. The reasons for the large differences in execution times for the different platforms will be explained in the remainder of this section. The slopes in the curves are due to the (quadrati-

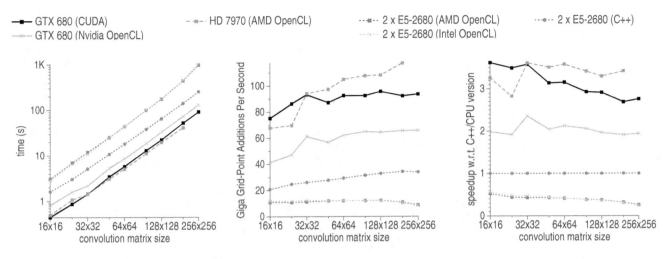

Figure 4: Performance of our new strategy for the W-projection algorithm.

cally) increased amount of work that is involved with larger convolution matrix sizes.

The middle graph of Figure 4 demonstrates the efficiency of our new work-distribution strategy. We express the efficiency in terms of *Giga Grid-Point Additions Per Second* (GGPAPS). Note that GGPAPS counts the number of updates in registers, not the number of updates to grid points in device memory. The number of "useful" GFLOPS per second is eight times the number of GGPAPS, since a complex multiply-add costs four real multiplications and four real additions (and maps well to fused multiply-add instructions).

6.1.1 The Nvidia GeForce GTX 680

We will first look at the performance of the CUDA version on a GTX 680. This is the only version for which the use of textures reduced the execution times; the benefits from the additional texture cache outweigh the overhead from extra instructions to do a texture lookup. Thus for this analysis, we enabled textures. We used the Nvidia visual profiler to study the behavior of our application.

For medium and large-size convolution matrices, it updates up to 93.6 billion grid points per second. This equals to 749 GFLOPS (24.2% of the theoretical peak performance), excluding all kinds of overhead. These overheads are substantial: for 256×256 convolutions, only 37% of all executed instructions are FPU instructions (fused multiply-adds) that operate on the visibility data. Most instructions (41%) are integer instructions used as loop variable or array index, the remainder are shared memory loads (7%), texture lookups (4.7%), comparisons that set predicates (4.7%), branch instructions (4.7%) and a few miscellaneous instructions. Only 0.094% of the executed instructions are atomic memory additions.

The new strategy successfully reduces the amount of device memory accesses: only 0.23% of all grid point updates need access to device memory. The measured device memory bandwidth is 53.0 GB/s (out of a maximum of 192 GB/s), of which 19.8 GB/s is due to grid point updates and 33.2 GB/s due to texture cache misses. The operational intensity (i.e., the amount of arithmetic operations per byte transferred to/from device memory) is 14.1 FLOPS/byte, which is on par with the peak GFLOPS/peak bandwidth (16.1 FLOPS/byte). The costs of transferring visibilities and UVW coordi-

nates from host memory through the PCIe bus to the GPU card are negligible, due to good overlap between computations and communication. A 87.2% texture hit rate is sufficient. The achieved occupancy is high (0.952): each multiprocessor runs two blocks of 1024 threads concurrently, using the full register file and nearly all shared memory.

Unfortunately, the profiler does not point us at the real bottleneck: the application seems neither compute bound, nor memory bound, or limited by PCIe bandwidth. The real culprit is the atomicity of the global memory additions, and the atomic aspect of this update is not covered by the profiler. Even though only 0.23% of all grid point updates result in an atomic memory update, the costs of these occasional updates are high: the atomic nature of these additions is responsible for 26% of the total run time. To remove the atomic nature of these updates, we could use a private grid per active block of compute threads if the device memory were somewhat larger (3–7 GB, depending on the convolution function size, assuming a 2048×2048 grid), but current GTX 680s are limited to 2 GB in size.

For the smallest convolution matrix sizes, the performance is also good, almost as good as for medium and large convolution matrices. This configuration requires quite different tuning parameters, though. With 16×16 matrices, each block has 256 threads, and we run 6 blocks per multiprocessor concurrently, yielding a measured occupancy of 0.694 (the theoretical maximum occupancy is 0.75). Increasing the number of concurrent blocks to 8 per multi-processor (for a theoretical occupancy of 1.00) did not improve performance anymore.

On the same GTX 680, the OpenCL implementation is clearly slower than the CUDA implementation. One reason for this is the fact that an atomic floating-point addition to device memory is natively supported in CUDA, and has to be implemented using an atomic compare-and-swap primitive in OpenCL, which must be repeated until it succeeds. With CUDA, an atomic floating-point addition is translated into a single, predicated, atomic add instruction in the binary executable of the GTX 680, while the binary executable of the OpenCL implementation requires seven instructions, including an even more expensive compare-and-swap. The performance impact is large: up to 55% of the performance difference between CUDA and OpenCL is caused by the absence of an atomic floating-point add in OpenCL. Unfortunately, even the new OpenCL 1.2 specification does not mention this as an extension. The remainder of the performance difference is explained by the fact that for these measurements, we did not use images (textures), as doing so increases the total runtime. The CUDA version uses 1D textures, but the current OpenCL 1.1 specification only supports 2D and 3D images. The benefits of using the texture cache does not outweigh the additional overhead of indexing a multi-dimensional image. OpenCL 1.2 will allow 1D images.

6.1.2   The AMD Radeon HD 7970

We will now discuss the results from the AMD HD 7970 GPU. In most cases, it is the fastest GPU, with a maximum performance of 117.4 GGPAPS. This is not surprising, since the HD 7970 has a 23% higher FPU peak performance, 37% more memory bandwidth, and an 18% higher maximum power consumption than GTX 680. However, for small convolution functions, the HD 7970 performs worse than the GTX 680. One reason for this is that the AMD OpenCL runtime does not (yet) overlap I/O and computations, even though we submit alternating I/O and compute commands to multiple queues (by multiple host threads). We saw this non-overlapping behavior in other applications as well. In contrast, the Nvidia runtime optimally overlaps I/O and computations on the GTX 680. If communication would have fully overlapped on the HD 7970, it would have achieved 79.3 GGPAPS, slightly more than the GTX 680. Fortunately, we found that the run time on the HD 7970 could be improved by mapping host memory into the GPU address space, letting the GPU cores read host memory. The other way around, mapping device memory into the host address space (an AMD extension), did not work for anything but impractically small buffers. The graph in Figure 4 shows the best obtained performance, hence for the version that maps host memory into the GPU address space.

A second cause for the lower performance of the HD 7970 on small convolution functions is the larger impact of the absence of support for native atomic floating-point additions. On this device, it is hard to estimate the performance if it would have supported atomic additions, but we see that the impact is high if we replace the atomic compare-and-swaps by non-atomic additions (yielding wrong results). The performance then increases from 67.8 to 84.9 GGPAPS for 16×16 convolutions. If I/O would also overlap with computations, the performance would further increase, up to 119.8 GGPAPS. Still, the new Graphic Core Next architecture used by the HD 7970 is a major leap forward over AMD's previous architecture: the HD 7970 runs our application between 5.0 and 5.6 times as fast as the older HD 6970. The gap between Nvidia's current Kepler architecture and its previous Fermi architecture is much narrower; the GTX 680 is 1.18–1.66 times as fast as the GTX 580, though it also reduces power consumption by ~25%.

6.1.3   The dual Intel Xeon E5-2680

On a dual Xeon E5-2680 CPU, our C++/AVX implementation runs highly efficiently. The performance varies between 20.8 and 33.9 GGPAPS. This corresponds to 48–79% of the FPU peak performance. The hand-written AVX intrinsics improved performance by a factor 2.3–3.4 times,

compared to compiler-vectorized code from the intel compiler. Thus, for CPUs, the old idea of adding convolved visibilities directly to the grid is not a bad idea, *provided that* the application uses hand-written AVX intrinsics and is optimized to restrict the working set size to something that fits in the L1 cache. Again, the latter cannot be done on a GPU, because there are too many threads in flight for the amount of cache that is available.

On a CPU, the OpenCL version is slower than the C++/AVX implementation. The AMD OpenCL compiler generates 4-word vector operations from the gridding kernel, as it does not see how it could generate 8-word vector operations. Without using 8-word vector operations, there is no way to keep up with the hand-written C++/AVX implementation. It does, however, accumulate grid updates in vector registers. A small penalty is paid for the use of atomic compare-and-swap instructions, but the penalty is at most 6%, lower than on the GPUs.

Intel's OpenCL runtime system performs similar to the OpenCL runtime from AMD, but only after turning off auto-vectorization: the auto-vectorizer creates code that aggressively spills vector registers to the stack, roughly doubling instead of reducing the execution times. Without auto-vectorization, the compiler does not attempt to collapse operations from multiple work items into a single vector instruction, but the compiler still can emit vector instructions, e.g., from float4 operations in a *single* work item. With auto-vectorization turned off, the performance is on par with the AMD OpenCL runtime, which is not surprising, because the generated code is highly similar.

6.1.4   CPUs vs. GPUs

Figure 4 (right) shows speedups with respect to the C++/AVX implementation on a dual Xeon E5-2680 CPU. The GPUs are 2.7–3.6 times faster than a pair of almost the fastest general-purpose CPUs currently available. The different architectures require different approaches. To obtain good performance on CPUs, one can rely on vector instructions and efficient caches. To obtain good performance on GPUs, one *must* reduce memory bandwidth consumption.

6.2   Comparison with other accelerator-based gridders

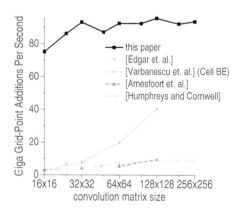

Figure 5: Comparison with other accelerator-based gridders.

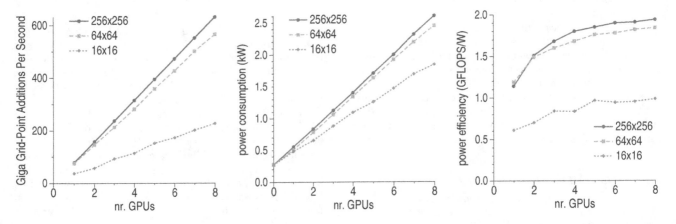

Figure 6: Multi-GPU scaling performance (left), power consumption (middle), and power efficiency (right) for W-projection gridding of different convolution matrix sizes, up to eight GTX 580 GPUs.

Below, we compare our results to those from all other accelerator-based gridders that we are aware of. Figure 5 graphically shows the performance of published results, multiplied with the estimated difference in hardware performance between the GTX 680 that we used and the hardware that the others used.[1]

The MWA gridder achieves 2.3 GGPAPS (130,186 baselines, 12 channels, a 24×24 convolution matrix, four polarizations in 1.57 seconds), using a Tesla C1060 GPU [5]. For the same size convolution matrix, our strategy runs 37.5 times faster (86.3 GGPAPS) on hardware that has 1.9 times the memory bandwidth. It must be noted, however, that the Tesla C1060 does not support atomic floating-point additions to device memory; to run our strategy on a Tesla C1060, a slower atomic compare-and-swap instruction must be used. On the other hand, their imager neither uses multiple W-planes, nor does it do oversampling, and this simplifies convolution matrix index calculations and allows the convolution matrix to fit entirely in the texture cache. Under these conditions (thus using atomic compare-and-swaps, a single convolution matrix, and no oversampling), our gridder still achieves 70.0 GGPAPS on a GTX 680.

The performance of the W-projection algorithm was also studied on a dual Cell BE by Varbanescu et. al. [11, 12]. They achieve 0.50–7.2 GGPAPS on hardware that has a quarter of the memory bandwidth. Unlike our work-distribution scheme, they sort visibilities to improve locality and search for visibilities contributing to a grid point. Obtaining good performance on the Cell BE is hard, because the SPUs cannot add values directly to main memory, but have to cache active parts of the grid in their local stores. Even though this architecture is extremely efficient in computing correlations [10], we think it is less suitable for gridding. Also, cache consistency has to be maintained in software by means of explicit DMAs, which places a notorious burden on the programmer.

Van Amesfoort et. al. [9] achieve 1.5–4.6 GGPAPS on a GTX 280, depending on the convolution matrix size. Corrected for the difference in hardware speeds, our work-distribution strategy is more than an order of magnitude faster. Also, our strategy allows grids that are at least 10×10 larger in size.

The gridder by Humphreys and Cornwell [6] is very much optimized to achieve maximum device memory bandwidth. However, since the number of device memory accesses is not reduced, their implementation peaks at 3.6 GGPAPS on hardware that has 1.67 times less bandwidth (a Tesla C2070 with ECC enabled). Again, the performance difference on comparable hardware is at least a factor of 12.5.

Although the other works were valuable early research contributions on accelerator-based gridding, our new strategy is convincingly faster than any other accelerated gridder. The difference is typically an order of magnitude.

6.3 Multi-GPU scaling and energy efficiency

We also studied the scaling behavior of this strategy for multiple GPUs in a single system, and determined the power efficiency. As we had only one GTX 680 (this architecture has just been released at the time of writing), we used a Tyan B7015 system with eight GTX 580 GPUs. Compared to the GTX 680, the GTX 580 has roughly half the computational power, the same memory bandwidth, and a 26% higher thermal design power. In practice, on the GTX 580 our application runs 40% slower for small convolution functions and 15–20% slower for large and medium sized convolution functions than on a GTX 680.

For these measurements, we used the CUDA implementation of the W-projection algorithm. We divided the work over the GPUs by partitioning the data set in time. This distribution is trivially parallel, thus these chunks are processed independently. Only at the very end of a run, the private GPU grids are transferred to host memory and added together.

On the B7015 system, the connections between CPU cores, host memories, I/O hubs, and GPUs involve multiple PCIe x16 V2.0 busses, PCIe switches, and Quick-Path Interface (QPI) links, which are non-uniform. To minimize contention,

[1] As the application is memory-I/O bound, we estimate the difference in hardware speed by dividing the peak memory bandwidth of the GTX 680 by the peak memory bandwidths of the devices used by others, plus a 50% safety margin in the advantage of the others, to make sure that we do not underestimate their performance.

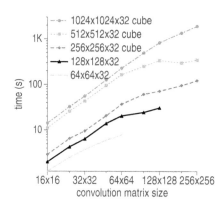 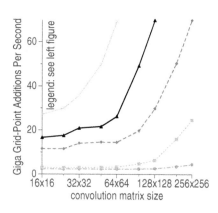 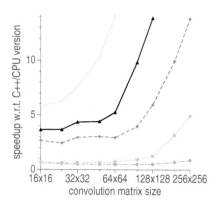

Figure 7: Performance of the interpolation algorithm on a GTX 680 GPU.

our prototype application allocates host memory on the CPU that is physically closest to the GPU.

With eight GPUs, the application runs no less than 131,072 threads concurrently in a single system! Figure 6 (left) shows the achieved amounts of GGPAPS for convolution matrices of different sizes, for up to eight GPUs. Except for very small convolution matrices, the speedups are perfect. Scaling for small matrices is still good, but with multiple GPUs and shared busses, there is some contention on the PCIe busses when the GPUs fetch visibilities and UVW coordinates from host memory.

A metered power-distribution unit accurately monitors the instantaneous voltage, current, and power factor of the whole system (including the power supply units). For runs with fewer than eight GPUs, we correct for the idle current of unused GPUs, but the power consumption of the rest of the system is included. Figure 6 (middle) shows that the system draws no less than 2.6 kW under heavy load. Still, the algorithm is highly energy-efficient on this platform, as the achieved amount of useful GFLOPS/Watt is as high as 1.94 (515 pJ/FLOP). For comparison: the C++ implementation on a dual E5-2680 CPU achieves at most 792 MFLOPS/Watt (1.26 nJ/FLOP), while the GTX 580 is from a 1.5 year older generation. We estimate the power efficiency of eight current-generation GTX 680s to be around 2.8 GFLOPS/Watt (360 pJ/FLOP). The middle graph also shows that convolving visibilities with a very small (16 × 16) matrix, where the amount of GFLOPS is lower than when convolving with large matrices, results in lower energy consumption. The power efficiency (right figure) is high, but not as high as for medium and large matrices.

6.4 Performance measurements for the interpolation algorithm

We finally measured the performance of the advanced gridder, that interpolates the convolution function weights that are stored in a 3D-texture. We only implemented the interpolation algorithm in CUDA, but there is no reason why it could not be implemented in OpenCL. OpenCL supports the use of hardware interpolation, but it would suffer from the absence of atomic floating-point additions to device memory. Figure 7 shows performance metrics on a GTX 680, for different texture sizes. For these measurements, we assume that the convolution function is symmetric in the U

and V directions, reducing the texture size by a factor of four.

The performance depends very much on the ratio between the sizes of the convolution matrix and the texture. When the convolution matrix is much smaller than the texture, the execution times rapidly increase. In that case, the texture is sparsely indexed, and the texture cache is less effective, because words read from the texture are not reused to compute the values of surrounding convolution matrix weights. However, if the convolution matrix size approaches the texture size, the convolution matrix weights are interpolated from texture entries that are at least partially cached in the texture cache. In that case, the performance is much closer to the performance of the standard W-projection algorithm.

The speedup with respect to the CPU version also depends much on the texture size and on the convolution matrix size, but is in some cases much higher than that of the W-projection algorithm. The performance of the CPU version depends less on the texture size than the GPU versions, but is, in fact, always poor, compared to the W-projection algorithm. With interpolation, the application is 5.4–6.5 times slower than our reference W-projection implementation that does not interpolate. This is not surprising, because the CPU has no dedicated interpolation hardware. The grids that are computed by the GPU version differ slightly from those of the CPU version, due to the limited interpolation accuracy of the GPU. The total powers on the grids, however, are equal in both versions.

The size of the texture has impact on the quality of the eventual image (see Section 7). Since we did not yet determine the impact, we do not know how small the texture can be made without losing too much accuracy.

7. FUTURE WORK

A future goal is to develop a GPU imager for the LOFAR radio telescope [13], and later, for the SKA. The ideas in this paper will be useful to achieve good performance. However, low-frequency telescopes like LOFAR need an even more advanced imaging algorithm (AW-projection), that corrects for direction-dependent effects as well. Essentially, this means that the convolution functions become time dependent and have to be recomputed for every five minutes of telescope data. Additionally, the convolution functions will be different for different polarizations.

An open issue is how interpolation of convolution weights in a 3D-texture affects astronomical data quality. As long as the texture contains at least as many entries as the number of oversampled convolution weights of the original W-projection algorithm, interpolation will likely give better results. Unfortunately, as we saw in the previous section, the run times increased by a factor of 6 when a texture is used that is much larger than the convolution matrix size. However, we expect that it is possible to use smaller textures. At least, the interpolation hardware of GPUs allows thinking about interpolation; on CPUs, this is prohibitively slow.

8. CONCLUSIONS

We presented a new work-distribution strategy for GPUs, that efficiently convolves radio-telescope data on a grid, a computationally expensive step in the pipeline that creates sky images from radio-telescope data. This strategy significantly reduces the number of device-memory accesses, by accumulating data as long as possible in registers. Unlike previous work-distribution strategies, this strategy neither relies on sorting input data, nor does it search for input data that contributes to some grid point, thus keeping the overhead low.

Performance measurements on various platforms show that the strategy is an order of magnitude faster than other proposed solutions for GPUs, corrected for differences in hardware speed. This order of magnitude improvement is what is necessary to be able to build the Square Kilometre Array. We compared CUDA and OpenCL implementations, and found that the OpenCL implementation suffers from the absence of an atomic floating-point addition to global memory. We also compared different architectures, and show that AMD's new Graphics Core Next architecture is highly competitive with Nvidia's Kepler architecture. Multi-GPU scaling on a system with eight GPUs is good for small-sized convolution matrices and excellent for large ones. The strategy is "green", we achieve almost 2 GFLOP/W (on previous-generation hardware).

Additionally, we showed how the hardware support for interpolations in three-dimensional textures can potentially improve the quality of the generated sky images. However, we also showed that the computational costs can be high, depending on size of the convolution matrix and the size of the texture that stores the convolution functions. Future research must make clear if interpolation or the traditional W-projection algorithm provides a better balance between computational costs and image quality.

Acknowledgments

We thank Chris Broekema, Ger van Diepen, Rob van Nieuwpoort, and the anonymous reviewers for their comments on a draft of this paper, and Tim Cornwell for a reference implementation of the W-projection algorithm. This work is supported by the SKA-NN grant from the EFRO/Koers Noord programme from Samenwerkingsverband Noord-Nederland, the Astron IBM Dome project, funded by the province Drenthe and the Dutch Ministry of EL&I, and the DAS-4 grant from the Netherlands Organization for Scientific Research (NWO). Intel kindly provided us with a dual Xeon E5 server.

9. REFERENCES

[1] U. Bordoloi. Image Convolution Using OpenCL — A Step-by-Step Tutorial, October 2009.

[2] T. Cornwell, K. Golap, and S. Bhatnagar. W-Projection: A New Algorithm for Wide Field Imaging with Radio Synthesis Arrays. In P. L. Shopbell, M. Britton, and R. Ebert, editors, *Astronomical Data Analysis Software and Systems (ADASS XIV)*, number 347 in ASP Conference Series, pages 86–95, Pasadena, CA, October 2004.

[3] P. E. Dewdney and et. al. SKA Phase 1: Preliminary System Description. *SKA Memo*, 130, November 2010.

[4] P. E. Dewdney, P. J. Hall, R. T. Schilizzi, and T. J. L. W. Lazio. The Square Kilometre Array. *Proceedings of the IEEE*, 97(8):1482–1496, August 2009.

[5] R. G. Edgar, M. A. Clark, K. Dale, D. A. Mitchell, S. M. Ord, R. B. Wayth, H. Pfister, and L. J. Greenhill. Enabling a High Throughput Real Time Data Pipeline for a Large Radio Telescope with GPUs. *Computer Physics Communications*, 181(10):1707–1714, 2010.

[6] B. Humphreys and T. Cornwell. Analysis of Convolutional Resampling Algorithm Performance. *SKA Memo*, 132, January 2011.

[7] V. Podlozhnyuk. *Image Convolution with CUDA*, June 2007.

[8] F. Schwab. Optimal Gridding of Visibility Data in Radio Interferometry. In *Proceedings of an International Symposium held in Sydney, Australia*, page 333. Cambridge University Press, August 1983.

[9] A. van Amesfoort, A. L. Varbanescu, H. J. Sips, and R. V. van Nieuwpoort. Evaluating Multi-Core Platforms for Data-Intensive Kernels. In *Proceedings of the ACM International Conference on Computing Frontiers*, pages 207–216, Ischia, Italy, May 2009. ACM Press.

[10] R. V. van Nieuwpoort and J. W. Romein. Using Many-Core Hardware to Correlate Radio Astronomy Signals. In *ACM International Conference on Supercomputing (ICS'09)*, pages 440–449, New York, NY, June 2009.

[11] A. L. Varbanescu. *On the Effective Parallel Programming of Multi-Core Processors*. PhD thesis, TU Delft, the Netherlands, December 2010.

[12] A. L. Varbanescu, A. S. van Amesfoort, T. Cornwell, A. Mattingly, B. G. Elmegreen, R. V. van Nieuwpoort, G. van Diepen, and H. J. Sips. Radioastronomy Image Synthesis on the Cell/B.E. In *EuroPar'08*, volume 5168 of *LNCS*, pages 749–762, Las Palmas de Gran Canaria, Spain, August 2008. Springer-Verlag.

[13] M. Vos, A. Gunst, and R. Nijboer. The LOFAR Telescope: System Architecture and Signal Processing. *Proceedings of the IEEE*, 97(8):1431–1437, August 2009.

GPU Merge Path - A GPU Merging Algorithm

Oded Green [*]
College of Computing
Georgia Institute of
Technology
Atlanta, GA, USA 30332
ogreen@gatech.edu

Robert McColl
College of Computing
Georgia Institute of
Technology
Atlanta, GA, USA 30332
rmccoll3@gatech.edu

David A. Bader
College of Computing
Georgia Institute of
Technology
Atlanta, GA, USA 30332
bader@cc.gatech.edu

ABSTRACT

Graphics Processing Units (GPUs) have become ideal candidates for the development of fine-grain parallel algorithms as the number of processing elements per GPU increases. In addition to the increase in cores per system, new memory hierarchies and increased bandwidth have been developed that allow for significant performance improvement when computation is performed using certain types of memory access patterns.

Merging two sorted arrays is a useful primitive and is a basic building block for numerous applications such as joining database queries, merging adjacency lists in graphs, and set intersection. An efficient parallel merging algorithm partitions the sorted input arrays into sets of non-overlapping sub-arrays that can be independently merged on multiple cores. For optimal performance, the partitioning should be done in parallel and should divide the input arrays such that each core receives an equal size of data to merge.

In this paper, we present an algorithm that partitions the workload equally amongst the GPU Streaming Multiprocessors (SM). Following this, we show how each SM performs a parallel merge and how to divide the work so that all the GPU's Streaming Processors (SP) are utilized. All stages in this algorithm are parallel. The new algorithm demonstrates good utilization of the GPU memory hierarchy. This approach demonstrates an average of 20X and 50X speedup over a sequential merge on the x86 platform for integer and floating point, respectively. Our implementation is 10X faster than the fast parallel merge supplied in the CUDA Thrust library.

Categories and Subject Descriptors

C.4 [**Computer Systems Organization**]: Special-Purpose and Application-Based Systems

---

[*]Corresponding author

Keywords

Parallel algorithms, Parallel systems, Graphics processors, Measurement of multiple-processor systems

1. INTRODUCTION

The merging of two sorted arrays into a single sorted array is straightforward in sequential computing, but presents challenges when performed in parallel. Since merging is a common primitive in larger applications, improving performance through parallel computing approaches can provide benefit to existing codes used in a variety of disciplines. Given two sorted arrays A,B of length $|A|,|B|$ respectively, the output of the merge is a third array C such that C contains the union of elements of A and B, is sorted, and $|C| = |A| + |B|$. The computational time of this algorithm on a single core is $O(|C|)$ [2]. As of now, it will be assume that $|C| = n$.

The increase in the number of cores in modern computing systems presents an opportunity to improve performance through clever parallel algorithm design; however, there are numerous challenges that need to be addressed for a parallel algorithm to achieve optimal performance. These challenges include evenly partitioning the workload for effective load balancing, reducing the need for synchronization mechanisms, and minimizing the number of redundant operations caused by the parallelization. We present an algorithm that meets all these challenges and more for GPU systems.

The remainder of the paper is organized as follows: In this section we present a brief introduction to GPU systems, merging, and sorting. In particular, we present Merge Path [8, 7]. Section 2 introduces our new GPU merging algorithm, GPU Merge Path, and explains the different granularities of parallelism present in the algorithm. In section 3, we show empirical results of the new algorithm on two different GPU architectures and improved performance over existing algorithms on GPU and x86. Section 4 offers concluding remarks.

1.1 Introduction on GPU

Graphics Processing Units (GPUs) have become a popular platform for parallel computation in recent years following the introduction of programmable graphics architectures like NVIDIA's Compute Unified Device Architecture (CUDA) [6] that allow for easy utilization of the cards for purposes other than graphics rendering. For the sake brevity, we present only a short introduction to the CUDA architecture.

To the authors' knowledge, the parallel merge in the Thrust

library [5] is the only other parallel merge algorithm implemented on a CUDA device.

The original purpose of the GPU is to accelerate graphics applications which are highly parallel and computationally intensive. Thus, having a large number of simple cores can allow the GPU to achieve high throughput. These simple cores are also known as stream processors (SP), and they are arranged into groups of 8/16/32 (depending on the CUDA compute capability) cores known as stream multiprocessors (SM). The exact number of SMs on the card is dependent on the particular model. Each SM has a single control unit responsible for fetching and decoding instructions. All the SPs for a single SM execute the same instruction at a given time but on different data or perform no operation in that cycle. Thus, the true concurrency is limited by the number of physical SPs. The SMs are responsible for scheduling the threads to the SPs. The threads are executed in groups called warps. The current size of a warp is 32 threads. Each SM has a local shared memory / private cache. Older generation GPU systems have 8KB local shared memory, whereas the new generation has 64KB of local shared memory which can be used in two separate modes.

In CUDA, users must group threads into blocks and construct a grid of some number of thread blocks. The user specifies the number of threads in a block and the number of blocks in a grid that will all run the same kernel code. Kernels are functions defined by the user to be run on the device. These kernels may refer to a thread's index within a block and the current block's index within the grid. A block will be executed on a single SM. For full utilization of the SM it is good practice to set the block size to be a multiple of the warp. As each thread block is executed by a single SM, the threads in a block can share data using the local shared memory of the SM. A thread block is considered complete when the execution of all threads in that specific block have completed. Only when all the threads blocks have completed execution is the kernel considered complete.

1.2 Parallel Sorting

The focus of this paper is on parallel merging; however, there has not been significant study solely on parallel merging on the GPU. Therefore we give a brief description of prior work in the area of sorting: sequential, multicore parallel sorting, and GPU parallel sorting [9, 11]. In further sections there is a more thorough background on parallel merging algorithms.

Sorting is a key building block of many algorithms. It has received a large amount of attention in both sequential algorithms (bubble, quick, merge, radix) [2] and their respective parallel versions. Prior to GPU algorithms, several merging and sorting algorithms for PRAM were presented in [3, 8, 10] . Following the GPGPU trend, several algorithms have been suggested that implement sorting using a GPU for increased performance. For additional reading on parallel sorting algorithms and intricacies of the GPU architecture (specifcally NVIDIA's CUDA), we refer the reader to [9, 4, 1] on GPU sorting.

Some of the new algorithms are based on a single sorting method such as the radix sort in [9]. In [9], Satish et al. suggest using a parallel merge sort algorithm that is based on a division of the input array into sub arrays of equal size followed by a sequential merge sort of each sub array. Finally, there is a merge stage where all the arrays are merged

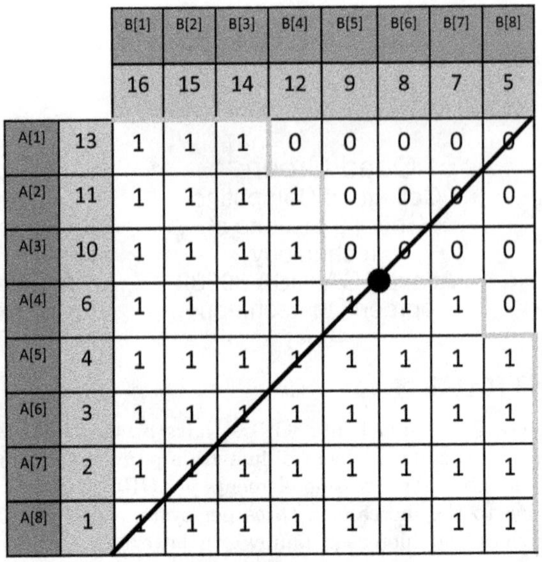

Figure 1: Illustration of the MergePath concept for a non-increasing merge. The first column (in blue) is the sorted array A and the first row (in red) is the sorted array B. The orange path (a.k.a. Merge Path) represents comparison decisions that are made to form the merged output array. The black cross diagonal intersects with the path at the midpoint of the path which corresponds to the median of the output array.

together in a pair-wise merge tree of depth $log(p)$. A good parallelization of the merge stage is crucial for good performance. Other algorithms use hybrid approaches such as the one presented by Sintorn and Assarsson [11], which uses bucket sort followed by a merge sort. One consideration for this is that each of the sorts for a particular stage in the algorithm is highly parallel, which allows for high system utilization. Additionally, using the bucket sort allows for good load balancing in the merge sort stage; however, the bucket sort does not guarantee an equal work load for each of the available processors and – in their specific implementation – requires atomic instructions.

1.3 Serial Merging and Merge Path

While serial merging follows a well-known algorithm, it is necessary to present it due to a reduction that is presented further in this section. Given arrays A, B, C as defined earlier, a simplistic view of a decreasing-order merge is to start with the indices of the first elements of the input arrays, compare the elements, place the larger into the output array, increase the corresponding index to the next element in the array, and repeat this comparison and selection process until one of the two indices is at the end of its input array. Finally, copy the remaining elements from the other input array into the end of the output array [2].

In [8], the authors suggests treating the sequential merge as though it is a path that moves from the top-left corner of an $|A| \times |B|$ grid to the bottom-right corner of the grid. The path can move only to the right and downwards. The reasoning behind this is that the two input arrays are sorted. This ensures that if $A[i] > B[j]$, then $A[i] > B[j']$ for all $j' > j$.

In this way, performing a merge can be thought of as the process of discovering this path through a series of comparisons. When $A[i] \geq B[j]$, the path moves down by one position, and we copy $A[i]$ into the appropriate place in C. Otherwise when $A[i] < B[j]$, the path moves to the right, and we copy $B[j]$ into the appropriate place in C. We can determine the path directly by doing comparisons. Similarly, if we determine a point on the path through a means other than doing all comparisons that lead to that point, we have determined something about the outcomes of those comparisons earlier in the path. From a pseudo-code point of view, when the path moves to the right, it can be considered taking the branch of the condition when $A[i] \leq B[j]$, and when the path moves down, it can be thought of as not taking that branch. Consequently, given this path the order in which the merge is to be completed is totally known. Thus, all the elements can be placed in the output array in parallel based on the position of the corresponding segment in the path (where the position in the output array is the sum of row and column indices of a segment).

In this section we address only the sequential version of Merge Path. In the following sections we further discuss the parallelization of Merge Path on an x86 architecture and its GPU counterpart.

We can observe that sections of the path correspond to sections of elements from at least one or both of the input arrays and a section of elements in the output array. Here each section is distinct and contiguous. Additionally, the relative order of these workspaces in the input and output arrays can be determined by the relative order of their corresponding path sections within the overall path. In Fig. 1, $A[1] = 13$ is greater than $B[4] = 12$. Thus, it is greater than all $B[j]$ for $j \geq 4$. We mark these elements with a '0' in the matrix. This translates to marking all the elements in the first row and to the right of $B[4]$(and including) with a '0'. In general if $A[i] > B[j]$, then $A[i'] > B[j]$ for all $i' \leq i$. Fig. 1, $A[3] = 10$ is greater than $B[5] = 9$, as are $A[1]$ and $A[2]$. All elements to the left of $B[4] =$ are marked with a '1'. The same inequalities can be written for B with the minor difference that the '0' is replaced with '1'.

Observation 1: The path that follows along the boundary between the '0's and '1's is the same path mentioned above which represents the selections from the input arrays that form the merge as is depicted in Fig. 1 with the orange, heavy stair-step line. It should be noted here that the matrix of '0's and '1's is simply a convenient visual representation and is not actually created as a part of the algorithm (i.e. the matrix is not maintained in memory and the comparisons to compute this matrix are not performed).

Observation 2: Paths can only move down and to the right from a point on one diagonal to a point on the next. Therefore, if the cross diagonals are equally spaced diagonals, the lengths of paths connecting each pair of cross diagonals are equal.

1.4 GPU Challanges

To achieve maximal speedup on the GPU platform, it is necessary to implement a platform-specific (and in some cases, card-specific) algorithm. These implementations are architecture-dependent and in many cases require a deep

understanding of the memory system and the execution system. Ignoring the architecture limits the achievable performance. For example, a well known performance hinderer is bad memory access (read/write) patterns to the global memory. Further, GPU-based applications greatly benefit from implementation of algorithms that are cache aware.

For good performance, all the SPs on a single SM should read/write sequentially. If the data is not sequential (meaning that it strides across memory lines in the global DRAM), this could lead to multiple global memory requests which cause all SPs to wait for all memory requests to complete. One way to achieve efficient global memory use when non-sequential access is required is to do a sequential data read into the local shared memory incurring one memory request to the global memory and followed by 'random' (non-sequential) memory accesses to the local shared memory.

An additional challenge is to find a way to divide the workload evenly among the SMs and further partition the workload evenly among the SPs. Improper load-balancing can result in only one of the SPs out of the eight or more doing useful work while others are idle due to bad global memory access patterns or divergent execution paths (if-statements) that are partially taken by the different SPs. For the cases mentioned, where the code is parallel, the actual execution is sequential.

It is very difficult to find a merging algorithm that can achieve a high level of parallelism and maximize utilization on the GPU due to the multi-level parallelism requirements of the architecture. In a sense, parallelizing merging algorithms is even more difficult due to the small amount of work done per each element in the input and output. The algorithm that is presented in this paper uses the many cores of the GPU while reducing the number of requests to the global memory by using the local shared memory in an efficient manner. We further show that the algorithm is portable for different CUDA compute capabilities by showing the results on both TESLA and FERMI architectures. These results are compared with the parallel merge from the Thrust library on the same architectures and an OpenMP (OMP) implementation on an x86 system.

2. GPU MERGEPATH

In this section we present our new algorithm for the merging of two sorted arrays into a single sorted array on a GPU. In the previous section we explained Merge Path [8] and its key properties. In this section, we give an introduction to parallel Merge Path for parallel systems. We also explain why the original Merge Path algorithm cannot be directly implemented on a GPU and our contribution development of the GPU Merge Path algorithm.

2.1 Parallel Merge

In [8] the authors suggest a new approach for the parallel merging of two sorted arrays on parallel shared-memory systems. Assuming that the system has p cores, each core is responsible for merging an equal n/p part of the final output array. As each core receives an equal amount of work, this ensures that all the p cores finish at the same time. Creating the balanced workload is one of the aspects that makes Merge Path a suitable candidate for the GPU. While the results in [8] intersect with those in [3], the approach that is presented is different and easier to understand. We use this approach to develop a Merge Path algorithm for

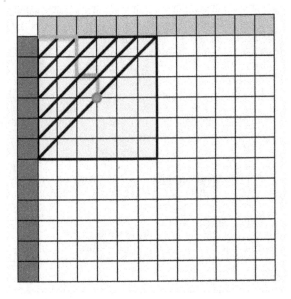

(a) Initial position of the window which.

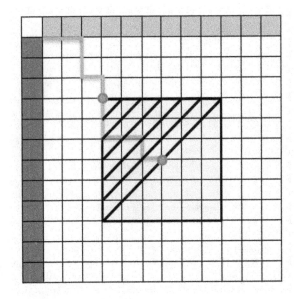

(b) New position of window(after completion of previous block).

Figure 2: Diagonal searches for a single window of one SM. (a) The window is in its initial position. Each SP does a search for the path. (b) The window moves to the farthest position of the path and the new diagonals are searched.

GPU. Merge Path, like other parallel merging algorithms, is divided into 2 stages:

1. Partitioning stage - Each core is responsible for dividing the input arrays into partitions. Each core finds a single non-overlapping partition in each of the input arrays. While the sub-arrays of each partition are not equal length, the sum of the lengths of the two sub-arrays of a specific partition is equal (up to a constant of 1) among all the cores. In Algorithm 1 and in the next section, we present the pseudo code for the partitioning and give a brief explanation. For more information we suggest reading [3, 7, 8] .

2. Merging stage - Each core merges the two sub arrays that it has been given using the same algorithm as a simple sequential merge. The cores operate on non-overlapping segments of the output array, thus the merging can be done concurrently and lock-free. Using the simple sequential mere algorithm for this stage is not well-suited to the GPU.

Both of these stages are parallel.

As previously stated, Merge Path suggests treating the sequential merge as if it was a path that moves from the top-left corner of a rectangle to the bottom-right corner of the rectangle ($|B|, |A|$). The path can move only to the right and down. We denote $n = |A| + |B|$. When the entire path is known, so is the order in which the merge takes place. Thus, when an entire path is given, it is possible to complete the merge concurrently; however, at the beginning of the merge the path is unknown and computation of the entire path through a diagonal binary search for all the cross diagonals

is considerably expensive $O(n \cdot log(n))$ compared with the complexity of sequential merge which is $O(n)$. Therefore, we compute only p points on this path. These points are the partitioning points.

To find the partitioning points, use cross diagonals that start at the top and right borders of the output matrix. The cross diagonals are bound to meet the path at some point as the path moves from the top-left to the bottom-right and the cross diagonals move from the top-right to the bottom-left. It is possible to find the points of intersection using binary searches on the cross diagonals by comparing elements from A and B (Observation 1), making the complexity of finding the intersection $O(log(n))$.

By finding exactly p points on the path such that these points are equally distanced, we ensure that the merge stage is perfectly load balanced. By using equidistant cross diagonals, the work load is divided equally among the cores, see [8]. The merging of the sub-arrays in each partition is the same as the standard sequential merge that was discussed earlier in this paper. The time complexity of this algorithm is $O(n/p + log(n))$. This is also the work load of each of the processors in the system. The work complexity of this algorithm is $O(n + p \cdot log(n))$.

2.2 GPU Partitioning

The above parallel selection algorithm can be easily implemented on a parallel machine as each core is responsible for a single diagonal. This approach can be implemented on the GPU; however, it does not fully utilize the GPU as SPs on each SM will frequently be idle. We present 3 approaches to implementing the cross diagonal binary search

Algorithm 1 Pseudo code for parallel Merge Path algorithm with an emphasis on the partitioning stage.

$A_{diag}[threads] \Leftarrow A_{length}$
$B_{diag}[threads] \Leftarrow B_{length}$
for each i **in** $threads$ **in parallel do**
    $index \Leftarrow i * (A_{length} + B_{length}) / threads$
    $a_{top} \Leftarrow index > A_{length} ? A_{length} : index$
    $b_{top} \Leftarrow index > A_{length} ? index - A_{length} : 0$
    $a_{bottom} \Leftarrow b_{top}$
    // binary search for diagonal intersections
    while true **do**
        $offset \Leftarrow (a_{top} - a_{bottom})/2$
        $a_i \Leftarrow a_{top} - offset$
        $b_i \Leftarrow b_{top} + offset$
        if $A[a_i] > B[b_i - 1]$ **then**
            if $A[a_i - 1] \leq B[b_i]$ **then**
                $A_{diag}[i] \Leftarrow a_i$
                $B_{diag}[i] \Leftarrow b_i$
                break
            else
                $a_{top} \Leftarrow a_i - 1$
                $b_{top} \Leftarrow b_i + 1$
            end if
        else
            $a_{bottom} \Leftarrow a_i + 1$
        end if
    end while
end for
for each i **in** $threads$ **in parallel do**
    $merge(A, A_{diag}[i], B, B_{diag}[i], C, i * length/threads)$
end for

followed by a detailed description. We denote w as the size of the warp. The 3 approaches are:

1. w-wide binary search.

2. Regular binary search.

3. w-partition search.

Detailed description of the approaches is as follows:

1. w-wide binary search - In this approach we fetch w consecutive elements from each of the arrays A and B. By using CUDA block of size w, each SP / thread is responsible for fetching a single element from each of the global arrays, which are in the global memory, into the local shared memory. This efficiently uses the memory system on the GPU as the addresses are consecutive, thus incurring a minimal number of global memory requests. As the intersection is a single point, only one SP finds the intersection and stores the point of intersection in global memory, which removes the need for synchronization. It is rather obvious that the work complexity of this search is greater than the one presented in Merge Path[8] which does a regular sequential search for each of the diagonals; however, doing w searches or doing 1 search takes the same amount of time in practice as the additional execution units would otherwise be idle if we were executing only a single search. In addition to this, the GPU architecture has a wide memory bus that can

bring more than a single data element per cycle making it cost-effective to use the fetched data. In essence for each of the stages in the binary search, a total of w operations are completed. This approach reduces the number of searches required by a factor of w. The complexity of this approach for each diagonal is: $Time = O(log(n) - log(w))$ for each core and a total of $Work = O(w \cdot log(n) - log(w))$.

2. Regular binary search - This is simply a single-threaded binary search on each diagonal. The complexity of this: $Time = O(log(n))$ and $Work = O(log(n))$. Note that the SM utilization is low for this case, meaning that all cores but one will idle and the potential extra computing power is wasted.

3. w-partition search - In this approach, the cross diagonal is divided into 32 equal-size and independent partitions. Each thread in the warp is responsible for a single comparison. Each thread checks to see if the point of intersection is in its partition. Similar to w-wide binary search, there can only be one partition that the intersection point goes through. Therefore, no synchronization is needed. An additional advantage of this approach is that in each iteration the search space is reduced by a factor of w rather than 2 as in binary search. This reduces the $O(log(n))$ comparisons needed to $O(log_w(n))$ comparisons. The complexity of this approach for each diagonal is: $Time = O(log_w(n) - log(w))$ and $Work = O(w \cdot log_w(n) - log(w))$. The biggest shortcoming of this approach is that for each iteration of that partition-search, a total of w global memory requests are needed(one for each of the partitions limits). As a result, the implementation suffers a performance penalty from waiting on global memory requests to complete.

In conclusion, we tested all of these approaches, and the first two approaches offer a significant performance improvement over the last due to a reduced number of requests to the global memory for each iteration of the search. This is especially important as the computation time for each iteration of the searches is considerably smaller than the global memory latency. The time difference between the first two approaches is negligible with a slight advantage to one or the other depending on the input data. For the results that are presented in this paper we use the w-wide binary search.

2.3 GPU Merge

The merge phase of the original Merge Path algorithm is not well-suited for the GPU as the merging stage is purely sequential for each core. Therefore, it is necessary to extend the algorithm to parallelize the merge stage in a way that still uses all the SPs on each SM once the partitioning stage is completed.

For full utilization of the SMs in the system, the merge must be broken up into finer granularity to enable additional parallelism while still avoiding synchronization when possible. We present our approach on dividing the work among the multiple SPs for a specific workload.

For the sake of simplicity, assume that the sizes of the partitions that are created by the partitioning stage are significantly greater than the warp size, w. Also we denote the CUDA thread block size using the letter Z and assume that $Z \geq w$. For practical purposes $Z = 32$ or 64; however, anything that is presented in this subsection can also be used with larger Z. Take a window consisting of the Z largest elements of each of the partitions and place them in local shared memory (in a sequential manner for performance benefit). Z is smaller than the local shared memory, and therefore the data will fit. Using a Z thread block, it is possible to find the exact Merge Path of the Z elements using the cross diagonal binary search.

Given the full path for the Z elements it is possible to know how to merge all the Z elements concurrently as each of the elements are written to a specific index. The complexity for finding the entire Z-length path requires $O(log(Z))$ time in general iterations. This is followed by placing the elements in their respective place in the output array. Upon completion of the Z-element merge, it is possible to move on to unmerged elements by starting a new merge window whose top-left corner starts at the bottom-right-most position of the merge path in the previous window. This can be seen in Fig. 2 where the window starts off at the initial point of merge for a given SM. All the threads do a diagonal search looking for the path. Moving the window is a simple operation as it requires only moving the pointers of the sub-arrays according to the (x, y) lengths of the path. This operation is repeated until the SM finishes merging the two sub-arrays that it was given. The only performance requirement of the algorithm is that the sub-arrays fit into the local shared memory of the SM. If the sub-arrays fit in the local shared memory, the SPs can perform random memory access without incurring significant performance penalty. To further offset the overhead of the path searching, we let each of the SPs merge several elements.

2.4 Complexity analysis of the GPU merge

Given p blocks of Z threads and n elements to merge where n is the total size of the output array, the size of the partition that each of the blocks of threads receives is n/p. Following the explanation in the previous sub-section on the movement of the sliding window, the window moves a total of $(n/p)/Z$ times for that partition. For each window, each thread in the block performs a binary diagonal search that is dependent on the block size Z. When the search is complete, the threads copy their resulting elements into independent locations in the output array directly. Thus, the time complexity of merging a single window is $O(log(Z))$. The total amount of work that is completed for a single block is $O(Z \cdot log(Z))$. The total time complexity for the merging done by a single thread block is $O(n/(p \cdot Z) \cdot log(Z))$ and the work complexity is $O(n/p \cdot log(Z))$. For the entire merge the time complexity stays the same, $O(n/(p \cdot Z) \cdot log(Z))$, as all the cores are expected to complete at the same time. The work complexity of the entire merge is $O(n \cdot log(Z))$.

The complexity bound given for the GPU algorithm is different than the one given in [8, 7] for the cache efficient Merge Path. The time complexity given by Odeh et el. is $O(n/p + n/\hat{Z} \cdot \hat{Z})$, where $\hat{Z}$ refers to the size of the shared memory and not the block size. It is worth noting that the GPU algorithm is also limited by the size of the shared memory that each of the SMs has, meaning that Z is bounded by the size of the shared memory.

While the GPU algorithm has a higher complexity bound, we will show in the results section that the GPU algorithm

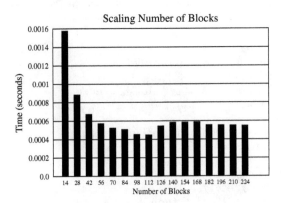

Figure 3: Merging one million single-precision floating point numbers in Merge Path on Fermi while varying the number of thread blocks used from 14 to 224 in multiples of 14.

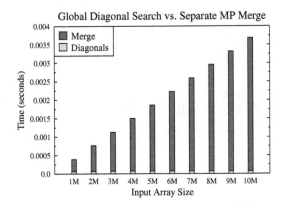

Figure 4: The timing of the global diagonal search to divide work among the SMs compared with the timing of the independent parallel merges performed by the SMs.

offers significant speedups over the parallel multicore algorithm.

2.5 GPU Optimizations and Issues

1. Memory transfer between global and local shared memory is done in sequential reads and writes. A key requirement for the older versions of CUDA, versions 1.3 and down, is that when the global memory is accessed by the SPs, the elements requested be co-located and not permuted. If the accesses are not sequential, the number of global memory requests increases and the entire warp (or partial-warp) is frozen until the completion of all the memory requests. Acknowledging this requirement and making the required changes to the algorithm has allowed for a reduction in the number of requests to the global memory. In the local shared memory it is possible to access the data in a non-sequential fashion without as significant of a performance degradation.

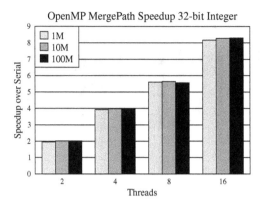

(a) 32-bit integer merging in OpenMP

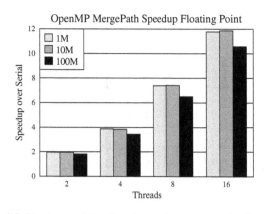

(b) Single-precision floating point merging in OpenMP

Figure 5: The speedup of the OpenMP implementation of Merge Path on two hyper-threaded quad-core Intel Nehalem Xeon E5530s over a serial merge on the same system.

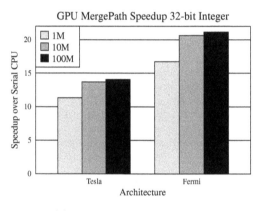

(a) 32-bit integer merging on GPU

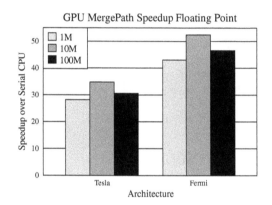

(b) Single-precision floating point merging on GPU

Figure 6: The speedup of the GPU implementations of Merge Path on the NVIDIA Tesla and Fermi architectures over the x86 serial merge.

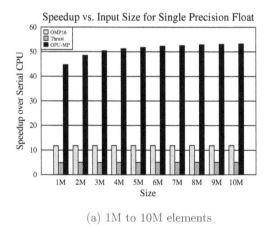

(a) 1M to 10M elements

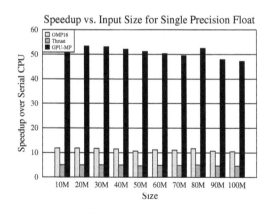

(b) 10M to 100M elements

Figure 7: Speedup comparison of merging single-precision floating point numbers using Parallel Merge Path on 16 threads, Merge Path on Fermi (112 blocks of 128 threads), and thrust::merge on Fermi. Size refers to the length of a single input array in elements.

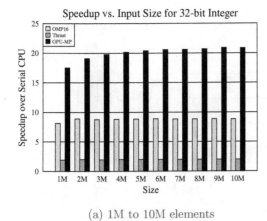

(a) 1M to 10M elements

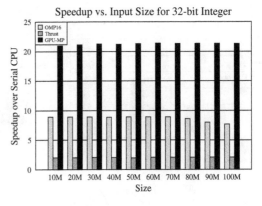

(b) 10M to 100M elements

Figure 8: Speedup comparison of merging 32-bit integers using Parallel Merge Path on 16 threads, GPU Merge Path on Fermi (112 blocks of 128 threads), and thrust::merge on Fermi. Size refers to the length of a single input array in elements.

2. The sizes of threads and thread blocks, and thus the total number of threads, are selected to fit the hardware. This approach suggests that more diagonals are computed than the number of SMs in the system. This increases performance for both of the stages in the algorithm. This is due to the internal scheduling of the GPU which requires a large number of threads and blocks to achieve the maximal performance through latency hiding.

3. EMPIRICAL RESULTS

In this section we present comparisons of the running times of the GPU Merge Path algorithm on the NVIDIA Tesla and Fermi GPU architectures with those of the Thrust parallel merge [5] on the same architectures and Merge Path on a x86 Intel Nehalem core system. The specifications of the GPUs used can be seen in Table 1, and the Intel multi-core configuration can be seen in Table 2. For the x86 system we show results for both a sequential merge and for OpenMP implementation of Merge Path. Other than the Thrust library implementation, the authors could not find any other parallel merge implementations for the CUDA architecture, and therefore, there are no comparisons to other CUDA algorithms to be made. Thrust is a parallel primitives library that is included in the default installation of the CUDA SDK Toolkit as of version 4.0.

The GPUs used were a Tesla C1060 supporting CUDA hardware version 1.3 and a Tesla C2070 (Fermi architecture) supporting CUDA hardware version 2.0. The primary differences between the older Tesla architecture and the newer Fermi architecture are (1) the increased size of the local shared memory per SM from 16KB to 64KB, (2) the option of using all or some portion of the L1 local shared memory as a hardware-controlled cache, (3) increased total CUDA core count, (4) increased memory bandwidth, and (5) increased SM size from 8 cores to 32 cores. In our experiments, we use the full local shared memory configuration. Managing the workspace of a thread block in software gave better results than allowing the cache replacement policy to control which sections of each array were in the local shared memory.

An efficient sequential merge on x86 is used to provide a basis for comparison. Tests were run for input array sizes of one million, ten million, and one hundred million elements for a merged array size of two million, twenty million, and two hundred million merged elements respectively. For each size of array, merging was tested on both single-precision floating point numbers and 32-bit integers. Our results demonstrate that the GPU architecture can achieve a 2x to 5x speedup over using 16 threads on two hyper-threaded quad-core processors. This is an effect of both the greater parallelism and higher memory bandwidth of the GPU architecture.

Initially, we ran tests to obtain an optimal number of thread blocks to use on the GPU for best performance with separate tests for Tesla and Fermi. Results for this block scaling test on Fermi at one million single-precision floating point numbers using blocks of 128 threads can be seen in Fig. 3. Clearly, the figure shows the best performance is achieved at 112 blocks of 128 threads for this particular case. Similarly, 112 blocks of 128 threads also produces the best results in the case of merging one million 32-bit integer elements on Fermi. For the sake of brevity, we do not present the graph.

In Fig. 4, we show a comparison of the runtime of the two kernels: partitioning and merging. It can be seen that the partitioning stage has a negligible runtime compared with the actual parallel merge operations and increases in runtime only very slightly with increased problem size, as expected. This chart also demonstrates that our implementation scales linearly in runtime with problem size while utilizing the same number of cores.

Larger local shared memories and increased core counts allow the size of a single window on the Fermi architecture to be larger with each block of 128 threads merging 4 elements per window for a total of 512 merged-elements per window. The thread block reads 512 elements cooperatively from each array into local shared memory, performs the cross diagonal search on this smaller problem in local shared memory, then cooperatively writes back 512 elements to the global memory. In the Tesla implementation, only 32 threads per block

Table 1: GPU test-bench.

Card Type	CUDA HW	CUDA Cores	Frequency	Shared Memory	Global Memory	Memory Bandwidth
Tesla C1060	1.3	240 cores / 30 SMs	1.3 GHz	16KB	2GB	102 GB/s
Fermi M2070	2.0	448 cores / 14 SMs	1.15 GHz	64KB	6GB	150.3 GB/s

Table 2: CPU test-bench.

Processor	Cores	Clock Frequency	L2 Cache	L3 Cache	DRAM	Memory Bandwidth
2 x Intel Xeon E5530	4	2.4GHz	4 x 256 KB	8MB	12GB	25.6 GB/s

are used to merge 4 elements per window for a total of 128 merged-elements due to local shared memory size limitations and memory latencies. Speedup for the GPU implementation on both architectures is presented in Fig. 6 for sorted arrays of 1 million,10 million, and 100 millions elements.

As the GPU implementations are benchmarked in comparison to the x86 sequential implementation and to the x86 parallel implementation, we first present these results. This is followed by the results of the GPU implementation. The timings for the sequential and OpenMP implementations are performed on a machine presented in Table 1. For the OpenMP timings we run the Merge Path algorithm using 2, 4, 8, and 16 threads on an 8-core system that supports hyper-threading (dual socket with quad core processors). Speedups are depicted in Fig. 5. As hyper-threading requires two threads per core to share execution units and additional hardware, the performance per thread is reduced versus two threads on independent cores. The hyper-threading option is used only for the 16 thread configuration. For the 4 thread configuration we use a single quad core socket, and for the 8 thread configuration we use both quad core sockets.

For each configuration, we perform three merges of two arrays of sizes 1 million, 10 million, and 100 million elements as with the GPU. Speedups are presented in Fig. 5. Within a single socket, we see a linear speedup to four cores. Going out of socket, the speedup for eight cores was 5.5X for integer merging and between 6X and 8X for floating point. We show a 12x speedup for the hyper-threading configuration for ten million floating point elements.

The main focus of our work is to introduce a new algorithm that extends the Merge Path concept to GPUs. We now present the speedup results of GPU Merge Path over the sequential merge in Fig. 6. We use the same size arrays for both the GPU and OpenMP implementations. For our results we use equal size arrays for merging; however, our method can merge arrays of different sizes.

3.1 Floating Point Merging

For the floating point tests, random floating point numbers are generated to fill the input arrays then sorted on the host CPU. The input arrays are then copied into the GPU global memory. These steps are not timed as they are not relevant to the merge. The partitioning kernel is called first. When this kernel completes, a second kernel is called to perform full merges between the global diagonal intersections using parallel merge path windows per thread block on each SM. These kernels are timed.

For arrays of sizes 1 million, 10 million, 100 million we see significant speedups of 28X & 34X & 30X on the Tesla card and 43X & 53X & 46X on the Fermi card over the sequential x86 merge. This is depicted in Fig. 6. In Fig. 7, we directly compare the speedup of the fastest GPU (Fermi) im-

plementation, the 16-thread OpenMP implementation, and the Thrust GPU merge implementation. We checked a variety of sizes. In Fig. 7 (a) there are speedups for merges of sizes 1 million elements to 10 million elements in increments of 1 millions elements. In Fig. 7 (b) there are speedups for merges of sizes 10 million elements to 100 million elements in increments of 10 millions elements. The results show that the GPU code ran nearly 5x faster than 16-threaded OpenMP and nearly 10x faster than Thrust merge for floating point operations. It is likely that the speedup of our algorithm over OpenMP is related to the difference in memory bandwidth of the two platforms.

3.2 Integer Merging

The integer merging speedup on the GPU is depicted in Fig. 6 for arrays of size 1 million, 10 million, 100 million. We see significant speedups of 11X & 13X & 14X on the Tesla card and 16 & 20X & 21X on the Fermi card over the sequenctial x86 merge. In Fig. 8, we directly compare the speedup over serial of the fastest GPU (Fermi) implementation, the 16-thread OpenMP implementation, and the Thrust GPU merge implementation demonstrating that the GPU code ran nearly 2.5X faster than 16-threaded OpenMP and nearly 10x faster on average than the Thrust merge. The number of blocks used for Fig. 8 is 112 blocks, similar to the number of blocks used in the floating point sub-section. We used the same sizes of sorted arrays for integer as we did for floating point.

4. CONCLUSION

We show a novel algorithm for merging sorted arrays using the GPU. The results show significant speedup for both integer and floating point elements. While the speedups are different for the two types, it is worth noting that the execution time for merging for both these types on the GPU are nearly the same. The explanation for this phenomena is that the execution time for merging integers on the CPU is 2.5X faster than the execution time for floating point on the CPU. This explains the reduction in the the speedup of integer merging on the GPU in comparison with speedup of floating point merging.

The new GPU merging algorithm is atomic-free, parallel, scalable, and can be adapted to the different compute capabilities and architectures that are provided by NVIDIA. In our benchmarking, we show that the GPU algorithm outperforms a sequential merge by a factor of 20X-50X and outperforms an OpenMP implementation of Merge Path that uses 8 hyper-threaded cores by a factor of 2.5X-5X.

This new approach uses the GPU efficiently and takes advantage of the computational power of the GPU and memory system by using the global memory, local shared-memory and the bus of the GPU effectively. This new algorithm would be beneficial for many GPU sorting algorithms including for a GPU merge sort algorithm.

5. ACKNOWLEDGMENTS

This work was supported in part by NSF Grant CNS-0708307 and the NVIDIA CUDA Center of Excellence at Georgia Tech.

We would like to acknowledge Saher Odeh and Prof. Yitzhak Birk from the Technion for their discussion and comments.

6. REFERENCES

[1] S. Chen, J. Qin, Y. Xie, J. Zhao, and P. Heng. An efficient sorting algorithm with cuda. *Journal of the Chinese Institute of Engineers*, 32(7):915–921, 2009.

[2] T. H. Cormen, C. E. Leiserson, R. L. Rivest, and C. Stein. *Introduction to Algorithms*. The MIT Press, New York, 2001.

[3] N. Deo, A. Jain, and M. Medidi. An optimal parallel algorithm for merging using multiselection. *Information Processing Letters*, 1994.

[4] N. K. Govindaraju, N. Raghuvanshi, M. Henson, D. Tuft, and D. Manocha. A cache-efficient sorting algorithm for database and data mining computations using graphics processors. Technical report, 2005.

[5] J. Hoberock and N. Bell. Thrust: A parallel template library, 2010. Version 1.3.0.

[6] NVIDIA Corporation. Nvidia cuda programming guide. 2011.

[7] S. Odeh, O. Green, Z. Mwassi, O. Shmueli, and Y. Birk. Merge path - cache-efficient parallel merge and sort. Technical report, CCIT Report No. 802, EE Pub. No. 1759, Electrical Engr. Dept., Technion, Israel, Jan. 2012.

[8] S. Odeh, O. Green, Z. Mwassi, O. Shmueli, and Y. Birk. Merge path - parallel merging made simple. In *Parallel and Distributed Processing Symposium, International*, may 2012.

[9] N. Satish, M. Harris, and M. Garland. Designing efficient sorting algorithms for manycore gpus. *Parallel and Distributed Processing Symposium, International*, 0:1–10, 2009.

[10] Y. Shiloach and U. Vishkin. Finding the maximum, merging, and sorting in a parallel computation model. *Journal of Algorithms*, 2:88 – 102, 1981.

[11] E. Sintorn and U. Assarsson. Fast parallel gpu-sorting using a hybrid algorithm. *Journal of Parallel and Distributed Computing*, 68(10):1381 – 1388, 2008. General-Purpose Processing using Graphics Processing Units.

SnuCL: An OpenCL Framework for Heterogeneous CPU/GPU Clusters

Jungwon Kim, Sangmin Seo, Jun Lee, Jeongho Nah, Gangwon Jo, and Jaejin Lee
Center for Manycore Programming
School of Computer Science and Engineering
Seoul National University, Seoul 151-744, Korea
{jungwon, sangmin, jun, jeongho, gangwon}@aces.snu.ac.kr, jlee@cse.snu.ac.kr
http://aces.snu.ac.kr

ABSTRACT

In this paper, we propose SnuCL, an OpenCL framework for heterogeneous CPU/GPU clusters. We show that the original OpenCL semantics naturally fits to the heterogeneous cluster programming environment, and the framework achieves high performance and ease of programming. The target cluster architecture consists of a designated, single host node and many compute nodes. They are connected by an interconnection network, such as Gigabit Ethernet and InfiniBand switches. Each compute node is equipped with multicore CPUs and multiple GPUs. A set of CPU cores or each GPU becomes an OpenCL compute device. The host node executes the host program in an OpenCL application. SnuCL provides a system image running a single operating system instance for heterogeneous CPU/GPU clusters to the user. It allows the application to utilize compute devices in a compute node as if they were in the host node. No communication API, such as the MPI library, is required in the application source. SnuCL also provides collective communication extensions to OpenCL to facilitate manipulating memory objects. With SnuCL, an OpenCL application becomes portable not only between heterogeneous devices in a single node, but also between compute devices in the cluster environment. We implement SnuCL and evaluate its performance using eleven OpenCL benchmark applications.

Categories and Subject Descriptors

D.1.3 [**PROGRAMMING TECHNIQUES**]: Concurrent Programming; D.3.4 [**PROGRAMMING LANGUAGES**]: Processors – Code generation, Compilers, Optimization, Runtime environments

General Terms

Algorithm, Design, Experimentation, Languages, Measurement, Performance

Keywords

OpenCL, Clusters, Heterogeneous computing, Programming models

1. INTRODUCTION

A heterogeneous computing system typically refers to a single computer system that contains different types of computational units. It distributes data and program execution among different computational units that are each best suited to specific tasks. The computational unit could be a CPU, GPU, DSP, FPGA, or ASIC. Introducing such additional, specialized computational resources in a system enables the user to gain extra performance. In addition, exploiting the inherent capabilities of a wide range of computational resources enables the user to solve difficult and complex problems efficiently and easily. A typical example of the heterogeneous computing system is a GPGPU system.

The GPGPU system has been a great success so far. However, in the future, applications may not be written for GPGPUs only, but for more general heterogeneous computing systems to improve power efficiency and performance. Open Computing Language (OpenCL)[9] is a unified programming model for different types of computational units in a heterogeneous computing system. OpenCL provides a common hardware abstraction layer across different computational units. Programmers can write OpenCL applications once and run them on any OpenCL-compliant hardware. Some industry-leading hardware vendors such as AMD[1], IBM[6], Intel[8], NVIDIA[20], and Samsung[22] have provided OpenCL implementations for their hardware. This makes OpenCL a standard parallel programming model for general-purpose, heterogeneous computing systems.

However, one of the limitations of current OpenCL is that it is restricted to a programming model on a single operating system image. The same thing is true for CUDA[12]. A heterogeneous CPU/GPU cluster contains multiple general-purpose multicore CPUs and multiple GPUs to solve bigger problems within an acceptable time frame. As such clusters widen their user base, application developers for the clusters are being forced to turn to an unattractive mix of programming models, such as MPI-OpenCL and MPI-CUDA. This makes the application more complex, hard to maintain, and less portable.

The mixed programming model requires the hierarchical distribution of the workload and data (across nodes and across compute devices in a node). MPI functions are used

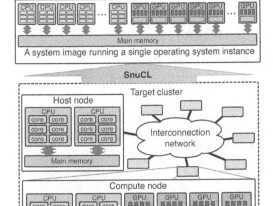

Figure 1: Our approach.

to communicate between the nodes in the cluster. As a result, the resulting application may not be executed in a single node.

In this paper, we propose an OpenCL framework called SnuCL and show that OpenCL can be a unified programming model for heterogeneous CPU/GPU clusters. The target cluster architecture is shown in Figure 1. It consists of a single host node and multiple compute nodes. The nodes are connected by an interconnection network, such as Gigabit Ethernet and InfiniBand switches. The host node executes the host program in an OpenCL application. Each compute node consists of multiple multicore CPUs and multiple GPUs. A set of CPU cores or a single GPU becomes an OpenCL compute device. A GPU has its own device memory, up to several gigabytes. Within a compute node, data is transferred between the GPU device memory and the main memory through a PCI-E bus.

SnuCL provides a system image running a single operating system instance for heterogeneous CPU/GPU clusters to the user as shown in Figure 1. It allows the application to utilize compute devices in a compute node as if they were in the host node. The user can launch a kernel to a compute device or manipulate a memory object in a remote node using only OpenCL API functions. This enables OpenCL applications written for a single node to run on the cluster without any modification. That is, with SnuCL, an OpenCL application becomes portable not only between heterogeneous computing devices in a single node, but also between those in the entire cluster environment.

The major contributions of this paper are the following:

- We show that the original OpenCL semantics naturally fits to the heterogeneous cluster environment.

- We extend the original OpenCL semantics to the cluster environment to make communication between nodes faster and to achieve ease of programming.

- We describe the design and implementation of SnuCL (the runtime and source-to-source translators) for the heterogeneous CPU/GPU cluster.

- We develop an efficient memory management technique for the SnuCL runtime for the heterogeneous CPU/GPU cluster.

- We show the effectiveness of SnuCL by implementing the runtime and source-to-source translators. We experimentally demonstrate that SnuCL achieves high performance, ease of programming, and scalability for medium-scale heterogeneous clusters.

The rest of the paper is organized as follows. Section 2 describes the design and implementation of the SnuCL runtime. Section 3, Section 4, and Section 5 describe memory management techniques, collective communications extensions to OpenCL, and code transformation techniques used in SnuCL, respectively. Section 6 discusses and analyzes the evaluation results of SnuCL. Section 7 surveys related work. Finally, Section 8 concludes the paper.

2. THE SNUCL RUNTIME

In this section, we describe the design and implementation of the SnuCL runtime for the heterogeneous CPU/GPU cluster.

2.1 The OpenCL Platform Model

The OpenCL platform model[9] consists of a *host* connected to one or more *compute devices*. A compute device is divided into one or more *compute units* (CUs) which are further divided into one or more *processing elements* (PEs).

An OpenCL application consists of a host program and kernels. A host program executes on the host and submits commands to perform computations on a compute device or to manipulate memory objects. There are three different types of commands: kernel-execution, memory, and synchronization. A *kernel* is a function and written in OpenCL C. It executes on a compute device. It is submitted to a *command-queue* in the form of a kernel-execution command by the host program. A command-queue is created and attached to a specific compute device by the host program. A compute device may have one or more command-queues. Commands in a command-queue are issued in-order or out-of-order depending on the queue type.

When a kernel-execution command is enqueued, an abstract index space is defined. The index space called NDRange is an N-dimensional space, where N is equal to 1, 2, or 3. An NDRange is defined by an N-tuple of integers and specifies the extent of the index space (the dimension and the size). An instance of the kernel, called a *work-item*, executes for each point in this index space. A work-item is uniquely identified by a global ID (N-tuples) defined by its point in the index space. Each work-item executes the same code but the specific pathway and accessed data can vary.

One or more work-items compose a *work-group*, which provides more coarse-grained decomposition of the index space. Each work-group has a unique work-group ID in the work-group index space and assigns a unique local ID to each work-item. Thus a work-item is identified by its global ID or by a combination of its local ID and work-group ID. The work-items in a given work-group execute concurrently on the PEs in a single CU.

2.2 Mapping Components

SnuCL defines a mapping between the OpenCL platform components and the target architecture components. A

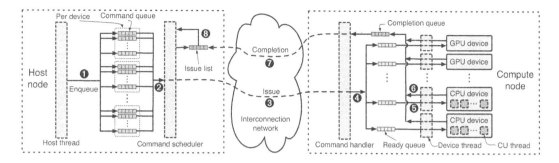

Figure 2: The organization of the SnuCL runtime.

CPU core in the host node becomes the OpenCL host processor. A GPU or a set of CPU cores in a compute node becomes a compute device. Thus, a compute node may have multiple GPU devices and multiple CPU devices. The remaining CPU cores in the host node other than the host core can be configured as a compute device.

Since OpenCL has a strong CUDA heritage[12], the mapping between the components of an OpenCL compute device to those in a GPU is straightforward. For a compute device composed of multiple CPU cores, SnuCL maps all of the memory components in the compute device to disjoint regions in the main memory of the compute node where the device resides. Each CPU core becomes a CU, and the core emulates the PEs in the CU using the work-item coalescing technique[15].

2.3 Organization of the SnuCL Runtime

Figure 2 shows the organization of the SnuCL runtime. It consists of two different parts for the host node and a compute node.

The runtime for the host node runs two threads: *host thread* and *command scheduler*. When a user launches an OpenCL application in the host node, the host thread in the host node executes the host program in the application. The host thread and command scheduler share the OpenCL command-queues. A compute device may have one or more command-queues as shown in Figure 2. The host thread enqueues commands to the command-queues (❶ in Figure 2). The command scheduler schedules the enqueued commands across compute devices in the cluster one by one (❷).

When the command scheduler in the host node dequeues a command from a command-queue, the command scheduler *issues* the command by sending a *command message* (❸) to the target compute node that contains the target compute device associated with the command-queue. A command message contains the information required to execute the original command. To identify each OpenCL object, the runtime assigns a unique ID to each OpenCL object, such as contexts, compute devices, buffers (memory objects), programs, kernels, events, etc. The command message contains these IDs.

After the command scheduler sends the command message to the target compute node, it calls a non-blocking receive communication API function to wait for the completion message from the target node. The command scheduler encapsulates the receive request in the command event object and adds the event object in the *issue list*. The issue list contains event objects associated with the commands that have been issued but have not completed yet.

The runtime for a compute node runs a *command handler thread*. The command handler receives command messages from the host node and executes them across compute devices in the compute node. It creates a command object and an associated event object from the message. After extracting the target device information from the message, the command handler enqueues the command object to the *ready-queue* of the target device (❹). Each compute device has a single ready-queue. The ready-queue contains commands that are issued but not launched to the associated compute device yet.

The runtime for a compute node runs a *device thread* for each compute device in the node. If a CPU device exists in the compute node, each core in the CPU device runs a *CU thread* to emulate PEs. The device thread dequeues a command from its ready-queue and launches the kernel to the associated compute device when the command is a kernel-execution command and the compute device is idle (❺). If it is a memory command, the device thread executes the command directly.

When the compute device completes executing the command, the device thread updates the status of the associated event to *completed*, and then inserts the event to the *completion queue* in the compute node (❻). The command handler in each compute node repeats handling commands and checking the completion queue in turn. When the completion queue is not empty, the command handler dequeues the event from the completion queue and sends a completion message to the host node (❼).

The command scheduler in the host node repeats scheduling commands and checking the event objects in the issue list in turn until the OpenCL application terminates. If the receive request encapsulated in an event object in the issue list completes, the command scheduler removes the event from the issue list and updates the status of the dequeued event from *issued* to *completed* (❽).

The command scheduler in the host node and command handlers in the compute nodes are in charge of communication between different nodes. This communication mechanism is implemented with a lower-level communication API, such as MPI. To implement the runtime for each compute node, an existing CUDA or OpenCL runtime for a single node can be used.

2.4 Processing Kernel-execution Commands

When a device thread dequeues a kernel-execution command from its ready-queue, it launches the kernel to the target device when the device is idle. When the target device is a GPU, the device thread launches the kernel using the vendor-specific API, such as CUDA if the GPU vendor is NVIDIA. When the target is a CPU device, CU threads (i.e., CPU cores) in the device emulate the PEs using a kernel transformation technique, called work-item coalescing[15]. Basically, the work-item coalescing technique makes the CU thread execute each work-item in a work-group one by one sequentially using a loop that iterates over the local index space in the work-group. This transformation is provided by the SnuCL OpenCL-C-to-C translator.

The CPU device thread dynamically distributes the kernel workload across the CU threads and achieves workload balancing between the CU threads. The unit of workload distribution is a work-group. The problem of work-group scheduling across the CU threads is similar to that of parallel loop scheduling for the conventional multiprocessor system because each work-group is essentially a loop due to the work-item coalescing technique. Thus, we modify the conventional parallel loop scheduling algorithm proposed by Li *et al.*[17] and use it in the SnuCL runtime.

In the SnuCL runtime, one or more work-groups are grouped together and dynamically assigned to a currently idle CU thread. The set of work-groups assigned to a CU thread is called a *work-group assignment*. To minimize the scheduling overhead, the size of each work-group assignment is large at the beginning, and the size decreases progressively. When there are N remaining work-groups, the size S of next work-group assignment to an idle CU thread is computed by $S=\lceil N/(2P) \rceil$, where P is the number of all CU threads in the CPU device. The CPU device thread repeatedly schedules the remaining work-groups until N is equal to zero.

2.5   Processing Synchronization Commands

OpenCL supports synchronization between work-items in a work-group using a *work-group barrier*. Every work-item in the work-group must execute the barrier and cannot proceed beyond the barrier until all other work-items in the work-group reach the barrier. Between work-groups, there is no synchronization mechanism available in OpenCL.

Synchronization between commands in a single command-queue can be specified by a *command-queue barrier* command. To synchronize commands between different command-queues, *events* are used. Each OpenCL API function that enqueues a command returns an event object that encapsulates the command status. Most of OpenCL API functions that enqueue a command take an *event wait list* as an argument. This command cannot be issued for execution until all the commands associated with the event wait list complete.

The command scheduler in the host node honors the type (in-order or out-of-order) of each command-queue and (event) synchronization enforced by the host program. When the command scheduler dequeues a synchronization command, the command scheduler uses it for determining execution ordering between queued commands. It maintains a data structure to store the events that are associated with queued commands and bookkeeps the ordering between the commands. When there is no event for which a queued command waits, the command is dequeued and issued to its target node that contains the target device.

3.   MEMORY MANAGEMENT

In this section, we describe how the SnuCL runtime manages memory objects and executes memory commands.

3.1   The OpenCL Memory Model

OpenCL defines four distinct memory regions in a compute device: global, constant, local and private. To distinguish these memory regions, OpenCL C has four address space qualifiers: `__global`, `__constant`, `__local`, and `__private`. They are used in variable declarations in the kernel code. Since OpenCL treats these memory regions as logically distinct regions, they may overlap in physical memory.

An OpenCL memory object is a handle to a region of the global memory. The host program dynamically creates a memory object and enqueues commands to read from, write to, and copy the memory object. A memory object in the global memory is typically a *buffer object*, called a *buffer* in short. A buffer stores a one-dimensional collection of elements that can be a scalar data type, vector data type, or user-defined structure.

OpenCL defines a relaxed memory consistency model. An update to a memory location by a work-item does not need to be visible to other work-items at all times. Instead, the local view of memory from each work-item is guaranteed to be consistent at synchronization points. Synchronization points include work-group barriers, command-queue barrier, and events. Especially, the device global memory is consistent across work-items in a single work-group at a work-group barrier, but there are no guarantees of memory consistency between different work-groups executing the kernel. For other synchronization points, such as command-queue barriers and events, the state of the global memory should be consistent across all work-items in the kernel index space.

3.2   Space Allocation to Buffers

In OpenCL, the host program creates a buffer object by invoking an API function `clCreateBuffer()`. Even though the space for a buffer is allocated in the global memory of a specific device, the buffer is not bound to the compute device in OpenCL[9]. Binding a buffer and a compute device is implementation dependent. As a result, `clCreateBuffer()` has no parameter that specifies a compute device. This implies that when a buffer is created, the runtime has no information about which compute device accesses the buffer.

The SnuCL runtime does not allocate any memory space to a buffer when the host program invokes `clCreate-Buffer()` to create it. Instead, when the host program issues a memory command that manipulates the buffer or a kernel-execution command that accesses the buffer to a compute device, the runtime checks if a space is allocated to the buffer in the target device's global memory. If not, it allocates a space to the buffer in the global memory.

3.3   Minimizing Memory Copying Overhead

To efficiently handle buffer sharing between multiple compute devices, the SnuCL runtime maintains a *device list* for each buffer. The device list contains compute devices that have the same latest copy of the buffer in their global memory. It is empty when the buffer is created. When the command that accesses the buffer completes, the host command scheduler updates the device list of the buffer. If the buffer contents are modified by the command, it empties the list

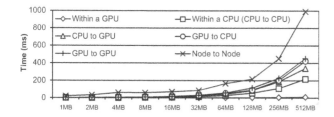

Figure 3: Memory copy time.

Table 1: Distance between compute devices

Distance	Compute devices
0	Within a device
1	a CPU and another CPU in the same node
2	a CPU and another GPU in the same node
3	a GPU and another GPU in the same node
4	a CPU and another CPU in the different nodes
5	a CPU and another GPU in the different nodes
6	a GPU and another GPU in the different nodes

and adds the device that has the modified copy of the buffer in the list. Otherwise, it just adds in the list the device that has recently obtained a copy of the buffer because of the command.

When the host command scheduler dequeues a memory command or kernel-execution command, it checks the device list of each buffer that is accessed by the command. If the target compute device is in the device list of a buffer, the compute device has a copy of the buffer. Otherwise, the runtime checks whether a space is allocated to the buffer in the target device's global memory. If not, the runtime allocates a space for the buffer in the global memory of the target device. Then it copies the buffer contents from a device in the device list of the buffer to the allocated space.

To minimize the memory copying overhead, the runtime selects a source device in the device list that incurs the minimum copying overhead. Figure 3 shows an example of the memory copy time in a node (Within a GPU, Within a CPU, CPU to CPU, CPU to GPU, GPU to CPU, and GPU to GPU) or between different nodes (Node to Node) of the target cluster. We vary the buffer size from 1 MB to 512 MB.

As the source of copying, the runtime prefers a device that has a latest copy of the buffer and resides in the same node as that of the target device. If there are multiple such devices, a CPU device is preferred. When all of the potential source devices reside in other nodes, a CPU device is also preferred to a GPU device. This is because the lower-level communication API does not typically support reading directly from the GPU device memory. It costs one more copying step from the GPU device memory to a temporary space in the node main memory.

To avoid such an unnecessary memory copying overhead, we define a distance metric between compute devices as shown in Table 1. Based on this metric, the runtime selects the nearest compute device in the device list of the buffer and copies the buffer contents to the target device from the selected device.

3.4 Processing Memory Commands

There are three representative memory commands in OpenCL: write (`clEnqueueWriteBuffer()`), read (`clEnqueueReadBuffer()`), and copy (`clEnqueueCopyBuffer()`).

When the runtime executes a write command, it copies the buffer contents from the host node's main memory to the global memory of the target device. When the runtime executes a read command, it copies the buffer contents from the global memory of a compute device in the device list of the buffer to the host node's main memory. A CPU device is preferred to avoid the unnecessary memory copying overhead. When the runtime executes a copy command, based on the distance metric (Table 1), it selects a nearest device in the device list of the source buffer from the target device. Then it copies the buffer contents from the global memory in the source device to the global memory in the target device.

3.5 Consistency Management

In OpenCL, multiple kernel-execution and memory commands can be executed simultaneously, and each of them may access a copy of the same buffer. If they update the same set of locations in the buffer, we may choose any copy as the last update for the buffer according to the OpenCL memory consistency model. However, when they update different locations in the same buffer, the case is similar to the false sharing problem that occurs in a traditional, page-level software shared virtual memory system[2].

One solution to this problem is introducing a multiple-writers protocol[2] that maintains a twin for each writer and updates the original copy of the buffer by comparing the modified copy with its twin. Each node that contains a writer device performs the comparison and sends the result (e.g., diffs) to the host who maintains the original buffer. The host updates the original buffer with the result. However, this introduces a significant communication and computation overhead in the cluster environment if the degree of buffer sharing is high.

Instead, the SnuCL runtime solves this problem by executing kernel-execution and memory commands atomically in addition to keeping the most up-to-date copies using the device list. When the host command scheduler issues a memory command or kernel-execution command, it records the buffers that are written by the command in a list called *written-buffer list*. When the host command scheduler dequeues a command, and the command writes to any buffer in the written-buffer list, it delays issuing the command until the buffers accessed by the dequeued command are removed from the written-buffer list. This mechanism is implemented by adding the commands that write to the buffers and have not completed their execution yet into the event wait list of the dequeued command. Whenever a kernel-execution or memory command completes its execution, the host command scheduler removes the buffers written by the command from the written-buffer list.

3.6 Ease of Programming

Assume that a user uses a mix of MPI and OpenCL as a programming model for the heterogeneous cluster. When the user wants to launch a kernel to an OpenCL-compliant compute device, and the kernel accesses a buffer having been written by another compute device in a different compute node, the user explicitly inserts necessary communication and data transfer operations in the MPI-OpenCL program. First, the user makes the source device copy the buffer into the main memory of its node using `clEnqueueReadBuffer()`, and sends the data to the target node using `MPI_Send()`. The target node receives the data from the source node using

Table 2: Collective communication extensions

SnuCL	MPI Equivalent
clEnqueueBroadcastBuffer	MPI_Bcast
clEnqueueScatterBuffer	MPI_Scatter
clEnqueueGatherBuffer	MPI_Gather
clEnqueueAllGatherBuffer	MPI_Allgather
clEnqueueAlltoAllBuffer	MPI_Alltoall
clEnqueueReduceBuffer	MPI_Reduce
clEnqueueAllReduceBuffer	MPI_Allreduce
clEnqueueReduceScatterBuffer	MPI_Reduce_scatter
clEnqueueScanBuffer	MPI_Scan

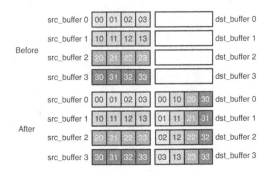

Figure 4: `clEnqueueAlltoAllBuffer()` operation for four source buffers and four destination buffers.

`MPI_Recv()`. Then, the user copies the data into the device memory by invoking `clEnqueueWriteBuffer()`. Finally, the user invokes `clEnqueueNDRangeKernel()` to execute the kernel.

On the other hand, SnuCL hides the communication and data transfer layer from the user and manages memory consistency all by itself. Thus, with SnuCL, the user executes the kernel by invoking only `clEnqueueNDRangeKernel()` without any additional data movement operations (`clEnqueueReadBuffer()`, `MPI_Send()`, `MPI_Recv()`, and `clEnqueueWriteBuffer()`). This improves software developers' productivity and increases portability.

4. EXTENSIONS TO OPENCL

A buffer copy command (`clEnqueueCopyBuffer()`) is available in OpenCL[9]. Although this can be used for point-to-point communication in the cluster environment, OpenCL does not provide any collective communication mechanisms that facilitate exchanging data between many devices. SnuCL provides collective communication operations between buffers. These are similar to MPI collective communication operations. They can be efficiently implemented with the lower-level communication API or multiple `clEnqueueCopyBuffer()` commands. Table 2 lists each collective communication operation and its MPI equivalent.

For example, the format of `clEnqueueAlltoAllBuffer()` operation is as follows:

```
cl_int clEnqueueAlltoAllBuffer(
    cl_command_queue *cmd_queue_list, cl_uint num_buffers,
    cl_mem *src_buffer_list, cl_mem *dst_buffer_list,
    size_t *src_offset_list, size_t *dst_offset_list,
    size_t bytes_to_copy, cl_uint num_events_in_wait_list,
    const cl_event *event_wait_list, cl_event *event)
```

The API function `clEnqueueAlltoAllBuffer()` is similar to the MPI collective operation `MPI_Alltoall()`. The first argument `cmd_queue_list` is the list of command-queues

that are associated with the compute devices where the destination buffers (`dst_buffer_list`) are located. The command is enqueued to the first command-queue in the list. The meaning of this API function is the same as enqueueing N independent `clEnqueueCopyBuffer()`s to each command-queue in `cmd_queue_list`, where N is the number of buffers. The meaning of this operation is illustrated in Figure 4.

5. CODE TRANSFORMATIONS

In this section, we describe compiler analysis and transformation techniques used in SnuCL.

```
__kernel void vec_add(__global float *A, __global float *B,
                      __global float *C) {
    int id = get_global_id(0);
    C[id] = A[id] + B[id];
}
```
(a)

```
int vec_add_memory_flags[3] = {
    CL_MEM_READ_ONLY, // A
    CL_MEM_READ_ONLY, // B
    CL_MEM_WRITE_ONLY // C
};
```
(b)

```
__global__ void vec_add(float *A, float *B, float *C) {
    int id = blockDim.x * blockIdx.x + threadIdx.x;
    C[id] = A[id] + B[id];
}
```
(c)

```
#define get_global_id(N) \
    (__global_id[N] + (N == 0 ? __i : (N == 1 ? __j : __k)))

void vec_add(float *A, float *B, float *C) {
    for (int __k = 0; __k < __local_size[2]; __k++) {
        for (int __j = 0; __j < __local_size[1]; __j++) {
            for (int __i = 0; __i < __local_size[0]; __i++) {
                int id = get_global_id(0);
                C[id] = A[id] + B[id];
            }
        }
    }
}
```
(d)

Figure 5: (a) An OpenCL kernel. (b) The buffer access information of kernel `vec_add` for the runtime. (c) The CUDA C code generated for a GPU device. (d) The C code for a CPU device.

5.1 Detecting Buffers Written by a Kernel

To keep shared buffers consistent, the SnuCL runtime performs consistency management as described in Section 3. This requires detecting buffers that are written by an OpenCL kernel. In OpenCL, each memory object has a flag that represents its read/write permission: `CL_MEM_READ_ONLY`, `CL_MEM_WRITE_ONLY`, and `CL_MEM_READ_WRITE`. Thus, the runtime may use the read/write permission of each buffer object to obtain the necessary information. However, this may be too conservative. When the memory object has `CL_MEM_READ_WRITE` and the kernel does not write to the buffer at all, the runtime cannot detect this.

Thus, SnuCL performs a conservative pointer analysis on the kernel source when the kernel is built. A simple and conservative pointer analysis[24] is enough to obtain the necessary information because OpenCL imposes a restriction on the usage of global memory pointers used in a kernel[9]. Specifically, a pointer to address space A can only be assigned to a pointer to the same address space A. Casting a pointer to address space A to a pointer to address space B ($\neq$ A) is illegal.

When the host builds a kernel by invoking `clBuildProgram()`, the SnuCL OpenCL-C-to-C translator at the host node generates the buffer access information for the runtime from the OpenCL kernel code. Figure 5 (b) shows the information generated from the OpenCL kernel in Figure 5 (a). It is an array of integer for each kernel. The ith element of the array represents the access information of the ith buffer argument of the kernel. Figure 5 (b) indicates that the first and second buffer arguments (A and B) are read and the third buffer argument (C) is written by kernel `vec_add`. The runtime uses this information to manage buffer consistency.

5.2 Emulating PEs for CPU Devices

In a CPU device, the SnuCL runtime makes each CU thread emulate the PEs in the CU using a kernel transformation technique, called work-item coalescing[15] provided by the SnuCL OpenCL-C-to-C translator. The work-item coalescing technique makes the CPU core execute each work-item in the work-group one by one sequentially using a loop that iterates over the local work-item index space. The triply nested loop in Figure 5 (d) is such a loop after the work-item coalescing technique has been applied. The size of the local work-item index space is determined by the array `__local_size` provided by the runtime. The runtime also provides an array `__global_id` that contains the global ID of the first work-item in the work-group.

When there are work-group barriers in the kernel, the work-item coalescing technique divides the code into work-item coalescing regions (WCRs)[15]. A WCR is a maximal code region that does not contain any barrier. Since a work-item private variable whose value is defined in one WCR and used in another needs a separate location for each work-item to transfer the variable's value between different WCRs, the variable expansion technique[15] is applied to WCRs. Then, the work-item coalescing technique executes each WCR using a loop that iterates over the local work-item index space. After work-item coalescing, the execution ordering of WCRs preserves the barrier semantics.

5.3 Distributing the Kernel Code

When the host builds a kernel by invoking `clBuildProgram()`, the SnuCL OpenCL-C-to-CUDA-C translator (we assume that the runtime in a compute node is implemented with the CUDA runtime) generates the code for a GPU and OpenCL-C-to-C translator generates the code for a CPU device. Figure 5 (c) and Figure 5 (d) show the code generated for a GPU and a CPU device, respectively. Then, the host command scheduler sends a message that contains the translated kernels to each compute node. The compute node stores the kernels in separate files and builds them with the native compiler for each compute device in the system.

6. EVALUATION

This section describes the evaluation methodology and results for SnuCL.

Table 3: The target clusters

	Host node	Compute node	
Processors	2 × Intel Xeon X5680	2 × Intel Xeon X5660	4 × NVIDIA GTX 480
Clock frequency	3.33GHz	2.80GHz	1.40GHz
Cores per processor	6	6	480
Memory size	72GB	48GB	1.5GB
Quantity	1	9	
OS	Red Hat Enterprise Linux Server 5.5		
Interconnection	Mellanox InfiniBand QDR		

Cluster A (a 10-node heterogeneous CPU/GPU cluster)

	Host node	Compute node
Processors	2 × Intel Xeon X5570	2 × Intel Xeon X5570
Clock frequency	2.93GHz	2.93GHz
Cores per processor	4	4
Memory size	24GB	24GB
Quantity	1	256
OS	Red Hat Enterprise Linux Server 5.3	
Interconnection	Mellanox InfiniBand QDR	

Cluster B (a 257-node CPU cluster)

6.1 Methodology

Target cluster architecture. We evaluate SnuCL using two cluster systems (Cluster A and Cluster B). Table 3 summarizes the target clusters.

Benchmark applications. We use eleven OpenCL applications from various sources: AMD[1], NAS[18], NVIDIA[19], Parboil[25], and PARSEC[3]. The characteristics of the applications and their input sets are summarized in Table 4. The applications from Parboil and PARSEC are translated to OpenCL applications manually. The applications from NAS are from SNU NPB Suite[21] that contains OpenCL versions of the original NAS Parallel Benchmarks for multiple OpenCL compute devices. For an OpenCL application written for a single compute device, we modify the application to distribute workload across multiple compute devices available. Especially, FT and MatrixMul use SnuCL collective communication extensions to OpenCL. Some applications are evaluated with two input sets. The smaller input set is used for Cluster A because a GPU has relatively small device memory and allows only the smaller input set for those applications. The larger input set is used for Cluster B to show its scalability in a large-scale cluster. All applications are portable across CPU and GPU devices. That is, we can run the applications either on CPU devices or GPU devices without any source code modification.

Runtime and source-to-source translators. We have implemented the SnuCL runtime and source-to-source translators. The SnuCL runtime uses Open MPI 1.4.1 as the lower-level communication API. The GPU part of the runtime is implemented with CUDA Toolkit 4.0[19]. We have implemented SnuCL source-to-source translators by modifying clang that is a C front-end for the LLVM[13] compiler infrastructure. The runtime uses Intel ICC 11.1[7], and NVIDIA's NVCC 4.0[19] to compile the translated kernels for CPU devices and GPU devices, respectively.

6.2 Results

Figure 6 shows the speedup (over a single CPU core) of each application with SnuCL when we use only CPU devices in Cluster A. The sequential CPU version of each application is obtained from the same source (Table 4). Each application from NAS is shown with its input set. The CPUs in the

Table 4: Applications used

Application	Source	Description	Input	Global memory size (MB)	Extension used
BinomialOption	AMD	Binomial option pricing	65504 or 2097152 samples, 512 steps, 100 iterations	2.0 or 64.0	
BlackScholes	PARSEC	Black-Scholes PDE	33538048 options, 100 iterations	895.6	
BT	NAS	Block tridiagonal solver	Class C (162x162x162) or Class D (408x408x408)	1982.1 or 30686.7	
CG	NAS	Conjugate gradient	Class C (150000) or Class D (1500000)	1102.6 or 20399.1	
CP	Parboil	Coulombic potential	16384x16384, 10000 atoms	4.1	
EP	NAS	Embarrassingly parallel	Class D (2^36)	0.8	
FT	NAS	3-D FFT PDE	Class B (512x256x256) or Class C (512x512x512)	2816.0 or 11264.0	AlltoAll
MatrixMul	NVIDIA	Matrix multiplication	10752x10752 or 16384x16384	1323.0 or 3072.0	Broadcast
MG	NAS	Multigrid	Class C (512x512x512) or Class D (1024x1024x1024)	3575.3 or 28343.7	
Nbody	NVIDIA	N-Body simulation	1048576 bodies	64.0	
SP	NAS	Pentadiagonal solver	Class C (162x162x162) or Class D (408x408x408)	1477.9 or 19974.4	

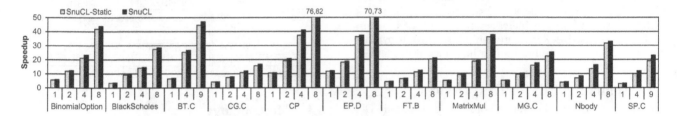

Figure 6: Speedup over a single CPU core using CPU devices on Cluster A. The numbers on x-axis represent the number of CPU compute devices.

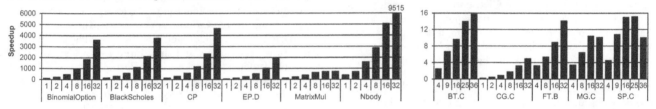

Figure 7: Speedup over a single CPU core using GPU devices on Cluster A. The numbers on x-axis represent the number of GPU compute devices.

compute nodes support simultaneous multithreading (SMT) that enables two logical cores per physical core. Thus, each compute node contains 24 logical CPU cores. In each compute node, two logical CPU cores are dedicated to the command handler and the CPU device thread. The remaining 22 logical CPU cores are configured as a CPU device. We vary the number of compute nodes (i.e., the total number of CPU devices in the cluster) from 1 to 8 in powers of two for all applications but BT and SP. We set the number of CPU devices to square numbers (1, 4, 9) for BT and SP because of their algorithms.

We also implement another SnuCL runtime (SnuCL-Static) that exploits a static scheduling algorithm (conventional block scheduling) for the kernel workload distribution for CPU compute devices. The device thread divides the entire work-groups into sets of $\lceil N/P \rceil$ work-groups, where N is the number of work-groups and P is the number of CU threads in the CPU device. The SnuCL runtime that uses the dynamic scheduling algorithm described in Section 2.4 is denoted by SnuCL in Figure 6.

All applications scale well in Figure 6. Our dynamic scheduling algorithm is quite effective. Static scheduling mechanisms used in SnuCL-Static ignore workload imbalance that occurs at run time due to variations in CPU cores. In addition, when the total workload is not evenly divisible for

all CPU cores, some CPU cores are not fully utilized resulting in load imbalance. Our dynamic scheduling mechanism solves this load imbalancing problem.

Figure 7 shows the speedup (over a single CPU core) when we use only GPU devices in Cluster A. Each compute node contains four GPU devices. We vary the number of GPU devices in the cluster from 1 to 36 in powers of two or square numbers. For BT, FT, MG, and SP, we cannot use fewer than four GPUs because of their memory requirement. Note that we use the same OpenCL application source code for both CPU devices and GPU devices.

When we use only GPU devices in the cluster, all applications but MatrixMul, MG and SP scale well. Since the communication overhead due to data movement (e.g., read/write and copy operations of buffers) dominates the performance of MatrixMul and SP, they do not scale well. The speedup of MG at 32 GPU devices is smaller than that at 16 GPU devices because its index space is not large enough to fully utilize all the 32 GPU devices and the communication overhead increases at 32 GPU devices.

When an application has enough data parallelism, its performance with GPU devices is better than that with CPU devices. On the other hand, the cost of data transfer between GPU devices is higher than that between CPU devices because of extra data transfer between the node

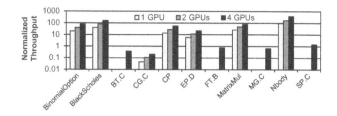

Figure 8: Normalized throughput of GPU devices over a CPU device.

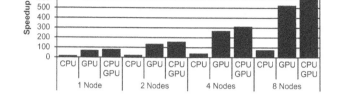

Figure 9: Exploiting both CPU and GPU devices for EP.

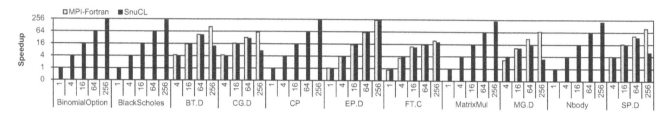

Figure 10: Speedup over a single node (a CPU compute device with four CPU cores) on Cluster B. The numbers on x-axis represent the number of nodes (CPU compute devices).

main memory and the GPU's device memory via the PCI-E bus. We see that applications with a low communication-to-computation ratio scales better in our cluster environment. A GPU device executes the kernel in MatrixMul 30 times faster than a CPU device but the GPU device has 30% longer data transfer time than the CPU device. With one GPU device, MatrixMul has a communication-to-computation ratio of 13%. As the number of GPU devices increases to 8 and 32, the ratio increases to 44% and 257%, respectively. On the other hand, a CPU device has 0.4% communication-to-computation ratio due to its lower communication overhead and slower computation than a GPU device. When the number of CPU devices increases to 8, the ratio increases to only 4.6%. This is the reason why MatrixMul scales better with CPU devices than with GPU devices.

Performance portability. In Figure 7, with GPU devices, the speedup of BT, CG, FT, MG and SP is three orders of magnitude smaller than that of other applications. These applications are from the NAS Parallel Benchmark suite that is originally targeting CPU systems, and note that we use the same OpenCL source code for both CPU devices and GPU devices. Since performance tuning factors, such as data placement, memory access patterns (e.g., non-coalesced memory accesses), the number of work-groups in the kernel index space, the work-group size (the number of work-items in a work-group), compute-device-specific algorithms, etc., between CPU devices and GPU devices are significantly different, an optimization for one type of device may not perform well on another type of device[16].

The kernels in BT, CG, FT, MG, and SP make the GPU devices suffer from non-coalesced memory accesses. Furthermore, they have many buffer-copy memory commands. The data transfer cost between GPU devices is much higher than that between CPU devices. Since the kernels in CG and MG have small work-group sizes that are not big enough to make all scalar processors (PEs) of a streaming multiprocessor (CU) in GPU devices busy, resulting in poor performance. On the other hand, for CPU devices, each CPU

core (CU) emulates the PEs. It executes each work-item in a work-group one by one sequentially using the work-item coalescing technique. Thus, the small work-group size does not affect the performance of the CPU devices.

Exploiting both types of devices. Figure 8 shows the normalized throughput (CPU execution time divided by GPU execution time) of one, two, and four GPU devices over a single CPU device within the same compute node for each application. The y-axis is in the logarithmic scale. BT, FT, MG, and SP have no throughput at one and two GPU devices because of their memory requirement.

An application that has similar performance between a CPU device and a GPU device can profit from exploiting both CPU devices and GPU devices in the cluster because our OpenCL implementation of the application is portable across both types of devices. If the user wishes more than 10 percent performance improvement using both types of devices, the normalized throughput between the faster device and slower device should be less than nine. However, one restriction is that the application should allow changing the number of devices used and the amount of workload distributed to each device.

Among those applications, only EP satisfies the condition. We distribute its workload between CPU devices and GPU devices based on the throughput. Figure 9 shows the speedup of EP when both types of devices are used. We vary the number of compute nodes from 1 to 8. Only one GPU device within each compute node (including one CPU device) is used for evaluation to manifest the difference. As we expected from the throughput, compared to the case of GPU devices only, the performance improvement of EP is 11.4% on average in Figure 9.

Scalability. To show the scalability of SnuCL, Figure 10 shows the speedups of all applications on Cluster B (a 257-node homogeneous cluster). For the applications from the NAS Parallel Benchmark (NPB) suite, it compares our OpenCL implementations with the unmodified original MPI-Fortran versions (MPI-Fortran) from NPB. We build

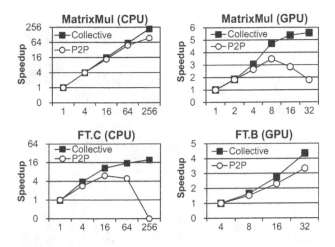

Figure 11: The performance of collective communication extensions. X-axis shows the number of compute devices.

the MPI-Fortran applications using Intel IFORT 11.1. Since BT and SP require the number of MPI tasks to be a square number while CG, FT, and MG require the number of tasks to be a power of two, we run 4 MPI processes per node for all applications (the Hyper-Threading mechanism is disabled for the CPU cores of Cluster B). For fair comparison, the SnuCL runtime configures a CPU device with 4 CPU cores per compute node. We vary the number of compute nodes from 1 to 256 in powers of four on x-axis. Y-axis shows the speedup in logarithmic scale over the OpenCL version on a single compute node.

All OpenCL applications scale well up to 64 nodes. The OpenCL applications from NPB show competitive performance with MPI versions. However, when the number of compute nodes increases to 256, some OpenCL applications from NPB show poor performance while MPI-Fortran versions still show good scalability. BinomialOption, BlackScholes, CP, EP, FT, MatrixMul, and Nbody still scale well on 256 nodes. They have a small number of commands that take long time to execute. Their communication-to-computation ratios are small and their scheduling overhead is negligible.

On the other hand, BT, CG, MG, and SP show performance degradation on 256 nodes. They have a large number of commands that take very short time to execute. For example, SP has the largest number of commands to be executed among the applications. Total 90,234,368 commands are enqueued and executed (with the Class D input) on 256 compute nodes while its total execution time is 1,813 seconds. This means that the host command scheduler schedules about 50,000 commands in a second. As the number of nodes increases, workload to be executed on each compute device decreases. However, the idle time of a compute device increases because command scheduling is centralized to a single host node and it takes time for the host node to schedule a new command when there are many nodes in the cluster. This makes compute devices less efficient, resulting in overall performance degradation on 256 nodes.

Collective communication extensions. The collective communication APIs in SnuCL are implemented with MPI collective operations. In addition, we use a depth tree

to implement the broadcasting mechanism[23] for GPU devices, rather than sending data directly from the source to the destination. Among the applications, MatrixMul uses `clEnqueueBroadcastBuffer()` and FT uses `clEnqueueAlltoAllBuffer()`. To compare performance, we implement another version (P2P) that uses `clEnqueueCopyBuffer()` instead of using the extensions. We evaluate the performance using Cluster A for GPUs and Cluster B for CPUs. Figure 11 shows the performance of SnuCL collective communication extensions to OpenCL (Collective). We see that Collective achieves much better performance than P2P as the number of compute devices increases.

As described in Section 4, `clEnqueueAlltoAllBuffer()` has an equivalent meaning of performing N independent `clEnqueueCopyBuffer()` to each device, where N is the number of buffers. To execute N independent commands concurrently, either the command queue should be out-of-order type or there should be N command queues per compute device. This makes the OpenCL program more complex and increases the scheduling overhead. Thus, SnuCL collective communication extensions provide the programmer with both high performance and ease of programming in the cluster environment.

7. RELATED WORK

There are some previous proposals for OpenCL frameworks[5, 14, 10, 11, 15]. Gummaraju *et al.*[5] present an OpenCL framework named Twin Peaks that handles both CPUs and GPUs in a single node. Twin Peaks executes SPMD style OpenCL kernels on a CPU core by switching contexts between work-items. They use their own lightweight `setjmp()` and `longjmp()` system calls to reduce the context switching overhead. Lee *et al.*[15] propose an OpenCL framework for heterogeneous multicores with local memory, such as Cell BE processors. They present work-item coalescing technique and show that it significantly reduces context switching overhead of executing an OpenCL kernel on multiple SPEs. Lee *et al.*[14] present an OpenCL framework for homogeneous manycore processors with no hardware cache coherence mechanism, such as the Single-chip Cloud Computer (SCC). Their OpenCL runtime exploits the SCC's dynamic memory mapping mechanism together with the symbolic array bound analysis to preserve coherence and consistency between CPU cores.

Some other prior work proposes GPU virtualization[10, 4, 11]. Kim *et al.*[10] propose an OpenCL framework for multiple GPUs in a single node. The OpenCL framework provides an illusion of a single compute device to the programmer for the multiple GPUs available in the system. Duato *et al.*[4] presents a CUDA framework named rCUDA. The framework enables multiple clients to share GPUs in a remote server. These approaches are similar to our work in that OpenCL or CUDA is used as an abstraction layer to provide ease of programming.

The work most similar to ours is an OpenCL framework presented by Kim *et al.*[11] in that it exploits remote GPUs in a GPU cluster without MPI APIs. SnuCL focuses on the heterogeneity available in the heterogeneous CPU/GPU cluster environment. Supporting both CPUs and GPUs in the cluster raises many challenging issues, such as dynamic scheduling, performance portability, buffer management, and minimizing data transfer overhead. They did not address these issues. Moreover, SnuCL provides collective communication extensions to OpenCL to achieve high performance and ease of programming. To our knowledge, our work is the first that shows OpenCL's portability and scalability on a heterogeneous CPU/GPU cluster.

8. CONCLUSIONS AND FUTURE WORK

In this paper, we introduce the design and implementation of SnuCL that provides a system image running a single operating system instance for heterogeneous CPU/GPU clusters to the programmer. It allows the OpenCL application to utilize compute devices in a remote compute node as if they were in the host node. The user launches a kernel to any compute device in the cluster and manipulates memory objects using standard OpenCL API functions. Our work shows that OpenCL can be a unified programming model for heterogeneous CPU/GPU clusters. Moreover, our collective communication extensions to standard OpenCL facilitate ease of programming. SnuCL enables OpenCL applications written for a single node to run on the cluster that consists of multiple such systems without any modification. It also makes the application portable not only between heterogeneous devices in a single node, but also between all heterogeneous devices in the cluster environment.

The experimental result indicates that SnuCL achieves high performance, ease of programming, and scalability for medium-scale clusters. For large scale clusters, SnuCL may lead to performance degradation due to its centralized task scheduling model. Our future work is to improve the scalability of SnuCL for large-scale clusters by introducing an effective distributed task scheduling mechanism.

9. ACKNOWLEDGEMENTS

This work was supported in part by grant 2009-0081569 (Creative Research Initiatives: Center for Manycore Programming) from the National Research Foundation of Korea. This work was also supported in part by the Ministry of Education, Science and Technology of Korea under the BK21 Project. ICT at Seoul National University provided research facilities for this study.

10. REFERENCES

[1] AMD. *AMD Accelerated Parallel Processing (APP) SDK*, 2011. http://developer.amd.com/sdks/amdappsdk/pages/default.aspx.

[2] C. Amza, A. L. Cox, S. Dwarkadas, P. Keleher, H. Lu, R. Rajamony, W. Yu, and W. Zwaenepoel. TreadMarks: Shared Memory Computing on Networks of Workstations. *Computer*, 29:18–28, February 1996.

[3] C. Bienia, S. Kumar, J. P. Singh, and K. Li. The PARSEC benchmark suite: characterization and architectural implications. In *Proceedings of the 17th international conference on Parallel architectures and compilation techniques*, PACT '08, pages 72–81, 2008.

[4] J. Duato, A. Pena, F. Silla, R. Mayo, and E. Quintana-Orti. rCUDA: Reducing the number of GPU-based accelerators in high performance clusters. In *Proceedings of the International Conference on High Performance Computing and Simulation*, HPCS '11, pages 224–231, 28 2010-july 2 2010.

[5] J. Gummaraju, L. Morichetti, M. Houston, B. Sander, B. R. Gaster, and B. Zheng. Twin peaks: a software platform for heterogeneous computing on general-purpose and graphics processors. In *Proceedings of the 19th international conference on Parallel architectures and compilation techniques*, PACT '10, pages 205–216, 2010.

[6] IBM. *OpenCL Development Kit for Linux on Power*, 2011. http://www.alphaworks.ibm.com/tech/opencl.

[7] Intel. Intel Composer XE 2011 for Linux. http://software.intel.com/en-us/articles/intel-composer-xe.

[8] Intel. *Intel OpenCL SDK*, 2011. http://software.intel.com/en-us/articles/vcsource-tools-opencl-sdk/.

[9] Khronos OpenCL Working Group. *The OpenCL Specification Version 1.1*, 2010. http://www.khronos.org/opencl.

[10] J. Kim, H. Kim, J. H. Lee, and J. Lee. Achieving a single compute device image in OpenCL for multiple GPUs. In *Proceedings of the 16th ACM symposium on Principles and practice of parallel programming*, PPoPP '11, pages 277–288, 2011.

[11] J. Kim, S. Seo, J. Lee, J. Nah, G. Jo, and J. Lee. OpenCL as a Programming Model for GPU Clusters. In *Proceedings of the 24th International Workshop on Languages and Compilers for Parallel Computing*, LCPC '11, 2011.

[12] D. B. Kirk and W.-m. W. Hwu. *Programming Massively Parallel Processors: A Hands-on Approach*. Morgan Kaufmann Publishers Inc., San Francisco, CA, USA, 2010.

[13] C. Lattner and V. Adve. LLVM: A Compilation Framework for Lifelong Program Analysis & Transformation. In *Proceedings of the international symposium on Code generation and optimization: feedback-directed and runtime optimization*, CGO '04, pages 75–86, 2004.

[14] J. Lee, J. Kim, J. Kim, S. Seo, and J. Lee. An OpenCL Framework for Homogeneous Manycores with no Hardware Cache Coherence. In *Proceedings of the 20th international conference on Parallel architectures and compilation techniques*, PACT '11, 2011.

[15] J. Lee, J. Kim, S. Seo, S. Kim, J. Park, H. Kim, T. T. Dao, Y. Cho, S. J. Seo, S. H. Lee, S. M. Cho, H. J. Song, S.-B. Suh, and J.-D. Choi. An OpenCL framework for heterogeneous multicores with local memory. In *Proceedings of the 19th international conference on Parallel architectures and compilation techniques*, PACT '10, pages 193–204, 2010.

[16] V. W. Lee, C. Kim, J. Chhugani, M. Deisher, D. Kim, A. D. Nguyen, N. Satish, M. Smelyanskiy, S. Chennupaty, P. Hammarlund, R. Singhal, and P. Dubey. Debunking the 100X GPU vs. CPU myth: an evaluation of throughput computing on CPU and GPU. In *Proceedings of the 37th annual international symposium on Computer architecture*, ISCA '10, pages 451–460, 2010.

[17] H. Li, S. Tandri, M. Stumm, and K. C. Sevcik. Locality and Loop Scheduling on NUMA Multiprocessors. In *Proceedings of the 1993 International Conference on Parallel Processing - Volume 02*, ICPP '93, pages 140–147, 1993.

[18] NASA Advanced Supercomputing Division. NAS Parallel Benchmarks version 3.3. http://www.nas.nasa.gov/Resources/Software/npb.html.

[19] NVIDIA. NVIDIA CUDA Toolkit 4.0. http://developer.nvidia.com/cuda-toolkit-40.

[20] NVIDIA. *NVIDIA OpenCL*, 2011. http://developer.nvidia.com/opencl.

[21] S. Seo, G. Jo, and J. Lee. Performance Characterization of the NAS Parallel Benchmarks in OpenCL. In *Proceedings of the 2011 IEEE International Symposium on Workload Characterization*, IISWC '11, pages 137–148, 2011.

[22] Seoul National University and Samsung. *SNU-SAMSUNG OpenCL Framework*, 2010. http://opencl.snu.ac.kr.

[23] M. Snir, S. Otto, S. Huss-Lederman, D. Walker, and J. Dongarra. *MPI-The Complete Reference, Volume 1: The MPI Core*. MIT Press, Cambridge, MA, USA, 2nd. (revised) edition, 1998.

[24] B. Steensgaard. Points-to analysis in almost linear time. In *Proceedings of the 23rd ACM SIGPLAN-SIGACT symposium on Principles of programming languages*, POPL '96, pages 32–41, 1996.

[25] The IMPACT Research Group. Parboil Benchmark suite. http://impact.crhc.illinois.edu/parboil.php.

clSpMV: A Cross-Platform OpenCL SpMV Framework on GPUs

Bor-Yiing Su
University of California, Berkeley
EECS Department
subrian@eecs.berkeley.edu

Kurt Keutzer
University of California, Berkeley
EECS Department
keutzer@eecs.berkeley.edu

ABSTRACT

Sparse matrix vector multiplication (SpMV) kernel is a key computation in linear algebra. Most iterative methods are composed of SpMV operations with BLAS1 updates. Therefore, researchers make extensive efforts to optimize the SpMV kernel in sparse linear algebra. With the appearance of OpenCL, a programming language that standardizes parallel programming across a wide variety of heterogeneous platforms, we are able to optimize the SpMV kernel on many different platforms. In this paper, we propose a new sparse matrix format, the *Cocktail Format*, to take advantage of the strengths of many different sparse matrix formats. Based on the *Cocktail Format*, we develop the *cl pMV* framework that is able to analyze all kinds of sparse matrices at runtime, and recommend the best representations of the given sparse matrices on different platforms. Although solutions that are portable across diverse platforms generally provide lower performance when compared to solutions that are specialized to particular platforms, our experimental results show that *cl pMV* can find the best representations of the input sparse matrices on both Nvidia and AMD platforms, and deliver 83% higher performance compared to the vendor optimized CUDA implementation of the proposed hybrid sparse format in [3], and 63.6% higher performance compared to the CUDA implementations of all sparse formats in [3].

Categories and Subject Descriptors

D.1.3 [**Programming Techniques**]: Parallel programming; C.1.2 [**Processor Architectures**]: Single-instruction-stream, multiple-data-stream processors (SIMD)

General Terms

Performance

Keywords

clSpMV, OpenCL, GPU, SpMV, Sparse Matrix Format, Autotuner, Cocktail Format

1. INTRODUCTION

In scientific computation, operations research, image processing, data mining, structural mechanics, and other fields, the system matrices are naturally sparse, and sparse matrix algorithms are required for analysis. Iterative methods are widely used to solve linear systems and find eigen decompositions. Many iterative methods are composed of sparse matrix vector multiplication (SpMV) operations with BLAS1 updates, such as the conjugate gradient method and the Krylov subspace methods [22]. Since the matrix size is orders of magnitude larger than the vector, the SpMV operations dominate the execution time of these iterative methods. In order to accelerate these iterative methods it is essential to optimize the SpMV kernel.

The SpMV kernel is notorious for its extremely low arithmetic intensity (the upper bound of the flop:byte ratio is 0.25, two flops for eight bytes on single precision floating point data type), and irregular memory access patterns [20]. The SpMV kernel is a pure memory bounded problem as shown in [21]. Although the peak floating point operations per second (FLOPS) of modern microprocessors are increasing rapidly, the maximum memory bandwidth is not improving at a similar pace. Therefore, the SpMV kernel usually performs poorly, achieving only 10% of the peak performance on single core cache based microprocessors [18]. Studies to improve performance of the SpMV kernel can be categorized into two directions: applying architecture specific optimizations, and applying new sparse matrix formats.

Interest in SpMV has increased with the advent of more powerful multi-core CPUs and many-core GPUs. Williams et al. [20] evaluates different optimization strategies on AMD Opteron X2, Intel Clovertown, Sun Niagara2, and STI Cell SPE. Bell and Garland [3] optimizes different SpMV kernels with different sparse matrix formats on Nvidia GPUs. Bordawekar and Baskaran [4] further optimizes the SpMV kernel with the Compressed Sparse Row (CSR) sparse matrix format on Nvidia GPUs. Choi et al. [6] implements Blocked Compress Sparse Row (BCSR) and Sliced Blocked ELLPACK (SBELL) formats on Nvidia GPUs.

Researchers have also proposed various sparse matrix formats with the goal of minimizing the memory footprint, and enforcing some regularity on the access pattern. Buluc et al. [5] uses the symmetric Compressed Sparse Block (CSB) and the bitmasked register block data structures to minimize the storage requirement of blocked sparse matrices. Monakov et al. [13] proposes the Sliced ELLPACK (SELL) format as an intermediate format between the CSR and the ELL format. Vázquez et al. [17] suggests the ELLPACK-R format that can preserve the data alignment requirement on Nvidia GPUs.

Different sparse matrices have different characteristics, and different microprocessors have different strengths. In order to achieve the best SpMV performance for a specific sparse matrix on a specific microprocessor, an autotuner is required to adjust the sparse matrix parameters and the platform parameters. The Optimized Sparse Kernel Interface (OSKI) library [18] is the state-of-the-art collection of sparse matrix operation primitives on single core cache based microprocessors. It relies on the SPARSITY framework [11] to tune the SpMV kernel. The major optimization strategy includes register blocking and cache blocking. Autotuning is used in [6,13] to find the best block sizes and the slice sizes of the given sparse matrices on Nvidia GPUs. Guo and Wang [10] also autotune the implementation parameters of the CSR SpMV implementation on Nvidia GPUs. Grewe and Lokhmotov [8] develop a code generator to generate CUDA and OpenCL code for SpMV kernels that can facilitate the autotuning process. However, the paper focuses on the generated CUDA code. For OpenCL code, only CSR SpMV results are presented. It is unclear how it will perform on other sparse matrix formats.

The micro-architectures of parallel microprocessors are increasing in their diversity. As a result, different hardware vendors develop their own languages to exploit parallelism in their architectures, such as SSE [15] and AVX [12] for x86, CUDA [14] for Nvidia GPUs, and Stream [1] for AMD GPUs. Fortunately, the leaders of the parallel computing industry have standardized parallel computations with OpenCL [16]. The goal of OpenCL is to make parallel code portable to heterogeneous platforms. With OpenCL, we can expect to develop an autotuner that can tune the SpMV performance on every existing parallel platform. This is the ultimate goal of the *cl pMV* project. However, the parallelization strategies on different platforms are different. In this paper, we show how the *cl pMV* framework can be used to tune the performance of SpMV on GPU platforms.

There are three major contributions of this work:

1. This is the first SpMV OpenCL work that covers a wide spectrum of sparse matrix formats (9 formats in total).

2. We propose a new sparse matrix format, the *Cocktail Format*, that takes advantage of the strengths of many different sparse matrix formats.

3. We have developed the *cl pMV* framework, the first framework that is able to analyze the input sparse matrix at runtime, and recommend the best representation of the given sparse matrix. It is also the first framework that can optimize the SpMV kernel across different GPU platforms.

The remainder of this paper is organized as follows. Section 2 introduces the new proposed *Cocktail Format*. Section 3 introduces the *cl pMV* framework in detail. Section 4 explains our platforms of choice, the supported 9 different sparse matrix formats, and the parallelization strategies on the target platforms. The experimental results are summarized in Section 5. Finally, the conclusions are given in Section 6.

2. THE COCKTAIL FORMAT

As stated in Section 1, many SpMV studies have developed novel sparse matrix formats. However, there is no one-size-fits-all solution. Every sparse matrix representation has its own strengths and weaknesses as explained in Section 4. The symmetric CSB, the bitmasked register block data structures in [5], the BCSR, and the SBELL data structures in [6] all assume dense blocks in the sparse matrix. The performance of the SELL format in [13] and the ELLPACK-R format in [17] relies on the variation of the numbers of nonzero per row in the sparse matrix. The experimental results in [3] also shows that the best SpMV results are heavily dependent on the choice of the sparse matrix format.

Based on the observation that different sparse matrix formats are good at different sparse matrix structures, we have developed the *Cocktail Format* to take advantages of different matrix formats. The *Cocktail Format* is a combination of many different sparse matrix formats. The *Cocktail Format* partitions a given matrix into several submatrices, each specialized for a given matrix structure. The trivial case finds a single best format for a given sparse matrix. The most complicated case is to partition the sparse matrix into many submatrices, and represent different submatrices using different formats. The list of sparse matrix formats in the *Cocktail Format* can be arbitrary. In *cl pMV*, we support 9 sparse matrix formats in 3 categories. The 3 categories and the 9 matrix formats are summarized as following, and will be further explained in Section 4:

- Diagonal based category: formats that store dense diagonals.
  - DIA: stores dense diagonals.
  - BDIA: stores a band of diagonals together.
- Flat category: formats that need a column index for every non-zero data point on the sparse matrix.
  - ELL: packs non-zeros into a dense matrix.
  - SELL: cuts the matrix into slices, and use different ELL settings for each slice.
  - CSR: the common compressed sparse row format.
  - COO: the common coordinate format.
- Block based category: formats that store dense blocks.
  - BELL: the blocked variant of the ELL format.
  - SBELL: the blocked variant of the SELL format.
  - BCSR: the blocked variant of the CSR format.

There exists works that partition a sparse matrix into many submatrices. However, the partitions are very restricted. Vuduc [19] partitions the sparse matrix into 2 to 4 submatrices with different dense block sizes. However, it only focuses on the BCSR format. If the number of dense blocks per row is regular, the BELL format will be a better choice. [3] partitions the sparse matrix into the ELLPACK portion and the COO portion. However, it does not take advantage of dense blocks in the matrices. The *Cocktail Format* is the first proposal that partitions the matrix into many different specialized regions.

3. THE CLSPMV FRAMEWORK

Based on the *Cocktail Format*, every sparse matrix can be partitioned into many submatrices. However, it is very challenging to find the best partitioning scheme of the given sparse matrix. Moreover, each sparse format can have many different parallelization strategies. Assuming the *Cocktail Format* is composed of k sparse matrix formats $f_1, f_2, \ldots, f_k$. $\bigcup_{i=1}^{k} f_i = F$. For a matrix format f_i, assuming there exists b_i implementations $p_{i1}, p_{i2}, \ldots, p_{i\ b_i}$. $\bigcup_{j=1}^{i} p_{ij} = P_i$. Let $t(A, f_i, p_{ij})$ be the execution time of the SpMV kernel using format f_i and implementation p_{ij} on matrix A. The matrix partitioning problem can be formulated as following:

- Problem *CMP* (*Cocktail Matrix Partitioning*): Given sparse matrix A, the k sparse formats in the *Cocktail Format*, the b_i implementations of format f_i, find k submatrices $A_1, A_2, \ldots, A_k$, and k implementations $L_1, L_2, \ldots, L_k$ such that $\sum_{i=1}^{k} A_i = A$, $L_1 \in P_1$, $L_2 \in P_2, \ldots, L_k \in P_k$, and the value of $\sum_{i=1}^{k} t(A_i, f_i, L_i)$ is minimized.

The CMP problem is a NP-complete problem. For a sparse matrix with n non-zeros, and the *Cocktail Format* with k formats, the size of the sample space is $O(k^n \times \max_{1 \leq i \leq k} b_i)$. If we allow single non-zero being covered by multiple formats, the sample space is even larger. Moreover, function $t(A, f_i, p_{ij})$ is nonlinear. The actual execution time will depend on the thread scheduler, system load, cache behavior, and many other factors.

3.1 Overall Structure of the clSpMV Framework

In addition to the CMP problem, we also need to compute the $t(A, f_i, p_{ij})$ function. When multiple implementations of a single sparse matrix format are available, most autotuners execute all implementations exhaustively to find the best implementation [8, 10, 13]. This strategy will give us the exact $t(A, f_i, p_{ij})$ value, but is very time consuming. For the *Cocktail Format*, the brute force search strategy will involve expensive reformatting the submatrices, because the submatrices may need to be adjusted frequently. The overhead is unacceptable. Some autotuners develop models of some specific architectures, and predict performance based on the models [6]. This strategy is applicable, but requires significant effort. For each platform we support, we need to develop its performance model. Then we need to apply the performance model on every implementation. Once a new platform is released, we need to go through the entire procedure again. For portability concerns, this is not the best strategy.

Following the philosophy of OSKI [18], the *cl pMV* framework is composed of two stages. The offline benchmarking stage and the online decision making stage. The goal of the offline benchmarking stage is to sample some performance data with different sparse matrix settings, and to provide a way of estimating the value of $t(A, f_i, p_{ij})$. The online decision making stage then solves the CMP problem.

3.2 The Offline Benchmarking Stage

The purpose of the offline benchmarking stage is to solve the performance approximation problem. Given a sparse matrix format f_i, and a corresponding implementation p_{ij}, the offline benchmarking stage will sample the execution time on different sparse matrix settings. The sparse matrix settings include matrix dimensions, total number of non-zeros, average number of non-zeros per row, variations of number of non-zeros per row, and so forth. The sample density controls the trade-offs between approximation accuracy and the offline benchmarking time. More data points with wider matrix settings will yield better approximation results, but it requires more offline benchmarking time. Given an arbitrary sparse matrix, the execution time can be approximated by interpolating nearby data points.

In our current implementation, we only consider matrix dimensions and average number of non-zeros per row, and benchmark on dense banded matrices. The performance benchmarking results for Nvidia GTX 480 and AMD Radeon 6970 are summarized in Figure 10 and Figure 11, and will be discussed in Section 5. When sampling on the matrix dimensions, we want to have representative data for the case that the processors are under-utilized most of the time, and the case that all processors are saturated. Therefore, we choose to use an exponential scale, ranging from 2^{10} to 2^{21}. When sampling on the number of non-zeros per row, we need to cover the case that the matrix is extremely sparse, to the case that every row has enough work to saturate all processors for a while. As will be discussed in Section 4, the parallelization strategies for different formats are different, so the sampling density of different formats are different. If the parallelization strategy is based on having different work items working on independent rows, having the number of non-zeros ranging from 1 to 64 should be enough. On the other hand, if the parallelization strategy is based on having multiple work items working on the same row, we will need hundreds to thousands non-zeros per row to saturate the processors.

For the 9 sparse matrix formats, we have 75 implementations in total, and we need to collect hundreds of sample points on each implementation. Including generating the sparse matrices with different dimensions and number of non-zeros per row, the offline benchmarking stages on both the Nvidia platform and the AMD platform take about half a day. However, it is a one-time cost. We only need to benchmark on a platform once, and the benchmarking results can be used to tune the performance of SpMV on as many sparse matrices as we want.

3.3 The Online Decision Making Stage

This stage solves the CMP problem by analyzing the input sparse matrix. We achieve this goal by collecting matrix features and enforcing partition policies.

Transforming a matrix from a format to another is very time and memory consuming. The *cl pMV* framework tries to explore the design space of 30 different formats (block based formats with different block dimensions are considered as different formats here), so it is infeasible to analyze the structures of all the matrix formats by converting to the formats. Instead we only collect statistical features that are representative of different matrix formats. When collecting features for diagonal formats, we maintain a histogram to count the number of non-zeros per diagonal. When collecting features for blocked formats, we maintain two histograms for each block dimension. One histogram counts the number of blocks per superrow. A superrow is defined on a blocked matrix as a submatrix of h rows, where h is the height of the block. The other histogram only counts the number of dense blocks per superrow. The definition of a dense block is given in the partition policies. The first histogram is used to estimate the execution time if we store the entire matrix using the blocked formats. The second histogram is used to estimate the execution time if we only store the dense blocks of the matrix using the blocked formats. When collecting features for flat formats, we maintain a histogram to count the number of non-zeros per row. The feature histograms are used to capture the characteristics of a matrix under different formats. In the partition policies, we also make our partition decisions based on the collected feature histograms.

The solution space of the CMP problem is enormous, so we use greedy policies to partition the sparse matrix. The policies are based on our analysis of the strengths and weaknesses of the formats as will discussed in Section 4. According to the 9 supported sparse matrix formats, we use the following policies:

- Priority of the categories: the priority of the 3 categories (the diagonal based category, the flat category, and the block based category) are decided by the maximum estimated performance of that category according to the current matrix settings explored in the offline benchmarking stage.

- Dense Diagonals: let g_d be the maximum GFLOPS the diagonal category can achieve under the current matrix settings. Let g_f be the maximum GFLOPS the flat category can achieve under the current matrix settings. A diagonal with dimension n_d is considered to be dense if its non-zero number e_d satisfies the following formula:

$$e_d > n_d \times \frac{g_f}{g_d}$$

- BDIA vs DIA: choose the maximum achievable GFLOPS in the following 3 cases: only using BDIA, only using DIA, using BDIA to represent thick bands and DIA to represent disjoint diagonals or thin bands.

- Dense Blocks: let g_d be the maximum GFLOPS the block category can achieve under the current matrix settings and the given block size. A block with size n is considered to be dense if its non-zero number e satisfies the following formula:

$$e > n \times \frac{g_f}{g}$$

- SBELL vs BELL vs BCSR: choose the maximum achievable GFLOPS in the following 3 cases: only using SBELL, only using BELL, only using BCSR.

- ELL and SELL vs CSR and COO: let the maximum achievable GFLOPS of ELL, SELL, CSR, and COO are g_{ELL}, g_{SELL}, g_{CSR}, and g_{COO}, respectively. Use CSR and COO if $m_c = \max(g_{CSR}, g_{COO}) > m_e = \max(g_{ELL}, g_{SELL})$. Otherwise, extract the ELL and SELL portion first, then represent the remaining non-zeros using CSR or COO.

- Extract ELL: let w be the ELL width (the definition of ELL width is given in Section 4), let c be the number of columns of the matrix, let $z(w)$ be the zero paddings when the ELL width is w, and let $e(w)$ be the non-zeros covered by the ELL format with width w. w is decided by solving the following problem:

$$\begin{aligned} \max \quad & w \\ s.t. \quad & (z(w) + e(w))/g_{ELL} < e(w)/m_c \\ & w \leq c \\ & w \in N \end{aligned}$$

The possible values of w is bounded by c, so we use brute force method to solve this problem.

- Extract SELL: the idea is the same as extracting ELL. The only difference is to consider the ELL width of each slice independently.

- ELL vs SELL: choose the one that has higher achievable GFLOPS value.

- CSR vs COO: the decision is based on the load balancing issue of CSR. Assuming there are u work groups in the CSR implementation. Let $nnz(i)$ be the number of non-zeros computed by work group i. For a matrix with n non-zeros, use the CSR format if the following rule is satisfied:

$$\frac{u \times \max\limits_{1 \leq i \leq u} nnz(i)}{g_{CSR}} < \frac{n}{g_{COO}}$$

- Merge small submatrices: merge a submatrix into another existing submatrix if such behavior results in better estimated performance.

The *Cocktail Format* is a superset over many single sparse matrix representations. Theoretically, the SpMV performance of the *Cocktail Format* should be at least the same as the SpMV performance of every format it covers. In practice, the performance depends on the policies of the *cl pMV* framework, and the accuracy of the estimated execution time (the value of the $t(A, f_i, p_{ij})$ function). This is a trade-off between analysis time and the SpMV performance. If we use more complicated policies and more accurate execution time estimates, we can find better matrix partitions, and achieve higher SpMV performance. However, it requires more analysis time. The analysis overhead of OSKI is about 40 SpMVs. *cl pMV* takes 1 SpMV for diagonal analysis, 20 SpMVs for block analysis of one block size, and 4 SpMVs for flat analysis.

Because the matrix analysis overhead is not trivial, *cl pMV* will be ideal for iterative methods that perform SpMV on a single sparse matrix for hundreds or thousands of times. Moreover, if the framework user is dealing with matrices with similar structures, one can perform full analysis on some exemplar matrices, and use the knowledge one gained from the experiments to speed up the analysis of future matrices. For example, if the exemplar matrices do not have any dense blocks, one can advise *cl pMV* to skip the analysis of the block based formats. To further reduce the analysis overhead, we can also follow the strategy used in [19]. Instead of analyzing the entire matrix, we can randomly sample the non-zeros of the matrix and make decision based on the samples. Since most of the analysis is based on counting (counting the number of non-zeros in a diagonal/in a block), we can also parallelize the analysis procedure to further reduce the overhead.

4. SPARSE MATRIX FORMATS AND PARALLELIZATION STRATEGIES ON GPU PLATFORMS

As introduced in Section 2 and Section 3, the *cl pMV* framework is an autotuner of the SpMV kernel across all platforms supporting OpenCL. It uses the *Cocktail Format* that combines many sparse matrix formats together. It also dynamically decides the representation of a given sparse matrix at runtime. The idea of the *Cocktail Format* and the idea of the *cl pMV* framework are platform independent. However, the optimized implementation of the SpMV kernel of every single format is platform dependent. In this section, we will discuss our platform of choice, and the optimized implementations of the 9 supported formats on the target platforms.

4.1 Target Platforms

The concept of the *Cocktail Format* is to take advantage of the strengths of a set of different sparse matrix formats. The idea of the *cl pMV* framework is to plug in many implementations of many SpMV kernels, performing analysis on the matrices, and to decide the best partition of the matrices. No matter what is the final decomposition of the matrices, the SpMV performance fully depends on the implementations of all supported formats. Because different platforms have different characteristics, there is no one-size-fits-all solution. To get the best performance, the implementations of the SpMV kernels should be platform dependent. Although many different platforms support OpenCL, they favor different parallelization strategies. For example, CPU based platforms favor coarse-grained parallelism, while GPU based platforms favor fine-grained parallelism. Because SpMV is a memory bounded problem [21], and modern GPU platforms have more memory bandwidth than DRAM, we decide to start by plugging in GPU-optimized SpMV kernels in our *cl pMV* framework. In the future, the *cl pMV* framework can support more platforms through more platform dependent implementations. Since we have decided to target GPU platforms, we will discuss the matrix formats and their corresponding parallelization strategies on GPU platforms in the following sections.

4.2 Diagonal Based Formats

$$B = \begin{bmatrix} 3 & 7 & 0 & 0 \\ 0 & 4 & 8 & 0 \\ 1 & 0 & 5 & 9 \\ 0 & 2 & 0 & 6 \end{bmatrix} \quad (1)$$

The diagonal based formats are the formats that capture dense diagonals. We will use matrix B in Equation (1) to explain the data structure of the formats in this category.

4.2.1 DIA Format

```
Offsets  =  [-2  0  1]
Data     =  [0  0  1  2,  3  4  5  6,  7  8  9  0]
```

Figure 1: The DIA format of matrix B.

As explained in [3], the diagonal (DIA) format is composed of two arrays, the Offsets array that stores the offsets of each diagonal, and the Data array that stores the dense diagonals. Figure 1 shows the DIA format of matrix B. The parallelization strategy of the DIA kernel is similar to [3]. Each work item is responsible for one row of the matrix. Because AMD platforms favor explicit vectorization by using the *float4* data type [2], we also implement the kernel that each work item being responsible for four rows of the matrix. Moreover, we implement kernels that use texture memory and kernels that do not use texture memory to store the multiplied vector. In the following we summarize the pros and cons of the DIA format:

- Pros: It does not need explicit column indices for each non-zero data. It has single-stride and aligned access on the matrix data. It also has single-stride access on the multiplied vector.
- Cons: It needs zero paddings in the Data array to ensure the lengths of all diagonals are the same. On

sparse diagonals, the zero padding overhead might be significant.

4.2.2 BDIA Format

```
Offsets  =  [-2  0]
BandPtr  =  [0  1  3]
Data     =  [0  0  1  2,  3  4  5  6,  7  8  9  0]
```

Figure 2: The BDIA format of matrix B.

The banded diagonal (BDIA) format is a variation of the DIA format. Instead of storing disjoint diagonals, it stores a band as a whole. This format is composed of three arrays. The Offsets array stores the offset of the first diagonal in each band. The BandPtr array stores the position of the first element of each band. In other words, the elements of band i are stored between BandPtr[i] and BandPtr[$i + 1$]. The Data array is exactly the same as the Data array in the DIA format. Figure 2 shows the BDIA format of matrix B.

The parallelization strategy of the BDIA is very similar to the DIA format. We have implementations where each work item is responsible for one matrix row, and have implementations where each work item is responsible for 4 matrix rows using the *float4* data type. The major difference between the DIA format and the BDIA format comes from the fact that the diagonals in a band are consecutive, so we can predict the vector sections that each work item is accessing. For example, assuming that the size of a work group is 128. Assuming that work item r to work item $r + 127$ in this work group are responsible for row r to row $r + 127$, respectively. Considering a band with d diagonals, and the offset of the first diagonal being o, the work item i will access vector elements $o+i, o+i+1, \ldots, o+i+d-1$. The entire work group will access vector elements $o+r, o+r+1, \ldots, o+r+127+d-1$. The consecutive vector section can be cached into the shared local memory. We have implemented kernels that use this caching strategy, and kernels that do not use this caching strategy. In the following we summarize the pros and cons of the BDIA format:

- Pros: It does not need explicit column indices for each non-zero data. It has single-stride and aligned access on the matrix data. It also has single-stride access on the multiplied vector. It can use shared local memory to cache the multiplied vector.
- Cons: It needs zero paddings in the data array to ensure the lengths of all diagonals are the same. On sparse diagonals, the zero padding overhead might be significant. Compared to the DIA format, it requires an additional BandPtr array.

4.3 Flat Formats

The flat formats are the formats that need explicit storage of the column indices of all non-zeros. We will use matrix B to explain the data structure of the formats in this category.

4.3.1 ELL Format

The idea of the ELLPACK (ELL) format [9] is to pack all non-zeros towards left, and store the packed dense matrix. Assuming the packed dense matrix has dimension $m \times n$. The ELL width of the matrix will be n, the width of the packed dense matrix. The ELL format is composed of two arrays, the `Col` array stores the column indices of all elements in the dense $m \times n$ matrix. The `Data` array stores the values of the dense $m \times n$ matrix. Figure 3 shows the ELL format of matrix B. The parallelization strategy is similar to [3]. Each work item is responsible for one row of the matrix. Considering platforms that favor explicit vectorization such as the AMD GPUs, we also have the implementation that each work item is responsible for 4 rows using the *float4* data type. Again, kernels using texture memory and kernels not using texture memory to cache the multiplied vector are all included. In the following we summarize the pros and cons of the ELL format:

```
Col  = [0 1 0 1, 1 2 2 3, 0 0 3 0]
Data = [3 4 1 2, 7 8 5 6, 0 0 9 0]
```

Figure 3: The ELL format of matrix B.

- Pros: The access pattern of the `Col` and the `Data` arrays is single-stride and aligned.
- Cons: Assuming the packed dense matrix has dimension $m \times n$, the ELL format needs zero paddings on every row that has number of non-zeros less than n. The zero paddings might introduce significant overhead. It requires random access on the multiplied vector.

4.3.2 SELL Format

```
SlicePtr = [0 4 10]
Col      = [0 1, 1 2; 0 2, 1 3, 3 0]
Data     = [3 4, 7 8; 1 2, 5 6, 9 0]
```

Figure 4: The SELL format of matrix B.

The sliced ELLPACK (SELL) format is proposed in [13]. The idea is to cut the original matrix into slices, and pack the slices into dense matrices with different dimensions. The SELL format is composed of three arrays. The `SlicePtr` array stores the beginning position of each slice. In other words, the elements of slice i are stored between `SlicePtr[i]` and `SlicePtr[i + 1]`. The `Col` array and the `Data` array are similar to the ELL format, storing the column indices and values of each element in the slices. Figure 4 shows the SELL format of matrix B with slice height 2. The semicolon in the array is used to separate different slices. Monakov et al. [13] uses autotuning to find the best slice height, reorders the matrix to further reduce the necessary zero paddings, and proposes the variable-height slice format. According to the experimental results in [13], the matrix reordering technique and the variable-height format only result in marginal improvements. Since these strategies might increase the complexity of the policies in the online decision making stage, current *cl pMV* does not include these approaches. Regarding the slice height, we develop kernels with slice heights equal to multiples of GPU alignment requirement (128 bytes). The parallelization strategy is the same as that in the ELL format. The only difference is that we need to cache the `SlicePtr` array in the local shared memory. In the following we summarize the pros and cons of the SELL format:

- Pros: The access pattern of the `Col` and the `Data` arrays is single-stride and aligned. It requires less zero paddings compared to the ELL format.

- Cons: It still needs zero paddings for each slice. The zero paddings might introduce significant overhead. It requires random access on the multiplied vector. It needs an additional `SlicePtr` array to store the slice positions.

4.3.3 CSR Format

```
RowPtr = [0 2 4 7 9]
Col    = [0 1, 1 2, 0 2 3, 1 3]
Data   = [3 7, 4 8, 1 5 9, 2 6]
```

Figure 5: The CSR format of matrix B.

The compressed sparse row (CSR) format is the most common sparse matrix format. It is composed of three arrays. The `RowPtr` array stores the beginning position of each row. In other words, the elements of row i are stored between `RowPtr[i]` and `RowPtr[i + 1]`. The `Col` array and the `Data` array are used to store the column indices and values of each non-zero. Figure 5 shows the CSR format of matrix B. [3] proposes two parallelization strategies for the CSR format. The scalar strategy will let one work item working on one row of the matrix. The vector strategy will let one warp of work items working on one row of the matrix. According to [3], the scalar strategy only outperforms the vector strategy when the number of non-zeros per row is small. However, when the number of non-zeros per row is small, the ELL format will be a better candidate. Therefore, we only have the vector strategy implemented in *cl pMV*. Again, implementations using texture memory and not using texture memory are both implemented. In the following we summarize the pros and cons of the CSR format:

- Pros: Need very few zero paddings.
- Cons: It might have unaligned access on both the `Col` array and the `Data` array. The access pattern on the multiplied vector is random. It might have load balancing problem if the number of non-zeros per row varies significantly.

4.3.4 COO Format

```
Row  = [0 0, 1 1, 2 2 2, 3 3]
Col  = [0 1, 1 2, 0 2 3, 1 3]
Data = [3 7, 4 8, 1 5 9, 2 6]
```

Figure 6: The COO format of matrix B.

The coordinate (COO) format explicitly stores the row indices. It is composed of three arrays. The `Row` array, the `Col` array, and the `Data` array store the row indices, the column indices, and the values of all non-zeros in the matrix, respectively. Figure 6 shows the COO format of matrix B. The parallelization strategy is the same as [3]. We are performing segmented reduction computation on the three arrays. However, the implementation in [3] requires three kernel launches. By padding zeros at the end of three arrays to match the work group size, we only need two kernel launches in our OpenCL implementation. In the following we summarize the pros and cons of the COO format:

- Pros: Need very few zero paddings. There is no load balancing problem. As shown in [3], it can deliver consistent performance regardless of the structure of the matrix.

- Cons: Has the worst memory footprint. It requires explicit indexing on both row and column indices. It needs random access on the multiplied vector.

4.4 Block Based Formats

$$C = \begin{bmatrix} 0 & 1 & 2 & 3 & g & h & i & j \\ 4 & 5 & 6 & 7 & k & l & m & n \\ 8 & 9 & a & b & o & p & q & r \\ c & d & e & f & s & t & u & v \end{bmatrix} \qquad (2)$$

The block based formats are the variations of the flat formats. Instead of storing each non-zero independently, we store a block contiguously. We are going to use matrix C in Equation (2) to show exemplars of block based formats. For block sizes, because AMD platforms always prefers the *float4* data type [2], while Nvidia platforms achieve similar performance on both *float* and *float4* data types, we decide to use block sizes that are multiples of 4. Moreover, when using texture memory to cache the multiplied vector, the OpenCL API always returns a *float4* value. If we do not use all the 4 elements in the returned value, memory bandwidth is wasted. Therefore, we choose block sizes with widths being multiples of 4. The block sizes supported by *cl pMV* are 1×4, 2×4, 4×4, 8×4, 1×8, 2×8, 4×8, and 8×8.

4.4.1 BELL Format

```
Col  = [ 0  0,   4   4   ]
Data = [ 0  1    2   3,   8  9  a  b,
         4  5    6   7,   c  d  e  f;
         g  h    i   j,   o  p  q  r,
         k  l    m   n,   s  t  u  v ]
```

Figure 7: The BELL format of matrix C. The block size is 2×4

The blocked ELLPACK (BELL) format is a variation of the ELL format. Instead of storing singular non-zeros, it stores a block of consecutive non-zeros. Each block only needs one column index, so the memory footprint is reduced. If the height of the block is larger than 1, the same data read from the multiplied vector can be reused across all the rows in the block. The BELL format is composed of two arrays. The Col array stores the column indices of the first elements from all blocks. The Data array stores the values of all blocks. Moreover, we need special arrangement to enforce single-strided memory access on the Data array. Because the 1×4 block is the smallest unit of all block sizes we support, the Data array is managed in a 2D fashion. The first dimension corresponds to the data of a 1×4 block. The second dimension corresponds to the number of 1×4 units in the block dimension. Figure 7 shows the BELL format of matrix C. The block size is 2×4, so there are two 1×4 units in the block. The Data array can be viewed as a 2×16 array. We store the first 1×4 unit of each block, and then store the next 1×4 unit of each block.

The parallelization strategy is similar to the ELL format. However, instead of letting one work item working on a row, we let one work item work on a superrow. Because the smallest unit of all block sizes is 1×4, we use the *float4* data

type in our implementation. In the following we summarize the pros and cons of the BELL format:

- Pros: We have single-stride data access on the Data array. The required memory storage of the column indices is reduced. If the block has height larger than 1, the segment of the multiplied vector can be cached in registers, and used across multiple block rows.
- Cons: It needs zero fillings in the blocks. It also needs zero paddings to make sure that the number of blocks per row are all the same. The fillings and paddings might introduce overhead.

4.4.2 SBELL Format

```
SlicePtr = [ 0   4   8   ]
Col      = [ 0   0,   4   4;   0   0,   4   4   ]
Data     = [ 0   1    2   3,   4   5    6   7,
             g   h    i   j,   k   l    m   n;
             8   9    a   b,   c   d    e   f,
             o   p    q   r,   s   t    u   v ]
```

Figure 8: The SBELL representation of matrix C. The block size is 1×4. The slice height is 2.

The sliced blocked ELLPACK (SBELL) format is proposed in [6]. Although the data arrangement in *cl pMV* is different from [6], the idea is similar. In *cl pMV*, the SBELL format is composed of three arrays. The SlicePtr array stores the beginning position of each slice. In other words, the elements of slice i are stored between SlicePtr[i] and SlicePtr[$i+1$]. The Col array stores the column indices of the first elements from all blocks. The Data array stores the values of all blocks. The data of a slice are stored consecutively. Like the case in the BELL format, in a slice, the data of a 1×4 unit are stored consecutively, and the data of multiple 1×4 units will be stacked into a large array. Figure 8 shows the SBELL format of matrix C, with block size 1×4 and slice height 2. Choi el al. [6] also rearranges the matrix rows to reduce the paddings of the SBELL format. Because we are using the SBELL format to represent only the portion of the matrix that is best for SBELL, we believe the remaining singular non-zeros will be taken care of by the flat formats. Therefore, we did not try to reorder matrix in our implementation. The parallelization strategy is similar to the BELL format. Each work item is responsible for a superrow. In the following we summarize the pros and cons of the SBELL format:

- Pros: We have single-stride data access on the Data array. The required memory storage of the column indices is reduced. If the block has height larger than 1, the segment of the multiplied vector can be cached in registers, and used across multiple block rows. It requires less zero paddings compared to the BELL format.
- Cons: It needs zero fillings in the blocks. It also needs zero paddings to make sure that the number of blocks per row in a slice are all the same. The fillings and paddings might introduce overhead. It also requires an additional SlicePtr array.

4.4.3 BCSR Format

The blocked compressed sparse row (BCSR) format is also discussed in [6]. The data arrangement in *cl pMV* is differ-

```
RowPtr  =  [   0    2    4    ]
Col     =  [   0    4,   0    4    ]
Data    =  [   0    1    2    3,   g    h    i    j,
               8    9    a    b,   o    p    q    r;
               4    5    6    7,   k    l    m    n,
               c    d    e    f,   s    t    u    v   ]
```

Figure 9: The BCSR format of matrix C. The block size is 2×4

ent, but the idea is similar. The BCSR format is composed of three arrays. The `RowPtr` array stores the beginning position of each superrow. In other words, the elements of superrow i are stored between `RowPtr`$[i]$ and `RowPtr`$[i + 1]$. The `Col` array stores the column indices of the first elements from all blocks. The `Data` array stores the values of all blocks. Like the case in the BELL format, the data of a 1×4 unit are stored consecutively, and the data of multiple 1×4 units will be stacked into a large array. Figure 9 shows the BCSR format of matrix C, with block size 2×4. The parallelization strategy is similar to the vector CSR strategy used in [3]. A warp of work items is responsible for a superrow. In the following we summarize the pros and cons of the BCSR format:

- Pros: The required memory storage of the column indices is reduced. If the block has height larger than 1, the segment of the multiplied vector can be cached in registers, and used across multiple block rows. It does not need to pad zero blocks at the end of each superrow.
- Cons: It needs zero fillings in the blocks. It might have unaligned access on the `Data` array. It might have load balancing problem.

5. EXPERIMENTAL RESULTS

We can evaluate the performance of *cl pMV* on different platforms, given the cross-platform capabilities of OpenCL. Nvidia and AMD are the major GPU vendors, so we evaluate the framework's performance on these two different platforms. Since both platforms achieve higher performance on single precision floating point data type, we use such data type in our experiments. In this section, we will first introduce the matrices we used for benchmarking, and then discuss the performance of *cl pMV* on Nvidia GTX 480 and AMD Radeon 6970. The code from our implementation is freely available at http://www.eecs.berkeley.edu/~subrian/clSpMV.html.

5.1 The Benchmarking Matrices

We use the 14 matrices in [20] as our benchmarking matrices. The same set of matrices is also used in [3,6,13]. The statistics of the matrices are summarized in Table 1. The # rows column, the # cols column, the # nnzs column, and the nnz/row column summarize the number of rows, the number of columns, the number of non-zeros, and the average number of non-zeros per row, respectively. Unfortunately, this set contains mostly regular matrices that are well-suited for single-format representation. Although the *cl pMV* is able to find the best single format to represent the matrices, it is hard to see how the *Cocktail Format* will further improve the performance. Therefore, we add 6 additional matrices from [7] in our benchmarking suite. We choose matrices

that has balanced portions of diagonals, dense blocks, and random singular non-zeros, matrices that has highly irregular distributions of the non-zeros, and matrices that have enough large number of non-zeros such that the overhead of launching multiple kernels will not be significant. The statistics of the 6 additional matrices are also summarized in Table 1.

Table 1: Overview of the sparse matrix benchmark.

Name	# rows	# cols	# nnzs	nnz/row
Dense	2K	2K	4M	2000
Protein	36K	36K	4.3M	119
FEM/Spheres	83K	83K	6M	72
FEM/Cantilever	62K	62K	4M	65
Wind Tunnel	218K	218K	11.6M	53
FEM/Harbor	47K	47K	2.37M	50
QCD	49K	49K	1.9M	39
FEM/Ship	141K	141K	3.98M	28
Economics	207K	207K	1.27M	6
Epidemiology	526K	526K	2.1M	4
FEM/Accelerator	121K	121K	2.62M	22
Circuit	171K	171K	959K	6
Webbase	1M	1M	3.1M	3
LP	4K	1.1M	11.3M	2825
circuit5M	5.56M	5.56M	59.5M	11
eu-2005	863K	863K	19M	22
Ga41As41H72	268k	268k	18M	67
in-2004	1.38M	1.38M	17M	12
mip1	66K	66K	10M	152
Si41Ge41H72	186k	186k	15M	81

5.2 Experimental Results on Nvidia GTX 480

We summarize the performance benchmarking results on the Nvidia GTX 480 platform in Figure 10. The x axis is the dimension of the matrix. On row 1 and 3, the y axis is the number of non-zeros per row. On row 2, the y axis is the number of dense blocks per superrow. The unit of the color-bar is in GFLOPS. Some performance numbers at the top-right corners are missing because the matrix storage size is larger than a pre-defined upperbound. Some performance numbers at the top-left corners are missing because the matrix is too dense to be considered as a sparse matrix. The performance of the diagonal based formats are benchmarked on dense diagonal matrices. Although each diagonal format has multiple implementations, the heat-map only shows the best achievable performance among all implementations. As expected, the performance increases with the increase in matrix dimension and number of non-zeros per row. The peak performance of the BDIA format is larger than that of the DIA format. When the number of non-zeros per row is very small, the DIA format will slightly outperform the BDIA format. The performance of the block based formats are benchmarked on dense diagonal blocked matrices. Due to the space limitations, only the performances of the 1×4 blocked matrices are included in the figure. Blocked matrices with other block dimensions follow the similar pattern. For the BELL and the SBELL formats, each thread is working on a superrow, we can get close to peak performance when there are 20 to 30 dense blocks per superrow. However, for the BCSR format, because a warp of work items is responsible for a superrow, we need more than 200 dense blocks per superrow to saturate the processors. The performance of the flat formats are benchmarked on dense diagonal matrices. The performance patters of the flat formats are very close to their blocked variations, but their peak achievable

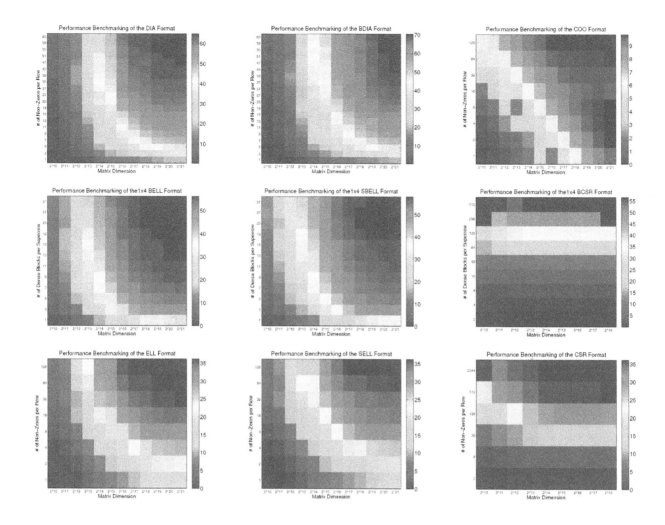

Figure 10: The performance benchmarking on the Nvidia GTX 480 platform. The x axis is the dimension of the matrix. On row 1 and 3, the y axis is the number of non-zeros per row. On row 2, the y axis is the number of dense blocks per superrow. The unit of the color-bar is in GFLOPS.

performances are significantly reduced. The COO performance is very stable while the dimension of the matrix is large enough. However, The peak achievable performance is the lowest among the 9 formats.

To evaluate the performance of *cl pMV*, we compare the performance with other implementations on the 20 benchmarking matrices. We first compare the performance with [3]. The released code of [3] is based on CUDA, and has SpMV kernels of the DIA, ELL, CSR, COO, and the HYB format. The HYB format in [3] is composed of ELL format and COO format. Therefore, the HYB format is a subset of our *Cocktail Format*. Although we also want to compare the performance of *cl pMV* with the SELL format in [13] and the blocked formats in [6], they did not release their code. As a result, we compare to our own OpenCL implementations of the SELL, BELL, SBELL, and the BCSR formats instead.

The experimental results are summarized in Table 2. The performance is measured by $\frac{2 \times nnz}{ExecutionTime}$ (GFLOPS). Sometimes using texture memory to cache the multiplied vector will result in higher performance, sometimes not. We evaluate both cases and only report the highest number in the

table. The NV HYB column lists the performance achieved by the CUDA code of the HYB format in [3]. The Best NV column lists the highest performance achieved among all the 5 implementations supported by [3], including DIA, ELL, CSR, COO, and HYB. The Best NV Format column lists the format that achieves the highest performance. The Best Single column lists the highest performance achieved among all single formats. Among all single format performances, the DIA, ELL, CSR, and COO performance is measured using the CUDA implementations from [3]; the BDIA, SELL, BELL, SBELL, and BCSR performance is measured using our own OpenCL implementations. Because we have multiple implementations of every single format as introduced in Section 4, such as different block sizes of the block based formats, only the highest performance numbers among all implementations are reported. The Best Single Format column summarizes the format that achieves the highest performance. The *cl pMV* column lists the performance achieved by *cl pMV* framework. The *cl pMV* Format column lists the decision made by *cl pMV*. The percentage numbers following the formats refer to the portions of non-zeros covered by the formats.

361

Table 2: The *clSpMV* performance on the selected 20 matrices, compared to implementations in [3], and all the single formats supported by *clSpMV* on Nvidia GTX 480. The highest achieved performance for each matrix is in bold.

Benchmark Name	NV CUDA			Single All		clSpMV	clSpMV
	NV HYB (GFLOPS)	Best NV (GFLOPS)	Best NV Format	Best Single (GFLOPS)	Best Single Format	clSpMV (GFLOPS)	clSpMV Format
Dense	8.38	32.63	CSR	**54.08**	BCSR	53.05	BCSR
Protein	15	23.17	CSR	35.84	SBELL	**35.86**	SBELL
FEM/Spheres	25.11	25.11	HYB	34.44	SBELL	**34.52**	SBELL
FEM/Cantilever	19.06	34.9	DIA	35.03	SBELL	**35.10**	SBELL
Wind Tunnel	25.07	25.07	HYB	**42.94**	SBELL	**42.94**	SBELL
FEM/Harbor	11.67	13.83	CSR	27.17	SBELL	**27.21**	SBELL
QCD	25.05	25.09	ELL	**30.93**	SELL	29.88	ELL
FEM/Ship	19.11	19.11	HYB	40.59	SBELL	**40.73**	SBELL
Economics	7.61	7.61	HYB	7.32	SELL	**10.59**	ELL(81%)COO(19%)
Epidemiology	24.02	24.02	ELL	25.36	SELL	**26.55**	ELL
FEM/Accelerator	9.35	9.35	HYB	**16.29**	SBELL	15.25	SELL
Circuit	7.35	7.35	HYB	7.72	SELL	**11.40**	ELL(84%)COO(16%)
Webbase	9.74	9.74	HYB	7.30	COO	**12.77**	ELL(64%)COO(36%)
LP	8.89	12.78	CSR	**12.99**	BCSR	12.98	BCSR
circuit5M	12.81	12.81	HYB	9.02	COO	**17.07**	DIA(9%)SELL(73%)COO(18%)
eu-2005	12.14	12.14	HYB	11.84	SBELL	**16.03**	SELL(85%)COO(15%)
Ga41As41H72	13.28	16.11	CSR	16.11	CSR	**16.80**	BDIA(18%)ELL(32%)CSR(50%)
in-2004	10.53	10.53	HYB	12.04	SBELL	**16.87**	SELL(79%)COO(21%)
mip1	10.8	18.92	CSR	18.92	CSR	**19.00**	SBELL(80%)SELL(17%)COO(3%)
Si41Ge41H72	12	17.68	CSR	17.68	CSR	**18.77**	BDIA(15%)ELL(27%)CSR(58%)

Table 3 summarizes the improvement ratios of *cl pMV* compared to all other implementations based on the performance numbers in Table 2. On average, *cl pMV* is 83% faster than the CUDA implementation of the proposed HYB format in [3]; 63.6% faster than all CUDA implementations in [3]; and 16.8% faster than all single formats supported by *cl pMV*.

For the 14 matrices from [20], most of them have regular structures, and the total number of non-zeros are small. Therefore, they favor single format representation. As shown in Table 2, most of the time *cl pMV* can successfully find the best single representations that match the results in the Best Single Format column. Even if the chosen format is not the same, the performance difference is very small. There are three matrices that the *cl pMV* matches the HYB format in [3]. The reason that *cl pMV* outperforms the CUDA implementation of the HYB format is due to three factors. First, the HYB format in [3] assumes that ELL format is 3 times faster than COO format. In contrast, *cl pMV* uses the more accurate offline benchmarking numbers. Second, the COO implementation in [3] needs three kernel launches, but *cl pMV* only needs two. Third, the number of work groups (or thread blocks) used by the COO implementation in [3] is fixed. However, *cl pMV* chooses the best work group size based on the offline benchmarking information.

For the 6 additional matrices from [7], *cl pMV* partitions them into many submatrices. *cl pMV* achieves significant improvements on three matrices (40% − 90% better performance), but small improvements on the other three matrices (0.4% − 6%). This is due to texture memory. Texture memory boosts CSR performance from 10 GFLOPS to 16 − 18 GFLOPS. Therefore, the data access pattern of CSR has very high hit rate on the texture cache. Though CSR performance is good, *cl pMV* achieves even greater performance. Theoretically, the *Cocktail Format* should outperform every single format. In practice, *cl pMV* uses good policies to find reasonable matrix partitions, represents them using the *Cocktail Format*, and achieves better performance compared to all other single formats.

Table 3: The improvement of *clSpMV* compared to the hybrid format in [3], the best implementations in [3], and the best single format implementations supported by *clSpMV*.

Benchmark Name	clSpMV Improvement		
	NV HYB	Best NV	Best Single
Dense	533.1%	62.6%	-1.9%
Protein	139.1%	54.8%	0.1%
FEM/Spheres	37.5%	37.5%	0.2%
FEM/Cantilever	84.2%	0.6%	0.2%
Wind Tunnel	71.3%	212.5%	0.0%
FEM/Harbor	133.1%	96.7%	0.1%
QCD	19.3%	19.1%	-3.4%
FEM/Ship	113.1%	123.4%	0.3%
Economics	39.2%	85.2%	44.7%
Epidemiology	10.5%	10.5%	4.7%
FEM/Accelerator	63.1%	97.5%	-6.4%
Circuit	55.1%	124.9%	47.6%
Webbase	31.1%	74.9%	74.9%
LP	46.0%	1.5%	-0.1%
circuit5M	33.3%	89.2%	89.2%
eu-2005	32.1%	82.4%	35.5%
Ga41As41H72	26.5%	4.3%	4.3%
in-2004	60.2%	86.8%	40.1%
mip1	75.9%	0.4%	0.4%
Si41Ge41H72	56.4%	6.2%	6.2%
Average	83.0%	63.6%	16.8%

5.3 Experimental Results on ATI Radeon 6970

The experimental settings on the AMD platform are very similar to that on the Nvidia platform. The performance benchmarking results are summarized in Figure 11. More performance numbers at the top-right corners are missing because the required matrix storage sizes of these sample points exceed 256 MB, the largest consecutive memory size allowed by the AMD OpenCL runtime. We are not aware of any SpMV project that targets AMD platforms, so we only compare *cl pMV* with the single format implementations supported by *cl pMV*. The results are shown in Table 4. On average, the performance of *cl pMV* is 43.3% higher than all the single format implementations. On the dense

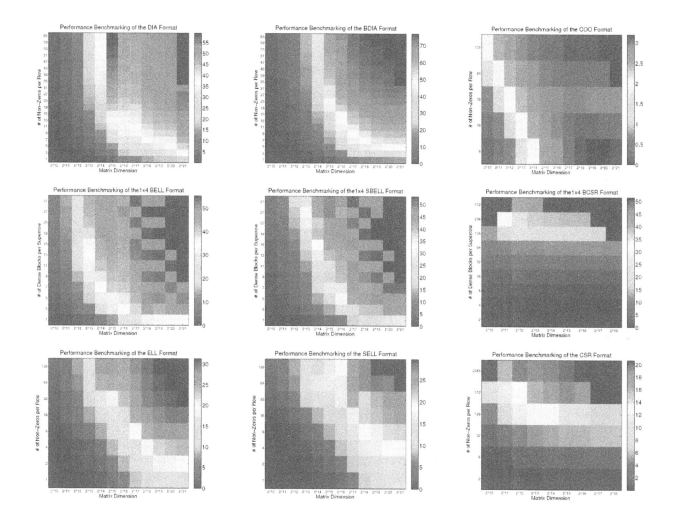

Figure 11: The performance benchmarking on the ATI Radeon 6970 platform. The x axis is the dimension of the matrix. On row 1 and 3, the y axis is the number of non-zeros per row. On row 2, the y axis is the number of dense blocks per superrow. The unit of the color-bar is in GFLOPS.

matrix and the LP matrix, *cl pMV* chooses the right single format, but the chosen block size is not optimal, and the performance is worse than the best single format. An offline benchmarking procedure with wider and denser sample points can give better execution time estimates, and enable *cl pMV* to find the best block size.

When comparing Table 2, Table 4, Figure 10, and Figure 11, we see that *cl pMV* makes decisions based on platform strengths. Since the BDIA format achieves significant higher performance than all other formats on the AMD platform, it favors BDIA format whenever possible. Moreover, the ELL performance on the AMD platform is significantly better than the COO performance, so the *cl pMV* increases the ratio of the ELL portion on the AMD platform.

6. CONCLUSION

In this paper, we have proposed a new sparse matrix format, the *Cocktail Format*, and the *cl pMV* framework, an OpenCL SpMV framework on GPU platforms. Theoretically, the *Cocktail Format* is a superset over all single sparse matrix formats, so its performance should be better than, or at least equal to all single formats. In practice, with the

help of the *cl pMV* framework, we have achieved 16.8% better performance than any single formats on the Nvidia GTX 480 platform, and 43.3% better performance on the AMD Radeon 6970 platform. Although solutions that are portable across diverse platforms generally provide lower performance when compared to solutions that are specialized to particular platforms, we achieved 83% better performance compared to the CUDA implementation of the proposed HYB format in [3]; and 63.6% better performance compared to all CUDA implementations in [3]. In conclusion, the *Cocktail Format* delivers better SpMV performance both theoretically and practically; *cl pMV* is a cross-platform framework that is able to choose the best representation of any given matrices, and deliver very high performance SpMV kernels.

7. ACKNOWLEDGMENTS

Thanks to Nadathur Satish for reviewing and commenting the clSpMV framework. Research supported by Microsoft (Award #024263) and Intel (Award #024894) funding, and by matching funding from U.C. Discovery (Award #DIG07 − 10227).

Table 4: The *clSpMV* performance on the selected 20 matrices, compared to all the single formats supported by *clSpMV* on AMD Radeon 6970. The highest achieved performance for each matrix is in bold.

Benchmark Name	Single All		*clSpMV*		Improvement
	Best Single (GFLOPS)	Best Single Format	*clSpMV* (GFLOPS)	*clSpMV* Format	
Dense	**46.85**	BCSR	41.85	BCSR	-10.7%
Protein	29.91	SBELL	**30.99**	BDIA(43%)SBELL(57%)	3.6%
FEM/Spheres	**31.85**	SBELL	31.44	SBELL	-1.3%
FEM/Cantilever	33.72	DIA	**35.93**	BDIA(90%)ELL(10%)	6.5%
Wind Tunnel	**35.23**	SBELL	34.51	SBELL	-2.0%
FEM/Harbor	**22.29**	SBELL	22.20	SBELL	-0.4%
QCD	24.84	SELL	**25.01**	BELL	0.7%
FEM/Ship	33.75	SBELL	**34.43**	SBELL	2.0%
Economics	4.87	SELL	**9.04**	ELL(88%)COO(12%)	85.9%
Epidemiology	22.51	ELL	**22.58**	ELL	0.3%
FEM/Accelerator	**15.83**	SELL	15.51	SELL	-2.0%
Circuit	3.06	COO	**8.40**	ELL(88%)COO(12%)	174.7%
Webbase	3.26	COO	**6.42**	ELL(70%)COO(30%)	97.0%
LP	**10.03**	BCSR	9.50	BCSR	-5.3%
circuit5M	3.21	COO	**8.06**	SELL(82%)COO(18%)	150.7%
eu-2005	3.01	COO	**8.19**	ELL(83%)COO(17%)	172.1%
Ga41As41H72	4.70	CSR	**6.93**	BDIA(18%)ELL(32%)CSR(50%)	47.5%
in-2004	3.04	COO	**7.42**	SBELL(28%)ELL(53%)COO(19%)	144.2%
mip1	8.27	BCSR	**8.28**	BDIA(20%)SBELL(62%)SELL(14%)COO(4%)	0.2%
Si41Ge41H72	10.81	SBELL	**11.10**	BDIA(15%)SBELL(85%)	2.7%
Average					43.3%

8. REFERENCES

[1] AMD. ATI Stream Computing User Guide, 2008.

[2] AMD. AMD Accelerated Parallel Processing OpenCL Programming Guide, 2011. http://developer.amd.com/zones/OpenCLZone.

[3] N. Bell and M. Garland. Implementing sparse matrix-vector multiplication on throughput-oriented processors. In *Proceedings of the Conference on High Performance Computing Networking, Storage and Analysis*, pages 18:1–18:11, New York, USA, 2009.

[4] R. Bordawekar and M. M. Baskaran. Optimizing sparse matrix-vector multiplication on gpus. *In Ninth SIAM Conference on Parallel Processing for Scientific Computing*, 2008.

[5] A. Buluc, and, S. Williams, L. Oliker, and J. Demmel. Reduced-bandwidth multithreaded algorithms for sparse matrix-vector multiplication. In *IEEE International Parallel and Distributed Processing Symposium (IPDPS)*, pages 721–733, may 2011.

[6] J. W. Choi, A. Singh, and R. W. Vuduc. Model-driven autotuning of sparse matrix-vector multiply on gpus. In *Proceedings of the 15th ACM SIGPLAN Symposium on Principles and Practice of Parallel Programming*, pages 115–126, New York, USA, 2010.

[7] T. A. Davis and Y. Hu. University of florida sparse matrix collection. 38(1), 2011. http://www.cise.ufl.edu/research/sparse/matrices.

[8] D. Grewe and A. Lokhmotov. Automatically generating and tuning gpu code for sparse matrix-vector multiplication from a high-level representation. In *Proceedings of the Fourth Workshop on General Purpose Processing on Graphics Processing Units*, pages 12:1–12:8, New York, USA, 2011.

[9] R. G. Grimes, D. R. Kincaid, and D. M. Young. Itpack 2.0 user's guide. Technical Report CNA-150, University of Texas, Austin, TX, USA, August 1979.

[10] P. Guo and L. Wang. Auto-tuning cuda parameters for sparse matrix-vector multiplication on gpus. In *International Conference on Computational and Information Sciences (ICCIS)*, pages 1154–1157, 2010.

[11] E.-J. Im, K. Yelick, and R. Vuduc. Sparsity: Optimization framework for sparse matrix kernels. *International Journal of High Performance Computing Applications*, pages 18:135–18:158, February 2004.

[12] Intel. Intel Advanced Vector Extensions Programming Reference. 2009. http://software.intel.com/en-us/avx.

[13] A. Monakov, A. Lokhmotov, and A. Avetisyan. Automatically tuning sparse matrix-vector multiplication for gpu architectures. *High Performance Embedded Architectures and Compilers*, pages 111–125, 2010.

[14] Nvidia. Nvidia cuda, 2007. http://nvidia.com/cuda.

[15] S. Thakkur and T. Huff. Internet streaming simd extensions. *Intel Technology Journal Q2*, 32(12):26–34, dec 1999.

[16] The Khronos OpenCL Working Group. OpenCL - The open standard for parallel programming of heterogeneous systems, 2011. http://www.khronos.org/opencl.

[17] F. Vázquez, G. Ortega, J. Fernández, and E. Garzón. Improving the performance of the sparse matrix vector product with gpus. In *IEEE 10th International Conference on Computer and Information Technology (CIT)*, pages 1146–1151, 2010.

[18] R. Vuduc, J. W. Demmel, and K. A. Yelick. Oski: A library of automatically tuned sparse matrix kernels. In *Proceedings of SciDAC 2005, Journal of Physics: Conference Series*, June 2005.

[19] R. W. Vuduc. *Automatic performance tuning of sparse matrix kernels*. PhD thesis, University of California, Berkeley, CA, USA, January 2004.

[20] S. Williams, L. Oliker, R. Vuduc, J. Shalf, K. Yelick, and J. Demmel. Optimization of sparse matrix-vector multiplication on emerging multicore platforms. In *Proceedings of the ACM/IEEE conference on Supercomputing*, pages 38:1–38:12, New York, USA, 2007.

[21] S. W. Williams, A. Waterman, and D. A. Patterson. Roofline: An insightful visual performance model for floating-point programs and multicore architectures. Technical Report UCB/EECS-2008-134, EECS Department, University of California, Berkeley, Oct 2008.

[22] S. Yousef. *Iterative methods for sparse linear systems*. Society for Industrial and Applied Mathematics, 2003.

Enabling and Scaling Matrix Computations on Heterogeneous Multi-Core and Multi-GPU Systems [*]

Fengguang Song
EECS Department
University of Tennessee
Knoxville, TN, USA
song@eecs.utk.edu

Stanimire Tomov
EECS Department
University of Tennessee
Knoxville, TN, USA
tomov@eecs.utk.edu

Jack Dongarra
University of Tennessee
Oak Ridge National Laboratory
University of Manchester
dongarra@eecs.utk.edu

ABSTRACT

We present a new approach to utilizing all CPU cores and all GPUs on heterogeneous multicore and multi-GPU systems to support dense matrix computations efficiently. The main idea is that we treat a heterogeneous system as a distributed-memory machine, and use a heterogeneous multi-level block cyclic distribution method to allocate data to the host and multiple GPUs to minimize communication. We design heterogeneous algorithms with hybrid tiles to accommodate the processor heterogeneity, and introduce an auto-tuning method to determine the hybrid tile sizes to attain both high performance and load balancing. We have also implemented a new runtime system and applied it to the Cholesky and QR factorizations. Our approach is designed for achieving four objectives: a high degree of parallelism, minimized synchronization, minimized communication, and load balancing. Our experiments on a compute node (with two Intel Westmere hexa-core CPUs and three Nvidia Fermi GPUs), as well as on up to 100 compute nodes on the Keeneland system [31], demonstrate great scalability, good load balancing, and efficiency of our approach.

Categories and Subject Descriptors

D.1.3 [**Programming Techniques**]: Concurrent Programming—*Parallel programming*; C.1.2 [**Processor Architectures**]: Multiple Data Stream Architectures (Multiprocessors)—*SIMD*

General Terms

Algorithms, Design, Performance

Keywords

Heterogeneous algorithms, hybrid CPU-GPU architectures, numerical linear algebra, runtime systems

[*]This material is based upon work supported by the NSF grants CCF-0811642, OCI-0910735, by the DOE grant DE-FC02-06ER25761, by Nvidia, and by Microsoft Research.

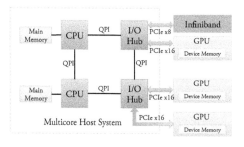

Figure 1: Architecture of a heterogeneous multi-core and multi-GPU system. The host and the GPUs have separate memory spaces.

1. INTRODUCTION

As the performance of both multicore CPUs and GPUs continues to scale at a Moore's law rate, it is becoming more common to use heterogeneous multi-core and multi-GPU architectures to attain the highest performance possible from a single compute node. Before making parallel programs run efficiently on a distributed-memory system, it is critical to achieve high performance on a single node first. However, the heterogeneity in the multi-core and multi-GPU architecture has introduced new challenges to algorithm design and system software.

Figure 1 shows the architecture of a heterogeneous multicore and multi-GPU system. The host system has two multicore CPUs and is connected to three GPUs each with a dedicated PCI-Express connection. To design new parallel software on this type of heterogeneous architectures, we must consider the following features: (1) Processor heterogeneity between CPUs and GPUs; (2) The host and the GPUs have different memory spaces and an explicit memory copy is required to transfer data between them; (3) As the performance gap between a GPU and its PCI-Express connection becomes larger, network is eventually the bottleneck for the entire system; (4) GPUs are optimized for throughput and expect a larger input size than CPUs which are optimized for latency [25]. We take into account these aspects and strive to meet the following objectives: a high degree of parallelism, minimized synchronization, minimized communication, and load balancing. In this paper, we present heterogeneous tile algorithms, heterogeneous multi-level block cyclic data distribution, an auto-tuning method, and an extended runtime system to achieve the objectives.

The heterogeneous tile algorithms build upon the previous tile algorithms [12], which divide a matrix into square

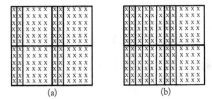

Figure 2: Matrices consisting of a mix of small and large rectangular tiles. (a) A 12×12 matrix is divided into eight small tiles and four large tiles. (b) A 12×12 matrix is divided into sixteen small tiles and two large tiles.

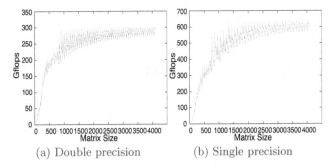

(a) Double precision   (b) Single precision

Figure 3: Matrix multiplication with CUBLAS 4.0 on an Nvidia Fermi M2070 GPU. (a) The max performance in double precision is 302 Gflops and the distance between the peaks is 64. (b) The max performance in single precision is 622 Gflops and the distance between the peaks is 96.

tiles and exhibit a high degree of parallelism and minimized synchronizations. A unique tile size, however, does not work well for both CPU cores and GPUs simultaneously. A large tile will clobber a CPU core, and a small tile cannot attain high performance on a GPU. Therefore, we have extended the tile algorithms so that they consist of two types of tiles: smaller tiles for CPU cores, and larger tiles for GPUs. Figure 2 depicts two matrices consisting of a set of small and large tiles. The heterogeneous tile algorithms execute in a fashion similar to the tile algorithms such that whenever a task computing a tile of [I, J] is completed, it will trigger a set of new tasks in [I, J]'s neighborhood.

We statically store small tiles on the host, and large tiles on the GPUs, respectively, to cope with processor heterogeneity and reduce redundant data transfers. We also place greater emphasis on communication minimization by viewing the multicore and multi-GPU system as a distributed memory machine. In order to allocate the workload to the host and different GPUs evenly, we propose a two-level 1-D block cyclic data distribution method. The basic idea is that we first map a matrix to only GPUs using a 1-D column block cyclic distribution, then we cut an appropriate size slice from each block and assign it to the host CPUs. Our analysis shows that the static distribution method is able to reach a near lower-bound communication volume. Furthermore, we have designed an auto-tuning method to determine the best size of the slice such that the amount of work on the host is equal to that on each GPU.

We design a runtime system to support dynamic scheduling on multicore and multi-GPU systems. The runtime system allows programs to be executed in a data-availability-driven model where a parent task always tries to trigger its children. In order to address the specialties of the heterogeneous system, we extend a centralized runtime system to a new one. The new runtime system is "hybrid" in the sense that its scheduling and computing components are centralized and resident in the host system, but its data, pools of buffers, communication components, and task queues are distributed for the host and different GPUs.

To our best knowledge, this is the first work to utilize multi-node, multi-core, and multi-GPU to solve fundamental matrix computation problems. Our work makes the following contributions: (i) making effective use of all CPU cores and all GPUs, (ii) new heterogeneous algorithms with hybrid tiles, (iii) heterogeneous block cyclic data distribution based upon a novel multi-level partitioning scheme, (iv) an auto-tuning method to achieve load balancing, and (v) a new runtime system to accommodate the features of the heterogeneous system (i.e., a hybrid of a shared- and distributed-memory system).

We conducted experiments on the Keeneland system [31] at the Oak Ridge National Laboratory. On a compute node with two Intel Westmere hexa-core CPUs and three Nvidia Fermi GPUs, both our Cholesky factorization and QR factorization exhibit scalable performance. In terms of weak scalability, we attain a nearly constant Gflops-per-core and Gflops-per-GPU performance from one core to nine cores and three GPUs. And in strong scalability, we reduce the execution time by two orders of magnitude from one core to nine cores and three GPUs.

Furthermore, our latest results demonstrate that the approach can be applied to distributed GPUs directly, and is able to scale efficiently from one node (0.7 Tflops) to 100 nodes (75 Tflops) on the Keeneland system.

2. MOTIVATION

2.1 Optimization Concerns on GPUs

Although computation performance can be increased by adding more cores to a GPU, it is much more difficult to increase network performance at the same rate. We expect the ratio of computation performance to communication bandwidth on GPUs will continue to increase, hence one of our objectives is to reduce communication. In ScaLAPACK [9], the parallel Cholesky, QR, and LU factorizations have been proven to reach the communication lower bound to within a logarithmic factor [7, 14, 17]. This has inspired us to adapt these efficient methods to optimize communication on the new multicore and multi-GPU architectures.

Another issue is that GPUs cannot reach their high performance until given a sufficiently large input size. Figure 3 shows the performance of matrix multiplication on an Nvidia Fermi GPU using CUBLAS 4.0 in double precision and single precision, respectively. In general, the bigger the matrix size, the better the performance is. The double-precision matrix multiplication does not reach 95% of its maximum performance until the matrix size $N = 1088$. In single precision, it does not reach 95% of its maximum until $N = 1344$. Unlike GPUs, it is very common for CPU cores to reach 90% of their maximum performance when $N \geq 200$ for matrix multiplications. However, solving a large matrix of size $N \simeq 1000$ by a single CPU core is much slower than dividing it into submatrices and solving them by multiple cores in parallel. One could still use several cores to solve the large

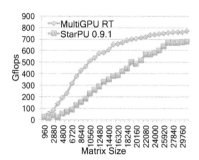

Figure 4: A comparison between our static scheduling approach and the dynamic scheduling approach of StarPU on Cholesky factorization (double precision) using three Fermi GPUs and twelve cores.

Algorithm 1 Heterogeneous Tile Cholesky Factorization

```
for t ← 1 to p do
    for d ← 1 to s do
        k ← (t - 1) * s + d /* the k-th tile column */
        Δ ← (d - 1) * b /* local offset within a tile */
        POTF2'(A_tk[Δ,0], L_tk[Δ,0])
        for j ← k + 1 to t * s /* along the t-th tile row */ do
            GSMM(L_tk[Δ+b,0], L_tk[Δ+(j-k)*b,0], A_tj[Δ+b,0])
        end for
        for i ← t + 1 to p /* along the k-th tile column */ do
            TRSM(L_tk[Δ,0], A_ik, L_ik)
        end for
        /* trailing submatrix update */
        for i ← t + 1 to p do
            for j ← k + 1 to i * s do
                j' = ⌈j/s⌉
                if (j' = t) GSMM(L_ik, L_tk[Δ+(j-k)%s*b,0], A_ij)
                else GSMM(L_ik, L_j'k[(j-1)%s*b,0], A_ij)
            end for
        end for
    end for
end for
```

matrix in a fork-join manner, but it will introduce additional synchronization overhead and more CPU idle time on multicore architectures [3, 11, 12]. Therefore, we are motivated to design new heterogeneous algorithms to expose different tile sizes suitable for CPUs and GPUs, respectively.

2.2 Choosing a Static Strategy

We have decided to use a static strategy to solve dense matrix problems due to its provably near-optimal communication cost, bounded tiny load imbalance, and lesser scheduling overhead [18]. In fact, the de facto standard library of ScaLAPACK [9] also uses a static distribution method on distributed-memory supercomputers.

We performed experiments to compare our static distribution strategy to an active project called StarPU [5] that uses a dynamic scheduling approach. Both our program and StarPU call identical computational kernels. Figure 4 shows the performance of Cholesky factorization in double precision on a Keeneland compute node with three Fermi GPUs and two Intel Westmere 6-core CPUs. Our performance data shows that the static approach can outperform the dynamic approach by up to 250%.

Dynamic strategies are typically more general and can be applied to many other applications. However, they often result in sophisticated scheduling systems that are required to make good decisions on load balancing and communication minimization on-the-fly. It is also non-trivial to guarantee that the on-the-fly decisions are globally good. Penalties for mistakes include extra data transfers, delayed tasks on the critical path, higher cache miss rate, and more idle time. For instance, we have found that StarPU sent critical tasks to slower CPUs to compute such that the total execution time has been increased. By contrast, a well-designed static method for certain domains can be proven to be globally near-optimal [18].

3. HETEROGENEOUS TILE ALGORITHMS

We extend tile algorithms [12] to heterogeneous algorithms and apply them to the Cholesky and QR factorizations. We then design a two-level block cyclic distribution method to support the heterogeneous algorithms, as well as an auto-tuning method to determine the hybrid tile sizes.

3.1 Hybrid Tile Data Layout

Heterogeneous tile algorithms divide a matrix into a set of small and large tiles. Figure 2 shows that two matrices are divided into hybrid rectangular tiles. Constrained by the correctness of the algorithm, hybrid tiles must be aligned with each other and located in a collection of rows and columns. Their dimensions, however, could vary row by row, or column by column (e.g., a row of tall tiles followed by a row of short tiles). Since we target heterogeneous systems with two types of processors (i.e., CPUs and GPUs), we use two tile sizes: small tiles for CPUs and large tiles for GPUs. It should be easy to extend the algorithms to include more tile sizes.

We create hybrid tiles with the following two-level partitioning scheme: (1) At the top level, we divide a matrix into large square tiles of size $B \times B$. (2) Then we subdivide each top-level tile of size $B \times B$ into a number of small rectangular tiles of size $B \times b$, and a remaining tile. We use this scheme because it not only allows us to use a simple auto-tuning method to achieve load balancing, but also results in a regular code structure. For instance, as shown in Fig. 2 (a), we first divide the 12×12 matrix into four 6×6 tiles, then we divide each 6×6 tile into two 6×1 and one 6×4 rectangular tiles. How to partition the top-level large tiles is dependent on the performance of the host and the performance of each GPU. Section 3.6 will introduce our method to determine a good partitioning.

3.2 Heterogeneous Tile Cholesky Factorization

Given an $n \times n$ matrix A, and two tile sizes of B and b, A can be expressed as follows:

$$
\begin{pmatrix}
\overbrace{a_{11} \ a_{12} \ldots A_{1s}}^{B} & \overbrace{a_{1(s+1)} \ a_{1(s+2)} \ldots A_{1(2s)}}^{B} & \ldots \\
a_{21} \ a_{22} \ldots A_{2s} & a_{2(s+1)} \ a_{2(s+2)} \ldots A_{2(2s)} & \ldots \\
\vdots & \vdots & \ddots \\
a_{p1} \ a_{p2} \ldots A_{ps} & a_{p(s+1)} \ a_{p(s+2)} \ldots A_{p(2s)} & \ldots
\end{pmatrix}, \text{ where}
$$

a_{ij} represents a small rectangular tile of size $B \times b$, and A_{ij} represents an often larger tile of size $B \times (B - b(s-1))$. Note that $\overbrace{a_{11} a_{12} \ldots A_{1s}}$ forms a square tile of size $B \times B$. We also assume $n = pB$ and $B > b$.

Algorithm 1 shows the heterogeneous tile Cholesky factorization. Here we do not differentiate a_{ij} and A_{ij} and always use A_{ij} to denote a tile. We also denote A_{ij}'s submatrix that starts from its local x-th row and y-th column, to its original

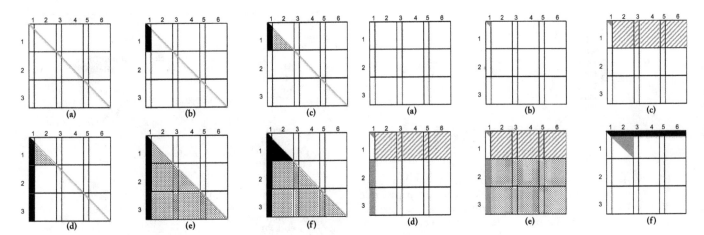

Figure 5: The operations of heterogeneous tile Cholesky factorization. (a) The symmetric positive definite matrix A. (b) Compute POTF2' to solve L_{11}. (c) Apply L_{11} to update its right A_{12} by GSMM. (d) Compute TRSMs for the two tiles below L_{11}. (e) Apply GSMMs to update all tiles on the right of the first tile column. (f) At the second iteration, we repeat performing (b), (c), (d), (e) on the trailing submatrix that starts from the second tile column.

Figure 6: The operations of heterogeneous tile QR factorization. (a) The matrix A. (b) Compute the QR factorization of A_{11} to get R_{11} and V_{11}. (c) Apply V_{11} to update all tiles on the right of A_{11} by calling LARFB. (d) Compute TSQRTs for all tiles below A_{11} to solve V_{21} and V_{31}. (e) Apply SSRFBs to update all tiles on V_{21} and V_{31}'s right hand side. (f) After the 1st iteration, we have solved the R factors on the first row with a hight equal to R_{11}'s size. At the second iteration, we repeat performing (b), (c), (d), (e) on the trailing submatrix.

bottom right corner by $A_{ij}[x, y]$. We denote $A_{ij}[0, 0]$ by A_{ij} for short. As shown in the algorithm, at the k-th iteration (corresponding to the k-th tile column), we first factorize the diagonal tile on the k-th tile column by POTF2', then solve the tiles located below the diagonal tile by TRSMs, followed by updating the trailing submatrix on the right side of the k-th tile column by GSMMs.

Figure 5 illustrates the operations to factorize a matrix of 3×3 top-level large tiles (i.e., $p = 3$), each of which is divided into one small and one large rectangular tiles (i.e., $s = 2$). The factorization goes through six ($= p \cdot s$) iterations, where the k-th iteration works on a trailing submatrix that starts from the k-th tile column. Since all iterations apply the same operations to A's trailing submatrices recursively, Fig. 5 only shows the operations of the first iteration.

We list the kernels called by Algorithm 1 as follows:

- POTF2'(A_{tk}, L_{tk}): Given a matrix A_{tk} of $m \times n$ and $m \geq n$, we let $A_{tk} = \binom{A_{tk1}}{A_{tk2}}$ such that A_{tk1} is of $n \times n$, and A_{tk2} is of $(m - n) \times n$. We also let $L_{tk} = \binom{L_{tk1}}{L_{tk2}}$. POTF2' computes $\binom{L_{tk1}}{L_{tk2}}$ by solving $L_{tk1} =$ Cholesky(A_{tk1}) and $L_{tk2} = A_{tk2}L_{tk1}^{-T}$.

- TRSM(L_{tk}, A_{ik}, L_{ik}) computes $L_{ik} = A_{ik}L_{tk}^{-T}$.

- GSMM(L_{ik}, L_{jk}, A_{ij}) computes $A_{ij} = A_{ij} - L_{ik}L_{jk}^T$.

3.3 Heterogeneous Tile QR Factorization

Algorithm 2 shows our heterogeneous tile QR factorization. It is able to utilize the same kernels as those used by the tile QR factorization [12], except that each kernel requires an additional GPU implementation. For completeness, we list them briefly here:

- GEQRT(A_{tk}, V_{tk}, R_{tk}, T_{tk}) computes $(V_{tk}, R_{tk}, T_{tk}) = \text{QR}(A_{tk})$.

- LARFB(A_{tj}, V_{tk}, T_{tk}, R_{tj}) computes $R_{tj} = (I - V_{tk}T_{tk}V_{tk}^T)A_{tj}$.

- TSQRT(R_{tk}, A_{ik}, V_{ik}, T_{ik}) computes $(V_{ik}, T_{ik}, R_{tk}) = \text{QR}\binom{R_{tk}}{A_{ik}}$.

- SSRFB(R_{tj}, A_{ij}, V_{ik}, T_{ik}) computes $\binom{R_{tj}}{A_{ij}}$ $= (I - V_{ik}T_{ik}V_{ik}^T)\binom{R_{tj}}{A_{ij}}$.

Similar to the Cholesky factorization, Fig. 6 illustrates the operations of the heterogeneous tile QR factorization. It shows a matrix of three tile rows by six tile columns. Again the algorithm goes through six iterations for the six tile columns. Since every iteration performs the same operations on a different trailing submatrix, Fig. 6 shows the operations of the first iteration.

3.4 Two-Level Block Cyclic Distribution

We divide a matrix A into $p \times (s \cdot p)$ rectangular tiles using the two-level partitioning scheme (in Section 3.1), which first partitions A into $p \times p$ large tiles, then partitions each large

---

Algorithm 2 Heterogeneous Tile QR Factorization

```
for t ← 1 to p do
    for d ← 1 to s do
        k ← (t - 1) * s + d  /* the k-th tile column */
        Δ ← (d - 1) * b  /* local offset within a tile */
        GEQRT(A_tk[Δ,0], V_tk[Δ,0], R_tk[Δ,0], T_tk[Δ,0])
        for j ← k + 1 to p * s  /* along the t-th tile row */ do
            LARFB(A_tj[Δ,0], V_tk[Δ,0], T_tk[Δ,0], R_tj[Δ,0])
        end for
        for i ← t + 1 to p  /* along the k-th tile column */ do
            TSQRT(R_tk[Δ,0], A_ik, V_ik, T_ik)
        end for
        /* trailing submatrix update */
        for i ← t + 1 to p do
            for j ← k + 1 to p * s do
                SSRFB(R_tj[Δ,0], A_ij, V_ik, T_ik)
            end for
        end for
    end for
end for
```

---

tile into s rectangular tiles. On a hybrid CPU and GPU machine, we allocate the $p \times (s \cdot p)$ tiles to the host and a number of P GPUs in a 1-D block cyclic way. That is, we statically allocate the j-th tile column to device P_x, where P_0 denotes the host system and $P_{x \geq 1}$ denotes the x-th GPU. We compute x as follows:

$$x = \begin{cases} ((\frac{j}{s} - 1) \mod P) + 1 & : \quad j \mod s = 0 \\ 0 & : \quad j \mod s \neq 0 \end{cases}$$

In other words, those columns whose indices are multiples of s are mapped to the P GPUs in a cyclic way, and the remaining columns go to all CPU cores on the host. Note that all CPU cores share the same set of small tiles assigned to the host, but each of them can pick up any small tile and compute on it independently.

Figure 7 (a) illustrates a matrix that is divided into hybrid tiles with the two-level partitioning scheme. Since we always map an entire tile column to a device, the figure omits the boundaries between rows. Figure 7 (b) displays how a matrix with twelve tile columns can be allocated to one host and three GPUs using the heterogeneous 1-D column block cyclic distribution. The ratio of the s-1 small tiles to their remainder controls the workload on the host and GPUs.

3.5 Communication Cost

We consider the hybrid CPU/GPU system a distributed memory machine such that the host system and the P GPUs represent $P + 1$ processes. We also assume the broadcast between processes is implemented by a tree topology in order to make a fair comparison between our algorithms and the ScaLAPACK algorithms [9].

On a system with P GPUs, and given a matrix of size $n \times n$, we partition the matrix into $p \times (p \cdot s)$ rectangular tiles. The small rectangular tile is of size $B \times b$ and $n = p \cdot B$. The number of words communicated by at least one of the processes is equal to:

$$\text{Words} = \sum_{k=0}^{p-1} (n - kB) B \log(P + 1) = \frac{n^2}{2} \log(P),$$

which reaches the lower bound of $\Omega(\frac{n^2}{\sqrt{P}})$ [20] to within a factor of $\sqrt{P} \log(P)$. We can also use a 2-D block cyclic distribution instead of the 1-D block cyclic distribution to attain the same communication volume as ScaLAPACK (i.e., $O(\frac{n^2}{\sqrt{P}} \log P)$ [7, 14]). The reason we use the 1-D distribution method is because it can result in less messages for the class of tile algorithms, and keep load balancing between processes as long as P is small. For distributed GPUs for which P is large, we indeed use a 2-D block cyclic distribution method.

The number of messages sent or received by at least one process in the heterogeneous tile QR (or Cholesky) factorization is equal to:

$$\text{Messages} = \sum_{k=0}^{p-1} (p - k) s \log(P + 1) = \frac{p^2 s}{2} \log(P).$$

The number of messages is greater than that of ScaLAPACK [7, 14] by a factor of $O(p)$, but the heterogeneous tile algorithms have a much smaller message size and exhibit a higher degree of parallelism. Note that we want to have a higher degree of parallelism in order to reduce synchronization points

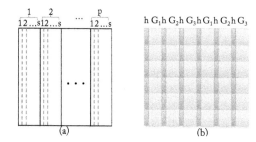

Figure 7: Heterogeneous 1-D column block cyclic data distribution. (a) The matrix A divided by a two-level partitioning method. (p, s) determines a matrix partition. (b) Allocation of a matrix of 6×12 rectangular tiles (i.e., p=6, s=2) to a host and three GPUs: h, G_1, G_2, and G_3.

and hide communications particularly on many-core systems [3, 4, 11].

3.6 Tile Size Tuning

Load imbalance could happen either between different GPUs, or between the host and each GPU. We use a 1-D block cyclic distribution method to achieve load balancing between different GPUs. Meanwhile we adjust the ratio of CPU tile to GPU tile to achieve load balancing between the host and the GPUs. We go through the following three steps to determine the best tile sizes to attain high performance:

1. We use the two-level partitioning scheme to divide a matrix assuming that we have known the top-level large tile size B (later we show how to decide B).

2. We use the following formula to estimate the best partition of size $B \times B_h$ to be cut off from each top-level tile of size $B \times B$:

$$B_h = \frac{\text{Perf}_{core} \cdot \#Cores}{\text{Perf}_{core} \cdot \#Cores + \text{Perf}_{gpu} \cdot \#GPUs} \cdot B$$

Perf_{core} and Perf_{gpu} denote the maximum performance of a dominant computational kernel (in Gflops) of the algorithm on a CPU core or on a GPU, respectively.

3. We start from the estimated size B_h and search for an optimal B_h^* near B_h. We wrote a script to execute the Cholesky or QR factorization with a random matrix of size $N = c_0 \cdot B \cdot \#GPUs$. In the implementation, we let $c_0 = 3$ to reduce the execution time. The script adapts the parameter of B_h to search for the minimal difference between the host and the GPU computation time. If the host takes more time than a GPU, the script decreases B_h accordingly. This step is inexpensive since the granularity of our fine tuning is 64 for double precision and 96 for single precision due to the significant performance drop when a tile size is not a multiple of 64 or 96 (Fig. 3). In all our experiments, it took at most three attempts to find B_h^*.

The top-level tile of size B in Step 1 is critical for the GPU performance. To find the best B, we search for the minimal matrix size that provides the maximum performance for the dominant GPU kernel (e.g., GEMM for Cholesky and SSRFB for QR). Our search ranges from 128 to 2048 and is performed only once for every new kernel library and every new GPU architecture.

Unlike Step 1, Steps 2 and 3 depend on the number of CPU cores and number of GPUs used in a computation. Note that there are at most ($\#Cores \cdot \#GPUs$) configurations on a given machine, but not every configuration is useful in practice (e.g., we often use all CPU cores and all GPUs in scientific computing applications). Our experimental results (Fig. 12) show that the auto-tuning method can keep the system load imbalance under 5% in most cases.

4. THE RUNTIME SYSTEM

We allocate a matrix's tiles to the host and multiple GPUs statically with the two-level block cyclic distribution method. After the data are distributed, we further require that a task that modifies a tile be executed by the tile's owner (either host or GPU) to reduce data transfers. In other words, the allocation of a task is decided by the task's output location.

Although we use a static data and task allocation, the execution order between tasks within the host or GPU is decided at runtime. For instance, on the host, a CPU core will pick up a high-priority ready task to execute whenever it becomes idle. We design a runtime system to support dynamic scheduling, automatic data-dependency solving, and transparent data transfers between devices. The runtime system follows the data-flow programming model, and drives the task execution by data-availability.

4.1 Data-Availability-Driven Execution

A parallel program consists of a number of tasks (or instances of compute kernels). It is the runtime system's responsibility to identify the data dependencies between tasks. Whenever identifying a parent-child relationship, it is also the runtime system's responsibility to transfer the parent's output data to the child.

Our runtime system keeps track of generated tasks in a list. The information of a task contains the input and output location of the task. By scanning the task list, the runtime system is able to find out which tasks are waiting for the finished task based on their input and output information. For instance, after a task is finished and has modified a tile [I,J], the runtime system searches the list for the tasks who want to read the tile [I,J]. Those tasks that were just found will be the children of the finished task. For instance, Fig. 8 shows that tasks 1-3 are waiting for the completion of task 0, and will be fired after task 0 is finished. In our runtime system, we use a hash table to speed up the matching between tasks by using [I,J] as hash keys.

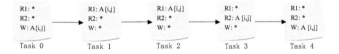

Figure 8: An example of solving data dependencies between tasks.

In essence, by solving data dependencies, our runtime system is gradually unrolling or constructing a DAG (Directed Acyclic Graph) for a user program. However, we never store the whole DAG or create it in one shot because whenever a task is finished, our runtime system can search for its children and trigger them on-the-fly dynamically. In addition, users do not need to provide communication codes to the runtime system, since the runtime system knows where the

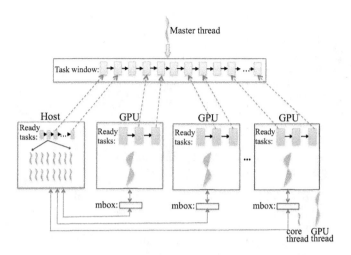

Figure 9: The runtime system for heterogeneous multicore and multi-GPU systems.

tasks are located based on the static allocation method, and will send data from the parent task to its children before actually notifying the children. This is why we call the scheme "data-availability-driven".

4.2 System Infrastructure

We extend the centralized-version runtime system of our previous work [29] to a new runtime system that is suitable for heterogeneous multicore and multi-GPU systems. The centralized-version runtime system works only on multicore architectures, and consists of four components (see Fig. 9 as if it had no GPUs):

- Task window: a fixed-size task queue that stores all the generated but unfinished tasks. It is an ordered list that keeps the serial semantic order between tasks. This is where the runtime system scans or searches for the children of a finished task.

- Ready task queue: a list of tasks whose inputs are all available.

- Master thread: a single thread that executes a serial program, and generates and inserts new tasks to the task window.

- Computational (core) threads: there is a computational thread running on every CPU core. Each computational thread picks up a ready task from the shared ready task queue independently whenever it becomes idle. After finishing the task, it scans the task window to determine which tasks are the children of the finished task, and fires them.

Figure 9 shows the architecture of our extended runtime system. Note that the master thread and the task window have not been changed. However, since the host and the GPUs own disjoint subsets of the matrix data and tasks, we allocate to the host and each GPU a private ready task queue to reduce data transfers. If a ready task modifies a tile that belongs to the host or a GPU, it is added to the host or the GPU's ready task queue accordingly.

We have also extended the computational threads. The new runtime system has two types of computational threads:

Table 1: Experiment Environment

	Host	Attached GPUs
Processor type	Intel Xeon X5660	Nvidia Fermi M2070
Clock rate	2.8 GHz	1.15 GHz
Processors per node	2	3
Cores per processor	6	14 SMs
Memory	24 GB	6 GB per GPU
Theo. peak (double)	11.2 Gflops/core	515 Gflops/GPU
Theo. peak (single)	22.4 Gflops/core	1.03 Tflops/GPU
Max gemm (double)	10.7 Gflops/core	302 Gflops/GPU
Max gemm (single)	21.4 Gflops/core	635 Gflops/GPU
Max ssrfb (double)	10.0 Gflops/core	223 Gflops/GPU
Max ssrfb (single)	19.8 Gflops/cores	466 Gflops/GPU
BLAS/LAPACK lib	Intel MKL 10.3	CUBLAS 4.0, MAGMA
Compilers	Intel compilers 11.1	CUDA toolkit 4.0
OS	CentOS 5.5	Driver 270.41.19

one for CPU cores and the other for GPUs. If a multicore and multi-GPU system has P GPUs and n CPU cores, the runtime system will launch P computational threads to represent (or manage) the P GPUs, and $(n-P)$ computational threads to represent the remaining CPU cores. A GPU computational thread is essentially a GPU management thread, which is running on the host but can invoke GPU kernels quickly. For convenience, we think of the GPU management thread as a powerful GPU computational thread.

We also create a message box for each GPU computational (or management) thread in the host memory. When moving data either from host to a GPU, or from a GPU to host, the GPU computational (or management) thread will launch the corresponding memory copies. In our implementation, we use GPUDirect V2.0 to copy data between different GPUs.

4.3 Data Management

It is the runtime system's responsibility to move data between the host and GPUs. The runtime system will send a tile from a parent task to its children transparently when the tile becomes available. However, the runtime system does not know how long the tile should persist in the destination device. Similar to the ANSI C function `free()`, we provide programmers with a special routine `Release_Tile()` to free tiles. `Release_Tile()` does not release any memory, but sets up a marker in the task window. While adding tasks, the master thread keeps track of the expected number of visits for each tile. Meanwhile the computing thread records the actual number of visits for each tile. The runtime system frees a tile if and only if: i) the actual number of visits is equal to the expected number of visits to the tile, and ii) `Release_Tile` has been called to free the tile. In our runtime system, each tile maintains three data members to support the dynamic memory deallocation: `num_expected_visits`, `num_actual_visits`, and `is_released`.

5. PERFORMANCE EVALUATION

We conducted experiments on a single node of the Keeneland system [31] at the Oak Ridge National Laboratory. The Keeneland system has 120 nodes and each node has two Intel Xeon hexa-core processors, and three Nvidia Fermi M2070 GPUs. Table 1 lists the hardware and software resources used in our experiments. The table also lists the maximum performance of `gemm` and `ssrfb` that are used by Cholesky and QR factorizations, respectively. In addition, we show our experiments with the Cholesky factorization using up to 100 nodes.

5.1 Weak Scalability

We use weak scalability to evaluate the capability of our program to solve potentially larger problems when more computing resources are available. In a weak scalability experiment, we increase the input size accordingly when we increase the number of CPU cores and GPUs.

Figure 10 shows the performance of Cholesky and QR factorizations in double precision and single precision, respectively. The x-axis shows the number of cores and GPUs used in the experiment. The y-axis shows Gflops-per-core and Gflops-per-GPU on a logarithmic scale. In each subfigure there are five curves: two "`theoretical peak`"s to denote the theoretical peak performance from a CPU core or from a GPU, one "`max GPU-kernel`" to denote the maximum GPU kernel performance of the Cholesky or QR factorization which is the upper bound of the program, "`our perf per GPU`" to denote our program performance on each GPU, and "`our perf per core`" to denote our program performance on each CPU core.

In the experiments, we first increase the number of cores from one to nine. Then we add one, two, and three GPUs to the nine cores. The input sizes for the double precision experiments (i.e., (a), (b)) are: 1000, 2000, ..., 9000, followed by 20000, 25000, and 34000. The input sizes for single precision (i.e., (c), (d)) are the same except for the last three input sizes which are 30000, 38000, and 46000. Figure 10 shows that our Cholesky and QR factorizations are scalable on both CPU cores and GPUs. Note that performance per core or performance per GPU should be a flat line ideally.

The overall performance of Cholesky factorization and QR factorization can be derived by summing up (perf-per-core $\times$ NumberCores) and (perf-per-gpu $\times$ NumberGPUs). For instance, the double precision Cholesky factorization using nine cores and three GPUs attains an overall performance of 742 Gflops, which is 74% of the upper bound and 45% of the theoretical peak. Similarly, the single precision Cholesky factorization delivers an overall performance of 1.44 Tflops, which is 69% of the upper bound and 44% of the theoretical peak. On the other hand, the overall performance of QR factorization is 79% of the upper bound in double precision, and 73% of the upper bound in single precision.

5.2 Strong Scalability

We use strong scalability to evaluate how much faster our program can solve a given problem if we are provided with additional computing resources. In the experiment, we measure the wall clock execution time to solve a number of matrices. Given a fixed-size matrix, we keep adding more computing resources to solve it.

Figure 11 shows the wall clock execution time of Cholesky and QR factorizations in both double and single precisions. Each graph has four or five curves, each of which corresponds to a matrix of a fixed size N. The x-axis shows the number of cores and GPUs on a logarithmic scale. That is, we solve a matrix of size N using 1, 2, ..., 12 cores, followed by 11 cores + 1 GPU, 10 cores + 2 GPUs, and 9 cores + 3 GPUs. The y-axis shows execution time in seconds also on a logarithmic scale. Note that an ideal strong scalability curve should be a straight line in a log-log graph. In Fig. 11 (a), we can reduce the execution time of Cholesky factorization in double precision from 393 seconds to 6 seconds for $N=23,040$, and from 6.4 to 0.2 seconds for $N=5,760$. In (b), we can reduce the execution time of QR factorization

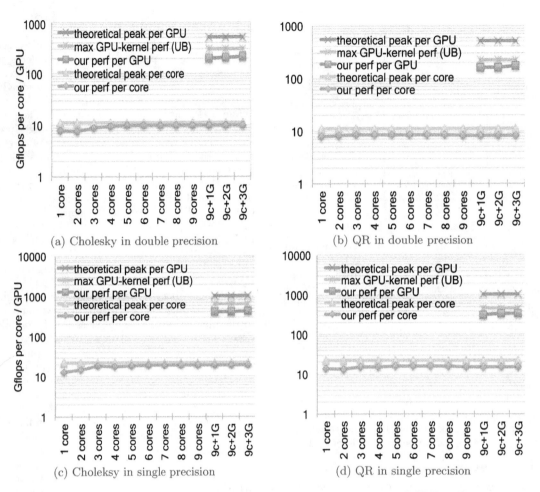

| (a) Cholesky in double precision | (b) QR in double precision |
| (c) Choleksy in single precision | (d) QR in single precision |

Figure 10: Weak scalability. The input size increases too while adding more cores and GPUs. The y-axis is presented on a logarithmic scale. OverallPerformance = (Perf$_{per\_core}$ * #cores) + (Perf$_{per\_gpu}$ * #gpus). Note that ideally the performance per core or per GPU should be a flat line.

in double precision from 1790 to 33 seconds for N=23,040, and from 29 seconds to 1 second for N=5,760. Similarly, (c) and (d) display performances for the single precision experiments. In (c), we reduce the execution time of Cholesky factorization from 387 to 7 seconds for N=28,800, and from 3.2 to 0.2 seconds for N=5,760. In (d), we reduce the execution time of QR factorization from 1857 to 30 seconds for N=28,800, and from 16 to 0.7 seconds for N=5,760.

5.3 Load Balancing

We employ the metric `imbalance_ratio` to evaluate the quality of our load balancing, where `imbalance_ratio` = $\frac{MaxLoad}{AvgLoad}$ [22]. We let computational time represent the load on a host or GPU. In our implementation, we put timers above and below every computational kernel and sum them up to measure the computational time.

Our experiments use three different configurations as examples: 3 cores + 1 GPU, 6 cores + 2 GPUs, and 9 cores + 3 GPUs. Given an algorithm, we first determine the top-level tile size, B, for the algorithm; then we determine the partitioning size, B_h^*, for each configuration using our auto-tuning method. We apply the tuned tile sizes to various matrices. For simplicity, we let the matrix size be a multiple of B and suppose the number of tile columns is divisible by the number of GPUs. If the number of tile columns is not

divisible by the number of GPUs, we can divide its remainder ($\leq$ NumberGPUs-1) among all GPUs using a smaller chunk size.

Figure 12 shows the measured imbalance ratio for double and single precision matrix factorizations on three configurations. An imbalance ratio of 1.0 indicates a perfect load balancing. We can see that most of the imbalance ratios are within 5% of the optimal ration 1.0. A few of the first columns have an imbalance ratio that is within 17% of the optimal ratio. This is because their corresponding matrices have too few top-level tiles. For instance, the first column of the `9Cores+3GPUs` configuration (Fig. 12 (c), (f)) has a matrix of three top-level tiles for three GPUs. We could increase the number of tiles to alleviate this problem by reducing the top-level tile size.

5.4 Applying to Distributed GPUs

Although this paper is focused on a shared multicore and multi-GPU system, we are able to apply our approach to distributed GPUs directly.

Given a cluster with lots of multicore and multi-GPU nodes, we first divide a matrix into $p \times p$ large tiles. Next, we distribute the large tiles to the nodes in a 2-D block cyclic way. Finally, after each node is assigned a subset of the large tiles, we partition each of the local large tiles into s-1

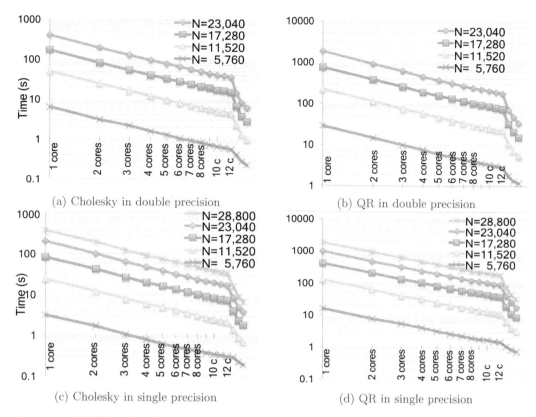

(a) Cholesky in double precision

(b) QR in double precision

(c) Cholesky in single precision

(d) QR in single precision

Figure 11: Strong scalability. An ideal strong-scalability curve were to be a straight line in a log-log graph. The last three ticks on the x-axis (after 12c) are: `11 cores + 1 GPU`, `10 cores + 2 GPUs`, and `9 cores + 3 GPUs`. The input size is fixed while adding more cores and GPUs. Both the x-axis and the y-axis are presented on a logarithmic scale.

small rectangular tiles and one large rectangular tile, and map them to the node's host and multiple GPUs using the two-level block cyclic distribution (in Section 3.4).

Our experiments with Choleksy factorization demonstrate that our approach can also scale efficiently on distributed GPUs. Figure 13 shows the weak scalability experiments on Keeneland using one to 100 nodes, where each node uses 12 cores and 3 Fermi GPUs. The single-node experiment takes as input a matrix of size 34,560. If an experiment uses P nodes, the matrix input size is $\sqrt{P} \times 34560$. The overall performance on 100 nodes reaches 75 Tflops (i.e., 45% of the theoretical peak). Also the workload difference on 100 nodes between the most-loaded node and the least-loaded node is just 5.2%. For reference, we show the performance of the Intel MKL ScaLAPACK library that uses CPUs only.

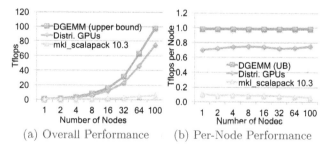

(a) Overall Performance (b) Per-Node Performance

Figure 13: Weak scalability of the distributed-GPU Cholesky factorization (double precision) on Keeneland.

6. RELATED WORK

There are a few dense linear algebra libraries developed for GPU devices. CUBLAS has implemented the standard BLAS (basic linear algebra subroutines) library on GPUs [26]. CULA [19] and MAGMA [30] have implemented a subset of the standard LAPACK library on GPUs. However, their current releases do not support computations using both CPUs and GPUs.

Quintana-Ortí et al. adapted the SuperMatrix runtime system to shared-memory systems with multiple GPUs [27]. They also recognized the communication bottleneck between host and GPUs, and designed a number of software cache schemes to maintain the coherence between the host RAM and the GPU memories to reduce communication. Fogue et al. presented a strategy to port the existing PLAPACK library to GPU-accelerated clusters [16]. They require that GPUs take most of the computations and store all data in GPU memories to minimize communication. Differently, we distribute a matrix across host and GPUs, and can utilize all CPU cores and all GPUs.

StarSs is a programming model that uses directives to annotate a sequential source code to execute on various architectures such as SMP, CUDA, and Cell [6]. A programmer is responsible for specifying which piece of code should be executed on a GPU. Then its runtime can execute the annotated code in parallel on the host and GPUs. Charm++ is an object-oriented parallel language that uses a dynamic load balancing runtime system to map objects to processors dynamically [21]. StarPU develops a dynamic load bal-

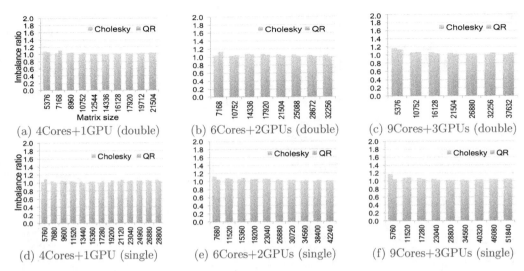

(a) 4Cores+1GPU (double) (b) 6Cores+2GPUs (double) (c) 9Cores+3GPUs (double)

(d) 4Cores+1GPU (single) (e) 6Cores+2GPUs (single) (f) 9Cores+3GPUs (single)

Figure 12: Load imbalance. The metric $imbalance\_ratio = \frac{MaxLoad}{AvgLoad}$. The closer the ratio is to 1.0, the better.

ancing framework to execute a sequential code on host and GPUs in parallel, and has been applied to Cholesky and QR factorizations [2, 1]. By contrast, we use a simple static distribution method to minimize communication and keep load balancing to attain high performance.

Fatica has implemented the Linpack Benchmark for GPU clusters by splitting the trailing submatrix into a single GPU and one CPU socket statically [15]. Yang et al. introduces an adaptive partitioning technique to split the trailing submatrix into a single GPU and individual CPU cores to implement Linpack [32]. Qilin is a generic programming system that can automatically map computations to GPUs and CPUs through off-line trainings [24]. Ravi et al. design a dynamic work distribution scheme for the class of Map-Reduce applications [28]. Differently, we use a heterogeneous multi-level 2D block cyclic method to distribute work to multiple GPUs, multiple CPU cores, and on many nodes.

There are also many researchers who have studied how to apply static data distribution strategies to heterogeneous distributed memory systems. Dongarra et al. designed an algorithm to map a set of uniform tiles to a 1-D collection of heterogeneous processors [10]. Robert et al. proposed a heuristic 2-D block data allocation to extend ScaLAPACK to work on heterogeneous clusters [8]. Lastovetsky et al. developed a static data distribution strategy that takes into account both processor heterogeneity and memory heterogeneity for matrix factorizations [23].

7. CONCLUSION AND FUTURE WORK

Designing new software on heterogeneous multicore and multi-GPU architectures is a challenging task. In this paper, we present heterogeneous algorithms with hybrid tiles to solve a class of dense matrix problems that have affine loop structures. We treat the multicore and multi-GPU system as a distributed-memory machine, and deploy a heterogeneous multi-level block cyclic data distribution to minimize communication. We introduce an auto-tuning method to determine the best tile sizes. We also design a new runtime system for the heterogeneous multicore and multi-GPU architectures. Although we have applied our approach to matrix computations, the same methodology and principles

such as heterogeneous tiling, multi-level partitioning and distribution, synchronization-reducing, distributed-memory perspective on GPUs, auto-tuning, are general and can be applied to many other applications (e.g., sparse matrix problems, image processing, quantum chemistry, partial differential equations, and data-intensive applications).

Our future work is to apply the approach to heterogenous clusters with an even greater number of multicore and multi-GPU nodes, and use it to build scientific applications such as two-sided factorizations and sparse matrix solvers. In our current approach, the largest input is constrained by the memory capacity of each GPU. A method to solve this issue is to use an "out-of-core" algorithm such as the left looking algorithm to compute matrices panel by panel [13].

Acknowledgments

We are grateful to Bonnie Brown and Samuel Crawford for their assistance with this paper.

8. REFERENCES

[1] E. Agullo, C. Augonnet, J. Dongarra, M. Faverge, H. Ltaief, S. Thibault, and S. Tomov. QR factorization on a multicore node enhanced with multiple GPU accelerators. In *IPDPS 2011*, Alaska, USA, 2011.

[2] E. Agullo, C. Augonnet, J. Dongarra, H. Ltaief, R. Namyst, J. Roman, S. Thibault, and S. Tomov. Dynamically scheduled Cholesky factorization on multicore architectures with GPU accelerators. In *Symposium on Application Accelerators in High Performance Computing*, Knoxville, USA, 2010.

[3] E. Agullo, B. Hadri, H. Ltaief, and J. Dongarrra. Comparative study of one-sided factorizations with multiple software packages on multi-core hardware. In *SC'09*, pages 20:1–20:12, 2009.

[4] K. Asanovic, R. Bodik, B. C. Catanzaro, J. J. Gebis, P. Husbands, K. Keutzer, D. A. Patterson, W. L. Plishker, J. Shalf, S. W. Williams, and K. A. Yelick. The landscape of parallel computing research: A view from Berkeley. Technical Report UCB/EECS-2006-183, EECS Department, University of California, Berkeley, December 2006.

[5] C. Augonnet, S. Thibault, R. Namyst, and P.-A. Wacrenier. StarPU: A unified platform for task scheduling on heterogeneous multicore architectures. *Concurr. Comput. : Pract. Exper., Special Issue: Euro-Par 2009*, 23:187–198, Feb. 2011.

[6] E. Ayguadé, R. M. Badia, F. D. Igual, J. Labarta, R. Mayo, and E. S. Quintana-Ortí. An extension of the StarSs programming model for platforms with multiple GPUs. In *Proceedings of the 15th International Euro-Par Conference on Parallel Processing*, Euro-Par '09, pages 851–862, 2009.

[7] G. Ballard, J. Demmel, O. Holtz, and O. Schwartz. Communication-optimal parallel and sequential Cholesky decomposition. In *Proceedings of the twenty-first annual symposium on Parallelism in algorithms and architectures*, SPAA '09, pages 245–252, 2009.

[8] O. Beaumont, V. Boudet, A. Petitet, F. Rastello, and Y. Robert. A proposal for a heterogeneous cluster ScaLAPACK (dense linear solvers). *IEEE Transactions on Computers*, 50:1052–1070, 2001.

[9] L. S. Blackford, J. Choi, A. Cleary, E. D'Azevedo, J. Demmel, I. Dhillon, J. Dongarra, S. Hammarling, G. Henry, A. Petitet, K. Stanley, D. Walker, and R. Whaley. *ScaLAPACK Users' Guide*. SIAM, 1997.

[10] P. Boulet, J. Dongarra, Y. Robert, and F. Vivien. Static tiling for heterogeneous computing platforms. *Parallel Computing*, 25(5):547 – 568, 1999.

[11] A. Buttari, J. Dongarra, J. Kurzak, J. Langou, P. Luszczek, and S. Tomov. The impact of multicore on math software. In *Proceedings of the 8th international conference on Applied parallel computing: state of the art in scientific computing*, PARA'06, pages 1–10, 2007.

[12] A. Buttari, J. Langou, J. Kurzak, and J. Dongarra. A class of parallel tiled linear algebra algorithms for multicore architectures. *Parallel Comput.*, 35(1):38–53, 2009.

[13] E. D'Azevedo and J. Dongarra. The design and implementation of the parallel out-of-core ScaLAPACK LU, QR, and Cholesky factorization routines. *Concurrency: Practice and Experience*, 12(15):1481–1493, 2000.

[14] J. W. Demmel, L. Grigori, M. F. Hoemmen, and J. Langou. Communication-optimal parallel and sequential QR and LU factorizations. LAPACK Working Note 204, UTK, August 2008.

[15] M. Fatica. Accelerating Linpack with CUDA on heterogenous clusters. In *Proceedings of 2nd Workshop on General Purpose Processing on Graphics Processing Units*, GPGPU-2, pages 46–51, 2009.

[16] M. Fogue, F. D. Igual, E. S. Quintana-ortŠ, and R. V. D. Geijn. Retargeting PLAPACK to clusters with hardware accelerators. FLAME Working Note 42, 2010.

[17] L. Grigori, J. W. Demmel, and H. Xiang. Communication avoiding Gaussian elimination. In *Proceedings of the 2008 ACM/IEEE conference on Supercomputing*, SC '08, pages 29:1–29:12, 2008.

[18] B. A. Hendrickson and D. E. Womble. The torus-wrap mapping for dense matrix calculations on massively parallel computers. *SIAM J. Sci. Comput.*, 15:1201–1226, September 1994.

[19] J. R. Humphrey, D. K. Price, K. E. Spagnoli, A. L. Paolini, and E. J. Kelmelis. CULA: Hybrid GPU accelerated linear algebra routines. In *SPIE Defense and Security Symposium (DSS)*, April 2010.

[20] D. Irony, S. Toledo, and A. Tiskin. Communication lower bounds for distributed-memory matrix multiplication. *J. Parallel Distrib. Comput.*, 64:1017–1026, September 2004.

[21] P. Jetley, L. Wesolowski, F. Gioachin, L. V. Kalé, and T. R. Quinn. Scaling hierarchical N-body simulations on GPU clusters. In *Proceedings of the 2010 ACM/IEEE International Conference for High Performance Computing, Networking, Storage and Analysis*, SC '10, pages 1–11, 2010.

[22] Z. Lan, V. E. Taylor, and G. Bryan. A novel dynamic load balancing scheme for parallel systems. *J. Parallel Distrib. Comput.*, 62:1763–1781, December 2002.

[23] A. Lastovetsky and R. Reddy. Data distribution for dense factorization on computers with memory heterogeneity. *Parallel Comput.*, 33:757–779, December 2007.

[24] C.-K. Luk, S. Hong, and H. Kim. Qilin: Exploiting parallelism on heterogeneous multiprocessors with adaptive mapping. In *Proceedings of the 42nd Annual IEEE/ACM International Symposium on Microarchitecture*, MICRO 42, pages 45–55, 2009.

[25] J. Nickolls and W. J. Dally. The GPU computing era. *IEEE Micro*, 30:56–69, March 2010.

[26] NVIDIA. CUDA Toolkit 4.0 CUBLAS Library, 2011.

[27] G. Quintana-Ortí, F. D. Igual, E. S. Quintana-Ortí, and R. A. van de Geijn. Solving dense linear systems on platforms with multiple hardware accelerators. In *Proceedings of the 14th ACM SIGPLAN symposium on Principles and practice of parallel programming*, PPoPP '09, pages 121–130, 2009.

[28] V. T. Ravi, W. Ma, D. Chiu, and G. Agrawal. Compiler and runtime support for enabling generalized reduction computations on heterogeneous parallel configurations. In *Proceedings of the 24th ACM International Conference on Supercomputing*, ICS '10, pages 137–146, 2010.

[29] F. Song, A. YarKhan, and J. Dongarra. Dynamic task scheduling for linear algebra algorithms on distributed-memory multicore systems. In *SC'09: Proceedings of the Conference on High Performance Computing Networking, Storage and Analysis*, pages 1–11, 2009.

[30] S. Tomov, R. Nath, P. Du, and J. Dongarra. MAGMA Users' Guide. Technical report, ICL, UTK, 2011.

[31] J. Vetter, R. Glassbrook, J. Dongarra, K. Schwan, B. Loftis, S. McNally, J. Meredith, J. Rogers, P. Roth, K. Spafford, and S. Yalamanchili. Keeneland: Bringing heterogeneous GPU computing to the computational science community. *Computing in Science Engineering*, 13(5):90 –95, sept.-oct. 2011.

[32] C. Yang, F. Wang, Y. Du, J. Chen, J. Liu, H. Yi, and K. Lu. Adaptive optimization for petascale heterogeneous CPU/GPU computing. In *Cluster Computing (CLUSTER), 2010 IEEE International Conference on*, pages 19 –28, sept. 2010.

An Optimized Large-Scale Hybrid DGEMM Design for CPUs and ATI GPUs

Jiajia Li, Xingjian Li, Guangming Tan, Mingyu Chen, Ninghui Sun
State Key Laboratory of Computer Architecture
Institute of Computing Technology, Chinese Academy of Sciences
Beijing, China
{lijiajia,lixingjian,tgm,cmy,snh}@ict.ac.cn

ABSTRACT

In heterogeneous systems that include CPUs and GPUs, the data transfers between these components play a critical role in determining the performance of applications. Software pipelining is a common approach to mitigate the overheads of those transfers. In this paper we investigate advanced software-pipelining optimizations for the double-precision general matrix multiplication (DGEMM) algorithm running on a heterogeneous system that includes ATI GPUs. Our approach decomposes the DGEMM workload to a finer detail and hides the latency of CPU-GPU data transfers to a higher degree than previous approaches in literature. We implement our approach in a five-stage software pipelined DGEMM and analyze its performance on a platform including x86 multi-core CPUs and an ATI $Radeon^{TM}$ HD5970 GPU that has two Cypress GPU chips on board. Our implementation delivers 758 GFLOPS (82% floating-point efficiency) when it uses only the GPU, and 844 GFLOPS (80% efficiency) when it distributes the workload on both CPU and GPU. We analyze the performance of our optimized DGEMM as the number of GPU chips employed grows from one to two, and the results show that resource contention on the PCIe bus and on the host memory are limiting factors.

Categories and Subject Descriptors

F.2.1 [**Numerical Algorithms and Problems**]: Computations on matrices; C.1.2 [**Multiple Data Stream Architectures (Multiprocessors)**]: Single-instruction-stream, multiple-data-stream processors (SIMD)

General Terms

Algorithms, Performance, Experimentation

Keywords

High Performance Computing, Heterogeneous Architecture, GPU, DGEMM

1. INTRODUCTION

Double-precision GEneral Matrix Multiplication (DGEMM) is a performance critical kernel found in many scientific and engineering applications. Since its performance depends on the underlying hardware, hardware vendors often provide optimized implementations of DGEMM within the BLAS library [8] (e.g. Intel MKL and AMD ACML). With the increasing popularity of GPUs and the high performance they make available, the need for GPU-optimized DGEMM implementations arise as well. DGEMM is compute-intensive and exhibits regular memory access patterns; these properties make it well suited to GPUs. Plenty of work in literature [7, 11–13, 16–23] has presented GPU-accelerated DGEMM implementations, but this work mostly focuses on optimizing computation and assumes that data can stay resident in GPU memory at all times. Unfortunately, realistic DGEMM applications exhibit operands that won't fit in GPU memory: this makes CPU-GPU data transfers crucial for the feasibility and the performance of the applications.

Optimizing CPU-GPU data transfers is non-trivial because these transfers occur through the PCIe bus, that acts as a bottleneck: while the GPU memory can deliver a throughput of up to 256 GB/s on a HD5970 GPU, a PCIe 2.0 bus only provides a peak bandwidth of 8 GB/s in each direction. Nakasato [13] reported that the floating-point efficiency of his DGEMM implementation decreased from 87% to 55% once he counted data-transfer overheads. A similar phenomenon occurs in the ACML-GPU library [2] released by AMD to accelerate BLAS functions on heterogeneous CPU-ATI GPU systems.

Software pipelining has been traditionally employed to mitigate the latency of data transfers through overlapping computation and transfers. Yang et al. [23] have developed a four-stage pipelined DGEMM algorithm that improves performance by about 30%. Automated approaches like the one proposed by Jablin et al. [10] simplifies the parallelization of workloads and handles CPU-GPU transfers automatically, but their performance still does not compare favorably with manual implementations. Therefore, the need is still strong to explore the full potential of manual data-transfer optimizations in critical kernels like DGEMM.

Multiple GPU boards can be employed on a single node in an attempt to achieve higher performance. We analyze the behavior of our optimized DGEMM on a multi-GPU node. The analysis shows that the performance increase comes at the cost of a lower floating-point efficiency (Section 4), even if there's no data dependence among tasks running on the different GPUs. We conclude that the efficiency loss is a result of resource contention on both the PCIe bus and host memory. We believe that our conclusions should guide the configuration and dimensioning of future CPU-GPU systems intended to tackle workloads similar to DGEMM with a high degree of efficiency.

In this paper we examine performance tuning of DGEMM on a heterogeneous system comprising x86 multi-core CPUs and ATI Cypress GPU chips. We develop a new software-pipelined design of the DGEMM kernel by identifying design choices that are performance-critical on the particular ATI GPU architecture, specifically the choices of memory addressing modes and the data placement in memory.

The main contributions of this paper are:

- We develop a new software pipelining design for the DGEMM kernel running on CPU-GPU heterogeneous architectures. The new design reduces the overheads of data movement by using the image addressing mode with low latency for dumping registers to GPU memory and employing fine-grained pipelining to hide CPU-GPU data transfer latencies. We generalize our five-stage design so that it can be employed in a general heterogeneous programming framework.

- We provide an optimized implementation of our design and evaluate its performance. Experimental results show that our implementation achieves 408 GFLOPS (88% efficiency) on one Cypress GPU chip, 758 GFLOPS (82% efficiency) on two Cypress GPU chips, and 844 GFLOPS (80% efficiency) on a system comprising two Intel Westmere-EP CPUs and one ATI $Radeon^{TM}$ HD5970 GPU. Compared with AMD's ACML-GPU v1.1.2, our DGEMM implementation improves performance by more than 2 times.

- We report a comprehensive experimental analysis showing that the major scaling bottleneck when multiple GPU chips are used is resource contention, especially PCIe contention and host memory contention. We show that it is difficult to further decrease the overheads by software means. We present recommendations on how to relax the resource contention in future hardware designs, that are beneficial on any heterogeneous architectures that integrate multiple CPUs and PCIe-attached accelerators.

The rest of the paper is organized as follows. In Section 2, we quantitatively analyze previous DGEMM implementation on the heterogeneous architecture. Our new software-pipelining algorithm is proposed in Section 3. Section 4 gives the performance results and the detailed analysis. Related work is presented in Section 5, and the conclusions in Section 6.

2. BACKGROUND AND MOTIVATION

2.1 The ATI GPU Architecture

The architecture we target in this work is a heterogeneous system based on ATI $Radeon^{TM}$ HD5970 GPU, which integrates two Cypress chips into one card. The Cypress chip contains several hundreds of computing units, a controller unit named ultra-threaded dispatch processor, memory controllers and DMA engines. The microarchitecture is customized with single-instruction-multiple-data (SIMD) and very long instruction word (VLIW) for high throughput of floating-point operations. It offers a peak performance

of 464 GFLOPS with double-precision floating-point operations at 725 MHz.

A notable feature related to software-pipelined design is its memory hierarchy exposed in ATI Compute Abstraction Layer (CAL) [4] system software stack. Figure 1 depicts the memory hierarchy in a CAL system on a heterogeneous CPU-ATI GPU architecture, i.e. local memory, remote memory and application space. The local memory is the high-speed memory on board of the GPU. The remote memory is the set of regions of host memory that are visible to the GPU. Both remote and local memory can be directly accessed by a GPU kernel, but with different latencies. A GPU kernel can directly write data from GPU registers into remote memory using a store instruction, although this operation has a much higher latency than a store on local memory. Remote memory is partitioned into a cached and an uncached portion. For example, in the ATI Stream SDK 2.2, the CAL system reserves 500 MB of cached memory and 1788 MB of uncached memory on an ATI $Radeon^{TM}$ HD5970 device. A good software-pipelining algorithm must place the shared data between CPU and GPU in carefully selected memory regions.

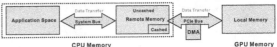

Figure 1: Memory hierarchy in CAL system between CPU and ATI GPU

2.2 Software Pipelining in DGEMM

In this section we describe an algorithmic framework for large scale DGEMM on a heterogeneous CPU-ATI GPU system, with initial data resident in CPU application space. DGEMM calculates $C = alpha \times A \times B + beta \times C$, where A, B, C are $m \times k, k \times n, m \times n$ matrices respectively. Since in most DGEMM applications the three matrices are too large to be held in GPU memory, they are partitioned into multiple sub-matrices to perform multiplication block-by-block. We assume the three matrices are partitioned as $A = \{A_1, A_2, \cdots, A_p\}$, $B = \{B_1, B_2, \cdots, B_q\}$, $C = \{C_1, C_2, \cdots, C_{p \times q}\}$, where p and q depend on GPU memory size. For simplicity of presentation, we take p=q=2 for example and the matrix multiplication is illustrated in Figure 2. The partition results in four independent sub-matrices of C which are calculated in parallel: $C_1 = A_1 B_1, C_2 = A_1 B_2, C_3 = A_2 B_1, C_4 = A_2 B_2$. For each sub-matrix multiplication we load its dependent sub-matrices A and B into GPU memory, then DGEMM kernel may further divide them into smaller ones for faster multiplication [6, 9, 14, 16, 17, 21] (e.g. register blocking). Yang et al. [23] developed a software-pipelining algorithm characterized by four-stage pipelining: $load1 \rightarrow load2 \rightarrow mult \rightarrow store$. Table 1 explains the related action of each pipelined stage.

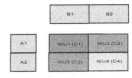

Figure 2: Work units split when p=q=2

Algorithm 1 outlines the four-stage software-pipelining DGEMM algorithm in [23]. The algorithm contains two stages for loading data to GPU local memory (*load1*, *load2*)

Table 1: The four pipelined stages in [23]

load1	copy both A and B from application space to remote memory
load2	copy both A and B from remote memory to local memory
mult	calculate C on GPU device and output them to remote memory
store	copy C from remote memory to application space

and one stage for storing data back to CPU application space (*store*). As data are arranged in different memory regions, the current software-pipelining algorithm loads input matrices A and B into cached remote memory. Thus data reuse can be exploited for executing multiplications. Take the example in Figure 2, if we schedule the execution of work units using the "bounce corner turn" [23], that is in the following order: $WU_1 = \{C_1 = A_1B_1\}, WU_2 = \{C_2 = A_1B_2\}, WU_3 = \{C_4 = A_2B_2\}, WU_4 = \{C_3 = A_2B_1\}$. Every two consecutive work units reuse one of the two input sub-matrices. The resulting sub-matrices of C are allocated to uncached remote memory because a finer blocked matrix multiplication algorithm can exploit register reuse, so that the results are written back for only one time. Another optimization is the usage of double-buffering strategy for overlapping multiplication with the write-back process. The algorithm partitions sub-matrices of C into many smaller blocks and writes two buffers in remote memory in an interleaved way. For each loop j in line 6-9 of Algorithm 1, the *store* dumps one buffer of a block $C_{i,j}$ into application space, while the *mult* calculates the next block $C_{i,j+1}$ and fills the results into the other buffer. Since the *mult* kernel is executed on GPU device in a non-blocking way, it proceeds in parallel with the *store* in every iteration.

Algorithm 1 Four-stage software-pipelining DGEMM algorithm in [23]

Partition: $A = \{A_1, A_2, \cdots, A_p\}, B = \{B_1, B_2, \cdots, B_q\}$,
$\qquad\qquad C = \{C_1, C_2, \cdots, C_{p \times q}\}$
Work units: $WU = \{C_1 = A_1 \times B_1, C_2 = A_1 \times B_2, ...\}$
$C_{i,j}$: *the sub-matrices of C_j*
//
1. bind remote memory for sub-matrices A,B,C
   //*pre-processing*
Allocate workunits using the "bounce corner turn" for exploiting data reuse
//*the for-loop is pipelined*
2. **for** each workunit wu_i **do**   //$i = 1, 2, \cdots, p \times q$
   //*load1*
3. copy either A_i or B_i from application space to remote memory
   //*load2*
4. copy either A_i or B_i from remote memory to local memory
   //*mult*
5. calculate $C_{i,1}$ on GPU device and output it to remote memory
6. **for** each block $C_{i,j}$ **do**   //$j = 2, 3, \cdots$
   //*store*
7. copy $C_{i,j-1}$ from remote memory to application space
   (also multiplied by beta)
   //*mult*
8. calculate $C_{i,j}$ on GPU device and output it to remote memory
9. **endfor**
   //*store*
10. copy the last $C_{i,j}$ from remote memory to application space
    (also multiplied by beta)
11. **endfor**

2.3 Motivation

We implement four-stage pipelined algorithm by modifying ACML-GPU library and profiling its execution on the heterogeneous CPU-ATI $Radeon^{TM}$ HD5970 GPU architecture. Figure 3 summarizes the time percentage of each stage in four-stage pipelined algorithm. As the time distributions of different problem scales show similar behavior, we take k=2048 as an example, and give the matrix order m (=n) in x axis. We learn that the *mult* kernel occupies the most percentage (about 70%) while the sum of the other three data transfer stages takes up about 30%. The experiments from both [23] and our implementation show that the four-stage software-pipelining algorithm improves performance

by about 30%. Intuitively, the overheads of data transfers should be totally hidden by multiplication kernel during the course of the pipelining execution. Our analysis of the pipelining execution reveals an extra data transfer which was not considered in previous software-pipelined designs.

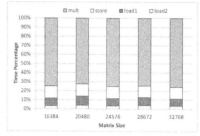

Figure 3: Time percentage of four-stage pipelining algorithm

The resources employed by the algorithm are host memory, GPU and PCIe bus. Operations on these three resources can typically proceed in parallel. Figure 4 outlines the resource usage in each stage of four-stage pipelining. Both *load1* and *store* employ the host memory, and *load2* only needs the PCIe bus to transfer data. The *mult* kernel performs DGEMM on the GPU, and then outputs the results to remote memory through the PCIe bus. The resource usage in each stage suggests straightforward software pipelining that overlaps the data transfers (*load1*, *load2*, *store*) with the *mult* kernel. This pipelining seems beneficial because the *mult* kernel becomes the bottleneck, as Figure 3 shows.

Note that the *mult* kernel in the four-stage pipelining directly stores data from registers to remote memory, causing data transfers through the PCIe bus at the end of each kernel execution. Although these store operations occur only once per kernel invocation, the total amount of data they transferred may be larger than that in *load2*. This happens for example in the DGEMM benchmark included in LINPACK [3] where A, B and C are matrices of size $m \times k, k \times n, m \times n$ respectively, and k is much smaller than both m and n. Therefore, the size of $C(m \times n)$ is larger than the size of A and B $(k \times (m + n))$. Besides, as described in Section 2.2 the latency of the data transfers in *load2* is reduced by exploiting data reuse. We profile the *mult* kernel taken from the four-stage pipelined algorithm and find its floating-point efficiency tops approximately at 50%, which is also observed in ACML-GPU v1.1.2 [2]. As we noted before, Nakasato achieved a maximum of 87% efficiency with a multiplication kernel that stores the results back to local memory in [13]. These results suggest that the difference between local and remote stores is critical to performance, and that the multi-threading performed implicitly by GPU hardware and the double buffering approach are not sufficient to hide such long latency. In summary, the efficiency gap between the four-stage pipelined algorithm and the *mult* kernel indicates that there is room for optimizing data movement in the *mult* kernel. Therefore, the software pipelining should be refined to achieve better overlap between computation and data transfers.

3. METHODOLOGY

According to the analysis above, we focus on the *mult* kernel of four-stage software-pipelining algorithm. We address the bottleneck represented by the long latency involved in writing back the result matrix to remote memory. Previous

	Host Memory	GPU	PCIe Bus
load1	X		
load2			X
mult		X	X
store	X		

Figure 4: Resource allocation in each stage of four-stage pipelined algorithm (Algorithm 1), "X" denotes the usage of resources

work [1, 2, 6, 9, 11–14, 16, 17, 19, 21–23] attempted to mitigate this latency via the architectural multi-threading provided by GPU hardware and the double-buffering approach. In this section, we provide instead a solution based on an improved software pipelining. We reduce the write-back latency by employing the image addressing mode available on ATI hardware, and by storing the C matrix to GPU local memory, adding a separate pipelining stage to write back the results to remote memory.

3.1 Addressing Mode

Two addressing modes are available to access GPU local memory: the image addressing mode and the global buffer addressing mode. In global buffer mode, kernels can access arbitrary locations in local memory. In image addressing mode, kernels can only address pre-allocated memory segments. The addresses of image reads are specified as 1D or 2D indices, and reads take place using the fetch units. The programmer must bind these pre-allocated memory segments to the fetch units. For a single kernel invocation, the number of images for reading and writing is 128 and 8, respectively. The maximum dimension of 2D addresses is 8192×8192 elements. Addresses must be contiguous as specified by the 1D or 2D mode and the reads must be invoked with dedicated instructions. Though the image addressing seems a bit complicated to perform, the latency it incurs is much less than the global buffer addressing.

Nakasato [13] described a detailed analysis of choosing blocking factors for DGEMM kernel implementation on Cypress GPU. Both his work and ACML-GPU library indicate that the optimal blocking algorithm calculates 4×4 sub-matrices in the kernel for satisfying requirements of memory bandwidth and registers. Our multiplication kernel adopts a similar blocking algorithm. Specifically, our kernel invokes 8 input and 8 output samplers using the image addressing mode instead of the global buffer addressing mode.

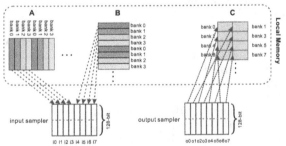

Figure 5: Data partition and sampler mapping of the new multiplication kernel in image addressing mode

As shown in Figure 5, two input matrices in local memory are partitioned into many banks which are loaded for multiplication by every four banks. Each column (row) of A (B) is one bank which is bound to a sampler. For example, every four banks of A are mapped to samplers i0-i3, and every four banks of B are mapped to samplers i4-i7. Since the width of a sampler is 128-bit and a 4×4 sub-block of C

matrix is calculated, the output C matrix is partitioned into many two-dimensional banks of 4×2. Algorithm 2 describes the kernel algorithm that calculates a 4×4 sub-block of C matrix in GPU local memory. In order to conserve registers, the algorithm splits banks of both A and B into two parts and loads them in two steps. The resulting sub-blocks of C are stored into local memory, instead of remote memory. Unlike the previous designs, we split the write-back into two stages: the first stores results to local memory, and the second transfers them to remote memory. In the next section, we will show how our new pipelining overlaps the local memory store with the other stages.

Algorithm 2 The algorithm of DGEMM kernel

```
bind banks of both A and B to input samplers
bind banks of C to output samplers
Registers: a[4], b[4], c[8]   //128-bit width
///////////////////////////////////////////
c[0 : 8]=0

for (k=0; k<K/4; k++) {
  //fetch four banks of two elements from A
  load a[0 : 3] ← bank_A[0 : 3][2k]
  //fetch two banks of four elements from B
  load b[0 : 3] ← bank_B[0 : 1][2k : 2k + 1]
  //multiplication
  c[0 : 8] + = a[0 : 3] × b[0 : 3]

  //fetch four banks of two elements from A
  load a[0 : 3] ← bank_A[0 : 3][2k + 1]
  //fetch two banks of four elements from B
  load b[0 : 3] ← bank_B[2 : 3][2k : 2k + 1]
  //multiplication
  c[0 : 8] + = a[0 : 3] × b[0 : 3]
} //end for
store c[0 : 8] → bank_C[0 : 8]
```

3.2 Five-stage Pipelining

In our multiplication kernel we output results to GPU local memory instead of remote memory, and a later transfer is required to write the results to remote memory. The difference with respect to previous approaches is the separation of this write-back transfer from the *mult* kernel into a new stage *store1*, which makes us design pipelining of five stages. This separation provides an opportunity to better utilize the DMA engine available in the hardware, and can perform data transfers asynchronously.

Algorithm 3 shows our five-stage pipelining, in which stage *mult* is split into stages *mult1* and *store1*, where *store1* transfers C results from local memory to remote memory. For clarity we rename the old *store* stage as *store2*.

With respect to resources, the *mult1* only occupies the GPU computing cores, whereas the *store1* only occupies the DMA engine. To better overlap with *mult1*, a sub-matrix of C output is divided into smaller ones to transfer. While *mult1* is running, several *store1* operations are executing at the same time. In our implementation, four *store1* stages are in parallel with *mult1* kernel due to the size of sub-matrices calculated. Thus, computation and DMA transfers can proceed in parallel in a fine granularity, similarly to what happens in the double-buffering scheme.

	Host memory	GPU	PCIe Bus
load1	X		
load2			X
mult1		X	
store1			X
store2	X		

Figure 6: Resource allocation in the new five-stage pipelined DGEMM

Figure 6 depicts the new resource allocation. The *mult1* no longer needs PCIe bus, and only uses GPU device. Therefore, *mult1* can now be executed in parallel with *load2* or *store1* without PCIe conflicts. Not only Algorithm 3 provides a finer-grained pipelining and alleviates the resource conflicts, but it also allows a faster kernel implementation.

3.3 Software Pipelining Design

We propose the use of our five-stage pipelined design not only in order to optimize DGEMM, but as a more general strategy to structure the execution of similar kernels. Our pipelining scheme could serve as the basis to create a reusable software-pipelining programming framework and runtime system, which can be used in a heterogeneous environment based on ATI GPUs. This section outlines how this framework could be implemented.

The framework will provide an API for the users to invoke a five-stage pipelining described in Table 2. Figure 7 illustrates the execution of this pipelining over time, where the five stages are represented with distinct colors. The bars inside the *exec* blocks represent the data transfer stages (*load1*, *load2*, *store1*, *store2*), which are overlapped by the *exec* kernel. As shown in this figure, except for the prologue and epilogue of the pipelining, data transfers are totally overlapped.

The framework will contain a runtime system that allows the users to describe properties of the data transferred (both input and output). These properties characterize the memory access patterns, i.e., whether data are contiguous and whether they are reused. Properties determine the data placement in each pipelining stage:

- For data accessed contiguously, the *exec* kernel should preferably use the image addressing mode, and the runtime system will correspondingly bind those data to the sampling fetch units.

- Those data that have been indicated as subject to reuse should be placed in cached remote memory regions for better reuse.

Algorithm 3 The five-stage software-pipelining DGEMM

Partition: $A = \{A_1, A_2, \cdots, A_p\}, B = \{B_1, B_2, \cdots, B_q\}$,
$C = \{C_1, C_2, \cdots, C_{p \times q}\}$
Work units: $WU = \{C_1 = A_1 \times B_1, C_2 = A_1 \times B_2, \cdots\}$
$C_{i,j}$: *the sub-matrices of* C_j
//
1. bind remote memory for sub-matrices A,B,C
//*pre-processing*
Allocate workunits using the "bounce corner turn"
//*the for-loop is pipelined*
2. **for** each workunit wu_i **do**   //$i = 1, 2, \cdots, p \times q$
//*load1*
3. copy either A_i or B_i from application space to remote memory
//*load2*
4. copy either A_i or B_i from remote memory to local memory
//*mult*
5. *DMAPipeline($C_{i,1}$)*
6. **for** each block $C_{i,j}$ **do**   //$j = 2, 3, \cdots$
//*store2*
7. copy $C_{i,j-1}$ from remote memory to application space
   (also multiplied by beta)
//*mult*
8. *DMAPipeline($C_{i,j}$)*
9. *endfor*
//*store2*
10. copy the last $C_{i,j}$ from remote memory to application space
    (also multiplied by beta)
11. *endfor*

Algorithm: DMAPipeline($C_{i,j}$)
$C_{i,j,k}$: *the sub-blocks of* $C_{i,j}$
//
//*the for-loop is pipelined*
//*mult1*
1. calculate $C_{i,j,1}$ in local memory
2. **for** each sub-block $C_{i,j,k}$ **do**   //$k = 2, 3, \cdots$
//*store1*
3. DMA transfer $C_{i,j,k-1}$ from local memory to remote memory
//*mult1*
4. calculate $C_{i,j,k}$ in local memory
5. *endfor*
//*store1*
6. DMA transfer the last $C_{i,j,k}$ from local memory to remote memory

---

An interesting experience from our DGEMM kernel optimization is that explicit double-buffering appears to be more

---

Table 2: The five stages in general software pipelining

load1	copy input data from application space to remote memory
load2	copy input data from remote memory to local memory
exe	perform kernel execution on GPU device and output data to local memory
store1	copy output data from local memory to remote memory
store2	copy output data from remote memory to application space

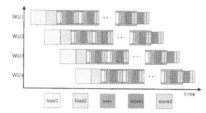

Figure 7: General software pipelining sketch

efficient for tolerating latency than multi-threading on current ATI GPU architectures, because of the long memory latency to be hidden. Therefore, it is worth implementing double-buffering for reading and writing data in each data transfer stage. In fact, the major source of performance improvement in our optimization is the identification of the inefficiency of the ATI GPU hardware in mitigating the latency due to remote writes. Therefore, we advocate an explicit orchestration of data transfer between local memory and remote memory with a software pipelining approach integrated in a programming framework, although it will increase the complexity of implementing runtime system.

4. EXPERIMENT RESULTS AND ANALYSIS

4.1 Experimental Setup

Our experiments were performed on the heterogeneous system comprising two Intel Xeon 5650 CPUs and one ATI $Radeon^{TM}$ HD5970 GPU. Table 3 summarizes the configuration parameters of our experimental platform. The CPU provides a peak double-precision performance of 128 GFLOPS. Its memory system is configured with a size of 24GBytes and an aggregated bandwidth of 31 GB/s. The GPU contains two Cypress chips and provides a peak arithmetic throughput of 928 GFLOPS (The calculation is shown below) in double-precision. Its memory size is 2 GBytes and peak memory bandwidth is 256 GB/s. The total double-precision peak performance of the heterogeneous system is 1056 GFLOPS.

GPU performance:
$928 GFLOPS =$
    $725 MHz(frequency) \times 2(\#DoublePrecisionFPRates)$
    $\times 320(\#StreamCores) \times 2(\#chips)$

Table 3: Configuration of the experimental platform

Processors	Xeon X5650	$Radeon^{TM}$ HD5970
Model	Westmere-EP	Cypress
Frequency	2.66GHz	725MHz
#chips	2	2
DP	128 GFLOPS	928 GFLOPS
DRAM type	DDR3 1.3GHz	GDDR5 1.0GHz
DRAM size	24GB	2GB
DRAM bandwidth	31.2 GB/s	256 GB/s
PCIe2.0	x16, 8 GB/s	
Programming	icc + openmpi	ATI Stream SDK 2.2

We evaluate multiple implementations of DGEMM on our experimental platform, and the abbreviations are described below in order of incremental optimizations:

- ACML-GPU: It is the ATI DGEMM library, which uses direct pipelining strategy among work units to hide the overheads caused by writing result C matrix from remote memory to application space. The *mult* kernel uses global buffer addressing mode.

- 4-stage pipelining: This is a DGEMM implementation of Algorithm 1. It improves ACML-GPU by overlapping the load operations of input matrices and using double-buffering strategy within a work unit better overlapping write-back of C matrix. It is realized according to [23].
- 5-stage pipelining: This is our new implementation that focuses on orchestrating the data placement through the memory hierarchy. It also selects a better addressing mode and data placement for the output C matrix.
- HDGEMM: While the above three implementations only exploit the arithmetic throughput of the GPU, this one implements a hybrid DGEMM, where CPU and GPU perform the workload cooperatively. This is also our best DGEMM implementation. It partitions matrices between the CPU and the GPU, and adaptively balances the workload between them using a strategy proposed in [23]. Our experiments use two processes, each comprising one computing element (CE) (one CPU and one GPU chip).

Table 4: DGEMM matrix dimensions and the corresponding storage sizes in Gigabytes used in the following experiments, and the number of work units

k \ GB	m=n				
	16384	20480	24576	28672	32768
1536	2.55	3.86	5.54	7.28	9.40
2048	2.68	4.03	5.64	7.52	9.66
4096	3.22	4.70	6.44	8.46	10.74
#workunits	6	12	12	20	24

Table 4 shows the matrices used in our experiments, with the order (m,n,k) and corresponding size in Gigabytes. We keep m equal to n because the difference between them has little effect on DGEMM performance. The size of k determines the amount of data reuse during reading the input matrices, which has a significant impact on performance. Therefore, three values of k are used to represent three data sets. Besides, the number of work units used in our experiments is given in the last row. Since we divide matrices in m and n dimension, the number of work units is independent of k size. In the sections below, we give the performance values for a particular k size by calculating the average performance over all the five values of m (n). As for detailed profiling, we always take k=2048 for example in default, and the matrix size in x axis represents different m (n) values.

4.2 Results

We first report the overall performance of the four DGEMM implementations on our experimental system. Figure 8 plots the performance and efficiency with different matrix sizes, as given in Table 4. The performance of DGEMM is measured in terms of GFLOPS i.e. the number of floating-point operations executed per second (in billions). Efficiency is defined as the ratio between the performance achieved and the machine's theoretical peak performance.

Each group of five bars represents the corresponding performance for each k value (k=1536, 2048, 4096 in the x axis) with five m (n) values, as shown in Table 4. The numbers on the left y axis are the floating-point performance in GFLOPS. From bottom up the segments of each bar indicate the performance increment. For each bar, the bottom segment represents the baseline program ACML-GPU, the

second one above represents performance improvement of the four-stage pipelining implementation over ACML-GPU, the third one shows performance improvement of five-stage pipelining over four-stage pipelining, the performance gains of hybrid CPU-GPU HDGEMM are depicted on the top. For simplicity, Figure 8 plots two efficiency lines (values shown in the right y axis), which correspond to the best GPU-only (5-stage-pipelining) DGEMM and HDGEMM respectively.

Our HDGEMM achieves a maximum performance of 844 GFLOPS and an efficiency of 80% (when <m,n,k> = <16384, 16384, 4096>) on the whole system with two Cypress GPU chips and two six-core CPUs. The 5-stage-pipelining DGEMM reaches a maximum performance of 758 GFLOPS and an efficiency of 82% (when <m,n,k> = <16384, 16384, 4096>) on two Cypress GPU chips. In a comparison against ACML-GPU, our five-stage pipelined implementation improves performance by a factor of 2 on average. HDGEMM further improves performance by 10%-20% by utilizing the computing power of multi-core CPUs.

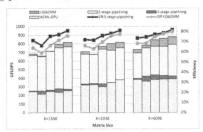

Figure 8: Our optimized DGEMM performance and efficiency on two GPUs and/or two CPUs

When k is fixed, all four implementations show an increase in both performance and efficiency with larger matrices. There are few cases with abnormal behavior (e.g. m=n=10240). It is because the matrix size is not a multiple of the optimal block size for data transfer and kernel execution. As we expected, comparing the average performance among different k sizes, the performance improvement of our five-stage pipelined implementation over ACML-GPU drops as the matrix scale becomes larger. When k is 1536, 2048 and 4096, the speedups are 2.9X, 2.1X, and 1.9X respectively. This is because the ratio of data transfer to kernel execution decreases with larger problem size. Since our software pipelined optimization focuses on data transfers, the performance improvements will be more obvious when data transfers take large portion of the implementation. On larger datasets, the computation absorbs a larger fraction of the DGEMM execution time, and the effect of data-transfer optimizations is less apparent. As Figure 8 shows, HDGEMM exhibits higher performance improvements with larger matrix sizes. That happens because the CPU delivers higher performance on large matrices, increasing the overall performance of HDGEMM.

In order to highlight the effect of the proposed optimizations in this work, we isolate sources of noise (e.g. bandwidth contention, which will be reported in the next section) that are present when multiple GPU chips are employed in the heterogeneous system. We perform experiments on one GPU chip and do not assign any computing load to CPU, which is only in charge of data transfers. Assuming k=2048, Figure 9 compares the performance of the three GPU-only DGEMM implementations, i.e., ACML-GPU, 4-stage pipelining, 5-stage pipelining. Compared with ACML-GPU, the 4-stage pipelining improves performance by about 30% through pipelining *store2* within a work unit and reusing data.

Our 5-stage pipelining implementation improves performance by 74% employing a better data placement, the image addressing mode, and a finer-grained pipeline. It explicitly leverages the DMA engine to pipeline the result write-back stage. Finally it achieves 408 GFLOPS with an efficiency of 88% on one Cypress GPU chip. This implementation only shows a 5% performance loss compared with an execution of the kernel without CPU-GPU transfers (94% efficiency). It demonstrates that our pipelining optimizations achieve almost complete success in mitigating data transfer latencies.

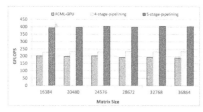

Figure 9: Performance improvements on one GPU chip

In Section 2, Figure 3 shows that the three data transfer stages (*load1*, *load2*, *store*) are responsible for about 30% of the total execution time (statistics do not include the implicit data transfer *store1* taking place in the *mult* stage). We refine the pipelining by separating *store1* from the *mult*. Our approach achieves a better pipelining. In fact, after counting the added *store1* stage, data transfers account for more than 40% of the total execution time. The new execution time fractions for each data transfer stage (*load1*, *load2*, *store1*, *store2*) are in Figure 10. Only the data transfer stages are given, and y axis represents the ratios between the time of each stage and that of the total data transfer. *Store1*, which takes about 55% of the total data transfer time, is the major part of the four data transfers.

From Figure 9, the performance improvement of the five-stage pipelining over the four-stage one is 74% on average; this number is larger than all the data transfer percentage of DGEMM (about 43%). This is because our optimizations improves not only data transfers, but also the performance of the multiplication kernel. Besides, Figure 9 shows that our optimized DGEMM performance is quite stable through all the matrix sizes. This property lays a good foundation for good scalability of our DGEMM implementation on multiple chips of both CPUs and GPUs. However, the stable trend on one GPU chip is different from that shown in Figure 8, where the HDGEMM efficiency line occurs below the 5-stage-pipelining line. We will discuss this phenomenon in the next section.

4.3 Analysis

Usually, DGEMM in CPU's math library can achieve a maximal efficiency of more than 90%. Our HDGEMM implementation on the heterogeneous system also achieves the maximal efficiency of 80%, counting data transfer between CPU and GPU. In this section we will investigate: (i) How much optimization room is left beyond our pipelining optimizations on such a heterogeneous architecture. (ii) What about the intra-node scalability of HDGEMM when scaling to multiple CPUs and GPUs. Note that we focus on multiple GPU chips on the same board that share the same CPU memory, because it is one trend that a heterogeneous system integrates multiple GPU chips or cards into one board

(node). Our analysis attempts to figure out some architectural constraints on the performance of our heterogeneous algorithm. One more point to be clarified is that we are not going to evaluate very large scale matrices distributed on many nodes. On one hand, a call to DGEMM routine usually happens after the higher level algorithm has partitioned the original problem size across nodes. Thus, each node executes DGEMM independently. On the other hand, our software pipelining optimization is customized to a tightly coupled a CPU-GPU heterogeneous architecture. Therefore, an evaluation on a large cluster system is out of the scope of this paper.

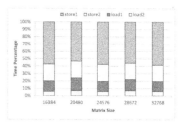

Figure 10: Time percentage of the four data transfer stages

4.3.1 Performance Gap

Among the five stages of the pipelining, the *mult1* stage determines the highest performance that DGEMM can achieve. Nakasato [13] optimized the DGEMM performance and reported the highest efficiency of 87% on an ATI HD5870 GPU that uses only one Cypress chip. Through the use of the image addressing mode (instead of the global buffer addressing mode) for the result matrix write-back, we achieve a higher efficiency of 94% on one Cypress chip.

Figure 11 compares the efficiency of the *mult1* kernel alone, the 5-stage pipelining implementation on one GPU chip, the 5-stage pipelining implementation on two GPU chips, and the HDGEMM implementation on a full system of two CPUs and two GPU chips. For each set of experiments, we show the average efficiency. DGEMM invokes the *mult1* kernel for multiple times in every execution, and the *mult1* kernel performance plotted is the average value over these times. Our optimized kernel only reads and writes GPU local memory, thus its performance has no relation to CPU resources. As shown in this figure the kernel's efficiency is over 90% (the best one is 94%), which is comparable to the floating-point efficiency of the CPU DGEMM library. The difference between the kernel and 5-stage pipelining is whether the data transfer between CPU and GPU is counted. Results show that, when running on one chip, the performance of the 5-stage pipelining implementation on one GPU is 6% lower than the kernel running alone, due to the data transfers. There are two reasons for the performance drop. First, the prologue and epilogue of the pipelining cannot be hidden, and they absorb around 3% of the total execution time (measured in our experiments). Second, as shown in Figure 6, there are still resource conflicts within the pipelining. During its execution, there is host memory contention between *load1* and *store2*, and PCIe bus contention between *load2* and *store1*.

When scaling within a node, contention of shared resources will limit performance. Figure 11 shows the intra-node scalability of HDGEMM with more GPUs and/or CPUs as well. Running 5-stage pipelining DGEMM on two GPU chips (5-

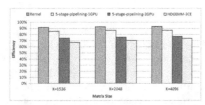

Figure 11: The scalability of our optimized DGEMM when scaling to multiple CPUs and/or GPUs

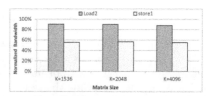

Figure 12: PCIe bandwidth of 5-stage-pipelining-2GPU normalized to that of 5-stage-pipelining-1GPU

stage-pipelining-2GPU), the efficiency drops by 11% with respect to 5-stage-pipelining-1GPU. Moreover, when we extend DGEMM to a system with two computing elements (HDGEMM-2CE), the efficiency further drops by 5% from 5-stage-pipelining-2GPU. We believe that resource contention is the main reason influencing DGEMM scalability. In the following sections, we will focus on HDGEMM intra-node scalability, and discuss host memory contention and PCIe contention in more details.

4.3.2 Contention on Multiple GPUs

Many state-of-the-art heterogeneous systems include accelerators (i.e., GPUs, ClearSpeed cards, Tilera) that are attached to the CPU through a PCIe bus that resides on the motherboard. Frequently there are multiple PCIe slots, each supporting one GPU board; moreover, some GPU boards host multiple GPU chips, e.g., the ATI $Radeon^{TM}$ HD5970 and the NVIDIA Tesla S1070. It is therefore valuable to analyze the scalability of our design on a system comprising multiple GPU chips.

As motherboards are concerned, the lane allocation among PCIe slots is different among models. Some motherboards support x16 + x16 combination, while others only support x8 + x8. If the combination is x16 + x16, there is no PCIe contention between different GPU boards, thus the intra-node scalability will not be influenced by PCIe contention. However, if a lane is divided between two GPU boards as in an x8 + x8 combination, which is more familiar, the PCIe usage is the same as two chips within one GPU board with an x16 slot.

In this paper, we focus on experimental conditions where PCIe contention exists, i.e., multiple GPU boards affected by the limited lane number, or multiple GPU chips within one GPU board. It makes sense to assume that the scalability on a system with multiple GPU chips on a board is similar to the one with multiple single-chip GPUs.

Due to the limitations of our experimental platform, we run two processes, each of which is in charge of one CPU and one GPU chip. The experiments profile the changes in available bandwidth from one GPU chip to two GPU chips, and analyze bandwidth contention between the two GPU chips to predict its scalability with more GPUs. For ease of comparison, each process of 5-stage-pipelining-2GPU runs with the same problem scale as that of 5-stage-pipelining-1GPU. From Figure 6, the bandwidth contention exists on both PCIe bus and host memory.

In order to focus on the bandwidth changes, the measured bandwidth of 5-stage-pipelining-2GPU is normalized to that of 5-stage-pipelining-1GPU. First, we consider PCIe contention during the execution of *load2* and *store1*. The reduction of average bandwidth is shown in Figure 12 with the normalized values in the y axis. As shown in this figure, *load2* and *store1* only achieve 89% and 56% of the PCIe bandwidth in 5-stage-pipelining-1GPU, respectively. We see

significant a decrease in *store1*, caused by higher frequency of PCIe request and larger amount of data to be transferred (the size of C is larger than that of A and B).

As we mentioned in Section 3, while *mult1* is running, several *store1* operations are executing at the same time (4 *store1* stages in our implementation). During *mult1* execution, the majority of PCIe bandwidth is consumed by *store1*, which reaches high occupancy even on one GPU chip. Therefore, when scaling to two GPU chips, PCIe bus contention becomes more severe. However, the bandwidth of PCIe bus available in the direction from the CPU to the GPU (*load2*) does not suffer as much as *store1*. That is because *load2* is pipelined with *mult1* among work units, so that the requests on the PCIe bus are not as frequent as *store1*. Besides, the size of matrices transferred by *load2* is $(m + n) \times k$, while the size of matrix transferred by *store1* is $m \times n$. Since k is much less than n in our experiment, the former puts less pressure on the PCIe bus.

In addition to PCIe bus contention, there is also contention on the host memory, since data is copied between the two regions of host memory (application space and remote memory). Figure 13 shows that the relative host memory bandwidth of *load1* and *store2* normalized to that of 5-stage-pipelining-1GPU. We find that *load1* and *store2* drop 8% and 14% bandwidth respectively, when scaling to two GPU chips. The reason is similar to that of PCIe contention, while the bandwidth reduction is smaller, because the frequency of *store2* is much less than that of *store1*.

Profiling shows that stages *load1*, *load2*, *store1* and *store2* are almost overlapped completely with *mult1* kernel in 5-stage-pipelining-1GPU. However, the bandwidth contention on the two GPU chips leads to an 11% efficiency loss: see 5-stage-pipelining-2GPU in Figure 11. Since two processes contend the shared resources (PCIe bus and host memory), some data transfers are prevented from overlapping with the *mult1* kernel. This reduces the performance. As the number of CPU or GPU chips increases, bus requests will become more frequent, decreasing efficiency even more because of resource contention. Our experimental results motivate the following two observations:

- Observation 1: **Due to the contention of PCIe bus, DGEMM hits its limitation on multiple GPUs with restricted number of lanes.** In DGEMM implementation, both *load2* and *store1* compete for PCIe bandwidth. As shown in Figure 10, these two phases occupy more than 60% of the total data transfer time. Our experimental results in Figure 12 show a significant decrease of bandwidth and 11% performance drop only scaling to two GPU chips. The situation would be worse if more GPUs share PCIe bandwidth.
- Observation 2: **DGEMM on multiple GPUs will not benefit much by improving host memory bandwidth.** Although both *load1* and *store2* consume host memory, it seems they are not quite sensitive to the contention from Figure 13. Besides, their

execution time is not the major part of the total data transfer time (Figure 10). For a small part of applications, the usage of pinned memory would help avoid both *load1* and *store2*. However, it is a must that no data rearrangement is required, and data should fit in the limited pinned memory space. Our work proves that data transfer overheads can also be mitigated by algorithmic optimizations with less limitation.

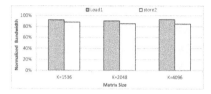

Figure 13: Host memory bandwidth of 5-stage-pipelining-2GPU normalized to that of 5-stage-pipelining-1GPU

4.3.3 Contention on Hybrid CPUs and GPUs

In our platform, the Intel Xeon CPU provides a peak arithmetic throughput of 128 GFLOPS, which contributes 12% of the whole system performance. CPUs should not be neglected when optimizing compute-intensive algorithms like DGEMM. In HDGEMM, matrices are first equally split into two parts, each of which is calculated by a distinct computing element (one CPU and one GPU). Within each computing element, we adopt the algorithm in [23] to partition the workload between the CPU and the GPU. HDGEMM-2CE improves the performance by 6% on average over 5-stage-pipelining-2GPU (see Figure 8), but its efficiency decreases by 5% (see Figure 11). In this section we explain why.

We profile the performance contributed only by CPU (denoted as CPU-HDGEMM) in Figure 14 when HDGEMM-2CE is executed. For comparison, we run a CPU-only DGEMM implementation (denoted as PureCPU), which calculates the same matrix size as CPU-HDGEMM in HDGEMM-2CE. From this figure, CPU-HDGEMM shows a performance loss of 22% compared to PureCPU. The comparison illustrates that HDGEMM prevents CPU from achieving its peak computing performance. We believe that CPU-HDGEMM performance is influenced by the GPU operations *load1* and *store2*. Data transfers to/from GPU share the same application space with CPU's DGEMM calculation. For the same reasons as discussed with 5-stage-pipelining-2GPU, host memory contention does not affect DGEMM performance in the GPU part of HDGEMM-2CE. However, the sharing of application space seriously influences DGEMM performance when executing on CPUs. We further observe that:

- Observation 3: **Host memory bandwidth is an important factor to HDGEMM performance.** As CPU arithmetic throughput increases, host memory contention will have greater impact on the overall performance of HDGEMM. Some applications might alleviate this contention by employing pinned memory.

Another minor reason for the efficiency degradation is the imbalanced workload partition between CPU and GPU. In our adopted partition strategy, a heuristic algorithm in [23] is used to search an appropriate split ratio between CPU and GPU, making the execution time difference less than a threshold. We take 0.1 seconds as the threshold in this paper, which is an empirically optimal value selected by multiple iterations of experiments. Figure 15 plots the execution

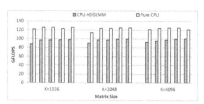

Figure 14: Comparison of performance that CPU contributes in HDGEMM and CPU-only DGEMM

time difference between CPU and GPU in different matrix sizes. We take CPU execution time as reference, and the time difference is calculated by $(time_{gpu} - time_{cpu})/time_{cpu}$. The slight imbalance leads to a little loss of the overall HDGEMM performance. However, as the difference is small, the performance degradation caused by load imbalance is not significant (about 1%).

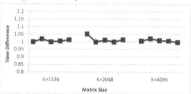

Figure 15: Relative time difference between CPU and GPU

5. RELATED WORK

The most related work includes both Nakasato's kernel optimization [13] and Yang's software-pipelining optimization [23]. Table 5 summarizes the optimization strategies used in the three DGEMM programs. All the optimizations improve performance over the baseline ACML-GPU library [2]. Until now, our DGEMM achieves the highest performance on the heterogeneous CPU and ATI GPU architecture. In addition, we disclose some experimental observations on the shared resources (PCIe bus and host memory) contention on a heterogeneous system.

Table 5: Comparison with [13] and [23]

	Nakasato [13]	Yang [23]	Ours
optimizations			
image addressing for C	no	no	yes
local memory for C	yes	no	yes
pipelining	no	four-stage	five-stage
data reuse	no	yes	yes
double-buffer in local memory	no	no	yes
double-buffer in remote memory	no	yes	yes
performance (maximal GFLOPS (floating-point efficiency))			
kernel	470 (87%)	248 (53%)	436 (94%)
one GPU chip	~300 (55%)	234 (50%)	408 (88%)
two GPU chips	-	438 (47%)	758 (82%)

Some other work optimized DGEMM assuming that the matrices have already been resident in GPU on-board memory. AMD's Accelerated Parallel Processing Math Libraries (APPML) v1.4 [1] in OpenCL language provides GPU-only DGEMM kernel, according to the test our kernel is more efficient than it. GATLAS auto-tuner in [11] makes use of auto-tuning method to increase the portability among different GPU architectures and is meant to be used in realistic applications. However, it still solves DGEMM which matrices are resident in GPU on-board memory. Thus, there is no direct way to call GATLAS in realistic applications so far with large datasets. V. Volkov and J. Demmel implemented one-sided matrix factorizations (LU, QR, etc.) on a hybrid CPU-GPU system in [21], they divided the factorization processes to CPU and GPU separately. Matrix-matrix multiplication in that case still uses data stored in

GPU memory without data transfer. MAGMA [14] develop a dense linear algebra library similar to LAPACK [5] for heterogeneous architecture, it has been implemented only for NVIDIA GPU so far. Therefore, our optimizations will provide a possible solution for MAGMA when extending to ATI GPU. Other math library implementations for heterogeneous architecture include hybrid Jacobi [20], model-based heterogeneous FFT [15], etc. Most of the work did not carefully optimize data transfer, but parallelized the computation on CPU with GPU computation instead. The software-pipelining approach may be a complement to improve the performance of hybrid libraries.

6. CONCLUSION

We analyze the state-of-the-art implementation of the DGEMM algorithm when running on a heterogeneous system comprising a CPU and an ATI GPU, and find sources of inefficiency. We propose a more optimized five-stage software-pipelined design, and provide an implementation that exploits the image addressing modes available on the ATI hardware. Our design mitigates better the latencies of CPU-GPU data transfers, delivering 408 GFLOPS (with 88% floating-point efficiency) on one Cypress GPU chip, 758 GFLOPS (82% efficiency) on two Cypress GPUs (i.e., the entire GPU board), and 844 GFLOPS (80% efficiency) on a system comprising two Intel Westmere-EP CPUs and an ATI $Radeon^{TM}$ HD5970 GPU. We show that the use of multiple GPUs on the same node increases the performance but achieves lower efficiency, due to the contention of shared resources, in particular the PCIe bus and the host memory. We believe that hardware designers should focus on reducing the cost of such contention instances if they desire their hardware to achieve higher degrees of efficiency with DGEMM-like workloads.

7. ACKNOWLEDGMENTS

We would like to express our gratitude to Dr. Daniele Paolo Scarpazza at D.E. Shaw Research for helping us revise this paper, and Dr. Udeepta Bordoloi for the comments. This work is supported by National 863 Program (2009AA01A129), the National Natural Science Foundation of China (60803030, 61033009, 60921002, 60925009, 61003062) and 973 Program (2011CB302500 and 2011CB302502).

References

[1] AMD Accelerated Parallel Processing Math Libraries.

[2] AMD Core Math Library for Graphic Processors.

[3] HPL - a portable implementation of the high-performance linpack benchmark for distributed-memory computers.

[4] ATI Stream SDK CAL Programming Guide v2.0, 2010.

[5] E. Angerson, Z. Bai, J. Dongarra, A. Greenbaum, A. McKenney, J. Du Croz, S. Hammarling, J. Demmel, C. Bischof, and D. Sorensen. LAPACK: A portable linear algebra library for high-performance computers. In Supercomputing '90. Proceedings of, pages 2 –11, nov 1990.

[6] J. Demmel, J. Dongarra, V. Eijkhout, E. Fuentes, A. Petitet, R. Vuduc, R. Whaley, and K. Yelick. Self-adapting linear algebra algorithms and software. Proceedings of the IEEE, 93(2):293 –312, feb. 2005.

[7] J. Dongarra, P. Beckman, T. Moore, et.al. The international exascale software project roadmap. Int. J. High Perform. Comput. Appl., 25(1):3–60, Feb. 2011.

[8] J. J. Dongarra, J. Du Croz, S. Hammarling, and I. S. Duff. A set of level 3 basic linear algebra subprograms. ACM Trans. Math. Softw., 16(1):1–17, Mar. 1990.

[9] K. Goto and R. Geijn. Anatomy of high-performance matrix multiplication. ACM Trans. Math. Softw., 34(3):12:1–12:25, May 2008.

[10] T. B. Jablin, P. Prabhu, J. A. Jablin, N. P. Johnson, S. R. Beard, and D. I. August. Automatic CPU-GPU communication management and optimization. In Proceedings of the 32nd ACM SIGPLAN conference on Programming language design and implementation, PLDI '11, pages 142–151, New York, NY, USA, 2011. ACM.

[11] C. Jang. GATLAS: GPU automatically tuned linear algebra software.

[12] Y. Li, J. Dongarra, and S. Tomov. A note on auto-tuning GEMM for GPUs. In Proceedings of the 9th International Conference on Computational Science: Part I, ICCS '09, pages 884–892, Berlin, Heidelberg, 2009. Springer-Verlag.

[13] N. Nakasato. A fast GEMM implementation on the Cypress GPU. SIGMETRICS Perform. Eval. Rev., 38(4):50–55, Mar. 2011.

[14] R. Nath, S. Tomov, and J. Dongarra. An improved MAGMA GEMM for Fermi graphics processing units. Int. J. High Perform. Comput. Appl., 24(4):511–515, Nov. 2010.

[15] Y. Ogata, T. Endo, N. Maruyama, and S. Matsuoka. An efficient, model-based CPU-GPU heterogeneous FFT library. In Parallel and Distributed Processing, 2008. IPDPS 2008. IEEE International Symposium on, pages 1 –10, april 2008.

[16] S. Ryoo, C. I. Rodrigues, S. S. Baghsorkhi, S. S. Stone, D. B. Kirk, and W.-m. W. Hwu. Optimization principles and application performance evaluation of a multithreaded GPU using CUDA. In Proceedings of the 13th ACM SIGPLAN Symposium on Principles and practice of parallel programming, PPoPP '08, pages 73–82, New York, NY, USA, 2008. ACM.

[17] S. Ryoo, C. I. Rodrigues, S. S. Stone, S. S. Baghsorkhi, S.-Z. Ueng, J. A. Stratton, and W.-m. W. Hwu. Program optimization space pruning for a multithreaded GPU. In Proceedings of the 6th annual IEEE/ACM international symposium on Code generation and optimization, CGO '08, pages 195–204, New York, NY, USA, 2008. ACM.

[18] M. Silberstein, A. Schuster, and J. D. Owens. Accelerating sum-product computations on hybrid CPU-GPU architectures. In W. W. Hwu, editor, GPU Computing Gems, volume 2, chapter 36, pages 501–517. Morgan Kaufmann, Oct. 2011.

[19] G. Tan, Z. Guo, M. Chen, and D. Meng. Single-particle 3d reconstruction from cryo-electron microscopy images on GPU. In Proceedings of the 23rd international conference on Supercomputing, ICS '09, pages 380–389, New York, NY, USA, 2009. ACM.

[20] S. Venkatasubramanian, R. W. Vuduc, and n. none. Tuned and wildly asynchronous stencil kernels for hybrid CPU/GPU systems. In Proceedings of the 23rd international conference on Supercomputing, ICS '09, pages 244–255, New York, NY, USA, 2009. ACM.

[21] V. Volkov and J. W. Demmel. Benchmarking GPUs to tune dense linear algebra. In Proceedings of the 2008 ACM/IEEE conference on Supercomputing, SC '08, pages 31:1–31:11, Piscataway, NJ, USA, 2008. IEEE Press.

[22] H. Wong, M.-M. Papadopoulou, M. Sadooghi-Alvandi, and A. Moshovos. Demystifying GPU microarchitecture through microbenchmarking. In Performance Analysis of Systems Software (ISPASS), 2010 IEEE International Symposium on, pages 235 –246, march 2010.

[23] C. Yang, F. Wang, Y. Du, J. Chen, J. Liu, H. Yi, and K. Lu. Adaptive optimization for petascale heterogeneous CPU/GPU computing. In Cluster Computing (CLUSTER), 2010 IEEE International Conference on, pages 19 –28, sept. 2010.

Author Index